INTERACTIVE 3D Application Development

USING EON PROFESSIONAL FOR CREATING 3D VISUALIZATIONS

Justice · Bergerud · Garrison · Cafiero · Churches
EON Reality, Inc.
and the
Kentucky Community and Technical College System

CONCEPT
Strategic Alliance Solutions for EON Reality, Inc., *Marly Bergerud*
Kentucky Community & Technical College System, *Jamie Justice*

PROJECT MANAGEMENT
Custom Editorial Productions, Inc., *Rose Marie Kuebbing*

WRITING & DEVELOPMENT
Custom Editorial Productions, Inc., *Rose Marie Kuebbing & Team*
EON Reality, Inc., *Dennis Cafiero & Lloyd Churches*
Kentucky Community & Technical College System, *Janet Garrison*

EDITING & PRODUCTION
Custom Editorial Productions, Inc.

COMPOSITOR
Macmillan Publishing Solutions

PRINTER
Printed and Bound in Malaysia for Imago

INTERNAL DESIGN & COVER DESIGN
Ramsdell Design

COVER ART SOURCE
Getty Images

ISBN 978-0-615-28492-7
ISBN 0-615-28492-2
10 9 8 7 6 5 4 3 2 1

EON Reality, Inc.
39 Parker St., Suite 100
Irvine, CA 92618

Kentucky Community
and Technical College System
300 N. Main St.
Versailles, KY 40383

Table of Contents

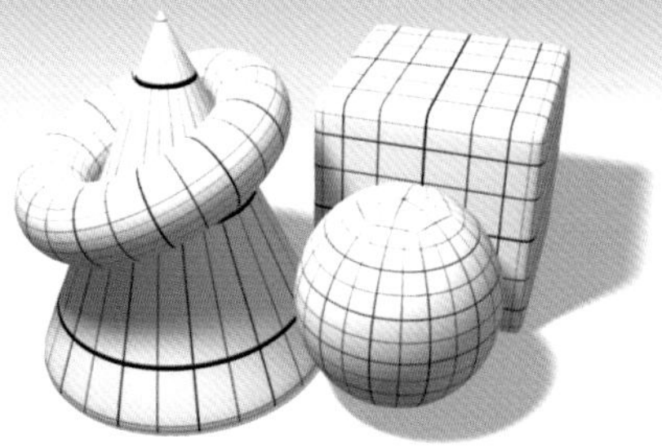

Module 9: Scripting and Dynamic Load 477

Lesson 9.1: Fundamentals of Scripting 478

Lesson 9.2: Using Scripts 519

Preface

Interactive 3D Application Development: Using EON Professional for Creating 3D Visualizations is a comprehensive guide for the development of a wide variety of interactive 3D applications. Users of this book will learn to easily and quickly manipulate the EON Professional software to develop exceptional interactive 3D simulations for use in numerous fields including business and industry, education and training, marketing, and research and development.

The compilation of this book has truly been a long, collaborative effort. Were it not for the vision of **Marly Bergerud**, President of Strategic Alliance Solutions and EON's Vice President, Education Development, the book you are reading would not exist. As an experienced educator and an accomplished author and co-author of more than twenty textbooks, Marly is passionate about the need to provide high-quality educational materials to foster the learning process. Recognizing a void within the 3D application training arena, Marly first approached me in early 2007 with the notion of creating a resource to provide instructional materials for 3D application development. I was at that time working feverishly to launch the KCTCS Interactive Digital Center and was instantly enthralled with Marly's idea. I could see innumerable ways in which a targeted book could benefit the KCTCS Visualization Technology program. Shortly thereafter, Marly and I began devoting countless hours to the development of our plan to revolutionize 3D educational learning.

Yet for any idea to take root, there must be stakeholders who believe in the vision, provide leadership, and champion the cause. For this project, we were fortunate to have the support of both KCTCS and EON Reality, Inc., which provided a rare collaboration between academia and a cutting-edge technology business. From KCTCS, assistance and leadership were supplied by **Dr. Michael B. McCall**, President; **Dr. Keith Bird**, Chancellor; **Dr. Jay Box**, Vice President; **Ken Walker**, Vice President; and **Tim Burcham**, Vice President. Their tremendous support, encouragement, and entrepreneurial spirit were essential in all aspects of the creation of the KCTCS Interactive Digital Center and in the completion of this book. From EON Reality, Inc., **Mats Johansson**, President and CEO, wholeheartedly embraced this learner-focused project. Mats played an essential role in the coordination of key EON technical resources and personnel to supplement and support the writing staff.

To help us turn our vision into reality, we enlisted the expertise of **Mary Lou Motl**, President of Custom Editorial Productions, Inc. (CEP), an editorial services company that specializes in book development and production. Marly had worked with Mary Lou and her staff on several previous publications, so working together again was a natural fit. **Rose Marie Kuebbing** of CEP promptly went to work assembling a team of dedicated professionals to undertake the challenge of researching and writing the content. Early in the process, Rose Marie and **Janet Garrison**, a professor at Maysville Community and Technical College (within the KCTCS), traveled to Sweden to work with the EON software developers and gain "behind-the-scenes" insight into the EON Professional software. There, they refined the table of contents and outlined initial chapter development, with input from Marly and me.

After Rose Marie and Janet returned from Sweden, the work began in earnest. Rose Marie and CEP team member **Beckie Middendorf** began writing the book, continually adjusting its framework to ensure that it accurately reflected the functionality of the software and the best practices for instructing others in application development. **Maria Townsley** from the CEP team followed closely behind, providing developmental and technical editing as the manuscript drafts were revised and finessed.

Although this book is an exceptional instructional tool, it is also a true developer's guide. All of the content was technically reviewed by two of the world's premier EON Professional content developers, **Dennis Cafiero** and **Lloyd Churches**, both with EON Reality. Dennis and Lloyd also contributed to the thematic units and designed many of the book's simulations and activities.

In addition to those who were previously mentioned, there were many others who contributed to the success of this project: **Marek Kozlak** with EON Reality–Poland, who provided 3D applications that were used in some of the activities; **Julie Hotchkiss** and **Jan Clavey** with CEP, who copyedited and proofread the manuscript, respectively; and the following members of the KCTCS Interactive Digital Center: **Mary Helen Hendrix**, IDC Director, who provided IDC staff and facilities support; **Ray Osborne** and **Mark McComb**, who created simulations and the lesson opener images; and **Leah Mason**, who reviewed and proofed final pages.

This endeavor was approached by all of its participants with enthusiasm and optimism; our combined perseverance has resulted in a unique and well-designed adjunct to 3D application education and training environments. My heartfelt gratitude extends to all who made this project their own. Your contributions are greatly valued and appreciated.

Jamie Justice, Director
Visualized Learning and Innovation
Kentucky Community and Technical College System

Introduction

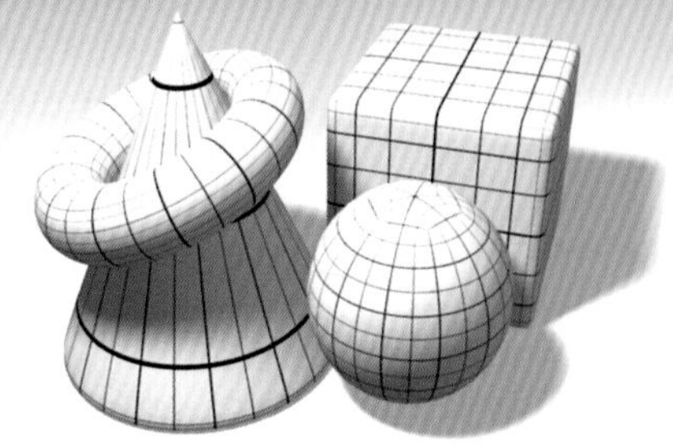

Interactive 3D Application Development: Using EON Professional for Creating 3D Visualizations will guide you through the application development process using EON Professional. This book contains interactive hands-on tutorials that will allow you to practice as you learn to use this very powerful software application. The content in the book is arranged in modules and developed in such a way that it enables you to choose specific topics to study on an as-needed basis. The modular design makes this book an indispensible tool for developing simplistic interactive objects as well as very high-end applications using EON Professional.

What Can You Achieve with This Book?

This book is designed for people who need to solve problems through the creation of interactive objects, basic interactive simulations, or fully developed 3D simulation applications using EON Studio or EON Professional. They may be new to or experienced in the use of application software for the development of interactive objects or 3D applications. This book also supports education and training programs as a resource that supplements instruction and helps individuals rapidly develop the knowledge and understanding required to create interactive, immersive 3D applications.

The design of this book is geared primarily toward all users of EON Professional. However, users of EON Studio software can use most of the hands-on activities within the book for training and technical support as well. Likewise, the book is designed for licensed users of the EON Professional software; however, you may complete many of the modules with a trial version of EON Studio.

If you are already familiar with EON Professional, this book will serve as a desk reference to provide solutions to common development challenges, tips and tricks, or specific skills that may need reinforcement. All users of this book will learn how EON Professional interacts with other software applications to fully unlock the development capabilities of EON Professional as a content creation tool.

What Are the Key Concepts in This Book?

This book provides comprehensive instruction in basic and advanced 3D application development using EON Professional. This practical, modularized, and hands-on approach enables you to create real-world solutions through simulations and step-by-step scenarios.

Some of the key concepts and operations covered in this book include the following:

- Using the EON Professional and EON Studio interface and creating your first simulation
- Fundamentals of EON Professional and 3D simulation development
- Importing 3D content from other applications and formats

- Object behaviors, object modification, and interactivity functions
- Viewports and cameras in EON Professional
- Creating user interfaces
- Adding sound and video to a 3D simulation
- Working with nodes and prototypes
- Integrating scripting into 3D simulations
- Running simulations on end user computers and distribution of EON applications

Licensing Information

EON is protected by a licensing system named FlexLM. This system requires you to provide your computer's host ID to EON Reality, which then uses it to generate a license file. You install the license by putting the file on your computer under C:\WINDOWS\FlexLM\. When you start EON software, EON verifies that the host ID from your computer matches the host ID in the license file and that the license file is authentic. If a valid EON Studio license is missing, EON will only run in Demo mode and you will not be able to save your content.

Host ID

A host ID is a number or series of numbers and letters from your computer's hardware that uniquely identifies your computer. You cannot choose or change your host ID. A host ID could be the Media Access Control (MAC) address (also known as the physical address or Ethernet address) from your network adapter or a serial disk number from your hard disk. If you replace the network card on your computer, then your license may stop working because the host ID was from a different network card.

There are several methods to retrieve your host ID. One method is:

1. Click Start > Run.
2. Type cmd in the Open text box and press Enter, or click OK.
3. Type getmac and press Enter.

The Physical Address displayed in the cmd.exe window is the host ID.

Another method to retrieve your host ID is to use the FlexLM License Manager. This software is installed with EON software and is accessed via the Control Panel of your computer. To use this method:

1. Open the Control Panel.
2. Double-click the FLEXlm License Manager icon.
3. Click the Diagnostics tab.
4. Click the Hostid's button to display the flexlm dialog box.

The dialog box shows the host ID next to "Internet =" and displays the serial disk number. Sometimes, you will have several host IDs because you have several network adapters. To avoid problems, it is best to provide all host IDs.

A third method to retrieve your host ID is to use a host ID tool that you can download from the support site. Directions for using a host ID tool can be found within its Help system.

License File

After you receive an EON license, place the EON Studio license file in the WINDOWS directory, which is usually located in C:\WINNT\FlexLM or C:\WINDOWS\FlexLM depending on whether you have Windows NT2000, Windows 98/XP/ME, or Windows Vista. The license file is typically named license.dat, so a default installation will expect that name. However, you can rename it anything you like as long as you tell the FlexLM License Manager which file it is. To do this, launch FlexLM License Manager from Control Panel, select the Setup tab, and next to License File, click the Browse button to select the license file.

If you open a license file in a text editor program, you will see that it consists of several features. The features depend on what products you have purchased or requested licenses for. There are separate license features for EON Studio and each EON module. If the license for an EON module is missing, the functionality may still be available if the module is checked in the Options > Modules dialog box. However, if a module is active but no license is available, the Save functionality is disabled.

You can have only one active license file at a time. If you have requested a license for one product and then later request another license for another product, you will need to copy the license features from one file to the other using Copy and Paste.

There are several license types. Normally, a license is "node locked," meaning it will only work for one computer. A floating (or network) license allows a set number of computers to be licensed by contacting the computer over a local area network. Licenses can also be temporary or permanent. Often, temporary licenses are provided until proof of purchase is obtained by the license-generating staff.

Note that attempts to change the system clock to increase a temporary license period will fail because FlexLM will detect this action. If this is attempted, it will no longer be possible to issue a temporary license for that computer.

Requesting a License from EON Reality

Request all license files from our support site, *support.eonreality.com*. You need to log on with a valid account and then select the Request License link.

EON Professional Licensing

EON Professional includes additional EON Studio modules that are licensed using the same FlexLM licensing system described previously. However, the EON Professional package also includes a separate tool named EON CAD.

EON CAD Module

For industrial users, EON Professional comes with an advanced computer-aided design (CAD) and 3D data exchange module for simple and fast optimization and conversion to native EON formats. Among the more than thirty supported formats in the base modules are AutoCAD, CADKEY, IGES, Maya, 3ds Max, LightWave, Autodesk® Softimage®, and Solidworks. In addition, users can benefit from features such as key frame support, automated normal correction, welding of vertices, geometry/surface reduction, and infinite variable adjustable tessellation while UV mapping and textures are maintained.

EON CAD is developed in cooperation with Right Hemisphere® and builds on the successful Deep Exploration™ product and the Polytools and CoreCAD modules, together with proprietary EON technology. The EON plug-in makes it possible to save CAD and DCC files in various EON formats. Also, you can add available native CAD extensions, such as MicroStation, CATIA, Alias, Unigraphics, Pro/ENGINEER, and STEP, with direct translation to EON's native EOZ or EOP formats, including batch conversion. EON CAD also allows you to view and optimize many 3D formats before exporting to EON format.

To use EON CAD, you require two licenses: an EON CAD license and a Deep Exploration license. The EON CAD license uses the FlexLM system, so there will be an EON CAD feature in the license.dat file. A Deep Exploration license requires a serial number and activation code that will be entered in a dialog box accessed under the Help menu.

You will need to activate the EON CAD module with a license key before you can use the tool to export content from the Right Hemisphere® Deep Exploration™ CAD Edition to a format that can be used by EON Professional. Without purchasing these additional license keys, you can view but not export content in the EON CAD window to EON. Deep Exploration also offers additional CAD format modules by purchasing additional activation codes, which you will need if you want to convert CAD formats to EON format.

Installing the EON Professional Software

To avoid problems during installation, uninstall any previous versions of EON Studio and reboot the computer before beginning a new installation.

To install EON software:

1. Insert the EON DVD. The EON Installation Launcher will be displayed automatically. If no display appears, go to step 2; otherwise proceed to step 5.
2. Choose Run from the Start menu.
3. Enter the file path to the autorun.exe file in the DVD drive, such as D:\autorun.exe in the dialog box.
4. Click the OK button.
5. Select the EON software you want to install by placing a check mark in the appropriate check boxes in the menu. (Some check boxes are dependent on the selected options, so they will automatically be checked.)
6. Click the Install now button to begin the installation.

The installation will proceed. You will see a dialog box when the installation is complete.

System Requirements

Runtime Requirements

The following table lists the runtime requirements for creating and viewing a simulation based on your operating system.

Operating System	Comments
Windows 95/98/ME	DirectX 6.1 or higher is required. To view Cg-based materials, DirectX 9.0b or later is required. However, note that the EON Rendering mode must be set to OpenGL. Cg-materials do not work in Direct3D mode.
Windows NT 4.0	Service Pack 3 or later must be installed.
Windows 2000/XP	To view Cg-based materials, DirectX 9.0b or later is required. However, note that the EON Rendering mode must be set to OpenGL. Cg-materials do not work in Direct3D mode.
Windows Vista	To view Cg-based materials, DirectX 9.0b or later is required. However, note that the EON Rendering mode must be set to OpenGL. Cg-materials do not work in Direct3D mode.

The following table lists the graphics card driver requirements for viewing a simulation. In general, it is recommended that you always use the latest driver for your graphics card.

Graphics Card Driver	Version
NVIDIA-based graphics cards	NVIDIA® ForceWare™ 53.03 or later. GeForce™ FX 5200 or higher is required to view simulations with Cg-materials.
ATI-based graphics cards	Catalyst™ 4.10 or later. Radeon™ 9500 or higher is required to view simulations with Cg-materials.
Other brands	Latest driver. The graphics card must support vertex and fragment shader object OpenGL extension.

Requirements for Application Development

The following table lists the operating system requirements for authoring time for a simulation using EON Studio.

Operating System	Comments
Windows® 95	Not supported.
Windows NT® 4.0	Not supported.
Windows® 98/ME/2000/XP	DirectX 9.0b or higher is required.
Windows Vista®	DirectX 9.0b or higher is required.

Additionally, the system must have 512 MB or more of system memory.

Web Browser Support

Internet Explorer® 6 and 7 as well as Mozilla® Firefox® 2 are supported web browsers. EON does not support Opera™, Safari®, or Google™ Chrome.

Features and Conventions in This Book

This book was created specifically to serve as a tool for learning to develop interactive 3D applications using EON Professional. Communicating these technical concepts and extensive procedural information presents challenges for the learner and instructors alike. To make this book as clear as possible, many unique features have been incorporated into the lessons.

The task-based approach correlates the skills and concepts explained in each lesson to a specific set of actions, allowing you to learn by doing. The following pages highlight the many features that contribute to your learning experience. The following list identifies key features in each lesson:

- Each lesson begins with an **Objectives** list. This is a list of the learning objectives that correlates to the skills covered in the lesson.
- Important technical vocabulary terms are listed at the beginning of each lesson in the **Key Terms** section. When these terms are defined in the lesson, they appear in bold italic type. The **Glossary** contains all of the key terms and their definitions.
- Each module (other than Module 1) features a **Storyboard**, typically within the first lesson. This feature provides an overview of 3D application development and orients you to the segment of that process covered within the given module.
- Frequently placed **Activities** provide opportunities for hands-on practice. Numbered steps give detailed, step-by-step instructions to help you learn application development skills. These Activities also show results in screen images to match what you should see on your computer screen.
- **Illustrations** and **screen images** provide visual feedback as you work through the exercises. These reinforce the key concepts, provide visual clues about the steps, and allow you to verify your progress.
- When the book instructs you to click a particular button on the Toolbar or to select a node or a prototype, an image of the **button** or of the **icon** is shown next to the text.
- Engaging **marginal reader aids** are located throughout the lessons to provide helpful hints (*Tips & Tricks*), point out items to watch out for or avoid (*Troubleshooting*), or guide you to locations where you can obtain more information within the book (*Cross-Reference*) or via the Internet (*Web Links*).
- The *Discuss* **in-line reader aid** encourages you to think beyond the information presented and to explore avenues of thought on your own.
- The **Best Practices** feature alerts you to the preferred methods used by professionals in the field. Although it is not mandatory or required, the information provided in these features tells you how various tasks are handled in real-world situations.
- Each lesson ends with a **Summary** list. This is a list of all of the skills covered in the lesson.
- Each module ends with a **Simulation**. The Simulation is a set of tasks, of increasing difficulty, that allows you to test your knowledge of the concepts covered within that module as well as all previous modules.

Lesson Features

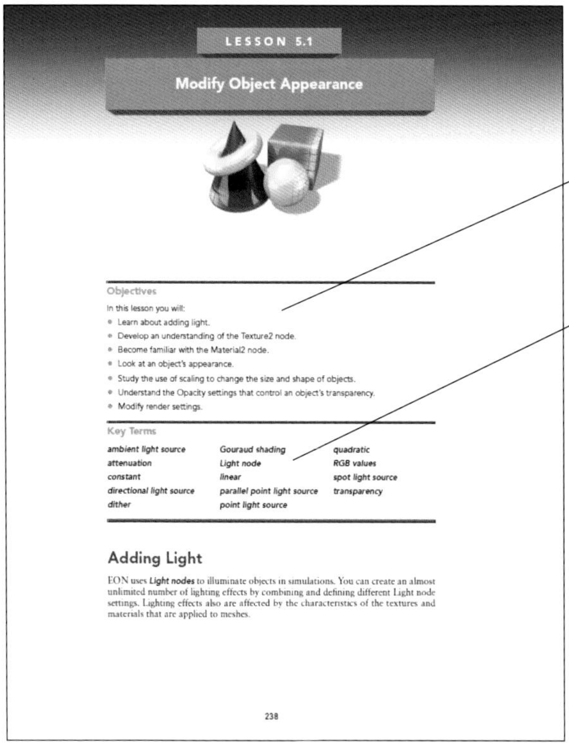
LESSON 5.1

Modify Object Appearance

Objectives

In this lesson you will:

- Learn about adding light.
- Develop an understanding of the Texture2 node.
- Become familiar with the Material2 node.
- Look at an object's appearance.
- Study the use of scaling to change the size and shape of objects.
- Understand the Opacity settings that control an object's transparency.
- Modify render settings.

Key Terms

ambient light source	*Gouraud shading*	*quadratic*
attenuation	*Light node*	*RGB values*
constant	*linear*	*spot light source*
directional light source	*parallel point light source*	*transparency*
dither	*point light source*	

Adding Light

EON uses ***Light nodes*** to illuminate objects in simulations. You can create an almost unlimited number of lighting effects by combining and defining different Light node settings. Lighting effects also are affected by the characteristics of the textures and materials that are applied to meshes.

238

Lesson Objectives

Key Terms

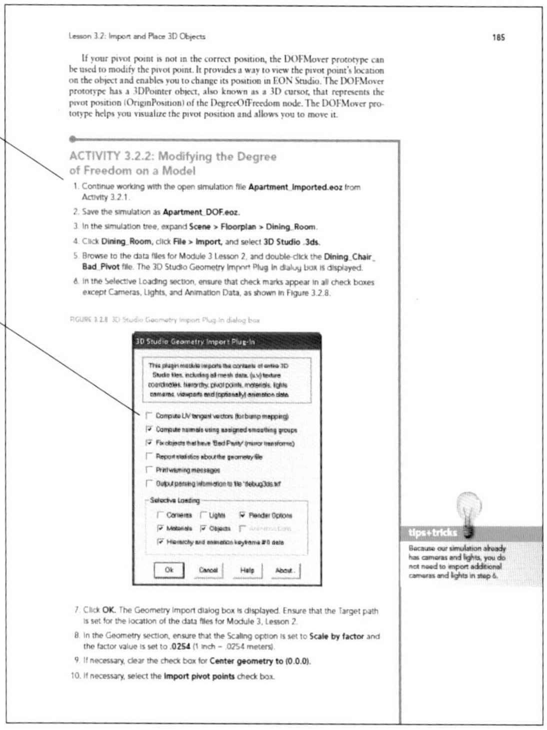
Lesson 3.2: Import and Place 3D Objects 185

If your pivot point is not in the correct position, the DOFMover prototype can be used to modify the pivot point. It provides a way to view the pivot point's location on the object and enables you to change its position in EON Studio. The DOFMover prototype has a 3DPointer object, also known as a 3D cursor, that represents the pivot position (OriginPosition) of the DegreeOfFreedom node. The DOFMover prototype helps you visualize the pivot position and allows you to move it.

ACTIVITY 3.2.2: Modifying the Degree of Freedom on a Model

1. Continue working with the open simulation file **Apartment_Imported.eoz** from Activity 3.2.1.
2. Save the simulation as **Apartment_DOF.eoz.**
3. In the simulation tree, expand **Scene > Floorplan > Dining_Room.**
4. Click **Dining_Room,** click **File > Import,** and select **3D Studio .3ds.**
5. Browse to the data files for Module 3 Lesson 2, and double-click the **Dining_Chair_Bad_Pivot** file. The 3D Studio Geometry Import Plug In dialog box is displayed.
6. In the Selective Loading section, ensure that check marks appear in all check boxes except Cameras, Lights, and Animation Data, as shown in Figure 3.2.8.

FIGURE 3.2.8 3D Studio Geometry Import Plug-In dialog box

7. Click **OK.** The Geometry Import dialog box is displayed. Ensure that the Target path is set for the location of the data files for Module 3, Lesson 2.
8. In the Geometry section, ensure that the Scaling option is set to **Scale by factor** and the factor value is set to **.0254** (1 inch – .0254 meters).
9. If necessary, clear the check box for **Center geometry to (0.0.0).**
10. If necessary, select the **Import pivot points** check box.

tips+tricks

Because our simulation already has cameras and lights, you do not need to import additional cameras and lights in step 6.

Hands-on Activity

Screen images

Web Links reader aid

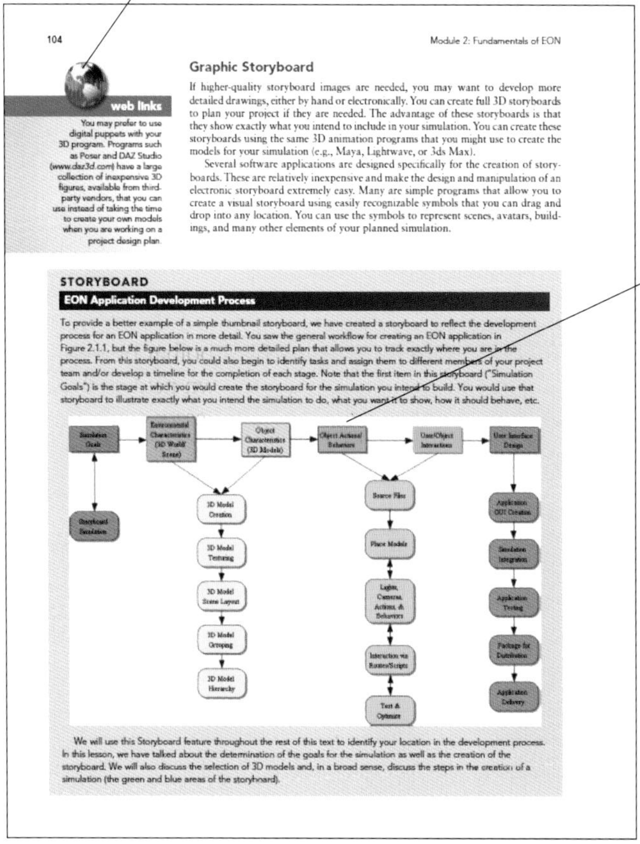
104 Module 2: Fundamentals of EON

Graphic Storyboard

If higher-quality storyboard images are needed, you may want to develop more detailed drawings, either by hand or electronically. You can create full 3D storyboards to plan your project if they are needed. The advantage of these storyboards is that they show exactly what you intend to include in your simulation. You can create these storyboards using the same 3D animation programs that you might use to create the models for your simulation (e.g., Maya, Lightwave, or 3ds Max).

Several software applications are designed specifically for the creation of storyboards. These are relatively inexpensive and make the design and manipulation of an electronic storyboard extremely easy. Many are simple programs that allow you to create a visual storyboard using easily recognizable symbols that you can drag and drop into any location. You can use the symbols to represent scenes, avatars, buildings, and many other elements of your planned simulation.

web links

You may prefer to use digital puppets with your 3D program. Programs such as Poser and DAZ Studio (www.daz3d.com) have a large collection of inexpensive 3D figures, available from third-party vendors, that you can use instead of taking the time to create your own models when you are working on a project design plan.

STORYBOARD

EON Application Development Process

To provide a better example of a simple thumbnail storyboard, we have created a storyboard to reflect the development process for an EON application in more detail. You saw the general workflow for creating an EON application in Figure 2.1.1, but the figure below is a much more detailed plan that allows you to track exactly where you are in the process. From this storyboard, you could also begin to identify tasks and assign them to different members of your project team and/or develop a timeline for the completion of each stage. Note that the first item in this storyboard ("Simulation Goals") is the stage at which you would create the storyboard for the simulation you intend to build. You would use that storyboard to illustrate exactly what you intend the simulation to do, what you want it to show, how it should behave, etc.

We will use this Storyboard feature throughout the rest of this text to identify your location in the development process. In this lesson, we have talked about the determination of the goals for the simulation as well as the creation of the storyboard. We will also discuss the selection of 3D models and, in a broad sense, discuss the steps in the creation of a simulation (the green and blue areas of the storyboard).

Storyboard

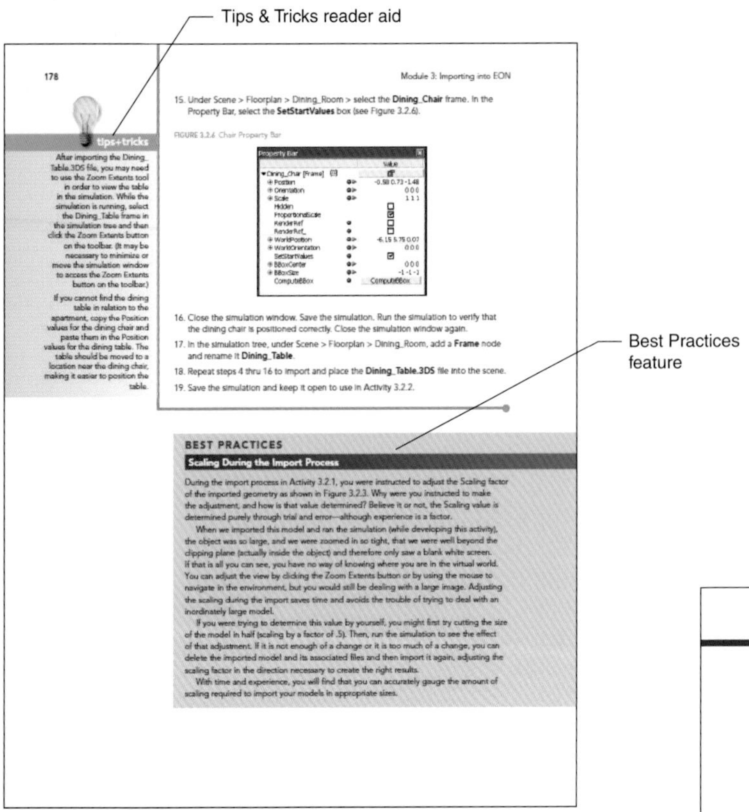

178 Module 3: Importing into EON

tips+tricks

After importing the Dining_Table.3DS file, you may need to use the Zoom Extents tool in order to view the table in the simulation. While the simulation is running, select the Dining_Table frame in the simulation tree and then click the Zoom Extents button on the toolbar. (It may be necessary to minimize or move the simulation window to access the Zoom Extents button on the toolbar.)

If you cannot find the dining table in relation to the apartment, copy the Position values for the dining chair and paste them in the Position values for the dining table. The table should be moved to a location near the dining chair, making it easier to position the table.

15. Under Scene > Floorplan > Dining_Room > select the **Dining_Chair** frame. In the Property Bar, select the **SetStartValues** box (see Figure 3.2.6).

FIGURE 3.2.6 Chair Property Bar

16. Close the simulation window. Save the simulation. Run the simulation to verify that the dining chair is positioned correctly. Close the simulation window again.
17. In the simulation tree, under Scene > Floorplan > Dining_Room, add a **Frame** node and rename it **Dining_Table**.
18. Repeat steps 4 thru 16 to import and place the **Dining_Table.3DS** file into the scene.
19. Save the simulation and keep it open to use in Activity 3.2.2.

BEST PRACTICES

Scaling During the Import Process

During the import process in Activity 3.2.1, you were instructed to adjust the Scaling factor of the imported geometry as shown in Figure 3.2.3. Why were you instructed to make the adjustment, and how is that value determined? Believe it or not, the Scaling value is determined purely through trial and error—although experience is a factor.

When we imported this model and ran the simulation (while developing this activity), the object was so large, and we were zoomed in so tight, that we were well beyond the clipping plane (actually inside the object) and therefore only saw a blank white screen. If that is all you can see, you have no way of knowing where you are in the virtual world. You can adjust the view by clicking the Zoom Extents button or by using the mouse to navigate in the environment, but you would still be dealing with a large image. Adjusting the scaling during the import saves time and avoids the trouble of trying to deal with an inordinately large model.

If you were trying to determine this value by yourself, you might first try cutting the size of the model in half (scaling by a factor of .5). Then, run the simulation to see the effect of that adjustment. If it is not enough of a change or it is too much of a change, you can delete the imported model and its associated files and then import it again, adjusting the scaling factor in the direction necessary to create the right results.

With time and experience, you will find that you can accurately gauge the amount of scaling required to import your models in appropriate sizes.

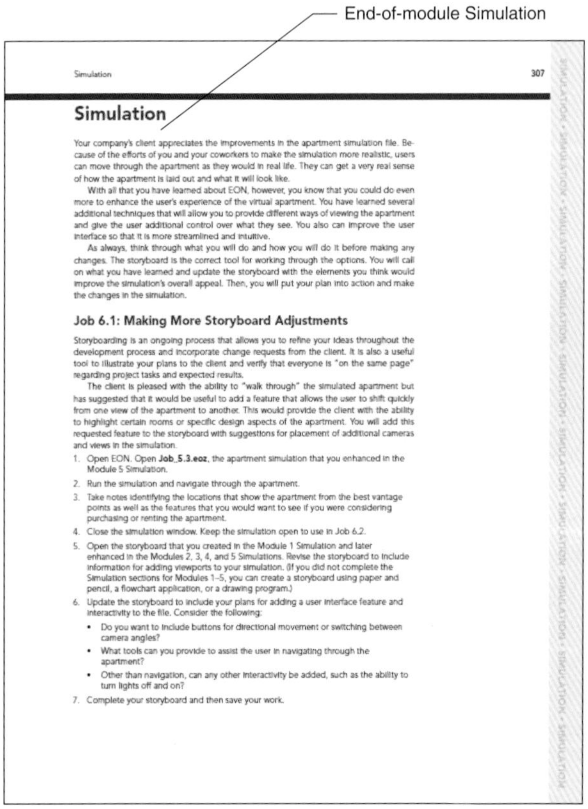

Simulation 307

Simulation

Your company's client appreciates the improvements in the apartment simulation file. Because of the efforts of you and your coworkers to make the simulation more realistic, users can move through the apartment as they would in real life. They can get a very real sense of how the apartment is laid out and what it will look like.

With all that you have learned about EON, however, you know that you could do even more to enhance the user's experience of the virtual apartment. You have learned several additional techniques that will allow you to provide different ways of viewing the apartment and give the user additional control over what they see. You also can improve the user interface so that it is more streamlined and intuitive.

As always, think through what you will do and how you will do it before making any changes. The storyboard is the correct tool for working through the options. You will call on what you have learned and update the storyboard with the elements you think would improve the simulation's overall appeal. Then, you will put your plan into action and make the changes in the simulation.

Job 6.1: Making More Storyboard Adjustments

Storyboarding is an ongoing process that allows you to refine your ideas throughout the development process and incorporate change requests from the client. It is also a useful tool to illustrate your plans to the client and verify that everyone is "on the same page" regarding project tasks and expected results.

The client is pleased with the ability to "walk through" the simulated apartment but has suggested that it would be useful to add a feature that allows the user to shift quickly from one view of the apartment to another. This would provide the client with the ability to highlight certain rooms or specific design aspects of the apartment. You will add this requested feature to the storyboard with suggestions for placement of additional cameras and views in the simulation.

1. Open EON. Open **Job_5.3.eoz**, the apartment simulation that you enhanced in the Module 5 Simulation.
2. Run the simulation and navigate through the apartment.
3. Take notes identifying the locations that show the apartment from the best vantage points as well as the features that you would want to see if you were considering purchasing or renting the apartment.
4. Close the simulation window. Keep the simulation open to use in Job 6.2.
5. Open the storyboard that you created in the Module 1 Simulation and later enhanced in the Modules 2, 3, 4, and 5 Simulations. Revise the storyboard to include information for adding viewports to your simulation. (If you did not complete the Simulation sections for Modules 1–5, you can create a storyboard using paper and pencil, a flowchart application, or a drawing program.)
6. Update the storyboard to include your plans for adding a user interface feature and interactivity to the file. Consider the following:
   - Do you want to include buttons for directional movement or switching between camera angles?
   - What tools can you provide to assist the user in navigating through the apartment?
   - Other than navigation, can any other interactivity be added, such as the ability to turn lights off and on?
7. Complete your storyboard and then save your work.

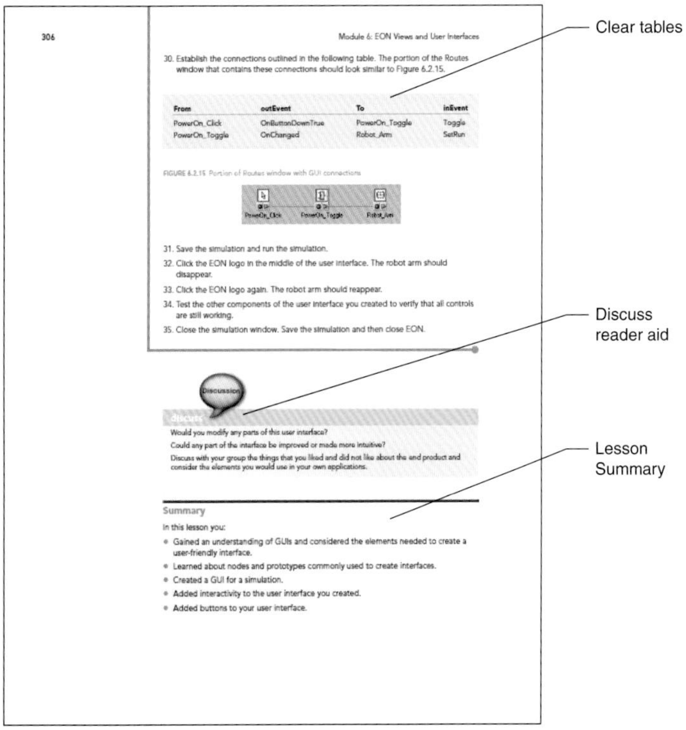

306 Module 6: EON Views and User Interfaces

30. Establish the connections outlined in the following table. The portion of the Routes window that contains these connections should look similar to Figure 6.2.15.

From	outEvent	To	inEvent
PowerOn_Click	OnButtonDownTrue	PowerOn_Toggle	Toggle
PowerOn_Toggle	OnChanged	Robot_Arm	SetRun

FIGURE 6.2.15 Portion of Routes window with GUI connections

31. Save the simulation and run the simulation.
32. Click the EON logo in the middle of the user interface. The robot arm should disappear.
33. Click the EON logo again. The robot arm should reappear.
34. Test the other components of the user interface you created to verify that all controls are still working.
35. Close the simulation window. Save the simulation and then close EON.

discuss

Would you modify any parts of this user interface?

Could any part of the interface be improved or made more intuitive?

Discuss with your group the things that you liked and did not like about the end product and consider the elements you would use in your own applications.

Summary

In this lesson you:

- Gained an understanding of GUIs and considered the elements needed to create a user-friendly interface.
- Learned about nodes and prototypes commonly used to create interfaces.
- Created a GUI for a simulation.
- Added interactivity to the user interface you created.
- Added buttons to your user interface.

Conventions Used in This Book

This book uses particular fonts, symbols, and heading conventions to highlight important information or to call your attention to specific items. For more information about the features in each lesson, refer to the Lesson Features on the previous pages.

Convention	Meaning
A sound with both position and orientation has a ***sound cone.***	Key terms appear in bold italic when they are defined in the lesson.
From the menu bar, choose **File > Import > 3D Studio .3ds.**	Any key you should press or any button or item on the screen you should click or select will appear in bold.
In the Property Bar, change the MaxWidth and MaxHeight to **16**.	Any text you are asked to key appears in bold.
Open **Activity_7.1.2.eoz** from the data files for Module 7 Lesson 1.	The names of data files and solution files will appear in bold for easy identification.
	*Tips & Tricks* provide helpful hints related to particular tasks and topics or alternative ways of accomplishing a particular task.
	*Troubleshooting* addresses common problems and pitfalls and, where applicable, provides solutions if you encounter these problems.
	*Cross-Reference* provides pointers to information discussed elsewhere within the book.
	*Web Links* provides pointers to additional information or avenues of study found on the Internet.
	*Discuss* reader aids provide queries to engage you in thinking further about what you are doing and what is possible.

Support for This Book

Although every effort has been made to provide accurate and detailed information in this book, we recognize that you may want to recommend corrections or changes or provide other user feedback. If so, please contact *so_idcteam@kctcs.edu.*

You may also contact EON Reality to order more copies of this book or for additional software or upgrades at:

EON Reality, Inc.
39 Parker St., Suite 100
Irvine, CA 92618
U.S.A.
Phone: +1 (949) 460-2000
Fax: +1 (949) 460-2004
Website for downloading software and licensing issues: *support.eonreality.com*
E-mail regarding book orders: *booksales@eonreality.com*

Downloads and Updates

To obtain additional information, downloads, or updates for the EON software or companion software, the web addresses listed below will be helpful.

Web site for EON's family of products and demos: *www.eonreality.com*
DirectX: *www.microsoft.com/directx/*
Windows NT Service pack: *www.microsoft.com/*
Adobe® Reader®: *www.adobe.com/*
Graphics cards and drivers:
www.nvidia.com
www.amd.com

Installing the Data Files

The enclosed CD provides easy access to all simulations and hands-on training content. When you begin working through the simulations and activities in this book, create a folder on your hard drive to save your work as you develop your skills with EON Professional.

You also may find it easier to work with the supplied files if you copy the data files from the CD to your hard drive before you begin your work. (This also provides a useful backup for the data files.) Simply create a folder on your local drive, insert the CD, and then use Windows Explorer to copy the data files from the CD to the desired folder on your local drive. The files are separated into folders based on the module and lesson in which they are used or, in the case of solution files, the lesson in which they are saved.

Once you have copied the data files to your local drive, you are ready to begin learning to use EON Professional using the activities outlined in this book. Use the solution files to check your work. You can also use any of these files as starting points for your own simulations and as samples to reference in your future work as an application developer.

HARALD SUND

MODULE 1

Getting Started with EON Studio

LESSON 1.1
Introduction to Interactive 3D Environments

LESSON 1.2
EON Studio Workspace

LESSON 1.3
Introducing EON Nodes and Basic Prototypes

LESSON 1.1

Introduction to Interactive 3D Environments

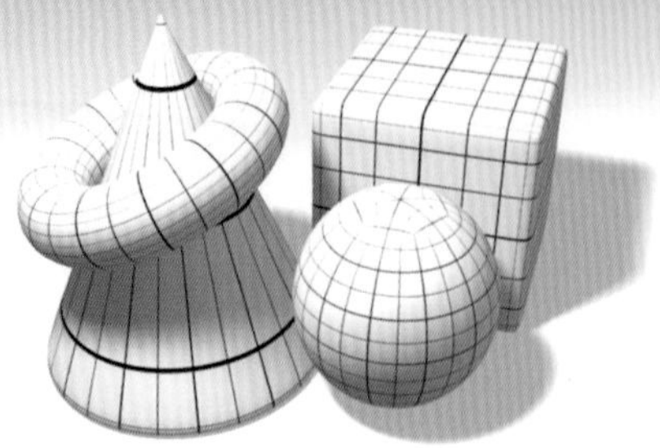

Objectives

In this lesson you will:

- Learn about visualization, simulation, and virtual reality.
- Develop an understanding of serious games and their role in the modern world.
- Consider EON Studio and EON Professional as authoring tools for 3D simulation.
- Understand the requirements for using EON Dynamic Load.
- Examine the available EON display systems.
- Become familiar with using navigation tools in the EON environment.
- Study the overall simulation development process.

Key Terms

animation
computer graphics
computer simulation
Computer-Assisted Virtual Environment (CAVE)
edutainment
face validation
immersive
mathematical models
multi-pass rendering
plug-in
serious game
virtual reality (VR)
visualization

Visualization and Simulation

Visualization, defined in the most basic way, is any technique in which an image is used to communicate a message. Within the confines of this definition, visualization has been around since the cavemen first decorated the walls of their homes with pictures and diagrams. A more modern understanding of visualization, however, is the use of visual imagery, diagrams, and animations as an effective way to communicate both abstract and concrete ideas. It impacts the way we work, play, and entertain ourselves. Entertainment, in fact, may be the most familiar application of three-dimensional (3D) visualization to most people. However, 3D visual content is rapidly evolving to improve the way we communicate, build, design, create, and teach. Visualization today has continually expanding applications in science, medicine, engineering, and education. This is primarily because of the introduction of computer graphics and the development of animation.

Various terminologies are used to describe visualization today—and many fields of study interact with and are a part of visualization. *Computer graphics, animation, simulation,* and *virtual reality* are some of the more common and broadly used terms that express methods of visualization, and these terms are often used synonymously. Another term that is gaining in popularity is *serious games.* These terms are each discussed in the following section, with examples that explain their differences and similarities.

Disciplines and Definitions

Computer simulation is the discipline of designing a model of an actual or theoretical physical scenario, executing the model on a digital computer, and in some cases analyzing the output. Simulations are similar to games in that they transport the user to another environment where the user controls the action. To understand simulation, it is useful to compare it with other fields such as computer graphics/animation and virtual reality. These fields all have much in common and often overlap.

- ***Computer graphics*** is the computational study of light and its effect on a geometric object. The use of computer graphics enhances the understanding of science, engineering, medicine, education, and business by enabling the generation, production, and display of synthetic renderings of natural objects with realism almost indistinguishable from photographs. Computer graphics aids in the production of images that range in complexity from simple line drawings to three-dimensional reconstructions of data obtained from computerized axial tomography (CAT) scans in medical applications.
- ***Animation*** is the use of computer graphics to generate a sequence of frames that, when viewed in rapid succession, produces the illusion of a moving picture.
- ***Virtual reality (VR)*** is a form of human-computer interaction in which a real or imaginary environment is simulated. A number of technologies are on the horizon that will provide an immersive environment or that of ***immersive*** human-computer interaction as found in various technological devices such as head-mounted displays (HMDs), position sensors, and data gloves. Another area, haptic computing, which adds the sense of touch to the simulated or virtual environment, is already being used in medical training and other critical content areas. Employing such devices, users are able to interact with and manipulate a virtual world. They travel within the simulated world, moving where they like and interacting with things by manipulating objects. If the virtual reality is successful, users feel that they are really present in the simulated world and that their experience in the virtual world matches what they would experience in a real environment like the one that has been simulated. This sensation is referred to as engagement, immersion, or presence—and it is this quality that distinguishes virtual reality from other forms of human-computer interaction.

Think of simulation as the "engine" behind the graphics and VR technologies. By creating simulations (creating a model, executing the model, and analyzing the output), you build the infrastructure necessary for other fields.

For computer animation, the ultimate test is that it "looks good" to the viewer. For computer simulations, however, this is only one component of validation (called ***face validation***). As long as you are not working in the fields of engineering or science, creating a geometric model that "looks good" as it undergoes motion is often satisfactory. However, if you are trying to validate a mathematical model, you must be concerned with more than mere looks.

Those working in virtual reality are more interested in the human-machine interaction and not so much with the mathematical models that actually create the artificial reality. For such models, however, computer graphics (for representing the geometry) and computer simulation (for representing the dynamic movements) are required.

Today, you can find simulations being used everywhere. If you talk with people from different walks of life who work in a variety of fields, you will undoubtedly find that they are using simulation at some point in their daily lives. For instance, someone working in wetlands restoration might utilize simulations of hydrology, population growth, and decay for wildlife species in a given geographic region; someone in astronomy might simulate the collision of galaxies and the formation of dark matter. Simulation allows these workers to explore their worlds without running extensive physical on-site experiments that tend to be expensive (both in time and money) or, in some cases, entirely impossible.

Simulations and Games

At the beginning of this discussion, we mentioned that simulations are similar to games. In both, the user controls the actions in another world by applying what they know. But simulations are different from games in three significant ways:

1. Instead of trying to win, as you would in a game, a user of a simulation takes on serious responsibilities—benefiting or suffering from the decisions made.
2. As users travel through a game, their progression is linear (moving along a clearly defined path). In a simulation, the user's progression is nonlinear, or branching—each new set of issues or problems is a direct result of decisions made earlier.
3. Simulations are governed by ever-changing and authentic relationships between several variables, whereas games are governed by rules that are not necessarily realistic.

Simulations embody the principle of *learn by doing*. The use of simulations is an activity that is as natural as a child who role-plays. Children learn to understand the world around them by simulating (with toys and figurines) their interactions with people, animals, and objects. Computer simulation is the electronic equivalent of this type of role-playing.

tips+tricks

In 2002, the Woodrow Wilson International Center for Scholars in Washington D.C. launched a Serious Games Initiative to encourage the development of games that address policy and management issues. More focused subgroups began to appear in 2004, including Games for Change, which focuses on social issues and social change, and Games for Health, which addresses health care applications.

The most recent avenue of simulations is the creation of serious games. A ***serious game*** is a software application developed with game technology and game design principles, but for a primary purpose other than pure entertainment. These are also called *instructional simulations* and *games for learning*, and they were originally pioneered by the military in the 1960s. Serious games have grown in popularity as the power and flexibility of computer technology has increased.

Long before the term *serious game* came into wide use (primarily after the Serious Games Initiative of 2002), games were being developed for purposes other than entertainment. They were used, on a limited scale, for training and education. But it was the growing technical abilities of games to provide realistic settings that led to a re-examination of the concept of serious games in the late 1990s. Additionally, the development of multiplayer gaming led to an increase in games being used in training.

There is no single definition of *serious games*, though they are generally considered to be games designed to run on personal computers or video game consoles that are used for training, advertising, simulation, or education. An alternate, more formal definition would be the application of game concepts, technologies, and ideas to non-entertainment applications.

What sets serious games apart from other games being designed is the focus on specific and intentional learning outcomes to achieve serious, measurable, sustained changes in performance and behavior. Also, games being designed for learning bring to the game world a new, complex area of design because they must organize game play to focus on changing the beliefs, skills, and/or behaviors of those who play the game while preserving the entertainment aspects of the experience. Serious games are being designed for audiences from elementary and secondary education to college, graduate school, and corporate training. They can be of any genre, and many of them are considered a kind of ***edutainment*** (educational entertainment or entertainment-education).

Models

To simulate a physical scenario, you will first need to create a computerized, 3D model that represents the real, physical object. Sometimes 3D models are referred to as ***mathematical models*** because they are made up of a set of XYZ coordinate values that represent the surface geometry of the physical objects being modeled.

After a model has been developed, the next task is to animate the model using computer-based authoring tools specifically designed for that purpose. The resulting application steps through time, one frame at a time, while constantly updating state, event, and XYZ positional coordinate values for each 3D model in the simulation.

Simulation of physical objects and scenes can be created with varying degrees of accuracy. And, accordingly, models are designed with varying levels of detail—the more detailed the model, the more detailed the output in the simulation. High-detail models can consist of a hierarchy of subcomponents, each of which is a complex 3D model itself. The kind of output you need for your simulation will suggest the type of model you will use and the process that will be required to produce changed beliefs, skills, and behaviors.

Why Simulate?

There are many methods of modeling situations that do not involve simulation. So why would you choose to utilize a simulation? One reason is simply the need for an engaging, compelling, interactive experience whether it is for learning or just entertainment. Another reason to do a simulation is the exploration of a concept, idea, or product. Yet another is the overwhelming evidence that people learn better and retain more when they can "do" something rather than just read about it or watch someone else.

Simulation is often essential in the following instances:

- The model is very complex with many variables and interacting components.
- The relationships of the underlying variables are nonlinear.
- The model contains random variables.
- The model output will be visual, as in a 3D computer animation.

The power of simulation is that—even for easily solvable linear scenarios—3D interactive, immersive learning, and exploration techniques can be used to solve a large variety of problems.

A simulation can have the look and feel of a game, but it can still be utilized in many nongame environments, including business and military operations. The games are intended to provide an engaging, self-reinforcing environment in which to motivate and educate players. Other purposes for these kinds of games include marketing and advertisement. Currently, the largest users of serious games are the U.S. government and various medical professionals. But other commercial sectors are actively pursuing development of these types of tools as well—and EON is paving the way as people find new uses for computer simulations every day.

Today there is substantial interest in games for learning in education and for professional training, particularly in health care, manufacturing, aerospace, energy, advertising, and public policy. In fact, many colleges and universities are now offering certificates and degrees specifically in serious game design.

Serious Games in the Real World

The concept of using simulations or games for education dates back before the days of computers. For centuries armies have honed their skills through war games. During times of more modern wars, air raid drills allowed citizens to practice their plans for personal safety. And many school children are drilled on what to do in the event of emergencies, such as natural disasters or intruders in the school. Each of these simulates a particular situation and allows people to prepare for the real events through practice in controlled situations. But the first serious game using computer technology is often considered to be Army Battlezone. This project, spearheaded by Atari in 1980, was designed to use the Battlezone tank game for military training. Figure 1.1.1 illustrates the early graphics and simulation of the Battlezone game at play.

web links

Over the years, Atari has continued to alter and improve on the Battlezone game. Today, in a much-altered form, it is available for modern gaming systems. For more information on the history of the game, to play an online version of an early arcade game, or to see the modern game, go to *www.atari.com*.

FIGURE 1.1.1 View from inside the tank in Atari Battlezone, circa 1980

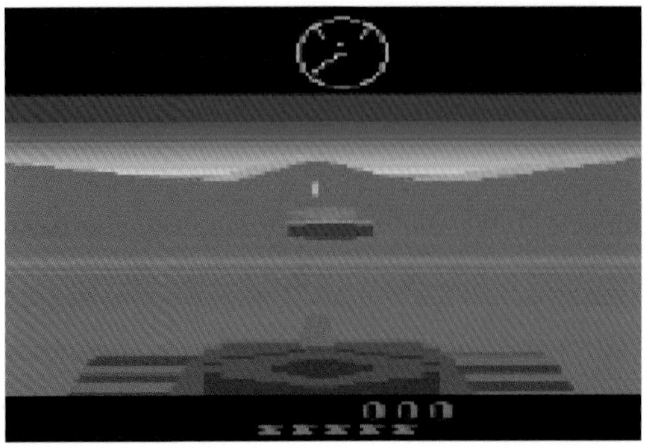

As we are all aware, games have the power to influence society—whether they are reality game shows on television, sporting events, or the latest craze that everyone is playing. Likewise, computer games are extending their influence into the serious business of military operations, medical education, emergency management training, and many other fields. Because of this, game technology is now bridging the gap between entertainment and work. Throughout the evolution of electronic and computer games, this gap existed because games were not seen as "serious" tools. But the incredible power of the personal computer, graphics cards, broadband Internet connections, intelligent software agents, accurate physics modeling engines, and accessible user interfaces is making it impossible to ignore the potential that these "toys" have in many real business world applications.

Traditional simulators often cost millions of dollars not only to develop, but also to deploy, and they generally require the purchase of specialized hardware. Because of this, in recent years, both business and military organizations have looked toward game developers to create low-cost simulations that are both accurate and engaging. Game developers' experience with game play and game design has made them prime candidates for developing these types of simulations.

Additionally, the cost of media for serious games is very low. Instead of volumes of media or computer hardware for high-end simulators, serious games can be packaged on a single DVD or CD-ROM, exactly like traditional computer and video games. Deploying these to the field requires nothing more than dropping them in the mail or posting them to a dedicated website.

Finally, although serious games are meant to train or otherwise educate users, they usually also strive to engage the player. In the course of simulating events and processes, many developers automatically inject entertainment and playability into their applications. Because most users are accustomed to seeing these attributes in their play, they are coming to expect it in their work as well.

As the people who initially experienced video games when they were children become the next generation of leaders in business, government, and the military, these technologies will continue to gain acceptance. The first generation of gamers are now entering the corner offices of the world, and they see these technologically powerful tools and techniques as not only acceptable, but also desirable.

Classifications and Subsets of Serious Games

The classification of serious games is something that has not yet been solidified. There are, however, a number of terms that are commonly used. These general terms and their definitions are listed in Table 1.1.1. The table is not all inclusive, but it does cover the major categories.

TABLE 1.1.1 Subsets of Serious Games

Serious Game Subset	Description
Advergaming	This is the practice of using video games to advertise a product, organization, or viewpoint. Often, a company provides interactive games on its website so that potential customers will be drawn to the game and spend time on the website where they will learn about the products the company offers. Some of these games are reworked arcade classics and others are new games developed exclusively for the company.
Edutainment	Also known as educational entertainment or entertainment-education, this is a form of entertainment designed to educate as well as to amuse. If the edutainment is successful, learning becomes fun because the teachers (or speakers) are both engaging and amusing. Edutainment typically uses some familiar form of entertainment such as television programs, computer or video games, films, music, websites, or multimedia software.
Games-based learning	Generally, these are games that are designed with a specific learning outcome in mind. Players need to retain and apply what they have learned about a specific subject in the course of the game play.
Edumarket games	These games are tools dedicated to communicating and educating people about social issues in particular.
Diverted or news games	These games discuss, in a direct way, political or geopolitical problems.
Simulations or simulation games	Also known as sim games, these are games that require the player to use a mixture of skill, chance, and strategy. They simulate aspects of real or fictional worlds or situations. Simulation games encompass a wide category that covers many titles such as MS Flight Simulator, SimCity, SimFarm, Civilization, RollerCoaster Tycoon, and The Sims. Simulation games are sometimes referred to as games of status or mixed games.
Persuasive games	These games are used as persuasion technology—a technology used to present or promote a point of view. These games are typically used in sales, diplomacy, politics, religion, military training, and management. Generally, these games are used to enhance a human face-to-face or voice interaction in order to sell to or persuade someone.
Organizational-dynamic games	These are serious games that teach and reflect the dynamics of organizations at three levels: individual behavior, group and network dynamics, and cultural dynamics. They are usually designed for the specific purpose of furthering personal development and character building, particularly in addressing complex organizational situations. They have a proven history of helping managers and decision makers better understand organizational dynamics, the diagnosis of organizational situations, and the impact of organizational interventions.

web links

An excellent example of an edumarket site is *www.food-force.com*, a website sponsored by the United Nations' World Food Program.

web links

Go to *www.newsgaming.com* for examples of diverted or news games. Two games offered here are "September 12th," a news game about the War on Terror, and "Madrid," a news game about terrorist attacks in Spain.

web links

An example of an organizational-dynamic game can be found at *www.calt.insead.edu/eis/*. In the EIS Simulation, participants working in groups are challenged to introduce an innovation in a division of the EuroComm corporation.

web links

The following websites provide some examples of advergaming:

Dyson, a United Kingdom bagless vacuum cleaner manufacturer, has two interesting puzzle games on its website, *www.dyson.co.uk/about/games/*.

Intel (*http://itmg2.intel.com/eng/*) has an IT manager game in which you play an IT manager who must manage the IT resources of a growing company.

Nurofen (ibuprofen), the leading analgesic brand in the United Kingdom, offers a game in which the players are in the shape of Nurofen Liquid Capsules with Nurofen branding. You race around the human body and try to be the first to reach the source of the pain. You must be a resident of the United Kingdom to play at *www.nurofen.co.uk/pinball/*.

A 3D real-time advergame developed for Toyota lets you get behind the wheel of a Yaris (*www.toyota.com/yaris/*) for a street-level tour of several cities. As you tour, you can win real prizes such as MP3 songs, city guides, and videos.

Examples of Serious Games

As we have discussed, serious games can be used to educate, instruct, and develop skills. Table 1.1.2 provides a sampling of some serious games.

TABLE 1.1.2 A Sampling of Serious Games

Serious Game Examples	Description
The Redistricting Game	Created by the University of Southern California Game Innovation Lab and available on the Internet, its goal is to teach people about congressional redistricting practices and options for reform.
Close Combat: First to Fight	This began as a United States Marine Corps training game and then was converted into a commercial game. It is now available for both Xbox and Microsoft Windows.
Dangerous Waters	Developed by a company that makes training simulators for various navies.
Darfur Is Dying	An online game by mtvU that simulates life in a Darfur refugee camp.
Food Force	A humanitarian video game available for personal computers. The United Nations' World Food Program designed this virtual world that includes food airdrops over crisis zones and trucks struggling up difficult roads under rebel threat with emergency food supplies.
Peacemaker	A commercial game simulation, designed for personal computers, that highlights the Israeli-Palestinian conflict. It was designed to promote dialog and understanding among Israelis and Palestinians, as well as anyone else in the world.
DoomEd	A single-player commercially available game for personal computers that combines scientific history and first-person shooter action. It explores bio-terrorism and World War II chemical experimentation.
Tactical Language & Culture Training System	A computer-based learning system that lets people quickly acquire functional knowledge of foreign languages and cultures. Current titles include Iraqi Arabic, Pashto, and French.
Re-Mission	Designed for personal computers, this 3D shooter game helps improve the lives of people living with cancer.
Full Spectrum Warrior	Began as a military training game that has been converted into a commercial game available for Xbox and Microsoft Windows.

Now that you have learned a bit about computer simulation and serious game terminology, take a few minutes to explore one of the many serious games that are available for learning and exploring a particular topic.

Activity 1.1.1: Exploring a Serious Game

1. If necessary, access the Internet and then open a browser application.
2. In the address field, key **www.redistrictinggame.org.**
3. Click **Play the Game.**
4. Read the brief description of each of the Missions that comprise the complete game.
5. Click **Basic** under Mission 1. Click **Click to Continue.** (You may need to install a more recent version of Adobe Flash. Follow the links and instructions given if this is necessary.)
6. Choose your party. In the next screen, click **Click to Continue.**

troubleshooting

You may see a message indicating that your browser is blocking pop-ups. If so, allow pop-ups in your browser to proceed with the game.

7. Read about your mission, click **Click to Continue,** then click **Begin Mission One.** You will see a map similar to the one shown in Figure 1.1.2.

FIGURE 1.1.2 Congressional district map

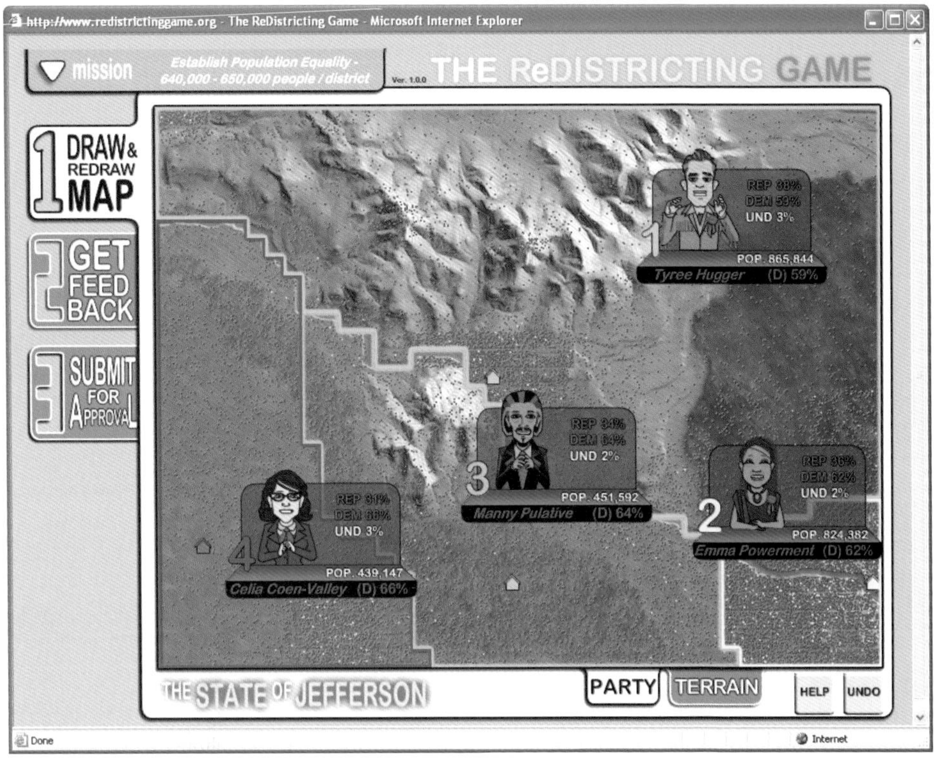

8. Redraw the district map to meet the population goals given for each district to complete your mission.
9. Click **2 Get Feedback** to see if your redistricting plan is likely to pass. Return to the map and redraw the district lines if it seems unlikely to pass.
10. Click **3 Submit for Approval** and watch to see if your redistricting plan passes.
11. Click **Fast forward to next election.** Note how the results of the election were impacted by the redistricting.
12. Click **Continue.**
13. Answer the survey questions and then click **Submit.**
14. If time permits, continue to explore the game by selecting another mission. If not, close the browser without saving the game.

Discussion

discuss

In what ways was this simulation effective? Would a report on how redistricting works be more or less effective as a tool for teaching?

What Does EON Bring to Simulation?

EON Reality, Inc. produces computer-based authoring software and multiple technology solutions for using the software. The software (primarily EON Studio and EON Professional) are tools for creating 3D interactive graphic simulations with which the viewer can interact. When viewers use the input tools on the computer to interact with these simulations, the results of their input are immediately reflected in the simulation.

The interactions made possible by EON can be:

- As simple as viewing a screen on which the simulation runs for the user to watch
- More complex, with the opportunity for the viewer to use input devices (keyboard, mouse, etc.) to manipulate the simulation showing on the screen
- Very complex, with the user utilizing VR peripherals such as touch-sensitive gloves and head-mounted displays to become part of the simulation

An individual using EON to build a simulation would import models and then position them, scale them appropriately, and add color, texture, and interactivity to the models. An EON user can interact in real time with the simulation.

Discussion

discuss

A user of a simulation might be a prospective customer or client who wants to "look into the future" with a real-time view of the product or design that she is negotiating to purchase. How would interaction with the simulation give the user an opportunity to make a better decision? How could it help with design creation before a product is actually completed?

EON Software

There are several different components that can comprise the EON software. The basic software components, which run on Microsoft Windows systems, are briefly outlined in Table 1.1.3. These will be described in greater detail in subsequent sections.

TABLE 1.1.3 EON Software Options

EON Software	Description
EON Studio	An authoring tool for developing interactive, 3D simulations
EON Professional	Builds on EON Studio but with a more robust set of modules, designed to meet specific developers' needs
EON SDK	A Software Development Kit (SDK) for constructing custom EON nodes and modules
EON Raptor	A plug-in for Autodesk's 3ds Max that provides fast viewing of large and complex content in real time
EON ICATCHER	An extension of EON Studio that includes features for interfacing with advanced display and integrated virtual reality (VR) systems. Common external devices and peripherals include: • Head-mounted displays (HMDs) • Gloves • I-glasses • Trackers • Quad-buffer stereo Also includes cluster visualization, which allows a simulation to be viewed on several monitors simultaneously, each one displaying a different viewpoint of the scene 

TABLE 1.1.3 EON Software Options *(continued)*

EON Software	Description
EON ICUBE	An extension of EON Studio that enables you to set up a multiwall immersive display system with up to six adjacent walls, forming a cube. It provides flawless image continuity in the corners and for perspective viewing 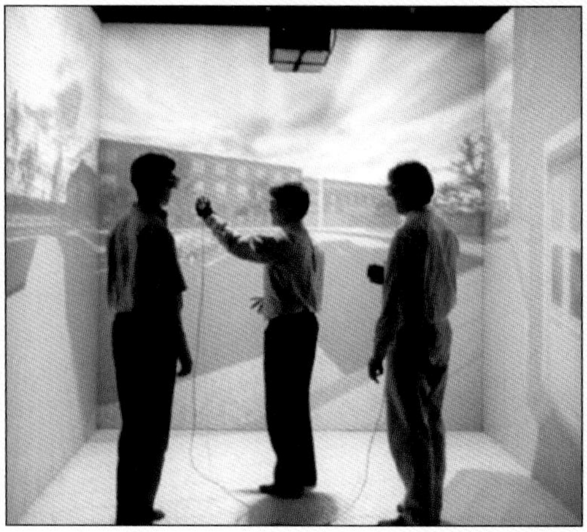

EON software gives you the ability to import predefined content from a multitude of sources and then add behavior and interactivity.

EON Studio

EON Studio is a complete graphical user interface (GUI)–based authoring tool for developing real-time 3D multimedia applications focused on sales/marketing, training/support, and visualization.

The development process includes importing 3D objects, usually originating from various modeling tools like 3D Studio Max (also known as 3ds Max) and LightWave 3D, or from computer-aided design (CAD) systems such as SolidWorks, ArchiCAD, or AutoCAD. EON Studio can import data in many different file formats.

After the model is imported, behaviors can easily be associated with the models through EON's intuitive graphical programming interface, simulation tree, node properties, event routing, scripting, or even compiled C++ code, using the EON SDK together with EON Studio. Figure 1.1.3 illustrates a model that has been brought into EON and is now being made into an interactive simulation.

tips+tricks

Scripting within EON Studio is based on either JScript (Microsoft's implementation of JavaScript) or VBScript (Visual Basic Script).

FIGURE 1.1.3 Using EON Studio to work with a model

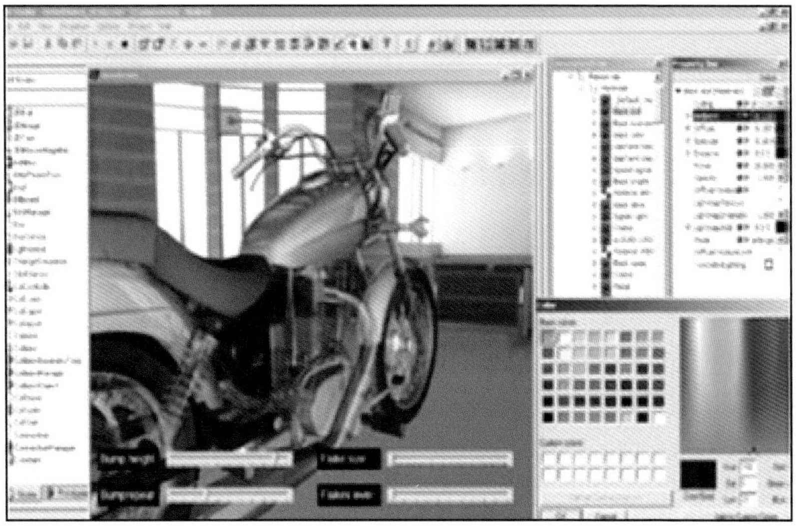

Finally, EON applications can be deployed over the Internet, as a standalone program on a CD-ROM, or at a kiosk. EON applications can also be integrated in other tools that support Microsoft's ActiveX components, such as Microsoft PowerPoint, Microsoft Word, Macromedia Authorware, Director, Shockwave, and Visual Basic.

EON Professional

EON Professional is an add-on product that extends EON Studio with four additional modules. These are each explained briefly in the following list and will be covered in more depth in later lessons.

tips+tricks

The terms mentioned here regarding advanced materials will be explained in later lessons.

- **Visual Effects:** The Visual Effects module of EON Professional creates real-time, ultra–high-quality, and flexible shading by taking advantage of the latest Cg (C programming language for graphics) shader technology available on the most recent generation of graphics cards—programmable graphics processing units (GPUs), which are also sometimes called visual processing units (VPUs). Advanced materials include Phong shading, bump mapping, darkmapping, cubical environment maps, high dynamic range (HDR) image-based lighting, leather, wood, fabric, and nonphotorealistic (NPR) hatch shading. Furthermore, completely custom materials can be created by writing your own Cg programs.
- **RPC Humans:** With this EON Professional human simulation module, you can import and use animated characters within EON Studio via remote procedure calls (RPCs) provided by ArchVision. This technology provides an easy way to visualize lots of human characters in an environment (without heavily taxing the rendering capacity) by using a billboard technique. EON Professional includes many RPC people and vegetation objects, and more can be purchased and imported from ArchVision. RPC humans in action can be seen in Figure 1.1.4.

FIGURE 1.1.4 Transportation terminal with animated people

- **Volume Shadows:** The Volume Shadows module adds dimension to the graphics in your EON applications by using realistic volume shadows that can be cast on any surface in the scene (including nonplanar). These can also be soft, volumetric shadows.
- **Physics Engine:** This EON Professional module adds lifelike animations to your EON applications using the correct laws of Newtonian physics.

These modules of EON Professional allow you to create a number of extremely detailed worlds. Figures 1.1.5 and 1.1.6 show just a couple of the possibilities of applications created with EON Professional.

FIGURE 1.1.5 Model in an artificial world

FIGURE 1.1.6 Real-world simulation

EON Professional also includes ***multi-pass rendering.*** With multi-pass rendering you can assign certain components to be a part of the initial scene (the first rendering) and then choose other effects to render as a second pass. This allows Cg shaders to create such effects as motion blur and distortion. For example, you could create the headlights of a car on the first pass and then, on the second pass, add a glow effect to the lights.

EON Dynamic Load

EON Dynamic Load enables developers to create highly configurable EON applications that load specific products or objects on demand (dynamically), thereby providing each user with a customized experience. Many objects are loaded dynamically at runtime from the Internet or a user's local disk, so they are not compiled within the simulation file and therefore decrease the overall size of the simulation file and reduce simulation load time.

The use of EON Dynamic Load requires a license to be purchased from EON Reality. There are four types of licenses to suit different situations:

- EON Server License
- Dynamic Load Stand Alone
- Licensed EDZ Application
- EON Studio License

Each of these allows downloading resources from different locations (local, Internet, or both). Some are valid for all users and some are just for a single user. And they are each implemented in different ways.

cross-reference

You will learn more about dynamic load and prototypes in Modules 8 and 9.

EON Display Systems

There are many different ways in which simulations created in EON can be displayed. The simplest, of course, is on a basic computer monitor. But there are other options for display that require the integration of computer software and VR hardware. Table 1.1.4 outlines some of the more common EON display options.

TABLE 1.1.4 EON Display Options

EON Display Systems	Description
Desktop Reality System	Allows natural interaction with the product through mouse or game controller movements
EON Artificial I	Allows users to experience 3D content appearing to float in space outside of the screen without the use of any glasses 
EON TouchLight	A bare-hand 3D interaction VR display system that allows users to interact with 3D objects without touching the screen 
Concave System	Curved screen that allows multiple users to fully immerse themselves in an all-surround stereoscopic virtual environment 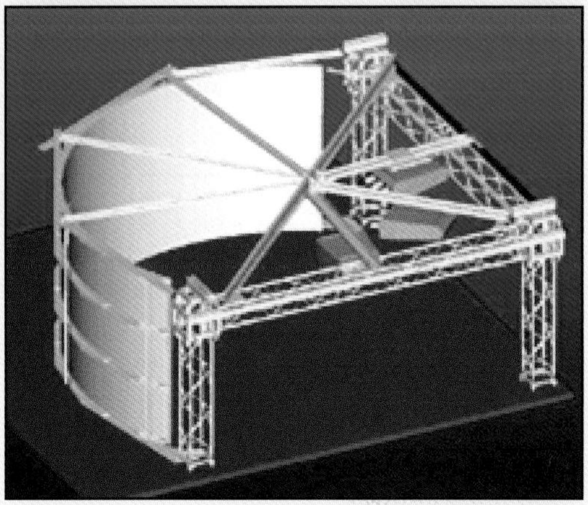

TABLE 1.1.4 EON Display Options *(continued)*

EON Display Systems	Description	
Head-Mounted VR–Immersive Reality System	Allows individuals to immerse themselves fully in the virtual environment through 3D imagery involving sight and motion. The user can navigate in the environment simply by using hand and head movements	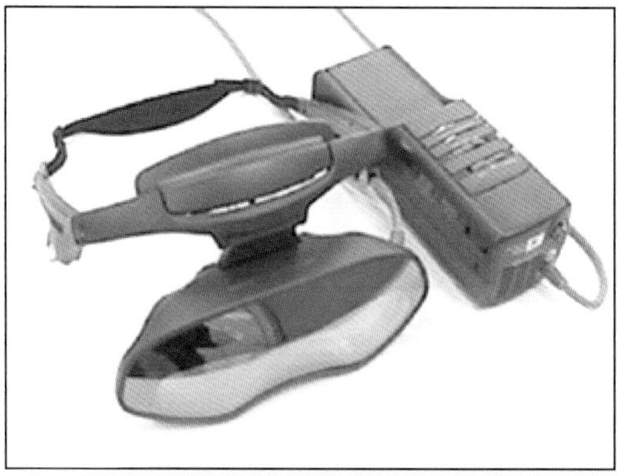
EON ICATCHER	The ultimate 3D stereo wall projection with realistic 3D imagery that is responsive to the user's actions	
Portable ICATCHER	An immersive stereoscopic turnkey display solution that uses an exclusive EON integrated hardware solution	
EON ICUBE	Multisided (3, 4, 5, or 6 walls) immersive environment in which participants are completely surrounded by virtual imagery and 3D sound	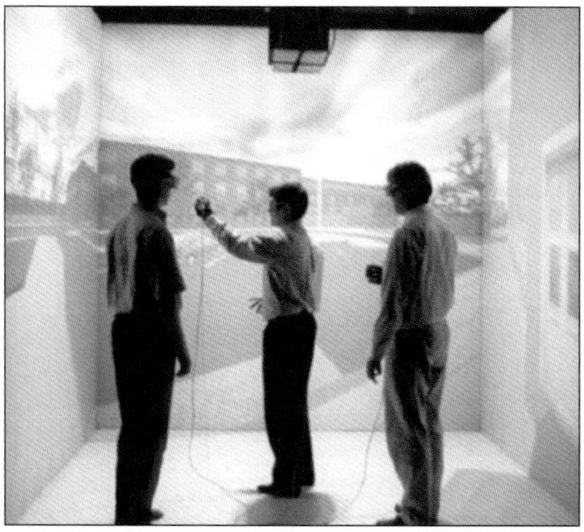

The EON ICUBE is what is commonly referred to as a ***Computer-Assisted Virtual Environment (CAVE)*** (a recursive acronym). This is an immersive, virtual reality environment where projectors are directed to three, four, five, or six of the walls of a room-sized cube.

Besides these impressive display systems, you can also publish an EON simulation to:

- Internet Explorer
- Microsoft PowerPoint
- Macromedia Director

tips+tricks

The first CAVE was demonstrated at the 1992 SIGGRAPH (Special Interest Group on Graphics and Interactive Techniques) conference.

EON Plug-Ins

A software ***plug-in*** is a small application that runs inside a larger application. EON has two optional plug-ins available:

- **Eon X:** A plug-in that is required for viewing an EON application within a website.
- **EON Raptor:** A plug-in for Autodesk's 3ds Max that gives you fast viewing of large and complex content in real time and allows you to save your 3D content in a format compatible with EON Studio/Professional. This is a free plug-in and is directly integrated into 3ds Max.

Navigating in EON Studio

Before you begin working in any software, you need to become familiar with the basics of the user interface—learning where various toolbars and windows are located. But, before we delve too far into all of the elements of the EON software, we thought it might be useful to get a little glimpse of an EON application in action. This will give you a better understanding of some of the options you can build into your own simulations.

When an EON application is running on a basic desktop system, you will typically be using a mouse, or perhaps a game controller, to navigate around the simulation. You can use these tools to move within the application, change your viewpoint, rotate the simulated object, and interact with the simulation in many other ways.

The obvious feature of a simulation is that it appears real and you can rotate and move the simulated object just as you would the real physical object represented by the 3D imagery.

The basic movements within EON and how they are accomplished with a mouse and keyboard are detailed in Table 1.1.5. Note that some of these movements are only possible in the EON simulation window or in the final published file. Some are not possible, for example, in the EON Viewer. Note also that the properties of the objects within a simulation can be changed from their defaults and could, therefore, behave differently if the creator of the simulation alters these settings.

TABLE 1.1.5 Navigating with a Mouse and Keyboard

Desired Movement	Description
Rotate	To be able to see the object from different directions, hold down the left mouse button and drag. The camera's orbit will change around its pivot position.
Zoom	To zoom in and out, hold down the right mouse button and drag. Alternately, you can press the Ctrl key and hold down the left mouse button and drag.
Pan	To pan the view, hold down the left and right mouse buttons simultaneously (or the middle mouse button) and drag. Alternately, you can press the Shift key and hold down the left mouse button and drag.

tips+tricks

Navigation can be done either with a three-button mouse or with various combinations of the mouse and the Ctrl and Shift keys.

Activity 1.1.2: Navigating in a Simulation

1. In a Windows Explorer window, browse to the data files for Module 1 Lesson 1.
2. From the file list, double-click **Activity_1.1.2.** This will launch EON Viewer. A simulation will automatically begin to play. You can choose to listen to the introduction or you can press **Esc.** After the introduction is complete (or you choose to skip it), your window should look similar to Figure 1.1.7.

FIGURE 1.1.7 Simulation in EON Viewer

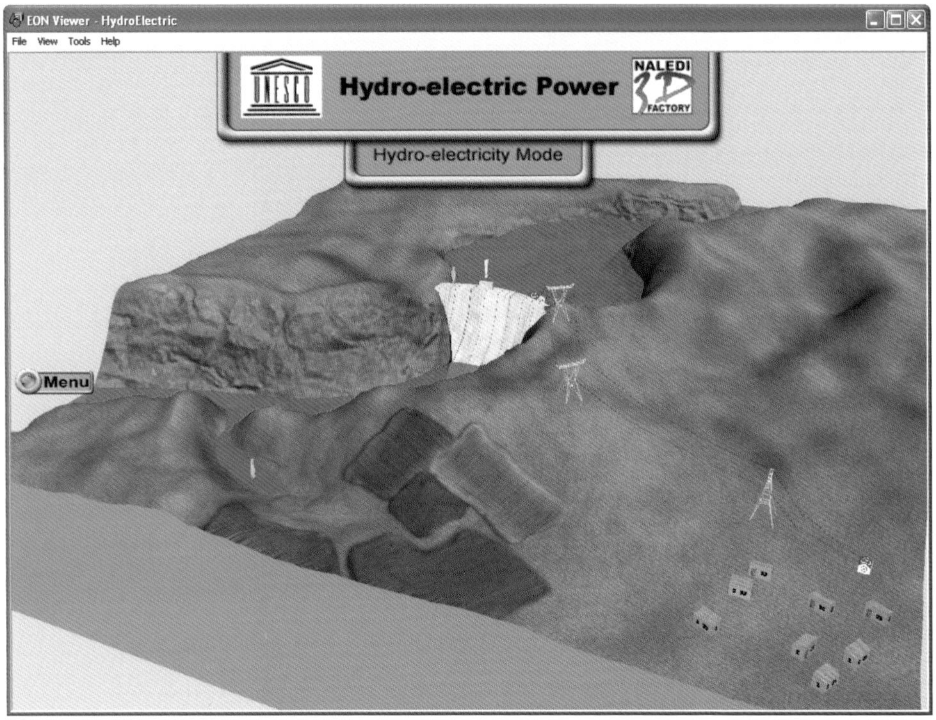

3. Click and hold the left mouse button while dragging the mouse. Drag left or right to spin the entire landscape around its axis, which appears to be in the center of the landscape, near the dam. Drag up and down to tilt the landscape. Continue to experiment with left-clicking and using the mouse to adjust your viewpoint of the simulation.
4. Click and hold the right mouse button while dragging the mouse up. As you drag, you zoom out (away from) the landscape.
5. Click and hold the right mouse button while dragging the mouse down. As you drag, you zoom in (nearer to) the landscape.
6. Hold down both the left and the right mouse buttons and move the mouse in any direction. The entire landscape pans in the direction of your movement.
7. Continue to practice moving around in the simulation. This will enable you to become more proficient in navigating a simulation. It also helps you better understand how users of a simulation that you create may move around.
8. Click the yellow exclamation point above the dam. This will open the sluice gate and cause "electricity" to flow (in the form of a yellow light) along the wires to the transformer plant. Additionally, a clock appears on the screen to indicate the passage of time. This is an example of how interactivity can be built into a simulation and how one event can be made to trigger other events.

troubleshooting

Some security software may present a warning about an outbound connection when you open this simulation. If this occurs, select the option to allow the opening of the file to continue.

9. Click the sluice gate again to close it and stop the electrical flow.
10. Click either one of the green, circling "I"s. This will trigger the playback of an audio recording that provides, in this case, useful information about the workings of a hydroelectric dam. For this simulation, the intent is educational, but audio can be applied to a simulation for a variety of purposes. (You may listen to the entire audio or press **Esc** to stop the recording and continue with the next step.)
11. Click the **Menu** button within the simulation. This will open a set of menu options for this simulation, as shown in Figure 1.1.8.

FIGURE 1.1.8 Menu options in a simulation

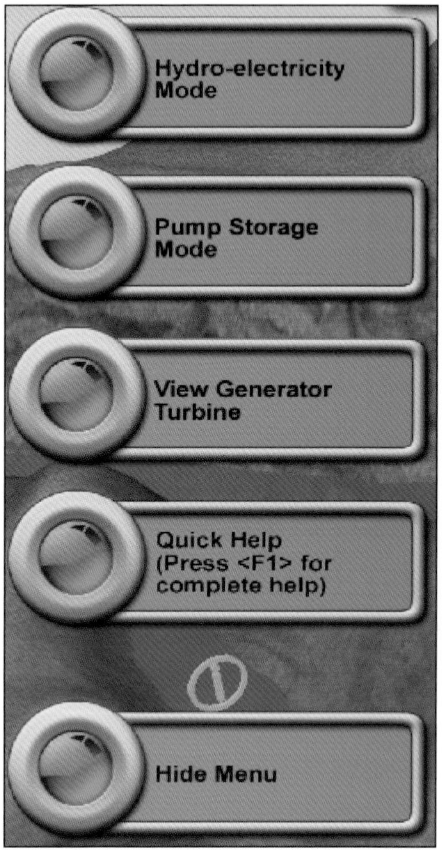

12. Click **View Generator Turbine.** Your view of the simulation is shifted to inside the dam.
13. Click the sluice gate (the yellow exclamation point) in the lower-right corner of the window and watch the turbine in action.
14. Click the sluice gate again to close it and stop the turbine.
15. Click the **Menu** button and then choose **Hydro-electricity Mode.** This will return you to the original viewpoint of the simulation.
16. As time permits, continue to explore the menus, viewpoints, and information available in this simulation. When you are finished, click the **Close** button on the EON Viewer window.

Discussion

discuss

The hydroelectric simulation is certainly a simulation of a limited "world" and is not the most advanced in terms of realism. But it does provide a small sampling of the capabilities of the simulations that can be created with EON. What features did you see in this simulation that you find helpful in a simulation? Were there any things in this simulation that you did not realize were possible? What elements might be more useful in a simulation created for education versus a simulation game?

Navigating with a Game Controller

In some instances you may have the option of using a joystick or other game controller with your desktop computer rather than a mouse and keyboard. If this is the case, you can still move around in the simulation, but you use the game controller to navigate in a different manner. Table 1.1.6 outlines the basic movements as they would be made with a traditional joystick. With so many different game controllers available today, it is impossible to say exactly which movements will be mapped to each control. Suffice it to say that you will have to read any directions provided or experiment with the controller to determine how to navigate within a particular application.

TABLE 1.1.6 Movements with a Joystick

Movement Type	Directions
Relative	1. Hold the joystick and press the assigned button (button 0).
	2. Push the stick forward and backward to move forward and backward.
	3. Push the stick left and right to rotate left and right.
Absolute	1. Hold the joystick and press the assigned button (button 1).
	2. Push the stick forward and backward to change pitch (to see up and down).
	3. Push the stick left and right to rotate left and right.

Pressing the button 0 is similar to clicking with the left mouse button. You must do so before you can move, and you should press the button before you move the stick forward or backward. This will ensure that you can move both backward and forward. If you press the button when the stick is already forward, then you can only move backward. Also note that the movement is relative—meaning that you move forward continuously as you hold the stick forward, and the more you press forward, the faster your speed will be.

The other joystick button (button 1) controls the pitch and heading. This movement is, however, absolute. This means that you rotate only when the stick moves. If you push the stick forward, you will pitch up, and as the stick returns to the center, the pitch returns to its previous position. This is true also for the left and right movements. Moving the stick left and right will rotate the simulation 90 degrees to the left and right. Moving the stick forward and backward will rotate pitch up and down to about 45 degrees. Note that, if you release the button before the stick is returned to the center, movement will stop immediately instead of returning to the place where the button was first pressed.

tips+tricks

The instructions given in Table 1.1.6 assume that the joystick is a standard two-axes, two-button joystick. Joysticks with additional axes or buttons will work, but you will need to determine the function of each button as you move through a simulation. There are no extra navigation functions for more advanced joysticks, unless special coding is added to the simulation to accommodate the capabilities of an advanced joystick.

tips+tricks

Note that EON also enables you to create applications that can be used with a Microsoft USB Xbox joystick. Throughout the remainder of this text, directions will be given as if you are working with a mouse and keyboard. You will need to refer to this section if you are working with a joystick.

EON Development Workflow

Simulation applications are built using EON Studio, but you will need other programs to create and edit 3D objects, textures, and sounds. Although some basic object editing is possible within EON Studio (for example, you can change an object's color or apply different textures to an object), you must prepare the texture and sound files you will need in your application beforehand.

Building an EON simulation involves three main activities:

- Importing and enhancing 3D graphic objects
- Defining behavioral properties for these objects
- Specifying how users will interact with these objects in the application

cross-reference

In Module 3 Lesson 2, you will learn how to import models, materials, and textures into EON.

Sound, light, and special effects can also be added to further enhance the realism of a simulation scene you create.

Most often, EON applications are intended for display outside EON Studio. Because EON adheres to Microsoft's ActiveX standard, you can view full-feature EON applications in documents created in ActiveX-compliant programs. Microsoft Internet Explorer, Macromedia Director, and Macromedia Authorware are a few examples of such programs.

You can display EON applications either by using EON Viewer or by inserting EonX (EON's ActiveX control) in a host application. The host application can be a Director publication, a web application, a PowerPoint presentation, or any other ActiveX-compliant host application.

cross-reference

You will learn more about optimizing and about distributing simulations in Module 11.

Simulation Creation Overview

We've covered a great deal of information in this first lesson, and much of it will probably make more sense when you start creating your own simulations. You may also find it useful to return to this lesson for reference as you work your way through later lessons.

In order to keep track of where you are in the process and where you are going next, you should first understand the overall simulation development process. Obviously, you begin with the EON Studio application—with which you can add behaviors, interactivity, scripting, and prototypes (see Figure 1.1.9).

FIGURE 1.1.9 Begin with EON Studio

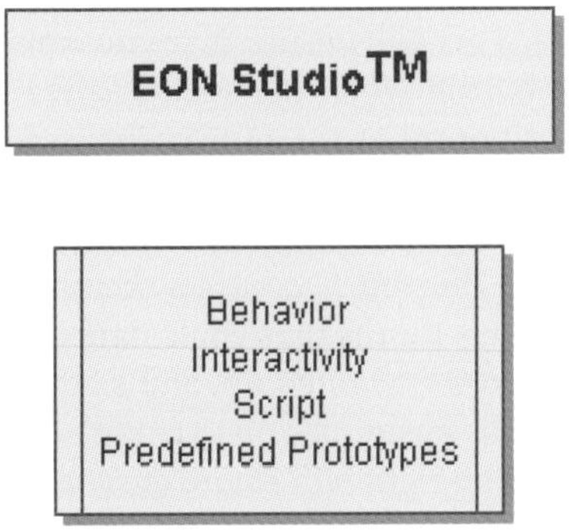

After EON Studio is running, you can import from a variety of other programs, including computer-aided design (CAD) and display data channel (DDC) files, as shown in Figure 1.1.10. You also can add sound and video elements in EON Studio. Note that behaviors, interactivity, and scripting can also be imported from these other applications.

FIGURE 1.1.10 Importing and adding objects in EON Studio

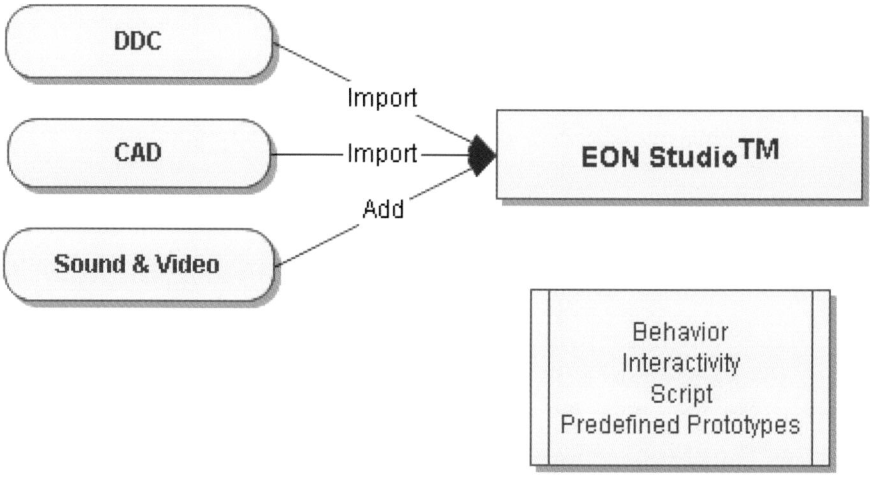

When you have added all of the components you need for your simulation, the file you create in EON Studio is saved as a source file with an EOZ extension. After the application is complete, EON Studio allows you to create a distribution file with an EDZ extension. Both EOZ and EDZ files can be used in EON Viewer and all host applications. (See Figure 1.1.11.)

FIGURE 1.1.11 Creating an EDZ file

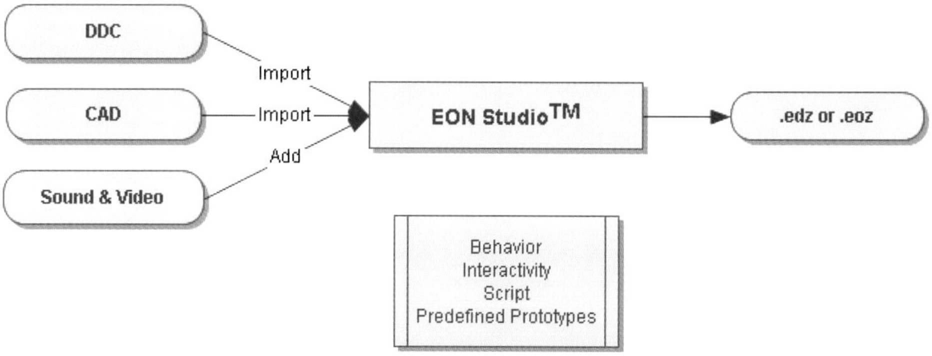

This EDZ file can be used in many different ways. As shown in Figure 1.1.12, you can publish it to the Internet, distribute it to standalone applications such as EON Viewer, or embed it in applications running ActiveX.

FIGURE 1.1.12 Distributing an EON simulation

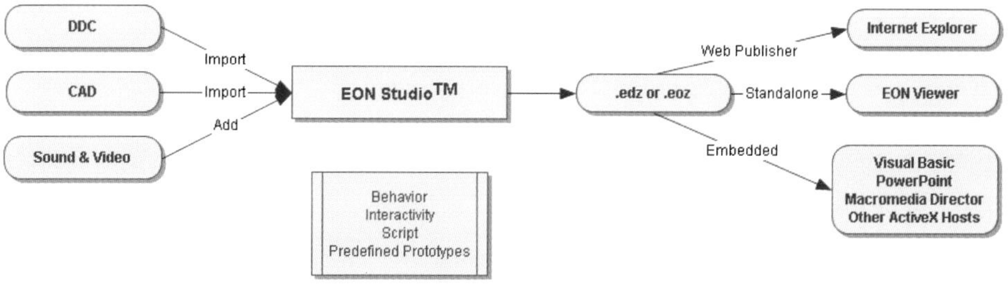

You could certainly stop at this point, with a very good simulation running in exactly the environment that you want. But, as the following figures illustrate, there are additional options and paths that you can choose to take.

By adding EON Professional (as shown in Figure 1.1.13), you can enhance your file with EON CAD capabilities.

FIGURE 1.1.13 EON Professional

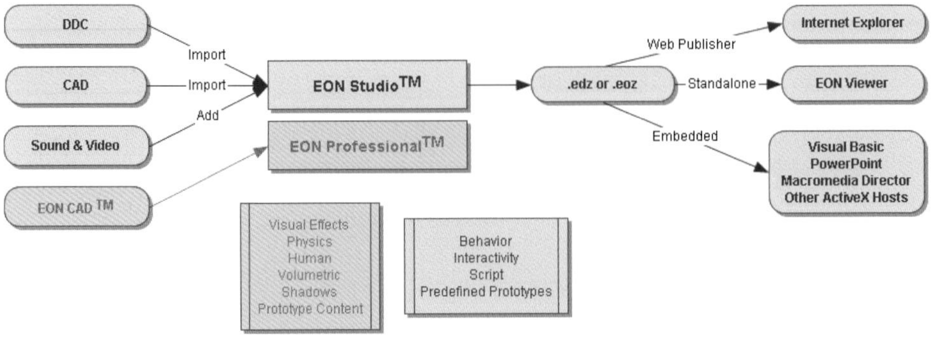

As Figure 1.1.14 illustrates, the addition of EON ICATCHER, ICUBE, or EON SDK allows a number of options for advanced distribution and display.

FIGURE 1.1.14 Advanced display options

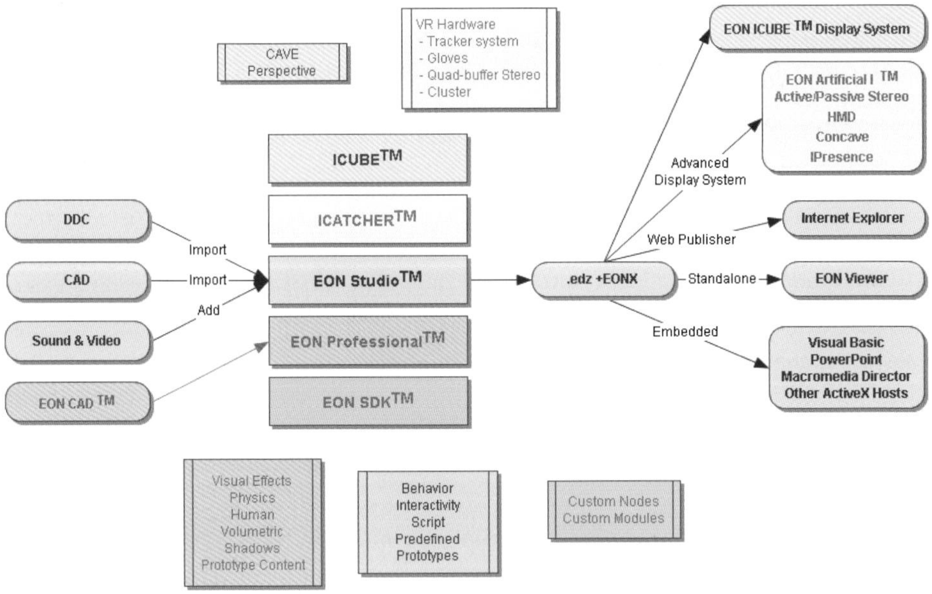

BEST PRACTICES

The Development Cycle

In all software development projects, a general order is typically followed. This is known as the software development life cycle (SDLC). This takes the product through investigation, analysis, design, implementation, and maintenance. It is a systems approach to problem solving and is made up of several phases, each comprised of multiple steps. This same process can readily be applied to the development of a simulation. The general steps to follow are:

- The *simulation concept* identifies and defines a need for the simulation.
- A *requirements analysis* analyzes the needs of the end users.
- The *architectural design* creates a blueprint for the simulation with the necessary specifications for the hardware, software, models, textures, and audio/video; it also specifies the required people resources (modelers and simulation developers).
- *Coding* and *debugging* create the models and simulations and verify the operation of each component.
- *Simulation testing* evaluates the simulation's actual functionality in relation to expected or intended functionality.

Following the SDLC guidelines helps ensure that a simulation is both fully planned and fully executed. Although this planning takes some time up front, it will undoubtedly save you much more time in the development of the simulation.

Summary

In this lesson you:

- Learned about visualization, simulation, and virtual reality.
- Developed an understanding of serious games and their role in the modern world.
- Considered EON Studio and EON Professional as authoring tools for 3D simulation.
- Understood the requirements for using EON Dynamic Load.
- Examined the available EON display systems.
- Became familiar with using navigation tools in the EON environment.
- Studied the overall simulation development process.

LESSON 1.2

EON Studio Workspace

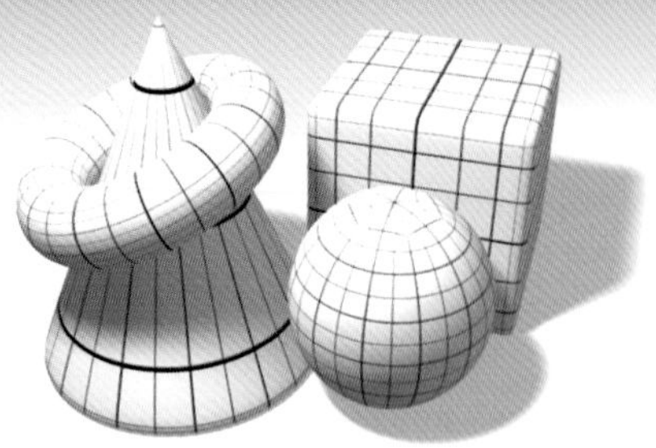

Objectives

In this lesson you will:

- Explore some basic EON Studio terms and concepts.
- Navigate the main EON Studio workspace and windows.
- Learn to use the EON Studio child windows and manipulate the windows to your needs.
- Begin exploring the EON toolbars and become familiar with some of the more commonly used features.
- Restore the EON Studio workspace layout to its default settings.
- Explore the various Help features available to you.

Key Terms

child windows
event
library
Multiple Document Interface (MDI)
node
prototype
referenced link
route
subtree

Every day you see 3D visual objects displayed on television, in video games, or in other applications that use visual objects. With advancements in computer technology and software, 3D technology is becoming easier to use and develop. As we have discussed, EON Studio is dynamic and powerful development software that allows you to create 3D interactive presentations that can be played online, in standalone applications, and on many types of display systems. This lesson is designed to help you learn to use the EON Studio software for simple program applications and presentations by introducing you to the primary display screens and basic functions of EON Studio.

EON Studio Terms

Before we can begin a discussion of the EON Studio workspace, we must discuss some of the basic terms that will be used throughout the rest of this text. A brief overview of these terms is provided here—enough information to begin to grasp the concepts behind them. We will introduce additional information as it becomes necessary for your simulation development, but the terms you need to know now are:

- Node
- Prototype

Basic Explanation of Nodes

Nodes are the building blocks used to create EON simulations. An EON simulation is constructed by arranging and connecting nodes to form a hierarchy of ***subtrees***. All child nodes under a subtree can then be manipulated and controlled as a unit. EON Studio has more than 100 nodes (many of which are shown in Figure 1.2.1) that you can use to add elements and features to your EON application. A unique assortment of properties is displayed in each node's properties window. By assigning specific values to these properties, a user can define how each node will perform in a simulation. All nodes also have a default name that reflects its particular functionality within a simulation.

FIGURE 1.2.1 Available nodes

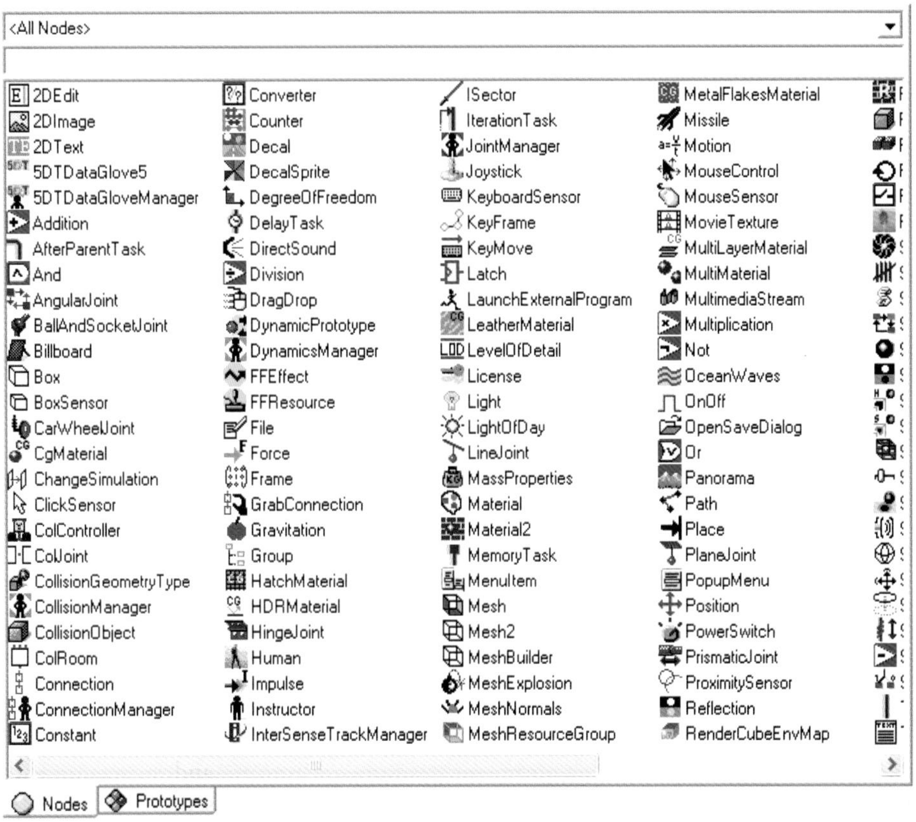

Basic Explanation of Prototypes

Prototypes are reusable, plug-and-play simulations that can be copied from the EON components library and placed into your own custom simulations. Each prototype contains its own internal simulation subtree and, optionally, a set of external fields (i.e., properties and events), depending on the prototype's purpose, which are used to pass values back and forth between the prototype and your simulation. After a prototype has been added to your simulation, you can manipulate and control its behavior by assigning specific values to its properties—just as you do with standard EON nodes. Some of the available prototypes are shown in Figure 1.2.2.

FIGURE 1.2.2 Available prototypes

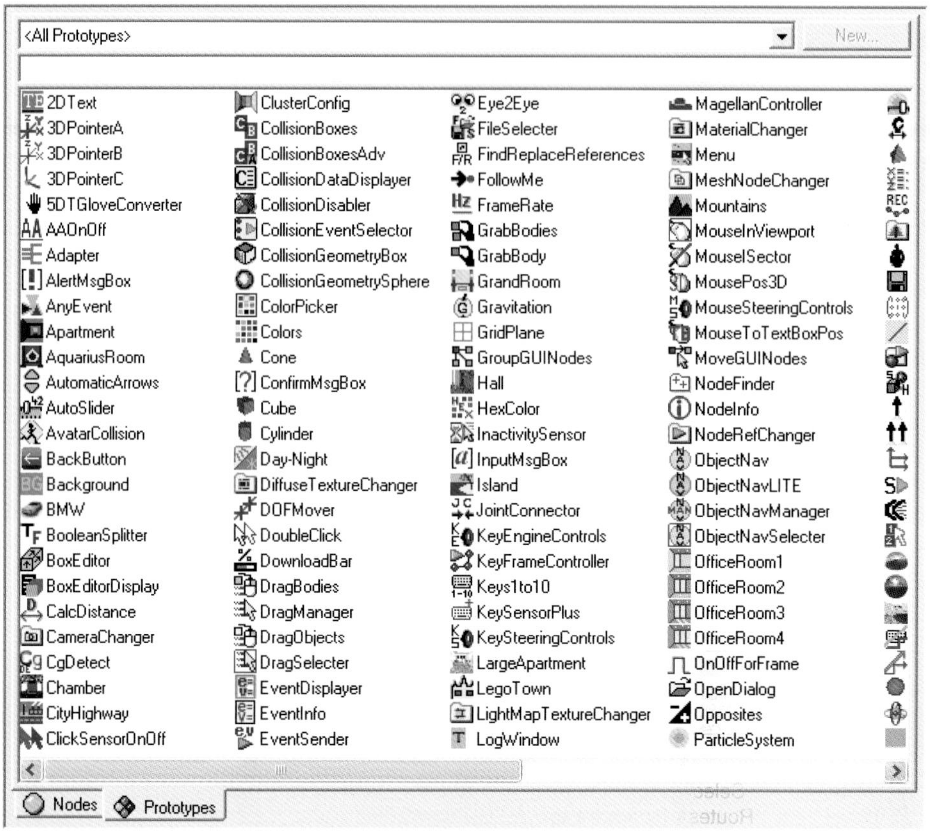

Multiple instances of a node or prototype can be used throughout the simulation tree. Each instance is assigned a unique system-generated name; however, you should always rename each instance with a more descriptive name.

cross-reference

The simulation tree will be discussed in greater detail later in this lesson.

With this basic understanding of the objects with which you will be working, we can proceed with our discussion of EON's user interface.

Main EON Studio Windows

When you open EON Studio, you will find a number of ***child windows*** within EON's main window. These windows are used for the different tasks you perform when constructing EON applications. The four most important windows are:

- Simulation Tree window
- Components window (Nodes or Prototypes)
- Routes window
- Property Bar

There are also a number of windows of lesser importance (because they are used less frequently or used only in certain circumstances). These include:

- Local Prototypes window
- Log window
- Find window
- Butterfly window

Additionally, there are numerous toolbars that put commonly used features and functionality in a convenient location for ease of use. Figure 1.2.3 illustrates many of these child windows and tools within the EON Studio interface, in their default locations.

FIGURE 1.2.3 EON Studio default workspace

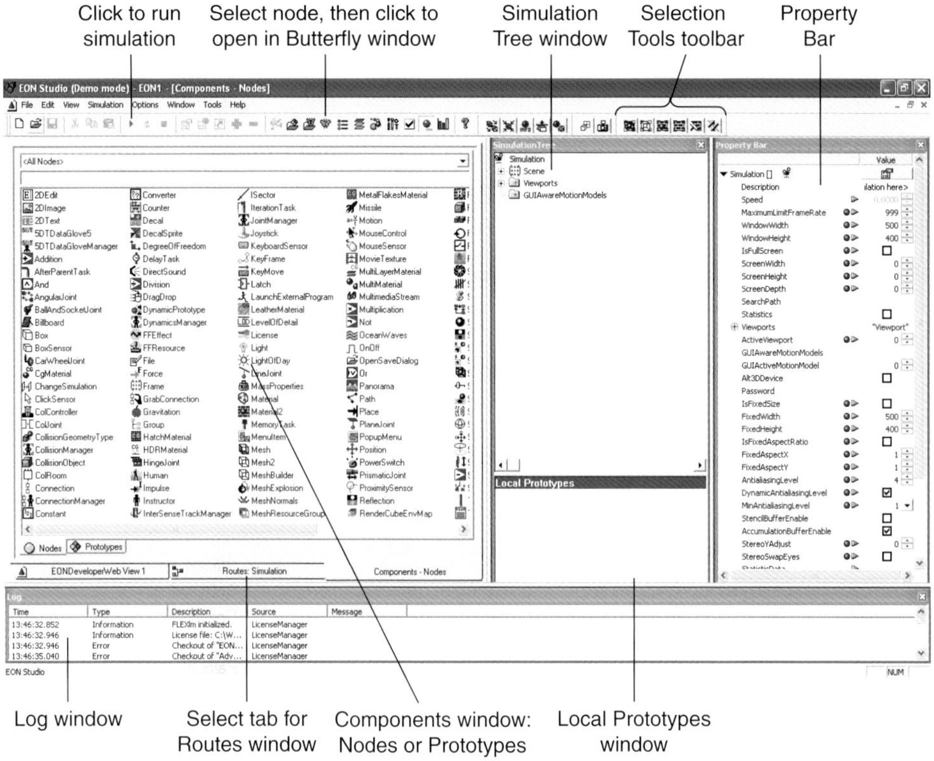

Basic Window Types

There are four basic types of windows in EON Studio. They are:

- Construction windows
- Library window
- Help windows
- Simulation window

Construction Windows

As mentioned earlier, an EON simulation is constructed by arranging and connecting basic node and prototype components. You will be building (or constructing) a simulation, and therefore it makes sense that some of the windows are viewed as "construction" windows. The construction windows are the Simulation Tree window and the Routes window.

The Simulation Tree window is where EON applications are built by arranging nodes into subtree hierarchies. An icon and a text name represent each node. Nodes with a plus sign next to them contain a subtree of additional nodes under them, which can be displayed by clicking the plus sign. Each node has a Property page that can be displayed by double-clicking the node.

The Routes window is a graphic editor for defining interactive, event-driven relationships between nodes. You define how information should be sent between nodes by creating routes between nodes. Routes are created by dragging nodes from the simulation tree hierarchy into the Routes window, where the node icons are

tips+tricks

Because you can work with both nodes and prototypes in a similar fashion, we will collectively refer to both components as "nodes" for the remainder of the book.

connected with lines or, more specifically, ***routes.*** After nodes are connected, they can exchange information or trigger events while the simulation is running.

cross-reference

See the "Components Window" section later in this lesson.

Library Window

The Components window contains all the available EON nodes arranged in a number of node ***libraries,*** such as Base nodes, Agent nodes, and so on. An easy way to build your EON application is to drag the node icons from the Components window to the place where you want them located in the Simulation Tree window. The Components window also contains a library of prototypes. Note that you can have several Components windows open at the same time.

Help Windows

Several windows within EON can provide helpful information concerning different aspects of a simulation:

- The Butterfly window displays an overview of the various routes for a selected node. Viewing nodes in the Butterfly window makes it easier to follow routes between indirectly linked nodes.
- The Find window is a search tool for locating nodes in the simulation tree.
- The Log window provides current information on EON Studio's internal operations. This feature is used for debugging and fine-tuning simulation behavior.

Simulation Window

The simulation window is used for running EON applications.

cross-reference

You will learn more about the components of a simulation in later lessons.

Simulation Tree Window

An important part of constructing a simulation is determining how the nodes are arranged in the simulation tree structure. The Simulation Tree window is the primary window for developing simulation solutions in EON Studio.

The simulation tree is built by copying nodes from a Components window. Figure 1.2.4 shows a simple simulation tree, and Table 1.2.1 details the default components of the simulation tree (numbered in Figure 1.2.4) for each newly created simulation file.

FIGURE 1.2.4 Simulation tree in the Simulation Tree window

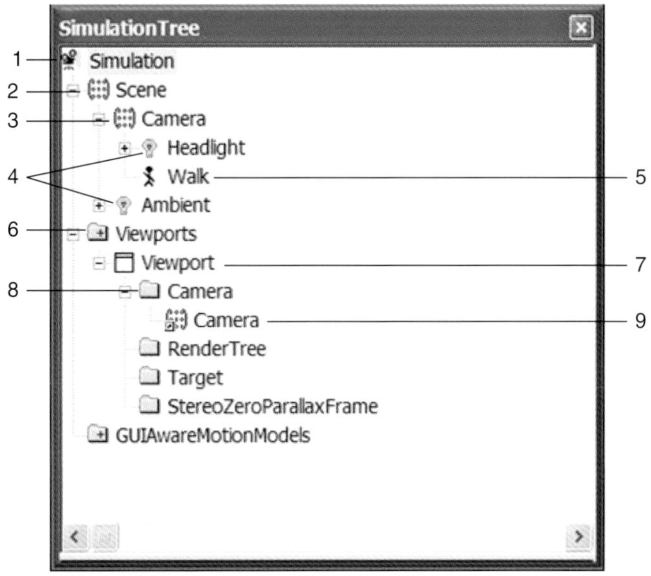

TABLE 1.2.1 Simulation Tree Components

Simulation Tree Component	Reference Number	Description
Simulation	1	The root node of an EON simulation.
Scene	2	The Scene node represents the world coordinate system. Use the Scene node to change background and fog effects. This is the simulation's main parent node.
Camera	3	This node serves as the simulation's camera. Its position determines what the viewer sees in the simulation window. By default, it contains a Light node and the Walk node.
Light	4	Light nodes are used to illuminate objects in the simulation. By default the simulation has two Light nodes (Headlight in the Camera node and Ambient Light), but five different lighting types are available.
Walk	5	The default Walk node is placed below the default Camera node and enables a user to stroll through the 3D environment by using the mouse.
Viewports folder	6	This folder can contain one or more Viewport nodes.
Viewport	7	A Viewport node defines the user's field of view and how the simulation is displayed in the simulation window. This node must be connected to a Frame node, defining the user's position in the simulation.
Camera folder	8	This Camera folder can store a single link to a frame that represents the simulation's camera position.
Camera shortcut	9	This is a referenced link to the Camera node.

tips+tricks

As in other hierarchical structures, you can expand or collapse the simulation tree to show or hide subcomponents. If there is a "+" sign next to an element, click the plus sign to expand the tree. If there is a "−" sign next to an element, click the minus sign to collapse, or hide, that section of the tree.

cross-reference

You will learn more about Frame nodes in Module 1 Lesson 3 and in subsequent modules.

Scene Frame

The Scene frame (a Frame node) contains all elements of the simulation and is the primary starting point of the simulation tree. The first items below the Scene frame are default commands and include the Camera frame and lighting.

Camera Frame

The collection of nodes and prototypes included in the Camera frame (a Frame node) enables default camera position, lighting, and user navigation controls for the scene. The Walk node, for example, controls the way you move in the scene. This enables you to move around objects in the simulation just as you would walk around something in the real world. The Camera frame is present in all simulations in EON. You will learn about other nodes and prototypes that can be placed in this frame and how they function in the development of the simulation later in this lesson.

Light Node

The Light node controls the lighting in the simulation. The color of the light can be changed as well as the type of lighting and its intensity. You can also choose to make the lighting directional, parallel point, point, or focused like a spotlight.

troubleshooting

If the Nodes and Prototypes tabs are not visible, it may be that another window is open in front of the Components window. You may have to select the Components tab to make it the visible window.

If the Components window is not open, you can open it by selecting Window from the menu bar and then selecting New Component Window. To get the windows to appear in the same arrangement as shown in Figure 1.2.5, you would also need to select View from the menu bar and then select Default Layout.

Components Window

The Components window is the second most frequently used window in the EON workspace. The Components window, as shown in Figure 1.2.5, holds the Nodes and Prototypes window tabs. From these windows you can locate specific content nodes or prototypes for developing simulation-based content.

FIGURE 1.2.5 Components window

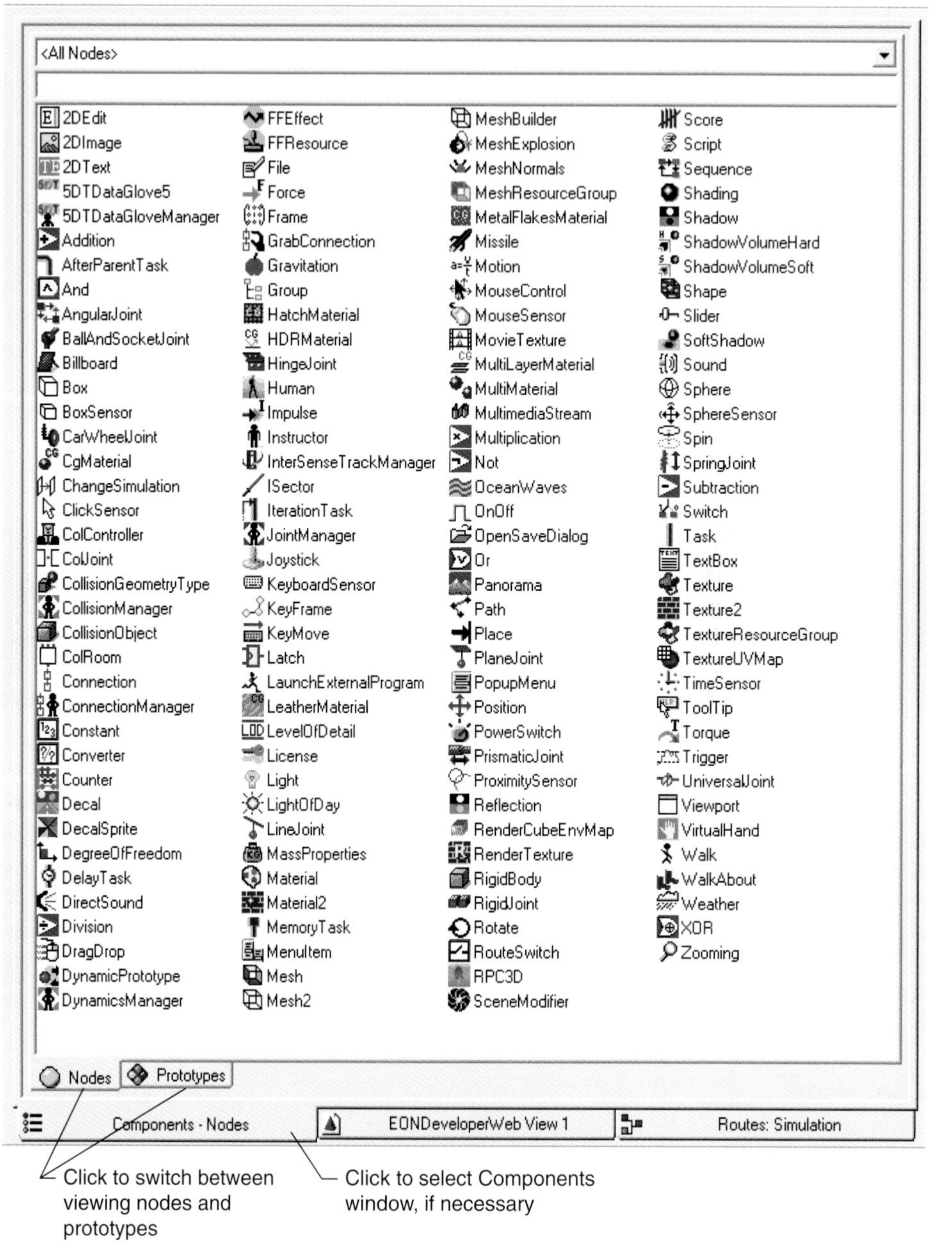

Placing Nodes and Prototypes in the Simulation Tree

Where you place the node within the simulation tree is a function of the type of node (or prototype). You can place nodes under the Scene frame, materials, resources, or a geometry-based object imported from a 3D model file.

There are several methods you can use to place a node or a prototype in the simulation tree:

- Drag and drop
- Double-click
- Pop-up window in the Simulation Tree window
- Copy as a link to reference an existing node

Drag and Drop

To access and use nodes and prototypes, select the node/prototype that you want to use in your simulation, click the node, and hold down the left mouse button to drag and drop the node to the correct location in the simulation tree.

Double-Click

To place a node or a prototype in a specific location in the simulation tree, first select (in the simulation tree) the frame or folder in which you want to place the component, and then double-click the node or prototype in the Components window. It will be placed automatically in the designated location.

Pop-Up Window in the Simulation Tree Window

Another method for placing a node (not a prototype) in the simulation tree is to first select (in the simulation tree) the frame or folder in which you want to place the component and then right-click. From the pop-up menu, select New, and then select the node category. Last, select the desired node.

Copy as a Link to Reference an Existing Node

If the node you want to use has already been placed in the simulation, you may find it simplest to create a ***referenced link.*** A referenced link is a shortcut within the simulation (like a shortcut in Microsoft Windows). This is the best method to employ if you want to reuse a node, including all of the property settings that have been changed from their defaults. To create a referenced link, right-click the node in the simulation tree and choose Copy as Link. Then select the location in the simulation tree where you want the linked node to be placed, right-click, and select Paste. The linked node will appear identical to the original one except that there is a small arrow in the corner of the linked node's icon.

tips+tricks

To rapidly locate specific nodes or prototypes within the Components window, enter the first letter of the node's name in the drop-down box or click the drop-down arrow and choose the node by category. Either method reduces search time.

Activity 1.2.1: Placing Nodes in the Simulation Tree

1. Open EON Studio or EON Professional.
2. If necessary, select the **Nodes** tab on the Components window.

tips+tricks

Holding a node or prototype that you want to insert above the destination frame or folder for a moment before dropping it will cause the subtree to expand automatically. This is useful if you need to place a component into a location that is not currently visible in the simulation tree.

tips+tricks

Hold down the Shift key to make the node focus shift to the newly inserted node. This makes it possible to quickly build a hierarchy.

3. Left-click the **2DImage** node and drag it until your cursor rests on the Scene frame; then release the mouse. The 2DImage node will be placed in the Scene frame, as shown in Figure 1.2.6. (The other elements within your Scene frame and the simulation may be collapsed. Those shown are all expanded.)

FIGURE 1.2.6 Node placed in the Scene frame using drag and drop

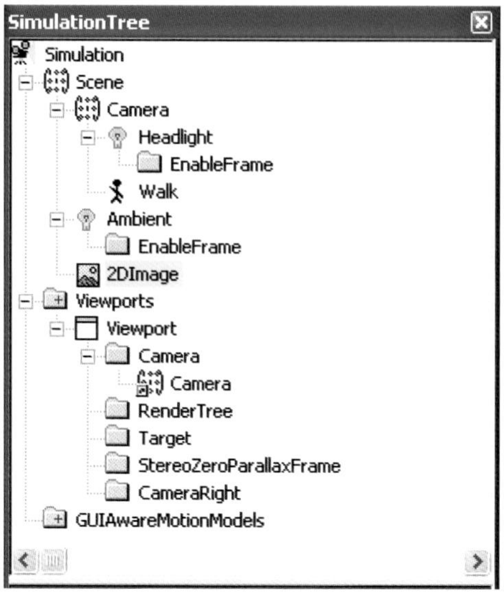

4. In the simulation tree, click the **Ambient** icon once.
5. In the Nodes panel, locate and double-click the **LightOfDay** node. This will place the LightOfDay node under the Ambient [Light] node, as shown in Figure 1.2.7. (The subtree will expand automatically to make the newly added node visible. Your other subtrees may still be collapsed.)

FIGURE 1.2.7 Node placed under the Ambient node by double-clicking

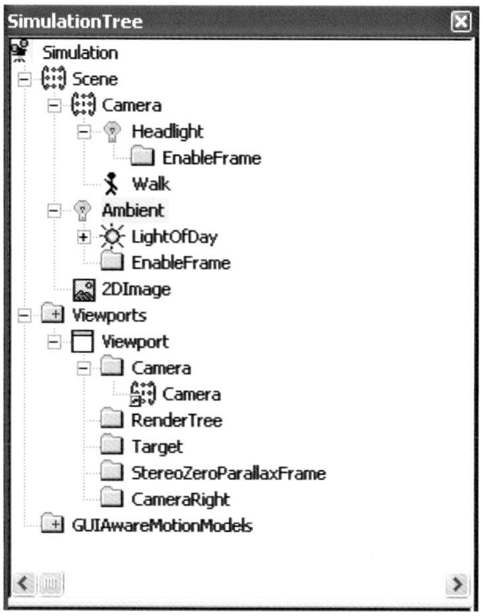

6. In the simulation tree, right-click the **Scene** frame. From the pop-up menu (shown in Figure 1.2.8), choose **New,** point to **SpecialFX Nodes,** and then select **Weather.** This places the Weather node in the Scene frame, as shown in Figure 1.2.9. (Some of your subtrees may be collapsed.)

FIGURE 1.2.8 Selecting a node from menus

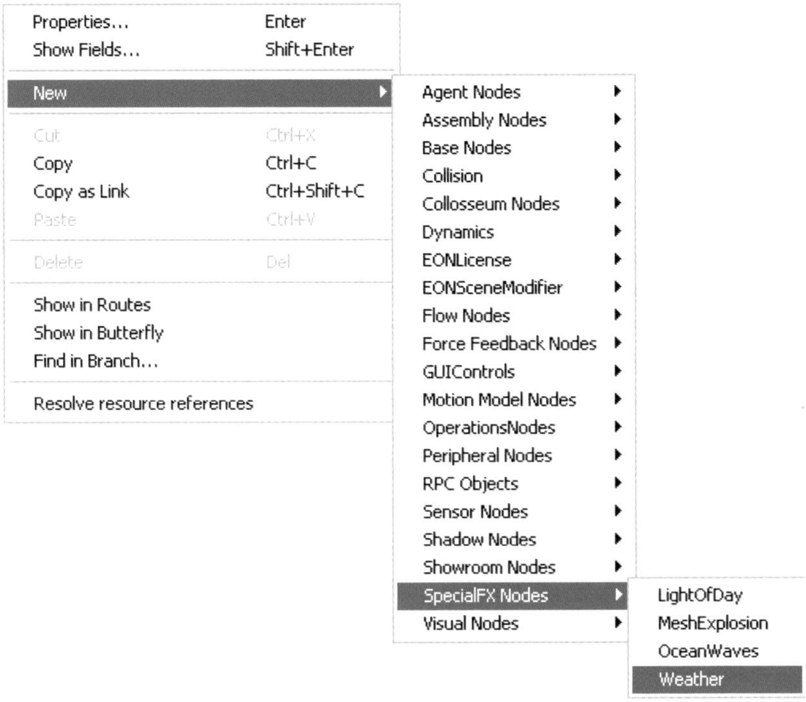

FIGURE 1.2.9 Node added by right-clicking

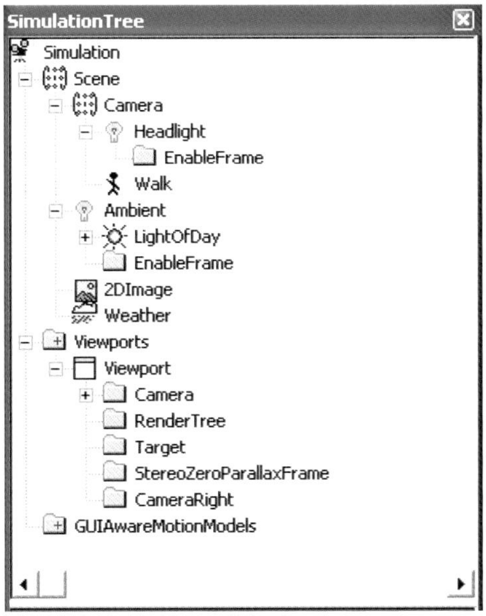

7. Right-click **2DImage** in the Scene frame of the simulation tree. Choose **Copy as Link** from the pop-up menu.

8. Right-click the **Camera** frame in the simulation tree. Choose **Paste** from the pop-up menu. A referenced link of 2DImage is added to the Camera frame as shown in Figure 1.2.10. You may need to expand the Camera frame node in order to see the referenced link node.

FIGURE 1.2.10 Referenced link node

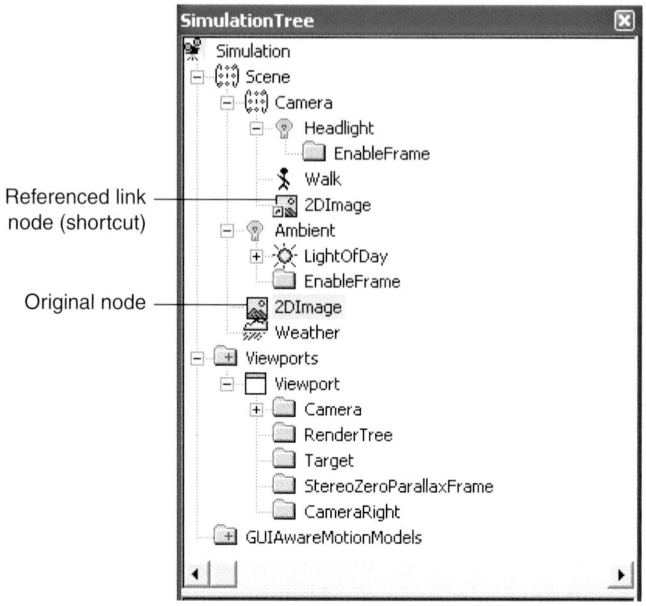

9. Close EON without saving the simulation.

The nodes used for the "simulation" in Activity 1.2.1 were just randomly selected as examples. They do not represent a good, working simulation. Use the Help system to find out more about each of these nodes. Based on what you have learned, why would Copy as Link never really be used with the 2DImage node?

Routes Window

The Routes window is where you connect nodes and define how they will behave when data is sent between them. By default this window is located to the left in the same window group as the Components window.

The Routes window provides a graphic representation of all defined routes. Connections between nodes are shown as lines that run from the triggering node's "out" field to the corresponding "in" field of the target node. Out fields (also called outEvents) are represented by a green arrow, and in fields (also called inEvents) are represented by a blue dot, as shown in Figure 1.2.11. If a specific node has several connections with two or more nodes, a black dot is displayed at the beginning of the connection line.

FIGURE 1.2.11 Sample Routes window

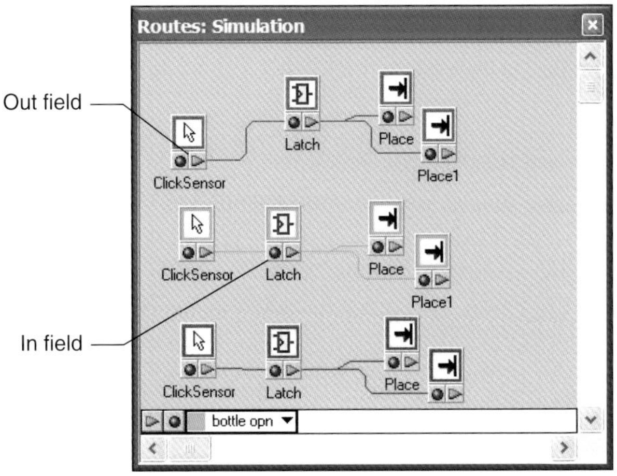

When you connect nodes in the Routes window, you are actually connecting node fields so data can flow from the source node's out field to the destination node's in field. Some fields may be used only for storing data related to object positions, whereas others may contain true/false states, to name just a few examples. Fields serve as connection points for routing data. When data is sent between two nodes, that data transaction is known as an ***event.***

You may only make connections between fields that are defined with the same data type. A route connection can be made between an eventOut field and an eventIn field as long as their data types are the same. Attempts to connect fields containing different data types are not allowed.

cross-reference

You will learn more about events as well as data types and eventIn and eventOut fields in the next lesson, Module 1 Lesson 3.

Adding Nodes to the Routes Window

Adding a node to the Routes window is a simple process. Left-click the node in the simulation tree and then drag and drop it into the Routes window.

Making Node Connections

After nodes have been placed in the Routes window, they need to be connected to one another to create functionality in the simulation. To establish a connection, click the arrow symbol at the lower-right corner of the source node. A pop-up menu displays, similar to that shown in Figure 1.2.12. (The options available in the out field pop-up menu depend on the node type. The menu shown in Figure 1.2.12 is for a ClickSensor node.)

FIGURE 1.2.12 OutEvent options for a ClickSensor node

OnRunFalse	SFBOOL
OnRunTrue	SFBOOL
OnRunChanged	SFBOOL
OnButtonDownFalse	SFBOOL
OnButtonDownTrue	SFBOOL
OnButtonDownChanged	SFBOOL
CursorOnObject	SFBOOL
changeCursor	SFBOOL
Button	SFINT32
Target	SFNODE
TargetPoint	SFVEC3F
TargetPointWorld	SFVEC3F
Continous	SFBOOL
Roots	MFNODE

Select an out field from the pop-up menu to display a connection line. Move the connection line to the destination node and click the symbol (the dot) at the node's

cross-reference

You will learn more about inEvents and outEvents in Module 2 Lesson 2.

lower-left corner. An in field pop-up menu displays, similar to the one shown in Figure 1.2.13. (The options available in the in field pop-up menu depend on the data type of the source node's outEvent. The menu shown in Figure 1.2.13 is for a Latch node.)

FIGURE 1.2.13 InEvent options for a Latch node

SetRun	SFBOOL
SetRun_	SFBOOL
Set	SFBOOL
Set_	SFBOOL
Toggle	SFBOOL
Clear	SFBOOL
Reset	SFBOOL
startValue	SFBOOL

Deleting Nodes from the Routes Window

If you have incorrectly placed a node in the Routes window, you can easily delete the node. Note that there is a difference between deleting nodes from the Routes window versus deleting them from the simulation tree. A node deleted in the Routes window will only be removed from the Routes window, but a node deleted in the simulation tree will be removed from the entire simulation, including the Routes window. In either case, the deletions cannot be undone.

There are several ways to delete a node. With the node selected in the Routes window:

- Select Edit > Delete.
- Right-click the node and select Delete from the pop-up menu.
- Press the Delete key on the keyboard.

tips+tricks

The confirmation dialog box will be disabled if you hold down the Shift key while pressing the Delete key.

In each case, a confirmation dialog box will appear if the node you are deleting has any connections that would be deleted with it. (Note that the connected nodes would remain in the Routes window.) Click OK to continue with the deletion.

If you want to delete a node as well as all the nodes that are connected to it, right-click the node and choose Select Related Nodes from the pop-up menu. All connected nodes will be highlighted. Use one of the deletion methods listed previously to delete all of the nodes and their connections.

Displaying Route Information

tips+tricks

In the Routes window, you can view the path of a specific node (where it is located in the simulation tree) by placing your mouse pointer over the node. The screen tip will show the location of the node (i.e., Simulation\Scene\ClickSensor).

At times it may be useful to see information about a specific route that you have created. This information includes the node that it is coming from, the out field property, the node that it is going to, and the in field property, as shown in Figure 1.2.14. There are two ways to view this information:

- Click the route to select it. The information displays at the bottom of the Routes window.
- Place your mouse pointer on the connection line. The information displays in a screen tip.

FIGURE 1.2.14 Viewing route information

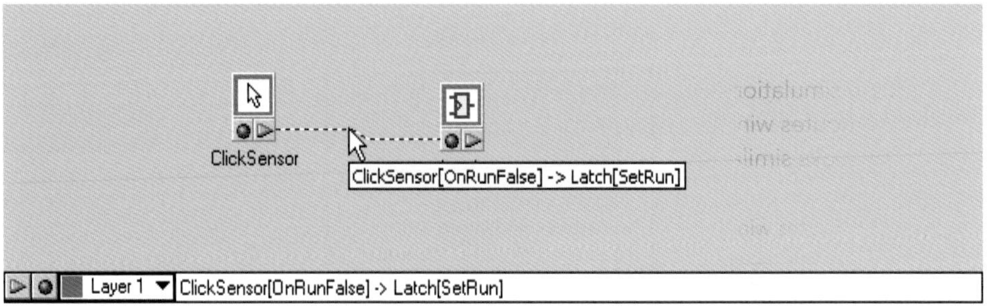

tips+tricks

When your simulations get more complex, you may find that there are situations where you have multiple lines on top of each other. To get information on the routes, you can click repeatedly on the lines. With each click, the display at the bottom of the Routes window is changed to another route. You can cycle through all of the overlapping lines by continuing to click.

Discussion

discuss

When and why do you think it could be helpful to use one of the described methods to locate route information?

Activity 1.2.2: Creating a Simple Simulation

1. Open EON.
2. If necessary, switch to the **Nodes** tab on the Components window, select the **Frame** node, and place it in the Scene frame in the simulation tree. Frame
3. Place each of the nodes or prototypes descibed in Table 1.2.2 in the **Frame** node in the simulation tree. When finished, your Simulation Tree window should look similar to Figure 1.2.15. (The actual order of the items within the frame depends on the order in which you add them.) Note that the Pyramid prototype is located on the Prototype tab of the Components window.

TABLE 1.2.2 Nodes and Prototype to Add to Frame Node

Node or Prototype?	Name	Icon	Action
Node	ClickSensor	ClickSensor	Detects when an object is left-clicked
Node	Latch	Latch	Sets and toggles true/false flag values
Node	Rotate	Rotate	Rotates the parent node on its vertical axis
Prototype	Pyramid	Pyramid	Creates a 3D model of a pyramid object

FIGURE 1.2.15 Simulation Tree window with nodes added

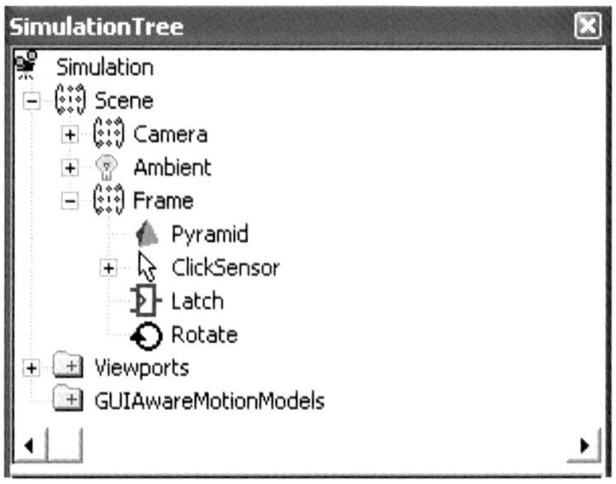

4. Switch to the Routes window.
5. From the simulation tree, drag and drop the **ClickSensor, Latch,** and **Rotate** nodes into the Routes window. If necessary, rearrange your nodes so that your Routes window looks similar to Figure 1.2.16.

FIGURE 1.2.16 Routes window with nodes added

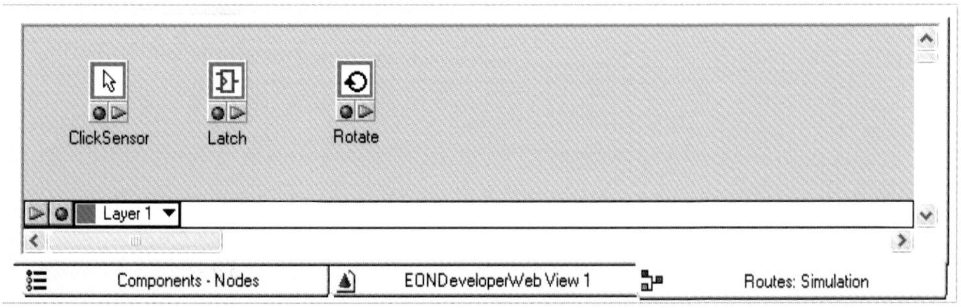

tips+tricks

To rapidly locate specific nodes or prototypes within the Components window, enter the first letter of the node's name in the text box above the icons. The list of nodes will be reduced to only those starting with the letter you keyed. You can also narrow your search by selecting the category of node or prototype from the drop-down list. You will learn more about these categories (also called libraries) in Module 1 Lesson 3 and later modules.

tips+tricks

If the Routes window tab is not visible next to the Components window tabs, select Window from the menu and then select Routes. You can also press Alt + 2 on the keyboard to display or hide the Routes window.

6. Click the **Out** field (green arrow) for ClickSensor.
7. From the pop-up menu, choose **OnButtonDownTrue.** A connection line with an arrow will appear.
8. Drag the connection arrow to the **In** field (blue dot) on the Latch node.
9. From the pop-up menu, choose **Toggle.** This completes the connection between the ClickSensor and the Latch nodes.
10. Click the **Out** field for Latch.
11. From the pop-up menu, choose **OnChanged.** A connection line with an arrow will appear.
12. Drag the connection arrow to the **In** field on the Rotate node.
13. From the pop-up menu, choose **SetRun.** Your completed Routes window should appear similar to Figure 1.2.17.

troubleshooting

Be sure to choose SetRun and not SetRun_. SetRun turns on the Rotate node, whereas SetRun_ has the opposite effect—it will turn off the Rotate node. Note that, in EON, the underscore usually indicates the negative or false action.

FIGURE 1.2.17 Completed connections

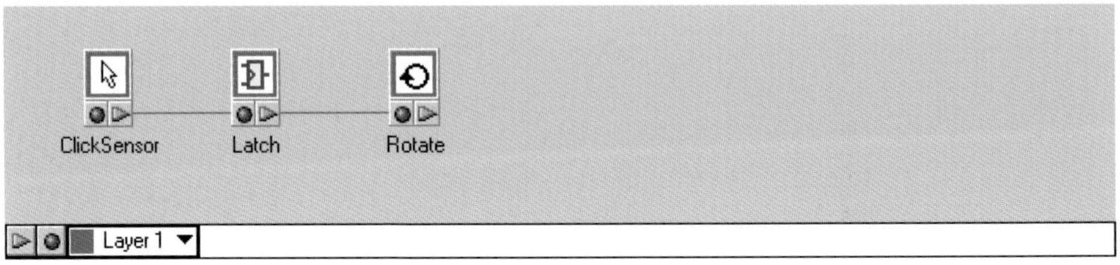

14. Save your simulation as **RotatingPyramid.**
15. Now that you have linked the nodes together in the Routes window, you can run the simulation. Click the **green arrow** on the toolbar, as shown in Figure 1.2.18. This will launch the EON simulation window, as shown in Figure 1.2.19. Notice that the pyramid is rotating when the simulation starts.

FIGURE 1.2.18 EON Toolbar

web links

Clicking the Start Simulation button actually compiles the simulation. This is very similar to compiling in a software application. Use the Internet to learn more about what it means to "compile" software in order to gain a better understanding of what is going on behind the scenes when you click the Start Simulation button.

FIGURE 1.2.19 EON simulation window

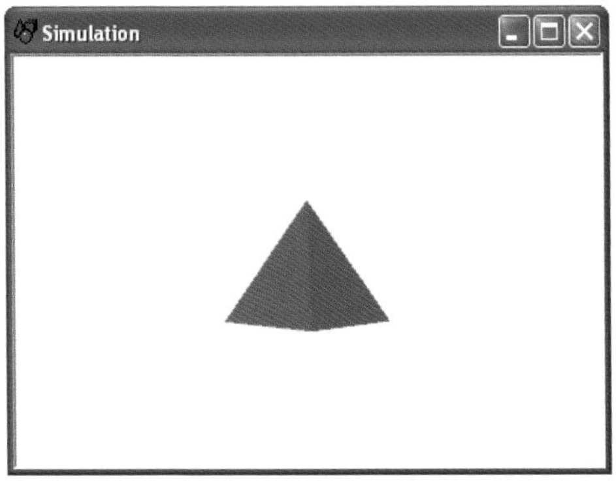

16. Move your cursor over the pyramid. The cursor changes from an arrow to a pointing finger. This indicates that a ClickSensor is attached to the object.
17. Click the pyramid. The spinning (rotating) will stop. Click the pyramid again. The spinning will resume. Note how clicking the object associated with a ClickSensor node toggles the Rotate action on and off.

18. Click the **Close** button (red **X**) in the upper-right corner of the simulation window to stop running the simulation and close the window. Save the simulation and keep it open to use in Activity 1.2.3.

Discussion

discuss

Why do you think you need to click the pyramid twice the first time in order to stop the rotation? How would the simulation behave differently if you choose to connect the route from the Latch to the Rotate nodes using SetRun_?

BEST PRACTICES

Routes Window Organization Using Layers

It is a good practice to organize the nodes in your Routes window in a neat and orderly way. Although it makes no difference in the functionality of the simulation you are creating, a well-organized Routes window can make a big difference in your ability (and the ability of others) to work within the simulation later.

As applications grow more complex, this area can become complicated and messy. Neatness will help you manage changes and will assist greatly in any debugging process.

If a simulation has several connecting routes, you can use the Layer view to organize your routes, making them easier to discern from one another. A *layer* is a group of routes and nodes in the Routes window that can be displayed separately.

New routes are assigned to the layer that is active when the connection is created. Note that only one layer can be active at a time.

To see and edit the layers, select the View menu and then select Layers. (You also can right-click anywhere in the Routes window and choose Layer Editor.) You will see a dialog box like that shown below.

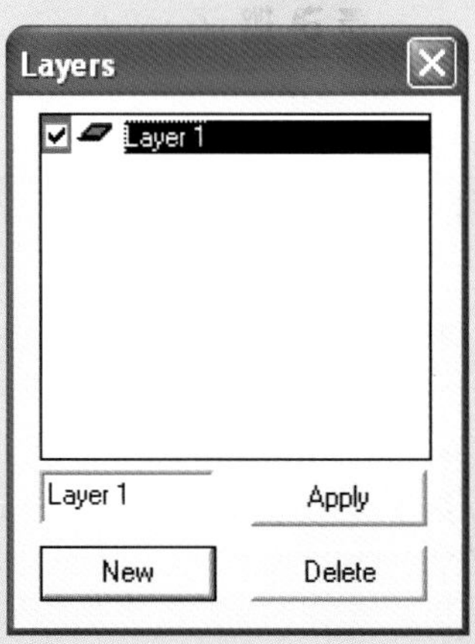

From the Layers dialog box, you can add, rename and hide/select layers, and assign layer colors. You should use different layer colors to improve legibility when the connecting routes displayed in the Routes window are complex. The layer color impacts the connecting route lines as well as the outline color of the icon for the node or prototype. To add a new layer with a specific color:

1. Enter a new layer name in the text field, found just above the New button.
2. Click the **New** button.
3. To specify a custom color, left-click the colored icon to the left of the layer name and select a new color from the color picker that appears.

A new route is assigned to the layer that is active when the connection is created or the node is placed. The new route will receive the color of the active layer. You select the active layer by choosing it from the [Layer] drop-down list at the bottom left of the Routes window. To change the color of a layer:

1. Choose **View** > **Layers** or right-click in the Routes window and choose **Layer Editor.**
2. In the Layers dialog box, select a different color. All nodes and routes in that layer will change to the newly selected color.

To change the layer that a route is assigned to:

1. Select the route. You can drag a selection box around all the nodes and routes you want to select, or you can Ctrl+click each item to be included.
2. Right-click one of the selected items and choose **Move to Layer** > **[Layer Name].**

The advantage to using layers is that it allows you to color-code your routes (and name them in ways that coordinate with portions of your simulation) so that you can more easily locate specific routes. It also gives you the option to hide layers so that you only view the specific parts of the simulation that you need. To hide a layer in the Routes window:

1. Open the Layers dialog box.
2. Clear the check box for the layer that you want to hide. All nodes and connections belonging to that layer will be hidden. (Note that the active layer cannot be hidden.)

When you hide a layer, it appears with hash marks instead of a solid color in the Layers drop-down list (bottom left of the Routes window), and you cannot switch a hidden layer to be the active layer.

A layer can be deleted if you no longer need or want to separate the nodes and routes within it. To delete a layer:

1. In the Layers dialog box, select the layer you want to delete from the list.
2. Click the **Delete** button and then click **OK** in the confirmation dialog box.

When you delete a layer, you do NOT delete the nodes, prototypes, and connections in that layer. Instead, everything in the deleted layer automatically becomes part of the default layer—which is the first layer in the list.

Last, if you use different layers and not all are currently displayed, you may notice gray-shaded node icons. This indicates that the gray-shaded node is linked in a layer that is not currently displayed.

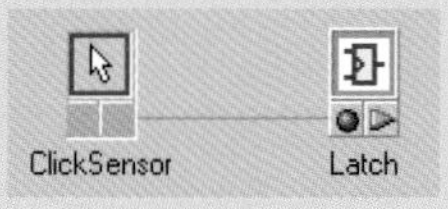

Other EON Studio Child Windows

As we mentioned at the beginning of this lesson, there are a number of child windows (windows within the main EON Studio window) that are used less frequently than the three main windows (Simulation Tree, Components, and Routes) that we have discussed to this point. These windows, however, are still extremely important to the overall simulation creation process and for learning to use EON with ease and efficiency.

Property Bar

All nodes have a preset collection of properties, or defining characteristics, that can be accessed and updated using the Property Bar for each node. The Property Bar view is available on the right side of the Simulation Tree window. This is where you can enter specific instructions to control size, shape, color, movement, and other properties that are available for the selected node. In the Property Bar, you can adjust coordinate settings, import files, set the node to be active or inactive, or perform other functions, depending on the node or prototype function. This will allow you to "fine-tune" your simulation. Figure 1.2.20 is an example of the properties available for the 2DImage node.

FIGURE 1.2.20 Property Bar for the 2DImage node

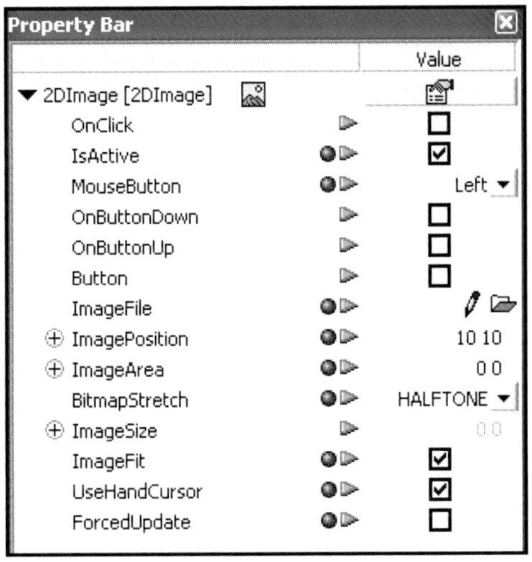

Activity 1.2.3: Changing Properties

1. Continue working with the open simulation file **RotatingPyramid.eoz** from Activity 1.2.2.
2. In the simulation tree, select the **Rotate** node. The properties for the Rotate command will appear in the Property Bar.
3. Click the check box next to the **active** property so that there is no check mark in the box. This alters the setting so that the pyramid will no longer rotate unless you click it.
4. Change the **LapTime** to a number between 5 and 10. (LapTime denotes how many seconds it takes to rotate one revolution. The closer to 10, the slower the rotation speed. You can experiment with this rotation speed.) You can change the value of the LapTime by either using the up and down arrows next to the field or by selecting the value in the field and keying a new value.
5. Click the **green arrow** (Start Simulation button) on the toolbar to run the simulation. This will launch the EON simulation window. Notice that now the pyramid is not rotating when the simulation starts.
6. Click the pyramid to start it rotating. Notice that its rotation speed is decreased from what it was when you first ran the simulation.
7. Repeat steps 4–6 if you would like to adjust the rotation speed again and then test any adjustments you make.
8. When you are satisfied with the rotation speed, close the simulation window. Save the simulation and keep it open to use in Activity 1.2.4.

tips+tricks

The Property Bar for the Rotate node also has an option to change the axis of rotation. That is something we will experiment with later.

BEST PRACTICES

Simulation Creation Overview

Up to this point, we have viewed and explored each separate window in EON. You must understand how these separate elements work together to create the simulation. As shown in the figure below, there is a basic four-step process for simulation creation.

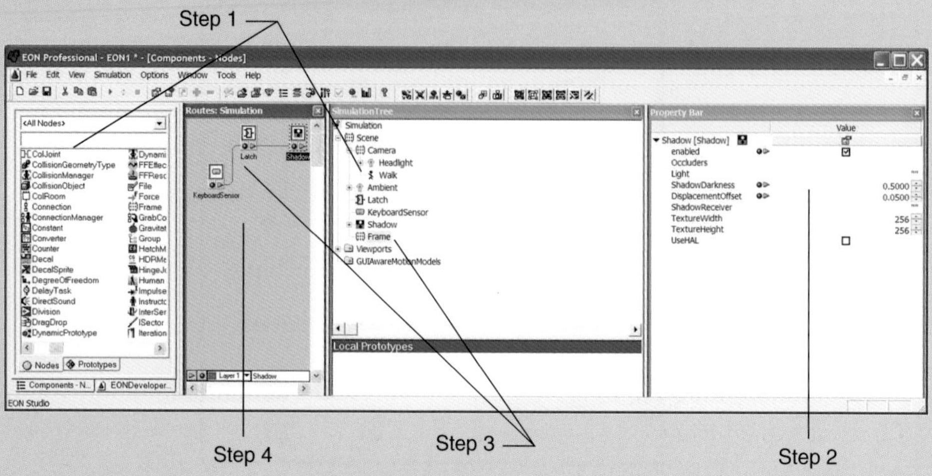

1. Add nodes (or prototypes) from the Components window to the simulation tree to create the desired subtree hierarchies.
2. Set node properties.
3. Drag and drop nodes from the simulation tree to the Routes window.
4. Connect nodes in the Routes window.

Keep these steps in mind as we move forward, because you will need to repeat them many times.

Log Window

The Log window, as shown in Figure 1.2.21, provides current information on EON Studio's internal operations. This feature is used for debugging and fine-tuning simulation behavior. It is especially useful when your simulation includes scripts or when you have created custom nodes.

FIGURE 1.2.21 Sample Log window

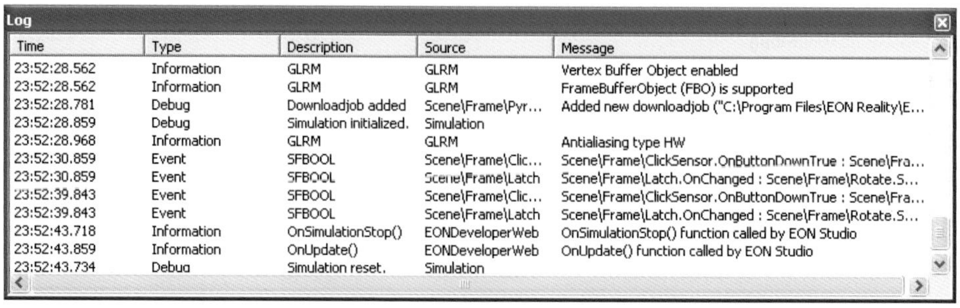

Time	Type	Description	Source	Message
23:52:28.562	Information	GLRM	GLRM	Vertex Buffer Object enabled
23:52:28.562	Information	GLRM	GLRM	FrameBufferObject (FBO) is supported
23:52:28.781	Debug	Downloadjob added	Scene\Frame\Pyr...	Added new downloadjob ("C:\Program Files\EON Reality\E...
23:52:28.859	Debug	Simulation initialized.	Simulation	
23:52:28.968	Information	GLRM	GLRM	Antialiasing type HW
23:52:30.859	Event	SFBOOL	Scene\Frame\Clic...	Scene\Frame\ClickSensor.OnButtonDownTrue : Scene\Fra...
23:52:30.859	Event	SFBOOL	Scene\Frame\Latch	Scene\Frame\Latch.OnChanged : Scene\Frame\Rotate.S...
23:52:39.843	Event	SFBOOL	Scene\Frame\Clic...	Scene\Frame\ClickSensor.OnButtonDownTrue : Scene\Fra...
23:52:39.843	Event	SFBOOL	Scene\Frame\Latch	Scene\Frame\Latch.OnChanged : Scene\Frame\Rotate.S...
23:52:43.718	Information	OnSimulationStop()	EONDeveloperWeb	OnSimulationStop() function called by EON Studio
23:52:43.859	Information	OnUpdate()	EONDeveloperWeb	OnUpdate() function called by EON Studio
23:52:43.734	Debug	Simulation reset.	Simulation	

Pop-Up Menu

You can right-click in the Log window to display a pop-up menu, as shown in Figure 1.2.22. From this menu, you have several choices, which are detailed in Table 1.2.3.

FIGURE 1.2.22 Log pop-up menu

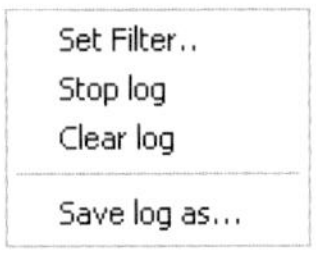

TABLE 1.2.3 Log Menu Options

Option	Action
Set Filter	Opens the Log Filter window. (Also accessible by choosing Set Log Filter from the Options menu or the Log Filter button on the toolbar.)
Stop log	Stops log entry.
Clear log	Removes all current log entries.
Save log as	Saves the contents of the Log window in a .txt file. The columns of the Log window are separated with tab characters.

Log data is not saved when you close the simulation. So, if there is any log entry that you would like to save for future reference, choose the *Save log as* option. The data will then be accessible for future reference.

Log Filter Window

To specify the type of information displayed in the Log window, select Set Log Filter from the Options menu, click the Log Filter toolbar button, or choose Set Filter from the pop-up menu in the Log window. This will open the Log Filter window, similar to that shown in Figure 1.2.23.

FIGURE 1.2.23 Log Filter window

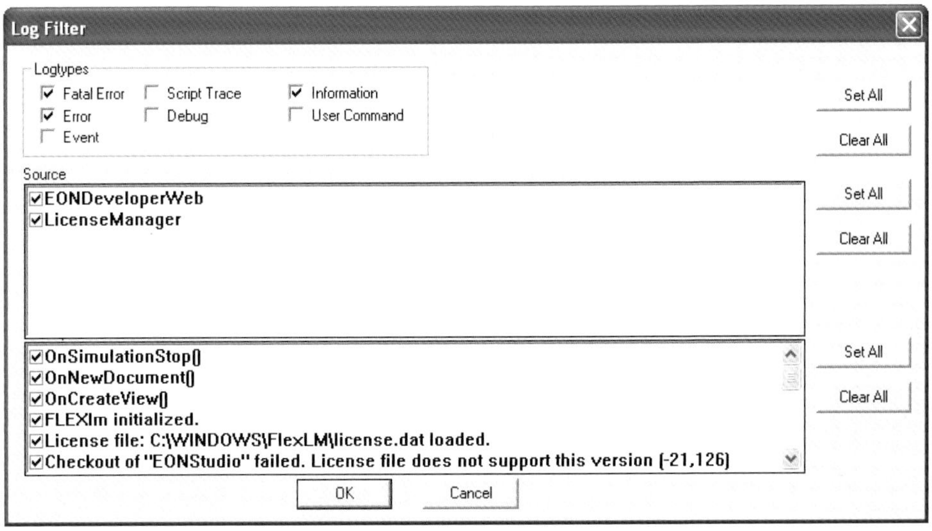

Within the Log Filter window, you can choose the type of information you want to see displayed in the log. Your basic choices of log types are outlined in Table 1.2.4.

TABLE 1.2.4 Log Types

Log Type	Description
Fatal Error	Displays fatal errors. Fatal errors are those that must be corrected before you can run your simulation.
Error	Displays less serious errors.
Event	Displays all events from the current simulation.
Script Trace	Used to check if a certain line in a script has been reached.
Debug	Displays debug messages of interest to developers creating custom nodes with EON Professional.
Information	Displays information from developers of an EON simulation to the user.
User Command	Displays user commands made during the simulation.

From the Log Filter window, you may also choose to display errors for selected portions of the program. You can make this selection in the Source section of the window. This gives you fine-grained control to display error messages when you are debugging a simulation. For either Logtypes or Source, you can use the Set All or Clear All buttons to quickly select or deselect your options.

Find Window

The Find window is a search tool you can use to locate nodes in the simulation tree. It is particularly useful when you need to change the properties for one or several nodes in a complex simulation. To open the Find window, choose Find from the Window menu or press Alt + 4. By default, the Find window opens in Floating mode and appears similar to Figure 1.2.24.

FIGURE 1.2.24 Find window

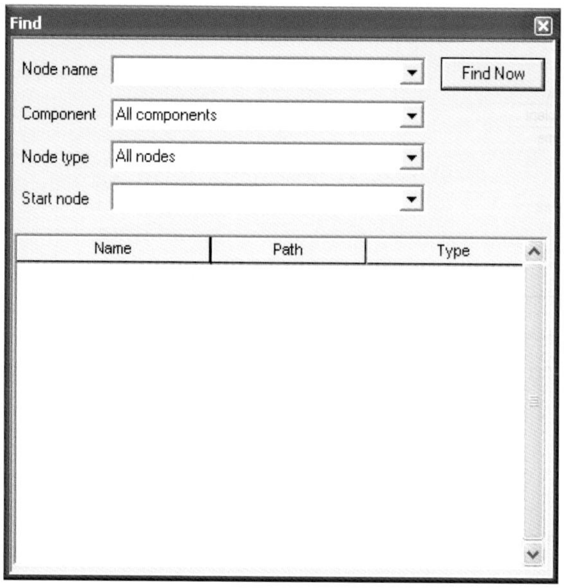

You can use this window to search using the search criteria options outlined in Table 1.2.5.

TABLE 1.2.5 Search Criteria in the Find Window

Criteria	Description
Node name	Use when searching for a specific node. Enter one or more characters of the name in the Node name field. Note that the entire text string for each node name is evaluated, regardless of the text string's position in the node name. For example, if you enter the letters "de," EON would find both the nodes Decal and LevelOfDetail.
Component	Defines the component group. The contents of the drop-down list correspond to the list in the Components window.
Node type	Defines the node type. Select the type from the drop-down list. If you have selected a component group in the Component drop-down list, only nodes that belong to the selected component group are available in the Node type drop-down list.
Start node	Defines where the search is started in the simulation tree. Enter the entire path manually, or select a node in the simulation tree and then drag and drop it into the *Start node* field.

cross-reference

You will learn more about the different groups and types of nodes in Lesson 3 of this module and as they are used in later lessons.

Searching for a Node

To search for a node, enter one or more of the search criteria into the Find window. When you click the Find Now button, the search results are displayed in a table at the bottom of the Find window, as shown in Figure 1.2.25.

FIGURE 1.2.25 Sample search results in the Find window

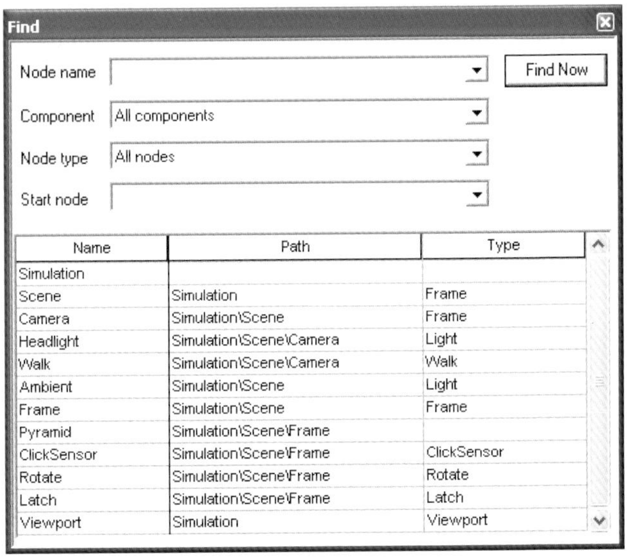

The basic search results table lists the information detailed in Table 1.2.6. Depending on the search criteria you enter and the results of the search, you may see additional fields displayed in your search results table.

TABLE 1.2.6 Search Results Fields

Search Result Field	Description
Name	This column is always visible, even if you scroll horizontally.
Path	The path to the node in the simulation tree.
Type	The node type.

If all detected nodes are of a single type (for example, if all are Frame nodes), the contents of fields from the Property Bar are displayed. For example, if Frame is selected for the Node type, the search results will show only frames, and all the properties that are common to all frames are shown in the Find window, as shown in Figure 1.2.26. Note that you may need to use the scroll bars or adjust the size of your Find window to see all of these fields.

FIGURE 1.2.26 Expanded search results fields

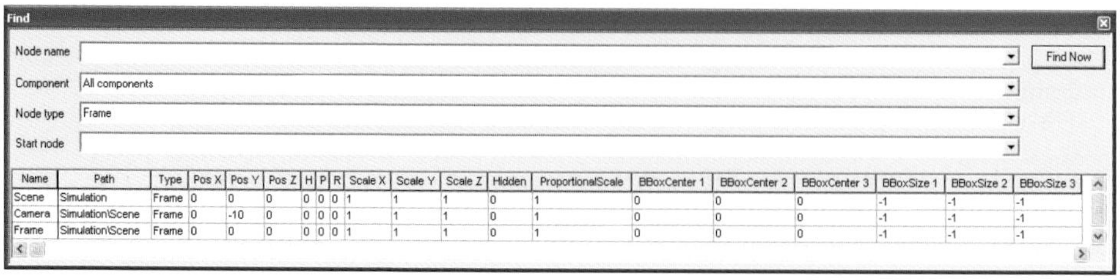

Note that multiple value fields are never displayed. Also, some fields may be displayed in the list, but the column heading may differ from the actual field names in the Property Bar. For example, the color fields Red, Green, and Blue are named Color1, Color2, and Color3 in the search results table.

Working with Search Results

To sort the results, click the column heading you want to sort by. Click the heading again to toggle the presentation between ascending and descending order based on that field.

To show a particular node's position in the simulation tree, double-click anywhere in that node's row in the search results table. The node on that row will be highlighted in the simulation tree.

In addition to viewing and locating nodes in the simulation tree, you can also edit property values directly in the search results table. Values in the node's Property Bar are updated automatically when changes are made in the Find window.

Multiselection

The Find window also supports multiselection. This means that you can select multiple cells and change their values in one sweep. To use this feature:

1. Select one column or row or a range of rows and columns.
2. Key a value and press Enter.
3. The keyed value will be written to all marked rows and columns.

If any marked field does not support the new value, the update is ignored for that field, but any fields that are valid will be updated with the new value.

When keying a new value, special syntax can be used to do arithmetic operations on the existing field value. The operations supported are addition (+=), subtraction (−=), multiplication (*=), and division (/=). For instance, if you want to increase every selected field value by 5, simply key +=5 instead of 5.

This syntax works for strings as well, but only addition and subtraction prefixes are used. The former will append the string after the existing string value in the field, and the latter will append it in front. For example, entering +=Test to a field containing FieldValue will result in a field containing FieldValueTest.

Activity 1.2.4: Using the Find Window

1. Continue working with the open simulation file **RotatingPyramid.eoz** from Activity 1.2.3.
2. Choose **Window > Find**. In the Node type field, select the drop-down menu. Scroll down and select **Frame.**
3. Click **Find Now.** (Your Find window should look similar to Figure 1.2.26 shown previously.)
4. In the Frame row, select the values for **Scale X, Scale Y,** and **Scale Z.**
5. Key **2** and then press **Enter.** The values under Scale X, Scale Y, and Scale Z in the Frame row will all change from 1 to 2.
6. Double-click anywhere on the **Frame** row. Notice that the Frame node is highlighted in the simulation tree and that the Frame properties are, consequently, shown in the Property Bar. Note that the values next to Scale are now 2 2 2. Your screen should appear similar to Figure 1.2.27.

FIGURE 1.2.27 Changes in the Find window reflected in the Property Bar

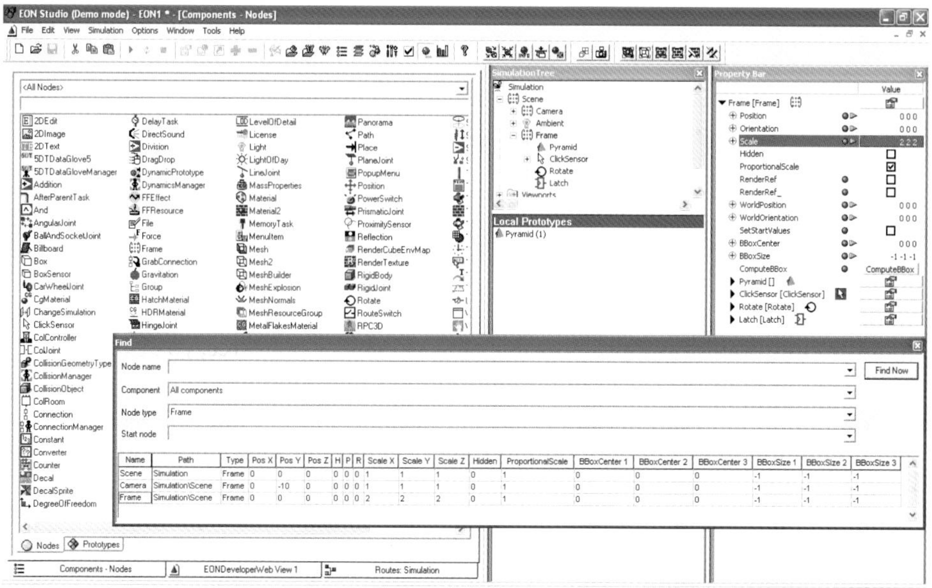

7. Click the **Close** button in the Find window.
8. Click the **Start Simulation** button to run the simulation. Notice that the pyramid is now twice the size as it was originally.
9. Click the pyramid to ensure that it still rotates and then close the simulation window.
10. Save the simulation and keep it open to use in Activity 1.2.5.

BEST PRACTICES

Ways of Viewing Windows

For some windows, you can set the window mode of a view (Floating, Docked, or MDI Child) by right-clicking the title bar to bring up the view context menu shown here. (For a window in MDI Child mode, right-click a workbook tab.)

Docked mode inserts the window into the main EON window, redistributing the space used by the other windows. *MDI Child* mode places the window as another tab next to the Components and Routes windows.

When you select *Floating* mode for a window, it will not automatically dock to the workspace again. To dock a window, right-click the window's title bar and choose the Docked or Docked to . . . Left/Right/Top/Bottom menu command.

Multiple Document Interface (MDI) windows are those that reside under a single parent window as opposed to situations in which all the windows are separate from each other.

Butterfly Window

The Butterfly window displays an overview of the various connections (routes) for a selected node and is another tool you can use to navigate and explore your simulation design. When you view nodes in the Butterfly window, you will find that it is easier to follow routes between indirectly linked nodes and to see how events will pass over the routes.

tips+tricks

Like the Find window, the Butterfly window opens by default as a floating window.

The Butterfly window displays the selected node as the central node in the window. The names and icons of the central (or selected) node and all connected nodes are displayed. Additionally, the names and types of all inEvents and outEvents connected to the central node are graphically illustrated, and you can see the names of the fields of the connected nodes. You will see nodes that send inEvents to the Butterfly window's central node displayed to the left, and to the right are the nodes that receive outEvents from the central node.

After you select (in the simulation tree) the node for which you want to see information, click the Show in Butterfly button on the toolbar. A window similar to the one shown in Figure 1.2.28 will display. Note that you can then select other nodes (as the Rotate node is selected in Figure 1.2.28) and shift the focus to the newly selected node as the central node.

FIGURE 1.2.28 Butterfly window

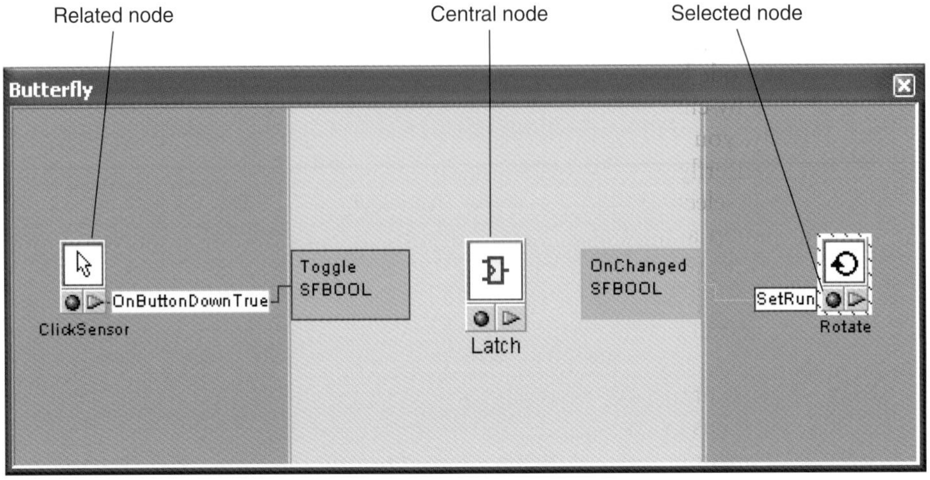

tips+tricks

Depending on the contents of the Butterfly window, you may have to resize it to see all of the information displayed.

In addition to using the Show in Butterfly button on the toolbar, there are two other ways you can display the Butterfly window:

- Right-click the node in the Routes window and select Show in Butterfly from the pop-up menu.
- Right-click the node in the Simulation Tree window and choose Show in Butterfly from the pop-up menu.

tips+tricks

The Butterfly window is a read-only display. You cannot make changes to the connections in this window.

Pop-Up Menus

If you right-click in the Butterfly window (not on a connection or node), you see a pop-up menu as illustrated in Figure 1.2.29.

FIGURE 1.2.29 Pop-up menu in Butterfly window

If you right-click a node in the Butterfly window, you will see a pop-up menu like that shown in Figure 1.2.30.

FIGURE 1.2.30 Pop-up node menu with a node selected in Butterfly window

The Follow Tree option (in either menu) means that the Butterfly window will show the node that the user clicks in the simulation tree. If you select the Follow Routes option, the node you select in the Routes view will be shown in the center of the Butterfly window.

When you select Properties from the pop-up menu with a node selected, the selected node's Property page opens. The Show in Tree option highlights the selected node in the simulation tree, and the Show in Routes option highlights the selected node in the Routes window. (If the Routes window is not already open, it will open when this option is selected.)

Navigating the Butterfly Window

You can change the focus of the Butterfly window so that a connected node becomes the new central node by using either the mouse or the arrow keys. Change the focus using the mouse by clicking a connected node to make it the central node.

Alternatively, you also can use the keyboard to change the focus. If you look closely at the Butterfly window, you will notice that one of the connected nodes is surrounded by a selection frame (hash marks). You can move this frame using the arrow keys. The up and down arrow keys move the frame vertically. The left and right arrow keys move the frame horizontally. If the selected node is to the left of the central node, press the left arrow key to make it the new central node. If the selected node is to the right of the central node, press the right arrow key to make it the new central node.

The previous central node is automatically selected after a focus shift, making it easy to shift the focus back to the previous central node. If the previous central node is to the left of the new central node, press the left arrow key to make it the central node again. If the previous central node is to the right of the new central node, press the right arrow key to put it back in the central position.

Activity 1.2.5: Using the Butterfly Window

1. Continue working with the open simulation file **RotatingPyramid.eoz** from Activity 1.2.4.
2. Select **Frame** in the simulation tree. Click the **Show in Butterfly** button on the Toolbar.
3. In the Butterfly window, choose one of the methods discussed earlier to display a node as the central node. Note that the selection frame is on the left side of the central node.
4. Press the **right arrow** key to move the selection frame to the right side of the central node.
5. To make ClickSensor the central node, click it in the simulation tree. The Butterfly window changes to reflect this selction, as shown in Figure 1.2.31. Notice that nothing is displayed to the left of the central node because there is no inEvent for the ClickSensor.

FIGURE 1.2.31 Central node shifted in Butterfly window

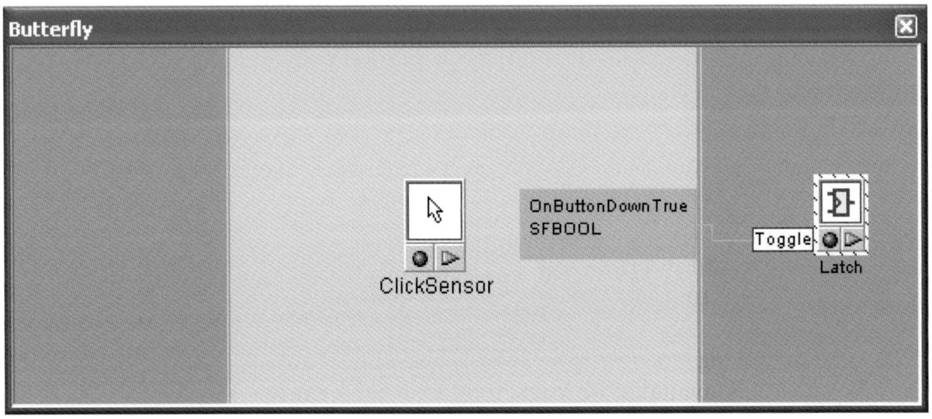

tips+tricks

The central node may be connected to another node via two or more different routes. If this is the case, a node icon is displayed for each route.

6. Click the **Latch** node in the Butterfly window to make it the central node again.
7. Right-click the **Latch** node in the Butterfly window and select **Show in Tree.** The Latch node is highlighted in the simulation tree.
8. Right-click the **ClickSensor** node in the Butterfly window and select **Show in Routes.** The Routes window opens (if necessary), and the portion that shows the ClickSensor is displayed with ClickSensor highlighted.
9. In the Routes window, click the **Rotate** node. The Butterfly window changes to reflect this selection, putting the Rotate node in the central position because the Follow Routes option is selected.
10. In the simulation tree, click the **ClickSensor** node. In the Butterfly window, ClickSensor becomes the central node because the Follow Tree option is selected.
11. Close the Butterfly window. Close EON without saving the simulation.

discuss

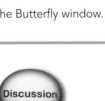

Navigating through the nodes and routes in the Butterfly window may seem a bit unnecessary at times. Can you think of situations in which this would be a useful tool when your simulations become more complex? Can you envision a time when it might prove difficult to locate a node or determine exactly what inEvents and outEvents are controlling the actions within a simulation?

Toolbars

In our limited exploration of the EON user interface so far, we have already used a few of the buttons on the toolbars. We will explore many more of these—and we will use some buttons repeatedly—as we move forward with our simulation creation. First, however, let's take a few moments to get a general overview of the toolbars and their available buttons.

By default, the button toolbars are displayed across the top of the EON window. The toolbars, as shown in Figure 1.2.32, include the standard Toolbar, the EON Zoom Extents Bar, the EONSelectionTools Bar, and the VisualNodesTools Bar. Additionally, the Status Bar is visible across the bottom of the EON window.

FIGURE 1.2.32 EON toolbars

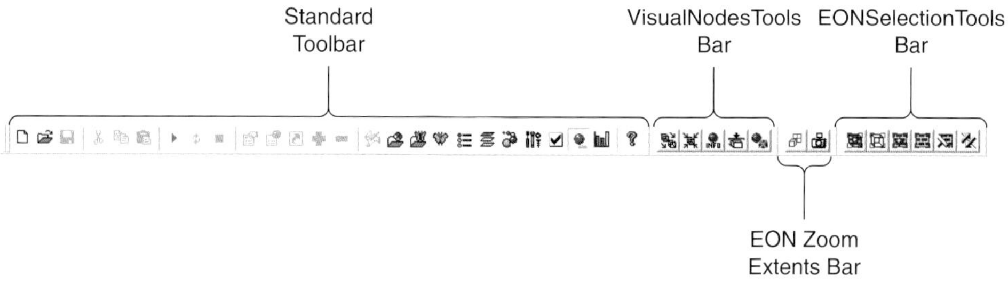

Each toolbar can be displayed or hidden by selecting or deselecting the toolbar name on the View menu (see Figure 1.2.33).

In the following sections, we will name and briefly describe the tools available on each toolbar. Their actual functions, however, will be detailed in later lessons when they are used.

If you are unsure of the name of a button, place your mouse pointer over the button for a few seconds to view the tooltip. The tooltip shows the name of the button and, consequently, provides clues about the use of the button.

FIGURE 1.2.33 View menu

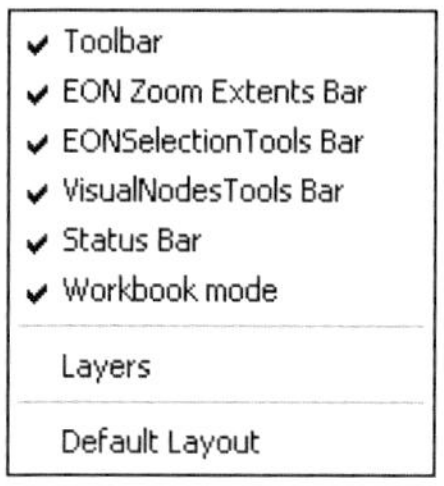

Toolbar

The primary EON Toolbar is shown in Figure 1.2.34. We have already used some of the tools available on this toolbar (Start Simulation, Show in Butterfly, and Log Filter), and we will use others as we progress in simulation creation.

FIGURE 1.2.34 Primary EON Toolbar

You are probably already familiar with the first set of buttons because they are common to many microcomputer applications: New, Open, Save, Cut, Copy, and Paste. The next three buttons control the running of the simulation. The remaining buttons help control what is displayed and how it is displayed. There is also a button to access the Help system, which we will discuss later in this lesson.

EON Zoom Extents Bar

Zoom Extents is a feature that enables you to quickly locate 3D objects in the simulation window. The camera is moved to make the selected object come into view completely. Figure 1.2.35 shows the buttons on the EON Zoom Extents Bar.

FIGURE 1.2.35 EON Zoom Extents Bar

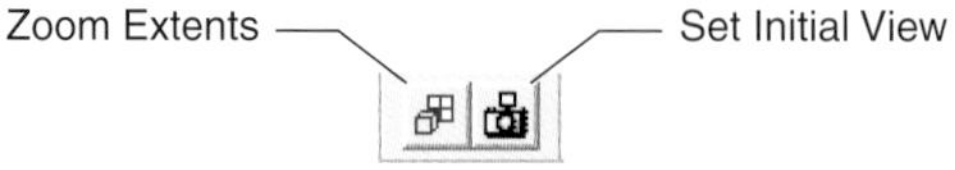

If you only want to set the Camera frame, the Set Initial View toolbar button will set the camera's start values. The Zoom Extents function only works on Frame, Prototype, and Shape nodes.

EONSelectionTools Bar

Selection tools make it easier to find objects in the simulation window and see where they are located in the simulation tree. The selection tools (shown in Figure 1.2.36) can also find and zoom in after an object is selected in the simulation tree.

tips+tricks

Note that selection tools only work with the new visual nodes. The selection tools do not work with EON Studio version 3.0 or earlier materials and textures, with the exception of the Mesh node.

FIGURE 1.2.36 EONSelectionTools Bar

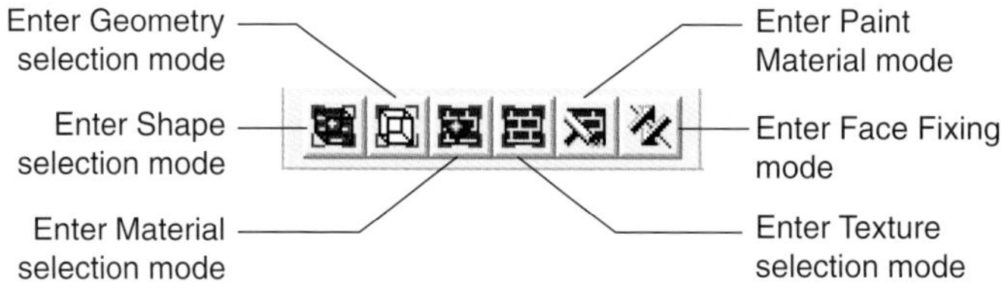

To support the Visual Nodes set, four selection tools are available on this toolbar. These tools are used to interactively select a Shape, Geometry (mesh), Material, or Texture node in the 3D simulation window simply by left-clicking the objects in the scene with the mouse.

A selection tool is active until you choose another selection tool or turn off the current tool by clicking it again. As long as the tool is active, whenever you click with the mouse in the 3D simulation window, the tool will try to select the subject (a shape, mesh, material, or texture, depending on the current selection tool) under the mouse cursor. If successful, the corresponding node in the simulation tree will be selected and selection brackets will appear around the selected object in the 3D window. Note that selection brackets are not displayed for texture and material selections.

When one of the selection tools is active (toolbar button depressed), the selection brackets will follow the selection made in the simulation tree. In other words, when you select another Shape node in the tree, the selection brackets will jump to the corresponding object in the 3D window. Note that because Material and Texture do not have selection brackets, this reverse selection feature only works for Mesh and Shape nodes.

tips+tricks

Selection, Paint, and Face Fixing tools require a modifier key (Alt) to activate.

VisualNodesTools Bar

The VisualNodesTools Bar, shown in Figure 1.2.37, contains five buttons that allow specific actions related to the Visual Nodes set. The buttons available are:

- Convert 3.1 Visual Nodes
- Merge shapes with the same material
- Display info of a node
- Make texture compression/resize permanent
- Remove duplicated resources

FIGURE 1.2.37 VisualNodesTools Bar

cross-reference

These features will be discussed further in Module 4 Lesson 2.

Status Bar

Across the bottom of the EON window is the Status Bar. This provides helpful information about what is going on in your simulation; combined with other tools such as the Log window, it can assist you in diagnosing errors and troubleshooting.

Returning to the Default Layout

The first time you start EON Studio, you will see a default layout of windows displayed in the EON main window. The default layout includes the following:

- The Simulation Tree window docked to the middle right
- The Components window displayed as an MDI window in Workbook mode on the left side
- The Property Bar available on the right side of the Simulation Tree window
- The Routes view located on the left side as another MDI window in Workbook mode
- The Find window is not visible but will open by default as a floating window, which makes it function like a dialog window
- The Butterfly window is not visible but will open by default as a floating window

Refer to Figure 1.2.3 at the beginning of this lesson to see the default workspace layout.

As you work on simulations, you may find it necessary to alter the workspace, expanding the size of different windows, closing some, and docking or undocking others. You may end up with a window that looks very dissimilar to the original layout. You can quickly restore the layout to the default workspace configuration by selecting Default Layout from the View menu.

Getting Help

Context-Sensitive Help (F1 Key)

Some views support context-sensitive help. This means you can bring up the correct Help page of a specific node/prototype by pressing F1 while the node/prototype is selected. The Components view, Simulation Tree window, and Property Bar support context-sensitive help.

The information that is displayed depends on which view you are in when you press the F1 key:

- If you are on the Nodes tab of the Components window, pressing F1 will present a Help page describing how to use the selected node.
- If you are on the Prototypes tab of the Components window, pressing F1 will present a Help page describing how to use the selected prototype.

web links

Because EON Studio is an ever-changing (and improving) product, you may encounter elements in your version of EON that simply have a link to online support where you can obtain more information. It is also possible that you might encounter an item that has not been documented yet. If this occurs, you can go to the support site and open a "ticket" (query) about that item. You should receive a response within 24 hours. After your question is answered, be sure to close the ticket.

These questions and their answers will be used to guide future development of online help and documentation.

- If you are in the Simulation Tree window or the Property Bar, pressing F1 will present a Help page describing the node and the fields found in the Property Bar for the selected node.

Help Topics

Another avenue for obtaining help is through the EON Help window. This can be accessed by clicking the Help Topics button on the Toolbar or by selecting Help Topics from the Help menu.

This opens the same window that is accessed using the F1 key, as shown in Figure 1.2.38. Rather than opening a specific topic (based on what is selected), however, it opens the "home" page from which you can generate your own search based on keywords, or you can browse through the entire Help system.

FIGURE 1.2.38 EON Help window

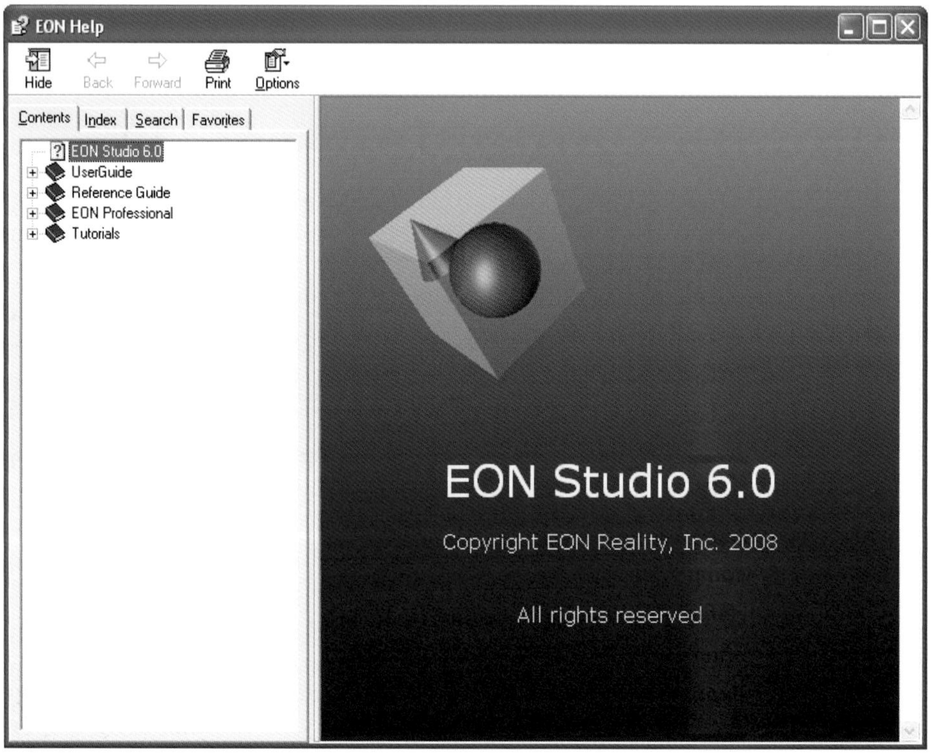

Summary

In this lesson you:

- Explored basic EON Studio terms and concepts such as nodes, prototypes, modules, and EON data types.
- Learned to navigate within EON Studio workspace and windows.
- Used the EON Studio child windows and toolbars to accomplish tasks.
- Explored the various Help features that enable you to get the most out of EON Studio.

LESSON 1.3

Introducing EON Nodes and Basic Prototypes

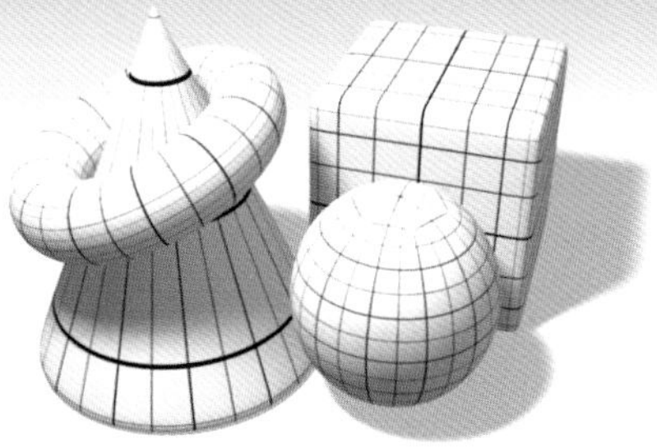

Objectives

In this lesson you will:

- Become aware of the different data types used in EON.
- Learn about the various types of fields used in EON.
- Explore node functions.
- Create simulations using some of the more commonly used nodes.
- Learn about basic prototypes and how to use them in simulations.

Key Terms

color field type
compound field type
default node fields
enumeration field type
exposedField
fields
floating point
inEvent
integer
numeric range field type
outEvent
prototype definition
prototype instance

An EON application is constructed by arranging and connecting EON nodes. EON Studio has more than one hundred predefined nodes that you can use to add elements and features to your EON application. A unique assortment of properties is displayed in each node's Property Bar. By entering information in the Property Bar, a user can define how the node will perform in a simulation. Each node also has a default name that reflects its particular task in a simulation. By changing the default name of a node, you can easily distinguish it from other nodes of the same type.

A node has no effect on a simulation until it is placed in an environment where it can interact with other nodes. As you learned in the previous lesson, interaction between nodes is made possible by arranging the nodes in the simulation tree hierarchy and by making connections in the Routes window or by enabling actions on the properties of the nodes. After nodes are connected to one another, they can exchange information while a simulation is running. The information a node receives results in an action of some kind—for example, an object may move or a sound or video file may play.

Data Types

All nodes contain information, or data. This data can be changed from the Property Bar or by receiving data from other nodes. The type of data a node can store, send, or receive depends on the node's predefined characteristics.

The data types used in EON are listed in Table 1.3.1. The name given to each data type reflects its function. The *SF* prefix denotes *single-field* data types. All SF data types also have *multiple-field* counterparts with the prefix *MF*. MF data types can store several SF values. For example, an *SFBool* (Boolean data type) has one field and can store a single true or false value; an *MFBool* has multiple fields and can store a list of true and false values.

TABLE 1.3.1 EON Data Types

Classification	Data Type	Description	Range
Integer	SFInt32	Whole number	[-2,147,483,648, 2,147,483,647]
Float	SFFloat	Floating point (a number with a decimal point)	[-3.4E-38, 3.4E 38]
Image	SFImage	Obsolete data type; not used by any node	
String	SFString	Text string	Not applicable
2D float vector	SFVec2f	Two-dimensional float vector, for example, in a coordinate system where X = 1.5 and Y = 1.5	[-3.4E-38, 3.4E 38]
3D float vector	SFVec3f	Three-dimensional float vector, for example, in a coordinate system where X = 1.5, Y = 1.5, and Z = 1.5	[-3.4E-38, 3.4E 38]
Boolean	SFBool	Boolean value; can be either true or false	0 or 1
Node	SFNode	Reference to a node	
Color	SFColor	Three floats for RGB (red, green, and blue values)	0–1
Time	SFTime	Double float representing seconds	
Rotation	SFRotation	Four floats: rotation around an axis in radians	

We will explore these data types further as we encounter them in our simulation development. For now, it is sufficient to recognize that there are different field types and that a node's data type dictates what data can be stored within, sent from, or received by that node.

web links

In computing, ***floating point*** refers to numeric values that have a decimal point (i.e., "real numbers"), whereas ***integer*** refers to numeric values that do not have a decimal point (i.e., "whole numbers"). For floating point numbers, the decimal point is not in a fixed position and can "float" to a specific position within the number as needed to accommodate the value being stored. All numeric values are stored in the computer's memory as a set of binary digits (or bits) that represent the order of magnitude (i.e., size or scale) for the number (real or whole number) being stored.

If you are unfamiliar with floating point usage, use the Internet to research the topic and learn more.

Fields

Nodes use ***fields*** to store data and to communicate with other nodes. Some fields are incorporated in all EON nodes. These fields, which are shown in Table 1.3.2, are the ***default node fields*** and are not, by default, shown in the Property Bar. (The Property Bar menu item, under the Options menu, can be used to check or uncheck the *Show all fields* setting.) Additionally, most nodes also have fields that are tailored to a node's particular function in a simulation.

TABLE 1.3.2 Fields in All EON Nodes

Field	Field Type	Data type	Description	Range
TreeChildren	Field	MFNode	List of child nodes and links	
Children	Field	MFNode	List of child nodes	
SetRun	inEvent	SFBool	Starts node if stopped	0/1
SetRun_	inEvent	SFBool	Stops node if running	0/1
OnRunFalse	outEvent	SFBool	True when the node is stopped	0/1
OnRunTrue	outEvent	SFBool	True when the node is started	0/1
OnRunChanged	outEvent	SFBool	True when the node changes state from running to stopped or vice versa	0/1

EON nodes use four field types:

- outEvent: These fields are used to send data.
- inEvent: These fields are used to receive data.
- exposedField: These fields are used to send and receive data.
- field: These fields are reserved for internal use.

Fields can serve as connection points for routing data between nodes in real time. (Recall that routes are created in the Routes window.) As you learned in Module 1 Lesson 2, an *event* occurs when data is passed between two nodes via a connecting route. An event can modify a receiving node's fields and, consequently, the node's behavior in a simulation.

An ***exposedField*** is an object property that can serve as both an ***outEvent*** and ***inEvent*** field. A route connection can be made between different field types (from an exposedField or outEvent field to an exposedField or inEvent field) as long as the data types are the same. The data types of the source and destination nodes must always match, regardless of the field type.

Another way of saying this is that exposedFields can be modified in the Routes window if the connected nodes have exposedFields with compatible data types. Event-driven programming within EON can also be accomplished using Script nodes as an alternative to using the Routes window.

cross-reference

You will learn more about scripting in Module 9.

tips+tricks

An event that sends data out of a node is called an outEvent, and an event that receives data into a node is called an inEvent. Events are used to facilitate changes to field values, external conditions, interactions between nodes, and so on. Events may even be sent over routes leading to points outside of the simulation tree to communicate with a host application such as a web application, Visual Basic program, or PowerPoint presentation.

Viewing Node Fields

As you may recall, a node's fields and their values can be readily seen in the Property Bar. However, you should note that it is also possible to view all of a node's fields, the field type, the data type, and the current values. Simply right-click a node in the simulation tree and choose Show Fields. This will open a Fields dialog box for the chosen node, as shown in Figure 1.3.1. This can be a useful diagnostic tool and may prove helpful as you begin to understand nodes and their interactions within a simulation.

tips+tricks

The terms inEvent and outEvent are used interchangeably with eventIn and eventOut as well as inField and outField. You may see each term used in your work with EON as well as with other programs. We will use inEvent and outEvent throughout this text.

tips+tricks

You can also access the Fields dialog box by selecting the desired node in the simulation tree and pressing Shift + Enter on the keyboard or selecting Edit > Show Fields from the menu.

FIGURE 1.3.1 Fields dialog box for the default Scene frame

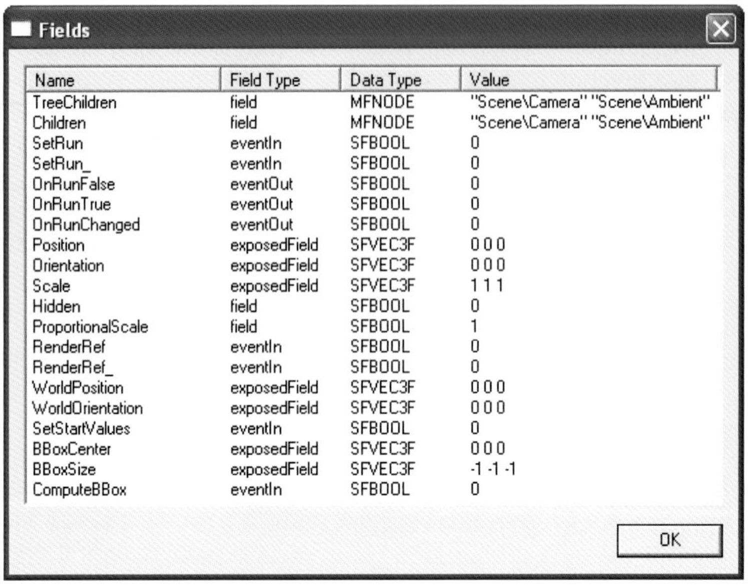

Fields

Name	Field Type	Data Type	Value
TreeChildren	field	MFNODE	"Scene\Camera" "Scene\Ambient"
Children	field	MFNODE	"Scene\Camera" "Scene\Ambient"
SetRun	eventIn	SFBOOL	0
SetRun_	eventIn	SFBOOL	0
OnRunFalse	eventOut	SFBOOL	0
OnRunTrue	eventOut	SFBOOL	0
OnRunChanged	eventOut	SFBOOL	0
Position	exposedField	SFVEC3F	0 0 0
Orientation	exposedField	SFVEC3F	0 0 0
Scale	exposedField	SFVEC3F	1 1 1
Hidden	field	SFBOOL	0
ProportionalScale	field	SFBOOL	1
RenderRef	eventIn	SFBOOL	0
RenderRef_	eventIn	SFBOOL	0
WorldPosition	exposedField	SFVEC3F	0 0 0
WorldOrientation	exposedField	SFVEC3F	0 0 0
SetStartValues	eventIn	SFBOOL	0
BBoxCenter	exposedField	SFVEC3F	0 0 0
BBoxSize	exposedField	SFVEC3F	-1 -1 -1
ComputeBBox	eventIn	SFBOOL	0

OK

Viewing Field Properties

In the Property Bar (found, by default, on the right side of the Simulation Tree window), the view is divided into two columns: field name and field value—as shown in Figure 1.3.2. You can adjust the column widths by dragging the divider in the header column (just as you would in any Microsoft Windows application).

FIGURE 1.3.2 Example Property Bar

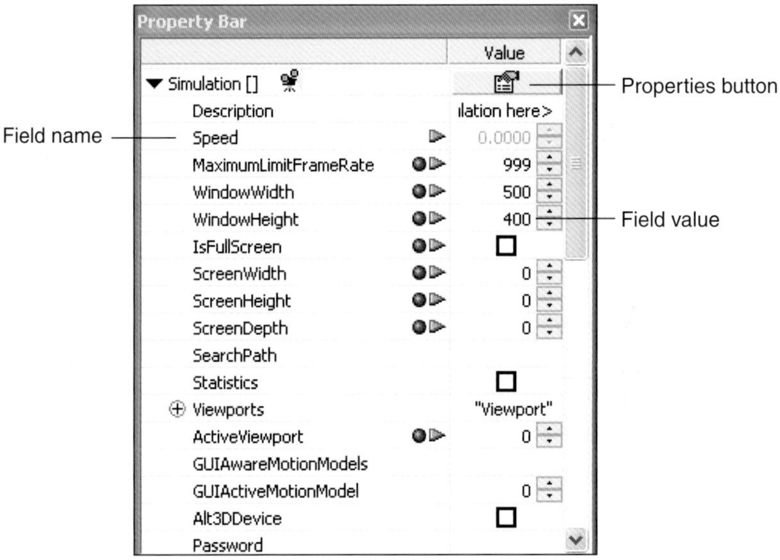

All fields available for editing within a node are shown in rows in the Property Bar. You can use the scroll bar on the window to see all of the options.

The view is updated with new content when the selection has changed (i.e., when you select a new node in the simulation tree). Also, when a simulation is running, the view is updated in real time.

In addition to fields, a row in the Property Bar can represent a node reference. This SFNode data type field occurs when a node contains children nodes or has fields that reference other nodes in the simulation tree. Instead of selecting the referenced node in the simulation tree, you can click the SFNode field and immediately view the fields of the referenced node inline (in the same Property Bar page). In the Property Bar, the text in square brackets next to the node's name identifies the node's type.

To open a Properties dialog box, you can click the Properties button in the Value column in the Property Bar (as shown in Figure 1.3.2). Like the Property Bar, the Properties dialog box (shown in Figure 1.3.3) allows you to view and modify an item's characteristics.

tips+tricks

All of the fields for a node are shown in the Property Bar except the seven default nodes listed in Table 1.3.2. These are not meant to be edited. To view them, you can enable the option *Show all fields* in the Property Bar Settings dialog box, which you access by selecting Options > Property Bar from the menu.

FIGURE 1.3.3 Simulation Properties dialog box

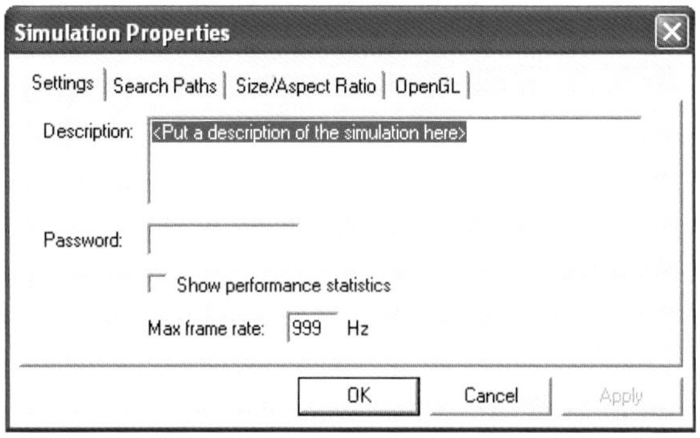

The differences between using a dialog box and using the Property Bar are immediately obvious. The dialog box presents the information in a more "user-friendly" manner than the Property Bar. Different types of data are separated into different tabs within the dialog box. Additionally, more information can be presented in the dialog box than what is visible in the Property Bar. For example, in the Description field of the Property Bar, the text that you see in the Value field is "ilation here>" or some portion of the text, depending upon the width of your Property Bar and the Value column within it. You need to select the value and scroll (using the mouse or arrow keys) to read all of the text. In the Simulation Properties dialog box, all the text, "<Put a description of the simulation here>," is immediately visible. You can also see other information, such as the units for values (i.e., the Maximum frame rate is in Hz), shown in the dialog box but not in the Property Bar.

Setting Field Values

The Property Bar is used to observe and adjust the values of the properties for each field within a node. Depending on the field type, how the values are adjusted varies. The various field types and the methods used to change the values are outlined in the following sections.

Text and Numeric Field Types

To set a new value for a text or numeric type field, simply find the field in the list and then click once on the Value column. The text or numeric value will be selected (highlighted) as shown in Figure 1.3.4 and, when you start keying, any characters you key will overwrite the previous value. There is no "undo" command. You must key the original value to undo your change. It is good practice, therefore, to note the original values before you make any changes so that you can return to them should you find that your edits are incorrect.

FIGURE 1.3.4 Editing a numeric value

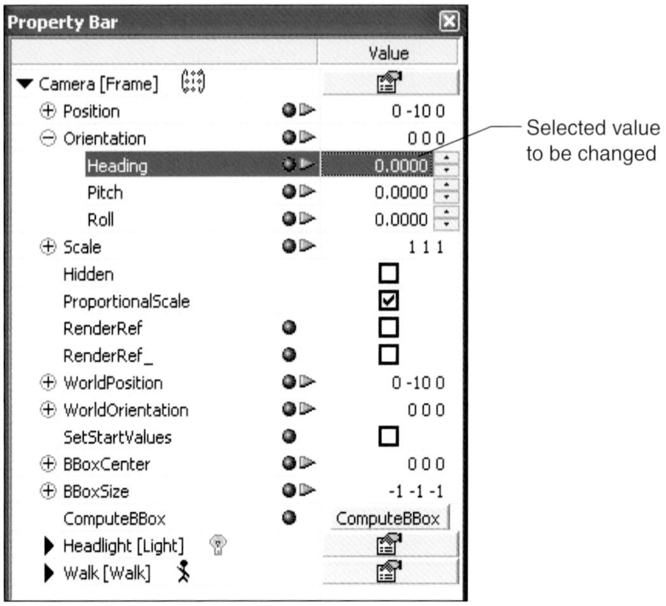

For numeric values, the number of digits allowed after the decimal point is set elsewhere. Therefore, you are limited to that number of characters. If you enter more than the specified number, the value will be rounded to the nearest decimal place.

If you do not want to replace the entire value (numeric or text), you can click on the value a second time to place an insertion point in the value, as shown in Figure 1.3.5. For numeric values, numbers to the right of the insertion point will be pushed over one place for each character entered but, again, the number will be rounded to the nearest decimal place allowed. In addition to highlighting and replacing the entire value or inserting values, you can also use the up or down arrow to increase or decrease numeric values.

FIGURE 1.3.5 Adding to a numeric value

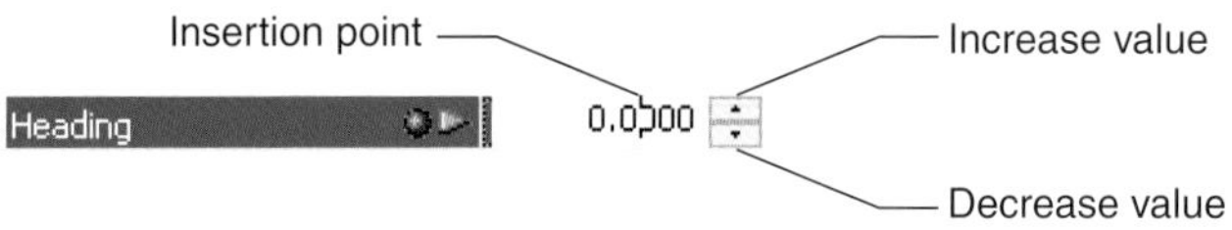

For text values, when you click a second time in the middle of the text string, the insertion point will appear at the desired location. The text will be deselected, and the cursor will be displayed as an insertion point. You can then key to add text to the string.

For numeric field types, you can click the up/down arrows to increase/decrease the value in discrete, predetermined increments. By holding down the up/down arrows and dragging the mouse, you can increase/decrease the field value continuously, as you would with a slider.

Boolean Field Type

To toggle a Boolean value, click to show the check mark in the box to set the value to true. Uncheck it to set it to false. See Figure 1.3.6 for examples of the true and false settings.

FIGURE 1.3.6 Setting Boolean values

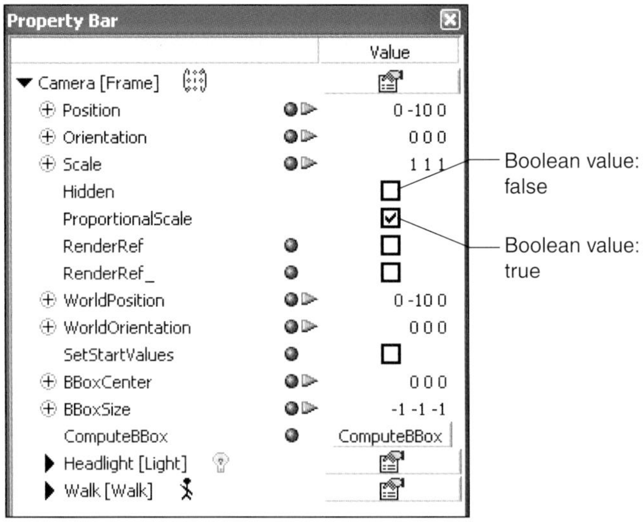

Filename Field Type

The Filename field is very similar to a text field, except that it has an additional Browse icon (as illustrated in Figure 1.3.7), which enables you to conveniently select a file through Microsoft Window's standard Open dialog box. You can choose to key the fully qualified file path and filename, or you can click the Browse icon to identify the correct file and its location more easily.

FIGURE 1.3.7 Identify a file and its location

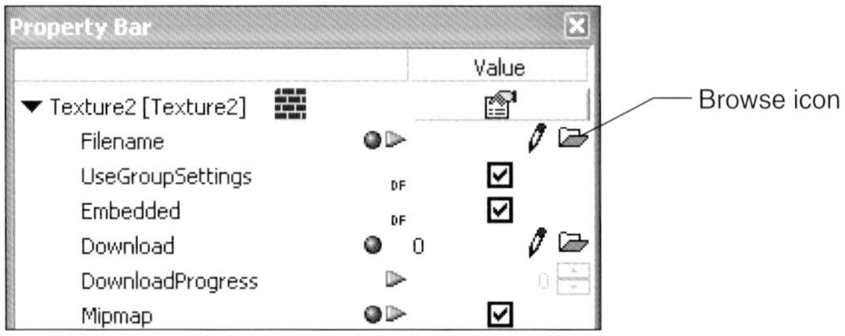

tips+tricks

The Property Bar is, by default, a narrow pane on the right side of the screen. To see a long filename or a long file path, you may need to expand the width of the Property Bar.

Enumeration Field Type

Some fields have a limited set of distinct values from which to choose. This is referred to as an ***enumeration field type.*** The Light node's Type field, for example, as shown in Figure 1.3.8, has only the following options: Ambient, Directional, Parallel Point, Point, and Spot. When such a field is encountered, the Property Bar will list the available options in a drop-down list. After you select a value from the list, the list will close. The value inside the square brackets shows the actual numeric value of the field.

FIGURE 1.3.8 Options for the Light node Type field

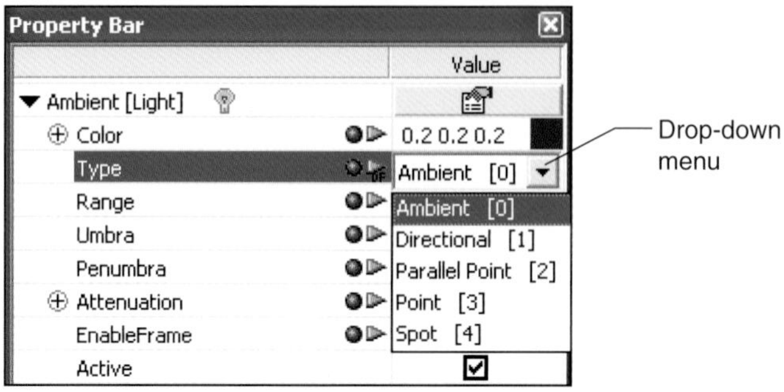

Numeric Range Field Type

Instead of a set of distinct values, some field values are continuous but within a limited range. In such cases, in addition to the ordinary numeric input box, a slider is available. This slider will appear beneath the selected field row if you click the down arrow, as shown in Figure 1.3.9. In these fields, identified as ***numeric range field type,*** you can drag the slider and see the current value being updated in the numeric input box. When you release the mouse button, the value will be applied to the field and the slider will disappear. To set a new value using the slider, click the down arrow button again.

FIGURE 1.3.9 Entering numeric values with a slider

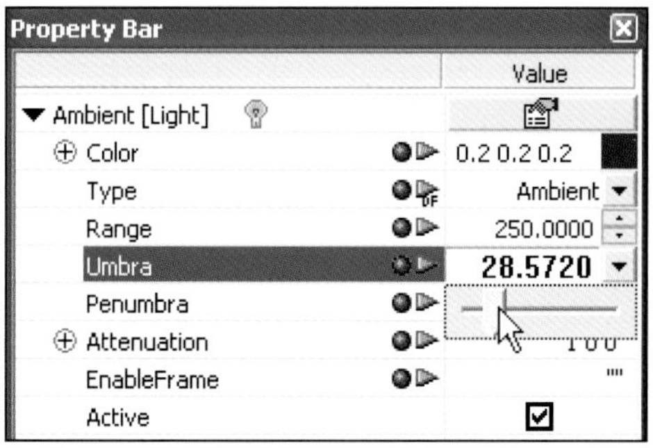

tips+tricks

For greater control in the selection of values using the slider, you can make the slider wider by increasing the width of the Property Bar.

Compound Field Type

Some fields, which use the ***compound field type,*** are a combination of several values. For example, an SFVec3F field would need to contain three values, separated from one another by a single space character. In such cases, a plus symbol beside the field name (see Figure 1.3.10) enables you to expand the individual members inside the compound field easily. When expanded, the individual members are each displayed on a separate row, and you can edit them as usual. When collapsed, the value of each member is displayed on the same row, separated by a space character. If you edit the values in this collapsed state, remember to add a space between each value.

FIGURE 1.3.10 Expanded and collapsed compound fields

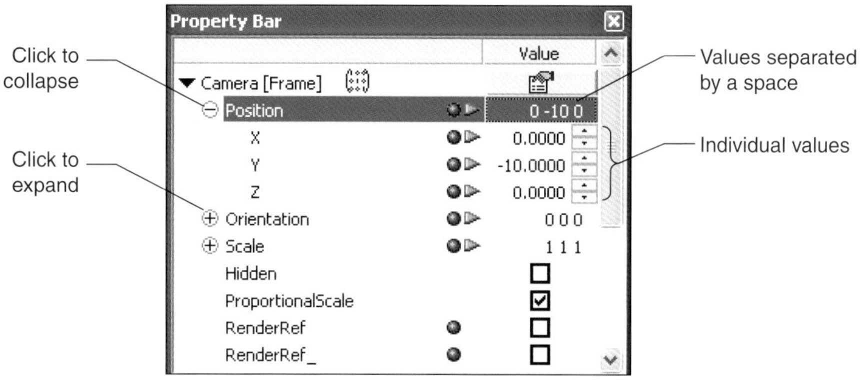

Color Field Type

Color field type is a special kind of compound field, used to store color values in RGB (Red, Green, Blue) format. In addition to changing the numeric values of each individual component, you can pick a color using Microsoft Windows' standard Color dialog box. As shown in Figure 1.3.11, you can click the colored square on the far right side of the field to open the Color dialog box. This square is always colored in the current value of the Color field. After the Color dialog box is open, you can select from the Basic color set, enter RGB values, or use the color pane to select an exact shade as well as adjust its intensity.

FIGURE 1.3.11 Changing the value of the Color field

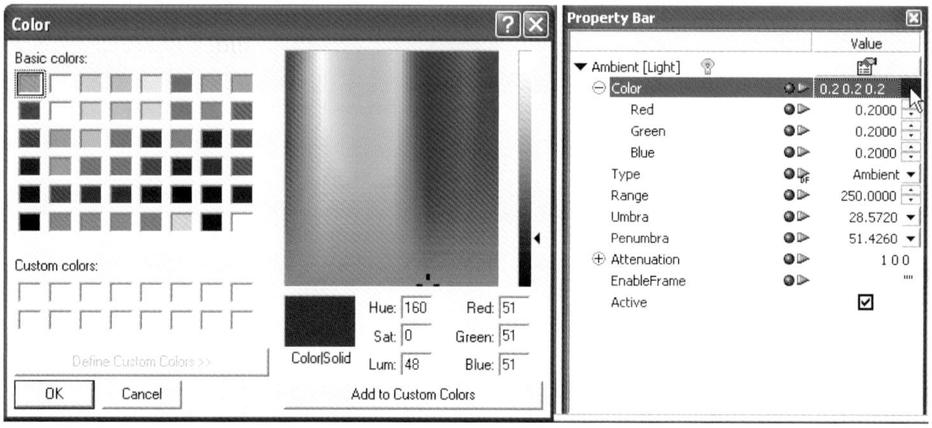

tips+tricks

Notice that the RGB values shown in the Color dialog box are not reflected in the Property Bar. Instead of the RGB number range of 0 to 255, the values in the Color field of the Property Bar are in the range from 0 to 1, with 0 being the darkest and 1 being the lightest. (This is how color codes are stored in OpenGL.) For example, an RGB value of 128 would register as 0.5 in the Property Bar.

web links

We will discuss OpenGL a bit more in future lessons, but a full discussion of OpenGL is beyond the scope of this text. If you are not familiar with OpenGL, you can learn much more about it by searching the Internet for information.

Property Bar Settings

The Property Bar has several settings that you can change. To access the Property Bar settings, choose Options from the menu bar and then select Property Bar. This opens the Property Bar Settings dialog box as shown in Figure 1.3.12. The options in this dialog box affect what you see and what you can adjust in the Property Bar.

FIGURE 1.3.12 Property Bar Settings dialog box

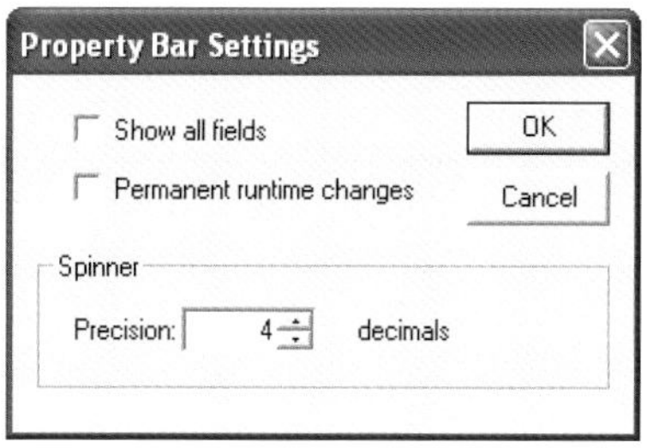

Show All Fields

If the *Show all fields* option is selected, the Property Bar will show all the fields of a node, including the default fields. Be careful if this option is selected because the default node fields typically do not need to be edited.

Permanent Runtime Changes

Most node field values are persistent, meaning that if you change their values while the simulation is running, they will retain the new values when the simulation is stopped (and restarted). However, some fields, such as the Position and Orientation fields of the Frame node, will revert to the original values (which were set when the simulation was in a stopped state). If you check the *Permanent runtime changes* option, all fields will retain the new values that are set while the simulation is running. (Note that all field values for prototypes are not persistent, and selecting this option will not retain changes made to those values during runtime.)

Spinner

The spinner value determines how many decimal places will be used in the numeric value fields. The setting affects values changed via distinct up/down increments as well as those changed via a slider. All the values shown in the preceding figures, for example, are precise to four decimal places (the default setting).

Activity 1.3.1: Viewing and Adjusting Field Properties

1. Open EON.
2. In the Simulation Tree window, click the + sign next to the Scene frame to expand the frame.
3. Right-click the **Camera** frame node and choose **Show Fields** to open the Fields dialog box.
4. Compare the fields shown in the Fields window to those shown in the Property Bar.

Discussion

discuss

Are all fields displayed in the Fields window shown in the Property Bar? If not, what field types are not shown? Why?

5. Click **OK** in the Fields dialog box to close it.
6. With Camera still selected, click the + sign next to Position in the Property Bar. This will expand the properties to show the X, Y, and Z values for the Camera's Position field.
7. Using the method you prefer, change the X value to **0.0059.**
8. From the menu bar, choose **Options** and then **Property Bar.** The Property Bar Settings dialog box opens.
9. Change the precision of the spinners used in the Property Bar to **2** decimals and then click **OK** to apply the setting and close the dialog box.
10. Click the + sign next to Position in the Property Bar to expand the properties for X, Y, and Z again. Note the value that is now displayed for X because the precision of the values in the Property Bar was changed from 4 to 2.

11. Click the **Properties** button next to Camera [Frame] in the Property Bar. The Frame Properties dialog box, as shown in Figure 1.3.13, appears.

FIGURE 1.3.13 Frame Properties dialog box

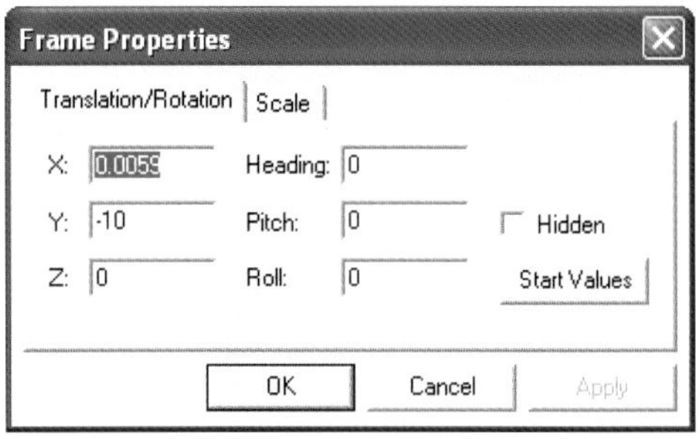

Discussion

discuss

Note that the precision of the values (4 decimal places) is maintained for the X value, which was input prior to changing the decimal places setting for the Property Bar. The adjustment you made only affects the display of values entered after the new decimal precision setting has taken effect. You can key entries with more or fewer decimal places. However, they will be formatted to display according to the currently selected decimal place default value. Why do you think this is the case?

12. Note that you can adjust the Position and Scale from within this dialog box. Changes made here will be reflected in the Property Bar. Click **OK** to close the Frame Properties dialog box without making any changes.
13. Continue to explore the Property Bar and the various methods of adjusting the values that we discussed in the previous sections. Keep the simulation open to use in Activity 1.3.2.

Nodes

More than one hundred different nodes are available in EON, each of which has its own unique properties. Node component names indicate the function or behavior that is achieved via the use of a node. After a node component is copied into the simulation tree, it is referred to as a node "instance" and is assigned a default node name patterned after the original node component name.

Figure 1.3.14 shows all of the nodes currently available in EON. Note that the category selection bar displays <All Nodes>. This indicates that all of the nodes are shown and, as you can see, they are listed in alphabetical order.

FIGURE 1.3.14 EON nodes

troubleshooting

Figure 1.3.14 represents the node list as of the printing of this text. Your list may contain additional nodes that are not shown here.

Your list of nodes will probably not display exactly like Figure 1.3.14. Depending on your screen size, you will likely only see a portion of the nodes initially. If this is the case, use the scroll bar to view the other nodes.

Discussion

discuss

Nodes are actually compiled versions of C++ code. How does using a tool such as a node make it easier to create a simulation than using C++ code?

Node Libraries

The Components window contains all EON nodes arranged in a number of node libraries, such as Base Nodes and Agent Nodes, to make it easier to locate a specific node or specific node types. You can use these node libraries to narrow your search. Each library contains nodes with similar functionality and application type. To view and select the node libraries, click the drop-down arrow next to the current library listing (<All Nodes> when you launch EON). You will see a list of options similar to the one shown in Figure 1.3.15.

troubleshooting

Your list of node libraries may appear different from that shown in Figure 1.3.15. The Modules option in the Options menu affects the contents of the Components Nodes and Prototypes windows. Additionally, your EON license may affect available modules because some modules are purchased separately. Your exact selection may vary depending on which options you have installed with EON and whether you are using EON Studio or EON Professional.

FIGURE 1.3.15 Node libraries

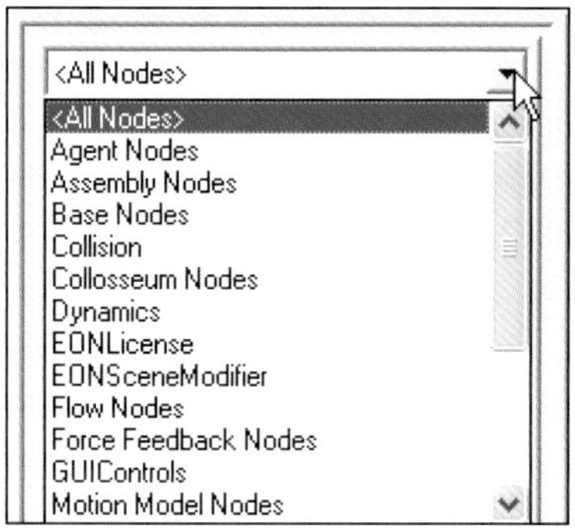

We will not list all of the nodes in each library, because you can easily view the libraries and the nodes they contain. Table 1.3.3 does, however, describe the libraries and, where necessary, provide basic information about the nodes in that library.

TABLE 1.3.3 Node Libraries

Node Library	Description	Examples
Agent Nodes	Provide interactive (input/output) and multimedia (motion and sound) features to simulations. Many Agent nodes work with rendered objects, such as Mesh nodes and Frame nodes. These movements are preset by the simulation designer and cannot be changed by the viewer.	Latch, Rotate, Spin, etc.
Assembly Nodes	Define connections and connection properties between objects; provide an interface to control each connection; and handle the motion of connected objects with respect to the properties in each connection.	Connection, Connection-Manager, and GrabConnection
Base Nodes	Provide basic simulation functions and therefore are used repeatedly and extensively. They contain instructions for basic simulation elements such as grouping nodes into subtrees and defining viewports, color, texture, light, etc.	Frame, DegreeOfFreedom, Viewport, Light, etc.
Collision	Provide a basic collision detection and response system. The system never initiates any motion on its own; it reacts to the motion of collision objects, such as avatars moving within the 3D space, and resolves subsequent collisions. Several collision-specific prototypes are also available.	CollisionGeometry-Type, Collision-Manager, and CollisionObject
Collosseum Nodes	Collosseum was a multiuser client server program that only remains part of EON Studio for backward compatibility. The three nodes that remain in this node library work to define rooms, to keep the users within rooms, and to let users move between rooms only in a defined manner.	ColController, ColJoint, and ColRoom

(continued)

tips+tricks

The License node must be programmed to handle a missing license and prevent the simulation from running. A customized notice for the user can also be displayed when a license is missing. To use the License node, use a feature name in the Feature field, a version in the Version field, and the LicenseNotOK outEvent to trigger a notice for a missing license. The License node looks for the license in the default directory for FlexLM.

TABLE 1.3.3 Node Libraries *(continued)*

Node Library	Description	Examples
Dynamics	*Available in EON Professional.* Include a complete set of joints for accurately portraying dynamics. These are used to simulate the laws of physics via rigid body property values. Such property values cause rigid bodies to react in a specified manner when they are placed in motion and exposed to gravity.	MassProperties, RigidBody, RigidJoint, etc.
EONLicense	Incorporates license protection into your EON applications. It uses the same FLEXlm licensing system as the EON software product line. License files are generated by EON Reality for a fee. License files can be temporary or permanent. Application files must be distributed in .edz format, or the user could open them in EON Studio or EON Professional and modify the EON application so it can be used without a license.	License
EONScene-Modifier	Modifies the background color and fog properties of the scene. Note that these properties cannot be changed using the Routes window because the Scene node has the same field interface as a Frame node. In authoring mode, you can double-click the Scene node to access these properties. In Runtime mode, however, you have to use this node to change the properties in real time.	SceneModifier
Flow Nodes	Control the sequence or "flow" of events within a simulation. Flow nodes provide an overview of the simulation flow and enable you to modify it. The flow tree resembles a flowchart used for structured programming. Large EON applications can have a complicated Routes window that makes it difficult to change the simulation. Using Flow nodes simplifies EON simulation development. During simulation runtime, you can monitor the status of each task. This helps you debug the simulation.	AfterParentTask, DelayTask, IterationTask, MemoryTask, and Task
Force Feedback Nodes	*Requires I-Force Studio.* Provide real-time, tactile feedback effects to users during simulation execution. EON Force Feedback nodes require Microsoft® DirectX 5 and support all DirectX compatible joysticks. The nodes themselves are not computationally intense; however, significant processor resources are required to control the force strength, direction, and duration of the joystick (or other supported hardware) in relation to the 3D environment in real time.	FFEffect and FFResource
GUIControls	Provide 2D graphical user interface (GUI) elements that overlay the 3D simulation window. They are positioned with 2D pixel screen coordinates. Because they are not part of the 3D space, they do not render inside a viewport.	2DImage, 2DText, PopupMenu, etc.
Motion Model Nodes	Provide controls that enable users to navigate a 3D scene, in real time, using a mouse or keyboard. User-controlled navigation is possible only if the simulation developer includes the appropriate motion model nodes.	Walk, KeyMove, and WalkAbout
Operations Nodes	Facilitate the inclusion of logic operations, calculations, and on/off functionality in a simulation application.	Addition, Subtraction, And, Or, Not, etc.
Peripheral Nodes	*Some of these nodes are available only in EON Professional, ICATCHER, and ICUBE.* Provide device drivers for selected interactive virtual reality (VR) hardware and incorporate routines to handle response timing, tracking, and synchronization.	5DT DataGlove, 5DTDataGlove-Manager, InterSenseTrack-Manager, and VirtualHand

(continued)

TABLE 1.3.3 Node Libraries *(continued)*

Node Library	Description	Examples
RPC Objects	Provide animated, plug-and-play simulation elements from externally defined object packages, such as EON Human. External remote procedure call (RPC) resources are optimized to reduce overhead within the application.	Human and RPC3D
Sensor Nodes	Provide "switches" that generate actions (called "events") in response to other actions occurring during real-time execution of a simulation.	ClickSensor, KeyboardSensor, MouseSensor, TimeSensor, etc.
Shadow Nodes	*Advanced shadow nodes available only in EON Professional.* Create dynamic shadows based on light sources within the simulation. EON Studio's SoftShadow node is well suited for the most common type of scene with shadows—where one or more objects cast shadows on a horizontal ground, plane, or floor. In particular, this node works well in scenes where one or more omnidirectional light sources light a scene from "outside."	SoftShadow and ShadowVolumeHard
Showroom Nodes	Improve the visual quality of simulations produced with EON Studio. The Showroom nodes provide the following effects: • Reflection mapping • Reflection • Shadows	MeshNormals, Reflection, RenderCube-EnvMap, Shading, and Shadow
SpecialFX Nodes	Complement simulations with special features for enhancing realism or adding dramatic effects.	LightOfDay, MeshExplosion, OceanWaves, and Weather
Visual Nodes	*Advanced cgShader materials are only available in EON Professional.* Provide support for adding and altering mesh (geometry), material, and texture components within a simulation. The old Visual nodes (Mesh, Texture, and Material in the Base Nodes library) were replaced by this new Visual Nodes set in EON Version 4. The old nodes are still included in current versions for backward compatibility, but they are obsolete. These new nodes will not interact with the old nodes, though EON Studio will not prevent you from trying to use the old ones.	Shape, Mesh2, Material2, Texture2, etc.

web links

EON Peripherals supports several different devices that are listed here. Use the URLs given to find out more about each of these devices.

PINCH® glove system from Fakespace, Inc. *(http://www.mechdyne.com)*

Flock of Birds® real-time motion tracker from Ascension Technology Corporation *(http://www.ascension-tech.com)*

FASTRAK® tracker system from Polhemus, Inc. *(http://www.polhemus.com)*

Magellan™ 3D Controller from Logitech, Inc. *(http://www.logitech.com)*

i-glasses™ from i-O Display Systems, LLC *(http://www.i-glasses.com)*

CrystalEyes® eyewear from StereoGraphics Corporation *(http://www.sharpertechnology.com/crystaleyeswseye.html)*

ProReflex™ motion capture camera from Qualisys AB *(http://www.qualisys.com)*

tips+tricks

OpenGL has replaced Direct3D in EON Studio and EON Professional. Previously incorporated Direct3D functionality has been left in the product for backward compatibility with legacy applications only.

tips+tricks

In EON, DirectX version 9.0b or higher is required for some SpecialFX nodes. Because DirectX does not support all features required by the SpecialFX module (an optional software component), you will not be able to run the Weather node on a system using DirectX.

tips+tricks

The change to the Visual Nodes set occurred in EON version 4. In that version, a tool called "Convert 3.1 to Visual Nodes" was added so that any existing old nodes could be quickly and easily converted to the new types. If you are working with an older EON application that was created with version 3.1 or earlier, you should convert the Visual nodes before you begin to make any changes.

BEST PRACTICES

DirectX, Direct3D, and OpenGL

Microsoft Direct3D is the 3D graphics application programming interface (API) within Microsoft DirectX. It is widely used for the development of computer games for Microsoft Windows, such as Xbox and Xbox 360. It is also used by other software applications for visualization and graphics tasks because of its ability to quickly render high-quality 3D graphics using DirectX-compatible graphics hardware. Because Direct3D is the most frequently used component of DirectX, it is common to see the names "DirectX" and "Direct3D" used interchangeably. But that is not a correct usage. DirectX is actually the whole collection of APIs for managing multimedia tasks on Microsoft platforms. In addition to Direct3D, some other components of DirectX are DirectDraw, DirectMusic, DirectPlay, DirectSound, and XInput.

With all of that said about Direct3D, as we noted previously, EON Reality has shifted to supporting OpenGL instead of Direct3D. OpenGL is a cross-language, cross-platform API that was developed by Silicon Graphics Inc. in 1992. It is widely used in CAD, virtual reality, scientific visualization, information visualization, flight simulation, and video games. The OpenGL interface consists of over 250 function calls that can be used to draw complex three-dimensional scenes from simple geometric shapes.

web links

Why has EON shifted from using Direct3D to using OpenGL? To learn more about the pros and cons of each API, search the Internet for "Direct3D versus OpenGL" or the "API wars."

discuss

After reading about Direct3D and OpenGL, discuss the factors you think went into EON Reality's decision to support OpenGL instead of Direct3D.

Node Functions

As we have already mentioned, interaction between nodes is made possible by arranging the nodes in the simulation tree hierarchy and by making connections in the Routes window. After nodes are connected to one another via routes, they can exchange information while the simulation is running. The information a node receives results in an action of some kind. For example, an object may move or change color, a sound or video file may play, and so forth.

As you have already begun to see, EON provides you with a variety of ready-to-use nodes. The nodes contribute different functions to the simulation. The basic functions of nodes are to:

- Set the scene and determine what will be displayed (establish the opening view of the scene for the audience)
- Select objects to use in the simulation scene (identify actors and props to be present in the scene)
- Control the appearance of objects (actors' appearance and prop design)
- Provide lighting (lighting types and locations)
- Add text (titles, captions, narratives, and credits)
- Manipulate media (multimedia effects—actors' voices, sounds, images, and video)
- Control moving objects (choreographed movement of actors and props)
- Add sensors (automated responses to specified events)
- Include controls (interactivity rules and constraints)
- Set the simulation performance (visual quality and response time requirements to provide satisfactory experience)

The majority of the nodes used for these functions are found either in the Agent Nodes library or the Base Nodes library.

The following section outlines some of the nodes that provide these basic functions to a simulation. (Note that this list includes only the fundamental nodes.) These nodes will be discussed in greater detail when they are first used, or if not used in our activities, you can find a complete list of nodes in the Appendix.

tips+tricks

Some of the more commonly used nodes are described in greater detail in the next section as well.

Simulation Scene

Some nodes define your "window" on the simulation scene. The following nodes determine what you will see by "setting the scene" for the simulation:

- Simulation
- Scene
- Viewport (defines size of view within the simulation window)
- Camera (defines what part of the scene is visible)

Objects in the Scene

The visual objects that appear in the simulation scene are displayed in either 3D or 2D. For example, the following components can serve as scene objects:

- Shape (Mesh2 node plus a Material2 node)
- TextBox node
- Decal node
- Panorama node

Appearance of Objects

An object's rendered appearance on the computer display is affected by several factors, including object surface characteristics (mesh geometry, diffuse color, texture, and specularity), object position in 3D space, and reflection of light within the environment. The following Visual nodes and Base nodes can be used to affect object appearance:

- Mesh2
- Texture2
- Material2
- Frame
- LevelOfDetail
- Light

2D Objects

2D objects are those that are placed on top of the rendered 3D view. These include:

- ToolTip
- 2DText
- 2DImage
- 2DEdit
- Slider
- FlashObject

Media

The following nodes are used to add multimedia effects to a simulation:

- MovieTexture
- DirectSound
- MultimediaStream

Moving Objects

The following nodes (found in the Agent Nodes library, except DegreeOfFreedom, which is a Base node) affect an object's position in 3D space. By using these nodes, various types of motion and behavior may be defined for a simulation's 3D objects. Motion characteristics are defined within a node's properties window.

- KeyFrame
- Place
- Motion
- Rotate
- Spin
- DegreeOfFreedom
- Gravitation

It is also possible to move objects by using standard input devices, such as the mouse or keyboard, by creating routes including combinations of the following Sensor nodes:

- ClickSensor
- KeyboardSensor

You can move a simulation's viewpoint through the 3D environment as well. The following prototype and Motion Model nodes enable this sort of simulation control:

- ObjectNav (prototype with multiple node variations available)
- Walk
- WalkAbout

Sensors

The following Sensor nodes are used to start and stop actions in response to activities occurring during the simulation:

- BoxSensor
- ClickSensor
- KeyboardSensor
- TimeSensor

Controls

These nodes are used to add control functions to the simulation. They activate other nodes when certain conditions are fulfilled.

- Counter
- Latch
- Trigger
- Sequence
- Switch

Counter, Latch, and Trigger nodes are found in the Agent Nodes library. Sequence and Switch nodes are found in the Base Nodes library.

cross-reference

EON also provides tools for designing nodes for specialized applications. Users with programming skills can write scripts to create a custom behavior or build new nodes using EON Professional and Visual C++. You will learn more about using scripts in Module 9.

Simulation Performance

These nodes reduce the size of a simulation file, thereby improving performance levels:

- LevelOfDetail (found in the Base Nodes library)
- ChangeSimulation (found in the Agent Nodes library)

Activity 1.3.2: Nodes and Functions

1. In the Components window, select the down arrow next to <All Nodes>. You will see the drop-down menu from which you can select one of the node libaries.
2. Select **Motion Model Nodes** from the drop-down list. Instead of showing all of the more than one hundred nodes, the Nodes panel now only shows the nodes in the Motion Model Nodes library, as shown in Figure 1.3.16.

FIGURE 1.3.16 Motion Model Nodes library

discuss

Are any of the Motion Model nodes already in use in the default simulation tree? Explore the simulation tree (by expanding nodes, if necessary) to see if any Motion Model nodes are in place and to determine where they are located.

3. Select the drop-down arrow again at the top of the Nodes panel and select **<All Nodes>** from the top of the list. The Nodes panel returns to showing all of the existing nodes.
4. In the text box just below the drop-down list, key the letter **r.** Instead of showing all of the nodes, the Nodes panel will display only those nodes whose names start with the letter R, as shown in Figure 1.3.17.

FIGURE 1.3.17 Nodes whose names start with R

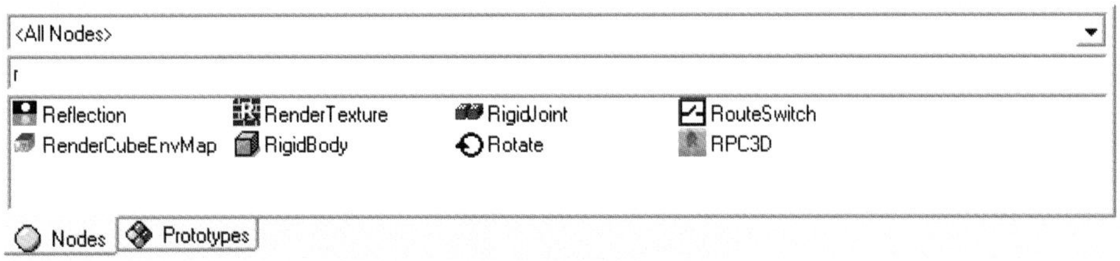

5. From the drop-down list, select **Agent Nodes.** Notice that only the Agent nodes whose names begin with the letter R are shown (only Rotate).
6. Delete the *r* from the text box. All of the Agent nodes are now visible.
7. Experiment with different ways to narrow your search and locate specific nodes. Pay special attention to the Agent Nodes and Base Nodes libraries because these are the ones you will most often need to access. When you are finished, restore the Nodes window to displaying <All Nodes>.
8. Close EON without saving the simulation.

troubleshooting

By default, the Nodes tab should be visible in the Components window. If it is not, make it the active tab in the Components window. If you do not know how to do this, refer to Module 1 Lesson 2.

Commonly Used Nodes

As you know, nodes are the building blocks used to create EON simulations. A node contributes varying effects to a simulation depending on the node's type, the values in its data fields, and the way it is connected to other nodes. From a programmer's perspective, a node is an object with functions (or methods) and data (or properties). Node properties store data for inEvents, outEvents, and exposedFields. Some properties can be altered during simulation runtime, whereas others can only be set by the simulation developer.

In this section, some of the most commonly used (and reused) nodes are described. These are nodes that we will practice using in activities and that you will find yourself using repeatedly as you build your own simulations. (Note that these nodes are listed in alphabetical order, not in any order of importance or frequency of use.)

2DText

The 2DText node (located in the GUIControls library) allows you to overlay text on top of the 3D-rendered EON window. The text is bounded within a 2D box-shaped area. The text color, background box color, box position (an XY value, in pixels, relative to the upper-left position of the window), box surface area, font, font size, font style, and alignment can be set through properties and changed in real time. The 2DText node also generates outEvents when you click in the box area. The events can be for a specific mouse button or for any mouse button. To hide the 2DText node from the start, set IsActive to false. The 2DText node must be triggered by an event at the start of the simulation before it will be visible. This trigger may be an outEvent from another node or may be set using a script. The 2DText node can then be set to trigger itself if you want it to remain visible for a specific length of time or under a specific set of conditions.

You can control word wrapping within a 2DText node by using the WordWrap and WordWrapTextHeight properties. If there is too much text for the size of the box, then the text will not be visible. However, when the AutoSize property is enabled, the width of the box will be set to exactly the width of the text as if it was all on one line. The height will be the height of one line of text. To see all the text when AutoSize is turned on, ensure that TextPosition is 0 0 and TextArea is 0 0.

2DImage

The 2DImage node (located in the GUIControls library) allows you to overlay bitmap (BMP) images on top of the 3D-rendered EON window. OutEvents are triggered when the end user clicks the image. The images can be positioned and the visible area (width and height) can be set. A 2DImage can also be scaled down. This allows you to load BMP textures, which makes this node a great tool for adding buttons quickly.

It is also possible to send new filenames to the ImageFile field to change the image. However, this relates only to files on the local hard disk or in the EON.eoz file and not to Internet URLs.

ClickSensor

The ClickSensor node (located in the Sensor Nodes library) detects when an object has been mouse-clicked in the simulation window. The ClickSensor node is typically placed under a Frame node or the DegreeOfFreedom node. If placed under a Frame node, all Mesh2 nodes that define objects sensitive to mouse clicks should also be placed under the same parent Frame node.

Converter

Converter

The Converter node (located in the Operations Nodes library) allows you to convert a field's data type. Single-value and multivalue data values can be accepted as input and output fields. You can, for example, convert an SFBool field to an SFInt32 field. This can be a very convenient tool to use.

troubleshooting

Be aware that not every data type can be converted to every other data type.

Counter

Counter

The Counter node (located in the Agent Nodes library), as the name implies, is used to count events. The counter value is an integer that may be decremented or incremented. Upper- and lower-limit values—and a trigger value—can be used to initiate an action by sending an event when the counter reaches a specified value.

troubleshooting

Note that 3D sound uses world coordinates for calculating attenuation and Doppler effects. To produce realistic sound, the simulation scale must be correct. This means that the *perceived* distance in a simulation must match the *actual* distance. Use the Scene node to adjust the simulation scale.

Also, note that hardware acceleration for 3D sound requires DirectX 6.0 or later.

DirectSound

DirectSound

The DirectSound node (located in the Agent Nodes library) plays a sound WAVE file using Microsoft DirectSound. WAVE (or WAV) is short for Waveform audio format. This file format, created by Microsoft and IBM, is now the standard for storing an audio bitstream on a PC.

Sounds can be played in either 2D or 3D. When played in 3D, sound direction is defined by the node's parent frame. Other 3D parameters can be adjusted on the 3D properties tab.

Frame

Frame

A Frame node (located in the Base Nodes library) serves as a container or parent for the nodes located below it, thereby enabling all child nodes to be manipulated as a unit. The Frame node performs translation, rotation, and scaling operations on all child nodes contained beneath it. Position values represent XYZ origin coordinates (in units) for the Frame node. Orientation values represent HPR (heading, pitch, and roll) coordinates (in degrees) for the Frame node. Scale values represent XYZ scaling values (in units) for the Frame node. To implement a simulation structure that is easier to maintain, Frame nodes are commonly used to create a hierarchy of subtrees consisting of groups of nodes that will behave as a unit.

Group

Group

The Group node (located in the Base Nodes library) allows the EON developer to arrange nodes in the simulation tree into groups. The Group node can be thought of as a container, and it is used simply as an aid for organization, so there are no properties or fields associated with it. Groups are similar to Frame nodes except that they do not contain position, orientation, or scale information.

cross-reference

You will learn more about using the Group node to organize your simulation tree in Module 2 Lesson 2.

KeyboardSensor

KeyboardSensor

This node (located in the Sensor Nodes library) detects when a specified key is pressed and generates events that can be routed to other nodes. KeyboardSensor nodes are typically placed under the Scene node.

KeyFrame

KeyFrame

This node (located in the Agent Nodes library) is used to move, rotate, and/or scale its parent node. The parent node must support translation and/or rotation.

Objects move through points entered in the Key Frame Properties dialog box or the Property Bar. Each entry consists of a time stamp, a position (X, Y, Z), an orientation (H, P, R), and a scale (SX, SY, SZ). From these entries, smooth movement and rotation are calculated so that objects reach each position with the object in the correct orientation at the time specified. Two alternative algorithms are available for traversing the path—Interpolate or Spline. The Interpolate algorithm will insert estimated locations between the points given. This provides very crisp movement. The Spline algorithm, on the other hand, does not try to interpolate any points between the points given but moves to the points given at the time designated. This provides smoother movement.

The KeyFrame node also has a unique Property page: Path Edit. Use the Path Edit page when the simulation is running to set values directly from this page and see updated position/orientation in the simulation window.

Latch

The Latch node (located in the Agent Nodes library) is triggered by receiving Boolean values as inEvents. False becomes true and true becomes false. The Latch node is useful for situations in which you need to toggle between true and false values. Its behavior is similar to a light switch (on and off).

Light

The Light node (located in the Base Nodes library) is used to illuminate objects. A Light node may light the entire scene or just a limited number of grouped nodes. The selected lighting type and color define lighting effects.

If the EnableFrame folder (under the Light node in the simulation tree) is empty, the Light node will illuminate the entire scene. If the EnableFrame folder contains a Frame node or a reference to a Frame node, only the objects beneath that Frame node will be illuminated.

New simulations have two default Light nodes: Ambient and Headlight. The Ambient node is actually a Light node with the Type field set to Ambient. It produces lighting effects similar to reflected sunlight. The light produced by this node has a light gray color, so it doesn't overwhelm the scene. The Headlight node is also a Light node, but its Type field is set to Directional. Because the Headlight is a child of the Camera, it shines straight ahead, away from the viewer.

troubleshooting

The Material2 node is a replacement for the Material node. The Material node remains in the software so that legacy applications are still functional. You should always use the Material2 node.

Material2

The Material2 node (located in the Visual Nodes library) should be used with other nodes in the Visual Nodes set. It represents a material in the scene. A Material2 node changes the colors, emissive parameters, and specular parameters of its parent Mesh2 node. To apply a material to a 3D object, you need to combine it with a geometry node (Mesh2) using the Shape node by copying the material as a link and placing that link below the Material folder in the Shape node.

cross-reference

You will learn more about a material's emissive and specular parameters in Module 4 Lesson 2.

Mesh2

Objects rendered within a 3D scene are based on Shape nodes, which in turn include references to Mesh2 and Material2 nodes. Mesh2 nodes (located in the Visual Nodes library) are created automatically when importing 3D objects in various formats. When an importer creates the resource database from a 3D file, it will create a Mesh2 node for each 3D object found in the file, store the 3D mesh data in a separate file, and then make the node reference this file. Compare this to how textures are stored in a similar way. However, unlike textures, the mesh data file (which has the extension .eog) can only be read and used in EON.

troubleshooting

The Mesh2 node is a replacement for the Mesh node. The Mesh node remains in the software so that legacy applications are still functional. You should always use the Mesh2 node.

MovieTexture

MovieTexture

Textures are images that can be used to supply details to a surface in a very cost-effective way (in terms of computation requirements). There are two types of texture resource nodes (located in the Visual Nodes library): Texture2 and MovieTexture. The difference between them is that the MovieTexture node uses a movie file as the image source, and the Texture2 node uses a simple static image file. Any movie format supported by the Microsoft DirectShow system (and thus able to be played by the Windows MediaPlayer) can be used in a MovieTexture node. Note that in addition to image, the MovieTexture node can optionally supply a sound track to the simulation. Conversely, you can choose to disable the video channel and use only the sound channel, for instance, to play a background tune in MP3 format.

The MovieTexture node must be referenced by a Material2 node to be visible in the scene. The Material2 node must be used by a Shape node as well.

troubleshooting

MultimediaStream The MovieTexture node is a replacement for the MultimediaStream node. The MultimediaStream node remains in the software so that legacy applications are still functional, but you should always use the MovieTexture node.

Place

Place

This node (located in the Agent Nodes library) places an object at a new position, either relative to the current location or at an absolute position. The Place node changes its parent node's position in the coordinate system (i.e., X, Y, Z, H, P, and R values) of the node directly above the Place node's parent in the scene hierarchy. The parent node of a Place node must support translation and/or rotation.

cross-reference

You will learn more about translation and rotation in Module 2 Lesson 1.

PopupMenu

PopupMenu

The PopupMenu node (located in the GUIControls library) provides the common context-sensitive menu or right-mouse button menu functionality that you are used to seeing in other Windows programs. It is totally configurable, so you can customize a menu to contain any elements you want.

You can have as many menu items as you wish. The MenuStrings field will hold all of the text for all of the menu items. You can enter text in this field by writing it in quotation marks. For example:

```
"This is menu option one" "This is menu option two" "This is menu
   option three" "This is menu option four"
```

An alternative method for entering text is to run the simulation and then use the Property Bar to enter one menu item at a time. You would key the text in the AddMenuString field and then press the Enter key. You can continue repeating this step until all of your menu items have been added.

To make your menu appear, connect a route to the ShowPopupMenu field. The pop-up menu will appear where the mouse cursor is located when the ShowPopupMenu command is received. Because you do not want floating menus linked to the location of the mouse, in most cases, it is recommended that you set a mouse click to make the menu appear. To do this, insert a MouseSensor node and connect its OnRightUp field to the PopupMenu node's ShowPopupMenu field. Alternatively, you can make a menu appear when the user clicks an object by connecting a route from ClickSensor's OnButtonDownTrue outEvent.

Discussion

discuss

What can you use the PopupMenu for? Commands to rotate an object, start an animation, provide information, hide an animation or parts of it, show prices, or change the color of the object are just a few of the possibilities. What other ways can you think of to use a menu within a simulation?

Rotate

Rotate

The Rotate node (located in the Agent Nodes library) rotates its parent around one axis (X, Y, or Z) or a combination of these. The origin for the rotation is the pivot point defined by the parent node, usually a frame. The parent node must support rotation. Rotation is specified by three values (X, Y, and Z). These determine the fraction of a 360° rotation around the respective axis to be completed during the LapTime value. The LapTime property is specified by the number of seconds it takes to make one rotation.

cross-reference

For information about using the Script Editor and available methods, see Module 9 Lesson 2.

SceneModifier

SceneModifier

This node (located in the EONSceneModifier library) is used to modify the scene's background color and fog properties. These properties cannot be changed using the routes because the Scene node has the same field interface as a Frame node. In authoring mode, you can double-click the Scene node to access these properties, but in Runtime mode, you must use this node to change the properties in real time.

web links

To use the Script node successfully, you must be familiar with either VBScript or JScript. To learn more about scripting, visit Microsoft's Scripting Technologies site at *http://msdn.microsoft.com.*

Script

Script

The Script node (located in the Base Nodes library) is the most versatile of all EON nodes. The Script node allows you to create custom nodes, using either VBScript or JScript. Both languages are included in the EON installation.

SphereSensor

SphereSensor

The SphereSensor node (located in the Sensor Nodes library) allows you to rotate an object using the mouse. It is located under the Frame node and affects the Frame node's orientation. The effect is similar to rolling a ball along a plane.

troubleshooting

Do not use the SphereSensor node under a DegreeOfFreedom (DOF) node. The SphereSensor node will not work in that location because position, head, pitch, and roll do not transform into world positions.

TextBox

TextBox

The TextBox node (located in the Agent Nodes library) adds a text box to the simulation that can provide information to the user. The text box can be moved within the 3D space, or it can have a fixed position and size. The text box's orientation is automatically adjusted in real time so that it always faces the viewer.

BEST PRACTICES

2DText versus TextBox

You might have noticed that there are two different nodes that, at a glance, appear to do the same thing. The 2DText node and the TextBox node both allow you to create text within a simulation. So what is the difference between the two, and when is one used versus another?

The 2DText node is placed on top of the whole simulation and is used when you want the text to overlay the entire simulation. The TextBox node has a specific location in the 3D world and is used when you want the text to be part of a specific component in the simulation.

Texture2

Texture2

As noted in the discussion of the MovieTexture node earlier in this lesson, textures are images that can be used to supply details to a surface in a way that is very cost effective (computationally). They can be placed on or wrapped around objects. A movie file is used as the image source for the MovieTexture node, but the Texture2 node (located in the Visual Nodes library) uses a static image file.

The Texture2 node supports several image formats including JPEG, JPEG2000, PNG, PPM, and DDS. If you have an image in a format that is not supported, you will need to convert it before the import procedure begins. Although many importers will automatically convert most of the common image formats to PNG or JPEG2000, to maintain maximum control, you should do the conversion yourself.

The Texture2 node must be referenced by a Material2 node to be visible in the scene. This Material2 node must be used by a Shape node as well.

TimeSensor

A TimeSensor node (located in the Sensor Nodes library) generates pulses at regular intervals. These pulses can be used to control the actions of other nodes.

ToolTip

The ToolTip node (located in the Agent Nodes library) lets you add help text to your simulation. The text you enter in the Text field will be displayed when the user clicks or points at the parent object (after an optional delay). Note that the ToolTip node must be placed under a Frame node that contains a Shape node.

Viewport

A Viewport node (located in the Base Nodes library) defines the user's field of view and how the simulation is displayed in the simulation window. The default Viewport node is located in the Simulation node's Viewports folder. A Viewport node has a Camera field that stores a reference to the Camera node. Remember that the Camera node determines what the observer sees in the simulation window. The Camera node is actually a normal Frame node that defines the user's position in the simulation. The simulation window can show several viewports at the same time, either side by side or with a small viewport on top of a large one.

Walk

The default Walk node is placed below the Camera node and enables a user to examine the 3D environment. The Walk node (located in the Motion Model Nodes library) implements the walk motion models found in many 3D environments.

The walking movement is controlled by pressing the left mouse button (default setting) and moving the mouse. Speed is proportional to mouse movement after the button is pressed. The maximum speed and assignment of the Walk mouse button can be modified.

This node affects its parent, so the parent must support translation and rotation. If you have a Camera node as a parent to a Walk node, you can examine a simulation by holding down the middle mouse button (default setting) while moving the mouse. This will turn the camera around, while still standing on the same spot. When the button is released, the orientation will stay in the last position, and you can continue or start walking using the left mouse button. If you want the viewpoint to snap back to the position it had before you initiated the turnaround navigation, hold down the Alt key before you release the mouse button.

If enabled, you can also go up and down along the z axis by holding down the right mouse button (default setting) while moving the mouse forward (up) and backward (down).

WalkAbout

The WalkAbout node (located in the Motion Model Nodes library) lets you navigate within your simulation using the keyboard. It also can be connected to a Camera node to change the view. Alternatively, you may connect a WalkAbout node to a Frame node to place an object.

troubleshooting

Texture The Texture2 node is a replacement for the Texture node. The Texture node remains in the software so that legacy applications are still functional. You should always use the Texture2 node.

Note that this node does not work with the ramp driver in Windows NT. Playing video files using the Windows NT ramp driver will terminate the simulation. You should convert the simulation to using a MovieTexture node if you need to play video files in Windows NT.

The Walkabout node moves another node if there is a reference to that node in the WalkAbout node's toMove folder. If the toMove folder (below WalkAbout) is empty, the Walkabout node moves its parent node.

General Guidelines for Using Nodes

You have already worked with several different nodes, and you are probably quickly developing your own set of useful mental notes from your experiences. However, before we delve too far into simulation development, we thought it might be useful to catalog some general guidelines for working with nodes.

- You can select only one node at a time, although the selected node may contain several child nodes.
- You may move and copy nodes between different simulation files.
- Certain nodes cannot be moved or copied. These are Simulation nodes and Scene nodes. (Note that the Viewport nodes cannot be moved from the Viewports folder, but they can be copied.)
- Some node types cannot be pasted under certain other node types.
- When you copy or move a node to a location that has a node of the same name, the copied or moved node will be renamed with a number suffix. For example, if you copy a Move node to a location that already contains a Move node, the copied version would become *Move1* because the name *Move* was already taken. If the name *Move1* is also in use, the name *Move2* would be assigned instead. This feature speeds copying of nodes to a common parent.
- If a node contains several children, moving or copying may be time consuming. Keep the cursor over the destination node until the crossed circle disappears and the node is highlighted.

In Module 1 Lesson 2, we explored the various methods for placing nodes in the simulation tree. In the following sections, we will describe some of the other common operations for working with nodes.

Copying and Moving Nodes

Various methods are available for copying and moving nodes in the simulation tree. Table 1.3.4 provides a basic outline of these methods.

TABLE 1.3.4 Methods for Copying and Moving Nodes

Method	Description
Copy nodes using drag-and-drop	To copy a node using drag-and-drop, hold the Ctrl key while dragging the node. Wait until the copied node is visible at its new location and then release the mouse button before releasing the Ctrl key.
Copy nodes using the Simulation Tree window's pop-up menu	To copy a node using the Simulation Tree window's pop-up menu, right-click the node to display the pop-up menu. Choose Copy, right-click the node that will be the parent of the copied node, and then choose Paste from the pop-up menu.
Copy nodes using the Toolbar	To copy a node using the Toolbar, select the node and click the Toolbar's Copy button. Select the node that will be the parent of the copied node and then click the Toolbar's Paste button.

(continued)

TABLE 1.3.4 Methods for Copying and Moving Nodes *(continued)*

Method	Description
Copy nodes using the keyboard	To copy a node using the keyboard, select the node and press Ctrl+C. Select the node that will be the parent of the copied node and then press Ctrl+V. When you paste nodes using a keyboard shortcut (Ctrl+V), the relevant destination node will be expanded, and the focus will be on the destination node (that is, the node where the new node is pasted).
Move nodes using drag-and-drop	To move a node using drag-and-drop, drag the node using the left mouse button and then drop it in the new desired location.
Move nodes using the Simulation Tree window's pop-up menu	To move a node using the Simulation Tree window's pop-up menu, right-click the node to display the pop-up menu. Choose Cut, right-click the node that will be the parent of the moved node, and then choose Paste from the pop-up menu.
Move nodes using the Toolbar	To move a node using the Toolbar, select the node and then click the Toolbar's Cut button. Select the node that will be the parent of the moved node and then click the Toolbar's Paste button.
Move nodes using the keyboard	To move a node using the keyboard, select the node and then press Ctrl+X. Select the node that will be the parent of the moved node and then press Ctrl+V.

Renaming Nodes

It is highly recommended that you adopt a standard naming convention and modify the default names of node and prototype instances to reflect their role or function within the simulation tree. Meaningful node and prototype names can serve as a means of self-documenting your simulation application.

When you insert a new ClickSensor node, for example, it is automatically named *ClickSensor*. If you insert several ClickSensor nodes under the same parent node, they are designated *ClickSensor*, *ClickSensor1*, *ClickSensor2*, and so on. These names are fine when you only have a few nodes, but when you have a simulation with many nodes, it may be difficult to keep track of which nodes perform which functions. For this reason, it is good practice to rename new nodes as they are inserted. To rename a node, select it in the Simulation Tree window, press the F2 key, key a name, and then press Enter on the keyboard.

troubleshooting

Names beginning with "!","/", "\","*",":" or a space are not allowed.

Changing Node Properties

In addition to the Property Bar located on the right side of the EON program window, you can view a node's Properties dialog box by double-clicking the node icon in the Simulation Tree window. You may also open a Properties dialog box by choosing Properties from either the Edit menu or from the pop-up menu displayed when you right-click a node icon in the Simulation Tree window. Yet another way is to select a node in the Simulation Tree window and then press the Enter key.

tips+tricks

Note that, in this case, the same result could be achieved by dragging another 2DText node to the scene. However, these two operations would produce different results if you have made edits to the node in the scene before you copy it.

tips+tricks

It is a good idea to keep node names as simple as possible and eliminate spaces within the names. You can use an underscore to separate words or format multiple words as one word. This simple organizational method will make the development of complex applications much easier.

Activity 1.3.3: Working with Common Nodes

1. Open EON to start a new simulation. If EON is already open, select **New** from the File menu.
2. From the Components window, select the **SceneModifier** node and drag and drop it under Scene in the simulation tree.
3. From the Components window, select the **2DText** node and drag and drop it under Scene in the simulation tree.
4. Right-click **2DText** in the simulation tree. Choose **Copy** from the pop-up menu.
5. Right-click the **Scene** frame in the simulation tree and choose **Paste.** A second 2DText node will appear in the scene. It is automatically named *2DText1*.
6. Select the **2DText** node in the simulation tree and then press **F2.** The node name text will become highlighted.
7. Key **Title** and press **Enter.**
8. Select the **2DText1** node in the simulation tree, press **F2,** key **Subtitle,** and press **Enter.** Your simulation tree should look like Figure 1.3.18.

FIGURE 1.3.18 Simulation tree in progress

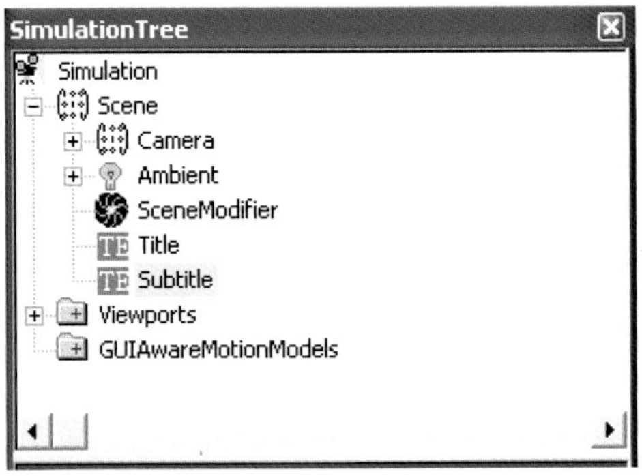

9. Select the **Title** node (in the simulation tree) and scrutinize the settings in the Property Bar. There are many fields with which you may be familiar from working with a word processor such as Font, FontSize, FontStyle, and WordWrap. Note that the TextColor is white and the BoxColor is black.
10. Click in the value field next to Text in the Property Bar. The existing word *Place* is selected. Key **The EON Professional CD.**
11. From the menu, select **File** > **Save As,** browse to your solution file storage location, key **TextAndImage** in the File name text box and then click **Save.**
12. Click the **Start Simulation** button (on the Toolbar) to run the simulation. Notice that the background of the entire simulation screen is black, as is the area behind the text. The text appears in white. Notice also that the text is located in the upper-left corner because the BoxPosition setting is 10 10. You do not see the subtitle text.
13. Stop the simulation (using either the **Close** button on the simulation window or the **Stop Simulation** button on the Toolbar).
14. Select **Title** in the simulation tree and then select the black box to the right of the BoxColor values in the Property Bar. This will open the Color dialog box.

tips+tricks

In the 2DText properties, the TextPosition value is an offset within the text box, whereas the BoxPosition value is an offset from the upper-left edge of the simulation window.

15. Choose the bright blue color, as shown in Figure 1.3.19. Click **OK** to accept the color selection.

FIGURE 1.3.19 Color dialog box

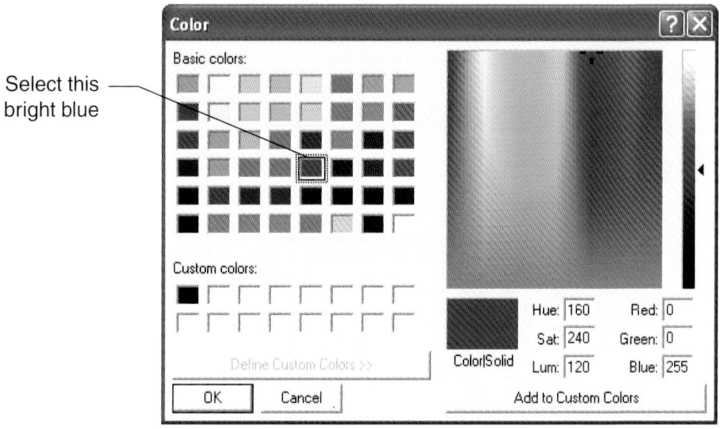

16. In the BoxPosition field in the Property Bar, select the first **10** (this is the value for X) and key **200.** (Be sure to keep a space between the X value and the Y value.)
17. Run the simulation and note the effects of the changes you have made. The area behind the text is blue, the rest of the background is black, and the Title text box has shifted from the upper-left corner of the simulation scene to the right by 200 pixels. This reveals the Subtitle text that was hidden under the Title text.
18. Decrease the size of the simulation window by dragging its borders but leave it open so that you can see the effects of the changes you will make in the Property Bar as you are making them. If necessary, drag the simulation window so that it is not covering either the Simulation Tree window or the Property Bar.
19. Select the **Subtitle** node in the simulation tree and change the Text value in the Property Bar to **Everything you need for your simulations.**
20. Change the subtitle's BoxPosition X value to **200** and change the Y value to **35.** This aligns the subtitle with the title and moves it below the title.
21. Change the subtitle's BoxColor to the same bright blue that we chose for the title and expand the BoxArea values. (Click the + sign next to the BoxArea field to display the spinners.) Change the [0] value to **300** so that all of the subtitile text can be seen.
22. Select the down arrow next to the FontStyle field. From the drop-down list, select **Italic [2].**
23. In the simulaton tree, select the **SceneModifier** node. In the Property Bar, change BackgroundColor to the same bright blue that you used as the background for the text.
24. Stop the simulation.
25. Add a **Frame** node under Scene in the simulation tree and rename it **Image.**
26. Add a **2DImage** node to the simulation tree, under the Image frame, and rename it **CD_Image.**
27. Select the **CD_Image** node. In the Property Bar, select the folder icon that appears in the ImageFile field. Browse to the data files for this lesson, select **EON_CD.bmp,** and click **Open.**
28. Expand the **ImagePosition** field and change the X value to **25** and the Y value to **75.** This places the image below the title and subtitle.

troubleshooting

If you are still not seeing all of the subtitle after you make the box position and color adjustments, you may need to stop the simulation and restart it. This should resolve any issues with viewing the subtitle.

29. Run the simulation. Resize the simulation window if necessary to display the entire image. It should look similar to Figure 1.3.20.

FIGURE 1.3.20 Simulation with text and an image

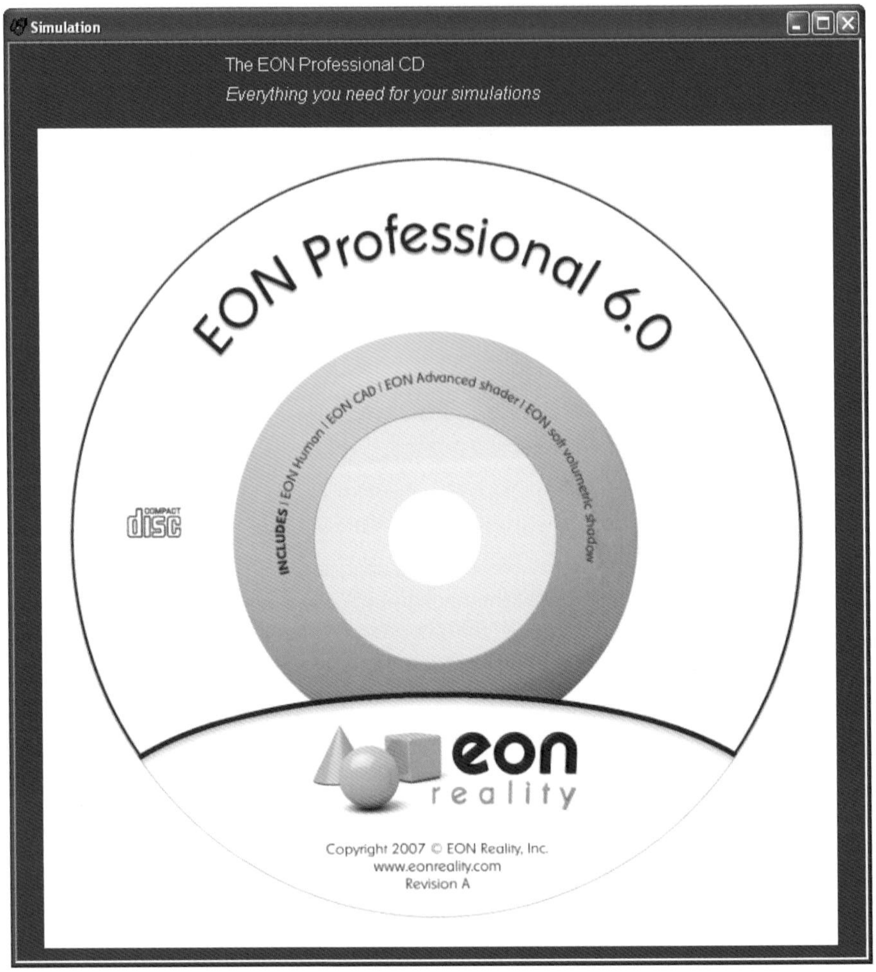

30. Close the simulation window. Save the simulation and then close EON.

Adding Prototypes to EON

Prototypes are reusable, plug-and-play simulation building blocks that can be copied from the Prototypes tab of the Components window and placed into your own custom simulations. A prototype works in a similar fashion to an object in object-oriented programming applications. Prototypes can be saved and used in other simulations just like nodes. You can also create your own prototypes.

In addition to being stored internally in the simulation file, prototype definitions can also be stored externally on a separate server and dynamically loaded into a running simulation over the Internet.

Each prototype component contains its own internal simulation subtree and may contain routing information and a set of external fields (i.e., properties) which, depending on the prototype's purpose, are used to pass values back and forth between the prototype and its parent simulation. A prototype can also contain other prototypes.

Prototypes make building simulations simpler because they eliminate the need to manually re-create equivalent simulation tasks over and over again. Prototypes are often described as "encapsulated" objects because their associated subtree, routes, and field information are stored separately within the prototype component's definition rather than locally and explicitly within the parent simulation tree.

Because the prototype's encapsulated subtree contains both nodes and routes, it is possible to reuse not only complex objects, based on EON nodes and other prototypes, but also the behaviors created in the Routes window and/or Script nodes for those objects. Because the inner details of prototypes are concealed, the parent simulation tree is a less complex, easier-to-maintain structure compared to a functionally equivalent collection of numerous local subtrees required to produce the same results as the selected prototype components.

Prototypes also affect how users work in the Routes window. Instead of creating routes between layers, routes are created between prototypes. This makes the Routes window easier to use, routes easier to follow, and the creation of routes more efficient.

cross-reference

You will learn more about using prototypes in Module 8.

Activity 1.3.4: Viewing Existing Prototypes

1. Open EON to start a new simulation. If EON is already open, select **New** from the File menu.
2. In the Components window, click the **Prototypes** tab. You will see the full set of prototypes, similar to the set shown in Figure 1.3.21.

FIGURE 1.3.21 Prototypes tab

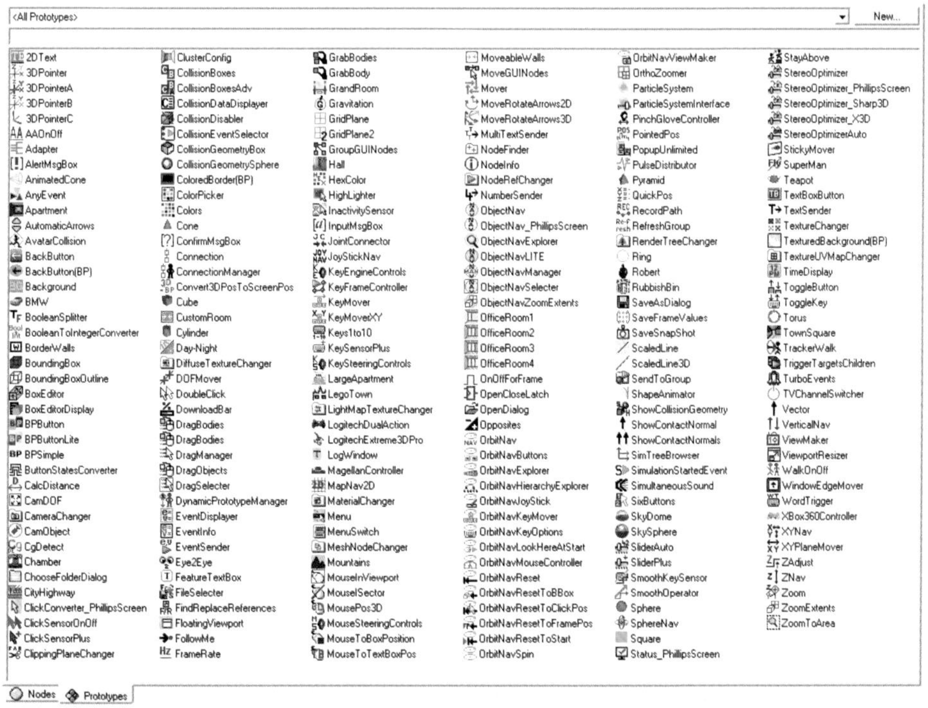

troubleshooting

You may need to resize your window or scroll to see all of the prototypes. Additionally, the exact set of prototypes you see may vary based on your version of the software and your specific installation.

3. Like nodes, prototypes are divided into libraries (or categories) of similar prototypes. Select the drop-down arrow next to <All Prototypes>. You will see a set of choices similar to that shown in Figure 1.3.22.

FIGURE 1.3.22 Prototype categories

4. Select **(3DShapes)** from the drop-down list. The set of visible prototypes is adjusted to show only the 3DShape prototypes.
5. Click the drop-down arrow again and select **<All Prototypes>** to make all the prototypes visible again.
6. In the text box below the <All Prototypes> drop-down menu, key **T.** Only the prototypes whose names begin with the letter T will be visible.
7. Select the letter **T** in the text box and delete it. All of the prototypes will be visible again. Keep the simulation open to use in Activity 1.3.5.

Definition and Instances

A prototype can be included in a simulation in two ways—as a ***prototype definition*** in the Local Prototypes window or as a ***prototype instance*** in the simulation tree shown in the Simulation Tree window. A prototype definition contains all necessary information to construct a prototype instance, including a subtree hierarchy containing nodes and/or other prototypes, routes, data fields with designated default values, and any required graphics resource files (such as image maps and textures).

The prototype definition is used as a template to create prototype instances in the simulation tree. The prototype definition is displayed as an icon in the Local Prototypes window, and the prototype instance is displayed as an icon within the simulation tree. Figure 1.3.23 shows the ToggleButton prototype in both the simulation tree (prototype instance) and the Local Prototypes window (prototype definition).

FIGURE 1.3.23 Prototype instance and definition

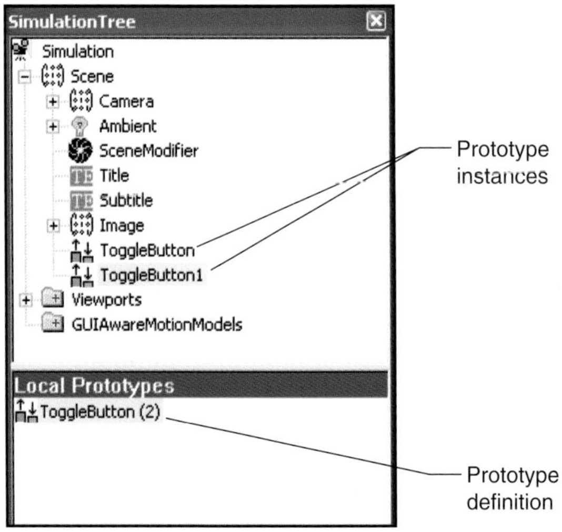

tips+tricks

Notice that the number in parentheses after the prototype definition reflects the number of times that prototype is used in the simulation tree. If the prototype is only in the Local Prototypes window and has not yet been placed in the simulation tree, the number in parentheses will be "0".

Adding Prototypes to the Scene

There are two fundamental methods for adding prototype definitions and instances to your simulation:

- Copy from the Prototypes window to the simulation tree in the Simulation Tree window
- Copy from the Prototypes window to the Local Prototypes window

Each of these methods is explored in greater detail in the following sections.

Copying Prototypes to the Simulation Tree Window

To create a prototype instance based on the prototype definition stored in the EON Components library, simply copy a prototype component directly from the Components window into the simulation tree in the Simulation Tree window. When a prototype instance is added to a simulation from the library, the prototype definition is also displayed in the Local Prototypes window, where all prototypes used in the current simulation are displayed. If the same prototype already exists in the simulation, this is indicated by a number in parentheses affixed to the prototype name. This index number increases for each identical prototype added to the simulation.

Copying Prototypes to the Local Prototypes Window

To create a prototype instance based on your own customized prototype definition stored in the Local Prototypes window of your simulation, copy the prototype definition from the Components library into the Local Prototypes window, customize the prototype, and then copy the prototype definition from the Local Prototypes window into the simulation tree in the Simulation Tree window. The new prototype instance will inherit all changes made to the local prototype. All changes to prototype definitions will be reflected in all prototype instances—no matter when the instances were created. However, changes to the exported field values of a local prototype definition will only affect new prototype instances created after the new changes were applied. Preexisting prototype instances will be unaffected.

As Figure 1.3.24 illustrates, after one or more prototype instances are created in the simulation tree, you can manipulate and control the behavior of each individual instance by assigning specific values to their exposedFields, just as you do with standard EON nodes.

FIGURE 1.3.24 Prototype definitions and instances

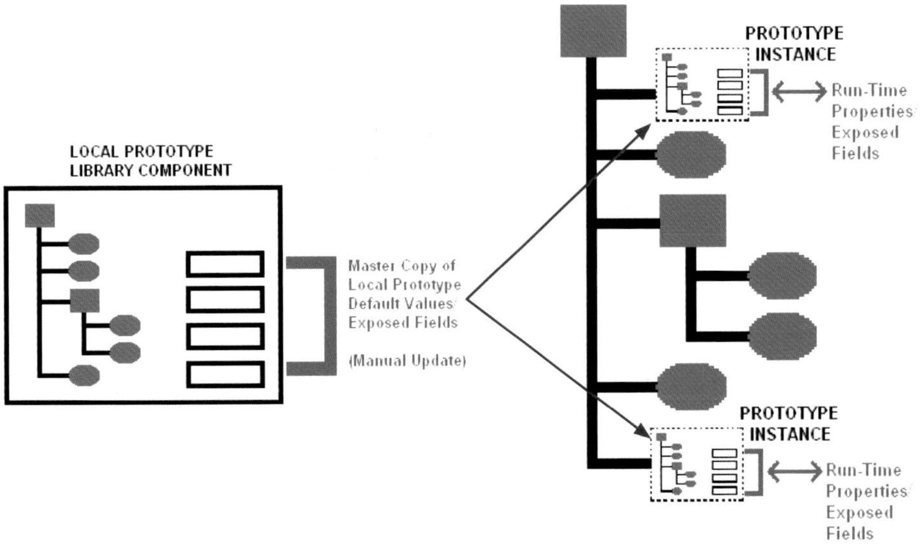

tips+tricks

A prototype can be modified before it is added to a simulation. You can drag a prototype to the Local Prototypes window, edit it, and then add it to the simulation when needed.

tips+tricks

When a prototype definition is copied from the EON Components library into the Local Prototypes window, a local copy of the prototype definition is stored within the simulation's .eoz file. You can customize this local definition without altering the original definition in the Components library. To modify the default values of the local prototype's external fields, simply double-click the local prototype definition's icon, select the Exported Fields tab, and make changes in the Value column.

cross-reference

You will have the opportunity to learn much more about existing prototypes as well as prototype creation and usage in Module 8.

Activity 1.3.5: Adding Definitions versus Instances

1. Continue working with the open simulation file from Activity 1.3.4.
2. If necessary, select the **Prototypes** tab in the Components window.
3. Select the **Teapot** prototype and drag it to the Local Prototypes window. You have just created a prototype definition for your simulation. Note, however, that there is no prototype instance. (See Figure 1.3.25.)

troubleshooting

If you do not see the Local Prototypes window, choose View from the menu and then select Default Layout. The Local Prototypes window should appear near the middle of the EON window. Alternatively, you could drag the Simulation Tree window's bottom border upward.

FIGURE 1.3.25 Prototype definition without instances

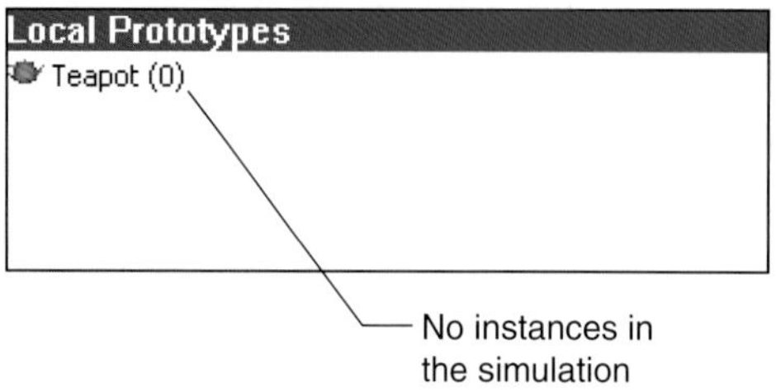

4. Double-click **Teapot (0)** in the Local Prototypes window. This will open the Prototype Definition Properties dialog box.
5. Select the **Exported Fields** tab. The dialog box will appear similar to that shown in Figure 1.3.26.

FIGURE 1.3.26 Prototype Definition Properties dialog box for the Teapot prototype

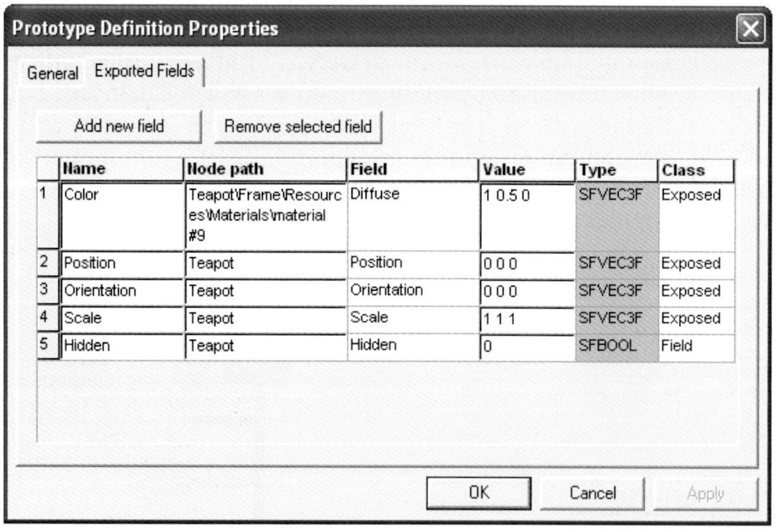

troubleshooting

In step 6, be sure to key a space between each value. You should key 0 [spacebar] 0 [spacebar] -20. This differentiates the values within the field. When you see a sequence of three separate values in this text, be sure to include the spaces between each value. Alternatively, if you are changing the values in the Property Bar, you can expand the field and then key each value separately.

6. Locate the Orientation field, select the numbers in the Value column and then key **0 0 -20.** Click **OK.** This will tilt the teapot on its side, as if it were being poured. The Teapot prototype definition in the Local Prototypes window is now different from the default Teapot prototype definition in the library.
7. Drag the **Teapot** from the Local Prototypes window to the Scene frame in the Simulation Tree window three times. You should now have three Teapot prototype instances in the Simulation Tree window and one prototype definition in the Local Prototypes window as shown in Figure 1.3.27.

FIGURE 1.3.27 Prototype instances and definition

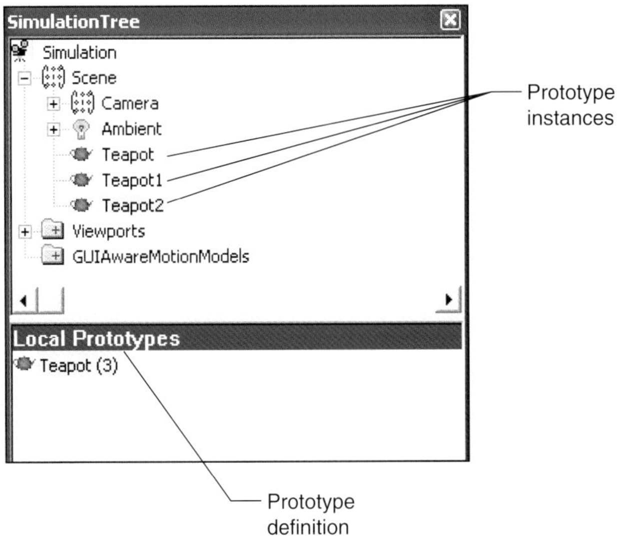

8. Select each **Teapot** in the simulation tree and note the Color field in the Property Bar for each. They are all an orange color. Note also that they are all positioned at 0 0 0 and that the orientation for each is 0 0 -20 as it was set in the definition before copying the prototype to the simulation.
9. Select the **Simulation** node in the simulation tree and then run the simulation. You only see one teapot because all three instances are located at exactly the same XYZ position in 3D space. Leave the simulation running for the next steps so that you can see the changes as you make them.
10. Change the name (using F2) of *Teapot* to **RedTeapot,** *Teapot1* to **BlueTeapot,** and *Teapot2* to **GreenTeapot.**
11. Select **RedTeapot** and change its color to red. You can do this by selecting the colored box and then selecting the color from the Color dialog box or by changing the values in the Diffuse field to **1 0 0.**
12. Change the colors for the BlueTeapot and the GreenTeapot. The Color values for blue are **0 0 1** and green are **0 1 0.** You will not see these color changes in the simulation because these two teapots are still behind the first (red) teapot.
13. Select **BlueTeapot** (in the simulation tree) and change the X value in the Position field to **2.** The blue teapot is now visible to the right of the red teapot.
14. Select **GreenTeapot** and change the X value in the Position field to **3.** The green teapot is still overlapping the blue teapot.
15. Change the X value in the green teapot's Position field to **4.** Now you now can see all three teapots as shown in Figure 1.3.28.

troubleshooting

Notice that, while the simulation is open, the name of the Color field is shown as *Diffuse*.

FIGURE 1.3.28 Three teapot instances

16. Stop the simulation. Look at the Position values for each of the teapots. Note that they have all returned to 0 0 0. Also note that the colors have reverted to the original orange color as well.
17. Select the **Simulation** node and run the simulation again to see that the teapots are again stacked on top of one another and colored orange. Stop the simulation.
18. Select **RedTeapot** and change its Color field to **1 0 0.**
19. Select **BlueTeapot** and change its color to **0 0 1** and the X value in its Position field to **2.**
20. Select **GreenTeapot** and change its color to **0 1 0** and the X value in its Position field to **4.**
21. Run the simulation and note that the teapots are now colored and positioned appropriately.
22. Close the simulation window. Save the simulation as **ColoredTeapots** and close EON.

troubleshooting

Some fields are not, by default, permanently changed if they are edited during runtime (when the simulation is running). The most prominent fields that are not permanently changed are the fields in the Frame and the DOF nodes. This helps you work out positioning and other details by allowing you to move objects temporarily. Changes made to prototypes during runtime are not affected by the *Permanent runtime changes* setting in the Property Bar Settings dialog box that we discussed earlier in this lesson. For these values to be retained, they must be changed when the simulation is not running.

Discussion

discuss

Why would it be helpful for the changes made to some fields (such as Position and Orientation) during runtime to be temporary? When would this be useful? Under what circumstances might you want to change the Property Bar setting so that those kinds of changes would be permanent?

troubleshooting

Note that, as long as there are instances of a prototype in the simulation tree, you cannot delete that prototype definition from the Local Prototypes window. A prototype definition can only be deleted if no instances are in use (i.e., the number in parentheses after the definition is "0").

BEST PRACTICES

Node Selection Before Running

Before you run a simulation, you should get into the habit of selecting either the Simulation node or the Scene node at the top of the simulation tree. If another node in the simulation is selected when you run the simulation, the Property Bar for that node may not be updated appropriately, and this can lead to some anomalies in the behavior of the field value selections and settings. If you select the node at the top of the tree, the Property Bar will be up to date when you edit the fields of a node further down in the tree.

Commonly Used Prototypes

Like the nodes, some prototypes are so useful that they are used frequently and in many different types of simulations. Certainly the other prototypes available are useful as well, but they may have more limited uses or may be specific to one field or one type of simulation. The prototypes described in the following sections are some of those that are widely used.

Camera Functions Prototypes

The Camera Functions library (shown in Figure 1.3.29) contains prototypes that can be used to modify the scene camera. The preferred placement of these prototypes varies. Some prototypes *must* be placed under the Camera frame, and some *must not* be placed under the Camera frame. Some can be placed anywhere, and some should be put under the Camera frame to reduce setup time. Read the Help provided with each prototype for more information.

FIGURE 1.3.29 Camera Functions library of prototypes

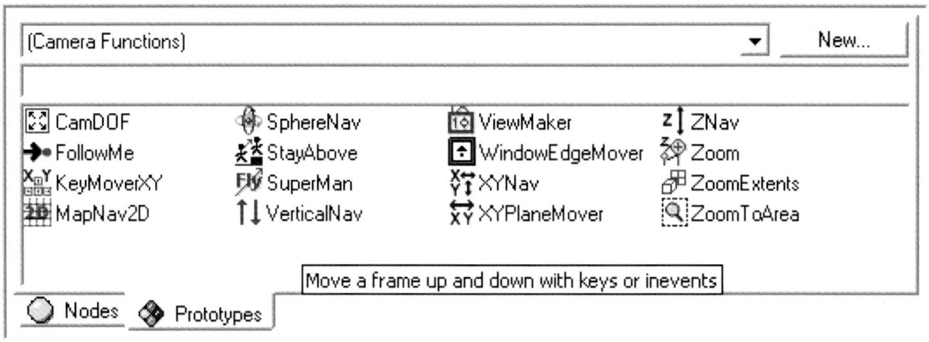

Several of the more commonly used prototypes are briefly described in Table 1.3.5.

TABLE 1.3.5 Commonly Used Camera Functions Prototypes

Prototype Name	Description	Icon
SuperMan	The SuperMan prototype provides a very realistic simulation of flight. After it is placed in the simulation, clicking the left mouse button accelerates the user forward through the simulation, and clicking the right mouse button accelerates backward. The maximum acceleration value is specified by the BaseSpeed property.	SuperMan
VerticalNav	The VerticalNav prototype allows a user to increase or decrease the height of a camera smoothly or in step amounts. This prototype needs to be placed below the Camera frame and in the Scene frame. After it is placed, up and down inEvents allow the keyboard or buttons to be routed to the prototype.	VerticalNav
Zoom	The Zoom prototype, which can be placed anywhere in the Scene frame, adjusts the field of view of the current viewport in the scene. It can be triggered by a keyboard value set in the ZoomKey field or by an inEvent.	Zoom

ObjectNav Prototypes

The ObjectNav prototypes are shown in Figure 1.3.30. Of these, the two most commonly used are ObjectNav and ObjectNavLITE, which allow rotation, zooming, and panning of the Viewport camera around a central point (PivotPoint). They can also limit the zoom distance and rotation angles for the camera. Table 1.3.6 details these prototypes.

FIGURE 1.3.30 Object navigation prototypes

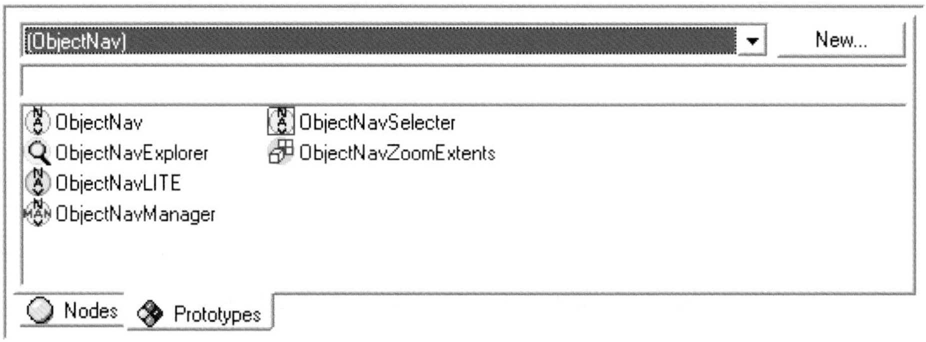

TABLE 1.3.6 Commonly Used Object Navigation Prototypes

Prototype Name	Description	Icon
ObjectNav	This prototype allows the user to rotate, zoom, and pan using the mouse. It has more than 70 exported fields to allow a variety of customization options.	ObjectNav
ObjectNavLITE	This prototype is the same as ObjectNav, but with only ten exported fields, providing a basic navigation tool that lets the user find the common settings more easily.	ObjectNavLITE

These prototypes should be placed under objects around which you want to rotate. The name of the camera Frame node must be noted in the Camera field for the prototype.

OrbitNav Prototypes

The OrbitNav prototypes are a new set of prototypes (released with EON version 6) that have been created as a better set of prototypes for navigating within a simulation (rather than using ObjectNav). There are 15 add-on prototypes that extend OrbitNav, as shown in Figure 1.3.31.

FIGURE 1.3.31 Orbit navigation prototypes

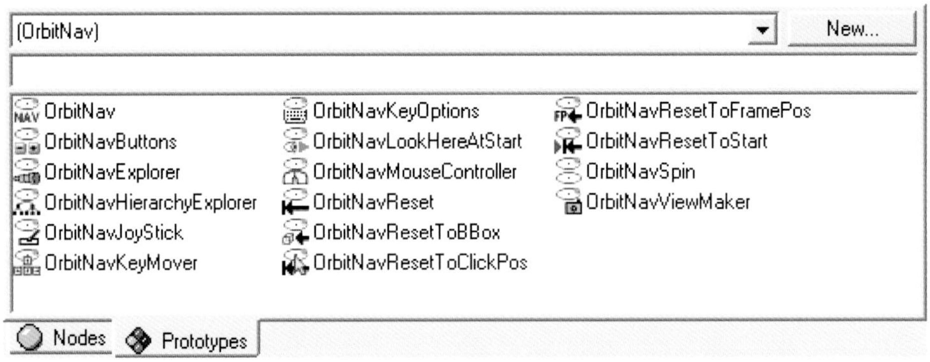

BEST PRACTICES

The Difference Between the OrbitNav and ObjectNav Prototype

The ObjectNav prototype developed earlier also rotates, zooms, and pans like OrbitNav, but the panning is different. With OrbitNav, panning will move the pivot point, but with ObjectNav, the pivot point stays inside the object. If it is important or desirable to have the pivot point stay inside the object, then use the ObjectNav prototype. Otherwise, the OrbitNav prototype is superior and recommended. The ObjectNav prototype has many fields that are difficult for all but the most experienced developers to use and understand. The approach the developers took with the OrbitNav prototype was to reduce the number of fields and to add more functionality by adding related prototypes whose fields can be understood in the context of the added function.

In most cases, all you need to do to use the OrbitNav prototype is put the prototype under the Camera frame. If a Walk node is under the Camera frame, then select Copy as Link for the Walk node and paste it in the OrbitNav's DisableWhenActive folder/field. With the prototype in place, you can use the left mouse button to rotate, the right mouse button (or Ctrl and the left mouse button) to zoom, and the middle mouse button to pan. (Alternatively, you can pan with Shift and the left mouse button or the left and right mouse buttons used together.)

OrbitNav also has a set of key functions that provide built-in navigation features as well. These are outlined in Table 1.3.7.

TABLE 1.3.7 OrbitNav's Key Functions

Key	Function
P	Show/hide PivotPoint with a 3D pointer object.
Spacebar	Turn on/off spinning (autorotate).
Esc	Reset (move the camera to position/orientation defined by reset fields).
O	Turn on/off OrbitNav. Often this means turning on/off the Walk node.
B	Backward (if pressed during a current action of rotate, zoom, pan, or spin, this will reverse the direction of the action).
Number pad keys: Plus (+) Minus (−) Multiply (*)	Speed-changing keys. If these keys are pressed during a current action of rotate, zoom, pan, or spin, they will increase (plus key) or decrease (minus key) the action's speed (or mouse sensitivity). The multiply key will restore the current action's speed to simulation start values.

Useful Functions Prototypes

The Useful Functions library of prototypes, as the name implies, contains many prototypes that you will find extremely useful. Figure 1.3.32 shows all of the Useful Function prototypes. Table 1.3.8 details some that you will likely begin using right away in your simulations.

FIGURE 1.3.32 Useful Functions library of prototypes

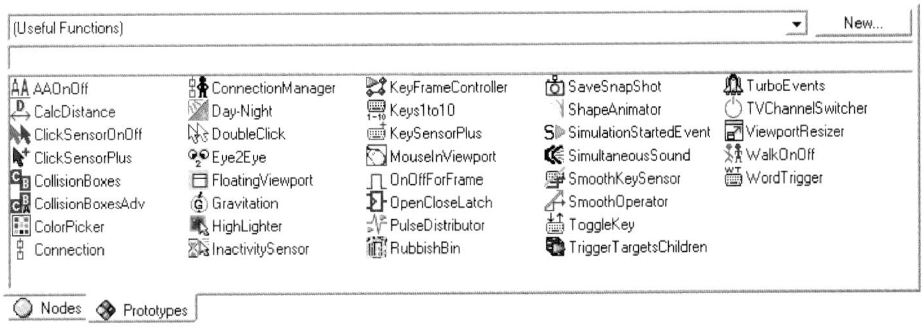

TABLE 1.3.8 Commonly Used Useful Functions Prototypes

Prototype Name	Description	Icon	Common Uses
Viewport Resizer	Can be placed anywhere in the scene. It contains two sets of viewport values (X, Y) that set the width and height of the viewport. Keyboard keys or inEvents are used to change the state.	ViewportResizer	
Eye2Eye	This prototype will affect the orientation of its parent node. It will cause this parent node (that is a Frame node) to "look at" another object. The other object/frame must also have an Eye2Eye prototype. Its purpose is to send its world position to the first prototype.	Eye2Eye	Make a spotlight aim directly at an object at all times. Establish a compass, where an arrow under the camera points north. Make the camera face an object all the time. Create a motion model so that the user can zoom in and out and go around the object while always looking at the object. Special effects, such as flowers leaning toward the sun as the sun moves over the sky.
Inactivity Sensor	Triggers an event after a set time of mouse inactivity. It is like a screen saver. When you don't move the mouse for a certain amount of time, it can start other selected events.	InactivitySensor	For demonstrations at an exhibition, you could run an animation or camera path when no one is moving the mouse. This activity could attract people to the display. If the application is a game or training application and a user did not move the mouse for a while, you could use sound to tell the user to do something or give the user a hint. After a period of inactivity, you could shut down the EON application by sending an event to the host program that can stop EON.
Smooth Operator	Sends out values that gradually change over time. Instead of changing certain values instantly (like an on-and-off switch), they can be changed smoothly (like a dimmer switch). The types of values that can be changed are float values and integer values.	SmoothOperator	Objects can fade away into nothing by sending the float values to the Alpha field of the Material2 node. Sounds can fade in and out, you can pan left and right, and the pitch can go up and down smoothly. An object's rotation or spin can accelerate and decelerate. You can alter the wavelength, amplitude, frequency, and modulation of the OceanWaves node.

Top Most-Used Prototypes

Obviously, the prototypes that you use most often will be dictated by the applications for which you are creating simulations. There are certainly some that you will find exceedingly useful and others that you never use at all. Table 1.3.9, however, contains the prototypes that current EON developers have found they use most often. We have discussed several prototypes previously. The others are ones that you should familiarize yourself with and keep in mind as you begin application development.

TABLE 1.3.9 Most-Used Prototypes

Prototype Name	Description	Icon
OrbitNav	Navigation system to rotate, pan and zoom. (See the section on OrbitNav prototypes for more details.)	OrbitNav
OrbitNavLookHereAtStart	Makes OrbitNav instantly look toward an object.	OrbitNavLookHereAtStart
ObjectNav	Rotate, zoom, and pan around a single object. (See the section on ObjectNav prototypes for more detail.)	ObjectNav
KeySensorPlus	A keyboard sensor plus three extra functions.	KeySensorPlus
Keys1to10	Sends OutEvents when you press keys 1 to 10.	Keys1to10
SimulationStartedEvent	Sends the event SimulationStarted when the simulation has started. The event is sent after all nodes have initialized.	SimulationStartedEvent
Cube	A cube object 2m wide.	Cube
Sphere	A sphere object 2m in diameter.	Sphere
Square	A square in the X-Z plane, 2m wide and 2m high.	Square
Chamber	Large, partly circular room with built-in lighting effects.	Chamber
Hall	A two-story hallway with beautiful lighting effects.	Hall

We will be using many of these prototypes in the activities of future lessons. You will become familiar with them and will learn to appreciate their usefulness.

cross-reference

You will learn more about these prototypes, and many others, in future modules, particularly Module 8.

Summary

In this lesson you:

- Became aware of the different data types used in EON.
- Learned about the various types of fields used in EON.
- Explored node functions.
- Created simulations using some of the more commonly used nodes.
- Learned about some basic prototypes and used them in simulations.

Simulation

As a new designer for the Contours Company, your first task is to become familiar with the processes and software commonly used by employees of Contours.

When a new project starts, those involved will hold one or more meetings to work through the storyboards for the project. They typically storyboard the development process for the models and simulations as well as the appearance and function of the final simulation.

To create their models, they use several different programs, including 3ds Max™ and Maya™, and you are already familiar with both of these applications from your previous modeling experience. But they also use EON Professional for all their 3D simulation applications. Because you have never used this program before, you will have to familiarize yourself with it.

Job 1.1: Creating a Storyboard

To begin your training process, you are asked to think about a project that will start soon. Contours' client would like the company to take an existing floor plan for an apartment and create a simulation that their potential customers can "walk through." This apartment should include some sample furniture. Your task is to create a general storyboard outlining the steps needed to create this apartment simulation. Think about necessary models, user interface options, features that might be important, and capabilities that the simulation should have. After each designer involved in the project has created a preliminary storyboard, you will meet and start brainstorming, using the work you have already completed as a starting point.

To complete your storyboard, you can use paper and pencil, a flowchart application, a drawing program, or any method you prefer. Use the medium that works best for you to get your ideas worked out.

Job 1.2: Exploring Some of EON's Basic Capabilities

The best way to learn what is possible with the EON simulation software is to work with completed simulations. If you have a chance to visit a facility equipped with an EON iCUBE or iCATCHER, you should definitely take the opportunity to do so. Personally experiencing either of these technologies in operation will give you the best sense of the full extent of the simulation software's capabilities. If that is not possible, you can open a completed simulation of an apartment on your local computer system.

1. Open EON. Open **Job_1.2.eoz** from the data files for the Module 1 Simulation. (Click **File** > **Open** and then browse to the data files for this module.)
2. Run the simulation by selecting **Start Simulation** (button with a green arrow) from the Toolbar.
3. In the simulation window, click and hold the left mouse button as you move the mouse to the right and left side of the simulation window. Notice how this allows you to pan around the room.
4. In the simulation window, click and hold the left mouse button as you move the mouse to the top and bottom of the simulation window. Notice how this allows you to zoom in and out.
5. Use the navigation techniques outlined in steps 3 and 4 to position yourself so that you are standing at the sink and looking toward the television.
6. Continue using the mouse to navigate around in the simulation.
7. Close the simulation window. Keep the simulation open to use in Job 1.3.

Discussion

discuss

Did this apartment simulation have things that you did not consider in your preliminary storyboard created in Job 1.1? Did your storyboard include things that were not in this simulation?

Job 1.3: Delving into a Simulation

Now that you have experienced a sampling of what can be done in EON, you can learn how such simulations are put together. Through what you have read about EON in this module, you have become familiar with some of the most commonly used nodes. Were any of those nodes used in the apartment simulation?

1. Continue working with the open simulation file **Job_1.2.eoz** from Job 1.2.
2. In the Simulation Tree window, expand the **Floorplan** frame to see the components that make up the floor plan for the apartment. Notice how the naming conventions used make it very easy to find different parts of the simulation.
3. Expand the **Kitchen** frame, the **Door_Cupboard_Main** frame, and the **_offset_** frame. What type of node is Door_Cupboard_MainShape?
4. Expand the **Geometry** folder under Door_Cupboard_MainShape. What type of node is used to create the geometry for the cupboard door?
5. Expand the **Material** folder under Door_Cupboard_MainShape. What type of node is used for the material of the cupboard door?
6. Continue exploring the simulation tree. Locate a Group node. What is it used to "group" together?
7. Run the simulation.
8. With the simulation window open, expand the **Resources** group and then the **Materials** group.
9. Select the **Walls** Material2 node.
10. In the Property Bar, select the color button for the Diffuse field.
11. Select a wall color of your choice in the Color dialog box and then click **OK.** Notice that the wall color in your simulation window changes to reflect the selection that you have made for your Diffuse lighting.
12. Close the simulation window. Close EON without saving the simulation.

After exploring an EON simulation just a little bit, you quickly realize that you have much to learn about the simulation development process! You ask your supervisor for more training and any learning materials and aids that she has available.

tips+tricks

Use the icons next to the text in the Simulation Tree window as a visual clue to the type of node used. You can look through the nodes in the Components window to find the matching type until you become familiar with them.

troubleshooting

If you choose a color from the color spectrum on the right side of the Color dialog box rather than choosing one of the preset colors on the left, you will need to click the Add to Custom Colors button before you click OK for the color change to take effect.

cross-reference

You will learn much more about the various types of lighting and how they affect the colors in your simulation in Module 5. You can use many techniques to change the appearance of objects in your simulation.

HARALD SUND

MODULE 2

Fundamentals of EON

LESSON 2.1

Fundamentals of Developing Interactive 3D Environments

LESSON 2.2

Organizing, Running, and Saving an EON Application

LESSON 2.1

Fundamentals of Developing Interactive 3D Environments

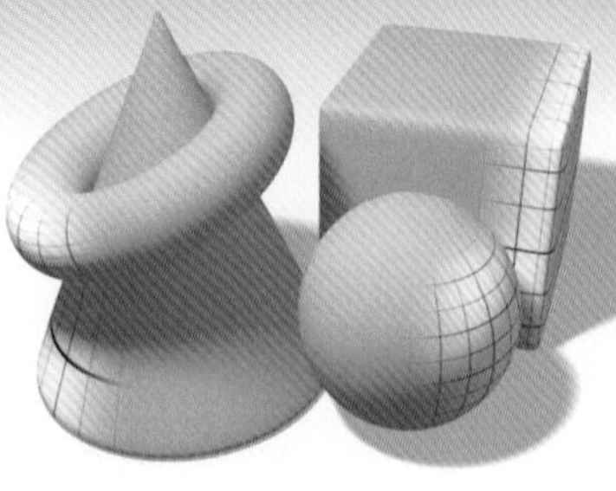

Objectives

In this lesson you will:

- Develop knowledge and an understanding of the typical application development workflow.
- Learn the basics of using a storyboard for project planning.
- Become familiar with a variety of external resources for obtaining elements used in your EON application.
- Define rendering.
- Consider the elements involved in establishing a virtual world.
- Begin to explore "level of detail" in the context of an EON application.
- Develop an understanding of coordinate systems within EON Studio and 3D projects in general.
- Develop the ability to move objects within the coordinate systems.

Key Terms

camera
camera coordinate
Cartesian coordinate system
clipping plane
culled
culling
external resource
field of view
frustum
heading
Hidden Surface Removal (HSR)
level of detail
local coordinate
pitch
project plan
rasterization
real-time rendering
rendering
roll
rotation
storyboard
texture mapping
thumbnail
translation
viewing frustum
viewing plane
viewport
world coordinate

EON provides the tools for building and viewing 3D worlds. Content such as text, images, movies, and sound (and all of their inherent 3D geometry) is integrated into those worlds. But where do all of the various content elements for such 3D worlds come from? How are they made able to mimic the real world? That is the fundamental work in developing an interactive, virtual environment, and that is what we will begin to explore in this lesson.

Workflow for Creating EON Applications

Simulations are built in EON Studio, but you will need other programs to create and edit 3D objects, textures, and sounds. Although some basic object editing is possible within EON Studio (for example, you can change an object's colors or apply different textures), the "raw materials" required for your simulations, such as 3D models, textures, and sound files, must be prepared in advance.

Building an EON simulation involves four main actions:

- Adding (importing) geometry to a scene and organizing the scene hierarchy
- Applying materials and enhancing 3D objects in a scene
- Defining behavioral properties for these objects
- Specifying how users will interact with objects in the simulation

To further enhance the realism of a simulation scene, you may also want to add sound, lighting, and special effects.

The last step in the process is distributing the application. Most EON applications are intended to be displayed outside of EON Studio. Because EON adheres to Microsoft's ActiveX standard, you can view full-feature EON applications in documents created in ActiveX-compliant programs. Microsoft Internet Explorer, Macromedia Director, and Macromedia Authorware are examples of such programs.

Figure 2.1.1 illustrates the general steps in the EON application workflow. The sections that follow provide more detail about each step.

FIGURE 2.1.1 Workflow for creating EON applications

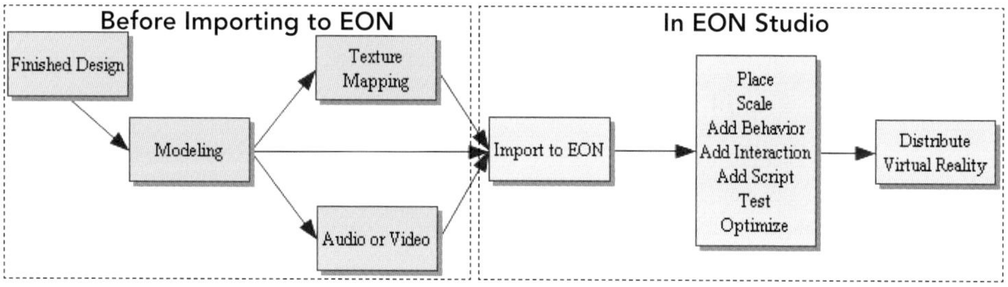

Before Importing to EON

Objects (particularly 3D objects), textures, audio, and video can be imported into EON. We will look more closely at where these files can come from later in this lesson. But right now, let's examine the steps involved in the other side of the equation—after an object is in your EON application.

In EON Studio

After being imported into EON's 3D environment, the objects, textures, sounds, and videos are available to be used in the simulation environment. However, many times, adjustments are needed before they fit into your virtual world. You can adjust the placement, scaling, behaviors, and interactions of objects within EON.

cross-reference

You will learn how to import and place 3D objects in Module 3 Lesson 2.

Placing and Scaling an Object

You may find the objects you have imported are not appropriately sized in relationship to one another. Part of creating a believable and realistic world is making sure

troubleshooting

If you cannot export objects from your modeling package in meters, you can change the measurement unit that EON uses for this model.

details like this are accurate. Therefore, you have the ability to position and scale imported 3D objects as needed in EON Studio.

When creating objects in a modeling application, make sure that you create your objects in the correct scale. EON's default unit is a meter. When exporting from your modeling package, it is important to set your units to meters.

Adding Behavior

After they are part of the simulation, the 3D objects are assigned behavioral properties that are appropriate for their role in the simulation. For example, an object can change positions after a specified length of time. This enables you to create animation and "movie" sequences—setting your objects to be in certain places on a given timeline.

cross-reference

You will learn more about scripting in Module 9.

Adding Interaction

One of the easiest ways for the user to interact with a simulation is by using the mouse. With basic techniques, the simulation can be configured so that users can navigate through the simulation environment and manipulate simulation objects by moving and clicking the mouse. You can also add more complex interactions that will enhance the user's experience with the simulation.

cross-reference

In Module 11, you will learn more about optimizing simulations.

Adding Script

By adding script, you can include functions that are not provided by the EON nodes. Scripting in EON is very similar to using Javascript and VBscript in hypertext markup language (HTML).

Testing and Optimizing a Simulation

Before distributing the EON application, you should test it and make sure it is optimized for runtime speed as well as download speed. You will find a variety of built-in tools for optimization (polygon reduction, texture compression, simulation statistics, and a log window) that you can use to test and optimize your simulation.

cross-reference

Module 11 discusses developing simulations with ActiveX interoperability as well as web-based distribution of simulations.

Distributing EON Applications

You can display EON applications by using EON Viewer or by inserting EonX (EON's ActiveX control) into a host application. The host application can be a Director multimedia production, a web application, an application framework, or a Microsoft PowerPoint presentation.

Interactive Media Storyboarding and Project Planning

As Figure 2.1.1 illustrates, you need a finished design before any 3D modeling occurs and well before you import anything into EON and create the simulation. What is meant by a finished design? Primarily, this means that you have a plan for what the finished product will include and the elements needed to create that finished product. It also means that you have considered some detail elements, such as how the user will interact with your simulation (i.e., mouse movement, menus, and/or command buttons) and what will exist in the worlds you create. In a nutshell, you need a project plan—a comprehensive blueprint for simulation construction.

A ***project plan*** can take many forms. It can be a written outline, a list, or a drawing. A very common technique used to plan a project of this nature is a storyboard. A ***storyboard*** is a graphic organizer. Typically, it includes illustrations, images, and some text displayed in sequence or in the relationships as they will appear in the finished product. A storyboard expresses, in some form, everything that will be seen, heard, or experienced by the application's end user. This might include what menu screens will look like, what pictures will be seen at what time and for how long, and what audio and text will be used.

The storyboarding process was originally developed during the early 1930s at the Walt Disney Company. Developed by a Disney animator, these first storyboards were generated to illustrate the concepts for Disney's short animated cartoons. The animator came up with the idea of drawing scenes on separate sheets of paper and then pinning them up on a bulletin board. This process allowed him to tell a story in sequence and, at the same time, allowed him to shift concepts around and insert others if he felt that the current plan wouldn't work.

Over the years, storyboards became popular in the creation of feature films, animated movies, and commercials. Almost all of these graphic products begin as a storyboard—a visual outline for the video production process. In recent years, storyboards have expanded into broad use by people who create websites and other interactive media projects during the design phases, including web development, software development, instructional design, and gaming.

Storyboards are used to outline the interactive events as well as the elements' audio and motion. They are particularly useful for detailing the user interfaces, navigation, links, and organization.

Discussion

discuss

A storyboard can also be used to outline the process of creating a simulation. Take a look at the workflow diagram in Figure 2.1.1 and consider how it provides the basis of a storyboard for creating a simulation. What other details would you want to add to that storyboard to make it more useful to your particular project? What other actions would you add?

web links

A quick Internet search for "storyboard software" will yield a variety of useful links. You should explore the software packages thoroughly before you make a purchase, however. There are all kinds of software available, but some are geared specifically toward film production (e.g., Storyboard Quick, FrameForge 3D Studio 2, and Adobe Director) and others are aids for writing a story or book (e.g., Inspiration and StoryBoard Pro). Make sure that, whatever software you choose, it will allow you to develop your storyboard to the level of detail that you need.

Storyboards have many benefits, including the chance for you to experiment with ideas and design changes before investing too much work in the details. For those working in groups, it allows everyone to brainstorm. Ideas can be put on pages of the storyboard and then arranged on a wall. This process of thinking visually generates more ideas and encourages everyone to participate. It has also been proven repeatedly that, in the long run, storyboarding saves time (and money)—which is why their use is so widespread. Some other advantages to consider:

- If there are any omissions or problems in the program, they may be easily spotted during the process of storyboarding. Discovering these problems or omissions at a later stage in the process could be extremely costly.
- The visual layout of a storyboard solidifies expectations for all parties concerned (potentially including a client) and clarifies exactly what is to be included in the final product.
- A storyboard helps everyone focus on the total content of the project—based on discussion of user interaction times and the overall size and scope of the final application.

Thumbnail Storyboard

Storyboards do not need to be fancy—often stick-figure drawings will do. The simplest storyboards are typically called ***thumbnail*** storyboards. These are rough sketches of what will be needed in each scene. You can make a simple thumbnail storyboard by hand using index cards or sticky notes. Then you will be able to sort and manipulate the cards or notes to develop the plan for your project. This is a good technique if you like to experiment with different layouts "on paper" before you create files. Or, if you prefer, you can achieve the same preliminary type of storyboard electronically using a simple flowchart and the drawing tools found in office suite software.

Graphic Storyboard

If higher-quality storyboard images are needed, you may want to develop more detailed drawings, either by hand or electronically. You can create full 3D storyboards to plan your project if they are needed. The advantage of these storyboards is that they show exactly what you intend to include in your simulation. You can create these storyboards using the same 3D animation programs that you might use to create the models for your simulation (e.g., Maya, Lightwave, or 3ds Max).

Several software applications are designed specifically for the creation of storyboards. These are relatively inexpensive and make the design and manipulation of an electronic storyboard extremely easy. Many are simple programs that allow you to create a visual storyboard using easily recognizable symbols that you can drag and drop into any location. You can use the symbols to represent scenes, avatars, buildings, and many other elements of your planned simulation.

web links

You may prefer to use digital puppets with your 3D program. Programs such as Poser and DAZ Studio (*www.daz3d.com*) have a large collection of inexpensive 3D figures, available from third-party vendors, that you can use instead of taking the time to create your own models when you are working on a project design plan.

STORYBOARD

EON Application Development Process

To provide a better example of a simple thumbnail storyboard, we have created a storyboard to reflect the development process for an EON application in more detail. You saw the general workflow for creating an EON application in Figure 2.1.1, but the figure below is a much more detailed plan that allows you to track exactly where you are in the process. From this storyboard, you could also begin to identify tasks and assign them to different members of your project team and/or develop a timeline for the completion of each stage. Note that the first item in this storyboard ("Simulation Goals") is the stage at which you would create the storyboard for the simulation you intend to build. You would use that storyboard to illustrate exactly what you intend the simulation to do, what you want it to show, how it should behave, etc.

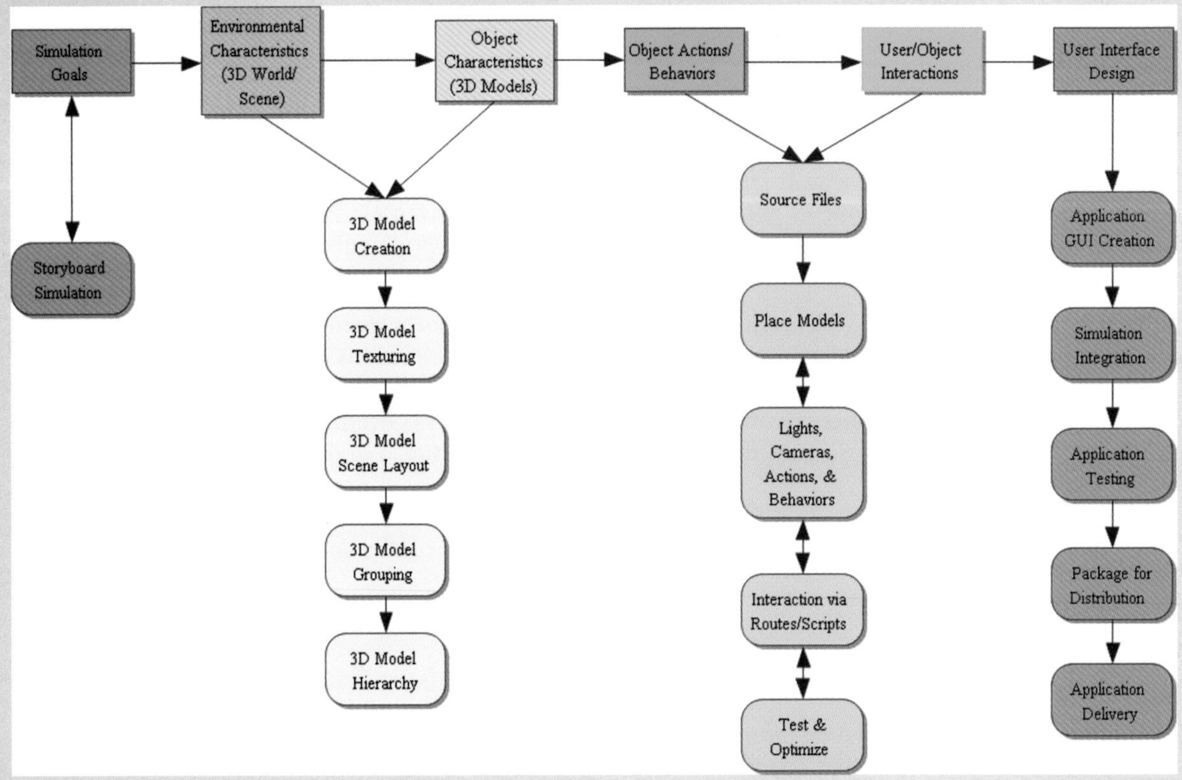

We will use this Storyboard feature throughout the rest of this text to identify your location in the development process. In this lesson, we have talked about the determination of the goals for the simulation as well as the creation of the storyboard. We will also discuss the selection of 3D models and, in a broad sense, discuss the steps in the creation of a simulation (the green and blue areas of the storyboard).

BEST PRACTICES

Developing an Intuitive User Interface

You may notice that one of the elements in the storyboard for the EON application development process is the User Interface Design. This is one area where graphic storyboarding can be immensely useful. If you invest the time in sketching the planned user interface, you can do some preliminary usability testing and get feedback from others about its functionality and possible improvements.

What makes a user interface "intuitive" to the user? Basically, it has to meet one of two conditions: It either needs to use terminology, icons, and/or structures that users are already familiar with so they immediately know what they need to do to operate the simulation. Alternatively, the design has to make it easy for users to learn what they need to operate the simulation, and this learning process has to be accomplished without the users being aware that they are being "trained" to use the system. The design has to help bridge the gap between what users already know and what they have to learn in an easy and natural way.

Entire texts are written on how to design good user interfaces—you will learn more about this topic in Module 4 Lesson 3—but keeping these basic concepts in mind should help you keep your users happy.

External Resources

We have mentioned importing objects, textures, sound, and video into EON several times. But we have not detailed exactly where those files come from or how they are obtained because the possible sources for these items are virtually limitless.

Each content element that comes from outside of EON is referred to as an ***external resource.*** These can be files you have created yourself (3D models, text, images, audio, or video), files obtained through free sources, or files that you have purchased. In this section, we will discuss a few ways of locating or creating the external resources that you need. You will want to explore these options as well as branch out and do your own research. Ultimately, you will develop your own set of preferred external resources and find ways of creating exactly what you need for your simulations.

Models

One way to add 3D objects to the EON application is by importing them from modeling programs. Some common 3D modeling programs are Maya, 3ds Max, Lightwave, Rhino, Softimage, and AutoCAD. There are certainly more 3D modeling programs available, but these are some of the current leaders in the field.

It is far beyond the scope of this text to provide instruction on how to use any of these modeling programs. You will have to explore these programs on your own (or perhaps with the assistance of a knowledgeable person who is already using one or more of them) to determine which program suits your needs. You might be able to download trial versions of the various software packages, or perhaps you can explore one or more products while taking a course in modeling or design.

web links

To explore some of the existing modeling programs, check out their websites.

Autodesk Maya: *www.autodesk.com/maya*

Autodesk 3ds Max: *www.autodesk.com/3dsmax*

Newtek Lightwave: *www.newtek.com/lightwave*

Rhino: *www.rhino3d.com*

Softimage: *www.softimage.com*

Although you would typically use one of these software applications to create your own 3D objects, some of the websites for these products may have download links for models, textures, and maps to support tutorials for their customers.

An alternate way for you to obtain 3D models is to purchase (or obtain free) pre-existing models. Again, an Internet search will reveal a myriad of sources for these models, but one good source is Turbo Squid (*www.turbosquid.com*). This site has less-detailed models available for free and professional-quality models available for purchase ranging from one dollar to much higher prices, depending on the level of detail. This site also has textures and maps available for purchase.

Materials and Textures

In the real world, objects are constructed of a variety of substances, commonly referred to as materials. Wood, metal, stone, and glass are a few examples of ordinary materials we encounter every day. The way light bounces off the surfaces of different types of materials can vary greatly. Smooth surface materials react differently to light than those that are bumpy or rough. They can also exhibit different levels of reflectivity, specularity, and transparency. Some materials have a uniform surface appearance, whereas others may be marked with a grain or a pattern.

tips+tricks

A good analogy for texture mapping is to think of it as a process similar to wrapping a box with gift wrap paper.

Bitmap images, referred to as textures, are used to add realistic surface characteristics to materials. ***Texture mapping*** allows you to add detail, surface texture, and color to a graphic or 3D model by adding one or more texture maps to a material and then applying that material to the surface area (a set of interconnected polygons) of the shape.

If you require a particular texture for a simulation object, you can scan or capture it with a digital camera to create a suitable photograph, edit it in a program (such as Adobe Photoshop), import the texture to EON or a 3D-modeling program, and then apply it to the object. Some textures are free or available for a fee from online sources.

Audio and Video Files

WAV and MIDI files from any source may be used with EON Studio. These files are edited in programs such as Creative Wave Studio, Microsoft Sound Recorder, or Audacity (open source). You can use these programs to edit, select, and mix sounds. The frequency, fade-in and fade-out, looping, length of play, and many other aspects also can be altered. When the sound or video file sounds correct, it can be imported.

Activity 2.1.1: Exploring an Online Model Source

1. If necessary, establish a connection to the Internet.
2. Open a web browser and key **www.turbosquid.com** into the address bar. Press **Enter.** You will see a screen similar to that shown in Figure 2.1.2.

FIGURE 2.1.2 Sample Turbo Squid window

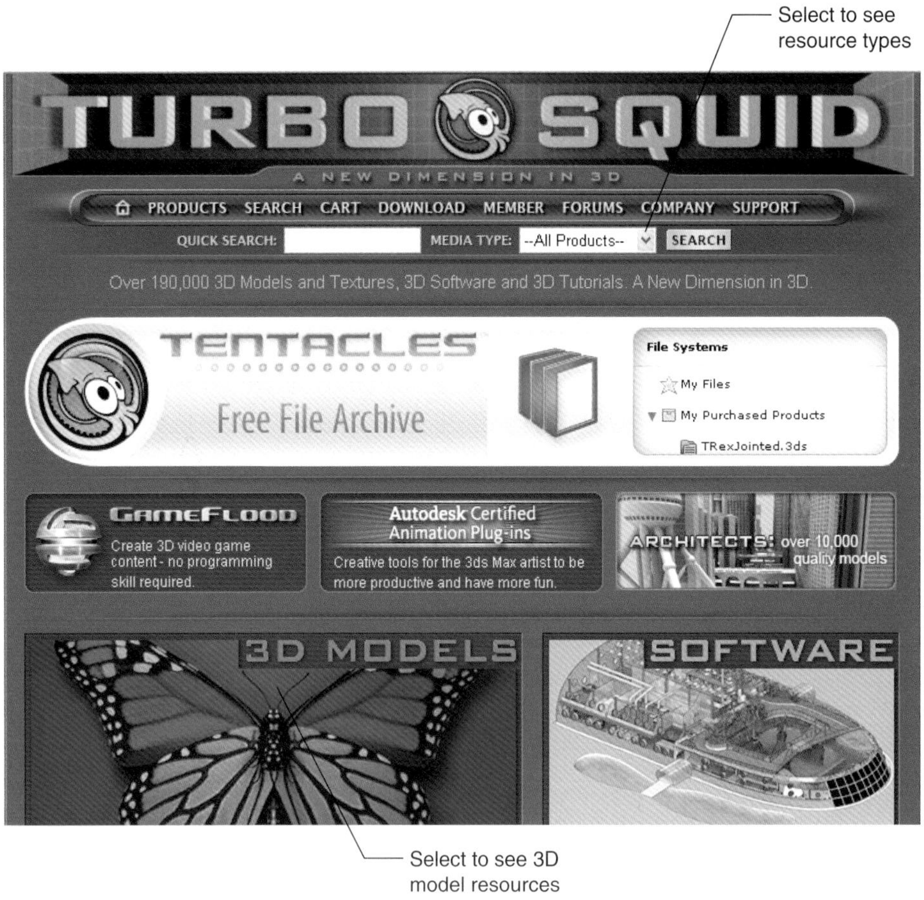

3. Select the down arrow next to **Media Type** to review the drop-down list of the different types of resources available from this site. Note that, in addition to 3D models, you can use the Quick Search tool to find materials, shapes, sounds, and texture maps available through this site.
4. Click the **3D Models** link on the home page. A page similar to the one shown in Figure 2.1.3 will appear. Note that while the Quick Search option is still available to find various media types, another navigation bar is displayed for the different media types, and you have the option to sort the 3D models by general categories.

FIGURE 2.1.3 Portion of the Turbo Squid 3D Models page

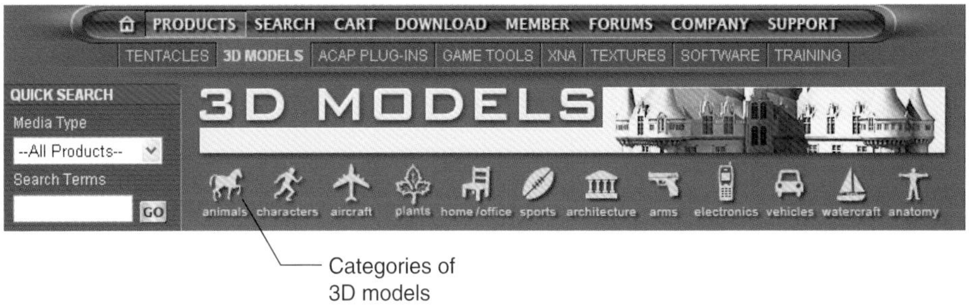

5. If necessary, scroll down until you see the link for free 3D models. It may say *Top Free 3D Models (see more…)*. Click this link. You will see a page with a wide variety of models, similar to Figure 2.1.4.

FIGURE 2.1.4 Free 3D models

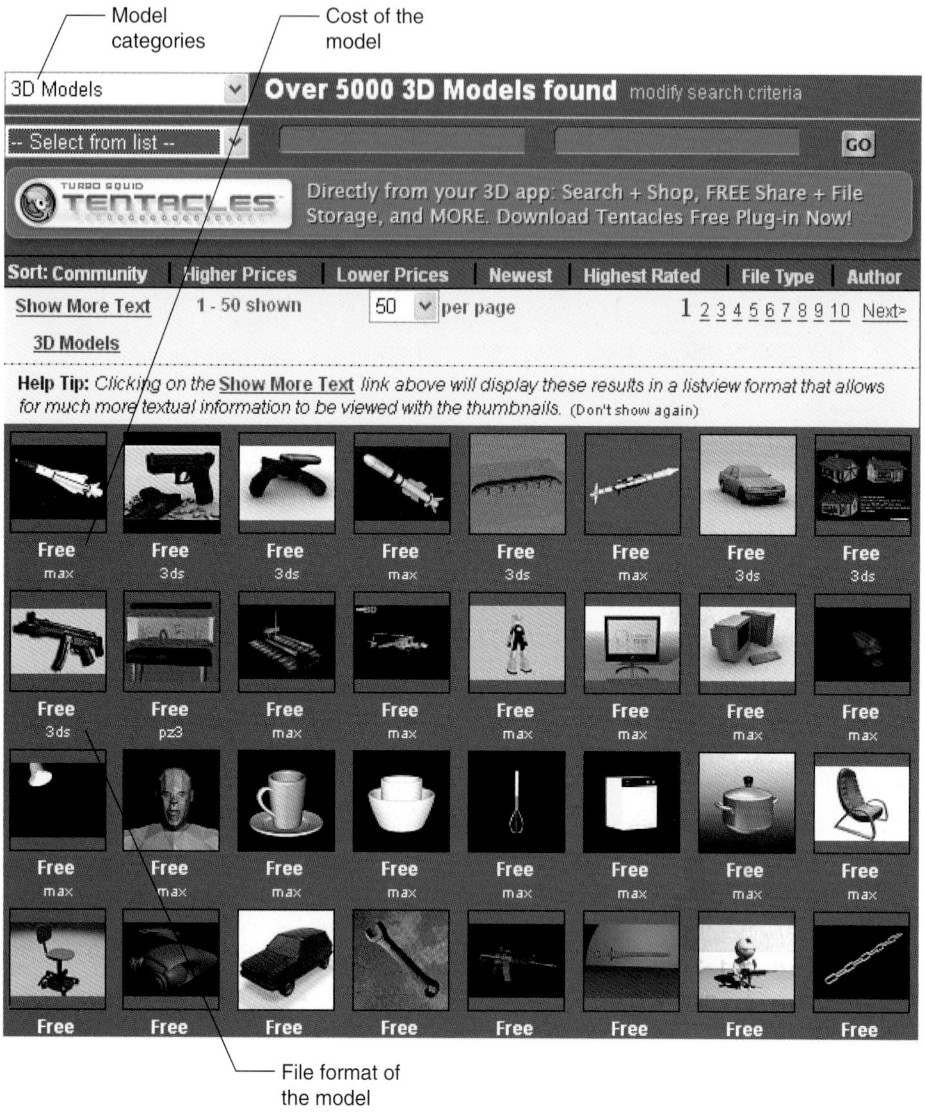

6. You could scroll through pages and pages of models, but note that it says *Over 5000 3D Models found* at the top of this page. It is far more efficient to use the sorting and searching tools available. Select the drop-down list of model categories at the top of the page.

7. Select **Animals** from the 3D models category list. In the second drop-down category, choose **Bird.** Click **Go.** The first page of models that fit these criteria will appear, as shown in Figure 2.1.5. (Note that your selection may vary greatly from what is shown here.)

FIGURE 2.1.5 Free models that meet search criteria

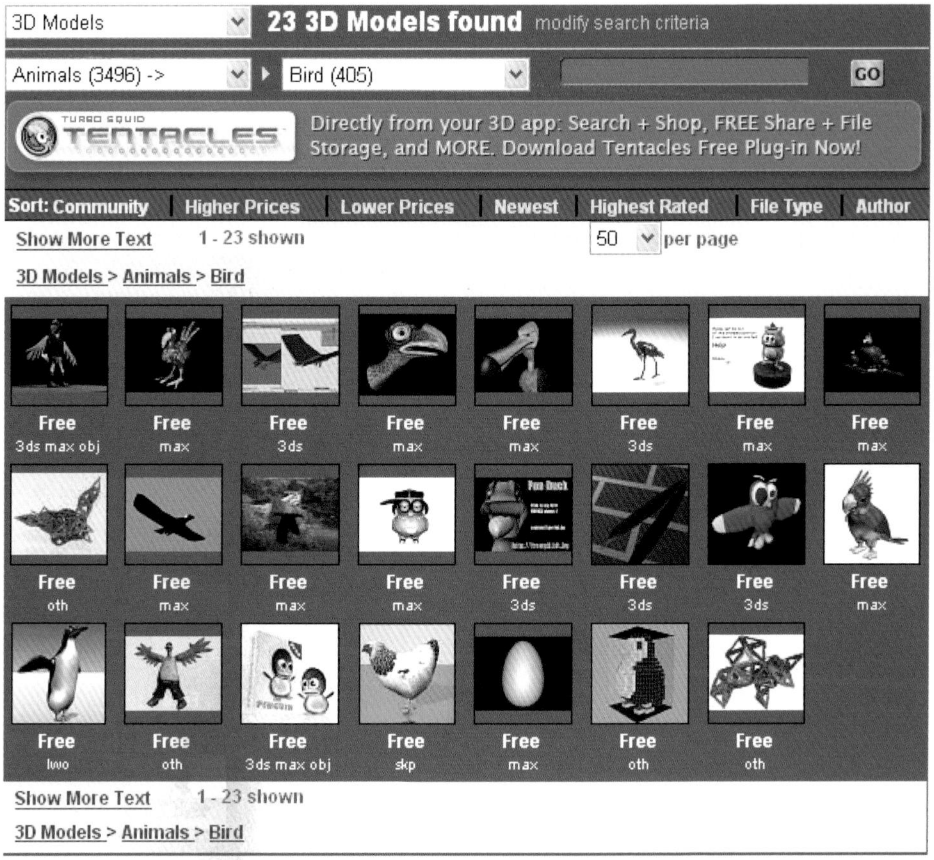

8. Click a model to view more details about it. Figure 2.1.6 is an example of one model. Note that information is provided about the model's creator; when the model was created; specifications about the model, including available file formats; and, if applicable, alternate views of the model. Below the figure (not shown in Figure 2.1.6) is a description of the model, provided by the creator. This often includes useful notes and other information that can help you select models for a simulation project.

FIGURE 2.1.6 Details about a selected model

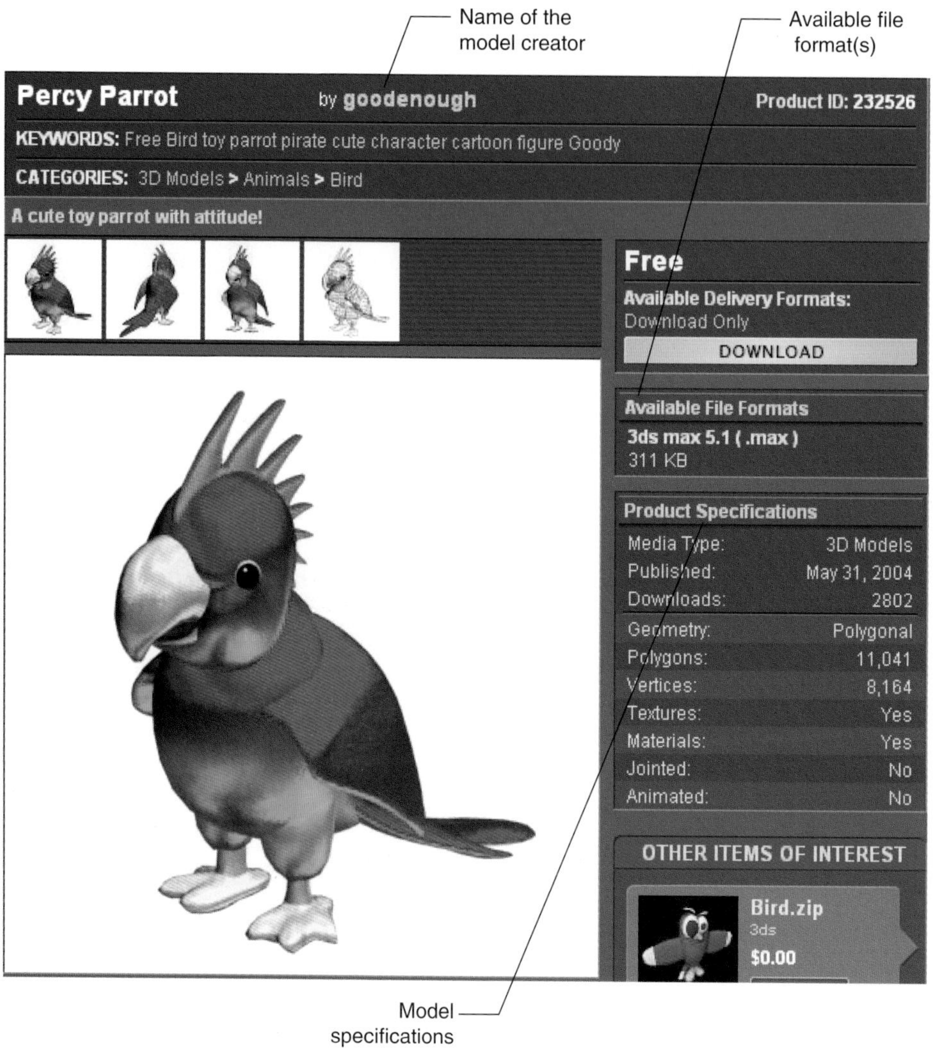

cross-reference

Note that the geometry type, the number of polygons, and the number of vertices are listed in the Product Specifications. You will learn about the significance of this information later in this module.

9. If allowed by your instructor or computer security settings, click the **Download** button. You will be asked to log in to Turbo Squid before you can download any files. Joining Turbo Squid is free, and you can decline to receive any e-mails or newsletters from the company. You will see a list of the products selected for download, similar to the one shown in Figure 2.1.7.

FIGURE 2.1.7 Products selected to download from Turbo Squid

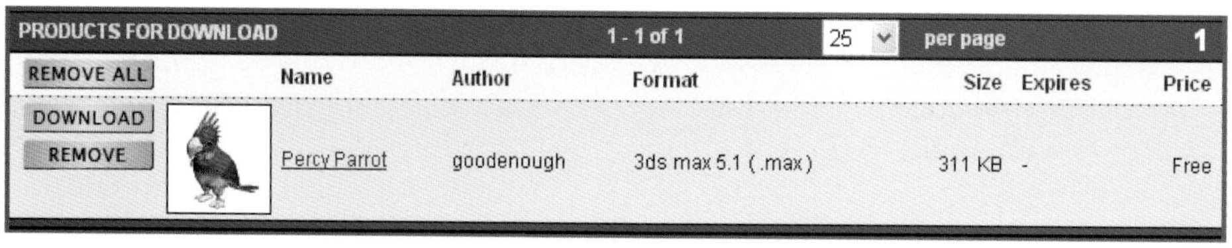

10. Click **Download.** Choose to save the file, and browse to select the location where you would like it saved. This should be the same location where you will save the simulations you create. Accept the name of the downloaded file or rename it to something descriptive for your needs and click **Save.**
11. After the download is complete, you can close Turbo Squid or spend more time exploring the available options and search functions.

Discussion

discuss

Turbo Squid, the 3D model resource that we explored in this Activity, is one of several such resources. How would you find other resources?

These online resources typically provide several ways to find just the right model. Other than previewing categories, what other methods could you use to find the best model?

Pros and Cons of External Resources

In EON, nodes such as Mesh2, Texture2, and MovieTexture use external resources. These nodes have a field named Embedded that indicates whether the resource is to be placed inside or outside the resulting distribution file. The Embedded flag has no effect on project files (.eoz or .eop) because all resources except dynamic prototypes are always embedded in the project files. However, when creating distribution files, the resources that are marked as external (Embedded = False) will be placed outside of the distribution file. These resources will be compiled like the embedded ones, but, as mentioned previously, they will be placed in a subfolder relative to the distribution file.

The main benefit of using external resources is to allow streaming downloads during simulation runtime. This reduces the file size and makes downloading much quicker.

Another benefit of external resources affects users who constantly update their objects but keep the same filename. For example, you have ten simulations that involve showing an avatar walking around. You want the same avatar in all of the ten simulations, and you want the ability to modify the avatar often. For example, you might want to update the geometry and textures of the avatar. You would make the changes to the model, and then, in EON Studio, you would make a new distribution file with external resources and copy those resources to a common folder for the ten .edz simulations that use it. This could be quicker than opening ten simulations in EON Studio, copying the new avatar into each file, and then saving them again.

Most simulation developers, however, think that the disadvantages of having external resources are greater than the advantages.

- It will be harder to move files to another location if you use external resources because they have to be contained in subfolders.
- Reusing a resource by inserting a Mesh2 node and browsing to insert the filename is time consuming. (Developers are more likely to copy objects [subtrees] between simulations.)
- When streaming, a progress bar displays a "Loading Resource" message and pauses the simulation while loading/initializing each new resource.
- You cannot determine the order in which objects are loaded or downloaded when streaming, whereas if you use dynamic load, you could determine when and therefore the sequence in which objects are downloaded.

tips+tricks

Note that loading is different from downloading. Loading pauses the simulation, whereas downloading does not. Downloading resources occurs in the background.

Resource Sharing

Resources such as geometries, textures, and prototypes can be shared between any number of simulations or prototypes. This means that you can build a repository of resources that can be reused at any time.

Streaming

To download resources asynchronously with a running simulation, you can add the resources to the simulation as they are downloaded. Currently, the nodes that support external resources are Mesh2, Texture2, MovieTexture, and the Dynamic prototype.

Streaming is a time-saving method that is used when it takes a long time to download a file from the Internet. If the file is small or if the speed of the user's connection is apt to be very fast, then it is not worth using external resources for streaming. If the resources are going to be external but placed on a local disk, then streaming could be slower than if the resources were inside the file.

Raptor

cross-reference

You will learn more about EON Raptor in Module 3 Lesson 2.

EON Raptor Web Studio is a plug-in for 3ds Max and Autodesk VIZ that allows real-time viewing of large models and the creation of interactive content for the Internet. Using EON Raptor, it is possible to create interactive real-time 3ds Max content with intuitive controls. Interactive behaviors also can be authored without additional programs outside 3ds Max. After animations have been created in 3ds Max, interactivity can easily be added and the animation can be published to the Internet using the wizard-driven web publisher provided in Raptor. The completed application can be published to a web page for viewing with a browser, or it can be exported as a standalone file for viewing with the free EON Viewer. It also can be exported to EON Studio for further editing.

tips+tricks

If the file will be edited in EON Studio, it should be saved as an .eoz project file.

With EON Raptor, you create the 3D model and animation in 3ds Max. EON Raptor allows real-time viewing of the 3D data at any time within 3ds Max. You can add interactivity to the model, and then use the Web Publisher Wizard to publish the model to the Internet or publish it to a CD-ROM. EON Raptor creates a highly compressed file format with support for user-customizable geometry and texture compressions. All 3ds Max content can be exported, including animations, lights, cameras, parent-child relationships, pivot points, and multimaterials.

Rendering

Originally, rendering was the term used for the process of an artist creating a scene. It began with hand-drawn sketches, drafting, and blueprints and then evolved into computer-perspective rendering, animation, and virtual reality. Today, the term has multiple meanings depending on whether you are working with real-time or offline computer graphics processing.

In computer graphics terms, ***rendering*** is the process of generating a two-dimensional (2D) snapshot image (or frame) of a 3D model. The 3D model is actually a comprehensive description that contains geometry, viewpoints, textures, lighting, and shading information. A single 2D-rendered image of a 3D model is often referred to as a digital image or, more precisely, as a raster graphics image (also known as a bitmap).

The term *rendering* also can refer to the offline process of converting an animated 3D model into a series of 2D image frames to produce a precompiled video file for subsequent viewing. Depending on the complexity of the 3D environment and associated scene animation, the offline rendering process can take several hours to complete.

Real-time rendering makes virtual reality possible through a 3D immersive experience. As opposed to offline rendering, real-time rendering is the immediate rendering and display of several frames per second, in rapid succession in real time, in response to the user's actions within the application. Although good real-time rendering still requires a lot of computer processing power, continual improvements in graphics cards and computers have dramatically improved real-time performance. In EON, you can adjust the frame rate (in the simulation tree's properties) to set the Maximum Frame Rate (in hertz), which allows you to use only the processing power needed to obtain the desired quality in your end product.

cross-reference

You will learn to modify the render settings and learn more about the benefits of adjusting these settings in Modules 4 and 5.

Establishing the Virtual World

It can take a lot of work to design high-performance 3D applications. Users have grown accustomed to large virtual worlds in which the smallest detail is accurate. For your EON application to be successful in this realm, you need to deal with many different types of operations including:

- Visibility determination—Determining which polygons are visible, given the current location of the camera. Objects outside the viewing area or obscured by other polygons should be clipped.
- Level of detail—Modeling distant objects with fewer details, and therefore fewer polygons, than close objects.
- Hidden Surface Removal—Drawing the polygons to ensure that the depth ordering of visible polygons is correct. Polygons associated with surfaces hidden behind other objects are eliminated from the final render list.
- ***Rasterization***—Converting 3D vector graphic shapes (based on the final list of visible polygons) into 2D raster images that can be drawn on a video display with minimal pixel redraw.

We will discuss each of these operations in more depth in the following sections and in even greater detail in later modules. But first, if you are new to creating 3D applications, you need to be familiar with a few basic concepts before delving into these topics.

The primary concept to keep in mind is that everything that will be rendered is based on the camera and the viewing plane. The ***camera*** has a specific position and orientation in the 3D world. The ***viewing plane*** represents the 3D area of the scene that is visible when viewed through the camera's lens.

A confined area of 3D space, known as a ***frustum***, typically refers to a rectangular pyramid shape that has been intersected by two planes: a near plane at the front boundary of the area and a far plane at the rear boundary of the area. In computer graphics, a frustum is built around the virtual camera's viewing plane and serves as a container for all visible objects within that view. The resulting confined area of 3D space is referred to as the ***field of view*** or the ***viewing frustum***. In EON, this field of view, or frustum, is called the ***viewport***. Figure 2.1.8 illustrates a 3D viewing frustum.

FIGURE 2.1.8 Viewing frustum (viewport)

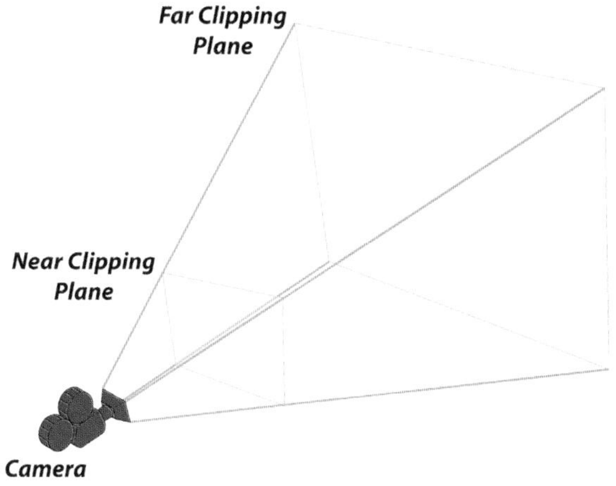

Objects closer to the camera than the near plane or beyond the far plane are not drawn. In some programs, the far plane is placed infinitely far away from the camera, so all objects within the frustum are drawn regardless of their distance from the camera. In EON, the FarClip is 100 meters away by default. To optimize the rendering speeds, it is best to increase the near clipping plane and reduce the far clipping plane to a reasonable distance. The relative position of the camera and the clipping planes are shown in the viewport diagram in Figure 2.1.8. You'll learn more about clipping planes later in this lesson.

Culling is the process of removing objects that lie completely outside the viewing frustum from the rendering process. Rendering these objects would be a waste of time because they are not directly visible. You usually increase the culling speed by reducing the bounding volumes of surrounding objects rather than by reducing the number of objects.

Visibility Determination

When you start creating larger virtual worlds, a significant portion of the polygons that make up the 2D snapshot images will probably never be visible from the camera position. Some fall completely outside the viewing area; others are completely obscured by other polygons. To use processor time efficiently, you need to have the data in the application organized to allow polygons to be ***culled*** (selectively removed) from what is being drawn. You cannot simply send everything to the hardware and expect it to draw fast enough to keep up. (The workload for the computer gets even larger if each polygon you draw also requires a texture to be loaded.)

Level of Detail

We have already touched on the fact that an object is actually comprised of polygons. Even a basic surface is made from a few vertices that make up a polygon. The number of vertices and surfaces in the scene directly determines the complexity of the model. Realistic lighting and shadows are essential for 3D models. Each of the vertices in a model requires a calculation to determine the effect of light at each point, which is then interpolated over the surface of the polygon to determine the precise pixel color for each point. Thus, more vertices and surfaces require more calculations to display the final 3D object—which can lead to decreased performance in real-time rendering.

Real-time rendering of simulation applications places demands on the computer processor and the graphic processor and consumes video memory and system random-access memory (RAM). If an extremely complex (hence, large) model is loaded, the processor will have to borrow virtual memory from the hard disk. If the polygon count and the number of textures are not well managed (i.e., maintained at the lowest numbers feasible while still providing the desired quality), the simulation's performance will suffer. A slow frame rate and memory overusage will cause the virtual reality to seem a lot less like "reality" because it will cease to operate in real time. You will see noticeable screen refreshes, and the movements will appear choppy.

All elements in the model collectively affect the performance of real-time rendering. As you begin to build simulations, keep the ***level of detail*** in mind. In computer graphics, accounting for level of detail involves decreasing the complexity of a 3D object representation as it moves away from the viewer or using other determining factors, such as the importance of a particular object or its position in the scene.

Consider several components when thinking about the simulation's level of detail, such as:

- The polygon face count of your model
- The use of textures and materials
- The clipping planes for your scene
- The boundaries for your scene

Model Polygon Face Count

The number of polygons in your model directly affects the level of detail in your simulation, as well as the time it takes to render your simulation. You must find the balance between these two, putting more detail (higher polygon face count) in elements that need it and reducing the detail where it is not necessary. Figure 2.1.9 is an example of a model in EON. This model (shown in Wireframe mode) illustrates how polygons (and vertices) make up a model. This particular model is made up of 3000 polygons.

FIGURE 2.1.9 Wireframe view of a model in EON

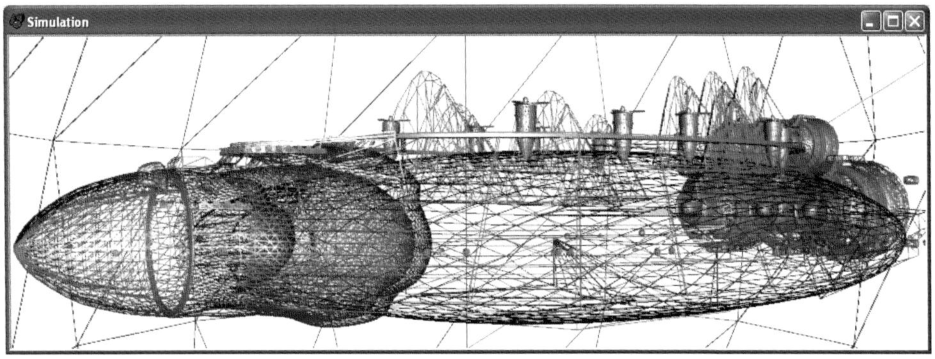

Figure 2.1.10 shows this same model as it might appear in a simulation with materials and textures applied to the polygon faces.

FIGURE 2.1.10 Model with textures applied to polygons

Using Materials and Textures

Although polygon count is significant to the overall size of an application, texture data, in general, tends to be far larger than the geometry data. Therefore, reducing material and texture data is one of the most effective ways to reduce the size of the entire simulation. The most obvious step is to remove any materials and textures that are not used in your simulation. Beyond that, controlling the resolution level of textures is a very good way to achieve smaller file sizes. You can select the appropriate resolution for a texture prior to bringing it into EON, based on the expected viewing size of the texture when used within the simulation and the relative importance of the texture to the overall appearance of the simulation.

cross-reference

These clipping planes are also referred to as *Z-clipping planes*. Clipping planes will be discussed in much greater detail in Module 6 Lesson 1.

Clipping Planes

From the viewpoint of the camera (the viewer), some objects are further away and some are closer. A ***clipping plane*** determines the contents of the rendered simulation based on the location of each object. There is a near clipping plane and a far clipping plane. As we discussed earlier, objects located between the camera and the near clipping plane are not rendered, and objects located beyond the far clipping plane are not rendered.

Bounding Planes

Bounding planes are a more general case of the clipping planes described previously. They differ from the standard near and far clipping planes in several ways:

- Bounding planes rotate, translate, and scale with the bounded objects. Clipping planes do not.
- Bounding planes are specified as part of a material definition and apply only to objects within that material.
- A bounding plane is specified by giving the coordinates of some point in the plane.
- By default, when an object is intersected by a clipping plane, the clipped portion of the object is not rendered at all. Thus, if an opaque object or surface is clipped, you will be able to see into the interior of the object. The default treatment of a bounding plane, however, is to slice the object and render a flat bounding surface. Therefore, if an opaque object or surface is cut by a bounding plane, you will see the flat surface instead of seeing inside the object.

tips+tricks

Ray tracing is an alternative method for generating an image in computer graphics. It works by tracing the path of light through the pixels of an image. Although this technique can produce incredible photorealism, it requires a much greater amount of computer processor time. Because of this, ray tracing is usually used only for applications in which the image can be rendered slowly and there is time for the rendering to occur before the image is needed. This is true for still images or for special effects that will be put into a video, for example. It does not work well for real-time applications (such as EON simulations) in which speed is critical.

Hidden Surface Removal

One of the first problems encountered in 3D computer graphics was the visibility problem—the issue of hiding elements that are not supposed to be seen from the current viewpoint. For example, an object that is behind a wall should be immediately removed from the rendering process. ***Hidden Surface Removal (HSR)***, also known as Hidden Surface Determination (HSD) or Visible Surface Determination (VSD), is the process used to determine which surfaces (or parts of surfaces) are *not* visible from a certain viewpoint. HSR is necessary to render images correctly in virtual reality.

Rasterization

Real-time applications need to respond immediately to user input. Therefore, 3D shapes need to be quickly rendered onto a 2D computer screen. The term *rasterization* refers to the process of converting 3D geometry (vector) data into a 2D bitmap image of individual pixels that can be mapped to the display screen.

A multistep rasterization algorithm takes a stream of vertices (the points that make up each polygon) and transforms them into 2D bitmaps for output to the display screen's frame buffer. Rasterization is fast compared with other rendering techniques, such as ray tracing, which is why rasterization is currently the most popular technique for producing real-time 3D computer graphics.

The Coordinate System

Another key component in understanding how to establish a virtual world is to have a firm grasp of the 3D coordinate system. Understanding the EON coordinate system is a fundamental skill required for developing interactive 3D simulations using the EON software.

The 3D ***Cartesian coordinate system*** used in EON products (and other 3D modeling and simulation packages) provides three physical dimensions of space: length, width, and height. Points within the 3D Cartesian coordinate system are referenced by their X (horizontal width), Y (horizontal depth/length), and Z (vertical height) values. The 3D XYZ coordinate system provides a perspective view with depth perception, whereas the traditional 2D XY coordinate system only provides a "flat" view.

If you are used to thinking of things in two dimensions—as you might see in an X-Y graph—then you may have to make a mental adjustment to the coordinates in a 3D system. (Refer to Figure 2.1.11 for a visual explanation.) You can think of X and Y as being located in the same positions on the graph as they would be on a flat sheet of paper that you are looking down on from above. You can then imagine the position of the Z coordinates as being located above the paper to add the third dimension.

FIGURE 2.1.11 2D XY coordinate system (left) and 3D XYZ coordinate system (right)

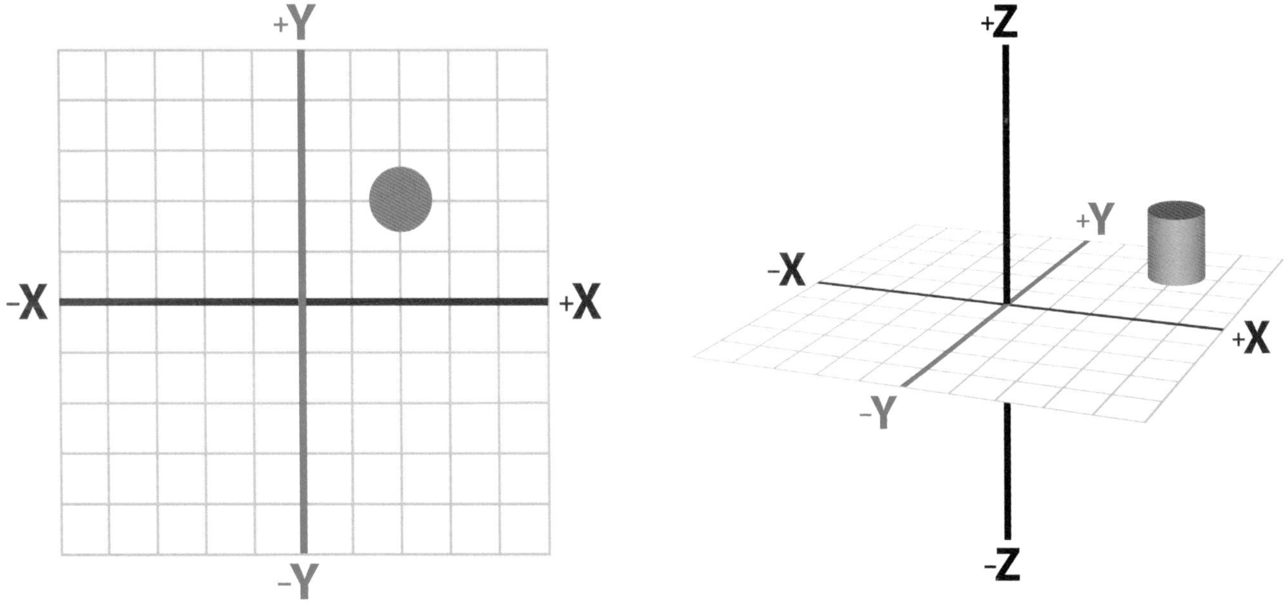

The XYZ coordinate system is used to position all objects in a 3D scene. The coordinate system provides a framework, or grid, for mapping 3D space and allows the precise placement of an object within that space by assigning it a set of location coordinates. Through the use of coordinates, you can align textures to objects, choreograph the movement of objects, and place text and backgrounds in specific areas of the scene.

When learning about coordinates, you should keep in mind that there are several different sets of coordinates at work within a 3D interactive simulation:

- Local coordinates
- World coordinates
- Camera coordinates

Local coordinates are the coordinates associated with an individual parent object and all of its associated child objects within the model's hierarchy. Each parent and child object is centered around a single internal point of origin known as a pivot point. Each parent and child object has its own local position and orientation coordinates that are automatically transformed into world coordinates by the EON software. For example, in EON, each Frame node is a local coordinate system in which the Frame's position and orientation controls (or transforms) the objects and child frames beneath it.

World coordinates are the standard, global coordinates that define an object's position and orientation within the virtual world environment. World coordinates serve as the common denominator for all object positions and orientations. World coordinates can be used to check for collisions between objects and to position objects in relationship to other objects during a real-time simulation.

To successfully render a scene, you need to select a point of observation and an orientation for the camera and define the view frustum by specifying values for the near and far clipping planes and the field of view. We always assume that the viewing rectangle is along the y axis (as shown in Figure 2.1.12), which simplifies the application design.

FIGURE 2.1.12 Camera coordinates in relationship to the EON coordinates

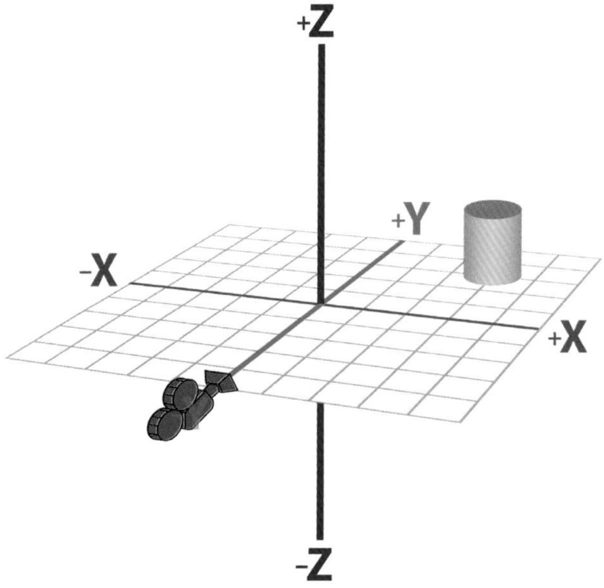

Given the camera's position and orientation—the ***camera coordinates***—you can calculate a transformation matrix that moves the point of observation to the origin and then rotates the coordinate system so that the camera is pointed down the y axis, with the z axis as the "up" direction for the camera.

Positioning 3D Objects in the Simulation Scene

An object's position in 3D space is determined by its translation and rotation values. Figure 2.1.13 illustrates the coordinate axis and the ways in which the position of an object can be adjusted. You will learn about translation and rotation in greater detail in the following sections.

FIGURE 2.1.13 EON coordinate system

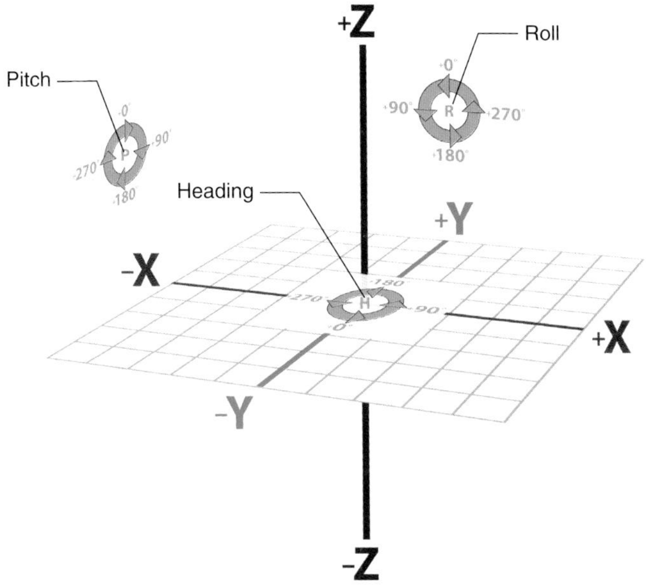

Translation

Translation refers to movement along an axis in a positive or negative direction and is expressed in (X, Y, Z) values. On the x axis (right to left), positive is to the right and negative is to the left. On the y axis, a positive coordinate is into the screen and a negative coordinate is out of the screen. On the z axis, positive is up and negative is down. Translation values of –1, 0, and 0, for example, would place an object one measurement unit to the left of the origin of coordinates.

Rotation

Rotation refers to rotation around an axis, as shown in Figure 2.1.13, and is expressed in H, P, and R values, representing heading, pitch, and roll. ***Heading*** (H) is the rotation around the z axis, ***pitch*** (P) is the rotation around the x axis, and ***roll*** (R) is the rotation around the y axis.

Rotation is specified in degrees within the 0° to 360° range (an entry of –90° is also valid—it is treated the same as 270°). If you were able to stand at the origin of the coordinate system and sight along the various translation axes, you would experience positive rotation in a counterclockwise direction. As an example, with heading, pitch, and roll values of 0°, 0°, and 340°, an object would be tilted slightly to the left, as shown in Figure 2.1.14.

FIGURE 2.1.14 Heading, pitch, and roll values of 0°, 0°, and 340°

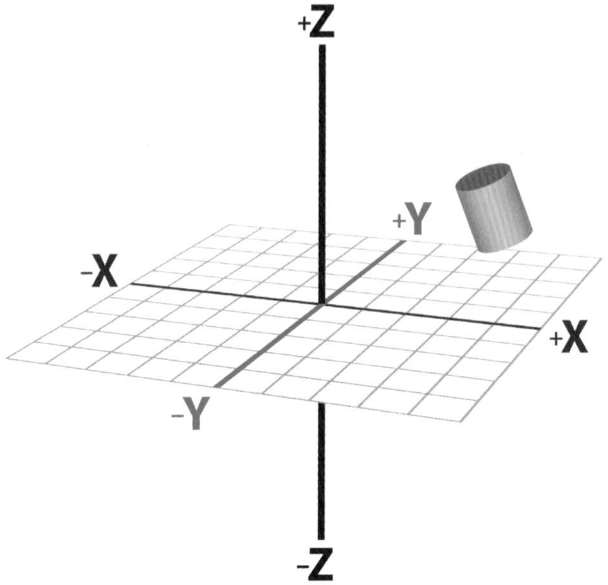

Another way of picturing rotation is to imagine that you are flying a virtual airplane along the coordinate system's y axis (into the screen in EON). In this case, you would see the following directional movement:

- Heading: A rotation around the z axis is positive when turning to the right and negative to the left.
- Pitch: Rotation around the x axis is positive when your plane dives and negative when it climbs.
- Roll: A rotation around the y axis is positive when you roll to the left and negative when you roll to the right. If you made a 180° roll, you would be flying upside down.

tips+tricks

In flight dynamics, the heading is referred to as the "yaw."

Using the KeyMove Node to Place Objects

KeyMove

The KeyMove node is an extremely useful node for simulation development. It provides an easy way to place an object correctly in the 3D world while the simulation is running. This allows you to visually position your model exactly where it should be and then determine the exact coordinates for that position—in translation (the Position property in EON) and rotation (the Orientation property in EON).

When you place the KeyMove node in the frame with a model, movement of the model is controlled by holding down a specific key on the keyboard and then using the arrow keys to move. The key you hold down directs the translational or rotational movement. The keys correspond to the model coordinates: X, Y, Z, H, P, or R. Use the up arrow key for higher values and the down arrow key for lower values.

tips+tricks

The KeyMove node provides a keyboard motion model and affects its parent node. The parent must support translation and rotation.

After you have the object positioned in the correct location, you can save the position coordinates as the object's starting values. The next time you run the simulation, the object will begin at those exact coordinates. If your intent is to move an entire object (with all of its child objects), place the KeyMove node under the parent frame within the scene hierarchy—not under a child object. The child object's coordinates are the local coordinates (relative to its parent), and the top-level parent frame's coordinates are the effective world coordinates for the entire object hierarchy. On the other hand, you can use the KeyMove node under a child object if your intent is to create movement of a subcomponent, such as a car door.

cross-reference

KeyMove is just one of several options for moving objects within a simulation. You will learn more about all of the "mover" options in Module 3 Lesson 2.

KeyMove Node Properties

The KeyMove node has properties that enable you to control the movement of the model more accurately within the simulation. The node's properties (accessible from the KeyMove Properties dialog box shown in Figure 2.1.15 or from the Property Bar) are Velocity and Angular Velocity.

FIGURE 2.1.15 KeyMove Properties dialog box

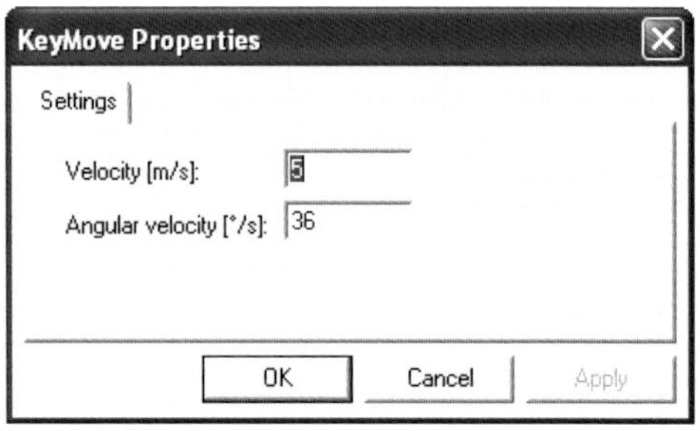

Velocity (measured in meters per second) determines the rate of change for the X, Y, and Z coordinates, and angular velocity (measured in degrees per second) determines the rate of change for H, P, and R coordinates.

cross-reference

Another method of movement using the camera positioning keys is explained in Module 6 Lesson 1.

Activity 2.1.2: Coordinate System Demonstration

1. Open EON to start a new simulation. If EON is already open, select **New** from the File menu.
2. Select the **Nodes** tab if necessary. Place a **Frame** node under Scene in the simulation tree and name it **CoordinateIllustration.**
3. Select the **Prototypes** tab and place the **3DPointer** prototype under CoordinateIllustration.
4. Select the **Nodes** tab and place a **Frame** node under CoordinateIllustration. Name it **Cube.**
5. Select the **Prototypes** tab and place a **Cube** prototype under the Cube frame.
6. Select the **Nodes** tab and place a **Frame** node under the Cube frame. Name the new Frame node **Cone.**
7. Select the **Prototypes** tab and place a **Cone** prototype under the Cone frame.
8. Select the **Nodes** tab and place a **Frame** node under the Cone. Name the new Frame node **Teapot.**
9. Select the **Prototypes** tab and place a **Teapot** prototype under the Teapot frame.
10. Place a **3DPointer** prototype under each of the frames: Cube, Cone, and Teapot.

11. Select the **Nodes** tab and add a **KeyMove** node to each of the Frames: Cube, Cone, and Teapot. Name the nodes **KeyMove_Cube**, **KeyMove_Cone**, and **KeyMove_ Teapot.** Your simulation tree should appear similar to the one shown in Figure 2.1.16.

FIGURE 2.1.16 Completed simulation tree

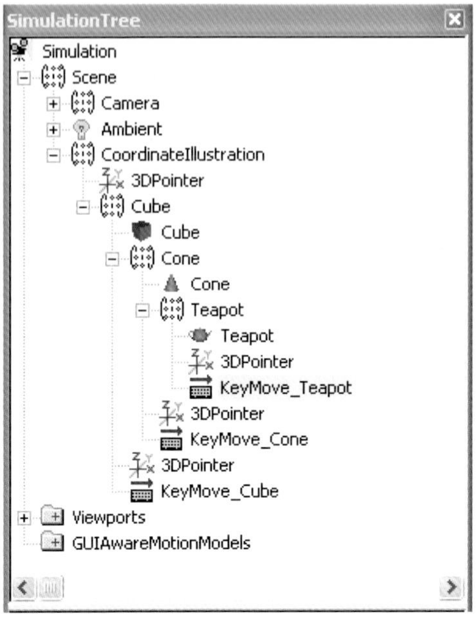

12. Run the simulation. Only the cube appears on the screen. The cone and the teapot are currently positioned behind the cube.
13. Hold down the **X** key and press the up arrow key a few times. Each time you press the arrow key, the position of the three objects shifts along the x axis. When you can see all three objects separately, stop pressing the up arrow key and release the X key. Your screen should appear similar to Figure 2.1.17.

FIGURE 2.1.17 Coordinates changed with KeyMove

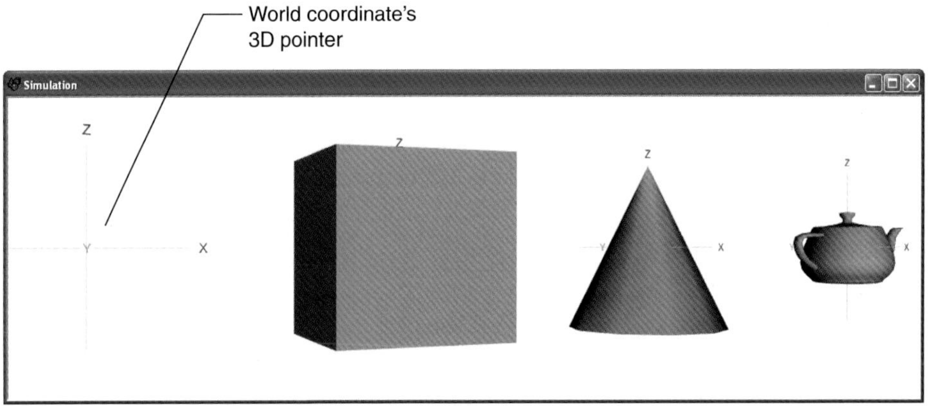

troubleshooting

When you spread the objects out along the x axis, you may find that some of the shapes are no longer visible. Enlarging the window will make the objects visible within the screen, but you might not be able to see all of the shapes. To see the elements that have shifted out of the view, use the mouse to scroll to the right or left until all shapes are visible.

14. If necessary, move the simulation window out of the way so that you can see the Property Bar and the simulation tree.
15. Select the **CoordinateIllustration** frame in the simulation tree. Note that the Position coordinates (shown in the Property Bar) are still 0 0 0. Note also that the WorldPosition coordinates have remained 0 0 0 as well. You did not change the position of the scene but simply the positions of the elements contained within the scene.

16. Select the **Cube** frame in the simulation tree. Note that the Position X coordinate has changed and that the WorldPosition X coordinate has changed to the same value. You have changed the position of the cube within the scene.
17. Select the **Cone** frame in the simulation tree. Note that the Position X coordinate has changed to the same value as the cube, but when you look at the X coordinate for the WorldPosition, it has changed to approximately twice the value of the local X coordinate.
18. Select the **Teapot** frame in the simulation tree. Note that the Position X coordinate has changed to the same value as the Cube frame and the Cone frame, but the WorldPosition X coordinate is approximately three times the value of the Cube frame position.
19. Continue to experiment with movement by using the KeyMove (using X, Y, Z, H, P, or R with the arrow keys) to adjust the position of the objects in the scene in relation to each other and in relation to the world coordinates. Try adjusting translational coordinates as well as rotational coordinates.
20. As you experiment with movement, be sure to note the differences in the local Position values versus the WorldPosition values of each object.
21. When you have the objects positioned exactly how you would like them, double-click the **Cube** frame in the simulation tree (or select the Properties button next to the Cube frame in the Property Bar). The Frame Properties dialog box appears, as shown in Figure 2.1.18. (The exact values within this dialog box will vary depending on where you have moved your objects.)

tips+tricks

If you make an adjustment that you do not like and have difficulty returning the objects to their previous position, you can close the simulation. Then run the simulation again, and the objects will return to 0 0 0 in the local Position and WorldPosition values.

FIGURE 2.1.18 Frame Properties dialog box

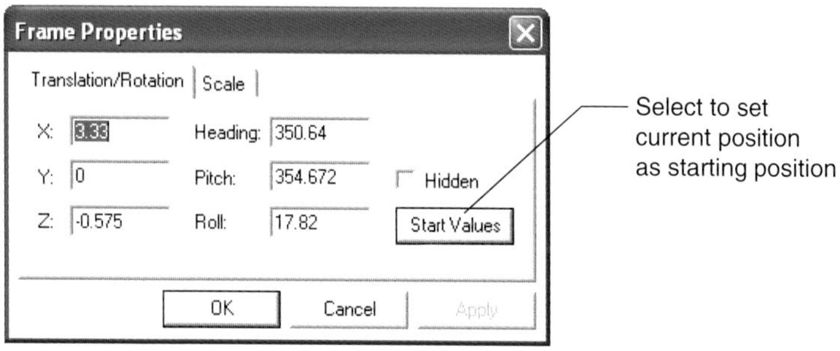

22. Select **Start Values** and then click **OK** to close the dialog box.
23. Repeat steps 21 and 22 to save the current position as the start values for the Cone frame and the Teapot frame.
24. Close the simulation window, and then start the simulation again. The objects will return to the positions where they were when you selected Start Values. Close the simulation window again.
25. Remove the KeyMove nodes and the 3DPointer prototypes from the simulation tree. After you have positioned the objects in your simulation, you no longer need the KeyMove nodes and 3DPointer prototypes in the simulation tree.
26. Save the simulation as **CoordinateExperiment.**
27. Run the simulation again. Note that the objects are now correctly positioned.
28. Try to use the X, Y, Z, H, P, or R keys with the arrow keys to move the objects. Because you removed the KeyMove nodes and the 3DPointer protoypes, none of the objects should be movable.
29. Close the simulation window. Close EON.

Discussion

discuss

How does this experiment help you to understand world coordinates (WorldPosition) versus local coordinates (Position)?

Does the 3DPointer make positioning objects easier?

Summary

In this lesson you:

- Developed knowledge and an understanding of the typical application development workflow.
- Learned the basics of using a storyboard for project planning.
- Became familiar with a variety of external resources for obtaining elements used in your EON application.
- Defined rendering.
- Considered the elements involved in establishing a virtual world.
- Began to explore "level of detail" in the context of an EON application.
- Developed an understanding of coordinate systems within EON Studio and 3D projects in general.
- Developed the ability to move objects within the coordinate systems.

LESSON 2.2

Organizing, Running, and Saving an EON Application

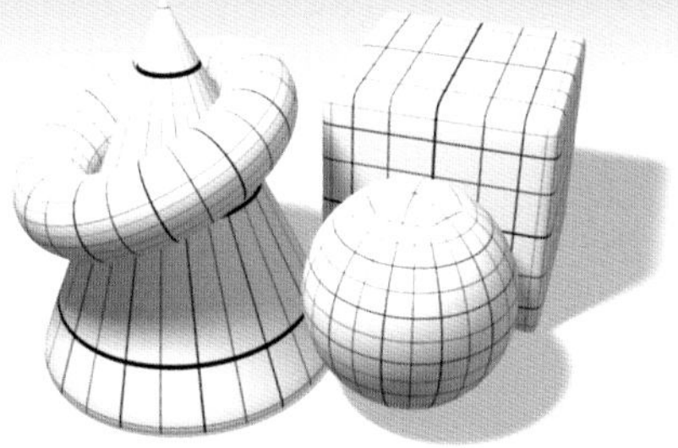

Objectives

In this lesson you will:

- Develop knowledge and an understanding of the organizational structure of the software and how to develop and manipulate objects, nodes, simulation commands, and scene parameters.
- Gain an understanding of node inEvents and outEvents and learn to use the Routes window to establish avenues for events coming into an EON simulation and going out of an EON simulation.
- Identify the options for saving an EON file for future development or for distribution.
- Differentiate between viewing an EON simulation in Normal Window mode or Full-size Window mode.
- Configure the render settings for an OpenGL driver and consider the tradeoffs in processor speed and quality of the rendering.

Key Terms

antialiasing
child node
EON Viewer
external field
external route
Full-size Window mode
graphical user interface (GUI)
logical hierarchy
Normal Window mode
OpenGL
parent node
positional hierarchy
SendEvent method
stereo

Simulation Tree and Node Hierarchy Relationships

In previous lessons, we completed activities in which we placed nodes into the simulation tree. We also touched briefly on using Frame nodes to group nodes and prototypes that we want to treat collectively—in other words, a process that makes it simpler to perform an operation (such as translation, rotation, or scaling) on all the nodes under a particular Frame node. We will explore the node hierarchy more completely so you understand the importance of the relationships between nodes in creating a successful simulation. Additionally, we will explore the situations in which you simply need to organize nodes and prototypes for the sake of organization—not to perform collective operations. For those situations, you can use the Group node. The Group node's sole purpose is to allow the EON developer to arrange nodes in the simulation tree; therefore, the Group node does not have any associated properties or fields.

A node that normally groups other nodes is called a ***parent node***. In EON, the most commonly used parent nodes are the Frame node and the Group node. Nodes that are placed under the parent nodes are called the ***child nodes***, or children. This parent-child relationship is a core principle in understanding the structure of the simulation tree and for developing a high-quality, well-documented, and easy-to-maintain application.

BEST PRACTICES

High-Quality Programming

No matter what programming language or software development tool you are using, you will find that certain fundamental principles are generally agreed on as necessary for a high-quality end product. Keeping these basic elements in mind as you develop your simulation in EON will reduce the costs of your application in terms of time (and money) required for debugging, developing the application further, and supporting the application's users. Experts have written entire books about the best ways to achieve quality programming, but the following elements are generally accepted as best practices by every programmer:

- **Portability:** Your application should work in various software and hardware environments. Although there may be basic requirements for operating the application, it shouldn't be linked to a setup that is too specific.
- **Reliability:** Simply put, the program needs to work correctly. This implies that you not only ensure correct coding and development, but that you also test the program completely and prevent typical errors.
- **Efficiency:** You must keep the use of system resources to a minimum. This includes the use of the computer processor, memory, devices, networks, and, to some extent, even the user.
- **Robustness:** This primarily refers to the interaction with the user. Your program should anticipate all expected input and be able to deal with unexpected input and situations.
- **Readability:** In a high-quality program, you must clearly define the purpose of the main segment (in the case of EON, the parent nodes) and of each subroutine (the child nodes) by using self-explanatory names and logical placement.

Efficiency and readability are two important benefits that result from a simulation tree that has a self-documenting, logical structure.

Although "logical design" may be difficult to grasp at first, you can ask yourself two simple questions as you lay out the plan for your simulation that will aid in developing a logical simulation tree structure. The questions are:

- *Which elements will depend on other elements?* For example, a hand is attached to an arm. It can rotate and move from a pivot point on the arm, but it does not move independently to an entirely different position in a room. In this analogy, the hand would be a child to the arm and would therefore be placed under it in the simulation tree.

- *Which elements are resources that might be used repeatedly?* For example, if you are creating a room with wooden tables and chairs in it, the wood-grain texture is a resource that might be used on multiple surfaces. Grouping all of your resources in one place and then linking objects to that location for the texture is the most efficient way to control the use (and reuse) of that resource.

You will learn many other tips and tricks as you go, but if you keep these two essential questions in mind, you will find that it is easier to tackle more complex applications.

Figure 2.2.1 is an example of a complex simulation with an excellent structure that makes it possible for someone (other than the original developer) to figure out—or at least make an educated guess—what the various components are and what purpose they serve within the application.

FIGURE 2.2.1 Hierarchical simulation tree structure

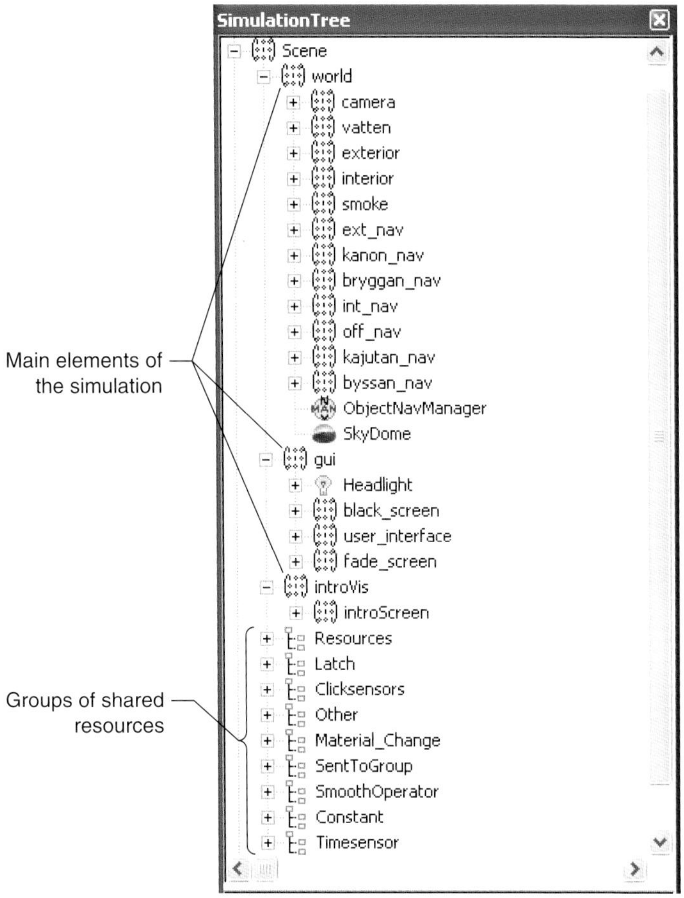

Do you notice anything unusual about the frame and group names in Figure 2.2.1? If you look closely, you will see that some of the names are not in English. If you are working collaboratively with people around the world or if the simulation could be used anywhere in the world, how important is it to lay out your simulation tree in a logical order?

cross-reference

As objects are imported into EON, additional hierarchy structures are appended to the simulation tree from the source model resource database via the use of an application-specific plug-in converter. All geometry is converted to polygon meshes, and all textures are converted to an EON-compatible format. You will see them as a hierarchy of Frame nodes and Mesh nodes under the Frame node from which you started the import procedure. You will learn more about importing in Module 3 Lesson 2.

Through the structural use of both Frame and Group nodes, you can see that the Scene frame contains the overall environment (world) as well as a ***graphical user interface (GUI)*** and an introductory screen (introVis). In Figure 2.2.1, note that many shared resource groups are managed separately, such as Latch, Material_Change, and Constant. If you wanted to make a change to something that appears when the simulation begins, for example, you would know exactly where to begin looking. When expanding any of these frames or groups, you should expect to see either basic node components that perform application tasks or additional levels of frames or groups that are used to organize the simulation tree further.

Using the Frame Node

Frames are used to group one or more nodes logically to maintain a suitable simulation structure. As you learned in Module 1 Lesson 3, the Frame node is a Base node that serves as a container (parent) for the nodes located below it. The Frame node enables all child nodes to be manipulated as a single unit. The Frame node properties that affect the translation and rotation of the frame are shown in Figure 2.2.2.

FIGURE 2.2.2 Translation/Rotation tab in the Frame Properties dialog box

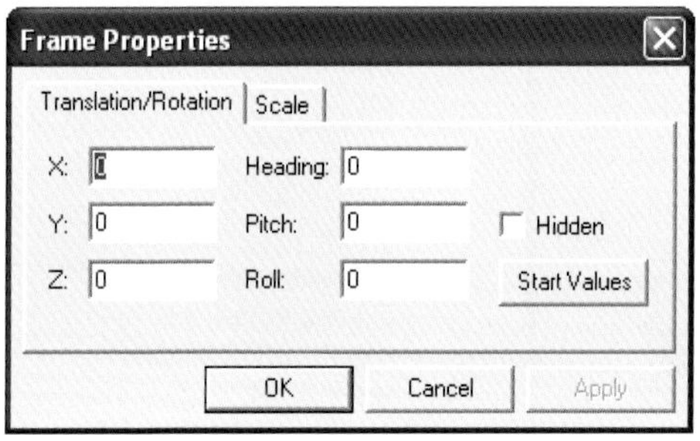

tips+tricks

Note that, in the case of the Scene frame, all of a simulation's Shape nodes are beneath the Scene node. So, selecting the Hidden option in the Frame Properties dialog box for the Scene will hide all objects in the simulation. Also note that simulation functionality can be disrupted when a hidden frame has child nodes that participate in processing events with other nodes outside of that frame (via inEvents or outEvents, which will be discussed later in this lesson).

These properties affect the child nodes contained within the frame, as shown in Table 2.2.1.

TABLE 2.2.1 Translation and Rotation Properties for Frame Nodes

Property Category	Description
Translation	Changes the X, Y, and Z values. Changing these values will change the position of all children of this node.
Rotation	Changes the Heading, Pitch, and Roll values for all children of this node.
Hidden check box	Selecting this option will hide all Shape nodes under this node. This is useful, for example, when an uncluttered scene is needed to orient and position objects.
Start Values button	Saves the current Translation, Rotation, Scale, and Hidden values as the values that the Frame node should now use at startup.

If you select the Scale tab in the Frame Properties dialog box, you will see the options shown in Figure 2.2.3.

FIGURE 2.2.3 Scale tab in the Frame Properties dialog box

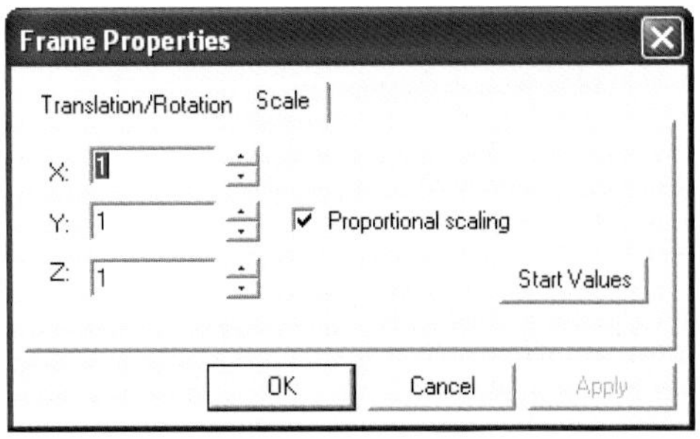

The Scale tab is used to set the X, Y, and Z scaling factors. The values set here adjust the scaling for all children in the frame by the given factor. The *Proportional scaling* option maintains the aspect ratio by changing all scale factors when one is modified. The Start Values button applies and saves the current Frame values (the same way as the Start Values button on the Translation/Rotation tab does).

If you look at the Property Bar for the Frame node (see Figure 2.2.4), you will notice that there are several additional fields available that are not accessible from the Frame Properties dialog box (besides the default node fields common to all EON nodes). These fields are explained in Table 2.2.2.

FIGURE 2.2.4 Frame node Property Bar

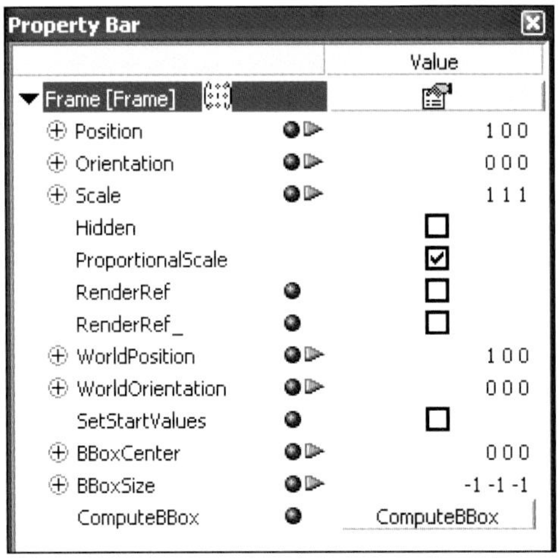

TABLE 2.2.2 World Position and Orientation Properties for Frame Nodes

Field Name	Description
RenderRef	Retained for backward-compatibility reasons. Do not use.
RenderRef_	Retained for backward-compatibility reasons. Do not use.
WorldPosition	Position of the Frame node in world coordinates (position of this Frame node relative to the Scene node).
WorldOrientation	Orientation of the Frame node in world coordinates (orientation of this Frame node relative to Scene node).

cross-reference

If you need to review any of the Frame properties or their impact on positioning objects within the scene, see the section titled "The Coordinate System" in Module 2 Lesson 1.

BEST PRACTICES

Using Multiple Displays to Develop in EON

A professional EON developer would normally use two displays simultaneously—one for running the simulation and the other for the EON workspace–integrated development environment. This allows the developer to access the Simulation Tree window and Property Bar easily without disrupting the running simulation. Otherwise, with only one display, they must reduce or minimize the simulation window to access the simulation tree and the Property Bar.

The figure below shows an EON developer's workstation.

A typical EON developer's workstation

Using the Group Node for Organization

You can use the Group node to organize all of the resources within your simulation tree—for example, you can place all textures in a group, all meshes in a group, and all materials in yet another group. Your simulation tree may contain the following basic structure:

```
Resources (a Group node)
   Materials (a Group node)
      Material A (a Material2 or MultiMaterial node)
      Material B (a Material2 or MultiMaterial node)
      ...
   Textures (a TextureResourceGroup node)
      Texture A (a Texture2 or MovieTexture node)
      Texture B (a Texture2 or MovieTexture node)
      ...
   Meshes (a MeshResourceGroup node)
      Mesh A (a Mesh2 node)
      Mesh B (a Mesh2 node)
      ...
```

As you can see, you can use a Group node to place all like resources in a scene together. In this example, you can see three resource groups beneath the Resources Group node: Materials, Textures, and Meshes. The Materials group is headed by an ordinary Group node, but the other two resource groups use special nodes: TextureResourceGroup and MeshResourceGroup. These special nodes are used because these groups require additional custom fields. The TextureResourceGroup and MeshResourceGroup nodes have specialized properties and fields just for textures and meshes, which can be edited, whereas a regular Group node does not include any editable properties.

In most cases, when you are importing geometry into an EON simulation, these groups are automatically created. But you need to pay attention to the structure of your simulation tree and to manage that structure so you can find resources when you are looking for them—and so others can work with and maintain your files.

Perhaps the best way to understand the concept of a good structure is to look at a well-organized simulation. In the following activity, you will open and examine the well-ordered application that we referred to at the beginning of this lesson.

cross-reference

You will learn more about the resource database and the TextureResourceGroup and MeshResourceGroup in Module 4 Lesson 2.

tips+tricks

Essentially, there are two ways to organize the simulation tree in EON: you can use a positional hierarchy or a logical hierarchy. In a ***positional hierarchy,*** elements are arranged in close proximity to the target element that they work with in the simulation. For example, a lamp may be turned on and off using a ClickSensor and a Latch. So the ClickSensor and the Latch would be placed in the same frame as the lamp. In a ***logical hierarchy,*** objects are placed according to their type or category. So, for example, a Latch would be grouped with other Latches in a resource group. Although a positional hierarchy may be preferred by some developers, the logical hierarchy is probably easier to debug and maintain over the long run.

Activity 2.2.1: Exploring the Monitor

1. Open EON. Open **Monitor.eoz** in the **Monitor** folder from the data files for Module 2, Lesson 2.
2. Expand the **Scene** frame. Notice that it contains three primary Frame nodes (*world, gui,* and *introVis*) and nine Group nodes.
3. Run the simulation and explore the various links, buttons, drop-down lists, and pull-up images.
4. After you have thoroughly explored the simulation, close the simulation window.
5. Expand the **gui** frame. Locate the button that provides the link to information about John Ericsson.
6. You may have noticed that the simulation transitioned smoothly from one screen to the next. Locate the nodes that make these smooth transitions possible.
7. You can see that many models were used to create this simulation. Locate the materials, textures, and meshes that were created when these models were imported.
8. Explore the frames, subframes, groups, and subgroups until you have a good sense of how this simulation was structured. Run the simulation again if you want to see how different items were used within the simulation.
9. Close the simulation window. Close EON without saving the simulation.

Discussion

discuss

What is the advantage of grouping items, such as ClickSensors and Latches like those that are grouped in the Monitor simulation? What naming conventions are employed in the names of the nodes and prototypes to make component identification easier?

Accessing and Changing Node Properties

Every node has a set of fields, referred to as properties, that are associated with it. As you learned in Module 1 Lesson 3, there are many different field types, and the way you edit the values associated with those fields varies by type. And as you have probably observed, there are multiple ways to access a node's properties.

- Right-click a node in the simulation tree. Choose Properties from the pop-up menu.
- Double-click a node in the simulation tree.
- With a node selected in the simulation tree, choose Properties from the Edit menu.
- With a node selected in the simulation tree, press the Enter/Return button on the keyboard.
- With a node selected in the simulation tree, select the Properties button at the top of the Value column in the Property Bar.

No matter which way you choose, you will see the same dialog box for a given node. The Properties dialog box usually shows all of the editable fields and values for the selected node. Note that each Properties dialog box is unique to the node selected.

The changes made within the Properties dialog box are reflected in the Property Bar. Likewise, changes in the values of the Property Bar will be shown in the Properties dialog box as well.

cross-reference

To review editing field values or Property Bar settings, go to Module 1 Lesson 3.

STORYBOARD

Node Properties and Routing in the Simulation Creation Process

Where does changing the node properties fit into the entire process of creating a simulation? If you recall the storyboard that we created in Module 2 Lesson 1, you can see where this task is located in the process:

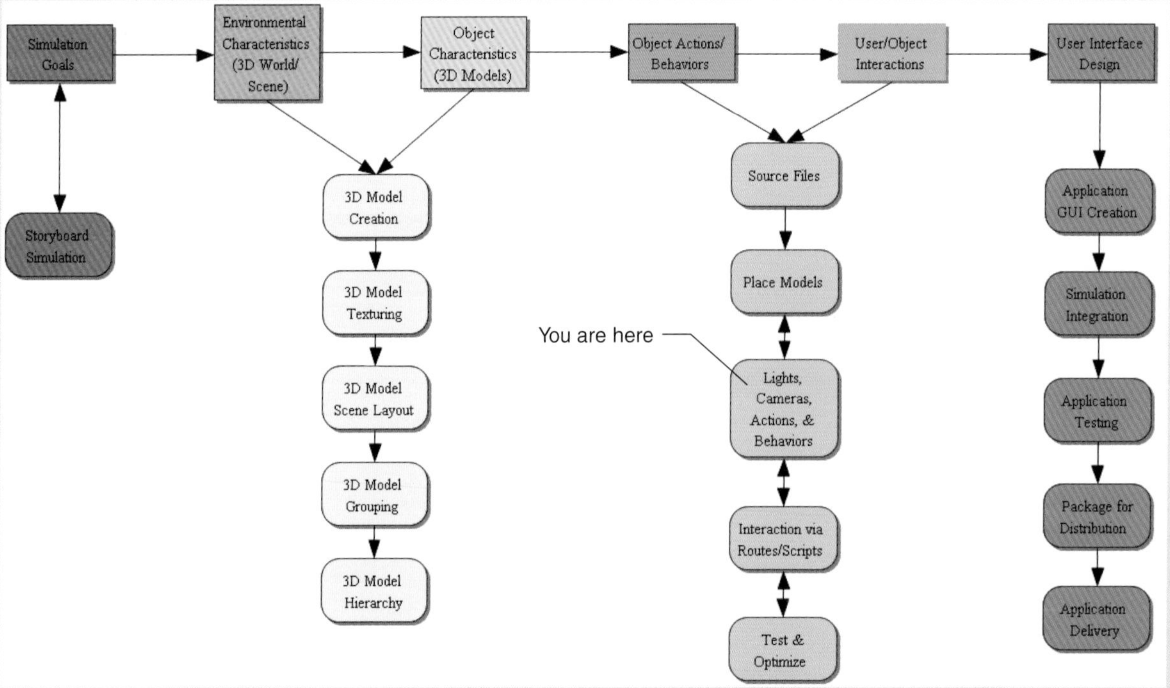

Changing the properties of the objects and nodes within the simulation falls into the "Lights, Cameras, Actions, & Behaviors" step when you are constructing your simulation.

Later in this lesson, we will also begin to learn about the next step, "Interaction via Routes/Scripts," as we discuss connecting nodes using the Routes window.

Connecting Nodes Using the Routes Window

After components are placed in the simulation tree, either manually or by importing 3D models, the resulting nodes and prototypes (which we will collectively refer to as simply "nodes" in this section) are separate entities that are independent of one another. To begin adding functionality and to bring order to the universe you are creating, you need to establish connections and associations between the nodes in your simulation tree. In EON, these connections are established with routes. Routes between nodes are made in the Routes window.

As you may recall from Module 1 Lesson 3, an event occurs when information is passed between two fields. An outgoing event is called an outEvent, and an incoming event is called an inEvent. Among other things, events signal changes to field values, external conditions, and interactions between nodes. Events may be sent over routes leading to or coming from points outside of the simulation tree.

To make a route, drag the nodes you want to connect to the Routes window. There they will be displayed as icons that resemble their respective node icons as shown in the Components window and the Simulation Tree window—the key difference being that each icon has an inEvent and an outEvent button at the bottom. You click the lower-right button (green arrow) of the source node to open the outEvent pop-up menu. The exact content of the outEvent menu varies depending on the node type. After selecting an outEvent, a connection line will appear. You click the lower-left button (blue dot) of the destination node and choose the desired inEvent from the pop-up menu to establish the connection. Once again, the exact content of the inEvent menu varies depending on the node type. Note that the route formed by the connected outEvent and inEvent must be of the same data type; otherwise, the application will issue an error.

If you want an EON application to communicate with other programs (i.e., a host application such as a web browser), you must establish external routes for sending and receiving events and external fields for storing data values associated with those events. ***External fields*** are user-defined variables created in the Routes window. After you create an external field, it is represented by an icon. An ***external route*** is a connection between an external field and an associated inEvent or OutEvent for a standard node. Routing to and from external fields is performed in the same manner as when connecting standard EON nodes in the Routes window.

Receiving External Data via inEvent Nodes

You use an inEvent to enable communication between an external ActiveX-compliant host application and an EON application. Before such communication can occur, you must create an inEvent node (with an inField to store the data sent from the external application) in the Routes window.

Activity 2.2.2: Creating an inEvent Node

1. Open EON to start a new simulation. If EON is already open, select **New** from the File menu.
2. Display the **Routes** window. Click the **inEvent** button in the lower-left corner of the Routes window, as illustrated in Figure 2.2.5. This will open the InEvent dialog box shown in Figure 2.2.6.

FIGURE 2.2.5 inEvent button in the Routes window

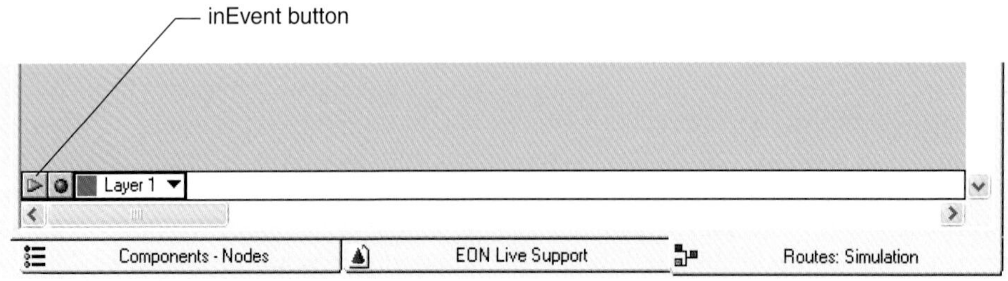

FIGURE 2.2.6 InEvent dialog box

3. Enter **SampleInEvent** in the Name text box. The name you choose in actual production applications should be descriptive to allow you to easily identify the external event.
4. Select **SFBOOL** if necessary as the type of inEvent from the drop-down list shown in Figure 2.2.7.

FIGURE 2.2.7 Types of inEvents possible

5. Click **OK.** The inEvent icon appears in the Routes window, as shown in Figure 2.2.8.

FIGURE 2.2.8 inEvent icon in the Routes window

6. Notice that the inEvent node in the Routes window only has an outEvent option for connecting to other nodes in the simulation. Click the **outEvent** button. The connection line appears, without showing a pop-up menu of outEvent options, because the triggering event was determined when the inEvent was created.
7. Click anywhere in the Routes window to stop attempting to make a connection because no other nodes are available in the Routes window.
8. Right-click the **SampleInEvent** icon in the Routes window and choose **Delete** from the pop-up menu. (Or you can select the icon and press the **Delete** key.) Keep the simulation open to use in Activity 2.2.3.

After an inEvent is established, you can use the EON ActiveX SendEvent method in the host application to send an event trigger and associated data to the inEvent's inField within your EON application. The inEvent's inField data is routed to all nodes that are programmed to be activated when that specific inEvent occurs.

cross-reference

The SendEvent method is explained in the section titled "Receiving and Sending Events" later in this lesson.

Sending Internal Data via outEvent Nodes

You use an outEvent to enable communication between an executing EON application and an external ActiveX-compliant host application. Before such communication can occur, you must create an outEvent node (with an outField for storing data to be sent to the external application) in the Routes window.

Activity 2.2.3: Creating an outEvent Node

1. Continue working with the open simulation file from Activity 2.2.2.
2. Display the **Routes** window. Click the **outEvent** button in the lower-left corner of the Routes window, as illustrated in Figure 2.2.9. This will open the OutEvent dialog box shown in Figure 2.2.10.

FIGURE 2.2.9 outEvent button in the Routes window

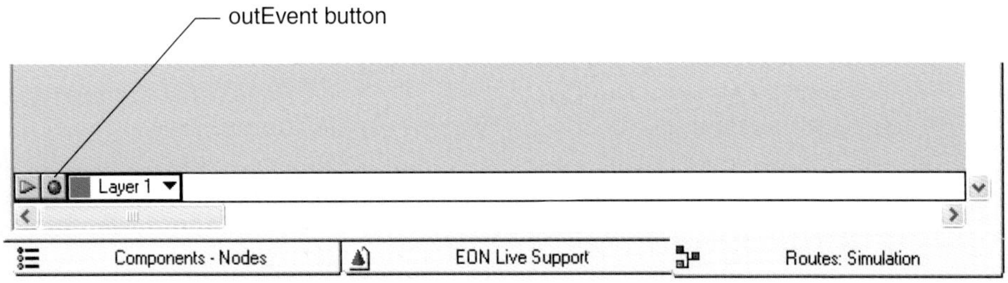

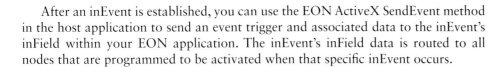

FIGURE 2.2.10 OutEvent dialog box

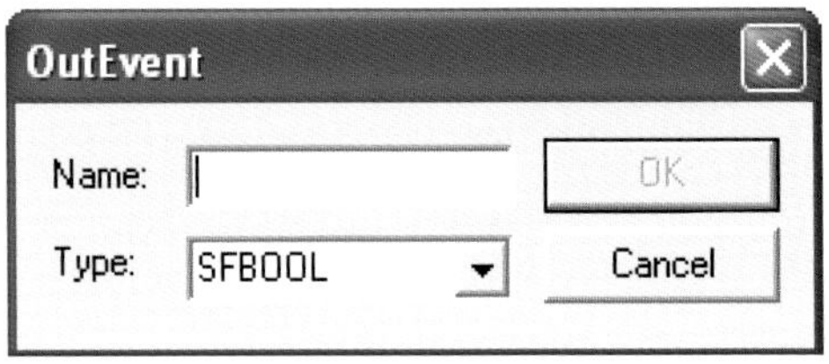

3. Enter **SampleOutEvent** in the Name text box. The name you choose in actual production applications should be descriptive to allow you to easily identify the event.
4. Select **SFBOOL** if necessary as the type of outEvent from the choices given. (The same choices were shown in Figure 2.2.7.)
5. Click **OK.** The outEvent icon appears in the Routes window, as shown in Figure 2.2.11.

FIGURE 2.2.11 outEvent in the Routes window

6. Notice that the outEvent node in the Routes window only has an inEvent option for connecting to other nodes in the simulation. You can route connections into it, but you cannot connect from it to another node in the simulation.
7. Right-click the **SampleOutEvent** icon in the Routes window and choose **Delete** from the pop-up menu. (Or you can select the icon and press the **Delete** key.) Keep the simulation open to use in Activity 2.2.4.

Receiving and Sending Events

In the previous sections, we discussed the specifics of setting up EON to accept an incoming event or to send an outgoing event. How those external events are handled within EON and how host applications process EON outEvents are the focus of this section. But first, you must understand the SendEvent method.

cross-reference

Running EonX applications on end-user computers and developing simulations with ActiveX interoperability are topics in Module 11.

SendEvent Method

The ***SendEvent method*** enables communication between an EON ActiveX control embedded within an external host application and a running EON application. To use this feature, one or more inEvent nodes must be created within the EON application using the method described in Activity 2.2.2. The SendEvent method (in the host application) triggers an inEvent within the running EON application and sends a value to its inField.

The SendEvent method has two parameters. The first parameter is a character string specifying the name of the event, and the event name must be an exact match with the corresponding inEvent node name in EON. The second parameter is the data value to be sent from the host application to the inField of the corresponding inEvent in EON. The data type of this value must be compatible with the inEvent node's data type in EON (for example, SFBool).

The SendEvent method has no effect if the EON application is not running. Likewise, the method has no effect if a nonmatching event name is used, the value is incompatible with the inEvent node's data type, or the external inEvent node is not routed or programmed to activate other nodes within the EON application.

Processing SendEvents Within an EON Application

Sending an event to an EON application is actually a fairly simple procedure. Take a look at the following example of calling a SendEvent method (using Jscript within the host application) for an EonX object named *MyEonX1* and an inEvent of the SFBool data type named *SampleInEvent*:

```
MyEonX1.SendEvent("SampleInEvent", true);
```

This statement sends an inEvent of data type SFBool with a value of true to the EON application where the event is recognized as *SampleInEvent*. As long as the name and data type match (this would match the inEvent we created in Activity 2.2.2) and the EON application is running, this would send the event to EON and trigger the events linked to that inEvent node.

troubleshooting

It is currently not possible to send events of data type SFIMAGE, SFNODE, and any of the MF data types.

Processing outEvents Within an External Host Application

The OnEvent function sends notifications to EonX controls in the host application that correspond with outEvents that occur within a running EON application. To use this feature, an outEvent node must be added to the EON application (as we did in Activity 2.2.3).

The OnEvent function that handles the outEvent will generally be named

```
controlname_OnEvent (e,v)
```

where *controlname* is the name of the embedded EonX control within the host application that handles the outEvent from the EON application, *e* is the outEvent name within the EON application, and *v* is the data value passed from the outEvent to the host application.

tips+tricks

The inEvent node created in EON would need to be further routed to another node to create effects.

Following is an example of JavaScript code within a web page that would be required to handle an outEvent from EON.

```
<script language="JavaScript" type="text/javascript">
<!--
function EON_OnEvent(e,v)
{
if (e=="cubeclicked") alert("You clicked the cube!");
}
//-->
</script>
```

If an outEvent is sent to the web page and there is no function called *EON_OnEvent(e,v)*, then you will get a JavaScript error of "Object Expected".

Following is an example of Visual Basic code for handling an outEvent from EON.

```
Private Sub EonControl_OnEvent(ByValmyevent As String, myvalue
As Variant)
      if myevent="productnumber" then Product.Text = myvalue
      if myevent="next" then ProductNr = ProductNr + 1
End Sub
```

tips+tricks

The following EON-supplied external script files must be included in a web page to provide support for the OnEvent function: **eonx_variables.js, eon_functions.js,** and **eon_functions.vbs.** You will learn more about how to use these files in Module 9.

Saving EON Project Files

Creating a good simulation will not matter if you do not save the files needed to access and use that simulation in the future. In the first few lessons, we saved our work several times. Saving your files is not complicated—it is simply a matter of using the File > Save menu command or clicking the Toolbar's familiar Save button. But what exactly are you saving when you use the Save command? In this section, we will examine what is being saved and how it is saved.

EON File Formats

When you select Save or Save As from the File menu, you will see only one choice for the type of file to save—an EOZ file. However, a number of other file formats are used for distributing completed EON applications as well as for saving new prototypes within an application. The types of EON file formats available include:

- EOZ
- EDZ
- EOP
- EDP

Each format is discussed in more detail in the following sections.

EOZ Files

When you select either the Save or Save As option, your simulation project is automatically saved in the EOZ file format. The resulting EOZ file is a standalone "work-in-progress" package that includes all nodes, prototypes (excluding dynamic load prototypes), and both internal and external project resources such as meshes, textures (.jpg, .png, etc.), sounds (.wav and .midi files), and movies (.avi, .mov, .wmv, and .mpg). As you can imagine, because all file resources are stored uncompressed and unoptimized, EOZ files can quickly develop into very large files. Not until you create an EDZ distribution file will the resources be compressed and optimized for size and performance. (See the following section on EDZ files.) From a developer's perspective, the EOZ file bundle makes it easy to move all work associated with a specific project to a new location on your storage devices without the fear of losing files or breaking links to files.

cross-reference

See Module 9 for more information about dynamic load prototypes.

EDZ Files

After all work on the project is complete, the EOZ file is condensed into an EDZ file format for distribution to end users. The following sequence of operations occurs when the Build Distribution File command (accessible from the File menu) is selected:

1. A distribution folder is created to store the distribution files. (The folder's name is the same as the EOZ file.)
2. All internal resource files are optimized, compressed, and then stored within an EDZ archive file, which is placed in the root of the distribution folder.
3. All external resource files are placed under the distribution folder in subfolders with appropriate names (resources, textures, etc.).

Because the resources within an EDZ file format are optimized and compressed, the resulting EDZ file size is much smaller than the original EOZ file, which ultimately improves the end user's experience by decreasing download time (if distributed via the web) and application load time.

An EDZ file cannot be opened for editing in EON Studio; it can be *viewed* only, whether in EON Studio, ***EON Viewer***, or in another host application that can interpret embedded EonX ActiveX controls, such as Microsoft Internet Explorer or Microsoft PowerPoint. EDZ files are secure and protected, making it a safe distribution format for clients who would like to protect their assets in the simulation file. For this reason, it is preferable to generate an EDZ file for distribution to the end users.

EOP Files

An EOP file is a project file for a prototype library. EOP files are essentially the equivalent of EOZ files, but they are used specifically for storing prototype libraries. Each EOP file contains one prototype library that, in turn, can contain a family or set of individual prototypes. For example, you may recall that the 3DShapes prototype library contains the following prototypes: Cone, Cube, Cylinder, Pyramid, Sphere, Square, Teapot, and Torus.

Each prototype within an EOP file is basically a miniature version of an EOZ simulation project file. Therefore, it can contain nodes, prototypes (excluding dynamic load prototypes), and both internal and external project resources such as meshes, textures, sounds, and movies. Like EOZ files, all resources within the EOP file are stored uncompressed and unoptimized. When you create an EDP prototype library distribution file, these resources will be compressed and optimized for size and performance. (See the following section on EDP files.)

When EON Studio is launched, all EOP files that reside within the default EON Studio PrototypeLibrary subfolder will display in the drop-down list located at the top of the Components—Prototypes window. You can create additional user-defined EOP files by selecting the New button at the top of the Components—Prototypes window.

cross-reference

See Module 8 for more information about creating your own prototypes and prototype libraries.

EDP Files

The EDP file is the distribution version of an EOP file. Like the EDZ file, the prototype library resources stored inside this file are protected, making EDP the preferred file format for distribution purposes. After a user-defined prototype is created, it will appear in the Local Prototypes window. Then, to create an EDP file, you simply right-click the prototype definition in the Local Prototypes window and choose the Build Distribution file option.

Internal and External Resources

Newer nodes within EON have an Embedded property that is used to control whether a resource is to be stored inside or outside of the distribution file. The Embedded property has no effect on EOZ or EOP project files because all resources (excluding dynamic prototypes) are always stored (i.e., embedded) internally within EOZ and EOP project files. However, when creating distribution files, those resources that are explicitly defined as external (Embedded = False/Unchecked) will be stored outside of the distribution file in subfolders beneath the project distribution folder.

There are two main reasons to enable the usage of external resources:

- Resource sharing
- Resource streaming

tips+tricks

The DynamicPrototype node is used for loading, unloading, and swapping EON prototypes while the EON application is running. Usually the content of an EON application is fixed, but this node enables content to be dynamic and changeable. Also, the content can be downloaded from a web server or from a local source. You must have a Dynamic Load license to use Dynamic Load. The PrototypebaseURL property (accessible from the Preferences option of the Options menu) identifies the URL from which dynamic load prototypes are retrieved.

Resource Sharing

Resources such as meshes (i.e., geometries), textures, movies, and prototypes can be shared by multiple simulation applications and prototypes. These resources can be collected and stored within a central repository to make them easier to access and re-use among multiple applications. Resources that a simulation obtains from a central repository are explicitly defined as external resources within individual applications. These external resources are downloaded on demand as the application loads just before runtime.

Resource Streaming

Resources can also be streamed on demand (i.e., downloaded dynamically after application load time) while the simulation application is running. By using EON Dynamic Load to enable resource streaming on demand, it is not only possible to download predefined resources (prototypes, geometries, textures, movies) and embed them in a 3D environment, but it is also possible to let the user decide which resources to download or unload at any time. This creates limitless combinations of 3D content in a running EON application. Currently, the nodes that support streaming of external resources include:

- Mesh2, geometry resources (EOG files)
- Texture2, texture resources (ETX files)
- MovieTexture, movie resources
- Dynamic Load Prototype, EOP files, and/or EDP files that are downloaded during simulation runtime. This is a special case because dynamic load prototypes are always external. They are never embedded inside an EOZ file, and they do not have an Embedded property to explicitly declare them as external resources.

cross-reference

See Module 9 for more information about resource sharing and streaming via Dynamic Load, resource search order, downloading, and loading.

Viewing the EON Application in Real Time

There are two ways to view a completed EON application: in Normal Window mode or in Full-size Window mode. (Note that we are referring to actually viewing the application, not just testing it within EON Studio while you are creating it.)

Normal Window mode is the default view and simply displays the EON simulation within a normal window. ***Full-size Window mode*** is used to maximize the simulation window to cover the entire desktop screen without any visible borders. Both views inherit their screen resolution from the current desktop resolution as defined by the Windows Display Properties settings.

EON Studio

To enable Full-size Window mode in EON Studio, select Simulation from the menu bar and then select Full-size Window Mode. Alternatively, you can press Ctrl + W or Ctrl + F on the keyboard.

EON Viewer

To enable Full-size Window mode in EON Viewer, select View from the menu bar and then select Full-size Window Mode. As with EON Studio, you can press Ctrl + W or Ctrl + F on the keyboard.

Configuration Setting for Rendering Engine

The rendered view quality and processing performance of your EON application are dictated by the choices you make in the Render Properties dialog box, as shown in Figure 2.2.12.

FIGURE 2.2.12 Render Properties dialog box

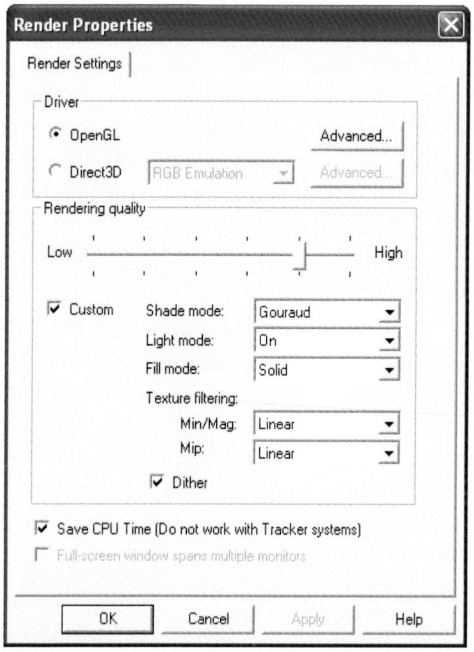

Activity 2.2.4: Exploring the Render Settings

1. Open EON to start a new simulation. If EON is already open, select **New** from the File menu.
2. Select **Simulation** from the menu bar and choose **Configuration.** This will open the EON Simulation Configuration dialog box as shown in Figure 2.2.13.

FIGURE 2.2.13 EON Simulation Configuration dialog box

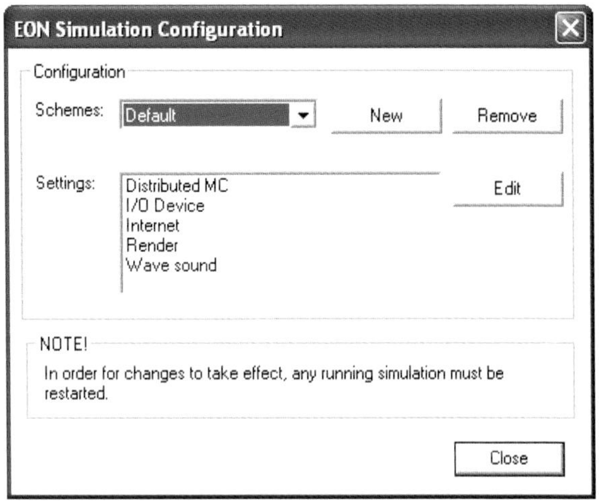

3. Select **Render** in the Settings list and then click **Edit.** This will open the Render Properties dialog box (see Figure 2.2.12).
4. Leave this dialog box open to explore as we discuss the available options in the next sections. When you have finished reading about the options and exploring them through the Render Properties dialog box, select **OK.**
5. Select **Close** in the EON Simulation Configuration dialog box.
6. Close EON without saving the simulation.

Driver Options

The options in the Driver section of the Render Settings tab address the capabilities of the graphics card driver. There are only two choices: ***OpenGL*** or Direct3D. EON no longer actively supports the development of Direct3D as a driver option because all modern graphics cards now support OpenGL; therefore, we will focus our discussion solely on OpenGL.

After you select OpenGL under the Render Settings tab, you can click the Advanced button to open the Advanced OpenGL dialog box shown in Figure 2.2.14.

FIGURE 2.2.14 Advanced OpenGL dialog box

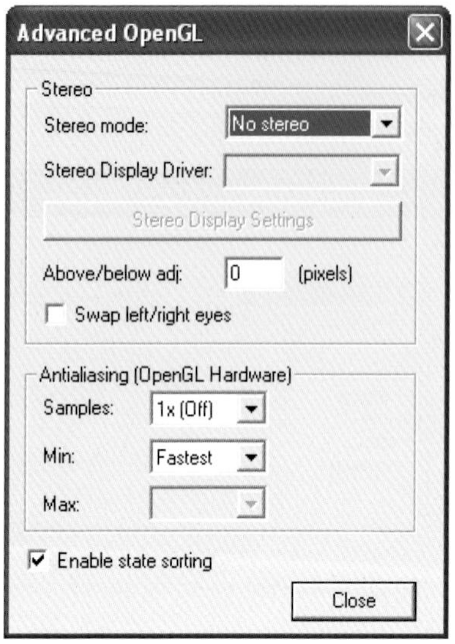

Stereo produces two individual pictures, one for each eye. Special hardware is required to deliver the two pictures to each eye individually. In the Stereo section of the dialog box, several options are available from the drop-down list next to Stereo mode. These options are detailed in Table 2.2.3.

tips+tricks

Selecting Quadbuffer in the Stereo section has no effect unless you have an OpenGL card that supports quad-buffer stereo. In addition, an ICATCHER Viewer license must be available on the computer to activate this stereo mode. Quadbuffer is commonly used with Passive- and Active Stereo–based systems.

TABLE 2.2.3 Stereo Mode Options

Stereo Mode Option	Description
No Stereo	The default setting—all stereo functionality is disabled.
Quadbuffer	Quadbuffer stereo generates a single output signal that contains two separate pictures: one for the left eye, and one for the right eye. This setting produces stereo effects in a window and increases stereo display resolution.
Above/Below	Draws the left eye to the top of the screen and the right eye to the bottom of the screen. Requires a sync-doubling emitter (StereoGraphics E-PC) to produce a stereo image. Selecting this option enables the Above/below adj setting, which is described in Table 2.2.4.
Interleaved	Somewhat similar to the Above/Below stereo option, but the left and right eye pictures are drawn every other line. The first line is left eye, the second line is right eye, the third line is left eye, and so on.

(continued)

TABLE 2.2.3 Stereo Mode Options *(continued)*

Stereo Mode Option	Description
Stereo Display	Selecting this option allows EON to create the stereo image using an external module—a stereo display driver. The stereo display drivers are then selected from the Stereo Display Driver drop-down list (below the Stereo mode selection). EON currently ships with five driver options: • Philips—To be used with Philips' stereo theater systems. • X3D—To be used with X3D's autostereoscopic displays. • Elumens—This is not a true stereo display, but it creates a spherical projection that can then be projected on the Elumens Dome Immersive display stations. Note that this driver requires an ICATCHER Viewer license. • Sharp—To be used with a Sharp3D display laptop for mobile autostereoscopic viewing. • ColorCodeDriver—To be used with the ColorCode 3D stereo system, a powerful and universal 3D stereo system. Selecting the Stereo Display mode enables the Stereo Display Settings button, which opens a dialog box with additional options you can configure for the selected driver.

troubleshooting

When using Above/Below Stereo mode, it is important to make sure that the above/below adjustment is set properly.

tips+tricks

Above/Below and Interleaved modes provide half of the vertical resolution for each eye. It can only be used for full-size applications. The advantage of the Above/Below and Interleaved Stereo modes is that they can be used with any OpenGL graphics card.

The Advanced OpenGL dialog box offers a number of other setting options and adjustments to the OpenGL properties. These are briefly described in Table 2.2.4.

TABLE 2.2.4 Advanced OpenGL Options

Advanced OpenGL Options	Description
Above/below adj	This setting affects the width of the black stripe at the center of the screen. It should be adjusted so that the left and right images properly overlap vertically. Positive values increase the distance between the viewports, which means that the right eye image is moved downward.
Swap left/right eyes	This option allows a user to switch the left/right eye when viewing an EON application in stereo.
Antialiasing (OpenGL Hardware)	The hardware antialiasing is enabled only if it is enabled in the Property Bar for the Simulation node.
Enable state sorting	If this option is selected, 3D objects with the same texture will be grouped and drawn together. Select this option if you suspect that the performance is negatively affected by textures.

tips+tricks

Other factors besides textures can negatively affect simulation performance. For example, performance may also be degraded by complex lighting. If other factors are at play, leave the *Enable state sorting* option unselected.

Antialiasing is one of the most important settings if you have a high-end graphics card. This allows you to set the sampling rate at four times the normal rate and the minimum and maximum settings at the highest levels. It also lets you set the render quality so that your image does not have jagged edges when moving in the simulation. Ultimately, it makes a much more realistic environment.

Rendering Quality Options

In the Rendering quality section of the Render Properties dialog box, you can set the rendering quality/speed from Low to High with the slider. Low provides maximum speed but lower visual quality. High provides optimal quality but may slow the simulation. With modern graphics adapters, we recommend using the setting for the highest quality.

The Custom check box, if selected, allows you to specify render quality settings in detail (rather than the broad Low to High setting). The custom choices are outlined in Table 2.2.5.

TABLE 2.2.5 Custom Rendering Quality Options

Category	Options	Description
Shade mode	Gouraud	Gouraud shading is generally used. Shading is blended so that objects appear more rounded. The individual planes of a ten-sided cylinder would not be visible as separate planes with Gouraud shading. This option requires more computing power than the Flat option.
	Flat	With flat shading, surface planes are easily distinguished from one another.
Light mode	On/Off	The light calculations can be turned on or off. When the Light mode is set to Off, meshes are displayed in the custom color.
Fill mode	Points	Displays just the dots at the corners of the polygons.
	Wireframe	No surfaces are displayed, just edges. The edges have the same colors as they would have if they were textured.
	Solid	Displays a solid surface.
Texture filtering: Min/Mag	Nearest	The texel with coordinates nearest the desired pixel value is used. This applies to both zooming in and zooming out.
	Linear	A weighted average is used of a 2 × 2 area of texels surrounding the desired pixel. This applies to both zooming in and zooming out.
Texture filtering: Mip	None	Mipmapping disabled.
	Nearest	Selects nearest mipmap level.
	Linear	Interpolates between the two nearest mipmaps.
Dither	Selected or not selected	Dither is used for color smoothing, which improves display quality. If your monitor has few colors (less than 24-bit display), this setting can be used to avoid color artifacts.

tips+tricks

Texel stands for texture element or texture pixel. It is the fundamental unit of texture space used in computer graphics.

tips+tricks

MIP is an acronym for the Latin phrase *multum in parvo,* which means "much in a small space." Mipmaps are precalculated, optimized collections of bitmap images that go with the main texture to increase rendering speed and reduce artifacts.

CPU Time

If the *Save CPU Time* option is enabled, EON will refresh the simulation window only when interactions or movements are taking place within the simulation window. If a user is not interacting with the simulation, the EON application uses minimal processor time. This allows EON to cooperate better with other central processing unit (CPU)–intensive software, but selecting this option also might interfere with some tracking systems, so it should be disabled when using such systems. To receive proper simulation statistics, such as rendering speed, this option must be turned off as well.

BEST PRACTICES

Hardware and Graphics Card Considerations

Beyond the general requirements for hardware and graphics cards that you will find in the Preface of this text, you should consider several other things when choosing the components for a system on which you will run EON.

Using an OpenGL graphics card will provide better performance when running EON on a Microsoft Windows platform. Although EON supported Direct3D in earlier versions, not all rendering features are available when running in this mode. Therefore, you should select OpenGL if at all possible.

Because of the introduction of programmable GPU (on the graphics card), several new advanced shading techniques can be used to create extremely realistic effects that were previously only available in an off-line rendering environment (batch process rendering of noninteractive animations).

In the more recent versions of EON, new Cg-based materials for ultra-high quality and flexible shading are available. To use and view these materials, a computer must be equipped with a graphics card with a programmable GPU, such as the NVidia FX 5200 or better or the AMD Radeon 9500 or better with vertex and pixel shader support.

The visual effects available in EON Professional create ultra-high quality and flexible shading by taking advantage of the latest Cg shader technology available on the latest generation of graphics card–programmable GPUs. Advanced materials include Phong shading, bump mapping, darkmapping, cubical environment maps, HDR image-based lighting, leather, wood, fabric, and NPR (nonphotorealistic) hatch shading. You can also create completely custom materials using the generic CgMaterial node by writing your own Cg programs.

Summary

In this lesson you:

- Developed knowledge and understanding of the organizational structure of the software and how to manipulate objects, nodes, simulation commands, and scene parameters.
- Developed an understanding of inEvents and outEvents and learned to use the Routes window to establish external communications for events coming into an EON simulation and going out of an EON simulation.
- Considered the options for saving an EON file for either future development or for distribution.
- Differentiated between viewing an EON simulation in Normal Window mode and Full-size Window mode.
- Configured the render settings for an OpenGL graphics card driver and considered the tradeoffs in processor speed and quality of the rendering.

Simulation

You have worked for Contours Company for several days and have taken every opportunity to get up to speed on their processes and the software applications that they use. To further your education, co-workers have pulled you into a project that they are developing that involves creating a simulation of a functional robotic arm. The client provided the model to use, and your co-workers have already imported that model and have begun simulation development. They are now at the point of making the model functional—meaning that the arm can pivot and rotate at the hinged points. You have just been learning about coordinates and pivot points in EON, so this is perfect timing.

Job 2.1: Thinking About the Storyboard

Because your co-workers have already begun this project, they are following a previously generated storyboard. However, to help you become familiar with their normal processes, they suggest that you develop your own storyboard that you can compare to their final product.

As you work on the storyboard, consider the known elements and the client's request. The client will provide the model and the specifications for the robotic arm. They do not need a fancy environment around the robotic arm—they simply want to highlight and illustrate its qualities and features. The robotic arm in the simulation must be able to move like a real robotic arm in every way. They also would like the simulation user to be able to turn the entire arm around and view it from any angle.

Create a storyboard for this simulation that outlines the steps through development and provides a thumbnail sketch of the final product's appearance.

Job 2.2: Exploring the Robotic Arm

Your first task is to explore the simulation to see what your co-workers have created already.

1. Open EON. Open **Job_2.2** from the data files for the Module 2 Simulation.
2. In the Simulation Tree window, expand the **Scene** frame. Notice the order and the structure of the frames and nodes under the Scene frame.
3. Expand the **Resources** group. Because the model for the robot arm was imported, the Resources group was automatically created with Materials, Textures, and Meshes folders.
4. Expand each of the groups under the Resources group and explore them further. Note that your co-workers named each element in a consistent and descriptive way, which makes it easier for you (or anyone who works on this simulation in the future) to determine the purpose of each element.
5. In the Scene frame, expand the **Robot_Arm** frame, the **Base_Cylinder** frame, the **DOF** node, the **Base_Cylinder_shapenode**, the **Base_CylinderShape**, and then the **Geometry** and **Material** folders so that you can see the Mesh2 node (Base_CylinderMesh) under Geometry and the Material2 node (Base_Cylinder) under Material. Notice that these are references (shortcuts) back to the actual material or mesh listed under Resources.
6. Run the simulation. Your simulation window should appear as shown in Figure 2.1.

tips+tricks

Recall that reference icons have a small arrow that resembles the arrow found on a Microsoft Windows shortcut icon.

FIGURE 2.1 Robotic arm simulation

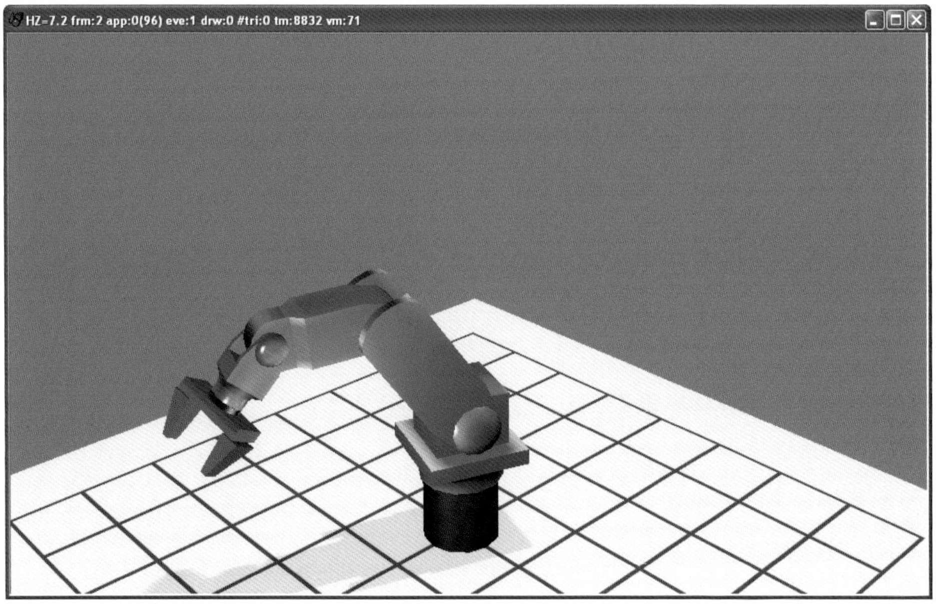

Discussion

discuss

Does the simulation match the simulation you envisioned for this product? Is it similar to the sketch in your storyboard?

7. Right-click and hold the mouse while dragging upward to zoom out and downward to zoom in. Zoom so that you can see the entire grid plane on which the robotic arm rests.
8. Press **Ctrl** and **Shift** at the same time (or, alternatively, press **P**). This will display the x, y, and z axes for the simulation.
9. Left-click and move the mouse to rotate and pivot around the robotic arm to view it from different angles.
10. Close the simulation window.
11. Continue exploring the Simulation Tree window until you understand the basics of this simulation.
12. Although you have made no changes to the simulation yet, you will make changes soon. Save the simulation as **Robotic_Arm_Moving** and keep it open to use in Job 2.3.

troubleshooting

Displaying the axis using P or Ctrl + Shift is a function of the ObjectNav prototype. If a simulation does not contain the ObjectNav prototype, these actions will not display the x, y, and z axes.

Job 2.3: Enhancing the Robotic Arm

Now that you are familiar with the existing robotic arm simulation, it is time to enhance the simulation so that it can move like a real robotic arm. First, you will study the structure of the simulation again. Then you will add the ability to rotate the pivot points using the KeyMove node.

1. Continue working with the open simulation file **Robotic_Arm_Moving.eoz** from Job 2.2.

2. In the Simulation Tree window, expand the following frames:

   Robot_Arm > **Base_Cylinder** > **DOF** > **Arm_Base** + **DOF** > **Arm_Section01** > **DOF** > **Arm_Section02** > **DOF** > **Arm_Section03** > **DOF** > **Clamp_Swivel_Base** > **DOF** > **Clamp_Unit_Motor**

discuss

What does the expansion of the Robot_Arm frame and its subframes illustrate? Do you see how this structure will allow you to select the separate parent pieces and child pieces and manipulate the positions?

3. Drag and drop the **KeyMove** node into the Arm_Base frame. Rename the node **KeyMove_Arm_Base**.
4. Run the simulation. Press and hold **X** while pressing the up or down arrow key. The robotic arm is actually moving off of its base, which is not something it would normally do.
5. Press and hold each of the following keys while pressing the up or down arrow key: **Y, Z, H, P,** and **R**.

discuss

Of the six directions of movement that you experimented with in steps 4 and 5, which of the movements would you expect a robotic arm to perform at that connection point?

6. Close the simulation window.
7. Select the **DOF** node under Arm_Base. In the Property Bar, notice that the movement of the arm is constrained in every direction except H.

discuss

If the DOF node is constrained in every way except H, why were you able to move the entire robotic arm off of its base?

8. Move the **KeyMove_Arm_Base** you inserted, placing it under the DOF found under the Arm_Base frame. Rename the node **KeyMove_Arm_BaseDOF**.
9. Run the simulation. Press and hold **X** while pressing the up or down arrow key. Press and hold each of the following keys while pressing the up or down arrow key: **Y**, **Z**, **H**, **P**, and **R**. Close the simulation.

tips+tricks

It is very important to establish a sensible naming convention and then stick with it. In many cases, you work with the default names from the imported models, which can be lengthy. You must decide whether to rename the imported items or to continue using the default names as you work with your simulation.

Regardless, you must make it clear that a specific node belongs with a specific frame, shape, node, and so on. In this case (step 8), because we will add more KeyMove nodes later, we want to make it clear which shape and node this KeyMove is associated with—and what it will control when it is used. Therefore, we keep "KeyMove" in the name to identify the type of node. We add "Arm_Base" to match the name of the frame under which it is found. (This is the original name that we gave it in step 3 when we placed it under the frame.) And then we add "DOF" to indicate that it is associated with the DegreeOfFreedom node located under Arm_Base.

Clear and concise naming also makes working within the Routes window later a much simpler task.

Discussion

discuss

With the KeyMove node placed under the DOF, how do the constraints work to make the movement of the arm more realistic? What does this demonstrate about parent-child relationships within the hierarchy of the simulation tree?

tips+tricks

Some of the DOF values have already been set for you to the appropriate constraints to limit movement to the direction and extent that are correct for the robotic arm.

10. Use the following table as a guide to add a KeyMove node to each frame indicated and rename the KeyMove as shown.

Place to Add KeyMove	Rename the KeyMove
Arm_Section01 > **DOF**	KeyMove_Arm_Section01DOF
Arm_Section02 > **DOF**	KeyMove_Arm_Section02DOF
Arm_Section03 > **DOF**	KeyMove_Arm_Section03DOF
Clamp_Swivel_Base > **DOF**	KeyMove_Clamp_Swivel_BaseDOF
Clamp_Unit_Motor > **Clamp_Finger_Left** > **DOF**	KeyMove_Clamp_Finger_LeftDOF
Clamp_Unit_Motor > **Clamp_Finger_Right** > **DOF**	KeyMove_Clamp_Finger_RightDOF

11. Save the simulation and then run the simulation.
12. Experiment with the KeyMove options. Close the simulation window.

Discussion

discuss

Which of the KeyMove options appear to be working correctly? Which do not seem to have any effect? Which work but allow the robotic arm to move in abnormal ways? Can you move the different segments of the arm in the way you desire?

tips+tricks

The KeyMove node does not have a Property option to be turned off or disabled at the start. To compensate for this, the TimeSensor node can be used to turn off the KeyMove nodes when the simulation starts. Then a ClickSensor can be used to allow the user to activate the portion of the arm to move.

13. Scroll down in the Simulation Tree window to see the SimulationStarted_TimeSensor node.
14. Display the **Routes** window. Locate the SimulationStarted_TimeSensor node.
15. Drag and drop each of the seven added KeyMove nodes from the Simulation Tree window into the Routes window. Try to keep them orderly as you place them in the window.
16. Select the **outEvent** (green arrow) on the SimulationStarted_TimeSensor and select **OnStartPulse** from the drop-down list. Drag the connection to the KeyMove_Arm_BaseDOF node's inEvent (blue dot) and select **SetRun_**. This establishes that when the simulation starts (OnStartPulse), the KeyMove for the Arm_Base is set to *not* run (SetRun_ means SetRun "false").
17. Repeat the outEvent connection from the SimulationStarted_TimeSensor to each of the KeyMoves, setting each to **SetRun_**. When complete, your Routes window should look similar to Figure 2.2.

FIGURE 2.2 Routes window with OnStartPulse connections to KeyMove nodes

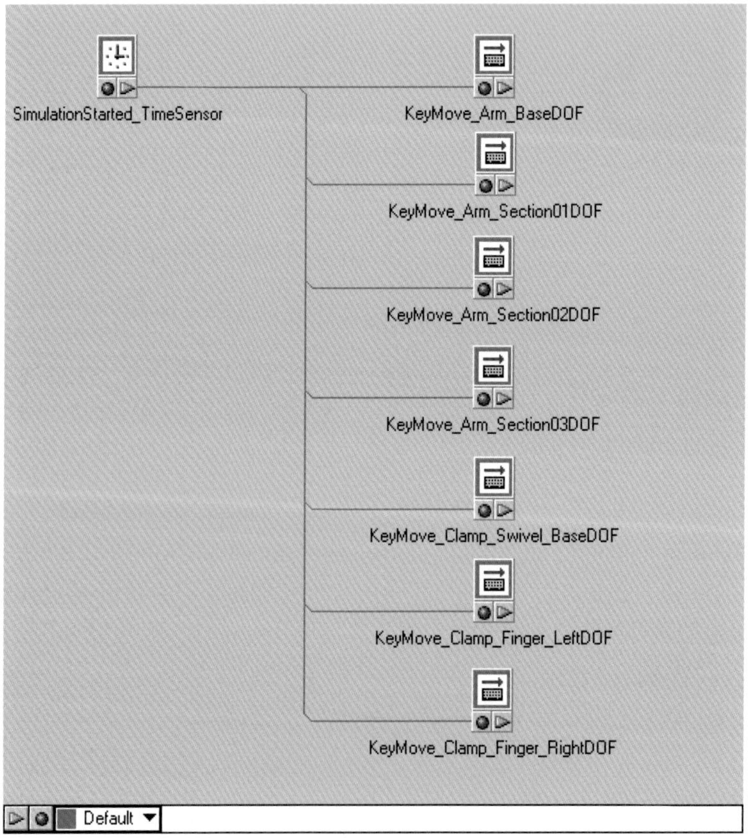

18. Save the simulation and then run the simulation.
19. Press and hold each of the following keys while pressing the up or down arrow key: **X**, **Y**, **Z**, **H**, **P**, and **R**. The robotic arm will not move in any way because all of the KeyMove nodes are set to "not run" when the simulation is started.
20. Close the simulation window and switch to the Components – Nodes window.

20. Double-click **ClickSensor_Arm_Base_MiddleClick**. Select **Middle** from the options in the ClickSensor Properties dialog box, as shown in Figure 2.6. Click **OK**.

FIGURE 2.6 ClickSensor Properties dialog box options

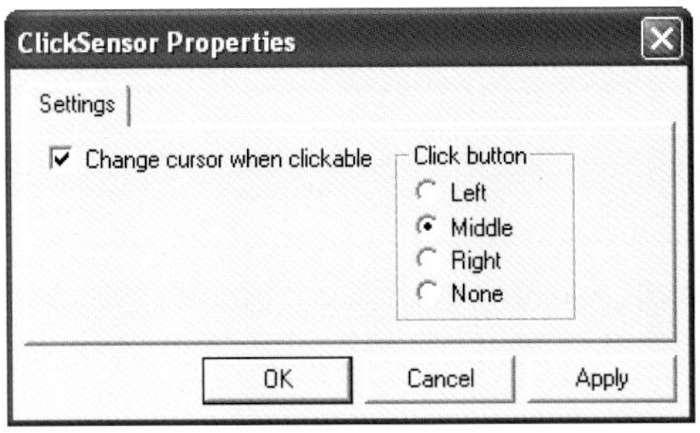

21. Double-click **ClickSensor_Arm_Base_RightClick**. Select **Right** from the options in the ClickSensor Properties dialog box and then click **OK**.
22. Double-click **Rotate_HeadLeft** in the Simulation Tree window. In the Place Properties dialog box, set the rotation (h in the Movement column) to **-15** and set the rotation time (h in the Time to move column) to **1**. Select the **Rel** (Relative) option for every value in the Type section of the dialog box. Click **OK**.
23. Double-click **Rotate_HeadRight** in the Simulation Tree window. In the Place Properties dialog box, set the rotation (h in the Movement column) to **15** and set the rotation time (h in the Time to move column) to **1**. Select the **Rel** (Relative) option for every value in the Type section of the dialog box. Click **OK**.
24. Drag the two new **ClickSensor** nodes and the three **Place** nodes to the Routes window.
25. Establish the connections outlined in the following table.

From	outEvent	To	inEvent
ClickSensor_Arm_Base_LeftClick	OnButtonDownTrue	Rotate_HeadLeft	SetRun
ClickSensor_Arm_Base_RightClick	OnButtonDownTrue	Rotate_HeadRight	SetRun
ClickSensor_Arm_Base_MiddleClick	OnButtonDownTrue	Reset_ArmBase	SetRun

26. Save the simulation and then run the simulation.
27. Right-click the square base on the robotic arm. The arm will rotate to the right. Left-click and it will rotate left. Now click with the middle mouse button, and the arm will reset to its original position.
28. Close the simulation window and make any other edits that you think are necessary or would enhance the appearance or functionality of the robotic arm.
29. Save the simulation and then close EON.

tips+tricks

The Movement column in the Place Properties dialog box correlates to Translation and Rotation values in the Property Bar. The Time to move column in the Place Properties dialog box correlates to TransTime and RotTime in the Property Bar.

tips+tricks

Notice that when you rename a node in the Simulation Tree window, it is automatically renamed in the Routes window.

HARALD SUND

MODULE 3

Importing into EON

LESSON 3.1

Model Export Considerations

LESSON 3.2

Import and Place 3D Objects

LESSON 3.1

Model Export Considerations

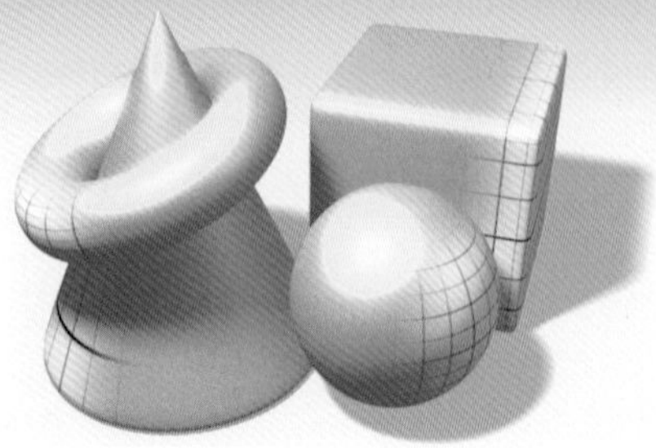

Objectives

In this lesson you will:

- Consider several important items that should be established within your model prior to importing it into EON.
- Discuss various methods of grouping and naming objects as well as establishing hierarchies before you import them into EON.
- Explore the positioning of pivot points and the impact they can have on an object's placement and behavior within a simulation.
- Develop an understanding of how geometry optimization can reduce the resources used by your simulation and increase the speed of loading the simulation.
- Discuss the benefits of establishing camera positions and animations in your modeling program versus in EON.
- Gain an understanding of the increased efficiency of setting lighting for your scene within your modeling program versus within EON.

Key Terms

flat hierarchy ***geometry optimization*** ***pivot point***

As you have undoubtedly begun to realize, there are many important considerations to keep in mind when you are designing and creating a simulation in EON. And, just as importantly, many aspects of modeling prior to importing into EON are significant as well.

Here are the six most important things to consider when modeling:

- Grouping
- Scene hierarchy and naming conventions
- Pivot points
- Geometry
- Camera views and animation
- Lighting

We will explore each of these items in greater detail in this lesson and look at some of the situations you may encounter when modeling in programs outside of EON. Then, in Module 3 Lesson 2, we will import and place 3D objects in EON.

Grouping, Hierarchy, and Naming

If you have worked with modeling programs, you may already be aware of the naming conventions that some of these programs use. As you create objects in a program such as 3ds Max, you will see that a ***flat hierarchy*** is created. By "flat," we mean that each object created is on the same level as each other object. For example, a table top and table legs are all parallel to each other, as is the vase that is placed on the table.

Establishing a hierarchy to provide an organizing structure for objects as you create them makes it easier for others to understand the model—both in the modeling program as well as in EON. To continue with the table example, it would be better to group the components of the table. Therefore, you would place the four table leg objects and the table top object together in a group.

Additionally, to aid in locating objects and understanding the models created, you should employ a naming convention that is easy to follow and sensible. For example, the default names of the table top and table legs that you would create for modeling a table may be named Box01, Box02, Box03, etc., as shown in Figure 3.1.1.

FIGURE 3.1.1 Default names applied to boxes used to create a table in 3ds Max

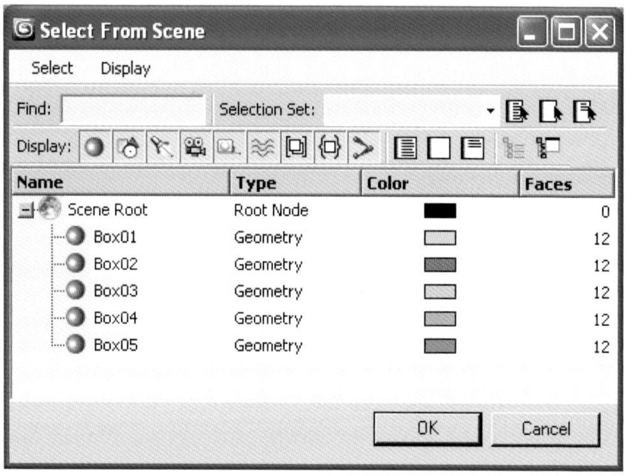

These names are not very useful or clear. However, if you rename and restructure as you go, you can create a much clearer and useful naming system, such as the following:

TableTop
TableLeg01
TableLeg02
TableLeg03
TableLeg04

This allows you to easily identify each object as well as which objects are used together to create an element in the model.

After you have created each individual object, all of these objects can be grouped together to form a single object. This allows you to keep all the elements together as you move the object around and makes it much easier to work with—both in the modeling program and when you import it into EON. In the table example, if the objects were not grouped, you would need to move the table top and then each individual leg, making sure that the objects are realigned perfectly. When grouped, your hierarchical structure and the number of objects that you need to deal with are greatly simplified. For the table example, grouping would change the scene hierarchy from the one shown in Figure 3.1.1 to the one shown in Figure 3.1.2.

FIGURE 3.1.2 Objects grouped and renamed for a table in 3ds Max

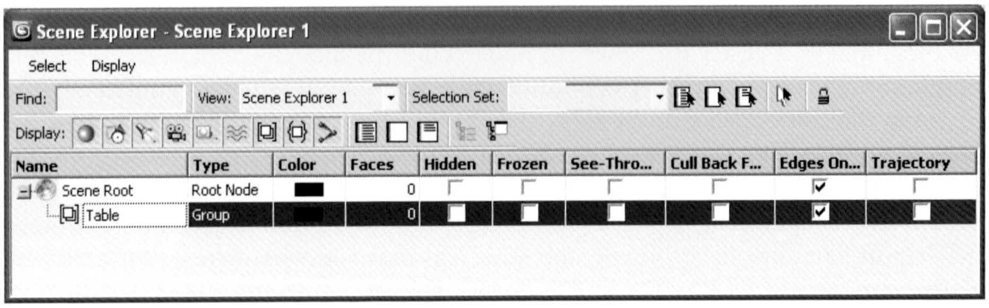

troubleshooting

Another important note about file naming concerns the names of textures. To avoid problems when importing 3ds Max files, restrict texture filenames to eight characters.

Objects that are part of the same item should be placed in the same group. Likewise, similar objects should be grouped together. This makes it easier to locate them and easier to apply treatments that should affect all items in a group.

When it comes to naming, you should also be conscious of using special characters in your names. Some special characters cannot be supported by EON. If one of these characters is encountered, EON will delete the character or replace it with an underscore. Depending on how you name objects, this could cause confusion or errors. Careful naming allows good data conversion.

Activity 3.1.1: Exploring Objects and Grouping

1. Open a modeling program. If you have several to choose from, select the one that you are most likely to use for your modeling. If you do not have a modeling program, download a trial version of a software package, such as 3ds Max or Maya.
2. Create a table using rectangular boxes for the table top and the legs, or create some other object that has multiple parts.
3. Look at the hierarchical structure of the scene you created. How many objects does it have? How are the objects named?
4. Rename the objects using descriptive names that make sense to you and to anyone who may work with this object in the future.
5. Group the objects together and give the group a descriptive name.
6. Save your work.
7. Close the modeling program.

Discussion

discuss

Although we will not step you through importing models until Module 3 Lesson 2, you could import the model you created as an extension project.

How is the object you created imported? Is the hierarchy that you established maintained? How could you improve the conversion that occurs when you import models into EON?

Pivot Points

A ***pivot point*** is a position in an object that serves as the center of rotation and as the position reference. The pivot point of an object is the location where all of the local axes come together. When an object rotates, it revolves around the pivot point. Most 3D software applications have a control that enables you to select the location of the pivot point or define multiple pivot points. If the object has multiple pivot points, you can define which point will be used for the rotation operations.

Discussion

discuss

How is the pivot point of an object similar to the origin point for the world coordinates axes discussed in Module 2 Lesson 1? How is it different?

Pivot points are, therefore, another important consideration for models created outside EON. Placing them in the correct area prior to importing your model into EON is critical for smoothly importing and placing models.

By default, the pivot point of an object will be at the center of the object, but that location is not correct for all objects. A door, for example, would need its pivot point on an edge, not in the center, to operate properly in the scene.

Activity 3.1.2: Exploring Pivot Points

1. Open EON. Open **Activity_3.1.2** from the data files for Module 3 Lesson 1.
2. Run the simulation.
3. Click the door on the left. Notice that it opens and closes as you would expect.
4. Click the door on the right. Does it open and close correctly?
5. Close the simulation window.
6. In the Components window, select the **Prototypes** tab.
7. Select **3DPointerA** in the Components window and drag it to the DoorCorrectPivot frame in the Simulation Tree window.
8. Select **3DPointerA** in the Components window and drag it to the DoorIncorrectPivot frame in the Simulation Tree window.

9. Save the simulation as **Door_Pivot_Points** and then run the simulation. Your simulation window should appear similar to Figure 3.1.3.

FIGURE 3.1.3 3DPointerA prototype used to illustrate pivot points

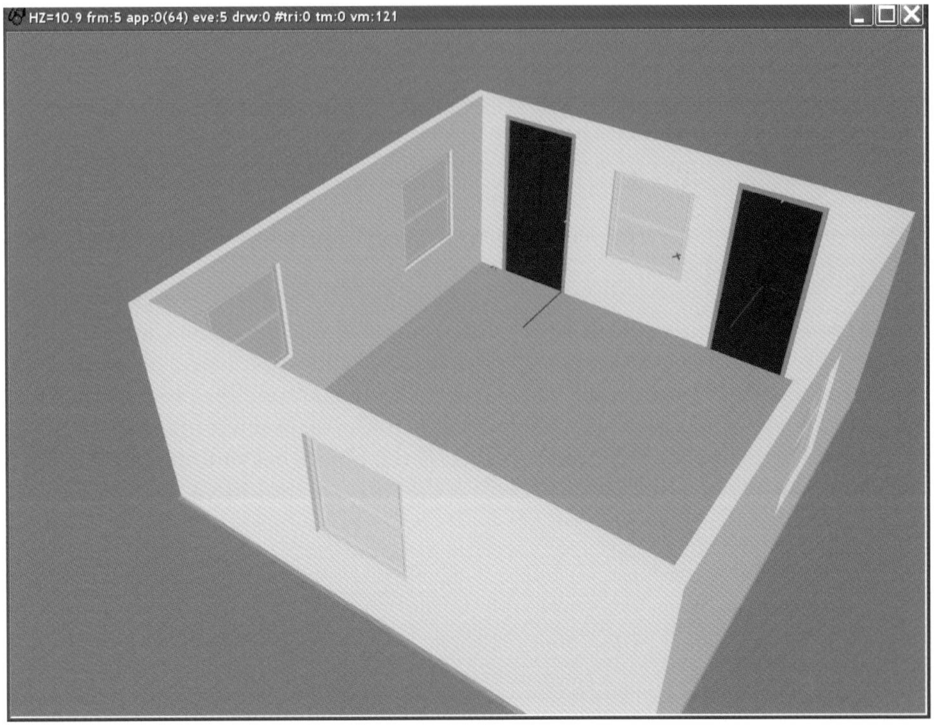

10. Based on the location of the 3D pointers, notice where the pivot points are located for each door.
11. Close the simulation window. Close EON.

As you can probably guess, one door swings correctly and the other does not, based on the pivot points set up in the model when it was created. If you encounter this sort of problem in an EON file, you have two options. If you have access to the original model, you can return to the modeling program, correct the pivot point location, re-import the model, and then create a new EON file. If this is not possible—because you do not have the original file or because valuable additions and changes have been made to the EON file since the model was imported—then you can make changes manually in EON to correct the pivot point error in the model using the DegreeOfFreedom node.

In most 3D modeling programs, the pivot point is adjusted on the object level or the group level. Some programs, like CATIA and SolidWorks, do not translate their pivot points to EON CAD. In these cases, you will have to establish the pivot points manually using the DegreeOfFreedom node in EON.

tips+tricks

The DegreeOfFreedom node has two purposes. First, as the name implies, it specifies the degree to which objects under the node can move or rotate. Second, it can be used to move the pivot position of objects under the DOF.

For example, you may have a frame with a Shape node under it and a Place node under the frame that rotates the frame. But you notice that the frame does not rotate around the correct pivot point.

The pivot point location of an object is saved with the object's geometry file. EON cannot view or change this internal value. Therefore, the pivot point cannot be changed in the Frame node properties in EON Studio. Instead, you must add a DegreeOfFreedom node (DOF) under the frame and then move the Shape node and the Place node, dropping them under the DOF node. This enables you to change the pivot position by setting the DOF node's origin position and origin orientation fields.

Setting the precise values for a DegreeOfFreedom node can be difficult because you cannot see the effect of changing the values until you apply rotation and view the action. You can use the DOFMover prototype, located in the Developer Tools prototype library, to visualize and move the pivot position.

Regardless of the modeling program you use, a Geometry Import dialog box appears during the import process. The one shown in Figure 3.1.4 is displayed for a model coming from 3D Studio, and Figure 3.1.5 illustrates the dialog box for a Lightwave model. The exact dialog box that appears depends on the type of file you are importing. As you can see, some importers automatically pick up data, such as the pivot points, and others do not.

FIGURE 3.1.4 Geometry Import dialog box for 3D Studio files

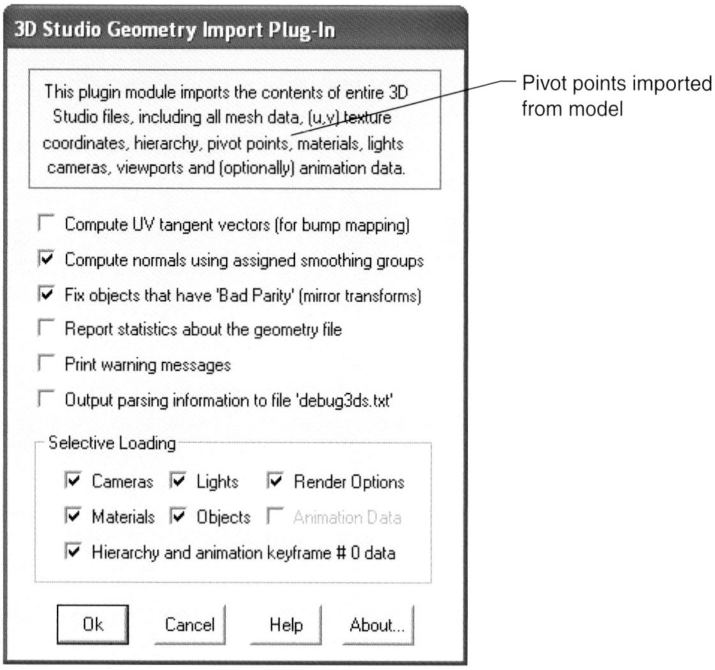

FIGURE 3.1.5 Geometry Import dialog box for Lightwave files

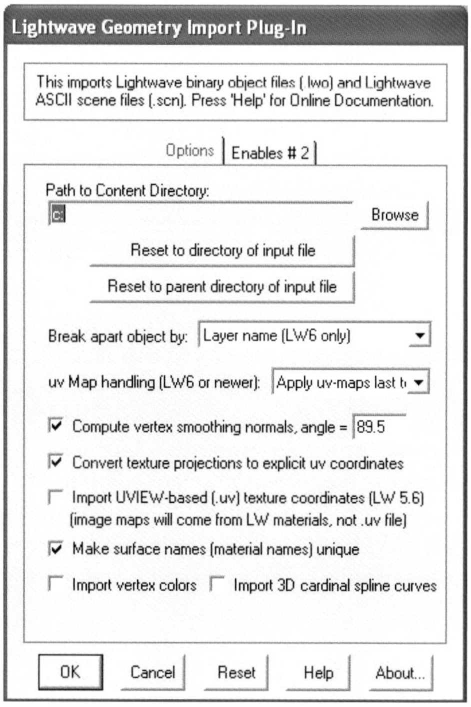

BEST PRACTICES

Textures

As you learned in Module 2, textures are used to add realistic surface characteristics to materials. These textures can be added in EON, but more often they are applied in the modeling program. When you import models with textures added, there are some things that you need to consider:

- Before you import models and their textures, verify that the textures are optimized for interactive simulations. Larger textures will decrease the performance of the simulation.
- If any of the textures you intend to use in your model are in TIF format, save them in JPG format.
- If a texture has transparency, then it should be saved as a PNG file type.
- When saving, verify that all the textures are located in the same general subfolder as your 3D model. Do not save textures in the Documents and Settings folder or on a network drive, for example.
- Although it is not required, it is a good practice to save all of your textures in one subfolder (within the same folder as your model) called Maps. This allows you to use the textures as a shared resource, and you can easily locate and access them for other models as needed.

Geometry Optimization

As you may recall from our discussion of polygon face count in Module 2 Lesson 1, the number of polygons in your model directly affects the level of detail in your simulation and the time needed to render your simulation. What can you do to strike a balance between time to render and the quality of your simulation? Reduce the number of polygons used to create your model by removing surfaces that you do not need. Additionally, combine objects that do not need independent animation (like the legs of a table).

In EON, each object is loaded separately, so separate table legs cause the program to "call" for each object every time it loads. As your simulation grows, this becomes a huge drain on system resources. Anything you can do to reduce the number of objects greatly enhances the loading speed. And even if you collapse multiple objects into one, you can still adjust surfaces independently as long as you set different names (IDs) for each in the modeling program.

The collective effort to reduce the size of the simulation is called ***geometry optimization.*** This includes decisions you make to remove unneeded surfaces and to group separate objects as one object. Geometry optimization also includes the choices you make to allow EON's algorithms to run when you select the GeometryCompressionLevel or the PolygonReductionLevel within the Property Bar. These options allow you to control the amount of optimization that is acceptable within your scene without affecting the scene's integrity.

You can also optimize a simulation by reusing objects. For example, if you have a building that consists of thirty columns modeled in detail, you do not need thirty identical geometry files. In EON, you can make thirty copies of a Shape node that reference a single Mesh2 node, and that will optimize file size and rendering performance.

Activity 3.1.3: Exploring Geometry Optimization

1. Open EON. Open **Activity_3.1.3** from the data files for Module 3 Lesson 1.
2. Expand the **Scene** frame in the Simulation Tree window. Notice the OptimizedRoom and UnOptimizedRoom frames.
3. Expand the **OptimizedRoom** and **UnOptimizedRoom** frames. In the OptimizedRoom, notice that the table and chairs are collapsed into one frame to organize and optimize the model.
4. Run the simulation. Your simulation window will look similar to the one shown in Figure 3.1.6.

FIGURE 3.1.6 Optimized Room

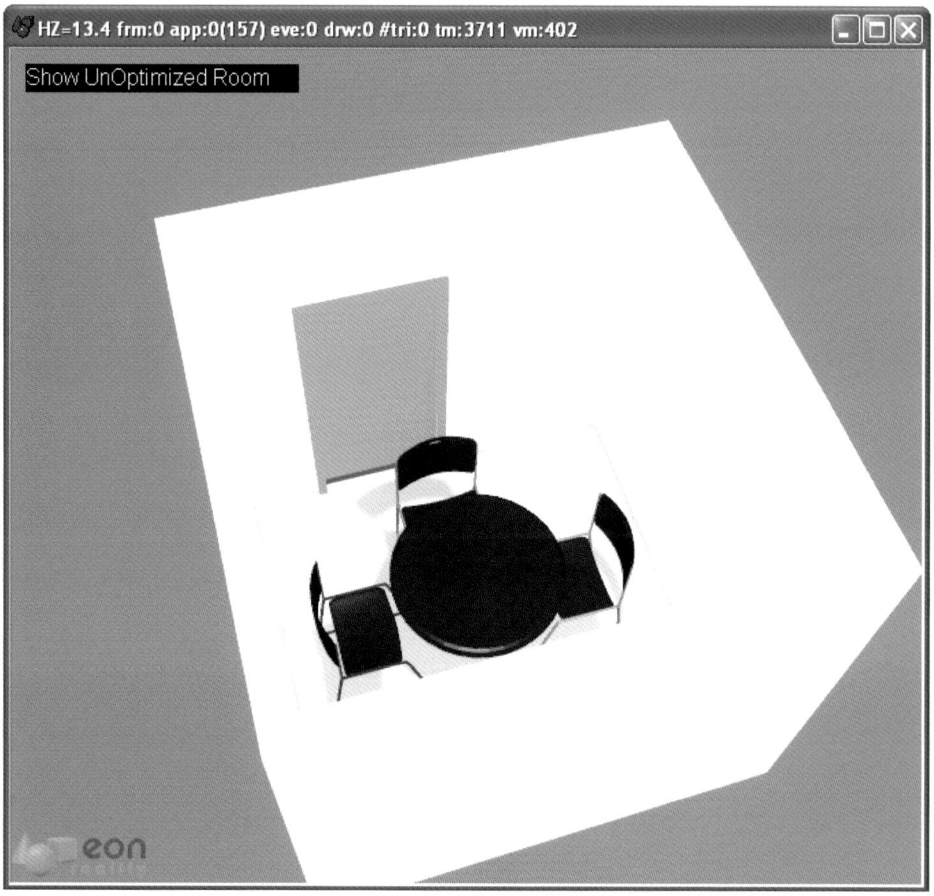

5. Click **Show UnOptimized Room** in the upper-left corner of the simulation window.
6. Adjust your view (using the left mouse button) so that you can see all the chairs and the table inside the room when looking from the top down into the room.
7. Adjust your view (using the left mouse button) so that you are looking at one of the walls from outside of the room.
8. Use the right mouse button to adjust your view to see the inside of the room.
9. Use the left mouse button to look around inside the room.
10. Click **Show Optimized Room** in the upper-left corner of the simulation window.
11. Use the left mouse button to look around inside the room.

Discussion

discuss

Do you notice any differences between the UnOptimized Room that you were first viewing and the Optimized Room you are looking at in steps 9 and 10?

12. Use the right mouse button to move outside of the room.
13. Rotate the image so that you are looking in from outside different walls. Your simulation window will look similar to the one shown in Figure 3.1.7.

FIGURE 3.1.7 View from outside the Optimized Room

Discussion

discuss

What differences do you see between the UnOptimized Room in step 7 and the Optimized Room when viewed from outside the room in steps 12 and 13?

tips+tricks

Note that the PolygonCount values are gray in the Property Bar because these values are read only. The values are outEvents determined when the simulation starts.

14. Close the simulation window.
15. In the Simulation Tree window, expand the following: **UnOptimizedRoom > Wall01 > Wall01Shape > Geometry**.
16. Select **Wall01Mesh**.
17. In the Property Bar, note the values in PolygonCountBeforeReduction and PolygonCountAfterReduction. The unoptimized walls have 112 polygons.

18. In the Simulation Tree window, expand the following: **OptimizedRoom > Wall02 > Wall02Shape > Geometry**.
19. Select **Wall02Mesh**.
20. In the Property Bar, note the values in PolygonCountBeforeReduction and PolygonCountAfterReduction. The optimized walls have only 36 polygons.

Discussion

discuss

Was the difference between the optimized walls and the nonoptimized walls in Activity 3.1.3 significant?

When a simulation is small, is it necessary to optimize the scene's elements?

When should you consider space constraints and geometry optimization?

21. Close EON without saving the simulation.

troubleshooting

If you look at the PolygonCount values before running the simulation, you will see that the values are 0 because these values are outEvents that are determined when the simulation is run.

Camera Views and Animations

Modeling programs typically have excellent mechanisms for establishing cameras and camera views as well as animating a scene. If possible, use these readily available tools. However, there are situations where this is not possible. For example, the model may have been created by someone else and imported into EON and you do not have access to the original model. Or, you may not have the same modeling program needed to make the edits. Or, so many additional changes have been made to the model since it was imported that you would not want to go back to the modeling program to alter the model, re-import it, and start creating the simulation all over again. In this type of situation, you want or need to make your adjustments in EON.

Camera Positions

Although you can set up camera positions within EON, it is much easier and more effective to do this in the modeling program. Establishing and adjusting cameras are common and simple functions in most modeling programs; these are more cumbersome tasks in EON because the modeling process is not its main focus and it was not designed for ease of camera positioning.

As much as possible, plan the camera views for your model and simulation in your 3D software. Within your modeling software, you can easily create and modify the position and orientation of multiple cameras—usually simply by selecting and dragging. EON does an excellent job of importing cameras so that the cameras set up in your modeling program will be directly imported into EON. They will be placed automatically into the appropriate folders, and you can adjust the cameras as needed after that.

cross-reference

You will learn more about EON cameras and viewports in Module 6 Lesson 1.

Animations

Animating your scene is easier in a modeling program than it is in EON. Most modeling programs allow you to move cameras easily and set them up on a timeline. For example, in 3ds Max, you can place the cameras on a timeline in the object-oriented interface. Then these elements would import directly into EON—automatically creating all the cameras and necessary property fields. Although you can achieve the same effect in EON, you would have to use the KeyFrame node and manually set the desired properties for every view based on the exact coordinates and times, which is a time-consuming process.

In a modeling program, if you find that the animation is not moving exactly as you expected, you can easily modify the position or orientation along a timeline and immediately see whether the changes had the desired impact. In EON, this would require guessing the correct values in the Property Bar and then running the simulation to see the effect of those changes. If the results are not right, then you would need to guess the exact coordinates and times again and rerun the simulation.

troubleshooting

EON does not currently support vertex animation, although some Cg materials applied to an object can modify vertices.

If you get animations working correctly in your modeling program, they directly translate to EON Studio as KeyFrame nodes when imported. Likewise, objects and groups can be animated and will be translated directly into EON. Scale, position, and orientation are supported.

Activity 3.1.4: Importing Camera Positions and Animation into EON

1. Open EON. Open **Activity_3.1.4** from the data files for Module 3 Lesson 1.
2. Expand the **Scene** in the Simulation Tree window. Notice that the Scene hierarchy contains a CameraTop frame and a CameraAnim frame in addition to the default ActiveViewportCamera frame. These frames hold the position information for cameras that were specified in your modeling program. Your simulation tree would look similar to this example immediately after you import a model with cameras. To use these values, you must transfer them to the default Camera frame in your simulation.
3. Select **CameraTop** and note the Position and Orientation values shown in the Property Bar.
4. Drag a **Place** node to the ActiveViewportCamera frame and rename it **CameraTopViewValues**.
5. With the **CameraTopViewValues** Place node still selected, expand the **Translation** field in the Property Bar. Enter the values from the CameraTop Position fields (noted in step 3) into the Translation fields.
6. With the **CameraTopViewValues** Place node still selected, expand the **Rotation** field in the Property Bar. Enter the values from the CameraTop Orientation fields (noted in step 3) in the the Rotation fields.
7. In the Simulation Tree window, expand the **CameraAnim** frame, select the **CameraAnimation** KeyFrame node below it, and drag the **CameraAnimation** KeyFrame to the ActiveViewportCamera frame.
8. Run the simulation. Notice that you are now viewing the room from the top because that is the camera position that you entered.
9. Close the simulation window.
10. Drag a **Frame** node into the Scene and rename it **LogicCreation**.
11. Drag a **KeyboardSensor** node into the LogicCreation frame and rename it **Key1_GoToCameraTop**.

12. Drag another **KeyboardSensor** node into the LogicCreation frame and rename it **Key2_PlayCameraAnim**. Your Simulation Tree window should look similar to Figure 3.1.8.

FIGURE 3.1.8 Simulation tree using cameras from modeling program

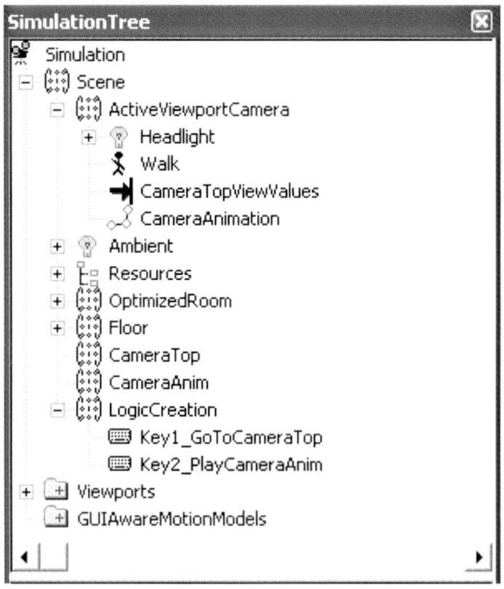

13. Display the **Routes** window.
14. Drag the **Key1_GoToCameraTop** and the **Key2_PlayCameraAnim** nodes from the Simulation Tree window to the Routes window, placing one below the other.
15. Drag the **CameraTopViewValues** node from the Simulation Tree window to the Routes window, placing it next to the Key1_GoToCameraTop node.
16. Drag the **CameraAnimation** node from the Simulation Tree window to the Routes window, placing it next to the Key2_PlayCameraAnim node.
17. Establish the connections outlined in the following table. Your Routes window should look similar to Figure 3.1.9.

From	outEvent	To	inEvent
Key1_GoToCameraTop	OnKeyDown	CameraTopViewValues	SetRun
Key2_PlayCameraAnim	OnKeyDown	CameraAnimation	SetRun

FIGURE 3.1.9 Routes window with KeyboardSensor nodes connected to camera positions

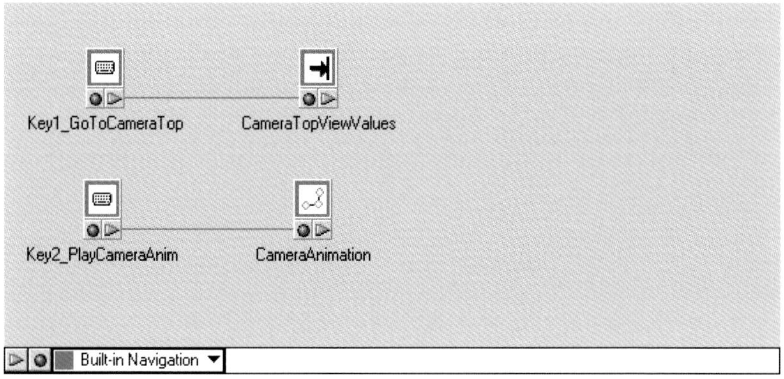

18. In the Simulation Tree window, expand the **LogicCreation** frame and select **Key1_GoToCameraTop**. In the Property Bar, select the drop-down list from the **keycode** field. Select **VK_1** from the list. This sets the KeyboardSensor to respond to the keystroke of 1.
19. In the Simulation Tree window, expand the **LogicCreation** frame and select **Key2_PlayCameraAnim**. In the Property Bar, select the drop-down list from the **keycode** field. Select **VK_2** from the list. This sets the KeyboardSensor to respond to the keystroke of 2.
20. Run the simulation. Your default position is the camera view from the top.
21. Press **2**. This triggers the animation (established in the modeling program) to run.
22. Explore this view by using the left and right mouse buttons to zoom in and out and move from side to side.
23. Press **2** again to repeat the animation.
24. Press **1**. This triggers the camera view from the top.
25. Explore this camera's angles and positions.
26. Close the simulation window. Save the simulation as **Cameraa_Animation.eoz** and then close EON.

Discussion

discuss

How does the ability to import cameras increase EON Studio's flexibility?

Can you think of a situation in which working within EON to adjust cameras and animations would be an easier task?

Lights

Like cameras, placing lights and adjusting lighting settings is also much easier in a modeling program than it is in EON Studio. Modeling programs are designed to allow you to move and set lighting parameters easily—usually using object-oriented methods. Although lighting can be set and adjusted in EON, it is another tedious and time-consuming endeavor.

Typically, when you import an object with lighting, you will see a Frame node that includes "omni" or "spot" in its name, as shown in Figure 3.1.10. These frames will have a Light node underneath them. After you have completed the importation process, you should regroup all of these frames and nodes into a group named Lights.

FIGURE 3.1.10 Imported lights in the simulation tree

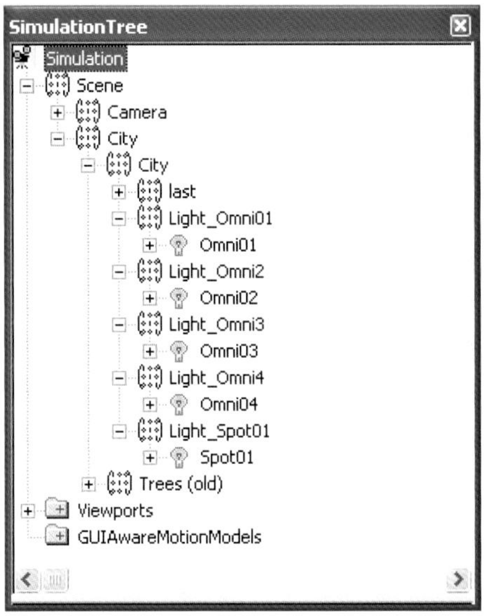

Summary

In this lesson you:

- Considered several important items that should be established within your model prior to importing it into EON.
- Discussed various methods of grouping and naming objects as well as establishing hierarchies for your models before you import them into EON.
- Explored the positioning of pivot points within models and the impact they can have on an object's placement and behavior within a simulation.
- Developed an understanding of how geometry optimization can reduce the resources used by your simulation and increase the speed of loading the simulation.
- Discussed the benefits of establishing camera positions and animations in your modeling program versus in EON.
- Gained an understanding of the increased efficiency of setting lighting for your scene within your modeling program versus within EON.

LESSON 3.2

Import and Place 3D Objects

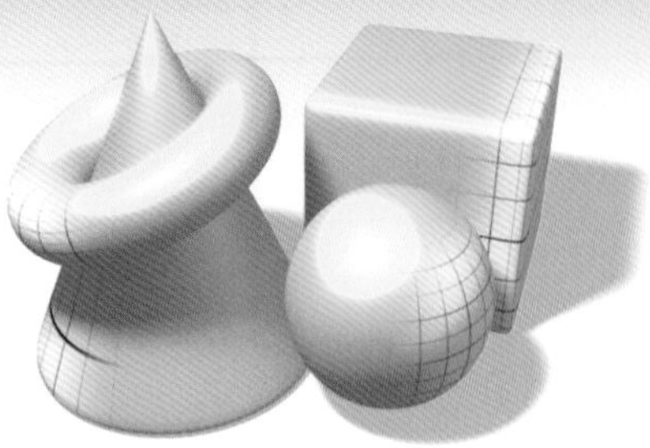

Objectives

In this lesson you will:

- Study the procedures for importing 3D objects into EON.
- Recognize import file formats that are compatible with EON.
- Discuss EON's file format importers.
- Understand how you can use EON Raptor™.
- Explore the basic considerations for importing VRML files.
- Look at the history of VRML.
- Learn how to import noncompatible 3D object file formats.
- Examine techniques you can use to position objects in EON.
- Develop an understanding of the DegreeOfFreedom node.
- Become familiar with how imported files can improve a simulation's appearance.

Key Terms

composability

DegreeOfFreedom node

DragManager prototype

DragSelector prototype

extensibility

file format importer

Mover prototype

MoveRotateArrows3D prototype

QuickPos prototype

Raptor

SaveFrameValues prototype

scalability

StickyMover prototype

Virtual Reality Modeling Language (VRML)

Procedures for Importing 3D Objects into EON

It is important to remember that only the simulation itself is built in EON. This means that any 3D model, image, sound, or video in your simulation must be imported into EON. The complete set of import procedures will differ depending on the file format you are importing, but the first steps are the same for all file formats:

1. Select a Frame node (parent to the imported object).
2. From the menu bar, Select File > Import.
3. Select the appropriate file format.
4. Select and open the 3D object file you want to import into EON.

tips+tricks

After you select a file and click Open, EON will begin building the simulation tree. During this phase, some information is logged in the EON Log window. You can view this information by selecting Windows > Log from the menu bar.

STORYBOARD

Node Properties and Routing in the Simulation Creation Process

As we delve deeper into the process of creating a simulation, we move on to new topics within our storyboard.

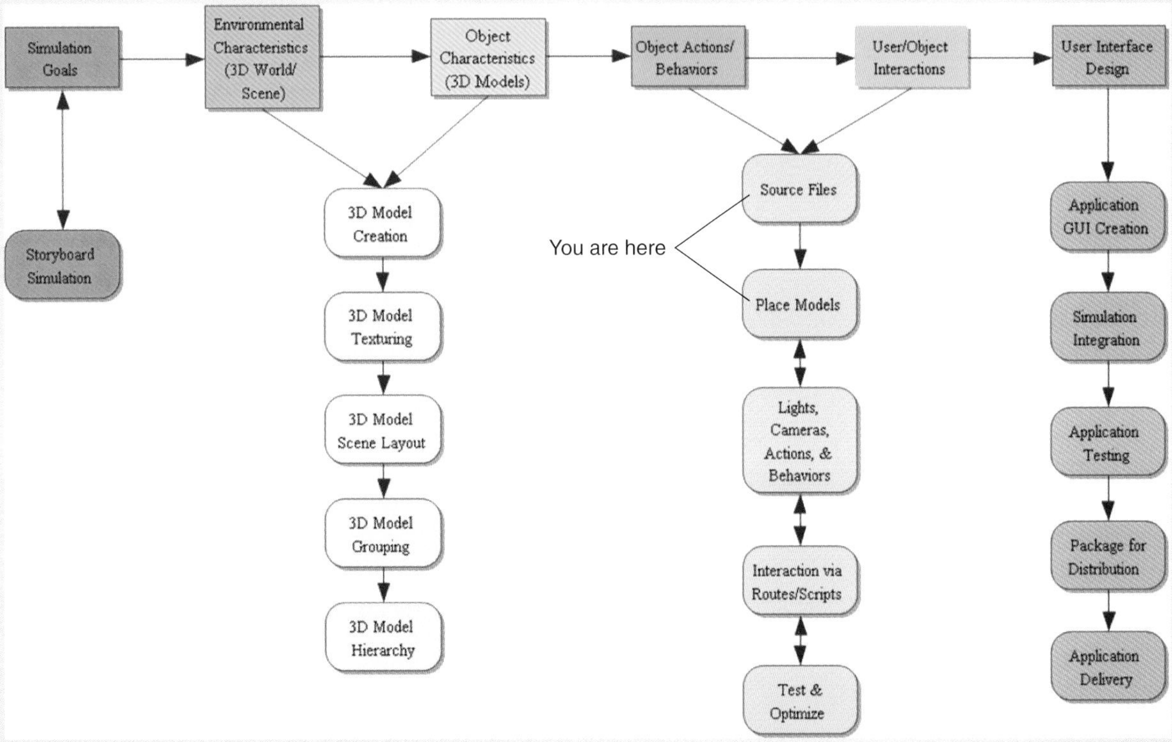

In this lesson, we will learn about importing source files, or 3D objects. We will also discuss the various methods that can be used to position, or place, these objects.

Importing Compatible 3D Object File Formats

Depending on the types of objects and files you import into EON, you should consider several things. The primary elements that you bring into EON are the 3D objects themselves, which are imported from modeling programs. When you import

3D models, the original files are converted to formats that are compatible with EON. Table 3.2.1 describes the 3D file formats supported by EON Studio.

TABLE 3.2.1 3D File Formats Supported in EON Studio

3D Objects	File Format
3D Studio (*.3ds)	Autodesk's 3D Studio's original native DOS file format. All Windows versions of 3D Studio can export files to the 3ds format for backwards compatibility and interchangeability. A 3ds filename can contain a maximum of eight characters.
3ds MAX (*.max)	Autodesk's 3D Studio Windows file format. EON Raptor is capable of reading the .max file format for 3D Studio (versions 6.0, 7.0, 8.0, 9.0, and 2008) and converting the contents into an.eoz file that can be edited in EON Studio.
ACIS & Solid Edge (*.sat, *.sab, *.par)	Any program based on the ACIS toolkit from Spatial Corp. can write ACIS SAT/SAB geometry files. Products that use ACIS are CADKEY, AutoCAD, Electric Image Modeler, triSpectives, MicroStation, Solid Edge (by Intergraph), and CorelCAD.
Okino transfer file format (*.bdf)	EON supports this format so that you can transfer any Okino files exported from the standalone PolyTrans tool to EON.
DWG (*.dwg)	The AutoCAD DWG file format is supported up to version 2005.
DXF ASCII/Binary (*.dxf)	The AutoCAD DXF file format is recognized by many applications and has become the de facto standard for interchanging 2D and 3D data.
IGES v5.3 (*.igs, *.iges)	The IGES format can be exported by many CAD and 3D software applications. This complex format has many varieties.
LightWave (*.lw, *.scn)	LightWave 3D (commonly known as LightWave), developed by NewTek, is a high-end computer graphics program.
OpenFlight (*.flt)	OpenFlight is an industry standard real-time 3D-scene description format developed, owned, and maintained by MultiGen, Inc. It was originally developed to provide database transportability within the visual simulation community.
Pro/Engineer .SLP (*.slp)	The Pro/Engineer SLP Render file format is generated by PTC's Pro/Engineer. It is a simple format, containing only triangles with vertex normals and a color for each triangle.
Softimage (*.hrc, *.dsc)	This is the native file format for Microsoft's Softimage.
SolidWorks (*.sldprt, *.sldasm)	This is the SolidWorks Part and Assembly file format.
Stereo Lithography .STL (.stl)	This is the STL file format that is typically used for rapid prototyping in CAD programs. It is a simple, triangle-based format.
trueSpace (*.cob, *.scn)	This is the file format used by Caligari trueSpace.
USGS DEM (*.dem)	This is the United States Geological Survey (USGS) digital elevation model (DEM) file format. Many 3D landscape files are available in this format on the Internet.
VRML 2.0 (*.wrl)/VRML 97(*.wrl)	VRML, short for Virtual Reality Modeling Language, is a specification for displaying 3D objects on the Internet. The first importer is provided by Okino. The second importer, developed by EON, provides the ability to import key frames.
WaveFront (*.obj)	The WaveFront OBJ (object) file format is used by WaveFront's Advanced Visualizer application to store geometric objects composed of lines, polygons, free-form curves, and surfaces.
XGL/ZGL (*.xgl, *.zgl)	The XML-based transfer file format is exportable from many popular CAD applications.

Using File Format Importer

Most formats, including 3ds Max (formerly 3D Studio MAX) and LightWave files, are loaded using a ***file format importer*** and inserted in the simulation tree. The import procedure for all imported formats is executed in two steps after the file is opened. First, the converter loads and converts the file to an internal database representation. In this step, the dialog box for loading the 3D file into the converter contains options specific for each format. In the second step, an EON hierarchy is built from the database created by the file format importer. Here, you enter the options for building the EON simulation tree. All geometry is converted to polygon meshes, and all textures are converted to an EON-compatible format. You will see them as a hierarchy of Frame nodes and Mesh nodes under the Frame node from which you started the import procedure.

Activity 3.2.1: Importing 3D Objects into an Existing Room

1. Open EON. Open **Activity_3.2.1.eoz** from the data files for Module 3 Lesson 2.
2. Save the file as **Apartment_Imported.eoz**.
3. View the simulation. Pan to view the empty dining room in front of the kitchen. Close the simulation window.
4. In the simulation tree, expand **Scene > Floorplan > Dining_Room**. With the Dining_Room frame selected, add a **Frame** node and rename it **Dining_Chair**.
5. With the Dining_Chair frame selected, choose **File > Import**. The Import menu will display, as shown in Figure 3.2.1.

FIGURE 3.2.1 Import menu

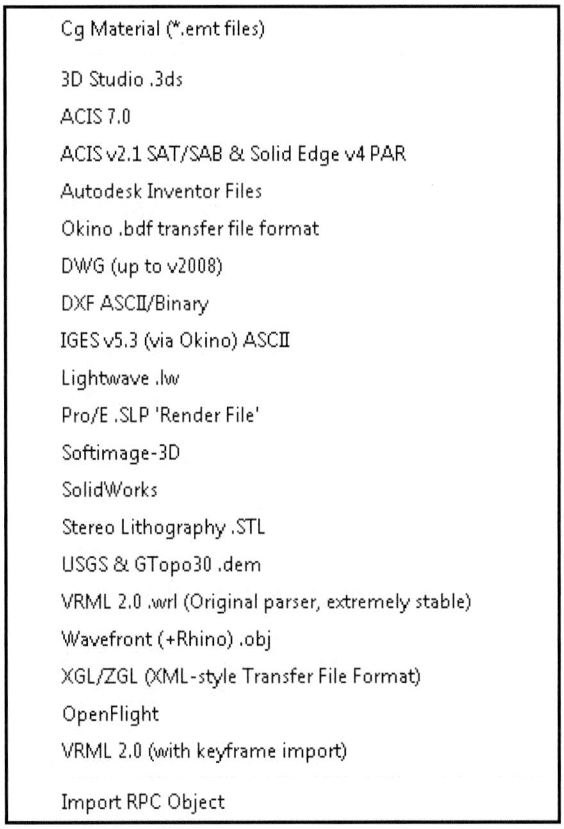
Cg Material (*.emt files)
3D Studio .3ds
ACIS 7.0
ACIS v2.1 SAT/SAB & Solid Edge v4 PAR
Autodesk Inventor Files
Okino .bdf transfer file format
DWG (up to v2008)
DXF ASCII/Binary
IGES v5.3 (via Okino) ASCII
Lightwave .lw
Pro/E .SLP 'Render File'
Softimage-3D
SolidWorks
Stereo Lithography .STL
USGS & GTopo30 .dem
VRML 2.0 .wrl (Original parser, extremely stable)
Wavefront (+Rhino) .obj
XGL/ZGL (XML-style Transfer File Format)
OpenFlight
VRML 2.0 (with keyframe import)
Import RPC Object

6. Select **3D Studio .3ds**.
7. Browse to the data files for this lesson and double-click the **Dining_Chair.3DS** file. The 3D Studio Geometry Import Plug-In dialog box appears, as shown in Figure 3.2.2. This dialog box provides import options for loading the file into the internal database

troubleshooting

This activity may require EON Professional. Depending on your configuration of EON modules, you may not be able to complete this activity.

format that will be displayed. Note that these options are specific to the import file format, in this case, 3D Studio. Verify that the settings match those in Figure 3.2.2.

FIGURE 3.2.2 3D Studio Geometry Import Plug-In dialog box

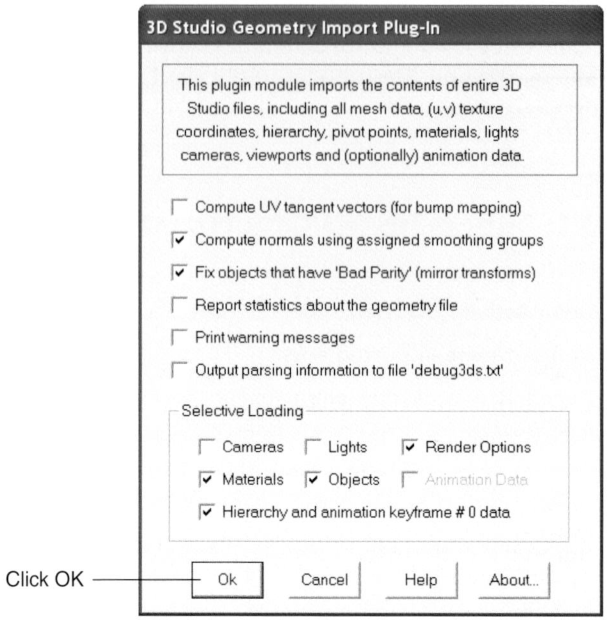

8. Click **OK**. The Geometry import dialog box is displayed. This dialog box allows you to define options for building the EON simulation tree. If necessary, click **Browse** to set the path to the location of the data files for this lesson. Verify that your settings match the ones shown in Figure 3.2.3.

FIGURE 3.2.3 Geometry import dialog box

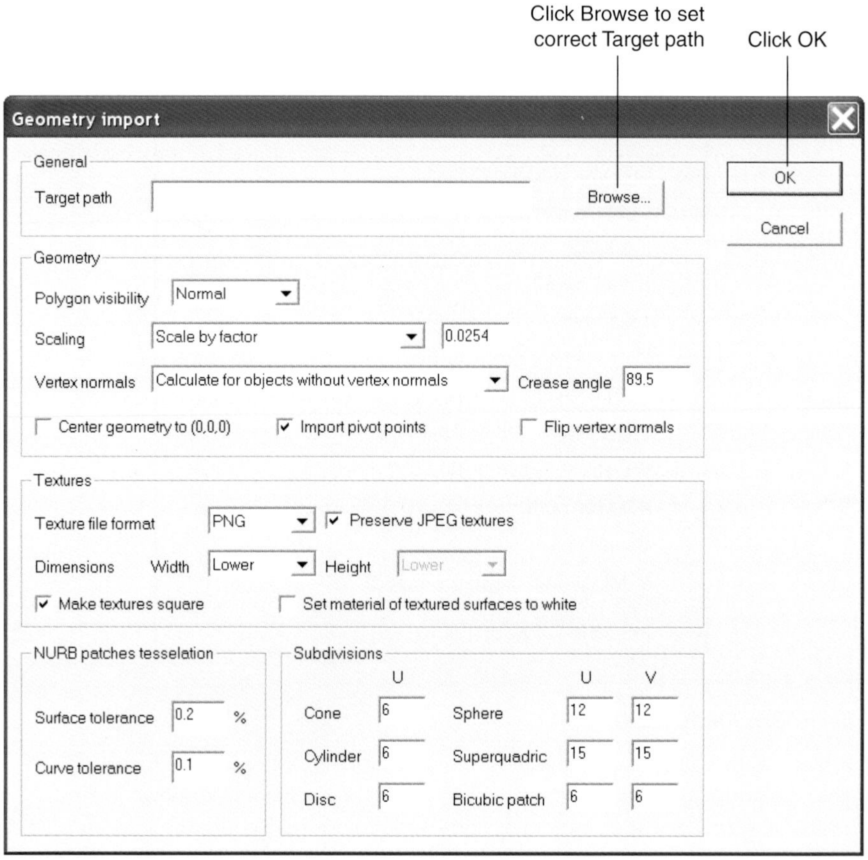

tips+tricks

From the Import file dialog box, you can choose to add search paths to files associated with the main file. These could be texture files, stored in a directory apart from the main file. Click the Add Path button. A dialog box is displayed that lets you browse to the directories that you would like to add to the search path. You can specify several directories by separating them with a semicolon (for example, C:\TEXTURES;C:\MORE_TEXTURES). If the importer cannot find a texture file, it will report this in the EON Studio Log window.

9. Click **OK**. The Import progress dialog box, shown in Figure 3.2.4, will be displayed as the objects are converted into an EON-supported format.

FIGURE 3.2.4 Import progress dialog box

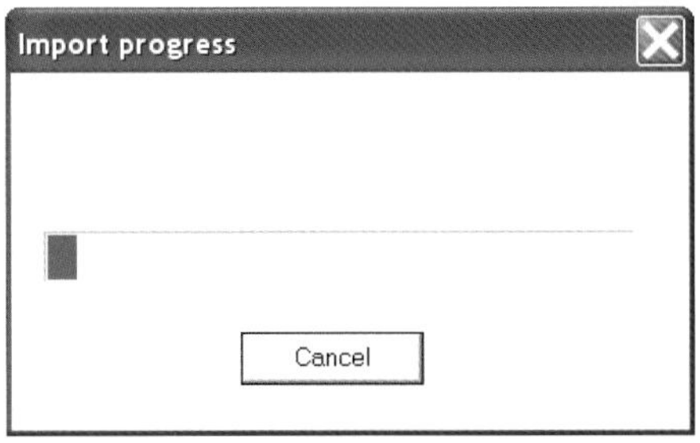

10. If the Material Name Collision dialog box appears as shown in Figure 3.2.5, read the description of each option and then click **Overwrite All** to continue.

FIGURE 3.2.5 Material Name Collision dialog box

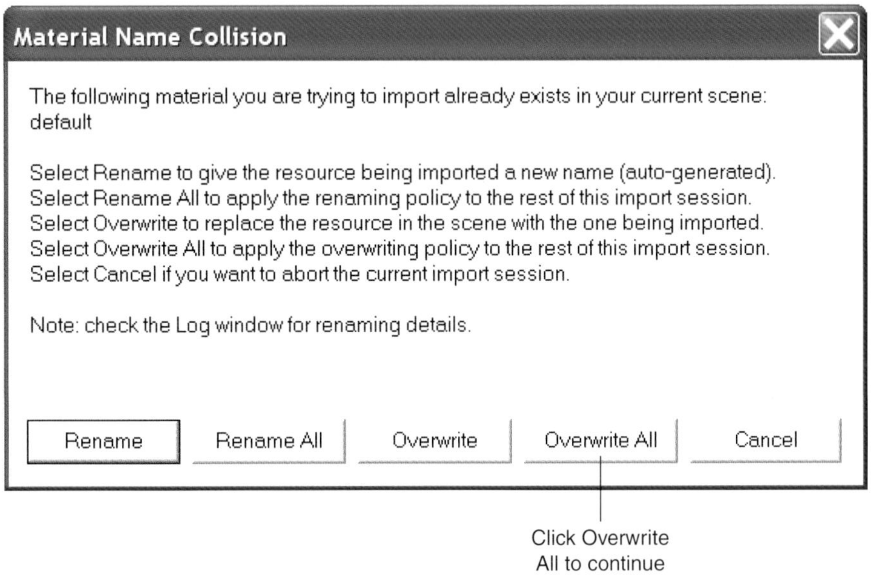

11. Under the **Dining_Chair** frame, add a **KeyMove** node.
12. Run the simulation.
13. Using the X, Y, and Z keys with the arrow keys, position the dining chair in the simulation.
14. Delete the **KeyMove** node when the dining chair is correctly positioned. You will no longer be able to use the arrow keys to move the dining chair.

troubleshooting

If the material you are importing already exists in your current scene, the Material Name Collision dialog box will be displayed (see Figure 3.2.5).

tips+tricks

After importing the Dining_Table.3DS file, you may need to use the Zoom Extents tool in order to view the table in the simulation. While the simulation is running, select the Dining_Table frame in the simulation tree and then click the Zoom Extents button on the toolbar. (It may be necessary to minimize or move the simulation window to access the Zoom Extents button on the toolbar.)

If you cannot find the dining table in relation to the apartment, copy the Position values for the dining chair and paste them in the Position values for the dining table. The table should be moved to a location near the dining chair, making it easier to position the table.

15. Under Scene > Floorplan > Dining_Room > select the **Dining_Chair** frame. In the Property Bar, select the **SetStartValues** box (see Figure 3.2.6).

FIGURE 3.2.6 Chair Property Bar

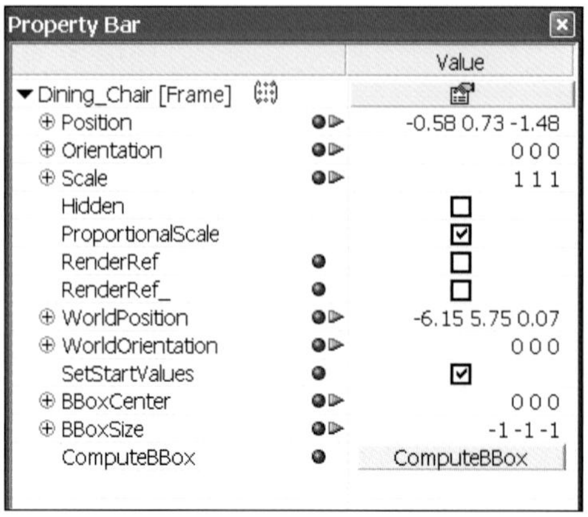

16. Close the simulation window. Save the simulation. Run the simulation to verify that the dining chair is positioned correctly. Close the simulation window again.
17. In the simulation tree, under Scene > Floorplan > Dining_Room, add a **Frame** node and rename it **Dining_Table**.
18. Repeat steps 4 thru 16 to import and place the **Dining_Table.3DS** file into the scene.
19. Save the simulation and keep it open to use in Activity 3.2.2.

BEST PRACTICES

Scaling During the Import Process

During the import process in Activity 3.2.1, you were instructed to adjust the Scaling factor of the imported geometry as shown in Figure 3.2.3. Why were you instructed to make the adjustment, and how is that value determined? Believe it or not, the Scaling value is determined purely through trial and error—although experience is a factor.

When we imported this model and ran the simulation (while developing this activity), the object was so large, and we were zoomed in so tight, that we were well beyond the clipping plane (actually inside the object) and therefore only saw a blank white screen. If that is all you can see, you have no way of knowing where you are in the virtual world. You can adjust the view by clicking the Zoom Extents button or by using the mouse to navigate in the environment, but you would still be dealing with a large image. Adjusting the scaling during the import saves time and avoids the trouble of trying to deal with an inordinately large model.

If you were trying to determine this value by yourself, you might first try cutting the size of the model in half (scaling by a factor of .5). Then, run the simulation to see the effect of that adjustment. If it is not enough of a change or it is too much of a change, you can delete the imported model and its associated files and then import it again, adjusting the scaling factor in the direction necessary to create the right results.

With time and experience, you will find that you can accurately gauge the amount of scaling required to import your models in appropriate sizes.

EON Raptor

EON ***Raptor*** is a 3ds Max file format importer that enables you to display and interact with 3ds Max content in real time with intuitive controls. Simple interactive behaviors can also be authored rapidly without leaving 3ds Max.

The completed application can be published to a web page for viewing with a browser, exported to a standalone file for viewing with the free EON Viewer application, or exported to EON Studio for further editing.

Using Raptor, the 3ds Max user can create interactive walkthroughs and design reviews within minutes, saving time and costs while offering a more flexible design tool due to its interactive nature.

Raptor provides the following features:

- Real-time 3D visualization
- Seamless integration with 3ds Max 6.0 or later
- Full-screen support
- Intuitive navigation and user interface
- Support for quick and easy content distribution over the Internet
- HTML templates for rapid web integration
- Highly compressed file format that supports customizable geometry and texture compressions
- Export function for all 3ds Max content, including animations, lights, cameras, parent-child relationships, pivot point, multimaterials, and so on
- Interactions created to trigger animations by clicking selected objects
- Radiosity solutions exported as light maps (texture baking) or vertex color data

tips+tricks

With a Frame node selected, from the menu bar, choose File > Import. Notice that two VRML options appear in the Import list, *VRML 2.0 .wrl (original parser that is extremely stable)* and *VRML 2.0 (with KeyFrame import)*. EON recommends using the second option, *VRML 2.0 (with KeyFrame import)* when importing a VRML file.

VRML

EON enables you to import and use VRML97 files (formerly VRML2.0) in your simulations. ***Virtual Reality Modeling Language (VRML)*** is most commonly referred to by its initials. VRML is a specification for displaying 3D objects on the Internet. Its designers intended VRML to become the standard language for interactive simulation within the World Wide Web—a sort of HTML for 3D content.

History of VRML

VRML was initially conceived in early 1994 at the first annual World Wide Web Conference in Geneva, Switzerland. A congregation of 3D enthusiasts began discussing the need for virtual reality interfaces to the World Wide Web. The term Virtual Reality Markup Language (VRML) was coined. The conference attendees envisioned it as a file format that would bring 3D to the masses. The word "Markup" was later changed to "Modeling" to reflect the graphical nature of VRML.

Shortly after the Geneva conference, the group created a mailing list to discuss the development of specifications for the first version of VRML. After much deliberation, list members agreed to use the Open Inventor American Standard Code for Information Interchange (ASCII) File Format from Silicon Graphics, Inc. (SGI) to form the basis of VRML. To streamline the design and implementation process, it was determined that VRML 1.0 would not support interactive behaviors. When planning VRML 2.0, the interface developers identified three additional requirements they thought were important to include: composability, scalability, and extensibility.

Composability deals with the interrelationships of components. For example, a user might create a virtual classroom and place it in a virtual school building. This school building could be placed on a street with other buildings, which could be placed in a city, which could be placed on a planet orbiting a sun. In this composition, each piece is independent. This means that someone can take that classroom and place it in a different building on a different street somewhere else on the planet because everything that makes it a classroom, such as the door, the light switch, and the teacher's desk, is contained within the classroom model.

web links

In December 1998, the VRML Consortium (formerly the VRML Architecture Group) expanded its charter and became the Web3D Consortium. Today, the Web3D Consortium is utilizing its broad-based industry support to develop the X3D (*.x3d) specification as a successor to VRML for communicating 3D on the web. You can find the latest 3D communication news and events at the Web3D Consortium website (*http://www.web3d.org*).

troubleshooting

The X3d (*.x3d) format is not supported directly within EON Studio, but can be imported through EON CAD.

Scalability allows worlds of arbitrary size to be created. Using VRML, it must be possible to see a galaxy, zoom in to see a star system, a planet, a city, a block, a house, a woman working in her garden, a plant in the garden, the fruit on the plant, and finally a bug eating the fruit. This would be difficult for the VRML developers to accomplish because of limits in the precision of computer hardware, but they realized it was important to prevent worlds from having arbitrary size or detail limits.

Extensibility provides an author with the ability to extend the language's capability to serve a special purpose. For instance, you could create multiuser worlds or add new geometric objects to VRML. The group decided that scripting was the best way to achieve the extensibility requirement.

In the fall of 1995, the VRML Architecture Group (VAG) was formed to steer the VRML 2.0 effort. At the time, designers from Sony and Mitra were collaborating to redesign the way VRML communicated animation and interaction data. It was widely agreed that the original SGI design and Sony/Mitra design had benefits and drawbacks, so engineers from SGI and the Sony/Mitra effort collaborated to redesign VRML's communication structure.

The first VRML-specific conference was scheduled for late 1995 in San Diego. A few weeks before the conference, Microsoft released a preliminary proposal for a language called ActiveVRML. This project, which was drastically different from any other proposal, was hyped as a competing proposal for VRML 2.0. In addition to Microsoft (ActiveVRML) and the SGI/Sony/Mitra collaboration (Moving Worlds), other groups submitted their own proposals for discussion, including Sun (HoloWeb), Apple (Out of This World), and others. A total of six proposals were discussed. The SGI/Sony/Mitra proposal had the widest support base, so the VAG agreed to use Moving Worlds as the basis for VRML 2.0.

In early 1997, VRML 2.0 was presented to the International Standards Organization (ISO), which oversees most of the specifications in use in the language computing community. By late 1997, a final ISO version, dubbed VRML 97, was approved.

Supported VRML Nodes

EON supports the PNG and JPG texture formats, with the following VRML97 nodes:

Appearance
Box
Cone
Cylinder
Extrusion
Elevation Grid
Group
Image Texture
IndexedFaceSet
Material
Pixel Texture
PositionInterpolator
OrientationInterpolator
Shape
Sphere
Texture Transforms
Transform

EON vs. VRML Coordinate Systems

EON's coordinate system is based on Open GL. Table 3.2.2 shows the relation between the coordinate system used for EON and the one used for VRML.

TABLE 3.2.2 Coordinate System Relationship Between EON and VRML

EON	VRML
X	X
Y	Z
Z	–Y

Importing Noncompatible 3D Object File Formats

Although not all 3D file formats are directly compatible with EON, often you can import the files within an EON simulation. To do so, you need access to the program originally used to create or edit the file. After you open the file in the original program, export the object in the 3ds Max file format. Now you can import the 3ds Max file using the EON file format importer.

Positioning Prototypes

EON provides several prototypes that can be used to help you position objects within a simulation.

tips+tricks

The MoveRotateArrows3D prototype is found in the Object Movers library.

MoveRotateArrows3D Prototype vs. DragManager and DragSelector Prototypes

Because of its quick and simple setup, reliability, and intuitive drag behavior, the ***MoveRotateArrows3D prototype*** is usually recommended for positioning objects. To use this prototype, place it under the Camera frame, specify a root node, and you will be able to move all child frames under the root node using drag and drop. Arrows will show the different directions in which the objects can be moved. This method is extremely useful for developers, as well as for planners who need to reposition objects within a simulation. After all objects have been moved to their final position, use the ***SaveFrameValues prototype*** to save the objects' placement.

tips+tricks

Remember that the SaveFrameValues prototype saves frame values as the simulation is closing. Therefore, set up which frame values should be saved before you run the simulation by copying frame references to the prototype's Frames field.

Although the MoveRotateArrows3D prototype is generally recommended, the ***DragManager prototype*** and ***DragSelector prototype*** contain many additional features that may be worth the extra setup time. For instance, this prototype has a scaling option that is not available in MoveRotateArrows3D. If you choose to use the DragSelector prototype, you must place it in every frame to which you will be dragging objects. You also must use a ClickSensor prototype and establish a route when using the DragSelector prototype.

Table 3.2.3 discusses the various features of the MoveRotateArrows3D prototype versus the DragManager and DragSelector prototypes.

TABLE 3.2.3 MoveRotateArrows3D Prototype vs. DragManager and DragSelector Prototypes

	DragManager and DragSelector Prototypes	**MoveRotateArrows3D**
Setup time	Longer. Every object you want to move must have its own DragSelector and ClickSensor. Also, a route must be connected between ClickSensor and DragSelector.	Shorter. Specify one root node so all child nodes can be moved.
Dragging	Not great. Dragging with a mouse is usually too fast or too slow because the speed is relative to the distance of the object from the camera. When the camera pitch is more than 45 degrees, however, the type of movement is changed; it is similar to the MoveRotateArrows3D prototype. This movement mode is called PlanMode; you are looking down on the objects.	Optimized. Dragging is like assuming there is a floor at the z level of the object, and the object moves in the direction that the mouse cursor points.
Objects that are same z level	These can be moved as usual.	No movement is possible. The camera height should be higher or lower than the object's height. Works better if the camera is looking down at the object. Camera pitch can be 0; height difference is more important.

(continued)

TABLE 3.2.3 MoveRotateArrows3D Prototype vs. DragManager and DragSelector Prototypes (continued)

	DragManager and DragSelector Prototypes	MoveRotateArrows3D
Arrows	No arrows used.	Arrows are optional, but are on by default. Arrows can show that an object is selected. If no arrows are used, the value of the MoveInXYUsingCSRoot field should be true.
Rotating	Can rotate in all directions (heading, pitch, and roll) by pressing keys. R (rotate) controls heading and pitch by default. (Rotate still requires dragging the mouse after you click the object.) R and X control heading. R and C control pitch. R and Z control roll.	Rotate by clicking the rotate arrows. The object rotates a certain interval per click. Pitch and roll are not possible.
Scaling	Only works with the old mesh nodes.	Not possible.
Show statistics	Yes. X, Y, and Z values shown as moving an object when the ShowStatistics field of DragManager is true.	No.
DOF limits	Yes. Limits position and orientation to within an area/angles. Off by default.	No.
Move in XZ plane	Yes. Press the Shift key.	No. An arrow enables you to drag in z direction.
Deleting object	Yes. Press the Delete key.	No.
Undo	Yes. Press the Backspace key.	No.
Restart	Yes. Press F12 to return all objects to their initial position.	No.
Customized settings	Yes. Each DragSelecter prototype can have different settings so that a particular object may not be moved or deleted but can be rotated and so on. Settings such as speed and DOF limits also can be customized.	No.
Buttons to control	Yes. Press F7 to view the buttons. Can limit movement to certain directions, delete, undo, reset, and simulate holding down keys including Shift, X, C, and Z.	No buttons.
Compatible with other prototypes	No.	Yes. The NodeToMove outEvent can be sent to other prototypes, such as the Mover prototype, so you can move the selected object in other ways like buttons or keys.
Walk interference	To stop the Walk node while dragging, you must connect a route from the Dragging field to the SetRun_field of the Walk node.	Add a reference to the Walk node in the DisableWhenMoving field.
Root node optional	Not applicable.	If you don't specify a root node, you can select which objects and frames should be moved by using a ClickSensor and SendToGroup prototype to send a frame reference to the NodeToMove field of the MoveRotateArrows3D prototype. OR Use the ClickSensorPlus prototype to send a different Frame node to the NodeToMove field. For example, instead of the root's child frame, it could be a grandchild or great-grandchild. Or, it could be the parent of the selected Shape node.

Mover Prototype

EON provides several additional positioning prototypes. For many users, the ***Mover prototype*** may be easier to understand. With this prototype, you can move objects by using the arrow keys. You do not need to use the combination of a letter key and an arrow key, like the KeyMove node.

- Use Ctrl + arrows to move up and down.
- Press Enter to toggle between a smooth motion and a step motion.
- Press End to toggle the arrow keys to control rotation. (Press Ctrl to roll.)

StickyMover Prototype

The ***StickyMover prototype*** enables you to move an object along a surface. The center of the object will contact the surface. Shift the pivot point if you need to contact the surface at a different point.

QuickPos Prototype

After the ***QuickPos prototype*** has been placed under the Camera frame, and a frame reference has been placed under it, you can press Q to display a box where the frame's position information can be viewed.

DegreeOfFreedom Node

When you import 3D models into EON, you do not always have the option of importing the pivot points. All the objects may come in with the same pivot position. To allow you to rotate objects around a new pivot position, use the DegreeOfFreedom node.

The ***DegreeOfFreedom node***, sometimes referred to as the DOF node, defines a local coordinate system that can be used to transform underlying geometries. The DegreeOfFreedom node also can limit the freedom of movements for its child nodes. Using the DegreeOfFreedom node can be confusing because the Property Bar contains OriginPosition and OriginOrientation fields as well as Position and Orientation fields (see Figure 3.2.7).

FIGURE 3.2.7 DegreeOfFreedom node Property Bar

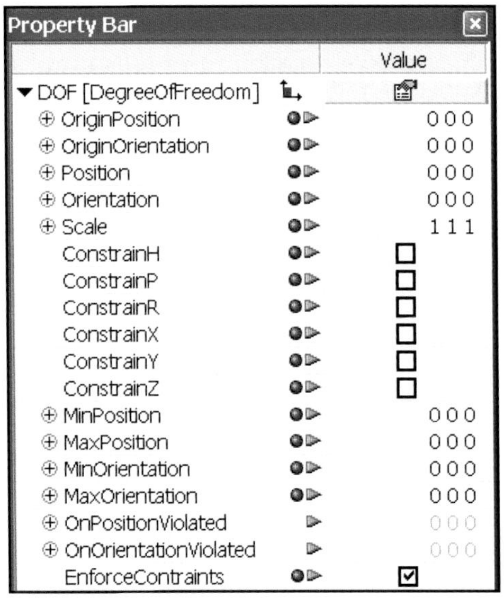

What is the difference? The Position and Orientation fields act like a normal frame and affect the position of objects under it. If you do not have any values in the Position and Orientation fields and then you change the OriginPosition and OriginOrientation fields, you will not see any difference in the position or orientation of the objects under the mesh. You only notice a difference when you start to rotate the objects by changing the Orientation field. Table 3.2.4 details the DegreeOfFreedom Property Bar fields.

TABLE 3.2.4 DegreeOfFreedom Node Property Bar Fields

DegreeOfFreedom Property Bar Fields	Description
OriginPosition	Specifies the location of the pivot point for meshes under the DOF node relative to the position of the parent frame.
OriginOrientation	Specifies the rotation of the axes for meshes under the DOF node relative to the orientation of the parent frame.
Position	Translation of underlying geometry. Same function as Position in the Frame node.
Orientation	Rotation of underlying geometry. Same function as Orientation in the Frame node.
Scale	Scaling of underlying geometry. Same function as Scale in the Frame node.
ConstrainH	When selected, Heading is constrained by values in MinOrientation and MaxOrientation.
ConstrainP	When selected Pitch is constrained by values in MinOrientation and MaxOrientation.
ConstrainR	When selected Roll is constrained by values in MinOrientation and MaxOrientation.
ConstrainX	When selected X position is constrained by values in MinPosition and MaxPosition.
ConstrainY	When selected Y position is constrained by values in MinPosition and MaxPosition
ConstrainZ	When selected Z position is constrained by values in MinPosition and MaxPosition.
MinPosition	Minimum Position values for X, Y, and Z.
MaxPosition	Maximum Position values for X, Y, and Z.
MinOrientation	Minimum Rotation values for H, P, and R.
MaxOrientation	Maximum Rotation values for H, P, and R.
OnPosition Violated	Sent if position constraints are violated. Each parameter tells the dimension (X, Y, or Z) in which the violation occurred, whereas the value of the parameter tells whether the violation was on the minimum or maximum side. Value = –1, MinPosition value was violated. Value = 0, no violation on this dimension. Value = 1, MaxPosition value was violated. Example: (0.0,1.0,0.0) means that the Y coordinate exceeded its maximum allowable value.
OnOrientation Violated	Sent whenever orientation constraints are violated. Works the same way as the OnPositionViolated event.
Force Constrained	When not selected a movement can be performed below or beyond the constrained values. The fields OnPositionViolated and OnOrientationViolated will be sent when position and orientation constraints are violated. When selected the movement cannot go below or beyond the constrained values.

If your pivot point is not in the correct position, the DOFMover prototype can be used to modify the pivot point. It provides a way to view the pivot point's location on the object and enables you to change its position in EON Studio. The DOFMover prototype has a 3DPointer object, also known as a 3D cursor, that represents the pivot position (OriginPosition) of the DegreeOfFreedom node. The DOFMover prototype helps you visualize the pivot position and allows you to move it.

Activity 3.2.2: Modifying the Degree of Freedom on a Model

1. Continue working with the open simulation file **Apartment_Imported.eoz** from Activity 3.2.1.
2. Save the simulation as **Apartment_DOF.eoz.**
3. In the simulation tree, expand **Scene > Floorplan > Dining_Room**.
4. Click **Dining_Room,** click **File > Import,** and select **3D Studio .3ds.**
5. Browse to the data files for Module 3 Lesson 2, and double-click the **Dining_Chair_Bad_Pivot** file. The 3D Studio Geometry Import Plug-In dialog box is displayed.
6. In the Selective Loading section, ensure that check marks appear in all check boxes *except* Cameras, Lights, and Animation Data, as shown in Figure 3.2.8.

FIGURE 3.2.8 3D Studio Geometry Import Plug-In dialog box

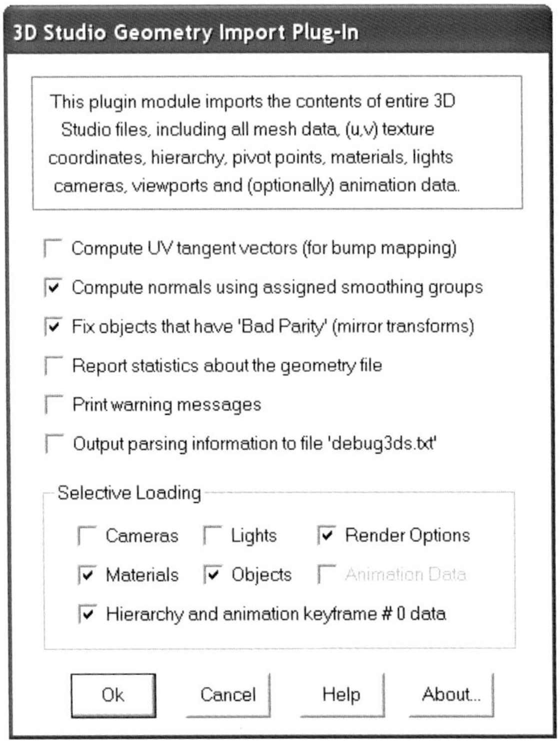

7. Click **OK.** The Geometry Import dialog box is displayed. Ensure that the Target path is set for the location of the data files for Module 3, Lesson 2.
8. In the Geometry section, ensure that the Scaling option is set to **Scale by factor** and the factor value is set to **.0254** (1 inch = .0254 meters).
9. If necessary, clear the check box for **Center geometry to (0.0.0).**
10. If necessary, select the **Import pivot points** check box.

tips+tricks

Because our simulation already has cameras and lights, you do not need to import additional cameras and lights in step 6.

11. In the Textures section, select the **Make textures square** check box, if necessary. The dialog box should now resemble Figure 3.2.9.

FIGURE 3.2.9 Geometry import dialog box

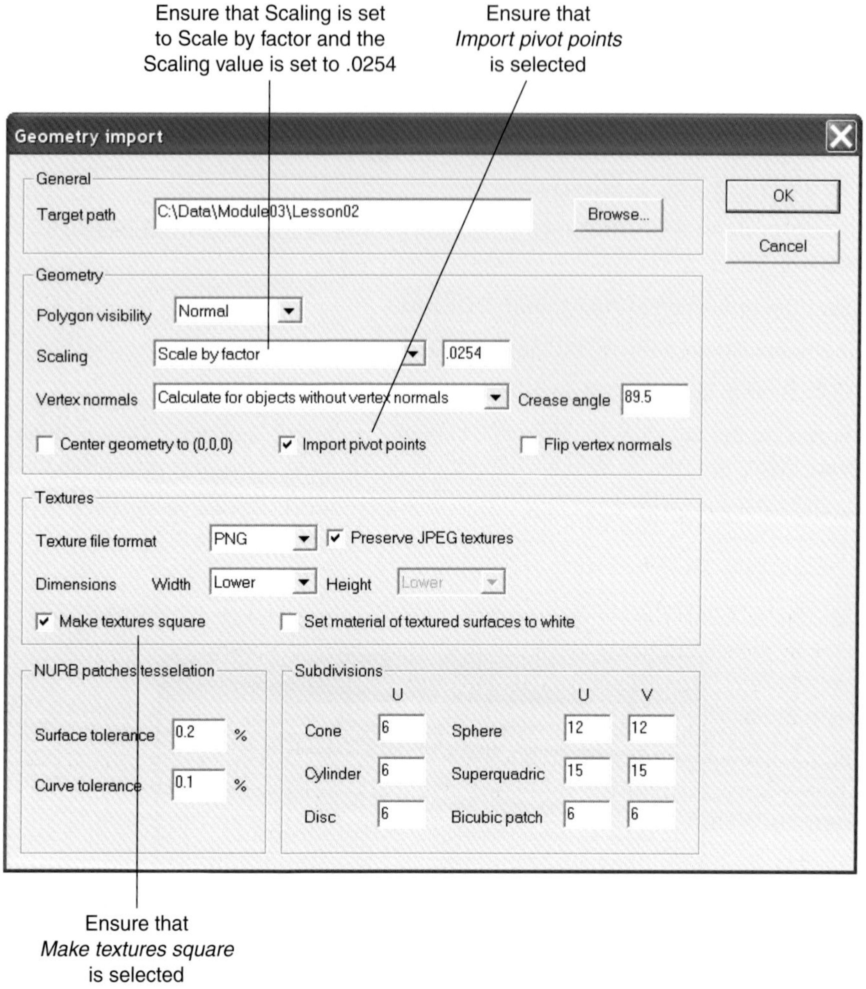

12. Click **OK** to accept the default settings for all other fields in the dialog box. The mesh file associated with the imported object will be converted into EON's internal geometry format (.eog), copies of any associated texture files will be stored within the EON simulation file, and the Import progress dialog box will be displayed.
13. If the Material Name Collision dialog box appears, click **Overwrite All.**
14. In the simulation tree, expand the following path: **Scene > Floorplan > Dining_Room > Dining_Chair_Bad_Pivot**.
15. In the Property Bar, enter the following coordinates for the Position properties of this node: **6.456 -3.622 -1.554**. Leave the Orientation values set at 0 0 0.
16. Save the simulation.
17. Run the simulation.

18. If necessary, click and drag the left mouse button to activate the Walk node and view the apartment area to the left of the kitchen. When the dining area is visible, note that you will now see two styles of dining chairs. Also note that Dining_Chair_Bad_Pivot simply needs to be rotated around the Z access (moving in the H orientation) to face the dining table.
19. Close the simulation window.
20. Drag and drop a **KeyMove** node under the Dining_Chair_Bad_Pivot frame. To avoid confusion, remember to use the Edit > Find option to delete other KeyMove nodes within your simulation.
21. Run the simulation.
22. Repeatedly use the KeyMove movement **H** command with the up and down arrow keys to modify the orientation of the Dining_Chair_Bad_Pivot frame. This will rotate the Dining_Chair_Bad_Pivot node around the z axis. You should immediately notice a problem. The pivot point for Dining_Chair_Bad_Pivot is not located near the dining chair; it seems as if the dining chair is tethered to a central pivot point via an invisible cord. Because the pivot point is not located within the object, it can be difficult to manipulate the location of the object in 3D space while attempting to rotate the object using a KeyMove operation. The solution is to override the original imported pivot point.
23. Close the simulation window.
24. Delete the **KeyMove** node from the Dining_Chair_Bad_Pivot frame.
25. Place a **DegreeOfFreedom** node under the Dining_Chair_Bad_Pivot frame.
26. Display the Components – Prototypes window. Place a **DOFMover** prototype under the DegreeOfFreedom node added in the previous step.
27. Drag the **Dining_Cha** frame from under the Dining_Chair_Bad_Pivot Frame node and drop it under the DegreeOfFreedom node you added in step 25. (All child nodes initially under the parent of a DegreeOfFreedom node must be moved under the DegreeOfFreedom node.)
28. Run the simulation.
29. Click the left mouse button, and drag your mouse in and toward the center of the apartment. You should see a 3D pointer axis and a yellow grid located between the kitchen counter and the couch in the living room. The origin of the 3D pointer represents the original pivot point for the Dining_Chair_Bad_Pivot object.
30. The DOFMover prototype has built-in KeyMove functions. Use the **X,Y,** and **Z** keys with the up and down arrow keys to relocate the 3D pointer over the center of the Dining_Chair_Bad_Pivot object.
31. Minimize (do not close) the simulation window and then click the **DegreeOfFreedom** node in the simulation tree. In the Property Bar, click the OriginPosition values, press **Ctrl + C** to copy this information, and then close the simulation window.
32. You will notice that the coordinate values for the OriginPosition property of the Dining_Chair_Bad_Pivot DOF node have returned to their previous value. Click the OriginPosition values again and then press **Ctrl + V** to paste the values you obtained in the previous step.
33. Save the file. Run the simulation. The Dining_Chair_Bad_Pivot object should be located near the dining table and facing the outside wall. Close the simulation.

tips+tricks

In step 22, you may need to click the Zoom Extents button to keep the dining chair visible within the simulation. (To access the Zoom Extents button on the toolbar, it may be necessary to minimize or move the simulation window.)

34. In the simulation tree, delete the **DOFMover** node. When the dialog box appears, click **Yes** to continue.
35. Place a **KeyMove** node under the DegreeOfFreedom node.
36. Run the simulation.
37. Repeatedly use the KeyMove movement **H** command, as well as the up and down arrow keys, to modify the orientation of the DegreeOfFreedom node. This will rotate the Dining_Chair_Bad_Pivot node around the z axis. As you can see, the dining chair now rotates as it should. Turn the dining chair so that it faces the dining table.
38. Minimize (do not close) the simulation window.
39. In the simulation tree, select the **Dining_Cha** frame, and then click in the Property Bar to select the **SetStartValues** check box.
40. In the simulation tree, select the **DegreeOfFreedom** node. In the Property Bar, select the Orientation coordinates with your mouse, press **Ctrl + C** to copy this information onto the Windows Clipboard, and then close the simulation window.
41. You will notice that the coordinate values for the Orientation property of the Dining_Chair_Bad_Pivot DOF node have returned to their previous values (0 0 0). Select the coordinate values in the Orientation field and then press **Ctrl + V** to paste the values you obtained in the previous step.
42. Save the simulation.
43. Run the simulation. You should see the dining chair facing the dining table.
44. Close the simulation window.
45. Delete the **Keymove** node under the DegreeOfFreedom node.
46. Save the simulation and then close EON.

tips+tricks

If you attempted to import the models more than once, you probably have multiple copies of the imported default camera and ambient light nodes. You may delete these extra nodes because they are not necessary. Delete all nodes under the Scene node that begin with Camera_default and defaultambient.

Your apartment now contains a dining table and one dining chair. However, the dining table material does not match the dining chair material. In the following activity, you will delete the material that was originally imported for the dining chair and replace it with the dining table material to create a more uniform appearance. You also will add three additional dining chairs to complete the dining set.

Activity 3.2.3: Copying and Placing Additional Dining Chairs

1. Open EON. Open **Activity_3.2.3.eoz** from the data files for Module 3 Lesson 2.
2. Save the file as **Apartment_Chairs.eoz.**
3. In the simulation tree, expand **Scene > Resources > Materials**.
4. Delete the Material2 node named **wood_oakgrtrt.** This material was imported for the dining chair. You will delete this material to replace it with the material used for the dining table to make the appearance of the dining table and chairs more uniform.

5. Right-click the MultiLayerMaterial node named **Dining_Table** and then select **Copy as Link,** as shown in Figure 3.2.10.

FIGURE 3.2.10 Copy as Link

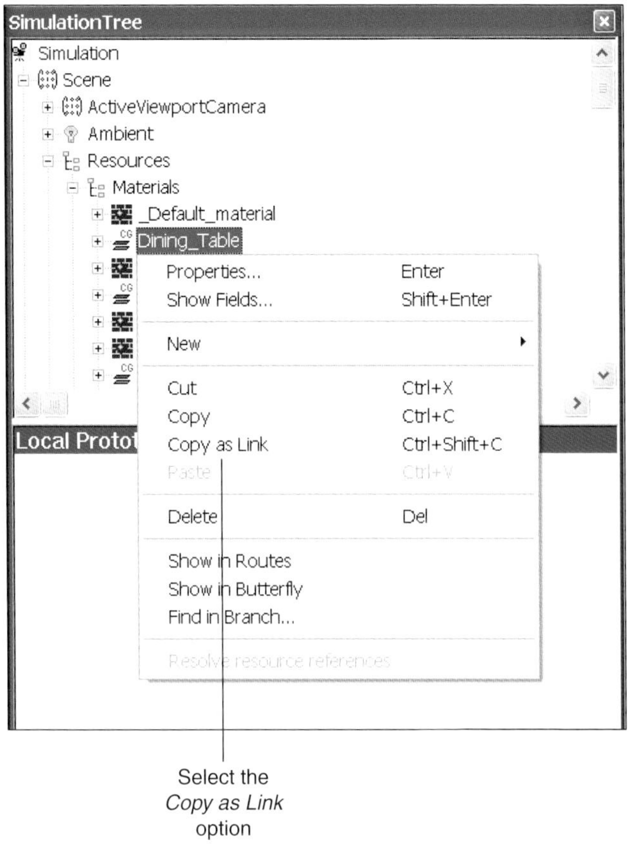

6. Collapse the **Resources** node.
7. Expand the following node path: **Scene > Floorplan > Dining_Room > Dining_Chair1 > Chair**.
8. For each child node under this path, expand the **DegreeOfFreedom** node and the associated Shape node.
9. Select the **Material** folder under each shape and paste the **Dining_Table** link.
10. Next, you will create a second dining chair. Right-click the **Dining_Chair_1** frame and select **Copy.**
11. Right-click the **Dining_Room** frame and then select **Paste.** You should have a new Dining_Chair2 frame.
12. Delete the **KeyMove** node from beneath the Dining_Chair1 frame.
13. Save the simulation.
14. Run the simulation. You will only see one dining chair because both Dining_Chair1 and Dining_Chair2 are located in the same exact 3D space, perfectly overlapping one another.
15. Now repeatedly use the KeyMove movement commands (**X, Y, Z**) with the up and down arrow keys to change the position of Dining_Chair2 so that it is located next to another side of the dining table. Use the KeyMove movement **H** command with the up and down arrow keys to modify the orientation of the Dining_Chair2 frame. This will rotate Dining_Chair2 around its z axis.

tips+tricks

As you can see, it is more efficient to make sure the correct materials are applied to the model before importing it rather than assigning materials to each piece of an object after it has been imported.

16. When you have Dining_Chair2 in the correct position, minimize the simulation window, select the **Dining_Chair2** node in the simulation tree, and, in the Property Bar, select the **SetStartValues** check box.
17. Close the simulation window.
18. In the simulation tree, right-click the **Dining_Chair_2** frame and then select **Copy.**
19. Repeat steps 11 thru 17 to create and move a third dining chair.
20. In the simulation tree, right-click the **Dining_Chair_3** frame and then select **Copy.**
21. Repeat steps 11 thru 17 to create a fourth dining chair.
22. Delete the **KeyMove** node from beneath the Dining_Chair_4 frame.
23. Close the simulation window. Save the simulation and then close EON.

tips+tricks

If you were unable to satisfactorily relocate the dining chairs, you may want to enter the following coordinates for the Position and Orientation properties before proceeding any further:

Dining_Chair1: Position (0.039 1.314 –1.554), Orientation (0 0 0)

Dining_Chair2: Position (0.46 0.063 –1.554), Orientation (101.232 0 0)

Dining_Chair3: Position (0.071 –0.859 –1.554), Orientation (180 0 0)

Dining_Chair4: Position (–0.555 0.063 –1.554), Orientation (275 0 0)

Improving Performance and Appearance

Images, sounds, and videos can be used to enhance an EON simulation. Like 3D models, these files also must be imported into EON. For example, if you require a particular texture for a simulation object, such as the fabric from your sofa, you can take a digital photo or scan a suitable photograph of the item, edit it in Adobe Photoshop, and then import the texture to EON or a 3D-modeling program to apply it to the object. Supported image file formats include:

*.dds
*.jpeg
*.ppm
*.jpg
*.png

tips+tricks

The *.dds file format is used for environment/cube maps.

Discussion

discuss

Most often, when you import an image into EON Studio, you intend to use that image as a background or a texture in your file. What design scenarios might warrant the use of an image as a background or a texture? In each of these scenarios, what images could you use?

tips+tricks

Recommended audio codecs for use with EON Studio include Wave (*.wav) and MP3 (*.mp3).

Sound files may also be used with EON Studio. Use programs such as Creative WaveStudio or Sound Recorder to edit, select, and mix sounds from these files. You can edit frequency, fade-in and fade-out, looping, length of play, and many other properties of the sounds. EON Studio relies on the audio codec installed on the local PC; thus, support is limited by the installed codec. Supported audio file formats include:

*.mp3
*.midi
*.wav
*.wma

tips+tricks

The MovieTexture node also may be used to play sounds.

Like audio support, video support in EON Studio also is limited by the video codec installed on the local PC. Supported video file formats include:

*.avi
*.mov
*.mp3
*.mpeg
*.mpg
*.wmv

> **tips+tricks**
> Generally, any video that can be played in Windows Media Player can be played in EON Studio.

Summary

In this lesson you:

- Studied the procedures for importing 3D objects into EON.
- Recognized import file formats that are compatible with EON.
- Discussed EON's file format importers.
- Understood how you can use EON Raptor.
- Explored the basic considerations for importing VRML files.
- Looked at the history of VRML.
- Learned how to import noncompatible 3D object file formats.
- Examined techniques you can use to position objects in EON.
- Developed an understanding of the DegreeOfFreedom node.
- Became familiar with how imported files can improve a simulation's appearance.

> **cross-reference**
> You will learn more about modifying an object's appearance in Module 5 Lesson 1.

Simulation

You have worked for Contours Company for several weeks and you are beginning to receive your own assignments. As your confidence with the company's processes grows and your EON skills expand, their trust in you also grows.

In the first week, you were asked to create a storyboard for an apartment that your co-workers were developing. Your supervisor gave you the floor plan and asked you to generate a storyboard outlining the tasks needed to create the apartment simulation. That project has moved forward and is ready for finishing touches and details, which they have asked you to provide.

Job 3.1: Creating a Storyboard

Contours' client requested a simulation that enables customers to "walk through" a floor plan for an apartment. Currently, the simulation includes sample furniture, light fixtures, and so on. Your task is to identify details that could improve the experience of walking through the apartment and make it more appealing to your client's customers.

1. Open EON. Open **Job_3.1.eoz** from the data files for the Module 3 Simulation.
2. Run the simulation. Navigate through the apartment and consider items that could be added or changed to improve each room.
3. List improvements that could be made.
4. Close the simulation window.
5. Open the storyboard that you created in the Module 1 Simulation. (If you did not complete the Module 1 Simulation, you can create a storyboard using paper and pencil, a flowchart application, or a drawing program.) Add details and enhancements to improve the overall experience based on your list of improvements. Think about models and textures as well as features and capabilities that the simulation needs.
6. Complete your storyboard and save your work.

Job 3.2: Importing Objects into the Apartment

Although the apartment in the simulation looks nice and seems realistic, it still appears to be bland and lacks visual interest. To improve the simulation experience, add objects to the scene.

1. Based on the list of improvements created in Job 3.1, find additional objects to import. Consider furniture and images for pictures and wall hangings. (You can create these objects in a modeling program, or you can find them at a website that offers free models as we discussed in Module 2.)
2. Open EON. Open **Job_3.1.eoz** from the data files for the Module 3 Simulation if necessary.
3. Import the models into the apartment and place them appropriately. Be creative.
4. Save the simulation as **Job_3.2**. Keep the simulation open to use in Job 3.3.

Job 3.3: Importing Textures into the Apartment

Undoubtedly, the additional objects have improved the apartment's appearance. However, you can make additional improvements by using more visually interesting and appealing textures.

1. Continue working with the open simulation file **Job_3.2** from Job 3.2.
2. Search the textures provided with EON Studio to find textures that could improve the apartment's wall surfaces, floors, furniture, and other decorative elements.
3. If you do not find textures you like in EON, search the Internet for free textures that you can download.

4. If necessary, import the textures into EON.
5. Create a new material for each set of curtains in the apartment. Use a different material in each room.
6. Choose a color scheme for each room based on the material used for the room's curtains. Change colors and textures for the walls and furniture as necessary to make the room attractive.
7. Save the simulation and then run the simulation.

Discussion

discuss

If time permits, allow others to explore the apartment you created. Do they like your selections?

Consider the client's needs. Although you want the apartment to look interesting and realistic, did you make too many choices based on your personal preferences without considering popular styles?

How can you make the apartment interesting and appealing while leaving it uncluttered so that it also invites potential tenants to imagine their own furniture, curtains, and pictures filling the space?

8. Close the simulation window and then close EON.

HARALD SUND

MODULE 4

Object Properties

LESSON 4.1
Object Fundamentals

LESSON 4.2
Visual Nodes Library

LESSON 4.3
3D Edit Tools

LESSON 4.1

Object Fundamentals

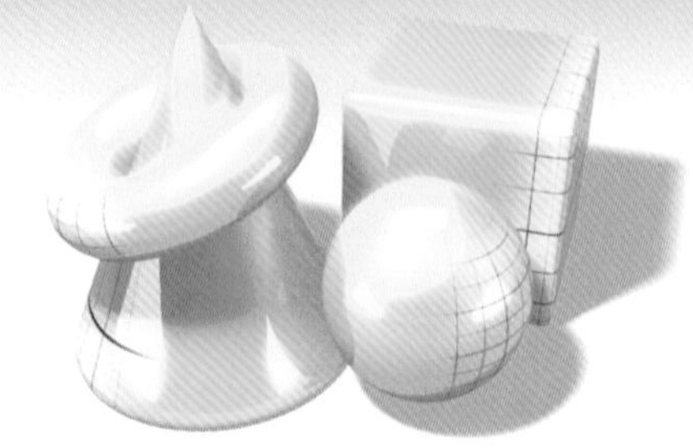

Objectives

In this lesson you will:

- Become familiar with the basics of textures and materials in modeling programs.
- Develop an understanding of texture mapping.
- Read about the texture projection method of texture mapping.
- Explore the fundamental elements of a shape: meshes and materials.
- Learn about the resource database created from the materials, textures, and meshes that comprise an imported model.
- Discuss the requirements for displaying a resource in your simulation.

Key Terms

compression	*opacity*	*texture*
diffuse color	*polygon reduction*	*texture coordinates*
map	*shape*	*texture projection*
material	*specularity*	
material definition	*surfacing*	

Texture and Materials Basics

Before delving any deeper into EON, you must understand the fundamental principles of objects. We have already discussed the wireframe (collection of geometries) that forms the basic structure of an object. But what about the surface of the object? How is an object's surface determined?

Surfacing is a good term to describe the actions that affect the appearance of a finished geometry when rendered. Surfacing consists of two layers. The first layer is called the ***material***, and every object must have a material applied. The material properties define the appearance of the object. They provide surface properties like ***diffuse color*** (the main color), ***opacity*** (transparency), reflectivity, roughness, ***specularity*** (highlights), and other less significant properties.

The term *material* that is used by virtually all 3D modeling programs comes from the idea that you can set an object's properties to create the illusion that an object is made of some recognizable material such as metal, glass, wood, or plastic. However, the *material* is actually a specific combination of parameter values. Whether the object looks like it is made from a real material or something never seen before does not matter.

The ***material definition*** is the set of values that are applied uniformly over the entire surface. To create variations in the material on a surface like you see in real-world materials, you could divide the surface into subsurfaces—each with its own material definitions. However, this method is very limited and extremely time consuming. The better way to create a more realistic surface is to add a second layer in the surfacing process. This layer is referred to as the ***map*** or ***texture***.

According to a typical definition found in a dictionary, *texture* is an object's perceptible or physical surface characteristics or appearance. A simpler explanation is that it is the look and feel of a surface. To create variation within a surface, you must apply a texture (or map) on top of the material. Textures laid on top of materials give objects complicated colors and other effects. A single object covered with a material can have several textures. For example, a round object with a gray material could have an image texture of stone, a texture to make the stone look bumpy, and a texture to make the stone deform in different ways. Textures are very powerful tools, and layering them can create a variety of interesting effects.

Often, the texture layer on the surface completely obscures the underlying material layer. The layer approach, which is common to all modeling programs, allows you to blend a texture with the underlying material. An underlying material value is always present—whether you see it or not—and then a texture is applied on top. (The one exception to this is the bump map, in which no underlying material is present.)

Texture Mapping

As you learned in Module 2 Lesson 1, texture mapping allows you to add detail, surface texture, and color to a graphic or 3D model by adding one or more texture maps to a material and then applying that material to the surface area (a set of interconnected polygons) of the shape. Put simply, texture mapping is a rendering technique for wrapping an image (the texture map) around a 3D object. These words (texture and mapping) can generate confusion. Originally, users created rough or textured effects by applying bitmap images to the surface of models. A common example is a picture of an orange applied to a sphere to create a pebbled effect. This became known as *mapping*. The word *texture* came to be used as a more general term over the years. Now, texture refers to any method of changing the material property, whether or not the effect looks like a surface texture.

To get a bitmap (which is a flat image) to map correctly to the surface of a 3D object is the most difficult part of texture mapping. To understand how this happens, you must understand ***texture coordinates***. All bitmaps used for texture maps are

tips+tricks

3D mapping is another term that is commonly used for texture mapping.

defined using the two coordinates U and V. As Figure 4.1.1 shows, the U coordinates run from left to right, and the V coordinates run from bottom to top. All values are between 0 and 1, which is the equivalent of 0 to 100 percent.

FIGURE 4.1.1 Coordinates of an image

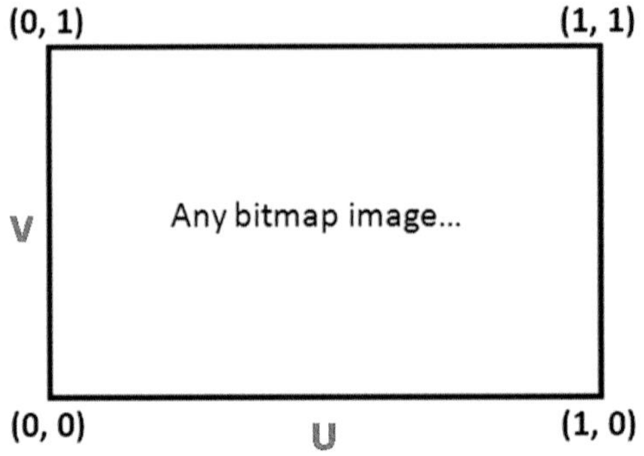

web links

Each modeling program handles basic texture mapping techniques a little differently. Use the Internet to explore some of the major modeling applications, such as 3ds Max, LightWave, and Softimage, and their texture mapping toolsets. You can download trial versions of the software or examine their online demonstrations and tutorials. In your opinion, which program provides the largest toolset (and, consequently, the greatest flexibility and control) for texture mapping? Which seems to be the most intuitive program?

Whether the bitmap image is a square or a rectangle does not matter. Regardless, the lower-left corner of the image is (0, 0) and the upper-right corner is always (1, 1). Every pixel on the bitmap is located at a given U and V coordinate point.

When the image is mapped to a model, each face of the model is assigned a certain region of the map. These texture coordinates plot every vertex (a corner point of a polygon) of every face on a model to UV coordinates on the bitmap. By default, the image is evenly distributed over the surface of the model. You can adjust the coordinates manually, but you must be careful about how you do it and consider the desired effect. If a relatively small section of the image is mapped to a large portion of the model, the image will appear stretched out and distorted. Conversely, if a large section of the image is mapped to a relatively small portion of the model, the image will appear compressed.

Although the explanation in the preceding paragraph may be a little confusing, the real point to understand is that you should use a modeling program for texturing whenever possible. If you do end up with an object without a texture in your simulation, then you will use the TextureUVMap node (which you will learn more about in Lesson 2 of this module). It offers four different mapping techniques and is referenced from the Material2 node.

Texture Projection

In the previous section, we asserted that the texture is automatically mapped evenly over the surface of the model. This may lead you to wonder how the associations between the vertex on the model and the pixels in the image are created. The most generally used method is texture projection.

troubleshooting

It can be tricky to position the textures precisely within EON, so we recommend that you do the texturing in a modeling program before importing it into EON.

Texture projection is a method in which the image is mathematically projected onto the object. Each coordinate in the image is assigned to the location on the model where it is "projected." Several different kinds of projection mapping consider the basic shape of the model to allow more accurate mapping. Depending on the program and the sophistication of its mapping techniques, you may have more or fewer options. In EON you can choose between planar (flat), cylindrical, spherical, and chrome—or customize the mapping entirely. When mapping an image/texture, use the projection type closest to the shape of the object.

Planar projection is the most frequently used projection method because it works well on many surfaces. The cylindrical and spherical methods also can provide respectable results with minimal effort. To understand the cylindrical method, think of the image as being rolled into a tube and then slid over the object. The spherical method is a bit more complex, but you can think of it like wrapping a present; certain parts fold over each other.

With this general understanding of materials and textures, you are ready to go further with EON. We will discuss these elements within EON in general terms in this lesson, and then, in Lesson 2 of this module, you will learn to edit these elements to create the exact surfaces for your objects.

Activity 4.1.1: Texture Example

To help you understand the texture mapping possibilities within EON, this simulation enables you to explore the parameters of the TextureUVMap node and how they work in different objects. Instead of toggling between the simulation window and the Property Bar to make adjustments, buttons and sliders are available in the simulation for changing field values. A variety of shapes are visible—and several different textures are available for mapping to those shapes—so you can get a good sense of how each of these options interacts to create a variety of effects.

1. Open EON. Open **Activity_4.1.1** from the data files for Module 4 Lesson 1.
2. Run the simulation. Your simulation window will appear similar to Figure 4.1.2. Notice that the texture shown in the upper-left corner (under *Click image below to choose texture*) is applied evenly over all surfaces. This is the effect of the Flat mapping type.

FIGURE 4.1.2 Texture mapping example

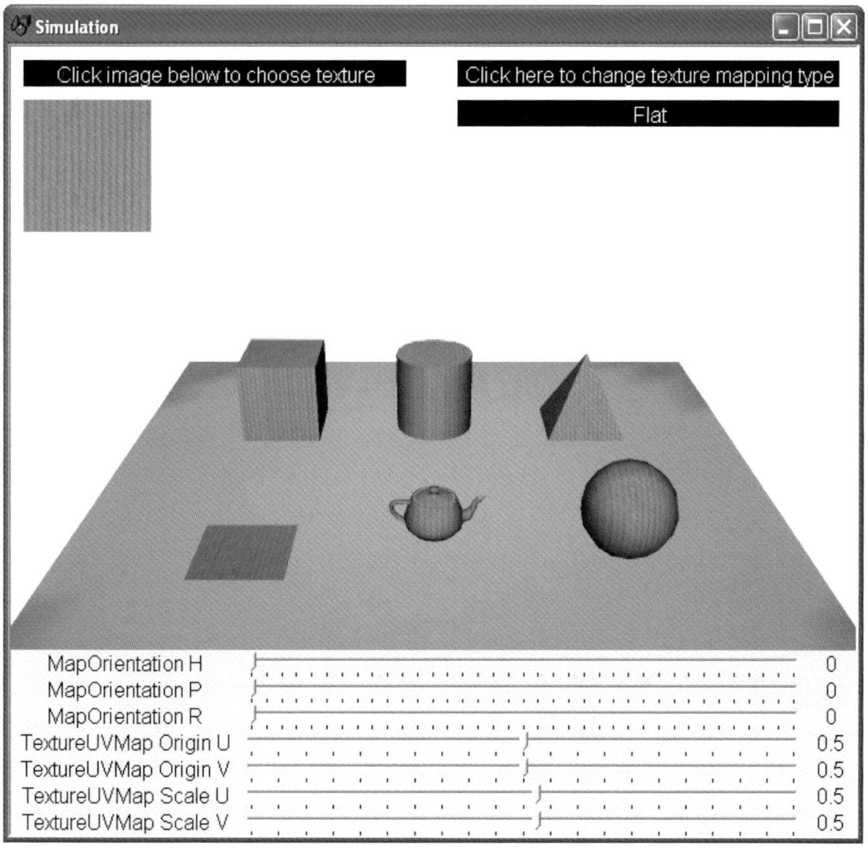

3. Click **Flat** or **Click here to change texture mapping type**. A pop-up menu appears from which you can select Flat, Cylinder, Sphere, or Chrome.
4. Select **Cylinder**. This changes the texture mapping style. The texture (shown in the upper-left corner) is applied to each object in a different way.
5. Click **Cylinder** or **Click here to change texture mapping type** to change the texture mapping type again and select **Sphere**.

6. Click again to change the texture mapping type and select **Chrome**.
7. Click again to change the texture mapping type and return to the **Flat** mapping type.

Discussion

discuss

As you toggled through the different texture mapping types, did any of them seem "right" or "wrong" for a particular shape? Certainly you can use these tools to create any look you want, but did any of them make a shape look more realistic?

8. Select the **TextureUVMap Scale U** slider and slide it to the left and to the right, stopping when you like the effect.
9. Select the **TextureUVMap Scale V** slider and slide it to the left and to the right, stopping when you like the effect.
10. Select the **TextureUVMap Origin U** slider and slide it to the left and to the right, stopping when you like the effect.
11. Select the **TextureUVMap Origin V** slider and slide it to the left and to the right, stopping when you like the effect.
12. Using the sliders, adjust the **MapOrientation H**, **MapOrientation P**, and **MapOrientation R** values to select values that create an effect that you like.
13. Toggle through each of the texture mapping types and use the sliders to experiment with adjusting the scale, origin, and orientation values.
14. Click the texture in the upper-left corner of the simulation window. Adjust the texture mapping types and adjust the orientation, origin, and scale to see the impact that these values can have on the selected texture.
15. Continue experimenting with the different textures, mapping types, and parameter settings to gain a better understanding of the interplay between each of these. As you experiment, determine the following:
    a. Which mapping type and parameter settings allow the rock wall texture to appear most realistic on the pyramid shape?
    b. Which mapping type and parameter settings allow the pebble texture to make the sphere look like a boulder?
    c. Which mapping type and parameter settings allow the striped texture to appear horizontally on the cube?
    d. Which mapping type and parameter settings allow the mosaic textures to appear centered on the flat square?
16. Continue experimenting until you find texture, texture mapping, and parameter settings that you like for the teapot.
17. Change your selections to find texture, texture mapping, and parameter settings that you like for the cylinder.

Discussion

discuss

As you experimented with the different textures, mapping types, and parameter settings, did you notice any situations in which the texture mapping dramatically changed the appearance of a texture to the point that it appeared to be a different texture entirely? For example, could you make the stone wall texture look like marble?

18. Leaving the simulation window open, position it so that you can see the simulation tree and the Property Bar in EON Studio.
19. In the simulation tree, expand **Scene > Objects > Resources** and select the **TextureUVMap** node.
20. In the Property Bar, expand the parameter fields for **UVOrigin**, **UVScale**, and **MapOrientation**.
21. In the simulation window, change the texture mapping type. Notice that the value in the Mode field in the Property Bar changes to reflect the change made in the simulation window.
22. In the simulation window, use the sliders to change the values for origin, scale, and orientation. Notice that the values in the corresponding UVOrigin, UVScale, and MapOrientation fields in the Property Bar change to reflect the settings selected in the simulation window.
23. Close the simulation window. Close EON without saving the simulation.

tips+tricks

The MapPosition field is another parameter within the TextureUVMap node that could be changed, but the effect is similar to changing the TextureUVMap Origin field, and so it is not available in this example.

STORYBOARD

Beyond Model Placement

After you import a model, many steps still are needed to create your simulation. Ideally, you included the appropriate textures and materials when you created your 3D model (prior to importing). However, you probably will encounter some situations requiring the addition or modification of textures and materials. You can make these changes after you place the model in the simulation as you work with lighting, cameras, and behaviors.

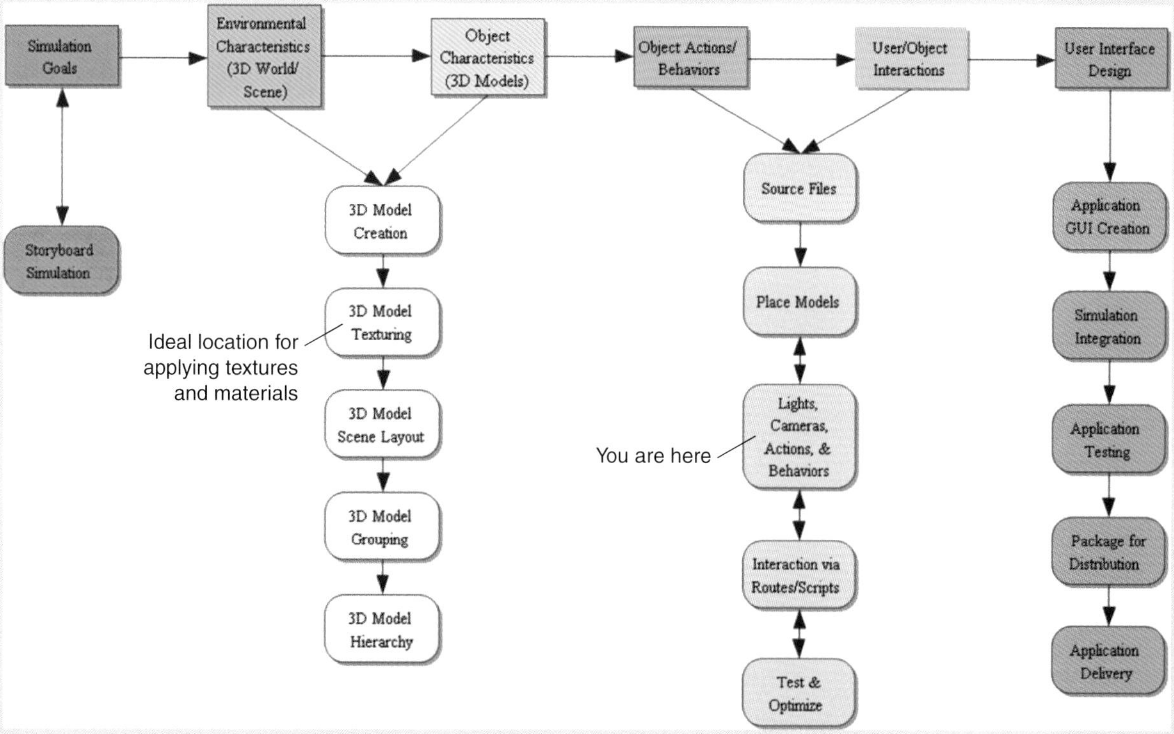

In this lesson, you will learn about working with textures, materials, and meshes in EON after a model has been imported.

Meshes and Materials in EON

In the previous section, you learned the distinction between a material and a texture and how they are applied to a basic geometric model. These elements are collectively referred to in EON as a ***shape***. To work with shapes effectively, you need to understand their basic structure.

Composition of a Shape

You need to understand what is involved in the composition of shapes because shapes are integral to creating simulations in EON. All 3D objects in EON are Shape nodes, which are comprised of a mesh (geometry) and a material. The Shape node combines the material (Material2 or MultiMaterial node) and the geometry (Mesh2 node) to form a visible 3D object in the simulation.

Meshes in EON

As you learned in Module 1 Lesson 3, the Mesh2 node is used with other nodes in the Visual Nodes library. It represents a geometry in the scene, storing the mesh data.

cross-reference

You can learn more about the associated mesh data file in Lesson 2 of this module.

A mesh defines a 3D object in terms of vertices, polygons, size, shape, and location, but a mesh does not define the object's appearance. When an importer creates the resource database from a 3D file, it will create a Mesh2 node for each 3D object found in the file, store the 3D mesh data in a separate file, and then add a reference to the 3D mesh data file. This is similar to how textures are stored. However, unlike textures, the mesh data file (which has the extension .eog) can only be read and used in EON.

To keep the data storage requirement to a minimum, a mesh in EON can be compressed and its polygon count reduced. ***Compression*** in EON is similar to JPEG image compression, in which you trade precision and quality for smaller data size. ***Polygon reduction*** means that you are actually reducing the number of polygons building up a mesh.

It is important to note that a mesh, by itself, does not generate any visible object in a scene. To make the mesh visible, you must combine it with a Material2 node in a Shape node.

BEST PRACTICES

Compression of Textures

To keep the size of your file as low as possible, you should compress data as much as possible. The trick is determining how much compression is enough and how much is too much.

The best way to achieve the maximum compression without adversely affecting your simulation is to push the compression values until you see a change in the quality of your texture. When you see a change, then you have gone too far and you need to back off. This process establishes the limit by identifying the maximum compression that is acceptable for your simulation.

If you are completely satisfied with the compression values, you can choose Make Compression Permanent from the Tools menu. Note, however, that you cannot undo this selection. You will not be able to make any other compression changes after selecting this option. Use this option only when you are completely sure that you will never edit the simulation.

Typically, you will make a copy of the simulation file that you are preparing for distribution. In the copied file, make the compression permanent before creating the distribution file. This maximizes the compression in the distributed copy, but you can return to your original file and make changes there if the simulation requires additional edits later.

cross-reference

We will talk more about compression in Lesson 3 of this module.

Materials in EON

Like the Mesh2 node, the Material2 node is used with other nodes in the Visual Nodes library. As you might guess, it represents a material in the scene. To apply a material to a 3D object, combine it with a geometry node (Mesh2) within the Shape node.

In addition to the Material2 node, you can use a MultiMaterial node. Some 3D modeling software supports multimaterials, which means a single mesh can be assigned many different submaterials—potentially one submaterial on each face of the mesh. EON supports this by creating a MultiMaterial node when such a multimaterial is encountered during the import process. Each submaterial in the multimaterial will be imported and created as well. Then the MultiMaterial node will contain references to these submaterials.

cross-reference

In addition to Material2 and MultiMaterial nodes, the Visual Effects module of EON Professional allows you to use shaders in your EON applications. Shaders, and Cg-based materials, are detailed in Lesson 2 of this module.

Resources Node in EON

A central concept of the EON system is the use of a resource database to facilitate sharing and instancing of geometry and texture data. As with so many other facets of EON, the database is simply a branch of the simulation tree. This means that you can organize the structure of this subtree as needed. However, when you create a model outside of EON, the geometry importers will automatically create a resource database tree like the following example.

```
Resources (a Group node)
   Materials (a Group node)
      Material a (a Material2 or MultiMaterial node)
      Material b (a Material2 or MultiMaterial node)
      ...
   Textures (a TextureResourceGroup node)
      Texture a (a Texture2 or MovieTexture node)
      Texture b (a Texture2 or MovieTexture node)
      ...
   Meshes (a MeshResourceGroup node)
      Mesh a (a Mesh2 node)
      Mesh b (a Mesh2 node)
      ...
```

As you can see, a Group node is used to group all resources in the scene. Beneath this Group node, three resource groups are inserted: Materials, Textures, and Meshes. Whereas the Materials group is headed by an ordinary Group node, the other two resource groups use special nodes because additional custom fields are needed for each.

cross-reference

You will learn about these groups and nodes in Lesson 2 of this module.

Making the Resource Visible

The nodes in the resource database tree are not visible until they are used by the Shape node. The Shape node combines a material (Material2, MultiMaterial, or a Cg-based material) and a geometry (Mesh2, Box, Sphere, etc.) to form a visible 3D object in the simulation. This structure creates a very powerful arrangement in which you can intermix different materials and meshes. For example, you can create five chairs of the same shape but different colors—or five different chairs with the same material setup. Furthermore, this system saves memory resources and downloading time because the simulation can share mesh and texture data (which typically accounts for 80–90% of the data size for a simulation).

Summary

In this lesson you:

- Became familiar with the basics of textures and materials in modeling programs.
- Developed an understanding of texture mapping.
- Read about the texture projection method of texture mapping.
- Explored the fundamental elements of a shape: meshes and materials.
- Learned about the resource database created from the materials, textures, and meshes that comprise an imported model.
- Discussed the requirements for displaying a resource in your simulation.

LESSON 4.2

Visual Nodes Library

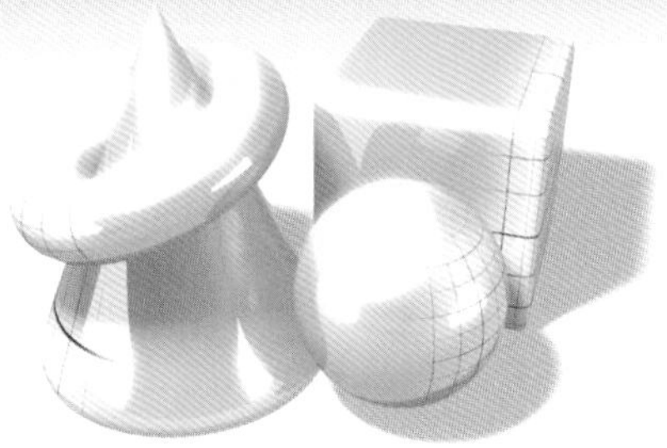

Objectives

In this lesson you will:

- Become familiar with the Visual Nodes library.
- Learn about the resource database created from the materials, textures, and meshes that comprise an imported model.
- Begin to explore the various types of lighting that affect your simulation.
- Experiment with creating your own materials, textures, and lighting and applying them to objects in a simulation.

Key Terms

ambient light	*emissive light*	*shader*
Cg	*light map*	*specular light*
diffuse light	*light mapping*	*Visual Nodes library*
DirectDraw Surface (DDS)	*multimaterial*	

Introduction to the Visual Nodes Library

To enhance the expressiveness and flexibility of the visual system, EON has a material-mesh system comprised of a set of nodes categorized the ***Visual Nodes library***. The nodes in this library, shown in Figure 4.2.1, are designed to be used together.

FIGURE 4.2.1 Visual Nodes library

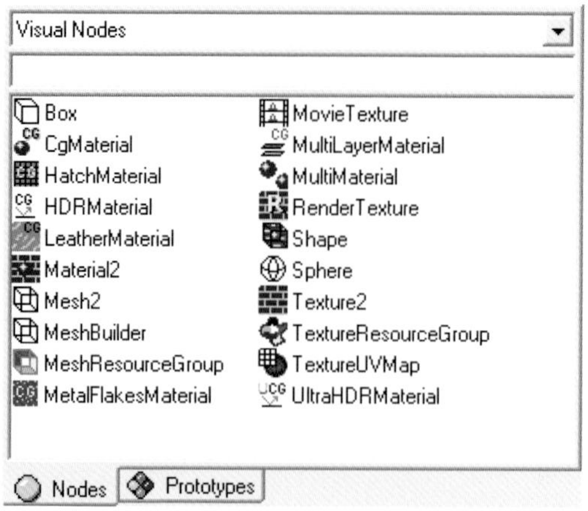

troubleshooting

Do not mix the Visual Nodes in this library with the older visual nodes in the same system. The old nodes (i.e., Material, Mesh, Texture, and Multimedia Stream nodes) remain in EON Studio for backward compatibility. EON will not prevent you from using them, but they will not work correctly if combined with those shown in Figure 4.2.1.

tips+tricks

Cg, which stands for "C for Graphics," is a high-level shading language developed by NVIDIA (in close collaboration with Microsoft) for programming vertex and pixel shaders. It is very similar to Microsoft's High Level Shader Language (HLSL). Based on the C programming language, it contains some features of C, modified to make Cg more suitable for programming graphics processing units. The Cg compiler outputs DirectX or OpenGL shader programs.

The list of Visual Nodes shown in Figure 4.2.1 includes several Cg-based materials. Most of these, except for HatchMaterial, are only available if you have installed EON Professional. (You can always access HatchMaterial and use it in the same way as the Material2 node.) The Cg-based materials are:

- CgMaterial
- LeatherMaterial
- HDRMaterial
- HatchMaterial
- MetalFlakesMaterial
- MultiLayerMaterial

The Visual Effects module of EON Professional enables the user to use shaders in the EON application. A ***shader*** is a programmable material—in other words, a procedural material. The material's appearance is defined by a short program in a language called ***Cg***. Cg is designed to allow you to control the various aspects of a material's appearance in a high-level programmatic way.

To take advantage of the free Cg programs that are available in various communities, EON Visual Effects allows you to import Cg programs and use them directly in EON by using the generic CgMaterial node. However, to empower you with even easier access to this exciting technology, several useful and state-of-the-art Cg scripts are shipped with EON Professional. Furthermore, several variants are provided as ordinary EON Material nodes so that you can drop them in to use them easily.

In this lesson, we will explore the Visual Node library in depth. We will discuss how resource groups can be used to reduce processor time. Additionally, we will look at the use of a light map with a material from the Visual Node library.

BEST PRACTICES

The DDS Texture Format

The Microsoft ***DirectDraw® Surface (DDS)*** graphics file format was established for use with the DirectX SDK (software developers' kit). This is a standard format used to store surface and texture data and cubic environment maps, with and without mipmap levels. (With textures whose size is divisible by powers of two, it is possible to save mipmap levels.) This image data is stored in Microsoft DirectX®.

The DDS file format is designed specifically for use in real-time rendering applications, such as 3D games. Use the DDS format to store textures, cubemaps, and mipmap levels. This format can store uncompressed and compressed pixel formats, and it is the preferred file format for storing DXTn compressed data. The format is supported by the DirectX Texture Tool, some third-party tools, and the Direct3D extensions (D3DX) library. Because most video cards natively support DXTn texture compression, use of this format can save memory on the video card.

DDS Texture Compression in EON allows increased speeds in rendering and performance because the DDS texture is read on the graphics card. Drivers can perform this compression on the fly. Thus, DDS reduces space (which leads to faster loading) without degrading the image. (Image degradation can occur when you try to recompress already-compressed formats like JPEG.)

The DDS file format is quickly becoming the preferred format for textures because it has both compression and mipmapping. With it, you can easily convert JPEG and BMP files into DDS, and you will clearly see the benefits of doing this. For example, a regular BMP texture file might be almost 800 KB in size. In the DDS file format, that same texture file would be less than 200 KB—with compressed mipmap levels and very little change in image quality.

tips+tricks

DXTn (also known as DXTC or S3TC) is a group of related image compression algorithms. These were originally developed by S3 Graphics Co., Ltd. for use in their Savage 3D graphics processor.

Resource Database

As you will recall from Lesson 1 of this module, EON uses a resource database to facilitate sharing and instancing of geometry and texture data. You can organize these resources in subtrees in any way you want. And, although models created outside of EON are automatically organized into resource database trees, you can adjust these as needed as well.

As you know, a Group node is used to group together all resources in the scene. Beneath this Group node, three resource groups can be found: Materials, Textures, and Meshes. The Materials group is headed by an ordinary Group node, and the other two resource groups use special nodes because additional custom fields are needed for each. You will learn about these groups and nodes in the following sections.

Materials

Materials, in general, are a list of structured commands and parameters that define the appearance and physical properties of the surfaces to which a specific material is applied. The Materials group contains every material available in the original model file. A Material2 node changes the colors, emissive parameters, and specular parameters of its parent Shape node.

Some 3D modeling software supports ***multimaterials.*** A multimaterial allows several materials to be assigned to a single mesh. One submaterial could, potentially, be assigned to each face of the mesh. Multimaterials are supported within EON by the creation of a MultiMaterial node when a multimaterial is encountered during the import process. The submaterials within the multimaterial will be created during importation as well. The MultiMaterial node will then contain references to these submaterials.

tips+tricks

You also can use the Material2 node to change to Wireframe mode.

The material nodes that you can use in your EON simulation are listed in Table 4.2.1, with a brief description of each. You will learn more about each of these materials as we encounter situations in which they are used.

TABLE 4.2.1 Material Nodes in the Visual Nodes Library

Material Node	Description	Icon
CgMaterial	The most generic Cg material node. It enables you to modify the Cg programs.	CgMaterial
HatchMaterial	Nonphotorealistic shading in hatch style.	HatchMaterial
HDRMaterial	Image-based lighting using high-dynamic range (HDR) images, such as cubemap. (The DiffuseCubemap is a folder below HDRMaterial in a simulation tree.)	HDRMaterial
LeatherMaterial	Creates realistic leather material using bump mapping.	LeatherMaterial
Material2	Material2 is used with other nodes in the Visual Nodes library. It represents a material in the scene. To apply a material to a 3D object, you must combine it with a geometry node (Mesh2) using the Shape node.	Material2
MetalFlakesMaterial	A metallic shader with flakes and environment reflections.	MetalFlakesMaterial
MultiLayerMaterial	A layered material node that permits you to combine a base color map, bump map, dark map, and environment map, in addition to the usual material properties, such as specular color and shininess. The maps are built on top of each other in a single rendering pass, resulting in optimal performance and quality.	MultiLayerMaterial
MultiMaterial	A node used when a multimaterial is encountered during the import process. Each submaterial in the multimaterial will be imported and created. Then the MultiMaterial node will contain references to these submaterials.	MultiMaterial
UltraHDRMaterial	Part of the EON Professional add-on, this node is like HDRMaterial, except that it adds shader information for the Shininessmap, DiffuseCubemap, and SpecularCubemap. (Each of these is a folder below the UltraHDRMaterial node.)	UltraHDRMaterial

tips+tricks

Notice that the Cg-based materials (which you will see only if you installed EON Professional) contain the letters "CG" somewhere in the icon.

Textures

Textures are images that you can use to supply details to a surface in a very cost-effective way (computation-wise). EON has two main texture resource nodes: Texture2 and MovieTexture. The difference between them is that the Texture2 node uses a simple static image file as the image source, and the MovieTexture node uses a movie file as the image source. You also may use the RenderTexture and the TextureUVMap nodes. Descriptions of the texture nodes follow.

Texture2

Texture2

The Texture2 node allows you to use static images as source files. Texture2 supports only five image formats: DDS, JPEG, JPEG2000, PNG, and PPM. Therefore, you should convert other image formats to JPEG or PNG before starting the import procedure. Many importers will automatically convert most of the common image formats to PNG or JPEG2000, but to maintain maximum control, you should do it yourself.

The Texture2 node must be referenced by a Material2 node to be visible in the scene. Also, the Material2 node must be used by a Shape node.

MovieTexture

As stated previously, the MovieTexture node uses a movie file as the image source. Any movie format supported by Microsoft's DirectShow system (which would be any movie that can be played by the Windows MediaPlayer) can be used in a MovieTexture node. Note that the MovieTexture node also can supply a sound track to the simulation. Conversely, you could choose to disable the video channel and only use the sound channel. This would allow you to play a background tune in MP3 format.

The MovieTexture node must be referenced by a Material2 node to be visible in the scene. Also, this Material2 node must be used by a Shape node.

troubleshooting

The MovieTexture node is a replacement for the MultimediaStream node. The MultimediaStream node remains in EON for backward compatibility, but it should not be used in new applications.

RenderTexture

This node is very similar to the Texture2 node, except a viewport provides the image data instead of an image file. It is used in a multipass rendering to store the intermediate result of the rendering.

To use this node, insert it into the simulation tree (typically the Resources branch if it exists). Then create a reference to the new RenderTexture node in the Target field of a chosen Viewport node. When you run the simulation, the chosen viewport will render the content into this texture instead of the display!

You can set the resolution and type using the following fields: Width, Height, Type, and Format. Furthermore, the RenderTexture node supports the usual rendering aspects of a texture, such as the use of mipmapping, and the tiling and filtering options with the Mipmap, WrapU, WrapV, WrapW, MinFilter, and MagFilter fields.

TextureUVMap

The TextureUVMap node is similar to the original Texture node (which is no longer used), but it is compatible with the new Visual Nodes library (Texture2, Material2, and Mesh2). It allows you to map a texture on an object manually using several standard projection types such as planar, cylindrical, and spherical.

When mapping an image or a texture, try to use the projection type closest to the shape of the object on which you want to map it. However, it can be tricky to position the textures precisely, so you should do the texturing in a modeling program before importing an object into EON.

tips+tricks

To get the best compression of the final EON distribution file (.edz) without losing information, use PNG texture for the original geometry, because JPEG2000 compresses best if the original texture has little or no compression.

TextureResourceGroup

In many applications, the textures can be manipulated and changed as a group. To support this workflow, a specialized group node named TextureResourceGroup is available. This node is always created by the importers to group all textures in the model. It contains all the common properties of the texture nodes, which are described in Table 4.2.2.

TABLE 4.2.2 Common Texture Node Fields

Field Name	Description
Embedded	If false, the image file will be placed outside of the distribution file.
QualityLevel	Controls the compression of the texture file when creating the distribution file. Its value ranges from 0 to 100, with 100 being the best quality (no compression).
MaxWidth	Limits the width of the texture to this size (in pixels). Enter 65536 to remove the limitation.
MaxHeight	Limits the height of the texture to this size (in pixels). Enter 65536 to remove the limitation.
OrginalSize	The total file size of all the texture resources in this group.
DistributionSize	The total estimated final file size after compression and size limitation of this group.

Unless the UseGroupSettings field of a Texture2 node is set to false, it will always use the values of these common fields on the TextureResourceGroup node instead of looking into each separate Texture2 node. This means you can change only one field, such as the QualityLevel, on the group node to change the QualityLevel of all Texture2 nodes below the TextureResourceGroup node. If you want to make individual adjustments on some nodes, uncheck the UseGroupSettings field for these nodes and make the changes only in the fields of these nodes.

Activity 4.2.1: Using the TextureResourceGroup Node and Textures

1. Open EON.
2. From the menu bar, choose **File > Import > 3D Studio .3ds**. This opens the Import file dialog box.
3. Browse to the data files for Module 4 Lesson 2 and select **Chair_Low Res**. Click **Open**.
4. Accept all the default selections in the 3D Studio Geometry Import Plug-In dialog box and click **OK**.
5. In the Geometry import dialog box, modify the Target path as needed to point to the data files for Module 4 Lesson 2. (The Target path must point to the location where the JPEG file for the texture is located.)
6. Select the drop-down arrow next to Scaling and select **Scale by factor** from the list if necessary. Change the Scaling value to **0.1**. Leave all other settings in this dialog box unchanged and click **OK**. After the import is complete, your simulation tree should look like the one shown in Figure 4.2.2.

FIGURE 4.2.2 Simulation tree after importing chair model

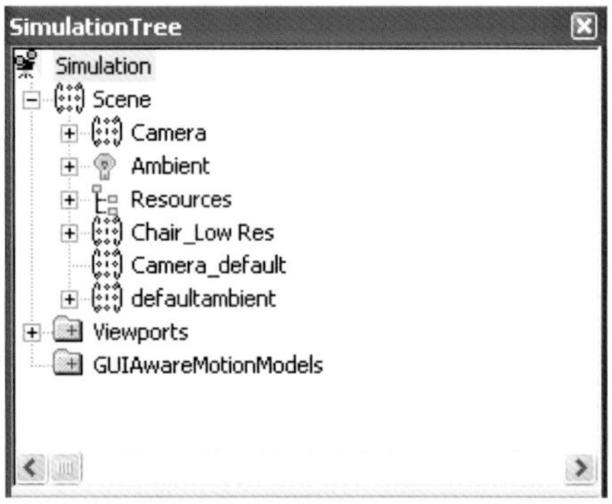

7. Run the simulation.
8. If you do not see anything, click **Zoom Extents** on the Toolbar to view the image in the simulation window. (You can also press the left mouse button and drag the mouse up or down to bring the image into view in the simulation window.) When the image is positioned correctly, click **Set Initial View** on the Toolbar to establish the image's position for future runs of the simulation. Your simulation window should look similar to Figure 4.2.3.

FIGURE 4.2.3 Chair model in the simulation window

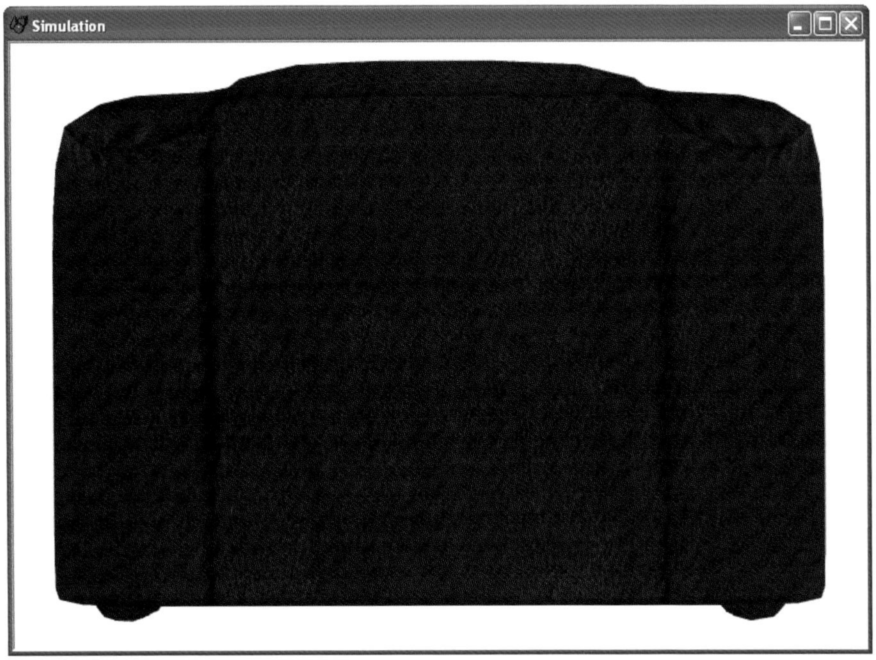

9. Leave the simulation running but drag it out of the way so that you can work in the Simulation Tree and Property Bar windows.
10. In the simulation tree, expand the **Resources** group.
11. Select **Textures** (the TextureResourceGroup node).
12. In the Property Bar, select the check box next to **PreviewCompression**. This will allow you to see the effect of the changes you make.
13. In the Property Bar, change the MaxWidth and MaxHeight to **16**. (Your simulation tree and Property Bar should appear as shown in Figure 4.2.4.) Note that, as you change the MaxWidth and MaxHeight values, the resolution of the texture on the chair changes. Instead of appearing to be black leather, it becomes a smooth black surface with much less detail.

FIGURE 4.2.4 Simulation tree and Property Bar after the chair's texture is modified

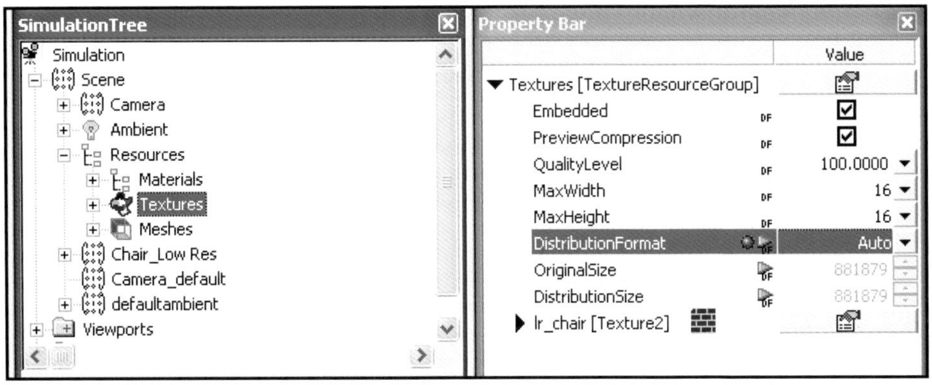

14. Expand **Textures** in the simulation tree and select the **lr_chair** Texture2 node.
15. In the Property Bar, uncheck **UseGroupSettings**. View the simulation window and note that the detail has returned to the texture of the chair in the simulation.

troubleshooting

Because PreviewCompression enables you to see changes in QualityLevel and Distribution format, it is not necessary for the changes you make to MaxWidth and MaxHeight in this activity. However, it is good practice to turn on this previewing function now so that you become accustomed to seeing the effect of your changes as you make them.

16. Change the MaxWidth and MaxHeight values to **256** each. View the simulation window and note that some, but not all, of the detail has been lost in the simulation.
17. Select the drop-down menu for DistributionFormat. You will see the choices shown in Figure 4.2.5.

FIGURE 4.2.5 DistributionFormat options

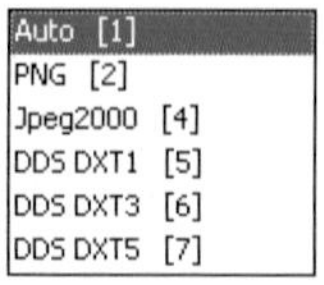

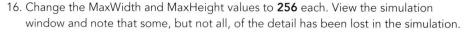

18. Select **DDS DXT3**.
19. Close the simulation window. Save the simulation as **ChairImport_LowRes** and then close EON.

Meshes

A mesh resource node contains the definition of a 3D model, but not the appearance (which is stored in the material resource node). When an importer creates the resource database from a 3D file, it will create a mesh node for each 3D object found in the file, store the 3D mesh data in a separate file, and then make the node reference this file.

Textures are stored in a similar way. However, unlike textures, the mesh data file (which has the extension .eog) can be read and used only in EON. Normally, the node and its associated mesh data file are treated as one entity because the file is embedded in the simulation file. However, sometimes it is useful to extract the mesh data file and store it somewhere else, preferably on a server. This enables the simulation to start and run immediately while the mesh data file (which can be huge) is streamed down from a server in the background. When it is downloaded, it will be initialized and loaded into the simulation window.

To reduce the need for data storage, you can compress a mesh in EON and reduce its polygon count. This compression is like JPEG image compression, in which you trade precision and quality for smaller data size, whereas polygon reduction means you actually reduce the number of polygons building up a mesh.

Mesh2

Mesh2

The Mesh2 node is a new version of the Mesh node, designed to be used with other nodes in the Visual Nodes library. It represents the geometry of a 3D object in the scene, storing the mesh data. To make the mesh visible, you must combine it with a Material2 node using the Shape node.

MeshBuilder

MeshBuilder

The MeshBuilder node is used to create a polygon-based geometry (mesh) dynamically. You can compare it with the Mesh2 node, which reads the geometry from a file when the simulation is rendered—meaning it cannot change during the simulation. Typically, the mesh data in MeshBuilder is filled from a Script node.

A mesh is built with polygons, and each polygon is built using three or more points. However, because many points in a mesh are usually shared by two or more polygons, polygons are built of indices to the points. Each polygon is specified with a series of 0-based indices into the Positions/Normals/Colors/TextureCoordinateX arrays and ends with −1 to close the polygon. Each polygon is defined in counterclockwise order. Each point, in addition to the 3D coordinates, can have normal colors and up to four texture coordinates.

tips+tricks

DDS DXT is the preferred distribution format because it delivers the best performance in the simulation. However, older graphics cards (i.e., some of those made prior to 2005) may not support this format. In those situations, select PNG or Jpeg2000. Selecting PNG creates a larger file and selecting Jpeg2000 creates the smallest file. Do not select Jpeg2000 if your image has transparent parts because they would no longer be transparent.

web links

To find out if your graphics card supports DDS, go to the website for your card and search for "DDS support."

troubleshooting

If you select a distribution format that is not supported by the graphics card on the system trying to run the simulation, the objects will appear dark green or black. (This also occurs if Cg graphics are not supported by the graphics card.)

tips+tricks

After you adjust the scaling, future imports will automatically default to the last scaling values set.

cross-reference

See Module 11 Lesson 1 for more information about streaming.

MeshResourceGroup

Similar to the procedure used for textures, importers will use a MeshResourceGroup node to group all meshes used in the 3D scene so that they can be manipulated easily as a group. This node has several fields that are common to the Mesh2 node. When one of these fields is modified, the new value will be applied to each of the Mesh2 nodes in this group. Polygon reduction is one such field. For each Mesh2 node within the group, you can choose whether to use the group settings or not.

Activity 4.2.2: Using the MeshResourceGroup Node

1. Open EON.
2. From the menu bar, choose **File > Import > 3D Studio .3ds**. This opens the Import file dialog box.
3. Browse to the data files for Module 4 Lesson 2 and select **Chair_High Res**. Click **Open**.
4. Accept all the default selections in the 3D Studio Geometry Import Plug-In dialog box and click **OK**.
5. In the Geometry import dialog box, verify that the Target path points to the data files for Module 4 Lesson 2. (The Target path must point to the location where the JPEG file for the texture is located.)
6. If necessary, select the drop-down arrow next to Scaling and select **Scale by factor** from the list. Change the Scaling value to **0.1** if necessary. Leave all other settings in this dialog box unchanged and click **OK**. After the import is complete, your simulation tree should look like the one shown in Figure 4.2.6.

FIGURE 4.2.6 Simulation tree after importing 3D Studio image

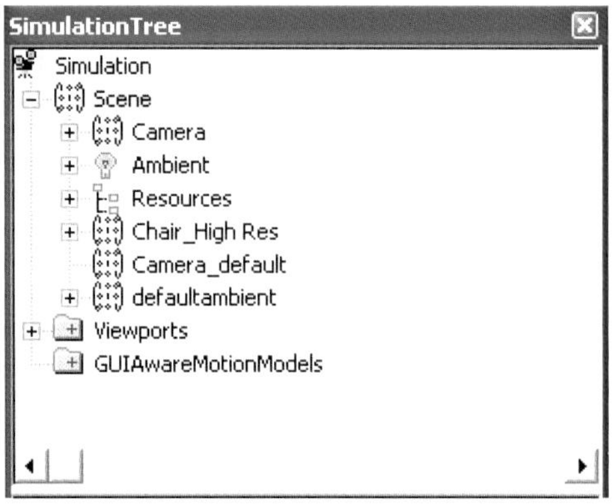

7. Run the simulation.
8. If you do not see anything, click the **Zoom Extents** button on the Toolbar to view the image in the simulation window. (You can also press the left mouse button and drag the mouse up or down to bring the image into view in the simulation window.) When the image is positioned correctly, click **Set Initial View** on the Toolbar to establish the image's position for future runs of the simulation.
9. Close the simulation window.
10. Run the simulation again to verify that it returns to the new initial view that you have set. Then close the simulation.
11. Switch to the **Prototypes** window and drag and drop the **OrbitNav** prototype into the Camera frame in the simulation tree.
12. Drag and drop the **OrbitNavResetToBBox** prototype into the Camera frame.

13. Right-click the **Walk** node in the Camera frame and choose **Copy as Link** from the pop-up menu.
14. Expand **OrbitNav** in the simulation tree.
15. Right-click **DisableWhenActive** and choose **Paste** from the pop-up menu.
16. Right-click the **Chair_High Res** frame and select **Copy as Link**.
17. Expand **OrbitNavResetToBBox** in the simulation tree, right-click **Frame**, and choose **Paste** from the pop-up menu. Your simulation tree should look like Figure 4.2.7.

FIGURE 4.2.7 Simulation tree with the OrbitNav prototype added

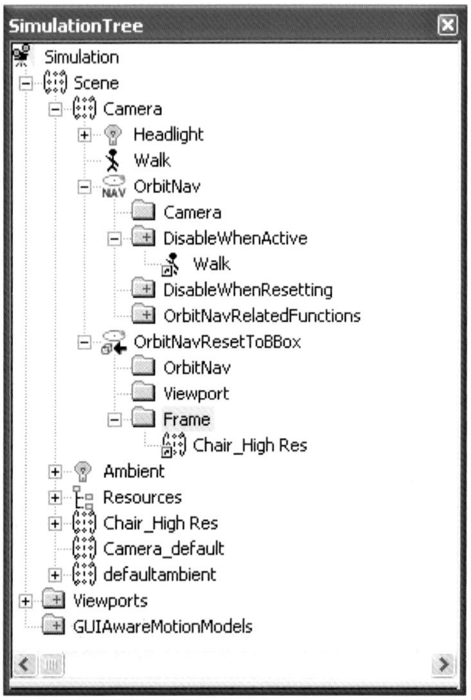

cross-reference

You will learn more about using the OrbitNav prototype in Module 5 Lesson 2.

18. Run the simulation again. Use your mouse to rotate the chair so that you can see the front of it. Set that view as your initial view.
19. Expand the **Resources** group in the simulation tree.
20. Select the MeshResourceGroup (named **Meshes** in the simulation tree).
21. Observe the values shown in the PolygonCountBeforeReduction field and the PolygonCountAfterReduction field of the Property Bar as shown in Figure 4.2.8.

FIGURE 4.2.8 Polygon counts displayed in the Property Bar

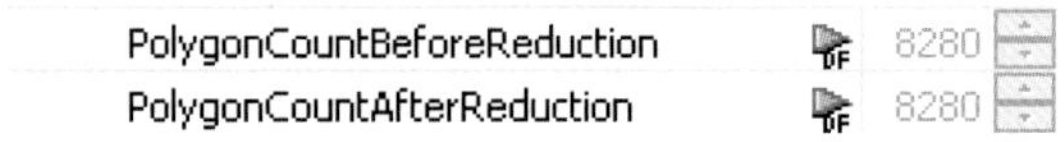

22. Select the **PolygonReductionLevel** field in the Property Bar and change the value to **50** (reducing the polygon count by 50%). Notice that the PolygonCountAfterReduction value changes, but you do not see a noticeable change in the appearance of the chair in the simulation window.
23. In the Property Bar, expand **Meshes** and select **Chair_High [Mesh2]** to view the Chair_High [Mesh2] properties. Notice that the PolygonCount values of the mesh were changed because it was included in the MeshResourceGroup.

24. Under Chair_High [Mesh2] in the Property Bar, clear the check box next to the **UseGroupSettings** option. Notice that the Chair_High's PolygonCountAfterReduction value now matches its PolygonCountBeforeReduction value.
25. Under Chair_High [Mesh2] in the Property Bar, change the PolygonReductionLevel to **80**.

Discussion

discuss

With the increased polygon reduction, do you notice any change in the chair in your simulation window? At what point does reducing the polygons begin to have an adverse effect?

26. Close the simulation window. Save the simulation as **ChairImport_HighRes** and then close EON.

cross-reference

Reducing textures and geometry data is one of the most effective ways to reduce the size of the entire simulation. You will learn more about optimizing resources in Module 11 Lesson 1.

Light Map Rendering

Light mapping is a computer graphics technique used to increase the speed of rendering 3D objects with complex lighting. Instead of calculating the impact of light sources on the 3D objects in real time, the contribution of the light sources are sampled and then mapped on the affected 3D objects as a texture (a ***light map***).

Note that the light map cannot be mapped on the objects statically because the shading caused by the lighting changes when the observer shifts position or the objects are translated. Instead, the mapping coordinates (texture coordinates) must be adjusted accordingly. However, for complex lighting, modifying these coordinates is faster than calculating the surface illumination based on the "real" light sources. Using light maps provides the advantage of more realistic specular (highlights) shading without sacrificing the rendering speed. Extremely reflective or very shiny surfaces benefit from being rendered with light maps.

Even though light maps offer superior shading for 3D objects, they have some limitations. First, the light sources must be static. Second, if your graphics card does not support multitexturing, the scene must be rendered in several passes, increasing the rendering time. Although multitexturing is an increasingly common hardware feature on the graphics card—designed to accelerate the job of mixing several textures together—EON does not use multitexturing when rendering light maps. Additionally, a technique to accelerate the drawing of polygons, known as Vertex Buffer Object (VBO), is disabled while rendering objects with materials that have light maps. This will affect the frame rate if the scene contains high-polygon models.

Several ways of using the light mapping technique in an EON simulation are available:

- Use the Material2 node if the object belongs to the new Visual Nodes system.
- Use the Shading node only if the object belongs to the old material system (before EON 4.0) and the simulation cannot be updated to a newer version of EON. This is not a preferred method.
- Write a custom shader that emulates the behavior of light maps in the Material2 node.
- Use the HDRMaterial node in EON Professional. This requires a set of three cubemap DDS textures instead of a single lightmap texture, so you cannot reuse the lightmap texture.

tips+tricks

The LightMapTexture field is in the Material2 node. In EON, the effect is similar to the Reflection field in 3ds Max. This field in the Material2 node determines the way in which light is applied to the texture.

cross-reference

You will learn much more about lighting, light maps, shading, and shadows in Module 5 Lesson 1.

Light Types

When working with 3D applications, you must understand several different types of light and the effect that each of these light options creates on the surface of rendered 3D objects. The terms we use to describe the lighting in simulations are derived from the effects that light produces on objects and the complex mathematical calculations needed to re-create these effects. These exact types of light do not actually exist in nature. The terms provide a way for us to define the light options. Remember that these options are not actually "light sources"—they are colors applied to the material of an object to make it appear "lit" in different ways.

In OpenGL, the common light types include the following options:

- Ambient light
- Diffuse light
- Specular light
- Emissive light

The following sections describe each type of light.

Ambient Light

The term ***ambient light*** is used to describe the color bouncing around the scene. Technically, ambient light is the average volume of light created by the emission of light from all of the light sources surrounding (or located inside of) the lit area.

As an example, when the sun's rays enter a room through a window, they directly hit some surfaces and then are reflected and scattered in different directions. This reflection and scattering has the impact of brightening the whole room. However, ambient light alone cannot accurately represent an object in 3D space because all points are evenly lit by the same color—making an object appear to be two-dimensional. Three-dimensional objects appear to be "flat" on the screen when lit by only ambient light.

Diffuse Light

Diffuse light is the light that has a specific position in space and comes from a single direction. It represents the directional light cast by a light source. Think of this light as the beam from a flashlight held slightly above the object. The diffuse color is typically the base color of the object that fills in the polygons of the mesh.

Typically, you use ambient light and diffuse light together to create objects that look more realistic. Together, these two lighting methods form the basis for making an object appear to be three-dimensional.

Specular Light

Specular light, sometimes referred to as *specular highlight* or *specular reflection*, provides the shininess of an object. Specular light is often white or light gray, and it is the "bright spot" on a curved surface. For example, if you create an illustration of a balloon, you make a lighter colored spot or semi-spherical shape on the side of the balloon to give it a rounded appearance. That spot is the result of specular light. The specular highlight is layered on the ambient light and diffuse light to enhance the object's 3D appearance.

Specular light, like diffuse light, is a directional light—meaning that it comes from one particular direction. However, unlike diffuse light, specular light reflects off the surface in a sharp, uniform way. The appearance of specular light is driven by the angle between the viewer and the light source. From the viewer's standpoint, specular light creates a highlighted area on the object's surface. The intensity of the specular light depends on the material the object is made of and the strength of the light source.

Emissive Light

Emissive light is different from the other lighting effects because it is the type of light emitted by the object, whereas the other three light types are used to describe a light source. The emissive light component is responsible for the ability of the object's material to reflect or absorb light. When applied to an object's material, emissive light simulates the light that is reflected off the object.

If you apply no other light sources, an object that has only the emissive light component applied will look the same as an object with only ambient light applied—it will appear flat or two-dimensional even though it is really three-dimensional. However, the way in which diffuse or specular light interacts with the surface of an object with only emissive light applied to it is different. If, for example, a sphere has a green emissive color and then you apply a red ambient light, a red diffuse light, and a white specular light, the resulting sphere will appear to have a yellowish surface. If the sphere did not have the green emissive color, it would have appeared red. But the light source color merges with the object's color (emissive color) to produce the yellowish surface. The specular light will appear white at the center of the object, but as it spreads from the center, it also merges with the green and red colors to create shades of yellow.

In the following activity, we will explore the interaction of textures, materials, and light maps.

tips+tricks

As you work through Activity 4.2.3, keep the following information in mind:

- The *mesh* defines the shape.
- The *material* fills the polygons of the mesh.
- The *texture* lays on the material and acts like a filter.

BEST PRACTICES

Keeping Resources Together

In Activity 4.2.3, expand the Scene, the Resources group, and the Meshes resource group. Note the mesh named Teapot01 contained in the Meshes resource group. Expand each Teapot frame, each Teapot shape, and the Geometry folder under each shape. Notice that each Teapot Shape node contains a link to the same Teapot01 mesh in the Resources group. This is an excellent illustration of conserving resource space by using only one mesh for several instances. The shape of each teapot will remain the same throughout this exercise; it is the material applied to each shape that changes.

Additionally, as you create materials in the activity, notice that you added the material to the Resources group before copying the material as a link to each teapot. These practices have the twofold benefit of allowing you to conserve resources and keeping all of your resources located in one place. As your simulations grow, this practice will become increasingly important to improve download and rendering speeds. It also makes it easier for you and your co-workers to manage and maintain the simulation.

Activity 4.2.3: Using Materials, Textures, and Light Maps

1. Open EON. Open **Activity_4.2.3** from the data files for Module 4 Lesson 2.
2. Run the simulation and notice that the simulation contains three white teapots. Close the simulation window.
3. Expand the **Resources** group to display the Materials group. Drag a **Material2** node into the Materials group.
4. Rename the Material2 node as **BasicBlue**.
5. With BasicBlue still selected, click the color swatch for the Diffuse color in the Property Bar. In the Color dialog box, select the blue color swatch that is in the first row, sixth column of the Color dialog box. Click **OK**. (The value for this color is 0 0.502 1.)
6. Change the Ambient color and the Specular color to white (**1 1 1**). Leave the Emissive color set to black (0 0 0).

7. Right-click **BasicBlue** in the simulation tree and select **Copy as Link**.
8. Expand the **Teapot1** frame until you see the Material folder. Right-click the **Material** folder and choose **Paste**.
9. Run the simulation. Your simulation window should appear similar to the one shown in Figure 4.2.9.

FIGURE 4.2.9 BasicBlue material applied to Teapot1

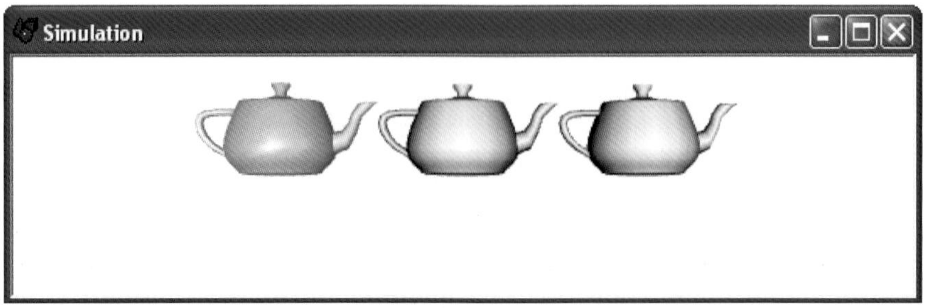

Discussion

discuss

You may see the selection handles around the teapot that you were working with because you have the Shape Selection tool toggled on. It does not affect the work you are doing; it simply lets you know which object is currently selected. When would you use these selection handles? How could they be useful to you while you are working in a simulation?

10. Close the simulation window. Drag a **TextureResourceGroup** node into the Resources group and rename it **Textures**.
11. Drag a **Texture2** node into the Textures group and rename it **Rockwall**.
12. With Rockwall still selected, select the folder icon next to the Filename field in the Property Bar. An Open dialog box will appear.
13. Browse to the location on your local hard drive where EON is installed (most likely C:\Program Files\EON Reality\EON Studio). Open the **MediaLibrary** folder and then the **Textures** folder. Select the **rockwall.png** texture and then select **Open**.
14. In the simulation tree, right-click **BasicBlue** in the expanded Materials group and select **Copy**.
15. Right-click the **Materials** group and select **Paste**. A copy of the BasicBlue material will be pasted into the group and named BasicBlue1.
16. Rename BasicBlue1 to **BasicBlueRockwall**.
17. Right-click **Rockwall** in the Textures group and choose **Copy as Link**.
18. Expand the **BasicBlueRockwall** material. Right-click **DiffuseTexture** and choose **Paste**.
19. Drag the **TextureUVMap** node into the DiffuseTextureUVMap folder under the BasicBlueRockwall material.
20. Right-click **BasicBlueRockwall** and choose **Copy as Link**.
21. Right-click **Material** under Teapot2. (Expand **Teapot2** and **Teapot02Shape**, if necessary.) Choose **Paste**.

22. Run the simulation. Your simulation window will appear similar to Figure 4.2.10.

FIGURE 4.2.10 Rockwall texture applied to the second teapot

23. Notice that the texture of the second teapot differs from the first teapot, but it does not exactly look like a rock wall because of the way in which the texture is mapped on to the surface of the teapot. With the simulation window still open, select **TextureUVMap** under Resource\Materials\BasicBlueRockwall\DiffuseTextureUVMap.
24. In the Property Bar, select the drop-down arrow next to Mode. Flat is the mode that was selected by default. The shape of the teapot much more closely resembles a sphere. Choose **Sphere** and observe the change in the teapot. Your simulation window should look like Figure 4.2.11.

FIGURE 4.2.11 Rockwall texture properly mapped to the teapot

Although the Rockwall texture is now applied to the teapot correctly, it still does not look like a rock wall. It appears to be a teapot that is painted to look like a rock wall. If you want the surface to really look like rocks, then you need to use a Cg shader material.

25. Close the simulation window. Drag a **MultiLayerMaterial** node to the Resources\Materials group and rename it **BasicBlueRockwallBump**.
26. Drag a **Texture2** node to the Textures group and rename it **RockwallNormal**.
27. With RockwallNormal still selected, select the folder icon next to the Filename field in the Property Bar and browse to locate the **rockwall_normal.png** texture in EON's Media Library. Select it and choose **Open**.
28. Expand **BasicBlueRockwallBump** (MultiLayerMaterial in the Materials resources). Do the following:
    a. Copy the **Rockwall** texture as a link from the Textures folder and paste it in BasicBlueRockwallBump's DiffuseTexture folder.
    b. Copy the **RockwallNormal** texture as a link from the Textures folder and paste it in BasicBlueRockwallBump's NormalMapTexture folder.
    c. Drag a new **TextureUVMap** node to the DiffuseTextureUVMap folder.

d. Set the TextureUVMap node's Mode to **Sphere** in the Property Bar.

e. Select the **BasicBlueRockwallBump** MultiLayer Material and, in the Property Bar, set the AmbientColor to **1 1 1**, the DiffuseColor to **0 0.502 1**, and the SpecularColor to **1 1 1**. (This matches the colors selected for the other materials.)

29. Right-click the **BasicBlueRockwallBump** MultiLayer Material and select **Copy as Link**. Paste it in the Material folder of Teapot3.

30. Run the simulation. Your simulation window should appear similar to Figure 4.2.12.

FIGURE 4.2.12 Texture with CG shaders for more realistic appearance

31. You can change the scale of the mapping of the texture onto the teapot. In the Resources\Materials group, expand the BasicBlueRockwallBump and the DiffuseTextureUVMap, if necessary. Select **TextureUVMap** and, in the Property Bar, change the UVScale values to **2 2**. Notice (in the simulation window) that the size of the rocks is now different between Teapot2 and Teapot3.

32. Close the simulation window. Drag a **Texture2** node into the Textures group and rename it **RockwallHeight**. Select the **Filename** folder in the Property Bar and browse to locate the **rockwall_height.png** texture in EON's Media Library. Click **Open**.

33. Right-click **RockwallHeight** in the simulation tree and choose **Copy as Link**. Right-click **DarkMapTexture** under the BasicBlueRockwallBump material and choose **Paste**.

34. Run the simulation. Your simulation window should appear similar to Figure 4.2.13. Notice that Teapot3 on the right seems to have deeper mortar lines between the rocks.

FIGURE 4.2.13 Texture with altered scale and dark mapping

35. Close the simulation window. Drag a **Texture2** node to the Textures group and rename it **CloudLightMap**.

36. With CloudLightMap selected, select the **Filename** folder in the Property Bar and browse to locate the **clouds_soft.jpg** from the data files for this lesson. Click **Open**.

37. Right-click **CloudLightMap** in the simulation tree and choose **Copy as Link**. Right-click the **LightmapTexture** folder under the BasicBlue material and choose **Paste**. Run the simulation. Your simulation window will appear similar to Figure 4.2.14.

FIGURE 4.2.14 A light map applied to Teapot1

38. Use your mouse (holding down the left button) in the simulation window to rotate the teapots. Notice that the rockwall textures remain fixed and the way the light reflects off of the rocks changes. On the other hand, the clouds on the first teapot are changing. This effect occurs because the clouds are a light map—meaning that they are a reflection on the teapot. The light source is behind the clouds, shining down on the teapot. Therefore, as the teapot moves, the clouds that are above it and their angle to the teapot are reflected differently.
39. Close the simulation window. Save the simulation as **TeapotTextures** and then close EON.

BEST PRACTICES

UV Maps in EON vs. UV Maps in Modeling Programs

View your final file for Activity 4.2.3 (TeapotTextures). If you rotate the teapots to view the back of the teapots, you can see a blurry area in the texture, as shown in Figure BP 4.2.1.

FIGURE BP 4.2.1 Texture mapping flaws

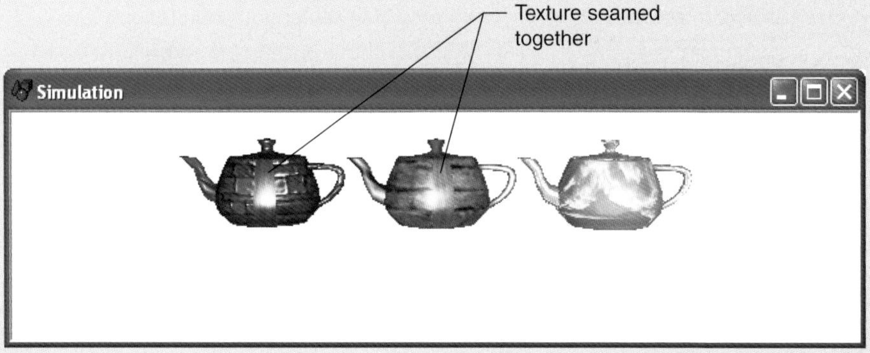

This blurry area is located where the edges of the texture that "wrapped" around the object meet—a sort of seam where the edges of the texture meet. Think of it like wrapping a gift. Sometimes the design at the edge of the wrapping paper matches at the seam on the bottom side, and sometimes it doesn't. EON attempts to fill in the design to make the texture from the two edges merge, but it doesn't always work perfectly.

A better way to approach mapping textures to a surface is to apply the texture in the modeling program—before it is brought into EON. Modeling programs are adept at accurately applying a texture to a surface. Although there are situations in which it is not possible to apply the texture in a modeling program (or there may be situations in which it does not matter), it is preferable to use your modeling program to make your simulation clean and accurate.

Figure BP 4.2.2 is an illustration of the same teapot that we used in the Activity 4.2.3 simulation. In this case, however, the rockwall texture was applied before the teapot was imported into EON.

FIGURE BP 4.2.2 Apply the texture map in a modeling program to prevent a "seam" on either side

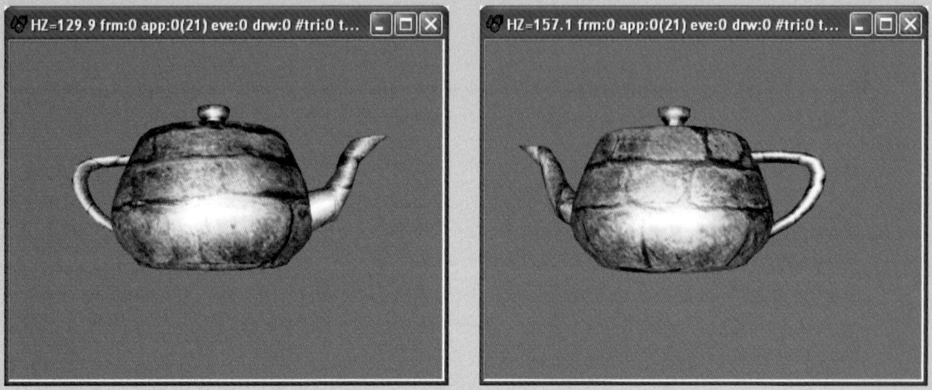

No matter which side of the teapot you look at, you cannot discern where the texture map starts and stops.

Summary

In this lesson you:

- Became familiar with the Visual Nodes library.
- Learned about the resource database created from the materials, textures, and meshes that comprise an imported model.
- Began to explore the various types of lighting that affect your simulation.
- Experimented with creating your own materials, textures, and lighting and applying them to objects in a simulation.

LESSON 4.3

3D Edit Tools

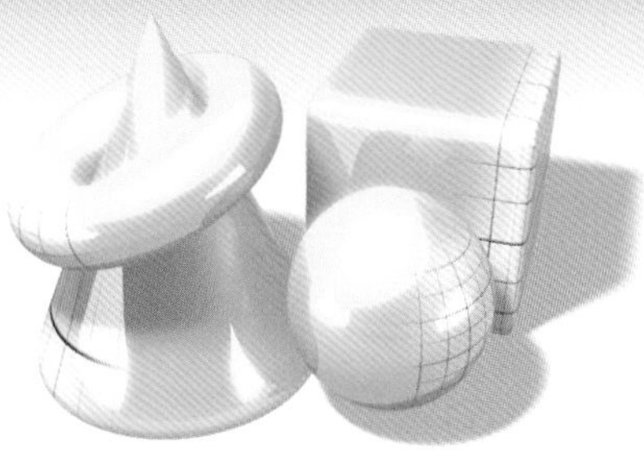

Objectives

In this lesson you will:

- Learn how to use the Zoom Extents tool.
- Understand how to use the Shape, Geometry, Material, and Texture selection tools.
- Develop an understanding of the Visual Nodes tools.
- Become familiar with the Face Fixing and Paint Material tools.

Key Terms

Convert 3.1 Visual Nodes tool	*Make texture compression/ resize permanent tool*	*Remove duplicated resources tool*
Display info of a node tool	*Material selection tool*	*Shape selection tool*
Face Fixing tool	*Merge Shapes with the same material tool*	*Texture selection tool*
Geometry selection tool	*Paint Material tool*	*Zoom Extents tool*

EON provides several 3D editing tools that will help you to enhance the overall look and performance of a simulation. Whether you want to locate an object, select a material, or repair a model, an EON tool can assist you with your task.

Zoom Extents Tool

Zoom Extents is a feature that enables you to quickly locate 3D objects in the simulation window. You can use the ***Zoom Extents tool*** to move the camera to allow the selected object to come into view completely.

cross-reference

Clipping planes and boundaries were briefly touched on in Module 2 Lesson 1, and both topics are discussed in greater detail in Module 6 Lesson 1.

If you inadvertently move the camera so that objects are further away than the camera's far clipping plane or objects are closer than the camera's near clipping plane, then objects may not be visible in the simulation window. If this happens, click the Zoom Extents button on the toolbar to reset the camera's position to a default location.

You can use the Zoom Extents tool to zoom out in the simulation window. While the simulation window is displayed, select a Frame node in the simulation tree and click the Zoom Extents button. The camera in the 3D simulation window zooms to display the element selected in the simulation tree. If a Frame node is selected in the simulation tree, all objects in the subtree beneath the Frame node will be displayed. If the geometry in the subtree spans a vast area, the camera may be pulled far away from the objects to display all of the objects.

The Zoom Extents tool also enables you to find 3D objects in the simulation window quickly. While the simulation window is displayed, select a prototype or Shape node in the simulation tree. The camera in the 3D simulation window zooms to display the object associated with the element selected in the simulation tree.

Activity 4.3.1: Using Zoom Extents

1. Open EON. Open **Activity_4.3.1.eoz** from the data files for Module 4 Lesson 3.
2. If the EON Zoom Extents Bar is not displayed, open the **View** menu and select **EON Zoom Extents Bar**.
3. Run the simulation. Notice that the simulation window is empty.
4. Move the simulation window if necessary so that you can access the simulation tree and the EON Zoom Extents Bar while the simulation window is displayed.
5. In the simulation tree, expand the **Floorplan** frame and then select the **Kitchen** frame. Click the **Zoom Extents** button.
6. In the simulation tree, expand the following frames: **Floorplan > Dining_Room > Dining_Table > _offset_**.
7. Click the **Dining_TableShape** node and click the **Zoom Extents** button.
8. Close the simulation window. Close EON without saving the simulation.

Selection Tools

Four selection tools are available on the EONSelectionTools Bar shown in Figure 4.3.1. You can use these tools to interactively select a shape, mesh, material, or texture by selecting the appropriate button from the toolbar and then clicking an object in the simulation window.

cross-reference

The Paint Material and Face Fixing tools are discussed later in this lesson.

FIGURE 4.3.1 EONSelectionTools Bar

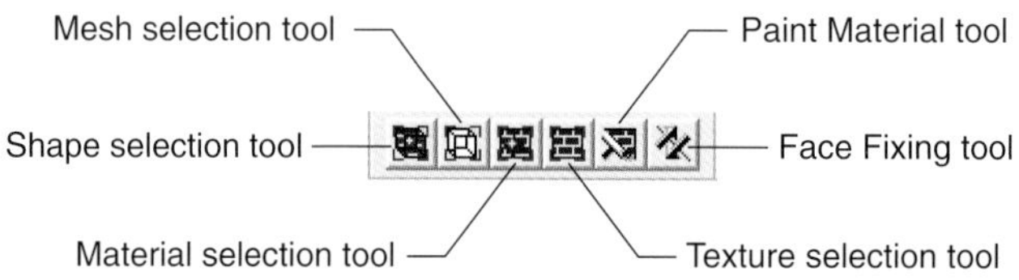

A selection tool is active until you click another selection tool or turn off the current tool by clicking it again. (A toolbar button that is not selected appears to be in a raised position.) While a selection tool is active, press the Alt key and click an object in the simulation window. The tool will try to select the subject (a shape, mesh, material, or texture depending on the current selection tool). If successful, the corresponding node in the simulation tree is selected, and selection brackets, which look like broken wireframe boxes, appear around the selected object in the simulation window. Note that selection brackets do not display for texture and material selections.

To use the selection tools, you must run the simulation. The selection is made in the simulation window. Therefore, the selection tools cannot be used when the simulation is stopped.

Click a selection tool and then click in the simulation window to activate the window if it is not already active. Next, press the Alt key and click an object in the simulation window to select its shape, mesh, material, or texture. To change your selection, press the Alt key and click a different object.

You can change to another selection tool by returning to the toolbar buttons and clicking the desired tool. Note that this deactivates the simulation window, so you must click in the simulation window before you can start selecting items again.

troubleshooting

The selection tools do not work with any materials or textures from the earlier 3.0 version of EON, with the exception of the old Mesh node. Therefore, your selection attempt will be unsuccessful if the simulation uses the older Material or Texture nodes rather than the newer Material2 and Texture2 nodes.

Shape Selection

The Shape selection tool is a great tool for locating an object in the simulation tree. It also makes it easier to find the Frame node, which is helpful when you need to modify the node.

To activate the ***Shape selection tool*** in EON, click the Enter Shape selection mode button on the toolbar. When this mode is active, press the Alt key and click an object in the simulation window to select the object's Shape node. The object is selected (marked with a yellow bounding box around the selected object) and the corresponding Shape node is selected in the simulation tree.

When the Shape selection mode is active, it also will work the other way—when an object is selected in the simulation tree, a yellow bounding box will appear around the object in the simulation window. When you select a shape and click the Zoom Extents button, the simulation window will zoom in on the object.

troubleshooting

In some cases, several Shape nodes use the same Mesh2 node, which means that the selection brackets will be displayed around several objects, even though you have clicked only one. This indicates which objects are currently sharing this particular geometry.

Geometry Selection

The Geometry selection tool is useful for reducing polygon count on a mesh that is selected in the scene. To activate the ***Geometry selection tool*** in EON, click the Enter Geometry selection mode button on the toolbar. When this mode is active, press the Alt key and click an object in the simulation window to select the Mesh2 node providing the object's geometry. Use the Geometry selection mode to identify the mesh in the Resource directory after the object is selected in the simulation window.

You also can select the Mesh2 node in the simulation tree. Objects using the mesh will be selected in the simulation window.

troubleshooting

If the object is using a MultiMaterial node (several material definitions in one mesh), the Material2 node of the actual submaterial under the mouse cursor (click position) is selected, not the MultiMaterial node. To select the MultiMaterial node, you have to use the simulation tree.

Material Selection

The Material selection tool can be used to locate and edit materials used in a simulation. To activate the ***Material selection tool*** in EON, click the Enter Material selection mode button on the toolbar. When this mode is active, press the Alt key and click an object in the simulation window to select the Material2 node providing the object's appearance. Use the Material selection tool to identify the material in the Resources group after selecting the object in the simulation window. You also can use this tool to edit the colors of various object parts quickly. Material selection mode works only from the simulation window to the simulation tree. Selection brackets are not displayed in the simulation window when Material selection mode is active.

troubleshooting

You cannot select the lightmap texture using the Texture selection tool. Instead, you must use the simulation tree or the Material selection tool to access the reference to the lightmap texture.

Texture Selection

The ***Texture selection tool*** is used to identify textures used in a simulation. To activate the Texture selection tool in EON, click the Enter Texture selection mode button on the toolbar. When this mode is active, press the Alt key and click an object that has textures mapped on its surface to select the corresponding Texture2 node. Like the Material selection tool, selection brackets are not displayed in the simulation window when using the Texture selection mode tool.

troubleshooting

The Texture selection tool currently works only on Material2 nodes.

Reverse Selection

When the Shape selection mode or the Geometry selection mode is active (indicated by the depressed toolbar button), the selection brackets will follow the selection made in the simulation tree. In other words, when you select another Shape node in the simulation tree, the selection brackets will jump to the corresponding object in the simulation window. Because Material selection mode and Texture selection mode do not display selection brackets, this reverse selection feature works only for Shape selection mode and Geometry selection mode.

troubleshooting

For Activities 4.3.2 through 4.3.5, EON recommends using a computer equipped with a NVIDIA or ATI Graphics Card driver. (You may see errors as you work through the activities if you are using a computer with the Intel Integrated Graphics driver.) Also, ensure that your computer has the latest version of Microsoft DirectX installed.

Activity 4.3.2: Using the Selection Tools

1. Open EON. Open **Activity_4.3.2.eoz** from the data files for Module 4 Lesson 3.
2. Run the simulation.
3. Click the **Enter Shape selection mode** button on the toolbar.
4. In the simulation tree, expand the following frames: **Scene > Toyota > Exterior > Car_Hood > Car_Hood_Frame > Hood**.
5. Press the **Alt** key and then click **HoodShape**, as shown in Figure 4.3.2. The car's hood is selected in the simulation window.

FIGURE 4.3.2 Select HoodShape in the simulation tree

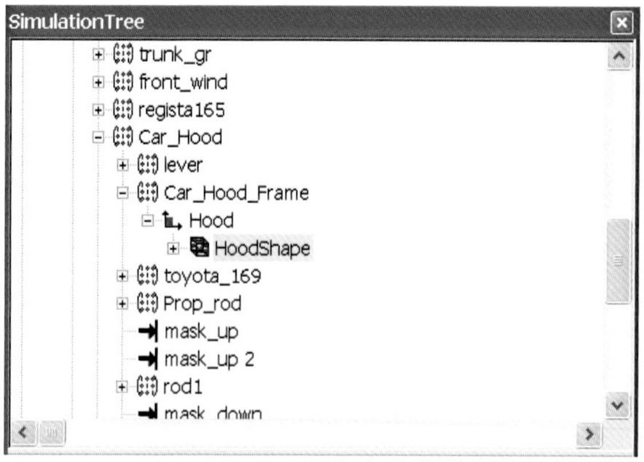

6. Select the **Enter Geometry selection mode** button on the toolbar.
7. Press the **Alt** key and click one of the wheel rims in the simulation window. Note the Mesh2 node selected in the simulation tree.
8. Close the simulation window.
9. In the Property Bar, clear the **UseGroupSetting** check box.
10. Also in the Property Bar, click the **PolygonReductionLevel** option and reduce the polygon count by 50%.
11. Run the simulation.

discuss

Why could a simulation have duplicated resources?

Activity 4.3.4: Removing Duplicated Resources

1. Open EON. Open **Activity_4.3.4.eoz** from the data files for Module 4 Lesson 3.
2. In the simulation tree, click **Scene**.
3. Click the **Remove duplicated resources** button on the VisualNodesTools Bar. The Select Nodes to Remove dialog box appears, as shown in Figure 4.3.9.

FIGURE 4.3.9 Select Nodes to Remove dialog box

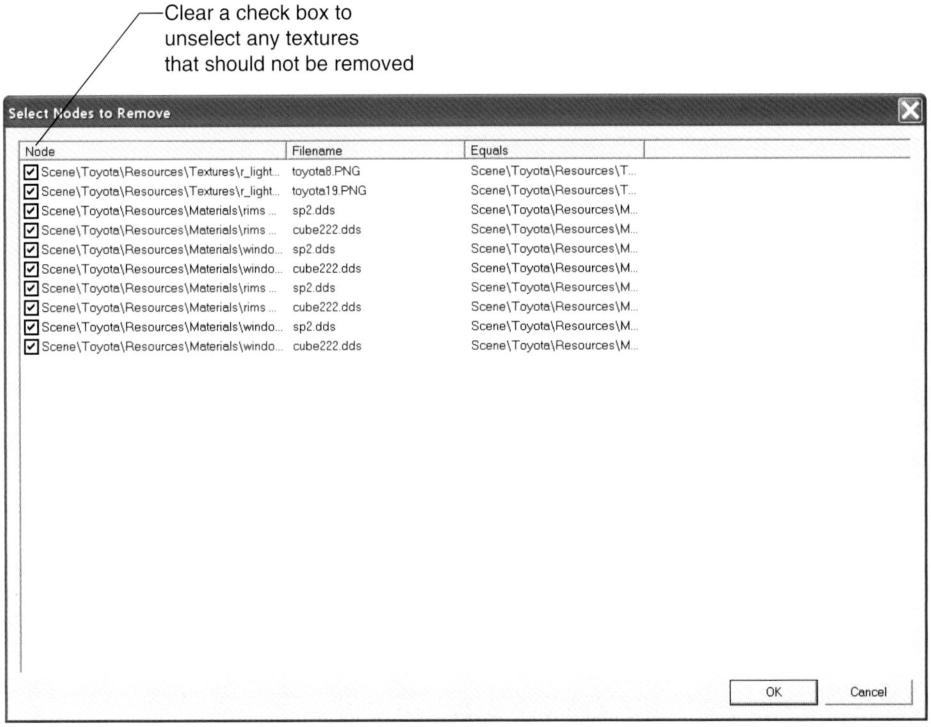

4. Examine the list of textures that will be removed. If necessary, you can clear the check box for each texture that you want to keep so you can change the textures in the future. Click **OK**.
5. Run the simulation.
6. Close the simulation window. Save the simulation as **Toyota_Resources.eoz** and then close EON.

Face Fixing Tool

Sometimes when importing certain types of 3D data, typically 3D CAD models, the face orientation is displayed incorrectly. This means some faces either are not visible (holes in the object) or are completely black (even if you increase the ambient light, the surface is still black). If this happens, you can use the ***Face Fixing tool*** in EON to make manual corrections to the faces.

First, activate the tool by clicking the Enter Face Fixing mode button on the EONSelectionTools Bar (see Figure 4.3.1). Next, start the simulation, if it is not already running, and click in the simulation window.

tips+tricks

Click the Enter Face Fixing mode button a second time to deactivate the tool.

Point the mouse cursor to the hollow surface or the black area and click the left mouse button while pressing the Alt key to fix the selected face. With each click, the "normals" of the selected face are reversed. You can click repeatedly until the face looks correct.

Paint Material Tool

EON allows you to use a simple point-and-click approach to assign materials to objects by using the ***Paint Material tool.*** To activate this tool, click the Enter Paint Material mode button on the EONSelectionTools Bar (see Figure 4.3.1). Next, start the simulation if it is not already running, and select a material in the simulation tree that you want to apply to an object.

tips+tricks

Click the Enter Paint Material mode button a second time to deactivate the tool.

Activate the simulation window and click the surface of the object you want to paint while pressing the Alt key. Instantly, the existing material will be replaced with the new one you selected in the simulation tree.

Activity 4.3.5: Using the Face Fixing and Paint Material Tools

1. Open EON. Open **Activity_4.3.5.eoz** from the data files for Module 4 Lesson 3.
2. Click the **Enter Face Fixing mode** button on the VisualNodesTools Bar.
3. Run the simulation.
4. Press the **Alt** key while you click all of the car's exterior panels.
5. Click the **Enter Paint Material mode** button on the VisualNodesTools Bar.
6. In the simulation tree, expand **Scene** and **MaterialOptions**. Select either the **Gold Paint** or **Silver Paint** option (see Figure 4.3.10).

FIGURE 4.3.10 MaterialOptions group

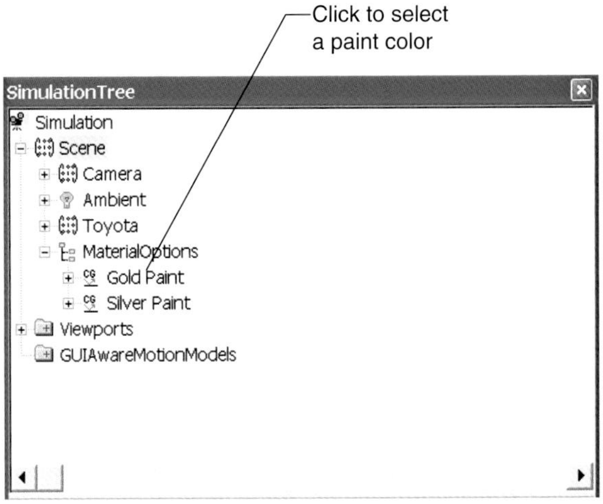

7. Press the **Alt** key while you click all of the car's exterior panels.
8. Close the simulation window. Save the simulation as **Toyota_Color.eoz** and close EON.

Summary

In this lesson you:

- Learned how to use the Zoom Extents tool.
- Understood how to use the Shape, Geometry, Material, and Texture selection tools.
- Developed an understanding of the Visual Nodes tools.
- Became familiar with the Face Fixing and Paint Material tools.

Simulation

Your employer, Contours Company, is impressed with your work, including the storyboard you created and the enhancements you made to the apartment simulation file. The client reviewed the apartment simulation and was pleased with the overall layout and object placement. However, the client has requested a few additional enhancements to certain objects in the apartment. Contours asked you to update your storyboard and include ideas for reducing the processing time for the simulation. Based on your understanding of various EON tools, you must fill the client's requests.

Job 4.1: Updating a Storyboard

Recently, you completed a storyboard for the client's apartment. You also created a simulation of the client's apartment, which provided the ability to "walk through" the apartment's floor plan. Later, you imported objects and textures into the simulation. Now, the client wants to reduce the processor requirements for the simulation and see the effects of a brighter color scheme throughout the apartment. Calling on your knowledge of the Visual Nodes library, resources, and various EON tools, update the storyboard to include ideas for reducing the simulation's processor time and brightening the apartment's color scheme. Keep in mind that you can change colors for all of the items in the apartment, including walls, furniture, curtains, and so on.

1. Open EON. Open **Job_3.2**, the apartment simulation you enhanced in the Module 3 Simulation.
2. Run the simulation and navigate through the apartment.
3. Using your knowledge of the Visual Nodes library shown in Figure 4.1 and the Resources group, take notes on ways to reduce processor requirements in the simulation.

FIGURE 4.1 Visual Nodes library

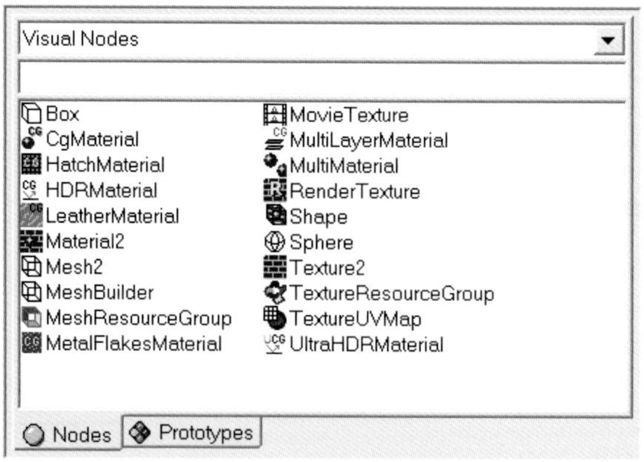

4. Apply your understanding of various EON tools, such as the tools on the EONSelectionTools Bar (shown in Figure 4.2), to determine how brighter colors could be applied throughout the apartment.

FIGURE 4.2 EONSelectionTools Bar

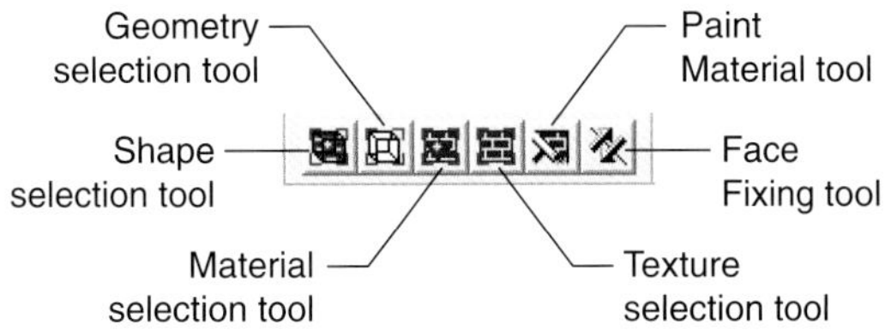

5. Close the simulation window.
6. Open the storyboard that you created in the Module 1 Simulation and enhanced in the Module 2 and 3 Simulations. (If you did not complete the Simulation sections for Modules 1 through 3, you can create a storyboard using paper and pencil, a flowchart application, or a drawing program.) Add information about reducing the processor requirements in the simulation file based on the notes you made as you navigated through the apartment. Consider the Visual Nodes library and the use of resources when updating the storyboard.
7. Include ideas for implementing a brighter color scheme throughout the apartment, and identify the object(s) you would recommend changing and the new colors you would suggest using.
8. Complete your storyboard and then save your work.

Job 4.2: Reducing Processor Time for the Apartment Simulation

In Job 3.2, you imported additional objects into the apartment simulation file to enhance the apartment's overall visual appeal. Unfortunately, the added objects probably increased the size of the simulation file, thus increasing the required processing time for the simulation file.

1. Review the observations you made in Job 4.1 for reducing processor time for the simulation file.
2. If necessary, open EON and then open **Job_3.2.eoz** (if you closed it in Job 4.1). Save the simulation as **Job_4.2.eoz**.
3. Apply your knowledge of the Visual Nodes library and resources to reduce the simulation's processing time.
4. Save the simulation and keep it open to use in Job 4.3.

Job 4.3: Brightening the Apartment Color Scheme

The client requested brighter colors throughout the apartment. Modify colors and use more visually interesting and appealing textures.

1. If necessary, open EON and then open **Job_4.2**, the simulation that you updated in Job 4.2.
2. Navigate to the living room in the apartment.
3. Use your knowledge of EON's 3D editing tools to select an object and apply a brighter color to the object.
4. Change the color(s) of other objects in the living room, maintaining a bright and consistent theme throughout.
5. Navigate to other rooms in the apartment and change colors to brighten the overall color scheme of each area.

tips+tricks

Because the client only indicated a preference for brighter colors applied throughout the apartment without specifying any exact color(s), you could provide several different samples for review. You may create multiple simulation files, each incorporating a slightly different color scheme throughout the apartment. For example, you could feature shades of red in one simulation, blues in a second simulation file, yellows in a third simulation file, and so on.

If time is short, you could produce the same effect within a single simulation file simply by introducing a different color in each room of the apartment. For example, use reds in the family room, blues in the kitchen, yellows in the bedroom, and so on.

6. Run the simulation.
7. Close the simulation window. Save the simulation and then close EON.

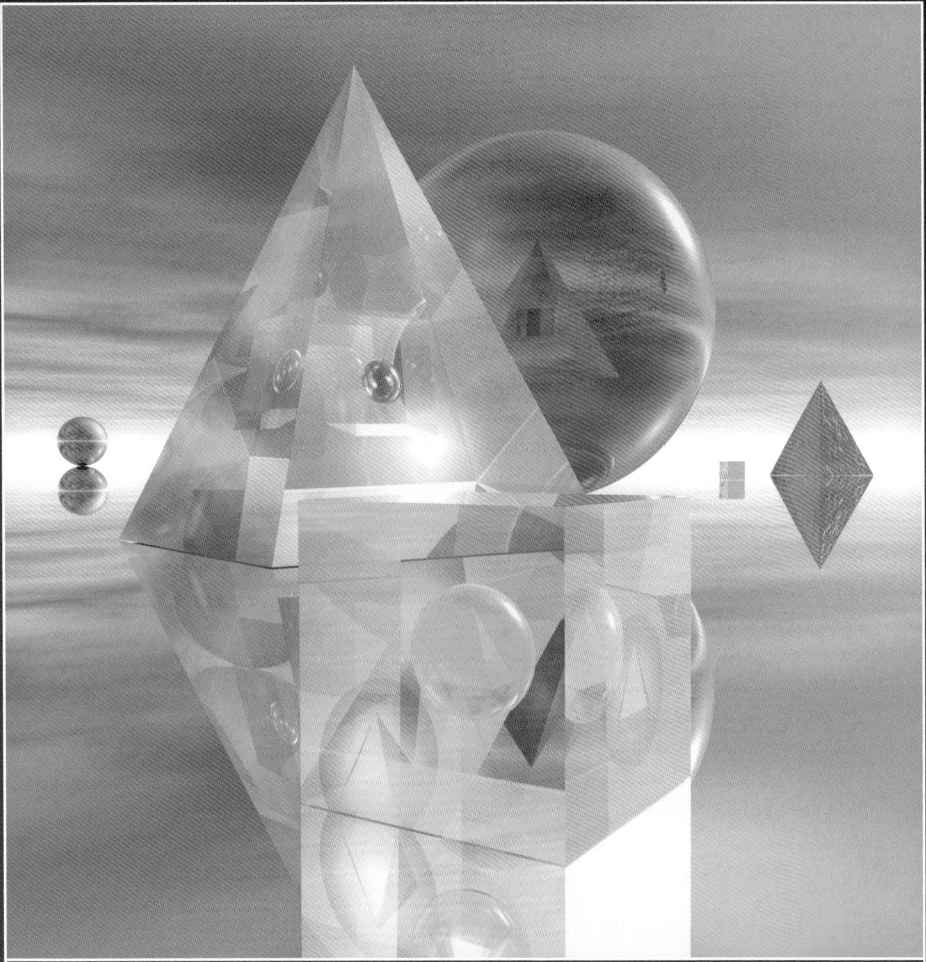

HARALD SUND

MODULE 5

Object Appearance, Behavior, and Interactivity

LESSON 5.1

Modify Object Appearance

LESSON 5.2

Add Behavior and Interactivity to Simulations

LESSON 5.1

Modify Object Appearance

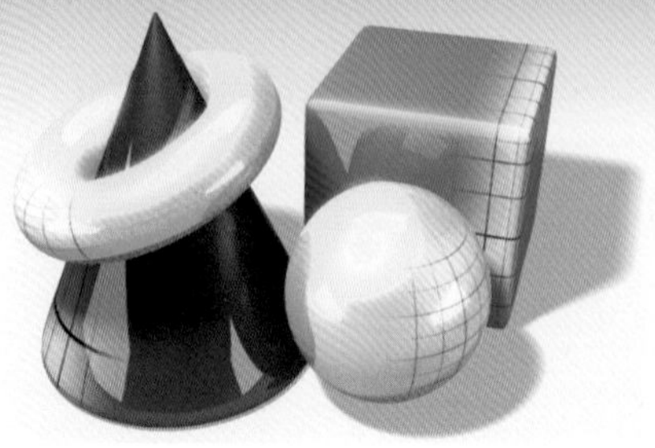

Objectives

In this lesson you will:

- Learn about adding light.
- Develop an understanding of the Texture2 node.
- Become familiar with the Material2 node.
- Look at an object's appearance.
- Study the use of scaling to change the size and shape of objects.
- Understand the Opacity settings that control an object's transparency.
- Modify render settings.

Key Terms

ambient light source	***Gouraud shading***	***quadratic***
attenuation	***Light node***	***RGB values***
constant	***linear***	***spot light source***
directional light source	***parallel point light source***	***transparency***
dither	***point light source***	

Adding Light

EON uses ***Light nodes*** to illuminate objects in simulations. You can create an almost unlimited number of lighting effects by combining and defining different Light node settings. Lighting effects also are affected by the characteristics of the textures and materials that are applied to meshes.

STORYBOARD

Lighting in the Simulation Creation Process

You have learned about proper model placement. Now you will study various lighting effects.

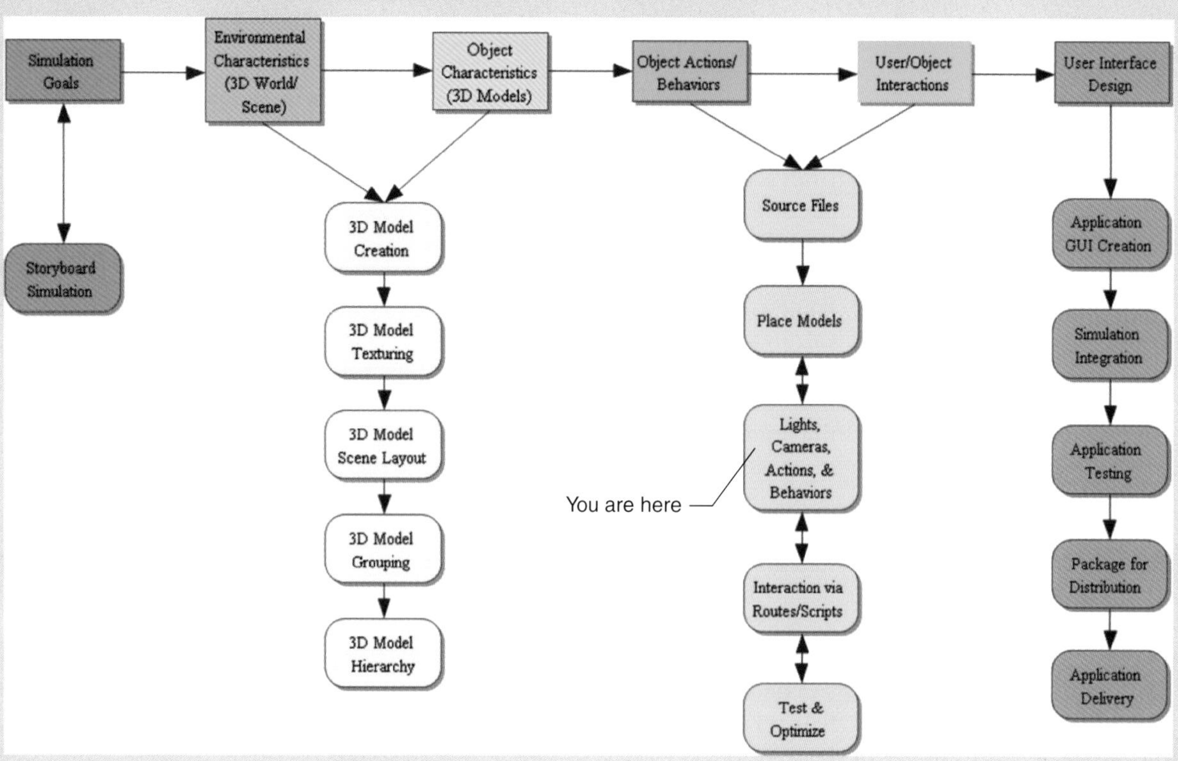

In this lesson, we will learn about the various lighting effects you can add to a simulation. We will discuss the Texture2 and Material2 nodes, scaling, transparency, and render settings.

Light Modes

EON has two Light modes—On and Off. When the Light mode is On, the objects in your simulation are illuminated by the Light nodes in the simulation tree. When the Light mode is Off, the Light nodes will not illuminate the simulation objects.

Light Node Parameters

As we discussed, Light nodes illuminate objects in a simulation. You can customize the appearance of the light and its effect on the objects in a simulation by modifying the Light node's settings or the parent Frame node's settings. These settings define the light type, light color, position, orientation, attenuation, and objects lit by the Light node. We will look at the Light node settings.

Light Types

Light nodes may be set to represent any of the following light types: ambient, directional, parallel point, point, and spot. The light type is determined by the source of the light.

- Ambient—An ***ambient light source*** appears to illuminate all objects with equal intensity in all directions, like indirect sunlight. You cannot control the position of an ambient light source.
- Directional—A ***directional light source*** is linked to a Frame node but appears to illuminate all objects with equal intensity in one direction, as if it were at an

infinite distance from the scene. Directional light sources are commonly used to simulate direct sunlight. This alternative is the best choice for maximum rendering speed. With directional light, the angle at which light is coming from is the same for all objects in the scene.

- Parallel Point—A ***parallel point light source*** has a position and radiates light in all directions. When this light strikes an object, the angle that it strikes is assumed to be parallel (like directional) for all faces in that object. Rendering-speed performance for parallel point light sources are nearly as high as with directional light sources. The parallel point falls somewhere between directional light and point light. With a parallel point light source, the angle at which light is coming from is the same for the whole object, but different for each other object. The angle of light is calculated as the angle between the position of the light and the bounding box center of the object (mesh). Therefore, it is called *parallel* because all the light rays hitting a certain object will be parallel.
- Point—A ***point light source*** radiates light equally in all directions. It requires the calculation of a new lighting vector for each facet it illuminates. For this reason, it is computationally more demanding than parallel point light sources. However, it produces more realistic lighting effects, and you should choose it when visual fidelity is your primary concern. With a point light source, the angle of the light is calculated between the point light source and each polygon of the mesh. This is why it is computationally intensive.
- Spot—A ***spot light source*** emits a cone of light and it illuminates only objects that are within this cone. Two angle values, called the *umbra* and the *penumbra*, define the variation of light intensity as a function of an angle. The umbra defines an inner "core" cone within which light is at full intensity. The penumbra cone surrounds the umbra cone and is less intense, with an illumination curve gradually decreasing in the interval between the umbra angle (where light is at full intensity) and the penumbra angle (where there is no light). Spot light is like point light in that the angle of the light is calculated between the spot light's position and the center of the polygon, but the light only affects objects within a cone and its intensity lessens as the distance from the light to the polygon increases.

Light Color

Light color is determined by ***RGB values***, which define the amount of red, blue, and green used in a color. You can modify RGB values in the Property Bar or on the Color tab of the Light Properties dialog box (both are shown in Figure 5.1.1). Enter color values in the Red, Green, and Blue fields.

tips+tricks

If you don't know the RGB value for the color you want, click the Change color button in the Light Properties dialog box. It will open a Color dialog box that allows you to click a displayed color to fill in the RGB values.

FIGURE 5.1.1 Set the light color in the Property Bar or in the Light Properties dialog box

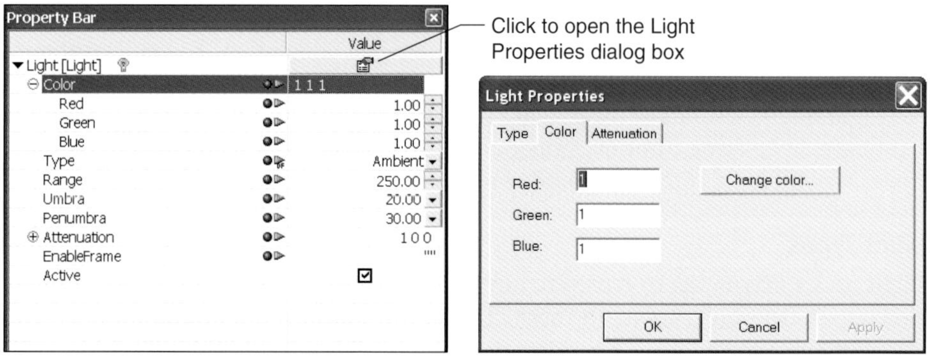

Light Position and Orientation

The position and orientation for most light sources is determined by the parent Frame node. You can modify these values in the Property Bar or on the Translation/Rotation tab of the Frame Properties dialog box (both are shown in Figure 5.1.2).

FIGURE 5.1.2 Set the light's position and orientation in the parent Frame node

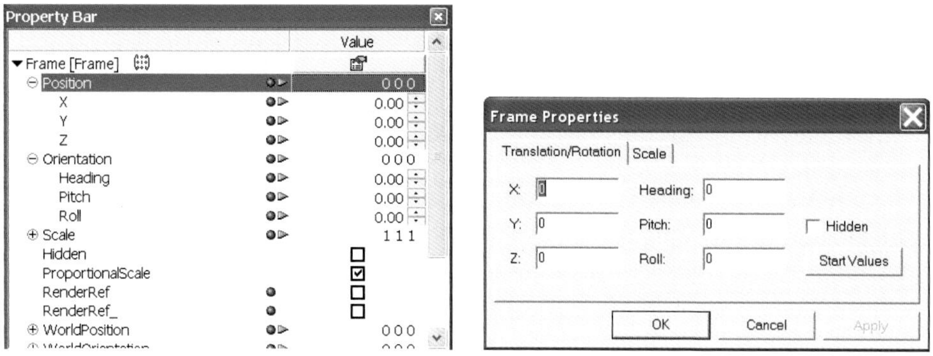

tips+tricks

The light's position will follow the default position of the parent Frame node.

Table 5.1.1 identifies the light sources that are affected by modifying the values in the Position and/or Orientation fields of their parent Frame nodes.

TABLE 5.1.1 Light Sources

Light Source Type	Position	Orientation
Ambient	NO	NO
Directional	NO	YES
Parallel point	YES	NO
Point	YES	NO
Spot	YES	YES

Attenuation

The amount of light that falls on real-world objects diminishes noticeably as a local light source moves away from the object. This is known as ***attenuation***. In EON, a local light source is one that has position. (See Table 5.1.1.) Use the settings on the Attenuation tab in the Light Properties dialog box shown in Figure 5.1.3 to reproduce this effect. Combine different coefficient values to customize attenuation for circumstances unique to your simulation.

FIGURE 5.1.3 Attenuation tab in the Light Properties dialog box

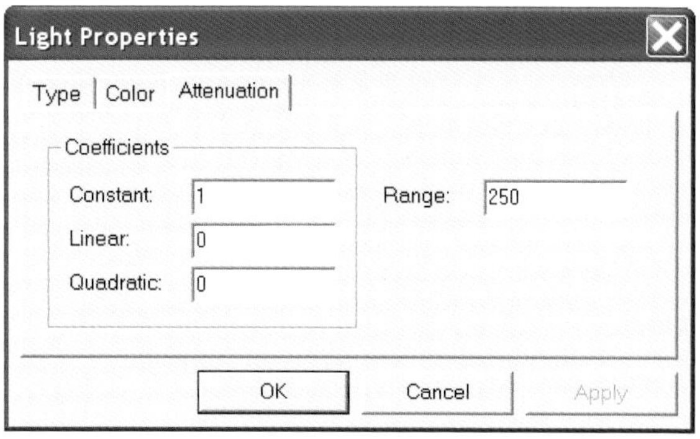

tips+tricks

The Range value is only valid for spot light sources. The three coefficients (Constant, Linear, and Quadratic) define how light intensity decreases in proportion to the distance from the light source.

- Constant—Light intensity decreases when the ***Constant*** value increases. The light intensity is constant in relation to the distance from the light source.
- Linear—When the ***Linear*** value increases, light intensity decreases faster in relation to the distance from the light source.

tips+tricks

Small coefficient values (values of magnitude of 0.01) give rise to considerable effects on light intensity.

tips+tricks

The EnableFrame folder does not affect ambient light types. Ambient light types will always affect the entire scene.

- **Quadratic**—The ***Quadratic*** value gives the curves a steeper slope than linear values and decreases light intensity faster (in relation to the distance) than linear values. A higher quadratic value decreases light intensity faster than a lower value.
- **Range**—The Range value specifies the distance from the light source at which light intensity is zero (no objects are illuminated by the light source).

Selective Lighting—The EnableFrame Folder

A Light node may illuminate the entire scene or a limited number of nodes. The contents of the EnableFrame folder (actually a graphic representation of the Light node's EnableFrame field) determine which objects in the simulation are lit.

If the EnableFrame folder is empty, its Light node will illuminate the entire scene. If the EnableFrame folder contains a Frame node or a reference to a Frame node, only the meshes beneath that Frame node will be illuminated. To add a reference to the EnableFrame folder, right-click a Frame node in the simulation tree and select Copy as Link from the pop-up menu. Return to the Light node, right-click the EnableFrame field, and select Paste.

Default Light Nodes

New simulations have two default Light nodes—Ambient and Headlight. The Ambient node is set to Ambient and produces lighting effects similar to reflected sunlight, whereas the Headlight node is set to Directional and produces lighting effects similar to a flashlight pointing straight ahead. The Headlight node follows the movement of the simulation's camera because it is placed below the Camera node in the default simulation tree.

Activity 5.1.1 Adding a Spot Light

1. Open EON. Open **Activity_5.1.1.eoz** from the data files for Module 5 Lesson 1.
2. Save the file as **Apartment_Spot.eoz**.
3. Expand **Scene** and **ActiveViewportCamera** and click **Headlight** in the simulation tree. The Property Bar should look like the one in Figure 5.1.4.

FIGURE 5.1.4 Property Bar for Headlight

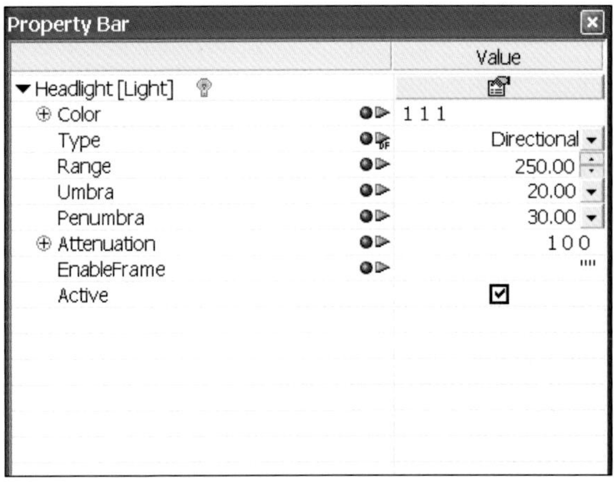

4. Clear the ***Active*** check box option to deactivate the Headlight Light node.
5. Run the simulation to see the effect of turning off the Headlight Light node.
6. Close the simulation window.

7. In the simulation tree, add a **Frame** node under the Scene frame and rename it **SpotLight**.
8. Add a **Light** node under the SpotLight frame. In the Property Bar, change the Type value to **Spot**.
9. In the simulation tree, add a **Cone** prototype and a **3DPointer** prototype under the SpotLight frame. Your simulation tree should resemble Figure 5.1.5.

FIGURE 5.1.5 Simulation tree with SpotLight frame added

10. In the simulation tree, select **Spotlight**. In the Property Bar, change Position to **–0.94 4.7 3.08** and change Orientation to **0 90 0**. Ensure that WorldPosition is set to **–0.94 4.7 3.08** and WorldOrientation is set to **0 90 0**.
11. In the simulation tree, select **Cone**. In the Property Bar, change Orientation to **0 –90 0** and Scale to **.25 .25 .25**.
12. Run the simulation to view the effect of the Spot light and then close the simulation window.
13. In the simulation tree, select **Light**. In the Property Bar, change Type to **Directional**. Run the simulation to view the effect of the Directional light and then close the simulation window.
14. In the simulation tree, select **Light**. In the Property Bar, change Type to **Ambient**. Run the simulation to view the effect of the Ambient light and then close the simulation window.
15. In the simulation tree, select **Light**. In the Property Bar, change Type back to **Spot**.
16. Save the simulation and then close EON.

Adding Textures

Textures are images that can be used to supply details to a surface in a way that is computationally efficient. EON has two types of texture resource nodes: Texture2 and MovieTexture. The difference between these two nodes is that the latter uses a movie file as the image source, and the former uses a simple static image file.

cross-reference

To review information about the Texture2 node, see Module 4 Lesson 2.

Texture2 Node Properties

The Texture2 node supports only five image formats: DDS, JPEG, JPEG2000, PNG, and PPM. Therefore, you should convert any foreign image formats to JPEG or PNG before the import process begins. The Texture2 node must be referenced by a Material2 node to be visible in the scene. Also, this Material2 node must be used by a Shape node.

Material2 Node

troubleshooting

Many importers will automatically convert most common image formats to PNG or JPEG2000, but to maintain maximum control, you should convert your file to the proper format yourself before importing it.

The Material2 node changes the colors, emissive parameters, and specular parameters of its parent Mesh node. The Material2 node is a new version of the Material node and it is used with other nodes in the Visual Nodes library. It represents a material in the scene. To apply a material to a 3D object, you must combine it with a geometry node (Mesh2 node) using the Shape node.

Object Appearance

troubleshooting

When importing a file with EON version 4.0 and newer, the new and enhanced Material2 node will be created and you can successfully use it with the new EON 4.0 nodes. Although you can open and view files containing the old Material node, you will find that many new functions do not work with the older node.

Objects in a simulation can be displayed in many ways. In EON applications, the variations are nearly unlimited. You can modify lighting, shading, object fill, colors, and textures. You can even play video clips on object surfaces.

A three-dimensional object created in a modeling program is often referred to as a *mesh*. A mesh is added to an EON application by referencing a geometry file from a Mesh2 node's Properties dialog box. The referenced mesh file defines the shape of a mesh. Meshes are made up of polygons. The shape of the modeled object determines the total number of polygons that comprise it; a complex object is usually made of more polygons than a simpler one. Mesh files use the .eog or .x file extension. Several sample mesh files are included in EON's Media directory. These files can be used in the EON applications you construct while you are learning EON. Later, when you begin applying your knowledge of EON to your own unique simulations, you can import mesh files created in other programs.

Scaling: Changing the Size of Objects

You can change the size of objects by changing the scale in the object's parent frame. You can use the parent frame's Frame Properties dialog box to change the scale. If the Proportional scaling check box is selected, then changing the scale of one dimension changes the other dimensions proportionally. If the check box is cleared, you can change one dimension of the object (its vertical or horizontal size) disproportionately to its other dimension, thus changing the shape of the object.

To skew an object, place two Frame nodes under each other and place a Shape node under the last Frame node. Then scale the first Frame node and change the orientation of the second Frame node.

Because a Frame node's scale settings affect all of the Frame node's child nodes, several objects can be rescaled simultaneously by changing the Scale factors in the Property Bar of their parent Frame node.

Shape Node

The main task of the Shape node is to combine a material and a geometry (mesh) to form a visible 3D object in the simulation. A mesh will not be visible until it is referenced by the Shape node.

Transparency

You can use different methods to make a visible object transparent. The Opacity field in the Material2 node can be used to control the ***transparency*** of the material. A value of 1.0 means the material is completely opaque, whereas a value of 0 means it is transparent. Or, you can use a .png file that has one color set to the transparent color, allowing you to see through those portions.

An entire mesh can have transparency properties by adding a Material2 node below the Mesh2 node in the simulation tree. On the Material2 node's Properties dialog box you can change the value of the Opacity field, which defines the degree of transparency for the entire mesh. An Opacity value of 1 (default) means the mesh is opaque and completely visible, and an Opacity value of 0 means that the mesh is totally invisible.

Activity 5.1.2: Material, Opacity, and Texture

1. Open EON. Open **Activity_5.1.2.eoz** from the data files for Module 5 Lesson 1.
2. Save the file as **Apartment_Opacity.eoz**.
3. Expand **Scene** and **ActiveViewportCamera**. Turn on the **Headlight** node.
4. Run the simulation.
5. Click the **Enter Material selection mode** button, press the **Alt** key, and select the curtain to the left of the front door in the scene.
6. Close the simulation window.
7. Expand **Resources > Materials > Curtains_Pattern** in the simulation tree, expand **DiffuseTexture**, and then select **Curtains_Pattern_Color**, as shown in Figure 5.1.6.

FIGURE 5.1.6 Curtains_Pattern_Color selected in simulation tree

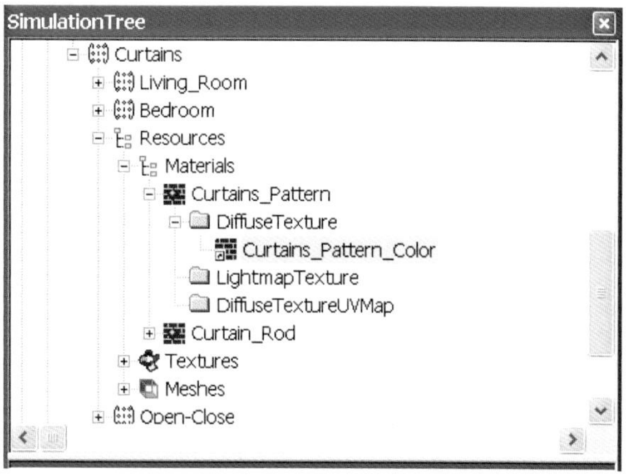

8. In the Property Bar, click the folder icon next to the Filename field, as shown in Figure 5.1.7.

FIGURE 5.1.7 Click the Filename folder icon in the Property Bar

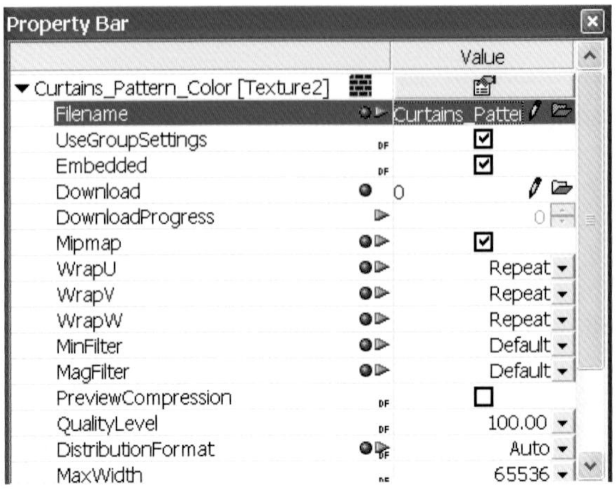

9. Browse to the data files for Module 5 Lesson 1 and double-click the **Curtains-White_Pattern_Color.dds** file.
10. Run the simulation and notice the color of the curtain. Close the simulation window.
11. In the simulation tree, click **Curtains_Pattern**.
12. In the Property Bar, click the white box next to **Diffuse** to display the Color dialog box. Click the red square and click **OK** to close the dialog box. The diffuse color of the material is changed to red.
13. Run the simulation and notice the color of the curtain. Close the simulation window.
14. In the Property Bar, adjust Opacity to **.1** and then run the simulation. Close the simulation window and change the Opacity to **.7**. Run the simulation again to see how the new Opacity value has affected the curtain and then close the simulation window again. Change the Opacity to **.9** and run the simulation to see the effect of this change.
15. Close the simulation window. Save the simulation and then close EON.

troubleshooting

Because EON offers better support (i.e., higher performance and visual quality) for OpenGL than for Direct3D, OpenGL is usually the best setting. If you are not sure that your card supports OpenGL, select this option anyway. EON also supports direct stereo viewing under OpenGL.

Modifying Render Settings

To improve the rendering quality of your EON application, select Configuration from the Simulation menu. The EON Simulation Configuration dialog box appears, as shown in Figure 5.1.8.

FIGURE 5.1.8 EON Simulation Configuration dialog box

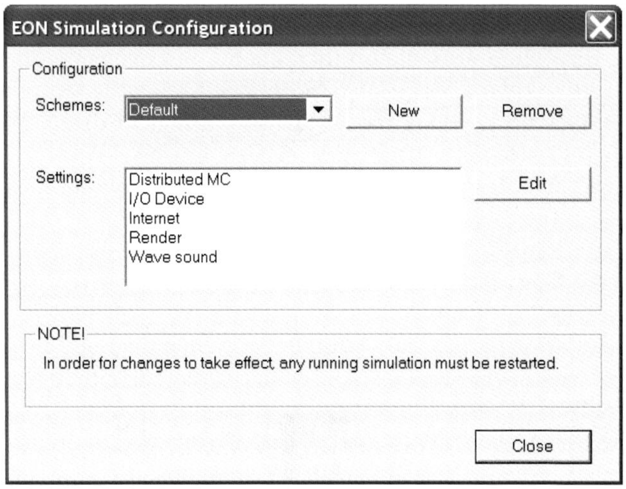

In the EON Simulation Configuration dialog box, select Render from the Settings list. Click Edit to open the Render Properties dialog box (see Figure 5.1.9).

FIGURE 5.1.9 Render Properties dialog box

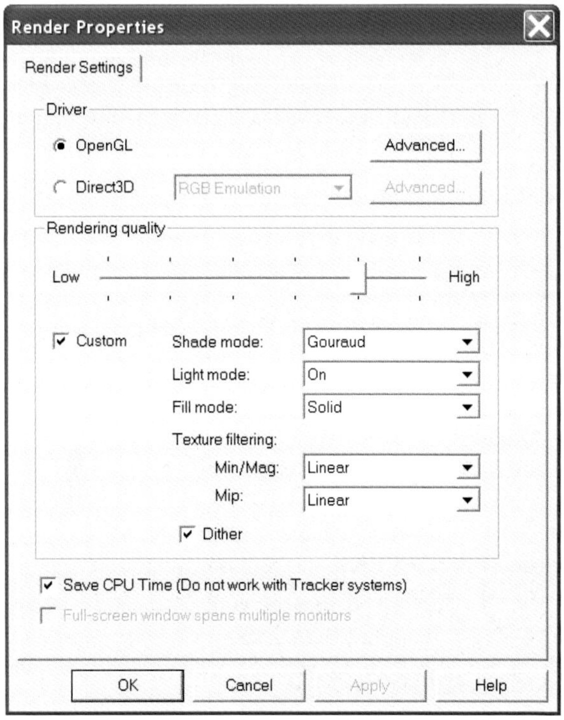

Driver

From the Render Properties dialog box, you can choose between the OpenGL and Direct3D graphics card drivers. OpenGL is recommended. However, you should select the one that is best supported by your graphics card. Direct3D rendering does not support most of the new functions added since version 4.0.

Rendering Quality

Set the render quality/speed with the slider. Low provides maximum speed but with lower visual quality. High provides optimal quality but may slow the simulation. If you have a modern graphics adapter, we recommend using the setting for the highest quality. Check Custom to specify render-quality settings in detail. Many fields will not be available if Custom is not selected.

For Shade mode, you can select Gouraud or Flat. ***Gouraud shading*** is generally used. The shading is blended so that objects appear more rounded. The individual planes of a ten-sided cylinder would not be visible as separate planes with Gouraud shading. With Flat shading, surface planes are easily distinguished from one another.

cross-reference

See the Light Modes topic at the beginning of this lesson for more information.

The light calculations can be turned on or off. When the Light mode is set to Off, meshes are displayed in the vertex color, which is the color they were given in the modeling program.

You can select from three fill options: *Points*, *Wireframe*, or *Solid*. The *Points* option displays only the dots at the corners of the polygons. If you select the *Wireframe* option, surfaces are not displayed. Only edges are displayed, and the edges have the same colors as they would have if they were textured. The *Solid* option will display a solid surface.

When a color cannot be displayed accurately in the current palette, you can ***dither*** the color. Dithering combines different color pixels to estimate the correct color. When you use the *Dither* option for color smoothing, the display quality of the color is improved. If your monitor has few colors (less than a 24-bit display), use this setting to avoid any visible defects.

If you enable the Save CPU Time option, EON will refresh the simulation window less often when the scene becomes static (no changes). This allows EON to cooperate better with other intensive working software. However, it might interfere with some tracking systems, so disable this option when using such systems. To receive proper simulation statistics (rendering speed and so on), this option must be turned off as well.

Activity 5.1.3: Render Settings

1. Open **EON**. Open **Activity_5.1.3.eoz** from the data files for Module 5 Lesson 1.
2. Select **Configuration** from the Simulation menu. The EON Simulation Configuration dialog box is displayed, as shown in Figure 5.1.10.

FIGURE 5.1.10 EON Simulation Configuration dialog box

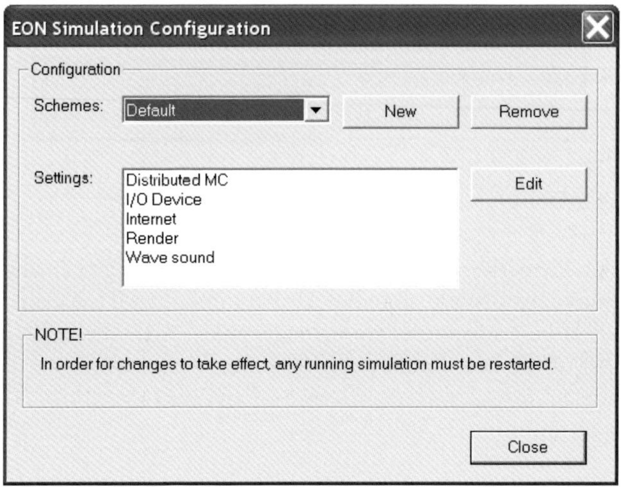

3. Select **Render** and click the **Edit** button. The Render Properties dialog box is displayed.
4. Select the **Custom** check box if necessary.
5. In the Render Properties dialog box, select **Wireframe** in the Fill mode field, as shown in Figure 5.1.11.

FIGURE 5.1.11 Render Properties dialog box with Wireframe selected

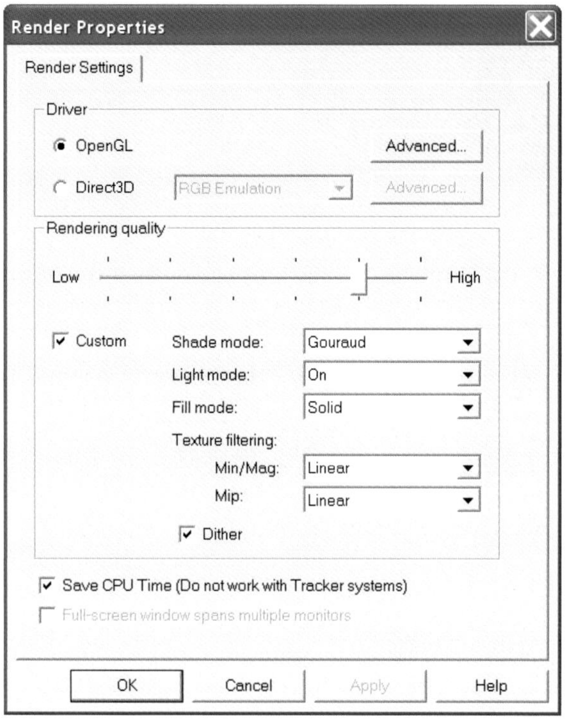

6. Click **OK** and then click **Close**.
7. Run the simulation.
8. Close the simulation window.
9. Open the Render Properties dialog box again. Select **Solid** in the Fill mode field. Click **OK** and then click **Close**.
10. Save the simulation and then close EON.

troubleshooting

Properties in the Render Properties dialog box are global properties for EON. This means that any setting changes you make in this dialog box will affect the appearance of every simulation in EON, not just the file you are currently working in. If you do not change the Fill mode field setting back to Solid, as instructed in step 9, all your simulations will continue to appear as Wireframe.

Summary

In this lesson you:

- Learned about adding light.
- Developed an understanding of the Texture2 node.
- Became familiar with the Material2 node.
- Looked at an object's appearance.
- Studied the use of scaling to change the size and shape of objects.
- Understood the Opacity settings that control an object's transparency.
- Modified render settings.

LESSON 5.2

Add Behavior and Interactivity to Simulations

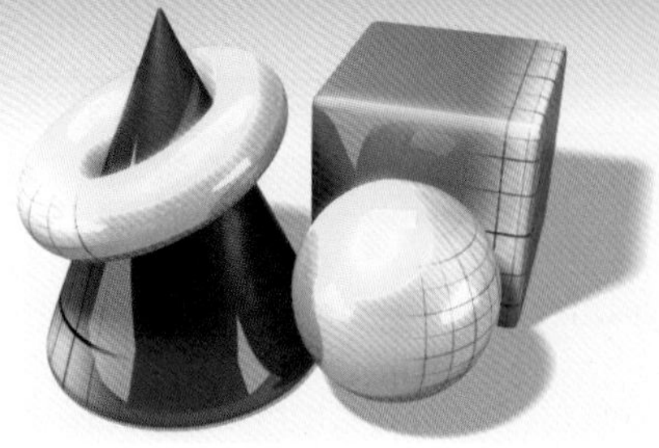

Objectives

In this lesson you will:

- Learn about adding motion.
- Become familiar with scene navigation using the camera.
- Study methods of movement.
- Discuss object movement in 3D space.
- Develop an understanding of handling collisions.

Key Terms

agent
bounding volume
BoxSensor node
ClickSensor node
CollisionManager node
CollisionObject node
Gravitation node
InactivitySensor prototype
ISector node
Joystick node
KeyboardSensor node
KeyFrame node
KeyMove node
Missile node
Motion node
MouseSensor node
Object Navigation model
OrbitNav prototype
Place node
ProximitySensor node
Rotate node
Spin node
sub stepping
SuperMan prototype
TimeSensor node
WalkAbout node
Walk Navigation model
Walk node

Adding Motion

You have learned a great deal about the many outstanding features available for creating and enhancing simulations in EON Professional. And you should now be able to recognize that simulations are often made up of several different objects. You also should understand that movement is one of the most useful features you can add to a simulation. EON allows you to add movement not only to an individual object, but also to a user's view within an environment. In either case, motion can bring an entire scene to life.

Scene Navigation Using the Camera

In EON Studio, you can use two basic ways of navigating: Object navigation or Walk navigation. Use the Object Navigation model for "Zoom/Rotate/Pan" navigation of an object. This navigation type is most suitable for visualization of a single object or a group of objects. Use the Walk Navigation model to move through an entire environment. Both models are explained in the following sections.

Object Navigation Model

The ***Object Navigation model*** allows you to zoom in or out and turn around the pivot point of the scene. You can change the scene's pivot, or rotation, point by pressing Ctrl and Shift simultaneously. The pivot point is represented by a 3D cursor showing the x, y, and z axes.

Walk Navigation Model

The ***Walk Navigation model*** allows you to navigate using an intuitive behavior that is similar to walking through the simulated environment. The Walk Navigation model is most suitable for performing a virtual walkthrough of a building or similar scenes that have an environment to explore. Press the left mouse button and drag vertically to move forward or backward. Drag horizontally with the left mouse button still pressed to control the heading.

To elevate the virtual walking plane, press the right mouse button and drag up or down. To look around, press the middle mouse button and drag the mouse. If you do not have a third mouse button, you can press Ctrl instead. To prevent the camera from returning to its initial orientation, press Alt before releasing the mouse button.

Methods of Movement

You can use several ways to move objects in a simulation. The nodes that produce the visible elements of a simulation can be moved by changing their parent Frame node's coordinates. These may be Shape nodes, Decal nodes, Light nodes (in cases where the light source type has position or orientation variables), or Camera nodes that determine the user's view in the simulation window.

OrbitNav Prototype

OrbitNav

Use the ***OrbitNav prototype*** for visualization of a single object or group of objects. This prototype provides a navigation system for rotating, zooming, and panning using a mouse. The pivot point is defined as the center of the screen. Therefore, panning moves the pivot point.

Walk Node

Walk

The ***Walk node*** implements the walk motion models found in many 3D environments. The Walk node is controlled by a mouse; each mouse button performs a different action. This node affects its parent, so the parent must support translation and rotation. The user controls movement by pressing the specified mouse button and moving the mouse. Speed is proportional to mouse movement after the button is pressed.

troubleshooting

Although the older ObjectNav prototype remains available, EON recommends using the new and improved OrbitNav prototype. The panning function is the main difference between these two prototypes. With OrbitNav, panning will move the pivot point. This means that rotation is always around the center of the screen, even after panning. With ObjectNav, the pivot point will stay inside the object. If you want the pivot point to stay inside the object, then use the ObjectNav prototype. Otherwise, the OrbitNav prototype is superior and recommended. The ObjectNav prototype is more complex; it has many fields or settings that are difficult for most users to apply and understand. The OrbitNav prototype was designed to reduce the number of fields and increase functionality by adding related prototypes whose fields can be understood in the context of the new function.

troubleshooting

Although you can choose to use a joystick instead of the mouse, the joystick no longer works directly through the Walk node. In addition, the collision-related fields no longer work in the Walk node.

The maxSpeed field in the Walk node is calculated as the speed reached from pressing the mouse button when the cursor is located in the middle of the simulation window and then dragging the cursor to the top of the simulation window. Similarly, the maxTurn field (rotation speed) is calculated as the number of degrees turned per second from pressing the mouse button when the cursor is located in the center of the simulation window and dragged to the side.

You can change which action is associated with a specific mouse button. By default, the left mouse button controls walking, the right mouse button raises or lowers the camera, and the middle mouse button rotates the view.

You can create a new type of joystick navigation by using the Joystick node under the Sensors group. By connecting the outEvents of the Joystick node to a script that then sends events to the Walk node fields named dX, dY, dZ, dH, dP, and dR, you will be able to create a different type of navigation. The Joystick node has support for advanced joysticks. You can use all axes and buttons.

Activity 5.2.1: Using ObjectNav, OrbitNav, and the Walk Node

1. Open EON.
2. Without making any changes, save the file as **Movement_Methods.eoz**.
3. Add a **Frame** node under Scene and rename the node **Grid**.
4. In the Property Bar, note that the Grid Position values are 0, 0, 0, the default values for new Frame nodes.
5. Under Grid, add the **GridPlane2** prototype and rename the prototype **GridPlane2_ Horizontal**.
6. Add a second **GridPlane2** prototype under Grid and rename the prototype **GridPlane2_Vertical**. See Figure 5.2.1.

FIGURE 5.2.1 Grid node in the Property Bar

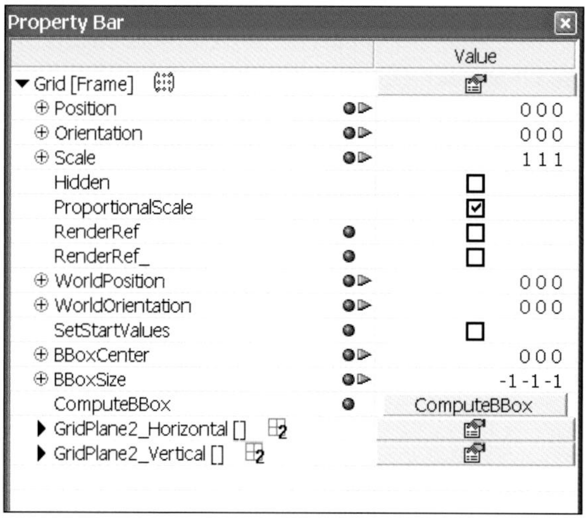

7. In the Property Bar, change the Position values for both of the added prototypes to **0**, **0**, **0**.
8. For GridPlane2_Vertical, in the Property Bar, change the Orientation values to **0**, **90**, **0**. This will change the pitch to 90 degrees.
9. For both of the GridPlane2 prototypes, in the Property Bar, change the Width and Height values to **20**.

10. Double-click **Camera** in the simulation tree. In the Frame Properties dialog box, change the settings as follows: X = **5.2**, Y = **−12.5**, Z = **1.8**, Heading = **345**, Pitch = **5** (see Figure 5.2.2). Click **OK** to close the dialog box.

FIGURE 5.2.2 Frame Properties dialog box for Camera

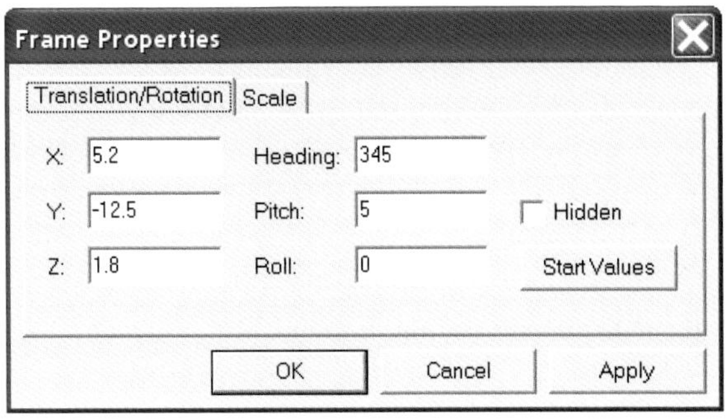

11. Add a **Frame** node under Scene and rename the node **Cube**.
12. Under the Cube frame, add the **Cube** prototye.
13. Run the simulation. Click the Cube to move forward and backward, right-click to rotate the head, and press the mouse's middle button to move up and down.
14. Close the simulation window.
15. Add the **ObjectNav** prototype under Scene.
16. Under Camera, delete the **Walk** node.
17. Under Scene, add the **OrbitNav** prototype. Make sure that **IsNotActive** is selected in the Property Bar and that **IsActive** is not selected.
18. Right-click **Camera** and choose **Copy as Link**. Also in the simulation tree, expand the **OrbitNav** node so you can see its Camera field, then right-click the **Camera** field, and then choose **Paste**.
19. Add a **KeyboardSensor** node under the Scene.
20. Double-click the **KeyboardSensor** node to open the KeyboardSensor Properties dialog box.
21. Click the drop-down arrow in the Virtual key name field and select **VK_1** to assign the 1 key, as shown in Figure 5.2.3. Click **OK** to close the dialog box.

FIGURE 5.2.3 KeyboardSensor Properties dialog box

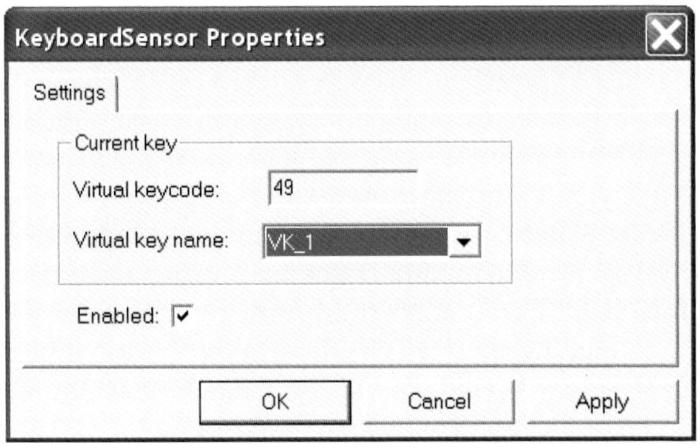

22. Add a **Latch** node under the Scene.
23. Display the **Routes** window. Drag the **KeyboardSensor** node, the **Latch** node, the **ObjectNav** prototype, and the **OrbitNav** prototype to the Routes window.

24. Establish the connections outlined in the following table and compare your Routes window to the one shown in Figure 5.2.4.

From	outEvent	To	inEvent
KeyboardSensor	OnKeyDown	Latch	Toggle
Latch	OnChanged	ObjectNav	IsNotActive
Latch	OnChanged	OrbitNav	IsActive

FIGURE 5.2.4 Routes window for Activity 5.2.1

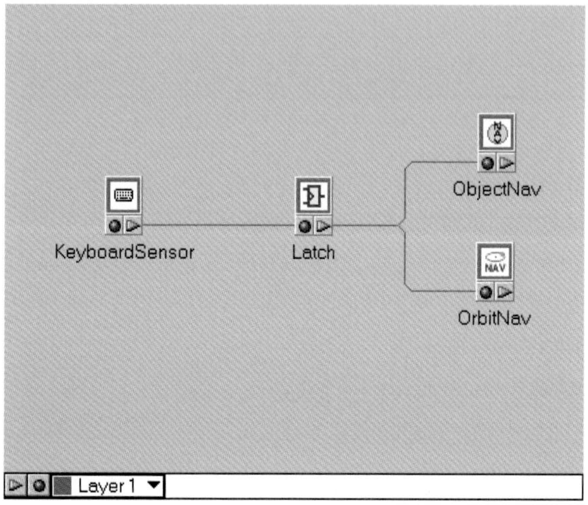

25. Select **ObjectNav** in the simulation tree. In the Property Bar, clear the **ReturnCamValues** check box, setting the field to false so that, when changing to OrbitNav, the camera is not returned to the location it occupied when ObjectNav was turned on.
26. Run the simulation.
27. Press **P** to show the pivot point in the simulation.
28. Press **1** to switch to the OrbitNav prototype navigation.
29. Press **P** again to see how the OrbitNav position of rotation is around the center of the screen instead of the center of the object.
30. Close the simulation window. Save the simulation and then close EON.

Joystick Node

Joystick

If you want to navigate using a joystick rather than a mouse, use the ***Joystick node***. You can make the joystick move in any frame by putting a reference to the frame in the Joystick's toMove field. If you place the Joystick node under your Camera node, you will be able to change the position of the camera by moving your joystick left, right, forward, and backward. You can change how the camera moves by changing the joystick mapping from XZ to XY to XYZ and by changing the motion type from absolute to relative.

For most users, the default behavior of the Joystick node is not suited to their needs because it changes only the Position field. However, by using the outEvent of the Joystick node and the outEvent of a Script node, you can create custom motion models that can use all of the features of modern, full-featured joysticks, including up to sixteen buttons, eight axes, and four point-of-view buttons. However, creating custom motion models is an advanced task. Fortunately, EON has some ready-made solutions.

In the JoyStick Related prototype library, you will see four prototypes: JoyStick-Nav, LogitechDualAction, LogitechExtreme3DPro, and XBox360Controller. The last three prototypes have a joystick in them, and they are named after specific joysticks or game controllers. The advantage of using these JoyStick Related prototypes is that all values sent out are between –1 and 1, and the field names of the outEvents are suitably named for that particular joystick or game controller.

The three prototypes named after specific joysticks will not move a frame alone. To make the camera move, you must add routes that connect them to the JoyStickNav prototype (for Walk navigation) or OrbitNavJoyStick (for Object navigation). OrbitNavJoyStick also requires the OrbitNav prototype itself. By connecting routes from and to different fields on the prototypes, you can create your own custom motion model. Try making the connections using some of the examples outlined in Table 5.2.1.

TABLE 5.2.1 LogitechExtreme3DPro and JoyStickNav Route Connections

From	outEvent	To	inEvent
LogitechExtreme3DPro	JoyStick_Xaxis	JoyStickNav	MoveX
LogitechExtreme3DPro	JoyStick_Yaxis	JoyStickNav	MoveY
LogitechExtreme3DPro	Throttle_Axis	JoyStickNav	MoveZ
LogitechExtreme3DPro	Handle_Twist	JoyStickNav	RotateHeading
LogitechExtreme3DPro	DirectionPad_Y	JoyStickNav	RotatePitch
LogitechExtreme3DPro	DirectionPad_X	JoyStickNav	RotateRoll
LogitechExtreme3DPro	Button_3_Down	JoyStickNav	ResetToStart
LogitechExtreme3DPro	Button_2_Down	JoyStickNav	ResetPitchRoll

tips+tricks

Even if you do not use one of the named joysticks, one of these prototypes could be useful, but you will need to determine which fields relate to the axes and buttons on the joystick you are using.

WalkAbout Node

WalkAbout

The ***WalkAbout node*** allows you to navigate within your simulation using the keyboard. This node can be connected to a Camera node to change the view. You may also connect a Walkabout node to a Frame node to place an object.

Discussion

discuss

Open **WalkAbout.eoz** from the data files for Module 5 Lesson 2 for a demonstration of the WalkAbout node. In what circumstances would this node be beneficial to a simulation?

KeyMove Node

KeyMove

The ***KeyMove node*** provides a keyboard motion model and affects its parent node. The parent must support translation and rotation. With this node, control movement by pressing X, Y, Z, H, P, or R while pressing the up arrow key for higher values or the down arrow key for lower values.

Discussion

discuss

Open **KeyMove.eoz** from the data files for Module 5 Lesson 2 for a demonstration of the KeyMove node. When might you choose to use this node in a simulation?

tips+tricks

When using the SuperMan prototype to fly around in a simulation, the heading and pitch will be combined, so it can be difficult to pull out of a roll. To avoid losing control, fly using small, circular mouse motions so that you can make course corrections more easily. To level off, press Ctrl. To restrain flight to the initial altitude, set the prototype's PitchActive field to 0 (False) so that pitch control is inactive.

SuperMan Prototype

Fly SuperMan

If you want users to be able to explore several levels of a simulation at varying heights or altitudes, use the ***SuperMan prototype.*** Unlike the Walk node, the SuperMan prototype can alter the simulation camera's position along the z axis at the same time as navigating a scene.

Discussion

discuss

Open **SuperMan.eoz** from the data files for Module 5 Lesson 2 for a demonstration of the SuperMan prototype. What are some benefits of using this node in a simulation?

tips+tricks

You can change the value in the BaseSpeed field during runtime (but not while the mouse buttons are pressed). Each time you press the plus or minus key on the numeric keypad, the BaseSpeed value is increased or decreased by one-eighth of the value of the TopSpeed field. Speed cannot be increased beyond the TopSpeed value. You can deactivate this function if you do not want the user to be able to make speed changes. An outEvent can be sent showing the new BaseSpeed value.

Using this prototype, you can press the left mouse button to accelerate forward and press the right mouse button to accelerate backward. Acceleration continues until the maximum speed specified in the BaseSpeed field is reached. You do not have to move the mouse to fly forward or to accelerate. Mouse movement is used only for steering. After the BaseSpeed is attained, you will continue flying at that speed until the mouse button is released. Speed will then gradually decrease to zero. If you want to stop immediately, press both mouse buttons at the same time. You can still look around while pressing both buttons.

This prototype is not ready to use until a few routes are established. First, you must insert a SuperMan prototype and a Walk node under the Camera node. Then, set the Walk node's maxSpeed and maxTurn fields to 0. Next, drag the Walk node and the SuperMan prototype to the Routes window. Make connections between the SuperMan prototype's dH, dP, and dY fields and the Walk node's dH, dP, and dY fields.

The SuperMan prototype provides a realistic simulation of flight. When turning, you can use pitch and heading to give the effect of rolling (or banking). Users can enjoy doing loops and flying upside down close to the ceiling or floor. You can even connect the outEvent dY field to change the pitch of a motor sound played during acceleration and deceleration.

Object Movement in 3D Space

Agents are the active nodes of a simulation. Agents provide motion, sound, and input/output features. Many agents work with rendered objects, such as Mesh nodes and Frame nodes. Many agents are members of the Agent Nodes set.

Several nodes affect an object's position in 3D space. Use these nodes to define various types of motion behavior for a simulation's 3D objects. Motion characteristics are defined on the nodes' properties windows.

Movement Along a Predefined Path

Movement can be initiated in two different ways. If you want movement to begin at simulation startup, select Active in the motion agent's properties window.

On the other hand, if you want movement to begin after the simulation has started, disable the Active option in the motion agent's properties window and control the movement with events. Movement begins when the motion agent's SetRun field receives a True event and stops when its SetRun_ field receives a True event. To move objects along a predefined path, use the following nodes.

Gravitation Node

Gravitation

The ***Gravitation node*** adds gravitational force to sibling nodes by modifying the parent Frame node's Z coordinate.

Discussion

discuss

Open **Gravitation.eoz** from the data files for Module 5 Lesson 2 for a demonstration of the Gravitation node. What type of simulation would call for the use of this node?

KeyFrame Node

KeyFrame

The ***KeyFrame node*** moves sibling nodes through predefined points, which consist of a timestamp, a position, and an orientation. The sibling nodes can move between the points with an abrupt or a smooth movement. The movement can be looped.

Discussion

discuss

Open **KeyFrameController.eoz** from the data files for Module 5 Lesson 2 for a demonstration of the KeyFrame node. What type of simulation might benefit from the use this node?

Missile Node

Missile

The ***Missile node*** moves sibling nodes as if they were missiles, with user-defined acceleration at the beginning of the movement. The sibling nodes continue to move with constant velocity when the "burn time" has ended.

Discussion

discuss

Open **Missile.eoz** from the Module 5 Lesson 2 data files for a demonstration of the Missile node. What are some practical applications for this node?

tips+tricks

When the Place node is finished with rotation and position, it sends an OnRunFalse message. This message signals that the action is complete and another event can be triggered.

Motion Node

The ***Motion node*** moves one or more sibling nodes with user-defined velocity and acceleration and rotates them with user-defined angular velocity and angular acceleration.

Place Node

The ***Place node*** moves sibling nodes to a new position and orientation within a user-defined time. The movement is performed either relative to the current position or relative to the origin (absolute).

discuss

Open **Place.eoz** from the data files for Module 5 Lesson 2 for a demonstration of the Place node. When might you choose to use this node in a simulation?

Rotate Node

The ***Rotate node*** rotates sibling nodes. The user defines the direction and lap time of the rotation.

discuss

Open **TeapotRotate.eoz** from the data files for Module 5 Lesson 2 for a demonstration of the Rotate node. You also can open **SmOp2-TeapotRotate.eoz** from the data files for Module 5 Lesson 2 for an additional demonstration. What are some benefits of using this node in a simulation?

Spin Node

The ***Spin node*** spins sibling nodes around the z axis at a given radius, speed, and height above the X–Y plane. The spinning object faces the spin center at all times.

Activity 5.2.2: Using a Single Place Node to Move an Object

1. Open EON.
2. Without making any changes, save the file as **Single_Place_Node.eoz**.
3. Add a **Frame** node under Scene and rename the node **Grid**.
4. Under Grid, add the **GridPlane2** prototype and rename the prototype **GridPlane2_ Horizontal**.

5. Add a second **GridPlane2** prototype under Grid and rename the prototype **GridPlane2_Vertical**. See Figure 5.2.5.

FIGURE 5.2.5 GridPlane2 nodes added to the Grid frame

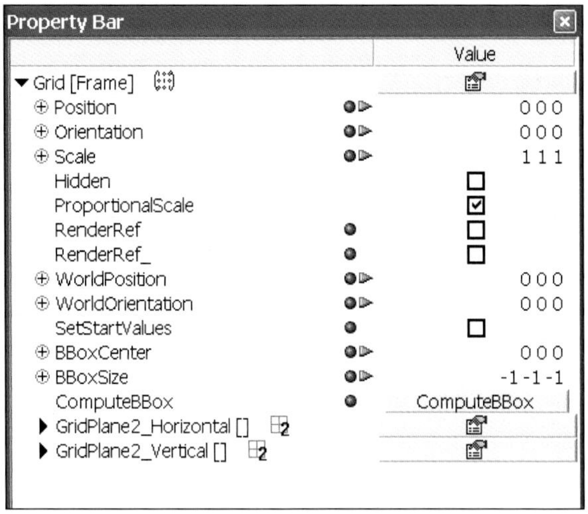

6. In the Property Bar, change the Position values for both of the added prototypes to **0**, **0**, **0**.
7. For GridPlane2_Vertical, in the Property Bar, change the Orientation values to **0**, **90**, **0**. This will change the pitch to 90 degrees.
8. For both of the GridPlane2 prototypes, in the Property Bar, change the Width and Height values to **20**.
9. Double-click **Camera** in the simulation tree. In the Frame Properties dialog box, change the settings as follows: X = **5.2**, Y = **−12.5**, Z = **1.8**, Heading = **345**, Pitch = **5** (see Figure 5.2.6). Click **OK** to close the dialog box.

FIGURE 5.2.6 Setting values in the Frame Properties dialog box for Camera

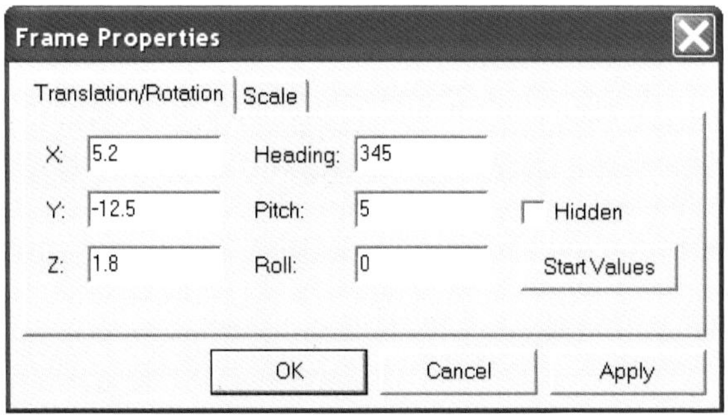

10. Add a **Frame** node under Scene and rename the node **Cube**.
11. Under the Cube frame, add the **Cube** prototye.
12. Under the Cube frame, add a **Place** node and rename it **MoveAbsolute**.
13. Double-click the **MoveAbsolute** node in the simulation tree. In the Place Properties dialog box, change Movement x to **2** and change Time to move x to **0**. Click **OK** to close the dialog box.
14. Under the Cube frame, add a **KeyboardSensor** node and rename the node **Key1_MoveAbsolute**.

15. Double-click the **Key1_MoveAbsolute** node in the simulation tree to open the KeyboardSensor Properties dialog box. Click the drop-down arrow in the Virtual key name field and select **VK_1** to assign the 1 key to the node. Click **OK** to close the dialog box.
16. Under the Cube frame, add a **Place** node and rename the node **MoveRelative**. Double-click the node to open the Place Properties dialog box. Under Type, change all values to **relative**. Change Movement x to **2** and change Time to move x to **5**. Make sure **No** is selected under Active, as shown in Figure 5.2.7, and then click **OK**.

FIGURE 5.2.7 MoveRelative Place Properties dialog box

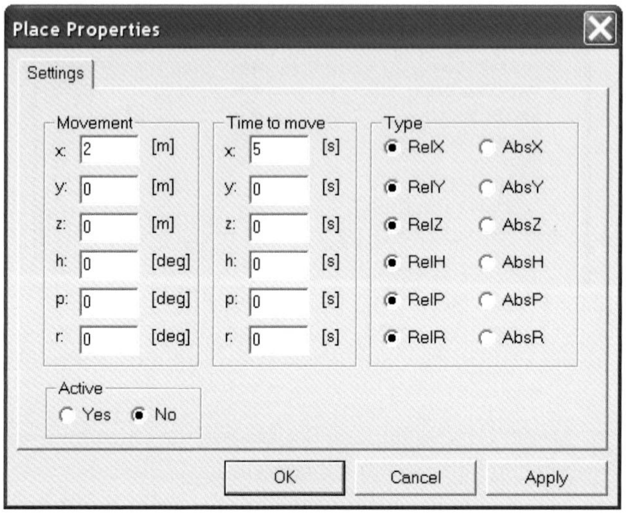

17. Under the Cube frame, add a **KeyboardSensor** node and rename the node **Key2_MoveRelative**.
18. Assign **VK_2** to the Key2_MoveRelative node.
19. For the MoveAbsolute and MoveRelative nodes, double-click to open the Place Properties dialog box and change Movement h to **90** and Time to move h to **5** (see Figure 5.2.8).

FIGURE 5.2.8 MoveAbsolute Place Properties dialog box

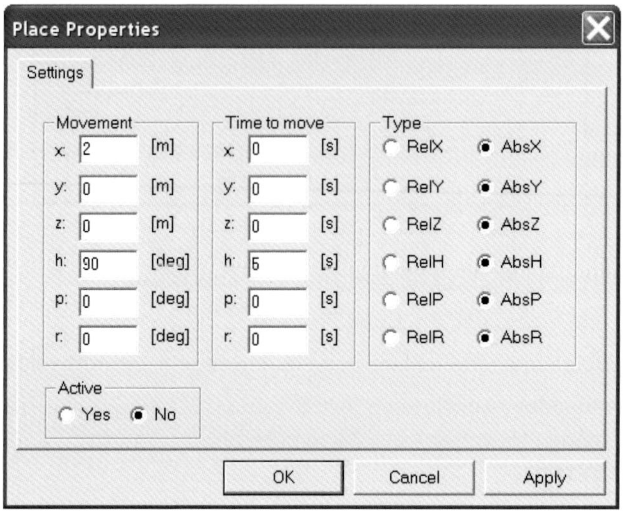

20. Display the **Routes** window. Drag the **MoveAbsolute** node, **MoveRelative** node, **Key1_MoveAbsolute** node, and **Key2_MoveRelative** node to the Routes window.
21. Establish the connections outlined in the following table.

From	outEvent	To	inEvent
Key1_MoveAbsolute	OnKeyDown	MoveAbsolute	SetRun
Key2_MoveRelative	OnKeyDown	MoveRelative	SetRun

22. Run the simulation. Press **1** and then press **2** to see the cube's movement within the simulation. Notice the difference between relative and absolute movement.
23. Close the simulation window. Save the simulation and keep it open to use in Activity 5.2.3.

Activity 5.2.3: Using a Series of Place Nodes to Move an Object

1. Continue working with the open simulation file created in Activity 5.2.2. Save the simulation file as **Series_Of_Place_Nodes.eoz**.
2. Under the Cube frame, add two **Place** nodes and rename them **MoveAbsolute_2** and **MoveAbsolute_3**.
3. Double-click the **MoveAbsolute_2** node to open its Place Properties dialog box. Change Movement x to **4**, Movement y to **2**, Time to move x to **3**, and Time to move y to **3**. Click **OK**.
4. Double-click the **MoveAbsolute_3** node to open its Place Properties dialog box. Change Movement x to **4**, Movement y to **2**, and Movement z to **2**. Change Time to move x to **3**, Time to move y to **3**, and Time to move z to **3**. Click **OK**.
5. Display the **Routes** window. Drag the **MoveAbsolute_2** and **MoveAbsolute_3** nodes to the Routes window.
6. Establish the connections outlined in the following table and compare your Routes window to the one shown in Figure 5.2.9.

From	outEvent	To	inEvent
MoveAbsolute	OnRunFalse	MoveAbsolute_2	SetRun
MoveAbsolute_2	OnRunFalse	MoveAbsolute_3	SetRun

FIGURE 5.2.9 Routes window for Activity 5.2.3

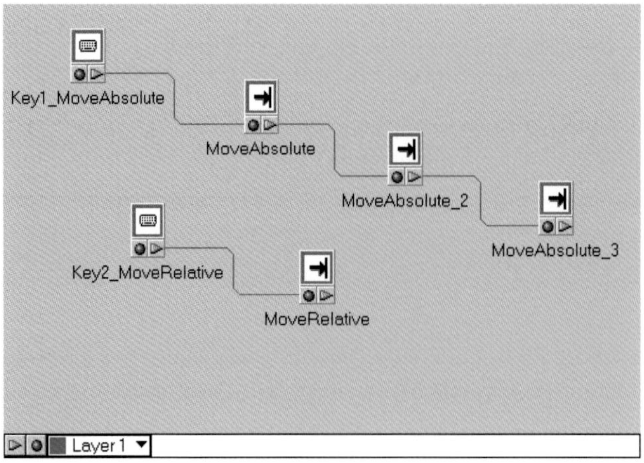

7. Run the simulation. Press **1** and then press **2** to see the cube's movement within the simulation. Notice the difference between the movement in this activity and the movement in Activity 5.2.2.
8. Close the simulation window. Save the simulation and keep it open to use in Activity 5.2.4.

Activity 5.2.4: Using a KeyFrame Node to Move an Object

1. Continue working with the open simulation file created in Activity 5.2.2 and modified in Activity 5.2.3. Save the file as **KeyFrame_Moves_Object.eoz**.
2. Under the Cube frame, add a **KeyFrame** node and rename the node **MoveAbsolute_ KeyFrame**.
3. Double-click the new node to open the KeyFrame Properties dialog box. Click the **Control points** tab and set the values as follows:

   Time **0.00**, x = **0**, y = **0**, z = **0**, h = **0**

   Time **5.00**, x = **2**, y = **0**, z = **0**, h = **90**

   Time **8.00**, x = **4**, y = **2**, z = **0**, h = **90**

   Time **11.00**, x = **4**, y = **2**, z = **2**, h = **90**

   The KeyFrame Properties dialog box should resemble Figure 5.2.10.

FIGURE 5.2.10 KeyFrame Properties dialog box – Control points tab

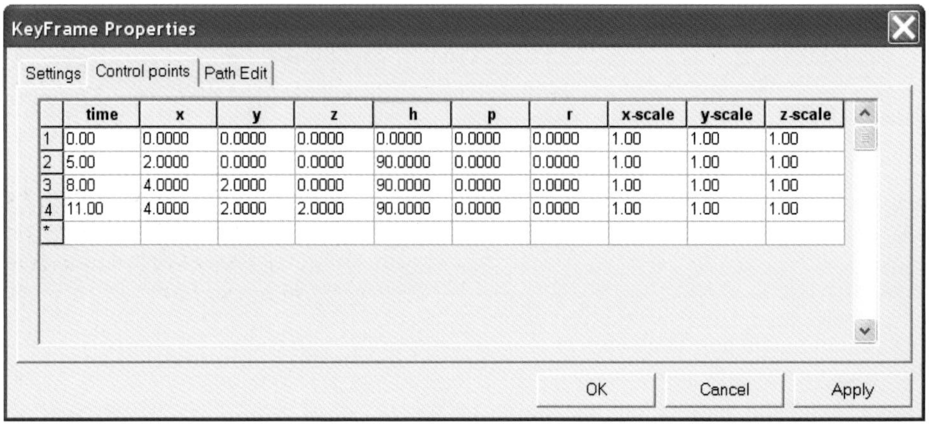

	time	x	y	z	h	p	r	x-scale	y-scale	z-scale
1	0.00	0.0000	0.0000	0.0000	0.0000	0.0000	0.0000	1.00	1.00	1.00
2	5.00	2.0000	0.0000	0.0000	90.0000	0.0000	0.0000	1.00	1.00	1.00
3	8.00	4.0000	2.0000	0.0000	90.0000	0.0000	0.0000	1.00	1.00	1.00
4	11.00	4.0000	2.0000	2.0000	90.0000	0.0000	0.0000	1.00	1.00	1.00
*										

4. Click the **Settings** tab, ensure **No** is selected under Active (see Figure 5.2.11), and then click **OK**.

FIGURE 5.2.11 KeyFrame Properties dialog box – Settings tab

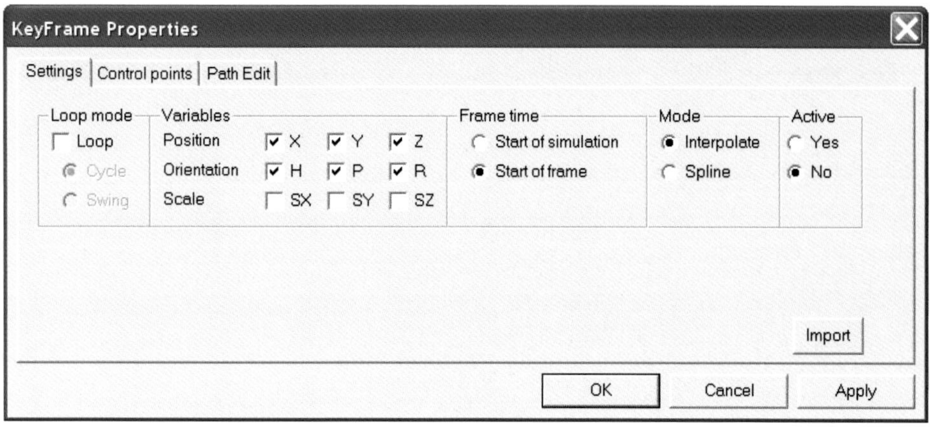

5. Under the Cube frame, add a **KeyboardSensor** node and rename the node **Key3_MoveKeyFrame**.
6. Assign **VK_3** to the Key3_MoveKeyFrame node.
7. Display the **Routes** window. Drag the **Key3_MoveKeyFrame** and the **MoveAbsolute_KeyFrame** nodes to the Routes window.
8. Establish the connections outlined in the following table.

From	outEvent	To	inEvent
Key3_MoveKeyFrame	OnKeyDown	MoveAbsolute_KeyFrame	SetRun

9. Run the simulation and press **3** to see the movement within the simulation.
10. Press **1** and notice the difference in movement.
11. Press **3** again.
12. Close the simulation window.
13. Under the Cube frame, add a **Place** node and rename the node **Reset_Cube**.
14. Double-click the node to open the Place Properties dialog box and change all values to **0** if necessary. Click **OK** to close the dialog box.
15. Under the Cube frame, add a **KeyboardSensor** node and rename the node **Key4_ResetCubeMove**.
16. Assign **Key4** to the Key4_ResetCubeMove node.
17. Display the **Routes** window. Drag the **Key4_ResetCubeMove** and the **Reset_Cube** nodes to the Routes window.

18. Establish the connections outlined in the following table and compare your Routes window to the one shown in Figure 5.2.12.

From	outEvent	To	inEvent
Key4_ResetCubeMove	OnKeyDown	Reset_Cube	SetRun
Reset_Cube	OnRunFalse	Move_Absolute	SetRun

FIGURE 5.2.12 Routes window with Key4_ResetCubeMove and Reset_Cube connected

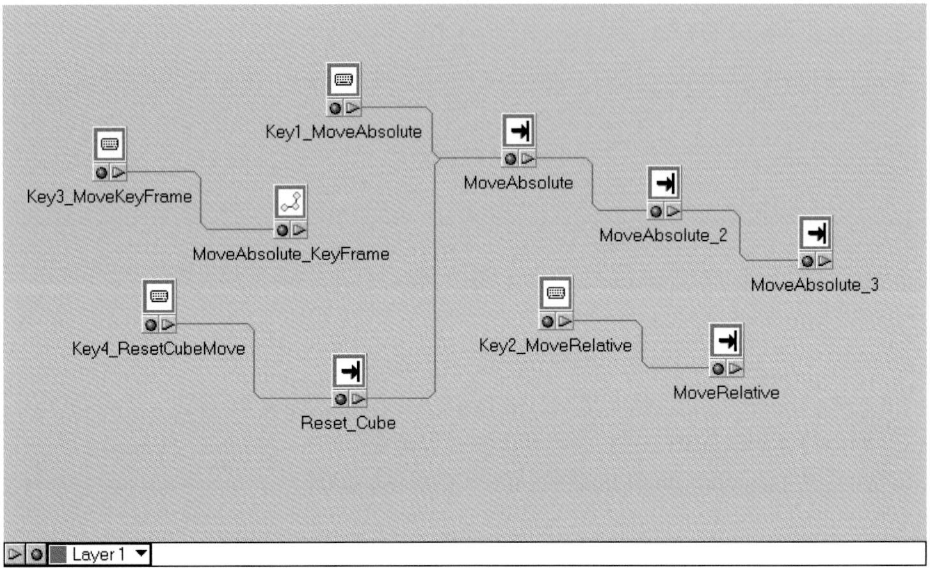

19. Run the simulation. Press **4** to see the cube's movement within the simulation.
20. Press **1** and notice the difference in movement.
21. Press **4** again.
22. Close the simulation window. Save the simulation and keep it open to use in Activity 5.2.5.

Discussion

discuss

You just practiced three distinct methods for moving an object within a simulation. Although similar, each process offers a slightly different approach. Did you find one particular method easier to understand than the others? Can you think of scenarios in which each particular method would work best?

Sensor Nodes

Use Sensor nodes or prototypes to generate events in response to actions occurring during the simulation. Sensor nodes are members of the Sensor Nodes set.

KeyboardSensor Node

KeyboardSensor

The ***KeyboardSensor node*** detects when a specified key is pressed and generates events that can be routed to other nodes. Use the KeyboardSensor node's Properties dialog box to identify the key that must be pressed. You used the KeyboardSensor node several times in the activities provided in this lesson.

ClickSensor Node

The ***ClickSensor node*** detects when an object has been clicked in the simulation window. The ClickSensor node should be placed under a Frame node. Shape nodes that are under this frame can be detected by the ClickSensor node. Alternatively, you can specify which frame or frames to use by placing node references in the Roots field of the ClickSensor node. If no roots are specified, the ClickSensor node's parent frame is the root.

ProximitySensor Node

The ***ProximitySensor node*** is activated when the Camera node is positioned within a specified radius. When activated, the ProximitySensor node can send events that may be used by other nodes.

tips+tricks

The ProximitySensor node is useful for triggering events such as explosions and doors opening.

TimeSensor Node

A ***TimeSensor node*** can generate pulses at regular intervals. These pulses can be used to control the actions of other nodes.

tips+tricks

Use the TimeSensor node to add delays in a simulation and trigger events at the beginning of a simulation.

MouseSensor Node

The ***MouseSensor node*** detects the position of the mouse cursor and mouse clicks. You can use the MouseSensor node to track the position of the cursor. This allows you to create functionality for zooming or to activate a function when the cursor is detected in a certain region of the screen.

ISector Node

An ***ISector node*** emits a sensor ray along the y axis of its parent frame and detects when the ray is intersected by 3D objects (Shape nodes or old Mesh nodes). If placed beneath a Camera node, the ISector node can detect specified objects that are in front of the camera.

The Root folder stores a link to a Frame node that will be a subtree. Only objects under that subtree will be checked for intersection with the sensor ray. If the Scene node is selected, all Shape nodes in the simulation will be checked.

If you want the ISector node to send an event when specific nodes intersect the sensor ray, place links to the targeted Shape nodes in the Targets folder. The TargetHit field is set to True when a target is hit.

BoxSensor Node

The ***BoxSensor node*** is activated when the simulation Camera node moves within a user-defined box. When activated, it posts events that can be used by other nodes.

Activity 5.2.5: Using a ProximitySensor Node to Move an Object

1. Continue working with the open simulation file created in Activity 5.2.2 and modified in Activity 5.2.3 and Activity 5.2.4. Save the file as **ProximitySensor.eoz**.
2. Under the Cube frame, add a **ProximitySensor** node.

3. Double-click the **ProximitySensor** node to open the ProximitySensor Properties dialog box. Change the Frames within radius to **5**, as shown in Figure 5.2.13.

FIGURE 5.2.13 ProximitySensor Properties dialog box

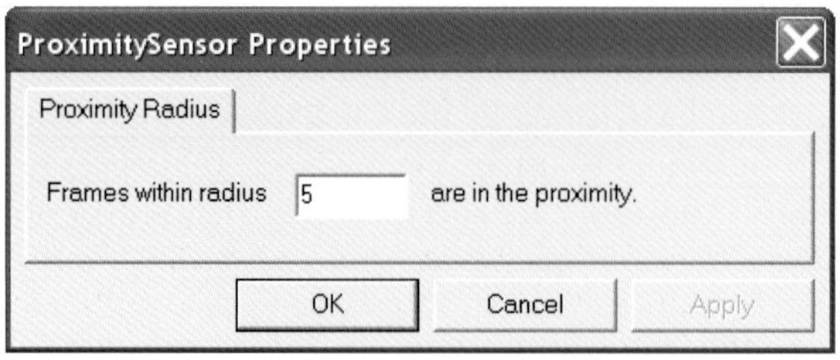

4. Display the **Routes** window. Drag the **ProximitySensor** node to the Routes window.
5. Establish the connections outlined in the following table and compare your Routes window to the one shown in Figure 5.2.14.

From	outEvent	To	inEvent
ProximitySensor	InProximityTrue	MoveAbsolute_KeyFrame	SetRun

FIGURE 5.2.14 Routes window for Activity 5.2.5

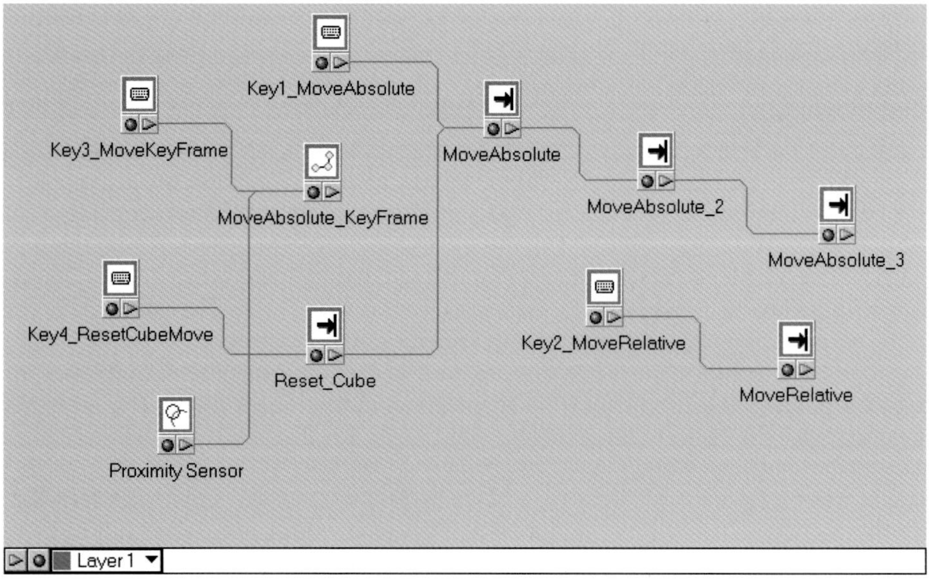

tips+tricks

"InProximityTrue" means that something is close to an object.

6. Run the simulation.
7. In the simulation tree, select the **Cube**.
8. Navigate toward the cube. Notice the cube's automatic movement as a result of the camera's proximity.
9. Close the simulation window. Save the simulation and then close EON.

Interactive Movement

To move an object interactively—using the mouse or keyboard as an input device, for example—you can use the MoveRotateArrows3D prototype and the Inactivity-Sensor prototype. The MoveRotateArrows3D prototype responds to a user moving the mouse or pressing a key on the keyboard. In contrast, the InactivitySensor prototype responds to a lack of movement from either device.

MoveRotateArrows3D Prototype

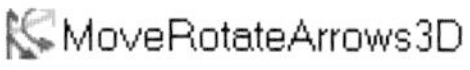

The MoveRotateArrows3D prototype gives you a simple system of moving and rotating objects by dragging and clicking arrows. If all of the objects you want to move are under the same Root frame, then this prototype also handles selection of objects. After a new object is clicked (selected), the arrows are moved to the selected object.

The arrows are shown centered on the object. Drag the straight arrows in the X, Y, or Z direction or drag the yellow box in the center to move in the X–Y plane. Click the pink curved arrows to rotate in the heading direction. Optionally, the rotation can be repeated if you continue to hold down the mouse button.

Although the arrows appear centered on an object, they are placed at a point that is one-tenth of the distance between the camera and the object. Advantageously, the arrows usually are visible on the object (rather than hidden inside it), making this prototype unsuitable for viewing in stereo displays.

InactivitySensor Prototype

The ***InactivitySensor prototype*** triggers an event after a set time of mouse inactivity. It is like a screen saver. When you do not move the mouse for a while, it can start other events you select.

This prototype is a good option for many different scenarios. You could run an animation or camera path on an exhibition demo computer when no one is moving the mouse, for example. This activity could attract people to the demo computer. If the application is a game or training application and a user did not move the mouse for a while, you could use sound to tell them to do something or give them a hint. After a period of inactivity, you could shut down the EON application by sending an event to the host program that can stop EON.

Handling Collisions

The Collision module provides basic collision detection and collision response. It is a reactive system because it never initiates any motion. Instead, it reacts to the motion of the collision objects and resolves collisions. The system simply reports data about collisions and/or resolves collisions. Specifically, the collision response should be feasible to use for avatars moving in an environment.

Base Nodes Overview

The two main nodes are the CollisionObject node and the CollisionManager node.

- The ***CollisionObject node*** holds properties and reports collisions for individual collision objects. These nodes are linked to a Frame node by adding a frame reference in the ObjectFrame field or by placing it below a Frame node, which identifies the frame as a collision object in the simulation.

- The ***CollisionManager node*** holds global properties for a set of collision objects between which collisions should be tested.

A collision object is linked to a collision manager by references. The collision object chooses its manager. A collision object that is not connected to a manager will automatically connect itself to the first manager it finds. If no manager exists, then it will create a default manager and connect to it. For example, in Figure 5.2.15, a collision object has been added to the Chair frame.

FIGURE 5.2.15 Collision object added to Chair frame

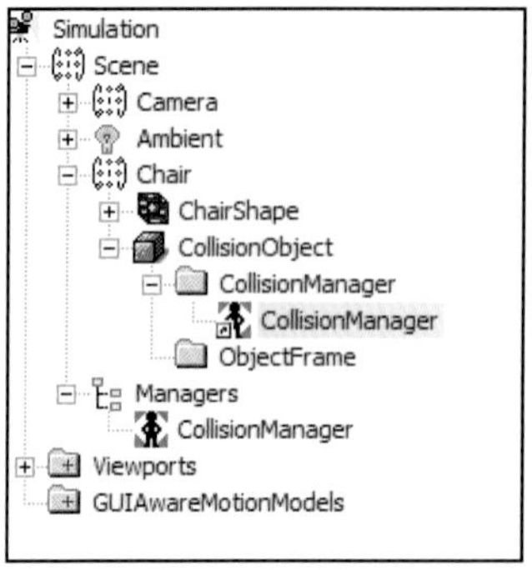

Normally, you do not need to set the references between the collision objects and the manager because it is handled automatically. Just add CollisionObject nodes to the frames in the simulation that should be included in the dynamics. Only when creating simulations with multiple managers will you need to choose which collision manager a collision object should belong to, and you do this by explicitly pointing to the specific manager in the CollisionObject node.

Collision objects can exist in the subtree of another collision object, but only if the "outer" object is immobile (static). The "outer" collision object will then exclude the geometry of the "inner" collision object. In Figure 5.2.16, the Scene is the "outer" object that contains the Chair as an "inner" object. The geometry of the Chair is excluded from the Scene object so that the Chair can interact or collide with the environment as expected.

FIGURE 5.2.16 The geometry of the Chair is excluded from the Scene object

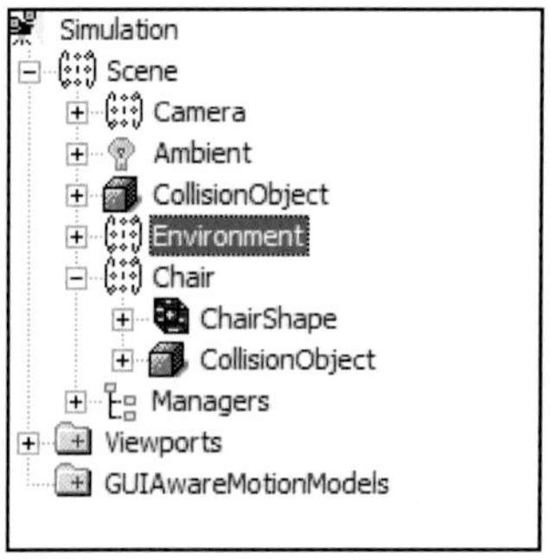

troubleshooting

It is important that the "outer" collision object is immobile. Moving the "outer" object will cause unpredictable behavior of the "inner" object.

Collision Geometry Types

For performance and stability, it is highly recommended that you use the simplest geometry possible in the collision system. This is a general rule in the area of simulating dynamics. In most cases, the results are no less satisfactory. With EON, it is easy to choose a simpler geometry based on the visual geometry. The basic principle is to generate a ***bounding volume*** around the visual geometry.

EON currently offers three types of bounding volumes:

- Bounding box
- Bounding sphere
- Convex hull

Bounding volumes can be adjusted to wrap individual geometries, or they can wrap entire hierarchies of frames and geometries. For example, in Figure 5.2.17, a bounding box was used around all the geometry of the Toaster but individual convex hulls were used around each geometry in the Table. The gray circles identify the objects surrounded by the bounding volume.

FIGURE 5.2.17 Bounding box around Toaster geometry and the individual geometries within the Table

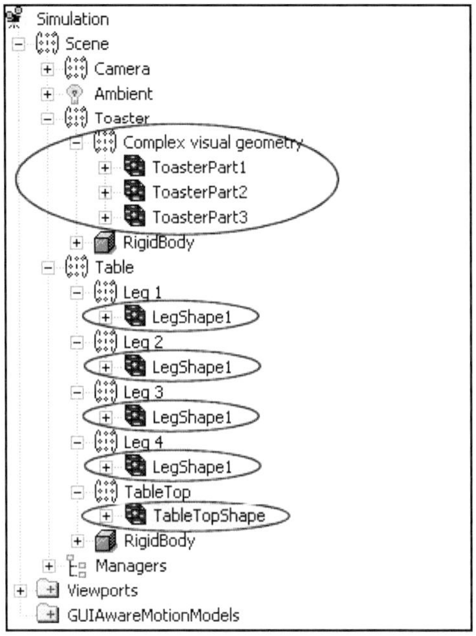

Naturally, choosing the most suitable bounding volume depends on the characteristics of the visual geometry and on the performance requirements of the entire simulation. A bounding box and a bounding sphere perform faster and require less memory than convex bounding volumes.

In some cases, it is not possible to use bounding volumes to simplify the collision geometry. Typically, a case might include terrain in which the nonconvex characteristics are important (bounding volumes are convex) or other large static environments cannot be wrapped in a bounding volume. In this case, you can use the visual geometry directly, also known as "Geometry as is."

Finally, another way to define a more suitable collision geometry is to simply create an alternative geometry in addition to the visual geometry in the collision

troubleshooting

Using general geometry directly is difficult in a dynamic simulation, especially in regard to stability and performance. Currently, using general geometry directly seems to work well for a static environment but not for moving objects. Also, the interaction between convex hull bounding volumes and "Geometry as is" is not currently supported, which means that these types of geometries will move through each other.

object. Using the geometry in Figure 5.2.18, assume that you did not find any bounding volume of the visual geometry that was suitable as a collision geometry for the car. Instead, you created another collision geometry in parallel to the visual geometry. With the CollisionGeometryType node, you can control which geometry will be used as collision geometry. The CollisionGeometryType node in the Visual Geometry frame declares that this subtree should be excluded from the collision geometry, leaving only the geometries in the Collision Geometry frame to be used as collision geometry.

FIGURE 5.2.18 Parallel collision geometry

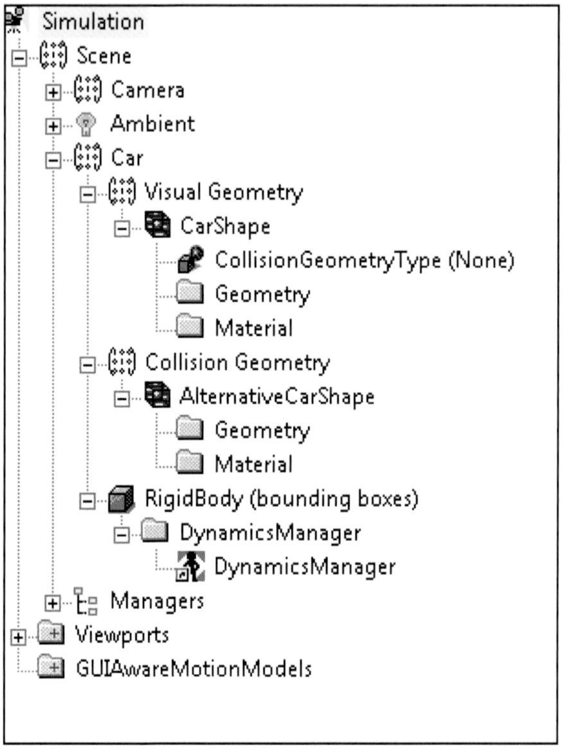

Discussion

discuss

Visualize a simulation that includes the objects found in your classroom. Can you identify objects within the room that would benefit from the utilization of a bounding volume? What type of bounding volume would you recommend using for each of these items? Could the use of bounding volumes help improve the performance and stability of such a simulation?

Collision Response

Collision response can be turned on and off with the CollisionResponse field in the CollisionObject node. The basic collision response (not using avatar abilities) will cause a moving object to slide along other objects. Collisions are resolved for one object at a time, and only the moving object is repositioned when responding to the collision. The collision response also can be adjusted to improve the collision response of an avatar moving in an environment, which is described in the section titled Avatar Abilities later in this lesson.

Sub Stepping

The motion of dividing an object into sub steps before resolution is referred to as ***sub stepping.*** Use sub stepping to avoid the problem that fast-moving objects can move through other objects without any detected collision. For example, setting the maximum sub step length of a car object to the length of the car will prevent the car from driving through walls even though it moves fast. This is a simple way to solve the problem, and it works well if the objects are not moving too fast. However, it does not solve the problem for very fast-moving objects like missiles or bullets because the number of sub steps required would be too high.

The SubStepPreference and SubStep fields in the CollisionObject node are used to configure sub stepping. With SubStepPreference, you can identify the SubStep value as a number or a length.

Penetration Depth

The CollisionObject node has two properties regarding penetration depth: MaxFinalPenetrationDepth and MaxIntermediatePenetrationDepth. MaxFinalPenetrationDepth sets the maximum allowed penetration depth in the final result of the collision resolve. MaxIntermediatePenetrationDepth sets the maximum allowed penetration depth while doing the collision resolve. These values should be balanced to the size of the object. Values that are too small might make the collision resolve slowly, but values that are too large might generate unexpected results.

Avatar Abilities

The basic sliding response is not enough to handle an avatar moving around in an environment. Two important features that have to be handled are the ability to step over obstacles or step up a stair and the ability to stand still on a slope without sliding while being able to smoothly slide along a wall.

The CollisionObject node has four avatar ability properties:

- StepUp
- FirmStep
- MaxIncline
- GravityDirection

GravityDirection defines "up" and "down." This value is used by the other avatar abilities. StepUp will make the collision object perform any motion as a step. For example, if StepUp is set to 0.5 and the collision object is moved 1.0 unit forward, then the collision system will perform that motion by

- moving the object 0.5 units in the negative gravity direction (step up).
- moving the object 1.0 units forward.
- moving the object 0.5 units in the gravity direction (step down).

FirmStep will make the collision object stand still on a slope by preventing the object from sliding for any motion that is directed down. MaxIncline defines the maximum incline that the avatar can climb and stand on.

Summary

In this lesson you:

- Learned about adding motion.
- Became familiar with scene navigation using the camera.
- Studied methods of movement.
- Discussed object movement in 3D space.
- Developed an understanding of handling collisions.

Simulation

The Contours Company client appreciates all of the time and effort you have spent improving the apartment simulation. Although the client is now satisfied that users will get a "real-life feel" for the apartment's overall layout, you realize that many of the apartment's features need proper lighting to look more realistic.

You decide to brainstorm to find methods of enhancing the client's visual experience of the virtual apartment. You have learned several techniques in EON that allow you to modify an object's appearance and position. You also can add behavior and interactivity to the simulation file. Calling on that knowledge, update the storyboard with the methods you think would increase the simulation's overall appeal.

Job 5.1: Continuing Progression of the Storyboard

By now, you realize that storyboarding is a process. You previously revised the client's storyboard, which originally provided only the ability to "walk through" the apartment's existing floor plan, by adding imported objects and textures. You also reduced the processing time of the simulation file and used EON's 3D editing tools to provide examples of brighter color schemes for the apartment. Once again, you need to update the storyboard. This time you will add ideas for further enriching the simulation file.

1. Open EON. Open **Job_4.2.eoz**, the apartment simulation you enhanced in the Module 4 Simulation.
2. Run the simulation and navigate through the apartment.
3. Take notes on the best methods for modifying the appearance and positions of objects in the apartment. Utilize the skills you learned in Module 5 Lesson 1 regarding lighting and textures.
4. Study the overall apartment layout and determine how you might incorporate behavior and interactivity in the simulation. Perhaps you could provide the client with the ability to navigate a predetermined path through the apartment with the simple click of a key.
5. Close the simulation window.
6. Open the storyboard that you created in the Module 1 Simulation and later enhanced in the Modules 2, 3, and 4 Simulations. Revise the storyboard to include information for modifying the appearance and position of various objects throughout the apartment. (If you did not complete the Simulation sections for Modules 1 through 4, you can create a storyboard using paper and pencil, a flowchart application, or a drawing program.)
7. Update the storyboard to include your plans for adding behavior and interactivity to the simulation.
8. Complete your storyboard and then save your work.

Job 5.2: Modifying the Appearance and Position of Objects in the Apartment

The apartment simulation currently contains a number of objects, including furniture, cabinets, curtains, and so forth. Adding the proper lighting and ensuring that each object is appropriately positioned will make the apartment look more realistic.

1. Refer to your notes from Job 5.1 about modifying the appearance and position of objects in the apartment.
2. If necessary, open EON and then open **Job_4.2.eoz** (if you closed it in Job 5.1). Save the simulation as **Job_5.2.eoz**.

3. Utilize your knowledge of lighting in EON to enhance the objects in the apartment. Remember that you can adjust the properties of lights in a simulation to achieve various effects. See Figure 5.1.

FIGURE 5.1 Light Properties dialog box

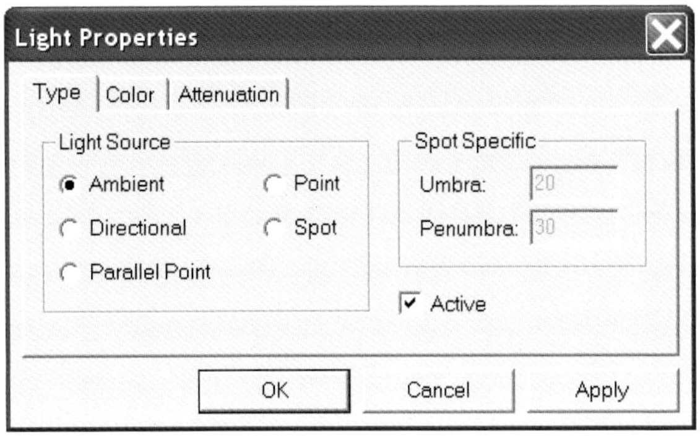

4. Draw on your understanding of positioning in EON to ensure that all of the objects are positioned correctly in the apartment.
5. Save the simulation and keep it open to use in Job 5.3.

Job 5.3: Incorporating Behavior and Interactivity in the Apartment Simulation

You know several different techniques in EON that will allow you to modify an object's appearance and position, as well as add behavior and interactivity to the simulation file. With the proper lighting and position of objects, you have produced a visually appealing apartment simulation. Now you will provide the ability to navigate automatically through the apartment. This will enhance the client's overall 3D experience of the apartment.

1. If necessary, open EON and then open **Job_5.2.eoz**, the simulation that you updated in Job 5.2.
2. Navigate to a starting point in the apartment, such as the front door in the living room.
3. Using your knowledge of movement in EON, create movement along a path through the apartment simulation.
4. Assign a key to commence the movement. See Figure 5.2.

FIGURE 5.2 Assign a key to initiate movement

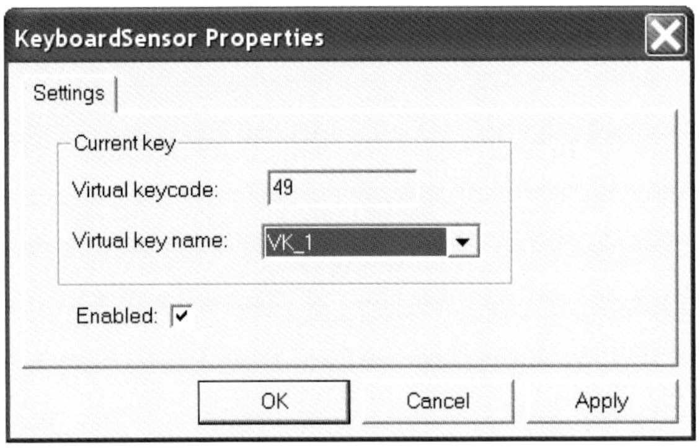

5. Based on the techniques you learned in Module 5 Lesson 2, select the best method for moving objects in the apartment.
6. Experiment with rearranging different pieces of furniture in each room of the apartment.
7. Save the simulation as **Job_5.3.eoz** and then run the simulation.
8. Use the key assigned in step 4 to navigate through the apartment. Note the new positions of the furniture in each room.
9. Close the simulation window. Close EON without saving the simulation.

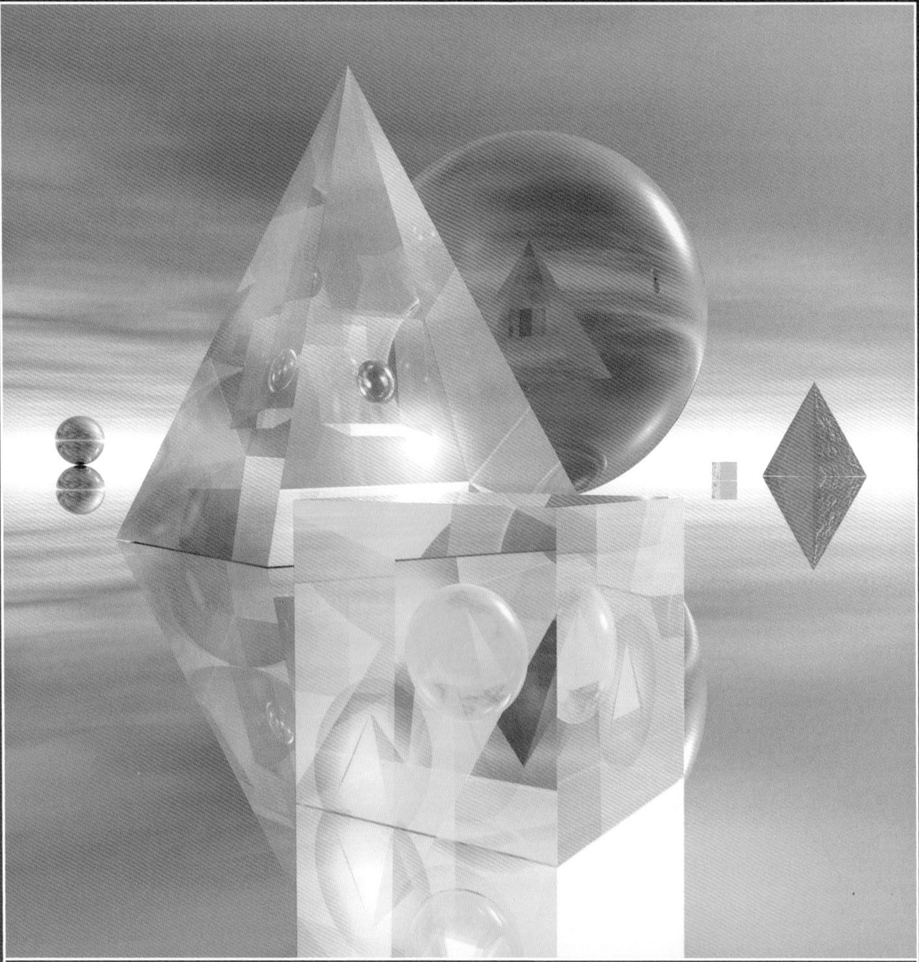

HARALD SUND

MODULE 6

EON Views and User Interfaces

LESSON 6.1
Viewports and Cameras

LESSON 6.2
User Interfaces

LESSON 6.1

Viewports and Cameras

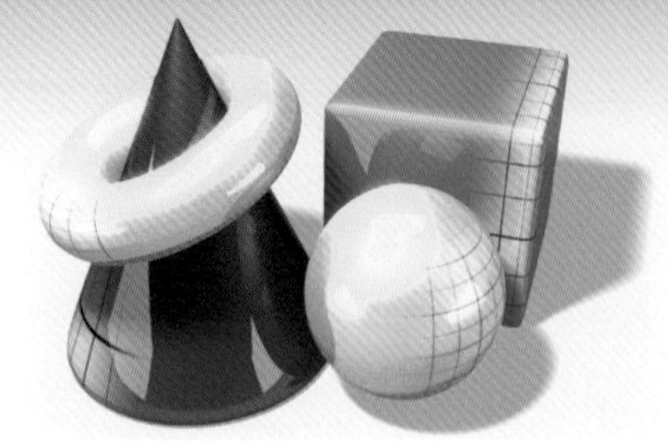

Objectives

In this lesson you will:

- Develop an understanding of viewports in EON.
- Learn about EON viewport elements.
- Become familiar with EON viewport properties.
- Discuss cameras in EON.

Key Terms

AvatarCollision prototype	*near clipping plane*	*Target node*
Camera node	*RenderTexture node*	*zero parallax*
far clipping plane	*RenderTree node*	

Understanding Viewports in EON

As you learned in Module 2 Lesson 1, the field of view, called a viewport, is the area that can be viewed from a camera. A viewport in EON is made up of camera reference information and property information for the field of view. This 3D viewport displays the current camera view of scene objects in a three-dimensional environment and allows you to move and rotate around all three axes to view the model from different angles.

STORYBOARD

Cameras

In EON, settings for the camera determine your view within a simulation.

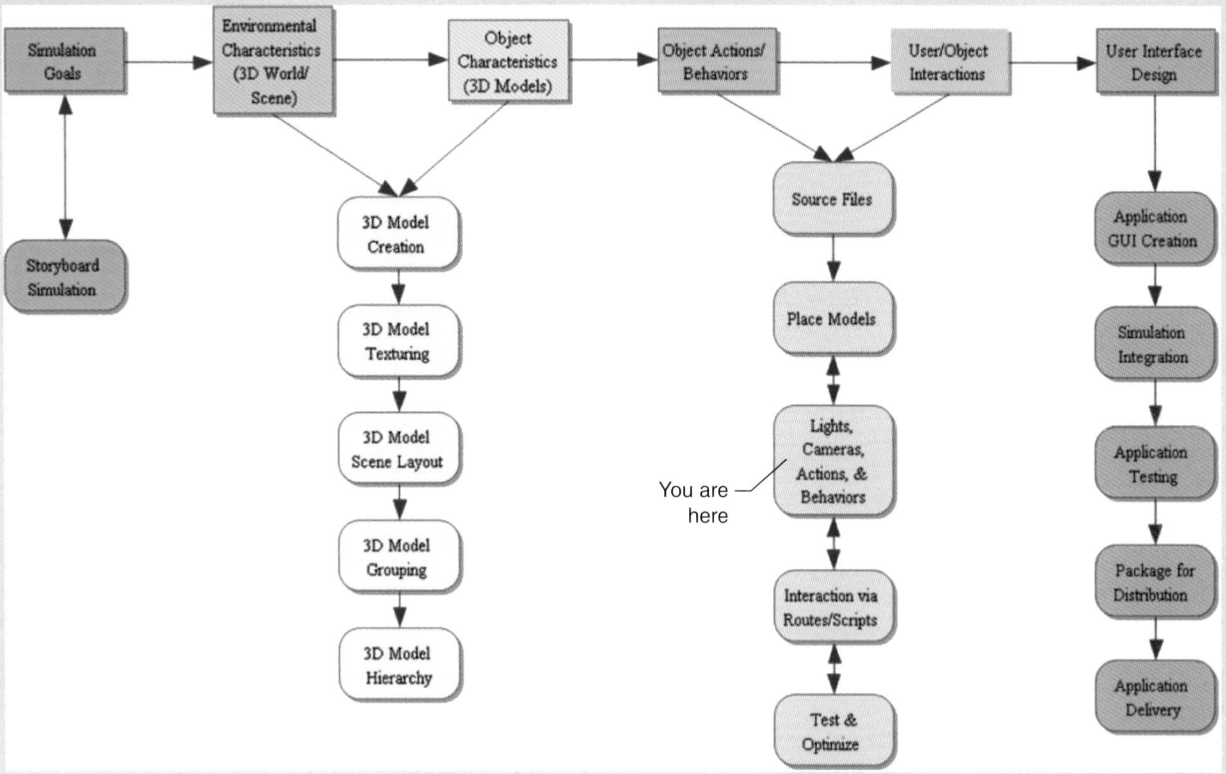

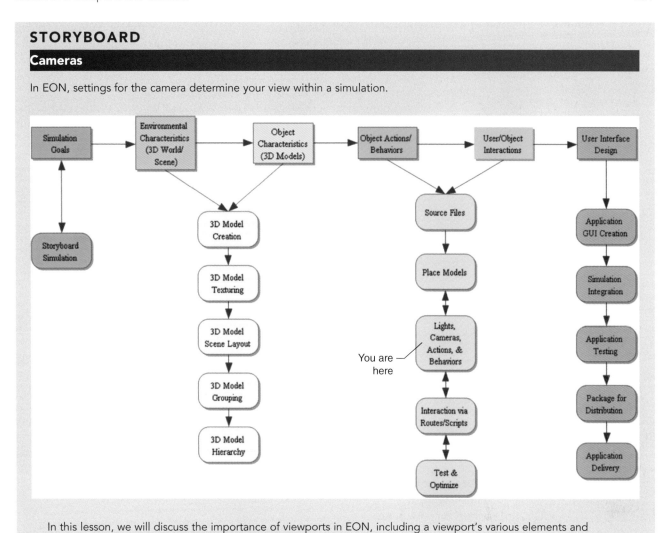

In this lesson, we will discuss the importance of viewports in EON, including a viewport's various elements and properties, and how they are reflected within the camera.

EON Viewport Elements

The EON simulation tree contains a Viewports folder, as shown in Figure 6.1.1.

tips+tricks

The plus sign next to the Viewports folder icon indicates that this folder is a graphic representation of a multiple value field used for storing lists of values.

FIGURE 6.1.1 Viewports folder in simulation tree

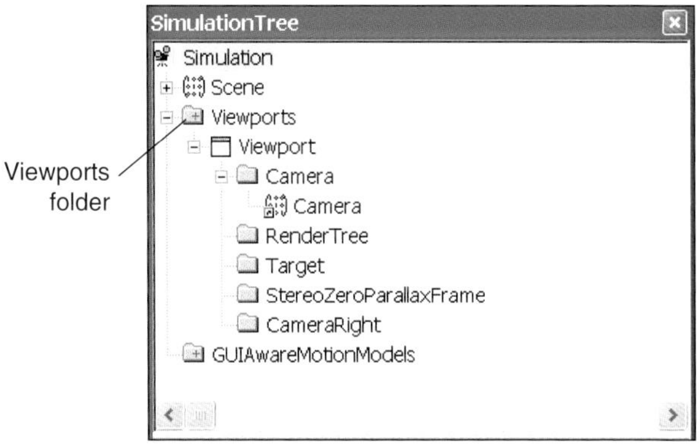

cross-reference

See Module 2 Lesson 1 for information about the field of view.

By default, an EON simulation opens with one Viewport node and one Camera node referenced in the Viewport node's Camera field. However, the simulation window can contain multiple viewports that can be overlaid on top of one another or placed on specific locations in the simulation area. In the Viewports folder, additional Viewport nodes can be placed for multiple view simulations.

A Viewport node defines the user's field of view and how the simulation is displayed in the simulation window. The Viewport node must be connected to a Frame node defining the user's position and orientation in the simulation.

Activity 6.1.1: Exploring a Viewport

1. Open EON to start a new simulation. If EON is already open, select **New** from the File menu.
2. Expand the following components in the simulation tree: **Viewports > Viewport > Camera**. Click the **Camera** node reference. Notice that the Camera frame holds the Position and Orientation information for the Viewport node when referenced in the Camera field.
3. Close EON without saving the simulation.

Camera Node

The ***Camera node*** contains the Position and Orientation fields that provide values for the Viewport node to render the 3D perspective of the viewing area. The Camera node is a Frame node that is linked to a Viewport node. The Camera node's Position and Orientation fields, the field of view, and the near and far clipping plane settings determine what the viewer sees in the simulation window.

RenderTree Node

The ***RenderTree node*** refers to the objects that will be rendered in the viewport. If the RenderTree field contains a reference to another node, EON will display only objects under that node in the viewport. If the RenderTree field is blank, everything will render.

Target Node

The ***Target node*** is used for Cg materials, for multi-pass rendering, and for the RenderTexture node. This node also applies to Cg shaders, which is a more advanced topic not covered in this text.

StereoZeroParallaxFrame Node

Stereo produces two individual pictures—one for each eye. ***Zero parallax*** is the distance from the eye to the plane where the images from the left and right eye coincide. In EON, you can control the zero parallax plane by setting it to a constant value in the Viewport node or by setting a reference to a frame in the StereoZeroParallax-Frame field that specifies the point that the plane goes through.

Use the StereoZeroParallaxFrame field to place the zero parallax plane at a specific object regardless of the position of the object or the camera. If this field is set, the value of the StereoZeroParallaxDistance field is ignored. If you want zero parallax in the center of an object, you can copy a link from the parent Frame node of the object to the Viewport node's ZeroParallaxFrame node field. The Zero Parallax reference is used for optimizing stereo for an object so that ideal 3D effects can be created for the simulation file.

CameraRight Node

Use the CameraRight folder for setting up custom eye separation for cameras in a viewport for rendering stereo. A user will see only the Camera Right camera when running a simulation in one of EON's stereo modes. This is an advanced topic and beyond the scope of this text.

RenderTexture Node

The ***RenderTexture node*** allows you to render a camera view to a texture and apply the texture to a material in the scene. To use the RenderTexture node, insert it in the simulation tree (typically the Resources branch if it is present in the simulation tree). Then it will be applied to a selected material's DiffuseTexture field. Next, create a reference to the new node in the Target field of a chosen Viewport node. If you run the simulation now, the chosen viewport will render the content into this texture instead of the display. You will use this primarily for multi-pass rendering effects when using Cg shaders in EON Professional.

Discussion

discuss

What scenarios might call for the use of the RenderTexture node?

EON Viewport Properties

The properties of the Viewport node allow you to specify a rectangular portion of the simulation window. The Viewport node's port can be thought of as a portal—a window through which you view a certain portion of the 3D world. The Viewport node's settings also define the viewing frustum, which is the shape of the 3D space defined by a field of view and near and far clipping planes. The Viewport node's properties determine where the viewport is positioned in the simulation window and which objects are displayed in the viewport window based on the camera's viewing area and distance from the objects that could be displayed.

Position

The position fields, X and Y, identify the X and Y start position relative to the upper-left corner of the simulation window. This field determines the viewport's relative position in the simulation window. The values can range from zero to one. The position (0,0) is located at the upper-left corner, and (0.5,0.5) is located at the center of the window.

Size

The size values, Width and Height, determine the viewport's relative size in the simulation window. The values can range from zero to one. A Width value of 0.5 sets the viewport to half of the simulation window's width.

troubleshooting

The sum of the position and size properties (for either X or Y) cannot be greater than 1. For example, if the X position value is 0.6, the Width value for X cannot be greater than 0.4. Likewise, if the Y position value is 0.3, the Width value for Y cannot be greater than 0.7.

Activity 6.1.2: Adding and Changing a Viewport

1. Open EON. Open **Activity_6.1.2.eoz** from the data files for Module 6 Lesson 1.
2. Run the simulation and notice the current viewport of the scene. Then close the simulation window.
3. In the simulation tree, add a **Frame** node under Scene.
4. Change the name of the new Frame node to **CameraTop**.
5. Double-click the **CameraTop** node to open the Frame Properties dialog box. Verify that the X value is **0**. Change the Y value to **1**. Change the Z value to **25**. Change the Pitch to **90** as shown in Figure 6.1.2. Click **OK** to close the dialog box.

FIGURE 6.1.2 Frame Properties dialog box for the CameraTop node

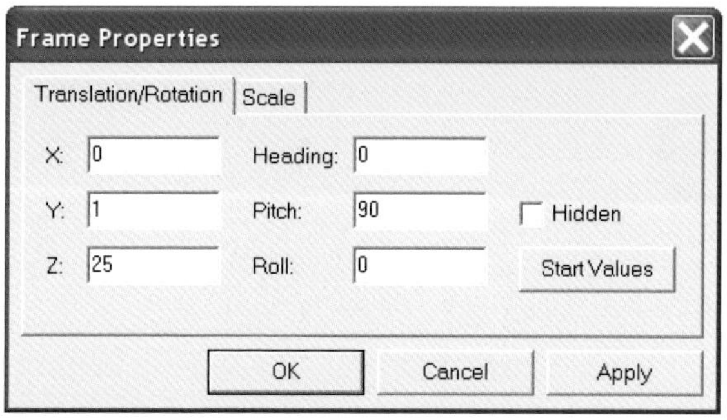

6. Add a new **Viewport** node under the Viewports folder.
7. Change the name of the new Viewport node to **TopView**.
8. Right-click the **CameraTop** node and select the **Copy as Link** option. Expand the **TopView** node in the simulation tree. Right-click the **Camera** folder under the TopView frame and select **Paste** from the drop-down menu.
9. Select the **TopView** node in the simulation tree. In the Property Bar, change the Width and Height values to **0.4**.
10. Run the simulation to see the viewports.
11. Close the simulation window.
12. Double-click the **TopView** node to display the Viewport Properties dialog box. Change the X value to **0.6** and change the Y value to **0.6**. Click **OK** to close the dialog box.
13. Run the simulation. Notice that the TopView viewport has moved to the lower-right corner.
14. Close the simulation window. Save the simulation as **Viewport.eoz** and keep it open to use in Activity 6.1.3.

Clipping Planes

Clipping planes, which are perpendicular to the camera, occupy the entire viewport. They can be used to prevent the processing of objects that are not within clear sight, thus preserving processing resources. Objects that are farther away than the distance of the ***far clipping plane*** are not drawn (see Figure 6.1.3). Objects closer than the distance of the ***near clipping plane*** are not drawn (see Figure 6.1.3).

FIGURE 6.1.3 Visualization of near and far clipping planes

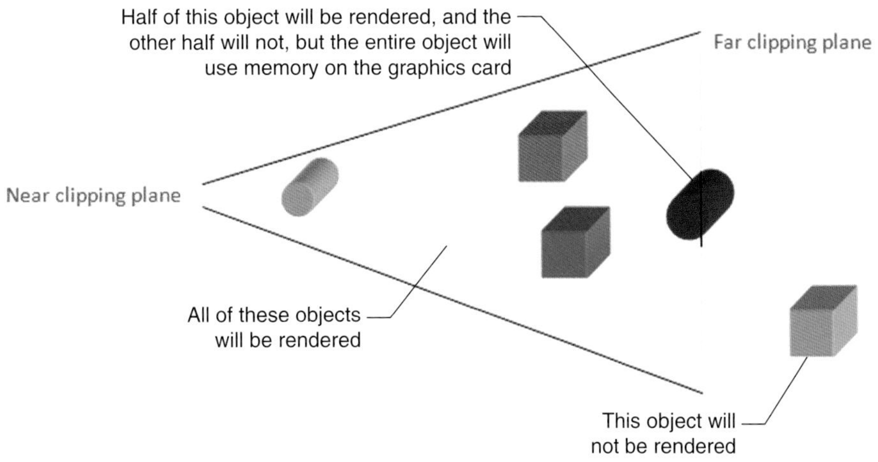

Field of View

The field of view value, which is stored in the FieldOfView field, determines the viewer's field of view in degrees. The default value is 53 degrees. For simulations of building interiors, 53 degrees is too narrow. If you broaden the field of view to 75 degrees, for example, the new field of view will allow you to see up to three walls of a room at the same time. The viewport perspective is altered, and you can now see more objects.

All of a Viewport node's properties affect the frame rate of the simulation. The more objects that are visible at any given time, the more calculations the computer must perform. For maximum performance, keep the far clipping plane near, the near clipping plane far, and the field of vision narrow.

Discussion

discuss

Why do you think an increase in the FieldOfView field value results in a slower simulation frame rate?

Activity 6.1.3: Adjusting a Viewport's Position

1. Continue working with the open simulation file **Viewport.eoz** from Activity 6.1.2.
2. Save the simulation as **Viewport_Position.eoz**.
3. Run the simulation. If necessary, move the simulation window so that you can access the Simulation Tree window and the Property Bar.
4. Select the **TopView** node in the Simulation Tree window and remove the check mark from the **Clear** check box in the Property Bar. Notice that the TopView viewport is no longer displayed in the simulation window.
5. Change the value in the NearClip field to **23** and notice that the TopView viewport is displayed again.
6. Close the simulation window. Save the simulation and keep it open to use in Activity 6.1.4.

Understanding Cameras in EON

In EON, cameras are EON Frame nodes that hold position and orientation information. Then, this information is passed on to the Viewport node. A camera (i.e., Frame node) can be moved around the scene dynamically to adjust the viewing perspective for the simulation by using EON motion nodes that move their parent frame including the Place node, KeyFrame node, Walk node, WalkAbout node, and the OrbitNav prototype. A camera also can be manually adjusted, although this method is not preferred.

Creating Camera Views in EON

If you want to set the camera position to your current location, click the Set Initial View button on the EON Zoom Extents Bar. Your current camera view will be displayed the next time you open the simulation.

As we just mentioned, camera views can be created by adding Motion Model nodes below the Camera frame. These nodes modify the position and orientation of the camera. A series of Place nodes can be placed below the Camera frame to create multiple camera views.

You can create ten views very simply by using the ViewMaker or OrbitNav-ViewMaker prototypes. Hold down the S key while pressing a number key to save the current view. To return to that view, press only the number key.

Activity 6.1.4: Creating Camera Views

1. Continue working with the open simulation file **Viewport_Position.eoz** from Activity 6.1.3.
2. Save the simulation as **Viewport_Camera.eoz**.
3. Under Scene\ActiveViewportCamera in the simulation tree, add three **Place** nodes. Change the names of the Place nodes to **Place_Camera1**, **Place_Camera2**, and **Place_Camera3**.
4. Double-click each new **Place** node to display its Place Properties dialog box. Select **No** under Active if necessary, as shown in Figure 6.1.4. Click **OK** to close the dialog box after making each change.

FIGURE 6.1.4 Place Properties dialog box

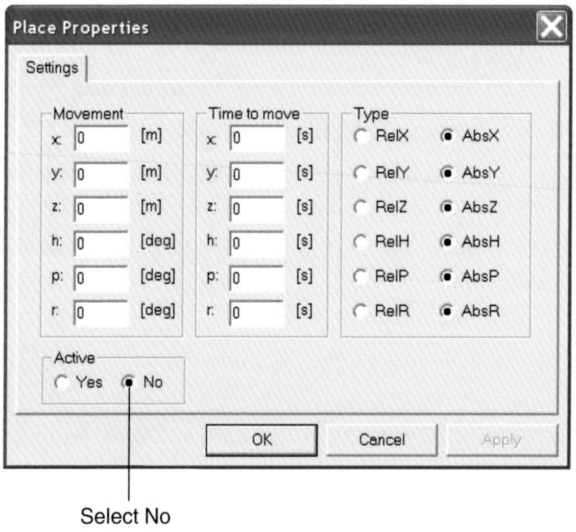

5. Double-click **Place_Camera1** to display the Place Properties dialog box. Under the Movement heading, make the following changes and then click **OK** to close the dialog box:

   x **5.6**

   y **–3.5**

   z **1.8**

   h **33**

   p **5**

6. Double-click **Place_Camera2** to display the Place Properties dialog box. Under the Movement heading, make the following changes and then click **OK** to close the dialog box:

   x **3**

   y **0.8**

   z **1.9**

   h **160**

   p **10**

7. Double-click **Place_Camera3** to display the Place Properties dialog box. Under the Movement heading, make the following changes and then click **OK** to close the dialog box:

   x **–3.6**

   y **2.6**

   z **1.8**

   h **145**

   p **5**

8. Under Scene, add a **Group** node. Change the name of the node to **Keys**.
9. Under the Keys group, add three **KeyboardSensor** nodes. Change the names of the nodes to **Camera1_Key1**, **Camera2_Key2**, and **Camera3_Key3**.
10. Display the **Routes** window. Existing routes for the simulation will be displayed. You will establish new routes in the following steps.
11. Drag the three KeyboardSensor nodes (**Camera1_Key1**, **Camera2_Key2**, and **Camera3_Key3**) to the Routes window.
12. Drag the three Place nodes (**Place_Camera1**, **Place_Camera2**, and **Place_Camera3**) to the Routes window.
13. Establish the connections outlined in the following table.

From	outEvent	To	inEvent
Camera1_Key1	OnKeyDown	Place_Camera1	SetRun
Camera2_Key2	OnKeyDown	Place_Camera2	SetRun
Camera3_Key3	OnKeyDown	Place_Camera3	SetRun

14. In the simulation tree, double-click **Camera1_Key1** to display the KeyboardSensor Properties dialog box. Select **VK_1** from the Virtual key name drop-down list. Verify that the **Enabled** check box is selected, as shown in Figure 6.1.5. Click **OK** to close the dialog box.

FIGURE 6.1.5 KeyboardSensor Properties dialog box

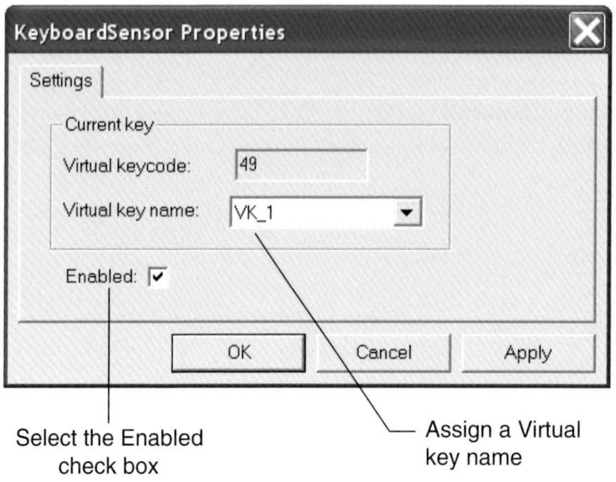

15. Repeat step 14, using the Virtual key name field to assign **VK_2** to the Camera2_Key2 node. Repeat step 14 again, using the Virtual key name field to assign **VK_3** to the Camera3_Key3 node.
16. Run the simulation. Press the **1** key, the **2** key, and then the **3** key. Each key should display a different location in the apartment.
17. Close the simulation window. Save the simulation and keep it open to use in Activity 6.1.5.

Collision on a Camera

The preferred method of setting up collision on a camera is by placing the ***AvatarCollision prototype*** in the Camera frame. The collision geometry of this prototype consists of four spheres that form a rough approximation of a human body. With this prototype, the physic engine, which is licensed from CM Labs, is used to calculate collision in the scene. It also uses EON CollisionObject nodes, which hold properties and report collisions for individual collision objects. Table 6.1.1 lists the AvatarCollision prototype fields available.

TABLE 6.1.1 AvatarCollision Prototype Fields

Field	Description
Enabled	Enable/disable the prototype.
ShowContactNormals	Show contact normals when the avatar is colliding.
GravityEnabled	Enable/disable gravity.
CameraPosition	Location of the camera. Four options are available: 0: Do not adjust camera position. Use currently set camera. 1: Position camera in the head of the avatar. Use internal camera or the camera defined in the Camera field. 2: Position camera behind the avatar. Use internal camera or the camera defined in the Camera field. 3: Position camera above the avatar. Use internal camera or the camera defined in the Camera field.
CollideWithScene	If set, a CollisionObject will automatically be placed in the scene at simulation start. Commonly, the avatar collides with the rest of the environment. Setting this flag will make this happen.
Camera	Camera to use instead of internal camera.
HideCollisionGeometry	Show/hide the collision geometry.
Scale	Change the size of the avatar. Using this property ensures that all affected properties are scaled properly.
StepUp	Height of the steps the avatar can take when stepping over obstacles.
Opacity	Opacity of the collision geometry.
AdaptiveCamera	Make the camera move closer to the avatar when objects are between the camera and the avatar. Also, adjust the opacity when the camera gets very close.
CameraDistance	Current distance between the camera and the avatar head when using AdaptiveCamera.
CurrentOpacity	Current opacity of the collision geometry when using AdaptiveCamera. Useful when setting opacity of visual avatar geometry.
ObjectFrame	The frame to be controlled by the AvatarCollision node. If empty, the parent frame will be used.
Jump	Make the avatar jump.
JumpSpeed	How fast/high the avatar can jump.
MaxFallSpeed	The maximum speed the avatar will reach when falling.
Gravity	The gravity in the world (z-axis).
CollisionManager	Detect and resolve collisions

tips+tricks

To better control the collision properties of the environment, clear the CollideWithScene check box in the AvatarCollision prototype, and place CollisionObject nodes as desired in the environment.

cross-reference

In Module 5 Lesson 2, you will find more information about handling collisions.

Activity 6.1.5: Using the AvatarCollision Prototype

1. Continue working with the open simulation file **Viewport_Camera.eoz** from Activity 6.1.4.
2. Save the file as **Viewport_AvatarCollision.eoz**.
3. Under Scene\ActiveViewportCamera, place an **AvatarCollison** prototype.
4. Run the simulation.
5. Using the mouse, try to move up—toward the ceiling—in the simulation window. Notice that you are automatically returned to the same position.

6. In the simulation tree, select the **AvatarCollision** prototype.
7. In the Property Bar, clear the **GravityEnabled** check box.
8. Using the mouse, try to move up in the simulation window again. Notice that you are able to move up in the simulation window.
9. Close the simulation window. Save the simulation and then close EON.

Summary

In this lesson you:

- Developed an understanding of viewports in EON.
- Learned about EON viewport elements.
- Became familiar with EON viewport properties.
- Discussed cameras in EON.

LESSON 6.2

User Interfaces

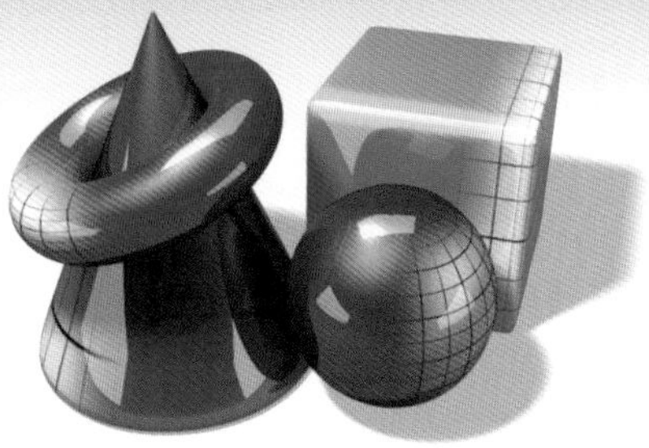

Objectives

In this lesson you will:

- Develop an understanding of graphical user interfaces (GUIs) and consider the elements needed to create a user-friendly interface.
- Explore nodes and prototypes commonly used to create interfaces.
- Create a GUI for a simulation.
- Add interactivity to a user interface, including buttons.

Key Terms

2DImage node
application-oriented user interface
BPButton prototype
fixed screen size
FlashObject node
haptic
object-oriented user interface (OOUI)
PopupMenu node
scalable screen interface
SixButtons prototype
Slider node
tactile interface
touch interface
usability
user interface

Understanding GUI

As you learned in Module 2 Lesson 2, the acronym GUI stands for graphical user interface. A GUI is a specific type of user interface through which people can interact with electronic devices such as computers, handheld devices (MP3 players, portable media players, gaming devices, etc.), household appliances, and office equipment. A GUI offers graphical icons and visual indicators rather than text-based interfaces, keyed command labels, or text navigation to represent the information and actions available to a user. You directly manipulate the graphical elements to perform an action.

To use a simulation effectively, users must be able to control the elements of the simulation. The ***user interface*** is the entire collection of elements that a user can access to complete a task. It can include visual clues, static or dynamic information that impacts decision making or leads the user to actions, and elements that are manipulated (touched, pressed, turned, clicked, etc.) to cause change.

web links

When speaking about a mechanical system, a vehicle, or an industrial system, the user interface is often referred to as the Human-Machine Interface (HMI). Prior to that, the original term was Man-Machine Interface (MMI). Use the Internet to search for these terms. Can you find any other terms that have been used in the past or that are presently used? What are the differences in meaning between these terms and our present-day usage of GUI?

Usability

The key to a good user interface is its ***usability***. Usability is the extent to which the design of the user interface accounts for the "human" element and how effective and efficient it makes operating the system. A well-designed user interface will require very little effort from the user to make changes in the system or to understand the information coming from the system. Ideally, interacting with the interface is effortless. The user should intuitively know what to do and how to do it.

User Interfaces

The term *user interface* refers to all the information a program presents to a user. This includes textual, graphical, and auditory information. It also refers to the keystrokes, computer mouse movements, touch screen selections, or other controller methods used to control the program. Today, GUI is the most common type of user interface.

Applications that use a GUI accept input via devices, such as a computer keyboard or a mouse, and provide graphical output on the computer monitor. At least two different principles are widely used in GUI design: ***object-oriented user interface (OOUI)*** and ***application-oriented user interface***.

web links

Usability testing is a separate field of study in software design. Use the Internet to learn more about usability testing and the elements that are commonly viewed as critical to a good and usable design.

Object-Oriented User Interfaces

In an OOUI, the user interacts only with objects that represent programming elements within the application. Drawing applications, for example, commonly have an OOUI. The user of the application can select an object, such as a circle or a line, alter its properties, such as color or size, and perform other actions, such as moving or copying the object.

Application-Oriented User Interfaces

With application-oriented user interfaces, the main component is the application itself. The user runs the application and then brings other files into the application to accomplish a task. The user must know which application is running, what type of files the application supports, and how the operating system organizes the files.

The application-oriented environment often is used for situations in which a few tasks must be completed over and over. These tasks usually must be done in a predefined sequence that is generally reflected in the application-oriented menu structure.

Other User Interfaces

As you have already learned, EON options provide many ways to interact with a computer in addition to interacting directly with the desktop computer. Two common nondesktop computing interfaces are ***tactile interfaces*** and ***touch interfaces***.

tips+tricks

Haptic technology refers to technology that interfaces with the user via the sense of touch by applying forces, vibrations, and/or motions to the user.

Tactile interfaces add to or replace other forms of output with ***haptic*** feedback methods. These interfaces are used in computerized simulators like those created with EON. Common devices and peripherals used for these interfaces are head-mounted displays, gloves, I-glasses, and trackers.

Touch interfaces are GUIs that use a touch screen display as a combined input and output device instead of the keyboard, mouse, and monitor. These are used in many places in the world, including many that you may be familiar with, such as self-service machines for banking or purchasing groceries.

Discussion

discuss

What elements make a GUI intuitive? Consider programs that you use frequently. What features do you find easy to use? What features do you have to search for repeatedly? Do you think your answers to these questions would be the same as the answers someone else might give?

Exploring Interfaces in EON

As you begin creating user interfaces for your simulations, you must consider the needs of the people who will use the simulation: What will they want to do? You also need to consider the best ways to provide those capabilities—while making the interface as intuitive as possible.

In the following activity, we are revisiting the robot arm that you worked with in earlier modules. This time, however, an interface has been added to allow the user to move the arm instead of clicking the arm parts (which was *not* a very intuitive interface). Three different graphical interfaces that function the same but were created differently are available, allowing you to explore each interface and determine its pros and cons.

Activity 6.2.1: Exploring Interfaces Created in EON

1. Open EON. Open **Activity_6.2.1_2DInterface.eoz** from the data files for Module 6 Lesson 2.
2. Run the simulation. This is a 2D GUI. Your simulation window should look like that shown in Figure 6.2.1.

FIGURE 6.2.1 Simulation window with a 2D interface

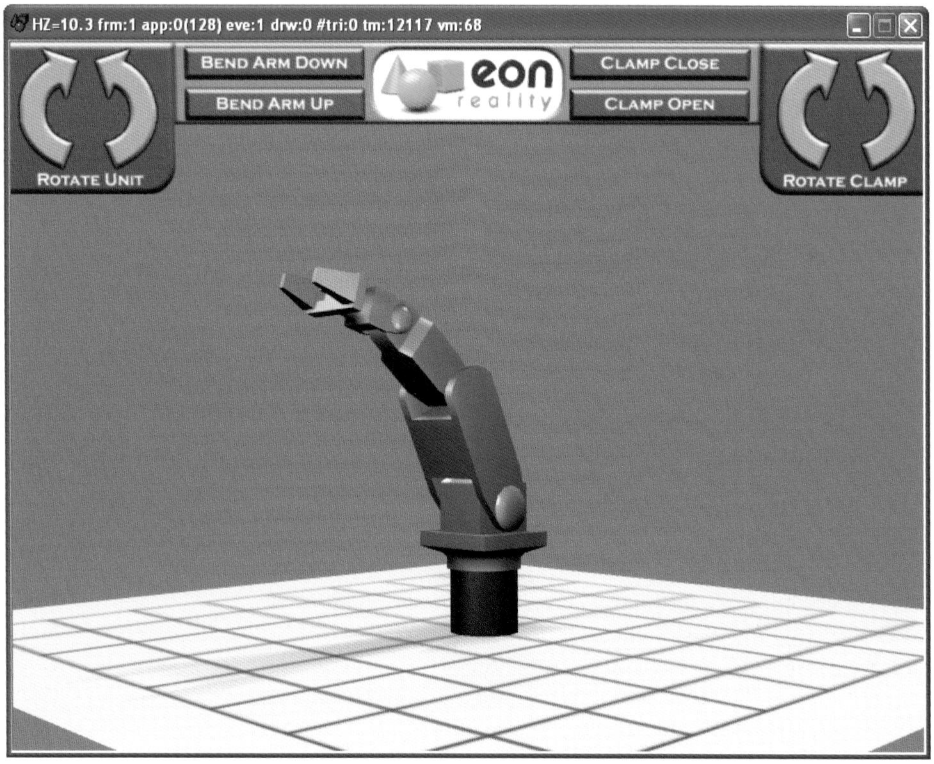

3. Experiment with the buttons on the interface.

Discussion

discuss

Was it easier to interact with this robot arm than it was to interact with the robot arm to which you added the KeyMove node?

Did you immediately understand how to move the arm?

Were you confused by any of the commands or did you see any unexpected results?

How do the Bend and Clamp buttons work?

Did you expect the Rotate Unit and Rotate Clamp areas of the display to act as a button on which you could click anywhere? Or did you understand that each arrow was a separate button?

These are all elements of usability.

4. Close the simulation window and expand the simulation tree so that you can see the contents of the Interface frame. Notice that each button in the interface is contained in a separate frame.
5. Expand the **Viewports** folder in the simulation tree and notice that a Viewport_ Interface folder was added to the Viewports folder.
6. Close EON without saving the simulation.
7. Open EON. Open **Activity_6.2.1_3DInterface.eoz** from the data files for Module 6 Lesson 2.
8. Run the simulation. This is a 3D GUI. The interface of your simulation window should look like that shown in Figure 6.2.2.

FIGURE 6.2.2 3D interface in the robotic arm simulation

9. Experiment with the buttons on the interface.

Discussion

discuss

Do you notice any differences in the way the 2D interface behaves versus the 3D interface?

Is one more visually appealing than the other?

If you were designing this interface, would you make any changes to the interface to enhance the 3D appearance? Is the 2D interface sufficient for the desired result?

10. Close the simulation window.
11. Expand the simulation tree so that you can see the components of the Interface frame. Does this look similar to or different from what you saw in the 2D interface simulation?
12. Expand the **Viewports** folder. Does it have a Viewport node for the interface?
13. Close EON without saving the simulation.
14. Open EON. Open **Activity_6.2.1_FlashInterface.eoz** from the data files for Module 6 Lesson 2.
15. Run the simulation. This is a Flash GUI. The interface of your simulation window should look like that shown in Figure 6.2.3.

FIGURE 6.2.3 Flash interface in the robotic arm simulation

16. Experiment with the buttons on this interface.

Discussion

discuss

Does the Flash interface cause the same actions as the 2D and 3D interfaces?

Do you notice any differences in the way the robotic arm behaves?

Of the three interfaces, which do you like the best?

17. Close the simulation window.
18. Expand the simulation tree so that you can see the components of the Interface frame. Notice that this frame contains only a FlashObject and a Script node.
19. Expand the **Viewports** folder. Notice that it does not have a Viewport node specifically for the interface.
20. Close EON without saving the simulation.

In addition to an interface's usability and intuitiveness, you also should consider its pros and cons, including how easy—or difficult—it is to create the interface and the impact the interface will have on system resources. Some of these considerations may have already become apparent to you as you worked through the previous activity. In Tables 6.2.1, 6.2.2, and 6.2.3, we outline the basic advantages and disadvantages of the three interfaces that we used in Activity 6.2.1. In the next section, you will begin to create your own interface.

TABLE 6.2.1 Advantages and Disadvantages of a 2D GUI

Pros and Cons of a 2D GUI	
Pros	**Cons**
Easy to create in Photoshop.	Suffers some quality loss when running in EON if the images are smaller than the simulation's target resolution.
Minimal polygon count impact.	Must use 3ds Max to create polygon shapes for the texture to appear.
Can use transparency.	Advanced interfaces can increase polygon count (but minimally).
No scripting required (although it can be used).	Requires additional viewports and configuration in EON.
	Requires further adjustment in EON for final placement (i.e., positioning in 3ds Max does not match positioning in EON).
	Animation is limited to MovieTextures only.
	Can require a cumbersome Routes window.
	Can have a large impact on Texture Memory usage while rendering, depending on the design.

TABLE 6.2.2 Advantages and Disadvantages of a 3D GUI

Pros and Cons of a 3D GUI	
Pros	**Cons**
Can be created in 3ds Max exclusively.	Affects polygon count more than 2D GUI (possibly significantly).
Can take advantage of transparency.	Requires additional viewports and configuration in EON.
GUI can be animated.	Requires further adjustment in EON for final placement (i.e., positioning in 3ds Max does not match positioning in EON).
Does not suffer from quality loss.	Can require a cumbersome Routes window.
No scripting required (although it can be used).	
Texture Memory impact (when rendering) is little to none, depending on the design.	

TABLE 6.2.3 Advantages and Disadvantages of a Flash GUI

Pros and Cons of a Flash GUI	
Pros	**Cons**
Simpler Routes window.	Does not support transparency.
No impact on polygon count.	Requires at least basic knowledge of Flash, ActionScript 2.0, and scripting in EON.
Little to no impact on Texture Memory usage when rendering.	Positioning is limited to the corners or the center.
Does not suffer from quality loss.	Flash Player must be installed on target machine.
Does not require additional viewports or positioning in EON.	
GUI can be animated.	

STORYBOARD

User Interface Development

As you reflect on the Storyboard, you will find that we have previously discussed almost all of the major components illustrated there.

In Module 2, we talked about the determination of the goals for the simulation as well as the creation of the storyboard itself. We also discussed the selection of 3D models and, in a broad sense, discussed the steps in the creation of a simulation. We explored changing the properties of the objects and nodes when constructing a simulation, which is part of the "Lights, Cameras, Actions, & Behaviors" stage, and began to learn about the "Interaction via Routes/Scripts" stage when we discussed connecting nodes using the Routes window.

In Module 3, we learned about importing source files, or 3D objects. We also discussed the various methods that can be used to position these objects—part of the "Place Models" stage. Module 4 explored working with textures, materials, and meshes in EON after a model has been imported. And in Module 5, you studied various lighting effects (Texture2 and Material2 nodes, scaling, transparency, and render settings).

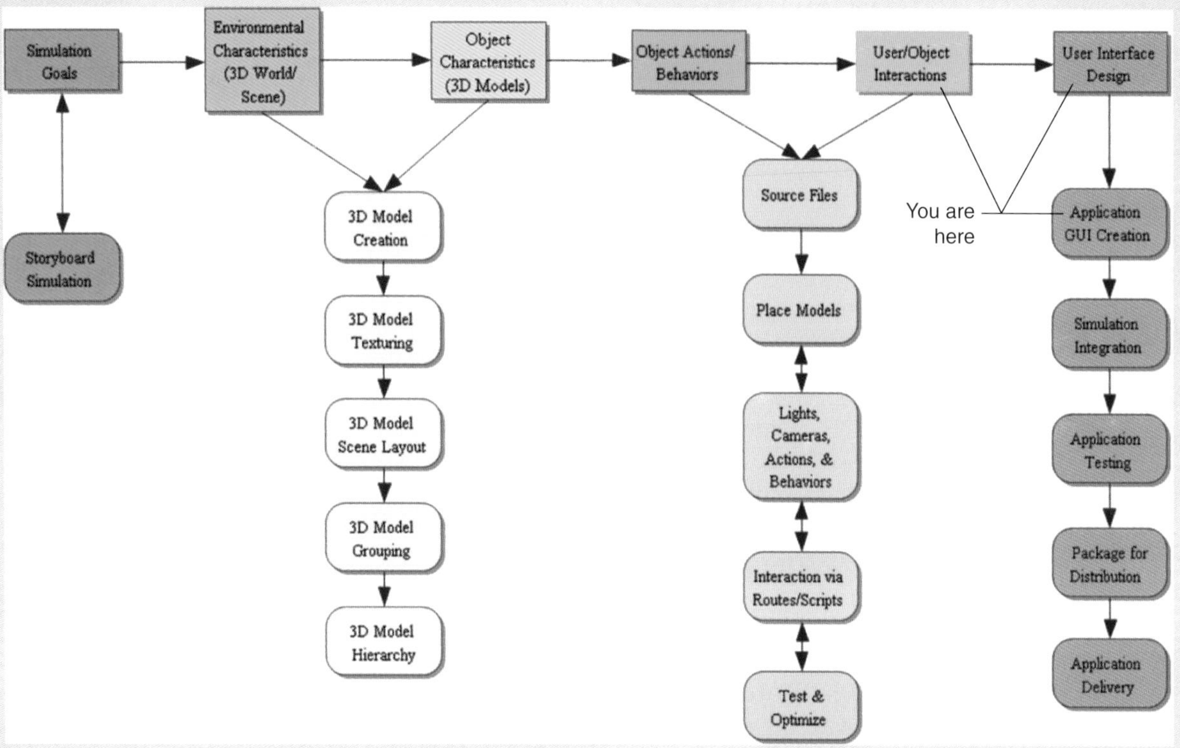

In this module, we will discuss "User/Object Interactions" and move into the last major area of the storyboard—the "User Interface Design" (blue section). Although complete user interface design instruction and usability testing are the subject of entire courses of study, this module will touch on the key components and provide basic instruction and considerations.

GUI Controls and Buttons Prototypes

As the tables in the previous section highlight, each type of interface has advantages and disadvantages. As you can imagine, you can make many choices and take different approaches to establish the right interface for the simulations you create. And you will likely find that what works well in one situation will not work as well in the next.

GUIControls Nodes

To begin creating and working with a user interface, you should be acquainted with several commonly used nodes. Because it is very common for EON users to need to create a user interface, a separate library of nodes is available for this task. The GUI-Controls nodes are shown in Figure 6.2.4. Familiarity with these nodes will make the task of creating a basic user interface much simpler. Although you can use the Help system to learn more about each of these nodes, we will detail four of the most commonly used nodes here.

FIGURE 6.2.4 GUIControls library of nodes

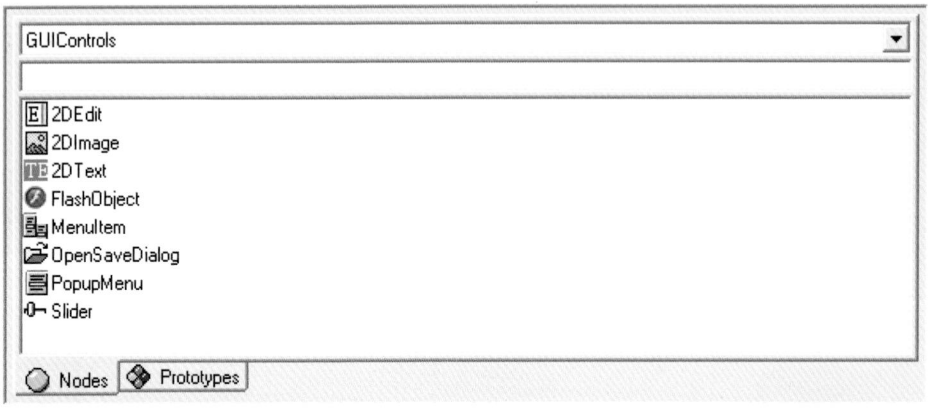

2DImage Node

2DImage

The ***2DImage node*** enables you to display bitmap images on top of the 3D-rendered EON window. It produces outEvents when you click the image. The images can be positioned, and the visible area (width and height) can be set. It also can be scaled down. Additionally, you can send new filenames to the ImageFile field to change the image. However, this relates only to files on the local hard disk or in the .eoz and not to Internet URLs.

Slider Node

Slider

The ***Slider node*** provides a vertical or horizontal slider control that appears on top of the 3D-rendered window. The moving part of the slider can be moved by dragging it with the mouse or by sending values to the SliderPos field.

The slider is one way for users to interact with the application, or it can be used to display a value on a scale. You can set minimum and maximum values on the slider, and you can choose to display small incremental markings that indicate the measurement scale at set intervals.

Additionally, you can set the position and area covered by the slider. When it is horizontal, the height should be set at 10, 15, 20, or 30, and when the slider is vertical, the width can be set at these same values. The size of the pointers depends on the height or width of the slider.

PopupMenu Node

PopupMenu

The ***PopupMenu node*** provides the context-sensitive menu and right mouse button menu functionality that are common to other Windows programs. You can have an unlimited number of menu items. The MenuStrings field will hold all the text for all the menu items. Enter the text for the menu items by enclosing it in quotation marks, for example, "This is menu one", "This is the second", "Number Three", "Fourth one", and so on.

An alternative method for entering text is to run the simulation and then use the Property Bar to enter one menu item at a time. To use the Property Bar, you key a menu item in the AddMenuString field and press Enter. Then you key another menu item and press Enter, repeating until all menu items have been entered. To make your menu appear, you must connect a route to the ShowPopupMenu field.

Because the menu will appear where the mouse cursor is located at the time, it is recommended that a mouse click trigger the menu to appear. To establish this, insert a MouseSensor node and connect the OnRightUp field to the ShowPopupMenu field. You could display the menu when the user clicks an object. This requires only a route from a ClickSensor's OnButtonDownTrue outEvent to the ShowPopupMenu field.

A PopupMenu node can be used to rotate an object, start an animation, or provide information. It also can be used to hide an object or parts of it. Other creative uses for a PopupMenu node include displaying an item's price and changing the color of an object.

Discussion

discuss

Can you think of places where pop-up menus are used in common programs? How do these menus typically behave? How does the use of familiar elements help the user?

FlashObject Node

FlashObject

The ***FlashObject node*** was designed to be a method for inserting media, but it also can be used to make an interface. In fact, FlashObject nodes are helpful when creating user interfaces. With this node, you can specify the values in the BoxPosition and BoxSize fields—and these can move and change while the simulation is running. Also, the object scales within the box size so that you do not lose any portion of the object regardless of the size of the screen. The FlashObject node always appears on top in a simulation window so it does not get lost behind other elements on the screen. Other features of the FlashObject node enable you to:

- Set variables and use the CallFunction field to send events.
- Use the FSCommand field to communicate with EON.

Buttons Prototypes

As more simulation applications are created, more prototypes are created to encapsulate good combinations of nodes and routes—capturing unique and useful tools for others to use. With each release of the EON software, more prototypes are added to the ever-growing collection to make the software more useful and to save time for other developers.

Figure 6.2.5 illustrates the Buttons library of prototypes. Again, although you can learn more about each of these by using the Help system, we will discuss two of the most useful Buttons prototypes here.

FIGURE 6.2.5 Buttons library of prototypes

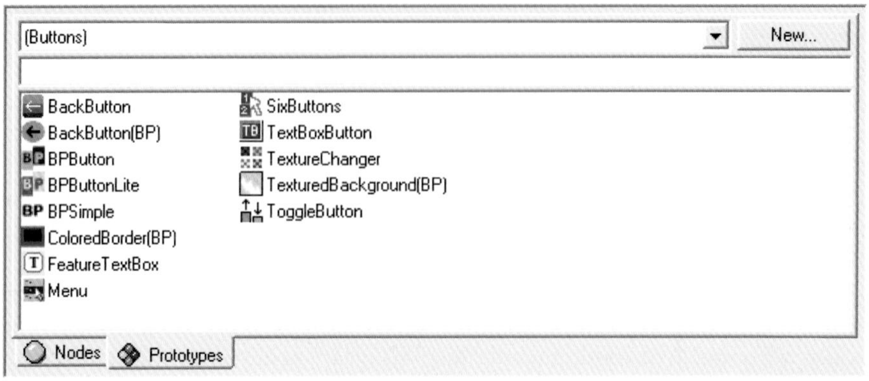

tips+tricks

The BP in the BPButton prototype name stands for "Box Positioned."

BPButton Prototype

BPButton

The ***BPButton prototype*** is a box-positioned button (image) placed under the Camera node. It is a 3D object, but it can be positioned like a 2D GUI object using pixel coordinates when it is under the Camera node. Therefore, it can be positioned in the same way as the GUIControls nodes such as 2DText, 2DImage, 2DEdit, and Slider.

The main features of the BPButton prototype include:

- Displays images as buttons/screens/GUI items/backgrounds.
- Uses the BoxPosition and BoxSize fields for positioning and sizing.
- Allows you to use your own texture node (with any .jpg, .png, or .ppm).
- Allows you to use outEvents, like OnButtonDown, or to send events directly.
- Enables you to change the appearance of the button with the MouseOverFX field.
- Enables you to move the button by dragging it.
- Allows you to show tooltips, animate (move) the texture, and launch external programs.
- Uses the IsActive field to control visibility.

SixButtons Prototype

SixButtons

The ***SixButtons prototype*** provides a set of six red and yellow buttons featuring all of the required supplementary functions. It is primarily intended to be used while you are creating a simulation as an alternative to the complexities of standard button construction. The buttons are already set up for event transmission. When you click one of these buttons, it moves in, and then it springs back when you release it. The buttons can change colors, make sounds, show tooltips, and send outEvents. In addition, you can specify that the buttons will be toggle buttons (toggle buttons do not spring back until they are reclicked). You also may specify whether toggle buttons should be "exclusive." An exclusive toggle button will not spring back until *another* toggle button is clicked.

Other features of the SixButtons prototype include:

- Allows you to change or disable tooltip text.
- Uses a keyboard-controlled button display (the default activation key is F6).
- Allows you to play sounds linked to button control.
- Provides the full range of button display options. Buttons may be arranged vertically or horizontally and can be displayed anywhere in the 3D environment (even closer to the simulation camera).
- Changes the button's color, depending on whether or not the button is depressed.

Although the SixButtons prototype is intended to be located under the Camera node, it can be used elsewhere (a useful option for any alternative applications you may discover). This prototype was originally developed as a testing tool, not for use on final products. The SixButtons prototype relieves you of the normal tasks of button construction—such as inserting KeyboardSensor nodes, Latch nodes, Place nodes, OnOff nodes, Counter nodes, and so on.

You can use several SixButtons prototypes in the same simulation, but remember to reposition them. Finally, you can edit the prototype and use your own geometry files if you do not like the button's appearance.

Creating an Interface in EON

In EON, you can use any one of a variety of ways to create interfaces. The method you select depends on the end product you want and how it will be used. The most important considerations are portability, scalability, and mobility.

Scalability is pivotal. Before you can make any determination about how you will build your interface, you must determine whether it will be a fixed screen–size interface or a scalable screen–size interface. The ***fixed screen size*** is the quickest interface to create, but it also looks more primitive. It can be created using 2DImage nodes and 2DEdit nodes if you need to enable the user to enter information. The 2DText prototype is available if you need multiple lines.

The ***scalable screen interface*** is the preferred interface and the type we will create in the following activities. A scalable interface enables you to create a professional-looking product that runs at different resolutions based on the client's display resolution. A user is not limited to a fixed resolution.

troubleshooting

Do not use the TextBoxButton prototype for creating a user interface. This prototype acts like a 3D object in the scene. It is made from the TextBox node and it does not scale. The TextBox node is relative to objects in the 3D space. It can be used for text in the scene, such as a road sign, but not for the interface.

BEST PRACTICES

Using Viewports for Interfaces

As you work with EON simulations, you will find that you can use multiple ways to achieve the desired result. However, in some instances, some methods are viewed as a better approach. For example, you can use viewports to create interfaces. The most direct way to place an interface over a scene is to stack viewports—with buttons in the second viewport. Also, keep in mind that you can use transparent viewports on top of your 3D window. In Activity 6.2.2, we will create a basic interface that uses the principle of stacked viewports to create an effective interface.

tips+tricks

The suggested graphic format for the user interface is either PNG or JPEG.

Activity 6.2.2: Creating an Interface

1. Open EON. Open **Activity_6.2.2.eoz** from the data files for Module 6 Lesson 2.
2. Run the simulation.
3. Experiment with the navigation features that you have come to expect in any user interface, such as clicking the object in the simulation, holding the left mouse button and moving left or right, and using the right mouse button to zoom in or out. Note that none of these features are enabled, and only the initial view is available.
4. Close the simulation window.

5. Expand the following elements in the Simulation Tree window: the **Scene** frame, the **Interface** frame, the **Main Scene** frame, the **Viewports** folder, and the **Viewport** node. Your Simulation Tree window should look like Figure 6.2.6.

FIGURE 6.2.6 Expanded Simulation Tree window

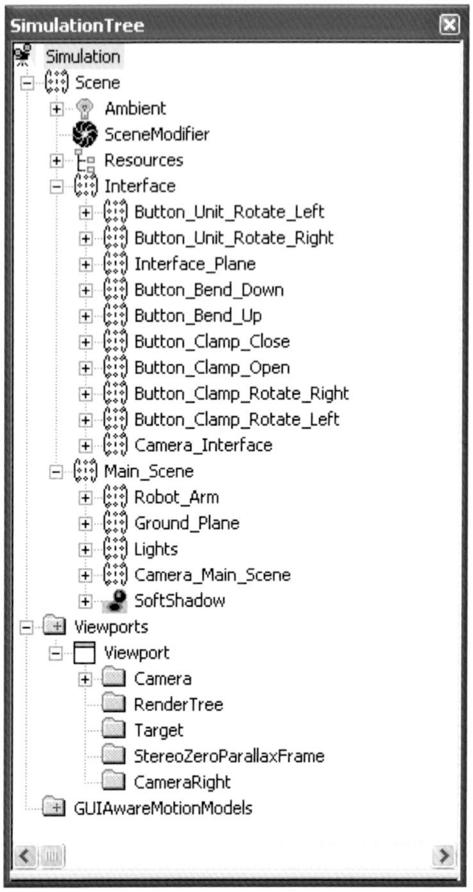

Discussion

discuss

Notice that all of the components for the interface have already been created for you. If time permits, explore these elements further and see whether you can determine how they will function, the nodes used to create them, and how the routes were established. Discuss the choices made for the interface with others in your group.

6. In the Simulation Tree window, right-click the **Main_Scene** frame and choose **Copy as Link**.
7. Right-click the **RenderTree** folder under the Viewport node and choose **Paste**.
8. Drag and drop another **Viewport** node from the Components window into the Viewports folder in the Simulation Tree window.
9. Rename the Viewport1 node **Viewport_Interface** and expand the node.
10. In the Simulation Tree window, right-click the **Camera_Interface** frame under the Interface frame and choose **Copy as Link**.
11. Right-click the **Camera** folder under the Viewport_Interface node and choose **Paste**.

12. Right-click the **Interface** frame under the Scene frame and choose **Copy as Link**.
13. Right-click the **RenderTree** folder under the Viewport_Interface node and choose **Paste**.
14. Select the **Viewport_Interface** node. Your simulation tree, with Viewports expanded, should look like Figure 6.2.7.

FIGURE 6.2.7 Simulation tree with stacked viewports

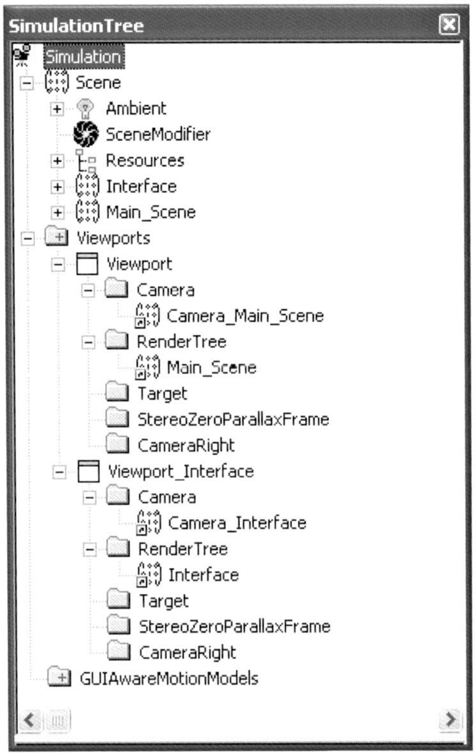

Discussion

discuss

Do you see how the stacked viewports will work in this simulation?

The first Viewport node, which is in the Scene frame by default, establishes the view of the simulation. The second Viewport node that we just added lays on the view of the robotic arm, and all of the buttons for the interface are rendered in the new viewport.

15. With the Viewport_Interface node still selected, in the Property Bar, select the drop-down arrow next to **ClearMode** and select **Depth** from the list.
16. Save your file as **MyInterface.eoz**.
17. Run the simulation.
18. Experiment with the interactive tools provided in the interface. Rotate the robotic arm, move it up and down, and open and close the clamp.
19. Close the simulation window. Keep the simulation open to use in Activity 6.2.3.

Discussion

discuss

Why is it important to have the components of the user interface established before they are copied to the Viewport_Interface?

Do you think the elements used in the interface were created in EON or in a modeling program and then imported?

Adding Interactivity to the Interface

After your interface is positioned and appears correctly, you must add the functionality to it. After all, an interface that looks good but does nothing would be of little use. Users expect to interact with the simulation through the interface you provide. In Activity 6.2.3, we will add interactivity to our simulation.

Activity 6.2.3: Add Interactivity to the Interface

1. Continue working with the open simulation file **MyInterface.eoz** from Activity 6.2.2.
2. Expand **Interface > Interface_Plane**. Drag and drop a **Place** node from the Components window into the Interface_Plane frame in the Simulation Tree window.
3. Rename the Place node **GUISlideOut**.
4. Double-click the **GUISlideOut** node to open the Place Properties dialog box. Change the values to match those shown in Figure 6.2.8.

FIGURE 6.2.8 Property values for the GUISlideOut Place node

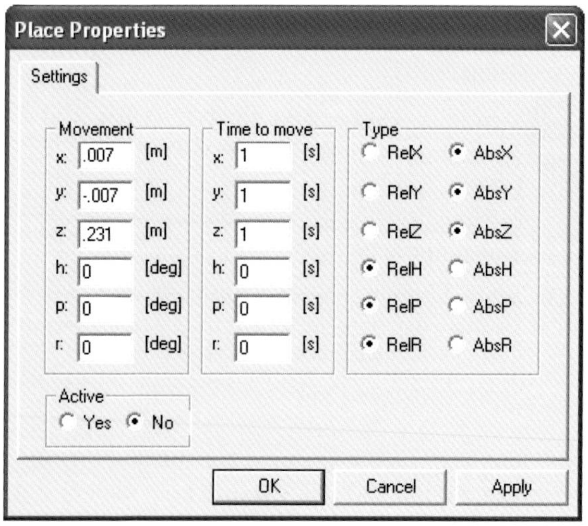

Discussion

discuss

Why do you think that the Active value is set to "No"?

If the values for heading, pitch, and roll are set to zero, does it matter whether they are relative or absolute values?

5. Click **OK** to accept all of these values.
6. Drag and drop another **Place** node from the Components window into the Interface_Plane frame in the Simulation Tree window.
7. Rename the Place node **GUISlideIn**.
8. Double-click the **GUISlideIn** node to open the Place Properties dialog box. Change the values to match those shown in Figure 6.2.9.

FIGURE 6.2.9 Properties for the GUISlideIn Place node

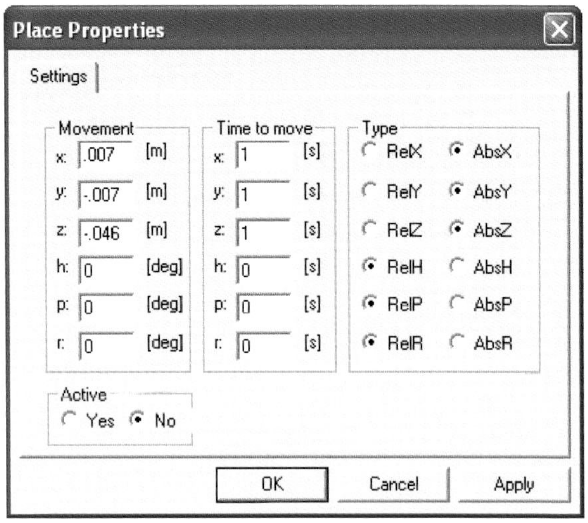

9. Drag and drop a **ClickSensor** node from the Components window into the Interface_Plane frame in the Simulation Tree window.
10. Rename the ClickSensor node **ShowGUI_Click**.
11. Drag and drop a **Latch** node from the Components window into the Interface_Plane frame in the Simulation Tree window.
12. Rename the Latch node **ShowGUI_Toggle**. The Interface frame of the simulation tree should look similar to Figure 6.2.10.

FIGURE 6.2.10 Interface frame of the simulation tree

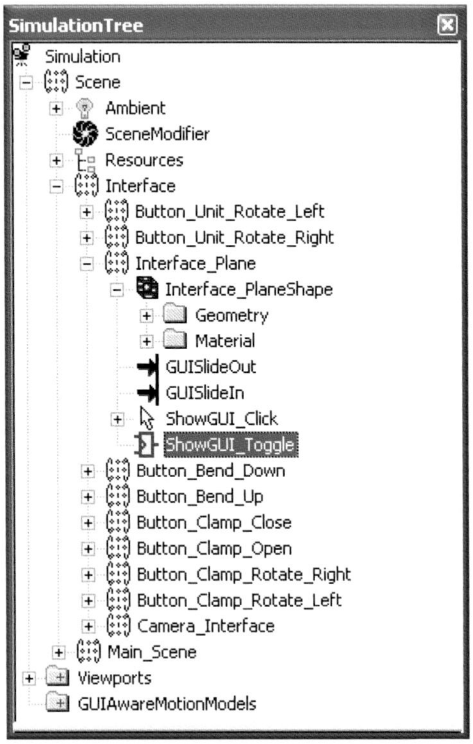

tips+tricks

If you were developing this simulation on your own, you would determine the values for the movement of x, y, and z by using a KeyMove node to determine the desired final positions.

13. Switch from the Components window to the **Routes** window.
14. Drag and drop **ShowGUI_Click, ShowGUI_Toggle, GUISlideOut,** and **GUISlideIn** into the Routes window.
15. Establish the connections outlined in the following table. The portion of the Routes window that contains these connections should look similar to Figure 6.2.11.

From	outEvent	To	inEvent
ShowGUI_Click	OnButtonDownTrue	ShowGUI_Toggle	Toggle
ShowGUI_Toggle	OnSet	GUISlideOut	SetRun
ShowGUI_Toggle	OnClear	GUISlideIn	SetRun

FIGURE 6.2.11 Portion of Routes window with GUI connections

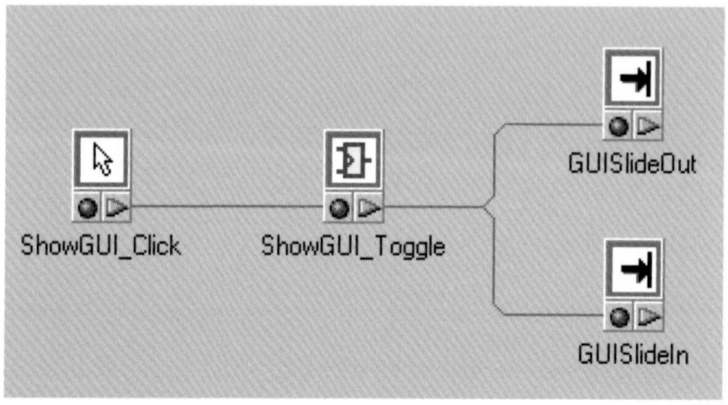

16. Save the simulation and then run the simulation.
17. Click any portion of the user interface area that is not linked to an action, such as where the words "EON Reality" are displayed or in the gray area surrounding the arrows. The button display should slide up out of view at the top of the display, leaving only a small section visible as shown in Figure 6.2.12.

FIGURE 6.2.12 Simulation window with user interface hidden from view

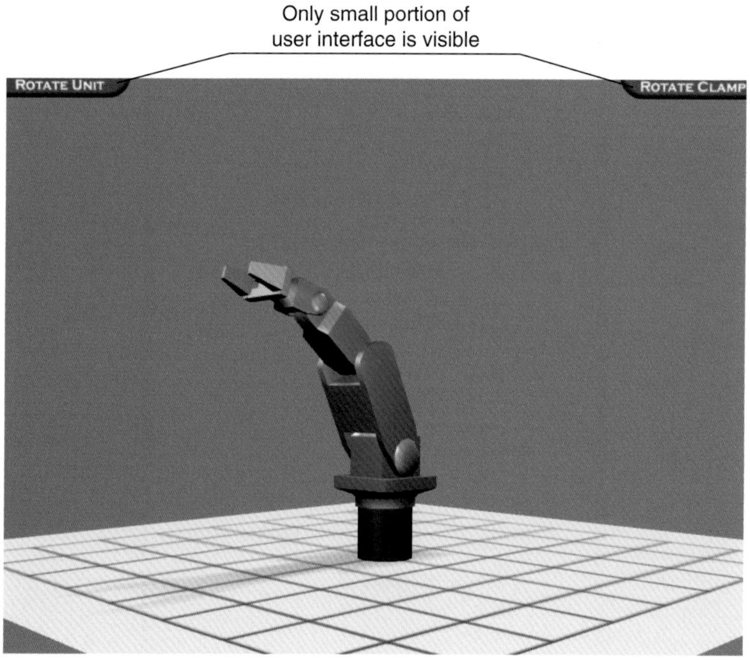

18. Click the visible section of the user interface to cause the entire interface to slide back into view.
19. Close the simulation window. Save the simulation and keep it open to use in Activity 6.2.4.

Discussion

discuss

What are some obvious advantages of having a user interface that can slide off the screen?

Can you think of any commonly used applications where you have seen this method employed?

Are there any disadvantages to having a user interface that is not always completely visible?

Have you ever been working in a program where you have "lost" a toolbar or some other user interface that you needed?

What do you think are the most important things to keep in mind if you choose to use this technique?

Add Buttons to the Interface

In addition to the interactivity provided by selecting or clicking certain items in a simulation, users often expect to use buttons to interact with the software application. These might be buttons that are displayed in the simulation or keystrokes on a keyboard. In either case, these buttons must be easy and intuitive like the other components of your interface—and they must be integrated seamlessly.

Activity 6.2.4: Add Buttons to the Interface

1. Continue working with the open simulation file **MyInterface.eoz** from Activity 6.2.3.
2. Switch to the **Components** window (from the Routes window).
3. Drag and drop a **Frame** node from the Components window into the Interface frame in the Simulation Tree window.
4. Rename the Frame node **PowerOn**.
5. In the Components window, click the **Prototypes** tab.
6. Drag and drop a **Cube** prototype from the Components window into the PowerOn frame in the Simulation Tree window.
7. With the Cube prototype still selected, set the Scale values in the Property Bar to **0.1 0.1 0.1**.
8. Click the **Nodes** tab in the Components window. Drag and drop a **KeyMove** node into the PowerOn frame.
9. Double-click **KeyMove** in the simulation tree to open the KeyMove Properties dialog box.
10. Set the Velocity to **0.1** and the Angular velocity to **10**. Click **OK** to close the dialog box.
11. Run the simulation.

tips+tricks

The adjustments to the KeyMove velocities in step 10 are not mandatory. These are simply suggested settings that will make it easier to fine-tune the adjustments in the following steps. Without some adjustment similar to this, the movements would be too gross to be able to place the cube in the desired location.

troubleshooting

In order to keep the changes you made in the Property Bar while the simulation was running, you must select the option to have runtime changes be permanent. You can alter this setting by selecting Options from the menu bar and then selecting Property Bar. This opens the Property Bar Settings dialog box, in which you can select the *Permanent runtime changes* option.

12. Use the KeyMove functionality (the keyboard keys X, Y, Z, H, P, and R in conjunction with the up and down arrows) to position the Cube prototype over the EON logo in the center of the user interface.
13. With the simulation still running, adjust the Scale values in the Property Bar for the Cube prototype to make the cube a rectagle the approximate size of the EON logo.
14. Click the cube in the simulation window again and make additional adjustments to the Cube prototype's position and orientation as needed.
15. Note the values in the Property Bar for Position, Orientation, and Scale and then close the simulation window.
16. Enter the values you noted and then run the simulation again. Verify that the placement of the cube is correct and make any adjustments by repeating steps 12–16 as necessary. Your simulation window should look similar to Figure 6.2.13.

FIGURE 6.2.13 Cube prototype sized and positioned in simulation

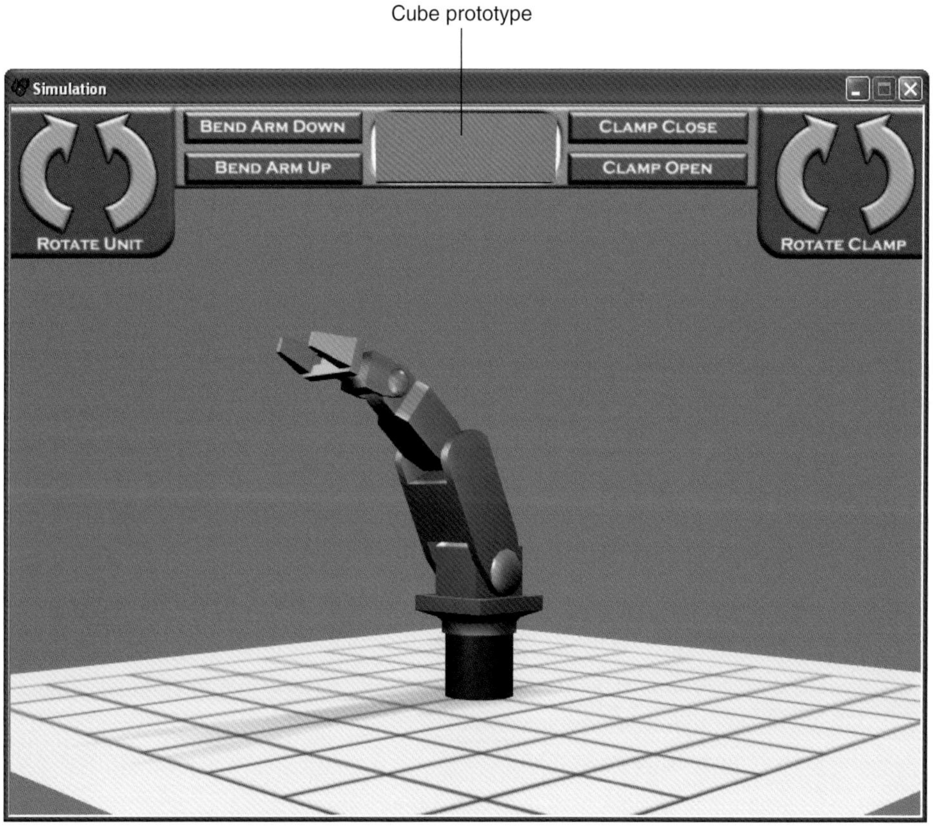

17. Close the simulation window.
18. In the Local Prototypes window, right-click **Cube(1)** and select **Properties**. This will open the Prototype Definition Properties dialog box.
19. Select the **Exported Fields** tab and then click **Add new field**. A new Unnamed1 field is added as shown in Figure 6.2.14.

FIGURE 6.2.14 New field added to the Cube prototype definition

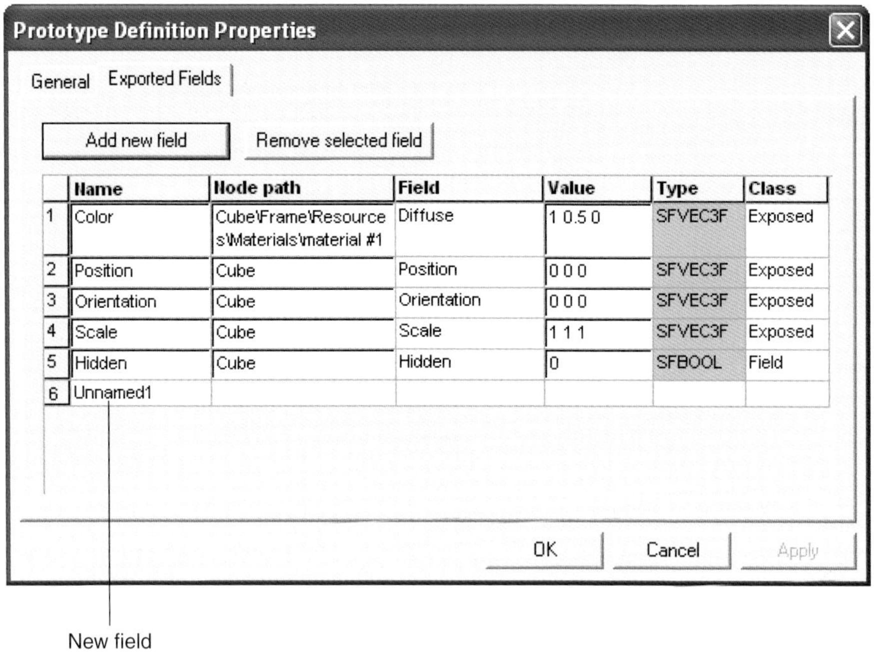

20. Rename the field **Opacity**.
21. Copy the Node path for the Color field and paste it into the Node path for the Opacity field.
22. Click in the Field column and select **Opacity** from the drop-down menu. Note that the Value, Type, and Class columns fill in automatically.
23. Click **OK** to save the addition of the new field to the prototype definition.
24. With Cube still selected in the simulation tree, you can now see the Opacity field in the Property Bar. Change the value for Opacity to **0**.
25. Run the simulation and note that the cube is no longer visible in the simulation window. Close the simulation window.
26. Drag and drop a **ClickSensor** node from the Components window into the PowerOn frame in the Simulation Tree window. Rename it **PowerOn_Click**.
27. Drag and drop a **Latch** node from the Components window into the PowerOn frame in the Simulation Tree window. Rename it **PowerOn_Toggle**.
28. Switch from the Components window to the **Routes** window.
29. Drag and drop **PowerOn_Click** and **PowerOn_Toggle** from the PowerOn frame to the Routes window. Drag the **Robot_Arm** frame from the Main_Scene frame to the Routes window.

30. Establish the connections outlined in the following table. The portion of the Routes window that contains these connections should look similar to Figure 6.2.15.

From	outEvent	To	inEvent
PowerOn_Click	OnButtonDownTrue	PowerOn_Toggle	Toggle
PowerOn_Toggle	OnChanged	Robot_Arm	SetRun

FIGURE 6.2.15 Portion of Routes window with GUI connections

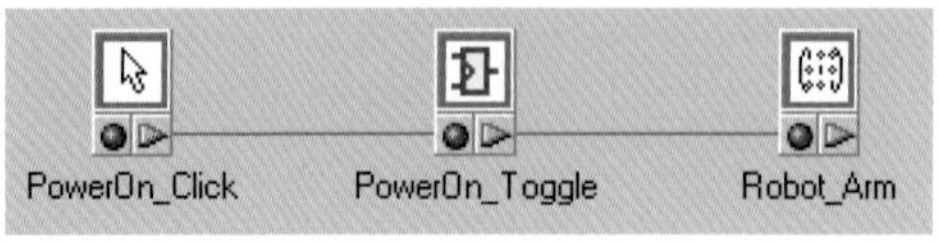

31. Save the simulation and run the simulation.
32. Click the EON logo in the middle of the user interface. The robot arm should disappear.
33. Click the EON logo again. The robot arm should reappear.
34. Test the other components of the user interface you created to verify that all controls are still working.
35. Close the simulation window. Save the simulation and then close EON.

Discussion

discuss

Would you modify any parts of this user interface?

Could any part of the interface be improved or made more intuitive?

Discuss with your group the things that you liked and did not like about the end product and consider the elements you would use in your own applications.

Summary

In this lesson you:

- Gained an understanding of GUIs and considered the elements needed to create a user-friendly interface.
- Learned about nodes and prototypes commonly used to create interfaces.
- Created a GUI for a simulation.
- Added interactivity to the user interface you created.
- Added buttons to your user interface.

Simulation

Your company's client appreciates the improvements in the apartment simulation file. Because of the efforts of you and your coworkers to make the simulation more realistic, users can move through the apartment as they would in real life. They can get a very real sense of how the apartment is laid out and what it will look like.

With all that you have learned about EON, however, you know that you could do even more to enhance the user's experience of the virtual apartment. You have learned several additional techniques that will allow you to provide different ways of viewing the apartment and give the user additional control over what they see. You also can improve the user interface so that it is more streamlined and intuitive.

As always, think through what you will do and how you will do it before making any changes. The storyboard is the correct tool for working through the options. You will call on what you have learned and update the storyboard with the elements you think would improve the simulation's overall appeal. Then, you will put your plan into action and make the changes in the simulation.

Job 6.1: Making More Storyboard Adjustments

Storyboarding is an ongoing process that allows you to refine your ideas throughout the development process and incorporate change requests from the client. It is also a useful tool to illustrate your plans to the client and verify that everyone is "on the same page" regarding project tasks and expected results.

The client is pleased with the ability to "walk through" the simulated apartment but has suggested that it would be useful to add a feature that allows the user to shift quickly from one view of the apartment to another. This would provide the client with the ability to highlight certain rooms or specific design aspects of the apartment. You will add this requested feature to the storyboard with suggestions for placement of additional cameras and views in the simulation.

1. Open EON. Open **Job_5.3.eoz**, the apartment simulation that you enhanced in the Module 5 Simulation.
2. Run the simulation and navigate through the apartment.
3. Take notes identifying the locations that show the apartment from the best vantage points as well as the features that you would want to see if you were considering purchasing or renting the apartment.
4. Close the simulation window. Keep the simulation open to use in Job 6.2.
5. Open the storyboard that you created in the Module 1 Simulation and later enhanced in the Modules 2, 3, 4, and 5 Simulations. Revise the storyboard to include information for adding viewports to your simulation. (If you did not complete the Simulation sections for Modules 1–5, you can create a storyboard using paper and pencil, a flowchart application, or a drawing program.)
6. Update the storyboard to include your plans for adding a user interface feature and interactivity to the file. Consider the following:
   - Do you want to include buttons for directional movement or switching between camera angles?
   - What tools can you provide to assist the user in navigating through the apartment?
   - Other than navigation, can any other interactivity be added, such as the ability to turn lights off and on?
7. Complete your storyboard and then save your work.

Job 6.2: Creating Additional Viewports and Cameras

As you explored the apartment simulation in Job 6.1, you developed a list of potential locations for cameras in the apartment—locations that would be useful and could highlight the positive or unique aspects of the apartment. Use the list that you refined as you created the storyboard to add viewports to the simulation.

1. Continue working with the open simulation file **Job_5.3.eoz** that you explored in Job 6.1.
2. Add at least two Viewport views to the simulation. (Add more if your work in the storyboard calls for more.) These camera views should be different from those created in the activities in Module 6 Lesson 1.

discuss

What are the differences between the needs of a potential renter/purchaser (the user of the simulation) and the needs of your client (the seller of the apartment)?

How can you balance the need to provide features that satisfy both the client and the user in your simulation?

3. Establish one of these new camera positions as the initial view for your simulation.
4. Add **Place** nodes and **KeyboardSensor** nodes to your simulation and establish a connection between them and each of the viewports you created.
5. Run the simulation and test the keystrokes to verify that they switch between camera views as designed.
6. Save the simulation as **Job_6.2.eoz** and keep it open to use in Job 6.3.

Job 6.3: Creating the Interface

tips+tricks

Consider using navigation buttons that look similar to those in the robotic arm simulation in Module 6 Lesson 2.

You added cameras to your simulation and established keystrokes for switching between the views. However, pressing keys on the keyboard is neither intuitive nor user friendly. Your next task is to create an interface that allows a user to navigate easily through the apartment and switch between the various viewports. (Base the interface on the storyboard modifications made in Job 6.1.)

1. Continue working with the open simulation file **Job_6.2.eoz** from Job 6.2.
2. Add buttons to navigate through the apartment.
3. Add buttons to switch between viewports. These buttons could contain text that indicates which view will be displayed, or they could contain a thumbnail snapshot of the view itself.

discuss

In terms of usability, are buttons with text or buttons with icons/images easier to understand?

If your audience is international, does that affect usability?

Are all icons internationally recognized?

4. Remove the connections between the cameras and the keystrokes and replace them with connections to the new user interface buttons.
5. Add a pop-up menu that allows the user to select a view from a list of all of the viewports.
6. Run the simulation and test the user interface to verify that users can switch between viewports using the buttons or the pop-up menu.
7. Close the simulation window. Save the simulation as **Job_6.3.eoz** and keep it open to use in Job 6.4.

Job 6.4: Adding Other Interactivity

The user interface that you created in Job 6.3 allows basic navigation in the apartment simulation. However, navigation is typically not the only function of the user interface. Often, many other features are accessible through the GUI. In this job, you will add other interactivity to the apartment simulation.

1. Continue working with the open simulation file **Job_6.3.eoz** from Job 6.3.
2. Using another viewport (and the Clear tag), connect the ceiling fan to a switch that the user can turn on and off.
3. Add a **Slider** node that allows the user to increase or decrease the speed of the fan.
4. Run the simulation and test all of the new interactive elements.

Discussion

discuss

Based on the information and various techniques you learned in Module 6, consider all of the user interface elements you added. Are the elements as user friendly as they could be? Could they be more intuitive? Do they allow the user to perform the needed actions? Does the simulation have too many interface elements? Can you present the user interface elements in a better way?

5. Close the simulation window.
6. Based on your answers to the discussion questions above, rearrange the GUI elements. Delete any GUI elements that are not necessary or useful.
7. Add any GUI elements that would be useful to someone exploring this apartment simulation.
8. Run the simulation. Retest all of the interface elements to confirm that the new features work and to verify that you did not disrupt the function of an element that you added in previous jobs.
9. Note anything that is not working or that could be improved.
10. Close the simulation window. Make any further changes if necessary and retest the simulation. Continue adjusting and testing the simulation until you are satisfied with the interface and interactivity of the apartment simulation.
11. Save the simulation as **Job_6.4.eoz** and then close EON.

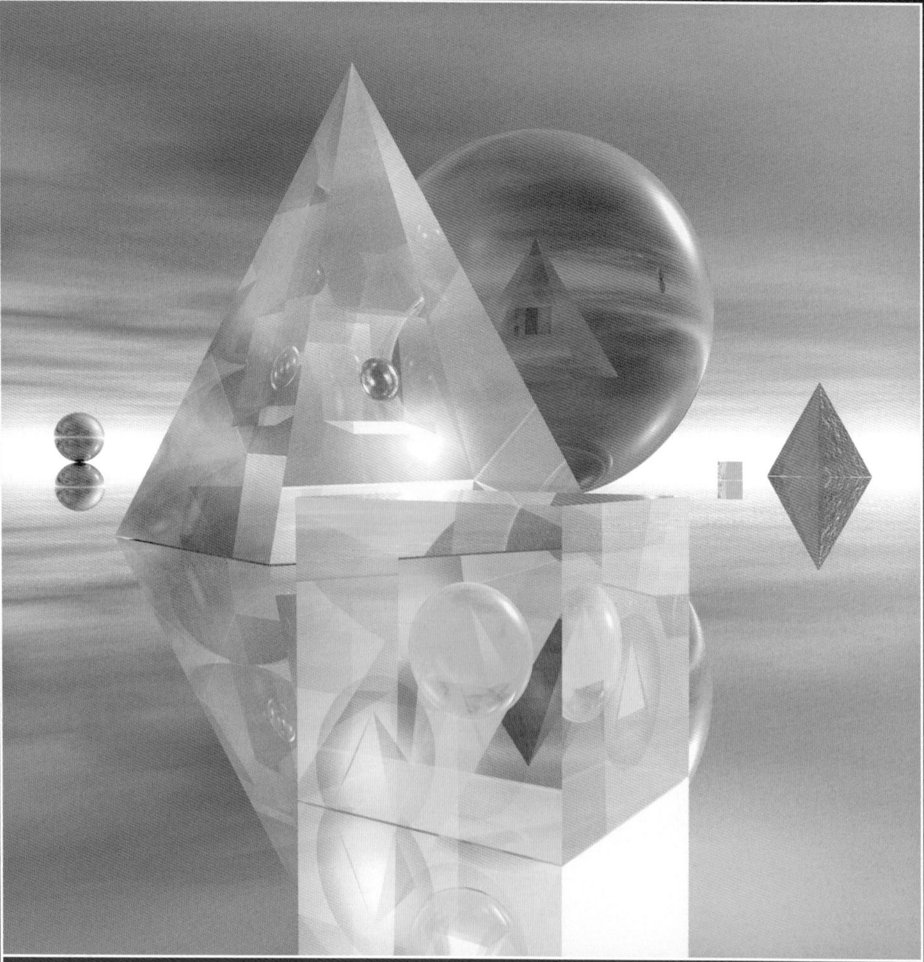
HARALD SUND

MODULE 7

Add Media

LESSON 7.1
Fundamentals of Media

LESSON 7.2
Adding Sound to a Simulation

LESSON 7.3
Adding Video to a Simulation

LESSON 7.1

Fundamentals of Media

Objectives

In this lesson you will:

- Consider the ways in which media is a part of our everyday lives and how it can be used to enhance a simulation.
- Learn the basic concepts that are important for working with sound in a simulation.
- Become familiar with the DirectSound node.
- Learn the basic concepts that are important for working with video in a simulation.
- Become familiar with the MovieTexture node.
- Consider the balance between quality and file size—a relationship that has a direct impact on simulation performance.

Key Terms

amplitude
attenuation
decibel (dB)
DirectSound node
DirectSound3D (DS3D)
DirectX Audio
Doppler effect
media
Microsoft DirectShow®
Microsoft DirectSound®
MovieTexture node
pitch
point source
sound cone
Sound node
tone
volume

Media in the Real World

Sound and video are collectively referred to as ***media***, and they help to make up the tapestry of the world in which we live. In all of our real-world experiences, sound is ever present and part of the complete package of our environment. Whether it is the sound of cars passing on the road or wind rustling the leaves on a tree, environmental sounds surround us; the real world is never completely silent. In most situations, multiple sounds play in our environments, such as the sound of a cricket in the garden, the neighbor's lawn mower running, an airplane passing overhead, and the soft hum of the computer fan on your laptop. A simulation without sound, therefore, would not seem "real."

Although video is not present in every real-world situation, it is certainly a component of many situations. How many times do you walk into a room where a television is playing? Have you ever passed a kiosk where a presentation is played automatically? Do you watch videos online or on a cell phone? These are just a few examples of situations in which you may want to enhance the experience in a simulation you are creating with the addition of video or sound.

Fortunately, applying sound and video to a 3D simulation is one of the simplest things to do in EON, and its impact on the realism of your simulation cannot be calculated. In this module, we will work with the nodes and prototypes that make adding sound and video an easy task.

STORYBOARD

Enhancing the Simulation

As you are aware, after you have imported and placed a model, you still have much to do to create your simulation. Building applications in EON is a process that generally involves the following tasks: importing 3D objects, adding sound and/or video, adding behavior, and adding interaction. Although most textures and materials were—ideally—included in your 3D model prior to importing, you may have needed to add or alter textures and materials as we discussed in earlier modules. You probably made additions and adjustments to the lighting, cameras, and behaviors of your simulation as well.

When enhancing your simulation, consider adding media (sound or audio). This, too, falls into the "Lights, Cameras, Actions, & Behaviors" segment of our storyboard.

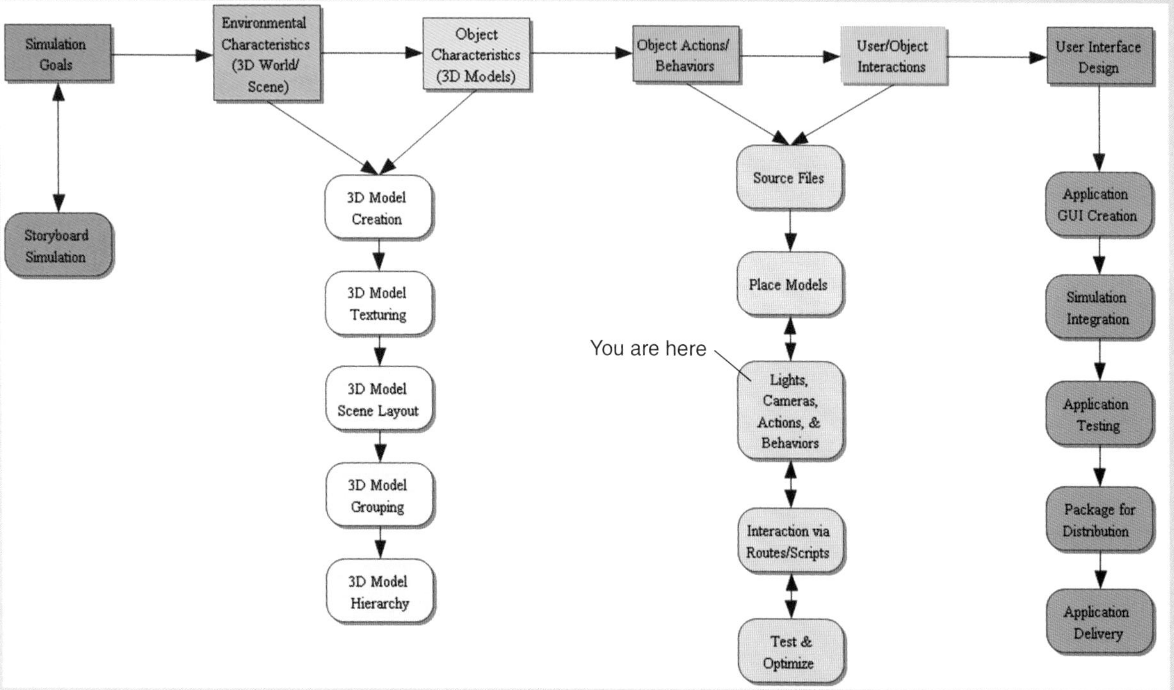

Note that you have been working on the same area of the storyboard in the last several modules because you have so many possibilities to learn about in this area. You can improve and enhance your simulation in countless ways to meet your specific needs. You may or may not need to use all of these features for any simulation, but you should know the available options to make an informed decision about what is best for your situation.

troubleshooting

The Sound node was replaced because it has a drawback. After the Sound node begins to play a file, it must be stopped by an inEvent before it can be started again. This was modified in the DirectSound node.

Media Nodes in EON

Several nodes support media in EON. The four media-type nodes are DirectSound, Sound, MovieTexture, and MultimediaStream.

The ***Sound node*** is an older EON node, but it is available because it is the only node that can play .midi sound files (in addition to .wav files). The ***DirectSound node*** can play only .wav files. The DirectSound node, however, is the only node that can play sound in 3D.

For video, the MultimediaStream node is used only for displaying an old Texture node in simulations developed in an earlier version of EON. The MovieTexture node supports many file formats and can run audio formats as well.

Keep the brief descriptions of these nodes in mind as you learn about the fundamentals of sound in an EON simulation. In the remainder of this lesson, we will learn more about sound and video in a 3D environment and about the application of these nodes in a simulation.

tips+tricks

Most sound formats (except .midi) can be played by the MovieTexture node with the EnableVideo property set to false and the SoundMode property set to 2D Sound.

Fundamentals of Sound

As mentioned previously, accurately rendering sound can significantly improve the realism of your simulation and make acoustic predictions possible for many real-life situations. For example, combined with visual input, the sound of a motor getting louder as a car approaches allows the user to gauge the rate at which the car is approaching and determine whether it is safe to step into the street or smarter to leap out of the way.

Although the science of sound can be quite complex, a few concepts will help you understand how sound works and how to use it in a simulation. In the real world, sound encounters interference, diffraction, and reverberation—all of which have an impact on what an individual can hear from a given position. The location, such as whether you are inside or outside, also has a major impact on the sound. And, if you are indoors, the room size (dimensions and volume) greatly influences the way in which sound travels and reaches the listener. Fortunately, EON offers a 3D sound option that allows you to replicate sounds in the real world very closely. But how do sounds behave in the real world? Before we can accurately simulate it, we need to understand how sound works in real life.

web links

Sound travels through air at a rate of 343 meters per second (m/s). This is commonly referred to as the "speed of sound." Exceeding this speed is known as "breaking the sound barrier" and will cause a sonic boom. Use the Internet to learn more about the cause of a sonic boom.

Sound from Science Class

As you may recall from science classes, sound waves are longitudinal waves produced by variations in air pressure. The sound source is actually a vibration that pushes molecules back and forth. When one molecule moves, it collides with the next one, which moves in turn. In this manner, the energy of a sound wave travels away from the source, through a series of molecule collisions, parallel to the direction of the wave. Note that these sound waves (molecular collisions) can occur in air, liquids, or solids—and sound waves actually move faster through liquids and solids than they do through air.

Frequency Is Pitch

Pitch is the frequency of a sound wave. Humans can hear frequencies between approximately 20 Hertz (Hz) and 15,000 Hz. Any sound wave with a frequency above 20,000 Hz is an ultrasonic wave, which cannot be heard by the human ear.

Amplitude Is Volume

The ***amplitude***, also known as ***volume***, of a sound wave is the amount of pressure placed on the source of the sound by air molecules. The more pressure, the harder the molecules will collide with each other and the farther they will travel. Amplitude is measured in atmospheres, and humans can detect changes in amplitude from less than one billionth of an atmosphere up through values one million times higher. Because this is such a wide range of values, the pressure is typically measured in terms of the intensity of the sound, or loudness, and the unit of measurement used is called a ***decibel (dB)***. Zero decibels correlates to the quietest sound, and sounds of 100 decibels or more are loud and annoying.

Sound Basics Help Understanding of 3D Simulations

The good news is that all of this information will ultimately enhance your understanding of what happens in your simulation, but you do not have to keep it all straight or determine these values yourself. The nodes that you will use in EON to bring sound into your simulation will automatically compensate for all of these sound variables.

Sound Attenuation

As we discussed, sound is the result of the disturbance of the eardrum by the impact of acoustic waves (vibration). The amount of energy contained in those waves (amplitude) and the time between the impact of consecutive waves (frequency or pitch) determine the strength of the disturbance (decibels). Although noise (annoying sound) is often thought of as simply being sounds with too much volume, this is only one type of noise; there are also others. A particular frequency or combination of frequencies may be low in volume but still be considered an annoyance. Therefore, "noise" is really the subjective interpretation of a physical phenomenon.

Sound ***attenuation*** is the conversion of the energy contained in acoustic waves into heat. This is accomplished by making the waves move other objects (work) at a frequency outside the range of human perception. If the objects themselves move at a frequency in the range that can be heard, the sound is simply transmitted. In real terms, attenuation translates to the following characteristics of sound:

- A gradual decline in volume as sound waves move through a medium
- A decrease in volume through air over distance
- A decrease in volume due to barriers like walls of different materials: wood, stone, foam, or other absorbers

The three most important considerations for sound attenuation are sound barriers, sound absorbers, and vibration dampers. Sound barriers are the obstacles that get in the way of sound such as walls, doors, and large objects in a room. Sound absorbers include foam padding, such as that found in furniture. They absorb some sound, but certainly not all of it. Vibration dampers would not come into play unless you are intentionally building a simulation where dampers are used, such as a sound studio.

Tone is the relative volume of different sound frequencies. The shape of sound is changed by barriers and direction, reducing the volume of some frequencies more than others. (This is commonly referred to as an *equalizer*.) Walls attenuate high frequencies more, which results in a muffled sound.

Orientation of Sound

Sound can be changed by the orientation of the sound source as well as the location of the sound observer. The most common example of this is explained by the ***Doppler effect*** (also referred to as the Doppler shift), which describes the change in frequency and wavelength of a sound wave coming from a moving object toward a stationary observer. A common example is that of a train blowing its whistle as it approaches a crossing and then continuing to sound the whistle as it moves through the crossing and continues down the track. As the train approaches, the frequency of the whistle is higher than the emitted frequency. As the train passes the observer, the frequency of the whistle is equal to the emitted frequency. As the train recedes from the observer, the frequency of the whistle is lower than the emitted frequency. In simplest terms, the Doppler effect is a change in pitch due to the relative movement of the sound source.

Of course, if the observer is not stationary, then the velocity of the observer and of the sound source are relative to each other and to the medium through which the waves are transmitted. Therefore, the total Doppler effect may result from motion of the source, motion of the observer, and/or motion of the medium.

Stereo Sound

People hear in stereo. Just as having two eyes is better for judging distances to objects, so is having two ears better for judging distances to sound sources. The sound that reaches each ear is slightly different in volume and tone. Your brain learns to interpret these differences to help you determine where sounds are coming from and how far away they are. (These are the fundamental elements applied in echolocation, which humans and many animals use to identify the location of objects in their environment.)

3D Sound in EON

With a basic understanding of how sound works in the real world, we can more readily understand the concepts and aims of 3D sound for the virtual world. We also can begin to see how the sounds we add to a simulation can be only an approximation of the sounds we hear in the real world.

Microsoft's DirectSound® Component of DirectX

To make use of the best technology currently offered, the DirectSound node available in EON uses the DirectSound software component of Microsoft's DirectX® library. This software component enables applications to produce sounds and music. It also provides the capabilities necessary for adding effects (i.e., echo and reverberation) to sound and for positioning sounds in 3D space—a feature that added a new dimension to virtual gaming when it became available. ***Microsoft DirectSound®*** is a mature application programming interface (API) that supplies many useful capabilities, such as the ability to play multichannel sounds at high resolution.

DirectSound3D (DS3D) is an addition to Microsoft's DirectX library system. It was introduced with DirectX 3 in 1996 and was intended to standardize 3D audio. DirectSound3D allows software developers to write to a single standardized audio programming interface instead of writing code for each audio card manufacturer. Starting with DirectX 8, which became available in 2000, DirectSound and DirectSound3D together became known as ***DirectX Audio.***

DirectSound Node

DirectSound

The DirectSound node in EON enables you to approximate the ways in which sound behaves in the real world very closely—particularly when you enable the 3D sound mode. Because the sound source and the observer (Camera frame) have position, orientation, and even speed, most of the aspects of 3D sound are automatically calculated. With 3D enabled, the DirectSound node controls pitch, Doppler effect, balance (pan), and muffled sounds behind the observer. If you use 2D sound, only the volume, pan, and pitch fields apply.

The attenuation of volume due to walls or 3D objects in the simulation is not factored into 3D sound automatically. For the basic 3D world in EON, we assume that the whole universe is air with no objects to muffle or bounce the sound against. Therefore, the volume is reduced smoothly over distance. We can control two areas as we create the simulation: the rate of attenuation of volume and the simulation of

web links

To learn more about the Doppler effect, named after Christian Doppler, and to gain a better understanding of how it applies to the way in which sound works in your simulation, use the Internet to research this term.

cross-reference

You will explore the property values of the DirectSound node more fully in Module 7 Lesson 2.

attenuation due to barriers. These are each discussed in greater detail in the following sections.

Note that, to fully appreciate 3D sound, it is important that you use stereo speakers or a headset. With this basic equipment, you can experience the different volumes and qualities made for the left and right ear. Interestingly, you do not need to use stereo sound files when working with 3D-enabled audio because the purpose of 3D audio is to create the stereo effect based on the orientation of the user. So, whether sound files are mono or stereo, they will be played, in effect, in mono—but you still get stereo sound because 3D is enabled in the DirectSound node.

Volume of Sound

Volume, in EON, is actually a combination of three volume values:

- Volume field (from the properties of the DirectSound node)
- Attenuation due to distance
- Attenuation due to sound cones

These three values are multiplied to calculate the final volume value that is applied at any particular moment within the simulation.

The Volume field can be directly manipulated to control the overall volume of the sound within the simulation. Distance attenuation and sound cone attenuation are each described in greater detail in the following sections.

Distance Attenuation of Volume

As you know, the further the listener is situated from the sound in any direction, the quieter the sound will be. Distance attenuation, therefore, is composed of two fields: MinDistance and MaxDistance. The MinDistance field is most important because it regulates the attenuation rate as well as the distance at which attenuation starts. The MaxDistance field is where attenuation stops.

The MinDistance variable is especially useful when an application must compensate for the variations in absolute volume levels of different sounds. For example, although a jet is much louder than a bee, for practical reasons, both must be recorded at similar absolute volumes because 16-bit audio does not have the capacity to accommodate such varying volume levels. A simulation can accurately use these sounds, however, by setting a minimum distance of 100 meters for the jet and 2 centimeters for the bee. With these settings, the jet would be at half volume when the listener was 200 meters away, but the bee would be at half volume when the listener was just 4 centimeters away.

Figure 7.1.1 illustrates the attenuation of sound over distance. The volume up to the MinDistance value would be 1. The volume at twice the minimum distance is 1/2 (or 0.5), and the volume at three times the minimum distance is 1/3 (or 0.333).

FIGURE 7.1.1 Sound volume attenuation over distance for different minimum distances

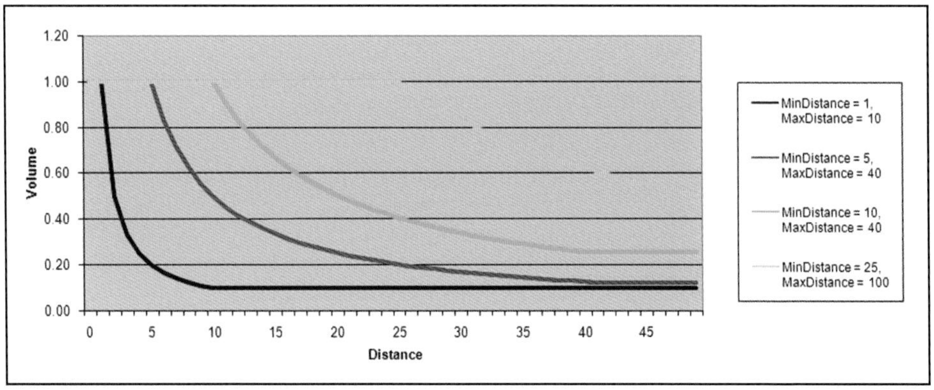

web links

Monophonic sound refers to the transmission of sound from a single source over a single channel. Stereophonic sound is sound from two sources transmitted over two channels. Use the Internet to learn more about the differences between monophonic and stereophonic sounds. Try to find samples of each so that you can hear the difference between them.

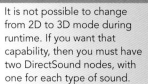

troubleshooting

It is not possible to change from 2D to 3D mode during runtime. If you want that capability, then you must have two DirectSound nodes, with one for each type of sound.

tips+tricks

The volume level at the distance identified in the MaxDistance property is applied to all locations that are farther away.

In the graph shown in Figure 7.1.1, the light blue line represents settings you might choose for louder sounds. Each subsequent line on the graph represents sounds that are not as loud as those above it. For example, if the light blue line represents the settings for a car, the green line might represent a loud stereo, the pink could represent a piano, and the dark blue line could represent the values for footsteps in the simulation.

Sound Cone Attenuation of Volume

To simulate sound attenuation caused by barriers, we set sound cones in certain locations within the simulation. A sound with position but no orientation is a ***point source***. A sound with both position and orientation has a ***sound cone***. The basic properties of a sound cone are illustrated in Figure 7.1.2.

FIGURE 7.1.2 Sound cone properties

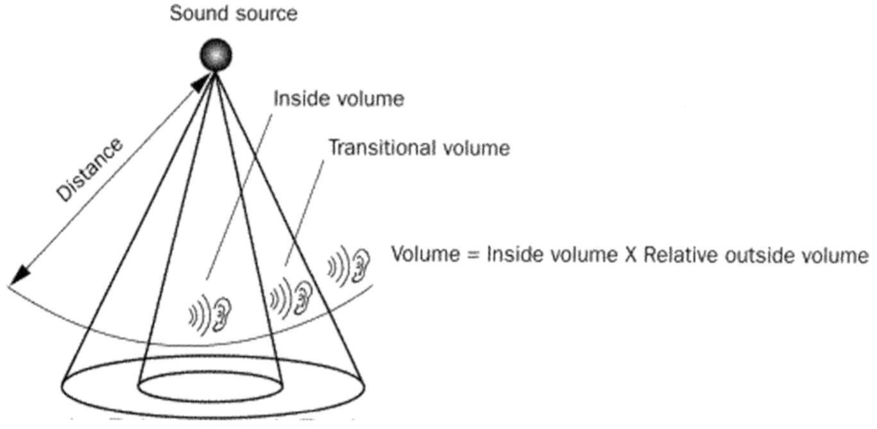

Properly designed sound cones can add dramatic effects to your simulation. For example, you could position a sound source in a room, setting its orientation toward a door. If you set the angle of the outside cone so that it extends just to the door's threshold (with the outside cone volume at 0), the sound source will not become audible until the user enters the room.

As a listener approaches a sound source, sound volume increases. Beyond a certain point, however, it is illogical for volume to increase; either the highest volume has been reached or the sound is of a type that would not seem realistic if it was louder. This is the minimum distance for the sound source. Similarly, the maximum distance for a sound source is the distance beyond which the sound is no longer heard.

In this way, sound cones are used to approximate real-world situations. By changing the angles of the sound cones, you can simulate situations in which volume changes quite quickly, such as when you pass an open door. This is a somewhat simplistic approach that is a long way from the complexities of sound in real life, but it can be quite useful in certain situations.

Three property values affect sound cone attenuation:

- InnerConeAngle
- OuterConeAngle
- OutsideConeVolume

Several additional items are worthy of note about sound cones. First, you should keep in mind that cones are directed in the positive Y direction. Second, the placement of the camera has a direct impact on the sound cone attenuation. If the camera is inside the inner cone or outside the outer cone, there is no sound cone attenuation. The volume value applied inside of the cone is 1, and the value applied outside of the cone is determined by the relative value in the OutsideConeVolume field. Last, cone angles can be greater than 180 degrees. When this is the case, they define areas that cannot correctly be referred to as cones.

Figure 7.1.3 shows the attenuation of sound caused by sound cones. Where the line is horizontal, there is no attenuation of sound volume. Where the line is slanting, the sound is attenuating.

FIGURE 7.1.3 Sound attenuation due to sound cones

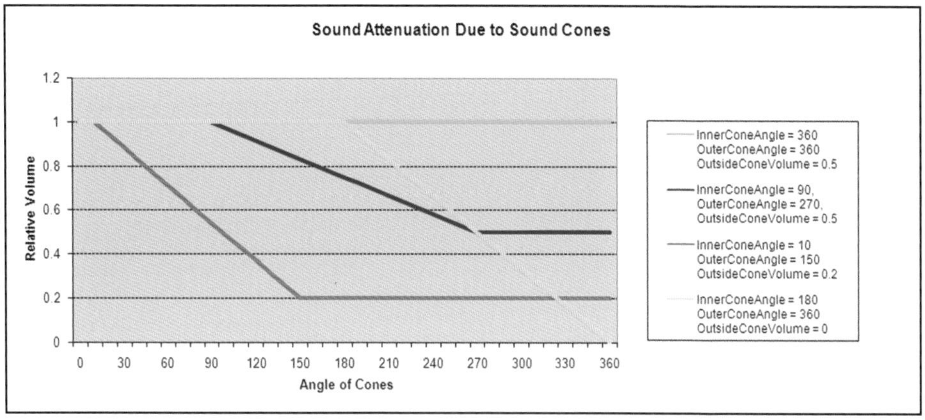

tips+tricks

To turn off sound cone attenuation, set the OutsideConeVolume property to 1.

To turn off sound outside the cones, set the OutsideConeVolume property to 0.

Activity 7.1.1: Listening to the Sound of a Passing Jet Plane

1. Open EON. Open **Activity_7.1.1.eoz** from the data files for Module 7 Lesson 1.
2. Run the simulation. You will see a simulation window like that shown in Figure 7.1.4.

FIGURE 7.1.4 Jet plane simulation

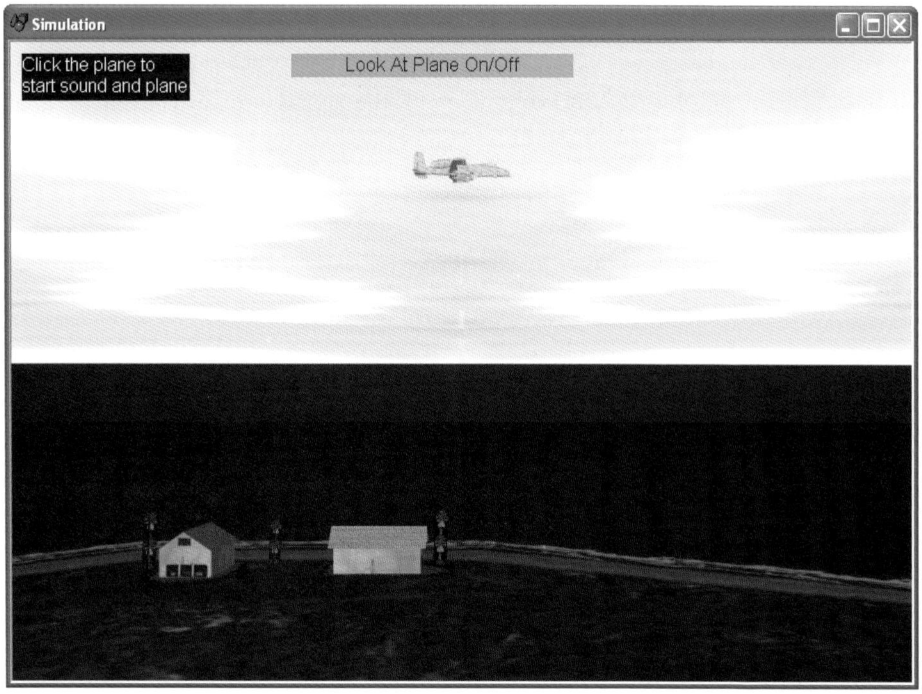

3. As the directions in the simulation indicate, click the plane to start both the sound and the plane's movement.
4. Listen to the entire sound simulation. Notice the Doppler effect as the plane approaches from the left, goes past, and recedes into the distance.

5. After the sound has receded, press the number **3** on the keyboard to move the camera to a different position. This view is from the ocean side of the buildings, as shown in Figure 7.1.5.

FIGURE 7.1.5 Different view of jet plane simulation

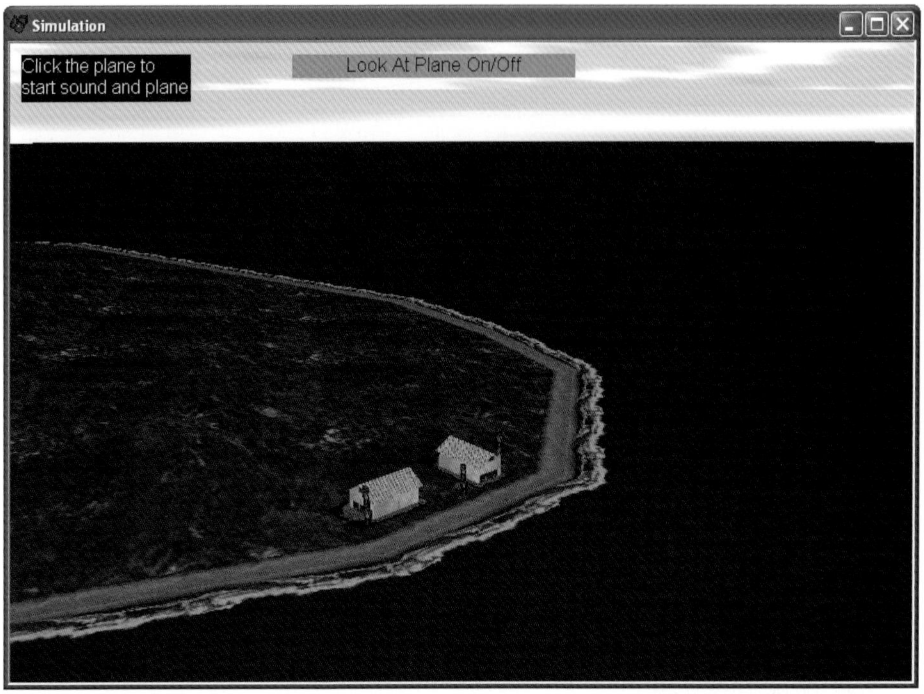

6. When the sound begins again, notice that the sound is now coming from the right because that is the direction from which the plane is now approaching relative to this new camera position.
7. Listen to the entire sound simulation. Note that the Doppler effect is again evident.
8. After the sound has receded, press the number **1** on the keyboard to move the camera to a new position. This is another oceanside view but is closer to the buildings, as shown in Figure 7.1.6.

FIGURE 7.1.6 Third view of jet plane simulation

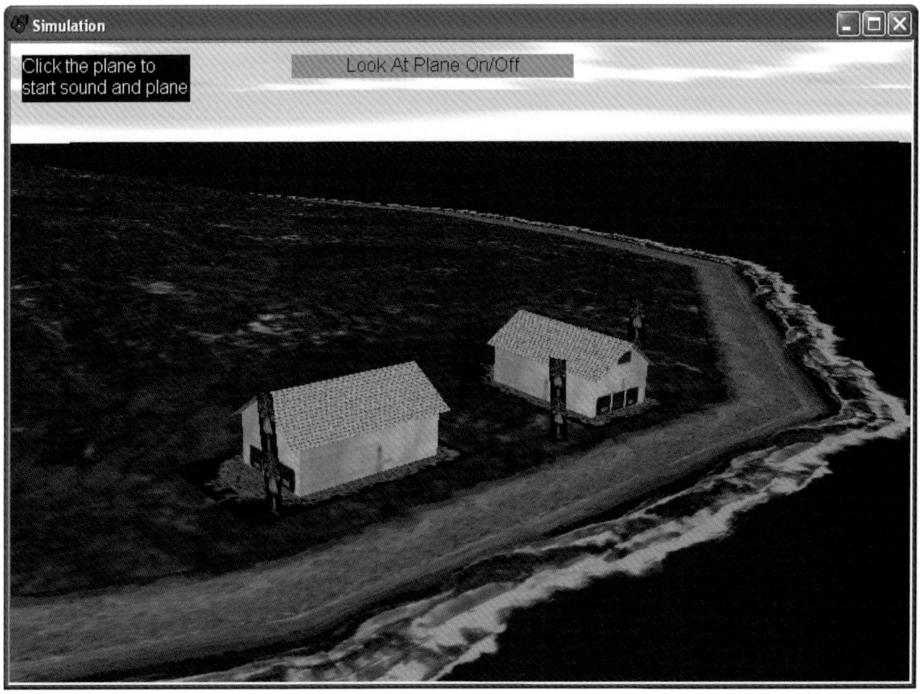

9. Listen to the entire sound simulation a third time. In this case, you will note that, because your view is closer to the ground and tighter to the buildings, you do not see the jet as it passes overhead. But the sound leaves no doubt about where the jet is coming from, when it is passing overhead, and the direction in which it is headed.
10. Click the red **Look At Plane On/Off** button at the top of the simulation. This turns on a function to make the camera look at the plane and track it as it approaches and passes by your location.
11. Listen to the entire pass of the plane. When it switches to approaching from the right again, press the **PageDown** key on the keyboard. This places the camera in a position directly behind the plane.
12. Press the **PageDown** key again to return to your previous view.
13. Close the simulation and then close EON.

tips+tricks

You may want to adjust your speaker volume to a lower setting before you press the PageDown key in step 11 because it can be very loud.

Discussion

discuss

What did you find most interesting about the simulation of the jet passing?

Did this simulation resemble the way a jet would sound as it flew past you in the real world?

Based on what you have already learned about sound, how do you think the simulation would sound if you were standing on the beach looking toward the ocean?

Would you be able to look up and see the jet passing overhead?

Fundamentals of Video

Videos are a great way to enhance your simulation and bring more realism to your scenes. Videos are commonplace in the real world; therefore, if you want your simulations to appear realistic, you should incorporate videos into them. Additionally, a video can be used in countless other ways. For example, you may have an instructional simulation that would benefit from a built-in video that demonstrates a specific operation. Or, you might want to use a video clip to introduce a virtual game. The possibilities are endless.

Fortunately, EON has a simple node that is used for adding video. The ***MovieTexture node*** uses a movie file as its image source. Any movie format supported by the ***Microsoft DirectShow***® system (meaning that it can be played with the Windows Media Player) can be used in a MovieTexture node.

Typically, movies or videos also contain sound, so the MovieTexture node also can supply the sound track for a simulation. Alternately, you can disable the video channel and use only the sound channel. In this way, you can use the MovieTexture node to play a background tune whether you are displaying the video or not.

troubleshooting

Note that the MovieTexture node does not play in 3D, even if you set the SoundMode property to 3D Sound.

File Types

The MovieTexture node can play all multimedia file types supported by DirectShow. DirectShow supports the following file types:

- MPEG-1
- MP3
- Windows Media Audio

- Windows Media Video
- MIDI
- AVI
- ASF
- WAVE

DirectShow also supports any other formats that have hardware and software support on your computer.

Microsoft DirectShow

Like the DirectSound node, the MovieTexture node in EON uses the Microsoft DirectShow API directly. DirectShow is a multimedia framework and API for software developers to perform various operations with media files or multimedia streams. Based on the Microsoft Component Object Model (COM) framework, DirectShow provides a common interface for media across many programming languages.

Activity 7.1.2: Exploring Video in a Simulation

1. Open EON. Open **Activity_7.1.2.eoz** from the data files for Module 7 Lesson1.
2. Run the simulation. You will see a simulation window like that shown in Figure 7.1.7.

FIGURE 7.1.7 Movie playing on television in the simulation

3. Notice that a movie (including audio) is playing on the television in the room.
4. After the movie has played through one time, adjust your view so that you can see the windows in the room.
5. Notice that clouds appear to be moving outside. These clouds are actually a movie playing.
6. Continue to explore the simulation and notice how the movie on the television continues to play no matter where you are in the simulation.
7. Close the simulation window and then close EON.

tips+tricks

Because this is a simple illustration, the television displays only one movie that is played on a continuous loop.

Discussion

discuss

As you moved around in the simulation in Activity 7.1.2, did you notice any changes in the volume of the sound from the television? Why or why not?

Would you expect the sound from the television to be different if you moved from the living room to the bedroom in this simulation?

In Module 7 Lesson 3, we will step you through the process of adding video elements to your simulation. We will experiment with the different ways to establish the video and then discuss the ways in which the video can be controlled with on/off switches, looping, and so on.

Quality vs. File Size

Like many forms of data in our modern technological world, the quality of the data file is directly correlated to the size of the data file. Not unexpectedly, this is true for sound and video files used in an EON simulation.

For this reason, you must consider several things. First and most importantly, you must consider where the simulation ultimately will be used. If the simulation will be distributed and accessed on the Internet, then it is critical that you keep the file sizes small. If, on the other hand, a simulation will be used on a standalone system, you can use larger files with higher resolutions.

The second consideration is the level of detail that is required in the file. For example, if you are playing a video on a small television in the corner of a room and the television is not likely to be the focus of the simulation, then you do not need the quality and resolution of the video file to be very high. On the other hand, if the simulation plays a video that provides important information, then it is critical that the quality of the file is high enough to adequately and clearly convey that information.

Obviously, the higher the quality, the larger your file will be—which directly affects the file size of the simulation. Before importing sound and video files into EON, you should optimize the files in every way possible. Maintain only the level of quality that is expressly needed for the way in which the file will be used. Keeping the file sizes of the individual components as low as possible will reduce the size of the simulation file and thus improve the loading time of the simulation.

Although the size of the overall simulation file and the loading time of the simulation can be affected by the size of the media files you use, sound and video do not affect the performance of the simulation as much as you might think. Because sound is separate from the 3D rendering process, it does not slow the rendering speed. Likewise, video does not have a major effect on the rendering process because only one frame of the video is sent to the rendering engine at a time. Therefore, EON can handle media files that are quite large without affecting rendering speed.

Summary

In this lesson you:

- Considered the ways in which media is a part of our everyday lives and how it can be used to enhance a simulation.
- Learned the basic concepts that are important for working with sound in a simulation.
- Became familiar with the DirectSound node.
- Learned the basic concepts that are important for working with video in a simulation.
- Became familiar with the MovieTexture node.
- Considered the balance between quality and file size—a relationship that has a direct impact on simulation performance.

LESSON 7.2

Adding Sound to a Simulation

Objectives

In this lesson you will:

- Develop an understanding of the use of sound in simulations.
- Learn about the DirectSound node's properties.
- Use the DirectSound node in a simulation.
- Become familiar with triggering the DirectSound node.
- Use the DirectSound node to configure a realistic sound effect.
- Explore the Sound node used to bring MIDI sounds into a simulation.
- Consider the use of the SimultaneousSound prototype to employ multiple DirectSound nodes at the same time.
- Learn how to use the SmoothOperator prototype with the DirectSound node.

Key Terms

loop

SimultaneousSound prototype

SmoothOperator prototype

Sound in a Simulation

In Module 7 Lesson 1, we discussed some of the basic concepts behind applying sound in a simulation. We also talked about the many different reasons for adding sound to a simulation. Above all, sound adds realism to your simulation.

In this lesson, we will delve into the specifics of adding sound to a simulation. We will explore the nodes that can be used to add sound (DirectSound node and Sound node), and then we will explore several prototypes that can be used in conjunction with or instead of these nodes to increase functionality.

DirectSound Node

DirectSound

As we mentioned in Module 7 Lesson 1, the DirectSound node plays a sound WAVE file using Microsoft DirectSound. Sounds can be played in 2D or 3D. If a sound is played in 2D, it is not linked to any position in the 3D environment. Two-dimensional sounds are not changed by EON; they sound the same when they are played in a normal media player. However, 3D sound is linked to a 3D position that is determined by the location of the DirectSound node in the simulation tree. When sound is played in 3D, the direction of the sound is defined by the node's parent frame. Other 3D parameters can be adjusted on the 3D node's Properties tab, which we will explore later.

Note that 3D sound uses world coordinates for calculating attenuation and the Doppler effect. To produce realistic sound, the simulation scale must be correct—meaning that the perceived distance in a simulation must match the actual distance. You can adjust the simulation scale in the Scene node when you create a simulation.

DirectSound Node Properties

The DirectSound node, like all nodes, has many properties that allow you to control and adjust the field values to produce exactly the effect that you want. For example, you can make a sound ***loop***, or repeat continuously, by selecting the Yes option for the Loop property. Although these properties can be modified directly in the Property Bar, you can use a dialog box that makes the properties easier to understand and edit. When you double-click the DirectSound node in your simulation tree, the dialog box shown in Figure 7.2.1 will appear.

FIGURE 7.2.1 General tab of the DirectSound Properties dialog box

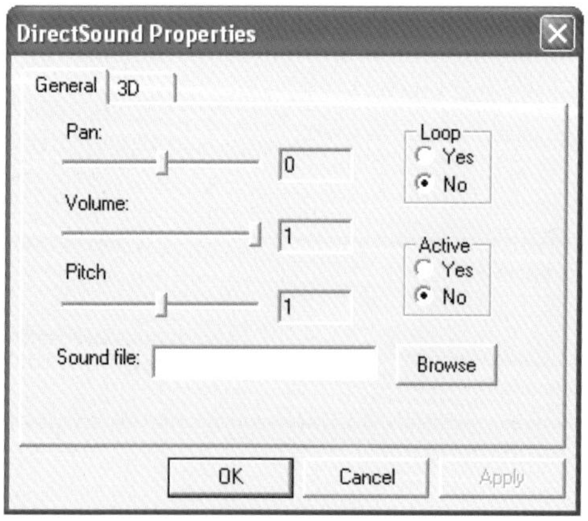

This dialog box has two tabs: General and 3D. Each tab contains the properties that control the way in which the sound will be played within the simulation. These are described in more detail in the following sections.

General Properties

The General properties tab, shown in Figure 7.2.1, contains the fields outlined in Table 7.2.1.

tips+tricks

Prepare or obtain any necessary sound files before creating the simulation. Sound files are not created in EON.

cross-reference

For a brief description of the Doppler effect or sound attenuation, see Module 7 Lesson 1.

web links

If you are not familiar with the Doppler effect or do not understand this principle, use the Internet to research this topic. This is an important concept to understand if you want the sounds in your simulation to behave as they would behave in the real world.

troubleshooting

Like EON Studio, hardware acceleration for 3D sound requires DirectX 5.0 or later.

troubleshooting

MultimediaStream

The MovieTexture node is a replacement for the older MultimediaStream node. The MultimediaStream node remains in EON so that legacy applications are still functional, but you should always use the MovieTexture node.

Discussion

discuss

As the pyramid moves out of view, what happens to the sound?

10. Continue pressing and holding the left mouse button and dragging in the same direction (toward either the left or right side of the simulation window) until the pyramid comes back into view on the opposite side of the simulation window.

Discussion

discuss

Did you know that the pyramid was close to coming into view before it was visible?

How does sound give us clues to enhance our perceptions and understanding of the world around us?

How does sound work with sight to guide our expectations?

11. Close the simulation window. Save the simulation and keep it open to use in Activity 7.2.3.

In both Activity 7.2.1 and Activity 7.2.2, the sound was set to Active and the Loop option was turned on. This means that the sound plays automatically when the simulation starts and it continues to play throughout the simulation.

So what do you do if you want a sound to start or stop at certain points within the simulation—perhaps triggered by a certain event or action? The DirectSound node, like other nodes, can be inserted into the Routes window and triggered by an outEvent from another node. The outEvent could come from a key stroke, a controller, or any action or event within the simulation. You also can trigger the DirectSound node from the same outEvent as another action so that a sound event and a visual event occur at the same time.

Activity 7.2.3: DirectSound Triggered

Before you begin this activity, copy **Sphere01.eog** from the data files for Module 7 Lesson 2 to the location where you will store your solution files.

1. If necessary, open EON and open the **DirectSound_Example02** simulation that you created in Activity 7.2.2.
2. Save the simulation as **DirectSound_Example03**.
3. In the simulation tree, double-click **DirectSound** to open the DirectSound Properties dialog box.
4. Select **No** for the Active option. This makes the DirectSound node inactive when the simulation starts, so it will no longer play automatically at startup. Click **OK** to close the dialog box.
5. Add a **Frame** node under the Scene and rename it **Exploding Sphere**.

6. With the Frame node still selected, set the Position in the Property Bar to **5 5 0**. This will place the contents of this frame to the right of the pyramid.
7. Add a **Shape** node, a **Mesh2** node, and a **Material2** node under the Exploding Sphere frame.
8. Expand the **Shape** node so that you can see the Geometry and Material folders under it.
9. To create a node reference, right-click the **Mesh2** node and select **Copy as Link**. Paste it under **Shape\Geometry**.
10. To create a node reference, right-click the **Material2** node and select **Copy as Link**. Paste it under **Shape\Material**.
11. Select the **Mesh2** node in the simulation tree. In the Property Bar, click the folder icon next to the Filename field. Select the **Sphere01.eog** file that you copied to your solutions folder before you started this activity.
12. Add a **MeshExplosion** node under the Shape node.
13. Double-click **MeshExplosion** to open the MeshExplosion Properties dialog box as shown in Figure 7.2.5.

FIGURE 7.2.5 Movement tab of the MeshExplosion Properties dialog box

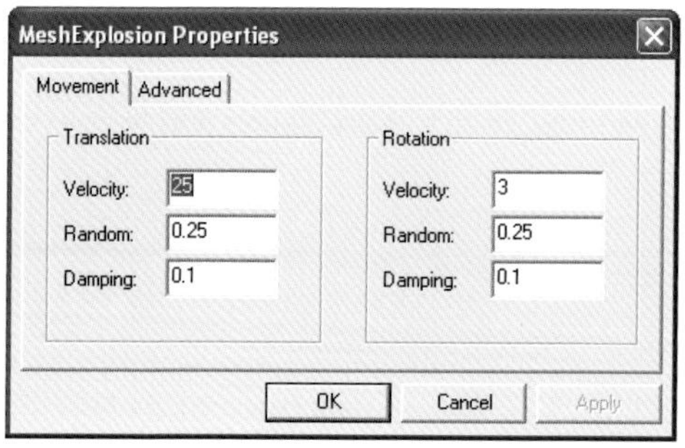

14. Select the **Advanced** tab and set the Gravity value to **0**. Leave all other parameters set to their default values as shown in Figure 7.2.6. Click **OK** to close the dialog box.

FIGURE 7.2.6 Advanced tab of the MeshExplosion Properties dialog box

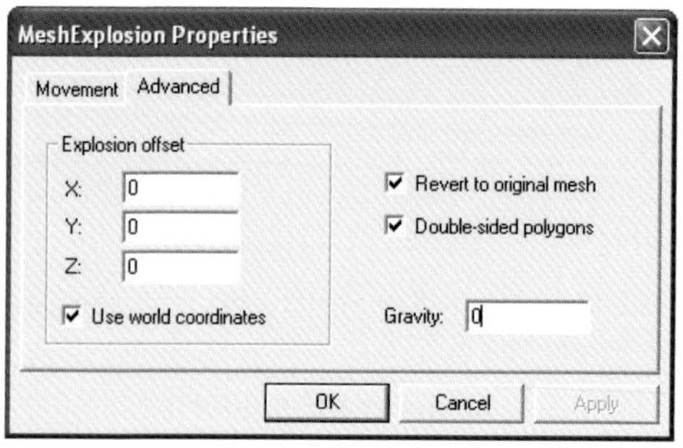

15. Add a **Latch** node to the Exploding Sphere frame. With the Latch node still selected, verify that the startValue check box in the Property Bar is cleared.
16. Add a **KeyboardSensor** node to the Exploding Sphere frame.
17. Double-click the **KeyboardSensor** node to open the KeyboardSensor Properties dialog box. From the drop-down list next to Virtual key name, select **VK_SPACE**. Verify that the **Enable** check box is selected. Click **OK** to close the dialog box.
18. Add a **DirectSound** node under the Exploding Sphere frame and rename it **DirectSound_Exploding**.

19. Double-click the **DirectSound_Exploding** node to open the DirectSound Properties dialog box.
20. From the General tab, click the **Browse** button to locate the **Activity_7.2.3.wav** file from the sound files for Module 7 Lesson 2, which you copied to your solutions folder in Activity 7.2.1. Select the file and click **OK** to close the Open dialog box. Verify that Loop and Active are set to **No**.
21. Select the **3D** tab and select the **Play this sound in 3D** check box.
22. Set Distances min to **10** and Distances max to **100**.
23. Click **OK**. Your completed simulation tree will look similar to Figure 7.2.7.

FIGURE 7.2.7 Simulation tree for DirectSound events

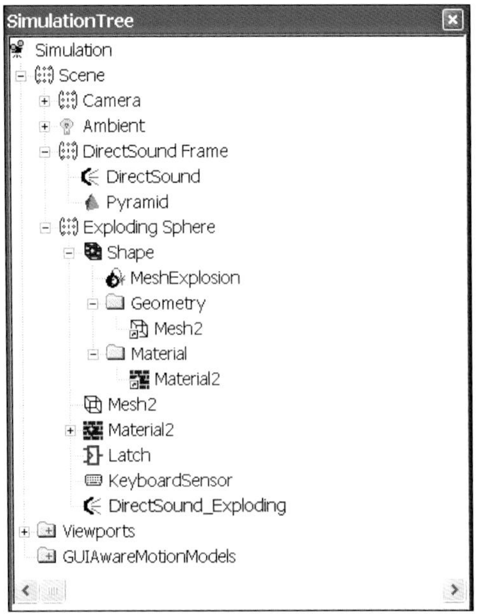

24. Display the **Routes** window. Drag and drop the following nodes into the Routes window: **KeyboardSensor**, **Latch**, **MeshExplosion**, and **DirectSound_Exploding**. Establish the connections outlined in the following table. Your completed Routes window should look similar to Figure 7.2.8.

Source Node	outEvent	Destination Node	inEvent
KeyboardSensor	OnKeyDown	Latch	Toggle
Latch	OnChanged	MeshExplosion	SetRun
Latch	OnChanged	DirectSound_Exploding	SetRun

FIGURE 7.2.8 Completed Routes window for DirectSound triggering

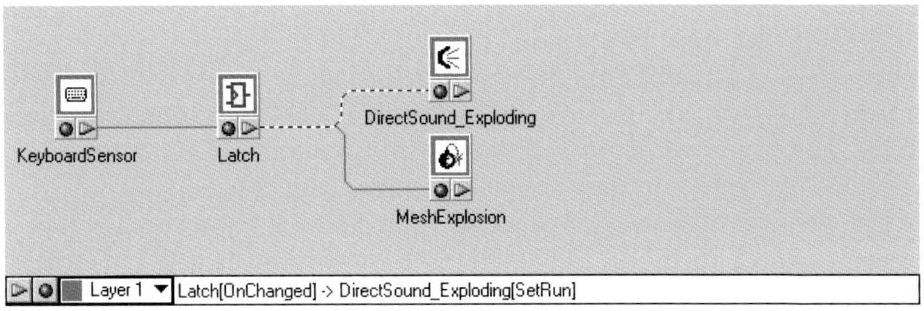

25. Run the simulation.
26. Press the spacebar to view and hear the results of your work. Note that you can press the spacebar again to display the sphere again, allowing you to repeat the explosion.
27. Close the simulation window. Save the simulation and then close EON.

Sound Node

Sound

The Sound node plays both WAVE and MIDI sound files. However, the DirectSound node is preferred if you are using WAVE files. Therefore, you should use the Sound node only if you intend to play MIDI sound files—which cannot be played with the DirectSound node.

Sound Node Properties

The Sound node's properties are accessible through the Sound Properties dialog box as well as through the Property Bar. The Sound Properties dialog box is shown in Figure 7.2.9.

FIGURE 7.2.9 Sound Properties dialog box

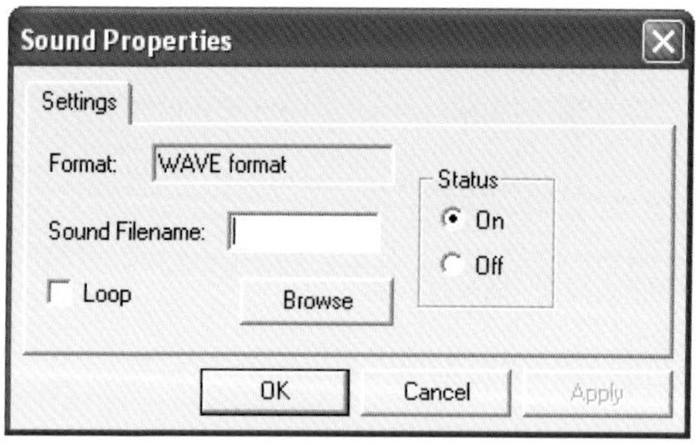

web links

Search the Internet for "free MIDI sounds" to locate sources for sounds that you might use in your own simulations.

The properties for the Sound node are relatively simple. The first option, Format, is not a field you can change. It simply identifies the type of file you select in the Sound Filename field. To choose a file, click the Browse button. From the Open dialog box that appears, you can navigate to locate the desired file. Within the Open dialog box, you can choose your file type from the Files of type drop-down menu, shown in Figure 7.2.10. Notice that you can choose either *Wave Files (*.wav)* or *MIDI Files (*.mid)*.

FIGURE 7.2.10 File type options for the Sound node

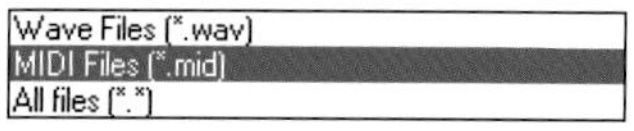

troubleshooting

Although the Sound node works well in EON Professional 6.0, it can be inconsistent in later versions. If you are using a later version of EON and are experiencing any difficulties, contact EON's technical support team.

Sound files can be played once or looped. Selecting the Loop check box will cause the file to loop, which uses the Microsoft Windows standard sound interface—the MCI driver. The benefit of the MCI driver is that all sound cards supported by Windows can play the sounds in your simulation without modification.

The last option in the Sound Properties dialog box is Status. The Status option indicates whether the sound should be played at simulation startup. On is the default selection. If you set the option to Off, then you must establish a trigger for the sound to play.

Activity 7.2.4: Creating a Sound Example

1. Open EON to start a new simulation. If EON is already open, select **New** from the File menu.
2. Add a **Frame** node under the Scene and rename the frame **Sound Frame**.
3. With the Sound Frame node still selected, set the values in the Position field of the Property Bar to **10 10 0**.
4. Set the values of the Orientation field to **225 0 0**. This sets the Heading to 225.
5. Add a **Sound** node to the Sound Frame.
6. Double-click the **Sound** node that you just placed. This will open the Sound Properties dialog box (refer to Figure 7.2.9).
7. Select the **Loop** check box.
8. Click the **Browse** button.
9. In the Open dialog box, select the **Files of type** drop-down list and choose **MIDI Files (*.mid)**.
10. Browse to the sound files for Module 7 Lesson 2, which you copied to your solutions folder in Activity 7.2.1, and select **Activity_7.2.4.mid**. Click **Open**. Your Sound Properties dialog box will look like Figure 7.2.11.

FIGURE 7.2.11 MIDI file selected in the Sound Properties dialog box

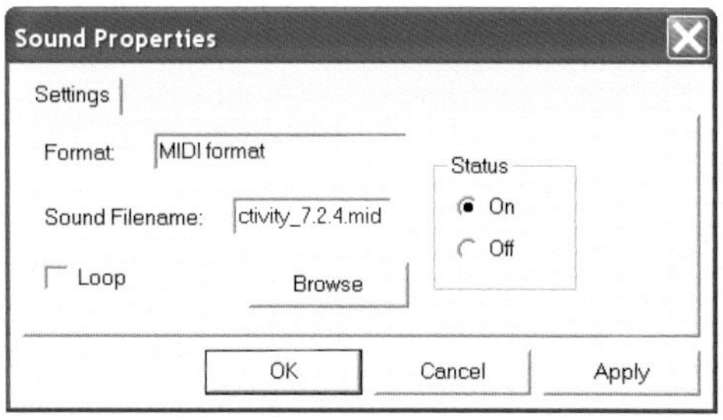

11. Click **OK** to accept the changes to the Sound node properties.
12. Run the simulation. You will see an empty simulation window and the sound will begin to play, looping continuously.
13. Press and hold the left mouse button and move toward one of the edges of the simulation window.

discuss

Do you notice any difference in the sound as you move toward the edge of the simulation window?

14. Move to another side or corner while holding down the mouse button.

discuss

As you move toward the opposite side of the simulation, did the sound change?

How is the behavior of the Sound node and the DirectSound node in the simulation the same or different?

Compare the results for step 14 in this activity with step 14 in Activity 7.2.1.

15. Close the simulation window. Save the simulation as **Sound_Example01**.
16. Add a **Cone** prototype to the Sound Frame node in the simulation tree.
17. Select the **Sound Frame** node and change the Position in the Property Bar to **0 0 0**. This places the cone and the sound in the middle of the scene.
18. Run the simulation. The sound begins to play.
19. Press and hold the left mouse button and drag toward the bottom of the simulation window so that you move away from the cone.

discuss

As you move away from the cone, what happens to the sound?

20. Press and hold the left mouse button and drag toward the top of the simulation window so that you move closer to the cone.

discuss

As you move toward the cone, what happens to the sound?

21. Press and hold the left mouse button and drag toward either the left or the right side of the simulation window.

discuss

As the cone moves out of view, what happens to the sound?

22. Continue pressing and holding the left mouse button and dragging in the same direction (toward either the left or right side of the simulation window) until the cone comes back into view on the opposite side of the simulation window.

Discussion

discuss

Did you know that the cone was close to coming into view before it was visible?

Compare the results of steps 19–22 of this activity with those of steps 7–10 of Activity 7.2.2.

23. Close the simulation window. Save the simulation as **Sound_Example02**.
24. Double-click the **Sound** node in the simulation tree. Change the Status to **Off**. This setting prevents the music from playing when the simulation starts.
25. Add a **ClickSensor** node and a **Latch** node to the Sound Frame node. Your simulation tree should look similar to Figure 7.2.12.

FIGURE 7.2.12 Completed simulation tree with a trigger for the Sound node

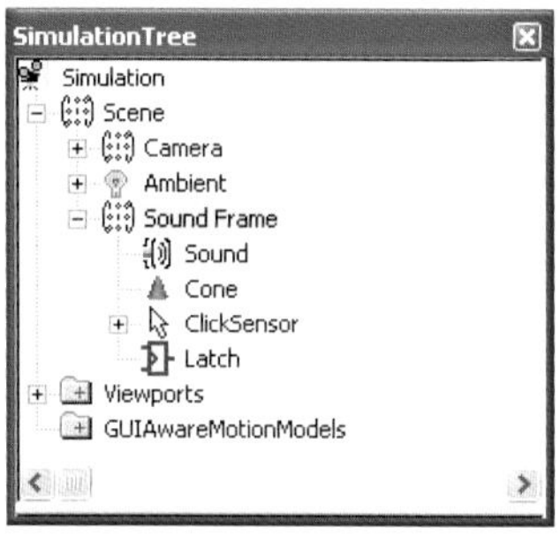

26. Display the **Routes** window.
27. Drag and drop the following nodes in the Routes window: **ClickSensor**, **Latch**, and **Sound**. Establish the connections outlined in the following table. Your completed Routes window should look similar to Figure 7.2.13.

Source Node	outEvent	Destination Node	inEvent
ClickSensor	OnButtonDownTrue	Latch	Toggle
Latch	OnChanged	Sound	SetRun

FIGURE 7.2.13 Completed Routes window for Sound triggering

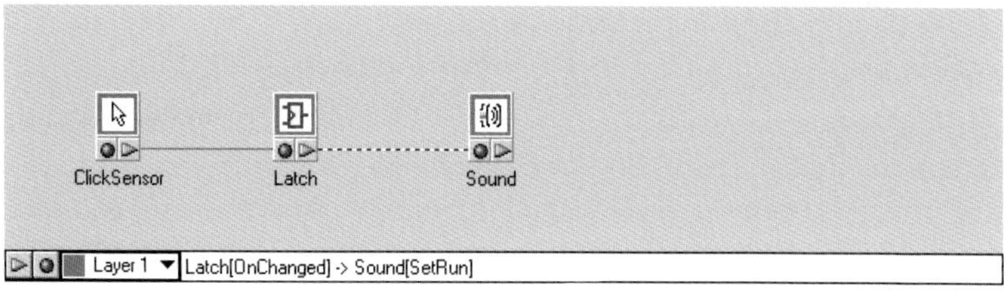

28. Run the simulation.

Discussion

discuss

When you run the simulation, is the MIDI file playing? Why or why not?

29. Click the cone to hear the results of your work. Note that you can click the cone repeatedly to cause the MIDI file to toggle between playing and not playing.
30. Close the simulation window. Save the simulation as **Sound_Example03** and then close EON.

Creating Realistic Sound

In Activity 7.2.4, you effectively placed a sound in a simulation using the Sound node. You saw how easily a basic sound file can be inserted into a simulation and played. However, this is not a very realistic simulation.

As we have discussed, the DirectSound node enables you to place and control the way in which a sound is heard within your simulation more accurately. In the next activity, we will illustrate a more realistic way of using sound by establishing a simulation in which you hear a mosquito humming.

Activity 7.2.5: Creating a Realistic Mosquito Sound

1. Open EON to start a new simulation. If EON is already open, select **New** from the File menu.
2. Select **Camera** under the Scene. In the Property Bar, set the Camera frame's Position to **0 -5 1.2**.
3. Add a **Cone** prototype under the Scene. This will point to our small mosquito.
4. Add a **Frame** node under the Scene and rename it **Mosquito Frame1**. In the Property Bar, set the frame's Position to **0 0 1.2**.
5. Add a **Frame** node under Mosquito Frame1 and rename the new frame **Mosquito Frame2**.
6. Add a **Sphere** prototype under Mosquito Frame2. In the Property Bar, set the Sphere prototype's Scale to **0.01 0.01 0.01**.
7. Add a **DirectSound** node under Mosquito Frame2 and rename it **Mozzie**. In the Property Bar, place a check mark in the **Active** and **Loop** check boxes.
8. Double-click **Mozzie** to display the DirectSound Properties dialog box. Click the **Browse** button. In the Open dialog box, browse to the sound files for Module 7 Lesson 2, which you copied to your solutions folder in Activity 7.2.1, and select **Activity_7.2.5.wav**. Click the **Open** button to select the file and close the Open dialog box. Click **OK** to close the DirectSound Properties dialog box.

9. Save the simulation as **Mosquito_Sound.eoz**. Your simulation tree should look like Figure 7.2.14.

FIGURE 7.2.14 Simulation tree with the DirectSound node added

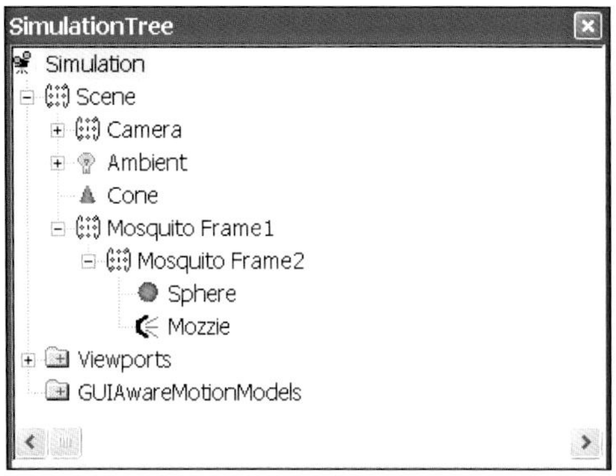

10. Run the simulation. Notice that it does not really sound like a mosquito yet. Close the simulation window.
11. Double-click the **Mozzie** prototype to display the DirectSound Properties dialog box. On the General tab, set the Pitch value to **4**.
12. Click the **3D** tab and place a check mark in the **Play this sound in 3D** check box. Set the Distances min to **0.08** and the Distances max to **2**. Set the Sound cone angles inner to **90** and the Sound cone angles outer to **270**. Set the Relative volume outside cones to **0.2**. The 3D tab of the DirectSound Properties dialog box should look like Figure 7.2.15.

FIGURE 7.2.15 3D tab in the DirectSound Properties dialog box for the Mozzie node

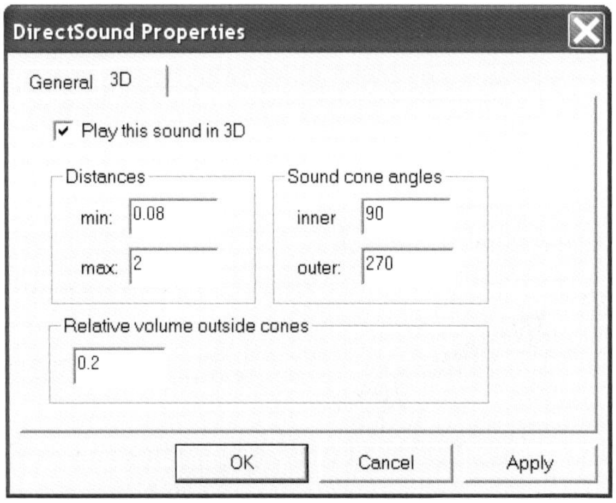

13. Click **OK** to close the dialog box. Changing the sound's pitch and making it 3D makes it sound more like a mosquito.
14. Run the simulation again. You can see the mosquito as a tiny sphere above the cone. Move closer to the sphere and then move past it. Notice how the sound changes.
15. Close the simulation window. Next, we will animate the mosquito to make more realistic (and annoying) mosquito sounds.
16. Add a **Place** node under Mosquito Frame2 and rename it **MoveRight**.

troubleshooting

If you do not hear the mosquito, adjust the volume of your computer. The Mozzie prototype's Volume property is already set to 1, which is the maximum value. You cannot increase the volume within the simulation, so you will need to increase your speaker volume. Remember to turn it down when you are done with this simulation.

17. Double-click the **MoveRight** node to open the Place Properties dialog box. Set the Movement x value to **0.2** and the Time to move x value to **0.5**. Set the Time to move y value to **2** seconds. Set the Active field to **Yes** if necessary. The Place Properties dialog box should look like Figure 7.2.16. Click **OK** to close the dialog box.

FIGURE 7.2.16 Place Properties dialog box for the MoveRight node

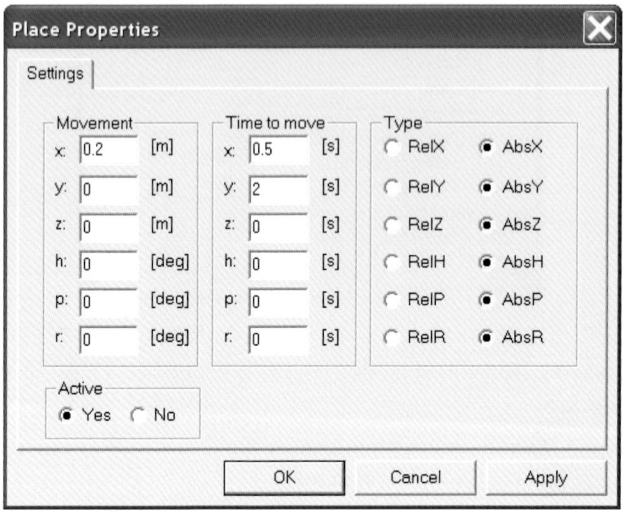

18. Right-click the **MoveRight** node and select the **Copy** option. Paste it under Mosquito Frame2 and rename it **MoveLeft**.
19. Double-click the **MoveLeft** node to open the Place Properties dialog box. Set the Movement x value to **-0.2**. Set the Active field to **No**. Do not change any other values. Click **OK** to close the dialog box.
20. Display the **Routes** window. Drag the **MoveRight** and **MoveLeft** nodes to the Routes window. Establish the connections outlined in the following table. Your completed Routes window should look similar to Figure 7.2.17.

Source Node	outEvent	Destination Node	inEvent
MoveRight	Done	MoveLeft	Start
MoveLeft	Done	MoveRight	Start

FIGURE 7.2.17 Routes window for Mosquito_Sound.eoz

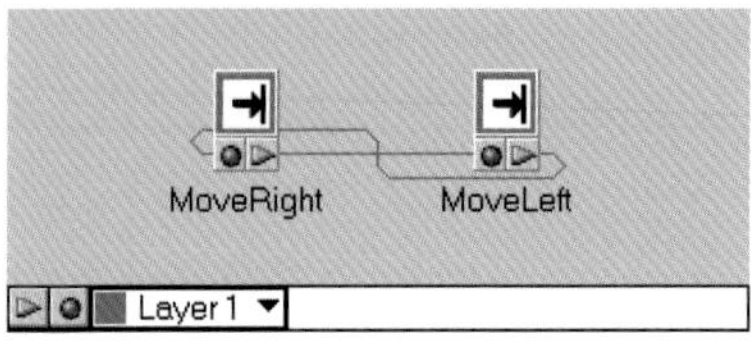

21. Add a **Rotate** node under Mosquito Frame1.

22. Double-click the **Rotate** node in the simulation tree to display the Rotate Properties dialog box. Set the Heading value to **1**, the Pitch value to **1.6**, and the Roll value to **0.2**. Set the Lap Time value to **1.75**. The Rotate Properties dialog box should look like Figure 7.2.18. Click **OK** to close the dialog box.

FIGURE 7.2.18 Rotate Properties dialog box

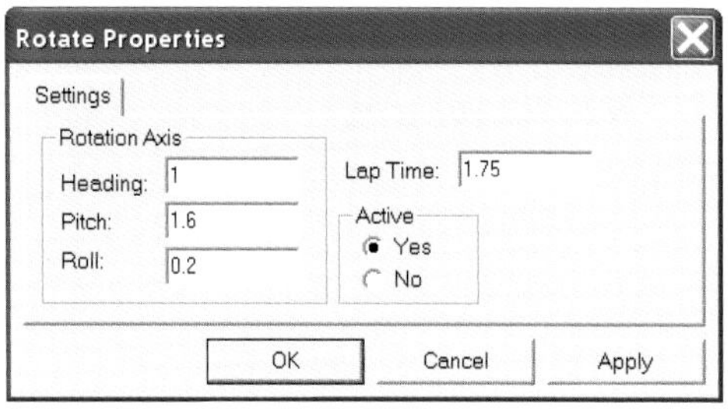

23. Save the simulation and then run the simulation. Move closer to the mosquito.

Discussion

discuss

Does it sound more like a mosquito buzzing around your head?

24. Close the simulation window.
25. Add a **Place** node under the Camera frame and rename it **Center**. In the Property Bar, set the Translation field to **0 0 1.2** and TransTime to **2 2 2**.
26. Add an **OnOff** node under the Center node.
27. Double-click the **OnOff** node to display the OnOff Properties dialog box. Verify that the Key value is **A**. Click **OK** to close the dialog box.
28. Save the simulation and then run the simulation. Press the **A** key to place the camera inside the area where the mosquito is moving.
29. Close the simulation window. Close EON.

SimultaneousSound Prototype

SimultaneousSound

The ***SimultaneousSound prototype*** provides an alternative to using only one DirectSound node. If a situation in your simulation calls for multiple sounds to be heard at the same time—an event that occurs constantly in real-world situations—then you can use the SimultaneousSound prototype. This prototype manages a set of DirectSound nodes, with each node started by a different trigger. So, triggering several starts in a short time will cause several sounds to run simultaneously.

The number of simultaneous sounds that can be run is determined only by the number of DirectSound nodes you place under it. You can run as many sounds as your situation requires.

Only a few parameters can be adjusted for the SimultaneousSound prototype itself. Most adjustments are made in the DirectSound nodes that are placed in the SimultaneousSound prototype. Figure 7.2.19 shows the Property Bar for the SimultaneousSound prototype before any sound nodes have been added to it.

FIGURE 7.2.19 Property Bar for SimultaneousSound prototype

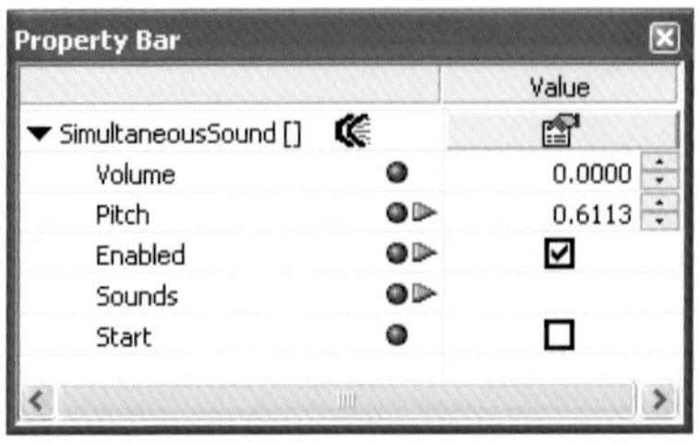

troubleshooting

Although the SimultaneousSound prototype works well in EON Professional 6.0, it can be inconsistent in later versions. If you are using a later version of EON and are experiencing any difficulties, contact EON's technical support team.

Enabled is selected by default—which is an override for all of the sounds that are placed within it. To disable all sounds at the same time, clear this check box. Start can be selected so that all of the sounds placed within the prototype will begin playing when the simulation starts.

Activity 7.2.6: Using the SimultaneousSound Prototype

1. Open EON to start a new simulation. If EON is already open, select **New** from the File menu.
2. Add a **Frame** node to the Scene and rename the frame **SimultaneousSound Frame**.
3. Add the **SimultaneousSound** prototype under the SimultaneousSound Frame.
4. Expand the **SimultaneousSound** prototype to display the Sounds folder, as shown in Figure 7.2.20.

FIGURE 7.2.20 Expanded SimultaneousSound prototype in the simulation tree

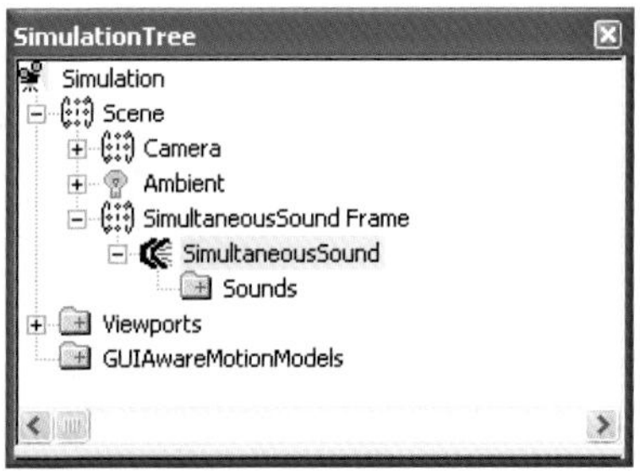

5. Add a **DirectSound** node to the Sounds folder under the SimultaneousSound prototype in the simulation tree. Rename the node **DirectSound01**.
6. Add another **DirectSound** node to the Sounds folder in the simulation tree. Rename the node **DirectSound02**.
7. Double-click **DirectSound01** to display the DirectSound Properties dialog box. On the General tab, choose **Yes** for Loop and **Yes** for Active. Click the **Browse** button. In the Open dialog box, browse to the sound files for Module 7 Lesson 2, which you copied to your solutions folder in Activity 7.2.1, and select **Activity_7.2.6a.wav**. Click the **Open** button to select the file and close the Open dialog box.
8. Select the **3D** tab and select **Play this sound in 3D**. Set Distances min to **10** and Distances max to **100**. Click **OK** to close the DirectSound Properties dialog box.

9. Double-click **DirectSound02**. On the General tab, choose **Yes** for Loop and **Yes** for Active. Click the **Browse** button. In the Open dialog box, browse to the sound files for Module 7 Lesson 2, which you copied to your solutions folder in Activity 7.2.1, and select **Activity_7.2.6b.wav**. Click the **Open** button to select the file and close the Open dialog box.
10. Select the **3D** tab and select **Play this sound in 3D**. Set Distances min to **10** and Distances max to **100**. Click **OK**. Your simulation tree should look like Figure 7.2.21.

FIGURE 7.2.21 Simulation tree with SimultaneousSound prototype

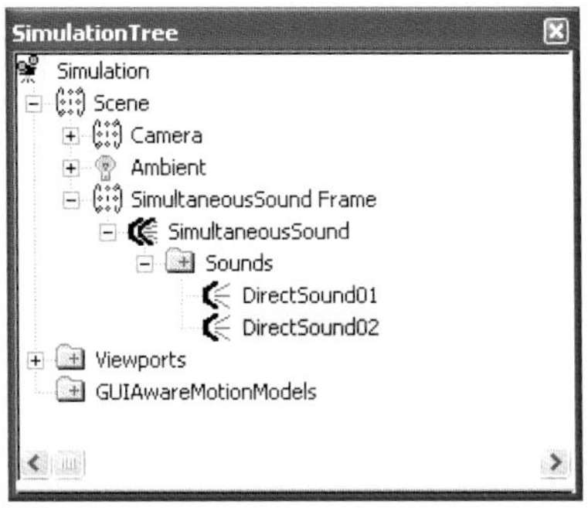

11. Run the simulation. You will hear the sound of water running in a stream as well as a beeping sound.
12. Close the simulation window. Save the simulation as **SimultaneousSound_Example** and then close EON.

Discussion

discuss

When could you use multiple sounds at the same time?

When would it be realistic to use the SimultaneousSound prototype?

Would you place sounds with an object in the scene or in a separate frame like the one we have in Activity 7.2.6?

SmoothOperator Prototype

SmoothOperator

The ***SmoothOperator prototype*** enables you to fade sound or objects in and out. This prototype sends out values that gradually change over time. Instead of changing certain values instantly, like an on/off switch, they can be changed smoothly. The SmoothOperator prototype can affect float values and integer values.

In EON Studio, you can use the SmoothOperator prototype to create the following effects:

- Objects can fade away into nothing by sending the float values to the Opacity field of the Material2 node.
- Sounds can fade in and out, pan left and right, and the pitch can go up and down smoothly.

- An object's rotation or spin can accelerate and decelerate.
- The wavelength, amplitude, frequency, and modulation of the OceanWaves node can be altered.

Figure 7.2.22 shows the Property Bar for the SmoothOperator. The SmoothOperator prototype will send out float values between two values. The two values are called State0Value and State1Value. For example, you can fade an object in and out by setting the State0Value to 0.1 and the State1Value to 0.99. You also can decide how long it should take to reach each state by setting the State0Time and State1Time values. These fields are described in Table 7.2.3. In Activity 7.2.7, we will step through an example of using the SmoothOperator prototype to manipulate sound. You can see, however, that this prototype could also be used in other situations.

FIGURE 7.2.22 Property Bar for the SmoothOperator prototype

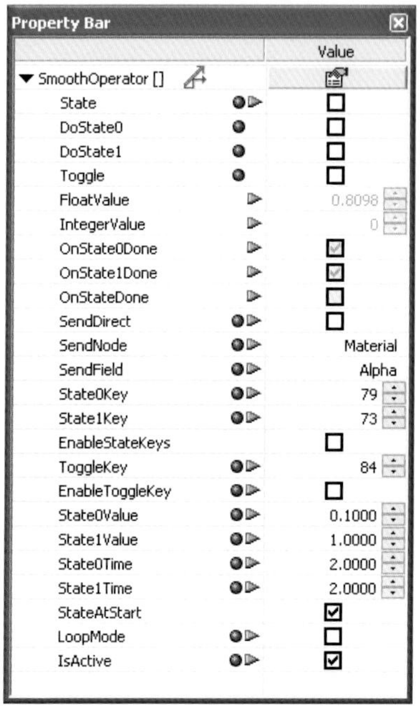

TABLE 7.2.3 SmoothOperator Values

Property	Description
State0Value	Enter the float value for State0 here. It can be more or less than State1. It also can be a negative number.
State1Value	Enter the float value for State1 here. It can be more or less than State0. It also can be a negative number.
State0Time	Enter the time it takes to reach State0Value here.
State1Time	Enter the time it takes to reach State1Value here.
StateAtStart	The FloatValue of one of the states is sent at the start of the simulation. Enter 0 (false) here for State0Value and enter 1 (true) for State1Value.
LoopMode	If LoopMode is true, then after a state is changed, it will continue to switch between the two states until LoopMode is set to false.
IsActive	If IsActive is false, then the prototype will not function. No values will be sent.

After you have set the state values and state times, then you can choose how to send the values. The prototype supports two methods of sending the values: events and keys.

Event Properties

The fields in the Property Bar enable you to set the inEvents and outEvents for the SmoothOperator prototype. Table 7.2.4 details the inEvents and Table 7.2.5 details the outEvents.

TABLE 7.2.4 inEvents for the SmoothOperator Prototype

Property	Description
State	An inEvent that accepts true and false. When true is received, State1Value is started, and when false is received, State0Value is started. The default value at start is the State0Value. Starting one state will immediately cancel the movement toward the other state.
DoState0	An inEvent that starts movement toward State0Value regardless of the value of the inEvent (true or false).
DoState1	An inEvent that starts movement toward State1Value regardless of the value of the inEvent (true or false).
Toggle	An inEvent that will start movement toward the other state. For example, if the last state reached was State1Value or movement toward State1Value is currently underway, then that movement is cancelled and movement is started toward State0Value.

TABLE 7.2.5 outEvents for the SmoothOperator Prototype

Property	Description
FloatValue	An outEvent that carries the smoothly changing value. Usually, the value is sent as many times per second as possible to produce a smooth transition. This outEvent is connected to other nodes in the Routes window.
IntegerValue	An outEvent that sends the value of the nearest integer of the FloatValue.
OnState0Done	When the FloatValue reaches State0Value, this outEvent sends true. It only sends true.
OnState1Done	When the FloatValue reaches State1Value, this outEvent sends true. It only sends true.
OnStateDone	This outEvent sends false when the OnState0Done outEvent is sent and false when the OnState1Done outEvent is sent.

Using Keys

In addition to inEvents and outEvents, the Property Bar also allows you to establish keys to control the action of the SmoothOperator prototype. Table 7.2.6 details the use of keys.

TABLE 7.2.6 Key Properties for the SmoothOperator Prototype

Property	Description
State0Key	This is the keycode of the key that will start movement toward State0Value. The default value is 79, which is the O key.
State1Key	This is the keycode of the key that will start movement toward State1Value. The default value is 73, which is the I key.
EnableStateKeys	The State0Key and State1Key are disabled by default. If you want to use them, then set the value of this field to true.
ToggleKey	This is the keycode of the key you select to start movement toward the other state. The default value is 84, which is the T key.
EnableToggleKey	The toggle key is not enabled by default. If you want to enable it, then set the value of this field to true.

Activity 7.2.7: Using the SmoothOperator Prototype

1. Open EON. Open the **DirectSound_Example01** simulation you created in Activity 7.2.1.
2. Expand the **Scene** and the **DirectSound Frame**.
3. Add the **SmoothOperator** prototype to the DirectSound Frame.
4. Display the **Routes** window. Drag the **SmoothOperator** prototype and the **DirectSound** node from the simulation tree to the Routes window. Establish the connection outlined in the following table.

Source Node	outEvent	Destination Node	inEvent
SmoothOperator	FloatValue	DirectSound	Volume

Next, decide how the states will change—either using keys or inEvents. There are three ways in which you can start changing the values: state keys, a toggle key, or sending events by connecting routes or writing scripts. In this activity, we will use the toggle key.

5. Select the **SmoothOperator** prototype in the simulation tree. Select the **EnableToggleKey** check box in the Property Bar.
6. Run the simulation. You can hear the water running.
7. Press **T**. The sound fades away to nothing.
8. Press **T** again. The sound fades in until it is full volume again.
9. Close the simulation window.
10. With the SmoothOperator prototype still selected, change the State0Time and the State1Time values to **3** in the Property Bar.
11. Run the simulation.
12. Press **T**. The sound fades away, but note that it takes longer before the sound is gone.
13. Press **T** again. The sound slowly returns to full volume.
14. Close the simulation window. Save the simulation as **SmoothOperator_Example** and then close EON.

Discussion

discuss

When would you use the SmoothOperator prototype?

Can you identify situations in which you might use the SimultaneousSound prototype and the SmoothOperator prototype together to make one sound slowly fade away while another becomes louder?

Summary

In this lesson you:

- Developed an understanding of the use of sound in simulations.
- Learned about the DirectSound node's properties.
- Used the DirectSound node in a simulation.
- Became familiar with triggering the DirectSound node.
- Used the DirectSound node to configure a realistic sound effect.
- Explored the Sound node used to bring MIDI sounds into a simulation.
- Considered the use of the SimultaneousSound prototype to employ multiple DirectSound nodes at the same time.
- Learned how to use the SmoothOperator prototype with the DirectSound node.

LESSON 7.3

Adding Video to a Simulation

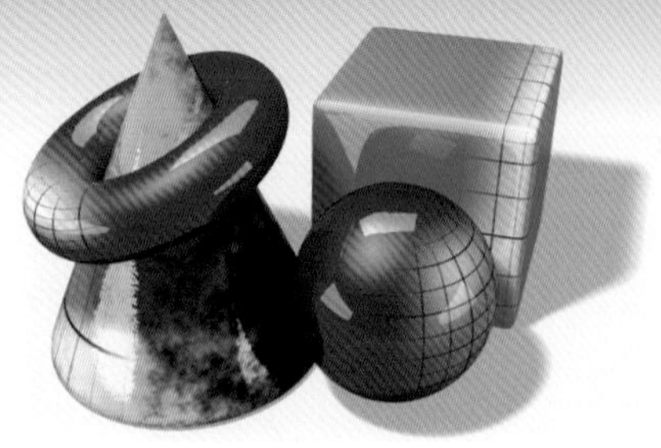

Objectives

In this lesson you will:

- Learn to use the MovieTexture node in a simulation.
- Become familiar with the MovieTexture node properties.
- Explore establishing events to control playing a movie.
- Begin to explore the use of the TVChannelSwitcher prototype to enable users to view multiple videos or images (including camera views) in the same location of the simulation.

Key Terms

node reference ***TVChannelSwitcher prototype***

Video in a Simulation

In Module 7 Lesson 1, we discussed some of the basic concepts behind applying video and other media in a simulation. We also talked about the many different reasons that you might want to add media to a simulation. Certainly, a video file is not needed in every simulation. You will undoubtedly encounter situations in which a video is the only way to achieve the results that you need, however.

In this lesson, we will explore the specifics of adding video to a simulation. First, we will explore the node that can be used for adding video (MovieTexture node), and then we will explore a prototype (TVChannelSwitcher) that can be used with this node to provide increased functionality.

16. Right-click **MovieTexture_Example1** in the Textures TextureResourceGroup in the simulation tree and select **Copy as Link**.
17. Scroll up in the simulation tree and right-click **Scene**. Select **Paste**. The MovieTexture_Example1 node is now in the simulation.
18. Run the simulation. Wait a moment until the movie begins to play.

Discussion

discuss

Do you hear the soundtrack?

Do you see the movie?

Why do you think the movie is running like this in the simulation?

From what you know about textures, what is missing from your simulation?

19. Close the simulation window.
20. Delete the **MovieTexture_Example1** node reference that you placed in the Scene frame.
21. Expand the **Resources** group node in the Simulation Tree window, if necessary.
22. Expand the **Materials**, **Material #945**, and **DiffuseTexture** folders under the Resources group node if necessary.
23. Delete the **TVScreen** Texture2 node reference. (Note that the original TVScreen node will remain in the Texture resources if you need it elsewhere in the simulation.)
24. Select the **MovieTexture_Example1** node (in the Textures group), right-click, and select **Copy as Link**.
25. Right-click the **DiffuseTexture** folder under **Material #945** and select **Paste**. Your Simulation Tree window should look like Figure 7.3.6.

tips+tricks

Technically, you do not need to perform step 24 because you already copied the MovieTexture_Example1 node as a link in step 16. Because you have not copied anything else since then, that node is still the copied node and it would be placed when you paste in step 25. We kept step 24, however, for clarity—and to ensure that the correct node is copied and pasted.

FIGURE 7.3.6 MovieTexture node placed in simulation

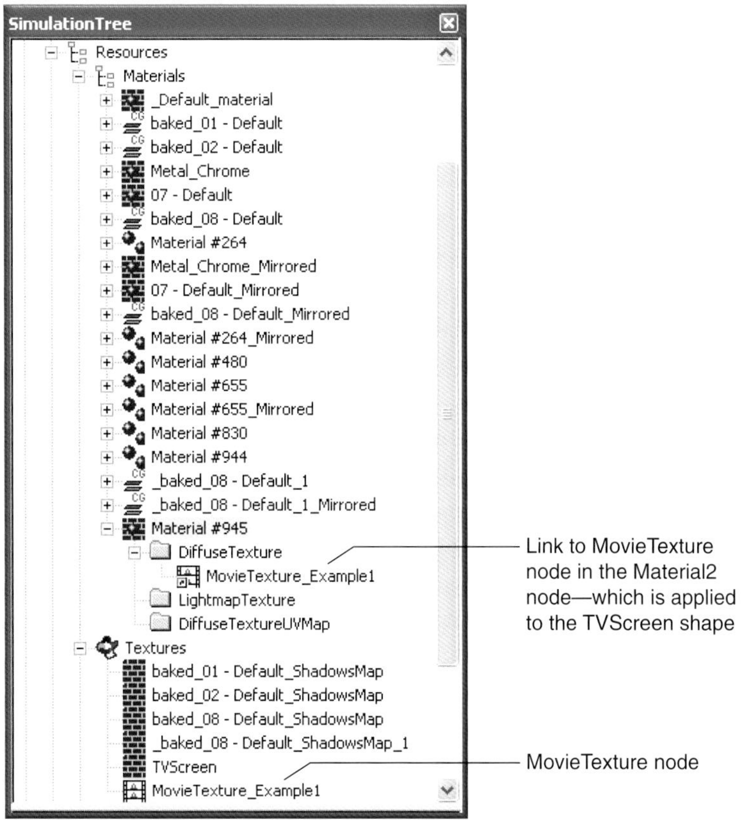

26. Run the simulation. The movie will start playing on the television screen on the wall. It will continue playing (looping) until you stop the simulation. Notice that the movie has a countdown before the skiing part begins.
27. Close the simulation window.
28. To start the movie where the skiing starts, select the **MovieTexture_Example1** node reference under Material #945\DiffuseTexture. Then set the StartTime field in the Property Bar to **9**.
29. Run the simulation and verify that the skiing part of the movie starts immediately.
30. Close the simulation window. Save the simulation as **MovieTexture_Example1** and keep it open to use in Activity 7.3.2.

BEST PRACTICES

Embedding Files

After you have saved your simulation, select the MovieTexture_Example1 node and observe the Property Bar. It will look similar to the following figure.

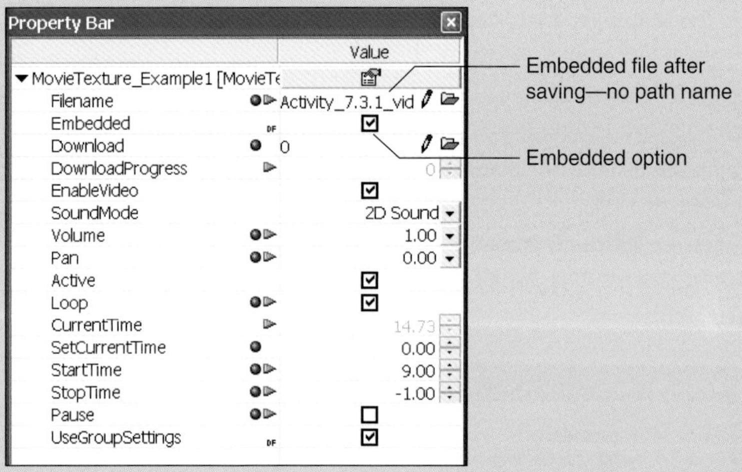

When you selected the file to be used, the pathway to that file was included. Because the Embedded check box was selected (set to true) by default, when you saved the file, it became a part of the EON file. Therefore, the Filename field no longer displays a path.

Embedding files is particularly important if you are saving to a location different from where the source file(s) is located or if you intend to transfer the EON file to different locations. You must make sure that all pertinent files either travel with the EON file or are still accessible following the same path.

troubleshooting

Although it is typically no longer an issue, you should note that the MovieTexture node does not work with the ramp driver in Windows NT. Playing video using the Windows NT ramp driver will terminate the simulation. You should use Open GL if you (or the person for whom you are creating a simulation) need to play video files in Windows NT.

MovieTexture Node in Context

In Activity 7.3.1, the video was set to Active and the Loop option was turned on. This means that the video begins to play automatically when the simulation is started and that it continues to play throughout the simulation. So what do you do if you want a video to start or stop at certain points within the simulation—perhaps triggered by a certain event or action?

The MovieTexture node, like other nodes, can be inserted into the Routes window and triggered by the SetRun inEvent. The trigger could be a keystroke, a controller, or any action or event in the simulation. You also can trigger the MovieTexture node at the same time as some other event is occurring.

Activity 7.3.2: Triggering the MovieTexture Node

1. If necessary, open EON and open the **MovieTexture_Example1** simulation that you created in Activity 7.3.1.
2. Add the **ClickSensor** node from the Components window to the simulation tree under the TV1 frame.
3. Double-click the **ClickSensor** node in the simulation tree. The ClickSensor Properties dialog box appears.
4. Verify that the **Change cursor when clickable** check box is selected. This changes the appearance of the cursor when you move it over a clickable object in the running simulation. Click **OK**.
5. If necessary, expand the **Resources** group and the **Textures** TexturesResourceGroup.
6. Select **MovieTexture_Example1**. In the Property Bar, clear the **Active** check box, changing its value to false. This prevents the movie from playing when the simulation starts.
7. Display the **Routes** window. Scroll to display a clear area of the Routes window if necessary.
8. Drag the **ClickSensor** node and the **MovieTexture_Example1** node to the Routes window.
9. Establish the connection outlined in the following table. This establishes that the movie will start when you click the television because the ClickSensor is placed below the TV1 frame. This section of the completed Routes window should look similar to Figure 7.3.7.

Source Node	outEvent	Destination Node	inEvent
ClickSensor	OnButtonDownTrue	MovieTexture_Example1	SetRun

FIGURE 7.3.7 Completed route for triggering the MovieTexture node

10. Run the simulation. Notice that the movie does not begin to play automatically and that the television screen is blank.
11. Move your cursor over the television screen. Notice that the cursor changes to the standard pointing hand icon to indicate that the screen can be clicked to initiate an action.
12. Click the television screen. The movie begins to play.

troubleshooting

It is not possible to drag a node reference (created using the Copy as Link feature) to the Routes window. In this case (step 8), you must drag the MovieTexture_Example1 node from the Textures TextureResourceGroup.

troubleshooting

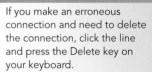

If you make an erroneous connection and need to delete the connection, click the line and press the Delete key on your keyboard.

discuss

Try clicking the screen again. Does it stop the movie?

From what you have learned, what node would you need to add to be able to start and stop the movie with each click?

13. Close the simulation window. Save the simulation as **MovieTexture_Example2** and keep it open to use in Activity 7.3.3.

Many Ways to Use the MovieTexture Node

With a little imagination, the MovieTexture node opens many possibilities. Try some of the following ideas:

- Create realistic running water in fountains, waterfalls, streams, and waves by applying movie textures to these objects.
- Make human models talk by replacing the face texture with a movie file.
- Simulate the rustling of leaves in trees.
- Simulate TV screens in a variety of situations, including computer monitors, security monitors, electronic notice boards, airport arrivals boards, advertising boards, and so on.
- Display instructional movies as a step in a training application. In this case, you can play movies on top of the 3D scene like a normal media player. Use a BPButton prototype so that you can set the pixel size and position of the video. For example, you could have the simulation play a movie of a person reading instructions in a small window on the scene.
- Because you do not have to use the video stream function of the MovieTexture node, you could create an MP3 player by downloading and playing .mp3 files from the Internet.
- Play sounds in formats other than the WAVE format.

A MovieTexture can be paused, which provides the opportunity to move to any frame in the movie. Using this feature, you could create a movie of a PowerPoint slide show. You would pause the movie when it starts. Then, each time you want to display a new slide, you would set the SetCurrentTime field of the MovieTexture node to move to a new slide. In this case, you should use high-quality video, but each slide would require only .2 seconds in the file because the slide is displayed while the movie is paused. If audio is not required, this could reduce the file size of the required images.

Note that you do not need to display movies in their full width and height. If you are replacing an object that had texture mapping showing only part of the texture, then only part of the movie will be visible. Also, movies can be tiled because they are textures. You could use the ability to tile textures to produce the impression of a bank of many television screens arranged in rows—the sort of display you might see in a retail store or a newsroom.

In some situations, movies can replace the need for time-consuming modeling and animation by showing moving objects. To maintain the 3D impression, this would be appropriate only when the movie is far from the camera. For example, a 3D theater model could show a movie containing performing actors on the stage backdrop.

tips+tricks

Remember that movies are applied to a Material2 node, so changing the color or opacity of the material will tint the movie or make it more transparent.

TVChannelSwitcher Prototype

TVChannelSwitcher

With the ***TVChannelSwitcher prototype***, you can click a TV shape to change the "channel." The channels can be links to different camera views from within the simulation or to movie files.

This prototype takes advantage of the feature that renders the scene displayed in a viewport to a texture node. You simply indicate the Shape nodes that should use the rendered texture and then indicate the camera views that are available. The user will click the shape to cycle through the cameras and display each camera's view on the shape, just like using a TV remote.

This prototype can handle unlimited shapes because it will create (copy) Viewport nodes inside. All shapes can show all cameras. If you want to use only certain cameras for a specific shape, then use another instance of this prototype.

Setting Up a TVChannelSwitcher Prototype

You can place this prototype anywhere in the simulation tree. When you place the TVChannelSwitcher prototype in the simulation tree and expand it, you will see the subfolders shown in Figure 7.3.8.

FIGURE 7.3.8 TVChannelSwitcher prototype expanded in the simulation tree

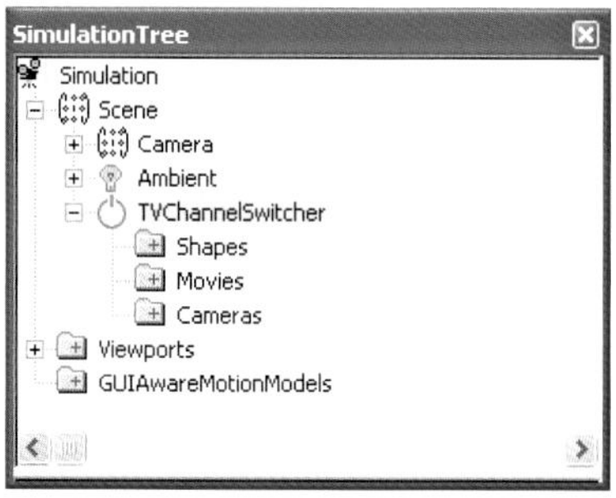

All Shape nodes that you specify will have a static texture when the simulation starts. The texture is black with a white circle and a cross, like a test signal on a TV. If you want a different start texture, then open the prototype and replace the OffTexture node. When a user clicks the start texture, it is replaced by a view from the first camera. You also can add movies by adding a MovieTexture node reference to the Movies field. Note that all of the movies will be cycled through before any camera views. None of the movies should be active when the simulation starts. They can become active only by the user clicking on the TV or shapes.

Fields

Other than entering values in the Shapes, Movies, and Cameras fields all of which are most easily edited in the simulation tree—the only fields to be altered for the TVChannelSwitcher prototype are the IsNotActive and IsActive fields in the Property Bar, as shown in Figure 7.3.9. When IsActive is false (check box not selected), it will restore the Shape nodes to their original appearance with their original textures. When it is true (check box selected), it will start by setting all shapes to the OffTexture, which is a black screen with a white circle and cross.

FIGURE 7.3.9 TVChannelSwitcher properties

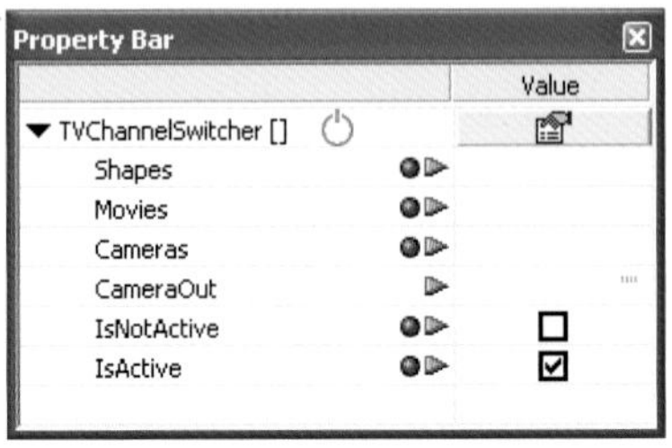

Activity 7.3.3: Using the TVChannelSwitcher Prototype

1. If necessary, open EON and open the **MovieTexture_Example2** simulation that you created in Activity 7.3.2.
2. Add the **TVChannelSwitcher** prototype to the Scene frame in the simulation tree.
3. Expand the **TV1** frame. Delete the **ClickSensor** node in this frame.
4. To create a node reference, right-click **TV1Shape** and select **Copy as Link**. Paste it under **TVChannelSwitcher\Shapes**.
5. Expand **Resources** and **Textures**. Right-click the **MovieTexture_Example1** node and select **Copy as Link**. Paste it under **TVChannelSwitcher\Movies**.
6. Save the simulation as **TVChannelSwitcher_Example.eoz**.
7. Run the simulation. Notice that the TV screen has a black screen with a white circle and cross. Click the TV screen to start the movie.
8. Close the simulation window.
9. Add a **Frame** node under the Scene frame and rename it **Camera2**.
10. Add a **Spin** node under the Camera2 frame.
11. Add an **AnimatedCone** prototype under the Camera2 frame.
12. Right-click the **Camera2** frame and select **Copy as Link**. Paste it under **TVChannelSwitcher\Cameras**.
13. Right-click the **ActiveViewportCamera** frame and select **Copy as Link**. Paste it under **TVChannelSwitcher\Cameras** also. Your simulation tree should look like Figure 7.3.10.

FIGURE 7.3.10 Simulation tree with the TVChannelSwitcher prototype

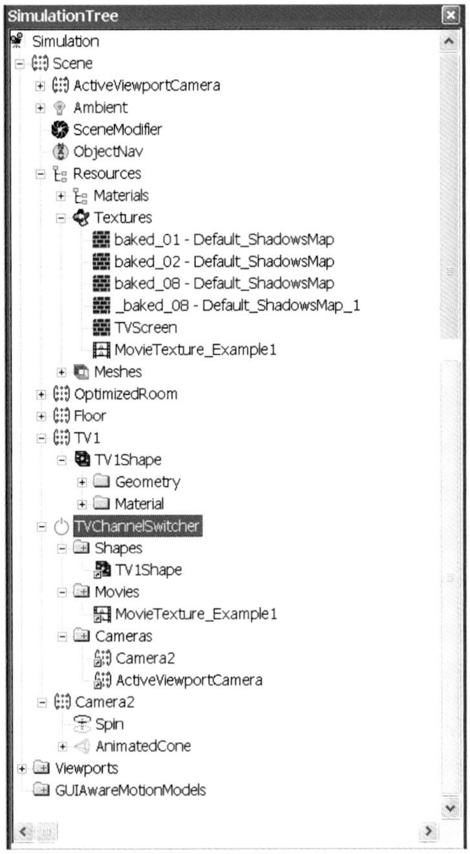

14. Save the simulation and then run it.
15. Click the TV screen to begin the movie of the skiers.
16. Click the TV screen a second time to display the Camera2 frame's current view. Zoom out using the right mouse button (right-click and drag the mouse up). Press the **C** key to display the animated cone. This helps you to understand where the Camera2 frame is currently located. If you continue to press the **C** key, you will observe that Camera2 is orbiting around the outside of the room.
17. Zoom back in closer to the room and click the TV screen a third time to display what your camera is seeing. Because you are seeing the TV screen as well, you will see the picture-in-a-picture effect.
18. Close the simulation window. Close EON.

troubleshooting

If you do not see the animated cone in step 16, zoom out further and press C again.

troubleshooting

If your system has an older video card and/or driver, the camera views may not be accurately displayed on the screen through the TVChannelSwitcher prototype as described in step 17. You can continue to change channels by clicking the screen, eventually returning to the movie.

Summary

In this lesson you:

- Learned to use the MovieTexture node in a simulation.
- Became familiar with the MovieTexture node properties.
- Explored establishing events to control playing a movie.
- Began to explore the use of the TVChannelSwitcher prototype to enable users to view multiple videos or images (including camera views) in the same location of the simulation.

Simulation

A co-worker recently demonstrated how easy it is to add multimedia to your EON simulation. Because you are still refining the details of the apartment simulation for your company's client, you start thinking about the ways that multimedia might be employed to make the simulation appear more true to life. Certainly, the client would be able to use a multimedia feature to enable potential owners or tenants to visualize themselves in that environment listening to music or watching television.

You call an impromptu meeting with your co-workers and brainstorm ways in which multimedia could enhance the experience of the virtual apartment. Everyone is excited about the prospects, and many different ways to use this feature are proposed. However, you know that you will have to choose carefully. Just because you have the ability to do something does not necessarily mean that it is a good thing to do. Too much multimedia could be overwhelming and could detract from the simulation instead of enhancing it.

Job 7.1: Adding to the Storyboard

As we have said before, storyboarding is an ongoing process. It allows you to continually refine your thought process and incorporate change requests from the client throughout the development of a project. It also allows you to present new ideas to the client for approval before investing too much time into developing something in your simulation.

You like some of the ideas that you and your co-workers suggested for using multimedia in the simulated apartment, but you realize that the client may have different ideas after considering the possibilities. Therefore, you need to update the storyboard again. This time, include suggestions for utilizing sound and video in the simulation.

1. Open EON. Open **Job_6.4.eoz**, the apartment simulation that you enhanced in the Module 6 Simulation.
2. Run the simulation and navigate through the apartment.
3. Take notes identifying the best locations for sound, video, or combined sound and video in the apartment. Consider the locations that would be most likely to have these elements in a real apartment.
4. Close the simulation window. Keep the simulation open to use in Job 7.2.
5. If possible, continue using the storyboard that you created in the Module 1 Simulation and later enhanced in the Modules 2 through 6 Simulations. Revise the storyboard to include information about adding multimedia to your simulation. (If you did not complete the Simulation sections for Modules 1 through 6, you can create a storyboard using paper and pencil, a flowchart application, or a drawing program.)
6. Complete your storyboard and then save your work.

Job 7.2: Adding Sound

As you explored the apartment simulation in Job 7.1, you developed a list of potential locations for adding sound in the apartment—locations where the user might expect to hear sounds and sites that your client would prefer.

After reviewing your suggestions by looking at your storyboard, the client selected the sounds to be added. The client would like the following sounds added to the simulation:

- A clock radio on the nightstand in the bedroom that plays when you touch it.
- A doorbell outside the main entrance that rings when it is pressed.
- A stereo located in the living room that is playing at the start of the simulation, which can be turned off when the stereo is touched.
- Additionally, the stereo sound should stop when the television is turned on, and vice versa.

Discussion

discuss

Consider how the sound will travel within each room and identify the sounds that can be turned on or off in the simulation.

Do you think it would be useful to use the SimultaneousSound prototype?

1. Continue working with the open simulation file **Job_6.4.eoz** that you explored in Job 7.1.
2. Add at least two or three sounds to the simulation. (Add more sounds if your work in the storyboard calls for additional sounds. You may substitute your own ideas for the listed suggestions.)

Discussion

discuss

What sounds might you expect when you walk into a real apartment?

Would the sounds that you hear when you walk into your home or a friend's home meet the needs of your client?

3. Establish routes in the simulation to ensure that each sound is activated and deactivated appropriately.
4. Run the simulation and test the sounds to verify that they work as designed.
5. Activate multiple sounds at the same time and note the results.
6. Note anything that is not working or improvements that could be made.
7. Close the simulation window. If any changes are necessary, make those changes and retest the simulation.

Discussion

discuss

Rather than having sounds activated and deactivated by selecting components in the simulation, would it make more sense to add user interface buttons to the simulation for sound control? Why or why not?

8. Save the simulation as **Job_7.2.eoz** and keep it open to use in Job 7.3.

Job 7.3: Adding Video

You added sound to your simulation and established the ways in which these sounds are activated and deactivated. Your next task is to add video elements to the apartment simulation. The elements you add can be based on the suggestions listed earlier or the notes you made when you were working on the storyboard in Job 7.1.

1. Continue working with the open simulation file **Job_7.2.eoz** from Job 7.2.
2. Add a video, with sound, that will play on a television in the living room of the apartment when the user clicks the television.

3. Add a video, with sound, that will play on a television in the bedroom of the apartment when the user clicks the television.
4. Use the TVChannelSwitcher prototype on one of these televisions to enable it to play different videos when the user clicks the television.
5. Run the simulation and test it to verify that users can play the videos on the televisions as expected.
6. Close the simulation window. Save the simulation as **Job_7.3.eoz** and keep it open to use in Job 7.4.

Job 7.4: Adding Multimedia to the GUI

The user interface that you created in the Module 6 Simulation allows basic navigation within the apartment simulation. However, navigation often is not the only purpose of the user interface. Typically, many other features are accessible through the graphical user interface (GUI). In this job, you will add sound controls to the GUI.

1. Continue working with the open simulation file **Job_7.3.eoz** from Job 7.3.
2. Add a Slider node that allows the user to increase or decrease the volume of the sound in each room.
3. Run the simulation and test the new slider.
4. Close the simulation window.

Discussion

discuss

Would it be beneficial to the client to have a video tour of the apartment available in a viewport of the GUI? Or is it better to enable each person to walk through the apartment at their own pace and in their own way?

What are the advantages and disadvantages of a video tour versus a self-guided tour?

5. Based on your answers to the Discussion questions, experiment with adding a video tour viewport to the GUI elements.
6. Review your GUI. Is it too cluttered or awkward? If you feel that some components are not necessary or are not particularly useful, delete them.
7. Add any other GUI elements that you think would be useful for controlling the multimedia features of the apartment.
8. Save the simulation as **Job 7.4.eoz** and then run the simulation. Retest all of the interface elements to be certain that all of the new features work and to verify that you did not inadvertently disrupt the functioning of a previously existing feature.
9. Make notes of anything that is not working or that could be improved.
10. Close the simulation window. If any further changes are necessary, make those changes and retest the simulation.
11. Close the simulation window. Save the simulation and then close EON.

HARALD SUND

MODULE 8

EON Prototypes

LESSON 8.1
Fundamentals of Prototypes

LESSON 8.2
Using EON-Supplied Prototypes

LESSON 8.3
Developing EON Prototypes

LESSON 8.1

Fundamentals of Prototypes

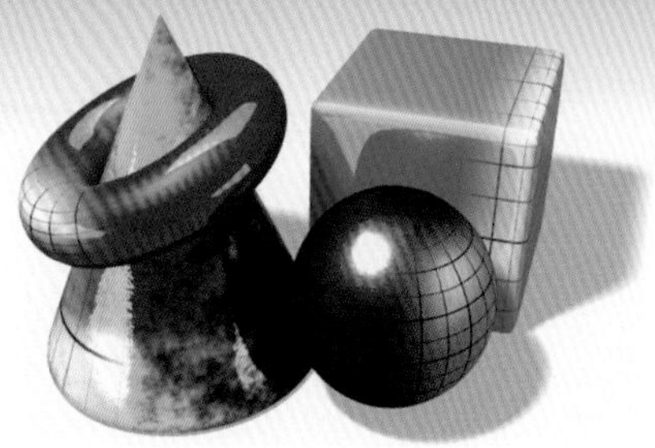

Objectives

In this lesson you will:

- Develop an understanding of prototypes and why prototypes are used.
- Learn about prototype definitions and prototype instances.
- Classify prototypes as object or functional prototypes.
- Explore the parts of a prototype and identify the parts that can be modified.
- Observe how prototypes work in EON.
- Learn what happens in a prototype when you run a simulation.

Key Terms

dynamic prototype

encapsulated

EON-supplied prototype

functional prototype

instance

Local Prototypes window

object-oriented programming

object prototype

prototype library

What Are Prototypes?

In the most basic terms, prototypes are simply reusable assets or objects. To save time and improve efficiency, programmers often will reuse sections of code from previously written applications. Such code is packaged into components, which are stored in a software library so they may be referenced and used by other applications. Prototypes resemble subroutines. In some programming languages, the definition (or declaration) of a reusable code component is commonly known as a function prototype, or simply a prototype.

The practice of code reuse has evolved over the years to take advantage of new features and functionality provided by ***object-oriented programming*** languages. With the object-oriented approach, new ***instances*** of objects based on prototypes (i.e., definitions) are created in memory during program execution.

Why Use Prototypes?

There are a number of good reasons to use prototypes. Some of them are:

- Facilitates reusability and portability between applications: Prototypes make it easier to recycle subtree constructions. Because these encapsulated subtrees contain nodes and routes, you can reuse complex objects and the behaviors created in the Routes window in EON.
- Simplifies development efforts: It is easier to interpret a complex simulation tree if it is divided into small, independent objects—the "divide and conquer" approach. A collection of independent prototypes is easier to manage than a complex collection of subtrees and their associated nodes, prototypes, and routes.
- Reduces time requirements: The use of prototypes simplifies simulation tree structure because prototypes appear as one node instead of many, and they only expose the fields you can set or connect. Prototypes greatly simplify how users work in the Routes window by hiding the routes between nodes that are contained inside a prototype. Instead of creating routes between layers, routes are created between prototypes. This makes the Routes window easier to use because routes are easier to follow, and you can create the routes more efficiently.
- Simplifies maintenance: Prototypes are easy to insert, and they allow multiple instances based on one shared definition. You can update multiple instances by changing only one prototype definition—a change in the prototype definition will affect all prototypes of that type in the simulation. You can make one change in a single location rather than expanding several subtrees to make the same changes in multiple locations.

What Is an EON Prototype?

From earlier modules you know that EON prototypes are reusable, plug-and-play, miniature simulations that can be copied from the Prototypes tab of the Components window and placed into your simulations. In Figure 8.1.1, the Prototypes tab in the Components window depicts some of the prototypes that are available in EON Professional 6.0. We will refer to these as the ***EON-supplied prototypes.***

FIGURE 8.1.1 EON-supplied prototypes

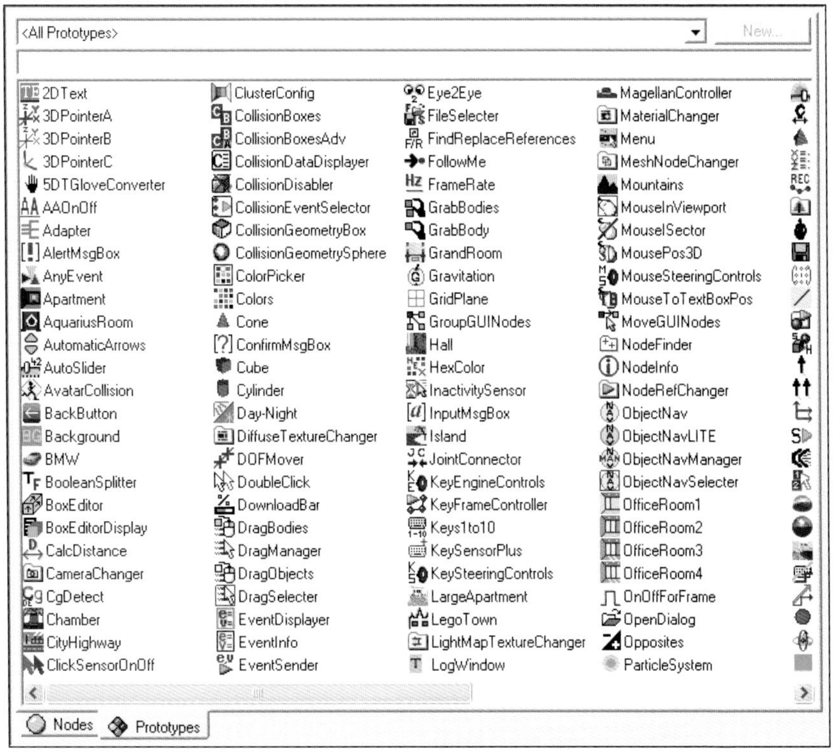

An EON prototype is actually an *encapsulated* simulation subtree that can be composed of various combinations of nodes, prototypes, and their routes. However, they are much more important than this simple definition might suggest because any EON user can create a prototype from scratch.

Prototypes in EON appear in three different areas and have three different names, as shown in Figure 8.1.2.

1. The *prototype definition* resides in the area below the simulation tree, which is known as the ***Local Prototypes window.***
2. One or more *prototype instances* can appear in the top section of the simulation tree.
3. ***Prototype libraries*** are displayed in the Components window in EON, enabling longer-term storage and easy access to many prototypes.

FIGURE 8.1.2 Prototype libraries, definitions, and instances

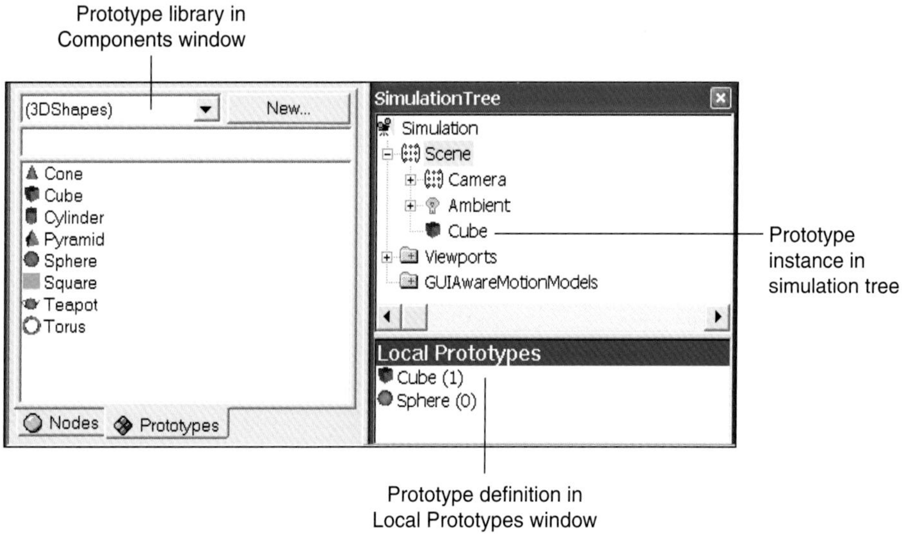

Prototype Definition vs. Prototype Instance

As you learned in Module 1 Lesson 3, a *prototype definition* in EON includes a set of properties, all components within a simulation subtree, and all associated routes between that subtree's components. Prototype properties include fields that store data to be used by the prototype and fields that facilitate communication between the prototype and simulation components external to the prototype.

An EON prototype is said to be ***encapsulated*** because it appears as one component in the simulation tree, although it actually contains various combinations of nodes, prototypes, and routes. Prototypes have a user-friendly plug-and-play appearance because they hide all of the complex details and inner workings via encapsulation.

A *prototype instance* can typically be used in the same manner as a standard EON node. Due to encapsulation, a prototype instance appears to be one object in the simulation tree with a name, an icon, and a set of properties or fields. Like a node, you can drag a prototype instance to the Routes window and connect routes from or to their fields. Also like a node, you can edit a prototype instance's field values in the Property Bar.

Prototype instances and nodes have an important difference. Nodes are based on internal C++ code that you *cannot edit*, whereas prototype instances are based on a prototype definition, which is a subtree of components (nodes and prototypes) and properties that you *can edit*.

Prototype Library Files

To enable you to reuse prototypes, store them in prototype library files that are external to the simulation file. The file format of a prototype library is similar to the simulation file. However, prototype library files have an .eop file extension rather than an .eoz file extension. You may be confused that an .eop file is called a prototype when in fact it has the capacity to hold multiple prototype definitions. The prototypes that you see in the Prototypes tab of the Components window are stored in .eop files. The names of the files are displayed at the top of the Components view without the .eop extension.

The EON-supplied prototypes are installed in C:\Program Files\EON Reality\EON Studio\PrototypeLibrary\. Figure 8.1.3 shows the contents of the OrbitNav prototype library in the Components window and a Windows Explorer view identifying the Windows folder where the OrbitNav.eop library file is located.

FIGURE 8.1.3 Prototype libraries are .eop files

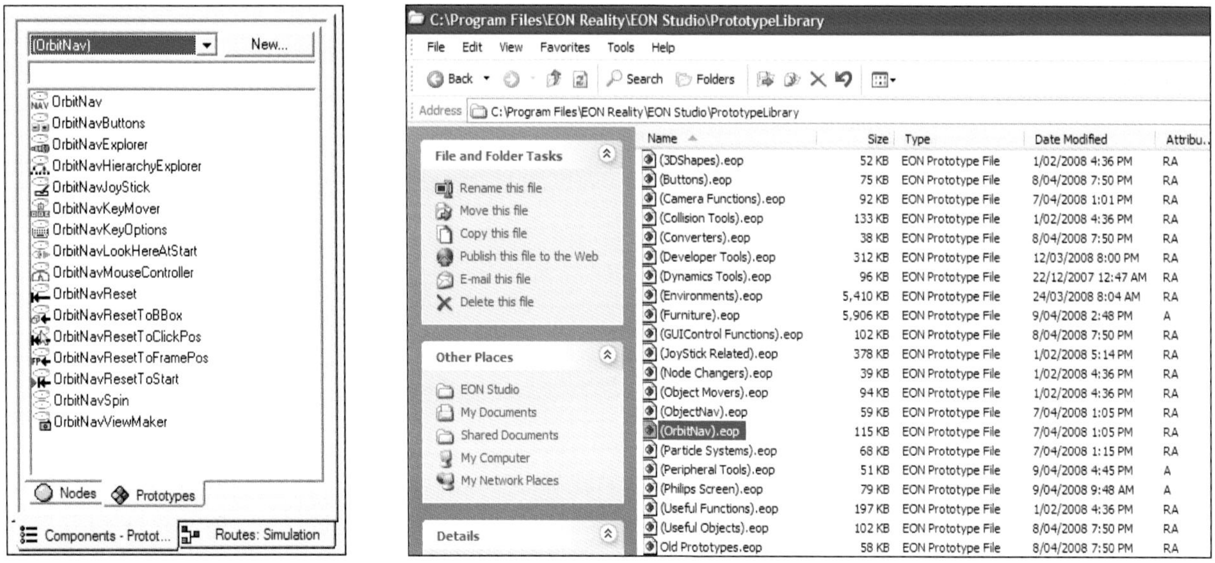

Activity 8.1.1: Installing a Prototype Library

1. Copy the **Top10Valued.eop** file from the data files for Module 8 Lesson 1 to a folder on your computer if necessary.
2. Open EON. Display the **Components** window if necessary.
3. Click the **Prototypes** tab in the Components window. Select **All Prototypes** in the drop-down list on the Prototypes tab to view all EON-supplied prototypes if necessary.

4. From the Options menu, choose **Preferences** to display the Preferences dialog box shown in Figure 8.1.4. Notice the path to the EON-supplied prototypes in the Search paths list.

FIGURE 8.1.4 Preferences dialog box

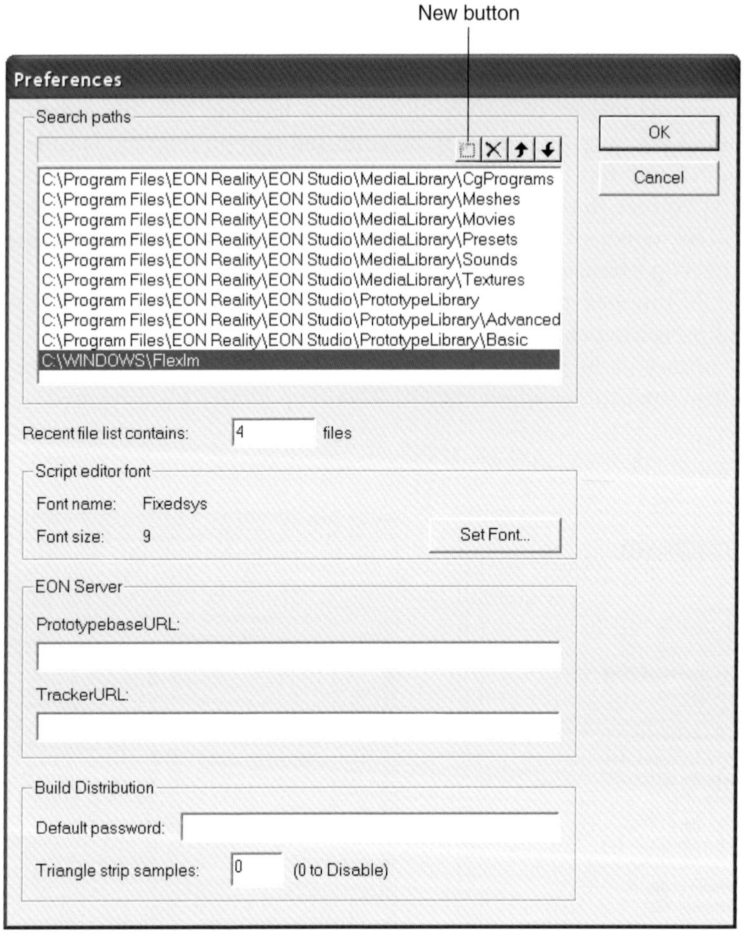

tips+tricks

In step 5, you could also key the search path to the folder containing the file. Do not, however, include the name of the file, such as Top10Valued.eop, as part of the path in the blank line. You must type only the path to the folder containing the file, stopping before the filename itself.

5. Click the **New** button above the Search paths list. You will see a blank line surrounded by a box at the bottom of the Search paths list. To the right of the blank line is a browse button that allows you to select the folder containing the Top10Valued.eop file on your computer. Click **OK** to close the dialog box.
6. From the drop-down list box in the Prototypes tab of the Components window, select **Top10Valued**. The prototypes in this prototype library are listed in the Components window.
7. Close EON without saving the simulation.

Object vs. Functional Prototypes

You can classify prototypes as object or functional prototypes. This classification will help you understand prototypes.

The main purpose of an ***object prototype*** is to store all the resources of a particular 3D object in one place. An object prototype includes the Frame nodes, Shape nodes, and resource nodes such as Mesh2, Texture2, MovieTexture, and DirectSound, which in turn reference geometry, image, movie, and audio files.

Typically, ***functional prototypes*** do not hold 3D objects. Instead, functional prototypes focus on providing specific functions such as navigation, making calculations, and converting or transforming data into a more usable form. They are like mini-programs. Frequently, they include a Script node as an important component. They may focus on working with objects, but the objects are usually not part of the prototype.

Most of the EON-supplied prototypes are functional prototypes. The main exceptions are the 3DShapes, Environments, and Furniture prototype libraries, which are solely objects.

Typically, object prototypes have a large file size because of the resource files they contain. Functional prototypes are small because they consist of only nodes and script.

tips+tricks

The Useful Objects library is different. Its prototypes could be classified as object and functional because they hold objects that are highly configurable.

Parts of a Prototype

The main part of a prototype definition is its subtree, which includes the nodes, field values, and routes between internal nodes. View the other parts of a prototype in the Prototype Definition Properties dialog box by double-clicking a prototype definition in the Local Prototypes window. See Figure 8.1.5.

FIGURE 8.1.5 Prototype Definition Properties dialog box

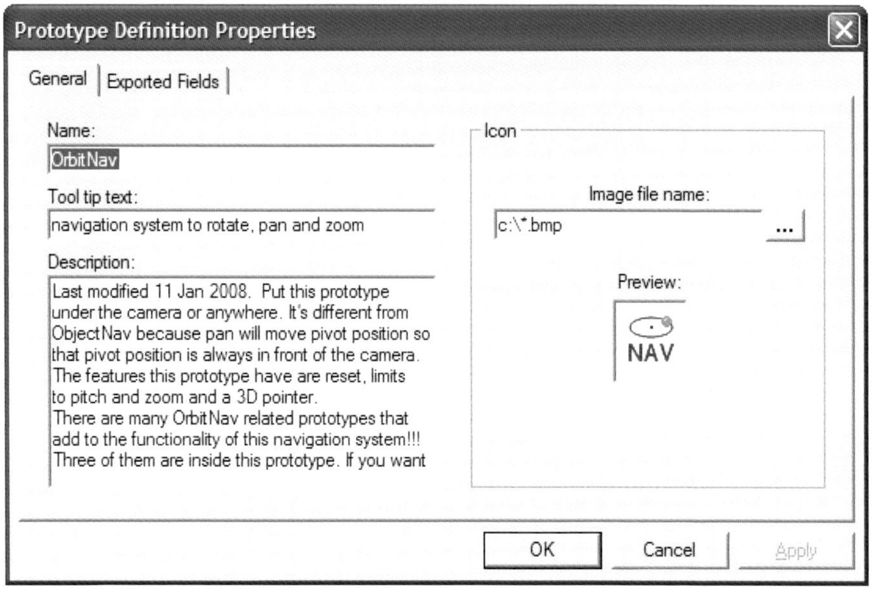

The Prototype Definition Properties dialog box enables you to verify and modify a prototype's characteristics.

- Name: This text is used as the default name of new prototype instances.
- Tool tip text: This short description of the prototype is displayed in the Prototypes tab of the Components window when the mouse hovers over the prototype's name.
- Description: This text box, which is larger than a tooltip text box, can store information such as how to set up the prototype, how to customize it, and the date that the prototype was last modified.
- Icon: This small bitmap image is always displayed next to the name of the prototype.
- Exported Fields tab: This list identifies the fields on various nodes within the prototype subtree that will be shown in the Property Bar for all instances of the prototype. All other fields of nodes inside the prototype are hidden. The exported fields allow you to *customize the instance* without *modifying the definition.*

Local Prototypes Window

The Local Prototypes window displays the prototypes that are stored locally in the simulation file. Prototype definitions are edited from the Local Prototypes window. Right-click a prototype definition icon in the Local Prototypes window to open a pop-up menu containing the commands described in Table 8.1.1.

TABLE 8.1.1 Pop-Up Menu Commands for the Local Prototypes Window

Command	Description
Build Distribution file	Saves a compressed copy of the prototype that can be used for dynamic load applications.
Clone	Creates an identical prototype in the Local Prototypes window.
Copy	Copies the selection and places it on the Clipboard.
Cut	Removes the selection and places it on the Clipboard.
Delete	Deletes the prototype definition from the current simulation. *Note:* You cannot delete a prototype definition if it has an instance in the simulation tree.
Insert in Tree	Inserts a prototype instance below the selected node in the simulation tree.
Open	Opens the Prototype Edit window.
Properties	Opens the Prototype Definition Properties dialog box.
If no prototype definition is currently selected, right-click in the Local Prototypes window to open the following pop-up menu:	
Compact view	Displays small prototype icons without a scroll bar.
List view	Displays small prototype icons with a scroll bar.
Normal view	Displays large prototype icons.
Paste	Inserts the contents of the Clipboard.

Open Source Development

All EON prototypes are open source. To see the contents of a prototype, right-click a prototype definition in the Local Prototypes window and choose Open, as shown in Figure 8.1.6. This displays the prototype's subtree in a new Simulation Tree window. You can open any of the EON-supplied prototypes to make modifications or learn how they work. Prototypes enable any user to extend the functionality of EON and to share it with colleagues or within online community forums.

FIGURE 8.1.6 Open the OrbitNav prototype to view how it works

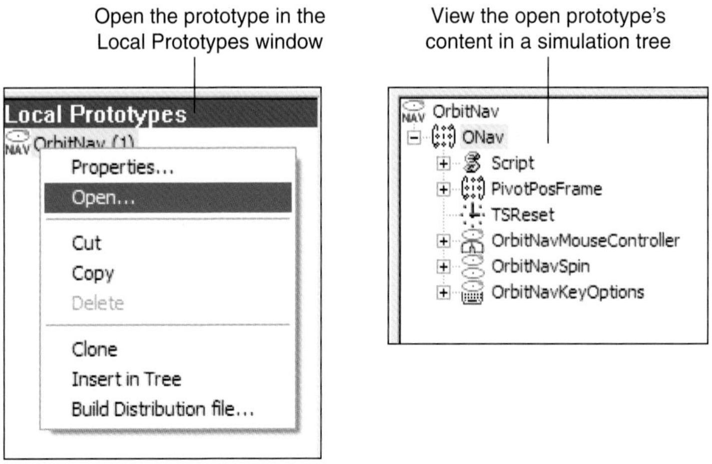

Dynamic Prototypes

EON has a DynamicPrototype node. This node is similar to a prototype instance, but it is not based on any prototype definition that exists in the simulation's Local Prototypes window. Instead, a ***dynamic prototype*** will be based on a prototype definition that is stored in an external prototype (.eop) library file. Therefore, we typically say that the DynamicPrototype node *loads* a prototype. The prototype file can be loaded from the local computer or downloaded over the Internet from any web server. "Dynamic" refers to the node's ability to *change* (during runtime) the prototype file that it loads by sending a new prototype name.

cross-reference

You will learn more about the DynamicPrototype node in Module 9 Lesson 3.

How Prototypes Work in EON

As you have seen in previous activities, you can add prototypes to an EON application by copying or dragging a prototype definition directly from the Prototypes tab of the Components window to one of two places: the Local Prototypes window or the Simulation Tree window. If you add a prototype to the Local Prototypes window, only the definition is added to the simulation file. If you add a prototype to the body of the simulation tree, a prototype instance is added to the simulation tree and a prototype definition is added to the Local Prototypes window. Figure 8.1.7 depicts each of these methods.

FIGURE 8.1.7 Two methods for adding prototypes to your simulation

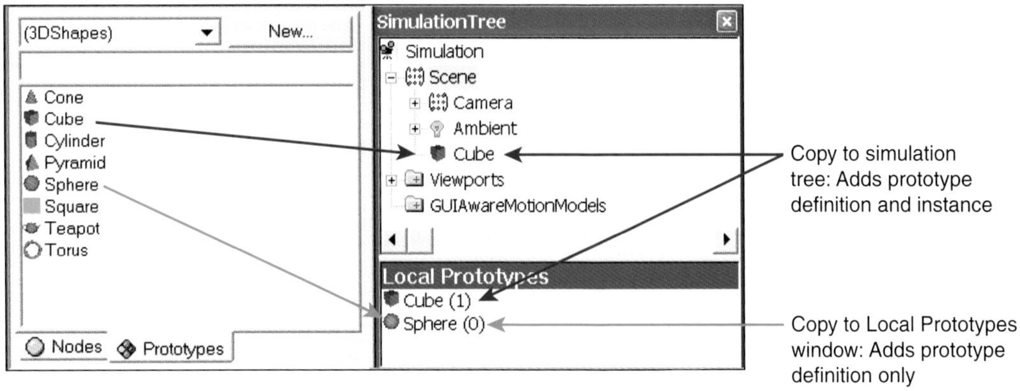

When a prototype is added to an application as a prototype instance or as a member of the Local Prototypes window, a copy of the prototype's definition is copied from a prototype library file into the computer's memory. When the simulation is saved, it is stored in the .eoz file. Before the simulation is saved, the Filename fields of all resource nodes like Mesh2 and Texture2 are modified to include the full path to the prototype library file. However, when the simulation is saved, these resource files are extracted from the prototype library file and inserted into the .eoz file and the Filename fields are changed to show the filename only (without a path).

You also can get a prototype definition into your application by copying it from another instance of EON Studio. You can copy a part of the simulation tree that has the prototype instance or copy the definition from the Local Prototypes window.

After the prototype definition is inside the .eoz file, it has no connection with the original definition in the prototype library file. You can use the local prototype definition in its original form or modify it to meet the needs of a particular application. Because the prototype definition in the Local Prototypes window is stored locally within the simulation's .eoz file, any modifications to the definition do not affect the prototype definition in the prototype library file from which the definition was originally copied.

tips+tricks

You also can create a prototype definition from scratch by dragging a Frame node to the Local Prototypes window. This will be covered in more detail in Module 8 Lesson 3.

tips+tricks

There are no limits to the number of instances and definitions you can have other than the limit of computer memory.

The Local Prototypes window, located in the lower portion of the Simulation Tree window, displays a list of the prototype definitions that have been added to the simulation's .eoz file. The index number in parentheses to the right of the prototype definition denotes the number of prototype instances that it has in the simulation tree. By dragging the prototype definition from the Local Prototypes window to the simulation tree, you can add more instances.

If a prototype definition has any exported fields, every instance based on it will have the same fields. If you drag the prototype definition from the Local Prototypes window to the simulation tree, the field values will be the same as the values in the Exported Fields list on the definition. If you copy an instance, the new instance will have the same values as the instance you copy. You can change the default field values in the Exported Fields list (except for outEvent fields) so that any new instances created by dragging the prototype definition to the simulation tree will inherit the new values.

Activity 8.1.2: Changing Default Values

1. Open EON. Open **Activity_8.1.2.eoz** from the data files for Module 8 Lesson 1.
2. Save the file as **Changing_Default_Values.eoz.**
3. Explore the simulation tree. Select the instance of the **OrbitNavReset** prototype under the Camera node. Note that the ResetZoom field has a value of 10.
4. Run the simulation and press **R** to trigger the OrbitNavReset function.
5. Close the simulation window.
6. In the Local Prototypes window, double-click the **OrbitNavReset** prototype to display the Prototype Definition Properties dialog box. Click the **Exported Fields** tab.
7. Change the ResetZoom field value to **20** if necessary and click **OK** to close the dialog box.
8. Notice that the OrbitNavReset instance already under the Camera node in the simulation tree does not change its ResetZoom value.
9. Drag the **OrbitNavReset** prototype from the Local Prototypes window to the Camera frame in the simulation tree to create another instance. The new instance is automatically named OrbitNavReset1. Notice that the ResetZoom value in this instance is 20.
10. In the Property Bar, change the value of the OrbitNavReset1 instance's ResetKey field to **T**.
11. Save the simulation and then run the simulation. Test the R and T keys.
12. Close the simulation window.
13. Copy the first instance, **OrbitNavReset,** and paste it in the Camera frame. The new instance is automatically named OrbitNavReset2. Notice that this instance, OrbitNavReset2, has the same values as the instance copied and not the default values from the prototype definition.
14. Change the value of the OrbitNavReset2 ResetPivotPos field to **0 20 0** in the Property Bar.
15. Click the **OrbitNavReset2** instance if necessary to display its properties in the Property Bar. Change the value of the ResetKey field to **Y**.
16. Save the simulation and then run the simulation. Test the R, T, and Y keys.
17. Close the simulation window. Keep the simulation open to use in Activity 8.1.3.

What Happens in a Prototype When You Run the Simulation?

To understand prototypes clearly, you must know what happens when you run the simulation. The prototype is involved in each stage: simulation startup, simulation runtime, and simulation shutdown.

Simulation Startup

When the simulation is started, the prototype definition's subtree is copied beneath each of its instances. The prototype instance is like a special node. The root node of the prototype definition's subtree is placed directly under the prototype instance node. From then on, the instance has no connection to the definition while the simulation is running. You cannot change the definition during runtime in a way that would instantly change all the instances based on it. You may be able to modify the subtree of a prototype definition while the simulation is running, but it has no effect until the simulation is stopped and started again.

After the subtree is copied beneath the instances, the field values stored in the prototype instances are sent to the various fields. This overwrites the definition's values, thereby customizing the copy. After this step, the simulation is running and a single simulation tree holds all of the nodes.

Simulation Runtime

During runtime, you cannot add prototype instances. For example, you cannot insert a prototype from the Components window into the simulation tree during runtime or drag a prototype definition from the Local Prototypes window to the simulation tree. If you attempt to do so, you will see a message telling you to stop the simulation and try again. Also, you cannot programmatically insert instances based on local prototypes. However, you can insert instances based on external prototype files by using the DynamicPrototype node.

cross-reference

You will learn more about the DynamicPrototype node in Module 9 Lesson 3.

During runtime, you cannot edit a prototype definition's properties, such as its name, tooltip, description, icon, and Exported Fields list. The Prototype Definitions Properties dialog box will open, but the properties will be disabled (they will appear shaded in the dialog box). If the prototype instance has routes connected to it, it passes on any values sent or received as if the routes were directly connected to the internal fields as listed in the prototype's Exported Fields list.

troubleshooting

For some prototypes, you can examine the nodes beneath a prototype instance during runtime. These prototypes must have exported fields of type SFNode or MFNode (the ones with yellow folders under them). However, this feature is not supported, and its use can lead to simulation instability if you try to edit internal values. Also during runtime, you can see exported field names on the prototype instance that change to the name of the internal field to which they are linked.

Simulation Shutdown

When the simulation is stopped, all nodes beneath prototype instances are deleted, and the instance is restored to the state it had before the simulation was run. Therefore, even if the instance's fields received new values during the simulation, these values are not saved. The field's values are restored to their previous state before runtime. This is a big difference when compared to most nodes, in which runtime field values persist after the simulation stops. This is one of the important distinctions you need to remember between nodes and prototypes. There is no point in editing a prototype instance's values during runtime—you must stop the simulation first and then edit the values.

Activity 8.1.3: Looking Inside a Prototype During Runtime

1. Continue working with the open simulation file **Changing_Default_Values.eoz** from Activity 8.1.2.
2. Expand the **OrbitNavReset2** node as shown in Figure 8.1.8.

FIGURE 8.1.8 Expanded OrbitNavReset2 instance before running the simulation

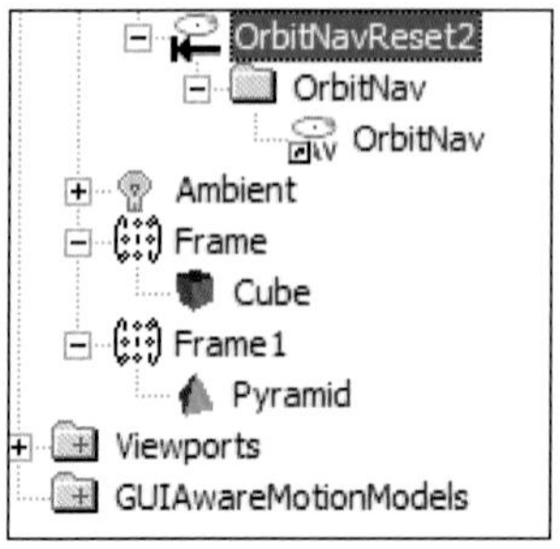

3. Run the simulation.
4. In the simulation tree, click the minus sign to the left of the OrbitNavReset2 icon to collapse the view.
5. Click the plus sign to the left of the OrbitNavReset2 icon to expand the view. As you can see, after starting the simulation, the top frame of the prototype definition has been copied beneath the OrbitNavReset2 instance.
6. Expand the **Frame** and **Script** nodes as shown in Figure 8.1.9. You can see that the prototype is made up of a Script node and two KeyboardSensor nodes.

FIGURE 8.1.9 Expanded OrbitNavReset2 instance while running the simulation

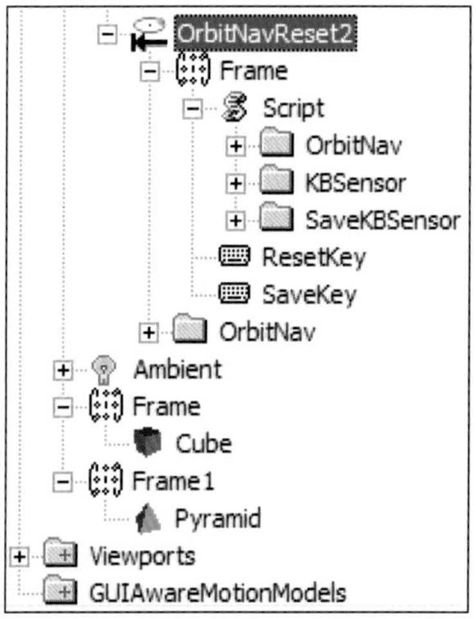

7. Click the **Camera** frame in the simulation tree.
8. Close the simulation window.
9. Click the **OrbitNavReset2** prototype instance again and notice the EnableResetKey field under the ResetKey field in the Property Bar.
10. Run the simulation and notice that the EnableResetKey field name has not changed.
11. Click the **Camera** frame and then click the **OrbitNavReset2** node.

12. Notice that the field name has changed. It has been refreshed to reveal the internal field name *enabled.*
13. Click the **Camera** frame again and close the simulation window.
14. In the Local Prototypes window, double-click the **OrbitNavReset** prototype to display the Prototype Definition Properties dialog box. Click the **Exported Fields** tab.
15. Scroll down to display the EnableResetKey field in the left column and note the connected field in the third column.
16. Click **OK** to close the dialog box. Close EON without saving the simulation.

Summary

In this lesson you:

- Developed an understanding of prototypes and why prototypes are used.
- Learned about prototype definitions and prototype instances.
- Classified prototypes as object or functional prototypes.
- Explored the parts of a prototype and identified the parts that can be modified.
- Observed how prototypes work in EON.
- Learned what happens in a prototype when you run a simulation.

LESSON 8.2

Using EON-Supplied Prototypes

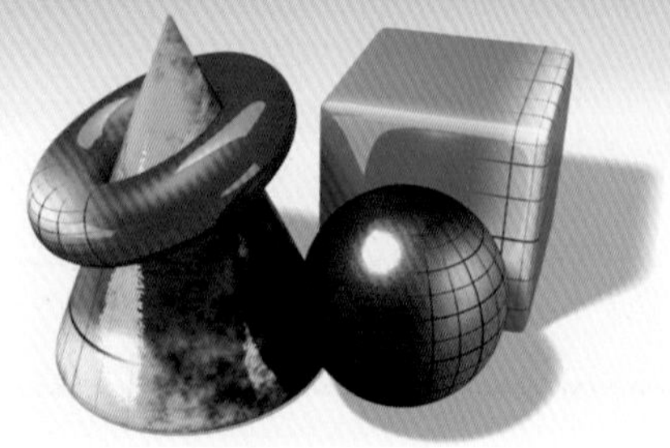

Objectives

In this lesson you will:

- Learn to recognize the EON-supplied prototypes.
- Familiarize yourself with the contents of the prototype libraries.
- Use and customize EON-supplied prototypes.
- Understand the common meaning for some field names.
- Learn about the most versatile and popular prototypes.

Key Terms

derivative prototype	***reset***
orthographic viewport	

Introduction to the EON-Supplied Prototypes

This lesson explores the many prototypes supplied with an EON installation. These prototypes are grouped into prototype libraries. You can recognize these libraries in the Components window because their names are displayed in parentheses, such as (Camera Functions).

Because EON has so many prototypes, it is impossible to explain how all of the prototypes work in this lesson. Instead, we will present an overview of the prototypes so you will learn where to look for certain types of functionality. We will take a closer look at some important prototypes and introduce you to many other useful prototypes. We also will look at some common field names to apply your knowledge to other prototypes.

How Are Prototypes Different from Nodes?

Nodes are individual building blocks, whereas prototypes are assemblies of nodes, merged into an encapsulated subtree and saved as a reusable component. Therefore, compared with nodes, prototypes typically have a more specialized purpose and function. Although a prototype looks the same as a node in the simulation tree and the prototype's field values can be customized like a node's field values, one important difference is that when a prototype's values are changed during runtime, those changes are not saved. When the simulation shuts down, a prototype instance's fields revert to the values they had before the simulation started.

cross-reference

To understand what prototypes are and how they work, see Module 8 Lesson 1. To learn how to develop your own prototypes, see Module 8 Lesson 3.

Most Versatile Prototypes

Obviously, the value and versatility of a prototype is subjective—it will vary from person to person and from time to time. The prototypes listed in Table 8.2.1 solve common problems and simplify complex functions. These prototypes, which offer extra functionality or introduce new capabilities, will be explained in greater detail later in this lesson.

TABLE 8.2.1 Top Ten Most Versatile Prototypes

Prototype Name	Description	Icon
BPButton	A box-positioned button placed under the Camera node.	
OrbitNav	Navigation system to rotate, pan, and zoom.	
OrbitNavHierarchyExplorer	Works with the OrbitNav prototype to hide/show shapes that are grouped in a hierarchy.	
MenuSwitch	Generates a pop-up menu, with names of the Frame nodes, that is used to control mutually exclusive visibility of the frames.	
RecordPath	Provides KeyFrame recording, editing, and saving functions.	
ShapeAnimator	Toggles visibility on/off for a series of shapes within a frame to produce an animated effect.	
MoveRotateArrows3D	Allows you to move and rotate an object by dragging or clicking a set of navigational "arrow" handles.	
PopupUnlimited	With script, easily creates pop-up menus with unlimited menu items.	
TVChannelSwitcher	Allows you to click a shape (such as a television) to change channels (movies or cameras) and automates usage of the RenderTexture node.	
ConnectionManager	Manages connections between a set of frames. Use it to snap objects into position and then move them as one object.	

Most Frequently Used Prototypes

The most frequently used prototypes include OrbitNav, OrbitNavLookHereAtStart, ObjectNav, KeySensorPlus, Keys1to10, SimulationStartedEvent, Cube, Sphere, Square, Teapot, Chamber, and Hall. We will look at several of these prototypes.

cross-reference

Review the commonly used prototypes in Module 1 Lesson 3.

The OrbitNav prototype is similar to the ObjectNav prototype, which was created for earlier versions of EON, but OrbitNav is now the preferred prototype. OrbitNav has a host of prototypes that work with it to extend its functionality. For example, the OrbitNavLookHereAtStart prototype, as the name implies, centers the camera on the frame containing a certain object at the start of a simulation. The OrbitNav prototype's zoom distance transitions (instantly or using a reset time value) from the camera's original position to a value equal to the world position of the frame containing the object.

The KeySensorPlus prototype is a replacement for the older KeyboardSensor node. It lets you specify a key by typing the character instead of selecting it from a list. This makes it much easier to see the key used in the Property Bar. It displays the character instead of the character's keycode (number).

The Keys1to10 prototype is a valuable time-saver. Instead of inserting ten different KeyboardSensor nodes or KeySensorPlus prototypes, the Keys1to10 prototype has outEvents for each key between 1 and 10. (The 0 key is used as the tenth key.) It also can send numbers between 1 and 10 and sum two values before sending a value.

The SimulationStartedEvent prototype sends an event at the start of a simulation. You may also use the OnRunFalse outEvent of a time sensor set to 0.1 seconds, but the SimulationStartedEvent is quicker and easier to understand in the Routes window because, as its name implies, it does one specific thing, whereas a TimeSensor node could be used for various purposes.

The Cube, Sphere, Square, and Teapot prototypes are 3D shape objects that are typically used for testing purposes. For example, you can add a cube and scale it to the shape of a pillar, use a sphere to show a clickable position, or use a square to display an image.

The Chamber and Hall prototypes are environments that you can quickly and easily insert in your simulation to test navigational features as you add them.

Derivative Prototypes

A ***derivative prototype*** is based on or derived from another prototype and typically maintains a close resemblance to the original prototype. For example, two prototypes may be identical except for the assigned prototype names and icons. A derivative prototype may be created to provide a new name and icon to effectively communicate an alternative use for the original prototype. A derivative prototype also may be created to provide a subtle change in functionality.

For example, the BPButton can be used to create a textured background, but users may not think of using it in that way. Therefore, the BPButton was cloned and then modified. Some of the fields that were not required were removed, some of the default values of the other fields were changed, and some fields were renamed. Then, the derivative prototype was packaged as TexturedBackground(BP) with a new name, icon, and description.

The following derivative prototypes have been created in EON:

- BackButton(BP), TexturedBackground(BP), ColoredBorder(BP), BPButtonLite, and BPSimple are derivatives of BPButton.
- MaterialChanger, CameraChanger, DiffuseTextureChanger, MeshNodeChanger, RenderTreeChanger, and TextureUVMapChanger are derivatives of NodeRefChanger.
- ObjectNavLITE is a derivative of ObjectNav.
- BoundingBoxOutline is a derivative of BoundingBox.

Prototype Libraries

Prototypes are categorized into prototype libraries. Some prototypes are difficult to categorize, so they may not seem to belong in any particular library. Most of the EON-supplied prototypes can be classified as either functional or object prototypes—functional prototypes perform an action and object prototypes mostly contain 3D objects. The library names in Table 8.2.2 followed by an asterisk (*) are object prototypes.

cross-reference

You can review information about functional prototypes and object prototypes in Module 8 Lesson 1.

TABLE 8.2.2 Prototype Libraries

Library	Description
3DShapes*	3D geometries, initially 2 x 2 x 2 meters in size, with customizable color, position, and size properties.
Buttons	Clickable user interface elements.
Camera Functions	Camera movement controls, including motion models.
Collision Tools	Functions used to set up collision geometry and use the CollisionObject node.
Converters	Changes one form of data into a different form that can be used in your simulation.
Developer Tools	Functions that help you develop simulations. Many are not used in the final EON application.
Dynamics Tools	Functions that work with the Dynamics nodes in EON Professional.
Environments*	Ready-to-use 3D models of various environments.
GUIControl Functions	Functions that are created using GUIControl nodes or that extend the usefulness of GUIControl nodes.
JoyStick Related	Functions that simplify the use of a joystick with well-named outEvents and a motion model function.
Node Changers	Functions that let you send node references to other nodes. NodeRefChanger is a generic prototype. All of the other prototypes in the library are derivatives of the NodeRefChanger prototype.
Object Movers	Functions that help you move objects, usually with a mouse and keyboard.
ObjectNav	Old navigation system used to rotate, zoom, and pan. The pivot point stays in the object.
OrbitNav	New navigation system used to rotate, zoom, and pan. The pivot position moves when panning. Many add-on functions are available.
Particle Systems	Functions that create particle system effects such as smoke, fire, bubbles, stars, fog, and so on.
Peripheral Tools	Functions that work with the Peripheral Nodes library that are related to external hardware.
Philips Screen	Functions that support features of the Phillips 3D autostereoscopic display hardware.
Useful Functions	Functions that cannot be categorized elsewhere. This group holds the most prototypes.
Useful Objects*	3D objects that are combined with other functions or are highly configurable.

troubleshooting

The libraries in your EON installation depend on your software version. New EON-supplied libraries can be added when EON is upgraded or updated. Newer versions of EON contain additional libraries, such as Furniture (object prototypes), Old Prototypes (a collection of prototypes that have been replaced by newer prototypes), and others.

Selecting a Prototype Library

As you learned in Module 1, if you know which library a prototype is in but you do not know the prototype's name, you can select the prototype library from the drop-down list at the top of the Components window to limit the prototypes displayed in the Components window. If you know the name of the prototype but not in which prototype library it is located, you can select All Prototypes from the drop-down list at the top of the Components window. You can use the text box under the drop-down

cross-reference

Review node libraries and prototype libraries in Module 1 Lesson 3.

list to filter the list. If you type an M in the text box, for example, the prototypes starting with the letter M are displayed. If you type more than one letter in the text box, the list will be filtered further, as shown in Figure 8.2.1.

FIGURE 8.2.1 Finding a prototype

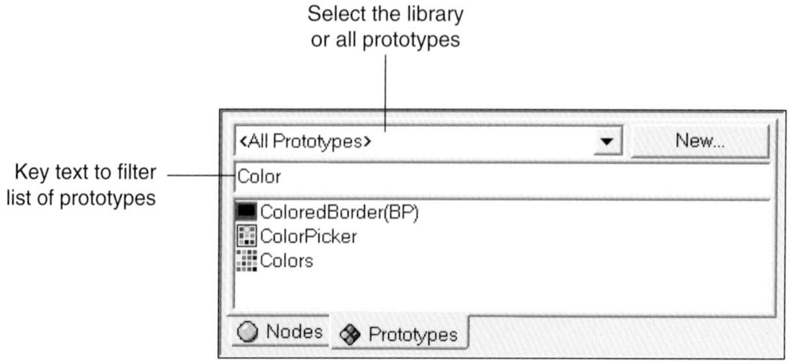

Using Selected Prototypes

The following sections contain information about several prototypes available in the EON prototype libraries. Explore the specified prototypes in the Components window, view the demonstration files identified in the Discuss sidebars, and consider how these prototypes might be used in your simulations.

Using Prototypes in the 3DShapes Library

Prototypes in the 3DShapes prototype library are very useful when you want to create test applications quickly. They reduce the need to import project-specific geometry when testing initial simulation functionality. Each 3DShapes prototype has Position, Orientation, and Scale fields that you can use to control their placement in 3D space rather than requiring separate parent Frame nodes for that purpose. This enables you to place one or more 3DShapes prototypes under a single Frame node.

Apart from their different shapes, the prototypes in the 3DShapes library are quite uniform. They are based on the new Mesh2 visual nodes and are scaled to fit into a 2 × 2 × 2-meter cube. Each prototype's origin is located in the center of its shape. By default, each 3DShapes prototype has orange material and identical values for the Position, Orientation, and Scale fields.

Using Prototypes in the Buttons Library

Prototypes in the Buttons library are graphical elements that a user clicks to perform an action. Buttons are important elements in many simulations.

The BPButton prototype is essentially a rectangular surface that accepts a texture and is positioned like a 2D element using pixel size and pixel coordinates. The BPButton must be placed under the Camera node, and it is always rendered facing the camera. The applied texture automatically scales to fit the BPButton when its BoxSize property is modified. The BPButton prototype has a BoxPosition field like a 2DText node. The BoxPosition field is the source of the *BP* part of the prototype's name. The BPButton is rich in extra features, which will be explored later in this lesson.

- Among other prototypes, the Buttons library contains the BPButton prototype and five derivatives of the BPButton prototype: BPButtonLite, BPSimple, ColoredBorder(BP), BackButton(BP), and TexturedBackground(BP).
- The BackButton prototype (not the BackButton(BP) prototype) was created long before the BPButton prototype. Although it is similar to the BPButton prototype, you cannot apply a texture to the older BackButton prototype.

- The PopupMenu node replaces the Menu prototype, which was based on the old TextBox node.
- The ToggleButton prototype simulates a button that appears to depress when the user clicks it. The button stays down until the user clicks it again. Therefore, it functions well as an On/Off button.

Activity 8.2.1: Using the BPButton Prototype

troubleshooting

This activity may require EON Professional. Depending on your configuration of EON modules, you may not be able to complete this activity.

1. Open EON. Open **Activity_8.2.1.eoz** from the data files for Module 8 Lesson 2.
2. Save the simulation as **BPButton.eoz**.
3. Add a **BPButton** prototype from the Buttons library to the Camera frame.
4. To create a node reference, right-click **Viewports\Viewport** and select **Copy as Link**. Paste it under **BPButton\ViewportNode**.
5. Save the simulation and then run the simulation.

Discussion

discuss

What is the default texture used by the BPButton prototype?

Would you use its default texture in a simulation?

6. Close the simulation window.
7. To create a node reference, right-click **TextureResourceGroup\home** and select **Copy as Link**. Paste it under **BPButton\Texture**.
8. Save the simulation and then run the simulation. Your simulation window should look like Figure 8.2.2.

FIGURE 8.2.2 BPButton with home texture

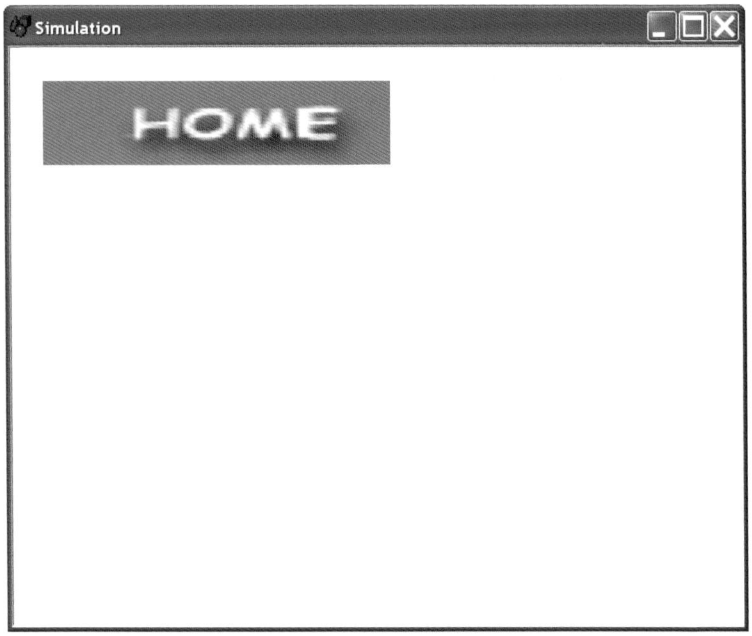

9. Close the simulation window.
10. Select the **BPButton** prototype in the simulation tree. In the Property Bar, set the BoxSize to **62 27** and set the BoxPosition to **5 5**.
11. Save the simulation and then run it. The texture on the button should appear more accurately proportioned, and the button should be closer to the upper-left corner of the simulation window.
12. Close the simulation window.
13. Select the **BPButton** prototype in the simulation tree again. In the Property Bar, place a check mark in the **EnableMouseOver** check box, setting the field to true. This setting enables you to modify the button's appearance when the user moves the mouse over the button in the simulation window. By default, the button's size is doubled. Also, you can change the button's opacity and texture.
14. To create a node reference, right-click **TextureResourceGroup\home_over** and select **Copy as Link**. Paste it under **BPButton\MouseOverTexture**. Your simulation tree should look like Figure 8.2.3.

FIGURE 8.2.3 Simulation tree with the BPButton prototype's appearance established

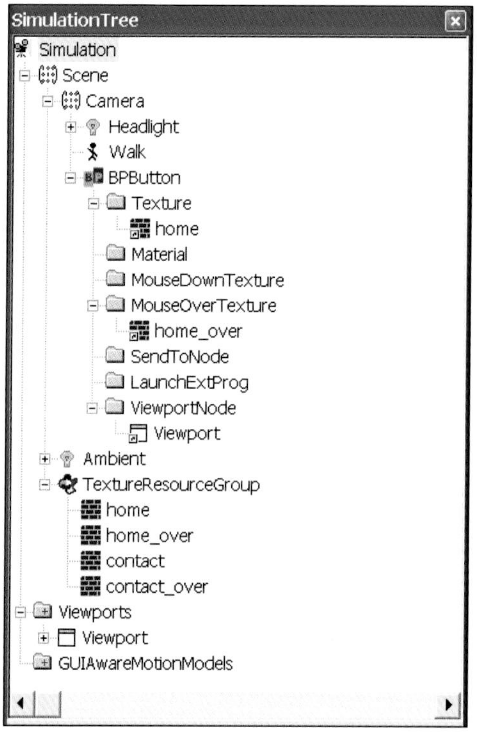

tips+tricks

The BPButton prototype contains a normal 3D object, a square, which is positioned and scaled so that it behaves like a 2D object. When the window's size changes, the 3D object normally changes size proportionally. However, the BPButton prototype senses changes to the window's size and adjusts the 3D object's position and size so that it continues to behave like a 2D object with fixed pixel position and pixel size.

15. Select the **BPButton** prototype in the simulation tree again. In the Property Bar, set the MouseOverSizeFactor to **1** so that the button will not change size when the user moves the mouse over the button.
16. Save the simulation and then run the simulation. Verify that the button's appearance changes correctly when you move the mouse over the button.
17. Select the **BPButton** prototype in the simulation tree again. In the Property Bar, clear the **RefreshEverySecond** check box, changing the field's value from true to false. Now BPButton will not refresh its window size, and the button will start to work like a normal 3D object.
18. Save the simulation and then run it. Press **Ctrl + F** to enter and exit Full-size Window mode (or change the size of the simulation window by dragging the edges).

Discussion

discuss

How does the button change when you adjust the size of the simulation window?

19. Close the simulation window.
20. Select the **BPButton** prototype in the simulation tree again if necessary. In the Property Bar, place a check mark in the **RefreshEverySecond** check box, changing its value back to true. Repeat steps 18 and 19. Notice that the refresh can be slow. Verify that the **RefreshEverySecond** check box is selected.
21. Add a **GrandRoom** prototype to the Scene frame.
22. Select the **Camera** frame. In the Property Bar, set its Position field to **0 -10 1.5**.
23. Add a **Place** node to the Camera frame and rename the Place node **MoveHome**. Set the values in the Translation field to **0 -10 1.5**. Set the values in the TransTime and RotTime fields to **1 1 1**. This sets the time to move for all directions (X, Y, Z, H, P, and R) to one second. Clear the check mark in the **Active** check box, setting the field to false. The Property Bar should look like Figure 8.2.4.

FIGURE 8.2.4 Property Bar for the MoveHome node

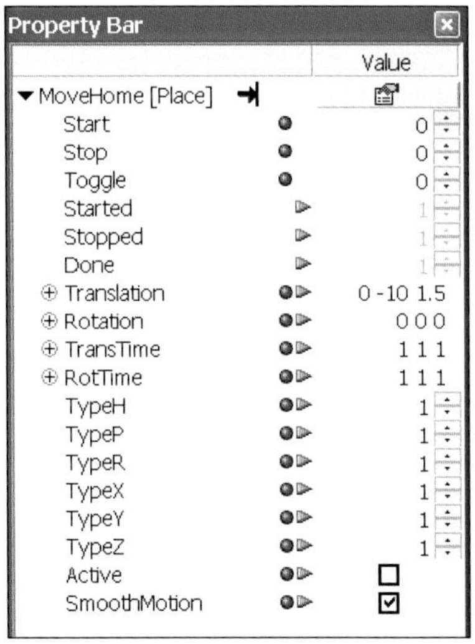

24. To create a node reference, right-click the **MoveHome** node and select **Copy as Link**. Paste it under **BPButton\SendToNode**. Now the Home button will move the camera to a "home" position.
25. Save the simulation and then run the simulation. Navigate to a new location. Click the **Home** button to verify that the camera moves to the initial location.
26. Close the simulation window.
27. Add the **ColoredBorder(BP)** prototype to the Camera frame and rename the prototype **Border**. ColoredBorder(BP) is a BPButton derivative that will display a border around the button.
28. To create a node reference, right-click the **Viewports\Viewport** node and select **Copy as Link**. Paste it under **Border\ViewportNode**.

tips+tricks

You can improve the refresh rate by creating routes between the Simulation node's WindowWidth and WindowHeight fields to the BPButton prototype's fields with the same name. When you have several BPButton prototypes, use the RefreshGroup prototype to improve the refresh rate.

tips+tricks

The distance from the camera of the BPButton can be controlled by five fields, which include PlaceAtFarClip and PlaceAtNearClip. By default, the PlaceAtNearClip field is true and the other is false. If both were false, then the DistanceFromCam field would determine the distance.

29. Display the **Routes** window. Drag the **BPButton** prototype and the **Border** node to the Routes window. Establish the connections outlined in the following table.

From	outEvent	To	inEvent
BPButton	AbsoluteBPOut	Border	BoxPosition
BPButton	BoxSizeOut	Border	BoxSize

30. Save the simulation and then run it. You will see a red rectangle displayed in front of the BPButton.
31. Close the simulation window.
32. In the Property Bar, set the Border node's DistanceFromNearClip field to **0.1**. Because the Home BPButton is at the NearClip, this setting places the border slightly behind the Home button.
33. Set the Border node's Color field to **black**.
34. Change the Border node's ExpandAllSidesBy value to **1**. By default, the border is 2 pixels wide because the default value of the ExpandAllSidesBy field is 2.
35. Place a check mark in the BPButton prototype's **EnableMove** check box, setting the field to true. Notice that the MoveMouseButton field's value is 1, meaning that you can use the middle mouse button to move the button.
36. Save the simulation and then run it. Drag the **Home** button using the middle mouse button. Notice that the Border remains with the button.
37. Close the simulation window.
38. Drag the **BPButton** prototype from the LocalPrototypes window to the Camera frame. Name the new prototype instance **ContactButton**.
39. To create a node reference, right-click **Viewports\Viewport** and select **Copy as Link**. Paste it under **ContactButton\ViewportNode**.
40. To create a node reference, right-click **TextureResourceGroup\contact** and select **Copy as Link**. Paste it under **ContactButton\Texture**.
41. To create a node reference, right-click **TextureResourceGroup\contact_over** and select **Copy as Link**. Paste it under **ContactButton\MouseOverTexture**.
42. Select the **ContactButton** prototype in the simulation tree. In the Property Bar, place a check mark in the **EnableMouseOver** check box, setting the field to true. Set the MouseOverSizeFactor to **1**. Set the BoxSize to **96 27**. Set the DistanceFromNearClip to **0.05**.
43. Display the **Routes** window. Drag the **ContactButton** prototype from the simulation tree to the Routes window. Establish the connection outlined in the following table.

From	outEvent	To	inEvent
BPButton	RelativeBPOut	ContactButton	BoxPosition

44. Set the ContactButton prototype's BPOffset field to **64 0**. The route established in the previous step placed the ContactButton in the same position as the BPButton. The BPOffset field moves the Contact button so that both buttons are visible.

45. Select the BPButton prototype instance in the simulation tree. In the Property Bar, place a check mark in the **ToggleCornerOnRightClick** check box to set the field to true.
46. Display the **Routes** window. Establish the connection outlined in the following table. Your Routes window should resemble Figure 8.2.5.

From	outEvent	To	inEvent
BPButton	Corner	ContactButton	Corner

FIGURE 8.2.5 Routes window with connections to position buttons

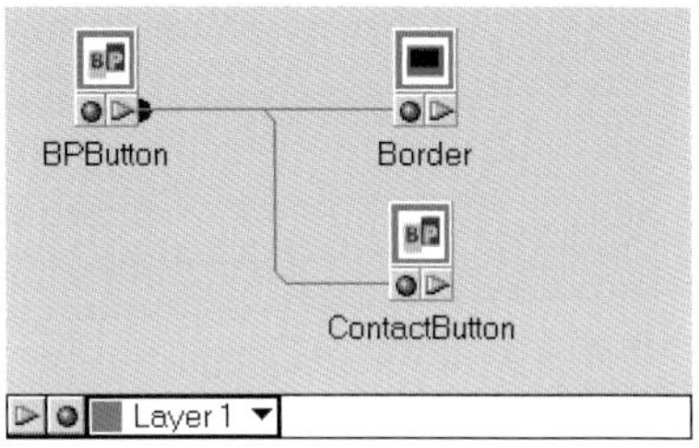

47. Save the simulation and then run it. Drag the **Home** button and verify that the Contact button moves with the Home button. Right-click the **Home** button. Notice that the Contact button may be displayed on the left or right side of the Home button because the BPOffset value is relative to the corner as well.
48. Close the simulation window. Close EON.

Using Prototypes in the Camera Functions Library

Prototypes in the Camera Functions library alter the orientation and position of the Camera frame. Motion Model nodes, such as the KeyMove and Walk nodes, are typically placed under a Camera frame to enable an end user to move the Camera frame using a keyboard or mouse. Many of the prototypes in the Camera Functions, OrbitNav, and ObjectNav libraries can be used in a similar manner. However, they include specialized features beyond basic Motion Model nodes.

- SphereNav prototype: Similar to the OrbitNav and ObjectNav prototypes, but the SphereNav prototype's rotation is around screen coordinates. Experiment with the prototypes to see the difference.
- MapNav2D prototype: Used for navigating within a 2D plane or orthographic viewport. An ***orthographic viewport*** is one without 3D perspective and is often referred to as a 2D view. Because orthographic viewports lack the perspective view, all objects appear to be the same size regardless of their actual distance from the camera.
- XYNav prototype: An alternative to the Walk node, except that the XYNav prototype cannot rotate the camera. It moves the camera in the X and Y planes relative to the direction that the camera is facing. Pressing the Z key allows you to switch to moving the camera in the X and Z planes.
- ZNav prototype: Similar to the XYNav prototype, but it only moves in the Z plane. You could combine the XYNav and ZNav prototypes with the Walk node so that you can use the LookAround function of the Walk node on the middle mouse button.

- SuperMan prototype: A flying motion model. You accelerate forward and backward by pressing and holding the left and right mouse buttons respectively until you reach a set maximum speed. You then steer by moving the mouse in a left or right direction.
- Zoom prototype: A quick way to zoom in or out. It is triggered by pressing the spacebar and the B key. This prototype does not move the Camera frame like others in this library. Instead, it alters the Viewport node's FieldOfView field.
- WindowEdgeMover and KeyMoverXY prototypes: These prototypes work with the XYPlaneMover prototype to move the camera. The WindowEdgeMover prototype senses when the mouse cursor is near the edge of a window and then sends events to the XYPlaneMover prototype to move the camera in the appropriate direction. The KeyMover prototype, like the WalkAbout node, enables you to use the four arrow keys to move the camera.
- StayAbove prototype: Senses the terrain or floor under the camera and ensures that the camera stays a certain distance above it. This is similar to the AvatarCollision prototype.
- ZoomToArea prototype: Enables you to select an area to zoom in on within an orthographic viewport simply by drawing a 2D box using the mouse. It is commonly used with other prototypes, such as MousePos3D and OrthoZoomer.

Using Prototypes in the Collision Tools Library

In the real world, you can usually assume that a physical table will support objects you place on it and that a wall will impede the motion of objects that come into contact with it. In computer-generated environments, the opposite is true. For a wall to impede motion, an algorithm must control and enforce such behavior in a simulation; otherwise, the object would be able to pass through the wall. Collision prototypes simplify the implementation of realistic collision behavior between objects in the simulation environment. This library is similar to the Developer Tools library, but it focuses specifically on collisions.

- AvatarCollision prototype: Can be placed directly below the Camera frame. The key to making this work and look realistic is to be certain that the size of the avatar fits the size of the environment. The AvatarCollision prototype has four spheres that represent the collision geometry. Functions enable an avatar to jump over small objects and walk up stairs. This prototype enables avatars to walk up a steep incline without automatically sliding down when you stop navigating. You should use a Walk or WalkAbout node to navigate with this prototype.
- CollisionGeometryBox and CollisionGeometrySphere prototypes: These prototypes can be used as collision objects instead of visible geometry. The ShowCollisionGeometry prototype enables you to show and hide the bounding box for collision geometries. It works on the CollisionGeometryBox and CollisionGeometrySphere prototypes as well as the RigidBody, CollisionObject, and Frame nodes.

Using Prototypes in the Converters Library

A simple converter receives a value in an initial data type format, converts the value to another data type format, and then outputs a new value in the converted data type format. For example, a prototype in this library could receive a Boolean value, such as true, and output a numeric value, such as 1. Some of the prototypes in the Converters library require several inEvents to calculate an output value for the outEvent.

- Adapter prototype: Converts SFVec3f into SFFloat data types and vice versa. The BooleanSplitter prototype enables you to send various outEvents. For example, it can send the false value when true or false is received.

- Convert3DPosToScreenPos prototype: Enables you to place a 2DText node on a 3D object. As you navigate in 3D, it will move the 2DText node's BoxPosition field.
- MouseToBoxPosition prototype: Enables you to display a 2DText field following the mouse cursor. The MouseToTextBoxPos prototype will perform the same function for the older TextBox node.
- MousePos3D prototype: Provides the position of the mouse cursor when using orthographic viewports. Its output is used by the MoveRotateArrows2D and ZoomToArea prototypes.

tips+tricks

Remember that EON also has the Converter node, which handles most data type conversions.

Using Prototypes in the Developer Tools Library

The prototypes in the Developer Tools library simplify the development of EON applications. Some of the prototypes are not intended to remain in the final EON application because they only assist in development tasks by assigning values to node properties or by displaying data necessary to ensure that program logic is correct.

- BoxEditor and BoxEditorDisplay prototypes: These prototypes are tools to help you create boxframes. A boxframe is simply a Frame node in which the frame's Position, Orientation, and Scale fields specify the location and size of a box or 3D space. Boxframes are used by the CollisionBoxes and CollisionBoxesAdv prototypes. These prototypes aim to keep the camera inside a box, but allow the camera to pass between overlapping boxes. It is an extremely efficient collision system, but it is limited because it can only keep the camera inside specific areas, not keep it outside of the specific areas.
- CgDetect prototype: Determines whether Cg Shaders are supported. This prototype can be used to show alternative materials.
- EventInfo prototype: A very useful testing and debugging tool. You can connect routes of any data type to it and it will display that data on the screen. This tells you when and what data is sent and can be used to identify the events that have occurred. Press the E key to display the data.
- EventSender prototype: Always a useful prototype to have in your simulation. Press the Insert key to display a dialog box that enables you to identify a frame that should be displayed or hidden. To hide something, add an underscore character after the frame's name. Also, you can send values to nodes. For example, enter Rotate,LapTime,5 to send 5 to the Rotate node's LapTime field.
- NumberSender, TextSender, MultiTextSender, and SendToGroup prototypes: Prototypes used to send data to nodes. Typically, a Boolean outEvent from a ClickSensor or KeyboardSensor node sends data, such as a number or text. You can use these prototypes to perform similar tasks.
- OrthoZoomer prototype: Enables you to zoom within an orthographic viewport. You can define the size, measured in meters, that should be displayed. It will adjust the Viewport node's FieldOfView field accordingly.
- QuickPos prototype: Will display a Frame node's Position, Orientation, and Scale values in a 2DText node. Press the Q key in the simulation window to display the information for 10 seconds.
- RecordPath prototype: Enables you to record, edit, and save KeyFrame animations. It is most suited for recording camera paths. It is a developer tool because you use the prototype only to develop or create the path. After the path is finished, the prototype is disabled or deleted. It is particularly useful for making paths for the humans from the Humans module of EON Professional. The RecordPath prototype is part of the EON Professional product package.

Activity 8.2.2: Using the RecordPath Prototype

1. Open EON to start a new simulation. If EON is already open, select **New** from the File menu.
2. Add the **TownSquare** prototype from the Environments library to the Scene frame.
3. Select the **Camera** frame. Set the Camera frame's Position value to **0 -10 2**.
4. Add a **KeyFrame** node to the Camera frame.
5. Add the **RecordPath** prototype from the Developer Tools library to the KeyFrame node.
6. Save the simulation as **RecordPath.eoz** and then run the simulation. Notice the menu button in the upper-left corner that enables you to access all of the functions of this prototype. See Figure 8.2.6.

FIGURE 8.2.6 Simulation window with the RecordPath prototype

7. Click the **Menu** button and select the **Record New Path** option. The Menu button will disappear.
8. Press the **spacebar** to start recording. Navigate around the town using the Walk node. When you are done, press the **spacebar** again. The Menu button reappears. The path has been recorded and put into the KeyFrame node. You can use the controls at the bottom of the simulation window to control the KeyFrame. Drag the **slider** to interactively explore the camera path.
9. Click the **Menu** button and choose **Trim Path**. This allows you to remove the first part and the last part of your path. Drag the **sliders** to adjust the start and end position and then click the **OK** button.
10. Click the **Menu** button and choose **Save Path** from the menu. Type a filename and click the **Save** button. The file is saved to a text file in the c:\ folder.

troubleshooting

If you click outside the simulation, you will not be able to save the path; you will have to record and trim again.

11. Click the **Menu** button and choose **Record Over Path**. Click the **H** button to record over the heading direction. Click **OK**. Press the **spacebar** to start and stop recording. The heading direction is not changed, but you can rotate the camera and the new heading values will be saved.
12. Click the **Play** button at the bottom of the window to see the path with the adjusted heading.
13. Click the **Stop** button at the bottom of the simulation window.
14. Close the simulation window. Save the simulation as **RecordPath.eoz** and then close EON.

tips+tricks

The Record Over Path function can be useful if you want different Orientation values for the Camera frame.

Using Prototypes in the GUIControl Functions Library

Most of the prototypes in the GUIControl Functions library build on or perform tasks similar to various nodes in the GUIControls node library. The prototypes within the GUIControl Functions library provide common graphic user elements such as dialog boxes, sliders, and pop-up menus.

- 2DText prototype: Very similar to the 2DText node. It enables the entry of multiple lines of text with explicit line breaks by using a designated new line character (the # character is the default).
- AlertMsgBox, ConfirmMsgBox, and InputMsgBox prototypes: These prototypes are similar to pop-up dialog boxes that tell the user something or ask the user for confirmation or data.
- OpenDialog, SaveAsDialog, and FileSelecter prototypes: These prototypes have been superseded by the OpenSaveDialog node.
- ChooseFolderDialog prototype: Uses an ActiveX control to show the standard Windows dialog box for choosing a folder.
- GroupGUINodes prototype: Can display, hide, and position a group of GUIControls nodes.
- MoveGUINodes prototype: Can be used to drag and drop various GUIControls nodes and the 2DText prototype by altering the BoxPosition field value.
- MenuSwitch prototype: Generates a pop-up menu of available frame names from which a user can select which frame is to be activated or made visible.
- SliderAuto prototype: A slider and a text box that will automatically resize itself to the full width of the simulation window. It can be placed at either the top or the bottom of the window.
- SliderPlus prototype: Has three visual elements in one: a label, a slider, and a generated value for the slider position. It is very useful for setting up slider-based GUIs.

Using Prototypes in the JoyStick Related Library

The prototypes in the JoyStick Related library simplify the use of joysticks for navigation. The outEvents are standardized so that the axis-type fields provide values that are between –1 and +1. An added advantage of these prototypes is that they have outEvent names based on popular commercial joystick and game controller products. The JoyStickNav prototype can be placed under the Camera frame. You can then connect routes from the JoyStick prototypes to the JoyStickNav prototype. Depending on the way you connect events, you can design different motion model support features.

Using Prototypes in the Node Changers Library

The NodeRefChanger prototype enables you to send node references to any node or prototype with an SFNode type field. The other prototypes in this library are derivatives of the NodeRefChanger prototype. They are basically the same as the

NodeRefChanger prototype, but some field names have been changed to enable the derived prototypes to complete specific precise tasks.

- CameraChanger prototype: Changes the Camera field of a Viewport node.
- DiffuseTextureChanger prototype: Changes the DiffuseTexture field of a Material2 node.
- LightMapTextureChanger prototype: Changes the LightMapTexture field of a Material2 node.
- MaterialChanger prototype: Changes the Material field of a Shape node.
- MeshNodeChanger prototype: Changes the Geometry field of a Shape node.
- RenderTreeChanger prototype: Changes the RenderTree field of a Viewport node.
- TextureUVMapChanger prototype: Changes the TextureUVMap field of a Material2 node.
- NodeRefChanger prototype: Uses the PageUp and PageDown keys to switch the node references, or you can use the inEvents named DoNodeRef1 through DoNodeRef6.

troubleshooting

Do not forget to zoom in before clicking the sofa or other shapes and materials. Zooming in ensures that you are selecting the correct item. If you do not zoom in first, you could be selecting a Shape or Material2 node for a transparent object between the camera and your intended target. For example, the ceiling or a light fixture suspended from the ceiling could be located in front of the camera, and you might inadvertently select it instead of the sofa.

Activity 8.2.3: Using the MaterialChanger Prototype

1. Open EON. Open **Activity_8.2.3.eoz** from the data files for Module 8 Lesson 2.
2. Save the simulation as **MaterialChanger.eoz** and then run the simulation. Notice the sofa in the furnished apartment. You will change the sofa's material in this activity.
3. Move the simulation window so that you can view the toolbars and the simulation window at the same time. In the simulation window, zoom in so that you are slightly above the surface of the sofa.
4. Click the **Enter Shape selection mode** button. Click anywhere inside the simulation window to give the focus to that window, and then press the **Alt** key while you click the sofa. A Shape node is selected automatically in the simulation tree.

5. Right-click the selected **Shape** node and click the **Copy as Link** option.
6. Close the simulation window.
7. Add a **NodeRefChanger** prototype to the Scene frame. Paste the Shape node reference into the NodeRefChanger prototype's **SendToNodes** field.

tips+tricks

Regardless of the complexity of the simulation tree or the language used to create a simulation, the selection tools can quickly locate shapes, geometries, materials, and textures.

Discussion

discuss

You could use a MaterialChanger prototype in step 7. Investigate the differences between the NodeRefChanger prototype and the MaterialChanger prototype. Why would you choose to use one of the prototypes?

8. Expand the **Shape** node. Expand its **Material** node, copy its node reference, and paste it into the NodeRefChanger's **NodeReferences** field. Your simulation tree should look like Figure 8.2.7.

FIGURE 8.2.7 Simulation tree with the NodeRefChanger prototype

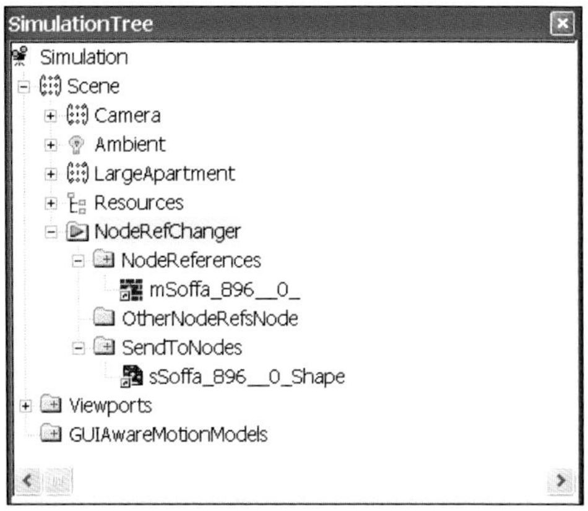

9. Save the simulation and then run it. While the simulation is running, you will choose more materials that could be used on the sofa.
10. Click the **Enter Material selection mode** button. 
11. Press the **Alt** key while you click the carpet under the coffee table. This selects a Material2 node in the simulation tree. Right-click the selected node and click the **Copy as Link** option. Paste it into the NodeRefChanger prototype's **NodeReferences** field.
12. Repeat step 11 to create a node reference for the floor material.
13. Close the simulation window. You have three Material2 node references in the NodeReferences field.
14. Select the **NodeRefChanger** prototype in the simulation tree. In the Property Bar, type **Material** in the SendToField field.
15. Expand the **NodeReferences** field in the Property Bar. We are preparing to send these Material2 node references to the Material field of a Shape node.
16. Save the simulation and then run it. Adjust the sofa's appearance by pressing the **Page Up** and **Page Down** keys to cycle through the list of values in the NodeReferences field.
17. Close the simulation window.
18. Add a **2DText** node to the Scene frame and rename the node **DoCarpet**. In the Property Bar, set the node's Text field to **Put carpet material on the sofa**.
19. Add another **2DText** node to the Scene frame and rename the node **DoFloor**. In the Property Bar, set the node's Text field to **Put floor material on the sofa**.
20. In the Property Bar, set the DoFloor node's BoxPosition field to **10 40** and set its BoxArea to **220 20**.
21. Display the **Routes** window. Drag the **DoCarpet** node, the **DoFloor** node, and the **NodeRefChanger** prototype to the Routes window. Establish the connections outlined in the following table.

From	outEvent	To	inEvent
DoCarpet	OnButtonDown	NodeRefChanger	DoNodeRef2
DoFloor	OnButtonDown	NodeRefChanger	DoNodeRef3

tips+tricks

You can repeat step 11 to collect an unlimited number of node references to Material2 nodes.

tips+tricks

The NodeRefChanger prototype will allow you to select a node reference in several ways. The default method is to press the Page Down key or Page Up key to cycle forward and backward through the list of node references in the NodeReferences field. Also, you can send an integer to the NodeRefNrIn field or send a node reference to the NodeRefIn field or send a Boolean value to one of the fields named DoNodeRef1 to DoNodeRef6.

tips+tricks

The DoNodeRef2 inEvent of NodeRefChanger tells the prototype to send the second node reference from the NodeReferences field to the Material field of the Shape node in the SendToNodes field.

22. Add a **Keys1to10** prototype to the Scene frame.
23. Display the **Routes** window. Drag the **Keys1to10** prototype to the Routes window. Establish the connection outlined in the following table. Your Routes window should resemble Figure 8.2.8.

From	outEvent	To	inEvent
Keys1to10	KeyNr	NodeRefChanger	NodeRefNrIn

FIGURE 8.2.8 Routes window with Keys1to10 prototype

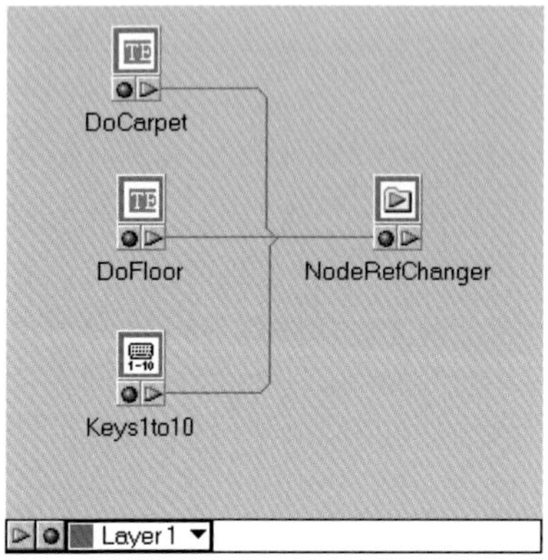

tips+tricks

If you have more than six materials, you must change the MaxNodeRefNr field in the NodeRefChanger prototype to identify the number of materials you have.

24. Save the simulation and then run it. Press the number keys to change the texture. If you press a number key that is higher than the number of material references available, nothing will happen.
25. Close the simulation window.
26. Add a new instance of the NodeRefChanger prototype in the Scene frame by dragging the **NodeRefChanger** prototype from the Local Prototypes window to the Scene frame. Name the new prototype instance **TVMaterialChanger**.
27. Save the simulation and then run it.
28. Click the **Enter Shape selection mode** button. Click anywhere in the simulation window to give the focus to that window. Press **Alt** and use the Shape selection tool to select the **TV screen** (not the TV box). Right-click the selected **Shape** node in the simulation tree and then select the **Copy as Link** option. Paste it in the TVMaterialChanger prototype's **SendToNodes** field.
29. Close the simulation window.
30. Add a **ClickSensor** node under the TV shape's parent frame, as shown in Figure 8.2.9.

FIGURE 8.2.9 Simulation tree with ClickSensor node added

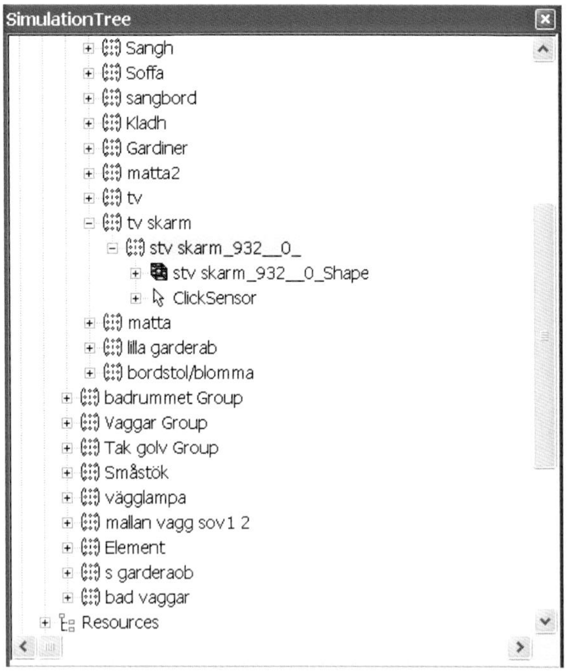

31. Display the **Routes** window. Drag the **ClickSensor** node and the **TVMaterialChanger** prototype to the Routes window. Establish the connection outlined in the following table.

From	outEvent	To	inEvent
ClickSensor	OnButtonDownTrue	TVMaterialChanger	Next

32. To create a node reference, right-click **Scene\Resources\Materials** and select **Copy as Link**. Paste it under **TVMaterialChanger\OtherNodeRefsNode** field. Note that 48 materials are available under Scene\Resources\Materials.
33. We want the prototype to use this node's children as the NodeReference list, so use the Property Bar to place a check mark in the **UseOtherNodeRefs** check box to set the field to true. Also in the Property Bar, verify that the OtherNodeRefsField is set to **Children**.
34. Select the **TVMaterialChanger** prototype. Clear the **EnableKeys** check box to set the value to false. This disables the keys on this prototype so that pressing the keys does not change both prototypes' values at the same time.
35. Set the SendToField field to **Material**.
36. Save the simulation and then run it. Clicking the TV screen should change the material displayed on its screen, enabling you to preview all of the materials in this file. The first material shown on the TV screen was not the original material because the NodeRefNrAtStart field is set to 1 and the SendNodeRefAtStart field is set to true.
37. Close the simulation window.
38. Select the **TVMaterialChanger** prototype. Set the NodeRefNrAtStart field to **30** and the MaxNodeRefNr field to **48** (this will enable you to cycle through all of the available material references).
39. Save the simulation and then run it. Verify that all of the modifications work.
40. Close the simulation window. Close EON.

tips+tricks

You can use a different method for preparing a list of Material2 nodes. Instead of copying node references to the NodeReferences field of the TVMaterialChanger, you can use the Materials Group node that has 48 Material2 children nodes.

tips+tricks

The KeyMover and Mover prototype combination is not the same as the KeyMove node. The KeyMover and Mover prototypes are similar to the OrbitNavButtons and OrbitNavKeyMover prototypes. The Mover prototype has a lot of MFNode fields that can hold references to 3D objects that act as buttons. This means you will not need to insert your own ClickSensor nodes.

Using Prototypes in the Object Movers Library

If you are creating a planning tool in which the user needs to move objects in 3D space, you have several options:

- MoveRotateArrows3D prototype: This prototype adds clickable, colored X, Y, Z, and H arrows to objects. The arrows extend from the center of the object. When the user drags or clicks an arrow, the object immediately responds by moving back and forth in the specified direction. A semi-transparent yellow box in the object's center allows the user to move the object in the XY plane. Pink curved arrows rotate the object in its heading direction.
- Mover prototype: Provides a simple way to position and rotate an object in the specific X, Y, Z, H, P, and R directions. The KeyMover prototype works with the Mover prototype by enabling the user to press the arrow keys to move the object.
- DragManager and DragSelecter prototypes: These prototypes work together to enable the user to drag and rotate objects. These prototypes are older; they were developed for earlier versions of EON Studio. Although they are rich in features, the drag method they use means that sometimes objects move too fast.
- PointedPos and StickyMover prototypes: These prototypes work together to move objects by placing them on the objects where the mouse is pointing. The MouseISector prototype is an older form of the PointedPos prototype.
- ZAdjust prototype: Similar to the StayAbove prototype, but it was defined for objects instead of the camera.

Using Prototypes in the ObjectNav Library

The ObjectNav prototype is a popular navigation system supported in previous versions of EON Studio to rotate, zoom, and pan. The OrbitNav prototype now supersedes the ObjectNav prototype. The two systems differ in that ObjectNav panning does not move the pivot position and OrbitNav panning does. Also, the ObjectNav prototype is not placed under the Camera frame. Instead, it can be placed under the Scene frame or a Frame node. The ObjectNav prototype's parent node is the location of the pivot position for rotation. Place this prototype under the object that you want to rotate around.

- ObjectNavLITE prototype: Identical to the ObjectNav prototype, but the number of fields and options has been reduced.
- ObjectNavManager prototype: Used to turn on and off several ObjectNav prototypes so that users can rotate around different objects.
- ObjectNavSelecter prototype: Enables you to choose different frames as the pivot position for a single ObjectNav prototype.
- ObjectNavZoomExtents prototype: Similar to the OrbitNavExplorer prototype because optimum zoom distances are calculated as you select different objects.

cross-reference

To review differences between the ObjectNav prototype and the OrbitNav prototype, see Module 1 Lesson 3.

Using Prototypes in the OrbitNav Library

The OrbitNav prototype provides a navigation system to rotate, zoom, and pan using the mouse. This library has prototypes that are designed to work with the OrbitNav prototype. They send events to the OrbitNav prototype, which has options to limit pitch and zoom.

- OrbitNavKeyOptions, OrbitNavMouseController, and OrbitNavSpin prototypes: These prototypes are already inside the OrbitNav prototype. Insert these prototypes only if you want to disable or customize the functions.

- OrbitNav-related prototypes: Many of these prototypes will move the camera in an action called ***resetting***. That is, the camera is moved without the user dragging the mouse. EON has many functions similar to resetting.
- OrbitNavReset prototype: Similar to a Place node because it holds only reset values that are sent to the OrbitNav prototype when triggered.
  - OrbitNavResetToStart prototype: Similar to the OrbitNavReset prototype except its reset values are automatically set to the values the OrbitNav prototype had when it started.
  - OrbitNavResetToClickPos prototype: Designed to get the position of the cursor when the mouse was clicked and use that location as the pivot position. Then orientation and zoom distances are calculated based on the current camera position.
  - OrbitNavResetToFramePos prototype: Obtains the pivot position of selected frames.
  - OrbitNavResetToBBox prototype: Obtains the pivot position of a selected frame's bounding box values and zooms in or out so that an object is fully in view without displaying more than necessary.
  - OrbitNavLookHereAtStart prototype: Similar to the OrbitNavResetToFramePos prototype, but it only happens when the simulation starts.
- OrbitNavButtons, OrbitNavKeyMover, and OrbitNavJoyStick prototypes: Enables you to use buttons, keys, and a joystick to rotate, zoom, and pan using inputs other than the mouse.
- OrbitNavViewMaker prototype: Allows you to save 10 camera positions and go to those positions by pressing the 1 to 0 keys. To save a position, hold down the S key and press a number. It is similar to the ViewMaker prototype in the Camera Functions library.
- OrbitNavExplorer prototype: Allows you to explore an object's parts. Right-click a part to hide all other objects. Right-click again to display all of the objects.
- OrbitNavHierarchyExplorer prototype: Enables you to probe deeper. Right-click to view fewer objects and middle-click to view more objects. With the OrbitNavExplorer and OrbitNavHierarchyExplorer prototypes, the OrbitNav prototype is reset so that the displayed objects are centered and the optimal zoom distance is calculated.

Using Prototypes in the Useful Functions Library

This library has a lot of diverse functions that cannot be grouped elsewhere. You can look at the prototypes to see the variety of functions in the library.

- ClickSensorPlus prototype: Has nine extra outEvents. Instead of only telling us the Shape node that was clicked, it also can tell us the related nodes, such as the Material2 node or its parent frame.
- CollisionBoxes prototype: A unique collision detection system that helps to keep the camera inside a group of overlapping bounding boxes. Although it is limited, it is a very efficient system that is rich with extra features.
- CollisionBoxesAdv prototype: Similar to the CollisionBoxes prototype except that the boxes can be freely rotated.
- KeySensorPlus, Keys1to10, ToggleKey, OnOffForFrame, SmoothKeySensor, and WordTrigger prototypes: Key-related prototypes in this library.
- MouseInViewport, ClickSensorOnOff, and Walk OnOff prototypes: These three prototypes are related. The last two prototypes turn off nodes when the mouse is outside a viewport.

- FloatingViewport prototype: Enables you to specify the viewport position and size in pixels. The ViewportResizer prototype will smoothly change the position and size of a viewport.
- OpenCloseLatch prototype: Useful when you have two Place nodes to open and close a door or drawer. Just place node references to the Place nodes in the OpenNode and CloseNode fields and connect a route to the Toggle inEvent.
- HighLighter prototype: Can change the material of any object that you mouse over or click.
- InactivitySensor prototype: Similar to a screen saver. It triggers a node or prototype when the mouse has not moved or been clicked for a set number of seconds.

Using Prototypes in the Useful Objects Library

This library contains objects that are useful tools for developing simulations. These prototypes can be used in a variety of situations.

- 3DPointer prototype: Useful when you are developing applications in which you need to visualize a position.
- AutomaticArrows prototype: Repositions the arrows when the window size changes, similar to the BPButton prototype.
- BoundingBox and BoundingBoxOutline prototypes: Similar to each other. Use them to indicate that an object is selected.
- Background prototype: Replaced by the TexturedBackground(BP) prototype in EON Professional.
- ScaledLine and ScaledLine3D prototypes: Similar to each other. They create a line between two positions that can be updated in real time. The ScaledLine prototype has a fixed Z component and is more suitable for orthographic viewports.
- MoveableWalls prototype: Used in orthographic viewports and is designed to send events to the CustomRoom prototype to change its size.
- GridPlane2 prototype: A better choice than the GridPlane prototype because you can specify the size and the gridlines are produced by a texture that you can replace.
- GridPlane prototype: Provides a simple 10 × 10-meter plane with intersecting gridlines resulting in 100 squares. The gridline color, background color, and scale can be modified, but the grid count cannot.

General Tips for Using EON-Supplied Prototypes

The following tips will help you work with the EON-supplied prototypes. Use this information to improve your efficiency and maintain consistency in your work.

Copying Node References to SFNode Fields

Many prototypes work with other nodes or are integrated with other nodes. To customize a certain prototype often requires telling the prototype which node to work with. This involves adding a node reference to one of the prototype's fields. To add a node reference, right-click a node and choose the Copy as Link option, right-click one of the yellow folders under the prototype instance in the simulation tree, and choose Paste from the drop-down menu. The node reference is displayed in the simulation tree, as shown in Figure 8.2.10.

4. Place a **Cube** prototype under the Cube frame. Click the **Cube** prototpe in the simulation tree. In the Property Bar, click the color swatch next to the Color field to display the Color dialog box. Click the blue swatch that is located in the fourth row from the top and the fifth column from the left. Note that the values in the Red and Green fields are 0 and the value in the Blue field is 255, as shown in Figure 8.2.17. Click **OK** to close the dialog box, setting the cube's color to blue.

FIGURE 8.2.17 Color dialog box

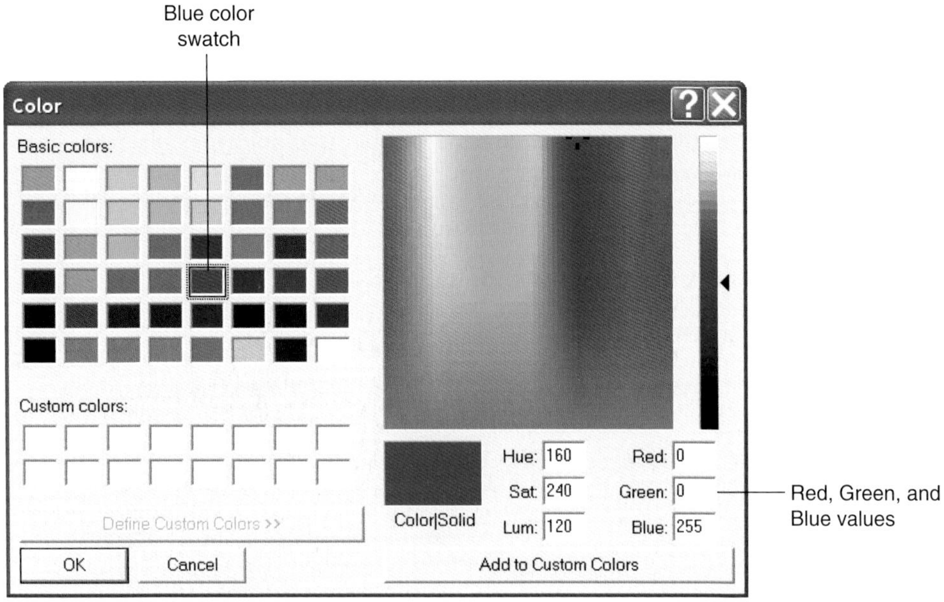

5. Place a **Pyramid** prototype under the Pyramid frame. Use the Color dialog box to change the Pyramid prototype's color to green.
6. Place a **Teapot** prototype under the Teapot frame. Do not change the teapot's color.
7. Place a **Torus** prototype under the Torus frame. Use the Color dialog box to change the prototype's color to purple (fourth row of the seventh column). Note that the Red and Blue values are 128 and the Green value is 0.
8. Select the **Cube** frame in the simulation tree. In the Property Bar, change the Cube frame's Position value to **-2 2 1**.
9. Select the **Pyramid** frame in the simulation tree. In the Property Bar, change the Pyramid frame's Position value to **2 2 1**.
10. Select the **Teapot** frame in the simulation tree. In the Property Bar, change the Teapot frame's Position value to **2 -2 0.5**.
11. Select the **Torus** frame in the simulation tree. In the Property Bar, change the Torus frame's Position value to **-2 -2 0.2** and change the Orientation value to **0 90 0**.
12. Save the simulation as **Environments_Objects.eoz** and keep it open to use in Activity 8.2.7.

In the previous activity, you added four objects. The prototypes for these objects enable you to change the object's color. You set the location of the objects by setting the Position value in the Property Bar.

In the next activity, you will add OrbitNav functions. Currently, when you start the simulation, the pivot position of the OrbitNav prototype is in the space above the grid. Because you want it to be centered on a certain object, you will place the OrbitNavLookHereAtStart prototype under the Objects frame.

Activity 8.2.7: Adding OrbitNav Functions

1. Continue working with the open simulation file **Environments_Objects.eoz** from Activity 8.2.6.
2. Place the **OrbitNavLookHereAtStart** prototype under the Teapot frame.
3. To create a node reference, right-click **Camera\OrbitNav** and select **Copy as Link**. Paste it under **OrbitNavLookHereAtStart\OrbitNav**. This prototype automatically uses its parent frame's position as the pivot position, calculates the zoom distance and orientation, and sends the values to OrbitNav immediately when the simulation starts.
4. Save the simulation as **Environments_Pivot.eoz** and then run the simulation. When the simulation starts, the teapot is displayed in the center of the simulation window. Close the simulation window.
5. Add the **OrbitNavExplorer** prototype to the Objects frame. Next, you will create node references for two of the OrbitNavExplorer prototype's exposed fields.
6. To create a node reference, right-click **Camera\OrbitNav** and select **Copy as Link**. Paste it under **OrbitNavExplorer\OrbitNav**.
7. To create a node reference, right-click the **Viewports\Viewport** node and select **Copy as Link**. Paste it under **OrbitNavExplorer\Viewport**. Your simulation tree should match the simulaton tree in Figure 8.2.18.

FIGURE 8.2.18 Simulation tree for Environments_Pivot.eoz with OrbitNavExplorer prototype

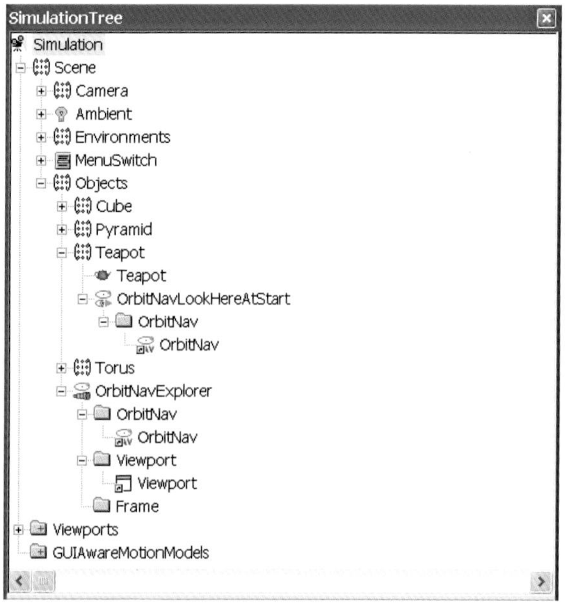

8. Save the simulation and then run it. Right-click one of the objects. Right-click the object again. Right-clicking an object will set the RenderTree field of the Viewport node so that only the object clicked will be displayed, as shown in Figure 8.2.19. When you right-click the object again, all of the objects are displayed. Each click also optimally resets the values in the OrbitNav's PivotPos, Orientation, and Zoom fields to view the selected object or all of the objects.

FIGURE 8.2.19 Only the clicked object is displayed

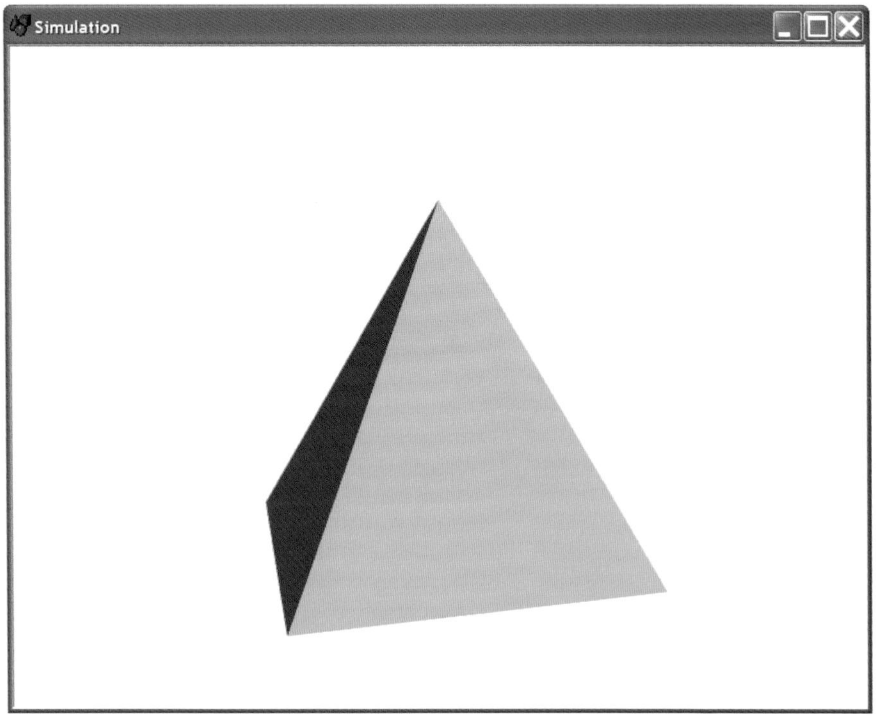

9. Close the simulation window.
10. Place the **OrbitNavResetToClickPos** prototype in the Camera frame. In the OrbitNavResetToClickPos prototype's OrbitNav field, create a node reference to the **OrbitNav** prototype under the Camera frame. (Review step 6 if you need assistance creating a node reference.)
11. In the OrbitNavResetToClickPos prototype's Roots field, create a node reference to the **Environments** frame and create a node reference to the **Objects** frame. Every time you hold down the Ctrl key and click the environment or one of the objects, the OrbitNav prototype will move into position so that the pivot position is at the point where you clicked.

12. Save the simulation and then run the simulation. Press the **Ctrl** key and click the blue **cube**. The pivot position is moved to the blue cube. Pan and move the camera to verify that the blue cube remains in the center of the simulation window, as shown in Figure 8.2.20.

FIGURE 8.2.20 Pivot point set in the blue cube

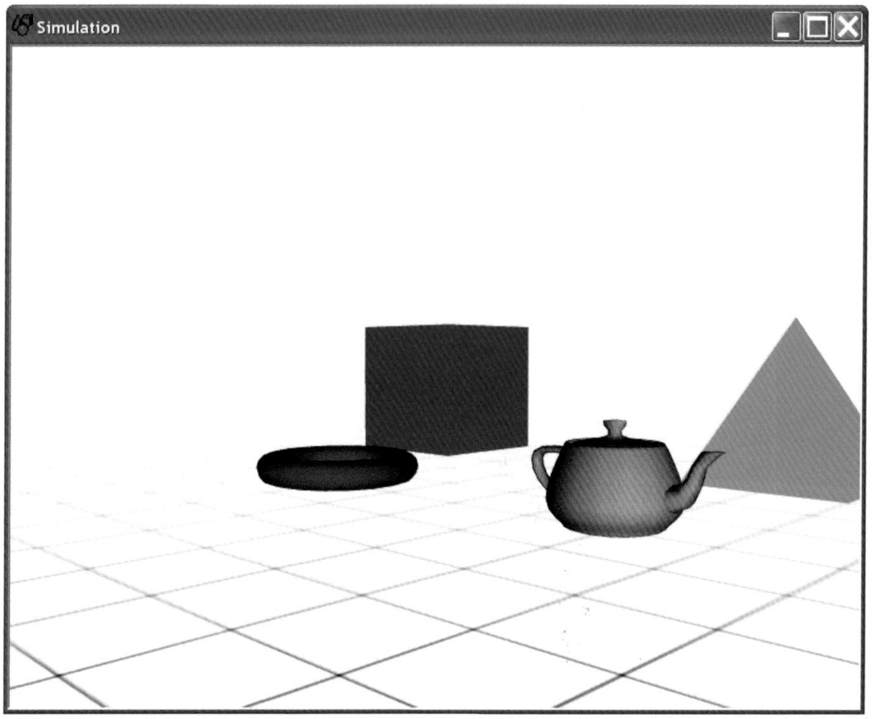

13. Close the simulation window. Keep the simulation open to use in Activity 8.2.8.

tips+tricks

You can press the P key to see a 3D pointer object that represents the pivot position inside the OrbitNav prototype. The 3D pointer moves when you press Ctrl and click a different object.

In the previous activity, you used prototypes and node references to enable the user to set a pivot position and determine which objects are displayed in the simulation window. In the next activity, you will add the ability to move the objects.

discuss

Consider the type of simulations you plan to develop in the future. Will users need the ability to display or hide objects in the simulation?

Activity 8.2.8: Moving Objects with the MoveRotateArrows3D Prototype

1. Continue working with the open simulation file **Environments_Pivot.eoz** from Activity 8.2.7.
2. Place the **MoveRotateArrows3D** prototype, which is stored in the Object Movers library, in the Camera frame. In the MoveRotateArrows3D prototype's RootNode field, create a node reference to the **Objects** frame. The children of this RootNode will be the frames that are moved.

3. In the MoveRotateArrows3D prototype's DisableWhenMoving field, create a node reference to the **OrbitNav** prototype under the Camera frame. This turns off navigation when you are dragging the objects.
4. Save the simulation as **Environments_Arrows.eoz** and then run the simulation.
5. In the simulation window, click the **teapot** to display arrows that will indicate how the object can be moved. Hover over an arrow to see the pointer change to a hand. Notice the light yellow area at the center of the arrows that enables you to drag the teapot in X and Y directions at the same time. See Figure 8.2.21.

FIGURE 8.2.21 Arrows displayed on the teapot

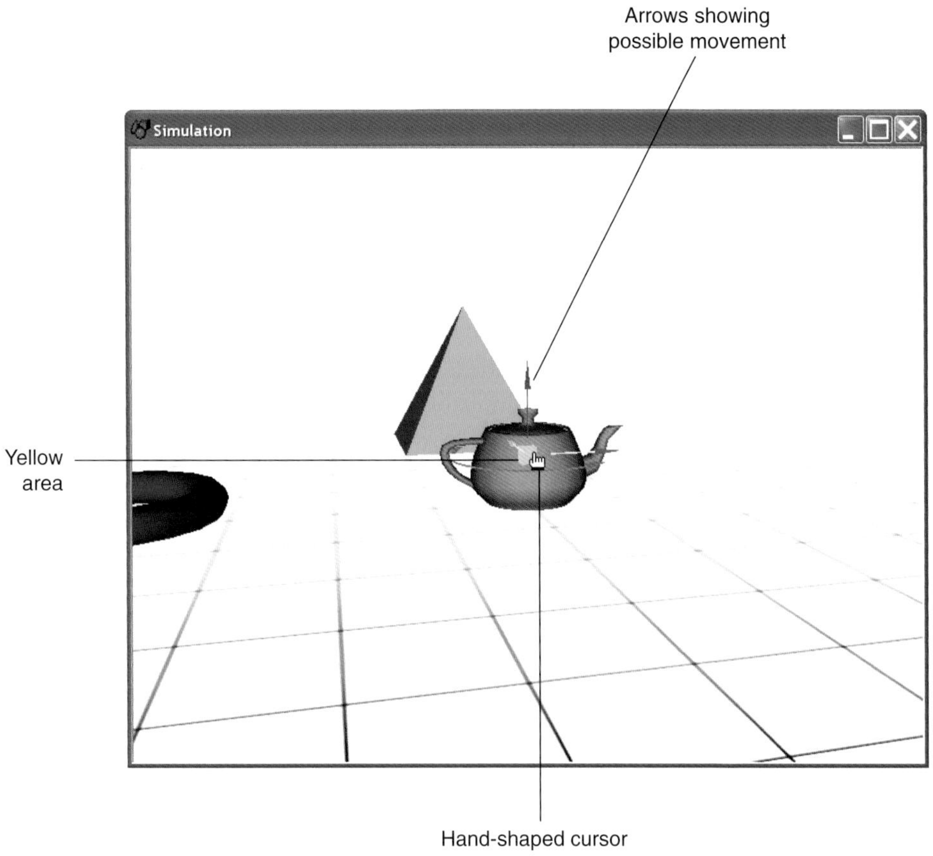

6. Drag the **teapot**. Notice that the camera is moving while you drag the teapot. The MoveRotateArrows3D prototype's DisableWhenMoving field turned off the OrbitNav prototype. This turned on the Walk node because it is no longer disabled by the node reference in the OrbitNav's DisableWhenActive field.
7. Close the simuation window. The following two steps will prevent camera movement while dragging an object.
8. Select the **MoveRotateArrows3D** prototype in the simulation tree. Remove the **OrbitNav** node reference in the DisableWhenMoving field.
9. Display the **Routes** window. Drag the **MoveRotateArrows3D** prototype and the **OrbitNav** prototype from the simulation tree to the Routes window. Establish the connection outlined in the following table.

From	outEvent	To	inEvent
MoveRotateArrows3D	Moving	OrbitNav	DisableInternalMouseController

tips+tricks

The arrows give the impression that they are inside the object but still visible. This is not actually the case. The arrows are about one-tenth of the distance between the camera and the object. The prototype's script constantly checks the position of the camera and the object. Then, it calculates the position, orientation, and scale needed to display the arrows. To see what happens when it is not checking the camera's position, clear the CheckIfCameraMoves check box. Try moving an object and then moving the camera. You will see that the arrows do not stay on the object. Avoid constantly checking these values if possible.

tips+tricks

Now it will not be necessary for the prototype to constantly check the camera's position. To optimize the MoveRotateArrows3D prototype, you could select the prototype in the simulation tree and clear the CheckIfCameraMoves check box in the Property Bar.

tips+tricks

It is better to hide the arrows when they are not needed.

The Internal Mouse Controller is a nested prototype in the OrbitNav prototype that receives mouse events and calculates values to send to the OrbitNav prototype.

10. Save the simulation and then run the simulation. Drag the **teapot** again. The camera should not move when you drag the object. Close the simulation window.
11. Select the **MoveRotateArrows3D** prototype in the simulation tree. In the Property Bar, click the **MoveInXYUsingCSRoot** check box, setting the field to true. The default settings require the user to click and drag an arrow to move the object, but setting the MoveInXYUsingCSRoot field to true enables the user to click and drag the object rather than an arrow.
12. To avoid constantly checking positions and calculating new values, establish routes that limit the simulation to calculating new values only when the camera moves. Drag the **Camera** frame to the Routes window. Establish the connections outlined in the following table.

From	outEvent	To	inEvent
Camera	Position	MoveRotateArrows3D	CamPosition
Camera	Orientation	MoveRotateArrows3D	CamOrientation

13. Place a **ClickSensor** node under the Environments frame. Select the **ClickSensor** node in the simulation tree if necessary. In the Property Bar, clear the **changeCursor** check box, setting the field to false.
14. Drag the **ClickSensor** node to the Routes window. Establish the connection outlined in the following table. Your Routes window should resemble Figure 8.2.22.

From	outEvent	To	inEvent
ClickSensor	OnButtonDownTrue	MoveRotateArrows3D	UnSelect

FIGURE 8.2.22 Routes window for Environments_Arrows

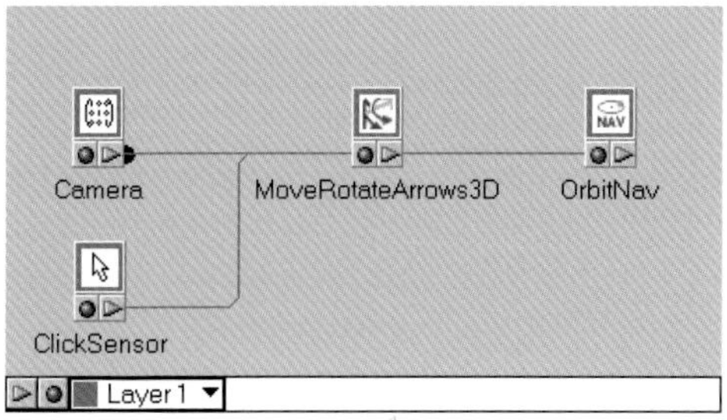

15. Save the simulation and then run it. Check the functions and verify that clicking the environment hides the arrows.
16. Close the simulation window. Keep the simulation open to use in Activity 8.2.9.

7. Copy the **StartCube** frame. Right-click the **Objects** frame and select **Paste** from the drop-down menu to paste a copy of the StartCube frame and its contents in the Objects frame. The pasted frame is automatically named StartCube1. Change its name to **EndCube**. Note that the Cube instance counter has been increased to 3 and the 3DPointer instance counter has been increased to 2.
8. Save the simulation as **Environments_Path.eoz** and then run the simulation. Note that the red cube in the StartCube frame occupies the same location as the red cube in the EndCube frame. Move the red cubes, placing the cubes so that they do not touch each other.
9. Close the simulation window.
10. Add a **ScaleLine3D** prototype under the Scene frame.
11. Display the **Routes** window. Drag the **ScaleLine3D** prototype, the **StartCube** frame, and the **EndCube** frame to the Routes window. Establish the connections outlined in the following table.

From	outEvent	To	inEvent
StartCube	Position	ScaledLine3D	StartPos
EndCube	Position	ScaledLine3D	EndPos

12. Save the simulation and then run it. Move the red cubes. When you move the cubes, note that there is a line between the two positions, as shown in Figure 8.2.27.

FIGURE 8.2.27 Line displayed between two positions in the simulation window

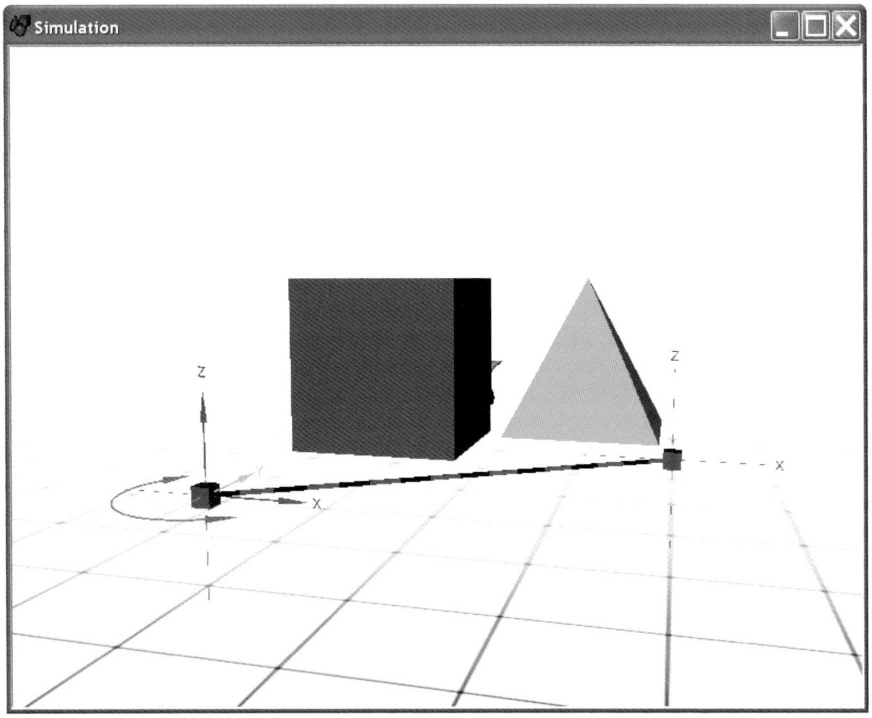

13. Close the simulation window.
14. Add a **BoundingBoxOutline** prototype under the Scene frame.

15. Display the **Routes** window. Drag the **BoundingBoxOutline** prototype from the simulation tree to the Routes window. Establish the connections outlined in the following table. Your Routes window should resemble Figure 8.2.28.

From	outEvent	To	inEvent
MoveRotateArrows3D	NodeToMove	BoundingBoxOutline	TargetNode
ClickSensor	OnButtonDownTrue	BoundingBoxOutline	MoveBBHome

FIGURE 8.2.28 Routes window for Environments_Path

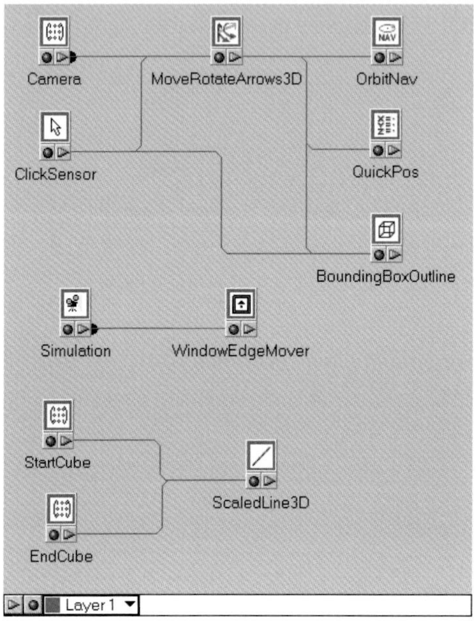

16. Save the simulation and then run it. Click the green **pyramid**. It is surrounded by a red bounding box. Click the **environment** to deselect the pyramid and hide the bounding box. Experiment by clicking other objects and clicking the environment.

17. Close the simulation window. Keep the simulation open to use in Activity 8.2.13.

In the previous activity, you used the ScaleLine3D prototype to display a path between two objects, and you used the BoundingBoxOutline prototype to identify which object in the simulation window had been clicked. These functions can be useful in many simulations. In the next activity, you will highlight objects as the user moves the pointer over them in the simulation window.

Activity 8.2.13: Highlighting Objects with Special Materials

1. Continue working with the open simulation file **Environments_Path.eoz** from Activity 8.2.12.

2. Add a **HighLighter** prototype, which is stored in the Useful Functions library, to the Scene frame.

3. In the HighLighter prototype's Roots field, create a node reference to the **Objects** frame.
4. Save the simulation as **Environments_Highlight.eoz** and then run the simulation. Move the mouse in the simulation window. The objects become red when the mouse moves over them.
5. Close the simulation window.
6. Add a **Material2** node to the Scene frame.
7. Select the **Material2** node in the simulation tree. In the Property Bar, click the color swatch next to the Ambient field to display the Color dialog box. Click the first color swatch in the second row and click **OK**. The Color dialog box is closed and the Ambient color is set to red.
8. Repeat step 7 to change the Diffuse, Specular, and Emissive values to **red**.
9. With the Material2 node still selected in the simulation tree, select **Wireframe** from the drop-down list for the Mode field.
10. In the HighLighter prototype's HighLightMaterial field, create a node reference to the **Material2** node.
11. Save the simulation and then run it. Move the mouse in the simulation window. The objects are displayed in Wireframe mode when the mouse moves over them.
12. Close the simulation window.
13. Add a new instance of the **HighLighter** prototype to the Scene frame by dragging it from the Local Prototypes window. The new instance is automatically named HighLighter1.
14. With the HighLighter1 prototype instance selected, click the **ClickToHighLight** check box, setting the field's value to true.
15. With the HighLighter1 prototype instance selected, click the **RequiresKey** check box, setting the field's value to true. Set the Key field to **shift** if necessary.
16. Save the simulation and then run it. Use the MenuSwitch pop-up menu to select the **TownSquare** option. Hold down the **Shift** key and click an object in the environment to highlight the object. When you move the mouse away and click in a different location, the highlight will be removed.
17. Close the simulation window. Close EON.

In the previous activity, you made it possible for the user to highlight an object in the simulation window. In this series of activities, you became familiar with several 3D prototypes and processes by practicing tasks, such as creating node references and adding routes in the Routes window.

Using 2D View Prototypes

In this set of activities, you will explore prototypes that are used in an orthographic viewport. You will use the MapNav2D prototype for navigation, the MoveRotateArrows2D prototype for moving objects, and the OrthoZoomer prototype to adjust the scale of the arrows, as well as the MousePos3D and the ZoomToArea prototypes.

cross-reference

Review viewports in Module 6 Lesson 1.

Activity 8.2.14: Setting Up an Orthographic Viewport

1. Open EON to start a new simulation. If EON is already open, select **New** from the File menu.
2. Add the **GridPlane2** prototype under the Scene frame.

3. Select the **GridPlane2** prototype in the simulation tree. In the Property Bar, set the prototype's Position field to **0 0 0**. Set its Width and Height fields to **1000**.
4. Select the **Camera** frame in the simulation tree. In the Property Bar, set the Camera frame's Position to **0 0 50** and Orientation to **0 90 0**. These values position the camera so that it is looking directly down on the grid.
5. Expand the **Viewports** folder and select the **Viewport** node in the simulation tree. Set the Viewport node's NearClip field to **10** and click the **Orthographic** check box, setting the field to true.
6. Save the simulation as **Viewport_Setup.eoz** and keep it open to use in Activity 8.2.15.

In the previous activity, you set up the viewport for 2D viewing and changed the default position of the camera. You also added a grid that will be displayed in the simulation window. In the following activity, you will explore a different motion model.

Activity 8.2.15: Adding the MapNav2D Motion Model

1. Continue working with the open simulation file **Viewport_Setup.eoz** from Activity 8.2.14.
2. Expand **Scene** > **Camera**. Delete the **Walk** node under the Camera frame.
3. Add the **MapNav2D** prototype, which is stored in the Camera Functions library, to the Camera frame.
4. In the MapNav2D prototype's Camera field, create a node reference to the **Camera** frame.
5. In the MapNav2D prototype's ViewportNode field, create a node reference to the **Viewport** node. Your simulation tree should resemble Figure 8.2.29.

FIGURE 8.2.29 Simulation tree with node references added in the MapNav2D prototype

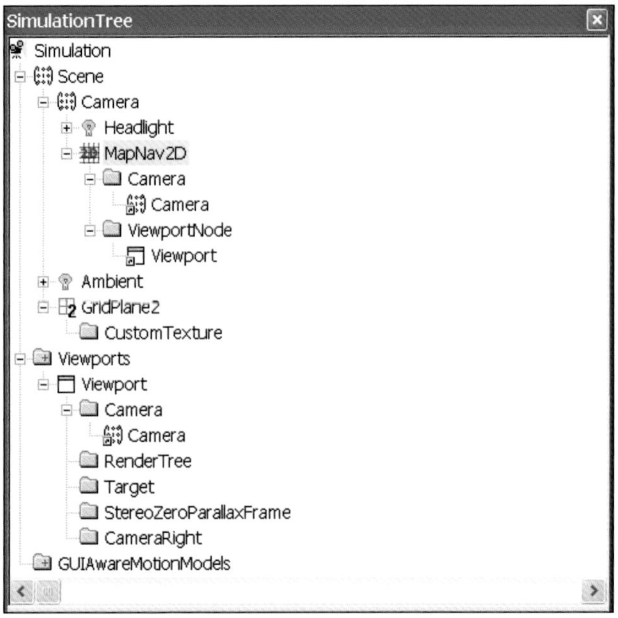

6. Display the **Routes** window. Drag the **Viewport** node and the **MapNav2D** prototype from the simulation tree to the Routes window. Establish the connection outlined in the following table.

From	outEvent	To	inEvent
Viewport	FieldOfView	MapNav2D	FOV

7. Save the simulation as **Viewport_2D_Motion.eoz** and then run the simulation. Explore the MapNav2D motion model to navigate. Try dragging with each mouse button.
8. Close the simulation window. Keep the simulation open to use in Activity 8.2.16.

In the previous activity, you added the MapNav2D prototype, replacing the default Walk node. You experimented to observe differences in navigation between the default model and the MapNav2D motion model. In the next activity, you will add objects so that differences in navigation and object movement will become more obvious.

Activity 8.2.16: Adding Objects to Move

1. Continue working with the open simulation file **Viewport_2D_Motion.eoz** from Activity 8.2.15.
2. Add a **Frame** node to the Scene frame. Change the name of the Frame node to **Objects**.
3. Add a **Frame** node to the Objects frame. Change the name of the new Frame node to **Frame1**.
4. Right-click the **Frame1** frame and select **Copy** from the drop-down menu. Right-click the **Objects** frame and select **Paste** from the drop-down menu. The pasted frame is automatically named Frame2. Right-click the **Objects** frame and select **Paste** from the drop-down menu again. The pasted frame is automatically named Frame3.
5. Add a **Cube** protototype to the Frame1 frame. Select the **Cube** prototype in the simulation tree. In the Property Bar, click the color swatch for the Color field to display the Color dialog box. Click the fifth square in the fourth row. Click the **OK** button to close the Color dialog box, setting the cube's color to blue.
6. Add a **Sphere** prototype to the Frame2 frame. Select the **Sphere** prototype in the simulation tree. In the Property Bar, click the color swatch for the Color field to display the Color dialog box. Click the third square in the third row. Click the **OK** button to close the Color dialog box, setting the sphere's color to green.
7. Add a **Teapot** prototype to the Frame3 frame.
8. Select the **Frame1** frame in the simulation tree. In the Property Bar, set the frame's Position field to **-4 0 0**.
9. Select the **Frame2** frame in the simulation tree. In the Property Bar, set the frame's Position field to **2 2 0**.
10. Select the **Frame3** frame in the simulation tree. In the Property Bar, set the frame's Position field to **2-2 0**.

11. Save the simulation as **Viewport_Add_Objects.eoz** and then run the simulation. View the new objects, as shown in Figure 8.2.30.

FIGURE 8.2.30 Objects displayed in the simulation window for Viewport_Add_Objects

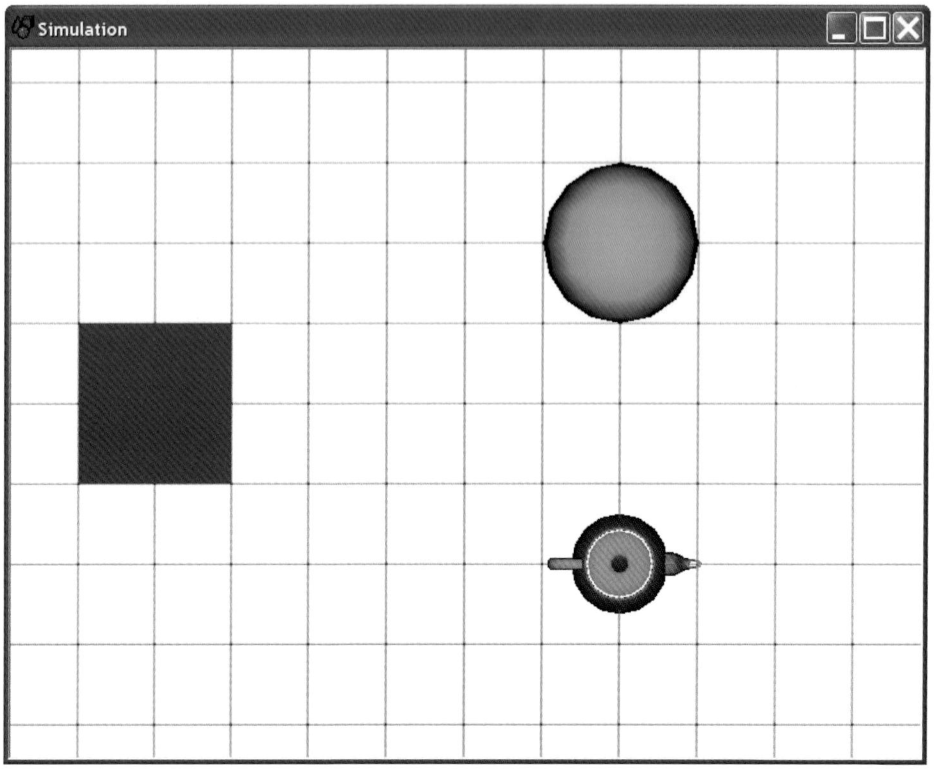

12. Close the simulation window. Keep the simulation open to use in Activity 8.2.17.

In the previous activity, you added three objects to the simulation. The camera is positioned to view the objects from above. In the next activity, you will add the MoveRotateArrows2D prototype to enable the user to move the objects and the camera.

Activity 8.2.17: Enabling Object Movement

1. Continue working with the open simulation file **Viewport_Add_Objects.eoz** from Activity 8.2.16.
2. Add a **MoveRotateArrows2D** prototype to the Camera frame.
3. In the MoveRotateArrows2D prototype's RootNode field, create a node reference to the **Objects** frame. The MoveRotateArrows2D prototype is designed to move the child frames of the RootNode you specify.
4. In the MoveRotateArrows2D prototype's DisableWhenMoving field, create a node reference to the **MapNav2D** prototype. This will turn off navigation while you are dragging objects.
5. In the MoveRotateArrows2D prototype's ViewportNode field, create a node reference to the **Viewport** node.
6. Add a **MousePos3D** prototype, which is stored in the Converters library, to the Camera frame. This calculates the 3D position of the mouse cursor so that it can be sent to the MoveRotateArrows2D prototype.

7. In the MousePos3D prototype's ViewportNode field, create a node reference to the **Viewport** node.
8. In the MousePos3D prototype's SendToNodes field, create a node reference to the **MoveRotateArrows2D** prototype. After routes are added, the MousePos3D protoype can send its position directly to the MoveRotateArrows2D prototype. The Camera frame in your simulation tree should look like Figure 8.2.31.

FIGURE 8.2.31 Simulation tree with the MoveRotateArrows2D and MousePos3D prototypes

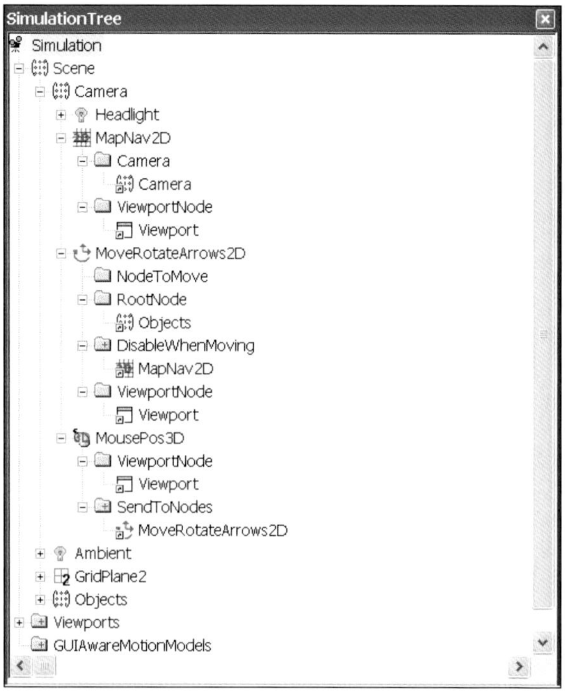

9. Display the **Routes** window. Drag the **Camera** frame, the **MoveRotateArrows2D** prototype, and the **MousePos3D** prototype to the Routes window. Establish the connections outlined in the following table. Your Routes window should resemble Figure 8.2.32.

From	outEvent	To	inEvent
Camera	Position	MoveRotateArrows2D	CamPosition
Camera	Position	MousePos3D	CamPos
Viewport	FieldOfView	MousePos3D	FOV

FIGURE 8.2.32 Routes added to send location values

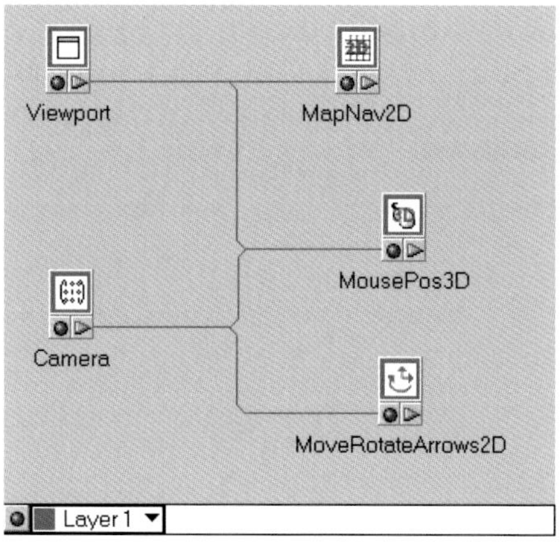

10. Save the simulation as **Viewport_Movement.eoz** and then run the simulation. Click an object to display the arrows. Click and drag an **arrow**. Drag the object in the middle of the arrows. Click and drag the pink **arrows** to change the rotation.
11. Close the simulation window. Keep the simulation open to use in Activity 8.2.18.

In the previous activity, you added prototypes and routes to enable the user to move the objects in the simulation. The color of all of the arrows can be customized. Also, you can hide all of the arrows and drag the objects in the XY plane.

Notice that the size of the arrows depends on how far you zoom in and out. It would be better to keep the size of the arrows constant when you change the zoom. One of the OrthoZoomer prototype's functions is to send new scale values to the arrows. In the next activity, you will add the OrthoZoomer prototype to the simulation.

Activity 8.2.18: Changing the Size of the Arrows

1. Continue working with the open simulation file **Viewport_Movement.eoz** from Activity 8.2.17.
2. Add an **OrthoZoomer** prototype from the Developer Tools library to the Scene frame.
3. To create a node reference, right-click **Viewports\Viewport** and select **Copy as Link**. Paste it under **OrthoZoomer\ViewportNode**.
4. To create a node reference, right-click **Camera\MoveRotateArrows2D** and select **Copy as Link**. Paste it under **OrthoZoomer\SendScaleTo**.
5. Select the **MoveRotateArrows2D** node and set its Size field to **2**.
6. Save the simulation as **Viewport_Arrow_Size.eoz** and then run the simulation.
7. Click an object to display the arrows. Zoom in and zoom out slowly. Notice that the arrows are changing size in intervals of one second because the OrthoZoomer has a function to refresh its viewport settings once per second. This is not often enough because the the MapNav2D prototype constantly changes the field of view. You can create a connection that will send the field of view values as they change.
8. Close the simulation window.
9. Display the **Routes** window. Drag the **OrthoZoomer** prototype to the Routes window. Establish the connection outlined in the following table. Your Routes window should resemble Figure 8.2.33.

From	outEvent	To	inEvent
Viewport	FieldOfView	OrthoZoomer	FOV

FIGURE 8.2.33 OrthoZoomer added to Routes window

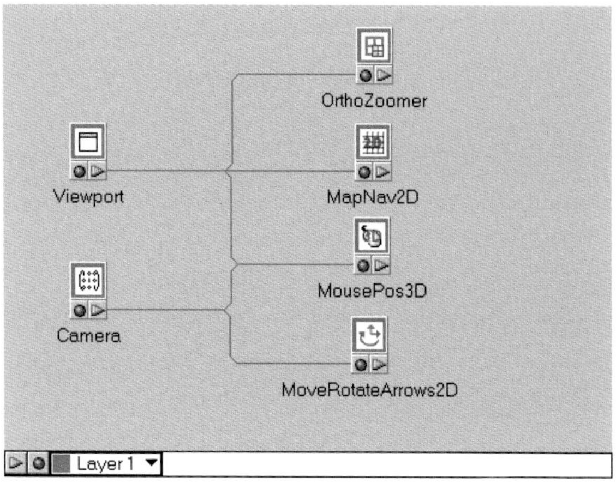

10. Save the simulation and then run it.
11. Click an object to display the arrows. Zoom in and zoom out slowly.
12. Close the simulation window.
13. Add a **ClickSensor** node to the Scene frame. In the Property Bar, set its changeCursor field to false by clearing the **changeCursor** check box.
14. To create a node reference, right-click the **GridPlane2** prototype and select **Copy as Link**. Paste it under the ClickSensor node's **Roots** folder.
15. Display the **Routes** window. Drag the **ClickSensor** node to the Routes window. Establish the connection outlined in the following table.

From	outEvent	To	inEvent
ClickSensor	OnButtonDownTrue	MoveRotateArrows2D	UnSelect

16. Save the simulation and then run it. Verify that the arrows are hidden when you click the grid in the simulation window.
17. Close the simulation window.
18. Select the **MoveRotateArrows2D** prototype in the simulation tree. In the Property Bar, place a check mark in the **SnapToGrid** check box to set the field to true.
19. Save the simulation and run it. Move one of the objects to observe the effect of selecting the SnapToGrid option.
20. Close the simulation window. Keep the simulation open to use in Activity 8.2.19.

In the following activity, you will use the ZoomToArea prototype. This function lets you draw a rectangle that becomes the viewing area. Therefore, the ZoomToArea prototype sends values to the Camera frame's Position field and sends zoom size information to the OrthoZoomer prototype, which sends values to the Viewport node's FieldOfView field.

Activity 8.2.19: Adding the ZoomToArea Function

1. Continue working with the open simulation file **Viewport_Arrow_Size.eoz** from Activity 8.2.18.
2. Add a **Group** node to the Scene frame and rename the Group node **ZoomFunctions**.
3. Add a **ZoomToArea** prototype from the Camera Functions library to the ZoomFunctions Group node.
4. To create a node reference, right-click the **OrthoZoomer** prototype and select **Copy as Link**. Paste it under **ZoomFunctions\ZoomToArea\OrthoZoomer**.
5. To create a node reference, right-click the **Camera** frame and select **Copy as Link**. Paste it under **ZoomFunctions\ZoomToArea\Camera**.
6. To create a node reference, right-click the **MapNav2D** prototype and select **Copy as Link**. Paste it under **ZoomFunctions\ZoomToArea\DisableWhenActive**.
7. To create a node reference, right-click the **ZoomToArea** prototype and select **Copy as Link**. Paste it under **MousePos3D\SendToNodes**. This transfers the 3D position of the mouse. Your simulation tree should look like Figure 8.2.34.

FIGURE 8.2.34 Simulation tree with ZoomToArea functionality

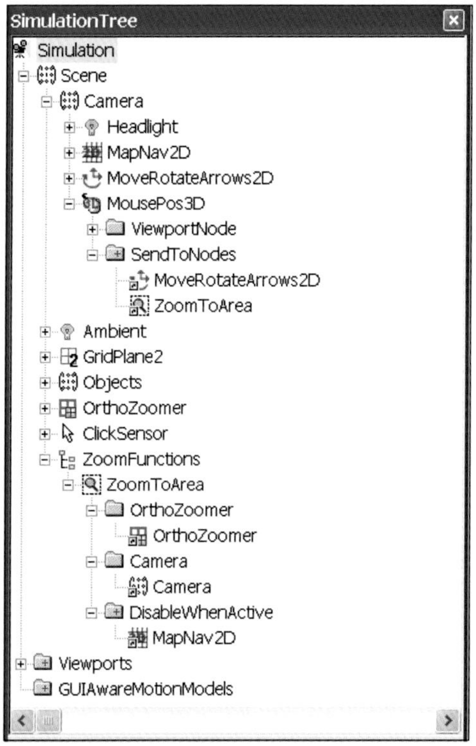

8. Save the simulation as **Viewport_ZoomToArea.eoz** and then run the simulation.
9. Press the **G** key and then click and drag the left mouse button to draw a rectangle. When you finish the rectangle, the view is instantly moved and zoomed to display only the area selected by the rectangle.
10. Close the simulation window. Keep the simulation open to use in Activity 8.2.20.

In the following activity, you will add a button and text about the ZoomToArea functionality. Users are more likely to use a function if they know it is available.

Activity 8.2.20: Adding a Button and Instructions for the ZoomToArea Function

1. Continue working with the open simulation file **Viewport_ZoomToArea.eoz** from Activity 8.2.19.
2. Add a **2DText** node to the ZoomFunctions group and rename the 2DText node **ZoomToAreaButton**.
3. In the Property Bar, set the ZoomToAreaButton node's Text field to **Zoom To Area**. Set the node's BoxArea field to **150 20** and set its TextAlignment field to **Left**.
4. Display the **Routes** window. Drag the **ZoomToAreaButton** node and the **ZoomToArea** prototype to the Routes window. Establish the connection outlined in the following table.

From	outEvent	To	inEvent
ZoomToAreaButton	OnButtonUp	ZoomToArea	GetReady

5. Save the simulation as **Viewport_ZoomToArea_Button.eoz** and then run the simulation. Notice that the ZoomToArea 2DText node is displayed in the upper-left corner of the simulation window.
6. Close the simulation window.
7. Add another **2DText** node to the ZoomFunctions group and rename the new 2DText node **ZoomInstructions**.
8. In the Property Bar, set the ZoomInstructions node's Text field to **Draw a rectangle to zoom to the area**.
9. In the Property Bar, set the ZoomInstructions node's BoxPosition field to **10 40**, set the BoxArea field to **150 75**, and set the TextAlignment field to **Left**. Clear the **IsActive** check box, setting the IsActive field to false.
10. Also in the Property Bar, click the BoxColor color swatch to display the Color dialog box. Select the blue swatch (fifth square in the fourth row) and click **OK** to close the Color dialog box. The Property Bar for the ZoomInstructions node should look like Figure 8.2.35.

FIGURE 8.2.35 Property Bar for the ZoomInstructions node

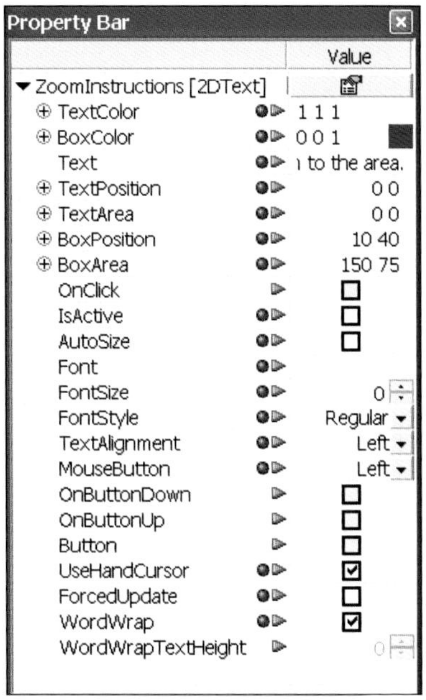

troubleshooting

If you cannot set the TextAlignment field to Left, you used the 2DText prototype rather than the 2DText node. Delete the 2DText prototype and return to step 2 to add the 2DText node.

11. Display the **Routes** window. Drag the **ZoomInstructions** node to the Routes window. Establish the connection outlined in the following table.

From	outEvent	To	inEvent
ZoomToArea	Active	ZoomInstructions	IsActive

12. Save the simulation and then run it. Test the Zoom To Area button.
13. Close the simulation window.
14. Add a **MouseToBoxPosition** prototype from the Converters library to the ZoomFunctions group. You will use the MouseToBoxPosition prototype to make the instructions follow the mouse cursor.
15. In the Property Bar, set the MouseToBoxPosition node's OffsetPos field to **20 20**.
16. Display the **Routes** window. Drag the **MouseToBoxPosition** prototype to the Routes window. Establish the connection outlined in the following table. Your Routes window should resemble Figure 8.2.36.

From	outEvent	To	inEvent
MouseToBoxPosition	BoxPosition	ZoomInstructions	BoxPosition

FIGURE 8.2.36 Routes window with the MouseToBoxPosition prototype

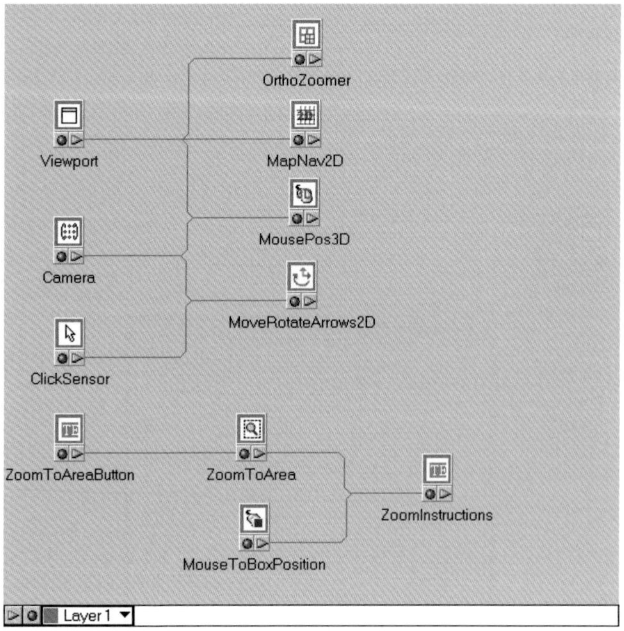

17. Save the simulation and then run it. Verify that the instructions move correctly while using the ZoomToArea function.
18. Close the simulation window. Keep the simulation open to use in Activity 8.2.21.

If you change the proportions of your simulation window by changing its width or height, some functions will no longer work correctly. Run the Viewport_ZoomToArea_Button.eoz simulation that you just created. Change the window size and test the simulation's functions. Notice that the navigation does not move at the correct speed when you drag with the left mouse button, the ZoomToArea instructions are not displayed in the correct location, and the ZoomToArea rectangle starts in the wrong position. These errors occur because certain prototypes do not have the latest values for the simulation window size. Instead of making routes between the simulation and all of these prototypes, you will use the RefreshGroup prototype. This prototype sends Refresh inEvents to the prototypes when the simulation window's width or height changes.

Activity 8.2.21: Refreshing Prototypes When the Simulation Window Size Changes

1. Continue working with the open simulation file **Viewport_ZoomToArea_Button.eoz** from Activity 8.2.20.
2. Save the simulation as **Viewport_Window_Size.eoz**.
3. Add a **RefreshGroup** prototype from the Developer Tools library to the Scene frame.
4. Display the **Routes** window. Drag the **Simulation** node and the **RefreshGroup** prototype instance to the Routes window. Establish the connections outlined in the following table. Your Routes window should resemble Figure 8.2.37.

From	outEvent	To	inEvent
Simulation	WindowWidth	RefreshGroup	WindowWidth
Simulation	WindowHeight	RefreshGroup	WindowHeight

FIGURE 8.2.37 Routes window with RefreshGroup prototype

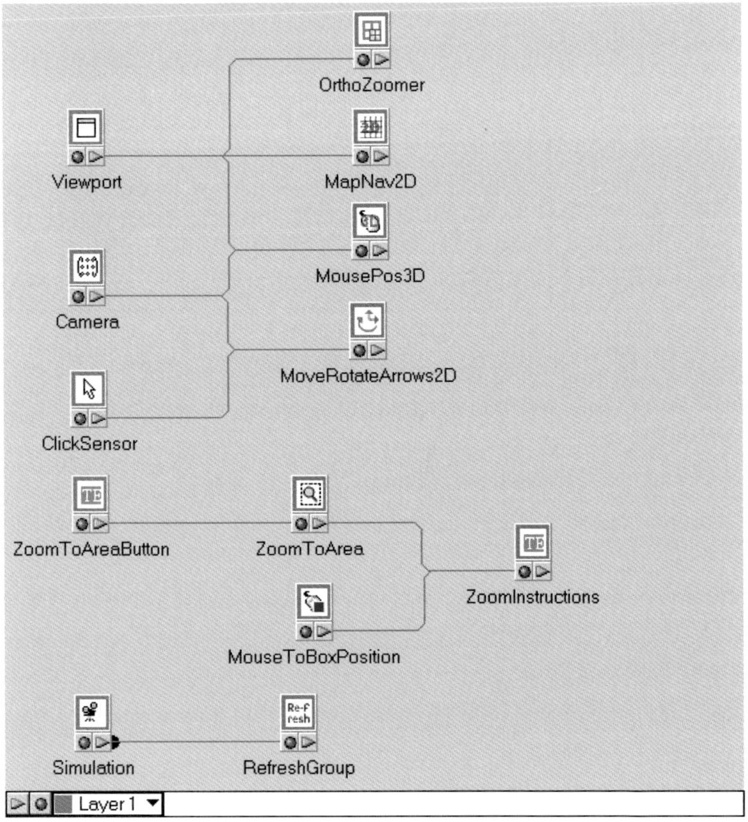

5. In the RefreshGroup prototype's RefreshThese field, create node references to the **MapNav2D** prototype in the Camera frame, the **MousePos3D** prototype in the Camera frame, the **OrthoZoomer** prototype in the Scene frame, and the **MouseToBoxPosition** prototype in the ZoomFunctions group. Your simulation tree should look like Figure 8.2.38.

FIGURE 8.2.38 Node references added to the RefreshGroup prototype

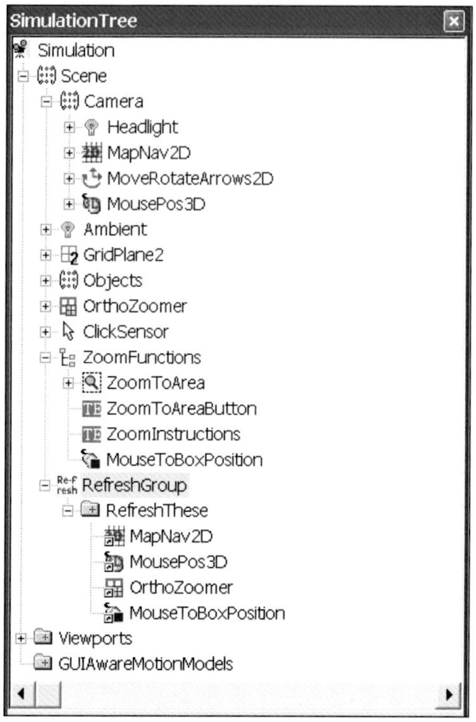

6. Save the simulation and then run it. Drag one **border** of the simulation window to change its proportions. Verify that all of the simulation's functions still work correctly.
7. Close the simulation window. Keep the simulation open to use in Activity 8.2.22.

A second viewport can add flexibility to a simulation. In the following activity, you will add a 3D viewport on the existing 2D viewport. The user will be able to hide or display the additional viewport.

Activity 8.2.22: Adding a 3D Viewport

1. Continue working with the open simulation file **Viewport_Window_Size.eoz** from Activity 8.2.21.
2. Save the simulation as **Viewport_3D.eoz**.
3. Add a **Viewport** node to the Viewports folder and rename the new Viewport node **Viewport3D**.
4. Add a **Frame** node to the Scene frame and rename the new Frame node **Camera3D**.
5. In the Property Bar, set the Camera3D frame's Position field to **0 -10 5** and set the Orientation field to **0 30 0**.
6. To create a node reference, right-click the **Camera3D** frame and select **Copy as Link**. Paste it under the Viewport3D node's **Camera** field.
7. Add a **Walk** node to the Camera3D frame.

8. Add a **Light** node to the Camera3D frame. In the Property Bar, set the Light node's Type field to **Directional**.
9. Add a **FloatingViewport** prototype to the Camera3D frame. In the Property Bar, set the prototype's PixelWidth field to **400**, set its PixelHeight field to **300**, and set its CornerPos field to **2**.
10. To create a node reference, right-click **Viewports\Viewport3D** and select **Copy as Link**. Paste it under **FloatingViewport\ViewportNode**.
11. To create a node reference, right-click **Camera3D\Walk** and select **Copy as Link**. Paste it under **FloatingViewport\DisableWhenMoving**.
12. Save the simulation and then run the simulation.
13. Notice the new viewport in the upper-right corner of the simulation window. Press the **F3** key to hide the viewport and press **F3** again to display the viewport. Press **F4** to move the viewport to a different corner. Click the middle mouse button and drag in the 3D viewport to move the viewport.
14. Try navigating in the two different viewports. It is difficult to navigate when MapNav2D and Walk are both active—you need to use only one at a time. To do this, you will enable the Walk node when the mouse is in the 3D viewport and enable the MapNav2D prototype when the mouse is not in the 3D viewport.
15. Close the simulation window.
16. Add a **MouseInViewport** prototype to the Camera3D frame.
17. To create a node reference, right-click the **Viewport3D** node and select **Copy as Link**. Paste it under the MouseInViewport prototype's **ViewportNode**.
18. Add the **WalkOnOff** prototype from the Useful Functions library to the Camera3D frame.
19. To create a node reference, right-click **Camera3D\Walk** and select **Copy as Link**. Paste it under the WalkOnOff prototype's **WalkNode**. The portion of your simulation tree that was modified in this activity should look like Figure 8.2.39.

FIGURE 8.2.39 Simulation tree with the Viewport3D node

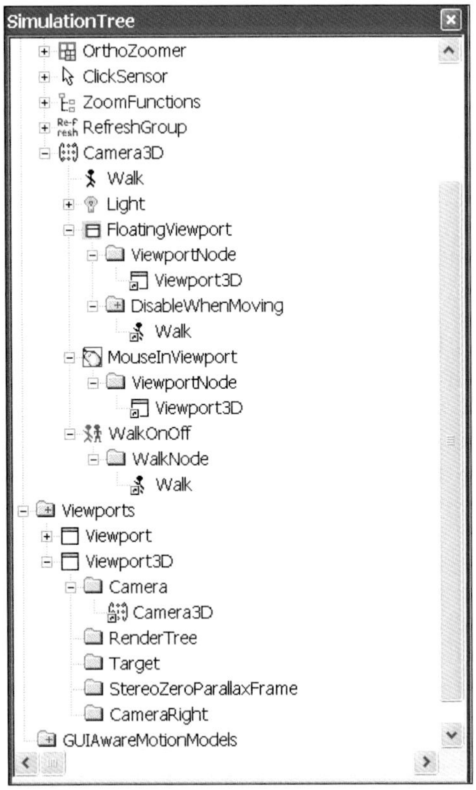

20. Display the **Routes** window. Drag the **MouseInViewport** and **WalkOnOff** prototypes to the Routes window. Establish the connections outlined in the following table. Your Routes window should resemble Figure 8.2.40.

From	outEvent	To	inEvent
MouseInViewport	MouseIn	WalkOnOff	MouseIn
MouseInViewport	MouseIn	MapNav2D	IsNotActive

FIGURE 8.2.40 Routes window with the MouseInViewport and WalkOnOff prototypes

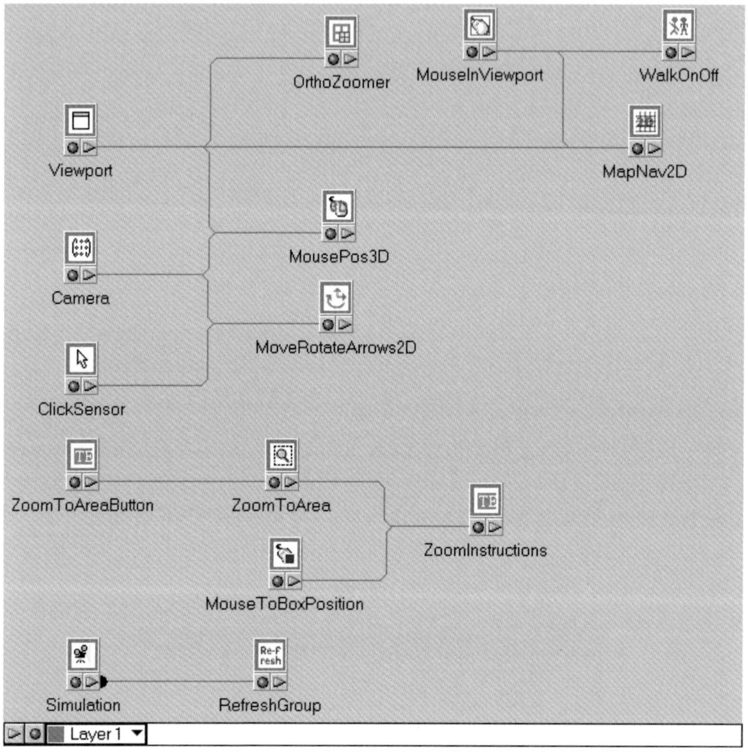

21. Save the simulation and then run it. Explore the differences in navigation.
22. Close the simulation window. Keep the simulation open to use in Activity 8.2.23.

In the final activity in this series, you will add a room that can be customized. The user will be able to drag lines in the main 2D viewport to resize the room displayed in the smaller 3D viewport.

Activity 8.2.23: Adding a Customizable Room

1. Continue working with the open simulation file **Viewport_3D.eoz** from Activity 8.2.22.
2. Save the simulation as **Viewport_Room.eoz**.
3. Add a **CustomRoom** prototype to the Scene node.
4. Add a **Frame** node to the Scene frame and rename the new Frame node **MovingWalls**. Set the MovingWalls frame's Position field to **0 0 10**.
5. Add a **MoveableWalls** prototype from the Useful Objects library to the MovingWalls frame.
6. To create a node reference, right-click the **CustomRoom** prototype instance and select **Copy as Link**. Paste it under the MoveableWall prototype's **SendToNodes**.
7. To create a node reference, right-click the **MoveableWalls** prototype and select **Copy as Link**. Paste it under the MousePos3D prototype's **SendToNodes**. The portion of your simulation tree that was modified in this activity should look like Figure 8.2.41.

FIGURE 8.2.41 Simulation tree with room added

8. Display the **Routes** window. Drag the **MoveableWalls** prototype to the Routes window and place it near the MapNav2D node. Establish the connection outlined in the following table. Your Routes window should resemble Figure 8.2.42.

From	outEvent	To	inEvent
MoveableWalls	Dragging	MapNav2D	IsNotActive

FIGURE 8.2.42 Routes window with MoveableWalls prototype

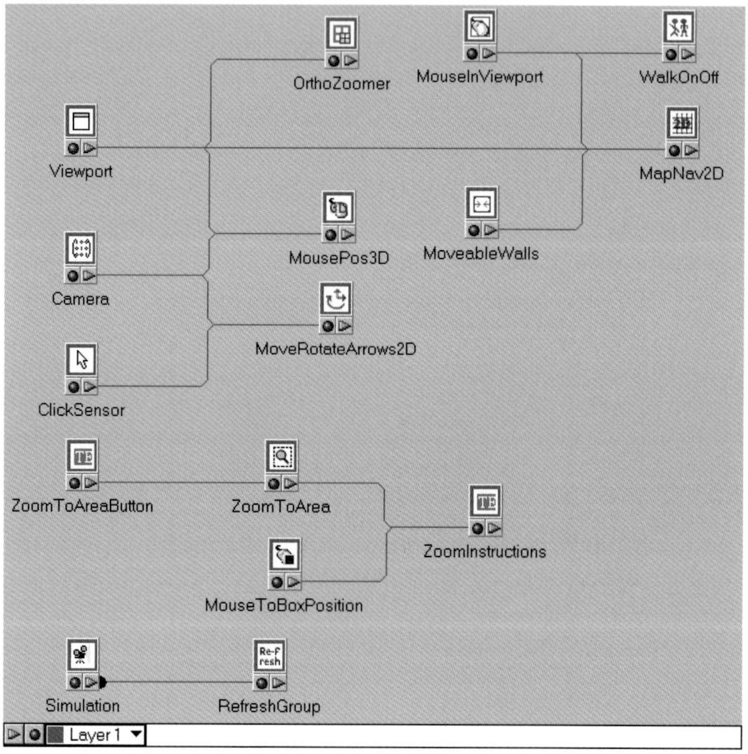

9. Save the simulation and then run it. In the 2D viewport, drag the blue **lines** with red corners to resize the room displayed in the 3D viewport.
10. Close the simulation window. Close EON.

Summary

In this lesson you:

- Learned to recognize the EON-supplied prototypes.
- Familiarized yourself with the contents of the prototype libraries.
- Used and customized EON-supplied prototypes.
- Learned about the common meaning for some field names.
- Learned about the most versatile and popular prototypes.

LESSON 8.3

Developing EON Prototypes

Objectives

In this lesson you will:

- Create, edit, and delete prototypes.
- Create a prototype library.
- Move prototypes from one library to another.
- Practice common tasks related to prototypes.
- Learn about the best practices to use when developing prototypes.

Key Terms

clone	*exported field*	*Resolve resource references*
customize	*instance counter*	*resource node*
default value	*nested prototype*	*SFNode field*

Developing prototypes is like object-oriented programming without writing any code. It is all done with nodes and routes. Very soon, you can enjoy the powerful features of prototypes that will save time, give you better control over prototypes, and help you understand your creations. Like any true discipline, however, you must learn design principles that will require dedication and experience to master.

Creating Prototypes

Regardless of whether it is supplied by EON or created by an end user, every prototype begins as a simulation subtree of nodes and prototypes and their associated routes. When a prototype is created, all associated subtree nodes are removed from the simulation tree and all associated routes are removed from the Routes window. The subtree nodes and routes are then encapsulated into a new prototype definition object. This object may be saved in a new or existing prototype library.

After the prototype is created, the new prototype will appear as a single object in the application. The new prototype has properties that can be edited in the same way as the properties of standard EON nodes.

In addition to creating new prototypes, existing prototypes within EON-supplied and user-defined prototype libraries can be updated and removed as necessary. Prototype libraries also can be installed from an external source for use in the local EON Studio installation.

Creation Methods

A simulation subtree is converted to a prototype by using one of the following three methods:

- **Drag-and-drop:** Drag the top node of the appropriate simulation subtree into the Local Prototypes window. The mouse pointer will indicate if your selection is valid.
- **Pop-up menu:** Right-click the top node of the appropriate simulation subtree and select Create prototype from the pop-up menu.
- **Copy/Paste:** Select the top node of the appropriate subtree and select Copy. Go to the Local Prototypes window, right-click in the window to open the pop-up menu, and select Paste.

Start Prototype Creation with a Frame

Any node below the root node of the simulation tree can technically serve as the starting point of a subtree. However, for a subtree to be converted into a prototype, the top node of the subtree must be a Frame node. If you copy a node that is not a Frame node and try to paste it in the Local Prototypes window, the Create Prototype alert window shown in Figure 8.3.1 will be displayed.

FIGURE 8.3.1 Create Prototype alert window

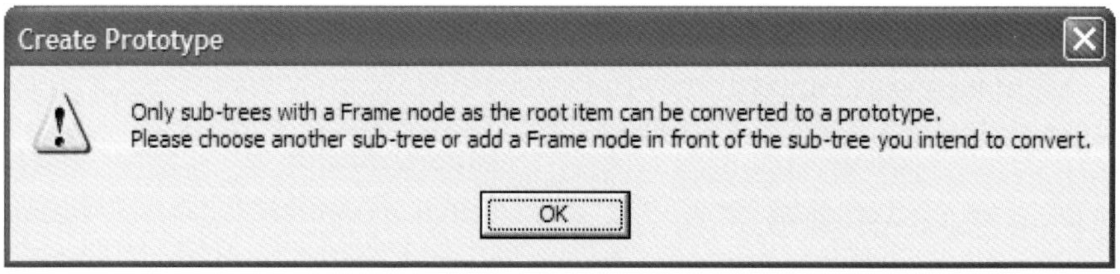

troubleshooting

You cannot use an easy undo command for the prototype creation process. Therefore, you should save your simulation before you create the prototype and then save the simulation with a new filename after you create the prototype.

Naming a New Prototype

After you create a prototype, the subtree in the simulation tree is replaced by a single prototype instance node with the default icon. The name of the subtree's top Frame node becomes the name of the prototype and the instance. If the Local Prototypes window already contains a prototype definition with that name, then the new prototype definition will get the same name, but an integer is added to the end of the name. For example, the top Frame node of a subtree is named Picture. If you drag the subtree to the Local Prototypes window, which already contains a prototype named Picture, dragging the Picture subtree to the Local Prototypes window will make a new prototype named Picture1.

Preserving Routes and Node References

When a prototype is made, all the routes that were connected between nodes within the subtree will be preserved. However, you cannot view the routes in the main Routes view for the simulation, which can be displayed in the Routes window. Instead, each prototype definition has it own Routes view that can be displayed in the Routes window.

When a route connects a node that will remain outside the prototype to a node that will be placed inside a prototype, EON will create an ***exported field*** for the new prototype definition. Exported fields are the fields or properties available to a prototype when it is used as an instance. They let users customize the prototype for use in a particular application, thereby increasing the usefulness of the prototype. This allows EON to create a new route automatically from the external node to the new prototype instance. The net effect is the preservation of the original route and any behavior caused by the connection.

Node references are similar to routes; they will be preserved if possible. If a subtree that will become a prototype has a reference to a node outside the subtree, EON will create an exported field and then place the node reference in the new prototype instance's exported field, which appears as a yellow folder under the prototype instance.

However, the reverse situation is handled differently. If a subtree that will become a prototype contains a node that is currently referenced by a node outside the subtree, then the link cannot be maintained. When you try to create a prototype that contains nodes used by other nodes outside the subtree, the SceneGraphModule alert window displayed in Figure 8.3.2 is displayed.

FIGURE 8.3.2 SceneGraphModule alert window

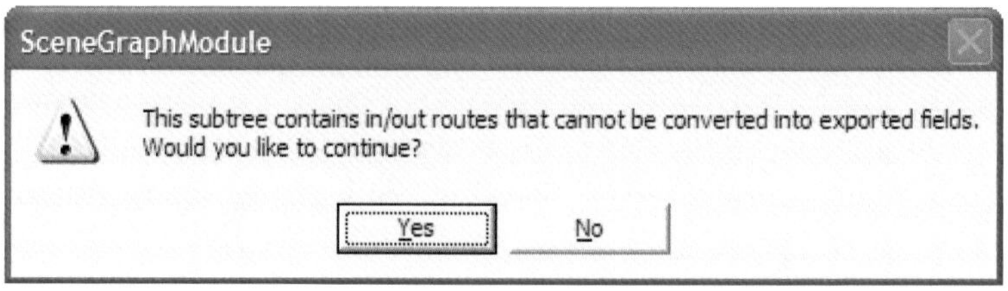

This can be reproduced in a new EON file by dragging the Camera Frame node to the Local Prototypes window. In this case, the Viewport node needs a reference to the Camera Frame node.

Resolve Resource References

You may recall that a 3D object is generally made up of a Shape node that has references to resource nodes. ***Resource nodes*** refer to geometry, image, sound, and video files. Usually, the resource nodes in a simulation are stored under a Group node named Resources that is separate from the Shape nodes. If you want to create a prototype for reusing a 3D object, then the prototype must include the resource nodes to see any objects. Potentially, it sounds like a lot of work to discover which resource nodes are required and which are not. You do not want to move all of the resources into the prototype because that would make the size of the prototype file unnecessarily large and also would remove the resources needed by other objects in the simulation.

Fortunately, the ***Resolve resource references*** function automates this process. Right-click the top Frame node in the prototype and choose Resolve resource references from the pop-up menu. This will create a Group node named Resources under the Frame node and place the copies of all the resource nodes required by the Shape nodes found in the selected subtree. The resources are grouped into the Materials, Textures, and Meshes folders under the new Resources Group node. Also, all of the Shape node's references are updated to point to these new resource nodes. The original resource nodes remain unchanged elsewhere in the simulation tree.

tips+tricks

If you have been using polygon or texture quality optimizations, you must disable them before you finish making your prototype. This refers to the PolygonReduction field in a Mesh2 node, the PreviewCompression field in a Texture2 node, and the QualityLevel field in a Texture2 node. This is important because you may forget these fields and wonder why the simulation takes longer to start.

troubleshooting

This activity may require EON Professional. Depending on your configuration of EON modules, you may not be able to complete this activity.

If you are making a 3D object prototype, you must move the required resource nodes or use the Resolve resource references function to place the required resource nodes under the top Frame node of the subtree before you create the prototype. If you do not place the resource nodes in the correct location before you create the prototype, you can copy the resource nodes into the prototype definition later. However, copying the resource nodes into the prototype later is more difficult because the references from the Shape nodes to the resource nodes will be missing; it is a lot of work to determine which resource nodes should be referenced by the Shape nodes and to copy and paste the required node references.

Activity 8.3.1: Creating Prototypes and Using the Resolve Resource References Function

1. Open EON. Open **Activity_8.3.1.eoz** from the data files for Module 8 Lesson 3.
2. Run the simulation. Examine the clock that has moving hands.
3. Close the simulation window.
4. Drag the **Clock** frame from the Scene frame in the simulation tree to the Local Prototypes window. A prototype named Clock (1) is created.
5. Click the plus symbol to the left of the prototype instance in the Simulation Tree window. This reveals a long list of SFNode fields. An ***SFNode field*** contains a reference to another node. In this simulation, the SFNode fields contain references to Mesh2 and Material2 nodes. EON automatically created these exported fields so that the simulation would continue to work after the Clock prototype was created.
6. Run the simulation again to verify that the clock is still displayed and then close the simulation window.
7. Delete the **Clock** prototype from the simulation tree and then add it again by dragging it from the Local Prototypes window to the Scene frame in the simulation tree. In the Property Bar, notice that all of the SFNode fields are now empty.
8. Run the simulation. Notice that the simulation window is blank because the prototype does not contain the resources it needs. This makes the prototype unsuitable for reuse. Setting up links to all of the resources referenced in the SFNode fields would require a lot of time and effort.
9. Close the simulation window. Close EON without saving the simulation.
10. Open EON. Reopen **Activity_8.3.1.eoz** from the data files for Module 8 Lesson 3. Reopening the data file discards your changes and allows you to start over with an unchanged data file. You already determined that it would require too much time to move all of the resource nodes to the Clock frame. Therefore, you will use the Resolve resource references function to place the resources in the prototype.
11. Expand the **Clock** frame. Right-click the **Clock** frame and select the **Resolve resource references** option. Notice that a Resources node containing meshes, materials, and textures is added to the Clock frame. Expand the frames under the Clock frame to find a Shape node in the simulation tree. Double-click the node reference under the Shape node to see that the resources are located under the new Resources group as shown in Figure 8.3.3.

FIGURE 8.3.3 Node reference for a Shape node in the Clock frame

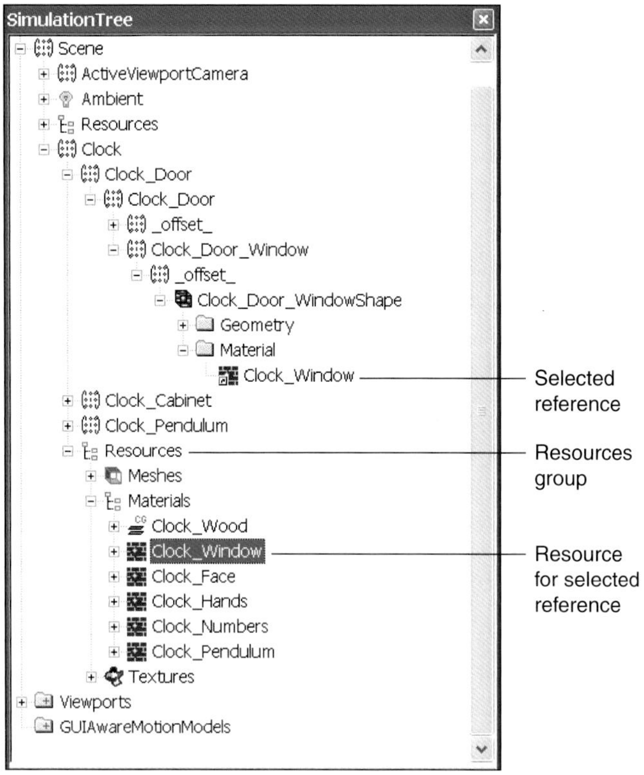

12. Drag the **Clock** frame from the simulation tree to the Local Prototypes window to create the prototype identified as Clock (1) in the Local Prototypes window.
13. Explore the **Scene** frame in the simulation tree. Notice that the Clock prototype replaced the Clock frame as shown in Figure 8.3.4. SFNode fields (yellow folders) are not displayed under the prototype instance because the resources are inside the prototype.

FIGURE 8.3.4 Clock prototype replaces the Clock frame

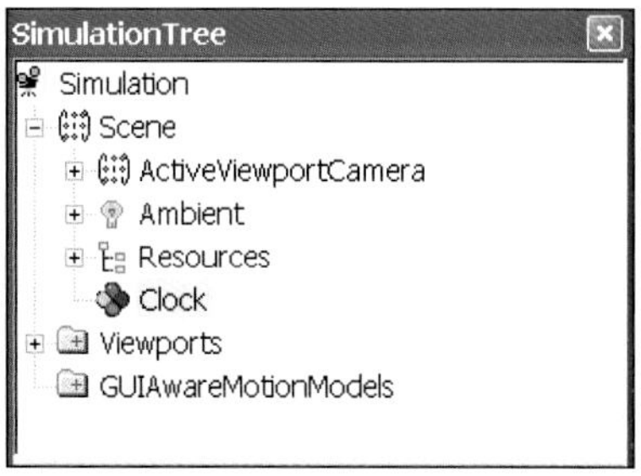

14. Delete the **Clock** prototype from the simulation tree and then add it again by dragging it from the Local Prototypes window to the Scene frame in the simulation tree.
15. Run the simulation. The clock is displayed because the Clock prototype contains the resources it needs.
16. Close the simulation window. Close EON without saving the simulation.

Nested Prototypes

In addition to nodes and routes, existing prototypes, which may contain other prototypes, can be encapsulated within new prototypes. We call prototypes within prototypes ***nested prototypes.*** The depth of the prototype's hierarchical structure is not limited. However, a prototype should be kept as small as possible to perform efficiently as a reusable object. In Figure 8.3.5, you can see that Prototype B includes Prototype A. In the Local Prototypes window for the main simulation tree, you can see that the instance count for Prototype A is zero, even though one instance of Prototype B (which contains a prototype called Prototype A) is present in the tree.

FIGURE 8.3.5 Nested prototypes

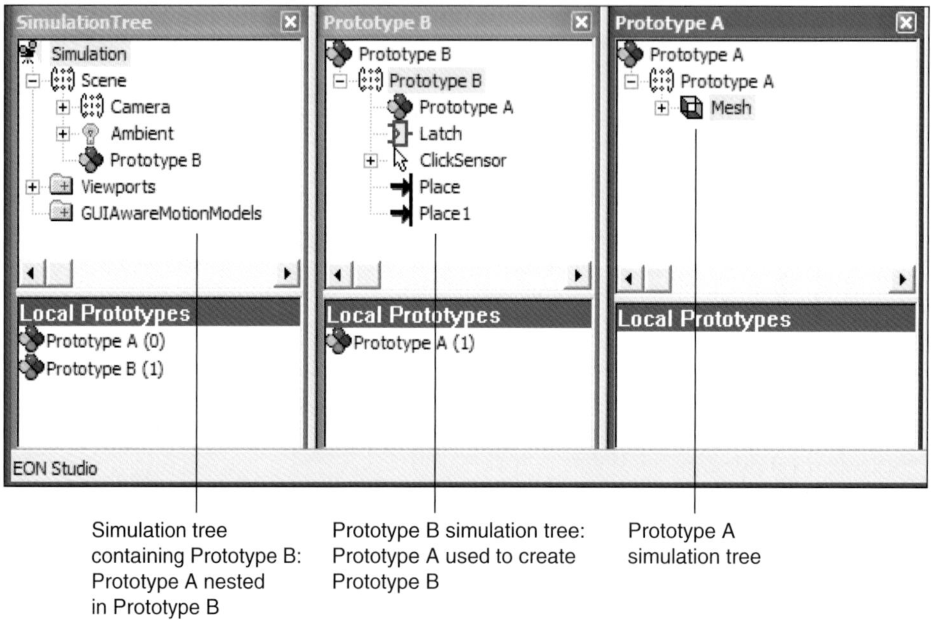

It is important to realize that the Prototype A in the Local Prototype window on the left no longer has any connection to the Prototype A in the Local Prototype window displayed in the middle. Because Prototype A is nested in the main simulation tree on the left, they have become separate prototype definitions. Deleting the Prototype A with zero instances does not delete the other Prototype A with one instance.

Adding or Inserting Prototype Instances

We have discussed the *creation* of prototype definitions. We will not use the terms *create* and *instance* together, such as *creating a prototype instance*, because you are not making a new thing. An instance is just a special node that says, "Put a copy of the definition here when you start the simulation." Instead, we should say that we *add* or *insert* a prototype instance in the same way as we add or insert a node. This is consistent because we do not create nodes either; we add or insert nodes into the simulation tree.

Insert a prototype instance into a simulation tree by using one of the following six methods:

- **Drag-and-drop from the library:** Drag the prototype definition from the prototype library to a node in the simulation tree. The mouse pointer will indicate if your selection is valid. When you release the mouse, a prototype instance is inserted under the selected node.
- **Copy a definition in the library:** Select a prototype in the prototype library and press Ctrl + C to copy the prototype. Select a node in the simulation tree and then press Ctrl + V or right-click the selected node and choose Paste. A prototype instance is pasted under the selected node.
- **Drag-and-drop from the Local Prototypes window:** Drag the prototype definition from the Local Prototypes window and drop it under a node in the simulation tree. The mouse pointer will indicate if your selection is valid. When you release the mouse, a prototype instance is inserted under the selected node.
- **Insert in the simulation tree:** Select a node in the simulation tree and then right-click a prototype definition in the Local Prototypes window. In the pop-up menu, choose Insert in Tree. A prototype instance is inserted under the selected node.
- **Copy a definition in the Local Prototypes window:** Select the prototype definition in the Local Prototypes window. Press Ctrl + C, use the Edit menu, or use the pop-up menu to copy the prototype. Select a node in the simulation tree. Press Ctrl + V, use the Edit menu, or use the pop-up menu to paste the prototype under the selected node.
- **Copy an instance in the simulation tree:** Select a prototype instance in the simulation tree. Press Ctrl + C, use the Edit menu, or use the pop-up menu to copy the prototype instance. Select a node in the simulation tree. Paste the prototype instance under the selected node by pressing Ctrl + V, using the Edit menu, or using the pop-up menu.

tips+tricks

Most of the methods listed here also will work between two EON Studio instances.

The first two methods will insert prototype instances and copy a definition from the prototype library to the Local Prototypes window. However, if the definition in the library is *mostly the same* as a definition that is already in the Local Prototypes window, then a new definition will not be added. Instead, the instance counter of the existing prototype definition will be increased by one. A prototype is *mostly the same* if only minor changes have been made, such as a modified value in an internal field. However, the local prototype is deemed *materially different* from the prototype definition in the library if an internal node has been removed or added. If the prototype is materially different, a new definition is added to the Local Prototypes window.

Editing Prototypes

You must understand the difference between changing prototype definitions and changing prototype instances. Using consistent terminology will help you remember the distinction. When you change a prototype instance, you will say that you are ***customizing*** a prototype. Use words such as *editing* and *modifying* to refer to changing the prototype definition.

To further understand the differences, consider this analogy to product manufacturing. In our manufacturing business, *product* equals *prototype*. Our factory is manufacturing an electric fan (an EON prototype). The first model is very simple, and the customer cannot do anything with the fan except plug it in to turn it on or unplug it to turn it off. This is like a prototype without any exported fields. In the next model, we want the customer to be able to choose the speed of the fan. Therefore, we add four buttons that enable the customer to *customize* the fan by selecting off, low, medium, or high. This is similar to allowing a user to select 0, 1, 2, or 3 in a prototype's exported field called FanSpeed. By pressing the buttons, the customer is not modifying the product because the fan is designed to respond to the buttons. Similarly, changing the exported field values is not modifying the prototype. Modifying the product would be like taking the fan apart so that the wiring is exposed and then changing the connections between the electric wires from one place to another place. In the same way, modifying a prototype would involve opening it and adding routes between internal nodes. You can see that giving a prototype an exported field is *modifying* the prototype, but changing the exported field's value is *customizing* the prototype.

Also, prototypes have ***default values,*** which are the values of the exported fields that a prototype is created with. Think of these as factory settings. Changing default values is not customization because the customer does not make the change. The change is made in the factory by the manufacturer (prototype developer).

Customizing Prototypes

Customizing a prototype is similar to customizing a node. You use the Property Bar or the Properties dialog box to see the fields and change the values. If you do not understand the purpose of a particular field, refer to the manual or the Help feature in EON.

Prototype instances have one major difference from nodes—if you change a field value during runtime, the change is not saved. When the simulation stops, the prototype instance's field values are reset to the values that they had before the simulation ran. You can change values during runtime, but the change will not have a permanent effect.

Editing Prototype Definitions

Editing a prototype can be divided into three parts: editing the subtree, editing the general properties, and editing the exported fields.

Editing the Subtree

To edit a prototype's subtree, you must open it to display the Prototype Edit window, which commonly refers to a window containing the simulation tree for a prototype. You can use one of the following four methods to open the prototype:

- **Pop-up menu:** Right-click a prototype in the Local Prototypes window and choose Open from the pop-up menu.
- **Shift and double-click:** Hold down the Shift key while you double-click a prototype in the Local Prototypes window.
- **Control + T:** Select a prototype instance in the simulation tree or its definition in the Local Prototypes window and then hold down the Ctrl key and press the T key.
- **Window menu:** Select a prototype instance in the simulation tree or its definition in the Local Prototypes window and then choose Window menu > Prototype > Open prototype.

tips+tricks

Prototypes cannot be opened and edited when they contain nodes that are not licensed on the computer used to perform the edits. A message will appear to explain this if you try to open one.

The Window menu also will have a list of all the open Prototype Edit windows that are available.

The Prototype Edit window is organized in the same way as the Simulation Tree window. A tree-like structure in the upper half of the window shows the current node hierarchy for the prototype, as shown in Figure 8.3.6. Any action that can be performed in the ordinary Simulation Tree window also can be performed in the Prototype Edit window. New nodes and prototypes, for example, can be added using the usual methods.

FIGURE 8.3.6 Prototype Edit window

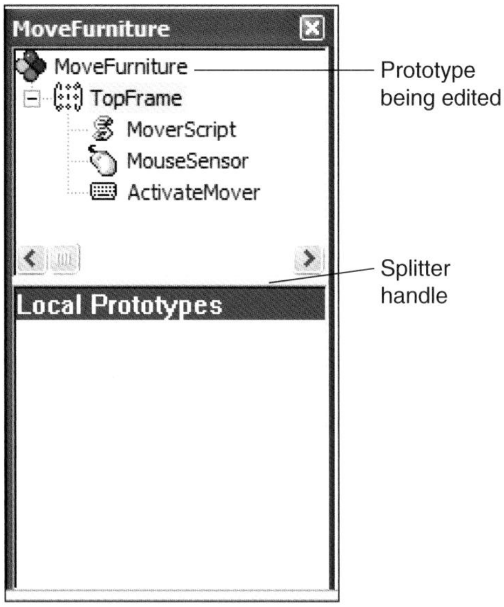

A prototype does not need to be added to a simulation tree before it can be modified. You can drag a prototype to the Local Prototypes window, edit the prototype, and then add it to the simulation tree by dragging it up to the Simulation Tree window from the Local Prototypes window.

A change in a prototype definition will affect all associated prototype instances except the values of the instance's exposed fields. You can update the values of the exposed fields of an instance in the same way as you would update normal nodes.

By using the splitter handle to split the window, you can view nested prototypes in the lower half of the window. This window is identical to the Local Prototypes window of the ordinary Simulation Tree window.

You can have nested prototypes, but be aware that they have no connection to other prototype definitions. You cannot create a never-ending loop. Nested prototypes can lead to inefficiencies because they are harder to maintain, but the encapsulation benefits can outweigh that problem.

Although a simulation can have many Prototype Edit windows (one for each prototype), it can have only one Routes window. The routes that are displayed in the Routes window depend on which Prototype Edit window or Simulation Tree window was last accessed or clicked. To see the internal routes for a prototype, open the prototype or click its Prototype Edit window. Because screen space is limited, the Routes window is not always displayed. To display the Routes window, you may need to click the Routes tab or select it from the Window menu.

The Routes window will show only nodes and routes for the last selected subtree or simulation tree. When you view a prototype subtree rather than the main simulation tree in the Routes window, the buttons for creating inEvents and outEvents are not shown. These buttons are not needed for prototypes because the exported fields serve that purpose.

Editing the General Properties

A prototype has only four general properties: name, tooltip, description, and icon. You edit the general properties in the Prototype Definition Properties dialog box shown in Figure 8.3.7. Use one of the following four methods to open the dialog box:

- **Double-click:** Double-click a prototype in the Local Prototypes window.
- **Pop-up menu:** Right-click a prototype in the Local Prototypes window and choose Properties from the pop-up menu.
- **Enter key:** Select a prototype in the Local Prototypes window and press the Enter key.
- **Edit menu:** Select a prototype in the Local Prototypes window and choose Properties from the Edit menu.

FIGURE 8.3.7 Prototype Definition Properties dialog box

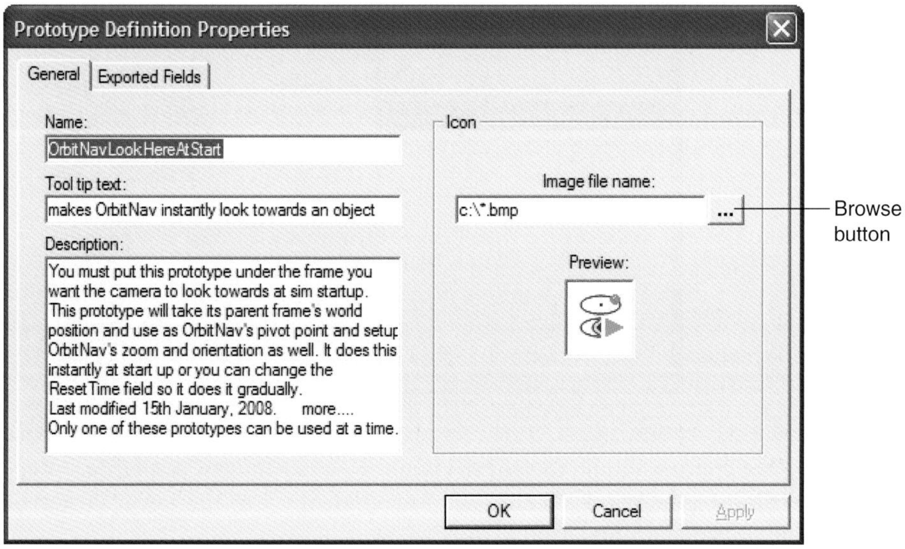

When you create a prototype, the name of the top frame in the prototype's simulation tree becomes the text for the name, tooltip, and description. A default icon is used. You can change these properties in the Prototype Definition Properties dialog box.

- **Name:** The default name for new instances. Note that changing a prototype's name does not change the names of its instances or sever the link between instances and their definition.
- **Tooltip text:** A short description of the prototype that is displayed in a tooltip when your mouse cursor hovers over the prototype in the Components window. This is a useful feature that allows you to see a brief overview of the different prototypes in a library.
- **Description:** This text is displayed only in this dialog box. Use this property to describe the prototype's purpose, how to set up the prototype, when it was last modified, and the important exported fields.
- **Icon:** An important visual element that provides a strong sense of individual identity. It is displayed next to the name of a prototype definition in the Local Prototypes window, next to prototype instances in a simulation tree, and in prototype libraries.

To change the icon, click the Browse button (a button with three dots next to the Image file name text field). This displays an Open dialog box that enables you to choose a new bitmap image. The icon's format must be a Windows bitmap (*.bmp). You can create an icon image easily with any graphics program, such as Paint or Photoshop.

The icon can be displayed in only one of two sizes: 16 × 16 pixels and 32 × 32 pixels. The larger size is displayed only in the Local Prototypes window in Normal viewing mode and in the Properties dialog box.

Although the icon can be displayed in only two sizes, the pixel size of the image can be any size. To avoid distortion, use a square (width equals height) image that is 16 × 16 pixels or 32 × 32 pixels. Do not use a large, detailed image because the detail will not be visible when it is reduced to fit into a 16 × 16 pixel space. On the other hand, using images smaller than 16 × 16 often results in blurry images when they are enlarged. Also, although you can use up to 24 colors, we recommend that you limit the icon to 16 colors to avoid distortion.

The size of the bitmap file does not matter because all images are resaved so that they all take the same amount of file space. Also, after an icon is inserted, it cannot be extracted, but it can be replaced.

In EON, the pixel in the upper-left corner is reserved for adding transparency to an icon. This means that all pixels that have the same color as the pixel in the upper-left corner will be transparent.

tips+tricks

If you are developing an object prototype, you can use a screen shot of the object in the simulation for your icon.

troubleshooting

If a prototype has fields of type SFNode or MFNode and you change the icon, the icon might be displayed on the SFNode's yellow folder under the prototype instance node. This will be corrected if you reload the simulation. This does not affect the simulation.

Activity 8.3.2: Creating a Prototype Icon

1. Open EON. Open **Activity_8.3.2.eoz** from the data files for Module 8 Lesson 3.
2. Run the simulation. Note that the object in the simulation looks small. Close the simulation window.
3. Double-click the **Simulation** node in the simulation tree to open the Simulation Properties dialog box.
4. Click the **Size/Aspect Ratio** tab.
5. Click the **Active** check box in the Fixed Size area. Enter **256** in the Width and in the Height fields as shown in Figure 8.3.8. Click **OK** to close the dialog box.

troubleshooting

This activity may require EON Professional. Depending on your configuration of EON modules, you may not be able to complete this activity.

FIGURE 8.3.8 Size/Aspect Ratio tab of the Simulation Properties dialog box

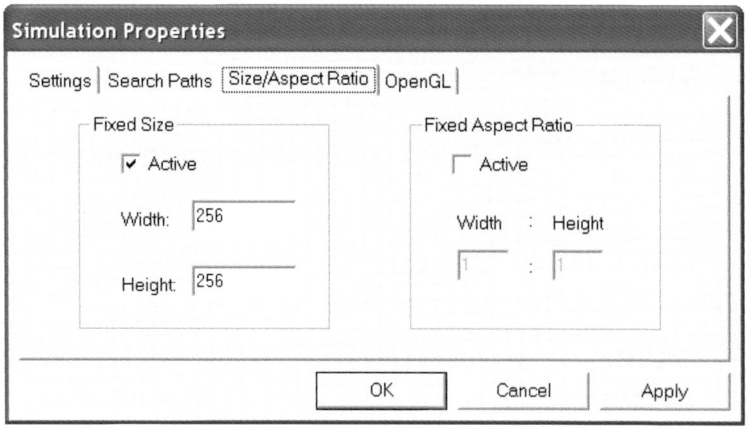

6. Save the simulation as **Resized_Clock.eoz** and then run the simulation. Note that the simulation window and the clock in the window are smaller.
7. Using OrbitNav navigation, zoom in by dragging the right mouse button until the clock object is as large as possible but the entire object is still visible.
8. Hold down the **Alt** key and press the **Print Screen** button on your keyboard.
9. Open your **Paint** program, which is usually found in Start > Programs > Accessories > Paint.
10. Press **Ctrl + V** to paste the screen shot.
11. Click the **Select** tool on the toolbar if necessary. The button for this tool looks like a rectangle with dashed lines.
12. Select the **clock** image by dragging the left mouse button from the upper-left corner of the image to the lower-right corner of the image. As you are dragging the mouse, you can see the size of the selected area in the lower-right corner of the Paint status bar. Try to select an area that is 256 × 256 pixels, as shown in Figure 8.3.9.

FIGURE 8.3.9 Select the clock image in Paint

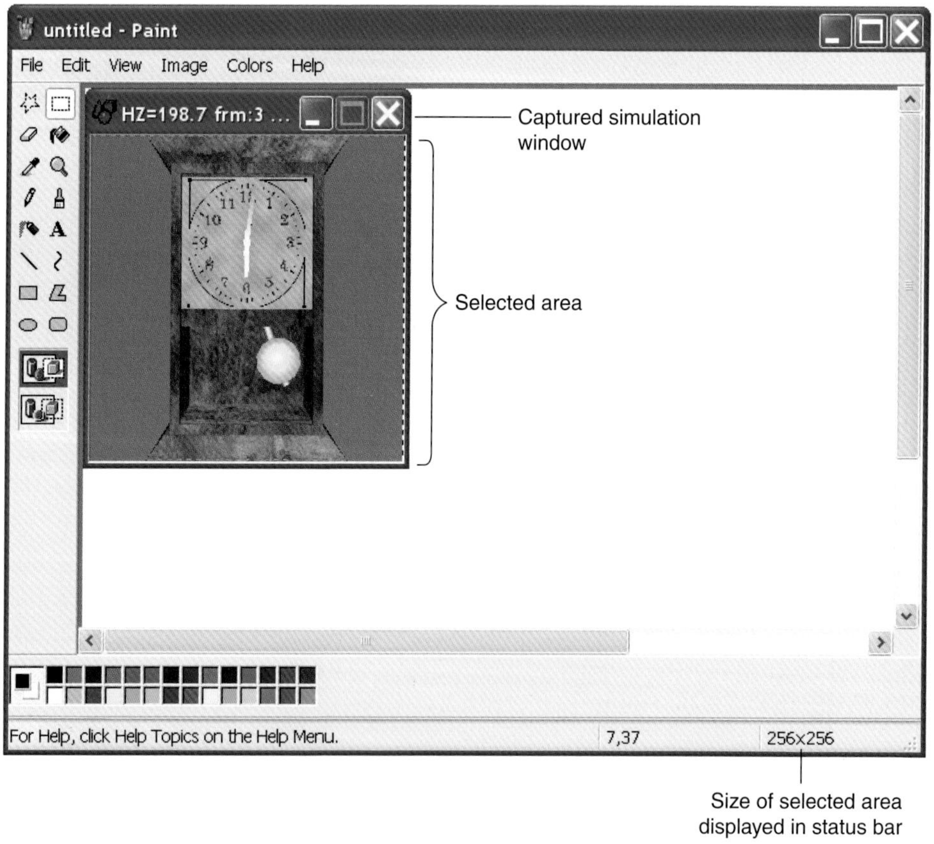

13. Press **Ctrl + C** to copy the selected area of the image.
14. Select **New** from the File menu. When asked if you want to save changes to the current file, click **No**. A new Paint window is opened.

15. Select **Attributes** from the Image menu to display the Attributes dialog box. Enter **256** in the Width and in the Height boxes. Click **OK** to close the dialog box. The size of the image area is adjusted.
16. Press **Ctrl + V** to paste the image.
17. Save the image as **Clock1.bmp**.
18. Close Paint and return to EON. Close the simulation window.
19. Double click the **Clock** prototype in the Local Prototypes window. The Prototype Definition Properties dialog box is displayed.
20. Click the **Browse** button next to the Image file name text field to display the Open dialog box. Browse to the Clock1.bmp file, select the **Clock1.bmp** file, and click the **Open** button. The Open dialog box is closed and the new icon is displayed in the Preview field of the Prototype Definition Properties dialog box.
21. Click **OK** to close the dialog box. The new icon is displayed in the Local Prototypes window. Expand the **Scene** frame in the Simulation Tree window to verify that the icon for the prototype instance has changed, as shown in Figure 8.3.10.

FIGURE 8.3.10 Updated icon in the Simulation Tree window and the Local Prototypes window

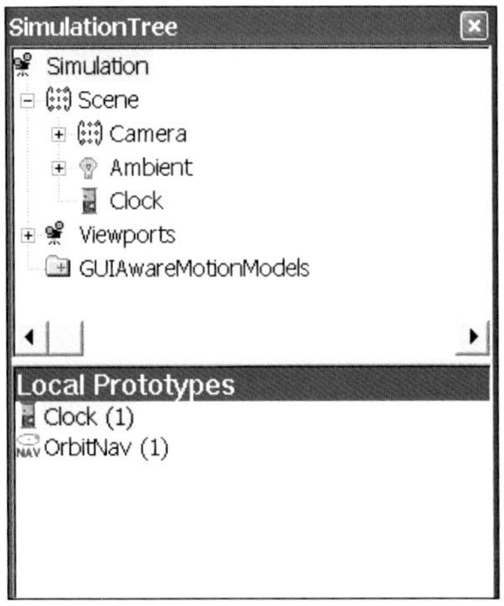

22. Save the simulation and then close EON.

Editing the Exported Fields

Another aspect of developing prototypes is editing a prototype's exported fields list. Typically, object prototypes do not have exported fields because the main purpose of an object prototype is to hold the 3D object and its resources. Usually, functional prototypes have many exported fields. The prototype developer decides which fields within a prototype they want to make available for easy access. Fields that users like to customize contain information about color, speed, position, size, and texture.

Opening the Exported Fields List

To edit the exported fields list, you must open the Prototype Definition Properties dialog box and then click the Exported Fields tab as shown in Figure 8.3.11. You also can open this tab directly by using one of the following four methods:

- **Double-click:** Double-click the root node of a Prototype Edit window.
- **Pop-up menu:** Right-click any node in a Prototype Edit window and choose Prototype Properties from the pop-up menu.
- **Enter key:** Select the root node of a Prototype Edit window and press the Enter key.
- **Edit menu:** Select the root node of a Prototype Edit window and choose Properties from the Edit menu.

FIGURE 8.3.11 Exported Fields tab for the OrbitNavResetToClickPos prototype

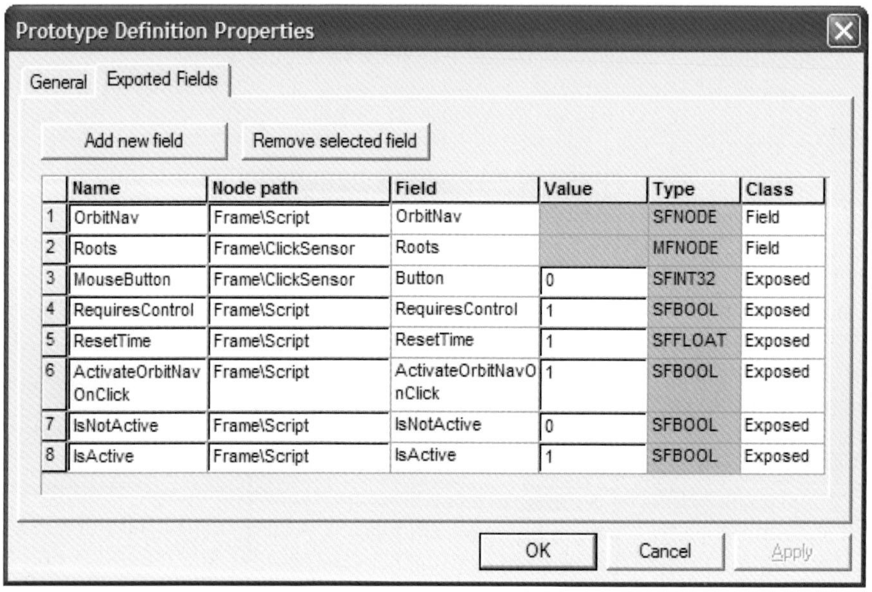

Columns in the Exported Fields List

The following information is displayed for each exported field:

- **Name:** The name of the field is displayed in the instance. It does not need to be the same as the internal field name. Choose names wisely to make your prototype easy to understand for other users.
- **Node path:** The absolute path to the node in a prototype subtree that has the field you are exporting.
- **Field:** The name of the field that you are exporting. If you selected a valid node in the Node path column, then this column will provide a drop-down list of all the fields contained in the selected node, and you are limited to this list. To find or select the field you want more quickly, press the letter key of the first letter of the field's name. For example, press B to find the Button field.
- **Value:** The initial value of the exported field. The Value column holds the prototype's default values (or factory settings). When you selected a field in the Field column, the current value of the selected field in the prototype was inserted. You can change this value.
- **Type:** Displays the selected field's data type (SFBool, SFInt32, SFFloat, etc.). This value is informational; you cannot change it.
- **Class:** The type of field that determines how the exported field can be connected in the Routes window. The four options are In, Out, Exposed, and Field. If the class is *In*, then routes can be connected only to the field. If the class is *Out*, then

troubleshooting

You cannot assign an initial value if the data type is SFNode or MFNode or the field type is an outEvent.

routes can be connected only from the field. If the class is *Exposed*, then routes can be connected to or from the field. If the class is *Field*, you cannot connect any routes to it. Depending on the class of the internal field, you may have only one or two options rather than the usual four options.

Adding, Changing, and Removing Exported Fields

Each row in this exported fields list contains information for one exported field. To add a new empty row to the list, click the Add new field button. To remove a row, select it by clicking a number in the left column and then click the Remove selected field button. You can remove several rows at the same time by clicking a number in the left column and dragging the mouse cursor down over additional rows.

You must obey the following rules when you are adding exported fields:

- Each exported field name must be unique. You cannot have two exported fields with the same name.
- You cannot use the default EON field names, which include SetRun, SetRun_, OnRunTrue, OnRunFalse, OnRunChanged, TreeChildren, and Children because you cannot have two exported fields with the same name.
- Names cannot have spaces. (Although you can use special characters, they are not recommended.)
- You cannot export the same field twice using different names.
- If you already have some prototype instances and you add a new exported field, then the exported field will immediately appear in the instance's field list. For example, the new exported field will be displayed in the Property Bar.
- If you remove an exported field, then the field will immediately disappear from the instances. Also, any routes that were connected to the removed field will be deleted without warning.
- If you rename an exported field, then any routes that were connected to the field will be deleted without warning. Renaming an exported field is similar to removing it and then adding a new one.
- If you rename or move a node that has an exported field within a prototype subtree, then the exported field *will not disappear*. The exported field will remain. If you look at the exported fields list, the node path in the Node path column has been updated accordingly.
- If you delete a node that had an exported field within a prototype, then the exported field and any connected routes will be deleted without warning.
- If you delete or rename an exported field of a Script node in a prototype, then the exported field and any connected routes will automatically be removed. You will see a warning message, but it says only that routes to the selected field may be lost.

Creating Exported Fields Automatically

Creating a prototype should not necessarily stop an EON application from working. EON can automatically convert routes into exported fields when you create a prototype. This maintains or preserves the behavior that the route provides.

If you think that adding exported fields manually is too challenging and you prefer to connect routes instead, then you could connect routes to all the fields that you want as exported fields before you create a prototype. EON can automatically create the exported fields for you.

When EON creates exported fields automatically, the name of the exported field will be the same as the name of the field inside the prototype. However, we cannot have two exported fields with the same name, so EON will rename the fields by adding an integer to the end of the name. Therefore, if your simulation has many Shape nodes that have references to external Material nodes, the exported fields will be named Material, Material1, Material2, and so on.

troubleshooting

Pressing Delete does not remove the selected rows; it only deletes the text in the rows.

tips+tricks

If a node is deep in a prototype subtree, making an exported field is more difficult because you must enter a long node path. To get around this, place the node temporarily under the root node, make the exported field, and then return the node to its correct location in the prototype subtree.

troubleshooting

You cannot change the name of an exported field by changing only the case of the first letter, such as changing the name from *position* to *Position*. If you try to make this change, the exported field will disappear! However, you can make the change in two steps. For example, change the name to *Pos* (changing the entire name rather than the case of the first letter). Then, open the list again and change the name to *Position*. In the exported fields list, the sequence of the fields will be changed, and the field will be displayed at the end of the list.

Also, when EON creates exported fields automatically, the default values for those fields will be the same values that the internal fields have when making the prototype.

On the same topic, a node reference is the value of an SFNode field. Although a node reference is not a route, it is similar because it is a link to a node instead of a link to a field in a node. Therefore, when you create a prototype, EON will also create exported fields for SFNode fields that have a value linking to a node that will be outside the prototype. Again, EON does this to keep the application working and to avoid disrupting the behavior set up by routes and node references.

However, EON cannot automatically fix a situation in which outside SFNode fields have references to nodes that are inside a prototype. In this situation, EON will warn you when you try to create a prototype. The message says, "*This subtree contains in/out routes that cannot be converted into exported fields. Would you like to continue?*" If you continue, these node references will be deleted.

tips+tricks

If you want to make all instances have the same value for a specific field, remove the exported field from the prototype definition and then add the exported field again. When you add the exported field, you can set its default value.

Editing Default Values

The default values are displayed in the Value column of the exported fields list. Think of these values as the factory settings. Try to set them to values that would suit the majority of users or the most common use for the prototype, or set them to values that you would most often require. If you spend more time optimizing the default values, you will spend less time customizing the prototypes when you reuse them later. You should understand the following items when you are working with default values:

- When you create a prototype that has an exported field, the field's default value will be the value of the field at the time the prototype was created.
- When you insert a new instance, it inherits all of the default values in the exported fields list.
- When you create an instance by copying another instance, the copy receives the values from the original instance.
- When you add a new exported field to a prototype definition, all instances receive the same default value.
- When you change a default value, it does not change the values of the instances already in the simulation. However, any new instances you insert by dragging the prototype definition to the simulation tree will inherit the new default values.

tips+tricks

Use the Find window to locate an instance in the simulation tree if you know the name of the instance. A more advanced method requires the NodeFinder prototype from the DeveloperTools library. Read the documentation for this prototype before you use it.

Deleting Prototypes

To delete a prototype definition from the Local Prototypes window, select the prototype definition and press the Delete key, or right-click the prototype definition and choose Delete from the pop-up menu. In both methods, a dialog box asks you to verify the action. Click Yes to confirm the deletion.

tips+tricks

If you delete a prototype from the Local Prototypes window and then select File > Save to save the .eoz file, the resource files that existed in the prototype are not removed from the .eoz file. To ensure that the resource files are removed, you must select File > Save As and enter a filename. You can choose the same filename and click Yes when a message informs you that the file already exists and asks if you want to replace the file.

Instance Counter

To delete a prototype definition, the instance counter must be zero. The ***instance counter*** is the number displayed in brackets at the end of the prototype's name. If you do not delete the prototype definition, it is saved as part of the simulation even if its instance counter is zero.

Deleting a Prototype Instance

To set the instance counter to zero, you must delete all of the prototype instances in the simulation tree. If you do not know where the instances are located in the simulation tree, you must search the simulation tree to find the prototype's icon. If more than one prototype definition has the same icon, click the instance; its prototype definition is highlighted in the Local Prototypes window.

Working with Prototype Libraries

Storing prototypes in prototype libraries (.eop files) allows you to access the prototypes quickly for reuse because prototype libraries are displayed in the Prototypes tab of the Components window. Also, libraries enable you to add multiple prototypes, which allows you to group several prototypes with similar or related functions. You also can use prototype libraries for moving subtrees between files instead of copying a prototype from one open EON window to another. When you create dynamic load applications, the resources you load must be inside a prototype library file.

Creating a Prototype Library

To create a new prototype library file, click the Prototypes tab in the Components window and click the New button in the upper-right corner, as shown in Figure 8.3.12.

FIGURE 8.3.12 Creating a new prototype library

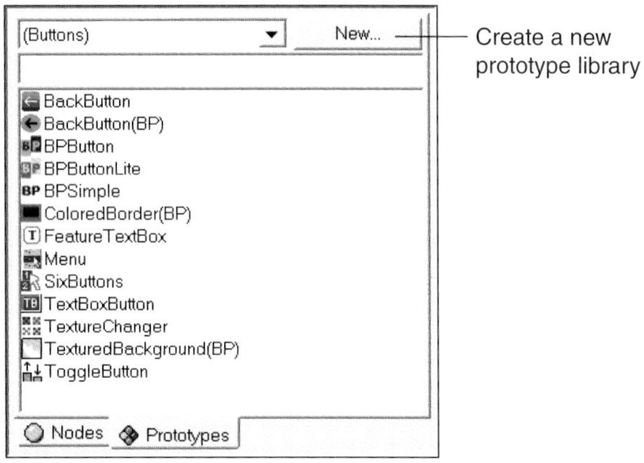

The New Prototype File dialog box is displayed. The New Prototype File dialog box, as shown in Figure 8.3.13, asks you where you want to save the file and allows you to name the file. It automatically adds the .eop extension to the end of the filename.

FIGURE 8.3.13 New Prototype File dialog box

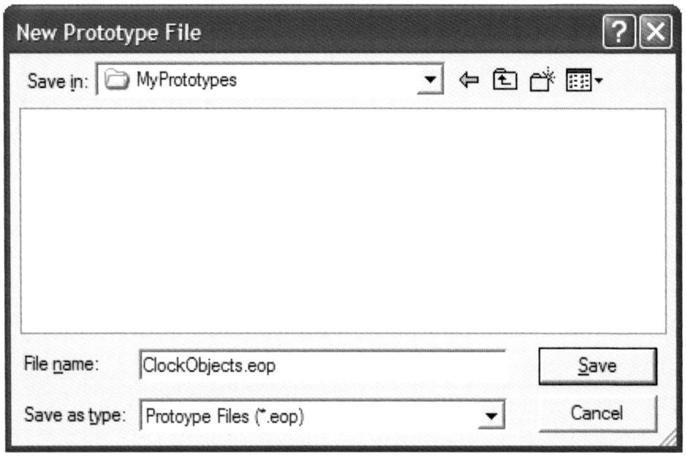

The filename you choose becomes the library's name, which is displayed at the top of the Components window, as shown in Figure 8.3.14. You can choose a prototype library from the drop-down list, limiting the prototypes displayed in the Components window. The file extension (.eop) is not displayed.

FIGURE 8.3.14 Prototype library selected in Components window

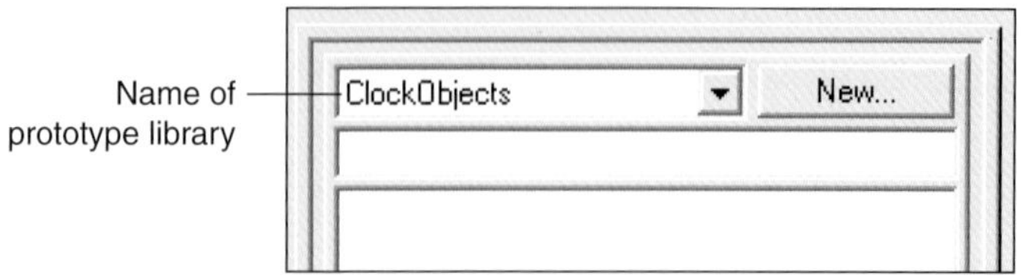

Storing Prototypes

It is convenient to save your prototypes in one folder separate from the EON-supplied prototypes. EON keeps a list of search paths that it uses to look for resources and prototype library files. Choose Preferences from the Options menu to view this list, as shown in Figure 8.3.15. When you create a prototype library file in a path that is not listed in the Preferences dialog box, EON will automatically add it to this list. The EON-supplied prototypes are installed in C:\Program Files\EON Reality\EON Studio\PrototypeLibrary.

FIGURE 8.3.15 Preferences dialog box

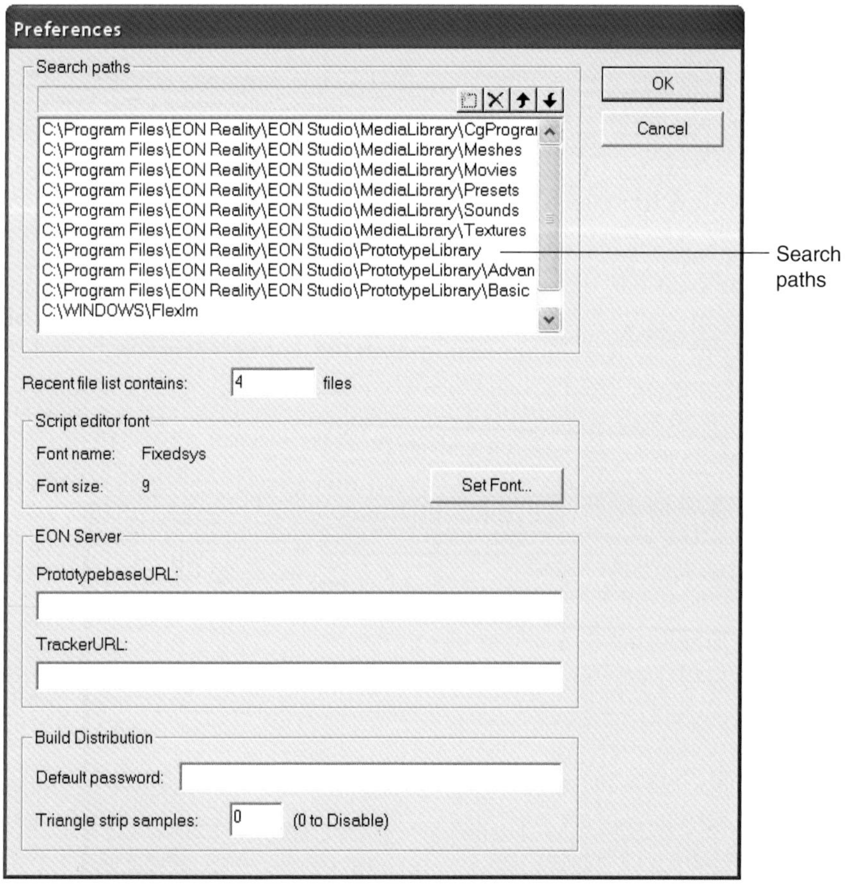

When you add or remove a path, EON refreshes the Components window so it shows all of the prototypes in those paths. However, if you have two EON Studio windows open, both Components windows will not be refreshed when you add or remove a path in one EON Studio window.

EOP File Format

The EOP file format is similar to the EOZ file format because it is a compressed file (zipped) containing information about nodes and resource files like geometry, image, video, and audio files. You can see the contents of the file by opening it with a compression utility program, such as WinZip®.

Adding Prototypes to a Library

Before you add a prototype definition to a prototype library, you must verify that the correct prototype library is displayed in the upper-left area of the Components window. Use the drop-down list to select the prototype library to which you want to add the prototype. If you just created a prototype library file, then it will already be selected. After you select the prototype library, use one of the following two methods to add a prototype to it. Repeat the procedure for each prototype you want to put in the prototype library file.

- **Drag-and-drop:** Drag the prototype definition from the Local Prototypes window to the Components window. The mouse pointer will indicate if your selection is valid.
- **Copy and Paste:** Select the prototype definition in the Local Prototypes window and press Control + C to copy the prototype or right-click the prototype definition and choose Copy. Next, click in the Components window and press Control + V to paste the prototype.

After you drop a prototype into a library, the prototype library file (.eop) is re-saved and all resource nodes in the prototype definition will be copied from the simulation file (.eoz) to the .eop file as well as the subtree information, exported fields list, general properties, and the icon. It may take several seconds to save the prototype library file. When it is complete, the prototype name and icon will appear in the Components window.

troubleshooting

If the prototype and icon do not appear, the .eop file has the read-only attribute turned on. EON-supplied prototypes are usually set to read-only. This attribute can be turned off in Windows Explorer by right-clicking a file, choosing Properties to open a dialog box, and clearing the Read-Only check box.

Removing Prototypes from a Library

To remove a prototype from a prototype library, select the prototype icon in the Components window, and press the Delete key. A confirmation dialog box is displayed. Click OK.

When you remove a prototype from a prototype library file, the resources are not removed from the prototype library file; only the EON subtree-related information is deleted because those resources also could be used by other prototypes in the library. To be sure that you do not have unnecessary resource files in .eop files, you should try to avoid deleting prototypes from libraries. Instead, you should create new prototype library files and move only the prototypes you want into them. You also could manually remove the resource files by opening the .eop file in a program like WinZip.

troubleshooting

If you recently deleted a prototype and then you load a new file or otherwise refresh the Components window and the prototype you deleted is displayed, then it was not really deleted. The prototype file probably has the read-only attribute turned on. You will have to turn off the read-only attribute by editing the properties of the prototype as explained previously and then delete the prototype again.

Moving Prototypes

You can move prototypes between libraries by dragging a prototype from a library in the Components window to the Local Prototypes window and then dragging it from the Local Prototypes window to another library. It is not possible to drag between two Components windows.

Deleting Prototype Libraries

EON does not have a way to delete .eop files. The only way to delete prototype library files is by using Windows Explorer.

EDP File Format

cross-reference

You can find more information about dynamic load in Module 9 Lesson 3.

Another type of prototype file is a distribution prototype file (.edp). It is similar to the .edz file format in that it is highly compressed and it cannot be edited. These files cannot be viewed in the Components window. Their only purpose is to be dynamically loaded in dynamic load applications. You can create a distribution prototype file by right-clicking a prototype definition in the Local Prototypes window and choosing Build distribution file.

Prototype Development Example

It will be easier to understand the process of creating a prototype, modifying a prototype, and storing it in a prototype library if you perform all of the actions we discussed. Therefore, in this series of activities, you will create a prototype of a clock with exported fields. When the prototype is complete, you will save it to a prototype library.

In the first prototype development activity, you will use the Resolve resource references function. After you create the new prototype, it will be displayed in the Local Prototypes window.

troubleshooting

This activity may require EON Professional. Depending on your configuration of EON modules, you may not be able to complete this activity.

Activity 8.3.3: Creating a Prototype

1. Open EON. Open **Activity_8.3.3.eoz** from the data files for Module 8 Lesson 3.
2. Run the simulation to view the clock.
3. Close the simulation window.
4. Right-click the **Clock** frame under Scene and choose **Resolve resource references**.
5. Right-click the **Clock** frame and choose **Create Prototype**.
6. Delete the **Resources** group under the Scene. It is not needed because the resources are now located in the prototype you created. Your simulation tree and Local Prototypes window should be similar to that shown in Figure 8.3.16.

FIGURE 8.3.16 Clock prototype created

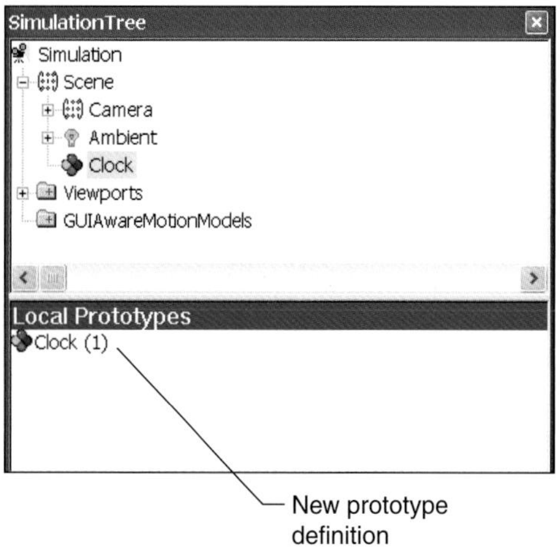

7. Save the simulation as **Clock_Prototype.eoz** and keep the simulation open to use in Activity 8.3.4.

Now you want the user of this prototype to be able to decide which parts of the clock should be displayed. Therefore, you will create exported fields for the Hidden field of the frames for the door, the cabinet, and the pendulum.

Activity 8.3.4: Adding Exported Fields to Hide Parts of an Object

1. Continue working with the open simulation file **Clock_Prototype.eoz** from Activity 8.3.3.
2. Right-click the **Clock** prototype in the Local Prototypes window and choose **Open**. The simulation tree for the Clock prototype is displayed on the left side of the EON window as shown in Figure 8.3.17. You should be able to see the Clock_Door, Clock_Cabinet, and Clock_Pendulum frames. Note the frame names and the paths to the frames because you will need to use them in the exported fields list.

FIGURE 8.3.17 Simulation tree for the Clock prototype

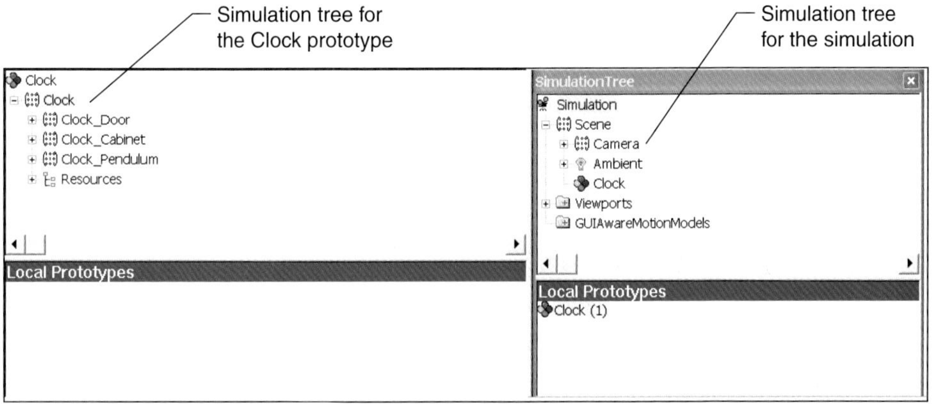

3. Double-click the **Clock** prototype in the Local Prototypes window to display the Prototype Definition Properties dialog box and then click the **Exported Fields** tab. This prototype does not have any exported fields yet.
4. Click the **Add new field** button. A blank line is displayed as shown in Figure 8.3.18.

FIGURE 8.3.18 Adding an exported field

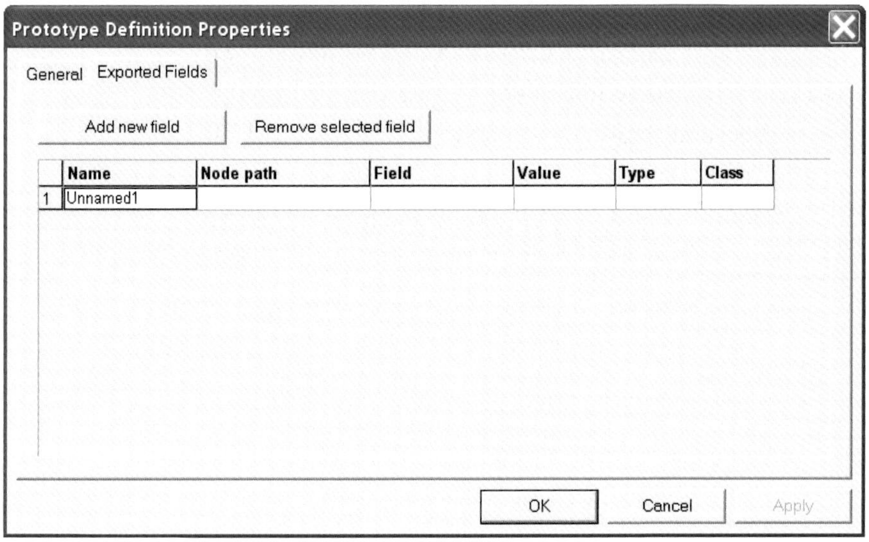

5. Key **HideDoor** in the Name field. Press **Tab** and enter **Clock\Clock_Door** in the Node path field. Choose **Hidden** from the drop-down list in the Field column.
6. Follow the same procedure to create fields named **HideCabinet** and **HidePendulum** by exporting the Hidden fields of **Clock_Cabinet** frame and **Clock_Pendulum** frame. Your Prototype Definition Properties dialog box should resemble Figure 8.3.19. Click **OK** to close the dialog box.

FIGURE 8.3.19 Exported fields to hide portions of the prototype added

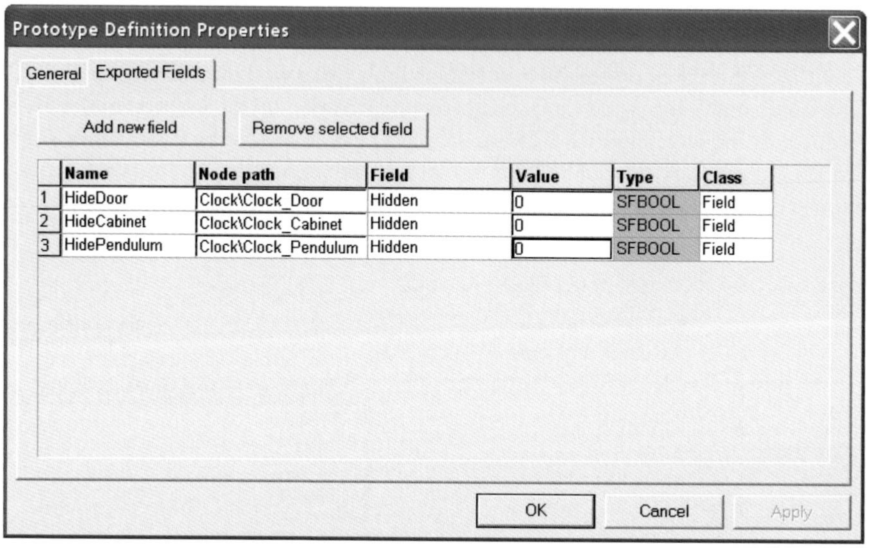

7. Save the simulation as **Clock_Hidden.eoz** and keep the simulation open to use in Activity 8.3.5.

In the previous activity, you added exported fields that will enable the user to display or hide parts of the Clock prototype. In the next activity, you will create a function to open and close the clock's glass door.

Activity 8.3.5: Adding inEvents to Open and Close the Clock's Door

1. Continue working with the open simulation file **Clock_Hidden.eoz** from Activity 8.3.4.
2. Right-click the **Clock** prototype in the Local Prototypes window and choose **Open**. The simulation tree for the Clock prototype is displayed in the left portion of the EON window.
3. In the Clock prototype simulation tree, expand **Clock** > **Clock_Door** > **Clock_Door**. Right-click the second **Clock_Door**, select **New** from the drop-down menu, select **Agent Nodes**, and then select **Place**. Change the name of the Place node to **Open**. Add a second **Place** node in the same location and change its name to **Close**.

4. Double-click the **Open** Place node to display its Place Properties dialog box. Under the Active heading, verify that the No radio button is selected. In the Type area, select **RelX**, **RelY**, and **RelZ**. Moving a relative distance of zero ensures that the position does not change. Under the Movement heading, set the h value to **150**. Under the Time to move heading, set the h value to **2** seconds. Your Place Properties dialog box for the Open Place node should match Figure 8.3.20. Click **OK** to close the dialog box.

FIGURE 8.3.20 Place Properties dialog box for the Open Place node

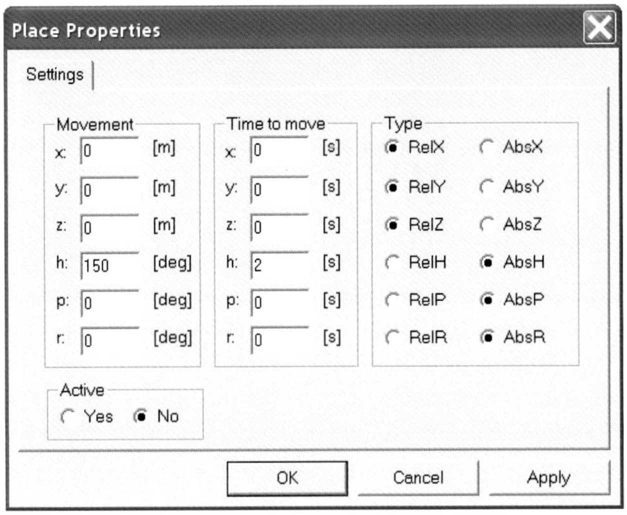

5. Double-click the **Close** Place node to display its Place Properties dialog box. Under the Active heading, verify that the No radio button is selected. In the Type area, select **RelX**, **RelY**, and **RelZ**. Under the Movement heading, set the h value to **0**. Under the Time to move heading, set the h value to **2** seconds. Your Place Properties dialog box for the Close Place node should match Figure 8.3.21. Click **OK** to close the dialog box.

FIGURE 8.3.21 Place Properties dialog box for the Close Place node

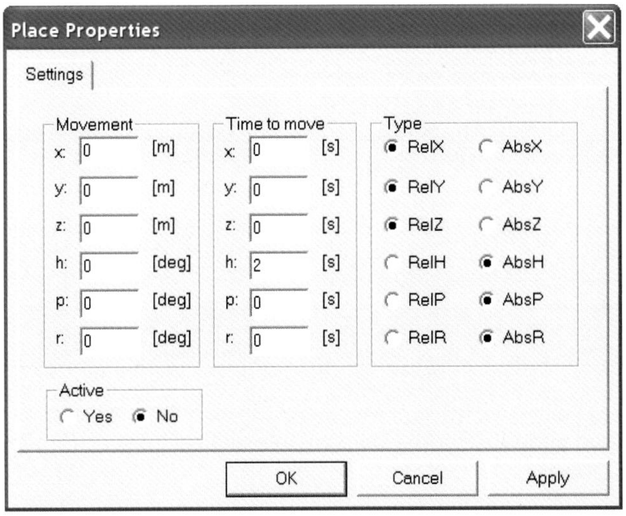

6. Now the user of the prototype must be able to trigger these Place nodes, so you will export the SetRun field on both Place nodes. First move the two **Place** nodes, placing them directly under the Clock root frame in the Clock prototype simulation tree. This will make it easier to create the exported field because the path to the field (which you need to type) is shorter. The relocated Open and Close Place nodes will be displayed in their new location as shown in Figure 8.3.22. Later, you will move the Place nodes back to the correct location—after you export the fields.

FIGURE 8.3.22 Relocated Open and Close Place nodes

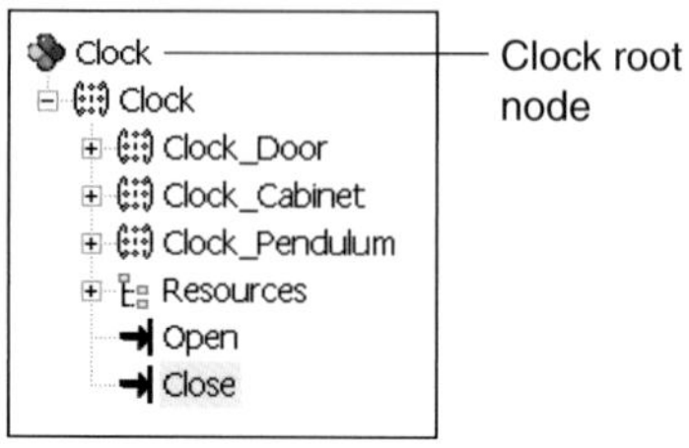

tips+tricks

Refer to Activity 8.3.4 if necessary to review adding exported fields.

7. Double-click the **Clock** root node in the Clock prototype's simulation tree in the left window to open the Prototype Definition Properties dialog box. Click the **Exported Fields** tab if necessary to view the exported fields list.
8. Add an exported field. Name it **OpenDoor** and enter **Clock\Open** in the Node path field. Choose **SetRun**, if necessary, from the drop-down list in the Field column.
9. Add another exported field. Name it **CloseDoor** and enter **Clock\Close** in the Node path field. Choose **SetRun** from the drop-down list in the Field column. Your Prototype Definition Properties dialog box should resemble Figure 8.3.23. Click **OK** to close the dialog box.

FIGURE 8.3.23 Exported fields to open the clock's door added

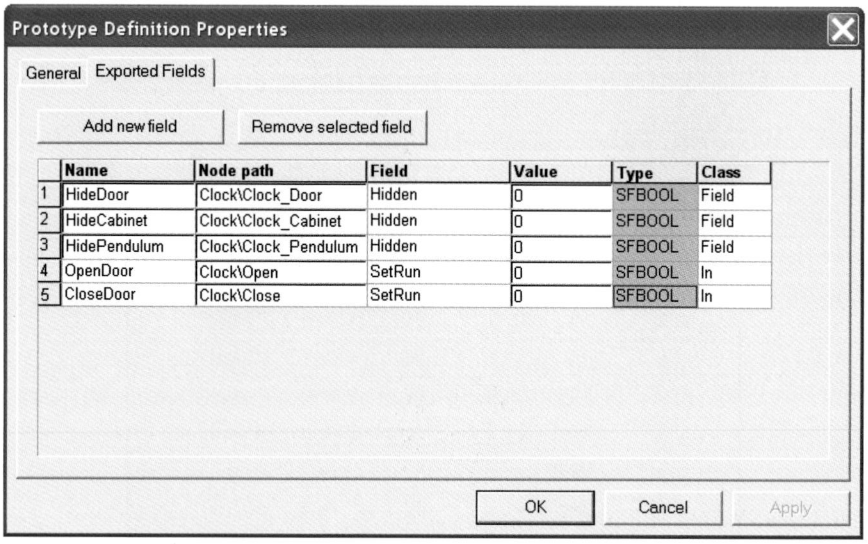

10. Move the **Open** and **Close** nodes back to their original locations in Clock\Clock_Door\Clock_Door\.
11. Open the Prototype Definition Properties dialog box to view the exported fields list again and confirm that the path to the nodes was automatically updated. Close the dialog box. In the next few steps, you will set up two 2DText nodes as buttons to open and close the door.

12. Return to the Simulation Tree window containing the main simulation tree. Insert a **2DText** node under the Scene frame and change its name to **OpenDoor**.
13. In the Property Bar, change the OpenDoor node's Text field to **Open Door**. Change its BoxArea to **100 20**.
14. Return to the Simulation Tree window containing the main simulation tree. Insert a **2DText** node under the Scene frame and change its name to **CloseDoor**.
15. In the Property Bar, change the CloseDoor node's Text field to **Close Door**. Change its BoxPosition fields to **120 10**.
16. Display the **Routes** window. Drag the two **2DText** nodes and the **Clock** prototype to the Routes window. Establish the connections outlined in the following table. Your Routes window should resemble Figure 8.3.24.

From	outEvent	To	inEvent
OpenDoor	OnButtonUp	Clock	OpenDoor
CloseDoor	OnButtonUp	Clock	CloseDoor

FIGURE 8.3.24 Routes that open and close the clock's door

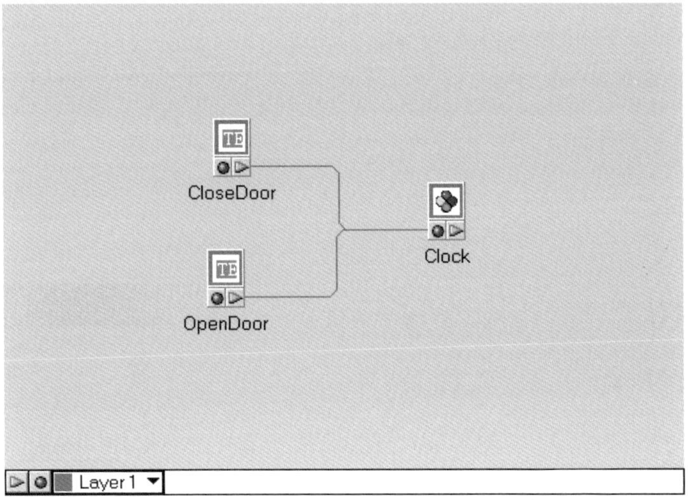

17. Save the simulation as **Clock_Door.eoz**.
18. Run the simulation and test the buttons.
19. Close the simulation window. Keep the simulation open to use in Activity 8.3.6.

Before you save this prototype to a library, set its general properties. General properties include the text displayed if your mouse hovers over the prototype and the icon that identifies the prototype.

troubleshooting

Break the lines of text as shown in step 5 so that all of the text is displayed.

Activity 8.3.6: Storing a Prototype in a Prototype Library

1. Continue working with the open simulation file **Clock_Door.eoz** from Activity 8.3.5.
2. Double-click the **Clock** prototype definition in the Local Prototypes window to display the Prototype Definition Properties dialog box.
3. Change the name to **PendulumClock**.
4. In the Tool tip text field, enter **a clock with moving pendulum and door**.
5. In the Description field, we can explain the Clock prototype's exported fields. Enter the following text:

   HideDoor, HideCabinet, and HidePendulum let you

   customize which parts of the clock should be visible.

   OpenDoor and CloseDoor are inEvents that rotate the

   clock's door so it opens and closes on demand.

   Last modified: October 31, 2008 (Use the current date.)
6. If you created an icon in Activity 8.3.2, select the icon file in the Image file name field. Your Prototype Definition Properties dialog box should resemble Figure 8.3.25. Click **OK** to close the dialog box.

FIGURE 8.3.25 General properties set

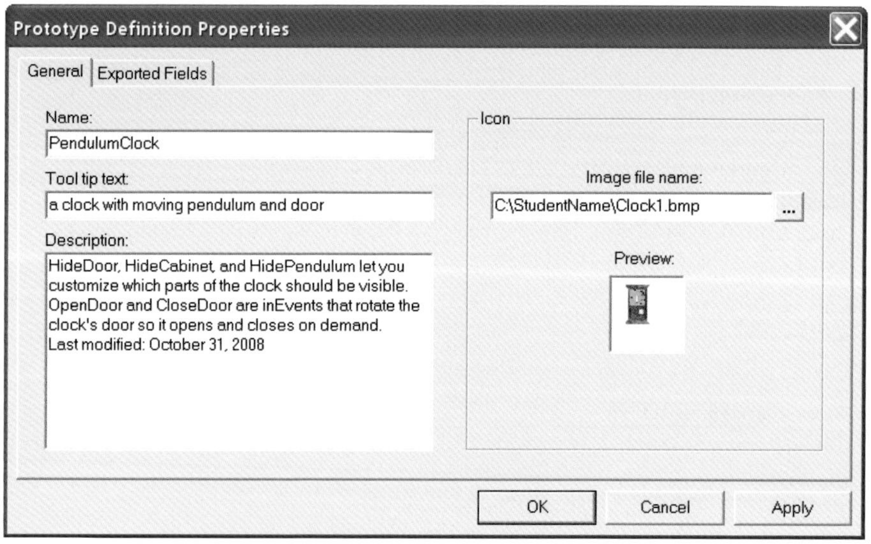

7. Save the simulation as **Clock_Prototype_Library.eoz**.
8. Display the **Components** window. Click the **Prototypes** tab. Click the **New** button on the Prototypes tab of the Components window. The New Prototype File dialog box is displayed.
9. Choose the folder you are using to save files for this lesson. Key **Clocks** in the File name field and click **Save**. This only creates an empty prototype library file, Clocks.eop, in which to store your prototypes. It does not contain a prototype yet. The empty Clocks prototype library is displayed in the Components window.
10. Drag the **PendulumClock** prototype from the Local Prototypes window to the Components window in which the Clocks prototype library is displayed. After a short delay, the prototype is saved and the icon and prototype name appear in the Components window, as shown in Figure 8.3.26.

FIGURE 8.3.26 PendulumClock prototype in the Clocks prototype library

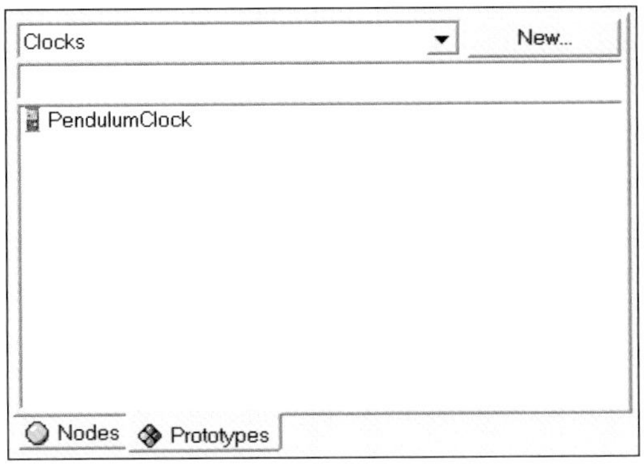

11. Save the simulation and keep it open to use in Activity 8.3.7.

In the previous activity, you created the Clocks prototype library and stored your PendulumClock prototype in it. In the next activity, you will add exported fields to move the minute and hour hands on the clock. Later, you will set default values for these fields.

Activity 8.3.7: Moving the Minute and Hour Hands

1. Continue working with the open simulation file **Clock_Prototype_Library.eoz** from Activity 8.3.6.
2. Select **PendulumClock** from the Window menu in EON, or right-click the **PendulumClock** prototype definition in the Local Prototypes window and select **Open** from the drop-down list to display the simulation tree for the PendulumClock prototype on the left side of the EON window.
3. Add two **Rotate** nodes under the root Clock frame of the PendulumClock prototype simulation tree. The Rotate and Rotate1 nodes are added to the PendulumClock simulation tree. You will move these nodes to the correct location later.
4. Change the name of the new Rotate node to **RotateHours**. In the Property Bar, set the Axis value to **0 1 0**. Clear the active check box.
5. Change the name of the new Rotate1 node to **RotateMinutes**. In the Property Bar, set the Axis value to **0 1 0**. Clear the active check box.
6. Double-click the **PendulumClock** prototype in the prototype's simulation tree to display the Prototype Definition Properties dialog box. Click the **Exported Fields** tab if necessary to view the prototype's exported fields.
7. Add an exported field and name it **HoursActive**. In the Node path field, enter **Clock\RotateHours** and then select **active** from the Field drop-down list.
8. Add an exported field and name it **MinutesActive**. In the Node path field, enter **Clock\RotateMinutes** and then select **active** from the Field drop-down list.
9. Add an exported field and name it **HoursLaptime**. In the Node path field, enter **Clock\RotateHours** and then select **LapTime** from the Field drop-down list.

10. Add an exported field and name it **MinutesLaptime**. In the Node path field, enter **Clock\RotateMinutes** and then select **LapTime** from the Field drop-down list. Your list of exported fields should resemble Figure 8.3.27. Click **OK** to save the new exported fields and close the dialog box.

FIGURE 8.3.27 Exported fields added to move the minute and hour hands

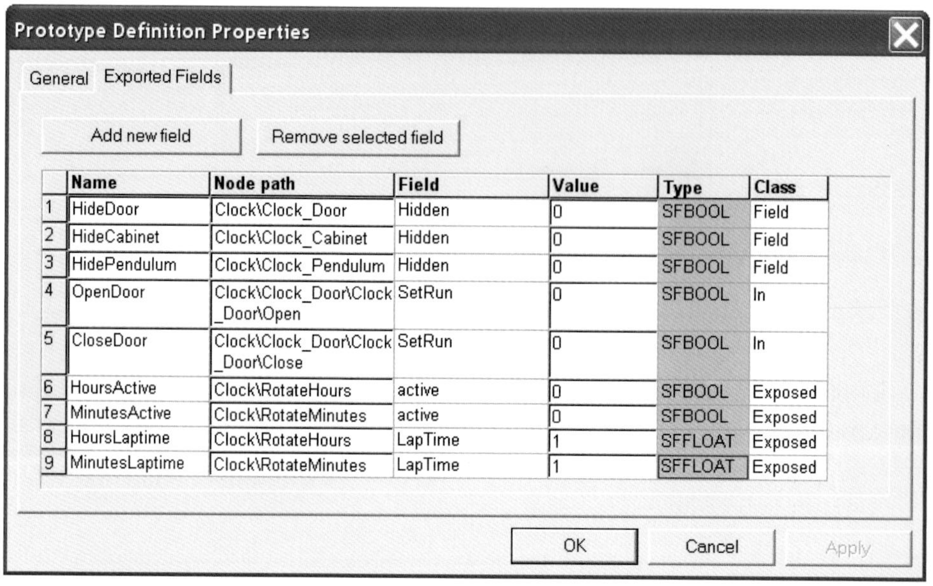

	Name	Node path	Field	Value	Type	Class
1	HideDoor	Clock\Clock_Door	Hidden	0	SFBOOL	Field
2	HideCabinet	Clock\Clock_Cabinet	Hidden	0	SFBOOL	Field
3	HidePendulum	Clock\Clock_Pendulum	Hidden	0	SFBOOL	Field
4	OpenDoor	Clock\Clock_Door\Clock_Door\Open	SetRun	0	SFBOOL	In
5	CloseDoor	Clock\Clock_Door\Clock_Door\Close	SetRun	0	SFBOOL	In
6	HoursActive	Clock\RotateHours	active	0	SFBOOL	Exposed
7	MinutesActive	Clock\RotateMinutes	active	0	SFBOOL	Exposed
8	HoursLaptime	Clock\RotateHours	LapTime	1	SFFLOAT	Exposed
9	MinutesLaptime	Clock\RotateMinutes	LapTime	1	SFFLOAT	Exposed

11. Move the **RotateHours** node to Clock\Clock_Cabinet\Clock_Hands\Clock_Hands_Hour\.

12. Move the **RotateMinutes** node to Clock\Clock_Cabinet\Clock_Hands\Clock_Hands_Minute\.

13. Click the **Clock** prototype instance in the Simulation Tree window to verify that your new exported fields are displayed in the Property Bar. Next, you will create a button to activate the hour and minute hands.

14. Display the **Prototypes** tab of the Components window. Drag a **ToggleButton** prototype from the Buttons prototype library, drop it under the Scene frame in the Simulation Tree window, and rename it **ActivateClock**.

15. In the Simulation Tree window, click the **ActivateClock** prototype. In the Property Bar, set the Text field to **Activate Clock** and change the value in the BoxPosition field to **10 40**.

16. Display the **Routes** window. Drag the **ActivateClock** prototype from the Simulation Tree window to the Routes window. Establish the connections outlined in the following table. Your Routes window should resemble Figure 8.3.28.

From	outEvent	To	inEvent
ActivateClock	ButtonDown	Clock	HoursActive
ActivateClock	ButtonDown	Clock	MinutesActive

FIGURE 8.3.28 Routes from ActivateClock to Clock prototype established

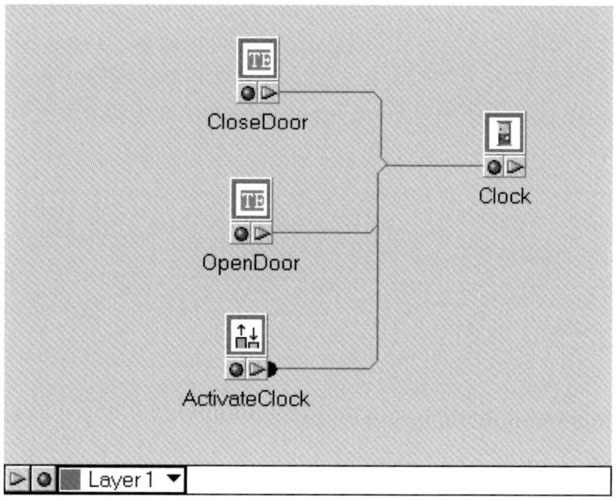

17. In the Clock prototype instance, set the HoursLaptime to **36** and set the MinutesLaptime to **3**.
18. Run the simulation and test your new button.
19. Close the simulation window. Save the simulation as **Clock_Moving_Hands.eoz** and keep it open to use in Activity 8.3.8.

In the previous activity, you used the ToggleButton prototype to provide a button that the user could click to make the clock's hands rotate. In the next activity, you will change the default value of the HoursActive and MinutesActive fields in the PendulumClock prototype. When you create instances of the PendulumClock prototype in the future, the clock's hands will be rotating when you start running the simulation.

Activity 8.3.8: Changing a Prototype's Default Values

1. Continue working with the open simulation file **Clock_Moving_Hands.eoz** from Activity 8.3.7.
2. Double-click the **PendulumClock** prototype definition in the Local Prototypes window and click the **Exported Fields** tab to display the prototype's exported fields list.
3. Change the value of the HoursActive field to **1** and change the value of the MinutesActive field to **1**. For this SFBool type field, the 1 value means true and 0 means false. Setting these values to 1 will make the hour and minute hands move when the simulation starts.
4. Change the HoursLaptime default value to **12** and the MinutesLaptime default value to **1** if necessary.
5. Click **OK** to close the dialog box and save these default values.
6. Save the simulation as **Clock_Default_Values.eoz** and keep it open to use in Activity 8.3.9.

In the previous activity, you set new default values for fields in the Pendulum Clock prototype. Remember that these changes will not affect the values of any current prototype instances; only new instances will be created with these values. In the next activity, you will update the PendulumClock prototype in the Clocks prototype library.

Activity 8.3.9: Updating a Prototype Library

1. Continue working with the open simulation file **Clock_Default_Values.eoz** from Activity 8.3.8.
2. First, we will update the prototype's description by adding information about the new fields. Double-click the **PendulumClock** prototype definition in the Local Prototypes window to display the Prototype Definition Properties dialog box.
3. Insert the following text into the Description field above the *Last modified: October 31, 2008* line of text:

   HoursActive and MinutesActive - When these fields are

   true, the clock's hands are rotating.

   MinutesLaptime and HoursLaptime - The number of

   seconds required for the hands to complete a lap/cycle.
4. Update the last modified date if necessary. Click **OK** to close the dialog box.
5. Save the simulation as **Clock_Update_Library.eoz**.
6. Display the **Prototypes** tab of the Components window. Select **Clocks** from the drop-down list of prototype libraries.
7. Select the **PendulumClock** prototype in the Components window and press the **Delete** key. The Delete Prototype dialog box is displayed. Click **Yes** to confirm the deletion. The Clocks prototype library is empty.
8. Drag the **PendulumClock** prototype from the Local Prototypes window to the Components window. The modified prototype is saved to the Clocks prototype library.
9. Save the simulation as **Clock_Update_Library.eoz** and keep it open to use in Activity 8.3.10.

troubleshooting

Break the lines of text as shown in step 3 so that all of the text is displayed.

Cloning a prototype is a way to create a new prototype based on an existing prototype in your simulation. When you ***clone*** a prototype, a new identical prototype definition is added to the Local Prototypes window. The name of the prototype will be the same as the original prototype, but the number 1 is added to the end of the name. Use the Clone option when you need to modify a prototype, but you also need to keep the original prototype. In the next activity, you will use cloning to create a prototype that consists of only the clock's face and hands.

Activity 8.3.10: Cloning to Create a New Prototype

1. Continue working with the open simulation file **Clock_Update_Library.eoz** from Activity 8.3.9.
2. Right-click the **PendulumClock** prototype in the Local Prototypes window and choose **Clone** from the drop-down menu. A new prototype named PendulumClock1 is displayed in the Local Prototypes window.
3. Change the name of the new prototype to **ClockFace**.
4. Right-click the **ClockFace** prototype and select **Open** from the drop-down menu to display the ClockFace simulation tree in the Prototype Edit window on the left side of the EON window.
5. Select the **Clock_Door** frame and press the **Delete** key. Click **Yes** when a small dialog box asks you to confirm the deletion.
6. Select the **Clock_Pendulum** frame and press the **Delete** key. Click **Yes** when a small dialog box asks you to confirm the deletion.
7. Under the Clock_Cabinet frame, delete the following frames: **Clock_Cabinet, Clock_Topper**, and **Clock_Base**.
8. Right-click the **Clock_Cabinet** frame and choose **Resolve resource references** from the drop-down menu.
9. Delete the **Resources** node that is located directly under the root Clock frame. Do not delete the Resources group in the Clock_Cabinet frame.
10. Double-click the **ClockFace** prototype in the Local Prototypes window to display the Prototype Definition Properties dialog box. On the Exported Fields tab, change the name of the HideCabinet field to **HideClock**. Click **OK** to close the dialog box.
11. Add a **Frame** node under the Scene node in the Simulation Tree window. In the Property Bar, set the X value in the Position field to **0.3**.
12. Drag the **ClockFace** prototype from the Local Prototypes window and drop it under the new frame. Your Simulation Tree window and Local Prototypes window should look similar to Figure 8.3.29. Each of the prototypes in the Local Prototypes window is used in the simulation.

FIGURE 8.3.29 Simulation containing the ClockFace prototype

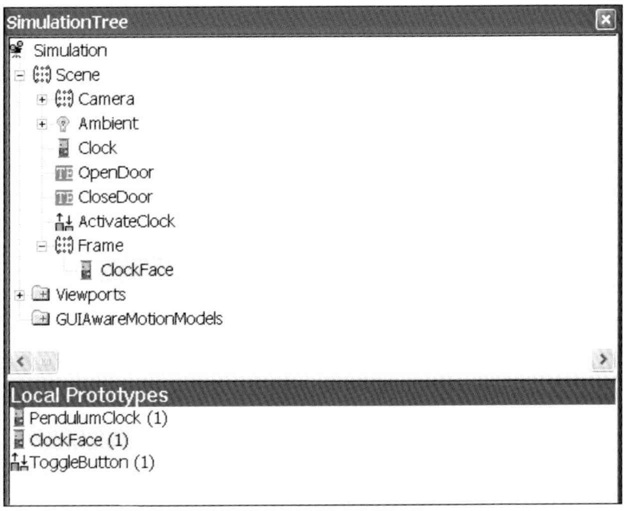

13. Run the simulation. The new clock face, the ClockFace prototype, is displayed to the right of the old clock. Close the simulation window.

tips+tricks

Do not forget to modify your new ClockFace prototype's tooltip, description, and icon to reflect the changes you made in the previous activities. Accuracy in these general properties helps you and other developers select and use the correct prototype.

discuss

Why are the hands of the new clock face rotating when the simulation starts?

14. Display the **Clocks** prototype library. Drag the **ClockFace** prototype into the Clocks prototype library. The Clocks prototype library should contain the ClockFace and PendulumClock prototypes.
15. Save the simulation as **Clock_Clone.eoz** and then close EON.

BEST PRACTICES

Developing Prototypes Using the Principles of Good Design

To promote prototype reusability and efficiency, we must develop prototypes that others can understand and set up quickly. The prototypes must work in predictable ways. Review the following principles or best practices for developing prototypes for yourself and a broader audience.

- **Design prototypes that are not too general or too specific.** Consider how others might use this prototype. If you make its use too general, then users may not understand its purpose. If you make it too specific, then you may miss the opportunity to use it for different purposes. This principle applies to many design areas including the name, field names, and the number of fields.
- **Use a descriptive prototype name.** The name of your prototype can be the hardest decision to make about your new prototype. The name cannot be too long, but it must capture the essence of the prototype's purpose.
- **Write an informative tooltip.** The tooltip is a very brief sentence or phrase that is often displayed with the prototype's name. It can help a user understand the prototype's purpose. It should be a clear, concise description that is not longer than the visible space in the Tool tip text field in the Prototype Definition Properties dialog box.
- **Use a distinctive icon.** It is very important not to use the default icon. Create a unique icon. Over time, the user will learn to recognize the prototype and its purpose. Continue editing and testing the icon until it is clear. Verify that it looks good in 16 × 16 and 32 × 32 sizes.
- **Add exported fields.** If you are making a functional prototype, you will probably need exported fields. Exported fields increase the amount that a prototype can be customized, thereby increasing its usefulness. Spend the time needed to add and test the exported fields. Consider the customizations that a user will want. Users rarely open a prototype to set internal field values, so you must make these values available on the exported fields list.
- **Do not have too many fields.** Exported fields are good, but too many exported fields make it difficult to write an overview of the important fields, which makes it difficult for the user to understand. If many exported fields are for the same node, then consider keeping that node outside the prototype and having a SFNode field to reference that node. If you have too many fields, consider splitting the prototype into two or more prototypes that support each other, or redesign the prototype for a more specific and more limited purpose.

- **Use descriptive field names.** The field names can be just as important as the prototype's name. Consider making them consistent with other fields, nodes, and prototypes. The more a certain field name is used, the more it acquires a defined meaning. Use a long field name rather than one that is short and meaningless or misleading.
- **Use mixed case for names.** When you create prototype names or field names, use uppercase for the name's first letter and certain other letters that are the first letter of words in the name. For example, instead of Orbitnavresettoclickpos, use OrbitNavResetToClickPos. This increases the readability and saves time for users scanning the fields. You cannot use spaces in field or prototype names, but consider using an underscore character instead.
- **Use appropriate field types.** The available field types are inEvent, outEvent, exposedField, and field. Although exposed fields give the user more flexibility, do not make it an exposed field if it does not make sense or it could not have an inEvent and an outEvent. Using the right field type helps the user understand how a field can be used. Use the field type when you don't want users to change a value during runtime.
- **Test all fields.** After you create the prototype and exported fields list, test the fields by connecting routes to them and changing values. Verify that changing the values has a predictable response and it does not create errors or unexpected behavior.
- **Write notes in the Description property.** Use the Description property of a prototype to document your prototype. Explain the purpose of the prototype and the way to set it up. Consider writing an explanation for fields that might not be obvious. Include the date that the prototype was last modified and update it when you make changes so users know if they have the right version of a prototype.
- **Set default values of exported fields.** To save time on customization, try to set the default values of exported fields to the optimum or most commonly used values.
- **Create the function before the prototype.** After you create a prototype, you cannot edit and save the nodes in the prototype during runtime. Often it is an advantage to change position in Frame nodes and text box settings while the simulation is running. Create the function first and then make it into a prototype.

Prototype Optimization Example

When creating prototypes, you must consider the prototype's purpose, possible problems you could encounter, and several potential solutions. The following example identifies the purpose, possible problems, and potential solutions.

- **Purpose:** You want many copies of an object that can be customized in color and position.
- **Problem:** Although a prototype would be good for this purpose, each instance would have a copy of all the resource nodes for the object instead of using one central set of resources. Resources use computer memory, so creating several instances that contain the same resources is a waste of computer memory.
- **Solution 1:** Design two prototypes. Use one prototype to hold the resources and use the second prototype to create multiple instances. The second prototype must reference the prototype that has the resources. Or, a script in each of the multiple instances of the second prototype must set the node references of the internal shape nodes.
- **Solution 2:** One prototype, using script, will copy internal nodes (excluding mesh and texture resources) and customize them. This method is easier if the customizing is done according to a formula. For example, you could position the copies in a pattern or use a random position generator.

Scripting for Prototypes

cross-reference

You will learn more about scripting in Module 9.

Scripting in EON is very useful. It increases the possibilities of what you can do and reduces the complexities of alternatives such as using operations nodes and routes. Scripting is used frequently with EON prototypes. The following tips will help you work with scripting and prototypes:

- **Use the Script node.** All advanced functional prototypes use a Script node and most exported fields are from the Script node.
- **Use IsActive and IsNotActive fields.** A precedent has been set with the EON-supplied prototypes to use fields named IsActive and IsNotActive to turn on and turn off the entire function of the prototype. These fields are created in a Script node and should appear as the last fields in your exported fields list. Although only one of these fields should be required, the other one makes it easier to connect routes without requiring the use of a Not node.
- **Design so setting up a prototype is easy.** The quicker a user can insert a prototype and see a result, the more likely they are to find a use for the prototype.
- **Avoid the need for routes.** Making routes takes time, and it is often quicker to create a node reference instead. Script can be used to send a value to a field of a node directly without routes. The EON-supplied prototypes often have fields called SendToNode, SendToField, and SendDirect that will send the main outEvent of the prototype to a node and field of your choice. You can set these up with script.
- **Instance placement.** We can use prototype instance placement to give meaning. The OrbitNav prototype is designed to send values to a Camera frame, and it has a Camera field that lets you copy and paste a node reference in that field. But, if you do not set this field, then it automatically selects the prototype instance's parent node as the Camera frame. This reduces the time needed to copy and paste node references. Scripting can set up this behavior. It can search for nodes and select the most likely node so users don't have to select a node. This typically applies to Simulation, Viewport, and Camera nodes.
- **Use Error Messages.** If a prototype is somewhat complex to set up and a user is missing a node reference or has not placed the prototype instance in a logical place, then consider showing the user an error message displayed in a pop-up dialog box or the Log window. You can do this using the Trace method to debug script. The error message should be displayed as soon as you run the simulation, and it should clearly indicate which prototype instance is sending the message.
- **Use multiple data types.** If the main purpose of a prototype is to calculate and output a value, then consider making the value available in different data types. For example, make a Float value also available in Integer, such as the SliderPlus prototype, which has SliderValue (SSFloat), IntegerValue (SFInt32), and Fraction (SFFloat) (range 0 to 1). This can reduce the need for inserting other nodes, such as a Converter node.
- **Use the same name for script and exported fields.** If most of your exported fields are coming from a Script node, then use the same name for your exported fields and your script fields. This is possible with script because you can decide the name of script fields but not of fields on other nodes. This will reduce confusion when scripting.

Rearranging the Sequence of Exported Fields

The sequence in which exported fields appear in the list is important because the sequence can make it easier for the user to understand the prototype's function and the options available. Use the following guidelines to sequence exported fields:

- Group related fields together.
- Group inEvents together and place them before outEvents.
- Place the fields that are customized more often before fields that are not needed as often.
- Place similar data types together.
- Place the IsNotActive and IsActive fields last because this is the custom with EON-supplied prototypes.
- It is not useful to list the fields in alphabetical order.
- Plan the sequence of your exported fields in a spreadsheet, but do not expect to be able to copy and paste from it.

Often, when you want to press a key to trigger an action as part of a prototype, you will use two fields. One field is used for the key, and one field enables the action or not. These fields are related, so place them next to each other. For example, the OrbitNavReset prototype has a ResetKey field and an EnableResetKey field that are located next to each other.

EON does not provide an easy way to rearrange the sequence of the exported fields list. Each new field is added to the end of the list. To rearrange fields, we delete the fields and add them again. They are automatically added at the end of the list, effectively resequencing the list. The following activity will show you how it is done most efficiently using copy and paste.

Activity 8.3.11: Rearranging Exported Fields

1. Open EON. Open **Activity_8.3.11.eoz** from the data files for Module 8 Lesson 3.
2. Expand the **Scene** frame. Double-click the **Frame** prototype, which is an instance of the MyPrototype prototype definition. Look at the order of fields in the Properties dialog box shown in Figure 8.3.30. Your goal will be to place the fields in numeric sequence. Click **OK** to close the Properties dialog box.

FIGURE 8.3.30 Properties dialog box for Frame prototype instance

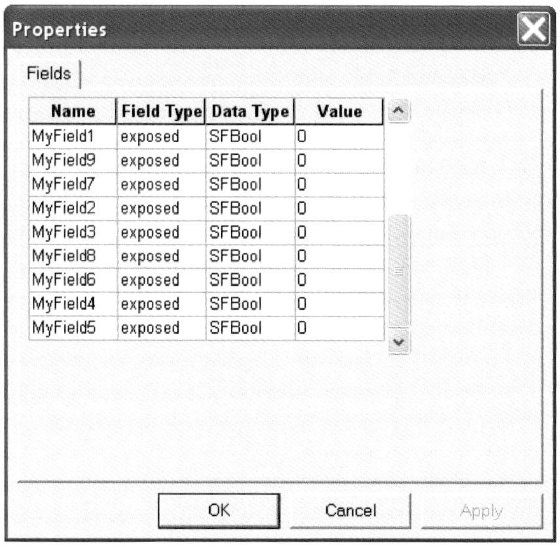

3. Double-click the **MyPrototype** prototype definition in the Local Prototypes window to display the Prototype Definition Properties dialog box.
4. Click the **Exported Fields** tab. Notice that MyField1 is in the correct position. The next field should be MyField2, which is in the fourth row. In the next few steps, you will copy and delete the rows between MyField1 and MyField2.
5. Click the number **2** in the left column and drag down one row. This selects the fields named MyField9 and MyField7.
6. Press **Control + C** to copy these two rows.
7. Click the **Remove selected field** button to delete the two rows.
8. Click **OK** to close the dialog box. This will ensure that the fields are deleted and the list is saved.
9. Double-click the **MyPrototype** prototype definition again and go to the exported fields list.
10. Click the **Add new field** button.
11. Select the row you just added by clicking the number in the left column.
12. Press **Control + V** to paste the two rows. Notice that you selected one row, but it pasted both rows. You can paste as many rows as you like this way.
13. Click **OK** to close the dialog box and then open it again. The first three fields are in the correct sequence. MyField4 should be next. Two fields are in the way, namely MyField8 and MyField6.
14. Select **MyField8** and **MyField6** and press **Control + C** to copy the fields.
15. Click the **Remove selected field** button.
16. Click **OK** to close the dialog box and then open it again.
17. Click the **Add new field** button.
18. Select the last row and press **Control + V** to paste the two rows.
19. Click **OK** to close the dialog box and then open it again. The first five fields are in the correct sequence.
20. MyField6 should be listed next, so select **MyField9**, **MyField7**, and **MyField8**. Copy the fields and then remove them.
21. Click **OK** to close the dialog box and then open it again.
22. Add a new row and paste the three fields.
23. Click **OK** to close the dialog box and then open it again. The first six fields are in the correct sequence. MyField9 should be moved to the end of the list.
24. Select **MyField9**. Copy the field and remove it.
25. Click **OK** to close the dialog box and then open it again.
26. Add a new row and paste the field.
27. Click **OK** to close the dialog box and then open it again. All of the fields should be in the correct sequence.
28. Click **OK** to close the dialog box.
29. Save the simulation as **Sequence_Fields.eoz** and then close EON.

Using Prototypes to Create or Delete Nodes

You may recall how prototypes work during runtime. At startup, a copy of the prototype definition is placed under each instance. At shutdown, the nodes under a prototype instance are deleted. If you combine this knowledge with the fact that nodes can be moved using script, then you can use prototypes to create and delete nodes.

A script in your prototype could move a subtree with a prototype to a location that is outside the prototype. When the simulation is shut down, then the nodes outside the prototype will remain in the simulation tree. You can use this fact to insert a customized object into your simulation tree. The OrbitNavViewMaker prototype moves a Script node to a location that is outside the prototype and saves all the viewing positions in it. This solution avoids the problem of prototype instance values created during runtime that are restored to pre-runtime values.

You can use this prototype feature in a different way—you also could move nodes in the simulation tree to a location in a prototype so that the nodes are deleted when the simulation shuts down.

Summary

In this lesson you:

- Created, edited, and deleted prototypes.
- Created a prototype library.
- Moved prototypes from one library to another.
- Practiced common tasks related to prototypes.
- Learned about the best practices to use when developing prototypes.

Simulation

Through your work at Contours Company, you have learned to use EON's nodes, prototypes, properties, and routes to create exactly the environment the client wants. Your knowledge has helped you appreciate the EON prototypes that have saved countless hours that you would have spent developing necessary functions if the prototypes were not available.

Job 8.1: Reviewing Your Simulation and Updating the Storyboard

As you know, a storyboard is a dynamic component of your simulation. As work progresses on the simulation, you continually refine your plan and incorporate change requests from the client by updating the storyboard. It also allows you to present new ideas to the client for approval before investing too much time in developing a feature in your simulation.

Your recent understanding of prototypes will not affect what the client sees at the end of the project. However, it directly affects what you are able to do and the amount of time it requires. In the workforce, where "time is money," this can have a major impact on a project. Any repetitive actions that you can avoid will save time, save money, and produce a better, more consistent product.

With that in mind, review your simulation file along with your storyboard and identify any locations where repetitive items could have been condensed into a single prototype. Use a unique symbol in your storyboard to identify the locations where developing a prototype would be the most efficient method of achieving the desired end result.

Discussion

discuss

Although it typically does not make sense to develop a prototype when the work has already been done, how can identifying the areas where you could have developed a prototype help you in the future?

Under what circumstances would it be beneficial to develop a prototype after the individual actions have already been completed?

1. If possible, continue using the storyboard that you created in the Module 1 Simulation and enhanced in subsequent simulations. Review the storyboard, looking for any obvious elements that are redundant.
2. Choose a unique identifier or symbol to use in your storyboard to indicate locations where you could develop a new prototype, and then create and use the new prototype.
3. Save your storyboard and keep it open.
4. Open EON and open the apartment file you enhanced in the Module 7 Simulation.
5. Search the simulation tree for redundant elements.
6. Take notes about any components of this simulation that could have been made into prototypes or any locations where an existing prototype would have reduced the necessary work.
7. Close the apartment file and return to the storyboard.
8. Use the unique identifier you chose in step 2 to indicate locations in the storyboard where an existing or new prototype could be useful.
9. Complete your storyboard using paper and pencil, a flowchart application, a drawing program, or any method you prefer, and then save the storyboard.

Job 8.2: Understanding Prototypes

Although you have learned a lot about prototypes in your recent work, you know there is more to learn. Your manager has asked you to review the existing prototypes in EON. As Figure 8.1 shows, EON has more than two hundred prototypes available for your use—and this number is growing with each new release of EON.

FIGURE 8.1 Prototypes currently available in EON Professional

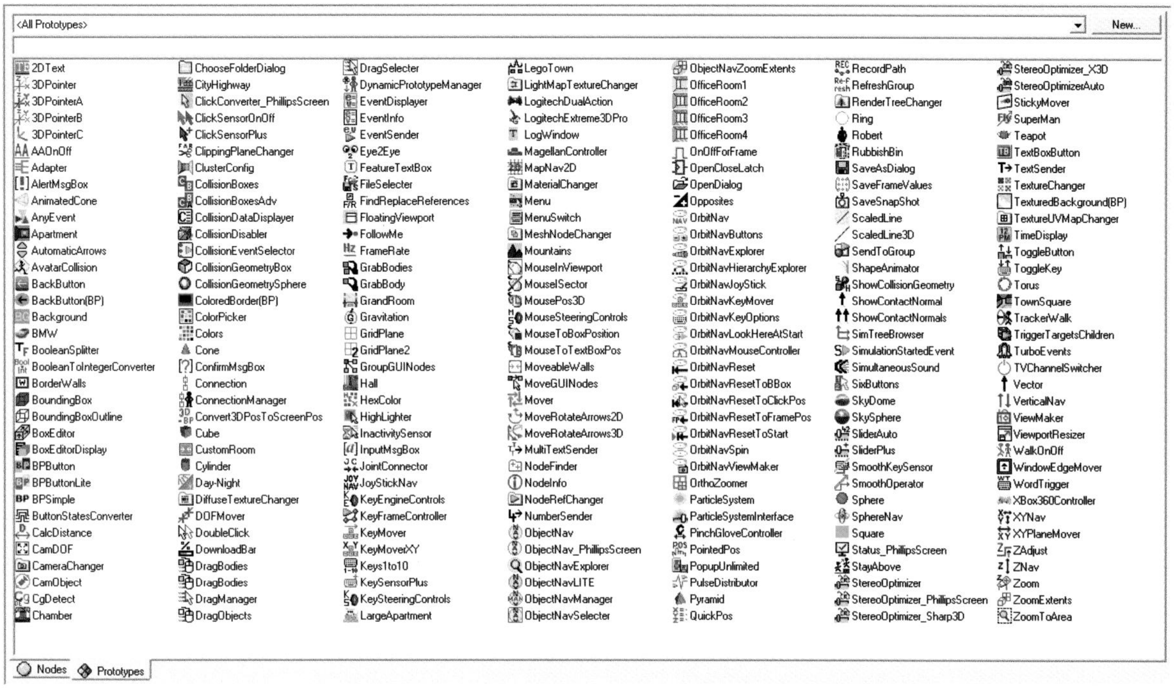

Your manager has asked you to explore at least ten prototypes that you have not used in your work with EON.

1. Use EON Help to find as much information as you can about the chosen prototypes.
2. Explore any available "Demo" files that illustrate the features of a prototype.
3. For each prototype you explore, write a brief report on what you learned about the prototype and the situations in which you think the given prototype would be most useful.
4. Look at the prototype libraries shown in Figure 8.2.

troubleshooting

Do not explore prototypes that are no longer current. Prototypes that remain only for backward compatibility can be found in the Old Prototypes library.

FIGURE 8.2 Prototype libraries

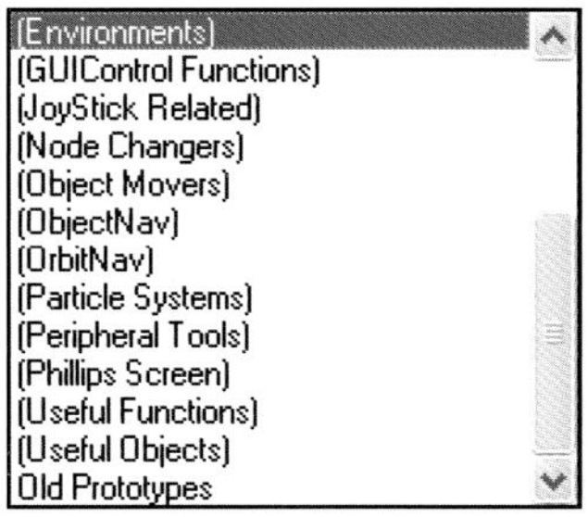

5. Explore at least one library and determine if it contains any prototypes that are designed to work together.
6. Write a report about a library, the prototypes it contains, and how the prototypes work together.

Discussion

discuss

Review the various libraries of prototypes. Does EON have a library that you think would be useful for certain types of simulations or user interfaces?

What library (or libraries), for example, would you look in if you were trying to develop a user interface?

7. If time permits, build a simple simulation that uses one of the prototypes you investigated.
8. When you finish reviewing the prototypes, writing your reports, and building a simple simulation using one of the prototypes, close EON.

Job 8.3: Using Prototypes

As you know, it is one thing to read about how something works and quite another to actually use it. Your manager is a firm believer in allowing her employees to take the time to learn as much as possible about the tools they are using—knowing that time spent exploring and learning a program saves the company's time and money in the end. It also gives her a more knowledgeable team of well-informed individuals who can use their experience with the tools to develop creative and unique ways to solve any problems a particular project may present.

Although the apartment simulation is already complete, you have identified some existing prototypes that could have been used in that simulation in place of the more time-consuming task of creating unique combinations of nodes and routes. Your manager would like you to use these existing prototypes to rework the simulation.

1. If necessary, open the storyboard and keep it available to refer to as you work.
2. If necessary, review what you have learned about the existing prototypes.
3. If necessary, open EON and the current apartment simulation.
4. Use at least one existing prototype to simplify the apartment simulation.

Discussion

discuss

Can you think of any ways to use prototypes to improve the functionality of the user interface?

5. Use at least two existing prototypes to add enhancements or features that did not exist in your simulation.
6. Run the simulation. Verify that the prototypes are working as expected. Make any necessary corrections or adjustments.
7. Close the simulation window. Save the simulation as **Job_8.3.eoz** and keep it open to use in Job 8.4.

Job 8.4: Developing Prototypes

In Job 8.1, you identified areas of your apartment simulation that would have benefited from the development of a prototype rather than repeatedly inserting the same combination of nodes and route connections. Although the simulation is already complete, your manager asked you to develop prototypes for these items because the prototypes could be used in the future, and it would be good practice for you.

1. Continue working with the open simulation file **Job_8.3.eoz** from Job 8.3.
2. If you need to review the items you identified in your storyboard as potential prototypes, open the storyboard and keep it available to refer to as you work.
3. If necessary, review what you have learned about developing your own prototypes.
4. Create at least two prototypes that will simplify common combinations of nodes and routes in the apartment simulation.
5. Create a library and move your new prototypes into that library.
6. Create icons for your new prototypes.
7. Use at least one of your new prototypes in your apartment simulation to replace existing nodes and routes.
8. Run the simulation. Verify that the prototypes are working as expected. Make any necessary corrections or adjustments.
9. Close the simulation window. Save the simulation as **Job_8.4.eoz** and then close EON.

HARALD SUND

MODULE 9

Scripting and Dynamic Load

LESSON 9.1
Fundamentals of Scripting

LESSON 9.2
Using Scripts

LESSON 9.3
Dynamic Load Applications

LESSON 9.1

Fundamentals of Scripting

Objectives

In this lesson you will:

- Develop an understanding as to why Script nodes are used.
- Become familiar with basic scripting concepts and terminology.
- Understand how scripting works in EON.
- Learn how to use the EON Script Editor.
- Use scripting to access field values.
- Trigger script functions using inEvents.

Key Terms

block	*host program environment*	*script*
bookmark	*JScript®*	*Script node*
code	*method*	*scripting*
EON Object Classes	*object*	*scripting language*
EON Software Development Kit (SDK)	*operator*	*statement*
event handler	*property*	*variable*
function	*scope*	*VBScript*

What Is Scripting?

Scripting involves writing instructions for a computer. In EON Studio, the instructions are typically about data manipulation—collecting data, performing operations on the data, and sending the result to objects such as nodes and fields. Before learning to use scripting in EON simulations, you should become familiar with the following terms:

- ***Scripting*** is the activity of writing code.
- ***Code*** is a loose term referring to the content of a script. Code is to a script as text is to a text document.

- ***Script*** refers to a collection of instructions to be carried out by a computer.
- A ***scripting language*** is a system of symbols, keywords, and syntax rules that is used to communicate instructions to a computer.

Why Use Scripting?

Use scripting to add functionality to your simulations. After you import the 3D models and resources into a simulation, you can add behaviors and desired functionality by using one or more of the following methods:

- Combining various nodes and prototypes within the simulation tree and connecting them via routes
- Developing new node library objects compiled from C++ code using the ***EON Software Development Kit (SDK)***
- Using EON Script nodes to create custom scripts

cross-reference

Script nodes are discussed in more detail later in this lesson.

The first method has already been addressed in earlier modules. The second method involves the use of the EON SDK. The EON SDK is a software development kit used to construct custom EON nodes and modules. The EON SDK, which is the same tool used by EON Reality to create standard nodes and modules, is beyond the scope of this book. In this lesson, we will turn our attention to using EON Script nodes to create custom scripts.

The possibilities available through scripting are limited only by your creativity and imagination. Scripting allows you to create simulations in EON that would not otherwise be possible by using only the nodes, prototypes, and routes identified in the first method of developing simulations. Many tasks that can be implemented using the first method are much quicker and easier to perform by using scripting:

- **Reduce the number of nodes.** Much of the functionality provided by nodes that provide control logic, such as the Latch, Counter, Switch, Trigger, File, PowerSwitch, and Score nodes, as well as all of the nodes in the Operations-Nodes library, can be replicated easily by a script. EON-supplied prototypes typically use script instead of control logic nodes. Important nodes that you cannot replace with scripting include nodes in the Sensor Nodes library such as the ClickSensor, KeyboardSensor, MouseSensor, and TimeSensor nodes.
- **Reduce routes.** If you use only nodes and routes, then your Routes window will become crowded and more difficult to use as your applications become larger and more complex. Even though you can use layers to organize routes and use the Butterfly window to follow routes, managing a large simulation's components can be difficult. A script can reduce routes because it can send values directly to fields without using routes. Also, a script can fetch values from other nodes without the need to connect a route between the node and the script. Usually, you can remove all of the routes except those that should trigger actions within the script. Therefore, when you use scripting, the typical Routes window will show a Script node that has many sensors going into it but no routes coming out of it.
- **Document functions.** Without script, you can describe the function you are creating only by using descriptive node names. If you use scripting, you can describe the function with text comments throughout the function. Also, all of the names you use for fields, objects, variables, and functions help to describe and document the functions you create.
- **Centralize functions.** Keeping code in one central location makes it easier to understand how a function works.

- **Access built-in functions.** Naturally, scripting enables you to do some things that nodes cannot do. A scripting language has built-in functions to simplify many actions. For example, built-in math functions can work with square roots, cosine values, and array handling. Other built-in functions provide text-handling capabilities. EON also provides some built-in functions that extend the base functionality of JScript and VBScript, such as the CopyNode, MessageBox, TransformPosition, and SaveSnapshot functions. The most useful functions that EON provides allow you to manipulate nodes and the values of the nodes' fields throughout the simulation tree.
- **Interact with external applications.** The ActiveX object provided by a scripting language enables you to do some amazing things such as communicate with databases, read and write to text and eXtensible Markup Language (XML) files, and read and write to the Windows registry.
- **Improve speed and efficiency.** Script is interpreted during runtime. This makes it perfect for quick development. Also, script does not require the installation of extra files on users' computers, which improves efficiency.

cross-reference

You will learn more about accessing external software in Module 9 Lesson 2.

This lesson will help you begin to develop your own scripts. Additional resources in EON Help include the EON Scripting Guide, the EON Scripting Reference, and the EON Scripting Examples subsections of the Scripting in EON section. Figure 9.1.1 displays the location of these resources in EON Help.

FIGURE 9.1.1 Scripting resources in EON Help

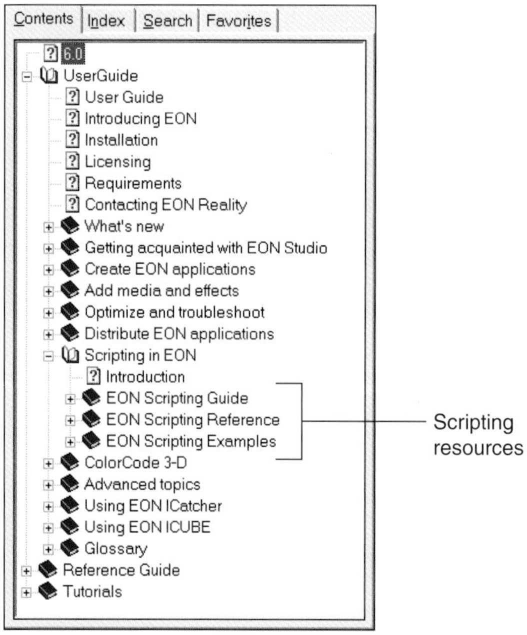

The EON Scripting Guide contains guidelines for the beginner as well as advanced users, such as program flow issues, differences between the supported script languages, and tips for debugging and troubleshooting. The EON Scripting Reference describes how EON implements script within its environment via scriptable objects (i.e., the EON Object Classes, which extend the supported scripting languages with additional functions), lists the methods available for each scriptable object, and provides usage examples. Finally, the EON Scripting Examples section provides some very useful script examples, which include accessing text files and databases.

STORYBOARD

Using Script in Simulation Development

Where does scripting fit into the process of creating a simulation? The storyboard will show you where this task is located in the process.

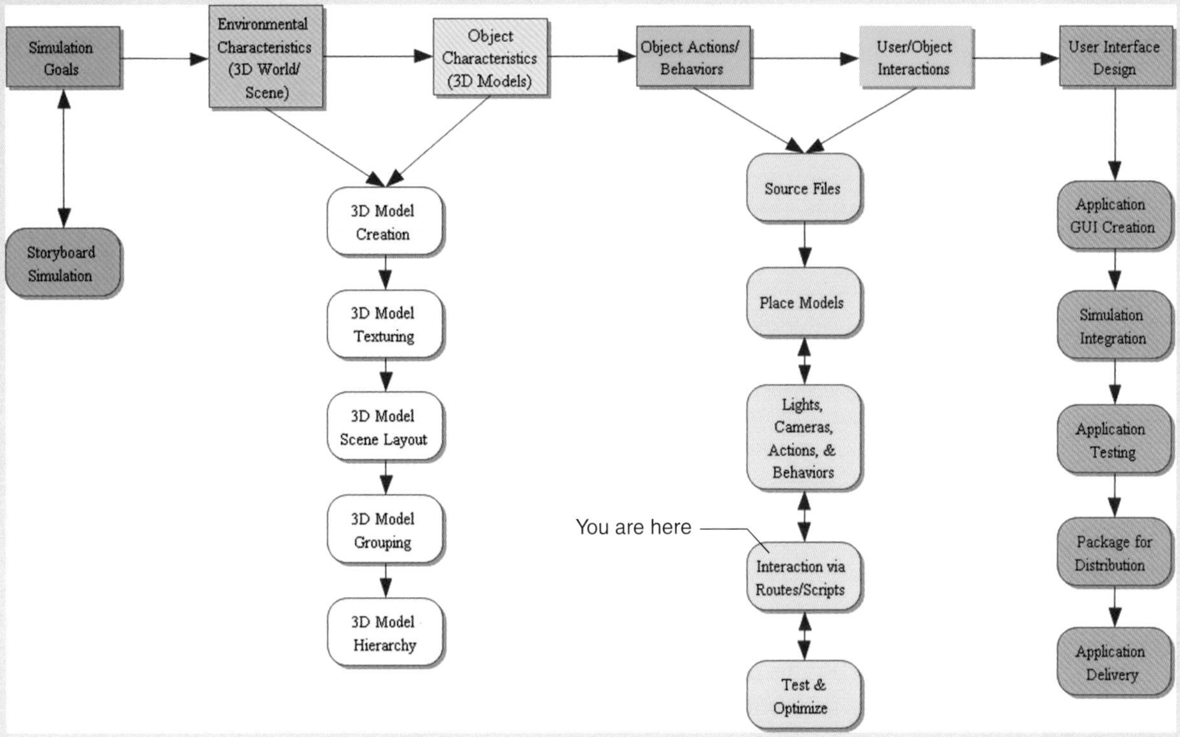

Scripting is part of the "Interaction via Routes/Scripts" step when you are constructing your simulation. In this lesson, we will begin to learn how scripting interacts with EON Studio to create simulations. Module 9 Lesson 2 provides practice using these skills.

Programming Concepts

Before we delve into scripting in EON, you should review some basic programming concepts to help you understand and use the information in this lesson. How does programming compare to scripting? What are the basic components of object-oriented programming?

Scripting vs. Programming

Code written in a conventional programming language, such as C++, must be compiled into machine code before it can be executed on a computer. Code written in a scripting language does not need to be compiled in advance; rather, it is interpreted and then immediately executed, one line at a time, within a ***host program environment.*** For example, code written in the HTML scripting language must be interpreted and executed within a web browser, which serves as its host program. Scripting in EON works in the same manner. Script code within a simulation must be interpreted and executed within either the EON Studio authoring tool or EON Viewer.

Additional subtle differences exist between scripting and conventional programming languages. However, as scripting languages become more powerful, the line that distinguishes a programming language from a scripting language may fade over time.

Object-Oriented Programming

JScript® and ***VBScript*** are the only scripting languages currently supported in EON Studio. JScript is the Microsoft implementation of JavaScript®, a scripting language used for client-side web applications. VBScript is a Microsoft scripting language that is based on the Visual Basic® programming language. VBScript is used for both client-side and server-side web applications and can be used within the Microsoft Windows® Script Host (WSH) environment. Like many modern programming languages, they support either object-based or object-oriented features. Basic concepts of object-oriented programming include objects, properties, methods, and events, which we will explain in more detail.

tips+tricks

Other terms commonly used for functions include subroutines or procedures. In JScript, blocks of program code are called functions because they must begin with the *function* keyword. In VBScript, they are called subroutines because they are enclosed between the *sub* and *end sub* keywords. In this book, the activities use JScript.

- An ***object*** is a group of related properties, methods, and events.
- A ***property*** is a data field that stores a value; the set of properties for an object collectively describes or defines its state for a specific moment in time. Some properties also may be objects themselves.
- A ***method*** is a function that belongs to an object. Typically, it is used to access and manipulate the associated object's properties.
- A ***function*** is a block of code (script or program statements) that performs a set of actions.
- An event is an incident that changes the value of one or more object properties (changing the object's state), which may provoke a programmed response. Examples of events include clicking an object or pressing a key on the keyboard. Events can trigger functions called event handlers.
- An ***event handler*** is a function that handles an event.

The following generic code shows how these concepts are usually implemented. To set the value of a property:

```
Object.Property = value
```

To call a method and send a value to the method:

```
Object.Method(value)
```

The first line of an event handler might be expressed like the following example:

```
Function Object_Event()
```

Because properties themselves can be objects, you can set the value of a property like this:

```
Object.Property.Property.Property = value
```

Because methods can return values, which can themselves be objects, you can set the value of a property. An object is returned by the call to the method and a value is assigned to a specified property of that object like this:

```
Object.Method().Property = value
```

The previous examples may be fine in theory, but in practice, the concepts may not seem as clear to you for several reasons:

cross-reference

The implementation of objects, properties, methods, and events in EON is explained later in this lesson.

- Properties can themselves be objects with properties.
- Events can occur when a property changes state.
- Event handlers can cause other properties to change state, which in turn trigger more event handlers.

How Scripting Works in EON

So far, you have learned some basic concepts of scripting and some reasons why you should use scripting. Now, we delve into how scripting is implemented in EON Studio. We start with the Script node and then discuss scripting languages, EON's extensions to the language, the definition of a field, and how events drive the simulation. We also will cover what you can and cannot do with scripting.

Script Node

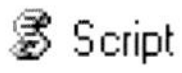

To use scripting in EON, you must insert a ***Script node***. A Script node, like all EON nodes, has a Properties dialog box, as shown in Figure 9.1.2. To display the Script Properties dialog box, double-click the Script node in the simulation tree.

FIGURE 9.1.2 Script Properties dialog box

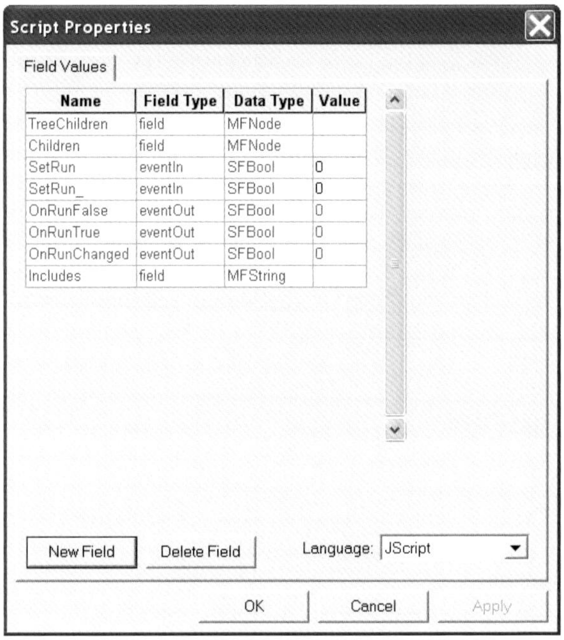

Unlike other EON nodes, the Script node initially does not have any fields other than the default fields that every node has. It is your job to create the fields. A Script node also has an associated page that you use to write script code. To access the associated page, select the Script node in the simulation tree and then click the Open Script Editor button on the main Toolbar displayed in Figure 9.1.3.

FIGURE 9.1.3 Open Script Editor button on the main Toolbar

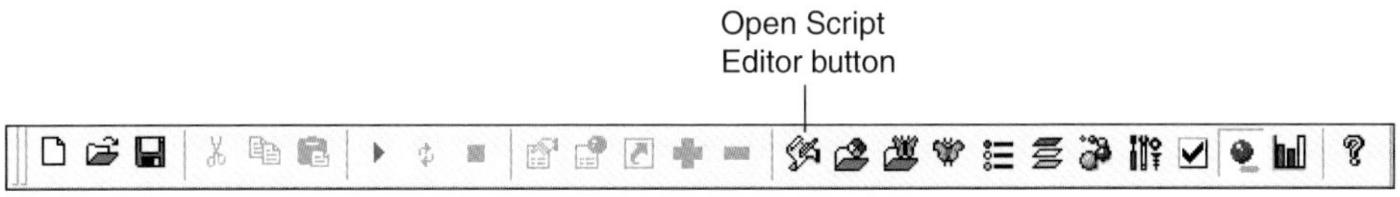

tips+tricks

To access the associated page used for entering script, you also can select the Script node and press Ctrl + E on your keyboard.

tips+tricks

Remember that you can customize the window layout in EON Studio. If you prefer to display the Script Editor window on the right side of the screen, simply change the layout.

cross-reference

You will learn more about using the Includes field in Module 9 Lesson 2.

web links

More resources about JScript and VBScript are available on Microsoft's website. Simply visit *www.microsoft.com* and enter either "JScript Reference" or "VBScript Reference" into the Search box. Keep in mind that EON is using version 5 of these languages, and online documentation might display information about a later version, which may have additional functions that do not work if you try them in EON Studio 6.0. Also, you will find it helpful to download the JScript.chm and VBScript.chm online help files onto your computer if they are available. The Reference documents list the objects and methods that are part of the language.

cross-reference

You will find more information about EON objects and their methods in Appendix B.

When you click the Open Script Editor button, the page associated with the selected Script node is displayed on the left side of the EON Studio window where the Components or Routes window is usually displayed. As shown in Figure 9.1.4, text is already displayed in the Script Editor window.

FIGURE 9.1.4 Script node consists of properties and a page for writing script

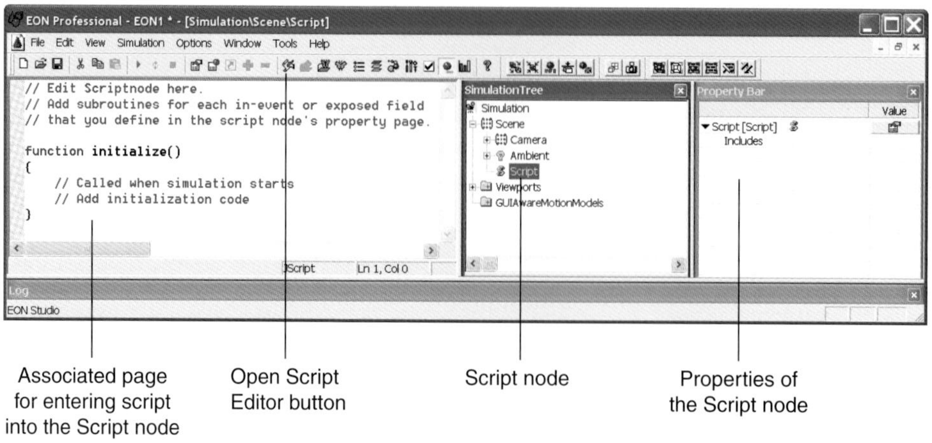

The script that you write in the Script Editor window is saved within the .eoz file. You cannot extract or access the script in any other way. Notice the Includes field in the Property Bar. This field is used for adding external scripts. When you save the .eoz file, any external script files listed in the Includes field will be copied into the .eoz file, like textures and other resource files.

Scripting Languages

The Script node supports two scripting languages: JScript (version 5) and VBScript (version 5). To use the Script node successfully, you must become familiar with JScript or VBScript. If you are not familiar with either scripting language, we recommend that you use JScript for the following reasons:

- JScript is the default language for the EON Script Editor.
- You can use JScript for scripting in web pages.
- JScript has more potential for portability across multiple operating system platforms. Currently, Windows Internet Explorer is the only web browser that provides native client-side support for VBScript.

EON Extensions to the Scripting Language

The EON authoring tools, EON Studio and EON Professional, and the EON Viewer host program environments enhance the functionality of JScript and VBScript by including support for ***EON Object Classes*** (i.e., EON Base Object, EON Node Object, and EON Field Object). These objects provide properties and methods for accessing and manipulating the simulation's environment, nodes, and fields in the nodes.

If you are familiar with scripting in web pages, HTML, and the JavaScript document object model, you will know that certain elements, such as window and location, and many of the HTML tags, such as <input>, <div>, <img>, and <p>, are treated as objects with properties and methods. When you use scripting in EON, these web page objects are not available. Instead, the nodes and their fields in the simulation tree are the available objects. These objects have methods. Table 9.1.1 provides a list of the methods.

TABLE 9.1.1 Methods of EON Objects and Events

Methods of the EON Base Object	Methods of the EON Node Object	Methods of the EON Field Object	Events
CopyNode	GetParentNode	GetName	On_FieldName
DeleteNode	GetFieldCount	GetType	initialize
Find	GetField	GetMFCount	shutdown
FindNode	GetFieldByName	SetMFCount	eventsProcessed
FindByProgID	GetIdOfName	GetMFElement	
FindAncestorNodeByName		SetMFElement	
FindAncestorNodeByProgID		AddMFElement	
FindAncestorSiblingNodeByName		RemoveMFElement	
FindAncestorSiblingNodeByProgID		Value (property)	
GetNodeName			
GetNodePath			
GetNodeProgId			
GetScriptTimeout			
SetScriptTimeout			
MakeSFColor			
MakeSFRotation			
MakeSFVec2f			
MakeSFVec3f			
MessageBox			
Trace			
Trace2			
TransformPosition			
TransformOrientation			
SaveSnapshot			

What Are Fields?

In strict object-oriented terminology, an EON field is an object. In practice, however, fields are known as properties and events as well. The following explanations try to reconcile this contradiction.

Fields Are Properties

EON commonly refers to its fields as properties because fields are displayed in a Properties dialog box and in the Property Bar. Also, the EON Field Object has only one property (the Value property), so it is easy to say the field is a property.

Fields Are Objects

In scripting, objects can have methods. The EON Field Object has seven methods. Therefore, it is an object.

Fields Are Events

In EON scripting, a field receiving a value is an event. We can write an event handler to respond to that event. Also, we define a field's type as an inEvent, outEvent, or exposedField in EON. Therefore, fields are often referred to as inEvents, outEvents, or events.

tips+tricks

Note that fields do not behave exactly like properties in a scripting sense because the syntax we need to access them is:

```
Node.GetFieldByName("Field name").value = 1
```

If a field was strictly a property, we should be able to do this:

```
Node.Fieldname = 1
```

Event-Driven Simulations

A Script node will not do anything until it receives an event. Thus, a script is event-driven. Earlier, we defined an event as something that happens to an object that can trigger an action to be performed. In EON, a Script node has only one type of event, which is a field of the Script node receiving a value. You could say that a Script node has the same number of events and fields because every field is capable of receiving a value.

In EON, all events initially occur in EON nodes such as ClickSensor, Keyboard-Sensor, TimeSensor, and so on. These events are passed through routes to other nodes. The Script node cannot sense these user inputs directly. These events must be collected by EON nodes and passed on to the Script node. Therefore, we say that a Script node receives an event from somewhere else. An event can propagate through many nodes and prototypes in a chain reaction before your Script node receives it.

A field can receive values through one of four methods:

1. A route is connected from a node to a field of the Script node.
2. Other scripts that you make or use send a value directly to a field of the Script node.
3. The script alters one of its own field values. This can occur only in response to an existing event.
4. In some rare circumstances, EON nodes can send values to fields, usually to the default SetRun field that exists for all nodes, including the Script node.

If you are designing an application in which an EON simulation is placed inside a host program, such as a web page or an Adobe Director® movie, then the host program can send events to EON. For the script to receive these events, a route must be connected from the external inEvent to an associated field of the Script node.

cross-reference

Other types of events include initialize(), which happens when the simulation starts; shutdown(), which happens when the simulation shuts down; and eventsProccessed, which will be explained in Module 9 Lesson 2.

tips+tricks

You may be familiar with events from the Hypertext Markup Language (HTML) used to create web pages. In HTML, some standard events are known as onclick(), onmouseover(), onkeypress(), onresize(), onload(), and so on. In EON, you create the event names by creating the fields of the Script node. For example, if you want to execute a script when the user clicks a cube in the simulation, you can create a field named Click or CubeClicked. Then, you must send a value to that field when the click occurs. It is not enough to create the field. You will need to connect a route from the ClickSensor node under a Cube prototype to the field of your Script node.

What Can a Script Do?

In a general sense, EON scripts can do almost anything. The only limit is your imagination. However, the following list of generic actions you can do with scripting in EON will give you some ideas about using the Script node. A Script node can:

- Access the values in its fields.
- Access the values in fields of other nodes and prototypes.
- Store the values of its fields or another node's fields for later use.
- Assign values to its outEvent fields that can affect other nodes via the simulation's routes. This feature provides much of the power of scripting.
- Bypass the simulation's routes and send a value directly to a field of a specific node.
- Copy nodes (including its child nodes).
- Access outside software through ActiveX controls.
- Send messages to the Log window using the Trace function, or it can send a message to a pop-up dialog box using the MessageBox function.
- Identify the names and types of fields in every node of the simulation tree.

What Cannot Be Done with Script?

Questions are frequently asked about the Script node's limitations. Within EON, scripting cannot perform several actions:

- Other scripts, within EON Studio or outside of EON Studio, cannot directly call functions in the Script node. They can only call functions indirectly by sending values to a Script node's fields.
- Although a Script node can be used to copy an entire node, it cannot create or copy individual node fields.
- A Script node cannot change the data type or field type of a field. For example, a script cannot change a field's type from inEvent to exposedField.

- A Script node cannot pause the simulation or make it end.
- A Script node does not have a function that can cause an EON simulation to be displayed in Fullscreen mode.
- A Script node cannot create 3D models, textures, or visible elements of itself. However, it can manipulate other EON nodes, such as the MeshBuilder and RenderTexture nodes, to perform this type of action.
- A Script node cannot access the position of vertices in 3D models.
- A Script node cannot insert seconds between statements of code. If you need a delay, you must trigger a TimeSensor node. When the time identified in the TimeSensor node has passed, the TimeSensor node must send an event to trigger the next action.

Creating Fields for the Script Node

As you have learned, the Script node must have fields that are capable of receiving values so that the script can respond to events. However, fields also are used to hold values that you will use. The fields might hold values related to speed, color, or position. Often, a Script node is used to hold node references.

To create a field, you must choose a name, a field type, and a data type. For some fields, you also need to enter an initial value for the field. The Script Properties dialog box, shown in Figure 9.1.5, is used to designate a scripting language, add fields, and delete fields within the Script node.

FIGURE 9.1.5 Field added in the Script Properties dialog box

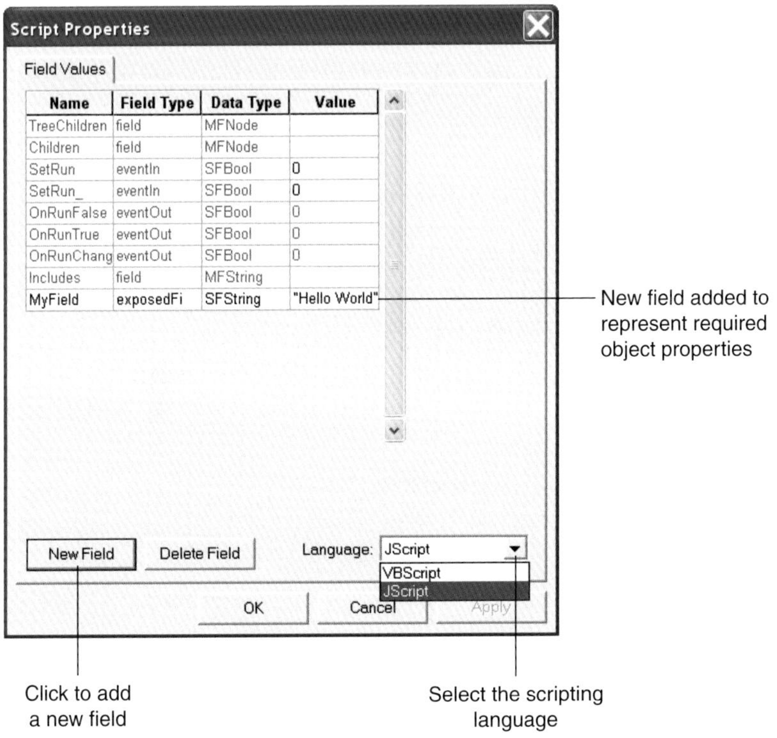

Like all fields, Script node fields must have a designated field type, which controls their ability to exchange data with other nodes, and an assigned data type, which indicates the type of data values that can be stored in the field. Choosing the right data type is important. To connect routes to your fields in the Script node, the data type must be the same as the field of the node to which you are connecting.

cross-reference

To review information about the default fields in every node, EON field types, and EON data types, refer to Module 1 Lesson 3.

SFNode and MFNode Data Types in a Script Node

cross-reference

To review information about using the SFNode and MFNode data types to create node references, refer to Module 8 Lesson 3.

As you may recall, the SFNode and MFNode data types are used to hold node references. When you create a field or an exposed field with the SFNode data type, you will see a yellow folder appear under the Script node, and when you create a field or exposed field with the MFNode data type, you will see a yellow folder appear under the Script node with a red plus sign (+) to denote the multifield nature of the MFNode data type. To place a node reference in one of these fields, you simply use the Copy as Link and Paste methods to place a shortcut to the node into the yellow folder beneath the Script node. Figure 9.1.6 displays the SFNode and MFNode fields that have been added to the Script node and the resulting folder icons in the simulation tree.

FIGURE 9.1.6 SFNode and MFNode fields added to a Script node

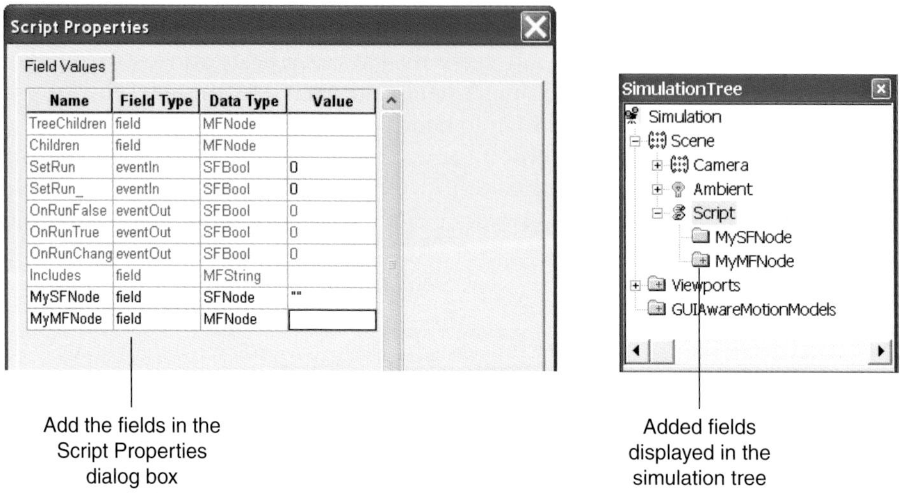

tips+tricks

The ClickSensor node has an outEvent named Target, which is an SFNode data type. It sends node references to Shape nodes that are clicked. After you have identified the Shape node, you can use the Script node to acquire references to the Shape node's Material2 node, and from that information, you can create a reference to its Texture2 node.

In the Script Properties dialog box, the value of a node reference is shown as a string representing the simulation path to the node. This does not mean that the value will be a string in your script—its value will be an EON Node Object.

In the following activity, you will set up three objects that the user can click to trigger the Script node. First, you will add fields to the Script node to accept these events.

Activity 9.1.1: Creating Fields

1. Open EON to start a new simulation. If EON is already open, select **New** from the File menu.
2. Save the simulation as **Fields_Added.eoz**.
3. Place three **Frame** nodes under the Scene and rename them **Cone_Frame**, **Cube_Frame**, and **Sphere_Frame**.
4. Place a **Cone** prototype under the Cone_Frame frame. Place a **Cube** prototype under the Cube_Frame frame. Place a **Sphere** prototype under the Sphere_Frame frame.
5. Run the simulation to view the scene. You will notice that all three shapes are stacked together because their position coordinates within the 3D space are identical.
6. Close the simulation window.
7. In the Property Bar, change the Cone_Frame frame's Position coordinates to **3 0 -2**. Change the Cube_Frame frame's Position coordinates to **0 0 2**. Change the Sphere_Frame frame's Position coordinates to **-3 0 -2**.

8. Run the simulation again to view the scene. Your simulation window should look like Figure 9.1.7.

FIGURE 9.1.7 Shapes displayed in the simulation window

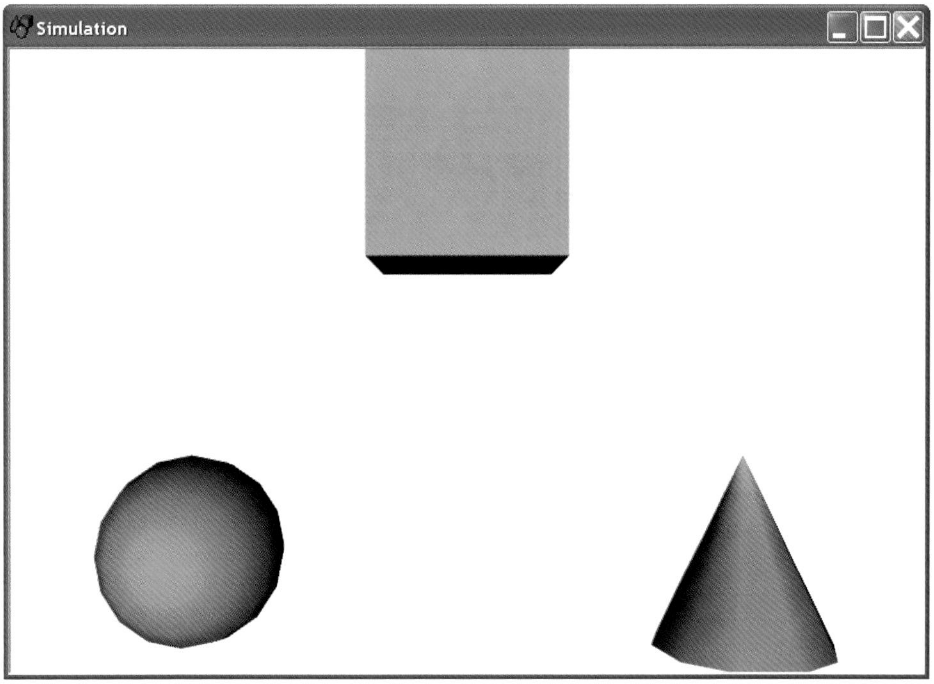

9. Close the simulation window.
10. Place a **ClickSensor** node under each of the three Frame nodes you added in step 3 and rename them accordingly as: **Cone_CS**, **Cube_CS**, and **Sphere_CS**.
11. Place a **Script** node under the Scene frame.
12. Double-click the **Script** node to open the Script Properties dialog box.
13. In the Language drop-down list, verify that **JScript** is selected.
14. Click the **New Field** button to add a row to the fields in the Script Properties dialog box. Modify the new field to match the first field displayed in Figure 9.1.8. Continue to add the remaining fields displayed in Figure 9.1.8. Notice also that the Sphere field is designed to hold a node reference. The value you entered is "Sphere." When you click OK, EON will use this text to search for a node named Sphere. If it finds a node with that name, it will create a node reference for you. If it does not find a node with that name, the field will remain empty, and you will need to add the node reference by using the Copy as Link method.

FIGURE 9.1.8 Fields added in the Script Properties dialog box

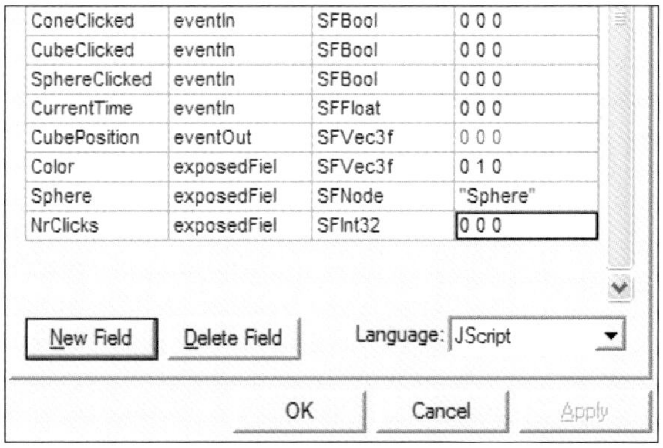

troubleshooting

JScript is a case-sensitive scripting language. Therefore, make sure your field names use mixed case as shown in Figure 9.1.8.

tips+tricks

Notice that the first four fields have values of 0 0 0 because the default value of a new field is 0 0 0 and you have not altered it. When you click the OK button, the values of these four fields will be 0. It takes the first value and ignores the others.

Notice that the CubePosition field has a value of 0 0 0 displayed in gray text. All eventOut fields are displayed in gray text to indicate that you cannot edit the value.

tips+tricks

Advanced users can edit the list of fields in another program, such as Microsoft Office Excel or Microsoft Notepad. Select the rows in the Script Properties dialog box. Paste the rows into Excel. Rearrange the sequence of the fields, copy the resequenced fields, and paste the fields back into EON. This provides you with a better way to organize your fields.

15. Click **OK** to close the Script Properties dialog box. Your simulation tree and Property Bar should look like Figure 9.1.9. Verify that the node reference has been added in the simulation tree.

FIGURE 9.1.9 Simulation tree and Property Bar after adding fields to the Script node

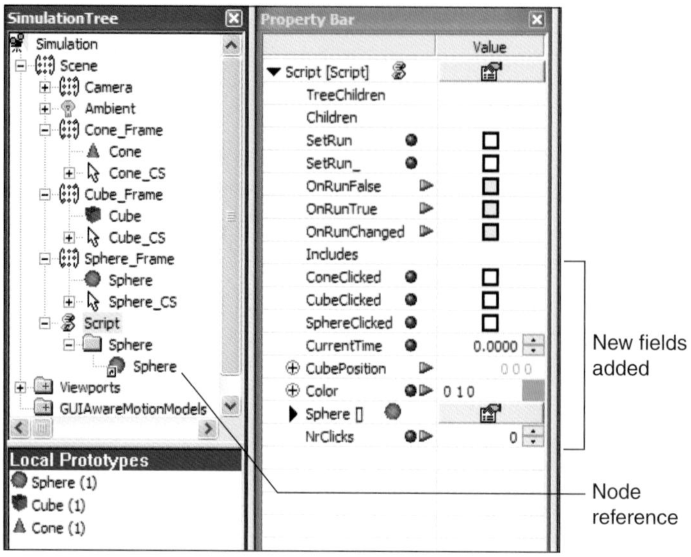

16. Save the simulation and keep it open to use in Activity 9.1.2. Congratulations! You have added several different types of fields to your first Script node. Some of these fields will be used as event handlers that will be developed in the next activity.

tips+tricks

Notice that the default fields for the Script node are displayed in the Property Bar. Showing or hiding default fields is an option. Select Property Bar from the Options menu to display the Property Bar Settings dialog box. Select or clear the Show all fields check box and click OK to change the setting.

BEST PRACTICES

Choosing Field Names

Choosing descriptive and meaningful names for your fields will make your scripts easy to read and will reduce errors in connecting routes to the wrong fields. When using node reference fields (SFNode), it may be appropriate to make the field's name the same as the node's name. Sometimes, the best field name could be the same as the name of the field that you intend to connect with routes. For example, connect the Simulation node's WindowWidth outEvent to a field named WindowWidth in your Script node. It is best to use mixed case for your field names. Start the field's name with a capital letter and capitalize any other words in the field name. For example, DisableWhenMoving and WalkSpeed use mixed case correctly. Later, when you are writing code, using a name with mixed case will help remind you that the name identifies a field and not a variable.

Event Handlers

In the event-driven world of real-time simulations, the flow of your simulation follows events as opposed to following a predefined linear program flow that is commonly found in conventional, procedural applications. This is an important point to remember because it means that a simulation is in a constant state of responding to events. When EON developers begin designing script code for an event handler, they identify the data and actions that must be performed in response to a state change during a simulation's frame rendering cycle. Therefore, in addition to storing data fields, a Script node is used to store the programming instructions to handle its events.

Events signal, among other things, changes to field values, external conditions, and interactions between nodes. The most common events are mouse clicks and key presses. External events may be sent over routes leading to or coming from locations outside of the simulation tree; they can originate from a host program, such as a web browser.

Creating Event Handlers for User-Defined Fields

As you saw in the example shown in Figure 9.1.5, the Script node has an exposedField named MyField. If the MyField property requires an action to be performed when its value changes, you will need to create an event handler. This is a function in your Script node's code area named function On_MyField(). If the Script node fields are created prior to launching the Script Editor, EON will automatically generate empty function code shells for all fields with field types of eventIn or exposedField. If you add the fields after you open the Script Editor window, then you will need to write the event handlers yourself. Always remember to include the On_ part of the function name. An example of a function code shell in JScript is shown in Figure 9.1.10.

FIGURE 9.1.10 Sample function code shell in JScript

```
function On_Myfield()
{
   < event handler statements here>
}
```

You can manually create event handlers for properties with field types of field and eventOut. However, you cannot connect routes to them. The event handlers for the field and eventOut field types are triggered when the associated fields receive new values from within the script itself or from another script. Therefore, an event handler can be triggered in two ways:

- Send a new value to a property field in a Script node through a route.
- Assign a new value to a property field through script code.

When an event occurs, execution control is temporarily transferred to the associated event handler. It is quite possible for a series of subsequent child events to be spawned by that initial event because the event handler code sends values to other fields in the local script, other scripts, or other nodes. This allows execution control to be passed down several levels of child events before returning to the original event at the top level. When all of the instructions in the top event handler have been completed, execution control shifts to the next top-level event and so on, until all top-level events have been handled. When all events have been handled, the frame will be rendered, and the next frame will start with nodes collecting new data that could lead to new events.

cross-reference

For more information about limitations placed on recursively triggered events, refer to Module 9 Lesson 2.

An event can recursively trigger itself. Therefore, developers should pay careful attention to the design of event handlers in order to minimize the depth of this event chain, including recursively triggered events. EON imposes restrictions on recursively triggered events to prevent simulation performance issues. Figure 9.1.11 graphically depicts how event handlers are invoked via user actions.

FIGURE 9.1.11 User actions invoke functions

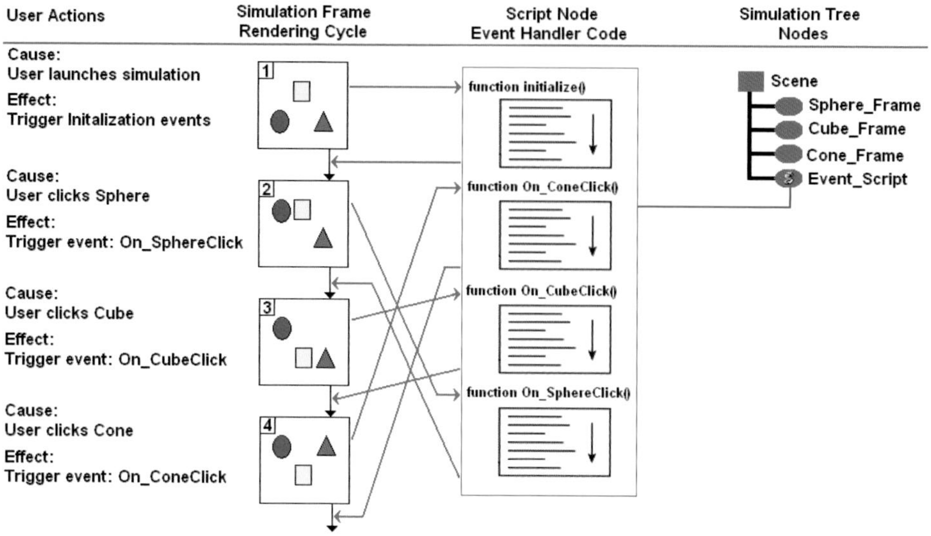

Now that you understand the fundamentals, it is time to start scripting—writing the code that tells the computer what to do. In the following activity, you will display a message box, write to the Log window, and make an object move smoothly. We have already created fields in our Script node. Now, we will connect events to the fields and write some event handlers (functions triggered by events).

Activity 9.1.2: Adding Event Handlers to Your First Script

1. Continue working with the open simulation file **Fields_Added.eoz** from Activity 9.1.1.
2. Save the simulation as **Event_Handlers_Added.eoz**.
3. Select the **Script** node and then click the **Open Script Editor** button on the toolbar to display the Script Editor window, as shown in Figure 9.1.12. Notice that the following function text has been added automatically for every field that you created of type eventIn or exposedField:

```
function On_ConeClicked()
{
   //TODO: Add your event handler code here
}
```

FIGURE 9.1.12 Event handlers are added automatically for fields with eventIn or exposedField selected in the Field Type column in the Script node

```
// Edit Scriptnode here.
// Add subroutines for each in-event or exposed field
// that you define in the script node's property page.

function initialize()
{
    // Called when simulation starts
    // Add initialization code
}

function On_ConeClicked()
{
    // TODO: Add your event handler code here
}

function On_CubeClicked()
{
    // TODO: Add your event handler code here
}

function On_SphereClicked()
```

4. Remove the comment in the ConeClicked() function and replace it with the following script code:

   ```
   eon.MessageBox("Hello World", "My first script");
   ```

   This code will display a pop-up message window containing the text Hello World. The title of the message box is My first script.
5. Run the simulation and click the cone. Nothing happens because the ConeClicked field of your script has not received the click event.
6. Close the simulation window.
7. Display the **Routes** window. Drag the **Cone_CS** node and the **Script** node to the Routes window. Establish the connection outlined in the following table.

From	outEvent	To	inEvent
Cone_CS	OnButtonDownFalse	Script	ConeClicked

8. Run the simulation and click the cone. The message window displayed in Figure 9.1.13 will appear on the simulation window. While the message window is visible, EON is paused; it does not continue any script or render any objects.

FIGURE 9.1.13 My first script message box

tips+tricks

The lines starting with double slashes are comments that will be ignored by the script interpreter.

9. Wait six seconds. When you do not click the OK button within six seconds, EON displays the message box shown in Figure 9.1.14 asking whether you would like to terminate the script.

FIGURE 9.1.14 EON script supervisor window

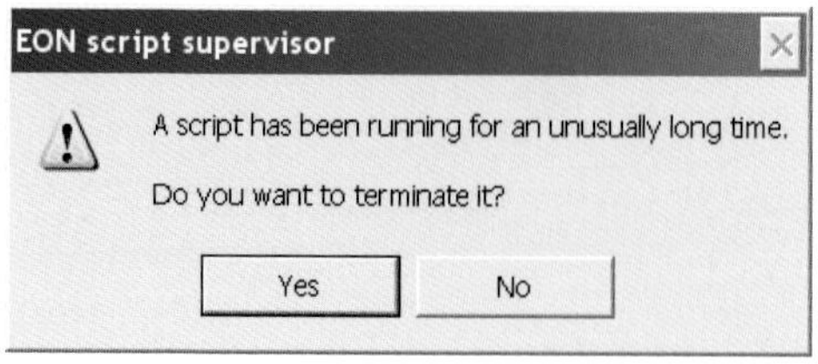

10. Click **No** in the EON script supervisor window. The message will disappear, but it will be displayed again in another six seconds. The EON script supervisor provides a way to terminate scripts caught in an endless loop or scripts that contain errors preventing the script from continuing. Without the EON script supervisor, you would have to terminate EON Studio or EON Viewer using the Windows Task Manager.
11. Click **OK** in the My first script message window to close the window.
12. Close the simulation window.
13. To display the Script Editor window again, click the **Script** node in the simulation tree and click the **Open Script Editor** button on the toolbar.
14. In the Script Editor window, add the following line before the MessageBox function:

    ```
    eon.setScriptTimeout(0)
    ```

    Add this line after the MessageBox function:

    ```
    eon.setScriptTimeout(6)
    ```

    This portion of the script code, displayed in Figure 9.1.15, effectively turns off the EON script supervisor temporarily.

FIGURE 9.1.15 Code that turns off the EON script supervisor

```
function On_ConeClicked()
{
    eon.setScriptTimeout(0)
    eon.MessageBox("Hello World", "My first script");
    eon.setScriptTimeout(6)
}
```

15. Run the simulation again. Click the cone to display the My first script pop-up window. Wait for six seconds to verify that the EON script supervisor does not interrupt the MessageBox function. Click **OK** to close the My first script message window.
16. Close the simulation window.
17. In the On_SphereClicked() function, replace the comment with the following text:

    ```
    eon.trace("sphere was clicked")
    ```

    The Trace function sends a message to the Log window in EON Studio. Information in the Log window can help you find errors in your simulation.

18. To see messages, select **Log** from the Window menu to display the Log window if it is not visible. Right-click in the **Log** window and choose **Set Filter**. The Log Filter dialog box is displayed. Select the **Script Trace** check box as shown in Figure 9.1.16. Click **OK** to close the Log Filter dialog box.

FIGURE 9.1.16 Log Filter dialog box

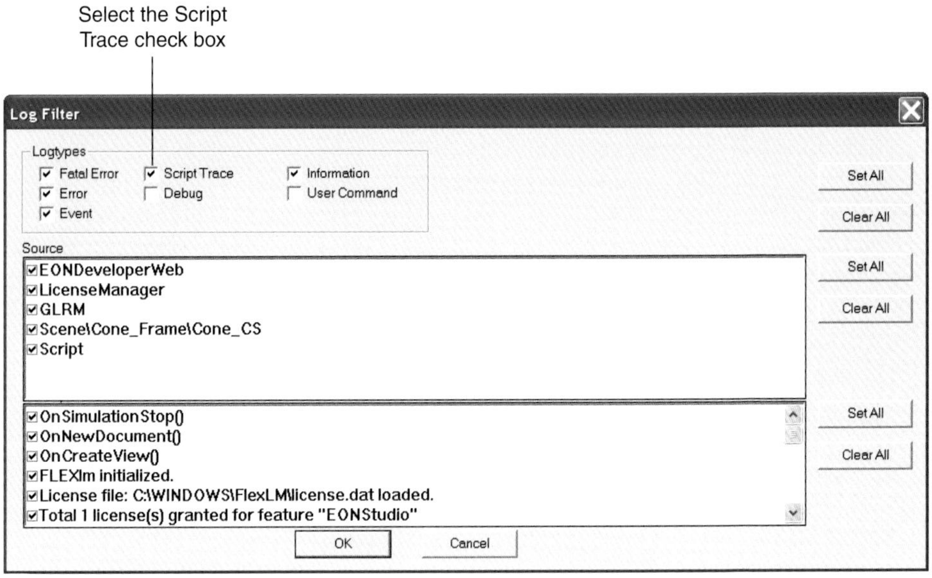

discuss

What would happen if you ran the simulation and clicked the sphere in the simulation window?

19. Display the **Routes** window. Add the **Sphere_CS** node to the Routes window. Establish the connection outlined in the following table. Your Routes window should look similar to Figure 9.1.17.

From	outEvent	To	inEvent
Sphere_CS	OnButtonDownFalse	Script	SphereClicked

FIGURE 9.1.17 Sphere_CS added to the Routes window

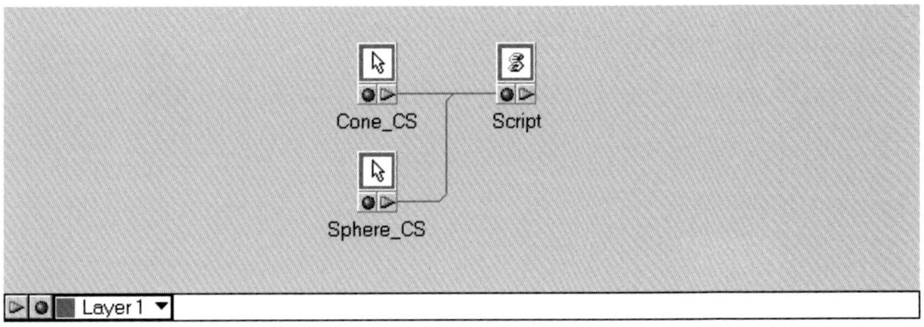

20. Run the simulation and then click the sphere. A new line of text appears in the Log window as shown in Figure 9.1.18.

FIGURE 9.1.18 Message in the Log window informs you that the sphere was clicked

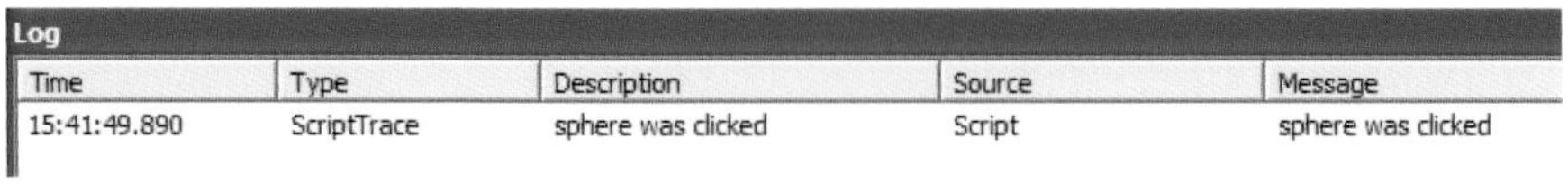

Log
Time
Type
Description
Source
Message
15:41:49.890
ScriptTrace
sphere was clicked
Script
sphere was clicked

21. Close the simulation window.

    For the next event, we will make the Cube move up and down smoothly by using the cosine wave. This is more complex because it involves several fields. Clicking the cube will start a TimeSensor that will send its CurrentTime value to the Script node. The CurrentTime is a special outEvent of the TimeSensor that is sent once every frame rendering cycle. When the script receives the time, it will use the JScript's math object to access the cosine function and create a Z value for the cube.

22. Add a **TimeSensor** node to the Scene frame. In the Property Bar, select the **LoopMode** check box, and clear the **Active** check box. Set the StopTime value to **100**. Your Property Bar should look like Figure 9.1.19.

FIGURE 9.1.19 Property Bar for the TimeSensor node

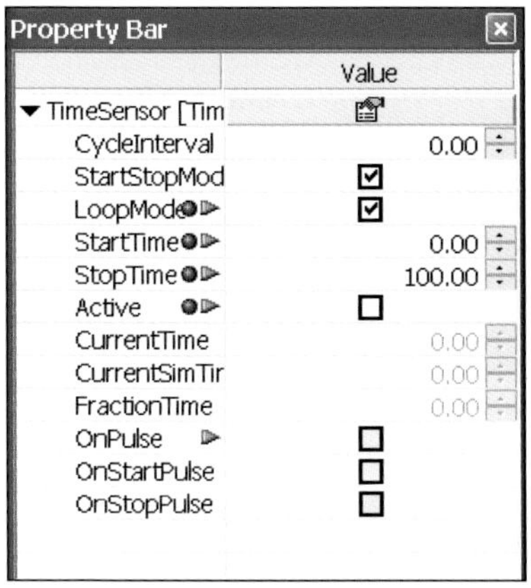

23. Display the **Routes** window. Drag the **Cube_Frame**, **Cube_CS**, and **TimeSensor** nodes to the Routes window. Establish the connections outlined in the following table. Your Routes window should look similar to Figure 9.1.20.

From	outEvent	To	inEvent
Cube_CS	OnButtonDownTrue	Script	CubeClicked
TimeSensor	CurrentTime	Script	CurrentTime
Script	CubePosition	Cube_Frame	Position

FIGURE 9.1.20 Routes window with connections added

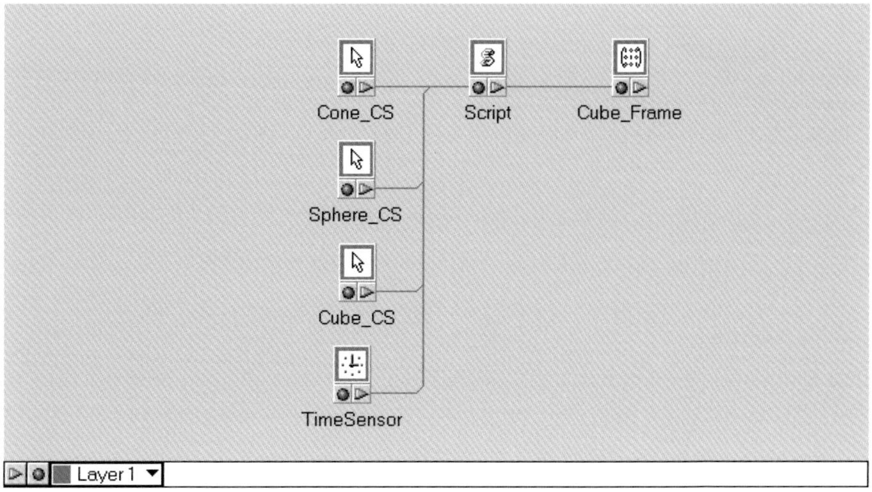

24. Display the **Script Editor** window. In the function for the cube, On_CubeClicked(), replace the comment with the following text:

    ```
    eon.findnode("TimeSensor").GetFieldByName("SetRun").value = true;
    ```

    This will send true to the SetRun field of the TimeSensor node.

25. In the function for the CurrentTime field, On_CurrentTime(), replace the comment with the following text:

    ```
    var t = CurrentTime.value;
    var z = 2*Math.cos(t*2);
    CubePosition.value = eon.MakeSFVec3f(0, 0, z);
    ```

    The first line gets the value of the CurrentTime field that was sent from the TimeSensor and stores it in a variable named *t*. The second line uses a built-in function in JScript to calculate the cosine value based on the time value and stores the result in the *z* variable. The third line makes a 3D positional vector value using *z* and assigns it to the eventOut field in our script named CubePosition. Because a route connects this field and the Position field of the Cube_Frame, the cube will be moved. Your Script Editor window should look like Figure 9.1.21.

FIGURE 9.1.21 Script added to the On_CurrentTime() function

```
function On_CurrentTime()
{
    var t = CurrentTime.value;
    var z = 2*Math.cos(t*2);
    CubePosition.value = eon.MakeSFVec3f(0, 0, z);
}
```

26. Run the simulation and click the cube. Notice that the cube moves up and down.
27. Close the simulation window.

tips+tricks

Step 24 demonstrates a quick way to send an event to a node without connecting a route. You may understand this better if you see it written in a longer way as follows:

```
var tsnode =
    eon.findnode
    ("TimeSensor")
var runfield =
    tsnode.GetFieldByName
    ("SetRun")
runfield.value = true
```

The findnode function returns an EON Node Object. The GetFieldByName() function returns a field object from a node object, and the .value portion of the script assigns a value to the Value property of the EON Field Object.

Discussion

discuss

Change 2 in the second line to a different number. How does this change affect the path of the cube?

troubleshooting

Be sure to remove the complete function, including the comment text and the closing bracket (}). Leaving part of the function text can create errors in your script.

28. In the On_SphereClicked() function, add the following text under the eon.trace line:

```
eon.findnode("Sphere").GetFieldByName("Color").value =
Color.value;
```

The Script node already had a color in its Color field. This step will send the color to the Sphere prototype when the user clicks the sphere, changing the sphere's color to green.

29. Run the simulation and click the sphere. The sphere's color should change to green.
30. Close the simulation window.
31. Delete the **On_Color()** event handler for the Color field. Because this field was used only to store a value and not as an event, you can safely remove this event handler.
32. Save the simulation and keep it open to use in Activity 9.1.3. Congratulations! Your first script has three event handlers—one that changes the color of a sphere, one that displays a message box, and one that moves an object smoothly.

Designing Scripts

To improve your skills in scripting, you will need to study the scripting language and the built-in objects and methods. But that is not all. To make useful scripts, you must have knowledge about the objects that are scriptable. In EON, the scriptable objects are the nodes, the prototypes, and their fields. You must know how to get events and data into your script and where you can send events and data to achieve the purpose of your script.

Scripting involves a design process. You must decide when to use a single script or multiple scripts. Using a single script might be efficient when you do not have many events, but the complexity increases as the number of events and the amount of code you write increases. To handle this complexity, you can use the "divide and conquer" approach. Try to divide your code into logical components and see whether you could move that code to a separate script. Each of these logical components should concentrate on doing one thing effectively and efficiently. The reduction of code in your main script makes it easier for you to understand and lets you concentrate on minimizing complexity.

In the previous activity, we handled three different events in three separate ways. The events do not really relate to each other. For example, you could have used three separate Script nodes. But more often, you will need to design your scripts to allow inEvents from many sources and combine data from multiple sources to create an integrated and useful function.

One reason for combining the three different events from our previous activity is to enable the three functions to be turned on or off as a group. There is no built-in way to turn your script on and off. Sending SetRun=false to your Script node will not stop the functions that are being executed. Therefore, you must design your script so that it behaves as if it is turned off, typically by using an IsActive field. The coding for this field typically involves exiting a function early or sending events to other nodes to turn them off.

In the next activity, we will add an IsActive field to turn off the script after three clicks.

Activity 9.1.3: Turning Off Your Script

1. Continue working with the open simulation file **Event_Handlers_Added.eoz** from Activity 3.2.1.
2. Save the simulation as **Turn_Off_Script.eoz**.
3. Double-click the **Script** node to open the Script Properties dialog box. Click the **New Field** button and add a new field named **IsActive**. Set the Field Type to **exposedField**, set the Data Type to **SFBool**, and set the Value to **1**. Click **OK** to close the dialog box.
4. Display the **Script Editor** window. Insert the following line of code as the first line in the On_ConeClicked(), On_CubeClicked(), On_SphereClicked(), and On_CurrentTime() functions:

   ```
   if (IsActive.value==false) return;
   ```

   This line says that if the IsActive field has a false value, then exit (return) the event handler. Return is a keyword that means program execution does not continue for that event handler. Next, we will make a function that will turn off the script after the user has clicked the objects in the simulation window three times. We will use the Script node's NrClicks field to count the clicks.
5. In the On_ConeClicked(), On_CubeClicked(), and On_SphereClicked() event handlers, add this line after the line checking the IsActive field:

   ```
   NrClicks.value = NrClicks.value + 1;
   ```

   This increments the value of the NrClicks field by 1 when the user clicks an object. This line of code creates an event, and program flow will immediately continue with the event handler for the NrClicks field. The On_ConeClicked() event handler portion of your script should look like Figure 9.1.22.

FIGURE 9.1.22 On_ConeClicked() function can increment the value in the NrClicks field

```
function On_ConeClicked()
{
    if (IsActive.value==false) return;
    NrClicks.value = NrClicks.value + 1;
    eon.setScriptTimeout(0)
    eon.MessageBox("Hello World", "My first script");
    eon.setScriptTimeout(6)
}
```

6. In the event handler for the NrClicks field, replace the comment with the following two lines:

   ```
   eon.trace("NrClicks = " + NrClicks.value);
   if (NrClicks.value>=3) IsActive.value = false
   ```

7. Run the simulation. Click the cube, the cone, and then the sphere. Click the cone again.

Discussion

discuss

Does the message box appear the second time you click the cone?

Why or why not?

8. Close the simulation window.

   The cube may have continued to move after the script was turned off. To stop the cube, we will stop the TimeSensor so it does not send events to the script. We will modify the function for the IsActive field, which is triggered internally by the second line in the On_NrClicks() function.

9. In the On_IsActive() function, replace the comment with the following lines. The On_IsActive() function portion of your script should look like Figure 9.1.23.

```
if (IsActive.value==false)
{
  // turn off the TimeSensor
  eon.findnode("TimeSensor").GetFieldByName("SetRun").value = false
  eon.trace("Script is now OFF")
}
```

troubleshooting

If the script does not have an On_IsActive() function shell, then create one yourself. EON will not create function shells after you have opened the Script Editor window.

FIGURE 9.1.23 On_IsActive() function

```
function On_IsActive()
{
            if (IsActive.value==false)
            {
                // turn off the TimeSensor
                eon.findnode("TimeSensor").GetFieldByName("SetRun").value = false
                eon.trace("Script is now OFF")
                }
}
```

10. Select the **Script** node in the simulation tree if necessary. In the Property Bar, select the **IsActive** check box, setting the field to true, and set the NrClicks field to **0**.
11. Run the simulation. Click the cube, the cone, and then the sphere.

Discussion

discuss

What happened when you clicked the sphere?

12. Close the simulation window. Run the simulation again.

Discussion

discuss

Can you click the objects now? Why or why not?

13. Close the simulation window.
14. Replace the comments inside the initialize() function at the top of your script page with the following lines of code. These lines will make the script active at the start of the simulation and will set the NrClicks field to zero. The addition to your script should look like Figure 9.1.24.

```
IsActive.value = true;
NrClicks.value = 0;
```

FIGURE 9.1.24 initialize() function

```
function initialize()
{
    IsActive.value = true;
    NrClicks.value = 0;
}
```

15. Run the simulation. Click the objects.

Discussion

discuss

What happens when you click the objects?

16. Close the simulation window.
17. To clean up the script, replace the three lines of comments at the top of the script with the following line.

```
// My First Script
```

18. Add the following two lines at the end of your script.

```
// Last modified April 30, 2009.
// by [put your name here]
```

19. Review your script. Add comments that explain specific lines of code or sections of code.

tips+tricks

Add comments before the line or section that you are explaining. This tells the reader what it will do before reading the code.

20. Compare your script to the script shown in Figure 9.1.25.

FIGURE 9.1.25 Script Editor window containing the complete script

```
// My First Script

function initialize()
{
    IsActive.value = true;
    NrClicks.value = 0;
}

function On_ConeClicked()
{
    if (IsActive.value==false) return;
    NrClicks.value = NrClicks.value + 1;
    // show a message
    eon.SetScriptTimeout(0);
    eon.MessageBox("Hello World", "My first script");
    eon.SetScriptTimeout(6);
}

function On_CubeClicked()
{
    if (IsActive.value==false) return;
    NrClicks.value = NrClicks.value + 1;
    // turn on the time sensor
    eon.findnode("TimeSensor").GetFieldByName("SetRun").value = true;
}

function On_SphereClicked()
{
    if (IsActive.value==false) return;
    NrClicks.value = NrClicks.value + 1;
    eon.trace("sphere was clicked");
    // change the sphere's color
    eon.findnode("Sphere").GetFieldByName("Color").value = Color.value;
}

function On_CurrentTime()
{
    if (IsActive.value==false) return;
    var t = CurrentTime.value;
    var z = 2*Math.cos(t*2);
    // send position to cube via CubePosition outevent
    CubePosition.value = eon.MakeSFVec3f(0, 0, z);
}

function On_NrClicks()
{
    eon.trace("NrClicks = " + NrClicks.value);
    if (NrClicks.value>=3) IsActive.value = false;
}

function On_IsActive()
{
    if (IsActive.value==false)
    {
        // turn off Timesensor
        eon.findnode("TimeSensor").GetFieldByName("SetRun").value = false;
        eon.trace("Script is now OFF");
    }
}

// Last modified April 30, 2009.
// by [put your name here]
```

cross-reference

Notice the keyword highlighting in this script. JScript language keywords and names of objects and functions are blue. Comments are red. String literals are green. EON functions are brown. You can determine which words are highlighted and select the highlighting color. Keyword highlighting is discussed later in this lesson.

21. Save the simulation and keep it open to use in Activity 9.1.4.

Using the Script Editor

In the previous section, you used the Script Editor to create a script. To increase your efficiency in writing code, you should become familiar with Script Editor features such as keyboard shortcuts, font settings, line numbers, bookmarks, and keyword highlighting.

Opening the Script Editor

Scripts are not defined when you add a Script node to the simulation tree. You must write scripts in the Script Editor, which is very similar to a text editor such as Microsoft Notepad or Microsoft WordPad. After selecting the Script node in the simulation tree, you can open the Script Editor in any of the following ways:

- Click the Open Script Editor button in the toolbar.

- Press Ctrl + E.
- Press Alt + 6.
- In the Window menu, select Script > Open Editor.

When you open the Script node for the first time, you will see that functions or subroutines, depending on the scripting language selected, have already been created for the eventIn and exposedField fields that you added to the Script node. The initialize function or subroutine is always present as well, as shown in Figure 9.1.26.

FIGURE 9.1.26 Script Editor window

```
// Edit Scriptnode here.
// Add subroutines for each in-event or exposed field
// that you define in the script node's property page.

function initialize()
{
    // Called when simulation starts
    // Add initialization code
}
```

While a simulation is running, you can open the Script Editor and edit the script, but the changes you make will not affect the simulation until it is restarted. Several Script Editor windows can be open simultaneously to display script for different Script nodes. All scripts that have been edited in the Script Editor are listed in the Window > Script submenu.

Editing in the Script Editor

The following topics will improve your ability to enter, organize, and edit script in the Script Editor window. After you master these skills, you will be a more efficient programmer.

Indenting Text

To make scripts easier to read, indent your code appropriately. You can indent lines by pressing the spacebar or the Tab key. Subsequent lines will have the same indentation automatically. Use the Backspace or Shift + Tab keys to cancel or remove indentation. You can indent many lines of code at the same time by selecting the rows and pressing the Tab key to increase indentation and Shift + Tab to reduce or remove indentation.

Using Shortcuts

Many of the shortcuts in the Script Editor window are standard for text editors. The EON Script Editor has unlimited Undo and Redo functions to help you enter script code. A powerful Find and Replace function helps you find and correct typing errors made in the Script Editor window. Additional keyboard shortcuts are listed in Table 9.1.2.

TABLE 9.1.2 Shortcut Keys for the EON Script Editor

Function	Shortcut
Cut	Ctrl + X
Copy	Ctrl + C
Paste	Ctrl + V
Undo	Ctrl + Z
Redo	Ctrl + Shift + Z
Select All	Ctrl + A
Find	Ctrl + F
Find Next	F3
Find and Replace	Ctrl + H
Column selection	Alt + Mouse selection
Select a row	Click left margin
Select a word	Double-click word
Select from cursor	Shift + click
General select	Drag mouse over text
Switch between open Script Editor windows	Ctrl + F6

Using Bookmarks

You can use a ***bookmark*** to find a certain paragraph in a script. Place the cursor anywhere within the desired line, click the right mouse button, and then select Toggle Bookmark. The bookmark is displayed as a blue dot to the left of the line, as shown in Figure 9.1.27.

FIGURE 9.1.27 Bookmark in a script

Bookmark

```
function On_ConeClicked()
{
    if (IsActive.value==false) return;
    NrClicks.value = NrClicks.value + 1;
    eon.setScriptTimeout(0)
    eon.MessageBox("Hello World", "My first script");
    eon.setScriptTimeout(6)
}
```

The Find function (Ctrl + F) can create bookmarks at every occurrence of a found word. Just click the Mark All button in the Find dialog box displayed in Figure 9.1.28. By default, the word in the Find What field is identified by the cursor's location in the script.

FIGURE 9.1.28 Find dialog box

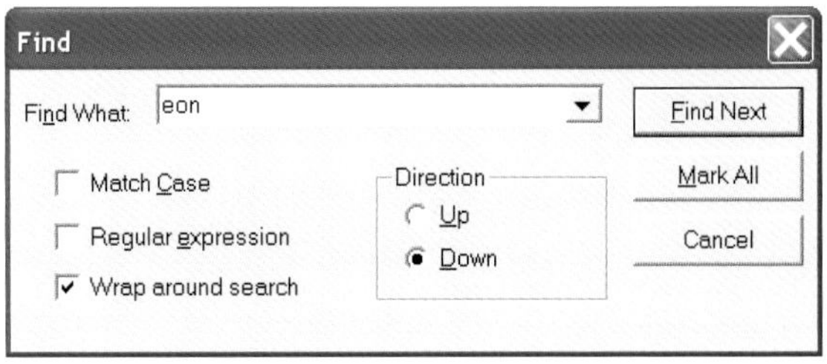

Identifying the Cursor's Position

The current position of the cursor (the line and column number) is indicated in the Status Bar at the bottom of the Script Editor window. This information is most useful when finding a line of code that contains an error. Generally, script errors are reported with a line number.

Changing the Font in the Script Editor

You can change the font used in the Script Editor so that it is larger or clearer for you to read. You might like to make it smaller to fit a typical line of code in the Script Editor window. Choose Preferences from the Options menu to display the Preferences dialog box. Click the Set Font button to open the Font dialog box displayed in Figure 9.1.29.

FIGURE 9.1.29 Changing the font preference for the EON Script Editor

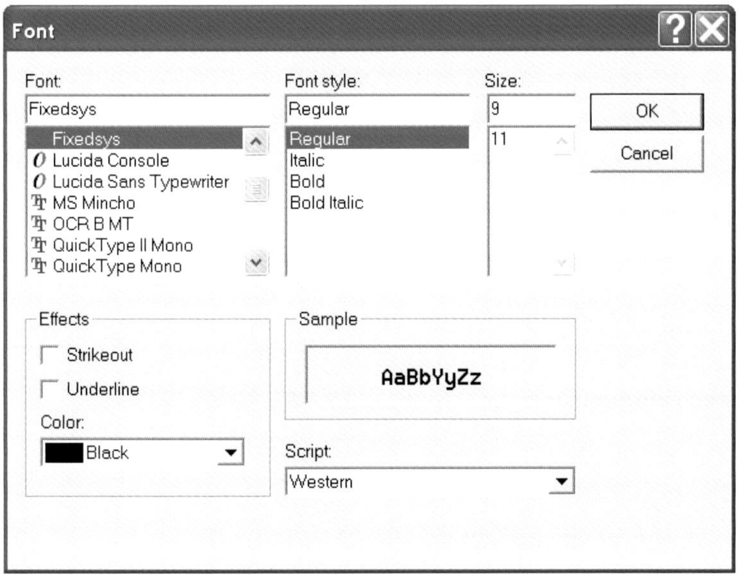

Highlighting Keywords

As you write script, keywords will be highlighted in different colors. This makes your scripts easier to read and understand. If you want to add new keywords or change text highlighting color preferences, you can modify the default definitions for VBScript and JScript in the files vbscript.ini and jscript.ini, respectively. These files are located in the Windows folder. Figure 9.1.30 displays a portion of the jscript.ini file.

FIGURE 9.1.30 Portion of the jscript.ini file

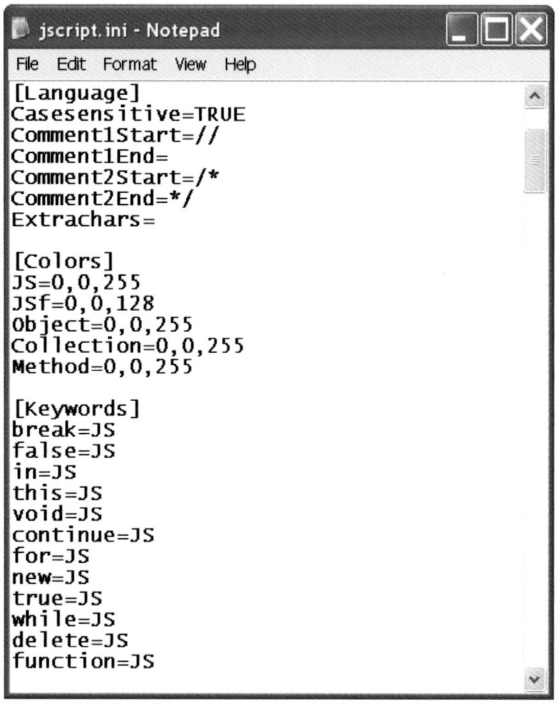

Activity 9.1.4: Modifying the Script Editor

1. Continue working with the open simulation file **Turn_Off_Script.eoz** from Activity 9.1.3.
2. Click the **Script** node and press **Ctrl + E** to open the Script Editor window.
3. From the Options menu, choose **Preferences** to display the Preferences dialog box displayed in Figure 9.1.31.

FIGURE 9.1.31 Preferences dialog box

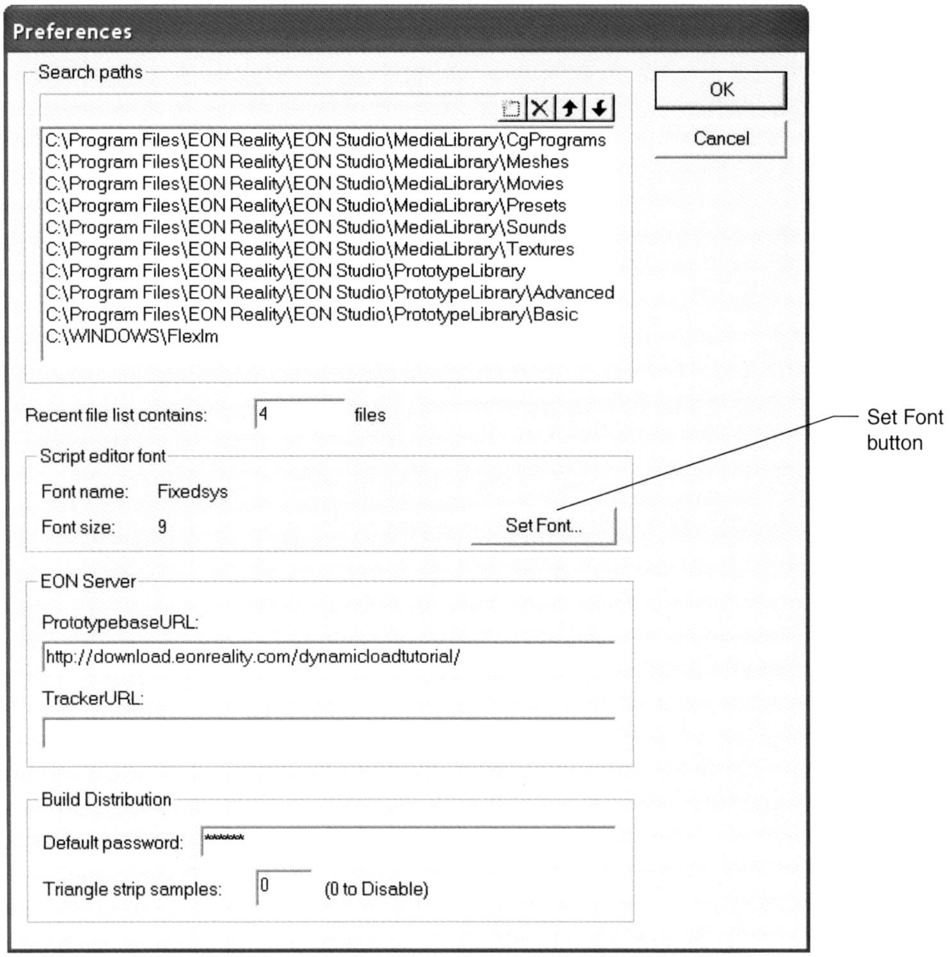

4. Click the **Set Font** button, which is identified in Figure 9.1.31. The Font dialog box is displayed.
5. In the Font field, select **Terminal**. In the Font style field, select **Bold** and select **9** in the Size field if necessary. Your Font dialog box should look like Figure 9.1.32.

FIGURE 9.1.32 Modified settings in the Font dialog box

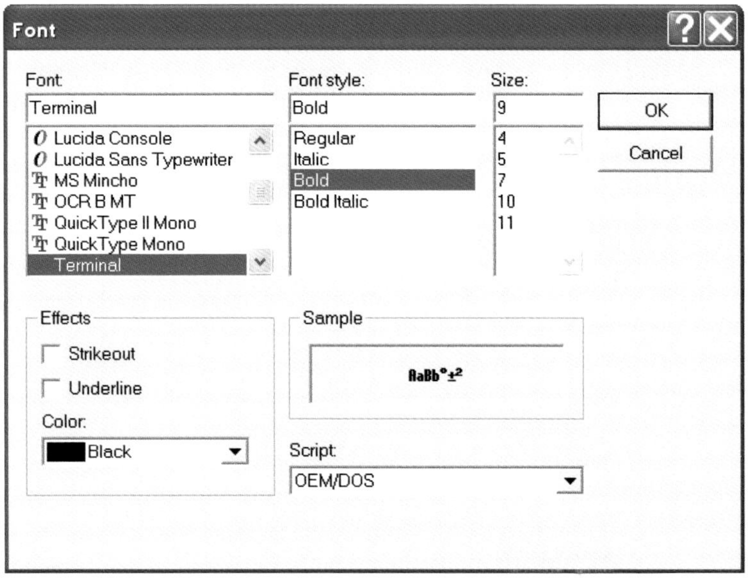

6. Click **OK** to close the Font dialog box. Click **OK** to close the Preferences dialog box. Notice the change in the font used in the Script Editor window as shown in Figure 9.1.33.

FIGURE 9.1.33 Modified font in the Script Editor window

```
function On_CubeClicked()
{
    if (IsActive.value==false) return;
    NrClicks.value = NrClicks.value + 1;
    eon.findnode("TimeSensor").GetFieldByName("SetRun").value = true;
}
```

troubleshooting

If you see a message that you cannot save the jscript.ini file, the existing file may have the Read-only attribute set. Right-click the file and select the Properties option to display information about the file. Clear the Read-only check box and click OK. Try again to save the file. If you still cannot save the file, verify that you are an administrator on your computer.

7. Open Notepad. Open **EON keyword highlighting.txt** from the data files for Module 9 Lesson 1.
8. Open another Notepad instance and open the **jscript.ini** file from C:\Windows\.
9. From the first file, **EON keyword highlighting.txt**, select and copy all of the text under the [keywords] row. Paste the text at the end of the **jscript.ini** file.
10. Scroll up to the top of the file in both Notepad windows. From the first file, **EON keyword highlighting.txt**, select and copy the line under the [Colors] row. Paste the text in the **jscript.ini** file, placing it as the last line in its [Colors] section.
11. Save the **jscript.ini** file.
12. Click in the **Script Editor** window. Notice that the names of EON methods are in brown text as shown in Figure 9.1.34.

FIGURE 9.1.34 Keyword highlighting modified

```
function On_ConeClicked()
{
    if (IsActive.value==false) return;
    NrClicks.value = NrClicks.value + 1;
    eon.setScriptTimeout(0)
    eon.MessageBox("Hello World", "My first script");
    eon.setScriptTimeout(6)
}
```

13. Click in the **Script Editor** window and then press the **Ctrl + F** keys. The Find dialog box is displayed.
14. In the Find What field, type **IsActive,** as shown in Figure 9.1.35, and then click **Find Next**. The dialog box is closed and the first instance of IsActive is highlighted in the Script Editor window.

FIGURE 9.1.35 Use the Find dialog box to locate specific text

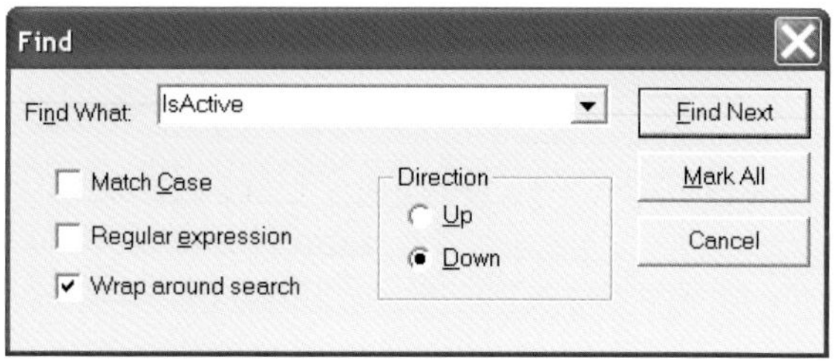

15. Press the **F3** key to find the next instance of IsActive.

Discussion

discuss

How many times does the word IsActive appear in the script?

16. Click in the first row of the script. Press the **Ctrl + H** keys to display the Replace dialog box.
17. In the Find What field, type **IsActive**. In the Replace With field, type **Active** as shown in Figure 9.1.36.

FIGURE 9.1.36 Replace dialog box

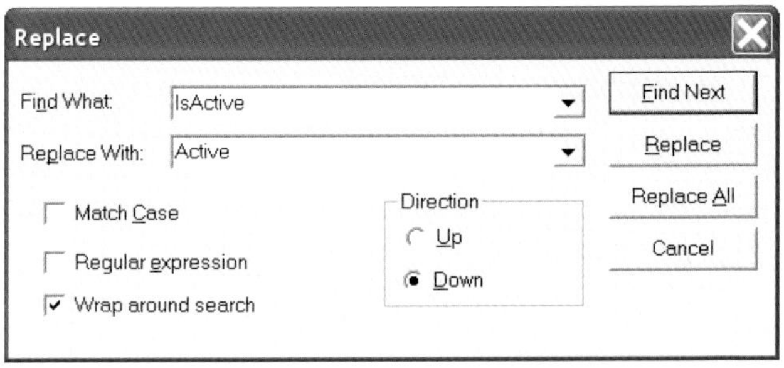

18. Click the **Find Next** button to select the first IsActive found in the script.
19. Click the **Replace** button to replace the selection with Active.
20. Click the **Cancel** button to close the dialog box.
21. Run the simulation. An error message is displayed, as shown in Figure 9.1.37.

FIGURE 9.1.37 Error message

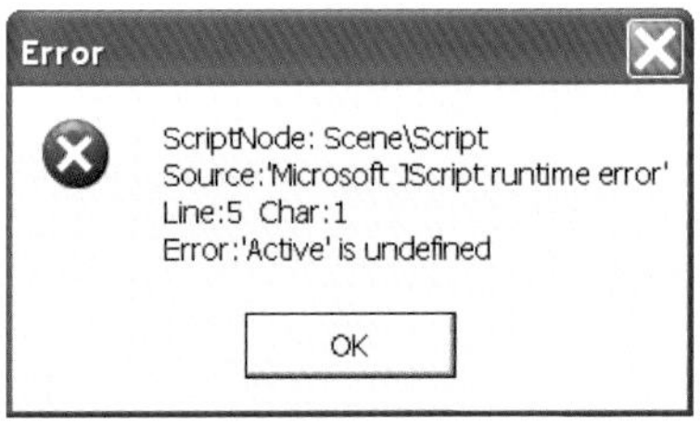

22. Note the error description and the line number and click **OK** to close the Error dialog box.
23. Close the simulation window.
24. In the Script Editor window, click a row of text. The line number is displayed in the Status Bar.

discuss

Will this function help you find the row where the error occurred?

25. Press **Ctrl + Z** to undo the last change made by the Replace function. Press **Ctrl + Shift + Z** to redo the change. Press **Ctrl + Z** to undo the change again.
26. Select the entire **On_ConeClicked()** function.
27. Press **Tab** three times. Notice the indentation.
28. Hold down the **Shift** key and press **Tab** three times to remove the indentation.
29. Close EON without saving the simulation.

Scripting Basics—JScript

In this section, you will be introduced to some basic scripting concepts. We recommend that you read the official scripting language reference for in-depth study or details about specific functions.

Statements

A ***statement*** in JScript is one line of code. You should use the semicolon to explicitly terminate a statement, but it is not compulsory. A group of statements enclosed in curly brackets { } is called a ***block***.

Among the most common types of statements are the if and else statements.

```
if (condition)
   statement1;
else
   statement2;
```

If you have more than one statement, then replace statement1 with a block. For clarity, it is best to always use block statements like this:

```
if (condition)
{
   statements
}
else
{
   statements
}
```

When you want to repeat some statements a certain number of times, you can use the for loop:

```
for (initialize; condition; increment statement)
{
statements
}

var num = 0
for (var i=0; i<10; i++)
{
   num = num + i
}
```

Variables

Variables are named memory locations that are used to temporarily store values needed for your script. Thoughtful use of descriptive and meaningful variable names makes your scripts easier to understand for you and others.

Declaring Variables

Variables are declared using the var statement like this:

```
var count;
var count = 0;
```

It is not compulsory to declare your variables. You can implicitly declare them by assigning a value like this:

```
pressure = 345;
```

Variable Scope

Variables have ***scope***, which refers to where they are visible. Variables can have local scope and global scope. Local scope variables are declared within a function statement. When the function terminates, the variable disappears so the computer memory storing the variable is released. Global variables will exist until the host program is shut down. Therefore, it is best to reduce your memory usage by using local variables when possible.

It is good programming practice to always declare your variables, especially local variables, so that you do not accidentally overwrite a global variable. If you consistently declare your local variables, it will be easier to recognize when you use a global variable within a local function because it will be the one that has not been declared. Global variables are those declared outside all of the functions of a script. It is good programming practice to declare all global variables at the top of your script.

In the following example, *count* is a global variable and *zoom* is a local variable.

```
var count = 0;
function initialize()
{
   var zoom = 8;
   eon.trace(zoom);
}
```

tips+tricks

In EON, every Script node is separate. Therefore, variables declared in one script are not available in another script, even if they are global variables. The only way variables in one script can get the values of variables in another script is by sending them via a Script node's fields.

Variable Data Types

JScript is a loosely typed programming language, which means you cannot declare the data type that a variable contains. A variable's type is defined by the value that you assign to it. Therefore, a variable's type can change as different values are assigned to it. This makes JScript a very flexible and easy language to use.

JScript has six data types: numbers, strings, Booleans, objects, null, and undefined. Table 9.1.3 describes the available data types.

TABLE 9.1.3 Data Types in JScript

Data Type	Description
Number	Consists of digits and symbols, such as + and -.
String	One or more characters or symbols, including numbers. When assigning literal strings, they must be enclosed within double or single quotation marks.
Boolean	Values that are either true or false.
Object	Variable holds references to a group of properties or methods, where properties are like variables and methods are like functions.
Null	Variable does not hold valid data. Some functions return null or you can explicitly assign null to any variable.
Undefined	Variable that has been declared, but a value has not been assigned to it.

web links

JScript has hundreds of reserved words that should not be used as variable names. Use the Internet to search for a list of variable names you should avoid.

To find out what the data type of your variable is, you can use the typeof operator.

```
var myvar = "hello"
eon.trace(typeof myvar)     // outputs [string] to the log view
```

Variable Naming Rules

When you name your variables, there are some hard rules and some strong recommendations. Use the following rules:

- Variables must start with a letter (a–z), an underscore (_) or a dollar sign ($).
- The next characters can be the same as the first character, but numbers (0–9) also are allowed.
- No other characters are allowed, including a space, period, !, @, #, *, and so on.
- Language reserved words cannot be used. This includes words such as var, if, else, while, for, true, false, function, return, and so on.

troubleshooting

JScript is a case-sensitive language. If you store a value in piperadius, for example, then you cannot retrieve it with pipeRadius.

To avoid possible errors and misunderstandings, avoid using names that are part of JScript's intrinsic objects, their properties, and methods. Avoid names such as Array, String, Object, Boolean, parseInt, cos, tan, getDate, getDay, and substring.

BEST PRACTICES

Lowercase Variable Names

To avoid problems caused by confusing a variable name with a script's field name, we strongly recommend that you use only lowercase names for variables and use only mixed case for the script's field names. If you mistakenly declare a variable using a name that matches the name of an existing field, you will not be able to access the field's value using the Fieldname.value syntax.

Operators

Operators are symbols that manipulate data values. Simple operators include addition, subtraction, multiplication, and division. Table 9.1.4 identifies some operators in JScript.

TABLE 9.1.4 Script Operators in JScript

Category	Operation	JScript
Math	Exponentiation	
	Multiplication, Division	*, /
	Integer division	
	Modulo division	%
	Addition, Subtraction	+, -
String	Concatenation	+
Relational	Equality	==
	Inequality	!=
	Less than	<
	Less than or equal to	<=
	Greater than	>
	Greater than or equal to	>=
Logical	And, Or, Not	&&, ||, !
Others	Assignment	=
	Increment, Decrement	++, --

One of the hardest things to understand is that + is used for addition and for joining strings together. To know which operation to carry out, JScript will look at the data types of the two values. If both values are numbers, it will add them. If both values are strings, it will join the strings. If one value is a string and the other value is a number, then the number will be converted into a string as shown in the following examples.

```
var a = "54" + "12"      // a = "5412"
var b = 54 + 12          // b = 66
var c = 54 + "12"        // c = "5412"
var d = 54 + false       // d = 54
var e = 54 + true        // e = 55
```

If you want to force a certain data type, then wrap it inside a String(), Number(), or Boolean(), as shown in the following examples.

```
var f = Boolean(54)      // f = true
var g = String(54)       // g = "54"
var h = Number("54")     // h = 54
var i = Number("abd")    // i = NaN (not a number)
```

Operator Precedence

Operators are evaluated in a particular sequence. Table 9.1.5 displays the sequence from highest to lowest. Within a row, operators have the same precedence and will be evaluated in left-to-right sequence.

TABLE 9.1.5 Operator Precedence

Operator	Description
. [] ()	Field access, array indexing, function calls
++ -- - ~ ! delete new typeof void	Unary operators, return data type, object creation, undefined values
* / %	Multiplication, division, modulo division
+ - +	Addition, subtraction, string concatenation
<< >> >>>	Bit shifting
< <= > >= instanceof	Less than, less than or equal, greater than, greater than or equal, instanceof
== != === !==	Equality, inequality, identity, nonidentity
&	Bitwise AND
^	Bitwise XOR
|	Bitwise OR
&&	Logical AND
||	Logical OR
?:	Conditional
= *OP*=	Assignment, assignment with operation
,	Multiple evaluation

Intrinsic Objects, Methods, and Properties

JScript has a built-in set of objects, methods, and properties. These are described as intrinsic. If you make your own objects, methods, and properties, they are described as user-defined. You should familiarize yourself with the intrinsic functions because JScript has many useful functions that could make your job much easier. Use intrinsic functions to process math, text, and dates and to convert data types. As mentioned previously, EON also extends the language with its own intrinsic objects and methods.

User-Defined Objects, Methods, and Properties

You can make your own objects, methods, and properties. Remember, properties are data fields attached to an object and methods are functions attached to an object. The following code shows how objects, properties, and methods are created.

```
var mychair = new Object() // object creation uses 'new' keyword
mychair.color = blue;       // added a property to the object
mychair.node = eon.findnode("Chair") // added another property
mychair.moveup = moveup;    // attaching the move function (seen
below) to our object
function moveup()
{
   var p = this.node.GetFieldByName("Position").value.toarray();
   var newpos = eon.MakeSFVec3f(p[0], p[1], p[2]+1);
   this.node.GetfieldByByName("Position").value = newpos;
}
```

User-Defined Functions

As you already know, event handlers are triggered when a data value changes. The On_PropertyFieldName() naming convention must be used for functions that serve as event handlers. However, there are instances when it is beneficial to create a function that is not tied to a specific event. These independent, user-defined functions can be explicitly called in your script code as needed by any number of event handlers.

It is more efficient to use a separate function for such tasks because it decreases the number of lines of code that must be included in each event handler. Future code maintenance is more efficient because only one copy of the code is stored in the reusable function. Note that these functions are given descriptive names according to the action they perform. In this example, the two functions call a user-defined function. Therefore, it is not necessary to write the code in each function.

```
function On_StartPosition()
{
   CalcDistance()
}

function On_EndPosition()
{
   CalcDistance()
}

function CalcDistance()
{
   var sp = StartPosition.value.toArray()
   var ep = EndPosition.value.toArray()
   var dsquared;
   dsquared = Math.pow(sp[0]-ep[0], 2)
   dsquared += Math.pow(sp[1]-ep[1], 2)
   dsquared += Math.pow(sp[2]-ep[2], 2)
   var distance = Math.sqrt(dsquared)
   Distance.value = distance   // assign to EON field called
Distance
}
```

Accessing EON Field Values

The way to access EON field values depends on the data type of the field. Data types can be divided into single field (SF) and multiple field (MF) type fields and then further divided into single value (e.g., SFBool) and multiple value (e.g., SFVec3f) data types, as shown in Table 9.1.6. The method of accessing a field value does not depend on the field type in the context of field, eventIn, exposedField, or eventOut.

TABLE 9.1.6 Relationship Between SF Fields and MF Fields

	Single Field	Multiple Field* (SFfield1, SFfield2, ... SFfieldn)
Single Value	SFBool	MFBool (SFBool*1*, SFBool*2*, ... SFBool*n*)
	SFFloat	MFFloat (SFFloat*1*, SFFloat*2*, ... SFFloat*n*)
	SFInt32	MFInt32 (SFInt32*1*, SFInt32*2*, ... SFInt32*n*)
	SFNode	MFNode (SFNode*1*, SFNode*2*, ... SFNode*n*)
	SFString	MFString (SFString*1*, SFString*2*, ... SFString*n*)
	SFTime	MFTime (SFTime*1*, SFTime*2*, ... SFTime*n*)
Multiple Values**	SFColor [r g b]	MFColor (SFColor*1*[r g b], ... SFColor*n*[r g b])
	SFRotation [x y z r]	MFRotation (SFRotation*1*[x y z r], ... SFRotation*n*[x y z r])
	SFVec2f [x y]	MFVec2f (SFVec2f*1*[x y], ... SFVec2f*n*[x y])
	SFVec3f [x y z]	MFVec3f (SFVec3f*1*[x y z], ... SFVec3f*n*[x y z])

*Multiple fields are simply arrays of single value or multiple value fields.

**Multiple values are simply single data values separated from one another by a space.

Single Field (SF) Type Fields

Single field type fields have a data type that starts with SF, such as SFBool, SFVec3f, SFFloat, and so on. The method used to access values depends on the data type. A single value field is accessed differently than a multiple value field. For example, a 3D position in EON (SFVec3f) is made up of an X, a Y, and a Z value. Therefore, it is a multiple value field, whereas the LapTime field of the Rotate node (SFFloat) is a single value field.

Single Value Fields

All fields of the Script node are like intrinsic objects; they exist without having to explicitly declare them in the script code. Also, all field objects have one property, the .value property. You can access the value of a script field and assign it to a variable like the following example:

```
var myvar = MyFieldName.value;
```

To assign a value to the Script node's field, use the following example. If MyFieldName was an eventOut type field connected by a route to another node, then this example would send the outEvent to the connected node:

```
MyFieldName.value = myvar;
```

In JScript, you can assign values of any data type to a variable, but EON fields have a strict data type that cannot be changed. If you try to assign a value to a Script node's field, JScript will try to convert the value into an EON data type. If it cannot be converted, a message will notify you of a Type Mismatch error.

Assume that the Script node has a field named Speed that has the exposedField field type and SFFloat data type. Then, the following example will generate an error:

```
var b = "abc"
Speed.value = b  // generates 'Type Mismatch' error.
```

Multiple Value Fields

Multiple value fields are fields of the data type SFVec2f, SFVec3f, SFColor, and SFRotation. When you use the FieldName.value with them, they return a VBArray, also known as a safe array. These arrays are not like JScript arrays. You cannot access them in the typical way in which you access arrays.

```
var p = Position.value
eon.trace(p[0])          // outputs 'undefined'
```

The previous mistake is often very difficult to find because an error message is not displayed. The only indication of an error is undefined data.

JScript offers a way to convert the VBArray into a normal array by using the toArray() function. This enables you to access these multiple value fields and place them into a normal array:

```
var p = Position.value.toArray()
eon.trace(p[0])  // outputs a number from the Position field.
```

If you want to store an SFVec3f value and then pass it unchanged to another SFVec3f field, you do not have to convert the value from VBArray to a JScript array. Therefore, the following example is possible:

```
var p = Pos1.value
Pos2.value = p
```

To assign a value to a multiple value field, the field will need to be a VBArray data type. However, JScript does not offer a method to create a multiple value field. Therefore, EON has added four functions that can create a variety of multiple value fields. The EON functions are named MakeSFVec3f, MakeSFVec2f, MakeSFColor, and MakeSFRotation. The following example assigns values to a Position field that is of data type SFVec3f:

```
Position.value = eon.MakeSFVec3f(0, -10, 2)
```

Often, you may want to move an object in your simulation. In the following example, you want to move an object 2 meters in the Z direction (upward). You need to get the position and then create a new position.

```
var p = Position.value.toArray()      // put position into a
normal array.
p[2] = p[2] + 2          // add 2 to the z value
var newpos = eon.MakeSFVec3f(p[0], p[1], p[2])     // create an
SFVec3f type value.
Position.value = newpos        // assign the SFVec3f to the
Position field.
```

Multiple Field (MF) Type Fields

Multiple field type fields are fields that can contain multiple instances of single field values. They are similar to arrays, but they are not handled in the same way as normal arrays in JScript. They are the fields that have a data type starting with MF such as MFFloat, MFNode, MFInt32, and so on. These types of fields can have zero to hundreds of instances of single field values. To access each single field value contained within a multiple field value, we need to use the methods of EON's Field Object, which are displayed in Table 9.1.7.

TABLE 9.1.7 Methods of the EON Field Object

Method	Description
GetMFElement(index)	Returns the value at the specified index. Use index 0 to get the first element.
SetMFElement(index, value)	Sets the value at the specified index.
GetMFCount()	Returns an integer representing the number of fields in a multiple field (MF) type field.
SetMFCount()	Sets the number of fields in a multiple field (MF) type field, thereby deleting or adding fields.
AddMFElement(value)	Adds a value to the end of the field.
RemoveMFElement(index)	Removes a specific element or value from a multiple-field (MF) type field.

In the following example, the Times field of data type MFFloat holds a series of times (in seconds). If we want to get the first time, then we use a statement such as the following:

```
t = Times.GetMFElement(0)
```

Often, we require a loop to iterate through all of the values of a multiple field data type. In the following example, we divide each of the Times values by 2.

```
for (var i=0; i<Times.GetMFCount(); i++)
{
   t = Times.GetMFElement(i) / 2;
   Times.SetMFElement(i, t);
}
```

To access the fourth X value within an MFVec3f field, use index number 3 because index numbers start with 0.

```
var p = Positions.GetMFElement(3).toArray()
var x = p[0]
```

Summary

In this lesson you:

- Developed an understanding as to why Script nodes are used.
- Became familiar with basic scripting concepts and terminology.
- Learned how scripting works in EON.
- Learned how to use the EON Script Editor.
- Used scripting to access field values.
- Triggered script functions using inEvents.

LESSON 9.2

Using Scripts

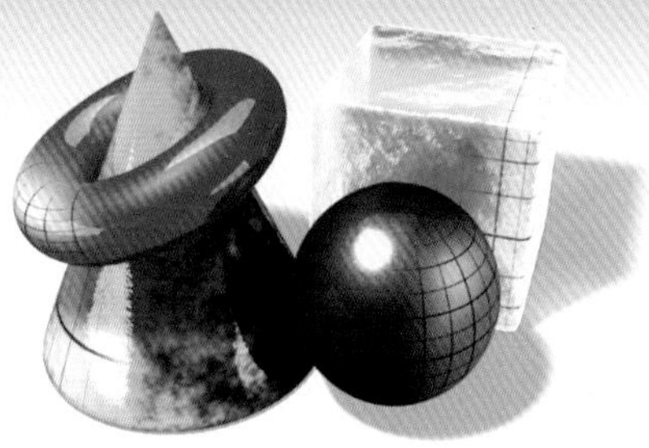

Objectives

In this lesson you will:

- Identify the stages of program flow for EON simulations.
- Copy and delete nodes.
- Include external script files in your simulation.
- Use script with the PopupUnlimited prototype.
- Access text files and databases.
- Learn about recursive functions and ActiveX controls.

Key Terms

call	*frame rate*	*recursive function*
eventsProcessed	*PopupUnlimited prototype*	*trigger*
file system object		

Program Flow in EON

Sometimes, scripting in EON requires an advanced understanding of how EON works. This section will briefly describe the program flow in EON and its implications for scripting.

Stages of Program Flow

EON is constantly performing a loop. Each loop represents one frame, as in frame rate. The ***frame rate*** tells you how many times the 3D view is rendered per second. In programming terms, the loop is:

```
do forever
{
read input sensors (e.g., time, mouse, keyboard, and other
hardware)
update nodes (each node calculates new field values if
necessary)
deliver data via routes and handle events (scripts are run here)
render
}
```

Figure 9.2.1 shows where the loop fits between the simulation's start and end. It also identifies the steps that are part of the loop.

FIGURE 9.2.1 Program flow in an EON simulation

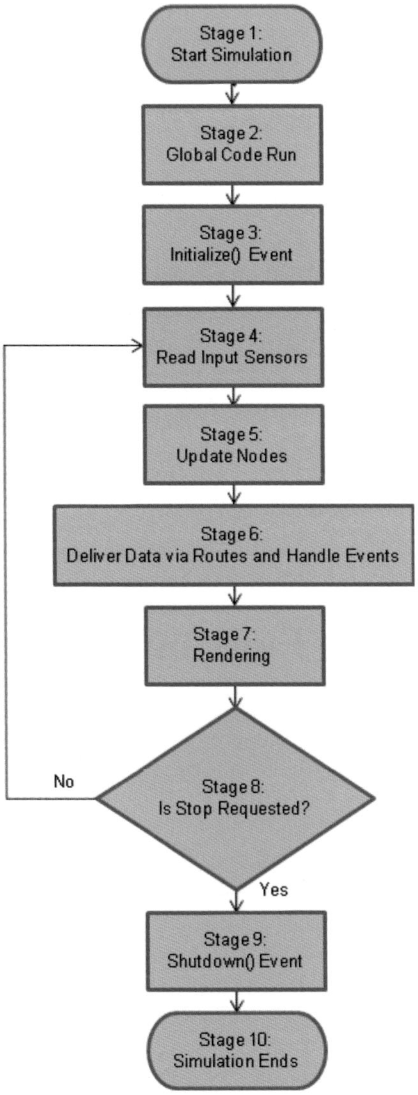

Stage 1: Start Simulation

When the simulation starts, the nodes are initialized. For the Script node, this means that the code is loaded. If the code has syntax errors, then error messages will be displayed. When a script error occurs, the Script node will not work for the duration of the simulation. The simulation must be restarted for the script to be loaded again. Any code you write while the simulation is running has no effect until the simulation is restarted. Also, note that it is not necessary to save the simulation for code changes to have an effect.

Stage 2: Global Code Run

Next, any code that is written outside functions will be executed. This is the only time this code is executed. Typically, you declare global variables at this time, but you can also call functions. However, you cannot trigger functions. This means that if you assign any values to fields at this stage, then the fields' event handlers are not triggered.

cross-reference

You will learn more about triggering events later in this lesson.

Stage 3: Initialize() Event

After global code runs, the initialize() functions in each Script node are triggered in simulation hierarchy order. If the initialize() code assigns values to other fields, then it can trigger other event handlers.

Stage 4: Read Input Sensors

Next, input sensors are read. This includes getting values from the clock, the location of the mouse, and any mouse buttons or keys that are pressed. If the simulation is using other hardware, such as tracking devices or peripheral devices for virtual reality applications, then these values will be read also.

Stage 5: Update Nodes

In this stage, some nodes use the input sensor data and calculate field values. Some nodes will work with other nodes and set their values. This does not include the Script node, which is only active during the next stage. During this stage, all fields that have been assigned a value will be flagged.

Stage 6: Deliver Data via Routes and Handle Events

In this stage, routes are delivered. A route is a connection (line) between two fields that allows values to flow from one field to the other field. All flagged fields of the eventOut or exposedField type that are connected by a route will, one by one, assign their values to the field at the end of the route. The order that routes are sent is inversely related to the order in which nodes were added to the simulation tree—that is, nodes that were added last send their routes first. To view a list of all routes within a simulation, right-click in the Routes window and then select the Text Dialog option from the pop-up menu.

When a field of a Script node receives a value from a route, we call that an event. If the event has an event handler, then it is started (triggered) immediately. The event handler code can assign values to other fields.

If the other fields have their own event handlers, then they are subsequently triggered and control moves immediately to the new event handler. Every event handler can assign values to fields and thereby trigger new event handlers. In this way, numerous event handlers may have started but may not have fully completed for a specific moment in time.

One route can trigger a chain reaction of many event handlers. When all event handlers are complete, data for the next route is delivered and events are handled. When all data from flagged fields have been delivered via the routes and events have been handled, the process will repeat if fields of the eventOut and exposedField type were assigned values in connection with the previously handled events.

tips+tricks

When a group of nodes is connected via routes in the Routes window, you might not see an output for every input. You should always view each route as an isolated transaction.

troubleshooting

To avoid possible never-ending loops, EON does not allow incomplete event handlers to be triggered again. Therefore, if a value is assigned to any field associated with a started but not completed event handler, then program flow continues in the current event handler that assigned a value to the field.

It is still possible to arrange routes in a circular fashion that would create an endless loop, but this does not occur because EON detects when a field has been flagged three times and does not allow it to be flagged a fourth time. EON Studio also remembers this field for subsequent frames and only allows it to be flagged once in the future. Therefore, in general, a route can be used no more than once per frame.

After all of the routes have been processed and their subsequent events handled, we then move on to the eventsProcessed stage. In this stage, the eventsProcessed() event handler in each Script node is triggered. Again, this can give rise to triggering more event handlers and more rounds of delivering data via routes. The eventsProcessed event is useful in optimizing simulation performance by limiting the number of times script functions need to be called. This is discussed more fully in the following sections.

Stage 7: Rendering

The Script node is not part of this stage. Scripting in EON does not involve itself with the deeper programming required to send data to graphics cards and so on. This is only done by the core EON software.

Stage 8: Is Stop Requested?

After rendering, we ask whether the user has chosen to close the simulation. If the user has not closed the simulation, then EON loops, returning to the Read Input Sensors stage.

Stage 9: Shutdown() Event

If the user has chosen to close the simulation, then the shutdown event is triggered. This event can be used to delete nodes, reset values, or save data to a text file. Code executed here can trigger other event handlers, but no more data is delivered via the routes.

Stage 10: Simulation Ends

After the simulation ends, you may notice that some fields have changed their values and remain that way in EON Studio. This is in contrast to prototype instances in which values are reset to the values held before the simulation started. This may have implications for your script. Therefore, you may want to have code within the initialize() or shutdown() event handlers that resets field values to the correct start values.

Program Flow Example

In the example displayed in Figure 9.2.2, the On_Click() event handler is triggered by a route from a ClickSensor node. As a result, other events are triggered.

FIGURE 9.2.2 Program flow example

```
function On_Click()
{
    eon.trace("Click at start =  " + Click.value)
    Num.value = 1;
    Num.value = 5;
    Num.value = 8;
    Eon.trace("Click at end = " + Click.value
}

function On_Num()
{
    eon.trace("Num = " + Num.value);
    Num.value = 3;
    Click.value = false;
}
```

The Log window prints:

```
Click at start = true
Num = 1
Num = 5
Num = 8
Click at end = false;
```

When Num is assigned 1, 5, or 8, it triggers the On_Num() event handler. When Num is assigned 3, it does not trigger the On_Num() event handler because the On_Num() event handler is currently started but not completed. If we change the Num.value = 3 to On_Num(), then we are calling and not triggering. This would lead to a never-ending loop.

If two ClickSensor nodes are under the same object with routes connected to On_Click(), then On_Click() will be triggered twice and the Log window output will be repeated.

Calling a Function vs. Triggering a Function

If you have a field named MyField in your script, then there are two ways to run the code in the On_MyField() function. One option is to ***call*** it directly using the following script code:

```
On_MyField()
```

The other option is to ***trigger*** it by assigning a value to it using the following script code:

```
MyField.value = 10
```

There is a significant difference between calling and triggering a function. You can call a function as many times as you like and the program flow shifts to the called function immediately; there are no exceptions. It can even call itself.

However, when assigning a value to the field, its associated function (event handler) is triggered and runs immediately. But if the event handler itself has a line of code that again assigns a value to its field, then the program flow does not move to the start of the event handler again. Even if the handler calls another function that assigns a value to the field, the handler does not run again. The rule is that event handlers that are triggered to start cannot be triggered again until they have completed. An event handler can trigger itself, but only if it was initially called and not triggered.

A function can call itself. These functions are called recursive functions and require special care in their design to prevent an endless loop.

cross-reference

You will learn more about recursive functions later in this lesson.

How to Make Global Variables and Functions

Some people may ask whether it is possible to make variables and functions in one script global so that they are available in other Script nodes. The short answer is no, but the long answer is yes.

Each Script node in EON is separate. The functions and variables in one script are not available to another script. Global scope applies to the Script node level only and does not extend beyond the Script node. The only way that scripts can communicate is via the fields of the Script nodes.

A function in a Script node can assign a value to a field in another Script node. When a value is assigned to a field, that is an event. An event may have an event handler, which is code inside the On_fieldname() function. Indirectly, you are calling a function in another script.

For example, Script1 has the following code:

```
eon.findnode("Script2").GetFieldByName("CalcDistance").value =
true;
```

Script2 has a field named CalcDistance and the following code:

```
function On_CalcDistance()
{
   statements here.
}
```

In effect, you have called a function in Script2.

Instead of storing values in variables, store them in fields. Then, they are available to all scripts, as shown in the following example:

```
myvar = eon.findnode("Script2").GetFieldByName("Count").value
```

You can call a function and get a return value. For example, if you have a function that calculates the area (width × height), you can send the parameters to fields and then trigger the CalcArea event handler, which places the answer in another field. Then, the original script collects the value. To set this up, Script1 would contain the following code:

```
eon.findnode("Script2").GetFieldByName("Width").value = 5
eon.findnode("Script2").GetFieldByName("Height").value = 3
eon.findnode("Script2").GetFieldByName("CalcArea").value = true
var area = eon.findnode("Script2").GetFieldByName("Result").value
```

Script2 would contain the four fields identified in Script1: Width, Height, CalcArea, and Result. It also contains the following code:

```
function On_CalcArea()
{
   Result.value = Width.value * Height.value
}
```

Program Flow with Script and a Frame Node

The previous example sends a value from one script to a second script and then gets another value from the second script. This also can work with the Frame node. The script can send a Position or Orientation value to a Frame node and then get the WorldPosition or WorldOrientation value from the Frame node. This can be done immediately without waiting for the next frame. It works in the opposite way as well; the script can send the WorldPosition and get a Position value. This shows that the Frame node has its own event handlers because something caused the WorldPosition value to change when the Position value was set. See the example in Figure 9.2.3.

FIGURE 9.2.3 Function to get the WorldPosition value

```
function GetWP()
{
    eon.findnode("myframe").GetfieldByName("Position").value = myposition.value
    wp = eon.findnode("myframe").GetFieldByName("WorldPosition").value.toArray()
    return wp;
}
```

The eventsProcessed Event

The ***eventsProcessed*** event is a special event in your script that will be triggered during every frame (related to frame rate) after all events have been processed, but only when at least one field of the script has changed its value since the last frame. Events referred to as "events processed" are those that occur after all routes have been sent and the nodes or scripts that receive those events have been processed or the scripts attached to the events have run. Thus, this event handler is called after events have been processed and before the scene is rendered.

This type of event is useful because it reduces the frequency of script code execution, thus optimizing the simulation so it runs faster. Sometimes, the inEvents to a Script node arrive more frequently than required by outEvents. Instead of making a new calculation every time the inEvent arrives, an eventsProcessed event will limit the number of times that the calculation will be performed to one. In addition, outEvents that set a position or somehow change what you see only need to be updated once per frame because rendering is done only once per frame. At other times, a script may have many inEvents that affect one outEvent. Instead of each inEvent calculating the outEvent when and if an inEvent value arrives, the eventsProcessed event handler will cut that back to one calculation that takes into account the several values of the different inEvents.

tips+tricks

EventIn fields receive values and store them, even if you do not have an event handler such as On_inevent() to handle them.

In a typical example, we have two Frame nodes and we want to render a line from one Frame node's position to the other Frame node's position. Both Frame nodes can be moving. We route the positions of the Frame nodes to our script. If we did not have the eventsProcessed event, we would write two event handlers, as shown in Figure 9.2.4.

FIGURE 9.2.4 Two event handlers required without eventsProcessed() event handler

```
function On_Position1()
{
    UpdateLine()
}
function On_Position2()
{
    UpdateLine()
}
```

If both positions have changed within a program (frame rendering) cycle, then both call the UpdateLine() function, which is a computationally expensive function of more than one hundred lines of code. It would be better to replace the two event handlers with the single eventsProcessed() event handler shown in Figure 9.2.5.

FIGURE 9.2.5 One eventsProcessed() event handler reduces computational expense

```
function eventsProcessed()
{
    UpdateLine()
}
```

As you complete the activities in this lesson, you will create a simulation that inserts and moves objects and saves the positions of the objects in text files. The first activity sets the scene.

Activity 9.2.1: Setting Up Navigation and a Floor

1. Open EON to start a new simulation. If EON is already open, select **New** from the File menu.
2. Add three **Frame** nodes under the Scene frame and rename them **Programming**, **Floor**, and **Objects**.
3. Add a **GridPlane2** prototype under the Floor frame. In the Property Bar, set its Position to **0 0 0**. Set its Width and Height fields to **1000**.
4. Select the **Viewport** node. In the Property Bar, set the FarClip field to **500**.
5. Select the **Camera** frame. In the Property Bar, set the frame's Position to **0 -20 5**.
6. Remove the **Walk** node under the Camera frame.
7. Add a **Frame** node under the Camera frame and rename it **Orbit Navigation**.
8. Add an **OrbitNav** prototype under the Orbit Navigation frame.
9. In the OrbitNav prototype's Camera field, create a node reference to the **Camera** frame.
10. Add an **OrbitNavLookHereAtStart** prototype under the Floor frame.
11. In the OrbitNavLookHereAtStart prototype's OrbitNav field, create a node reference to the **OrbitNav** prototype. Your simulation tree should look like Figure 9.2.6.

FIGURE 9.2.6 Simulation tree for ObjectEditor_Setup

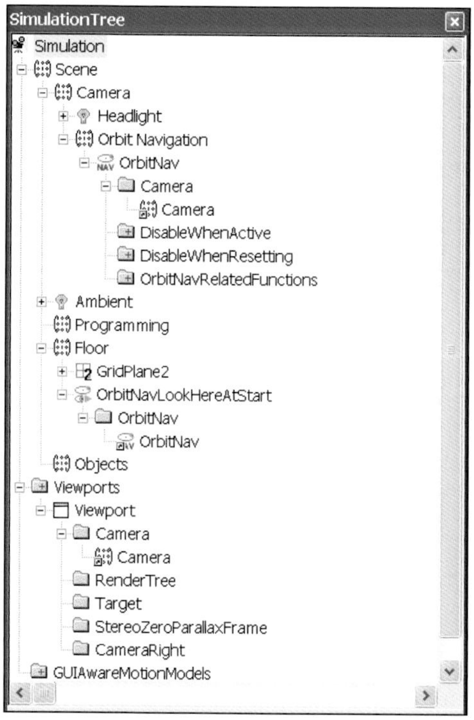

12. Save the simulation as **ObjectEditor_Setup.eoz**.
13. Run the simulation. You will see that only a grid is displayed.
14. Close the simulation window. Keep the simulation open to use in Activity 9.2.2.

In the previous activity, you set the scene for the remaining activities. In the following activity, you will add objects that can be manipulated in activities later in this lesson.

Activity 9.2.2: Adding Objects to Copy

1. Continue working with the open simulation file **ObjectEditor_Setup.eoz** from Activity 9.2.1.
2. Add a **Frame** node under the Camera frame and rename it **ObjectsToCopy**. In the Property Bar, set its Position to **0 2 0.5**. Set its Scale to **0.1 0.1 0.1**.
3. Add three **Frame** nodes under the ObjectsToCopy frame. Rename the new Frame nodes **CubeFrame**, **PyramidFrame**, and **SphereFrame**.
4. In the Property Bar, set the CubeFrame frame's Position to **-3 0 0**. Set the SphereFrame frame's Position to **3 0 0**.
5. Add a **Cube** prototype under the CubeFrame frame. In the Property Bar, set its Color to **0 0 1** (blue) and set its Position to **0 0 1**.
6. Add a **Pyramid** prototype under the PyramidFrame frame. In the Property Bar, set its Position to **0 0 1**.
7. Add a **Sphere** prototype under the SphereFrame frame. In the Property Bar, set its Color to **1 1 0** (yellow) and set its Position to **0 0 1**. Your simulation tree should look like Figure 9.2.7.

FIGURE 9.2.7 ObjectsToCopy frame added to the simulation

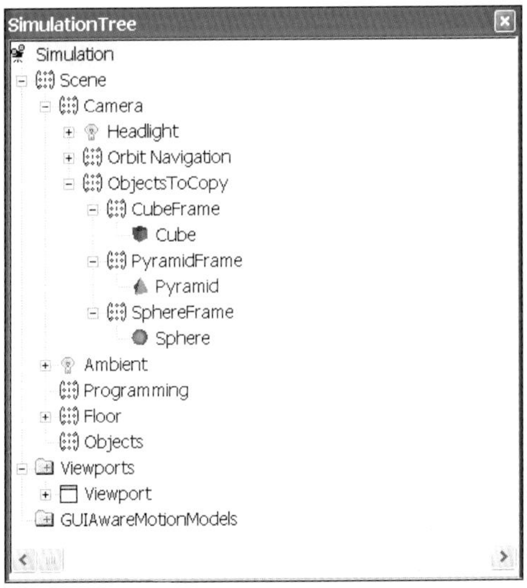

8. Save the simulation as **ObjectEditor_ObjectsToCopy.eoz**.
9. Run the simulation. Notice that when you move the camera, the three objects do not appear to move at all because they are under the Camera frame and move with the camera.
10. Close the simulation window. Keep the simulation open to use in Activity 9.2.3.

tips+tricks

You also can change the color of an object by clicking the color swatch to display the Color dialog box, which provides the ability to view and select specific shades of colors.

Copy and Delete Nodes

The ability to copy nodes in EON has exciting potential. Script can create copies at lightning speed. If you also use scripting to change those copied nodes, you can complete complex tasks quickly, such as creating objects arranged in patterns or populating an area with trees. The example in Figure 9.2.8 contains script code that will copy the specified shapes and objects.

FIGURE 9.2.8 Example of script code to copy objects

```
var shape = eon.findnode("Shape1");
var objects = eon.findnode("Objects");
eon.CopyNode(shape, objects");
```

Deleting nodes provides a way to clean up your simulation tree and remove any resource nodes, thereby freeing computer memory. The example in Figure 9.2.9 contains script code that will delete a node.

FIGURE 9.2.9 Example of script code used to delete a node

```
eon.DeleteNode(eon.findnode("Shape2"));
```

troubleshooting

If time is critical and you are already familiar with scripting, you may want to copy the script from the solution file provided for this activity.

Activity 9.2.3: Copying Objects with Script

When this activity is complete, you will be able to copy an object by clicking it and then clicking again to place the copy on the floor at the point where you clicked.

1. Continue working with the open simulation file **ObjectEditor_ObjectsToCopy.eoz** from Activity 9.2.2.
2. Save the simulation as **ObjectEditor_Copy.eoz**.
3. Add a **Script** node under the Programming frame and rename it **MainScript**.
4. Double-click the **MainScript** node to display the Script Properties dialog box. Click the **New Field** button to add the first field in the following table. Add the remaining fields, as shown in Figure 9.2.10. Click **OK** to close the dialog box.

Name	Field Type	Data Type	Value
NodeToCopy	exposedField	SFNode	
Destination	exposedField	SFNode	
CS_Floor	exposedField	SFNode	
FloorClicked	exposedField	SFBool	0

FIGURE 9.2.10 Fields added in the Script Properties dialog box

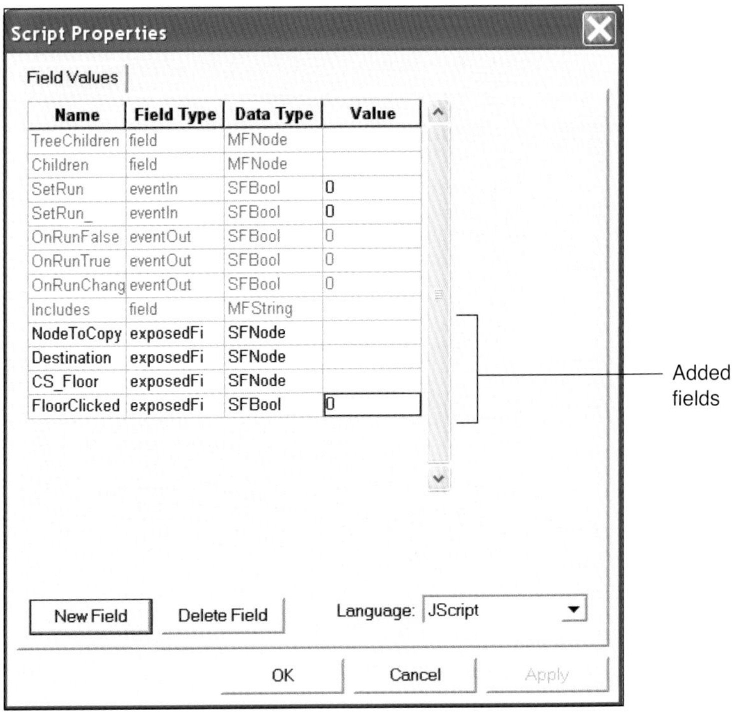

tips+tricks

In the Script Properties dialog box, you can use several keyboard shortcuts that enable you to choose the field type and data type. Press Tab to move to the next column. Instead of typing the entire data type of SFFloat, you can type SFF and press Tab; EON will automatically choose SFFloat. Try using other abbreviations, such as SFN for SFNode and SFIn for SFInt32. Also, you can type ex in the Field Type column and press Tab instead of typing exposedField.

5. In the MainScript node's NodeToCopy field, create a node reference to the **CubeFrame** frame.
6. In the MainScript node's Destination field, create a node reference to the **Objects** frame.
7. Add a **ClickSensorPlus** prototype under the ObjectsToCopy frame. This will sense which object we want to copy.
8. In the ClickSensorPlus prototype's Roots field, create a node reference to the **ObjectsToCopy** frame.
9. In the ClickSensorPlus prototype's SendRefFieldToNode field, create a node reference to the **MainScript** node.
10. In the Property Bar, set the ClickSensorPlus prototype's RefField to **Sibling** if necessary.
11. In the Property Bar, set the ClickSensorPlus prototype's SendToField field to **NodeToCopy**. Now, the ClickSensorPlus prototype will send a node reference to the NodeToCopy field of the MainScript node. It will be one of the frames under the ObjectsToCopy frame, meaning that it is a sibling.
12. Add a **ClickSensor** node under the Floor frame and rename it **CS_Floor**.

13. In the Script node's CS_Floor field, create a node reference to the **CS_Floor** ClickSensor node. The portion of your simulation tree modified in this activity should look like Figure 9.2.11.

FIGURE 9.2.11 Simulation tree with the ClickSensor node added

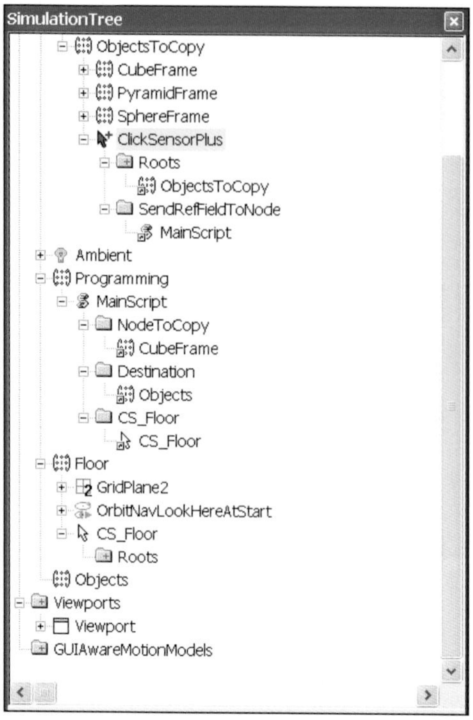

14. Display the **Routes** window. Drag the **CS_Floor** ClickSensor node and the **MainScript** node to the Routes window. Establish the connection outlined in the following table.

From	outEvent	To	inEvent
CS_Floor	OnButtonDownFalse	MainScript	FloorClicked

15. Select the **MainScript** node in the simulation tree. Click the **Open Script Editor** button on the Toolbar to display the Script Editor window.

16. Delete the event handler shells for the On_NodeToCopy(), On_Destination(), and On_CS_Floor() functions. We will not need them in the script. After the shells are removed, your Script Editor window will look like Figure 9.2.12.

FIGURE 9.2.12 Script Editor window after removing unnecessary functions

```
// Edit Scriptnode here.
// Add subroutines for each in-event or exposed field
// that you define in the script node's property page.

function initialize()
{
    // Called when simulation starts
    // Add initialization code
}

function On_FloorClicked()
{
    // TODO: Add your event handler code here
}
```

17. Add script code inside the On_FloorClicked() function so that the On_FloorClicked() function looks like Figure 9.2.13. After the eon.CopyNode method, we would need a reference to the new object, which will be the last child node of the Destination frame. Therefore, we set the *treech* variable to the TreeChildren field of the Destination frame. This gives us the last element in *treech*. After we have the node reference, we want it to have the position we clicked. The CS_Floor node provides the values in its TargetPointWorld field. Finally, we trigger the SetStartValues field so that the object's position will be saved until we run the simulation again.

FIGURE 9.2.13 On_FloorClicked() function in the Script Editor window

```
function On_FloorClicked()
{
    eon.CopyNode(NodeToCopy.value, Destination.value);
    var treech = Destination.value.GetFieldByName("TreeChildren");
    var node = treech.GetMFElement(treech.GetMFCount()-1);

    // give position clicked to new object
    node.GetFieldByName("Position").value = CS_Floor.value.GetFieldByName("TargetPointWorld").value
    node.GetFieldByName("SetStartValues").value = true;
}
```

18. Save the simulation. Verify that the **Objects** frame in the simulation tree is empty.
19. Run the simulation. Click the blue cube and then click the floor. Click the yellow sphere and then click the floor. Click the pyramid and then click the floor. The objects are copied and then pasted on the floor in the location you clicked, as shown in Figure 9.2.14.

FIGURE 9.2.14 Copied objects pasted in new locations

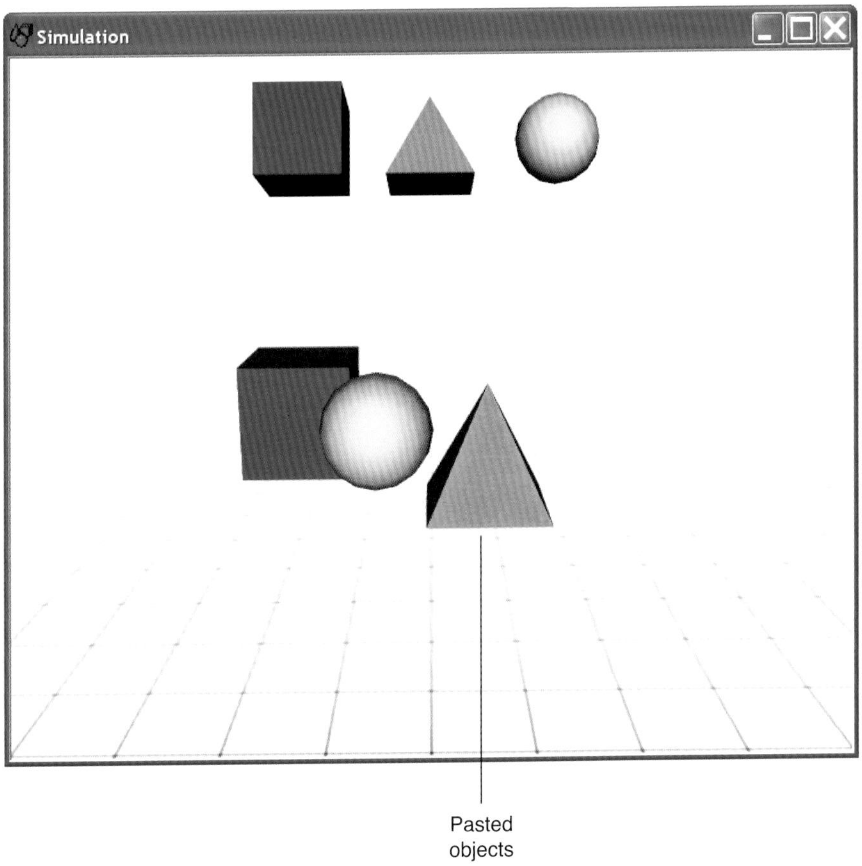

troubleshooting

If the simulation does not work correctly, verify the spelling and the case of the script code you typed.

20. Close the simulation window.
21. In the simulation tree, expand the **Objects** frame. As shown in Figure 9.2.15, all of the objects that you pasted have been copied to the Objects folder.

FIGURE 9.2.15 Pasted objects in the Objects frame

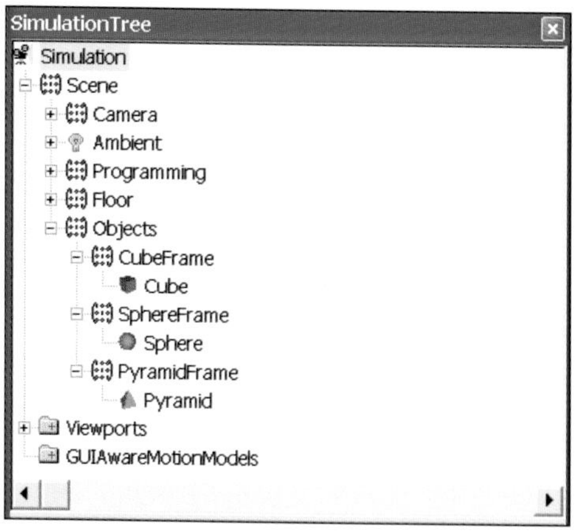

22. Run the simulation again. Notice that the pasted objects are still displayed.
23. Close the simulation window.
24. Insert the script code shown in Figure 9.2.16 after the On_FloorClicked() function. This new DeleteAllObjects() function deletes all nodes under the Objects frame when we close or open the simulation. This function can be triggered on initialize() and shutdown().

FIGURE 9.2.16 DeleteAllObjects() added in the Script Editor window

```
function DeleteAllObjects()
{
    // get a reference to the TreeChildren field
    var treech = Destination.value.GetFieldByName("TreeChildren");
    // keep deleting until there are no nodes left.
    while (treech.GetMFCount()>0) eon.DeleteNode(treech.GetMFElement(0));
}

function shutdown()
{
    DeleteAllObjects();
}
```

25. Add the **DeleteAllObjects()** function call to the initialize() function as shown in Figure 9.2.17. With this addition, the objects will be removed when the simulation starts, whether or not we get a script error and the shutdown event does not run.

FIGURE 9.2.17 Function call added to the initialize() function

```
function initialize()
{
    DeleteAllObjects();
}
```

26. Run the simulation again.

Discussion

discuss

Are the pasted objects still displayed?

Why or why not?

27. Paste several objects again.

Discussion

discuss

With the simulation window still open, expand the Objects frame in the simulation tree. Does it contain any objects?

Why or why not?

28. Close the simulation window.

Discussion

discuss

Will the Objects frame ever contain objects?

Will pasted objects be displayed when you run the simulation again?

Why or why not?

29. Save this simulation and keep it open to use in Activity 9.2.4.

Including External Script Files

EON allows the use of external script files. Instead of writing all of the script code in the Script Editor window, you can write some or all script code in an external program, save it to a text file, and then include it in a Script node by using the Includes field. You just add the name of the file in the Script node's Includes field, which is a default field for every Script node. When you save your .eoz file, the external script files will be copied and placed inside the .eoz file.

The reasons you might want to use the Includes field are:

- **To enable the easy reuse of common script functions.** Over time, you may realize that you are using the same functions again and again, copying them from previous simulations to your current simulations. If you have several functions like this, then you may want to place them together in one file that can be included in your current Script node.

- **To reduce the amount of script that must be saved.** Script nodes can share included files with other scripts. Instead of copying Script nodes and doubling the amount of script code to be saved, only one instance must be saved. This reduces file size, but the effect is minimal because text takes very little space compared to textures and geometry. Also, text can be compressed quite well. The main advantage can be that updating one external script will update all Script nodes that share that external script file. However, this last advantage also can be achieved by prototypes. You can have many instances of a prototype that have just one Script node. When you change that Script node, all prototype instances change.
- **To allow you to use an external program to edit the script.** You could use an external script editor, copy the script code, and paste it into the Script node every time you make a change. However, it is more efficient to use the Includes field; you just save the file in the external editor and then run the simulation. As an additional benefit, some external editors provide advanced features that may increase productivity for experienced programmers.

tips+tricks

Occasionally, you may need to update an external script. If you saved your EON simulation, then the script that was external is now internal, saved inside the .eoz file. If you made some changes to a script and want to replace the one inside your EON simulation, you must complete several steps.

1. Delete the filename of the script from the Includes field.
2. Select File > Save As (not Save) and choose a filename for the simulation file. If the name you select is the same as the current filename, a message will ask whether to replace the existing file. Choose Yes.
3. Add the filename to the Includes field of the Script node again.
4. Select File > Save to save the script inside the EON application.

Keeping Included Scripts External

A standalone file is one that does not depend on or use files from outside sources. Normally, all .eoz files are standalone files. Updating an external script becomes frustrating if you plan to use an external editor constantly. Fortunately, you can save an .eoz file that will not make a standalone file. Instead, another command that is separate from the Save command, named Make StandAlone, will copy all external resources to the .eoz file. To access this function, you will need to change a setting in the Windows Registry.

1. Click the Windows Start Menu and then select Run.
2. Type regedit in the Open field and click OK to open the Registry Editor program.
3. Find the following path: HKEY_CURRENT_USER\Software\EON Reality\EON\6.0\EON Studio\Preferences.
4. In the right panel, double-click the ForceMakeStandAlone option, change the value from 1 to 0, and then click OK.
5. Close the Registry Editor application.
6. Close EON Studio and open it again. In the File menu, you will see the Make StandAlone command. The Save and Save as commands will no longer make a standalone file.

tips+tricks

You may change the ForceMakeStandAlone setting back to 1 at any time.

If you make this change, saving a simulation will no longer include the external script files. This means that you can continue to save the external file in your external editor as well as save the EON application. However, before you send this EON application to someone else, you must make it a standalone file by using the Make StandAlone command. If you do not make it a standalone file, then other people will not be able to view the file because the absolute paths to the external resources will be missing on the other person's computer.

troubleshooting

The registry is a part of the Windows operating system that stores settings for many programs. Installation programs usually install these settings. Editing the registry is an unconventional way of changing settings, and it is not recommended often because modifying the registry may cause your computer to stop working.

Working with the Includes Field

The code of a script that is included by the Includes field behaves like code that precedes the code in the EON Script Editor window. If you have several included scripts, they are inserted in order. This order may be important to understand. For example, if you have declared a function in an included script and then declare it again in the Script node's code, then the latter code in the Script node will be the one that applies.

When you get error messages with a line number, the line number can refer to any of the included scripts. If each included script has 100 lines and the simulation has four included scripts, the line error will be less than a hundred. It does not add the number of lines to provide an accurate location within all of the script code. If you have an error in line 47, for example, it could be in line 47 in any of the four included scripts.

Using Script and the PopupUnlimited Prototype

The ***PopupUnlimited prototype*** is part of the EON Professional package. This prototype does nothing by itself. But when it is used with a script, the PopupUnlimited prototype enables you to create pop-up menus with multiple levels and unlimited menu items. The items can have check marks and separators. The items also can be disabled individually. The only outEvent is SelectedMenuTag, which should be connected via routes to your script. This prototype is dependent on using menus created by script code. Unlimited MenuItems nodes are created on demand using the eon.copynode method, which copies a single menu item inside the prototype to a store node, which is also inside the prototype. Because they are inside a prototype, the nodes are removed on shutdown. The prototype has a script within it that creates an object and has some methods. You can use these methods to create and display the menus. The methods shown in Table 9.2.1 are available.

TABLE 9.2.1 Methods to Create and Display Menus

Method	Description
clear()	Clears the menu items made last time.
additem(parentid, text, tag, checked, disabled)	Adds a menu item and returns the ID of the menu item, which can be used to place other menu items under it. The tag is text that will be returned by the SelectedMenuTag event.
addseperator()	Adds a menu item that is a horizontal line instead of text.
show()	Displays the pop-up menu at the mouse cursor's location.

The advantage of creating menus with script is that the menus will be dynamic. The menus are created by script each time the user clicks a button to display the menu, which means that the menu can reflect the current circumstances, such as changing the check mark next to menu items, changing the disabled state, and displaying or hiding menu items. You can access databases and display a menu item for each row of a table in a database. After you use this method a few times, you will see it is a very simple and powerful tool for creating menus.

Activity 9.2.4: Creating Pop-up Menus

In this activity, we will use script to create a File menu to access typical functions in a standard Windows File menu such as New, Open, Save, and Save As. Later, we will make these options functional in another activity.

1. Continue working with the open simulation file **ObjectEditor_Copy.eoz** from Activity 9.2.3.
2. Save the simulation as **ObjectEditor_Menu.eoz**.
3. Add a **2DText** node under the Programming frame and rename it **MENU**. In the Property Bar, set its Text field to **MENU**. Set its BoxArea to **100 25**. Set the Font to

troubleshooting

If time is critical and you are already familiar with scripting, you may want to copy the script from the solution file provided for this activity.

Arial. Set the FontSize to **25**. Set the FontStyle to **Bold** and set the TextAlignment to **Center**. Your Property Bar should look like Figure 9.2.18.

FIGURE 9.2.18 Property Bar for the MENU 2DText node

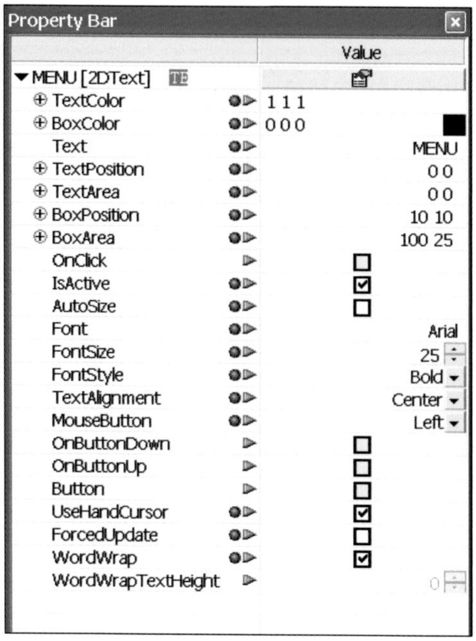

4. Add the **PopupUnlimited** prototype under the Programming frame.
5. Double-click the **MainScript** node to display the Script Properties dialog box. Click the **New Field** button to add the first field in the following table. Add the remaining fields listed in the table so that the dialog box on your screen looks similar to the one shown in Figure 9.2.19. Click **OK** to close the dialog box.

Name	Field Type	Data Type	Value
PopupUnlimited	exposedField	SFNode	
ShowMainMenu	eventIn	SFBool	0
SelectedMenuTag	eventIn	SFString	""

FIGURE 9.2.19 Fields added in the Script Properties dialog box

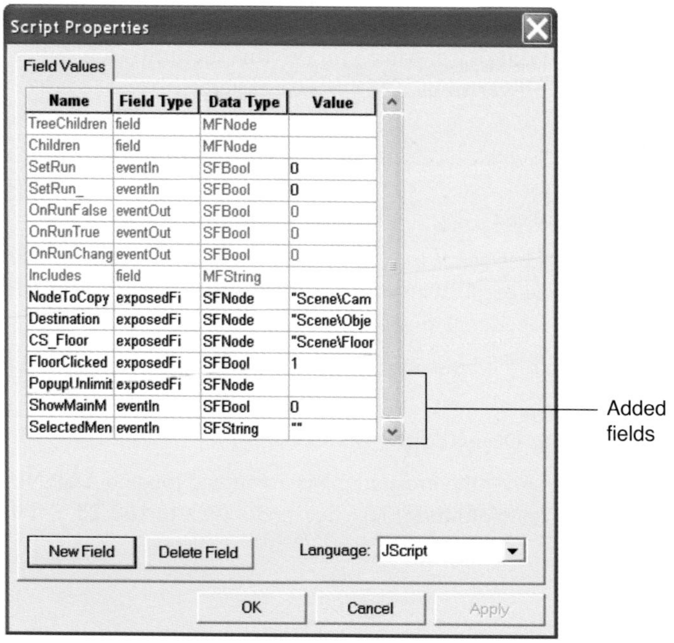

6. In the MainScript node's PopupUnlimited field, create a node reference to the **PopupUnlimited** prototype.
7. Display the **Routes** window. Drag the **PopupUnlimited** prototype and the **MENU** 2DText node to the Routes window. Establish the connections outlined in the following table. Your Routes window should resemble Figure 9.2.20.

From	outEvent	To	inEvent
PopupUnlimited	SelectedMenuTag	MainScript	SelectedMenuTag
MENU	OnButtonUp	MainScript	ShowMainMenu

FIGURE 9.2.20 Routes window with PopupUnlimited prototype and MENU node added

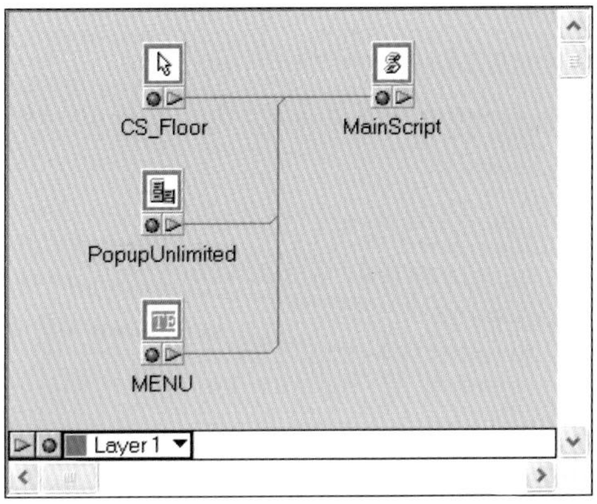

8. In the Local Prototypes window, right-click the **PopupUnlimited** prototype and select **Open** from the context menu. The subtree for the PopupUnlimited prototype is displayed, as shown in Figure 9.2.21.

FIGURE 9.2.21 Nodes in the PopupUnlimited prototype

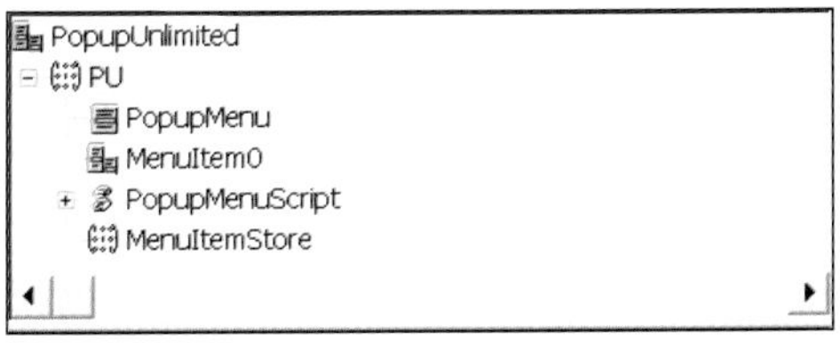

9. Click the **PopupMenuScript** node and then click the **Open Script Editor** button on the Toolbar to display the script in the PopupMenuScript node. This script is designed to be added to your main script. We will add it to our script as an Includes file.
10. Click in the Script Editor window if necessary. Press **Ctrl + A** to select the entire script text and then press **Ctrl + C** to copy it.

11. Open Notepad by clicking the Windows **Start** button, **All Programs**, **Accessories**, and then **Notepad**. Press **Ctrl + V** to paste the text, as shown in Figure 9.2.22.

FIGURE 9.2.22 Script pasted in a Notepad window

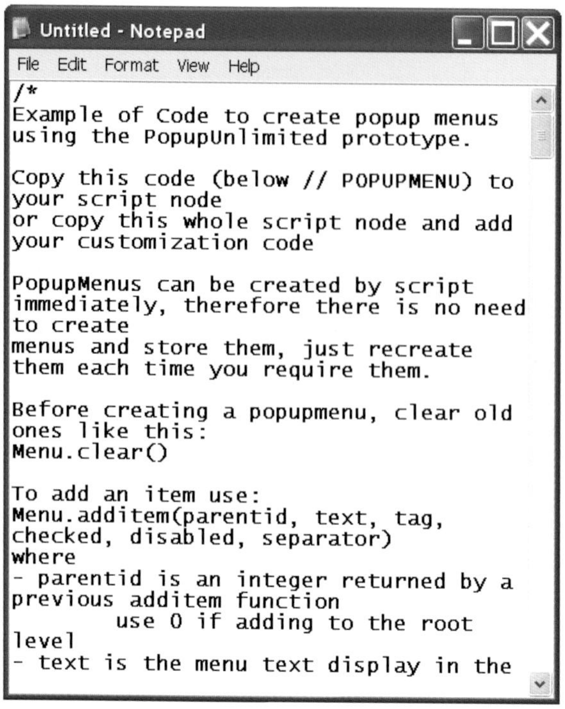

troubleshooting

Verify that the file is correctly saved as popupmenu.js and not as popupmenu.js.txt.

12. Save the file as **popupmenu.js** in the folder where your simulation is currently saved. The .js extension identifies the file type as JScript.
13. Read the **popupmenu.js** file to learn what it does and how you can work with it. Close the file.
14. In the Simulation Tree window, select the **MainScript** node. In the Property Bar, enter **popupmenu.js** in the Includes field, as shown in Figure 9.2.23.

FIGURE 9.2.23 File entered in the Includes field in the Property Bar for the MainScript node

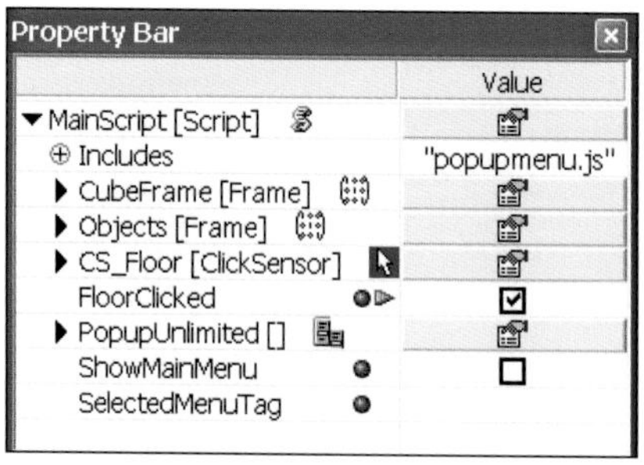

15. Save the simulation. The external file we created is saved inside the ObjectEditor_Menu.eoz file.
16. Close the **PopupMenuScript** and the **PopupUnlimited** prototype if necessary.
17. Select the **MainScript** node in the simulation tree and then click the **Open Script Editor** button on the Toolbar to display the Script Editor window.

18. If EON created an event handler for the PopupUnlimited field, as shown in Figure 9.2.24, delete it.

FIGURE 9.2.24 Delete the On_PopupUnlimited() function

```
function On_PopupUnlimited()
{
    // TODO: Add your event handler code here
}
```

19. Move the cursor to the top of the Script Editor window. Delete the three comment lines at the top of the script and replace them with the statement shown in Figure 9.2.25. This statement declares a global variable, named *Menu*, which will let us access the properties and methods of the object we declare in the external script included through the Includes field. The PopupUnlimited prototype is referenced here. Although only one menu item node is identified in the prototype, our included script can copy it as many times as necessary. Because it is inside a prototype, the menu items are removed when the simulation is shut down. Using this script, we can add menu items in order and the menus are created in the split second that the On_ShowMainMenu() event handler is triggered.

FIGURE 9.2.25 Global variable declared

Added global variable

```
var Menu = new PopupMenu(PopupUnlimited.value);
function initialize()
{
    DeleteAllObjects();
}
```

20. Add the script code shown in Figure 9.2.26 to the On_ShowMainMenu() event handler. This creates a File menu to access commands such as New, Open, Save, Save As, Properties, and Exit. The files we save will contain the type of object and its position. Properties will display information about the saved file, such as the number of bytes in the file and when the file was last saved. Exit will not do anything, but it makes the menu look more complete.

FIGURE 9.2.26 Script code added to the On_ShowMainMenu() function

```
function On_ShowMainMenu()
{
    Menu.clear()
    //Menu.additem(parentid, text, tag, checked, disabled, separator)
    //Menu.addseparator(parentid);

    // file menu
    var file_menu = Menu.additem(0, "File");
    Menu.additem(file_menu, "New", "file_new");
    Menu.additem(file_menu, "Open", "file_open");
    Menu.addseparator(file_menu);
    Menu.additem(file_menu, "Save", "file_save");
    Menu.additem(file_menu, "Save As", "file_saveas");
    Menu.addseparator(file_menu);
    Menu.additem(file_menu, "Properties...", "file_properties", false, true);
    Menu.additem(file_menu, "Exit", "file_exit", false, true);

    Menu.show()
}
```

21. Add the script code shown in Figure 9.2.27 to the Script Editor window after the On_ShowMainMenu() event handler.

FIGURE 9.2.27 On_SelectedMenuTag() function added to the MainScript

```
function On_SelectedMenuTag()
{
    eon.trace(SelectedMenuTag.value)
}
```

troubleshooting

We will use the trace method to display messages in the Log window. To ensure that script trace messages are shown, verify that the Log window is visible, then right-click in the Log window and choose Set Filter. In the Log Filter dialog box, select the Script Trace check box. Also, clear the other log type check boxes, especially the Event log type. Click OK to close the dialog box.

22. Save the simulation and then run the simulation. The new Menu button is displayed in the simulation window.

23. Click the **Menu** button, select **File**, and select one of the commands, as shown in Figure 9.2.28.

FIGURE 9.2.28 Simulation window with Menu button

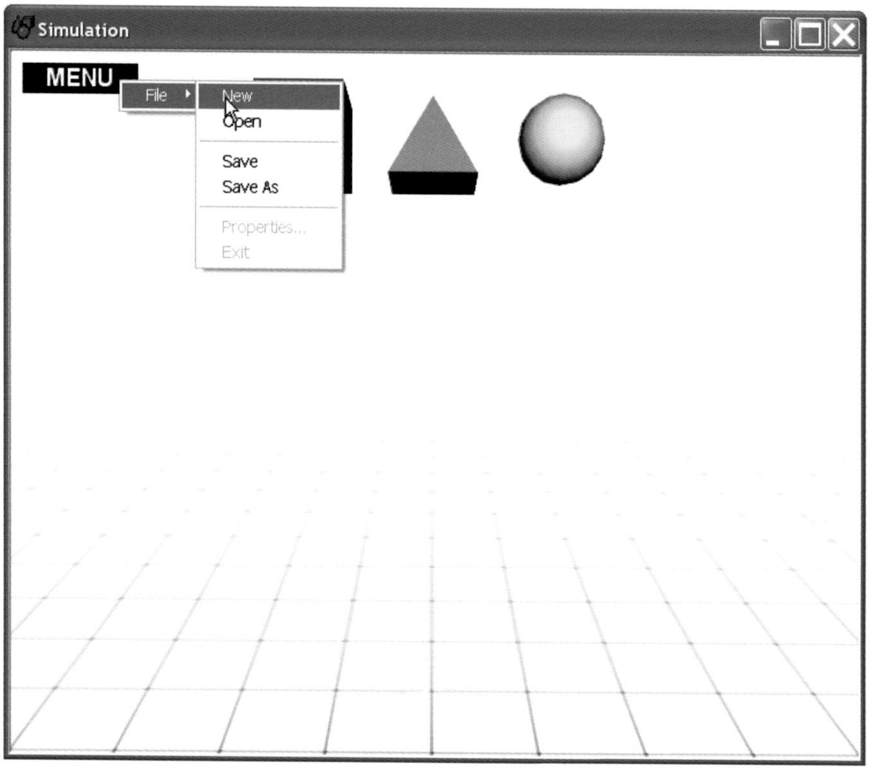

Discussion

discuss

Are script trace messages displayed in the Log window?

How could these messages help you?

24. Close the simulation window. Keep the simulation open to use in Activity 9.2.5.

The On_ShowMainMenu() function added in step 20 of the previous activity uses the additem() method:

```
Menu.additem(parentid, text, tag, checked, disabled, separator)
```

This method has several arguments; only the first two arguments are compulsory. The parentid argument identifies which menu item to place the new menu item under. The text argument is the text displayed on the menu item. The tag argument is very important because it identifies the information that will be sent to the script to indicate which command the user selected. The checked argument (true/false) determines whether a tick (check mark) is displayed to the left of the item. The disabled argument (true/false) determines whether the menu item is shown in gray text, indicating that the option cannot be chosen. The separator argument determines whether the text should be replaced with a line. The whole function returns a value, which can be stored in a variable so that new menu items can be added under it.

When the Menu.show() method is called, the pop-up menu will appear at the mouse cursor's current location. (That is why it is called a pop-up menu.) If the user clicks outside the Menu button, then the menu disappears and no events are sent. If the user clicks a menu item, then the PopupUnlimited prototype sends an event to our MainScript that is handled by the On_SelectedMenuTag() event handler.

In the following activity, we will add an Edit menu that has two options regarding editing: Continue Copying and Enable Moving. Continue Copying will refer to the function that creates a new object when you click the floor. After a while, the user will want to click the floor to navigate without creating more objects, so they should be able to turn off the Continue Copying option. The Enable Moving function will refer to the MoveRotateArrows3D prototype that lets the users move the objects after they are created. Check marks will be displayed next to the active menu items. The current value will be saved in two new fields.

tips+tricks

Instead of using the separator argument, we normally use another method to make a separator that only requires a parentid, as shown in the following example:

```
Menu.addseparator
   (parentid);
```

Activity 9.2.5: Adding the Edit Menu and Handling Its Events

1. Continue working with the open simulation file **ObjectEditor_Menu.eoz** from Activity 9.2.4.
2. Save the simulation as **ObjectEditor_EditMenu.eoz**.

troubleshooting

If time is critical and you are already familiar with scripting, you may want to copy the script from the solution file provided for this activity.

3. Double-click the **MainScript** node to display the Script Properties dialog box. Click the **New Field** button to add the first field in the following table. Add the remaining field, as shown in Figure 9.2.29. Click **OK** to close the dialog box.

Name	Field Type	Data Type	Value
ContinueCopying	exposedField	SFBool	0
EnableMoving	exposedField	SFBool	0

FIGURE 9.2.29 Two fields added in the Script Properties dialog box

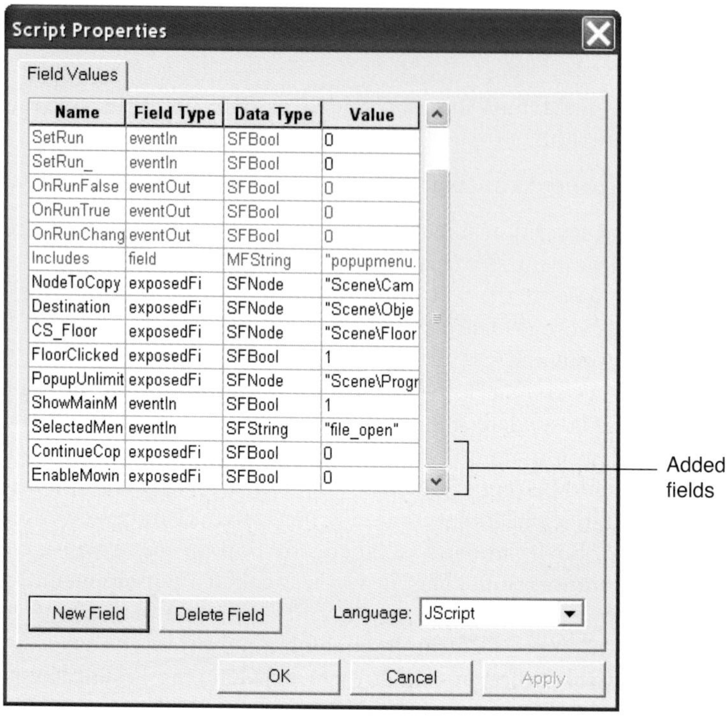

4. Select the **MainScript** node in the simulation tree and then click the **Open Script Editor** button on the Toolbar to display the Script Editor window.

5. Add the script code shown in Figure 9.2.30 in the On_ShowMainMenu() event handler just above the Menu.show() line. Note that the fourth parameter of the additem method can be true or false; a true value displays a tick (check mark) next to the menu item.

FIGURE 9.2.30 Edit menu added in Script Editor window

```
    // edit menu
    var edit_menu = Menu.additem(0, "Edit");
    Menu.additem(edit_menu, "Continue Copying", "edit_copying", ContinueCopying.value);
    Menu.additem(edit_menu, "Enable Moving", "edit_moving", EnableMoving.value);

    Menu.show()
}
```

6. Save the simulation and then run the simulation. Select the new menu items and verify that the edit_copying and edit_moving tag values appear in the Log window.

7. Close the simulation window.

8. Add script code to the On_SelectedMenuTag() event handler just after the eon.trace line, modifying the function as shown in Figure 9.2.31. This function uses a switch statement in JScript, which is appropriate when we have many different values

coming in. The switch statement is easier to use than numerous if statements. The first line in the split() function will split a string into an array, and it uses the underscore to represent where the string should be split. This means that the "edit_copying" tag will be broken into "edit" and "copying." The switch statement then triggers different case statements based on the first element of the array, in this case, "edit." The if statement toggles the field values of ContinueCopying and EnableMoving.

FIGURE 9.2.31 Switch statement added in Script Editor window

```
function On_SelectedMenuTag()
{
    eon.trace(SelectedMenuTag.value)
    t = SelectedMenuTag.value.split("_");
    switch(t[0])
    {
        case "edit" :
            if (t[1]=="copying") ContinueCopying.value = !ContinueCopying.value
            if (t[1]=="moving") EnableMoving.value = !EnableMoving.value
            break;
    }
}
```

9. Save the simulation and then run the simulation. Select the menu items and confirm that the tick next to the menu option changes each time you click the option.
10. Close the simulation window.
11. Add the new global variable, *copynexttime*, at the beginning of the script after the existing global variable, *Menu*, as shown in Figure 9.2.32. This global variable is used to implement the ContinueCopying feature. We want to remember to copy the next time the user clicks the floor after clicking one of the three objects. The new *copynexttime* global variable will be set to true after a click on an object and set to false after we have copied an object.

FIGURE 9.2.32 New global variable added in the Script Editor window

```
var Menu = new PopupMenu(PopupUnlimited.value);
var copynexttime = false;
```

12. In the Script Editor window, add the event handler shown in Figure 9.2.33 for the NodeToCopy field before the On_FloorClicked() event handler.

FIGURE 9.2.33 On_NodeToCopy() function added in the Script Editor window

```
function On_NodeToCopy()
{
    copynexttime = true;
}
```

13. In the Script Editor window, add script code to the On_FloorClicked() event handler, modifying the function as shown in Figure 9.2.34.

FIGURE 9.2.34 Script code added to the On_FloorClicked() function

```
function On_FloorClicked()
{
    if (!ContinueCopying.value && !copynexttime) return;
    copynexttime = false;
```

14. Save the simulation and then run the simulation. Test this function by selecting the **Continue Copying** menu item, adding objects, selecting the menu item again, and adding objects.

Discussion

discuss

Are objects copied and pasted in the simulation window?

15. Close the simulation window.
16. Add a **MoveRotateArrows3D** prototype from the Object Movers prototype library to the Camera frame. To enable you to move the selected objects, we will use the added MoveRotateArrows3D prototype. However, we will disable the arrows and enable the user to click and drag the objects.
17. In the MoveRotateArrows3D prototype's RootNode field, create a node reference to the **Objects** frame.
18. In the MoveRotateArrows3D prototype's DisableWhenMoving field, create a node reference to the **OrbitNav** prototype.
19. In the Property Bar, clear the **EnableArrowX**, **EnableArrowY**, **EnableArrowZ**, **EnableArrowHplus**, **EnableArrowHminus**, and **EnableBoxXY** check boxes, setting the fields to false. Select the **MoveInXYUsingCSRoot** check box, setting the field to true.
20. Double-click the **MainScript** node to display the Script Properties dialog box. Click the **New Field** button to add the field in the following table. Click **OK** to close the dialog box.

Name	Field Type	Data Type	Value
MoveRotateArrows3D	exposedField	SFNode	

21. In the MainScript node's MoveRotateArrows3D field, create a node reference to the **MoveRotateArrows3D** prototype.
22. Select the **MainScript** node in the simulation tree and then click the **Open Script Editor** button on the Toolbar to display the Script Editor window.
23. Add script code in the Script Editor window, adding the On_EnableMoving() function as shown in Figure 9.2.35. With this code, changing the EnableMoving field in the On_SelectedMenuTag() event handler immediately triggers this event handler before continuing. This code directly sends an event to the prototype to turn it on or off.

FIGURE 9.2.35 Script added to the On_EnableMoving() event handler

```
function On_EnableMoving()
{
    MoveRotateArrows3D.value.GetFieldByName("IsActive").value = EnableMoving.value;
}
```

24. Save the simulation and then run the simulation. Copy and paste objects. Select **Menu > Edit > Enable Moving**. Move objects in the simulation window.

Discussion

discuss

When you start the simulation, can you move objects when the EnableMoving field is false?

25. Add two lines of script code after the DeleteAllObjects() line in the initialize() function, modifying the initialize() function as shown in Figure 9.2.36. This sets the EnableMoving field to true when the simulation starts.

FIGURE 9.2.36 Modify the initialize() function in the Script Editor window

```
function initialize()
{
    DeleteAllObjects();
    EnableMoving.value = true;
    ContinueCopying.value = false;
}
```

26. Save the simulation and then run the simulation. Verify that you can move objects as expected.
27. Close the simulation window. Keep the simulation open to use in Activity 9.2.6.

In the previous activity, you added an Edit menu with the Continue Copying and Enable Moving options. You added script code that enabled you to move objects after they are pasted in the simulation window.

In the following activity, we will use the OrbitNavViewMaker prototype in the View menu. Usually, this prototype uses the number keys (1–9 and 0) to trigger the OrbitNav prototype to move the camera into positions that were saved earlier. The user can press the S key and a number key to save the current camera position. Later, the user can return to that position by pressing the number without another key. Here, however, we will use the menu to go to views, save views, and name the views. We will store the names in an array.

Activity 9.2.6: Adding the View Menu and Handling Its Events

1. Continue working with the open simulation file **ObjectEditor_EditMenu.eoz** from Activity 9.2.5.
2. Save the simulation as **ObjectEditor_ViewMenu.eoz**.
3. Add the following line of script code at the beginning of the script after the *copynexttime* variable line. This declares a global variable to hold our array of view names.

```
var viewarr = new Array()
```

troubleshooting

If time is critical and you are already familiar with scripting, you may want to copy the script from the solution file provided for this activity.

4. Add the function shown in Figure 9.2.37 to the end of the script. It will assign empty string values to ten array elements.

FIGURE 9.2.37 ClearViewArray() function added in the Script Editor window

```
function ClearViewArray()
{
    for (var i=1; i<11; i++)
    {
        viewarr[i] = "";
    }
}
```

5. Add the following line of script code at the end of the initialize() function. This statement calls the ClearViewArray function from our initialize() function.

   ```
   ClearViewArray();
   ```

6. Add the script code shown in Figure 9.2.38 in the On_ShowMainMenu() function just before the Menu.show() line. The View menu will have three menu items, which will each have ten submenu items. We will use for loops to create the many menu items.

FIGURE 9.2.38 Script code added to the On_ShowMainMenu() function

```
    // view menu
var view_menu = Menu.additem(0, "View");
var goto_view_menu = Menu.additem(view_menu, "Go to View...")
var save_view_menu = Menu.additem(view_menu, "Save Current View to...")
var rename_view_menu = Menu.additem(view_menu, "Rename View...")

// goto view menu
for (var i=1; i<11; i++)
{
    Menu.additem(goto_view_menu, viewarr[i] + "\t" + i, "view_" + i)
}

// save view menu
for (var i=1; i<11; i++)
{
    Menu.additem(save_view_menu, viewarr[i] + "\t" + i, "saveview_" + i)
}

// rename view menu
for (var i=1; i<11; i++)
{
    Menu.additem(rename_view_menu, viewarr[i] + "\t" + i, "renameview_" + i)
}
```

tips+tricks

Review the code to ensure that you understand how the array is utilized. The menu items will display the names of the views if they have names. The tag parameter uses an integer that represents a view number.

tips+tricks

View information is stored in a Script node named StoredViewsScript. The OrbitNavViewMaker prototype's StoredViewsScript field should hold a reference to this Script node. If this field is left blank and the prototype does not find a Script node named StoredViewsScript, then the prototype will create a Script node (copy from inside itself) when you run the simulation.

7. Save the simulation and then run the simulation. Select the three different types of View menu items and watch the Log window for results.
8. Close the simulation window. Next, you will start to implement the commands for the View submenu.
9. In the simulation tree, add an **OrbitNavViewMaker** prototype under the Orbit Navigation frame.
10. In the OrbitNavViewMaker prototype's OrbitNav field, create a node reference to the **OrbitNav** prototype in the Orbit Navigation frame.
11. Run the simulation and then close the simulation window. The StoredViewsScript node is displayed under the Orbit Navigation frame.

12. In the OrbitNavViewMaker prototype's StoredViewsScript field, create a node reference to the **StoredViewsScript** node in the Orbit Navigation frame. Your simulation tree should look like Figure 9.2.39.

FIGURE 9.2.39 StoredViewsScript node created in the OrbitNavigation frame

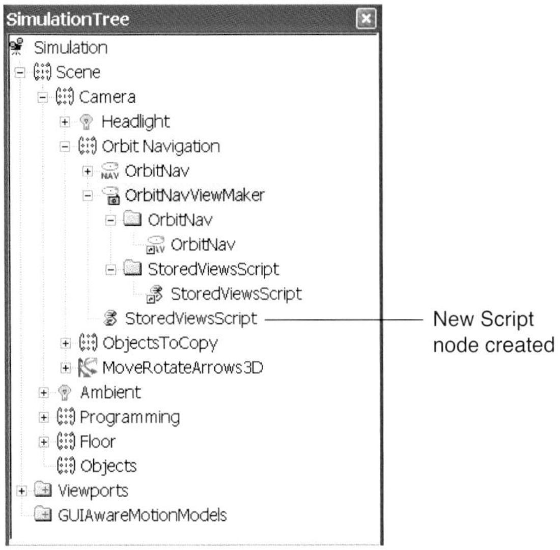

13. Double-click the **MainScript** node to display the Script Properties dialog box. Click the **New Field** button to add the field in the following table. Click **OK** to close the dialog box.

Name	Field Type	Data Type	Value
OrbitNavViewMaker	exposedField	SFNode	

14. In the MainScript node's OrbitNavViewMaker field, create a node reference to the **OrbitNavViewMaker** prototype.
15. Select the **MainScript** node in the simulation tree and then click the **Open Script Editor** button on the Toolbar to display the Script Editor window.
16. Add the script code shown in Figure 9.2.40 to the On_SelectedMenuTag() event handler just before the end of the switch statement, after the edit menu code.

FIGURE 9.2.40 Script code added to the On_SelectedMenuTag() function

Existing script code

```
        case "edit" :
            if (t[1]=="copying") ContinueCopying.value = !ContinueCopying.value
            if (t[1]=="moving") EnableMoving.value = !EnableMoving.value
            break;
        case "view" :
            OrbitNavViewMaker.value.GetFieldByName("ViewNr").value = t[1];
            break;
        case "saveview" :
            OrbitNavViewMaker.value.GetFieldByName("SaveViewNr").value = t[1];
            break;
        case "renameview" :
            RenameViewNr.value = t[1];
            break;
```

Added script code

17. Save the simulation and then run the simulation. Test the **Go to View** and **Save Current View to** menu commands. The Rename View option will not work because we do not have a RenameViewNr field yet.
18. Close the simulation window.
19. Double-click the **MainScript** node to display the Script Properties dialog box. Click the **New Field** button to add the first field in the following table. Add the remaining fields, as shown in Figure 9.2.41. Click **OK** to close the dialog box. You will use these three new fields when renaming a view. Also, you will need the InputMsgBox prototype and our script, which will set some fields, trigger the InputMsgBox to open, and send the result back to our script.

Name	Field Type	Data Type	Value
RenameViewNr	exposedField	SFInt32	0
InputMsgBox	exposedField	SFNode	""
ResultText	eventIn	SFString	""

FIGURE 9.2.41 Three fields added in the Script Properties dialog box

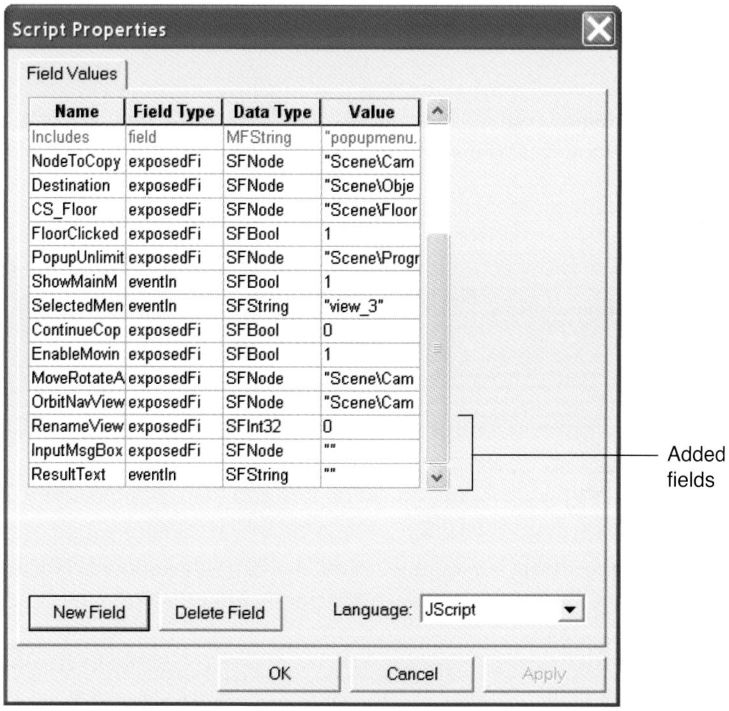

20. Add an **InputMsgBox** prototype from the GUIControl Functions prototype library under the Programming frame.
21. In the MainScript node's InputMsgBox field, create a node reference to the **InputMsgBox** prototype.
22. In the InputMsgBox prototype's SendToNode field, create a node reference to the **MainScript** node.
23. Select the **MainScript** node in the simulation tree and then click the **Open Script Editor** button on the Toolbar to display the Script Editor window.

24. Add the event handler code shown in Figure 9.2.42 at the end of the script. In the On_SelectedMenuTag() event handler, a change to the RenameViewNr field triggers an event handler used to configure the InputMsgBox prototype. Notice how we get the current name of a view from the array and use it as the default text of the InputMsgBox. The last line is an inEvent that triggers the input box to appear.

FIGURE 9.2.42 On_RenameViewNr() event handler added to the script

```
function On_RenameViewNr()
{
    InputMsgBox.value.GetFieldByName("Caption").value = "Rename View";
    var msg = "Enter a new name for this view.#The current name is shown below.";
    InputMsgBox.value.GetFieldByName("Message").value = msg;
    InputMsgBox.value.GetFieldByName("DefaultText").value = viewarr[RenameViewNr.value];
    InputMsgBox.value.GetFieldByName("ShowMessage").value = true;
}
```

25. Add the **On_ResultText()** event handler shown in Figure 9.2.43 at the end of the script. It is triggered when the InputMsgBox prototype sends the name to the ResultText field of the MainScript.

FIGURE 9.2.43 On_ResultText() event handler added to the script

```
function On_ResultText()
{
    if (ResultText.value=="") return;

    // puts the name of the view entered by user into the array
    viewarr[RenameViewNr.value] = ResultText.value;
}
```

26. Save the simulation and then run the simulation. Test all of the View functions.
27. Close the simulation window. Keep the simulation open to use in Activity 9.2.7.

Accessing Text Files

Through an ActiveX control, you can access the file system and create, save, and open text files. You will be able to take your application to a new level by saving data in any format you choose.

First, create a variable to hold a reference to a FileSystemObject ActiveX control object called the ***file system object***, as shown in the following example.

```
var fso = new ActiveXObject("Scripting.FileSystemObject")
```

To know whether a file exists, use the FileExists method, as shown in the following example.

```
if (!fso.FileExists(Filename.value)) return;
```

To create a file, use the CreateTextFile method, as shown in the following example.

```
var ts = fso.CreateTextFile(Filename.value, true);
```

Then, add text to the file, as shown in the following example.

```
ts.WriteLine("Hello World");
```

And then close the file, as shown in the following example.

```
ts.Close();
```

web links

There are many more objects, methods, and properties that you can use to access text files in your scripts. You can read about them in online documentation. Search for FileSystemObject on the Internet.

troubleshooting

If time is critical and you are already familiar with scripting, you may want to copy the script from the solution file provided for this activity.

Activity 9.2.7: Implementing the File Menu Functions

In Activity 9.2.4, we created a File menu but did not create a way to handle its events. In this activity, we will save the type and positions of objects to a text file that can be opened later. To open or save a file, the user must choose a filename. Instead of the OpenSaveDialog node, we will use the FileSelecter prototype to get the name of the file.

1. Continue working with the open simulation file **ObjectEditor_ViewMenu.eoz** from Activity 9.2.6.
2. Save the simulation as **ObjectEditor_FileMenu.eoz**.
3. Double-click the **MainScript** node to display the Script Properties dialog box. Click the **New Field** button to add the first field in the following table. Add the remaining fields, as shown in Figure 9.2.44. Click **OK** to close the dialog box. These three new fields will be used to make the File menu operational. The FileSelecter field will hold a reference to the FileSelecter prototype, which is similar to a dialog box that asks the user to select a file.

Name	Field Type	Data Type	Value
DoOpen	exposedField	SFBool	0
FileSelecter	exposedField	SFNode	
Filename	exposedField	SFString	""

FIGURE 9.2.44 Three fields for the File menu added in the Script Properties dialog box

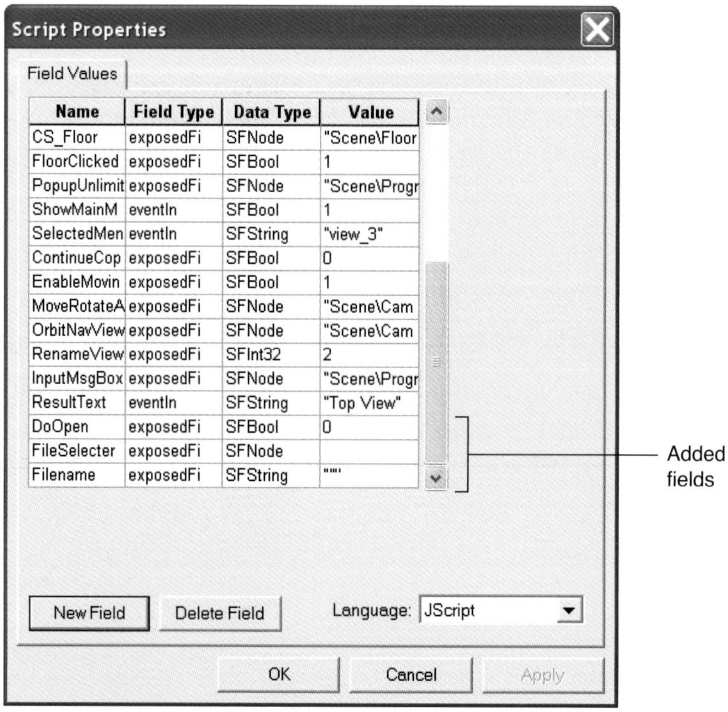

4. Add a **FileSelecter** prototype from the GUIControl Functions prototype library to the Programming frame. In the Property Bar, set the prototype's Extension field to **.dat** and set its DefaultFilename field to **plan1**.
5. In the MainScript node's FileSelecter field, create a node reference to the **FileSelecter** prototype.
6. In the FileSelecter prototype's SendToNode field, create a node reference to the **MainScript** node.
7. Select the **MainScript** node in the simulation tree and then click the **Open Script Editor** button on the Toolbar to display the Script Editor window.
8. Add the script code shown in Figure 9.2.45 to the On_SelectedMenuTag() at the start of the switch statement. This script code calls a new function named FileMenuResult() to handle the related features.

FIGURE 9.2.45 Script code added to call the FileMenuResult() function

Added script code

Existing script code

```
        case "file" :
            FileMenuResult(t[1]);
            break;
        case "edit" :
            if (t[1]=="copying") ContinueCopying.value = !ContinueCopying.value
            if (t[1]=="moving") EnableMoving.value = !EnableMoving.value
            break;
```

9. Add the function shown in Figure 9.2.46 to the end of the script. When File > New is selected, the initialize() function is called. This shows that event handlers also can work as functions to be called at any time, even when they are not events. Initialize() deletes the current objects and clears the view array. It also should clear the Filename field.

FIGURE 9.2.46 FileMenuResult() function added

```
function FileMenuResult(result)
{
    switch (result)
    {
        case "new" : initialize(); break;
        case "open" :
            DoOpen.value = true;
            FileSelecter.value.GetFieldByName("Mode").value=2;
            FileSelecter.value.GetFieldByName("TitleBarText").value="Open a file";
            FileSelecter.value.GetFieldByName("SaveBtnText").value="Open";
            FileSelecter.value.GetFieldByName("ShowDialog").value=true;
            break;
        case "save" :
            DoOpen.value = false;
            if (Filename.value!="")
            {
                On_Filename()
                break;
            }
        case "saveas" :
            DoOpen.value = false;
            FileSelecter.value.GetFieldByName("Mode").value=1;
            FileSelecter.value.GetFieldByName("TitleBarText").value="Save As";
            FileSelecter.value.GetFieldByName("SaveBtnText").value="Save";
            FileSelecter.value.GetFieldByName("ShowDialog").value=true;
            break;
        case "properties" :
            ShowProperties();
            break;
    }
}
```

10. Add the following line of script code to the end of the initialize() function.

```
Filename.value = "";
```

11. Add the event handler shown in Figure 9.2.47 to the end of the script. The File > Open option will set some text values of the FileSelecter and open the FileSelecter for the user to write or select a file. The File > Save option will trigger On_Filename(), which you have not added yet. If the Filename field is empty, the program flow will continue with the "saveas" case because program flow would not encounter the break statement. The "saveas" code is similar to the "open" code because it uses the FileSelecter to get a filename. The FileSelecter will then send the Filename to the MainScript's Filename field, which will trigger this event handler. This event handler receives the filename when saving and opening. Therefore, we have set the DoOpen field previously so we know whether we should open or save a file.

FIGURE 9.2.47 On_Filename() function added to the end of the script

```
function On_Filename()
{
    if (Filename.value=="") return;
    if (DoOpen.value) OpenFile();
    else SaveFile();
}
```

12. Add the **SaveFile()** function shown in Figure 9.2.48 to the end of the script. This function accesses the file system and creates a text file. Our saved files have one line of data for each object that we created. The data will be the object type (Cube, Pyramid, Sphere) and its position. The script loops through the child nodes of the Objects node and identifies the name of the child frame to determine the object type. It rounds the position values to 3 decimal places to minimize file size, and it separates all values with the equals (=) character. The *ts* variable holds a TextStream object that allows the addition of text to a file with its WriteLine() method.

FIGURE 9.2.48 SaveFile() function added to the end of the script

```
function SaveFile()
{
    var fso = new ActiveXObject("Scripting.FileSystemObject");
    var ts = fso.CreateTextFile(Filename.value, true);

    // we will loop through the children nodes of the Objects frame.
    var treech = Destination.value.GetFieldByName("TreeChildren")
    var node, obj_type
    for (var i=0; i<treech.GetMFCount(); i++)
    {
        node = treech.GetMFElement(i)
        // look at node name to determine what type of object it is
        var nodename = eon.GetNodeName(node)
        if (nodename.substring(0, 4)=="Cube") obj_type = "Cube"
        if (nodename.substring(0, 4)=="Pyra") obj_type = "Pyramid"
        if (nodename.substring(0, 4)=="Sphe") obj_type = "Sphere"

        // get position and round values
        p = node.GetFieldByName("Position").value.toArray()
        x = Math.round(p[0]*1000)/1000;
        y = Math.round(p[1]*1000)/1000;
        z = Math.round(p[2]*1000)/1000;

        // save it to the file.
        ts.WriteLine(obj_type + "=" + x + "=" + y + "=" + z);
    }

    // close the file.
    ts.Close()
}
```

13. Save the simulation and then run the simulation.
14. In the simulation window, add some objects and move the objects. Click the **Menu** button, select **File**, and then select the **Save** option as shown in Figure 9.2.49. Click the **Save** button. The file will be saved to your C drive's root folder unless you choose otherwise in the FileSelecter prototype's FolderPath field.

FIGURE 9.2.49 Save function in the simulation window

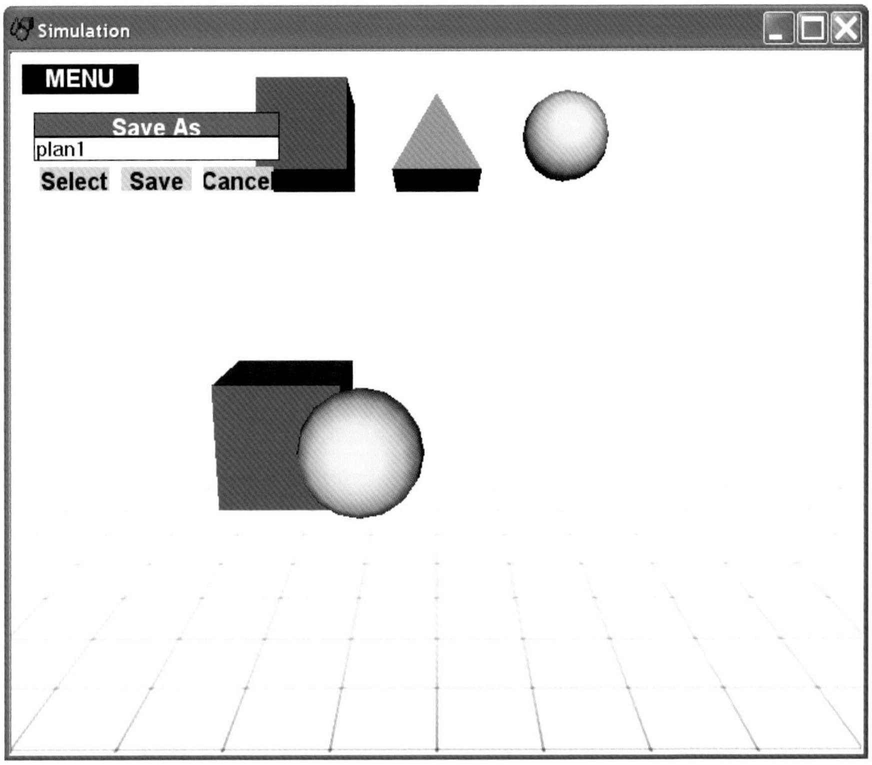

15. Close the simulation window.
16. Using Notepad, open the saved file and inspect it. Like the sample file shown in Figure 9.2.50, it will contain object names and positions.

FIGURE 9.2.50 Sample plan1.dat file

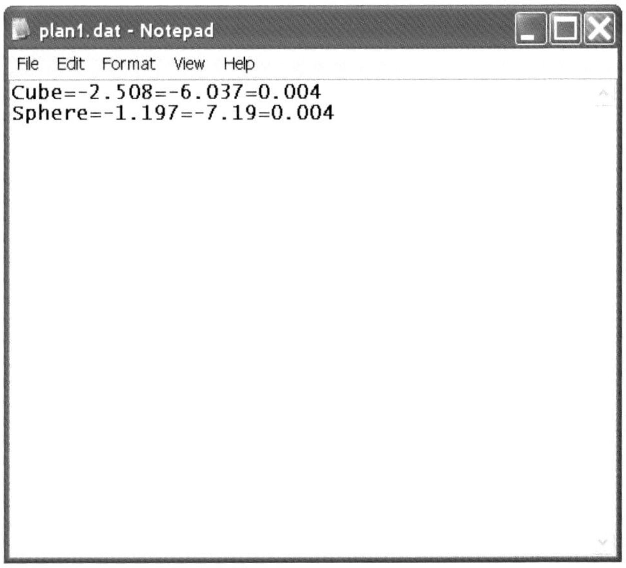

tips+tricks

Note that this activity does not save the names or positions of saved views, but you are encouraged to try this exercise yourself.

17. Close Notepad.
18. Add the **OpenFile()** function shown in Figure 9.2.51 to the end of the MainScript node's code. The *ts* variable holds a TextStream object that can read lines of text from the text file. The ReadLine() method returns a line of text and moves an internal pointer to the next line. The split("=") function splits the line of text into an array so that we can access the first array element as the object type and the next three as X, Y, and Z values of its position.

FIGURE 9.2.51 OpenFile() function added to the end of the script

```
function OpenFile()
{
    var fso = new ActiveXObject("Scripting.FileSystemObject");
    var ts = fso.OpenTextFile(Filename.value, 1, false);

    // first remove anything that already exists
    DeleteAllObjects();
    ClearViewArray();

    // loop through rows of text file.
    var t, node, newpos, treech
    while (!ts.AtEndOfStream)
    {
        // Read a line and put it into an array
        t = ts.ReadLine().split("=")
        // find a node to copy
        node = eon.findnode("ObjectsToCopy!" + t[0] + "Frame");

        // copy a node to Objects frame
        eon.CopyNode(node, Destination.value);
        treech = Destination.value.GetFieldByName("TreeChildren");
        node = treech.GetMFElement(treech.GetMFCount()-1);

        // set its position
        newpos = eon.MakeSFVec3f(t[1], t[2], t[3]);
        node.GetFieldByName("Position").value = newpos;
        node.GetFieldByName("SetStartValues").value = true;
    }
    ts.Close()
}
```

19. Display the **On_ShowMainMenu()** event handler in the Script Editor window. We created a "Properties" menu item, but set it to disabled. (Refer to Figure 9.2.26.) Replace that line now with the three lines of script code shown in Figure 9.2.52. The *dis* variable holds the disable parameter. Now, we will only disable properties if we do not have a filename selected.

FIGURE 9.2.52 Script code using the *dis* variable

```
    if (Filename.value=="") dis = true
    else dis = false
    Menu.additem(file_menu, "Properties...", "file_properties", false, dis);
```

20. Add the **ShowProperties()** function shown in Figure 9.2.53 to the end of the script.

FIGURE 9.2.53 ShowProperties() function added to the end of the script

```
function ShowProperties()
{
    if (Filename.value=="") return;
    var fso = new ActiveXObject("Scripting.FileSystemObject");
    var fn = Filename.value;
    if (!fso.FileExists(fn)) return;
    var f = fso.GetFile(fn);

    var msg = "Here are some properties of the current file:\n";
    msg += "Path: " + f.Path + "\n";
    msg += "File: " + f.Name + "\n";
    msg += "Type: " + f.Type + "\n";
    msg += "Size: " + f.Size + " bytes.\n";
    msg += "Last modified " + f.DateLastModified;

    eon.SetScriptTimeout(0);
    eon.MessageBox(msg, "File Properties");
    eon.SetScriptTimeout(6);
}
```

21. Save the simulation and then run the simulation. Click the **Menu** button, select **File**, and select **Open**. In the Open a file box, you will see the plan1 default text displayed. Click the **Select** button to display a list of the available files. Select **plan1.dat**. Click the **Open** button to open the file. The objects displayed at the time the file was saved will be displayed in the positions they occupied at the time the file was saved.
22. Click the **Menu** button, select **File**, and select **Properties**. The File Properties dialog box shown in Figure 9.2.54 is displayed. It contains information about the open file. Click **OK** to close the dialog box.

tips+tricks

You can open any file you saved when you ran the simulation earlier.

FIGURE 9.2.54 File Properties dialog box

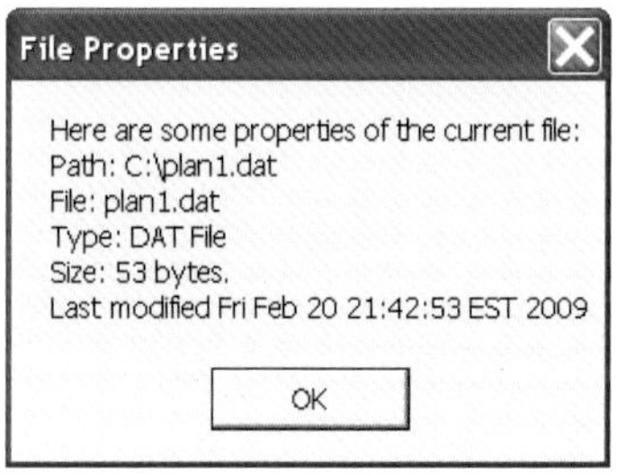

23. Close the simulation window. Keep the simulation open to use in Activity 9.2.8.

In Activity 9.2.8, we will accomplish four tasks:

- Eliminate a script error that occurs when you move an object and then select File > New.
- Add a Delete function to the simulation.
- Eliminate an error that adds extra copies when you try to rotate an object.
- Identify the object that is selected for copying.

troubleshooting

If time is critical and you are already familiar with scripting, you may want to copy the script from the solution file provided for this activity.

Activity 9.2.8: Finishing the Application

1. Continue working with the open simulation file **ObjectEditor_FileMenu.eoz** from Activity 9.2.7.
2. Save the simulation as **ObjectEditor_Finish.eoz**.
3. Run the simulation. Add a cube and then drag the cube to a new position.
4. Click the **Menu** button, select **File**, and select **New**. You will see the first of two script error messages from two scripts within the MoveRotateArrows3D prototype, as shown in Figure 9.2.55. This prototype is constantly checking the position of selected nodes, and it was not expecting a node to disappear. The File > New function will delete all objects, so we must tell the MoveRotateArrows3D prototype to unselect the node before we delete the node.

FIGURE 9.2.55 Error dialog box containing the first script error message

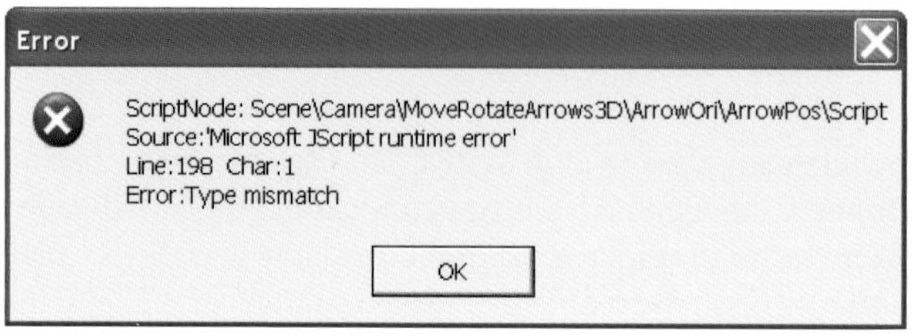

5. Click **OK** to close the first error message and display the second error message, shown in Figure 9.2.56. Click **OK** to close the second error message.

FIGURE 9.2.56 Error dialog box containing the second script error message

6. Close the simulation window.
7. Select the **MainScript** node in the simulation tree and then click the **Open Script Editor** button on the Toolbar to display the Script Editor window.
8. In the DeleteAllObjects() function, add the script code shown in Figure 9.2.57 at the beginning of the function.

FIGURE 9.2.57 Script code added to the DeleteAllObjects() function

```
// Unselect any existing object before deleting it.
MoveRotateArrows3D.value.GetFieldByName("UnSelect").value = true;
```

9. Save the simulation and then run the simulation. Repeat steps 3 and 4 to verify that the error no longer occurs.

10. Close the simulation window.

    We have a function to delete all objects using the File > New function, but not a way to delete a single object. We will create a right-click context menu to delete an object.

11. Drag the **ClickSensorPlus** prototype from the Local Prototypes window to the Programming frame. Rename the prototype **CS_Objects**. In the Property Bar, set its Button field to **2**, which means it senses when the right mouse button is pressed. Clear the **SendDirect** check box, setting the field to false.

12. In the CS_Objects prototype's Roots field, create a node reference to the **Objects** frame.

13. Double-click the **MainScript** node to display the Script Properties dialog box. Click the **New Field** button to add the first field in the following table. Add the remaining field and click **OK** to close the dialog box.

Name	Field Type	Data Type	Value
ShowContextMenu	eventIn	SFBool	0
CS_Objects	exposedField	SFNode	

14. In the MainScript node's CS_Objects field, create a node reference to the **CS_Objects** prototype.

15. Display the **Routes** window. Drag the **CS_Objects** prototype to the Routes window. Establish the connection outlined in the following table.

From	outEvent	To	inEvent
CS_Objects	OnButtonDownFalse	MainScript	ShowContextMenu

16. Select the **MainScript** node in the simulation tree and then click the **Open Script Editor** button on the Toolbar to display the Script Editor window.

17. Add the function shown in Figure 9.2.58 at the end of the script in the Script Editor window.

FIGURE 9.2.58 On_ShowContextMenu() function added to the end of the script

```
function On_ShowContextMenu()
{
    Menu.clear();
    Menu.additem(0, "Delete", "delete_object", false, false);
    Menu.show();
}
```

18. Save the simulation and then run the simulation.
19. Add a sphere. Right-click the sphere to display the Delete menu item. Select the **Delete** option. You should see the "delete_object" text in the Log window. The object is not deleted.
20. Close the simulation window.
21. Add the script code shown in Figure 9.2.59 to the end of the switch statement in the On_SelectedMenuTag() event handler. Notice that we tell the MoveRotateArrows3D prototype to unselect so that we avoid the type of script error we identified earlier. Then, we get a node reference of the object that the user right-clicks from the ClickSensorPlus prototype, and we delete that node.

FIGURE 9.2.59 Script code added to the On_SelectedMenuTag() event handler

```
case "delete" :
    MoveRotateArrows3D.value.GetFieldByName("UnSelect").value = true;
    node = CS_Objects.value.GetFieldByName("Sibling").value;
    eon.DeleteNode(node);
    break;
```

22. Save the simulation and then run the simulation. Add a pyramid and verify that you can delete the object using the right-click pop-up menu.
23. Click the **Menu** button, select **Edit**, and then select the **Continue copying** option. Click the floor to insert an object. Now, rotate the view. When you release the mouse button, you will see that an object has been added to the scene. This is probably not what a user expects. They either want to rotate the view or add an object, not both. We will add a condition to the function that currently adds objects when clicking the floor. It should add an object only if the mouse position when the mouse button is pressed is the same as the mouse position when the mouse button is released. If the mouse position has changed, then we assume the user is trying to rotate the view.
24. Close the simulation window.
25. Add a **MouseSensor** node to the Programming frame. It has a cursorPosition field to check the position of the mouse when the button is pressed and when the button is released.
26. Double-click the **MainScript** node to display the Script Properties dialog box. Click the **New Field** button to add the first field in the following table. Add the remaining field, as shown in Figure 9.2.60. Click **OK** to close the dialog box.

Name	Field Type	Data Type	Value
MouseSensor	exposedField	SFNode	
SaveMousePos	exposedField	SFVec2f	0 0

FIGURE 9.2.60 Final fields added in the Script Properties dialog box

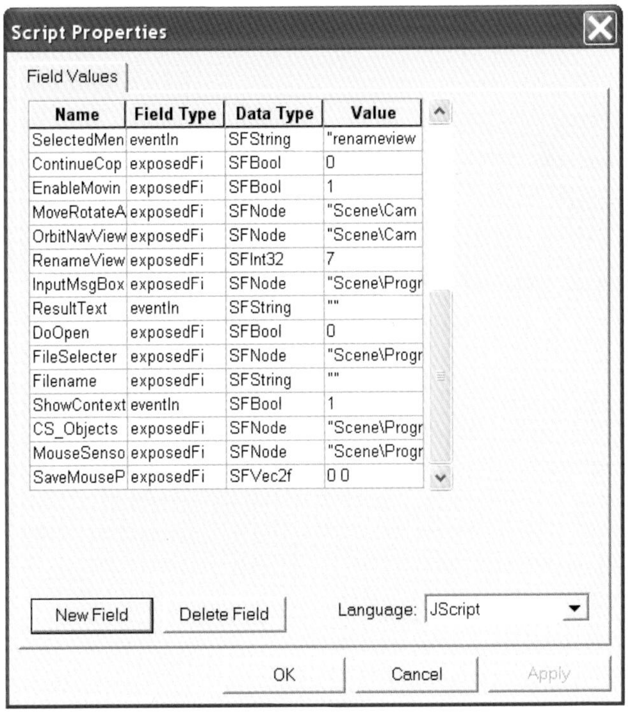

27. In the MainScript node's MouseSensor field, create a node reference to the **MouseSensor** node.
28. Display the **Routes** window. Currently, the FloorClicked inEvent receives an event only when the mouse is released. Instead of using the OnButtonDownFalse event that only sends true when the mouse button is released, we will use OnButtonDownChanged, which sends true when pressed and false when released.
29. Delete the route from the CS_Floor node to the MainScript node.
30. Establish the connection outlined in the following table.

From	outEvent	To	inEvent
CS_Floor	OnButtonDownChanged	MainScript	FloorClicked

31. Add the script code shown in Figure 9.2.61 to the beginning of the On_FloorClicked() event handler. This code modifies our On_FloorClicked() event handler so that when true is received, the script saves the mouse position and exits; when false is received, it compares the current mouse position with the saved mouse position and exits if they are different.

FIGURE 9.2.61 Script code added to the beginning of the On_FloorClicked() event handler

```
function On_FloorClicked()
{
    if (FloorClicked.value)
    {
    SaveMousePos.value = MouseSensor.value.GetFieldByName("cursorPosition").value
    return;
    }

    // compare saved mouse position with current position
    // and exit if they are different.
    var sp = SaveMousePos.value.toArray();
    var mp = MouseSensor.value.GetFieldByName("cursorPosition").value.toArray();
    if (sp[0]!=mp[0]  || sp[1]!=mp[1]) return;
```

tips+tricks

Remember that the .toArray() method is required to convert the SFVec2F data type to a regular JScript array.

32. Save the simulation and then run the simulation. Click the **Menu** button, select **Edit**, and then select the **Continue Copying** option. Click an object to copy and then click the floor. Rotate the view.

Discussion

discuss

Does an object appear when you release the mouse button?

Which part of the script determines when an object is added?

33. Close the simulation window.
34. Add a **HighLighter** prototype from the Useful Functions prototype library to the Camera\ObjectsToCopy frame. Users like to see something happen when they click the screen, providing instant feedback. The HighLighter prototype can change the material of the object selected to copy when users click it.
35. In the HighLighter prototype's Roots field, create a node reference to the **ObjectsToCopy** frame.
36. Select the **HighLighter** prototype in the simulation tree if necessary. In the Property Bar, select the **ClickToHighlight** check box, setting the field to true. No scripting is required for this feature.
37. Save the simulation and then run the simulation. Test the new highlighting functionality.

Discussion

discuss

How can you test the highlighting functionality?

38. Close the simulation window.
39. Select the **MainScript** node in the simulation tree and then click the **Open Script Editor** button on the Toolbar to display the Script Editor window.
40. Clean up your script by removing any empty event handlers. Remember that these are automatically created by EON Studio if you add the fields before opening the Script Editor.
41. Add the following comment to the beginning of your script.

```
// Object Editor Script
```

42. Add the following comment to the end of your script:

```
// Last modified [place today's date here].
// by [place your name here].
```

43. Save the simulation. Close EON. Congratulations! You have completed a major scripting project.

The following suggestions could help you extend this script.

- Save the names and positions of the views to the file.
- Hide the Menu button when the FileSelecter or InputMsgBox dialog boxes are displayed.
- Add an Insert menu to choose which object to copy, and insert the menu at the center of the scene.
- Find a way to copy only the Shape nodes and Frame nodes rather than the Cube, Pyramid, and Sphere prototypes. Then, set the geometry and material node references. Copying that does not include copying resource nodes uses far less memory.
- Add an Insert menu that inserts multiple objects arranged in a particular way.
- Add a Copy Object feature to the Edit menu that will place a copy that is two meters to the right of the selected object.
- Allow multiple selection and then select a Group function from the Edit menu. Move the selected object under a new Frame node that can be moved as one unit.

Discussion

discuss

The favorites.js, getkeycode.js, and getorient.js JScript files are located with the data files for Module 9 Lesson 2. Explore these scripts to determine what they do. Would you find these scripts useful in the future?

How to Move Nodes

Although EON provides methods to copy and delete nodes, it does not offer a way to move them to rearrange the simulation tree. Moving nodes, especially Shape nodes, can be a way to group 3D objects and then move them as one unit. Use the function shown in Figure 9.2.62 to move a node to a new parent node.

FIGURE 9.2.62 MoveNodeToNewParent() function

```
function MoveNodeToNewParent(node, newparent)
{
    var OldParent = node.GetParentNode()
    var OldTreeCh = OldParent.GetFieldByName("TreeChildren")
    for (var i=0;i<OldTreeCh.GetMFCount();i++)
    {
        if (node==OldTreeCh.GetMFElement(i))
        {
            childnr = i
            break;
        }
    }
    var NewTreeCh = newparent.GetFieldByName("TreeChildren")
    var NewCh = newparent.GetFieldByName("Children")
    NewTreeCh.AddMFElement(node)
    NewCh.AddMFElement(node)
    OldParent.GetFieldByName("Children").RemoveMFElement(childnr)
}
```

troubleshooting

Moving nodes can cause EON to close unexpectedly. Therefore, nodes should be moved only by users with advanced knowledge and experience.

Recursive Functions

Recursive functions are those that call themselves. They can be very useful and powerful functions. They also can lead to infinite loops if not designed carefully. They can be quite useful in traversing hierarchical structures, including the simulation tree in EON Studio. In the example shown in Figure 9.2.63, we use a recursive function to produce a list of node names found in the simulation.

FIGURE 9.2.63 Sample recursive function

```
function initialize()
{
    SaveNodeNames()
}


function SaveNodeNames()
{
    var simnode = eon.findnode("Simulation")
    var t = GetNodeNames(simnode, 0)
    SaveToFile(t);
}


function GetNodeNames(node, indent)
{
    var str = getindent(indent) + eon.GetNodeName(node) + "!"

    var treech = node.GetFieldByName("TreeChildren")
    for (var i=0; i<treech.GetMFCount(); i++)
    {
        str = str + GetNodeNames(treech.GetMFElement(i), indent + 1)
    }
    return str
}

function getindent(nr)
{
    var str = "";
    for (var i=0; i<nr; i++)
    {
        str = str + "   ";
    }
    return str;
}

function SaveToFile(str)
{
    var fso = new ActiveXObject("Scripting.FileSystemObject");
    var ts = fso.CreateTextFile("c:\\nodelist.txt", true);
    a = str.split("!")
    for (var i=0; i<a.length; i++)
    {
        ts.WriteLine(a[i]);
    }
    ts.Close();
}
```

ActiveX Controls

Scripting allows you to access the objects, methods, and properties of other software through ActiveX controls. We have already observed the use of ActiveXObject's FileSystemObject method in accessing the file system and text-based files. Several more types are available.

Figure 9.2.64 demonstrates how you can use the Common Dialog ActiveX control to show a color picker like the one used in the ColorPicker prototype in the Useful Functions library.

FIGURE 9.2.64 Sample script using the Common Dialog ActiveX control

```
dlg = new ActiveXObject("MSComDlg.CommonDialog");
dlg.ShowColor()
```

web links

Full documentation of Windows Script Host can be found at Microsoft's MSDN library, or you can search the Internet for more information.

You can use the Windows Scripting Host ActiveX control to do a variety of things such as starting programs, accessing the registry, or sending keystrokes. Figure 9.2.65 demonstrates a sample script that starts a program.

FIGURE 9.2.65 Sample script that starts the Windows Calculator program

```
// start Calculator program
var wsh = new ActiveXObject("WScript.Shell");
wsh.Exec("calc");
```

The registry is a database that stores information needed to configure and use computer applications and hardware. Figure 9.2.66 demonstrates a sample script that accesses your computer's registry.

FIGURE 9.2.66 Sample script that accesses your computer's registry

```
// access registry
var Reg = new ActiveXObject("WScript.Shell")
var filename = Reg.RegRead("HKEY_CURRENT_USER\\Software\\EON
Reality\\EON\\6.0\\EON Studio\\Recent File List\\File1")
eon.trace("First file in EON Studio's recent file list is");
eon.trace(filename);
```

Sending a keystroke can perform a variety of tasks, such as starting an action. Figure 9.2.67 demonstrates a sample script that sends a keystroke.

FIGURE 9.2.67 Sample script that sends a keystroke

```
// send the space bar keystroke
var shell = new ActiveXObject("WScript.Shell")
shell.AppActivate("EON");
shell.SendKeys(" ");
```

Accessing Databases

Scripts also can be used to access a database. In the example shown in Figure 9.2.68, we access a Microsoft Access database named members.mdb, extract names and scores, and display them in the Log window.

FIGURE 9.2.68 Script that accesses a database

```
function AccessDatabase()
{
    // create a connection object
    var conn = new ActiveXObject("ADODB.Connection");
    // create a recordset object
    var rset = new ActiveXObject("ADODB.Recordset");

    // establish connection with database file
    var dbpath = "C:\\members.mdb"
    var db = "Provider=Microsoft.Jet.OLEDB.4.0;Data Source=";
    db += dbpath + ";Persist Security Info=False";
    conn.Open(db);
    with (rset)
    {
        ActiveConnection = conn;     //recordset uses conn object
        CursorType = 3; //adOpenStatic
        CursorLocation = 3; //adUseClient
        LockType = 2;    //adLockPessimistic
    }

    // select data and print to Log Window
    rset.Source = "Select firstname, score from Scores";
    rset.Open();
    var name, score
    for (var i=0; i<rset.RecordCount; i++)
    {
        name = rset.Fields("firstname").value
        score = rset.Fields("score").value
        eon.trace(name + "'s score was " + score);
        rset.MoveNext()
    }
    rset.Close();
}
```

discuss

The Microsoft Access database named members.mdb used in the sample script displayed in Figure 9.2.68 is located with the data files for Module 9 Lesson 2. Use the script to extract names and scores and display them in the Log window. How could you use the script in the future?

Additional Functions

You can find more ActiveX controls that perform some very useful functions. If you have Microsoft Visual Studio, look under the Projects menu to view References and Components. Many ActiveX controls are listed, and some may work in EON.

Remember that scripting in EON is not all about writing code. Much preparation is needed to send the right events to your script. You still need to add nodes and prototypes, set their fields, create fields on the Script node, and connect routes to them.

To learn scripting well, you should try the examples presented in this module. Do not be afraid to experiment with variations of the activities provided in this lesson.

Summary

In this lesson you:

- Identified the stages of program flow for EON simulations.
- Copied and deleted nodes.
- Included external script files in your simulation.
- Used script with the PopupUnlimited prototype.
- Accessed text files and databases.
- Learned about recursive functions and ActiveX controls.

LESSON 9.3

Dynamic Load Applications

Objectives

- Understand EON Dynamic Load and its advantages.
- Learn where to set the PrototypebaseURL in host applications.
- Use the DynamicPrototype node to download prototypes from the Internet.
- Use the Download field of the Texture2 node to download photos from the Internet.
- Add a download bar to an EON Dynamic Load application.
- Create a simple download bar using 2DText nodes.
- Understand the licensing requirements for EON Dynamic Load.

Key Terms

Dynamic Load Stand Alone license
DynamicPrototype node
EON Dynamic Load license
EON Server license
host application
host ID
licensed EDZ application
PrototypebaseURL
session

Introduction to EON Dynamic Load

EON Dynamic Load makes it possible to load, unload, and swap EON resources (prototypes, geometries, textures, and movies) dynamically during runtime (while an EON application is running). Normally, the content of an EON application is fixed and cannot be changed after the application is run. However, this feature allows an application to change its content—making it a dynamic application. Content can be retrieved from the local hard drive, a local server, or a server accessed via the Internet.

STORYBOARD

Distributing and Delivering EON Content

EON Dynamic Load spans several items in the storyboard.

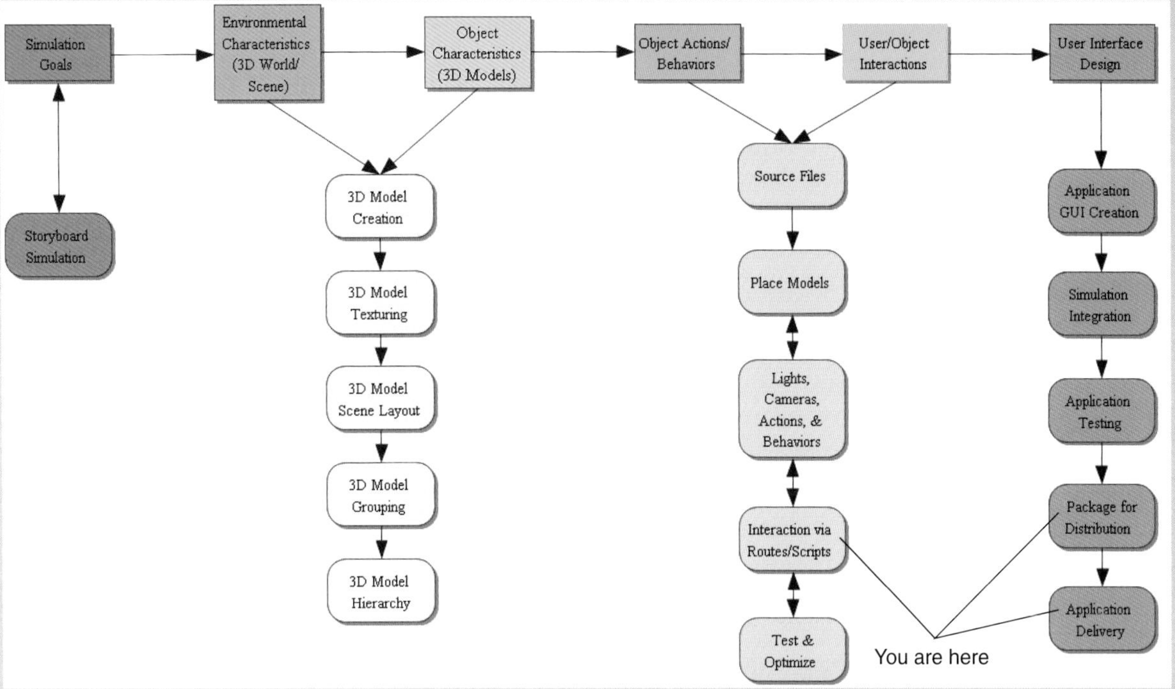

Looking at our storyboard, it is difficult to see where EON Dynamic Load fits. In a way, it is about packaging files for distribution because 3D content files will be packaged as prototypes and placed on a local hard drive, a local server, or a web server. In another way, it is about application delivery because EON Dynamic Load is a method of delivering content to the user. However, EON Dynamic Load is mainly about user interactions, showing and hiding content by setting up routes.

Advantages of Using EON Dynamic Load

EON Dynamic Load provides two key benefits that allow you to create different applications. Compared to the standard system, EON Dynamic Load provides the following benefits:

- EON applications can be configured and changed during runtime.
- Large EON applications can be downloaded in smaller parts on demand when they are needed.

tips+tricks

The EON Dynamic Load feature is also called EON Server by EON Reality. Additional licensing requirements apply to applications that use EON Dynamic Load services.

Configurable EON Applications

Using EON Dynamic Load makes it possible to download predefined resources (prototypes, geometries, textures, and movies) and embed them in a 3D environment. EON Dynamic Load also makes it possible to let the user decide which resources to download; the user also can unload any resource they choose. This creates limitless combinations of the 3D content in a running EON application. Because the resources may be used in different EON applications, it makes reuse highly feasible.

Because prototypes are self-contained units, they can be reused easily in future EON applications, reducing development time and enhancing the conformity of the developed applications. EON Dynamic Load can use an unlimited number of resources. For example, you can choose to provide a very large catalog of 3D objects for configuration.

Distribution of Large EON Applications

Because Internet bandwidth is limited, it can take a long time to download some EON applications. If the EON application is larger than a megabyte (MB), people may find it too time-consuming to download. The EON Dynamic Load service enables you to split the EON application into smaller prototypes and download only the prototypes that the application needs. Each prototype can contain any EON functionality. All interactivity embedded in the prototype will function immediately when it is downloaded.

Instead of recompiling the EON application when a new object is created, the new object is made into a prototype and the prototype's name is entered into a list or database that is external to the EON application. Using a specific sequence for downloading the prototypes ensures that the 3D environment will be built in an attractive way.

Examples of Applications

The following examples of EON Dynamic Load applications have one thing in common—they handle large volumes of content in a systematic way. Often, this is more important than downloading the content over the Internet. Many applications are designed to load objects from the local computer.

- Office configurator: Select a number of furniture pieces in a web catalog, add them to an EON application as prototypes, place them, select colors, and so on to create a new customized office/room.
- House configurator: When building a new house, the buyer selects options such as wallpapers, floors, kitchen cabinets, and so on. All of these decisions can be made on the Internet and saved with the order information.
- Car configurator: See how your car and the price of the car change when you select different options.
- Boat configurator: Boats are usually luxury items that have many options that can be configured in 3D.
- Large buildings/constructions: Download large buildings or constructions in small parts so that the user can see the 3D environment grow when more details are downloaded.
- Virtual worlds/cities: If you have a very large area to display, such as a city, an island, or other multiuser environments, use EON Dynamic Load to display only objects in the vicinity of the user. Download is controlled by nodes that sense how far the user's point of view (camera) is from objects such as buildings, trees, cars, and other terrain features.
- E-learning: Create a large E-learning application, which can be downloaded from the Internet when needed.

How could you use EON Dynamic Load in your situation?

Running an EON Dynamic Load Application

There are five requirements to run an EON Dynamic Load application:

1. An EON application (.eoz or .edz file) that uses the DynamicPrototype node or similar nodes.

2. Files, such as EON prototypes, textures, geometries, and movies, that can be dynamically loaded into the EON application.
3. A location, called the ***PrototypebaseURL***, where the required files are hosted. This can be a web server, a local server, or a user's local hard disk.
4. One of several types of EON Dynamic Load licenses that can be purchased from EON Reality, Inc.
5. A ***host application*** that can have an embedded EON application and the PrototypebaseURL property set. This is usually a web page run on a web browser, such as Internet Explorer or Mozilla Firefox, but it can be any ActiveX-compliant software, even EON Viewer.

Activity 9.3.1: Running a Simple Dynamic Load Application

As preparation for this activity, EON Reality has created prototypes (requirement 2), placed the prototypes on their web server at *http://download.eonreality.com/dynamicloadtutorial/* (requirement 3), and registered this PrototypebaseURL with their EON License server (requirement 4). Requirements 2, 3, and 4, which are described previously, have been met.

1. To open EON Viewer, click the Windows **Start** button and select **All Programs > EON Reality > EON Studio 6.0 > EON Viewer**. This will be our host application.
2. Choose **Options** from the Tools menu to display the Options dialog box.
3. Set the PrototypebaseURL to **http://download.eonreality.com/dynamicloadtutorial/**, as shown in Figure 9.3.1. Click **OK** to close the dialog box. This completes requirement 5.

FIGURE 9.3.1 PrototypebaseURL set in the Options dialog box

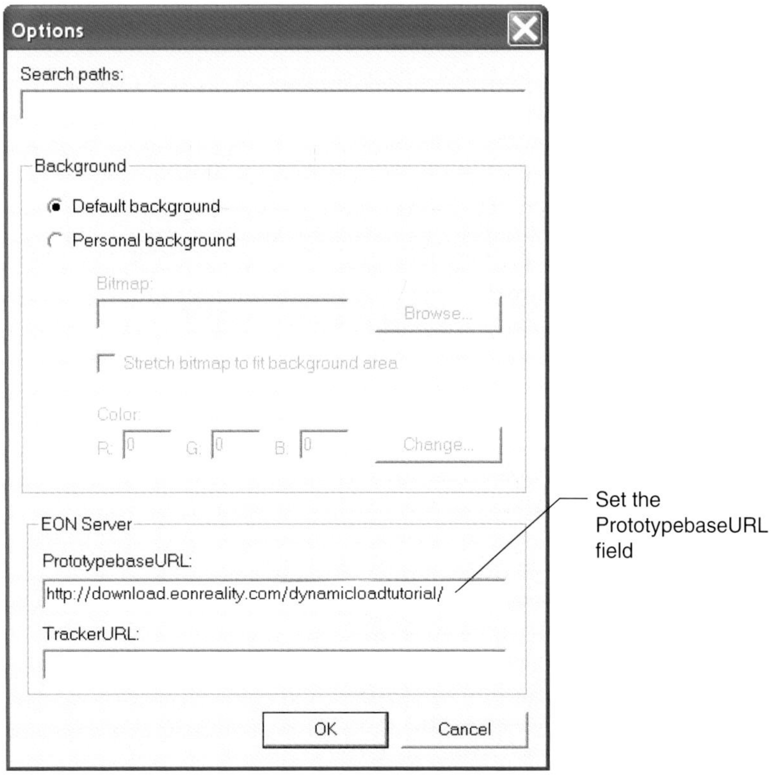

4. Using EON Viewer, open **Activity_9.3.1.edz** from the data files for Module 9 Lesson 3. The application will download the data file. This completes requirement 1. All five requirements described previously now have been met.

5. To download and display a prototype, click the green **Click to Download** button on the left. Select the **Choose a prototype** option and click **bookcase.eop**. Notice the custom download bar that appears. This download bar, displayed in Figure 9.3.2, was designed to appear only while a prototype is downloading, so you will not see it if you select the same prototype from the pop-up menu again because the prototype is stored in your Internet cache folder. When the download bar indicates that the download is complete or the prototype is loaded from your Internet cache folder, you will see the bookcase displayed.

FIGURE 9.3.2 Application is downloading a prototype

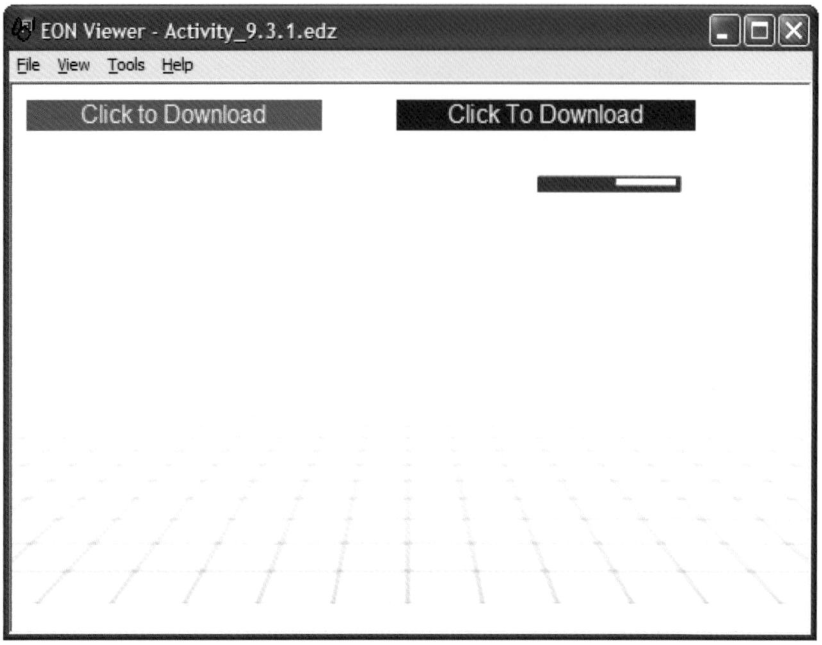

tips+tricks

After a prototype has been downloaded, it exists in your Internet Temporary Files folder, so the prototype will load very quickly when you select it again.

6. Zoom in and navigate as needed to see the bookcase more clearly, as shown in Figure 9.3.3.

FIGURE 9.3.3 Bookcase prototype displayed

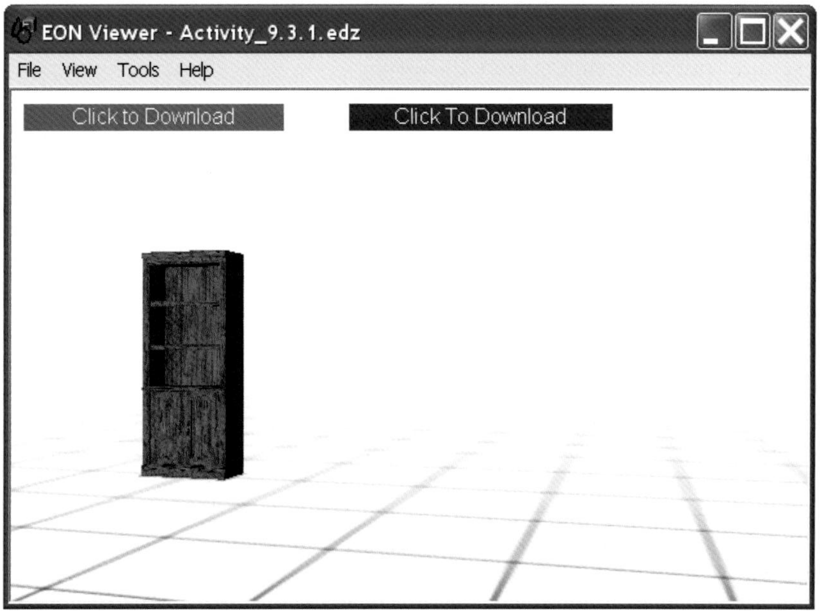

7. Close EON Viewer.

discuss

Compare the time needed to download the bookcase.eop file to the time needed to download a larger prototype.

Understanding Web-Based Dynamic Load Applications

Typically, EON Dynamic Load applications are web-based. To explain how they work, we will divide the discussion into authoring time—when the applications is being created—and runtime—when the application is being used.

Authoring Time

During authoring time, all components of the EON Dynamic Load application are created and placed on servers. The components are the dynamic objects, which include EON prototype files, texture files, product information texts, and an EON application embedded in an HTML page. The most important node in this EON application is the DynamicPrototype node, which will load any EON prototype dynamically.

cross-reference

We will discuss the DynamicPrototype node later in this lesson.

Runtime

When you enter an EON Dynamic Load–enabled website, an HTML page that includes an EonX window is opened. The objects on the web page, such as the text and buttons for the graphical user interface (GUI) and script to communicate with the EonX control, are downloaded first. Next, the EonX control downloads the premade EON application, which usually contains a 3D environment for displaying the 3D objects. This application also defines navigational behaviors.

When you select an object to display in 3D, a script in the web page will determine which prototype to load and sends an SFString event into the EON application. This event is routed to the DynamicPrototype node, which triggers it to download the prototype specified by the event.

When the download is complete, the DynamicPrototype node will delete any existing subtree beneath it and then dynamically create a new subtree that has the same content specified in the prototype file. This includes any meshes, textures, lights, and routes that were defined in the authoring stage.

Setting the PrototypebaseURL Property

The PrototypebaseURL property is an EonX property that identifies the location from which resources (primarily prototypes) are dynamically loaded. The location can be on the Internet or on your hard disk or local area network (LAN). If the resources are located on the Internet, then they must be accessible by the http: protocol (not ftp, https, or other protocols). The PrototypebaseURL is a base directory, and all resources that are dynamically loaded must reside in this base directory or in subdirectories below this base directory.

To ensure that prototypes and other resources are found by the EON Dynamic Load application, the path specified in the PrototypeName field of the Dynamic-Prototype node or the path specified in the Download field of the Mesh2, Texture2, or MovieTexture node must be relative to the PrototypebaseURL. Adding the path in these fields to the PrototypebaseURL will make an absolute path. See the following examples.

- http://www.mycompany.com/prototypes/
- http://download.eonreality.com/dynamicloadtutorial/
- C:\airnetplanner\prototypes\
- \\Worker\media\

Different host applications have different ways to set the PrototypebaseURL property. We will discuss the methods used to set this property in EON Studio, EON Viewer, and web pages.

EON Studio

While developing and testing your EON Dynamic Load application, you must set the PrototypebaseURL in EON Studio. Open the Options menu and choose Preferences to display the Preferences dialog box. Use this dialog box to set the PrototypebaseURL field as shown in Figure 9.3.4.

FIGURE 9.3.4 Preferences dialog box with PrototypebaseURL field

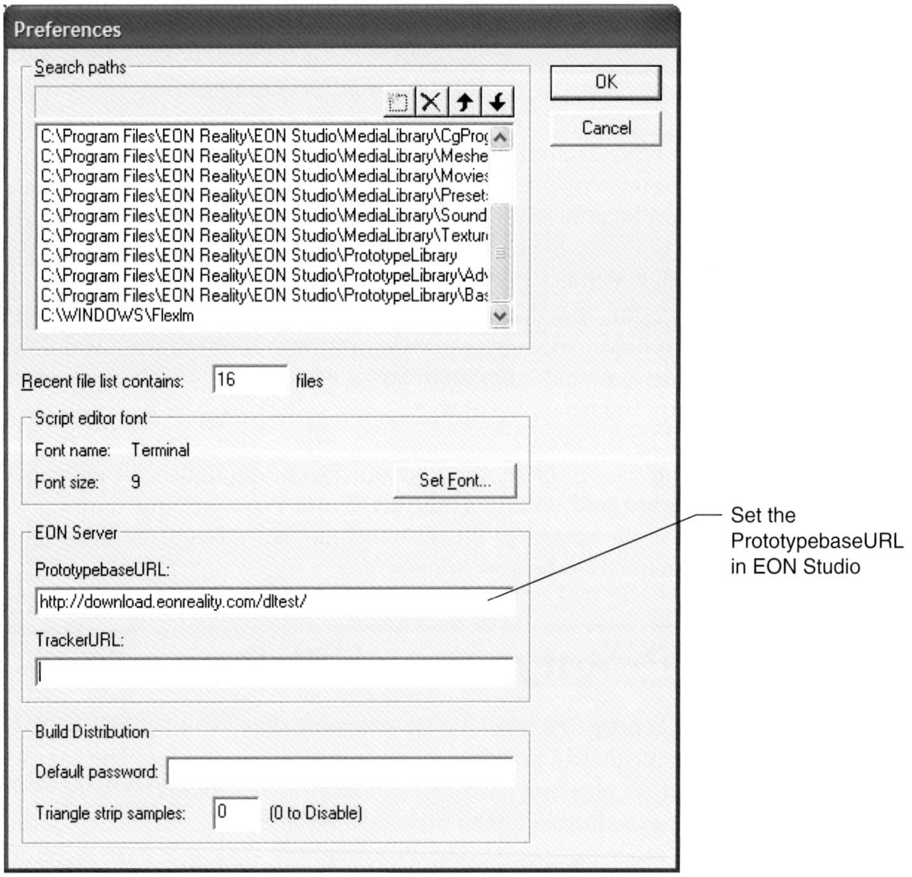

EON Viewer

To view the application in EON Viewer, you must set the PrototypebaseURL property. To set this property, close the simulation and then choose Options from the Tools menu. This displays the Options dialog box that enables you to set the PrototypebaseURL value, as shown in Figure 9.3.5.

FIGURE 9.3.5 Options dialog box in EON Viewer

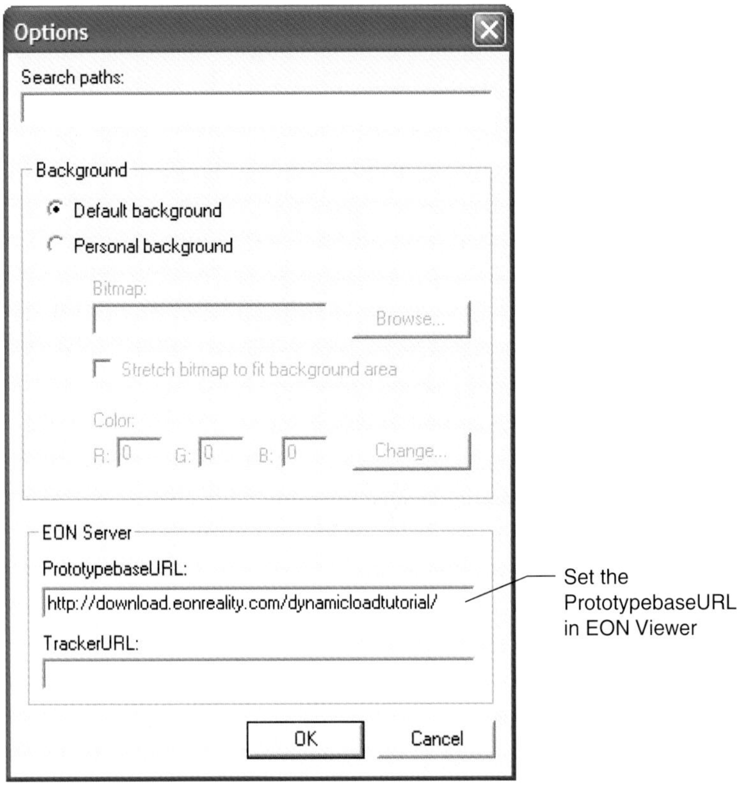

cross-reference

You will learn more about the EON Web Publisher Wizard in Module 11 Lesson 2. Editing the eonx_variables.js file is otherwise beyond the scope of this text.

Web Pages

The EON Web Publisher Wizard creates the eonx_variables.js file. This file contains several EonX variables, including eonxPrototypebaseURL, as shown in Figure 9.3.6. You can edit the variable in the eonx_variables.js file or set it in the web page before calling the EONInsert() function.

FIGURE 9.3.6 Extract of the eonx_variables.js file with the PrototypebaseURL selected

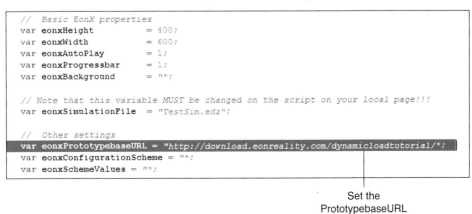

```
//  Basic EonX properties
var eonxHeight            = 400;
var eonxWidth             = 600;
var eonxAutoPlay          = 1;
var eonxProgressbar       = 1;
var eonxBackground        = "";

// Note that this variable MUST be changed on the script on your local page!!!
var eonxSimulationFile  = "TestSim.edz";

//  Other settings
var eonxPrototypebaseURL = "http://download.eonreality.com/dynamicloadtutorial/";
var eonxConfigurationScheme = "";
var eonxSchemeValues = "";
```

Set the PrototypebaseURL for a web page

Creating a Dynamic Load Application

Making an EON Dynamic Load application requires knowledge of the nodes that can download new resources, how to make the resource files (prototypes), and how to send events from host applications to the right nodes. We will discuss the Dynamic-Prototype node and nodes that download resources. Also, we will walk through creating an EON Dynamic Load application and using these nodes.

tips+tricks

The DynamicPrototype node will be disabled (it will not download or initialize) if it is under a hidden Frame node.

DynamicPrototype Node

The most important node in this type of EON application is the ***DynamicPrototype node*** that can download, load, unload, or swap any EON prototype during runtime (dynamically). This node has a PrototypeName field that holds the name of the prototype file to be downloaded and loaded. This field can be set during authoring time or it can be left empty and filled with a prototype filename during runtime. It is always possible to change the PrototypeName field during runtime. When the DownloadAutomatic and InitializeAutomatic fields are true, you only need to change the PrototypeName field to load a new prototype. If the DownloadAutomatic and InitializeAutomatic fields are false, then you must use the StartDownload and Start-Initialize inEvents to trigger download and initialization.

The PrototypeName field should include the path to the EON prototype relative to the PrototypebaseURL. For example, if the resource is at the absolute position of http://www.mycompany.com/prototypes/furniture/armchair1.eop and the PrototypebaseURL is http://www.mycompany.com/prototypes/, then the text sent to the PrototypeName field should be "furniture/armchair1.eop".

When the PrototypeName field is changed and the DownloadAutomatic field is true, then the prototype is downloaded to your Internet Explorer's cache folder. During download, the DynamicPrototype node can display progress by using the Downloaded outEvent (SFFloat), DownloadProgress outEvent (SFInt32 number between 0 and 100), and IsDownloading outEvent (SFBool). Use these values to show a download bar to the user.

After download, the next step is initializing, which is also called loading. If the InitializeAutomatic field is true, the prototype is loaded immediately when the download is complete. During loading, any existing prototype within the Dynamic-Prototype will be unloaded, and then the prototype is added as a subtree under the DynamicPrototype node. During this process, the EON application will pause and the progress bar will display a message that says "Loading Resource." The length of the pause depends on the file size of the prototype being loaded. When loading is complete, the prototype's objects are visible, and the IsRunning outEvent is set to true.

tips+tricks

You can use script to access nodes inside the DynamicPrototype node.

Triggering the UnInitialize inEvent unloads a prototype, which includes removing it from memory.

The "Loading Resource" message in the progress bar is not displayed in EON Studio.

troubleshooting

If you download prototypes that contain scripts, then the initialize() function in them is not triggered.

If you move nodes from a DynamicPrototype node to a new parent node, they may disappear and reappear because moved resources will be reloaded.

Activity 9.3.2: Creating a Dynamic Load Application

1. Open EON to start a new simulation. If EON is already open, select **New** from the File menu.
2. Select the **Camera** frame. In the Property Bar, set the Position to **0 -10 5**. Expand the **Orientation** field and set the Pitch value to **20**.
3. From the Useful Objects prototype library, add a **GridPlane2** prototype under the Scene frame and set its Position to **0 0 0**.
4. Add a **DynamicPrototype** node under the Scene frame.
5. Add a **2DText** node under the Scene frame and rename it **ChooseObject**. Set its Text field to **Choose an Object** and its TextAlignment field to **Center**.
6. Add a **PopupMenu** node under the Scene frame.

troubleshooting

Do not dynamically load a prototype that has an exported field if the field exported is already an exported field of a nested prototype.

7. Under the PopupMenu, add three **MenuItem** nodes and rename them **cabinet.eop**, **desk.eop**, and **office_chair1.eop**, respectively.
8. Display the **Routes** window. Drag the **ChooseObject** node, **PopupMenu** node, and **DynamicPrototype** node to the Routes window. Establish the connections outlined in the following table. Your Routes window should resemble Figure 9.3.7.

From	outEvent	To	inEvent
ChooseObject	OnButtonUp	PopupMenu	ShowPopupMenu
PopupMenu	SelectedMenuString	DynamicPrototype	PrototypeName

FIGURE 9.3.7 Routes window with the PopupMenu node added

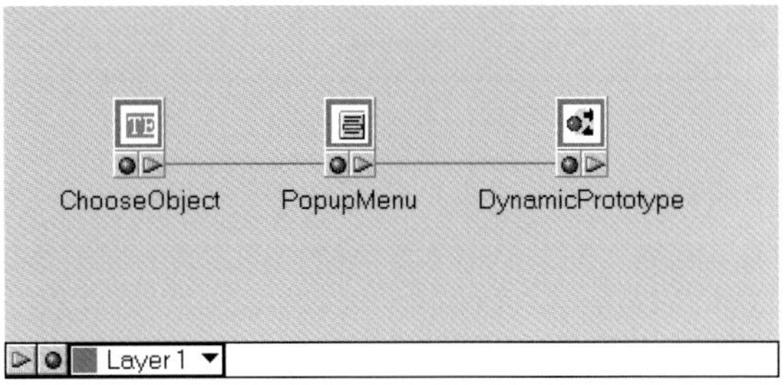

9. Save the simulation as **Dynamic_Load.eoz**.
10. Select **Preferences** from the Options menu to display the Preferences dialog box. In the PrototypebaseURL field, type **http://download.eonreality.com/dynamicloadtutorial/** as shown in Figure 9.3.8. Click **OK** to close the dialog box.

FIGURE 9.3.8 PrototypebaseURL set in the Preferences dialog box

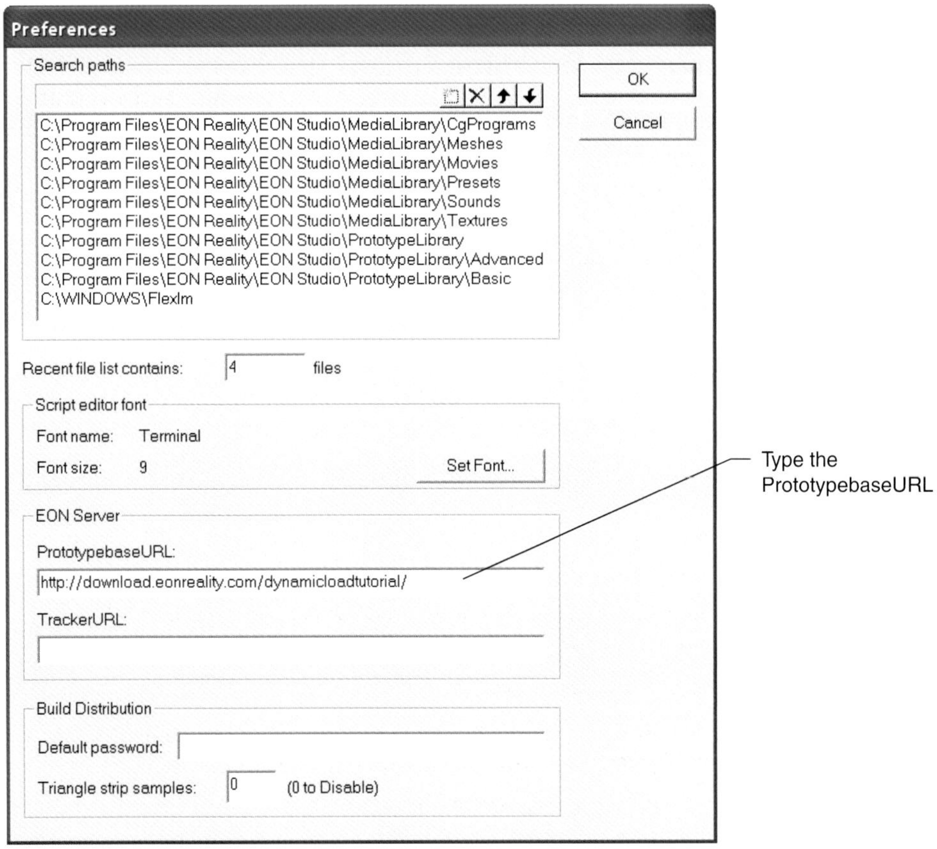

11. Save the simulation and then run the simulation. Click the **Choose Object** button and then select **cabinet.eop** from the list. The object is displayed in the center of the scene, as shown in Figure 9.3.9.

FIGURE 9.3.9 Downloaded prototype

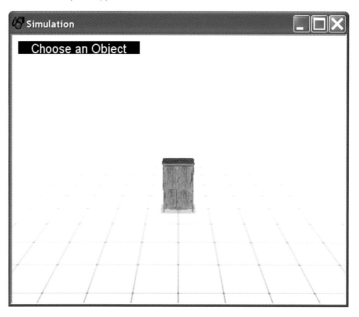

12. Close the simulation window. Close EON. You will download additional prototypes in later activities.

tips+tricks

The DownloadProgress field sends an integer between 0 and 100, which could be used to show a download progress bar.

The old Texture node also supports EON Dynamic Load by changing the value in its Filename field. It does not have the Download or DownloadProgress fields.

You can hide the progress bar by setting the EonX property named Progressbar to 0.

Nodes That Have the Download Field

Three other nodes support EON Dynamic Load: Texture2 node, Mesh2 node, and MovieTexture node. These nodes have fields named Download (SFString), Download-Progress (SFInt32 0-100) and Filename (SFString). During authoring time (design time), only the Filename field is set. During runtime, you can send a new resource name to the Download field to cause the resources to download and initialize. Like the DynamicPrototype node, the Download field must have a path that is relative to the PrototypebaseURL. Download and initialization are always automatic for these nodes. When download is complete, initialization begins. The EON application is paused and a progress bar displays the Loading Resource message. The length of the pause depends on the file size of the resource. When initialization is complete, the new resource becomes visible and the Filename field changes to reflect the new file that is running.

Activity 9.3.3: Dynamically Loading Textures

1. Open EON. Open **Activity_9.3.3** from the data files for Module 9 Lesson 3.
2. Save the simulation as **Dynamic_Textures.eoz**. Run the simulation. In this activity, you will dynamically load three photo textures and display them using the BPButton prototype. Currently, the BPButton prototype displays a default image in the simulation window.
3. Close the simulation window.
4. Expand **Scene > Camera**. Select **BPButton**. In the Property Bar, set the BoxPosition to **10 40** and set the BoxSize to **640 480**.
5. Under the Camera node, add a **Texture2** node.
6. To create a node reference, right-click the **Texture2** node and select **Copy as Link**. Paste it under **BPButton\Texture**.
7. From the DeveloperTools prototype library, add a **MultiTextSender** prototype under the Scene frame. In the Property Bar, set the Text07 field to **hillviews.jpg**. Set the Text08 field to **koala.jpg**. Set the Text09 field to **tasmania.jpg**.
8. To create a node reference, right-click the **Texture2** node and select **Copy as Link**. Paste it under **MultiTextSender\SendToNode**.
9. In the Property Bar, set the MultiTextSender prototype's SendToField field to **Download**.
10. From the Converters prototype library, add a **BooleanToIntegerConverter** prototype under the Scene frame. Your simulation tree should look like Figure 9.3.10.

FIGURE 9.3.10 Simulation tree with BooleanToIntegerConverter added

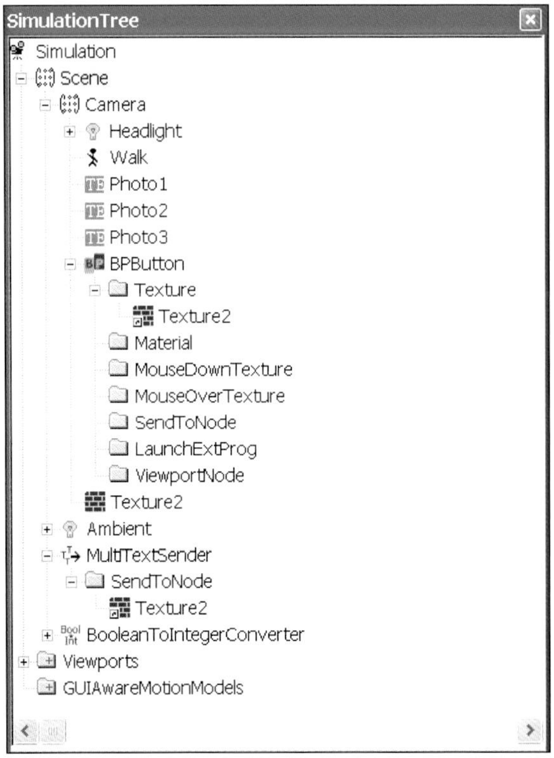

11. Display the **Routes** window. Drag the **BooleanToIntegerConverter** prototype to the Routes window. Establish the connections outlined in the following table. Your Routes window should resemble Figure 9.3.11.

From	outEvent	To	inEvent
Photo1	OnButtonUp	BooleanToIntegerConverter	B07
Photo2	OnButtonUp	BooleanToIntegerConverter	B08
Photo3	OnButtonUp	BooleanToIntegerConverter	B09

FIGURE 9.3.11 Routes window with BooleanToIntegerConverter prototype added

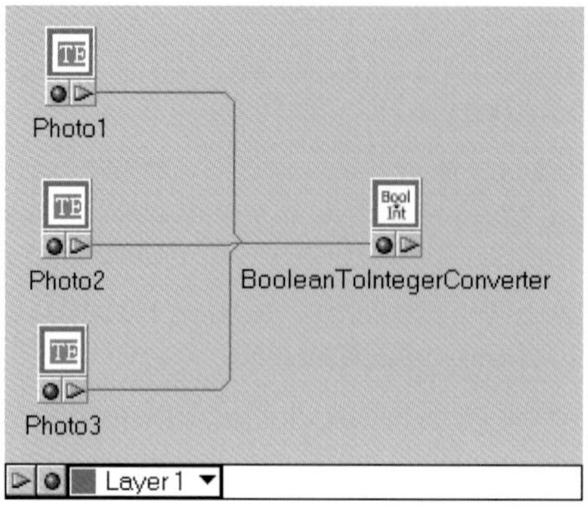

troubleshooting

The photos are located at the PrototypebaseURL, which is a web server address. You must have an Internet connection to download the photos.

12. To create a node reference, right-click the **MultiTextSender** node and select **Copy as Link**. Paste it under **BooleanToIntegerConverter\SendToNodes**.
13. Set the BooleanToIntegerConverter prototype's SendToField field to **SendTextNr**.
14. Save the simulation.
15. Select **Preferences** from the Options menu. Set the PrototypebaseURL to **http://download.eonreality.com/dynamicloadtutorial/** if necessary. Click **OK** to close the dialog box.
16. Run the simulation. Click the **Hill View** button at the top of the simulation window to load the photo. The simulation may pause briefly while the photo is downloading and loading. Your simulation window should look like Figure 9.3.12.

FIGURE 9.3.12 Hill View photo displayed in the simulation window

17. Click the remaining buttons to display the remaining photos.
18. Close the simulation window. Save the simulation and then close EON.

Adding Download Bars to Your Application

In the previous activity, you probably experienced some delay between the time you clicked a button and the appearance of the photo. This delay can be very confusing if you do not explain it to the user. The appearance of the progress or download bar instantly tells the user that the click had an effect and it will take time to see a result. In the following activity, you will add a download bar for the Dynamic_Load.eoz simulation you created in Activity 9.3.2.

Activity 9.3.4: Adding a Download Bar

1. Open EON. Open **Activity_9.3.4.eoz** from the data files for Module 9 Lesson 3. This data file is identical to the Dynamic_Load.eoz simulation file you created in Activity 9.3.2.
2. Save the simulation as **Add_Download_Bar.eoz**.
3. Under the Camera frame, add a new **Frame** node and rename it **DownloadBarFrame**. In the Property Bar, set its Position value to **0 1.2 0.4** and set its Scale value to **0.25 0.25 0.25**.
4. Under the DownloadBarFrame frame, add a **DownloadBar** prototype from the Useful Objects prototype library. Your simulation tree should look like Figure 9.3.13.

FIGURE 9.3.13 Simulation tree with the DownloadBar prototype added

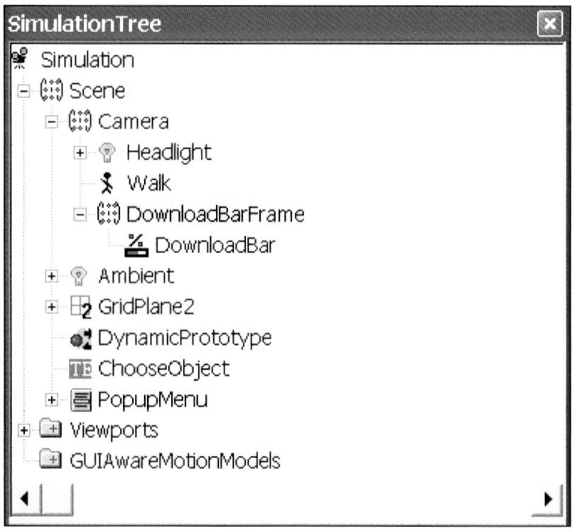

5. Display the **Routes** window. Drag the **DownloadBar** prototype to the Routes window. Establish the connections outlined in the following table. Your Routes window should resemble Figure 9.3.14.

From	outEvent	To	inEvent
DynamicPrototype	IsDownloading	DownloadBar	IsActive
DynamicPrototype	Downloaded	DownloadBar	Downloaded

FIGURE 9.3.14 Routes window with the DownloadBar prototype added

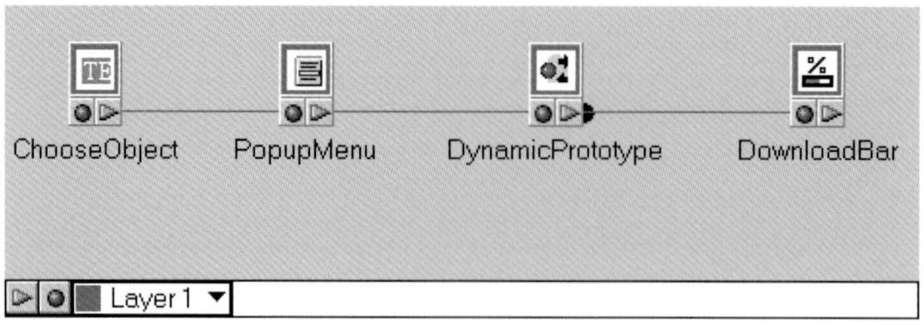

6. Save the simulation and then run the simulation.
7. Click the **Choose Object** button and then select **desk.eop** from the list. The object is displayed in the center of the scene, as shown in Figure 9.3.15.

FIGURE 9.3.15 Desk prototype displayed in the simulation window

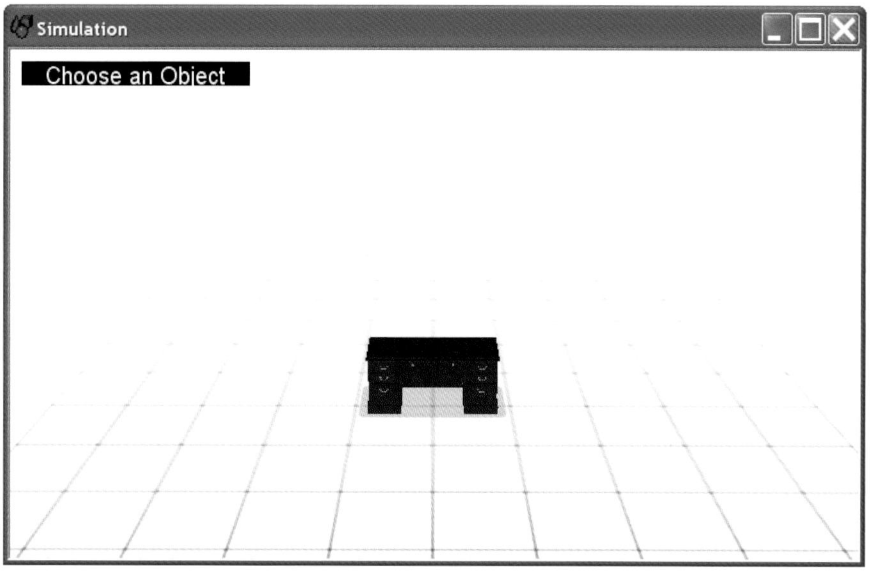

troubleshooting

If you do not see your download bar or if it does not appear to change, the prototype may have already been downloaded to your Internet cache folder or the prototype was downloaded too quickly to see the download bar.

8. Close the simulation window. Close EON. You will download the third prototype in the next activity.

In the previous activity, you used a prototype to add a download bar. In the following activity, you will start with the same Activity_9.3.4.eoz simulation file that you used in Activity 9.3.4. However, you will create a download bar instead of using the DownloadBar prototype.

Activity 9.3.5: Creating Your Own Download Bar

1. Open EON. Open **Activity_9.3.4.eoz** from the data files for Module 9 Lesson 3. This data file is identical to the Dynamic_Load.eoz simulation file you created in Activity 9.3.2.
2. Save the simulation as **Create_Download_Bar.eoz**.
3. Under the Camera frame, add a new **Frame** node and rename it **DownloadBarFrame**.
4. Under the DownloadBarFrame frame, add a **2DText** node and rename it **TextForeground**. In the Property Bar, set its BoxColor value to **0 0 1** (blue). Set the Text field to **Downloading...** and set the TextPosition to **5 0**. Set the BoxPosition to **10 40**. Set the BoxArea to **150 20**. Clear the **IsActive** check box, setting the value to false. Also clear the **UseHandCursor** check box. The Property Bar for the TextForeground node should look like Figure 9.3.16.

FIGURE 9.3.16 Property Bar for TextForeground node

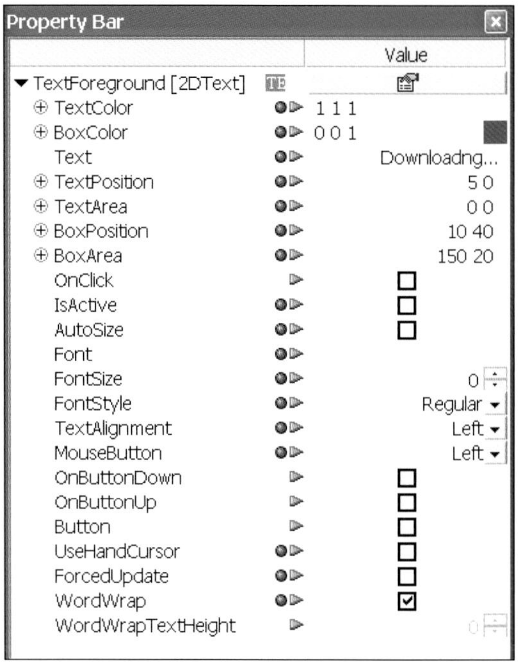

5. Right-click the **TextForeground** node and select the **Copy** option. Right-click the **DownloadBarFrame** node and select the **Paste** option. Rename the copy **TextBackground**. In the Property Bar, set the BoxColor value to **0 0 0** (black).
6. Add a **Multiplication** node under the DownloadBarFrame. In the Property Bar, place a check mark in the **AutoTrigger** check box, setting the field to true. Set the InitialValue2 field to **150**.
7. Add a **Converter** node under the DownloadBarFrame frame. Place a check mark in the **AutoTrigger** check box to set the field to true. Set the YIn field to **20**.

8. Display the **Routes** window. Drag the **Multiplication** node, **Converter** node, **TextForeground** node, and **TextBackground** node to the Routes window. Establish the connections outlined in the following table. Your Routes window should resemble Figure 9.3.17.

From	outEvent	To	inEvent
DynamicPrototype	Downloaded	Multiplication	InValue1
Multiplication	OutValue	Converter	Xin
Converter	2DVectorOut	TextForeground	BoxArea
DynamicPrototype	IsDownloading	TextForeground	IsActive
DynamicPrototype	IsDownloading	TextBackground	IsActive

FIGURE 9.3.17 Routes window with the connections for the download bar established

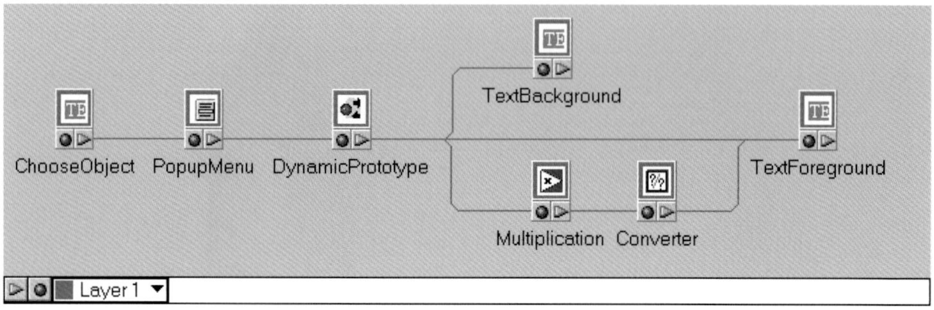

troubleshooting

Clearing your Internet cache removes your browser history (the websites you have visited), cookies (text files placed on your computer by web servers to identify you as a unique visitor), and passwords saved by the browser. Clearing your cache enables you to download a prototype a second time. If you do not clear your cache, the browser will display the prototype that is saved in the cache rather than downloading it again from the website.

9. Save the simulation.
10. Clear your **Temporary Internet Files** folder, often referred to as the Internet cache. To clear the Internet cache, open Internet Explorer and choose **Internet Options** from the Tools menu to display the Internet Options dialog box. On the General tab, click the **Delete** button under the Browsing history section to display the Delete Browsing History dialog box. Click the **Delete Files** button under the Tempory Internet Files section. Click **Yes** in the small Delete Files dialog box to confirm the deletion. The Delete Browsing History window is displayed while the files are deleted. Click the **Close** button to close the Delete Browsing History dialog box and then click **OK** to close the Internet Options dialog box.
11. Returning to EON Studio, select **Preferences** from the Options menu. Set the PrototypebaseURL to **http://download.eonreality.com/dynamicloadtutorial/** if necessary. Click **OK** to close the dialog box.
12. Save the simulation and then run the simulation.
13. Click the **Choose Object** button and then select **office_chair1.eop** from the list. When you choose an item to download, you should see the blue text grow and cover the black text while the object is downloading. The object is displayed in the center of the scene, as shown in Figure 9.3.18.

FIGURE 9.3.18 Desk prototype displayed in the simulation window

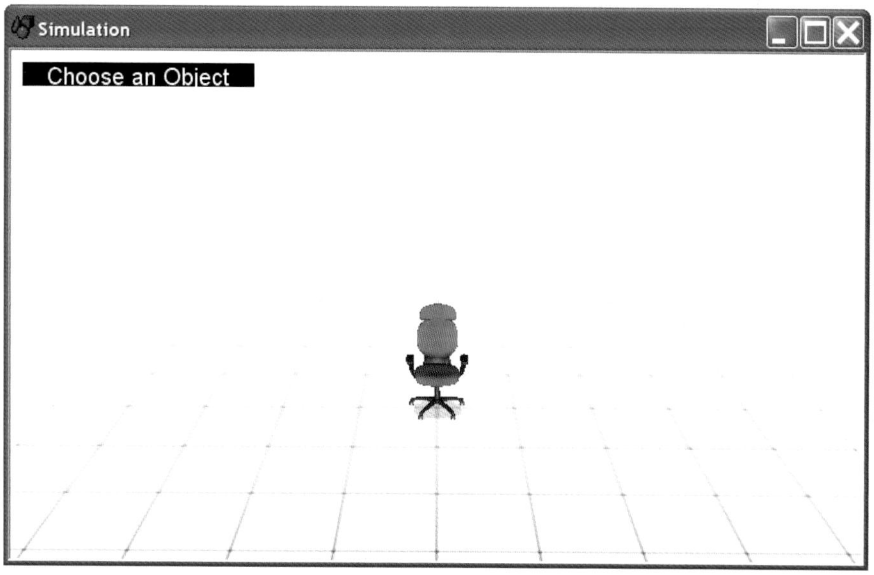

14. Display the two prototypes you downloaded in previous activities.

Discussion

discuss

Are the prototypes downloaded from the website or loaded from your Internet cache?

15. Close the simulation window. Close EON.

tips+tricks

Although it is possible to design functional prototypes that are dynamically loaded, it is not common because their file size is small and only a few instances are required.

tips+tricks

Place only one prototype in an .eop file. Although a prototype file (.eop file) is designed to contain several prototypes, this is not acceptable for prototypes that must be dynamically loaded. If you try to load a prototype, then only one of the possible prototypes would appear and you cannot control which prototype is displayed.

Configurable EON Dynamic Load Applications

To get the full benefit of EON Dynamic Load, the user should choose the resources that are downloaded and shown in the EON application. EON supports some GUI controls, such as text buttons and pop-up menus, that the user to choose a resource to download. However, it is more likely that a web page displays buttons and other GUI elements that control the EON application via script in the web page or the EON application.

Licenses for EON Dynamic Load

To access the significant benefits that the EON Dynamic Load function provides, you must purchase one of the several available types of ***EON Dynamic Load licenses*** from EON Reality, Inc. The available types of licensing methods include the EON Server license, a Dynamic Load Stand Alone license, and a licensed EDZ application.

troubleshooting

When the EON Dynamic Load function is not licensed, text banners are displayed in the simulation window at regular intervals (10 seconds off, 2 seconds on) in random position. The banners contain messages such as *Dynamic Load License missing* and *For Evaluation Purposes Only*. However, the EON Dynamic Load function will continue to work regardless of the licensing status so that you can develop and test EON Dynamic Load applications before they are published.

EON Server License

The ***EON Server license*** is a client-server–based solution for licensing the EON Dynamic Load function. You can obtain the EON Server license by registering the PrototypebaseURL used by the application with EON Reality, Inc. EON Reality's administrators add the PrototypebaseURL to a database on the EON server. When a user visits a web page that has an EON application and its PrototypebaseURL property is set, then the EonX control attempts to contact the EON server to verify that the value of the PrototypebaseURL is a registered site. If it is not registered, then the user will see text banners in the simulation window. If it is registered, then the EON server records that another session has been used against that PrototypebaseURL.

For this type of license, the user must have an Internet connection and the application owner must have a valid license that has a set number of sessions (e.g., 20,000) or unlimited sessions within a time frame (e.g., one year). A ***session*** is a start of an EON application, usually when the end user goes to a web page containing an EON application.

If you see text banners when using EON Dynamic Load with an EON Server license, check the following items:

- Is a PrototypebaseURL set for the EON application?
- Is the value of PrototypebaseURL registered with EON Reality, Inc. on the EON server?
- Are the resources to be downloaded located on the PrototypebaseURL?
- Does the license have remaining sessions or has your EON Server license expired?

Dynamic Load Stand Alone License

The ***Dynamic Load Stand Alone license*** is used for computers that stand alone—that is, they are not connected to the Internet. For this type of EON Dynamic Load application, a server is not contacted to verify a license and prototypes are not downloaded from a server. Instead, the resources are dynamically loaded from a local hard disk and the PrototypebaseURL property's value will be a path on the local computer or LAN.

To get a license, you will need to send the host ID of the computer to EON Reality, Inc. and request a Dynamic Load Stand Alone license. A ***host ID*** is a unique number and/or letters found in network cards or hard disk drives that can identify a specific computer. EON Reality will send you a text file named license.dat that must be placed on the computer in the C:\Windows\FlexLM folder. The license.dat file will contain a feature named DynamicLoadStandAlone and the host ID of the particular computer. Each license.dat file is unique and works only on one computer. After you install this license on your computer, it will work for all EON Dynamic Load applications you run on that computer.

This license will be suitable for running EON Dynamic Load applications on a laptop without an Internet connection. For example, this license enables traveling salespeople to use a configurator application to show merchandise to their customers without relying on the Internet.

Licensed EDZ Application

Another way to license EON Dynamic Load is to insert it into the EON application itself. Only EON Reality staff can do this. If you want a ***licensed EDZ application***, send your source EON application (.eoz file) to EON Reality so the staff can insert a license while building a distribution file (.edz format). After this file is created, it cannot be modified. The EDZ file format means that it cannot be opened in EON Studio for editing. A licensed EDZ application will work for all users and for EON Dynamic Load from a web server or local disk.

Choosing the Correct Type of License

Table 9.3.1 summarizes the differences among the license types. Use this information to select the correct type of license for your situation.

TABLE 9.3.1 Types of EON Dynamic Load Licenses

	EON Server License	Dynamic Load Stand Alone License	Licensed EDZ Application
Resources Download From	Internet	Local disk	Internet or local
Valid For	All users	Users of a single PC	All users
Implemented By	Register PrototypebaseURL on the EON server	Install license.dat file based on unique host ID	EON Reality staff inserts a license into the application

Summary

In this lesson you:

- Learned to understand EON Dynamic Load and its advantages.
- Learned where to set the PrototypebaseURL in host applications.
- Used the DynamicPrototype node to download prototypes from the Internet.
- Used the Download field of the Texture2 node to download photos from the Internet.
- Added a download bar to an EON Dynamic Load application.
- Created a simple download bar using 2DText nodes.
- Learned to understand the licensing requirements for EON Dynamic Load.

Simulation

Now that you have worked on several different projects at Contours Company, you are familiar with many of the nodes and prototypes available in EON. You have learned to adjust the properties of the nodes and prototypes to get the look and feel you want in your simulation. You have used routes to create exactly the simulation you and your client desire.

This core knowledge has helped you appreciate the EON prototypes when developing a simulation. You have learned to rely on the streamlined way in which many simulations can be created. However, as you continue to work on more projects that have become increasingly complicated, you have begun to encounter situations in which none of the existing EON nodes or prototypes, no matter how you combine and configure them, will produce the exact results that you need. For these problematic simulations, a co-worker suggested that you learn about using scripting in EON. At your request, your manager agreed to allot some time for you to learn more about scripting.

To improve your understanding of scripting and how it can be an asset in creating simulations, you will review the simulation on which you have been working. Then, you will use your new knowledge of scripting to enhance the simulation.

Job 9.1: Reviewing Your Simulation Storyboard

Storyboards are a dynamic component of any simulation. You have continually refined your storyboard as work progressed on the simulation. You have used the storyboard to plan and incorporate change requests and present new ideas to the client.

However, the recent knowledge you have gained about scripting will not directly affect what the client sees in the end product. Scripting affects the amount of time required to produce the simulation. Scripting enables you to do more with your simulation in less time.

With that in mind, review your simulation file and your storyboard to identify any locations where scripting might enable you to complete a series of actions in a simpler, more direct way. Use a unique symbol in your storyboard to identify the locations where scripting would be a more efficient method of achieving the desired result.

Discussion

discuss

Although it typically does not make sense to go back and write script for work that has already been completed, how can identifying the areas where you could have used scripting help you in the future?

What circumstances would make it beneficial to develop a script after the simulation has already been completed?

1. If possible, continue using the storyboard that you created in the Module 1 Simulation and enhanced in subsequent simulations. Review the storyboard to find any locations where a script might be utilized.
2. Choose a unique identifier or symbol to indicate locations where you could develop a script and mark the appropriate locations in your storyboard.
3. Save your storyboard and keep it open.
4. Open EON and open **Job_8.4.eoz**, the apartment file you enhanced in the Module 8 Simulation.

5. Search the simulation for areas where scripting might be used.
6. Take notes about any components of this simulation that could have been improved by scripts or any locations where a script would have reduced the necessary work.
7. Return to the storyboard. Close EON.
8. In the storyboard, use the unique identifier chosen in step 2 to indicate locations where you can use scripting.
9. Complete your storyboard using paper and pencil, a flowchart application, a drawing program, or any method you prefer, and then save the storyboard.

Job 9.2: Understanding Scripting

Although you have learned a lot about scripting in your recent work, you are aware that there is much more to learn. You have wondered how certain EON-supplied prototypes work and realize that most of them use scripting. Now you want to investigate how they use scripting to learn how to create your own scripts.

1. Open EON to start a new simulation. If EON is already open, select **New** from the File menu.
2. Choose a few prototypes that you have wondered about or prototypes that might be helpful for your simulation. Place the prototypes in your simulation tree.
3. Open each prototype, select the **Script** node in the prototype, and look at the field names. Then, open the **Script Editor** window and examine the script code.
4. Try to understand what the script is doing in each statement. When you encounter new statement structures, look in your scripting documentation to read about how they work.
5. To investigate a new statement structure further, create a test script in a new file that uses the script code structure that is new to you.
6. Examine which EON methods are commonly used in the script. Identify functions that could save time for you in simulations you develop in the future.
7. Close EON.

Job 9.3: Using Scripts

Your manager encourages employees to learn the software they are using thoroughly. This policy gives her a more knowledgeable team of designers who can apply creative solutions to any problems encountered.

Although the apartment simulation is already complete, you identified some areas where scripting could have been used instead of the nodes and routes in the simulation. Your manager would like you to use scripts to rework the simulation.

1. If necessary, open the storyboard and keep it on hand as you work.
2. If necessary, review what you have learned about scripting.
3. If necessary, open EON and **Job_8.4.eoz**, the current apartment simulation.
4. Create at least one script to simplify the apartment simulation.

Discussion

discuss

Can you think of any ways to use scripts to reduce the number of routes?

5. Use at least two scripts to add enhancements or features that did not exist in your simulation.
6. Run the simulation. Verify that the scripts are working as expected. Make any necessary corrections or adjustments.
7. Close the simulation window. Save the simulation as **Job_9.3.eoz** and then close EON.

Job 9.4: Using EON Dynamic Load

You recently learned about EON Dynamic Load. Now, you want to focus on using EON Dynamic Load to increase the flexibility of your apartment simulation. A house configurator is one of the suggested applications for EON Dynamic Load. You believe that the client would be enthusiastic about providing potential buyers with the ability to select different features, such as cabinets and appliances. With a few selections, a buyer could see the combined effect of many choices. This feature could reduce the number of changes your client has to make when finishing the apartment because a buyer may change his or her mind about original customization choices. The improved simulation will allow buyers to see how several different customization options will look before making a final choice.

1. Review the five requirements to run an EON Dynamic Load application.
2. Collect or create several 3D models of some type of appliance, such as a refrigerator or a stove. Make these models into prototypes. (This meets requirement 2.)
3. Store these prototypes in a location that can serve as a PrototypebaseURL. (This meets requirement 3.)
4. Verify that the PrototypebaseURL is registered with the EON License server. (This meets requirement 4.)
5. Create an EON distribution file that uses the DynamicPrototype node or similar nodes to download the prototypes you created or collected. Save the distribution file as **Job_9.4.edz**. (This meets requirement 1.)
6. View **Job_9.4.edz** in EON Viewer. (This meets requirement 5.)

Discussion

discuss

Do you want to challenge your skills? Modify the **Job_9.3.eoz** simulation file to use EON Dynamic Load to download the prototypes of appliance models. Use script to enable the user to display one of the models of the appliance in the correct location in the apartment.

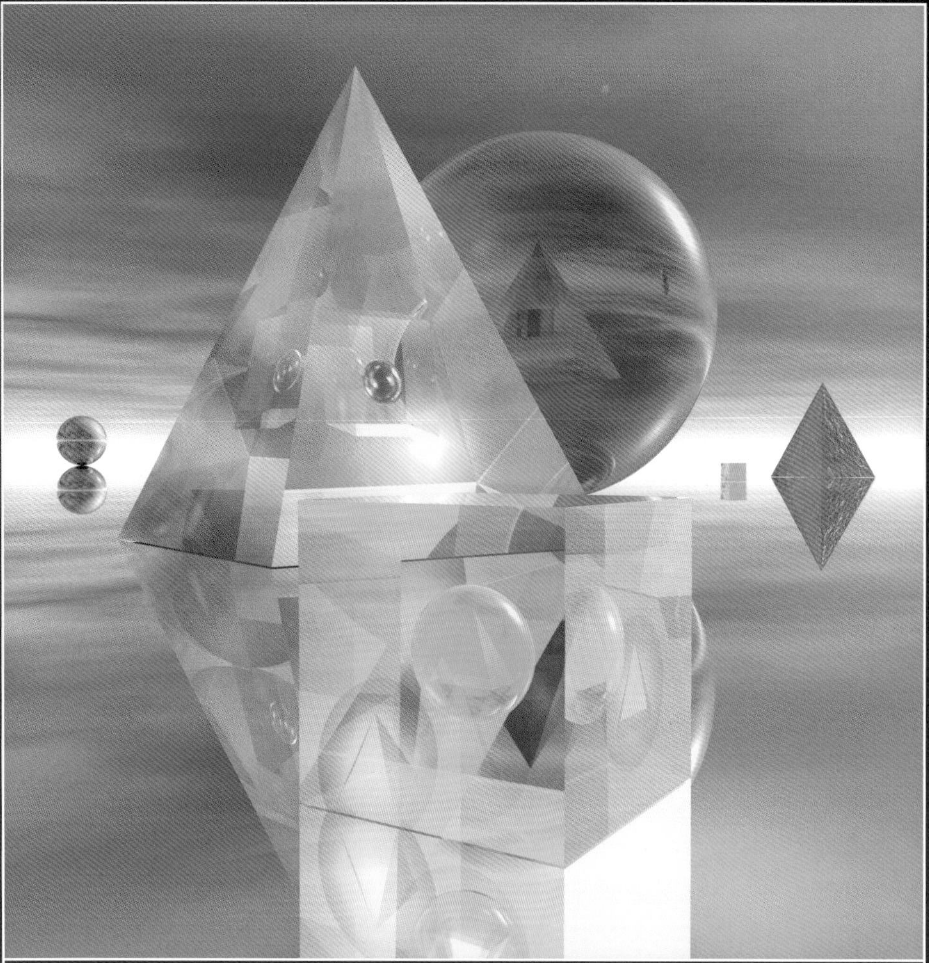

HARALD SUND

MODULE 10

Working with Advanced Nodes and Prototypes

LESSON 10.1
Creating User-Driven Simulations

LESSON 10.2
Data Manipulation

LESSON 10.1

Creating User-Driven Simulations

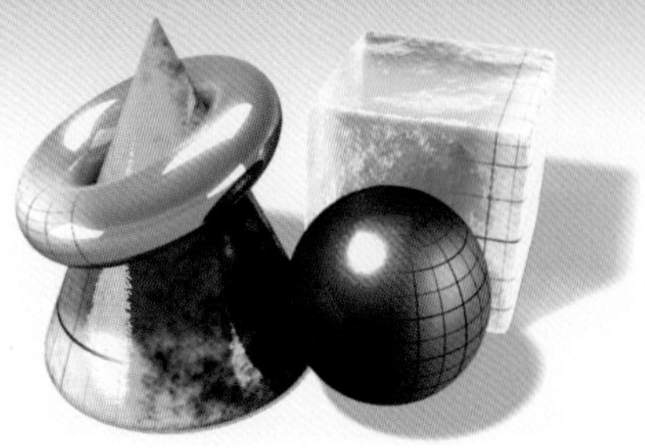

Objectives

In this lesson you will:

- Learn about creating user-driven simulations.
- Understand which nodes are used to control the responses or flow in a simulation.
- Become familiar with logic control nodes such as the And, Or, XOR, and Not nodes.
- Learn the basic rules common to nodes in the Flow Nodes library.
- Use nodes in the Flow Nodes library to create a simple user training exercise.

Key Terms

AfterParentTask node	***logic control nodes***	***task***
And node	***MemoryTask node***	***Task node***
Counter node	***Not node***	***toggle***
cycle	***Or node***	***Trigger node***
DelayTask node	***PowerSwitch node***	***user-driven simulation***
IterationTask node	***Sequence node***	***XOR node***
Latch node	***Switch node***	

Creating User-Driven Simulations

A ***user-driven simulation*** is an interactive simulation in which the user's actions and decisions determine the application's responses. As a simulation designer, you create the logic structures that enable and disable certain responses at different times. These logic structures are built in EON by adding nodes, creating routes, and setting field values. This lesson explores some of the nodes that can be used to create the logic structures you need to limit input and deliver responses.

If you want to create a complex interactive simulation, the Script node is the best solution. However, if you do not know scripting or your simulation responses follow a set sequence like a training course, your simulation would benefit from the structured logic system provided by the Flow Nodes library.

Long or complex interactive simulations use many routes, which makes it difficult to get an overview of the simulation flow. Nodes in the Flow Nodes library drastically reduce the number of routes required in the following ways:

- They limit the possible responses.
- They send events to nodes that have node references in the flow nodes' fields.
- They are arranged in sequence in the simulation tree.

Logic Control Nodes

Several nodes, shown in Figure 10.1.1, could be described as ***logic control nodes***. These nodes help you create logic structures, control the simulation flow, and activate other nodes when certain conditions are met. More detailed descriptions of these nodes follow.

FIGURE 10.1.1 Logic control nodes

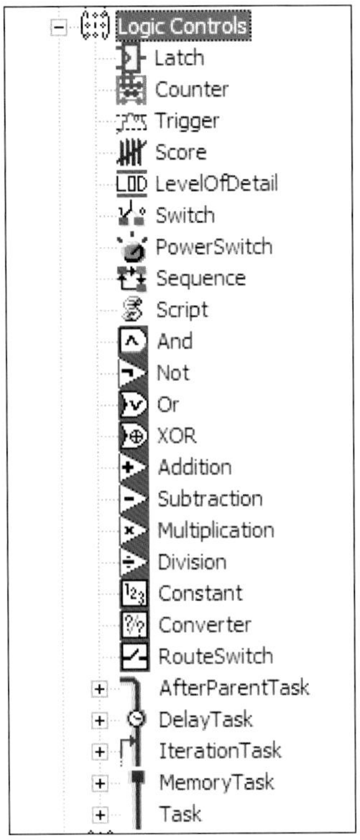

Counter Node

The ***Counter node*** triggers another node when its counter value reaches a specified value. It receives inEvents that increment and decrement the counter's value. The Counter node has upper and lower limits. When a limit is reached, it can stop at that limit or ***cycle***, which means to continue at the opposite limit.

Latch Node

The ***Latch node*** holds a Boolean value and receives inEvents to set its Boolean value to true, clear its value to false, or ***toggle*** its value. Toggling a value switches it between two values, such as swapping true to false or false to true. When the Latch node receives values, it sends Boolean outEvents that can be used to trigger other nodes.

PowerSwitch Node

The ***PowerSwitch node*** is a more versatile version of the Switch node (described in an upcoming section). It has extra inEvents so that you can trigger certain child nodes with Boolean inEvents instead of using the integer value inEvent. It also has the extra ActivateNone inEvent to hide all child node objects. It does not insist that only one object is visible when the simulation starts. However, when it receives an inEvent, it will ensure that only one object is visible. The Switch node does not ensure that only one object is displayed, so more than one object can be displayed if a different node makes it visible. Finally, while the Switch node can have only Frame nodes under it, the PowerSwitch node accepts all nodes.

Sequence Node

A ***Sequence node*** activates one of its children in a predetermined sequence at specified intervals. The sequence can be used to implement special effects, such as flashing lights.

Switch Node

The ***Switch node*** is used to switch among children in a subtree. For example, if one of a node's two children is visible and the other is not, changing the value of the Switch node hides the visible child and displays the other child. Many objects can appear under a Switch node, and the Switch node will ensure that only one object is visible at a time. You can send a value to the Switch node to tell it which object to display.

Trigger Node

The ***Trigger node*** signals when a value is outside a specified interval. When the value is changed, the node will compare the changed value with the specified interval and send events accordingly.

Activity 10.1.1: Using a Sequence Node

1. Open EON. Open **Activity_10.1.1.eoz** from the data files for Module 10 Lesson 1.
2. Save the simulation as **Sequence.eoz**.
3. Run the simulation to view the scene and then close the simulation window.
4. Under the Scene frame, add a **Sequence** node.
5. Expand the **Scene** frame if necessary. Move the **Cone**, **Cylinder**, **Cube**, and **Teapot** frames under the new Sequence node, in order as listed here.
6. Under the Scene frame, add a **KeyboardSensor** node and rename it **Key1_StartSequence**.
7. Double-click the **Key1_StartSequence** node to display the KeyboardSensor Properties dialog box. In the Virtual key name field, select **VK_1** from the drop-down menu and ensure that Enabled is selected (see Figure 10.1.2). Click **OK** to close the dialog box.

FIGURE 10.1.2 KeyboardSensor Properties dialog box

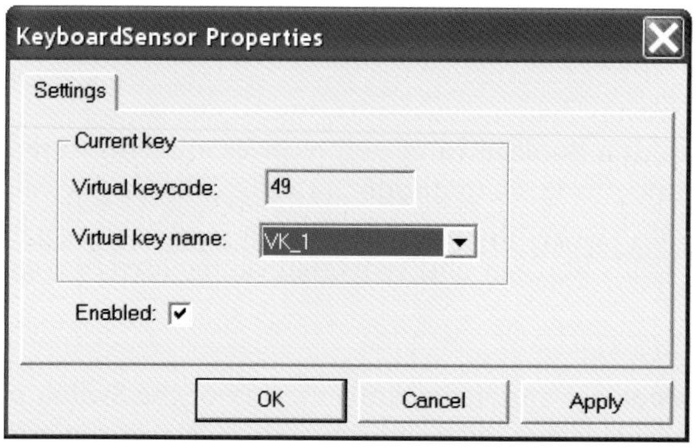

8. Display the **Routes** window. Drag the **Key1_StartSequence** node and the **Sequence** node to the Routes window. Establish the connection outlined in the following table.

From	outEvent	To	inEvent
Key1_StartSequence	OnKeyDown	Sequence	SetRun

9. Click the **Sequence** node in the simulation tree to view the node's properties in the Property Bar. Check to make sure that your settings match those shown in Figure 10.1.3.

FIGURE 10.1.3 Sequence node Property Bar

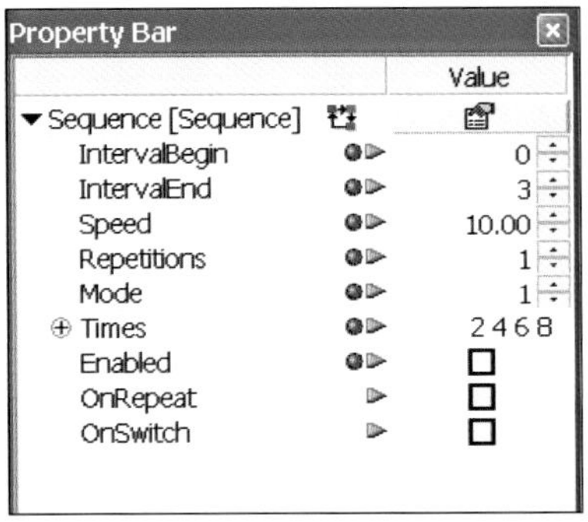

10. Run the simulation. Press the **1** key on your keyboard. Notice the sequence of the objects as they appear in the simulation window.
11. Close the simulation window. Save the simulation and keep it open to use in Activity 10.1.2.

When you run the simulation and press the 1 key, the four objects in the scene (cone, cylinder, cube, and teapot) are sequentially displayed. In the following activity, you will add a Counter node to stop the sequential display after it is repeated three times. The Counter node will then trigger the presentation of a 2DText node in the scene.

Activity 10.1.2: Adding a Counter Node

1. Continue working with the open simulation file **Sequence.eoz** from Activity 10.1.1.
2. Save the simulation as **Counter.eoz**.
3. Under the Scene frame, add a **Counter** node and a **2DText** node. Rename the 2DText node **SequenceRan3Times**.
4. Click the **SequenceRan3Times** node to display its properties in the Property Bar. In the Text field, click the word **Place** and type **Congratulations the Sequence Ran 3 Times**. In the BoxArea field, click **200** and type **300** to increase the size of the text box.

5. Clear the **IsActive** check box if necessary (see Figure 10.1.4).

FIGURE 10.1.4 SequenceRan3Times node Property Bar

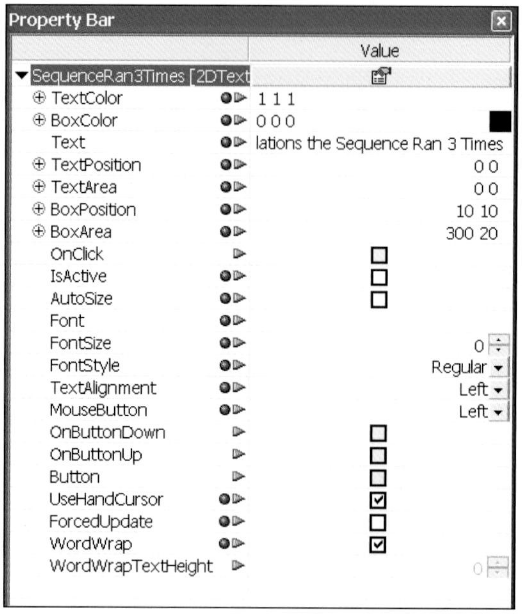

Discussion

discuss

Why should you clear the IsActive check box?

6. Display the **Routes** window if necessary. Drag the **Counter** node and the **SequenceRan3Times** node to the Routes window. Establish the connections outlined in the following table.

From	outEvent	To	inEvent
Sequence	OnRunFalse	Counter	Increment
Counter	OnIntervalEnd	SequenceRan3Times	SetRun

7. In the Simulation Tree window, double-click **Counter**. Set the values in the Counter Properties dialog box to match those shown in Figure 10.1.5. Click **OK** to close the dialog box.

FIGURE 10.1.5 Counter Properties dialog box

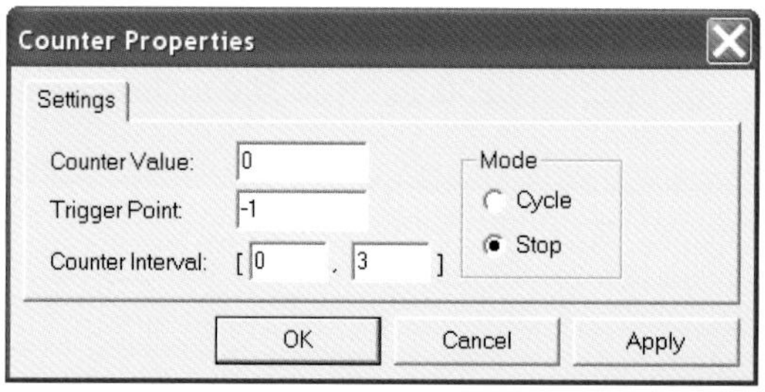

8. Run the simulation. Press the **1** key on your keyboard to start displaying the sequence of shapes.
9. After the teapot appears, press the **1** key.
10. Repeat step 8. After the third sequence has completed, notice the text that appears in the upper-left portion of the simulation window.
11. Close the simulation window. Save the simulation and then close EON.

troubleshooting

Move the simulation window if necessary to see the Simulation Tree window and the Property Bar while the simulation is running. Select the Counter node in the simulation tree and observe its Value field in the Property Bar. The number in the Value field will increase by one each time the sequence is completed.

And, Or, XOR, and Not Nodes

The And, Or, XOR, and Not nodes allow you to perform logic operations in an EON application.

tips+tricks

The And, Or, XOR, and Not nodes do not have any editable properties.

And Node

The ***And node*** compares two Boolean inEvents and sends a Boolean outEvent. The value of the outEvent will be true only if both inEvents are true. Table 10.1.1 displays how the value of the outEvent depends on the values of the two inEvents.

TABLE 10.1.1 And Node Values

InValue1	InValue2	OutValue
True	True	True
True	False	False
False	True	False
False	False	False

Or Node

The ***Or node*** compares two Boolean inEvents and sends a Boolean outEvent. If any inEvents are true, the value of the outEvent will be true. Table 10.1.2 displays how the value of the outEvent depends on the values of the two inEvents.

TABLE 10.1.2 Or Node Values

InValue1	InValue2	OutValue
True	True	True
True	False	True
False	True	True
False	False	False

XOR Node

The ***XOR node*** compares two Boolean inEvents and sends a Boolean outEvent. If the two inEvents have different values, the value of the outEvent will be true. Table 10.1.3 displays how the value of the outEvent depends on the values of the two inEvents.

TABLE 10.1.3 XOR Node Values

InValue1	InValue2	OutValue
True	True	False
True	False	True
False	True	True
False	False	False

Not Node

The ***Not node*** inverts a Boolean inEvent. If the inEvent is true, the value of the out-Event will be false, and the other way round.

Activity 10.1.3: Using the And, Or, XOR, and Not Nodes

1. Open EON. Open **Activity_10.1.3.eoz** from the data files for Module 10 Lesson 1.
2. Save the simulation as **Logic.eoz**.
3. Run the simulation to view the scene and then close the simulation window.
4. Under the Scene frame, add a **Frame** node and rename the node **Logic**.
5. Under the Logic frame, add a **Not** node and a **2DText** node. Change the name of the 2DText node to **CubeNotSpinning**.
6. In the Property Bar, set the Text field of the CubeNotSpinning node to **Cube is NOT Spinning!** (see Figure 10.1.6).

FIGURE 10.1.6 CubeNotSpinning Property Bar

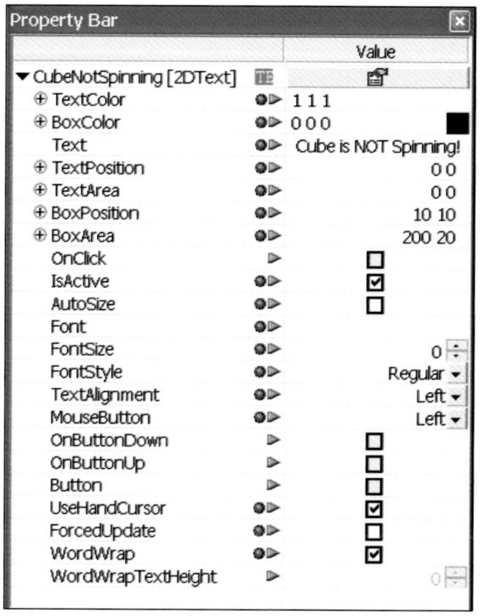

7. Display the **Routes** window. Drag the **Not** and **CubeNotSpinning** nodes to the Routes window. Establish the connections outlined in the following table.

From	outEvent	To	inEvent
Rotate_Cube	OnRunChanged	Not	InValue
Not	OutValue	CubeNotSpinning	IsActive

8. Run the simulation and notice the message that appears. Click the **cube** to start it spinning and notice that the message disappears from the simulation window.
9. Close the simulation window.
10. Under the Logic frame, add an **XOR** node and a **2DText** node. Change the name of the 2DText node to **OnlyOneObjectSpinning**.
11. In the Property Bar, set the Text field of the OnlyOneObjectSpinning node to **Only One Object Spinning**. Set the BoxPosition field to **10 30** and clear the **IsActive** check box (see Figure 10.1.7).

FIGURE 10.1.7 OnlyOneObjectSpinning Property Bar

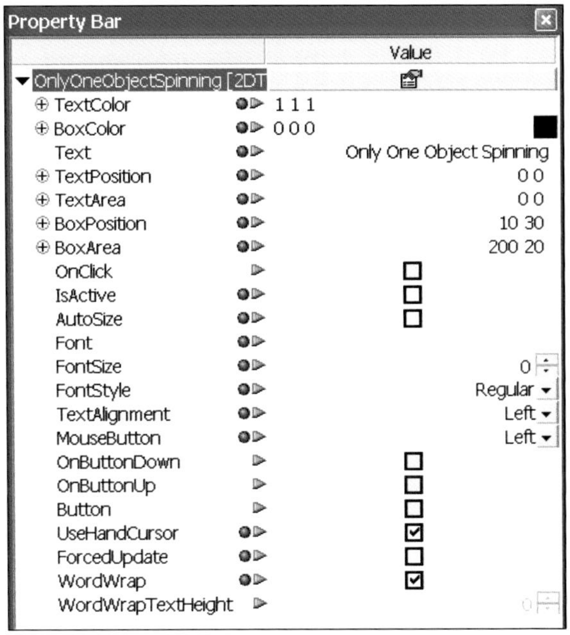

12. Display the **Routes** window. Drag the **XOR** and **OnlyOneObjectSpinning** nodes to the Routes window. Establish the connections outlined in the following table.

From	outEvent	To	inEvent
Rotate_Cube	OnRunChanged	XOR	InValue1
Rotate_Pyramid	OnRunChanged	XOR	InValue2
XOR	OutValue	OnlyOneObjectSpinning	IsActive

13. Run the simulation. Click the **cube** and notice the message that appears.
14. Close the simulation window.
15. Under the Logic frame, add an **And** node and a **2DText** node. Change the name of the 2DText node to **BothObjectsSpinning**. In the Property Bar, set the Text field to **Both Objects Spinning**. Set the BoxPosition field to **10 50** and clear the **IsActive** check box (see Figure 10.1.8).

FIGURE 10.1.8 BothObjectsSpinning Property Bar

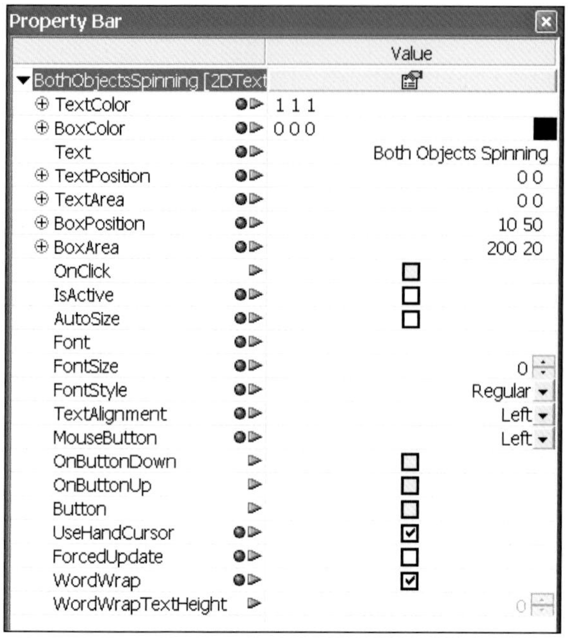

16. Display the **Routes** window. Drag the **And** and **BothObjectsSpinning** nodes to the Routes window. Establish the connections outlined in the following table.

From	outEvent	To	inEvent
Rotate_Cube	OnRunChanged	And	InValue1
Rotate_Pyramid	OnRunChanged	And	InValue2
And	OutValue	BothObjectsSpinning	IsActive

17. Run the simulation. Click the **cube**, then click the **pyramid** and notice the message that appears.
18. Close the simulation window.
19. Under the Logic frame, add an **Or** node.
20. Display the **Routes** window. Drag the **Or** node and the **LightFrame** frame to the Routes window. Establish the connections outlined in the following table.

From	outEvent	To	inEvent
Rotate_Cube	OnRunChanged	Or	InValue1
Rotate_Pyramid	OnRunChanged	Or	InValue2
Or	OutValue	LightFrame	SetRun

21. Run the simulation. Click the **cube** or the **pyramid** and notice the spotlight that appears on the object.
22. Close the simulation window. Save the simulation and then close EON.

Flow Nodes

When dealing with large EON projects that have a lot of interactivity, the Routes window can become very complex. When the Routes window has many tightly connected nodes, it becomes difficult to see an overall picture of the simulation's flow. This makes it difficult to correct errors or make changes to the simulation. Traditionally, large EON projects have been developed with the aid of script or an external application to control the flow of events in the simulation, but the Flow nodes offer an alternative. Flow nodes greatly simplify certain types of EON simulation development, such as training applications.

cross-reference

You will learn more about scripting in Module 9.

As the name suggests, Flow nodes are used to ensure that tasks are completed in a specific sequence. Each one of the Flow nodes are individually called ***tasks.*** The general idea is that only one task can be done at a time. When one task is completed, the next task is started.

tips+tricks

The basic rule for all Flow nodes: a task cannot be completed if it has not been started.

For example, one task could be that the user must click a door. To complete this task, we set up a route between a ClickSensor on the door and the Flow node so that the OnButtonDownTrue outEvent is connected to the Flow node's RequestCompleted inEvent. If the flow has not reached this particular Flow node yet, then the RequestCompleted inEvent is ignored. But if the Flow node had been started, then the RequestCompleted inEvent would have succeeded, and the next Flow node would be started automatically. Most likely, the next Flow node would trigger a Place node to open the door.

One of the main advantages of using Flow nodes is the total overview of the simulation flow that they provide. Flow nodes can be arranged hierarchically so that larger tasks can be divided into many smaller tasks. The depth of the simulation tree is unlimited for these nodes. When a Flow node is started, the flow moves to the first child task. When all child tasks have completed, the parent task is completed. The part of the simulation tree consisting of Flow nodes bears a close resemblance to a flowchart or a table of contents. The application designer should rename the Flow nodes to reflect the task that needs to be completed. Some of the higher levels of the Flow node hierarchy can be used to group lower levels of tasks, as shown in Figure 10.1.9.

FIGURE 10.1.9 Sample Flow node hierarchy

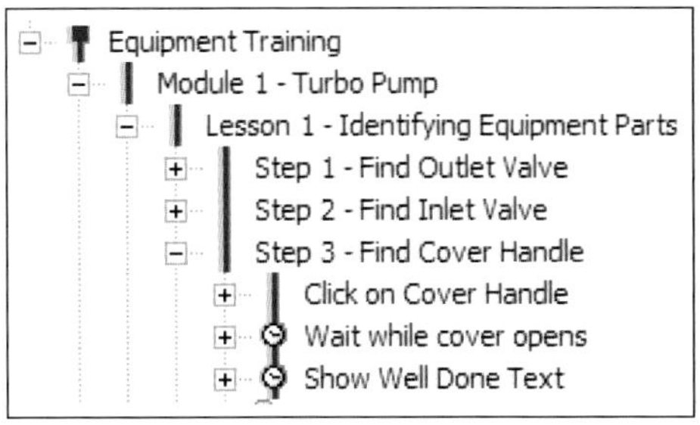

Another advantage of using Flow nodes is the reduction of routes. It is important to understand how Flow nodes continue the simulation's flow automatically. You do not require routes between Flow nodes to start the next task when the previous task is completed. Because Flow nodes are not hard-wired with routes, you can change the flow and redesign your application by moving a few nodes in the simulation tree.

You also can reduce the use of the Routes window by using the four fields that appear as four folders under each Flow node, as shown in Figure 10.1.10.

FIGURE 10.1.10 Fields in a Flow node

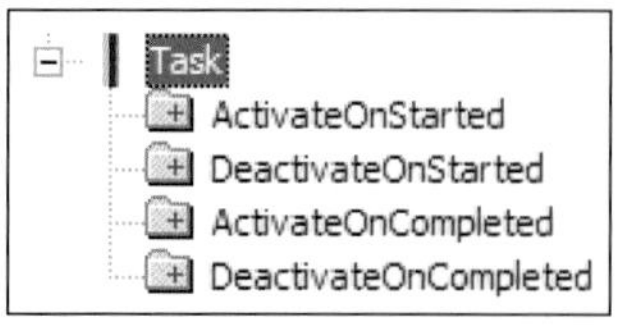

All Flow nodes can activate or deactivate an unlimited number of nodes when tasks are Started or Completed, as shown in Figure 10.1.11. Place node references to the nodes you would like to activate or deactivate in the appropriate folder under the relevant task. Activate means that it sends True to the SetRun field. Deactivate means that it sends False to the SetRun field. This means that routes are not needed between the Started field in a Flow node and the SetRun field in other nodes.

FIGURE 10.1.11 Multiple node references in a Flow node

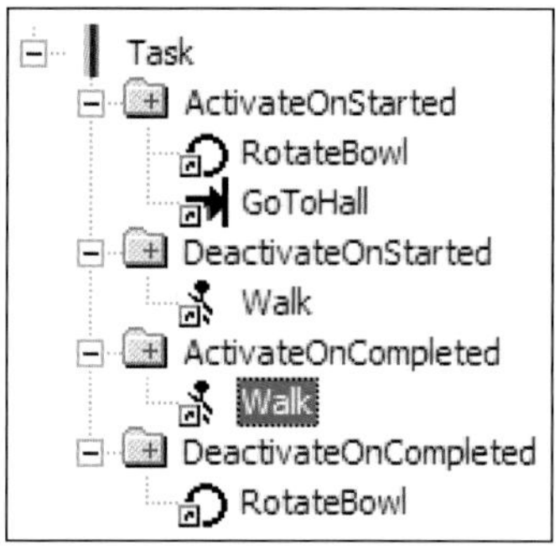

Flow Node Basics

EON has five different Flow nodes, which are described in Table 10.1.4. Although it would be possible to use only the Task node, the extra four nodes perform one extra automatic function each, which reduces the need for manually connecting routes between other nodes and the Task node.

TABLE 10.1.4 Flow Nodes

Flow Node	Description	Icon
AfterParentTask node	The ***AfterParentTask node*** starts when the parent task has been completed. It is used for selecting paths (comparable to an IF statement in a programming language) or to divide the flow into two or more paths. This enables control of nonlinear simulation flow.	
DelayTask node	The ***DelayTask node*** starts when either its parent task or the task directly above it is completed. The DelayTask node can be used as a task that waits for an event to occur or for grouping several child tasks. The only difference between this node and the Task node is that the DelayTask node registers itself as completed a set number of seconds after it starts. This node is ideal for tasks that take a certain amount of time to perform, or for restricting the maximum time allocated for the completion of child tasks.	
IterationTask node	The ***IterationTask node*** starts when either its parent task or the task directly above it is completed. This node repeats its child tasks a fixed number of times (comparable to a FOR loop in a programming language). Iteration can be stopped at any time by using the RequestCompleted event. If an infinite number of repetitions are required, set the Iterations field to –1.	
MemoryTask node	The ***MemoryTask node*** always starts automatically. Although the MemoryTask node can be used simply as the task starting the simulation flow (by placing the MemoryTask at the top of a task sub-branch), its intended use is to store important states (comparable to global variables in a programming language). Because the MemoryTask node is always started, it will always be sensitive to RequestCompleted events.	
Task node	The ***Task node*** starts when either the task of its parent node or the task of the node directly above it is completed. The Task node can be used for a task that waits for an event to occur, as well as for grouping several child tasks.	

Each Flow node has a RequestStart and RequestCompleted inEvent. The term *Request* in the field name implies that you cannot always force a task to start or complete. The result of the request depends on the state of the task as shown by its IsStarted and IsCompleted fields.

All Flow nodes have three states or modes:

- Reset: (IsStarted = false, IsCompleted=false)
- Started: (IsStarted = true, IsCompleted=false)
- Completed: (IsStarted = true, IsCompleted=true)

At any point during simulation runtime, you can monitor the status of each task to determine how far the simulation has advanced, which tasks have been completed, and which tasks remain. To check the status, select a Flow node and look at the IsStarted and IsCompleted check boxes in the Property Bar. This provides an efficient method for debugging the simulation.

tips+tricks

All Flow nodes must change state in sequence, changing from Reset to Started and then changing from Started to Completed. However, all Flow nodes can be Reset at any time.

Automatically Changing a Flow Node's State

The following rules govern how Flow nodes change their state automatically, without using routes. The first five rules apply to all Flow nodes. The last four rules apply to the Flow node specified in the rule.

1. All tasks are set to Reset when the simulation starts.
2. A task is set to Started when it is the first child of a parent task that is set to Started.
3. A task is set to Started when the sibling task above it is set to Completed AND the parent task above it is set to Started.
4. A task is set to Completed when ALL its child tasks are set to Completed.

tips+tricks

Manually changing the state of one Flow node can trigger the state of other Flow nodes to change automatically.

tips+tricks

In the IterationTask node, the child tasks will only be completed once if the Iterations field is 0. You can use a Counter node and increment the counter when the last child task is Completed. When the Counter reaches its trigger value, it should send the RequestCompleted event to the IterationTask node.

5. A task is set to Reset when a parent task or higher is set to Reset.
6. The MemoryTask is set to Started immediately after it is set to Reset.
7. The AfterParentTask is set to Started when its parent task is set to Started even if it is NOT the first child.
8. The DelayTask is set to Completed a certain number of seconds after it is set to Started.
9. The IterationTask is set to Reset when all its child tasks are set to Completed OR it is set to Completed when all its child tasks have been set to Completed a certain number of times.

Manually Changing a Flow Node's State

You can change the state of a Flow node manually by using routes. If a Flow node's state is changed manually, it will perform the same actions it would perform if its state was changed automatically. Use the following routes to change a Flow node's state manually.

- Reset a task by sending false to the RequestStart inEvent at any time.
- Start a task by sending true to the RequestStart inEvent when in the Reset state.
- Complete a task by sending true or false to the RequestCompleted inEvent when in the Started state.

tips+tricks

The most common mistake users make when using Flow nodes is that they fail to remember the second part of rule 3: A task is set to Started when the sibling task above it is set to Completed AND the parent task above it is set to Started.

Therefore, do not start with a MemoryTask node followed by a sibling task under it. The flow cannot continue automatically from one task to the next sibling task because they do not have a parent task above them. Instead, the next task should be the first child of the MemoryTask node.

Using the Flow Nodes

Generally, the only routes we connect to Flow nodes are connected to the Request-Completed inEvent when users perform an action. Usually, we do not need to use routes to the RequestStart inEvent because we rely on the flow (or automatic behavior) to start a Flow node.

The MemoryTask node has two main functions. The first function, as its icon implies, is to start the flow. The MemoryTask node starts automatically when it is reset. Because all tasks are set to Reset at the start of the simulation, the node is always set to Started. You will not need to start the flow manually if you use the MemoryTask node. Place the next task as a child node to the MemoryTask node because flow can only continue if Started parent tasks exist.

The second function of the MemoryTask node is to remember what has been done until a later time. Because the MemoryTask nodes are always set to Started, they are always sensitive to RequestCompleted inEvents. Therefore, if you place a MemoryTask node as a child task to a parent task, then it is set to Started even if its parent is not set to Started. A user could complete this task at any time; however, if its parent is not set to Started, flow will not continue to the next task. Instead, the flow started by this MemoryTask node is halted until the parent is set to Started. When the parent is set to Started, it searches its child tasks. If any of the child tasks are set to Completed, it will start the next task—that is, it will remember that a task is completed and will not require that the task be done again. Of course, if the user has not done that task yet, it must be done now.

The AfterParentTask node starts when its parent task is set to Started, even if it is not the first child. You can use the AfterParentTask node to divide the flow into two or more paths. If a simulation has two or more tasks that could be started and completed in any sequence, then multiple tasks can be started with the AfterParentTask node. This enables control of nonlinear simulation flow or multiple simultaneous flows.

For example, the user has a task to remove a panel from a piece of equipment, which requires removing four screws. When the user clicks a screw, we could display an animation of the screw rotating and lifting. Because it is not important that these four screws are removed in a certain sequence, we can use the AfterParentTask to set them all to Started tasks. In the simulation tree shown in Figure 10.1.12, the parent task is named Remove Panel, and the four child tasks are named Screw 1, Screw 2, Screw 3, and Screw 4. The first child, Screw 1, is set to Started automatically, but the other three children are not set to Started unless we make them AfterParentTask nodes.

FIGURE 10.1.12 Simulation tree for removing screws to remove a panel

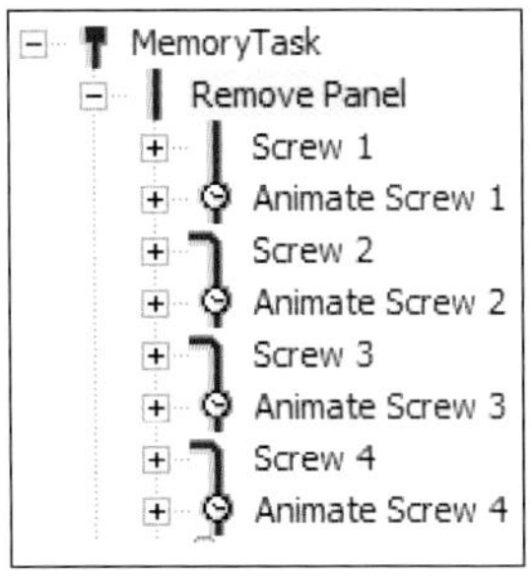

The previous example represents AND logic because the user has to click all of the screws before proceeding to the next task. Another option is the OR logic, in which any one of the four Started tasks is set to Completed and forces the parent to be set to Completed. However, no Flow node breaks rule number 4, so this requires OR logic. You would need to connect a route between the Completed outEvent of the child task to the RequestCompleted inEvent of the parent task.

The DelayTask node completes itself after a certain number of seconds. Set the number of seconds in the DelayTask node's Time field, which can be used to delay the flow. For example, use the DelayTask node to wait for the user to watch an animation or read a message. Alternatively, use the DelayTask node to set a time limit for a user to perform an action, such as click a cube. Either the user clicks the cube within five seconds, or the flow continues without the user clicking the cube.

Often, you want to combine the OR logic with the DelayTask node. For example, you could ask a user to click a cube within five seconds. If the user succeeds, then you display one message. If the user fails, then you display a different message, as shown in Figure 10.1.13.

FIGURE 10.1.13 Display success or failure message

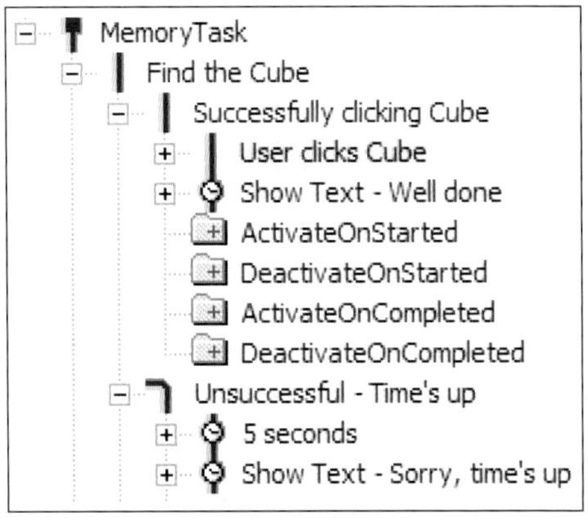

This example breaks the flow into two paths: a successful path and an unsuccessful path. The AfterParentTask node is used so that two tasks are Started under the Find the Cube task. If the user clicks the cube, a route from the ClickSensor to the User clicks Cube task will set that task to Complete and the next task, Show Text – Well done is activated. However, while the "Well done" text is displayed, the 5 seconds task might be set to Complete and the "Sorry, time's up" message might be displayed. We must connect a route from the User clicks Cube Completed outEvent to the Unsuccessful – Time's up RequestCompleted inEvent. By completing this task, the child task named Sorry, time's up will not start because its parent will not be in the Started state. Similarly for the unsuccessful path, if the five-second time limit has been passed and we are displaying the "Sorry, time's up" text, then we do not want the user to click the cube and see the "Well done" text. A route from the 5 seconds Completed outEvent to the Successfully clicking Cube node's RequestCompleted inEvent will prevent the flow from continuing to display the "Well done" text.

The IterationTask node repeats its child tasks a fixed number of times, and it is comparable to a FOR loop in programming language. Iteration can be stopped at any time by using the RequestCompleted inEvent. If an infinite number of repetitions are required, the Iterations field should be set to –1. The IterationTask node bends rule 4, stating that a task is set to Completed when ALL its child tasks are set to Completed because it will be set to Completed only when it has fulfilled its number of repetitions.

Activity 10.1.4: Adding the Required Flow Nodes

1. Open EON. Open **Activity_10.1.4.eoz** from the data files for Module 10 Lesson 1.
2. Under the Scene frame, add a **MemoryTask** node and rename it **Training To Identify Shapes**.
3. Under the MemoryTask node, add a **Task** node and rename it **WelcomeText – Click To Begin**.
4. Under the MemoryTask node, add an **IterationTask** node and rename it **Repeatable Lesson**. Set the Iterations field to **−1** (repeatable forever).
5. Under the MemoryTask node, add a **Task** node and rename it **ShowText – The End**.
6. Under the Repeatable Lesson node, add a **Task** node and rename it **Click on Cube**.
7. Under the Repeatable Lesson node, add a **DelayTask** node and rename it **ShowText – Well Done1**. Set the Time field to **3** seconds.
8. Under the Repeatable Lesson node, add a **Task** node and rename it **Click BOTH Pyramid AND Teapot**.
9. Under the Repeatable Lesson node, add a **DelayTask** node and rename it **ShowText – Well Done2**. Set the Time field to **3** seconds.
10. Under the Repeatable Lesson node, add a **Task** node and rename it **Start Again?**
11. Under the Click BOTH Pyramid AND Teapot node, add an **AfterParentTask** node and rename it **Click on Pyramid**.
12. Under the Click BOTH Pyramid AND Teapot node, add an **AfterParentTask** node and rename it **Click on Teapot**. Your simulation tree should resemble Figure 10.1.14.

FIGURE 10.1.14 Flow nodes added

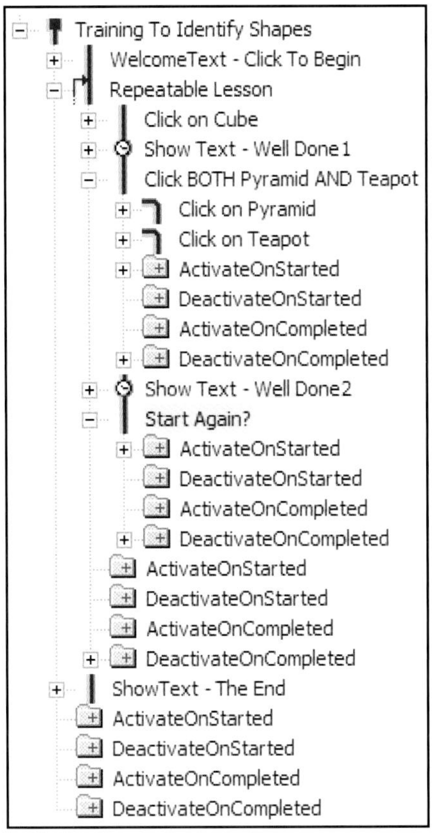

13. Save the simulation as **Flow.eoz** and keep it open to use in Activity 10.1.5.

In the previous activity, you added Flow nodes to a simulation. These Flow nodes will control the simulation's flow—its progress through the simulation. In the next activity, you will insert node references to control other nodes in the simulation without creating routes in the Routes window.

Activity 10.1.5: Adding Node References to Activate and Deactivate Nodes

1. Continue working with the open simulation file **Flow.eoz** from Activity 10.1.4. The node references created in this activity will be placed under folders in the Scene\Training To Identify Shapes folder.
2. To create node references, right-click **Text Messages\ClickToBegin** and select **Copy as Link**. Paste it under **Welcome Text – Click To Begin\ActivateOnStarted** and under **Welcome Text – Click To Begin\DeactivateOnCompleted**. This displays the text at the start and hides it when the task is completed.
3. To create node references, right-click **TextMessages\Step1_ClickCube** and select **Copy as Link**. Paste it under **Repeatable Lesson\Click on Cube\ActivateOnStarted** and under **DeactivateOnCompleted** in the same location. This displays the text *Click on the Cube* while waiting for the user to click the cube.
4. To create node references, right-click **Text Messages\Step1_WellDone** and select **Copy as Link**. Paste it under **Repeatable Lesson\Show Text – WellDone1\ActivateOnStarted** and under **DeactivateOnCompleted** in the same location.

5. To create node references, right-click **Objects\CubeFrame\Rotate_Cube** and select **Copy as Link**. Paste it under **Repeatable Lesson\Show Text – WellDone1\ActivateOnStarted** and under **DeactivateOnCompleted**. These two steps display the text *Well done, the cube is spinning* for three seconds. It also turns on and turns off the spinning of the cube.
6. To create node references, right-click **Text Messages\Step2_ClickPyramidAndTeapot** and select **Copy as Link**. Paste it under **Repeatable Lesson\Click BOTH Pyramid AND Teapot\ActivateOnStarted** and under **DeactivateOnCompleted** in the same location. This displays instructions that tell the user to *Click on the Pyramid AND the Teapot!* while waiting for the user to complete the two child tasks.
7. To create a node reference, right-click **Objects\PyramidFrame\Rotate_Pyramid** and select **Copy as Link**. Paste it under **Repeatable Lesson\Click BOTH Pyramid AND Teapot\Click on Pyramid\ActivateOnCompleted**.
8. To create a node reference, right-click **Objects\TeapotFrame\Rotate_Teapot** and select **Copy as Link**. Paste it under **Repeatable Lesson\Click BOTH Pyramid AND Teapot\Click on Teapot\ActivateOnCompleted**. Your simulation tree should now resemble Figure 10.1.15.

FIGURE 10.1.15 Node references added

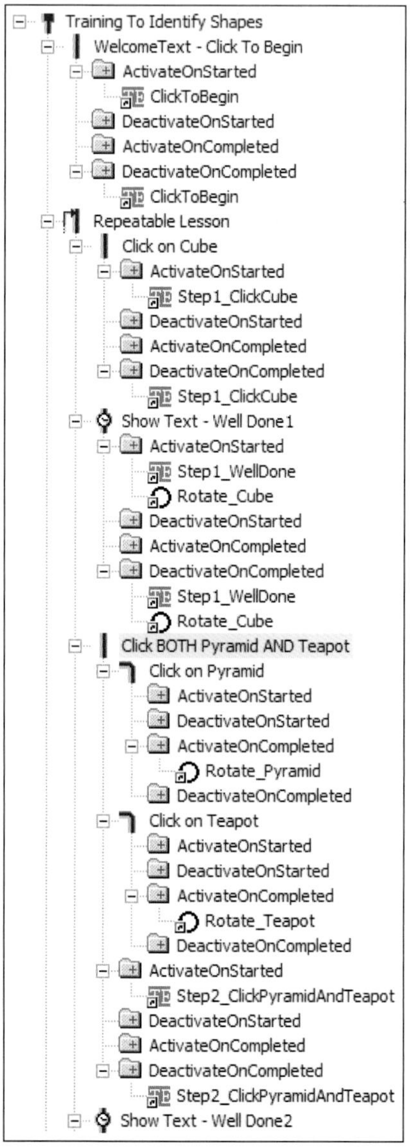

9. To create node references, right-click **Text Messages\Step2_WellDone** and select **Copy as Link**. Paste it under **Repeatable Lesson\Show Text – Well Done2\ActivateOnStarted** and under **DeactivateOnCompleted** in the same location. This displays text for three seconds.
10. To create a node reference, right-click **Objects\PyramidFrame\Rotate_Pyramid** and select **Copy as Link**. Paste it under **Repeatable Lesson\Show Text – Well Done2\DeactivateOnCompleted**.
11. To create a node reference, right-click **Objects\TeapotFrame\Rotate_Teapot** and select **Copy as Link**. Paste it under **Repeatable Lesson\Show Text – Well Done2\DeactivateOnCompleted**. These two steps turn off the spinning of the objects after three seconds. Next, we will ask the user a question and we will display two buttons for the user to choose from—a Yes button and a No button.
12. To create node references, right-click **Text Messages\StartAgainText** and select **Copy as Link**. Paste it under **Repeatable Lesson\Start Again\ActivateOnStarted** and under **DeactivateOnCompleted** in the same location.
13. To create node references, right-click **Text Messages\YesText** and select **Copy as Link**. Paste it under **Repeatable Lesson\Start Again\ActivateOnStarted** and under **DeactivateOnCompleted** in the same location.
14. To create node references, right-click **Text Messages\NoText** and select **Copy as Link**. Paste it under **Repeatable Lesson\Start Again\ActivateOnStarted** and under **DeactivateOnCompleted** in the same location.
15. To create node references, right-click the text messages identified in steps 12 through 14 (**StartAgainText, YesText, NoText**) and select **Copy as Link**. Paste each node reference under **Repeatable Lesson\DeactivateOnCompleted**.
16. To create a node reference, right-click **Text Messages\TheEnd** and select **Copy as Link**. Paste it under the **Show Text – The End\ActivateOnStarted**. Your simulation tree should now resemble Figure 10.1.16.

FIGURE 10.1.16 Additional node references

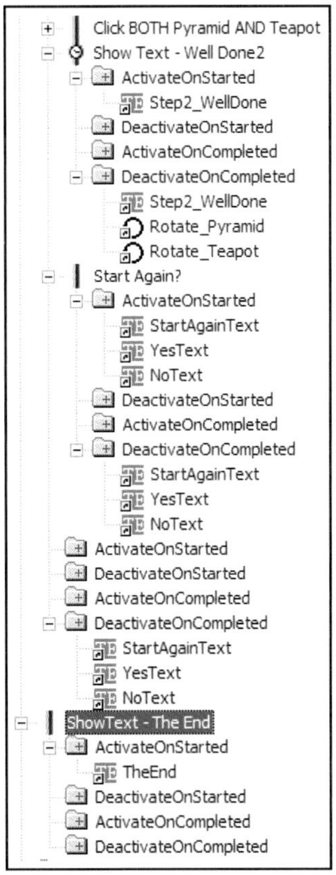

17. Save the simulation and keep it open to use in Activity 10.1.6.

In the previous activity, you added node references that tell the Flow nodes what to do when they are triggered. For the flow to continue, the user must click text boxes or objects. Each click will complete one task, which triggers the next task.

Activity 10.1.6: Connecting Routes to Tasks

1. Continue working with the open simulation file **Flow.eoz** from Activity 10.1.5.
2. Open the **Routes** window. Drag the following nodes from the simulation tree to the Routes window.

   TextMessages\ClickToBegin

   Training To Identify Shapes\WelcomeText – Click To Begin

   Objects\CubeFrame\ClickSensor_Cube

   Training To Identify Shapes\Repeatable Lesson\Click on Cube

   Objects\PyramidFrame\ClickSensor_Pyramid

   Training To Identify Shapes\Repeatable Lesson\Click BOTH Pyramid AND Teapot\Click on Pyramid

   Objects\TeapotFrame\ClickSensor_Teapot

   Training To Identify Shapes\Repeatable Lesson\Click BOTH Pyramid AND Teapot\Click on Teapot

   TextMessages\YesText

   Training To Identify Shapes\Repeatable Lesson\Start Again?

   TextMessages\NoText

   Training To Identify Shapes\Repeatable Lesson
3. Establish the connections outlined in the following table. Your Routes window should resemble Figure 10.1.17.

From	outEvent	To	inEvent
ClickToBegin	OnButtonUp	WelcomeText – Click To Begin	RequestCompleted
ClickSensor_Cube	OnButtonDownTrue	Click on Cube	RequestCompleted
ClickSensor_Pyramid	OnButtonDownTrue	Click on Pyramid	RequestCompleted
ClickSensor_Teapot	OnButtonDownTrue	Click on Teapot	RequestCompleted
YesText	OnButtonUp	Start Again?	RequestCompleted
NoText	OnButtonUp	Repeatable Lesson	RequestCompleted

FIGURE 10.1.17 Routes window for Flow.eoz

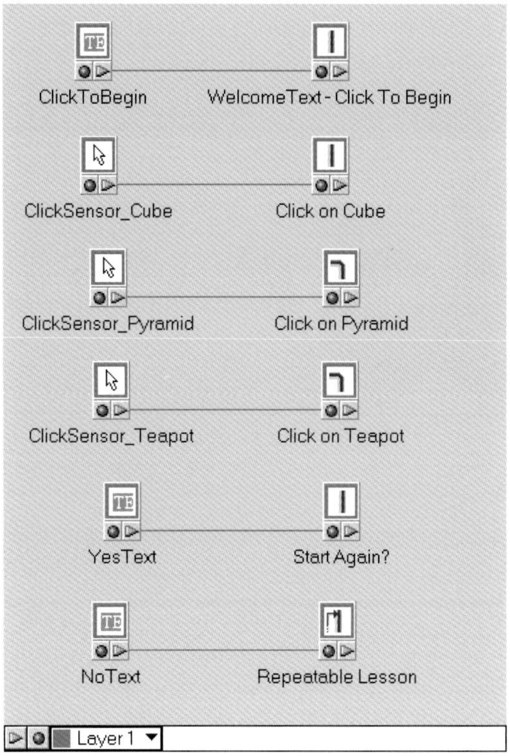

4. Run the simulation and test the options.
5. Close the simulation window. Save the simulation and then close EON.

If the user clicks the Yes text, we complete the StartAgain task, which means all of the child tasks of Repeatable Lesson are completed and the Repeatable Lesson will repeat because it is an IterationTask node. However, if the user clicks the No text, we will directly complete the Repeatable Lesson task and flow continues to the end.

Summary

In this lesson you:

- Learned about creating user-driven simulations.
- Understood which nodes are used to control the responses or flow in a simulation.
- Became familiar with logic control nodes such as the And, Or, XOR, and Not nodes.
- Learned the basic rules common to nodes in the Flow Nodes library.
- Used nodes in the Flow Nodes library to create a simple user training exercise.

LESSON 10.2

Data Manipulation

Objectives

In this lesson you will:

- Become familiar with nodes and prototypes that can convert data types.
- Learn how to manipulate data using new nodes and prototypes.

Key Terms

Adapter prototype
Addition node
BooleanSplitter prototype
BooleanToInteger-Converter prototype
Colors prototype
Constant node
convert
Convert3DPosToScreen-Pos prototype
Converter node
data manipulation
Division node
GroupGUINodes prototype
HexColor prototype
MousePos3D prototype
MouseToBoxPosition prototype
MouseToTextBoxPos prototype
Multiplication node
Opposites prototype
RouteSwitch node
Subtraction node

Data Manipulation in EON

In this lesson, we look at nodes that can assist you in converting and manipulating data. To ***convert*** data usually refers to changing the data type of information. Data types can be Boolean (SFBool), Number (SFFloat), Integer (SFInt32), Text (SFString), Vectors (SFVec2f or SFVec3f), and a few others. As you know, you can only connect routes between fields that have the same data type. If you want to connect fields that have incompatible data types, you must convert one of the data types so that the two fields have the same data type.

The term *converting* can have a more general meaning than simple data type conversion. For example, we could receive data from multiple sources and perform calculations before sending the data in a form that is more useful. In this situation, converting could be described as ***data manipulation***. Data manipulation can be as simple as using the Addition node to add two float values or as complex as using the Convert3DPosToScreenPos prototype, which uses about nine sources of data—although most of the incoming values do not change often.

tips+tricks

Converters can help you avoid using scripts.

Converters

In EON, several converters are prototypes that are grouped in the Converters library. The nodes that can be classified as converters are members of the OperationsNodes library. The following sections provide details about these useful prototypes and nodes.

Adapter Prototype

The ***Adapter prototype***, which converts data types such as SFFloat to SFVec3F, prevents problems caused by the need to share different types of data. For example, use this prototype to convert the mouse position (SFVec2F data type) into the position of an object, which uses an SFVec3F data type. Or, use the Adapter prototype to convert a time of type SFFloat into the Z position of an object, which has a data type of SFVec3F.

GroupGUINodes Prototype

By grouping your GUIControl nodes with the ***GroupGUINodes prototype***, you can change the BoxPosition field, and all the nodes in the group will be moved while keeping their relative positions.

tips+tricks

If you need to hide and show a group of GUI nodes, you do not need to create routes for each GUI node. Instead, simply place the nodes in the GroupGUINodes prototype and then connect one route to the GroupGUINodes prototype's IsNotActive or IsActive field to hide or show all nodes in the group.

Discussion

discuss

Can you think of scenarios in which you might use this prototype? Discuss various circumstances in which this prototype would be advantageous.

Activity 10.2.1: Creating Three Sliders to Manipulate the Color of a Cube

1. Open EON. Open **Activity_10.2.1.eoz** from the data files for Module 10 Lesson 2.
2. Save the simulation as **Three_Sliders.eoz** and then run the simulation. Notice the cube, which you can rotate around with OrbitNav.
3. Close the simulation window.
4. Add a **Frame** node under the Scene and rename the node **ColorSliders**.

5. Drag a **SliderPlus** prototype from the Local Prototypes window and drop it under the ColorSliders frame. Change the prototype instance's name to **SliderPlus-Red**.
6. In the Property Bar, place a check mark in the **UseGreyBGColor** check box.
7. Set the StartValue to **0.5**.
8. Set the LabelText value to **Red**. Your Property Bar should resemble Figure 10.2.1.

FIGURE 10.2.1 SliderPlus-Red Property Bar

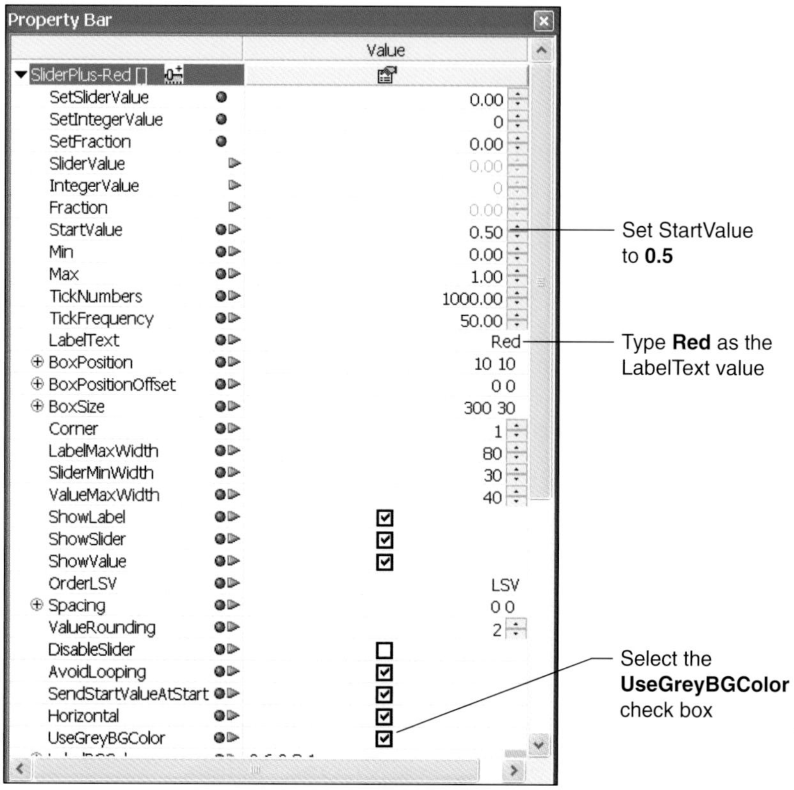

9. Run the simulation to view the added slider.
10. Close the simulation window.
11. Copy the **SliderPlus-Red** prototype in the simulation tree, paste it under the ColorSliders frame, and rename the new prototype instance **SliderPlus-Green**.
12. In the Property Bar, change the LabelText to **Green** and set the BoxPosition to **10 40**.
13. Copy the **SliderPlus-Red** prototype in the simulation tree, paste it under the ColorSliders frame, and rename the new prototype instance **SliderPlus-Blue**.
14. In the Property Bar, change the LabelText to **Blue** and set the BoxPosition to **10 70**.
15. Save the simulation and then run the simulation. Notice the three sliders, as shown in Figure 10.2.2.

FIGURE 10.2.2 Simulation window after adding the slider bars

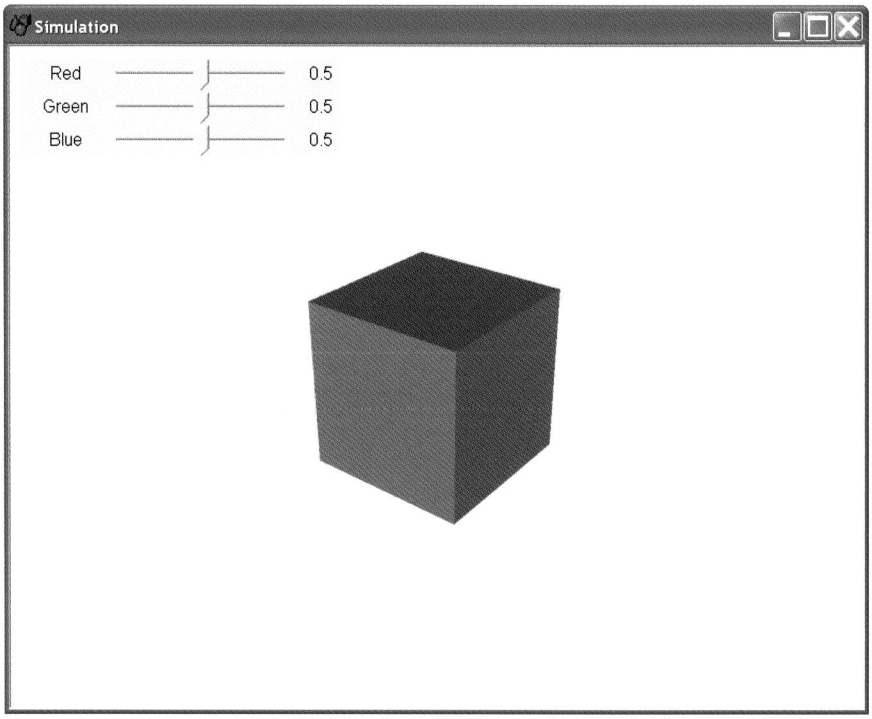

16. Close the simulation window.
17. Drag an **Adapter** prototype from the Local Prototypes window and drop it under the ColorSliders frame.
18. Display the **Routes** window. Drag the three **slider** prototype instances, the **Adapter** prototype, and the **Cube** prototype to the Routes window. Establish the connections outlined in the following table. Your Routes window should resemble Figure 10.2.3.

From	outEvent	To	inEvent
SliderPlus-Red	SliderValue	Adapter	X_In
SliderPlus-Green	SliderValue	Adapter	Y_In
SliderPlus-Blue	SliderValue	Adapter	Z_In
Adapter	XYZ_Out	Cube	Color

FIGURE 10.2.3 Routes window after routes are connected

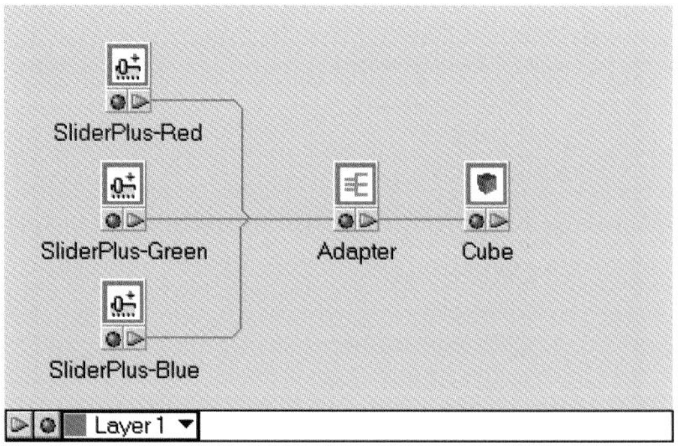

tips+tricks

This activity has a second set of three sliders that change the scale of the cube. Instead of starting from scratch, you can save time and effort by copying the existing set of sliders and then using a GroupGUINodes prototype.

troubleshooting

If you run the simulation immediately after step 26, the scale sliders are hidden behind the color sliders. Adding the GroupGUINodes prototype enables you to group the scale sliders and then move the sliders as a group.

19. Save the simulation and then run the simulation. Drag the sliders to see the color of the cube change.
20. Close the simulation window.
21. Copy the **ColorSliders** frame, paste it under the Scene, and rename it **ScaleSliders**.
22. Under ScaleSliders, rename the three SliderPlus prototypes **SliderPlus-X**, **SliderPlus-Y**, and **SliderPlus-Z**.
23 Change the LabelText field of the sliders to **Scale X**, **Scale Y**, and **Scale Z**, respectively.
24. If necessary, rearrange the elements in the Routes window so that they are neat and easy to follow.
25. In the Routes window, select the route from the newly added Adapter prototype to the Color field of the Cube prototype and then press the **Delete** key. The Delete dialog box, as shown in Figure 10.2.4, will be displayed. Click **OK** to continue.

FIGURE 10.2.4 Delete dialog box

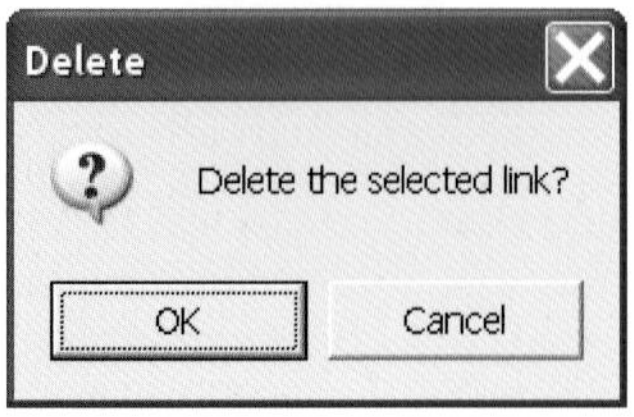

26. Establish the connection outlined in the following table.

From	outEvent	To	inEvent
Adapter	XYZ_Out	Cube	Scale

27. Insert the **GroupGUINodes** prototype under the ScaleSliders frame.
28. To create a node reference, right-click the **ScaleSliders** frame and select **Copy as Link**. Paste it under the **NodesInGroup** folder of the GroupGUINodes prototype. Your simulation tree should resemble Figure 10.2.5.

FIGURE 10.2.5 Simulation tree after adding node reference to GroupGUINodes prototype

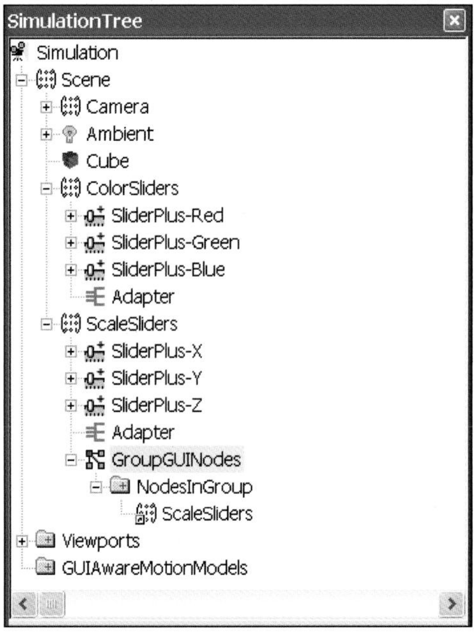

29. In the Property Bar, set the GroupGUINodes prototype's BoxPosition field to **350 0**.
30. Save the simulation and then run the simulation. Test the new sliders.
31. Close the simulation window. Close EON.

Addition, Subtraction, Multiplication, and Division Nodes

The ***Addition node***, ***Subtraction node***, ***Multiplication node***, and ***Division node*** manipulate data. Each node has two float values (InValue1 and InValue2 fields) that they use to perform a mathematical operation. They place the result in the OutValue field.

Each node has a Trigger and an AutoTrigger field. If AutoTrigger is set to true, then the OutValue is calculated when new values are received for the InValue1 or the InValue2 field. If AutoTrigger is false, then you must send a Boolean value to the Trigger field so that it will calculate and send the OutValue (SFFloat). For example, you could connect a route from a ClickSensor node's OnButtonDownTrue field to the Trigger field.

You should be aware of some differences among the nodes to use them successfully for data manipulation. In the Division node, the InValue1 and InValue2 fields are named Numerator and Denominator. In the Subtraction node, InValue2 is subtracted from InValue1.

tips+tricks

When using the Division node, an operation will not be executed if the denominator equals zero. Instead, an outEvent will not be sent and an error message will be displayed in the Log window.

Discussion

discuss

What are some potential simulations in which the Addition node, Subtraction node, Multiplication node, or Division node could be useful?

BooleanSplitter Prototype

The ***BooleanSplitter prototype*** enables you to send true or false. You can split a Boolean so it only sends out true or only sends out false. Fields with an underscore after the name send out false only. For example, OnTrueFalse_ will send false when either true or false is received.

BooleanToIntegerConverter Prototype

The ***BooleanToIntegerConverter prototype*** accepts 50 Boolean inEvents and sends a number between 1 and 50 as one integer outEvent. This prototype could be used as an alternative to the Constant node or the NumberSender prototype.

Colors Prototype

The ***Colors prototype*** is a very simple prototype. It is a converter that allows you to change colors easily. It converts inEvents of type Boolean into SFColor or SFVec3F outEvents. It has 26 color inEvents. You connect routes to the inEvents, which have names representing colors, and you connect the outEvent, named Color, to an appropriate node such as a Material2, Light, Shading, or LightOfDay node.

Constant Node

The ***Constant node*** sends a value stored in the Value (SFFloat) field when it receives the Trigger inEvent (SFBool). Therefore, it converts a Boolean inEvent to a number outEvent. The NumberSender prototype in the DeveloperTools library does the same thing but also offers the number as an integer (SFInt32).

Convert3DPosToScreenPos Prototype

With the ***Convert3DPosToScreenPos prototype***, you can position 2D elements over moving 3D objects. This prototype uses values from several sources, calculates values, and places them in the BoxPosition field. It needs nine values, but seven of the values do not change often. You can send the Refresh inEvent to the prototype so that it will retrieve the seven pieces of data it needs from the Simulation node and Viewport node, or you can connect routes directly to the relevant fields on this prototype. The camera position and the positions of the moving 3D objects change more often, so these values should be sent in by routes.

Activity 10.2.2: Positioning a Text Label on a Moving 3D Object

1. Open EON. Open **Activity_10.2.2.eoz** from the data files for Module 10 Lesson 2.
2. Save the simulation as **Position_Label.eoz** and then run the simulation. It has a sphere orbiting another sphere, similar to Jupiter orbiting the sun. Locate these nodes in the simulation tree.
3. Close the simulation window.
4. Add a **Frame** node under Scene and rename the node **Logic**.
5. Add a **2DText** node under the Logic frame and set its Text field to **Jupiter**.
6. Also in the Property Bar, set the BoxArea field to **60 20** and the TextAlignment to **Center**. Your Property Bar should resemble Figure 10.2.6.

FIGURE 10.2.6 Property Bar for 2DText node

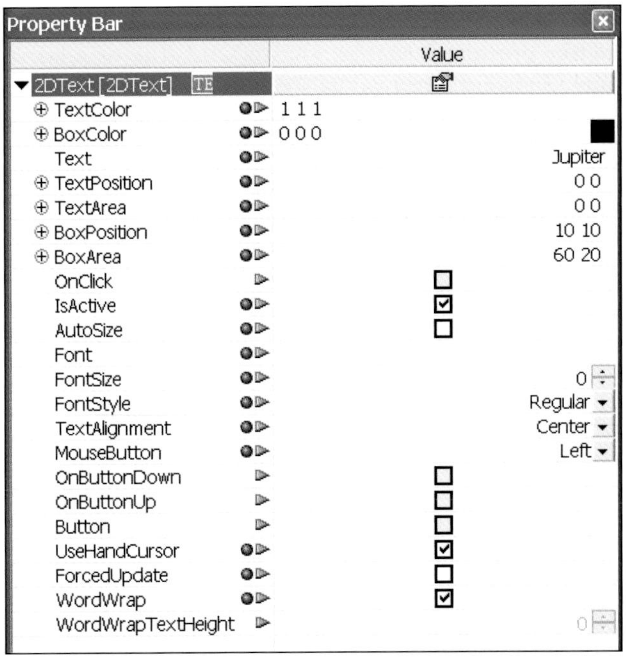

7. Add a **Convert3DPosToScreenPos** prototype under the Logic frame.
8. To create a node reference, right-click **Sun\JupiterOrbiting** and select **Copy as Link**. Paste it under **Logic\Convert3DPosToScreenPos\Pos3DFrame**.
9. To create a node reference, right-click **Viewports\Viewport** and select **Copy as Link**. Paste it under **Logic\Convert3DPosToScreenPos\ViewportNode**.
10. To create a node reference, right-click **Logic\2DText** and select **Copy as Link**. Paste it under **Logic\Convert3DPosToScreenPos\SendToNodes**. Your simulation tree should resemble Figure 10.2.7.

FIGURE 10.2.7 Simulation tree after adding node references

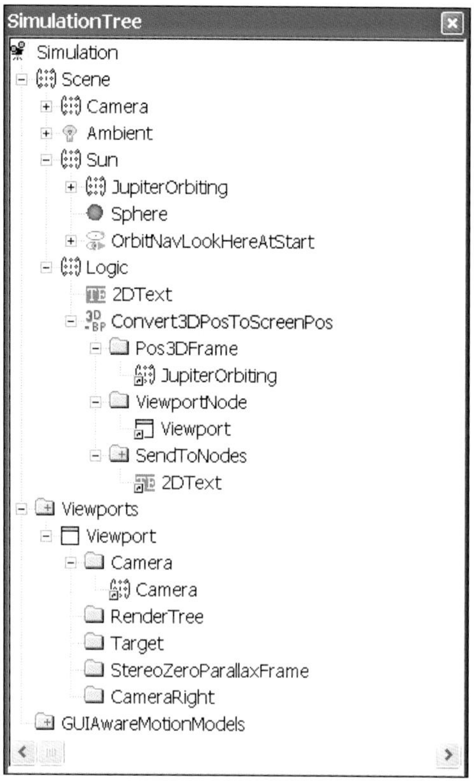

11. Display the **Routes** window. Drag the **Convert3DPosToScreenPos** prototype to the Routes window. Establish the connections outlined in the following table. Your Routes window should resemble Figure 10.2.8.

From	outEvent	To	inEvent
JupiterOrbiting	Position	Convert3DPosToScreenPos	Pos3D
Camera	Position	Convert3DPosToScreenPos	CamPos

FIGURE 10.2.8 Routes window after adding routes to the Convert3DPosToScreenPos prototype

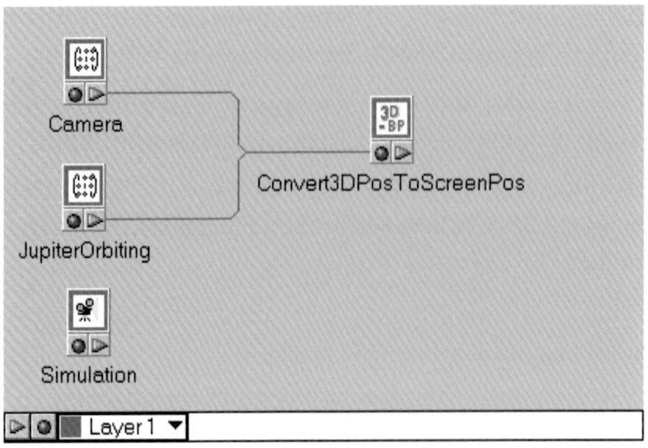

12. Save the simulation and then run the simulation. View the results.
13. Close the simulation window.
14. Select the **Convert3DPosToScreenPos** prototype in the simulation tree. In the Property Bar, change the BPOffset field to **-30 -30**. This moves the 2DText node slightly higher and to the left.
15. Run the simulation. View the results.
16. Close the simulation window. Save the simulation and keep it open to use in Activity 10.2.3.

Converter Node

The ***Converter node*** allows the conversion of a field's data type. For example, an SFBool field can be converted to an SFInt32 field, or an SFString field can be converted to an SFFloat field. Almost all of EON's data types are supported, although some conversions are not used.

HexColor Prototype

The ***HexColor prototype*** converts colors into a hexadecimal string for HTML use and vice versa. This simple prototype has only one Script node that converts a color of data type SFVec3f into a string, which is the hexadecimal equivalent of that color for use primarily in a web page. It also receives hexadecimal strings, which it converts to SFVec3f data types.

This prototype is useful in a configuration simulation. It allows the user to choose the exact color to be used on a Web page and to see it in the EON application. It is also useful for EON applications that enable you to choose the color within EON. This prototype can report which colors were chosen to the web page.

MousePos3D Prototype

The ***MousePos3D prototype*** provides the 3D coordinates that identify the position of the mouse cursor when using orthographic viewports. An orthographic viewport shows no depth, so this prototype produces the X and Y values and you provide the Z value. The prototype generates two outEvents—MousePos3D and MousePos2D. The first is most useful because it has the data type SFVec3f, which can be used to position objects by sending it to a Frame node's Position field.

cross-reference

For more information about an orthographic viewport, see Module 8 Lesson 2.

This prototype makes it possible to move and rotate objects. You can move the camera of a normal viewport to a position represented in the orthographic viewport. You also can measure an area covered while dragging the mouse.

This prototype is flexible because it considers the many other variables that affect the outEvent's value. They are the Viewport node's X, Y, Width, Height, NearClip, and FieldOfView fields; the Simulation node's WindowWidth and WindowHeight fields; and the Camera node's Position field. All of this information is external to the prototype and has to be sent in or collected. The only variable generated internally by the prototype is the MouseSensor node's nCursorPosition field.

MouseToBoxPosition Prototype

The ***MouseToBoxPosition prototype*** converts mouse position to BoxPosition (pixel values). It gives the position of the mouse using the BoxPosition outEvent. Use this prototype to position some of the GUIControl nodes, such as the 2DText node, so that the 2DText node follows the mouse cursor.

MouseToTextBoxPos Prototype

The ***MouseToTextBoxPos prototype*** converts mouse position into text box position for variously sized viewports. This makes it possible for you to position a TextBox node at the location the user clicks. It also makes it possible to move a text box by dragging the mouse. The values will continue to be correct regardless if the viewport changes position or size.

Opposites Prototype

The ***Opposites prototype*** is a simple prototype that sends the opposite of any data it receives. If it receives true, it sends false. If it receives 25, it sends –25. If it receives "some text," it sends "txet emos." If it receives a color, it sends the inverse color, and so on.

For example, use this prototype to open a set of double doors in a wide doorway. For both doors to open in the same direction, they rotate on hinges placed on opposite sides of the doorway. Instead of using Place nodes for both doors, you can link the orientation of one door via the Opposites prototype.

RouteSwitch Node

The ***RouteSwitch node*** enables you to forward inEvents of most data types and map them to outEvents of the same data type. You can then control whether the inEvents should be forwarded by setting the Connected field to true or false.

Activity 10.2.3: Placing a Text Label at the Cursor Position

1. Continue working with the open simulation file **Position_Label.eoz** from Activity 10.2.2.
2. Save the simulation as **Click_Label.eoz**.
3. Add a **2DText** node under the Logic frame and rename the node **HelloText**.
4. In the Property Bar, set the Text field to **Hello**, the BoxArea field to **60 20**, and the TextAlignment to **Center**.

5. Under the Logic frame, insert a **MouseToBoxPosition** prototype from the Converters prototype library. Your simulation tree should resemble Figure 10.2.9.

FIGURE 10.2.9 Simulation tree after adding the MouseToBoxPosition prototype

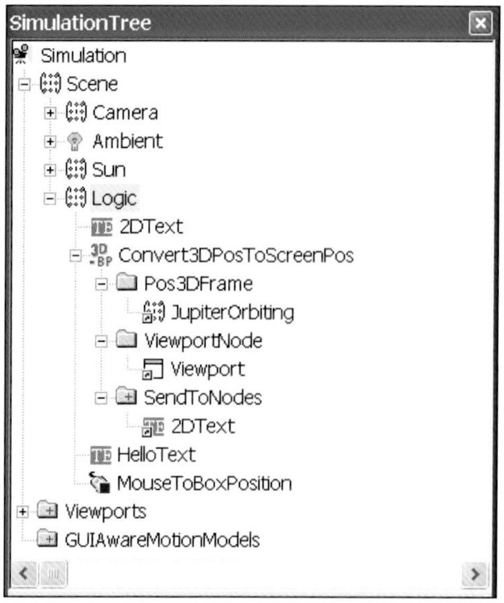

6. Display the **Routes** window. Drag the **MouseToBoxPosition** prototype and the **HelloText** node to the Routes window. Establish the connection outlined in the following table.

From	outEvent	To	inEvent
MouseToBoxPosition	BoxPosition	HelloText	BoxPosition

7. Save the simulation and then run the simulation. The text box should follow the mouse cursor.
8. Close the simulation window.
9. Select the **MouseToBoxPosition** prototype in the simulation tree. In the Property Bar, set the OffsetPos value to **-60 -20** so that the mouse cursor is not in the way of the text (see Figure 10.2.10).

FIGURE 10.2.10 Property Bar for the MouseToBoxPosition prototype

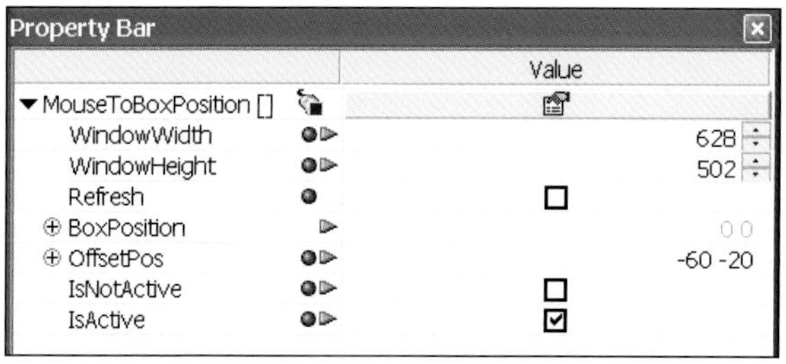

10. Delete the last route, which was added in step 6.
11. Under the Logic frame, add a **MouseSensor** node and a **RouteSwitch** node. Your simulation tree should resemble Figure 10.2.11.

FIGURE 10.2.11 Simulation tree after adding the MouseSensor node and the RouteSwitch node

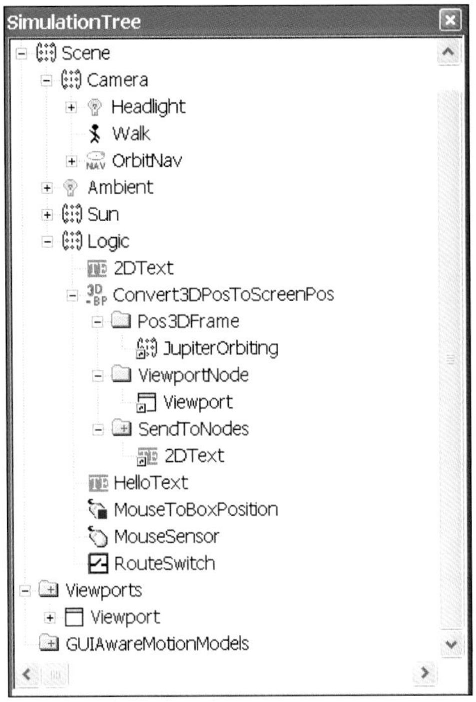

12. Display the **Routes** window. Drag the **MouseSensor** node and the **RouteSwitch** node to the Routes window. Establish the connections outlined in the following table.

From	outEvent	To	inEvent
MouseSensor	rb	RouteSwitch	Connected
MouseToBoxPosition	BoxPosition	RouteSwitch	2DVectorIn
RouteSwitch	2DVectorOut	HelloText	BoxPosition

13. Save the simulation and then run the simulation. When you click the right mouse button, the text box is displayed at the location you clicked.
14. Close the simulation window. Keep the simulation open to use in Activity 10.2.4.

The prototypes used in Activity 10.2.4 need the correct WindowWidth and WindowHeight values to calculate their output. These prototypes must be informed if the simulation window's size changes. The RefreshGroup prototype was designed to send refresh signals to other prototypes when the window size changes.

Activity 10.2.4: Creating a Text Box That Follows the Mouse Cursor

1. Continue working with the open simulation file **Click_Label.eoz** from Activity 10.2.3.
2. Save the simulation as **Follow_Label.eoz**.
3. Add the **RefreshGroup** prototype from the Developer Tools library to the Logic frame.
4. Display the **Routes** window. Drag the **RefreshGroup** prototype to the Routes window. Establish the connections outlined in the following table.

From	outEvent	To	inEvent
Simulation	WindowWidth	RefreshGroup	WindowWidth
Simulation	WindowHeight	RefreshGroup	WindowHeight

troubleshooting

If the arrow is not displayed in the lower-left corner of the icon, you moved the prototype instead of creating a node reference. If this happens, move the MouseToBoxPosition prototype back to the Logic frame and try again to create the node reference.

5. To create a node reference, right-click the **Convert3DPosToScreenPos** prototype and select **Copy as Link**. Paste it under the **RefreshThese** folder of the RefreshGroup prototype.
6. In the simulation tree, press the **Ctrl** and **Shift** keys while dragging the **MouseToBoxPosition** prototype from the Logic folder to the RefreshThese folder under the RefreshGroup prototype. This creates a node reference to the prototype, indicated by the arrow in the lower-left corner of the icon representing the node reference.
7. Add a **Frame** node under the Camera frame. Double-click the **Frame** node to open the Frame Properties dialog box and set the Y value to **2** (see Figure 10.2.12). Click **OK** to close the dialog box.

FIGURE 10.2.12 Frame Properties dialog box

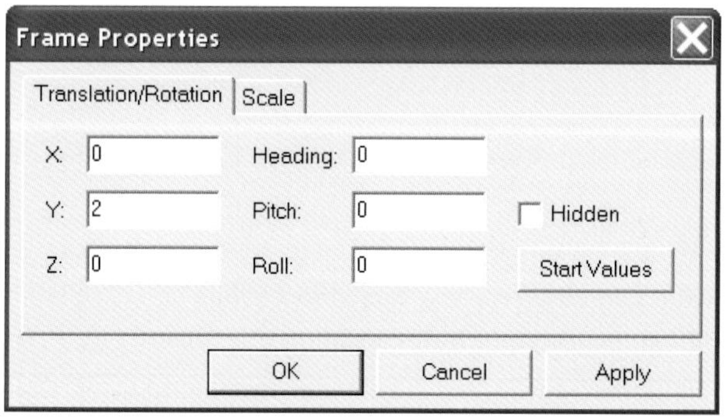

8. Add a **TextBox** node under the Frame node. In the Property Bar, set the Text field to **Welcome**, set the FontSize to **160**, and place a check mark in the **Fixed** check box to set its value to true.
9. Under the Frame node, add a **MouseToTextBoxPos** prototype from the Converters prototype library.
10. Display the **Routes** window. Drag the **MouseToTextBoxPos** prototype and the **TextBox** node to the Routes window. Establish the connection outlined in the following table.

From	outEvent	To	inEvent
MouseToTextBoxPos	M2TextBoxPos	TextBox	FixedPos

11. Save the simulation and then run the simulation. Notice that the mouse cursor covers the *Welcome* text.
12. Close the simulation window.
13. Delete the route created in step 10.
14. Under Frame, add an **Addition** node. In the Property Bar, set the InitialValue2 to **0.02** and place a check mark in the **AutoTrigger** check box.
15. Under Frame, add two **Adapter** prototypes and rename them **Adapter1** and **Adapter2**. Your simulation tree should resemble Figure 10.2.13.

tips+tricks

Change the name of the second Adapter to Adapter2 first. If you try to change the name of the first Adapter to Adapter1, it will conflict with the default name of the second Adapter.

FIGURE 10.2.13 Simulation tree after adding the Adapter prototypes

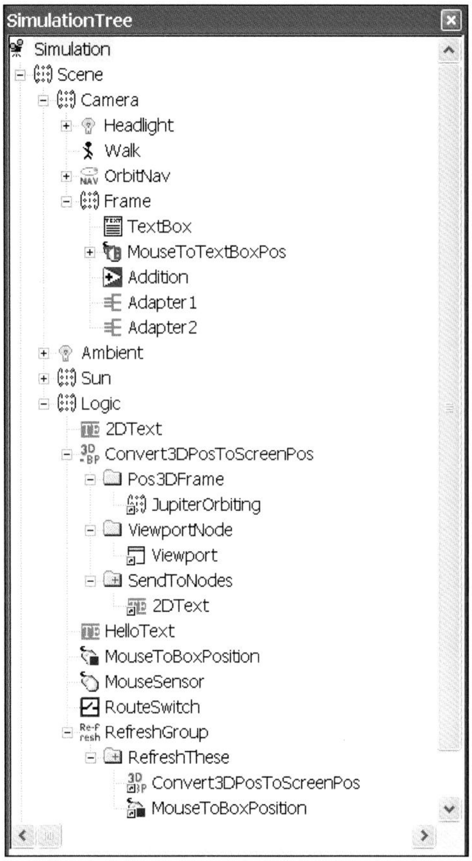

16. Display the **Routes** window. Drag the **Addition** node and the **Adapter1** and **Adapter2** prototypes to the Routes window. Establish the connections outlined in the following table.

From	outEvent	To	inEvent
MouseToTextBoxPos	M2TextBoxPos	Adapter1	XY_In
Adapter1	X_Out	Addition	InValue1
Addition	OutValue	Adapter2	X_In
Adapter1	Y_Out	Adapter2	Y_In
Adapter2	XY_Out	TextBox	FixedPos

17. Save the simulation and then run the simulation. Notice that the text is slightly to the right of the mouse cursor.
18. Close the simulation window. Close EON.

In the following activity, you will add the ability to switch between objects using a pop-up menu.

Activity 10.2.5: Creating a Pop-up Menu to Switch Between Objects

1. Open EON. Open **Activity_10.2.5.eoz** from the data files for Module 10 Lesson 2.
2. Save the simulation as **Popup_Menu.eoz**.
3. Run the simulation. Currently, the ClickSensor and Counter nodes enable you to switch the object (a cube, cylinder, or sphere) that is displayed by clicking the displayed object.
4. Close the simulation window.
5. Add a **2DText** node under the SwitchingLogic frame. In the Property Bar, set the node's Text field to **Choose an object**.
6. Add a **PopupMenu** node under the SwitchingLogic frame.
7. Add three **MenuItem** nodes under the PopupMenu node.
8. Rename the MenuItem nodes to **Cube**, **Cylinder**, and **Sphere**, respectively. Your simulation tree should resemble Figure 10.2.14.

FIGURE 10.2.14 Simulation tree after renaming MenuItem nodes

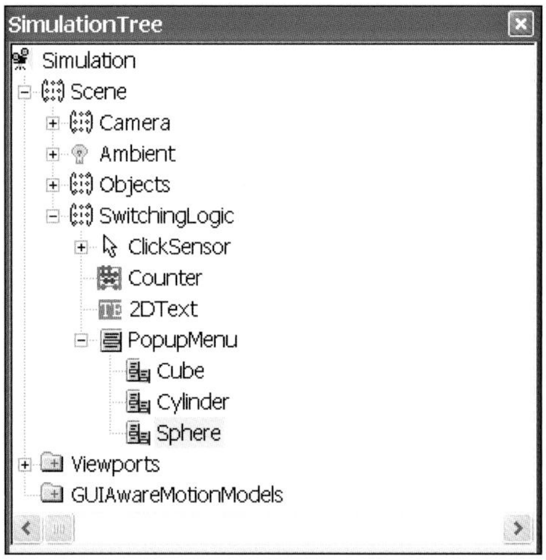

9. Display the **Routes** window. Drag the **2DText** node and the **PopupMenu** node to the Routes window. Establish the connections outlined in the following table.

From	outEvent	To	inEvent
2DText	OnButtonUp	PopupMenu	ShowPopupMenu
PopupMenu	SelectedMenuId	Switch	Value

10. Save the simulation and then run the simulation. Test the pop-up menu.
11. Close the simulation window.
12. Delete the route from the PopupMenu node to the Switch node created in step 9.
13. Add a **Subtraction** node under the SwitchingLogic frame. In the Property Bar, set the node's InitialValue2 field to **1**. The value in the InitialValue2 field is subtracted from the value in the InValue1 field before sending the OutValue.

troubleshooting

Immediately after completing step 13, drag the **Subtraction** node to the Routes window and attempt to make the following route:

Click the **PopupMenu Out** button and select **SelectedMenuId**. Click the **Subtraction In** button and select **InValue1**.

You could not make this connection because the data types are incompatible. One is SFInt32 (an integer), and the other is SFFloat (normal number). To solve this problem, you need to use the Converter node.

14. Under the SwitchingLogic frame, add a **Converter** node and rename it **Converter_IntegerToFloat**.
15. Display the **Routes** window. Drag the **Converter_IntegerToFloat** node and the **Subtraction** node to the Routes window. Establish the connections outlined in the following table.

From	outEvent	To	inEvent
PopupMenu	SelectedMenuId	Converter_IntegerToFloat	IntIn
Converter_IntegerToFloat	FloatOut	Subtraction	InValue1

16. Under the SwitchingLogic frame, add another **Converter** node and rename it **Converter_FloatToInteger**. Your simulation tree should resemble Figure 10.2.15.

FIGURE 10.2.15 Simulation tree after adding a second Converter node

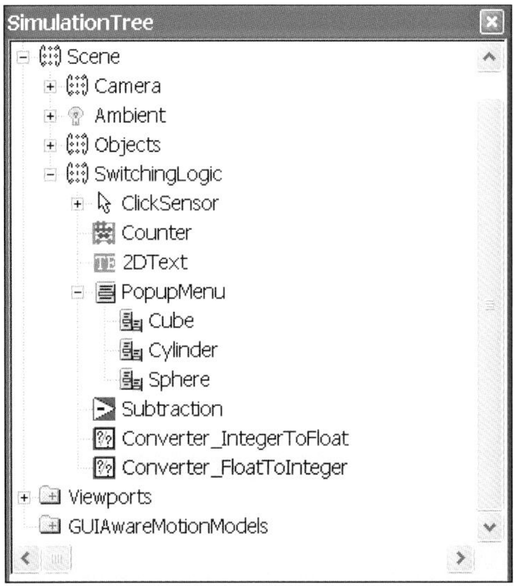

troubleshooting

While running the simulation in step 10, click the **Choose an object** button. Do you notice a problem? Selecting Cube will display the cylinder, selecting Cylinder will display the sphere, and selecting Sphere will not change anything. This happens because the numbers are sent by the PopupMenu node. The SelectedMenuId number sends 1 for the first Cube MenuItem, but the Switch node needs to receive a 0 to display the cube. To solve this problem, you must subtract one from the SelectedMenuId before sending the value to the Switch node.

17. Display the **Routes** window. Drag the **Converter_FloatToInteger** node to the Routes window. Establish the connections outlined in the following table. Your Routes window should resemble Figure 10.2.16.

From	outEvent	To	inEvent
Subtraction	OutValue	Converter_FloatToInteger	FloatIn
Converter_FloatToInteger	IntOut	Switch	Value

FIGURE 10.2.16 Routes window with final connections

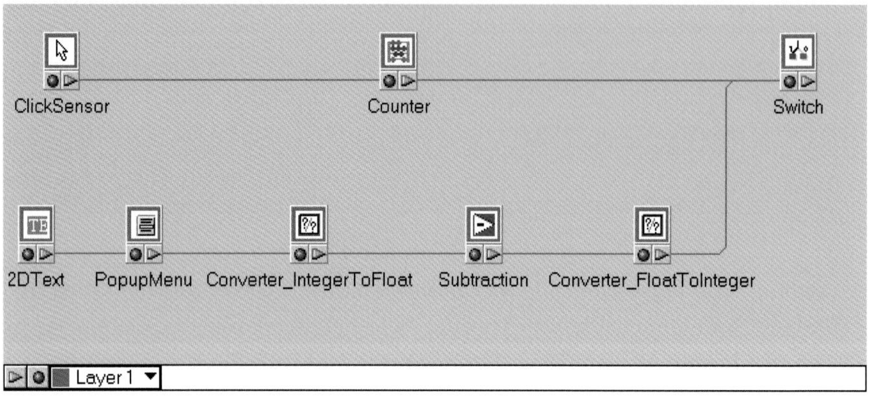

18. In the Property Bar of the **Converter_IntegerToFloat** node, the **Converter_FloatToInteger** node, and the **Subtraction** node, place a check mark in the **AutoTrigger** check box.
19. Save the simulation and then run the simulation. Click the **Choose an object** button.
20. Close the simulation window. Keep the simulation open to use in Activity 10.2.6.

In the previous activity, you set up a pop-up menu to enable the user to choose a shape from the menu. It works, but EON has a faster method for setting up a pop-up menu—the MenuSwitch prototype. Using this prototype is faster because no extra nodes and routes are required. You will explore this method in the next activity.

Activity 10.2.6: Adding a Pop-up Menu Using the MenuSwitch Prototype

1. Continue working with the open simulation file **Popup_Menu.eoz** from Activity 10.2.5.
2. Save the simulation as **Popup_MenuSwitch.eoz**.
3. Delete the **2DText**, **PopupMenu**, **Subtraction**, and two **Converter** nodes from the SwitchingLogic frame.
4. Add a **MenuSwitch** prototype from the GUIControlFunctions prototype library to the SwitchingLogic frame.
5. To create a node reference, right-click the **Switch** node in the Objects frame and select **Copy as link**. Paste it under the **Roots** folder of the MenuSwitch prototype.

6. Save the simulation and then run the simulation. Right-click an object to display the pop-up menu.
7. Close the simulation window.
8. Expand **Scene > Objects > Switch**. Change the name of the Cube frame to **A red cube**. Change the name of the Cylinder frame to **A green cylinder**. Change the name of the Sphere frame to **A blue sphere**.
9. Save the simulation and then run the simulation. Notice that the names of the Frame nodes are used by the MenuSwitch (see Figure 10.2.17).

FIGURE 10.2.17 Pop-up menu created using the MenuSwitch prototype

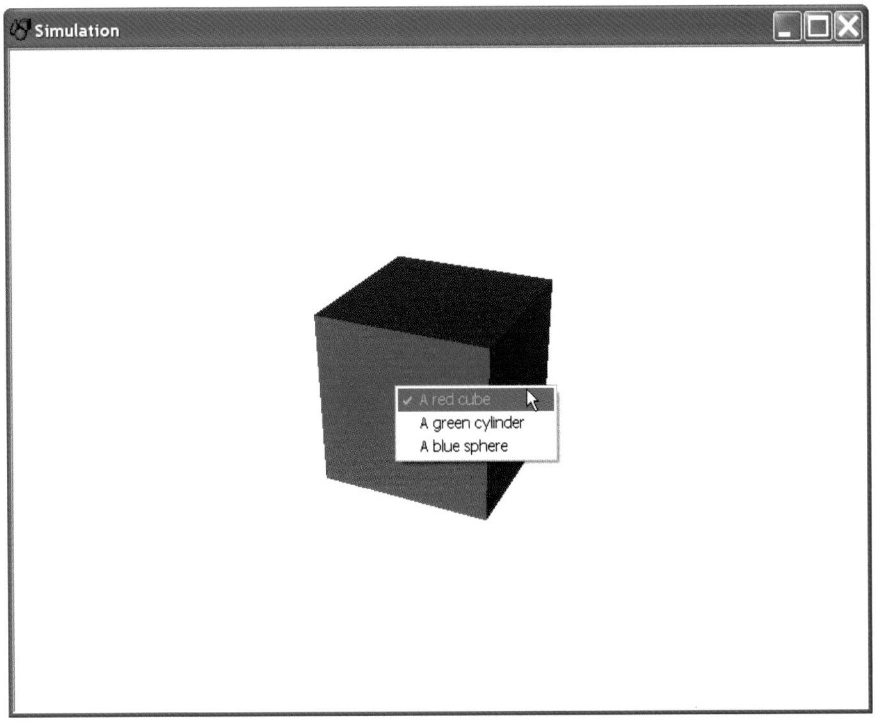

10. Close the simulation window. Close EON.

Discussion

discuss

Which method did you prefer for setting up a pop-up menu? Why?

Summary

In this lesson you:

- Became familiar with nodes and prototypes that can convert data types.
- Learned how to manipulate data using new nodes and prototypes.

Simulation

Congratulations! You are the only designer employed by Contours Company who is familiar with the basic skills required to create user-driven simulations and to carry out data manipulation. Your supervisor proposed that you create a sample simulation to train other company designers in these useful skills. For this task, the supervisor has requested that you keep each story line simple and straightforward, using basic shapes and elementary scenarios.

Job 10.1: Brainstorming

Using the knowledge you gained in Module 10, brainstorm to devise at least three scenarios in which you could incorporate your new skills. In one of the scenarios, you must include at least one EON Converter node or prototype.

1. Open each of the activity files you created in Module 10 Lesson 1.
2. Run and navigate each simulation (see Figure 10.1).

FIGURE 10.1 Logic.eoz simulation window from Activity 10.1.3

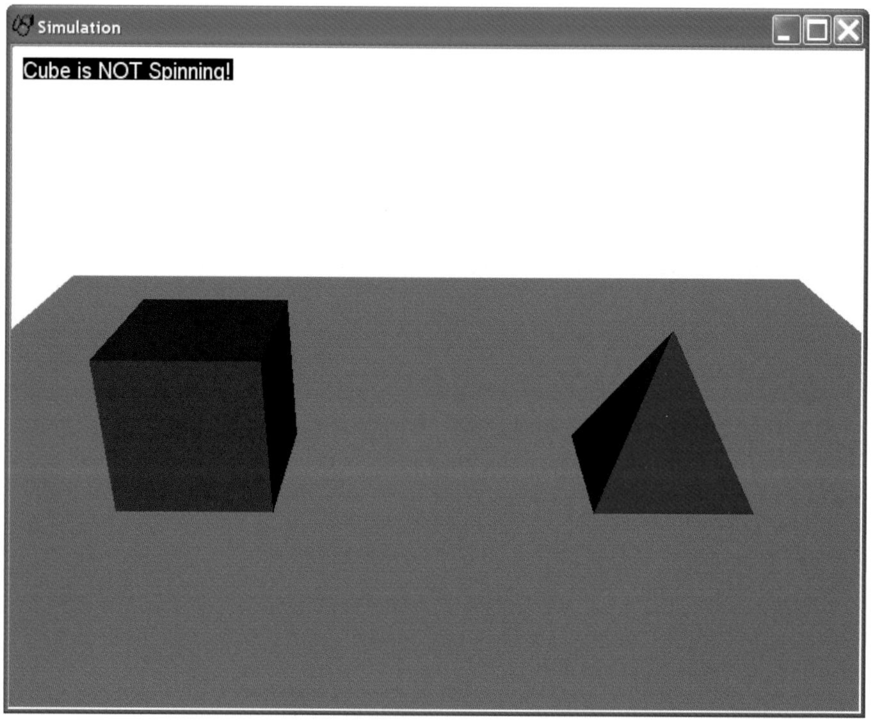

3. Navigate to the simulation tree of each file (see Figure 10.2).

FIGURE 10.2 Logic.eoz simulation tree from Activity 10.1.3

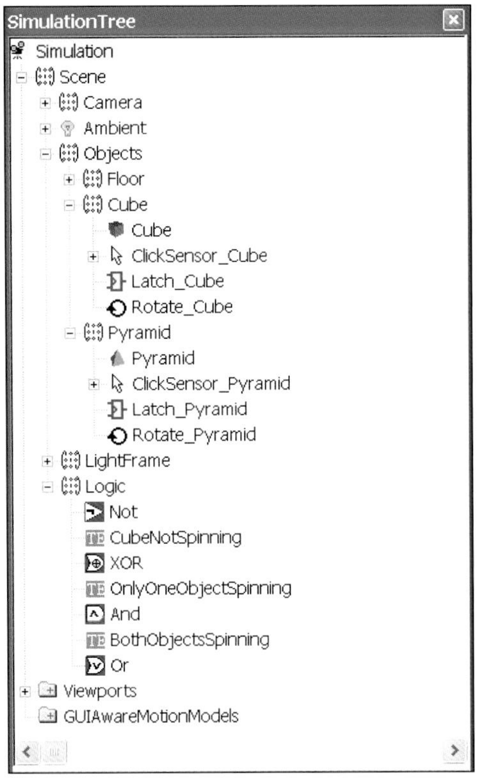

4. Take notes on the nodes that were used to create each simulation. Include information about the purpose of each node. If you need a quick refresher about a particular node, click the node in the simulation tree and press the **F1** key to display context-sensitive information in the EON Help window, as shown in Figure 10.3.

FIGURE 10.3 EON Help window for the And, Or, XOR, and Not nodes

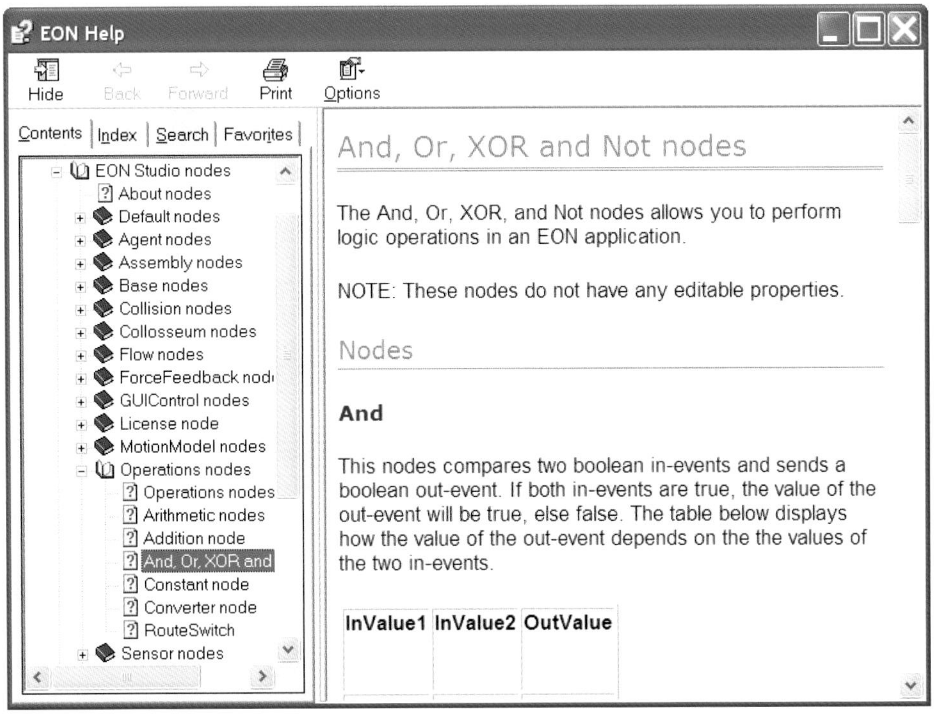

5. When you finish reviewing the contents of the EON Help window, close the window.
6. Close each simulation window. Close EON.
7. Run and navigate each simulation you created in Module 10 Lesson 2.
8. Review the simulation tree of each simulation.
9. Observe the nodes and prototypes that were used to create each simulation and add information to the notes you began taking in step 4. Like the notes you recorded previously, include information about the purpose of each node or prototype, reviewing the information available in the EON Help feature if necessary.
10. Close each simulation window. Close EON.
11. Brainstorm to create three storyboards documenting three different simulations you could write to train other designers. The simulations should be user-driven activities using basic shapes and data manipulation. Remember that one of the simulations must incorporate at least one EON Converter node or prototype.

Discussion

discuss

How did you decide which EON Converter node or prototype to include in your simulation?

Job 10.2: Creating a User-Driven Simulation

In Module 10 Lesson 1, you learned that a user's actions can be used to drive a simulation. Using your knowledge of this concept, create a user-driven simulation based on one of the storyboards you created in Job 10.1. Remember to keep the simulation simple, using basic shapes to represent more complex objects. Include a label to reference which object each shape represents. For example, you could use a shape to represent anything from a single chair to an entire office building. Be creative.

1. If necessary, take a few minutes to review the observations you documented in Job 10.1 that relate to the nodes used to create user-driven simulations. Make sure the storyboards you created for these simulations are also available for reference.
2. Create a simulation based on one of the storyboards you created in Job 10.1 and save the file as **Tutorial.eoz**.
3. Applying the information that you recorded in your notes, create the user-driven simulation you think would best serve as a tutorial for other designers.
4. Save the simulation and then run the simulation.
5. Close the simulation window. Keep the simulation open to use in Job 10.3.

Discussion

discuss

What are a few of the tips and tricks you would pass along to designers who are learning to create user-driven simulations for the first time?

Job 10.3: Performing Data Manipulation

In Module 10 Lesson 2, you learned that EON provides several nodes and prototypes that you can use to convert one type of data into a different—and more useful—form of data. Relying on your understanding of this subject, add data manipulation to the Tutorial.eoz simulation you created in Job 10.2, or create a different simulation from a storyboard you created in Job 10.1.

1. Continue working with the open simulation **Tutorial.eoz** from Job 10.2.
2. Save the simulation as **Tutorial_Data_Manipulation.eoz**.
3. Before continuing, review your notes and the storyboards you created in Job 10.1 that relate to data manipulation.
4. Incorporate at least one node or prototype to manipulate data.
5. Save the simulation and then run the simulation.
6. Close the simulation window. Close EON.

troubleshooting

Depending on the storyboard you chose to work with in Job 10.2, it might not make sense to perform data manipulation on the Tutorial.eoz simulation. If that is the case, create a second user-driven simulation file based on one of the other storyboards that you created in Job 10.1.

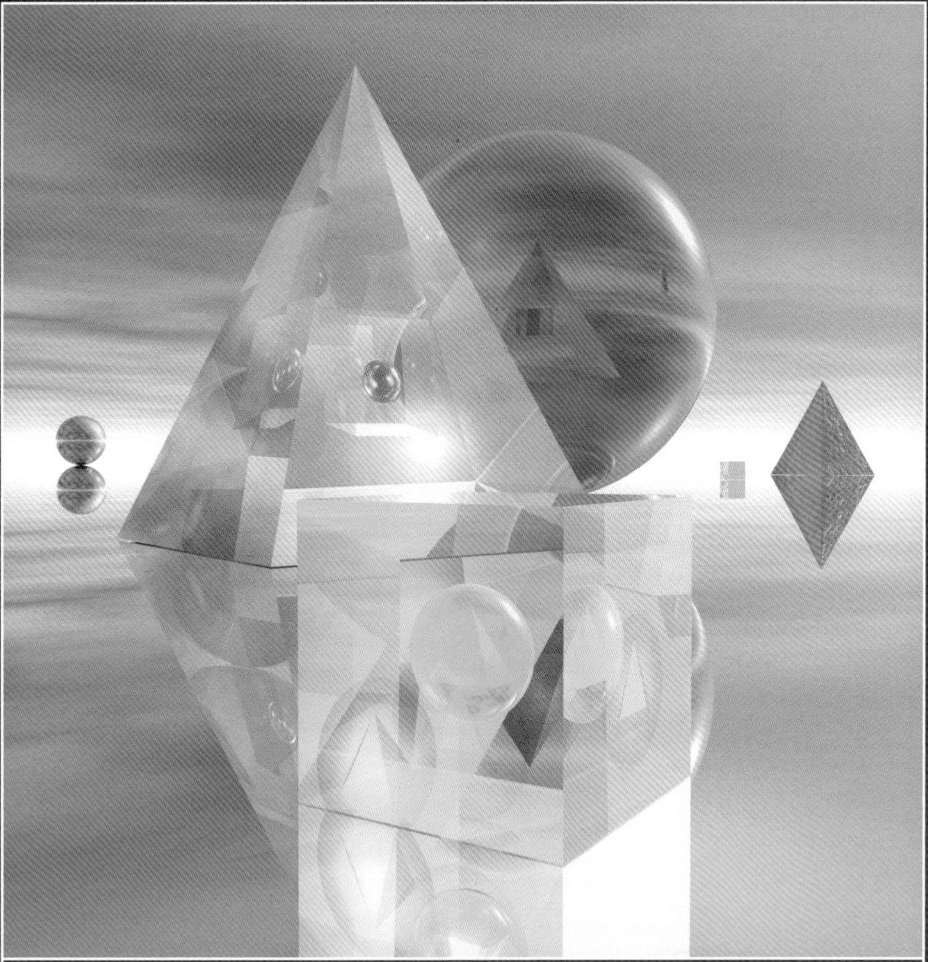
HARALD SUND

MODULE 11

Running Simulations on End User Computers

LESSON 11.1
Building Distribution Files

LESSON 11.2
Web Publishing and Runtime Installation

LESSON 11.1

Building Distribution Files

Objectives

In this lesson you will:

- Learn about the compilation process.
- Create a distribution file.
- Learn how to optimize geometry.
- Learn how to reduce file size with compression.
- Create a compiled prototype file.
- Understand external resource files.
- Determine when to use streaming and dynamic loading.
- Create a password-protected distribution prototype.

Key Terms

compilation
distribution file
downloading
dynamic load
geometry compression
loading
lossless
NURBS
password-protected private resource
private resource
public resource
resource sharing
streaming
tessellated
texture compression

Introduction to Simulation Distribution

In this last module, we consider how simulations will run on end user computers. What files will the end user need and how will the files be delivered? This lesson looks at building distribution files, which includes the topics of geometry and texture compression, as well as the advantages of making some resources external. The next lesson looks at publishing to a web page and the software that must be installed on the end user's computer before the simulation can run.

STORYBOARD

Building Distribution Files

Now that you know how to create simulations, it is time to move to the next logical topic in the storyboard.

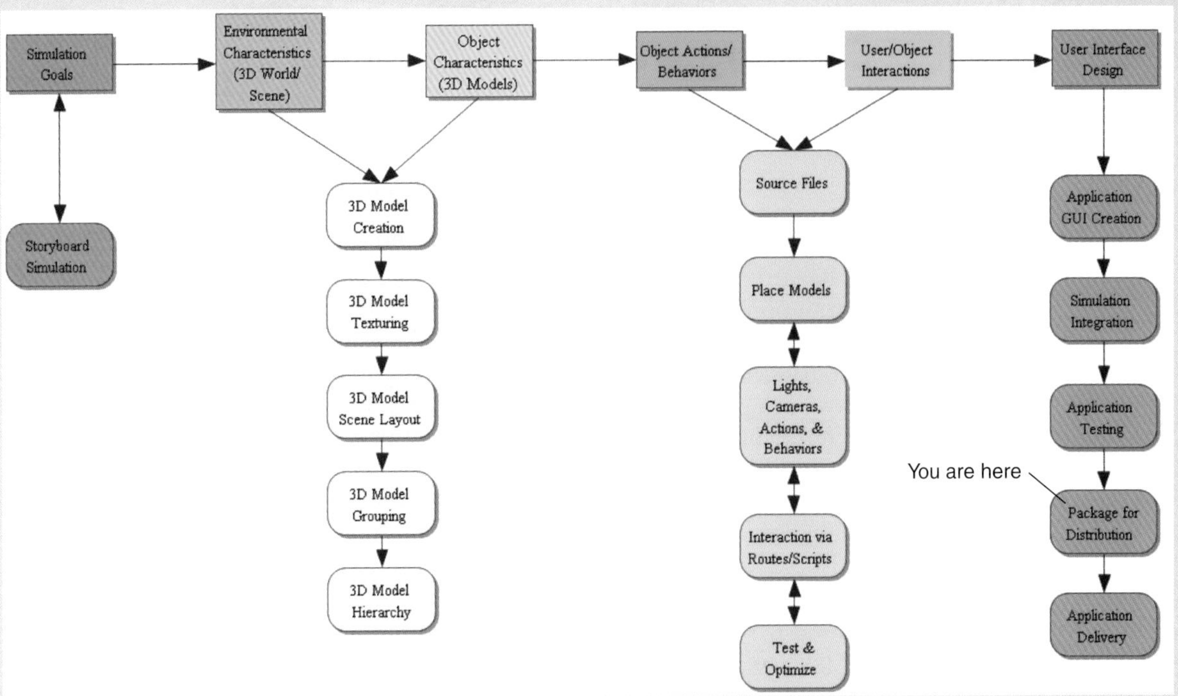

In this lesson, we will learn about the compilation process and how to create a distribution file. We will discuss how to optimize geometry, reduce file size, and create a compiled prototype file. We will talk about external resource files and how to determine when the use of streaming and dynamic loading is warranted. Finally, we will cover password-protected distribution prototypes.

Distribution File Format

In the previous lessons, you saved simulations in the .eoz file format. These files also could be called project files or source files. They are editable in EON Studio and include all of the resource files that are used. The .eoz files can be used by the end user as well as the simulation developer. However, another file format, called the ***distribution file***, is used specifically for the end user because it cannot be edited in EON authoring software. The distribution file, identified by the .edz file extension, is created through a compilation process. ***Compilation*** is an irreversible process that performs tasks such as polygon reduction, geometry compression, texture compression, and removal of other unnecessary information.

Why Should You Create Distribution Files?

Distribution files provide several advantages over the use of source files.

1. Only distribution files offer the optimization features of permanent polygon reduction, geometry compression, and texture compression.
2. Distribution files can be significantly smaller in size if the optimization features are enabled.
3. Distribution files protect the models, media, and programming from being copied by others for use in other applications.

4. Only distribution files allow specified resources to be external to the distribution file so they can be loaded after the application has started. This feature is called *streaming*.
5. External resources can be shared among many distribution files so that many simulations are updated by changing just one resource file.

Creating a Distribution File

When you choose to create a distribution file, several operations are automatically performed behind the scenes. During the Build Distribution File process, resources are compiled and inserted into an .edz file that can be viewed only in the EON runtime software, an EON standalone viewer, or a web browser. This makes it a safe distribution format for clients who would like to protect a simulation file's assets.

Regardless of the size or complexity of a simulation file, the process for creating a distribution file in EON is quite simple. With the simulation file open in EON, select File from the menu bar and then choose the Build Distribution File option. EON automatically performs the compilation process and creates the distribution file. You can view a progress bar during the process.

By default, the filename of the distribution file will be the same as the project file, but it has the file extension .edz instead of .eoz. Also by default, the file will be placed in a subfolder of the folder where the project file was located. The subfolder's name will be the same as the project file without the .eoz ending.

These two default settings can be modified by changing the DistributionFilename field in the Simulation node. The default value of this field is *${Project.Directory}\${Project.Name}\${Project.Name}.edz*, where *${Project.Directory}* is replaced with the path to the project file and *${Project.Name}* is replaced by the project filename without the .eoz extension. Instead of this default value, you could use an absolute path and filename so that it updates a certain file on your computer or a shared network drive.

Activity 11.1.1: Creating a Distribution File

1. Open EON. Open **Activity_11.1.1.eoz** from the data files for Module 11 Lesson 1.
2. Save the simulation as **Earth.eoz**.
3. From the Menu Bar, select **File > Build Distribution File**. The Compiling simulation dialog box is displayed (see Figure 11.1.1) during the compilation process. When the dialog box disappears, the compilation process has concluded and the distribution file has been created.

FIGURE 11.1.1 Compiling simulation dialog box

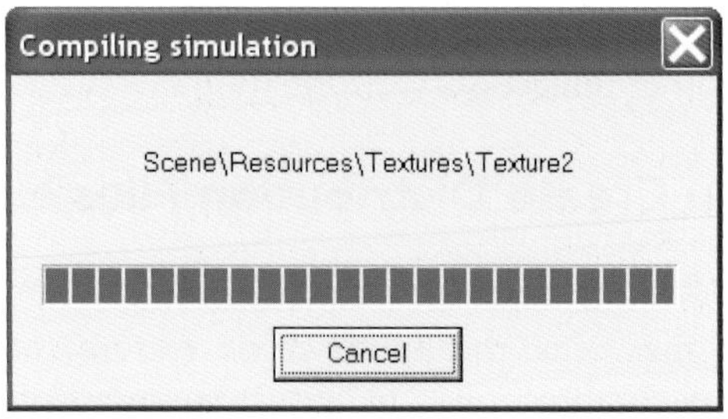

4. Navigate to your solution files for Module 11 Lesson 1 and notice that a new file folder, shown in Figure 11.1.2, has been created. Also note the size of the original Earth.eoz file, which is 1,316 KB.

FIGURE 11.1.2 EON distribution file folder

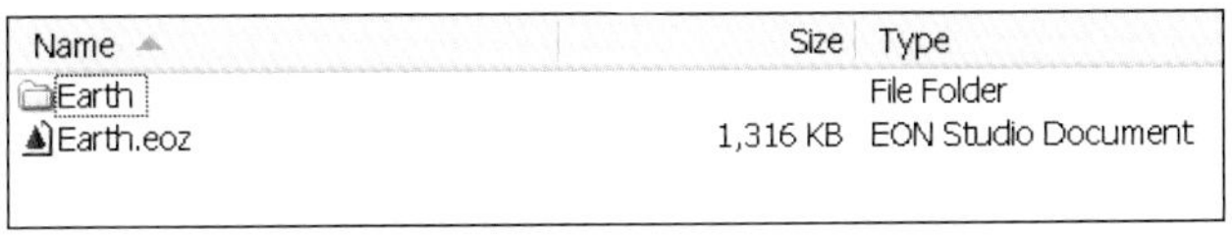

5. Double-click the **Earth** file folder. The new Earth.edz file appears (see Figure 11.1.3). Notice that the size of the .edz file is significantly smaller than that of the original .eoz file.

FIGURE 11.1.3 EON distribution file

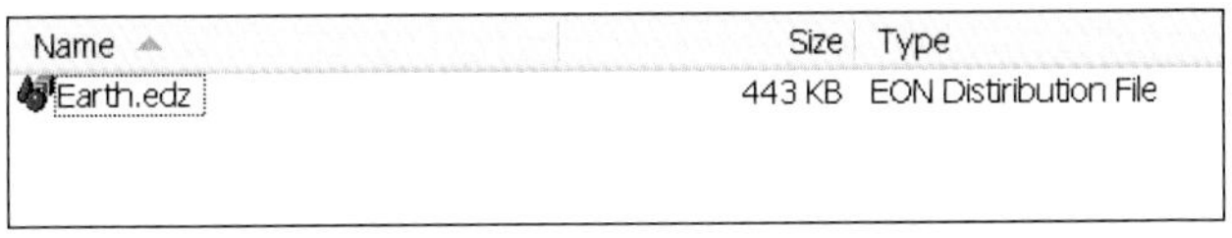

6. Close your browser window. Close EON without saving the simulation.

Optimization Features

Three areas of optimization can be applied to distribution files. They are polygon reduction, geometry compression, and texture compression and conversion. The overall goal of these processes is to reduce the file size and make the simulation perform as fast as possible without noticeably affecting quality. There is often a trade-off between visual quality on one side and rendering speed and file size on the other.

Polygon reduction removes an approximate percentage of the polygons in a 3D model. It does this in a way that tries to preserve the basic shape as much as possible so that new larger polygons may replace many smaller ones. ***Geometry compression*** does not cut away any polygons, but it reduces the precision of the data used to define a polygon and other geometry data. For example, a position might be reduced from 23.3458904 to 23.346. Both of these methods should be applied for maximum effectiveness.

Texture compression results from changing a texture's maximum width and height in pixels, changing its format, and changing its quality level. Textures can be saved to the DDS DXT format, but these textures are only visible on modern graphics cards, such as NVIDIA GeForce 5200 or later and ATI Radeon 9500 or later.

Using distribution files enables you to provide different versions to different end users. For example, you can create one version that has highly compressed textures for older, low-end computers and another version that has moderately compressed textures in the DDS DXT format for fast new computers.

You can preview the compression settings in EON Studio. However, if you open the project source file in EON Viewer or another host application, there is no compression of geometry or textures. After changing the compression settings and creating the distribution file, you should undo these changes so that the source file can run quickly. After removing the compression settings, you can continue to work with the simulation's .eoz file, modifying the simulation or using different compression settings to create another distribution file.

Texture compression and polygon reduction can significantly increase the startup time of project files in EON Studio. Therefore, if you continue to work with the simulation file, it is better to remove the compression settings. However, the distribution files that run in runtime software load quickly because the resources will already be compressed. For these reasons, use compression settings to create the distribution file.

Polygon Reduction

Polygon reduction can be applied to any mesh data for a Mesh2 node, but it is most effective on large, dense geometry files and CAD models with tessellated NURBS objects. ***NURBS*** (non-uniform rational B-spline) represents a mathematical model commonly used in computer graphics for generating and representing curves and surfaces. ***Tessellated*** NURBS have a checkered or tiled appearance. The fields used for polygon reduction are identified in Figure 11.1.4.

FIGURE 11.1.4 Mesh2 node's fields used for polygon reduction

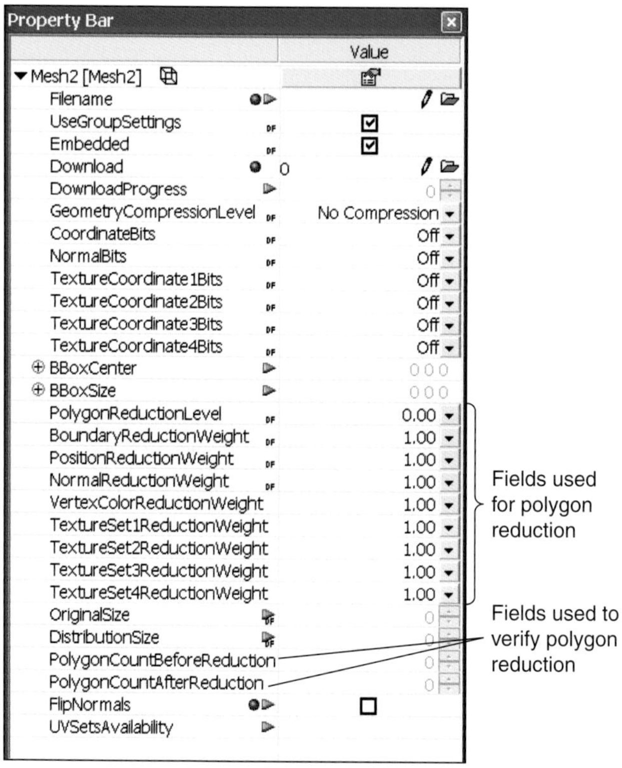

tips+tricks

If you run the source file in EON Viewer or another host application, the reduction settings are ignored. You can only preview the reduction effects in EON Studio.

To reduce the polygons of a specific 3D model:

1. Select the appropriate Mesh2 node (using the selection tools on the EONSelectionTools Bar or via the simulation tree).
2. Using the Property Bar, clear the UseGroupSettings check box of a geometry node if you want to set individual reduction settings for this geometry file. If this check box is checked, all reduction settings on this node are ignored.

3. Set the desired polygon reduction level using the PolygonReductionLevel field. This value identifies the percentage of the original polygon count that should be removed. For example, the value of 0 means no reduction at all, whereas a value of 100 means reduce as much as possible.
4. If the simulation window is open, the reduction will be applied to the chosen geometry node immediately and the effect is displayed in the simulation window. However, changes might not be visible if the reduction is small (or the geometry data is dense and can be reduced very well so the reduction is not obvious). In fact, the goal is to avoid any visible degradation while pushing the reduction level as high as possible. Visible degradation can be detected in shape changes, missing polygons, and uneven lighting effects.
5. To verify that the polygon count has been reduced, check the difference between the values in the PolygonCountBeforeReduction and PolygonCountAfterReduction fields. Note that the DistributionSize figure is adjusted as well to reflect the savings in storage requirements. Note that this figure is only an estimate because the final size cannot be determined until all data size–saving techniques have been applied to the model, which happens when creating a distribution file of the simulation.
6. If you make adjustments to the reduction level when the simulation window is not open, the reduction will be applied the next time that you start the simulation. The fields identified in the previous item are only updated during runtime.
7. To fine-tune how polygons are removed, use the reduction weight parameters. Each of the components comprising a 3D mesh has a weight value, as shown in Table 11.1.1. A higher weight value means that this component is more important, and it will not be reduced as much as other components that have lower weights.

tips+tricks

It is not always possible to reduce polygons to the requested level for all objects. Sometimes the topology or edge connection in the model prevents the reduction engine from making additional reductions.

TABLE 11.1.1 Reduction Weight Parameters

Parameter	Mesh2 Field Name
Vertex coordinates	PositionReductionWeight
Vertex normals	NormalReductionWeight
Vertex colors	VertexColorReductionWeight
Edges	BoundaryReductionWeight
Texture coordinates	TextureSet1ReductionWeight

tips+tricks

The TextureSet2ReductionWeight, TextureSet3ReductionWeight, and TextureSet4ReductionWeight fields are used for meshes that contain multiple UV sets. Polygon reduction supports up to four sets of UVs.

Geometry Compression

In the Mesh2 node, the GeometryCompressionLevel field controls the amount of compression. Eight preset levels range from 1 (lowest compression) to 8 (highest compression). Also, you can choose no compression (−1) and Custom (0). When you choose Custom, the fields named CoordinateBits, NormalBits, and TextureCoordinate1Bits will determine the compression level. Geometry data consists of positions (coordinates), orientations (normals), and texture coordinates. This data can be stored using between 3 and 31 bits precision. Geometry compression can be applied to any mesh data of Mesh2 type, even though it is most effective on large, dense geometry files. The fields used for geometry compression are identified in Figure 11.1.5.

FIGURE 11.1.5 Mesh2 node's fields used for geometry compression

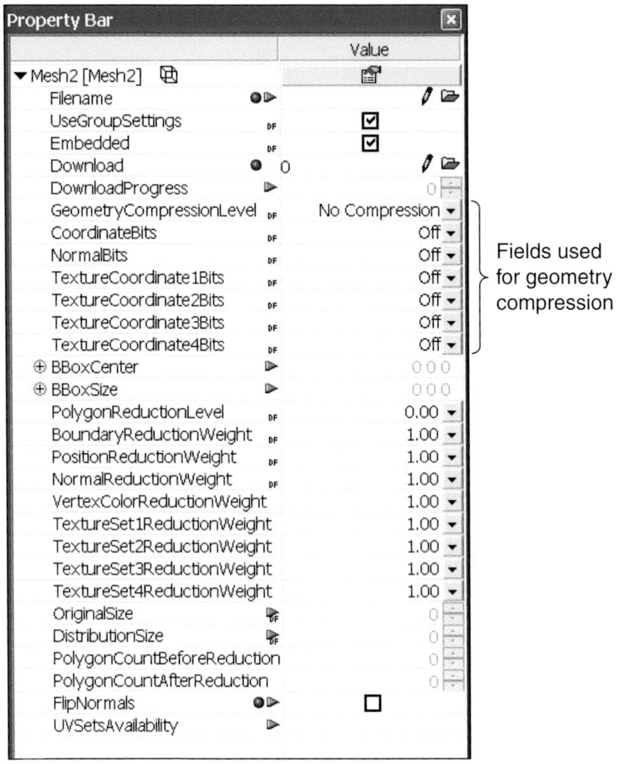

tips+tricks

The TextureCoordinate2Bits, TextureCoordinate3Bits, and TextureCoordinate4Bits fields are not used in version 6 of EON Studio.

To compress a specific 3D model:

1. Select the appropriate Mesh2 node (using the selection tools on the EON-SelectionTools Bar or via the simulation tree).
2. Using the Property Bar, clear the UseGroupSettings check box of a geometry node if you want to set individual compression settings for this geometry file. If this check box is checked, all compression settings on this node are ignored.
3. Set the desired overall compression level using the GeometryCompressionLevel field. You also can customize the compression by setting GeometryCompression-Level to Custom and then adjusting the compression level of individual geometry components through the CoordinateBits, NormalBits, and TextureCoordinate-1Bits fields. The numeric values in these fields control the number of bits that are used to store the respective geometry components. Allocating more bits for a component provides better accuracy but creates a larger data file.
4. If the simulation window is open, the compression will be applied to the chosen geometry node immediately and the effect is displayed in the simulation window. However, changes might not be visible if the compression is set to a low level (or the geometry data can be compressed very well). In fact, the goal is to avoid any visible degradation while pushing the compression level as high as possible.
5. To verify that the geometry data has been compressed, check the difference between the values in the OriginalSize and DistributionSize fields, which should be positive. Note that the DistributionSize figure is only an estimate because the actual reduction in size cannot be determined until a final compression is done on the underlying geometry file (which happens when creating a distribution file of the simulation).
6. If you make adjustments to the compression when the simulation window is not open, the compression will be applied the next time that you start the simulation. The OriginalSize and DistributionSize fields are only updated during runtime.

Texture Compression and Conversion

Texture optimization is an important part of the development of interactive 3D simulations. If you do not ensure that the total memory size needed for textures is less than the memory size of the graphics card, then the simulation will be slow, and some textures may appear black. A texture can be converted to a different format. The texture's maximum pixel width and height can be changed. If the texture uses the JPEG 2000 format, you can change the texture's quality level.

EON supports several texture formats: JPG, PNG, PPM, JPEG 2000, and DDS/DXT. When you need to convert a texture to a different format, consider your needs and the advantages and disadvantages of each format.

In general, the JPEG 2000 format appears to compress better than the other formats, creating the smallest file size, followed by DDS/DXT. The largest files often use the PNG format; however, this is not always the case. If the QualityLevel value of 100 is not changed, then JPG files can be larger than the original file. Therefore, when you convert the format to JPEG 2000, set the QualityLevel field to a value that is less than 100. If your texture format is DDS/DXT, then the texture will not be converted or compressed at all.

To compress a texture, you can set its maximum pixel width or pixel height to a value that is less than its current width or height. Generally, when you lower the pixel size, the image looks more pixelated. If you are using the JPEG 2000 format, then a lower quality level will produce a blurry image that uses fewer colors. The PNG and DDS/DXT formats do not use the QualityLevel field. The image type for the PNG and DDS/DXT formats is ***lossless***, meaning that image quality is not lost for a certain pixel size in the image.

JPEG 2000 compression is better than JPG compression; it produces a smaller file with the same quality as the JPG format or the same file size with better quality. The PNG, JPG2000, and DDS/DXT formats support alpha channels.

DDS/DXT textures have an advantage because you do not need to decompress the textures before sending them to the graphics card. This means that the textures can be sent immediately, allowing applications to start much faster. They also take less RAM space on the graphics card than decompressed textures using the JPG, PNG, and JPEG 2000 format. The DDS/DXT format has several variations, but the general rule is to use the DDS DXT1 format for nontransparent textures and use the DDS DXT5 format for transparent textures. Using this technology creates a dramatic change in graphics card memory usage.

Texture compression or conversion is applied to the Texture2 node. The fields used for texture compression or conversion are identified in Figure 11.1.6.

troubleshooting

The PPM format does not have any useful advantages for simulations. Therefore, the format is supported but it is not offered as a conversion option.

troubleshooting

Textures using the DDS/DXT format do not work on all computers. Only newer computers with a modern graphics card will support these types of textures. Use NVIDIA GeForce FX5200 or later or ATI Radeon 9500 or later and always use the latest official graphics card drivers.

FIGURE 11.1.6 Texture2 node fields used for texture compression or conversion

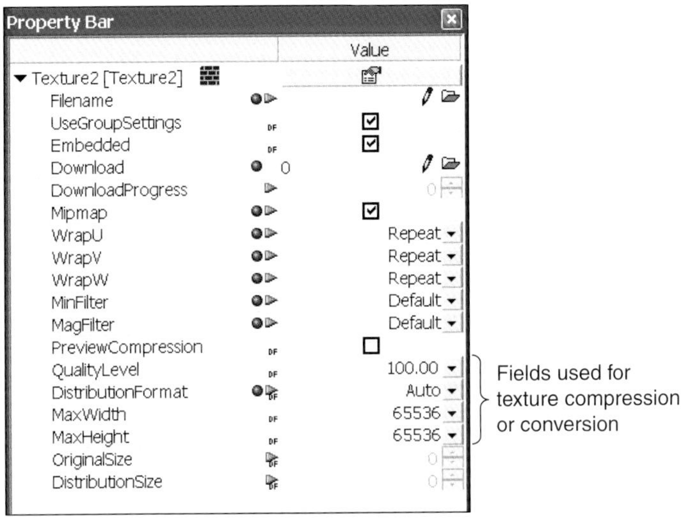

troubleshooting

After you change compression settings in the Property Bar, it may take some time before EON converts and compresses the textures. During this time, the simulation is paused and appears frozen or unresponsive. Also, additional startup time may be needed for texture compression and conversion.

tips+tricks

When you convert a PNG format texture to DDS/DXT, the actual distribution size is usually half of the displayed value.

tips+tricks

You cannot preview compression when you run the source file in EON Viewer.

To compress or convert a texture:

1. Select the appropriate Texture2 node (using the selection tools on the EONSelectionTools Bar or via the simulation tree).
2. Using the Property Bar, clear the UseGroupSettings check box if you want to set individual compression settings for this texture file. If this check box is checked, all compression settings on this node are ignored.
3. Set the desired distribution format in the DistributionFormat field. If Auto is selected, then EON will choose the format based on the current texture format and the other compression settings. Do not select DDS DXT1 if your texture has transparent parts; instead, use the PNG, JPG2000, or DDS DXT5 format.
4. Set the values in the MaxWidth and MaxHeight fields to reduce the size of the texture and thereby compress it.
5. If you are converting to JPEG 2000, then set the QualityLevel field to a value between 1 and 100, in which 1 is the lowest quality and 100 is the best quality.
6. You can see the effects of compression and conversion if the simulation window is open and the PreviewCompression check box is checked. Your goal is to avoid any visible quality degradation while compressing the textures as much as possible. If no effect is detected, verify that the UseGroupSettings check box is unchecked, the PreviewCompression check box is checked, and you are looking at the correct texture. Generally, you should reduce the values in the MaxWidth and MaxHeight fields first and then reduce the value in the QualityLevel field.
7. To verify that the textures have been compressed, check the difference between the values in the OriginalSize and DistributionSize fields. Note that the value in the DistributionSize field is only an estimate.
8. If you make adjustments to the compression level when the simulation window is not open, the reduction will be applied the next time that you start the simulation. The DistributionSize field is only updated during runtime.

Discussion

discuss

Why would you optimize a file?
Can you think of situations when file optimization should not be used?

Distribution Prototype Files

The advantages of compilation can be applied to your dynamic load applications. The resources in prototypes also can be compressed and protected. Distribution prototypes have the .edp file extension, and they can be dynamically loaded only by a distribution file. The method of creating distribution prototype files is different from normal prototypes. You do not use the New button in the Components window. Instead, you right-click a prototype in the Local Prototypes window and choose the Build Distribution file option from the pop-up menu. A Distribute Target File dialog box is displayed that allows you to choose a location for the saved file. By default, it saves the file in a subfolder of the folder that contains the .eoz file. The subfolder's name will be the same as the prototype's name.

Activity 11.1.2: Creating a Distribution Prototype for Dynamic Load

1. Open EON. Open **Activity_11.1.2.eoz** from the data files for Module 11 Lesson 1.
2. Save the simulation as **Office.eoz**.

3. In the Local Prototypes window, right-click the **OfficeChair1** prototype and choose the **Build Distribution file** option from the pop-up menu to display the Distribution Target File dialog box shown in Figure 11.1.7. Click **Save** to save the distribution file to the default location. In this activity, the default location is the OfficeChair1 folder, which is created when this file is saved. The OfficeChair1 folder will be created in the folder containing the Office.eoz file you created in step 2.

FIGURE 11.1.7 Distribution Target File dialog box for the OfficeChair1 prototype

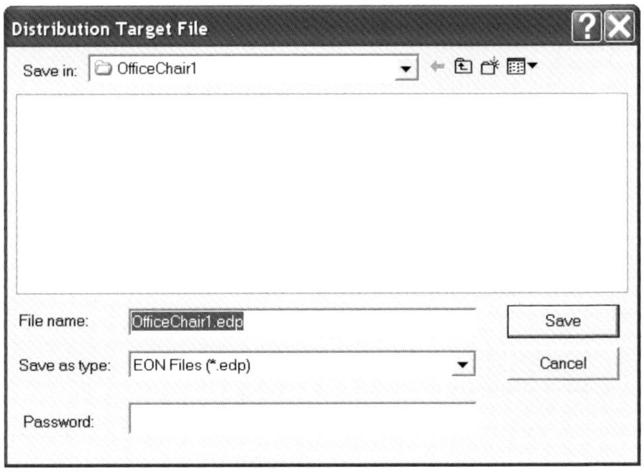

4. Expand **Scene > Office > Chair** in the simulation tree. Delete the **OfficeChair1** prototype from the simulation tree and the Local Prototypes window.
5. Add a **DynamicPrototype** node under the Chair frame in the simulation tree. In the Property Bar, set its PrototypeName field to **OfficeChair1.edp** as shown in Figure 11.1.8. The PrototypeName field will display the entire path to the OfficeChair1.edp file.

FIGURE 11.1.8 DynamicPrototype node added to the simulation tree

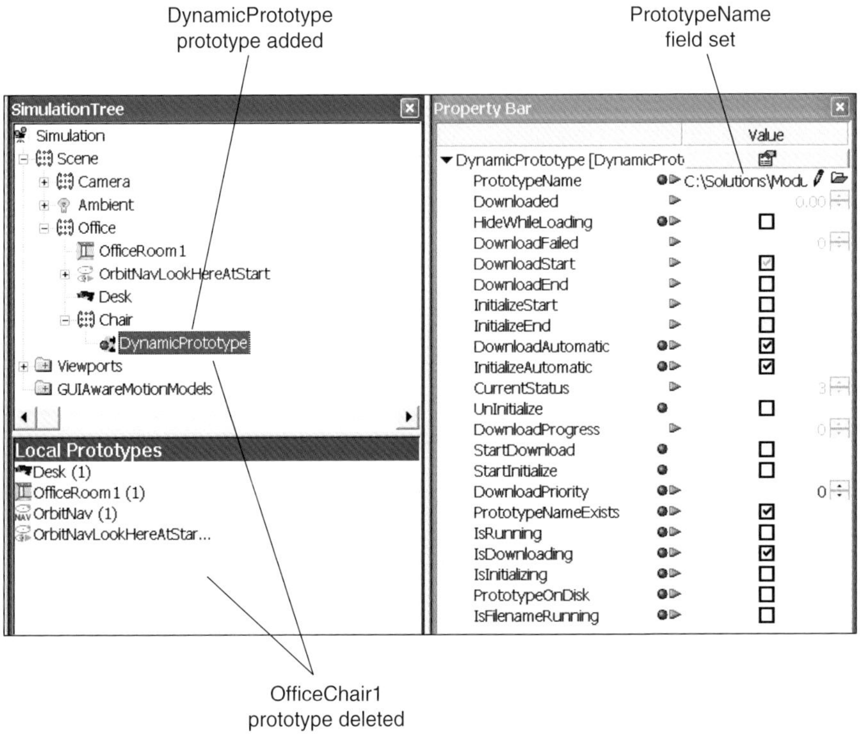

6. Save the simulation.

troubleshooting

EON looks for the distribution prototype file in the default location first. If the distribution prototype file is not in the default location, browse to the correct location. The location on your computer may differ from the location displayed in Figure 11.1.8.

7. To build a distribution file, select **Build Distribution File** from the File menu. You will see a small Compiling simulation window while the distribution file is created, as shown in Figure 11.1.9. The message window is closed when the distribution file has been created.

FIGURE 11.1.9 Compiling simulation window

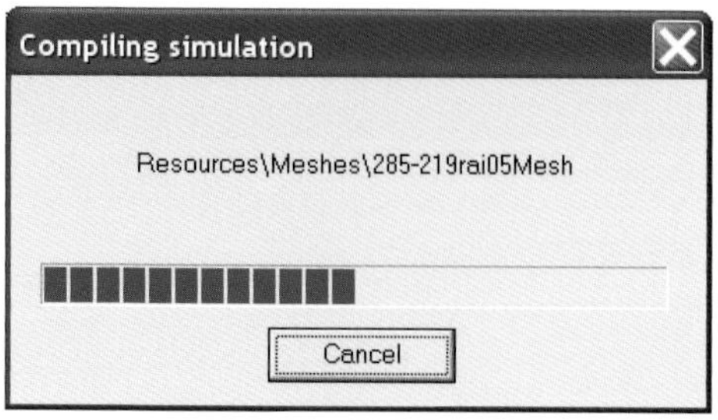

troubleshooting

The location of EON Viewer may differ if you are using a different version of EON Studio.

8. Close EON without saving the simulation.
9. Open EON Viewer by clicking the Windows **Start** button and selecting **All Programs > EON Reality > EON Studio 6.0 > EON Viewer**.
10. From the menu bar, select **Tools**, and then click **Options** to display the Options dialog box, as shown in Figure 11.1.10.

FIGURE 11.1.10 Options dialog box for EON Viewer

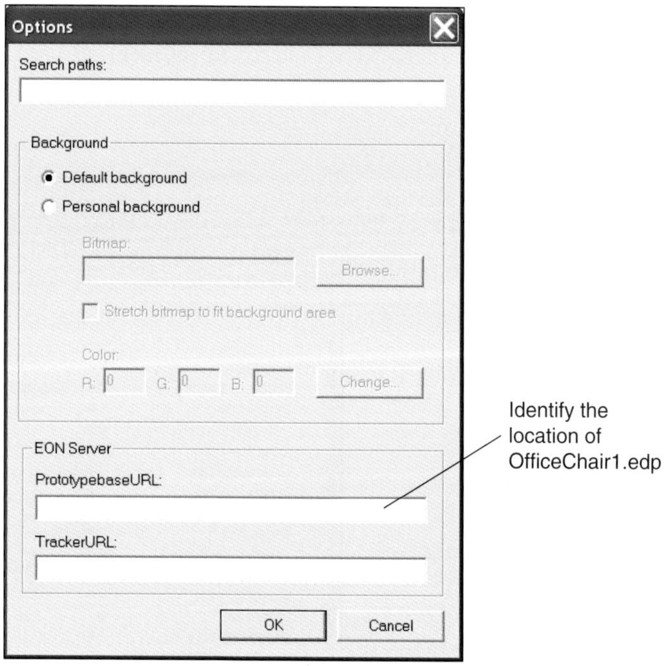

tips+tricks

The PrototypebaseURL field does not have an associated Browse button to navigate to the prototype distribution file. Open a Windows Explorer window and browse to the prototype distribution file. Copy the path from the Address field at the top of the Windows Explorer window. Close the Windows Explorer window and paste the path in the PrototypebaseURL field in the Options window.

11. Set the PrototypebaseURL field to the location of the prototype distribution file and then click the **OK** button.

12. Select **Open** from the File menu to display the standard Windows Open dialog box. Browse to the **Office.edp** file you created in step 7 as shown in Figure 11.1.11.

FIGURE 11.1.11 Options dialog box for EON Viewer

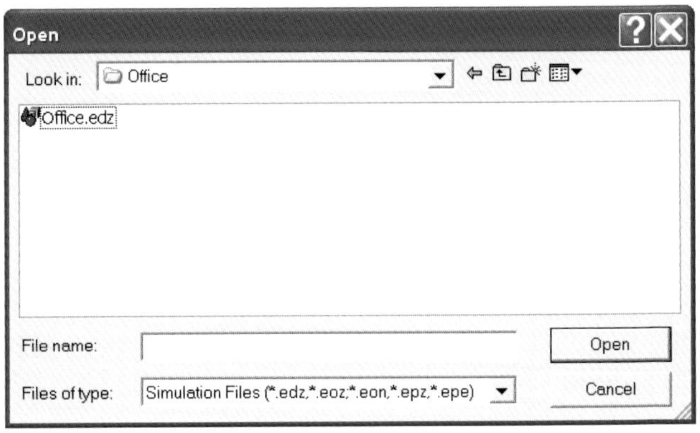

13. Select the **Office.edz** distribution file and click the **Open** button. The simulation, including the office chair (OfficeChair1.edp), is displayed, as shown in Figure 11.1.12.

FIGURE 11.1.12 Office.edz displayed in EON Viewer

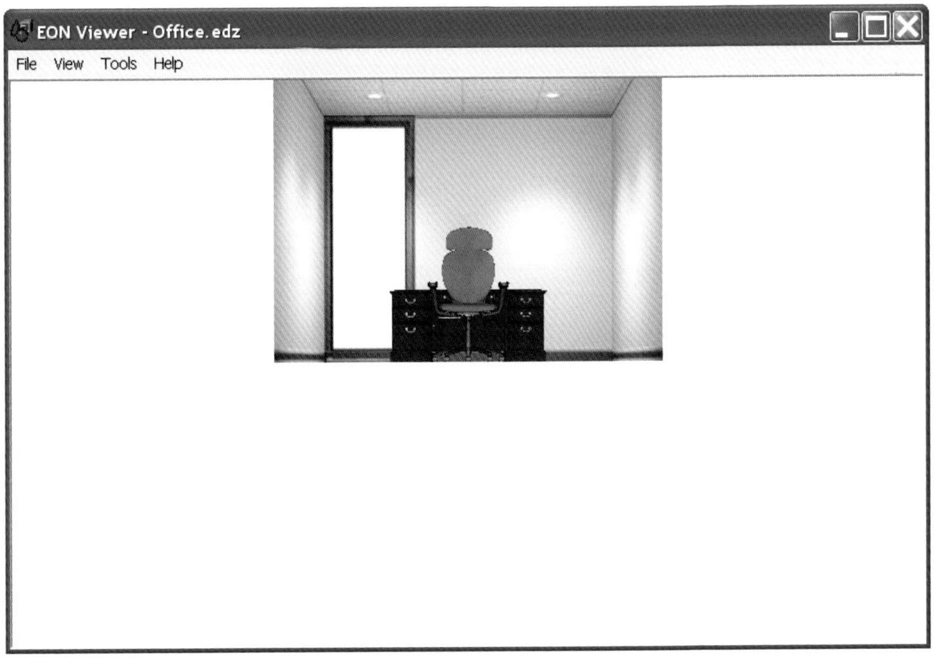

14. Zoom in to see the office more clearly. Mouse over different parts of the chair. Click the chair when the cursor looks like a hand to see a text message displayed. Explore all of the parts of the chair and the desk.
15. Select **Exit** from the File menu to close the EON Viewer.

External Resource Files

Before you create distribution files, you can make some or all of the resources external. This enables two important features: streaming and resource sharing.

Nodes that use resources, such as textures and meshes, have an Embedded field that indicates whether the resource will be placed inside or outside the resulting distribution file. The Embedded flag has no effect on a project file; all resources except dynamic prototypes are always embedded inside the simulation file. However, when creating a distribution file, the resources that are marked as external (Embedded is false) will be placed outside the distribution file. External resources will be compiled just like embedded resources, but they will be placed in a folder relative to the distribution file.

The Mesh2, Texture2, and MovieTexture resource nodes have the Embedded field that allows them to be external resources. If you want any other types of resources to be external, they must be in a prototype that is loaded by the DynamicPrototype node. Resources that can be in a prototype include resources used by nodes such as the DirectSound, Sound, 2DImage, Panorama, and Decal nodes. The old Mesh and old Texture nodes could also be included in a prototype.

Follow these steps to make a specific resource external:

1. Select the Mesh2, Texture2, or MovieTexture node that references the resource that is to be external.
2. Using the Property Bar, clear the UseGroupSettings check box because we want to set individual embedded settings for this resource file. If this field is checked, the Embedded field on this node is ignored and the Group node's Embedded field is followed.
3. Using the Property Bar, clear the Embedded check box, as shown in Figure 11.1.13.

FIGURE 11.1.13 MovieTexture node settings to create an external resource

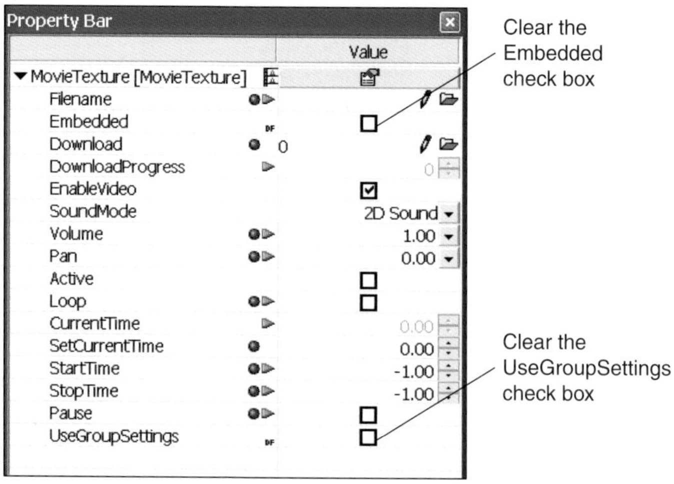

When you create a distribution file, external resources are compiled and placed relative to the distribution file. They are placed under two subfolders. The first subfolder is named resources. The second folder, depending on the type of resource, has one of three possible names: geometries, textures, or movies.

When you run a distribution file, the EON runtime software searches for the external resources relative to the distribution file, as described previously, or relative to the PrototypebaseURL, which can be specified in a host application.

cross-reference

Resource sharing is discussed later in this lesson.

tips+tricks

When performing the Save or Save As function on a simulation file, all references to external resources are resolved and the external resources are copied into the simulation project file. Simulation files (.eoz files) are always saved as standalone files. This means that they do not rely on any external resources.

troubleshooting

If you have already saved an EON simulation file, deleted resource type nodes (such as Mesh2, Texture2, and MovieTexture), and selected the Save option, the deleted resources are not removed from the .eoz file. To remove the resources, you must choose the Save As option, which creates a new .eoz file and takes only what it needs from the old file. You can use the Save As option and choose the same filename, replacing the old file. If you think your file is larger than it should be, use the Save As function to ensure that all unnecessary resources have been removed.

troubleshooting

In EON Studio version 6, textures can be compressed *or* external, but they will not load if they are compressed *and* external.

Resource Streaming and Loading

Streaming is the ability to download and load external resources after the simulation has started. The main reason for streaming is to reduce the time needed to start a simulation. Starting time consists of two parts: the time required to download the distribution file from the Internet and the time required to load the simulation from its file into the computer's memory. By removing resources from the main distribution file that are not immediately required when the simulation starts, the size of the distribution file is smaller and, therefore, requires less time to download. Having fewer resources also reduces the amount of time needed for loading or initialization. The removed resources will be external resources that will start downloading when the application starts. While external resources are downloading, the user can begin to use the simulation.

Example of Streaming

In the following example of streaming, a simulation of a house is stored on the Internet. The simulation resources are divided into four parts:

1. Exterior walls, windows, and roof
2. Internal walls, doors, and floor
3. House contents, such as furniture and appliances
4. Home surroundings such as the terrain, trees, and landscaping

Rather than making one large standalone .edz file, we could create a small distribution file that contains only the resources for the first part (the external walls, windows, and roof). All of the other resources could be external resources that are streamed in after the application starts. This enables the user to see the part that is important when the simulation starts (the outside part of the house). While they explore, additional parts are downloading. These parts will start to appear if they are in the user's field of view. By the time the user is ready to explore the interior of the house, the relevant resources have been downloaded and loaded.

Deciding to Use Streaming

Streaming is advantageous only if your simulation is downloaded over the Internet where download time is an issue. If your simulation is small or the end user's Internet connection is fast, streaming is not needed.

Downloading is the process of getting the resource from the Internet to your computer's local disk (Internet Cache folder). ***Loading*** is the process of moving the resource from the local file to the computer's memory. Downloading can be done without disturbing a running simulation, and we can see the progress of downloading by utilizing the DownloadProgress field of the resource nodes. During the second loading process, the simulation pauses and a message is displayed in a bar at the bottom of the simulation window that says "Loading Resource." This can disrupt the user's experience, so consider this factor when you are deciding if or how many resources to make external.

Another consideration is the number of times the user is likely to use the simulation. Streaming is advantageous only when the simulation is viewed for the first time. When the simulation is viewed again, the resources will already be in the user's Internet Cache folder, eliminating the need to save time when downloading resources. Instead, the application appears to start, but it immediately pauses the simulation to load external resources. For the same reason, streaming is not recommended for simulations that have a local distribution file. In fact, it can take longer to load external resources than it does to load internal resources because external resources have the extra overhead of searching for the resources and displaying the Loading Resource message for every resource.

Another consideration is the total download time from the Internet, which will tend to be longer if you have many files instead of just one file, even if the combined total file size in each situation is the same. This is caused by the increased overhead for each file.

Streaming vs. Dynamic Load

Resources can be loaded using two different methods: streaming or dynamic load. Streaming involves loading statically bound resources in which the reference to a resource is set in a saved simulation or prototype. Loading begins immediately after the simulation has downloaded and occurs in no particular order.

cross-reference

For more information about the EON Dynamic Load license, see Module 9 Lesson 3.

Dynamic load involves loading dynamically bound resources in which the reference to a resource is set or changed while a simulation is running. This type of loading lets you identify the resources, decide the sequence for downloading and loading resources, and determine whether resources will be loaded at all. This powerful type of resource loading requires an EON Dynamic Load license. Note that dynamic loading will work without a license, but text will pop up regularly in the simulation window declaring that the simulation is missing a license.

Streaming does not require a license. A DynamicPrototype node, whose PrototypeName field was set while authoring the simulation to download a prototype immediately, will load the prototype automatically. This is known as streaming. It does not require an EON Dynamic Load license.

Sharing and Protecting Resources

Resource sharing is the use of specified external resources by multiple simulations. You can build a repository of resources that can be reused at any time. The most important advantage of resource sharing is the time-saving ability to update a resource once in a single location to affect every simulation using the resource without recompiling all of the simulations that use that resource. All simulations will use the updated resource.

The other advantage affects simulations downloaded from the Internet. If a user is using multiple simulations that share one resource, then they only need to download the resource once. From then on, the resource will be in the user's Internet Cache folder. This means that users will not need to wait for the resource to download a second time.

Protecting Resources from Unauthorized Use

Another reason to create distribution files is to protect your digital assets from being used in unauthorized ways. This includes 3D models, textures, script code, and other media, such as sound and video. Some companies like to keep product specifications confidential. Although they are willing to show the product in a certain simulation, they do not want to allow detailed exploration of the model by a competitor. Additional reasons for preventing access to the resources in an EON simulation include the protection of intellectual property and complying with confidentiality or licensing agreements. Also, scripts in your simulations might include passwords to databases or server applications connected to your simulation.

A distribution file can only be used by the EON runtime software. No other software can open this file, not even EON Studio. In contrast, the source simulation project file (.eoz) allows access to all of the resources it contains. The .eoz project file can be opened in EON Studio, EON Professional, WinZip, and the EON runtime software. The geometry inside an .eoz project file is saved in EON's own format (.eog), but all of the texture, sound, and video resources used are well-known image, sound, and video file formats. Anyone could open the .eoz file to extract resources and code or see how the simulation is constructed.

If you do not want others to use these resources in their own simulations, then you should create a distribution file. Creating a distribution file will compile the file in an irreversible process that prevents all access. No special settings are required. It is automatic for all distribution files.

tips+tricks

The .eoz project file can be password protected. Enter the password in the Password field of the Simulation node. When you try to open a password-protected simulation, a dialog box asks for the password. If the password is not entered, the simulation opens in Locked mode. Locked mode does not allow access to the simulation tree or the Routes window, but it does allow you to run the simulation.

Discussion

discuss

What are other reasons for protecting resources from unauthorized users?

Controlling Access to External Resource Files

The distribution file (.edz) is protected, but what protects the external resources that the distribution file uses? EON offers ways to protect the external resources as well, but the method depends on the format of the external resources. External resources can be categorized into three groups: public resources, private resources, and password-protected private resources.

Public Resources

Public resources are external resource files that can be opened in software other than the EON runtime software. They include prototype library files (.eop, not .edp) and movie files. EOP files are in the same category as .eoz files and can be opened and editied in EON Studio. Movie files can be opened and edited in movie-editing software. Dynamically loaded prototype library files (.eop) are external resources that are in the same category as .eoz files because they can be opened in EON Studio and WinZip. This means that the files are public.

Private Resources

Private resources are external resource files that are private to the EON runtime software. Private resources can be used only by the EON runtime software. When you create a distribution file, the resources you choose to be external will be compiled as well. Therefore, they can be used only by the EON runtime software. This includes resources referenced by the Mesh2 and Texture2 nodes. External compiled geometry will be in the .eogz file format. Textures can be in the .etxz or .jpgz format.

Distribution prototypes are compiled into the .edp format and can only be dynamically loaded by distribution files in EON runtime software. These files are also private resources.

tips+tricks

The exceptions to the rule pertaining to external resource file access control are the movie resources used by the MovieTexture node. If these resources are made external, they will remain public resources and their file format will not be changed. To protect movie resources, keep them as embedded resources or put them inside a distribution prototype.

Password-Protected Private Resources

Private resources offer a great deal of protection for your digital assets, but one area is not protected. Although these resources can be used only in EON runtime software, this does not stop other users from creating their own EON simulations in the distribution format that reference external resources that have the same filename as yours. This would allow them to use the resources in ways that you did not intend, such as examining models and textures in close detail. To prevent unauthorized use of your private resources, you can protect them with a password.

To use this feature, choose Preferences from the Options menu to display the Preferences dialog box, as shown in Figure 11.1.14. Specify a password in the Default Password field located in the Build Distribution area of the dialog box and click the OK button. When you build a distribution file, the default password will be saved as part of the file format of any external resources. These ***password-protected private resources*** will load only if referenced by a distribution file that has a matching password in the ResourcePasswords field of its Simulation node. The ResourcePasswords field can specify multiple resource passwords that give the distribution file permission to use any password-protected resource containing a password in the resource that matches any one of the passwords in the distribution file.

FIGURE 11.1.14 Preferences dialog box

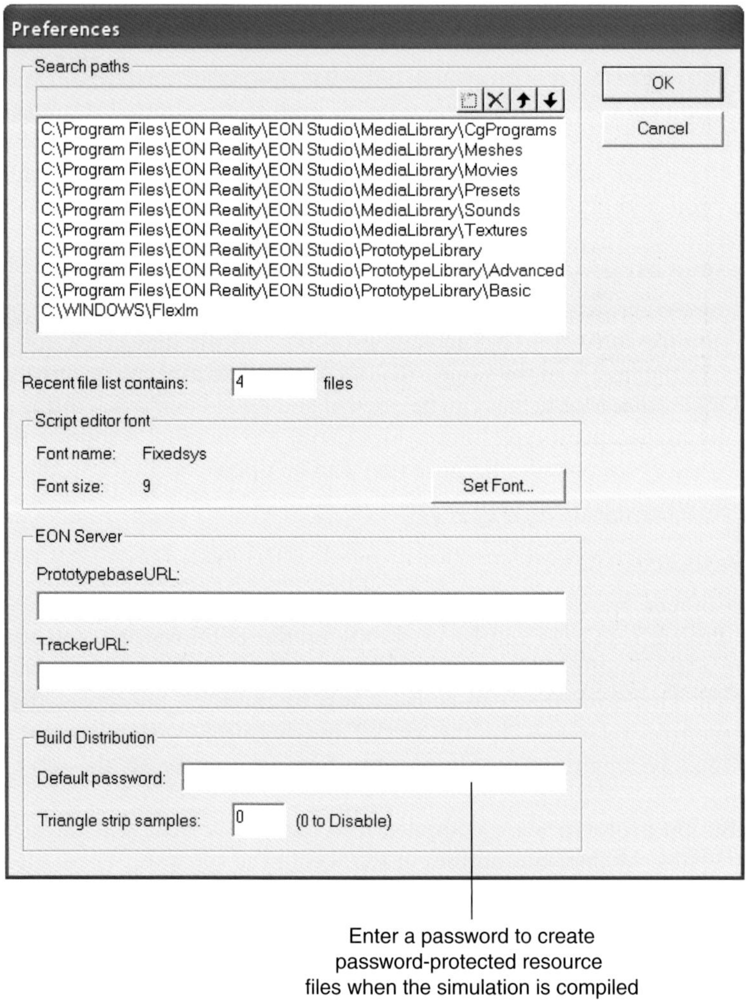

Activity 11.1.3: Password-Protecting an External Resource

1. Open EON. Open **Activity_11.1.3.eoz** from the data files for Module 11 Lesson 1.
2. Expand **Scene > Teapot > Frame > Resources > Meshes**. Select the **Teapot01** node. In the Property Bar, clear the **Embedded** check box and clear the **UseGroupSetttings** check box as shown in Figure 11.1.15. Clearing these check boxes sets the fields to false and identifies this Mesh2 node as an external resource.

FIGURE 11.1.15 Teapot1 node identified as an external resource

3. Save the simulation as **MyTeapot.eoz**.
4. Before you create a distribution file, you will choose a password. Select **Preferences** from the Options menu to display the Preferences dialog box. In the Build distribution section, set the default password by typing **cheers** in the Default password field as shown in Figure 11.1.16. Click the **OK** button. This will protect all of the external resources created by the build distribution file process.

troubleshooting

This activity may require EON Professional. Depending on your configuration of EON modules, you may not be able to complete this activity.

FIGURE 11.1.16 Default password set

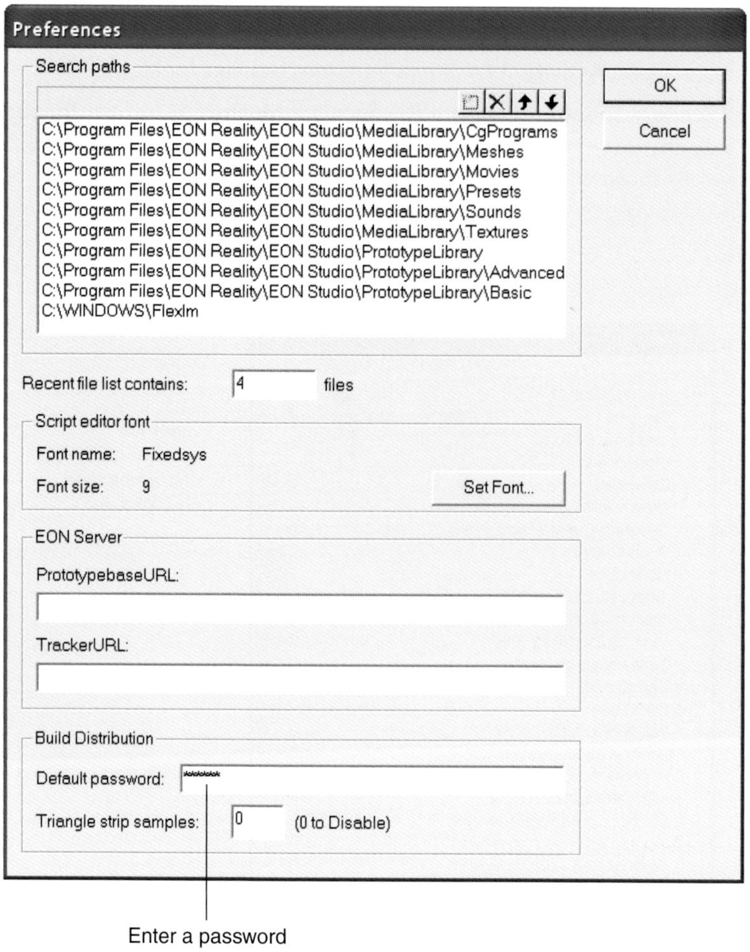

5. Select **Build Distribution File** from the File menu. The MyTeapot.edz distribution file and the Teapot01.eogz external resource file are created.
6. Browse to the MyTeapot.edz distribution file. Confirm that the Teapot01.eogz external resource file is in the resources\geometries subfolder.
7. Without closing EON Studio, open the **MyTeapot.edz** distribution file in EON Viewer. The teapot is missing because the MyTeapot.edz distribution file does not have the *cheers* password stored in it.
8. In the EON Viewer window, select **Exit** from the File menu to close EON Viewer.
9. Return to EON Studio. Select the **Simulation** node in the simulation tree. In the Property Bar, add the **cheers** password to the ResourcePasswords field as shown in Figure 11.1.17.

STORYBOARD

Delivering an EON Application

After you have created and packaged your EON application, you can distribute it to other users.

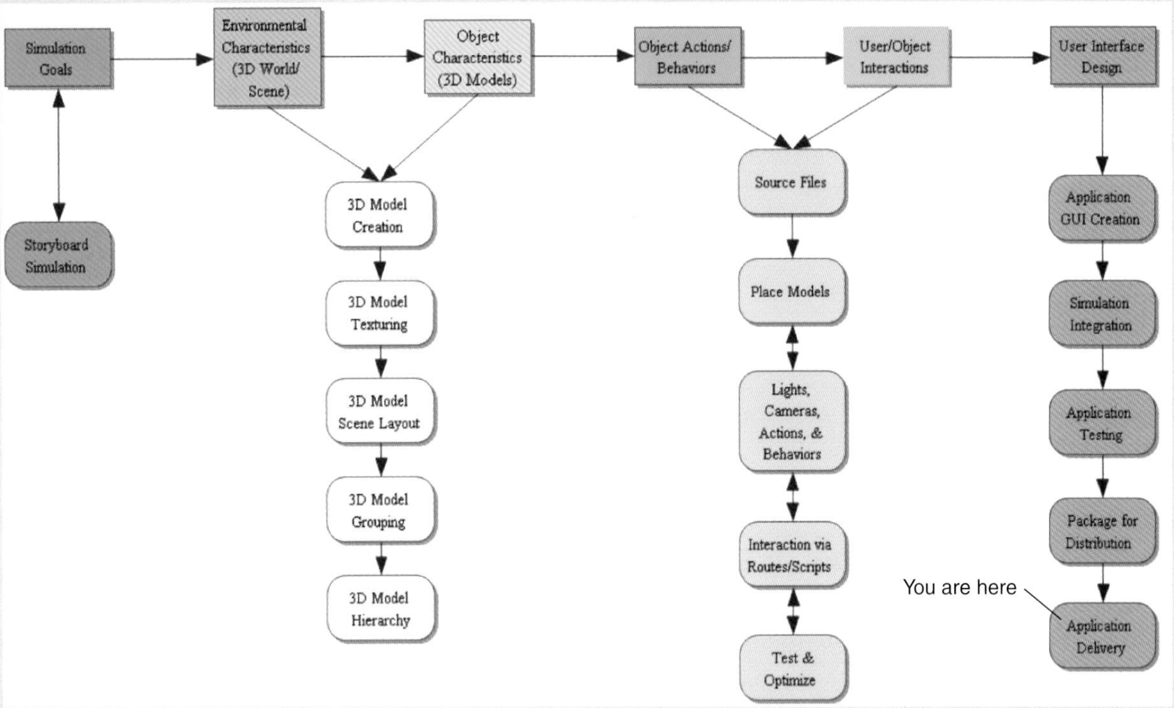

In this lesson, we will learn about creating web distribution files using the EON Web Publisher Wizard and discuss the requirements for viewing an EON simulation on an end user's computer. We will cover downloading the EON Viewer installation package from EON Reality's web server and examine basic functionality of the EON Dependency Walker application.

Step 1: Select a Template

The first step in the EON Web Publisher Wizard instructs you to select a ***Web Publisher template*** from a list of templates, as shown in Figure 11.2.1. The template determines the functionality and appearance of the web publication. A description and preview image are provided for each template to help you determine which template best suits your needs. You also can choose to create your own template.

tips+tricks

If you are familiar with HTML and scripting, you can create your own templates.

tips+tricks

Some templates have images that describe the type of navigation an EON application provides. Unless you intend to delete the images, you must verify that they are compatible with your application.

tips+tricks

The EON Web Publisher Wizard guides you through a series of choices that determine how your web publication will look and behave. The choices that you make can be saved to appear automatically as the default settings. To activate this feature, select the *Remember my last settings* check box.

FIGURE 11.2.1 Available templates in the EON Web Publisher Wizard

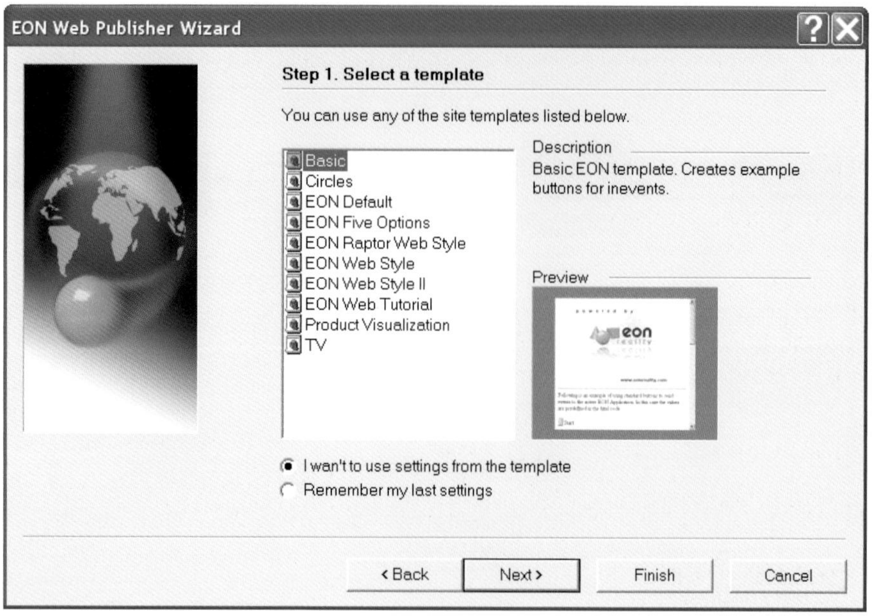

Step 2: Select Events

Next, the wizard displays a list of all of the inEvents and/or outEvents in your EON application, as shown in Figure 11.2.2. These are also known as ***external events.*** The wizard can add default controls (buttons) for the events you select. This is intended to demonstrate to the web developer how events are sent and received.

FIGURE 11.2.2 External events displayed in the EON Web Publisher Wizard

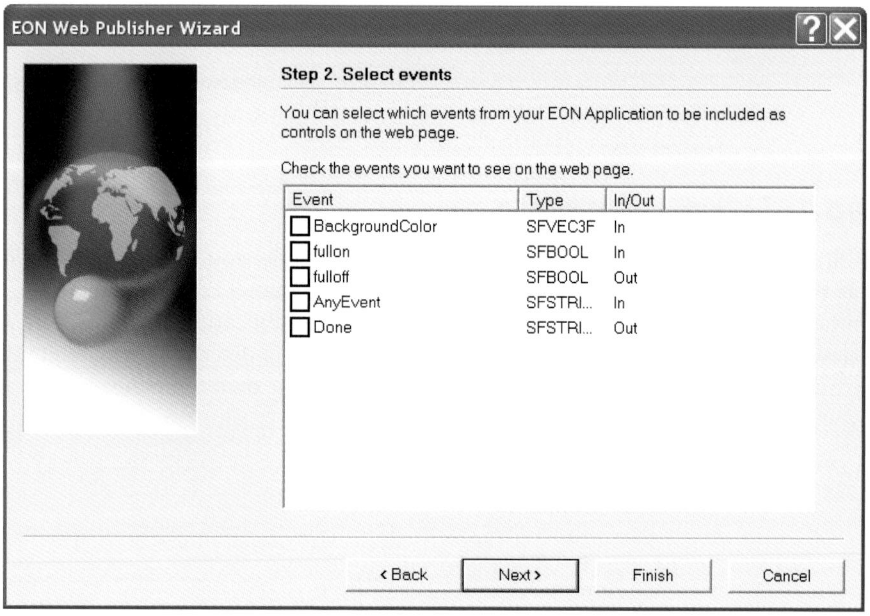

The controls may not be attractive enough to keep in the web publication as they currently appear. Also, only dummy values are sent with the events and may not be appropriate for your web application.

Choose the inEvents and/or outEvents for which you want buttons and text fields created. Up to three types of buttons are demonstrated for each inEvent, and one text field shows the value of each outEvent.

Step 3: Configure Background

Next, the wizard prompts you to configure the appearance of the background. You can choose to keep the default background settings (see Figure 11.2.3), or you can select Custom, which allows you to change the background image and color. You could, for example, set the background color to match your company's color or the background of the content on your web page. Or, you could choose to have your company's logo display as the background image.

FIGURE 11.2.3 Configure the background in the EON Web Publisher Wizard

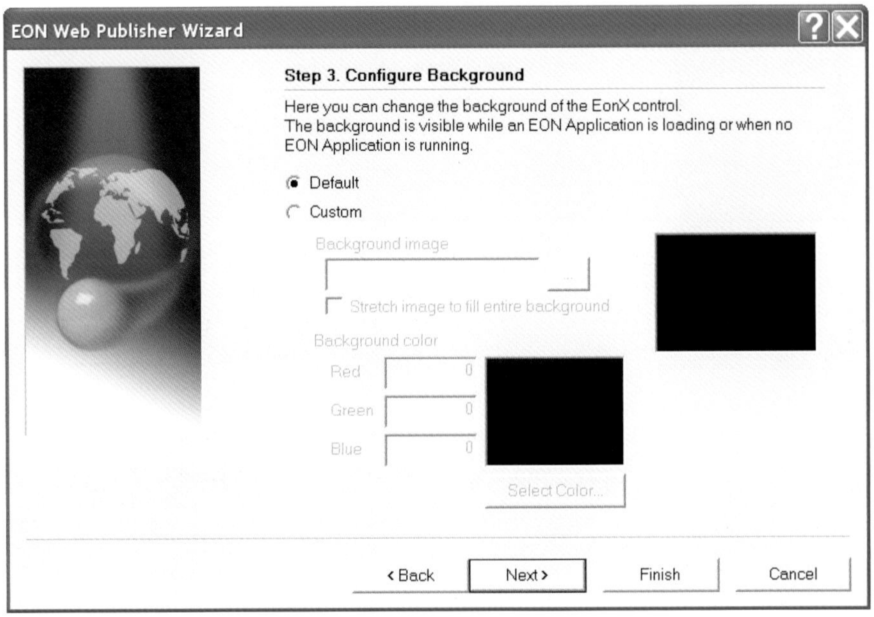

The background is visible while an EON application is downloading or when an EON application is not running. The EON background, as shown in Figure 11.2.4, is displayed by default while an EON application is downloading.

FIGURE 11.2.4 Default background displayed before a simulation is loaded

troubleshooting

Not all templates support events. The controls for the events will only be inserted if the template has the tags required by the web publisher. Four of the templates (EON Default, EON Five Options, Basic, and TV) have controls for inEvents and outEvents. The EON Five Options template has five pages, however, and only one page has the inEvent and outEvent controls. The other templates do not have the controls because they would affect the appearance of the web page and the publication would look unfinished.

troubleshooting

Some data types cannot be used on a web page, so they are not supported by the EON Web Publisher: SFNODE, SFIMAGE, MFBOOL, MFCOLOR, MFFLOAT, MFIMAGE, MFINT32, MFNODE, MFROTATION, MFSTRING, MFTIME, MFVEC2F, and MFVEC3F. Events of these types will not be listed.

Discussion

discuss

How could a company use the background options to market their business?

Step 4: Web Page Configuration

Next, the wizard prompts you to configure the web page, including the web page title, EON window size, AutoPlay settings, and progress bar. See Figure 11.2.5.

FIGURE 11.2.5 Configure the web page in the EON Web Publisher Wizard

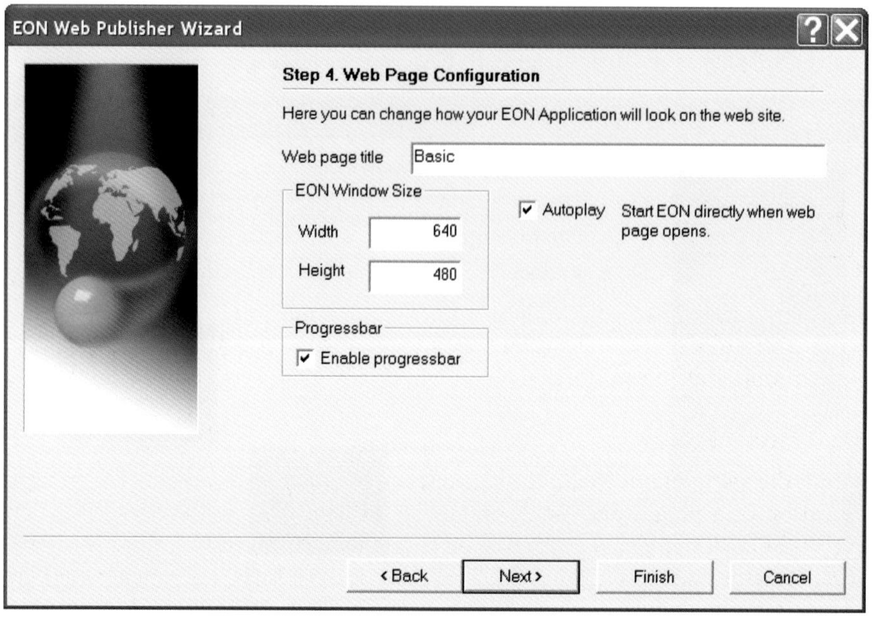

troubleshooting

Enter only numbers in the EON Window Size fields of the Web Page Configuration window. If you enter percentages or text in either field, JavaScript errors will appear on your web page.

In the Web page title field, enter the text that you want to appear in the browser's title bar. For some templates, this text also will appear as a heading on the web page. In the EON Window Size field, enter the size of the display window in pixels. If the Autoplay check box is checked, the EON application will start immediately when the web page opens. This setting is recommended. When the Progressbar option is enabled, a progress bar will be displayed when files are being downloaded and loaded. This setting is recommended so it is easier to tell that the EON application is active.

Step 5: Where Do You Want to Store Your New Site?

Next, the wizard prompts you to choose a location on your computer for saving the files it will create, as shown in Figure 11.2.6. In the Result Folder field, type the path or browse to the folder in which you want to store published files. The default location includes the My Documents folder in the path. It is better to browse to a folder to avoid creating folders in an unwanted location or to avoid typing errors.

FIGURE 11.2.6 Select a storage location in the EON Web Publisher Wizard

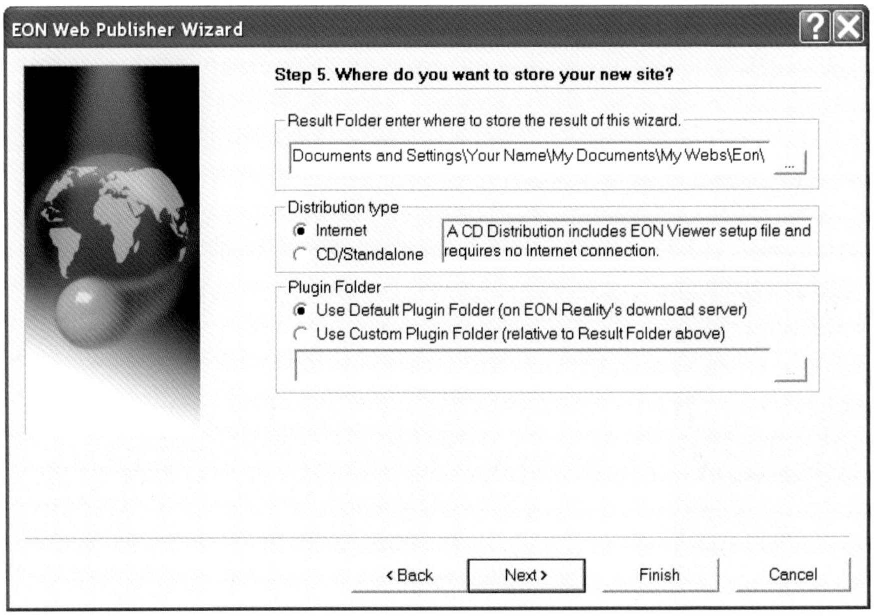

troubleshooting

EON web files, such as eon_function.js, eon_functions.vbs, and eonx_variables.js, will be copied to the same folder as the published files. The wizard will insert values into the eonx_variables.js file while it creates the web publication.

You can choose between Internet or CD distribution: the CD distribution option copies the Redist folder (the folder that contains EON runtime files and file packages) to a subfolder of the Result folder. The Plugin Page folder is required for the CD distribution option, so its path is fixed.

Default Plugin Folder

Selecting the Use Default Plugin Folder option is highly recommended. It represents the location of a plugin page with up-to-date information and the latest version of EonX on EON Reality's website. Based on the default settings of these templates, a viewer who does not have EonX installed will be asked to click a link to go to this plugin page.

tips+tricks

You should use an absolute path only when you write a URL that starts with *http*. For example, to use a folder directly under the Website folder, simply type **plugin** in this field. This is recommended if you do not use the Default Plugin Folder on EON Reality's website.

Custom Plugin Folder

If you want to use a custom Plugin folder, then one will be created for you in a location that is relative to the folder you selected in the first field. To place the files in the Website folder with the published files, simply leave the field empty. If you use a relative path such as ../../, then a folder will not be created. Instead, the plugin files will be deposited in the folder that is two folders above the Website folder. If you use a relative path such as ../../plugin/, then a folder named Plugin will be created under the folder that is two folders above the Website folder.

Step 6: Summary

The last page of the wizard, shown in Figure 11.2.7, displays a summary of the decisions that you made in the previous steps, allowing you to verify that they are correct. Select the *Preview in browser* option to display your new publication in your Internet browser when you click the Finish button.

FIGURE 11.2.7 Selection summary in the EON Web Publisher Wizard

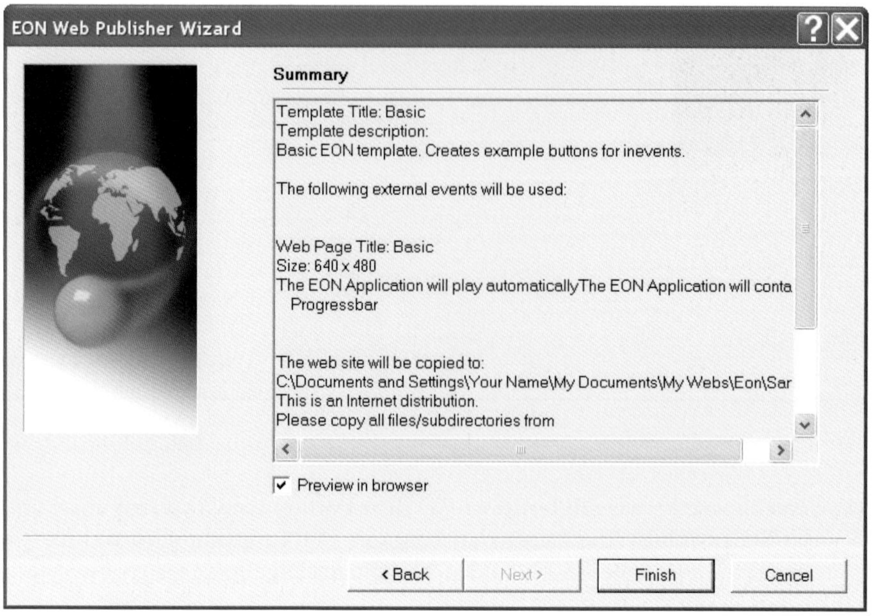

troubleshooting

This activity may require EON Professional. Depending on your configuration of EON modules, you may not be able to complete this activity.

troubleshooting

Before you can start the EON Web Publisher Wizard, you must save the simulation file. If you have not saved your simulation file, you will be prompted to save it when you start the wizard.

troubleshooting

You must build a distribution file before you can start the EON Web Publisher Wizard. If you have not created a distribution file, you will be prompted to create the file when you start the wizard.

Activity 11.2.1: Creating a Web Distribution File

1. Open EON. Open **Activity_11.2.1.eoz** from the data files for Module 11 Lesson 2.
2. Save the simulation as **Earth_Web.eoz**.
3. Select **Build Distribution File** from the File menu.
4. Select **Create Web Distribution** from the File menu. The EON Web Publisher Wizard opens. The Welcome screen is displayed (see Figure 11.2.8).

FIGURE 11.2.8 EON Web Publisher Wizard Welcome screen

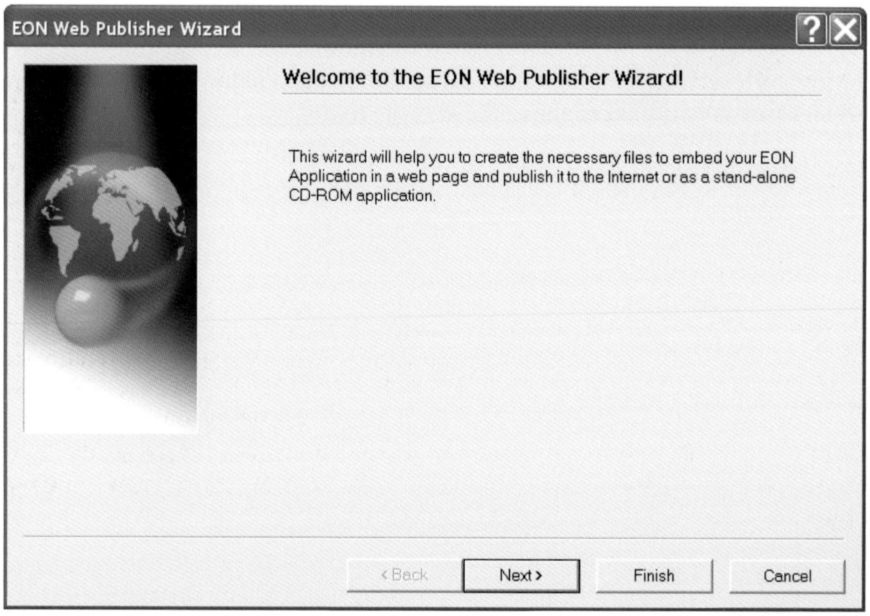

5. Click **Next** to continue. The Step 1. Select a template page is displayed (see Figure 11.2.9), prompting you to select a template.

FIGURE 11.2.9 Step 1. Select a template page of the EON Web Publisher Wizard

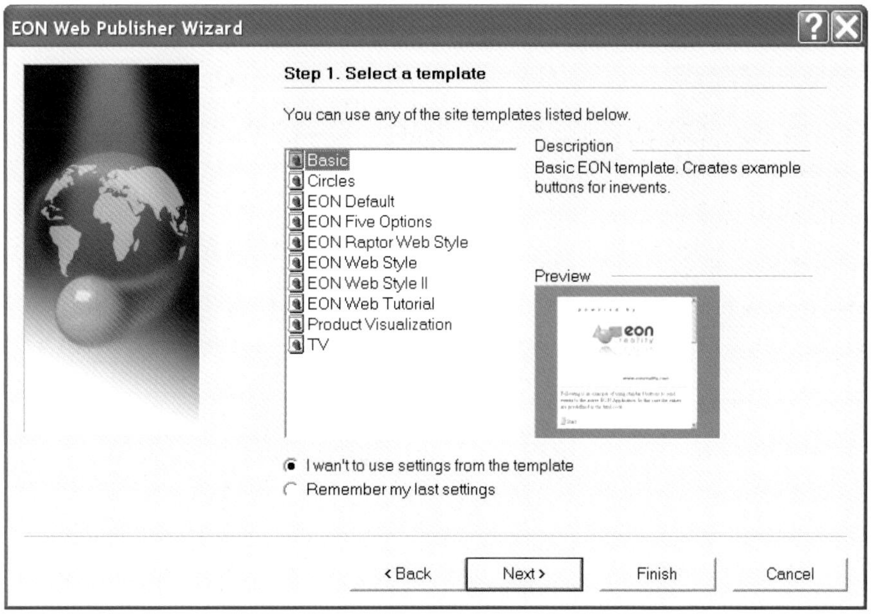

6. Keep the default settings and click **Next** to continue. The Step 2. Select events page appears (see Figure 11.2.10), displaying a list of all inEvents and/or outEvents in your EON application. Because this application does not have inEvents or outEvents, the list is empty.

FIGURE 11.2.10 Step 2. Select events page of the EON Web Publisher Wizard

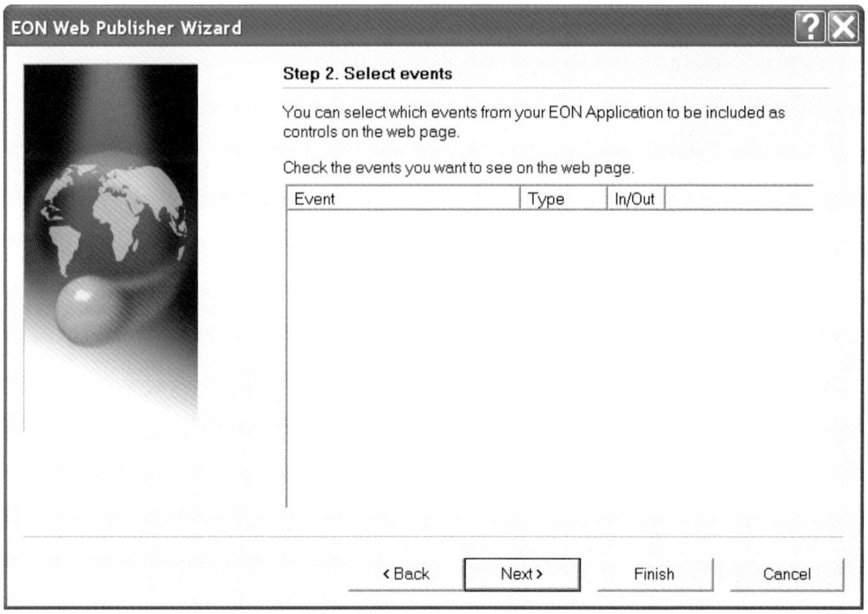

7. Click **Next** to continue. The Step 3. Configure Background page appears (see Figure 11.2.11), prompting you to configure the appearance of the background.

FIGURE 11.2.11 Step 3. Configure Background page of the EON Web Publisher Wizard

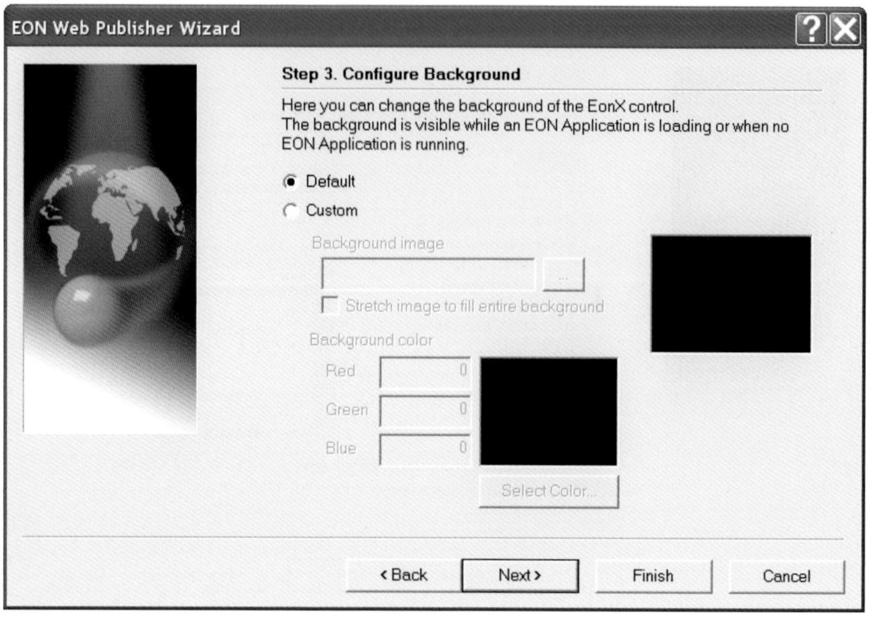

8. Keep the default settings and click **Next** to continue. The Step 4. Web Page Configuration page appears, prompting you to configure the web page. Enter **Earth Web** in the Web page title field, as shown in Figure 11.2.12.

FIGURE 11.2.12 Step 4. Web Page Configuration page of the EON Web Publisher Wizard

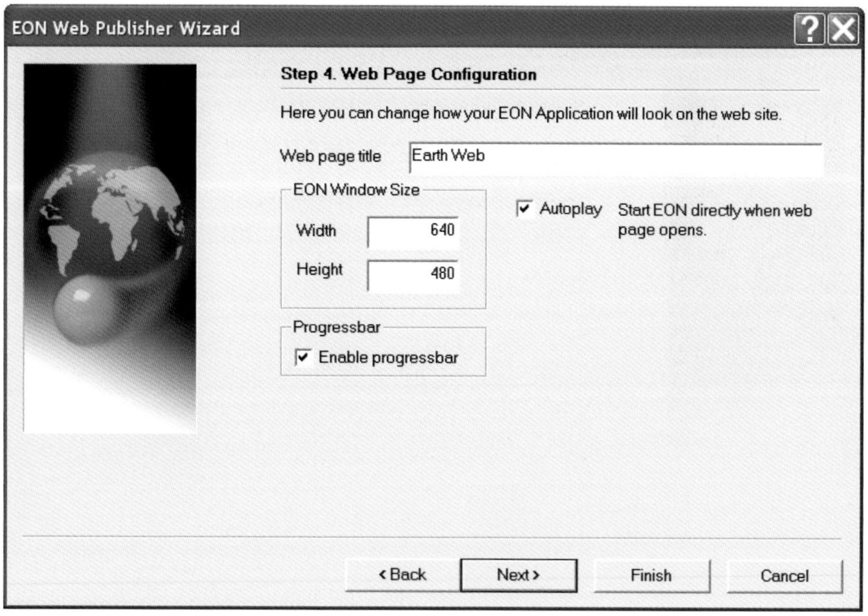

9. Keep the remaining default settings and click **Next** to continue. The Step 5. Where do you want to store your new site? page appears, prompting you to set where you want to store your new site. Click the button next to the Result Folder field and then browse to the location of your solution files for this lesson. The destination will be displayed in the Result Folder field, as shown in Figure 11.2.13.

FIGURE 11.2.13 Step 5. Where do you want to store your new site? page of the EON Web Publisher Wizard

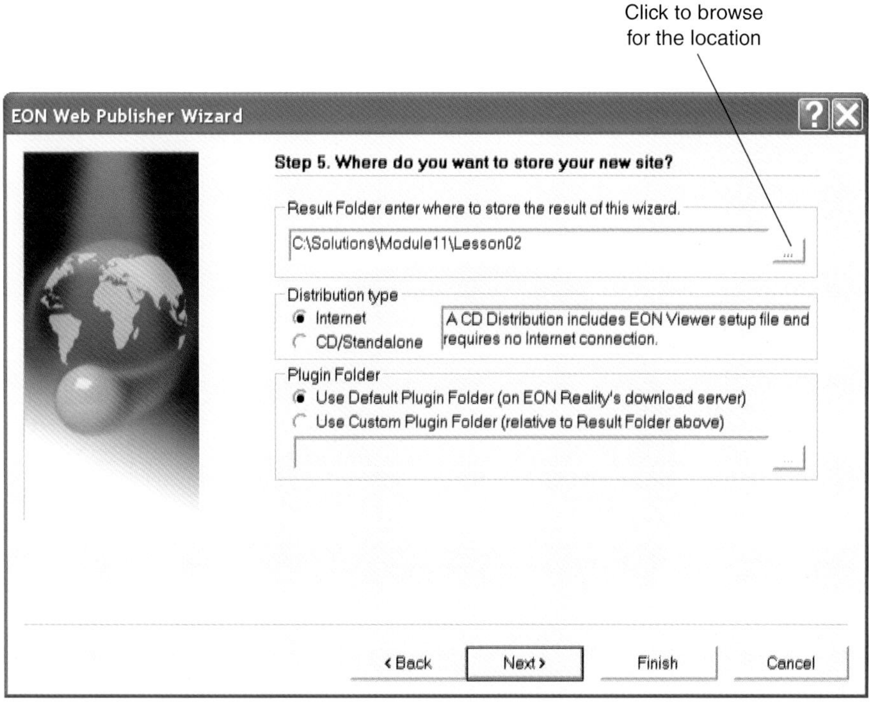

troubleshooting

The location identified in the Result Folder field may differ on your computer.

10. Keep the remaining default settings and click **Next** to continue. The Summary page appears (see Figure 11.2.14), displaying a summary of the decisions made in the previous steps.

FIGURE 11.2.14 Summary page of the EON Web Publisher Wizard

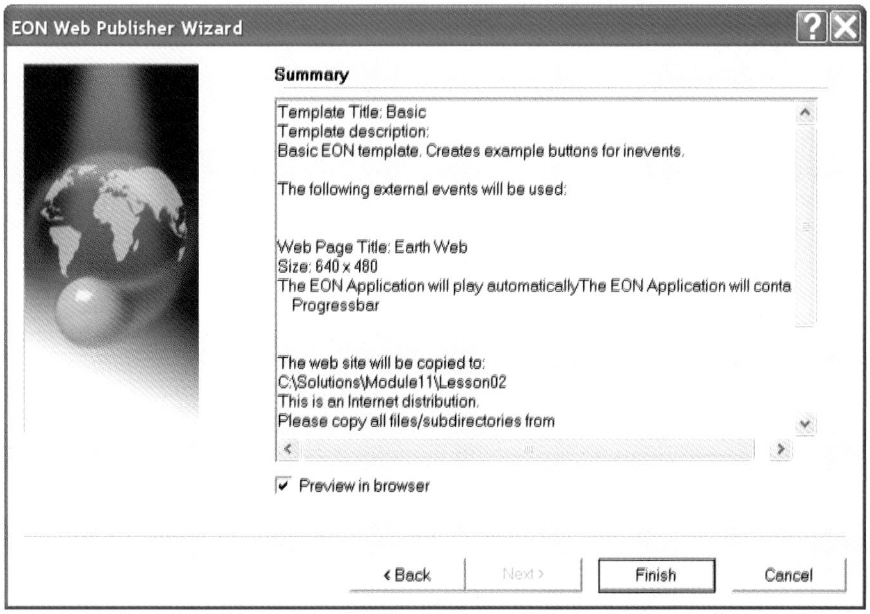

11. Check to make sure the settings are correct and then click **Finish** to continue. Because the Preview in browser check box is selected, your web browser opens to display the EON application, as shown in Figure 11.2.15.

FIGURE 11.2.15 Preview in web browser

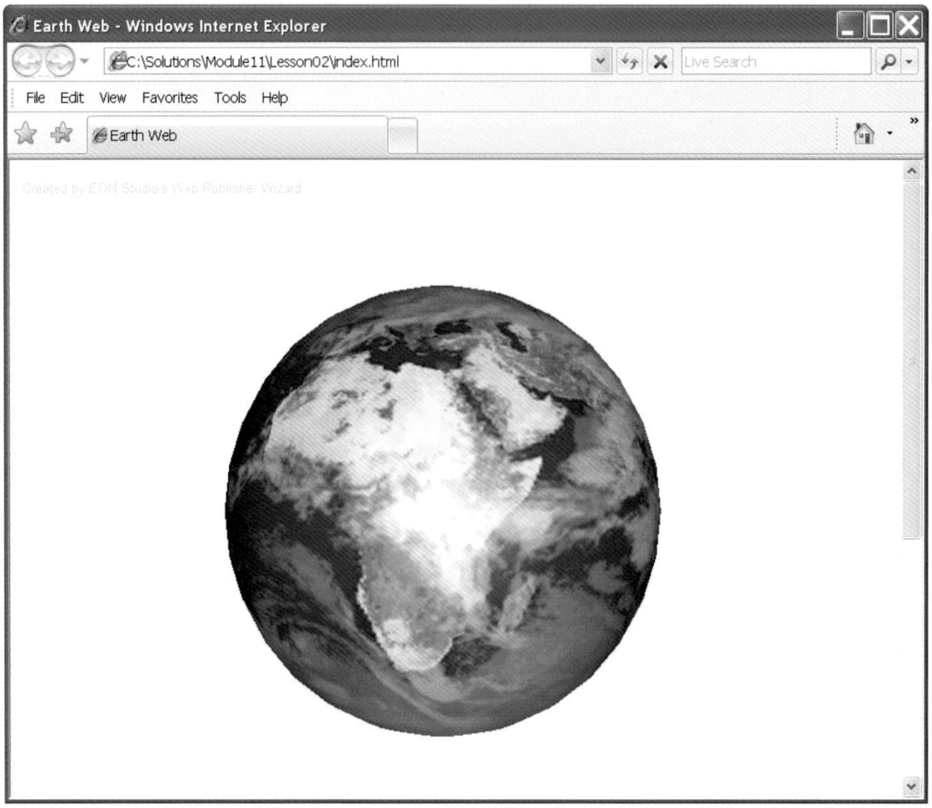

12. Close your web browser. Close EON.

tips+tricks

You can replace this distribution file with a different EON simulation that does not have to be a distribution file; it can be an .eoz file. You must change a line in the index.html file that says eonxSimulationFile = "newsimulationfilename.eoz". The new simulation will appear in the browser in the place of the previous one and any buttons created will *not* be changed. The buttons will work only if the file happens to have the same external events. You can save time by changing the simulation file rather than running the Web Publisher again with the same settings.

discuss

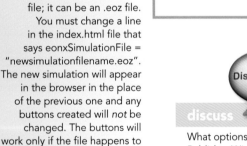

What options do you think users are most likely to change as they step through the EON Web Publisher Wizard, and which defaults are they most likely to keep? Why?

After you complete the wizard, several files will be located in the target folder. The files will include the EON application file in distribution file format.

You can move your published files to a web server using your File Transfer Protocol (FTP) program. But before you move the files, you can edit the web pages manually. In fact, most users use the EON Web Publisher Wizard to create a web page that is a starting point for a web application, and then they examine how the files work rather than publishing to a web server immediately.

Running EON Simulations on End User Computers

Before any EON application can be viewed on a computer, you must use the ***EON Viewer setup*** installation program to install the EON runtime software. The EON Viewer installation program includes all software needed to run most EON simulations.

Two Installation Programs

EONViewer_6.0.0.exe is the EON Viewer installation file. It also comes in a lighter version named EONViewerWebInstall_6.0.0.exe, which is suited for web applications in which download time is an issue. The smaller installation program, EONViewerWebInstall_6.0.0.exe, does not install all of the EON components, but the EonX control will download any additional components automatically if they are required by an application.

EON Applications on the Internet

If a user opens a web page that has an embedded EON application and the user has never installed EON software, then JavaScript code will direct the user to a plugin page to download the EON Viewer setup package. After downloading the package and running the installation program, the user can return to the web browser, refresh the web page, and view the EON application.

troubleshooting

If a newer version of EON is available, then the 6_0_0 portion of the URL will be replaced with 6_1_0 or 7_0_0 and so on.

Activity 11.2.2: Viewing the Default Plugin Page

1. Open your web browser and type **http://download.eonreality.com/eonx/6_0_0/plugin/eonx_plugin_page.html** to go to the default plugin page on EON Reality's web server, as shown in Figure 11.2.16.

FIGURE 11.2.16 EON 3D Viewer Download Center—Download Now

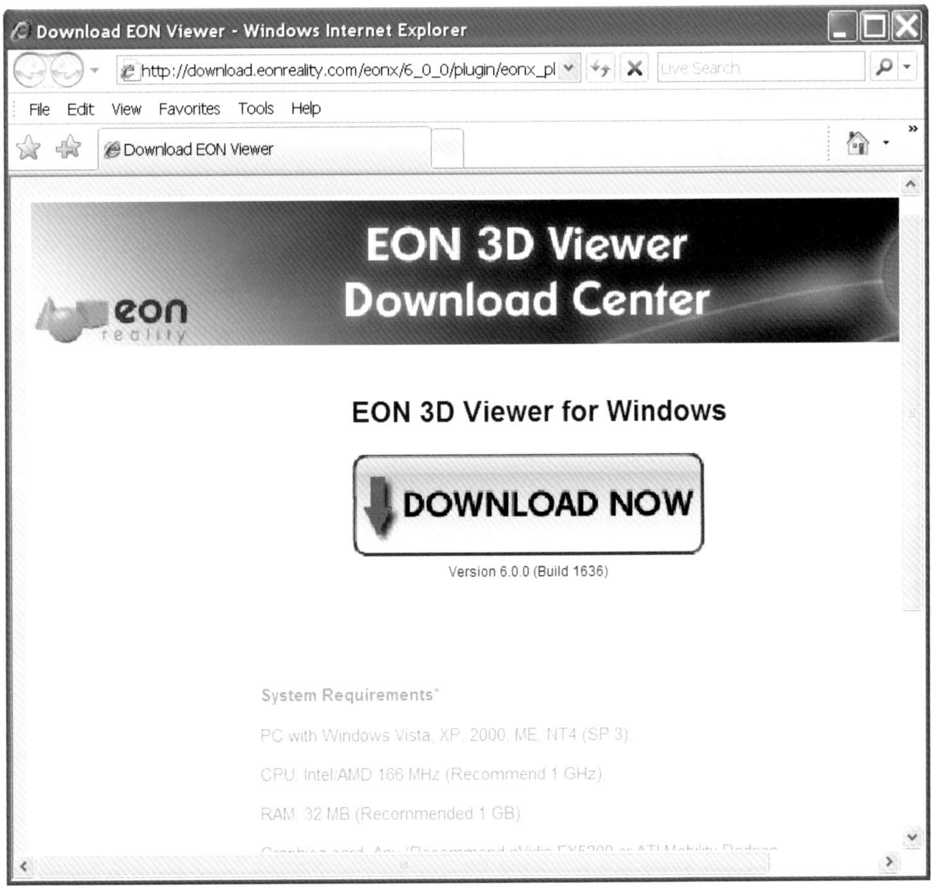

troubleshooting

Do not run the installation program if you already have EON software installed.

2. Click the **DOWNLOAD NOW** button. The EON 3D Viewer Download Center page appears, as shown in Figure 11.2.17.

FIGURE 11.2.17 EON 3D Viewer Download Center—Start Downloading

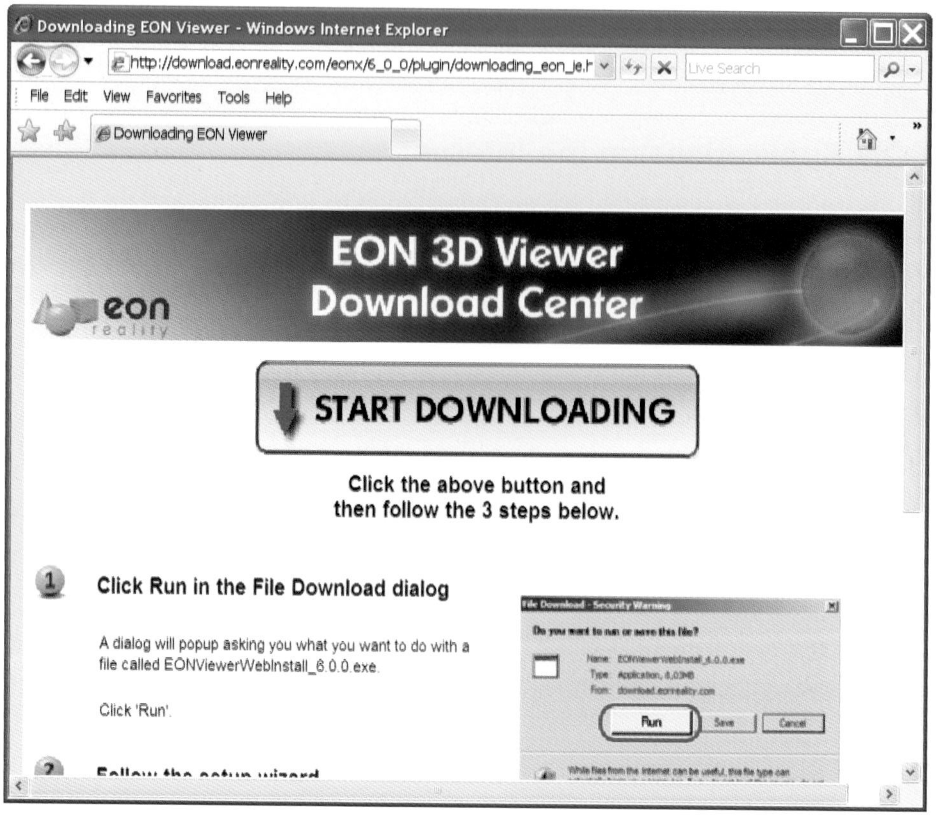

3. Read the information provided about downloading the necessary files, running the setup wizard, and viewing an EON application. Click the **START DOWNLOADING** button to begin downloading the file.

troubleshooting

Depending on your browser, the EON Viewer installation package may start to download automatically after you click the DOWNLOAD NOW button in step 2.

CD/DVD Distribution

If you are creating a CD or DVD distribution file through the EON Web Publisher Wizard, it creates a folder named Redist. This folder provides the EON runtime software.

tips+tricks

The only file that is required in the new Redist folder is the EONViewer_6.0.0.exe file. All of the other files in this folder were previously required by older browsers for an automatic installation process that is no longer recommended. Because these files are no longer necessary, they can be safely removed from the folder.

What Is EonX?

The EON Viewer installation program installs EonX. ***EonX*** is an ActiveX control used to display and control EON applications from other programs. EonX is required to display EON applications through any software other than EON Studio. EonX enables you to distribute EON applications over the Internet, in Microsoft PowerPoint presentations, in Adobe Director movies, or in a customized Visual Basic program.

What Is an ActiveX Control?

An ***ActiveX control*** places the necessary program code into a specific package to facilitate insertion into other programs known as host applications. If we did not have an ActiveX control, then each host program would have to be programmed by its developers to display an EON application. Instead, programmers create ActiveX-compliant programs that can accept the ActiveX standard. EON adheres to Microsoft's ActiveX standard so you can insert EON applications into documents created in ActiveX-compliant programs. Microsoft Internet Explorer, Microsoft PowerPoint, and Adobe Director are examples of ActiveX-compliant programs that can host EonX. Other examples of ActiveX controls include Adobe Flash and Adobe Shockwave.

tips+tricks

EonX is referred to as a *control* because it is a type of ActiveX control. It is referred to as a *plugin* because Internet browsers use extra programs called plugins. It is referred to as an *Xtra* because Director's extra programs are called Xtras. It is referred to as a *component* because Visual Basic programs have extra programs called components. EonX is referred to as an *object* because Microsoft Office uses extra programs called objects.

Where Does the EON Viewer Setup Program Place Its Files?

The EON Viewer setup program places files in several locations:

- Most of EON's runtime software will be placed in the C:\Windows\EON folder.
- Some files will be placed in the C:\Windows\System32 folder, including EonControlPanel.cpl, which enables EON simulation configuration via the Control Panel.
- The EONViewer.exe program will be placed alone in C:\Program Files\EON Reality\EON Studio.
- If you have Mozilla Firefox 2, the EonXPlugin.dll plugin file will be placed in the application's Plugins folder, such as C:\Program Files\Mozilla Firefox\Plugins.

All EON applications and external resources downloaded from the Internet will be saved to your normal Internet Cache folder. This includes .eoz, .edz, .eop, .edp, .eogz, etxz, and .jpgz files.

System Requirements

The system requirements can change depending on the content of the EON simulation. More polygons, textures, and complex calculations require a better graphics card, more RAM, and increased processor speed.

- PC with Windows Vista, XP, 2000, ME, or NT4 (SP 3).
- CPU: Intel/AMD 166 MHz (recommended 1 GHz).
- RAM: 32 MB (recommended 1 GB).
- Graphics card: Any (recommended NVIDIA FX5200 or ATI Mobility Radeon X300 with latest drivers). Simulations with DDS/DXT textures require the recommended graphics card.
- Browser: Internet Explorer 6, Internet Explorer 7, or Mozilla Firefox 2.
- Internet connection (to download extra components when needed if you have used the WebInstall package).

Discussion

discuss

Does your home computer meet the basic requirements for viewing an EON simulation?

When Does a User Need an EON License?

The end user will require a license for the EON application only if they will view the application through a special display system, such as the various types of stereoscopic displays and the ICUBE. Normal viewing of applications, especially on the Internet, is free.

Uninstalling EON Runtime Software

Use your computer's Add or Remove Programs option, located in the Control Panel, to remove the EON Viewer and all of its components. This is the most effective method of ensuring that all of the EON Viewer's components are safely removed.

EON Dependency Walker

The EON software has been produced in many versions. Generally, all EON simulations created in earlier versions can be viewed in the latest version, but few simulations saved in later versions can be opened in old software. When you save an EON simulation in EON Studio, it becomes dependent on certain components of the currently installed version.

You can view the components and component versions that an EON application requires in the ***EON Dependency Walker*** program. This program is generally accessible from the Start menu or at C:\Program Files\EON Reality\EON Studio\EonDepends.exe. Missing or old versions of components are highlighted with a red or yellow dot. Green dots identify components available in your EON software, as shown in Figure 11.2.18. This program is useful when you are troubleshooting simulations that do not open because they were created with beta release files or with the developer's own components created through the EON Software Development Kit (SDK).

FIGURE 11.2.18 EON Dependency Walker results

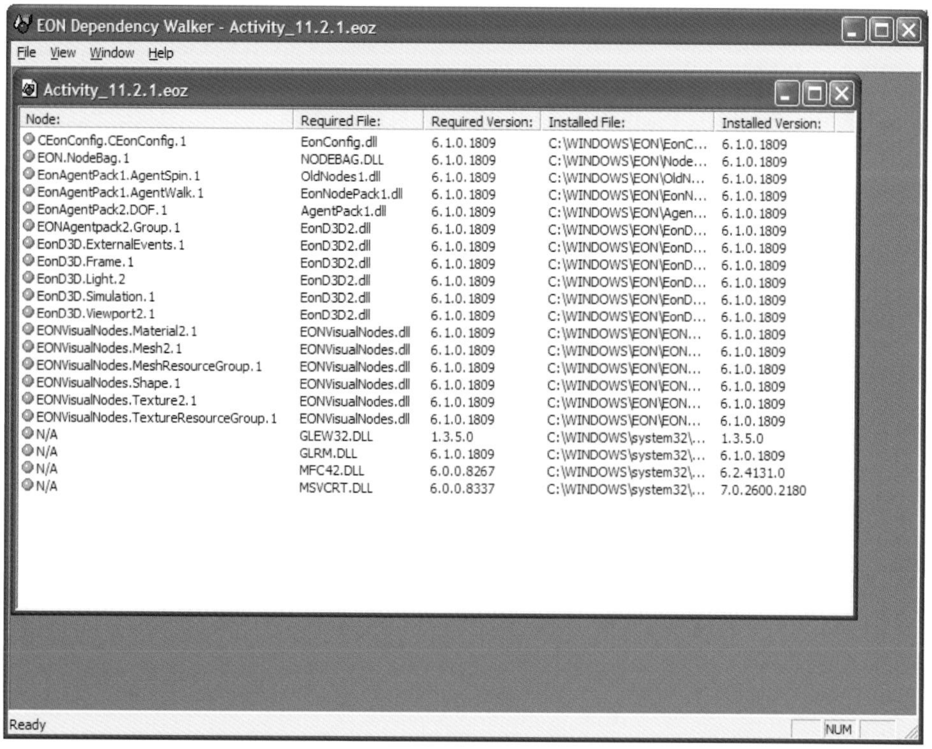

Summary

In this lesson you:

- Used the EON Web Publisher Wizard to create a web distribution file.
- Learned the requirements for viewing an EON simulation on an end user's computer.
- Learned how to download the EON Viewer installation package from the default plugin page on EON Reality's web server.
- Understood the functionality of the EON Dependency Walker application.

Simulation

Now that you have honed your design and creation skills in EON, it is time to share your work with others. Choose a simulation file that you would like to distribute to your colleagues. Because many of your co-workers do not have access to EON software, you decide to build a distribution file that they can access on their computers with EON Viewer software available from the EON download site. Your company also would like to give users the ability to view a simulation via their website, but they want to ensure that any external resources are protected.

Job 11.1: Outlining the Procedure for Downloading the EON Viewer Installation Package

Review all of the activities you completed for each lesson in this book and select a simulation that you can distribute to your colleagues and other users via the Internet. Applying the skills you acquired in Module 11 Lessons 1 and 2, brainstorm to choose the file distribution and web publishing options you will use.

1. Examine all of the simulation files you have created so far.
2. Choose the simulation you want to share with others.
3. Review Module 11 Lesson 1.
4. Take notes about the procedures for creating distribution files, including available optimization features and resource protection options you may want to employ.
5. Review Module 11 Lesson 2.
6. Take notes on creating a web distribution file, including the EON Web Publisher Wizard options you plan to use and the end user requirements for viewing an EON simulation.
7. Write a short step-by-step outline for downloading the EON Viewer installation package that you can distribute to users with your simulation file. An example outline is shown in Figure 11.1.

FIGURE 11.1 Example outline

Downloading EON Viewer Installation Package
Step-by-Step Outline

1. Open your web browser and go to http://download.eonreality.com/eonx/6_0_0/plugin/eonx_plugin_page.html. The EON 3D Viewer Download Center page is displayed. If a newer version of EON is available, then the 6_0_0 portion of the URL will be replaced with 6_1_0 or 7_0_0 and so on.
2. Verify that your computer meets the listed system requirements for running the EON 3D Viewer software.
3. Click the **DOWNLOAD NOW** button. The next EON 3D Viewer Download Center page appears.
4. Read the information provided about downloading the necessary files, running the setup wizard, and viewing an EON application.
5. Click the **START DOWNLOADING** button to begin downloading the software. The EON Viewer installation program includes all software needed to run most EON simulations.

Job 11.2: Creating Distribution Files

In Module 11 Lesson 1, you learned that you can easily create distribution files for simulations in EON. You also discovered that users can view your simulation distribution files even if they do not have EON software loaded on their computers. Create a distribution file for the simulation you selected in Job 11.1.

1. If necessary, take a few minutes to review the observations you documented in Job 11.1 relating to the procedures and options available when creating a simulation distribution file.
2. Open EON. Open the simulation file you plan to distribute and save it as **Job_11.2.eoz**.
3. Use the information recorded in your notes to create a simulation distribution file. The distribution file will be saved as **Job_11.2.edz** in the Job_11.2 folder by default (see Figure 11.2).

FIGURE 11.2 Job_11.2.edz file saved by default to the Job_11.2 folder

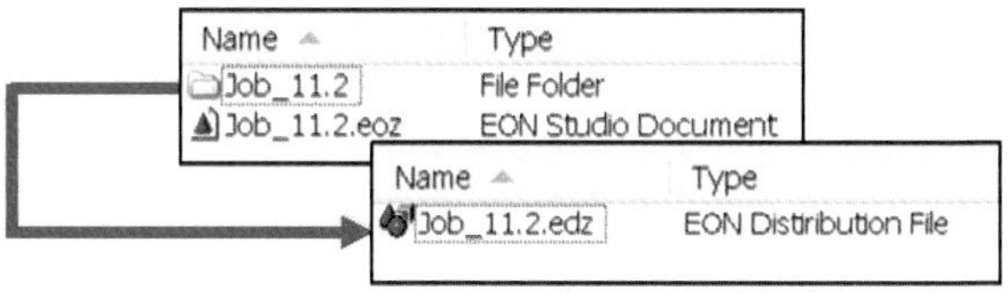

4. Close the simulation. Close EON.

Job 11.3: Creating a Web Distribution File

While completing Module 11 Lesson 2, you learned about the procedures for creating a web distribution file. Use the **Job_11.2.eoz** and **Job_11.2.edz** files created in Job 11.2 to produce a web distribution file.

1. Open EON. Open the **Job_11.2.eoz** file created in Job 11.2.
2. Before continuing, refer to your notes from Job 11.1 and review the remarks concerning web distribution files.
3. With the skills you learned in Module 11 Lesson 2, use the EON Web Publisher Wizard to create a web distribution file (see Figure 11.3).

FIGURE 11.3 Use the EON Web Publisher Wizard to create a web distribution file

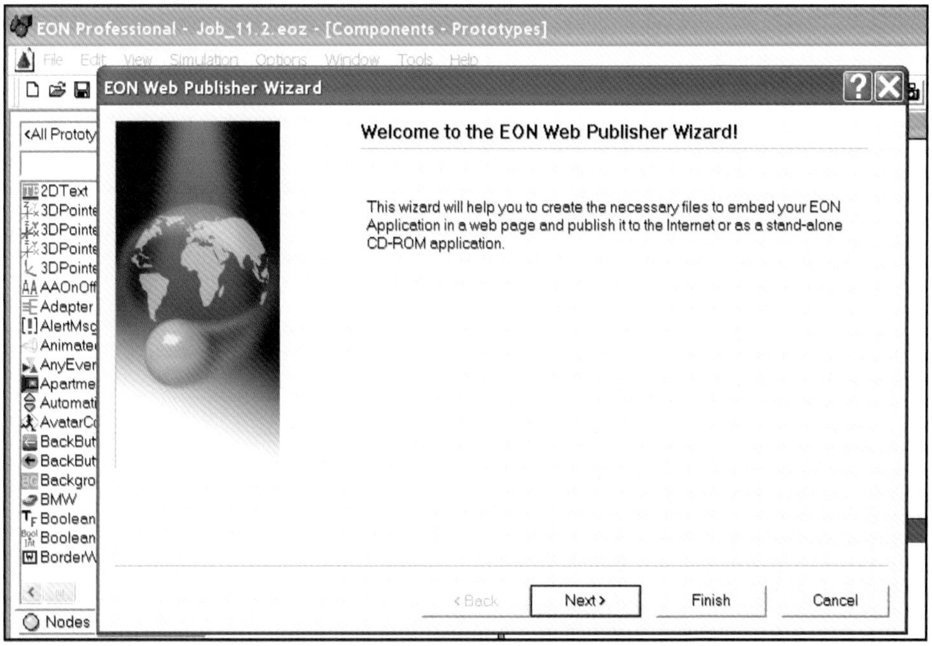

4. View the simulation in a web browser.
5. Close the web browser and then close EON.

discuss

You are planning to distribute the Job_11.2.edz file via the Internet, but what are some other methods you could use to distribute simulation files to end users?

APPENDIX A

EON Prototypes

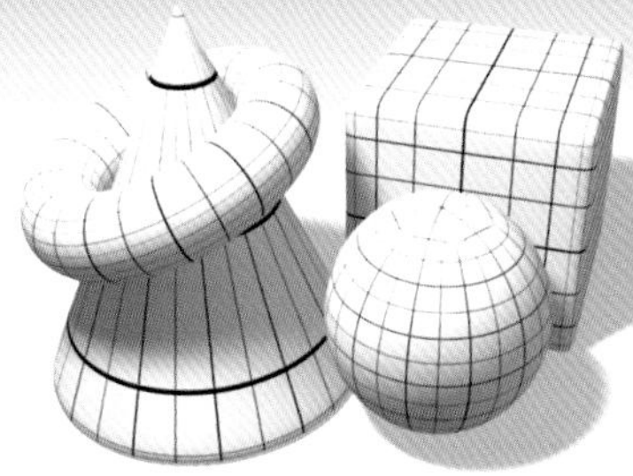

This appendix contains tables listing the EON prototypes for EON Studio 6.0 and EON Professional 6.0. These tables provide a central location for viewing and learning basic information about the available prototypes. To make this appendix easier to use, the prototypes are divided into tables based on their libraries.

EON Studio 6.0 has 164 prototypes found in 17 libraries. EON Professional contains an additional 89 prototypes and four additional libraries. In the tables of this appendix, the prototypes that are exclusive to EON Professional are shown in blue text. The prototypes that are available in both EON Studio and EON Professional are shown in black text.

The descriptions that are provided in the tables of this appendix are intentionally brief—usually mirroring the tooltip that you would find in EON. They are designed to provide only the most basic information. If you require more information on a given prototype, refer to the EON Help system. The most direct way to obtain help for a prototype would be to select the prototype in the Components window and then press the F1 key. This will take you directly to information about the selected prototype. Within the Help system, you will find a detailed explanation of the prototype and its main features. You also will find information about the property fields and values for the prototype, as well as useful information about requirements for using the prototype and the best way to set up the prototype. As always, consult the online Help and the EON Reality support site (*www.eonreality.com/support*) if you need more information about an individual prototype. You also can find new sample simulations that demonstrate prototype usage at the support site under the Downloads link.

tips+tricks

Prototypes and libraries can be added every time EON Studio is updated. The available libraries and the content of your libraries may differ from the libraries documented in this appendix.

troubleshooting

The prototype libraries have been rearranged in EON Professional 6.0 because new prototypes were added. Therefore, you may not find the old prototypes where they used to be in previous versions. If you are unable to locate a prototype that you seek, choose the <All Prototypes> option in the list of prototype libraries and search for the prototype in the complete alphabetical listing.

TABLE A.1 3D Shapes Library

Prototype	Icon	Description
Cone		A cone object that is 2 meters wide and 2 meters high.
Cube		A cube object that is 2 meters wide.
Cylinder		A cylinder object that is 2 meters in diameter and 2 meters high.
Pyramid		A pyramid object that is 2 meters wide and 2 meters high.
Sphere		A sphere object that is 2 meters in diameter.
Square		A square in the X–Z plane that is 2 meters wide and 2 meters high.
Teapot		A teapot object that is 2 meters wide.
Torus		A donut shape that is 2 meters wide and 2 meters high.

TABLE A.2 Buttons Library

Prototype	Icon	Description
BackButton		Back button with auto-positioning and auto-scaling functions.
BackButton(BP)		A ready-to-use box-positioned (BP) Back button
BPButton		A box-positioned (BP) button placed under the camera.
BPButtonLite		A box-positioned (BP) button placed under the camera that has fewer features than the BPButton prototype.
BPSimple	BP	A box-positioned (BP) button that works with EON Dynamic Load prototypes.
ColoredBorder(BP)		A rectangle that acts as a border when placed behind a 2DText node or other object.
FeatureTextBox		Shows a title and description in a rounded text box.
Menu		Pop-up menu, context menu, or right-mouse button menu.
SixButtons		Six ready-made buttons with all the features you need.
TextBoxButton		Sends outEvents when you mouse-over or click a text box.
TextureChanger		Up to six "texture buttons" that download and swap textures.
TexturedBackground(BP)		Uses your texture as the viewport's background (BPButton).
ToggleButton		A color-changing On/Off button.

Prototypes shown in blue are available only in EON Professional.

TABLE A.3 Camera Functions Library

Prototype	Icon	Description
CamDOF		Limits camera position and sends values for the Position and Orientation fields.
FollowMe		Allows camera to follow a moving object.
KeyMoverXY		Enables use of arrow keys to trigger the XYPlaneMover prototype.
MapNav2D		Used for moving within orthographic viewports.
SphereNav		Rotates, zooms, and pans around screen coordinates.
StayAbove		Stays above the ground and follows the terrain.
SuperMan		Fly motion model.
VerticalNav		Moves a Frame node up and down with keys or inEvents.
ViewMaker		Makes up to ten viewing locations by saving your current position.
WindowEdgeMover		Triggers the XYPlaneMover when the cursor approaches the edge of the simulation window.
XYNav		Enables mouse navigation in X–Y plane with new cursors.
XYPlaneMover		Enables movement in any direction in the X–Y plane.
ZNav		Enables mouse navigation in the Z plane with new cursors.
Zoom		Zooms in and out using keys or the mouse.
ZoomExtents		Moves camera into position to view the target object.
ZoomToArea		Zooms into an area selected by drawing a box.

TABLE A.4 Collision Tools Library

Prototype	Icon	Description
AvatarCollision		Handles collisions between an avatar and the environment.
CollisionDataDisplayer		Displays collision data in a text box.
CollisionDisabler		Disables/enables collision between two groups of collision objects.
CollisionEventSelector		Selects one collision event from an array of collision events.
CollisionGeometryBox		Provides a simple box collision geometry.
CollisionGeometrySphere		Provides a simple sphere collision geometry.
ShowCollisionGeometry		Shows/hides collision geometries.
ShowContactNormal		Shows selected contact normals for a CollisionObject.
ShowContactNormals		Shows all contact normals of a CollisionObject.

Prototypes shown in blue are available only in EON Professional.

TABLE A.5 Converters Library

Prototype	Icon	Description
Adapter		Converts data types (e.g., SFFloat to SFVec3F).
BooleanSplitter		Sends true or false when needed.
BooleanToIntegerConverter		Converts a maximum of fifty Boolean inEvents to one integer outEvent.
ButtonStatesConverter		Converts a string of 0s and 1s to Boolean outEvents.
Colors		Converts Boolean inEvents to colors.
Convert3DPosToScreenPos		Obtains Position values from a Frame node and sends BoxPosition values; positions 2D elements over moving 3D objects.
HexColor		Converts colors into a hexidecimal string for HTML use and vice versa.
MousePos3D		Converts the mouse Position value into 3D Frame node Position values for orthographic viewports.
MouseToBoxPosition		Converts the mouse's position to BoxPosition (pixel values).
MouseToTextBoxPos		Converts the mouse's position into a text box Position value for variable-sized Viewport nodes.
Opposites		Values sent to this prototype are converted to the opposite value; e.g., true becomes false.

TABLE A.6 Developer Tools Library

Prototype	Icon	Description
AnyEvent		Use to have a web page send any event to EON.
BoxEditor		Tool to visualize a box while you move, rotate, and scale it.
BoxEditorDisplay		Text box that displays outEvents of the BoxEditor prototype.
CgDetect		Detects support for Cg shaders.
ClippingPlaneChanger		Changes the far and near clipping plane via sliders, etc.
ClusterConfig		Calculates the view plane coordinates for a three-screen Cluster Visualization.
DOFMover		Shows, moves, and saves origin, position, and orientation for the DegreeOfFreedom node; use it to visualize and move the pivot position without moving the objects under a DegreeOfFreedom node.
DynamicPrototypeManager		Advanced features for downloading prototypes.
EventInfo		Displays latest event information in a 2DText node or TextBox node; replaces Event Displayer prototype.
EventSender		Write an event that is sent in runtime.
FindReplaceReferences		Finds or finds and replaces specified references in the selected subtrees.
FrameRate		Calculates frame rate.

(continued)

Prototypes shown in blue are available only in EON Professional.

TABLE A.6 Developer Tools Library (*continued*)

Prototype	Icon	Description
MultiTextSender		Sends up to fifty pieces of text via routes or directly.
NodeFinder		A tool to find nodes and add them to MFNode fields.
NodeInfo		Displays information about a node; allows browsing of the simulation tree.
NumberSender		A simple tool to send numbers via routes.
OrthoZoomer		Lets you zoom an orthographic viewport using FOV (field of view value).
QuickPos		Displays the camera's position when the Q key is pressed.
RecordPath		KeyFrame recording, editing, and saving functions.
RefreshGroup		Refreshes a group of prototypes when a window's size changes.
SaveFrameValues		On shutdown, saves a Frame node's Position, Orientation, and Scale values as start values.
SendToGroup		Sends an event to a group of nodes at the same time.
SimTreeBrowser		Allows you to view the simulation tree node information and change field values.
StereoOptimizer_Sharp3D		Useful for optimizing stereo settings for the Sharp3D screen.
StereoOptimizer_X3D		Useful for optimizing stereo settings for X3D screens.
StereoOptimizerAuto		Useful for optimizing stereo settings of the Viewport node; replaces the StereoOptimizer prototype.
TextSender		A simple tool to send text via routes.

TABLE A.7 Dynamics Tools Library

Prototype	Icon	Description
DragBodies		Provides DragObjects support for use on dynamic bodies that can move with a camera; also available from the Object Movers library.
GrabBodies		Moves bodies with a "hand."
GrabBody		Grabs a rigid body using a rigid joint.
JointConnector		Connects two joint attachment points in runtime.
KeyEngineControls		Controls the drive of a CarWheelJoint with keys.
KeySteeringControls		Controls the steering of a CarWheelJoint with keys.
MouseSteeringControls		Controls the steering of a CarWheelJoint with the mouse.

Prototypes shown in blue are available only in EON Professional.

TABLE A.8 Environments Library

Prototype	Icon	Description
Apartment		A large unfurnished apartment with orange walls.
BMW		A BMW car using Cg shaders.
Chamber		A large, partly circular room with beautiful lighting effects.
CityHighway		A major inner-city highway, complete with bridges and buildings.
GrandRoom		A magnificent, well-lit room with polished floorboards.
Hall		A two-story hallway with beautiful lighting effects.
LargeApartment		A furnished apartment that includes bedrooms and a bathroom.
LegoTown		A small town square made of LEGO pieces.
MountainDome		A desert environment surrounded by mountains.
Mountains		A simple mountain environment with one texture.
OfficeRoom1		Small office room that is 3.0 × 3.6 meters.
OfficeRoom2		Medium office room that is 3.6 × 4.8 meters.
OfficeRoom3		Large office room that is 4.8 × 6.0 meters.
OfficeRoom4		Large office room that is 8 × 10 meters.
SkyDome		A 360-degree background made with a high-resolution photo.
SkySphere		An image on the inside of a sphere for use as a sky background.
TownSquare		A paved city center area with large stone buildings.

TABLE A.9 Furniture Library

Prototype	Icon	Description
Bookcase		Wooden bookcase with cupboard doors that open.
Cabinet		Wooden cabinet with doors and parts that move.
ComputerDesk		Steel and glass computer desk with moving keyboard shelf.
Desk		Wooden desk with six drawers that open.
DeskAndHutch		Wooden desk and hutch with many moving parts.
Lockers		Six steel lockers with doors that open and close.
LowCabinet		Low wooden cabinet with shelves and glass doors.
OfficeChair1		Gray swivel office chair with adjustable height.
OfficeChair2		Beige swivel office chair with adjustable height.
OfficeChair3		Black leather office chair with adjustable height.
TV_Cabinet		Wooden TV cabinet with storage shelves.

Prototypes shown in blue are available only in EON Professional.

TABLE A.10 GUIControl Functions Library

Prototype	Icon	Description
2DText		A 2DText node with "#" as the new-line character.
AlertMsgBox		Displays a message with an OK button.
ChooseFolderDialog		Displays a dialog box that lets the user choose a folder.
ConfirmMsgBox		Displays a question with OK and Cancel options.
FileSelecter		Opens a dialog box that allows the user to enter or select a filename.
GroupGUINodes		A time-saving function that moves and hides GUI nodes as a group.
InputMsgBox		Displays a question and returns text input by the user.
LogWindow		Adds text to a 2DText node.
MenuSwitch		Uses a pop-up menu to switch geometries.
MoveGUINodes		Drag-and-drop nodes that have BoxPosition-type fields.
OpenDialog		Displays an Open dialog box that enables a user to select a filename.
PopupUnlimited		Used with script to create a pop-up menu with unlimited menu items.
SaveAsDialog		Displays a Save As dialog box that enables a user to enter or select a filename.
SliderAuto		An automatically positioned slider that outputs fraction, float, or integer values.
SliderPlus		Displays a slider plus a label and the slider's value.
TimeDisplay		A 2D text box that displays the current system time.

TABLE A.11 JoyStick Related Library

Prototype	Icon	Description
JoyStickNav		Accepts joystick outEvents to create Walk node–like navigation.
LogitechDualAction		Provides outEvent support for the Logitech® Dual Action™ Gamepad.
LogitechExtreme3DPro		Provides outEvent support for the Logitech® Extreme™ 3D Pro joystick.
XBox360Controller		Provides outEvent support for the Xbox 360™ Controller (joystick).

Prototypes shown in blue are available only in EON Professional.

TABLE A.12 Node Changers Library

Prototype	Icon	Description
CameraChanger		Changes the Camera field of the Viewport node.
DiffuseTextureChanger		Changes the DiffuseTexture field of a Material2 node.
LightMapTextureChanger		Changes the LightmapTexture field of a Material2 node.
MaterialChanger		Changes the Material field of a Shape node.
MeshNodeChanger		Changes the Geometry field of a Shape node.
NodeRefChanger		Changes the SFNode type field of any node or prototype.
RenderTreeChanger		Changes the RenderTree field of the Viewport node.
TextureUVMapChanger		Changes the DiffuseTextureUVMap field of the Material2 node.

TABLE A.13 Object Movers Library

Prototype	Icon	Description
DragBodies		Provides DragObjects support for use on dynamic bodies that can move with a camera; also available from the Dynamics Tools library.
DragManager		Allows drag-and-drop movement of objects; use with DragSelecter prototype.
DragObjects		Allows drag-and-drop movement of objects.
DragSelecter		Drag-and-drop selector; use with the DragManager prototype.
KeyMover		Uses keys to control the Mover prototype.
MouseISector		Provides the position at which the mouse is pointing.
Mover		Simple motion model that requires buttons or keys.
MoveRotateArrows2D		Moves and rotates objects by dragging and clicking arrows in an orthographic viewport.
MoveRotateArrows3D		Moves and rotates objects by dragging or clicking arrows.
PointedPos		Provides the 3D position at which the mouse is pointing.
StickyMover		Moves objects that stick to any surface.
ZAdjust		Adjusts the Z value of an object to follow the floor level.

Prototypes shown in blue are available only in EON Professional.

TABLE A.14 ObjectNav Library

Prototype	Icon	Description
ObjectNav		Rotates, zooms, and pans around a single object.
ObjectNavExplorer		Useful to zoom in and out on parts of an object.
ObjectNavLITE		Rotates, zooms, and pans around a single object; has fewer fields than the ObjectNav prototype.
ObjectNavManager		Turns off an ObjectNav prototype when a new one turns on.
ObjectNavSelecter		Selects this node's parent for ObjectNav prototype's PivotPosition field.
ObjectNavZoomExtents		Performs a "ZoomExtents" on a Frame node and resets the ObjectNav prototype so that the target is in the center of the screen view; zooms in on the target object using automatically calculated PivotPosition and ZoomDistance values.

TABLE A.15 OrbitNav Library

Prototype	Icon	Description
OrbitNav		Provides a navigation system to rotate, zoom, and pan using a mouse.
OrbitNavButtons		Enables rotate, zoom, and pan-type navigation using buttons or inEvents.
OrbitNavExplorer		Zooms in and out on parts of an object.
OrbitNavHierarchyExplorer		Hides/shows shapes that are grouped in a hierarchy.
OrbitNavJoyStick		Enables use of a joystick to rotate, zoom, and pan by converting joystick values into rotate, zoom, and pan values.
OrbitNavKeyMover		Uses arrow keys to rotate, zoom, and pan; arrow keys trigger inEvents of the OrbitNavButtons prototype.
OrbitNavKeyOptions		Alters OrbitNav prototype properties; uses keys to reset, spin, turn on/off, adjust speed, etc.
OrbitNavLookHereAtStart		Points camera at a selected target when simulation starts; makes OrbitNav prototype instantly look toward an object.
OrbitNavMouseController		Allows the mouse to manipulate OrbitNav prototype; rotates, pans, and zooms using the mouse buttons.
OrbitNavReset		Sets camera position via OrbitNav prototype's reset method.
OrbitNavResetToBBox		Resets OrbitNav prototype using bounding box size and center; resets OrbitNav prototype so that the target is in the center of the screen's view.
OrbitNavResetToClickPos		Faces camera at point where mouse was clicked; centers the camera's view on the clicked position.
OrbitNavResetToFramePos		Resets OrbitNav prototype to look at the position of a Frame node.
OrbitNavResetToStart		Resets OrbitNav prototype properties to values at simulation start; saves the OrbitNav prototype's start values for resetting later.
OrbitNavSpin		Auto-rotates camera in the heading direction; makes OrbitNav prototype rotate without a user controlling it.
OrbitNavViewMaker		Creates and saves ten predefined camera viewing positions by saving the current position.

Prototypes shown in blue are available only in EON Professional.

TABLE A.16 Particle Systems Library

Prototype	Icon	Description
ParticleSystem		Creates particle effects such as smoke, clouds, bubbles, fire, and stars.
ParticleSystemInterface		Use with the ParticleSystem prototype to configure it.

TABLE A.17 Peripheral Tools Library

Prototype	Icon	Description
MagellanController		Contains a 3DMouseMagellan and extends it with additional features.
PinchGloveController		Splits some common gestures into independent gestures.
TrackerWalk		Offers Walk node–like navigation using a tracker system.

TABLE A.18 Phillips Screen Library

Prototype	Icon	Description
ClickConverter_PhillipsScreen		Workaround for ClickSensors on Phillips stereo screens.
ObjectNav_PhillipsScreen		Middle mouse button disabled for use by PhillipsCS.
Status_PhillipsScreen		Access registry to determine whether Phillips Screen is active.
StereoOptimizer_PhillipsScreen		Change near and far clipping plane via sliders or other user interface tools.

TABLE A.19 Useful Functions Library

Prototype	Icon	Description
AAOnOff		Enables and disables AntiAliasing.
CalcDistance		Measures distance traveled while holding down a key.
ClickSensorOnOff		Activates a ClickSensor node only while inside a viewport.
ClickSensorPlus		A ClickSensor plus nine outEvents.
CollisionBoxes		Collision detection system to keep a camera inside a group of boxes.
CollisionBoxesAdv		Collision detection system to keep a camera inside a group of rotated boxes.
ColorPicker		Opens a dialog box to choose a color and then sends the color value as an outEvent.
Connection		Sends connection data to the ConnectionManager prototype.
ConnectionManager		Manages unlimited connections between Frame nodes.

(continued)

TABLE A.19 Useful Functions Library (*continued*)

Prototype	Icon	Description
Day-Night		Day and night lighting.
DoubleClick		Sends outEvents when you double-click an object.
Eye2Eye		Makes an object/camera look/stare at another object.
FloatingViewport		Moves a viewport; keeps the size of the viewport the same when the size of the window changes.
Gravitation		Applies gravitation motion to a Frame node.
HighLighter		Changes the material of Shape nodes on mouse over.
InactivitySensor		Triggers an event after a set time of mouse inactivity.
KeyFrameController		Slider and buttons used to play/pause/stop a KeyFrame node.
Keys1to10		Sends outEvents when you press keys 0 to 9; press 0 to send the value 10.
KeySensorPlus		A keyboard sensor plus three functions.
MouseInViewport		Tells you whether the mouse pointer is inside a viewport.
OnOffForFrame		Hides and displays a frame when a key is pressed.
OpenCloseLatch		Versatile latch with open/close terminology.
PulseDistributor		Sends pulses to a group of nodes in sequence.
RubbishBin		Moves objects to a "rubbish bin" that will be deleted on shutdown.
SaveSnapShot		Saves a .png image of EON to disk when Ctrl + S keys are pressed.
ShapeAnimator		Animates by quickly switching on/off shapes.
SimulationStartedEvent		Sends an event when the simulation starts running.
SimultaneousSound		Plays sounds simultaneously when multiple DirectSound nodes are started in a short period of time.
SmoothKeySensor		Sends continuous key-down events without delay between the first and the second event.
SmoothOperator		Changes float values gradually.
ToggleKey		A key that turns a node on and off.
TriggerTargetsChildren		Triggers nodes under Shape nodes (targets) detected by an ISector.
TurboEvents		Prepares the EON file for EON Turbo Generator.
TVChannelSwitcher		Click TVs (shapes) to change channels (cameras or movies).
ViewportResizer		Resizes and moves a viewport.
WalkOnOff		Activates Walk node only while inside a viewport.
WordTrigger		Used to trigger an event by typing a word.

Prototypes shown in blue are available only in EON Professional.

TABLE A.20 Useful Objects Library

Prototype	Icon	Description
3DPointer		X, Y, and Z axes rods; useful to show pivot position.
AnimatedCone		Shows a position by scaling a cone up and down.
AutomaticArrows		Green arrows with auto-positioning and auto-scaling function.
Background		Displays or manipulates a background image or file.
BorderWalls		Generates a border when given X, Y, W, and H values.
BoundingBox		Shows a selected object; when given a node, the prototype will surround the objects in the node with a transparent box.
BoundingBoxOutline		Shows a selected object; when given a node, the prototype will surround the objects in the node with a completely transparent box.
CamObject		Works as a flat object representing the camera in 2D viewports.
CustomRoom		Used to makes a custom-sized room.
DownloadBar		Shows download progress.
GridPlane		A plane with grid lines; the color of the grid lines can be changed.
GridPlane2		A plane with grid-line textures.
Helicopter		Sikorsky Helicopter MH60.
MilitaryFuelTruck		M978 HEMTT 2500 Gallon Refueler.
MoveableWalls		Move and resize this 2D representation of walls; drags walls in an orthographic (2D) viewport; can be used with CustomRoom prototype.
Ring		A red wireframe ring with a 1-meter radius.
Robert		Picture of a man walking away from you.
ScaledLine		Displays a line between two specified positions in a 2D viewport.
ScaledLine3D		Displays a line between two positions.
TurboPump		Industrial pump with transparent and moving parts.
Vector		Used to visualize vectors; four vectors are used in slightly different ways.

TABLE A.21 Old Prototypes Library

Prototype	Icon	Description
3DPointerA		Use the newer 3DPointer prototype.
3DPointerB		Use the newer 3DPointer prototype.
3DPointerC		Use the newer 3DPointer prototype.
EventDisplayer		Use the newer EventInfo prototype.
StereoOptimizer		Use the newer StereoOptimizerAuto prototype.

Prototypes shown in blue are available only in EON Professional.

APPENDIX B

EON Scripting Reference

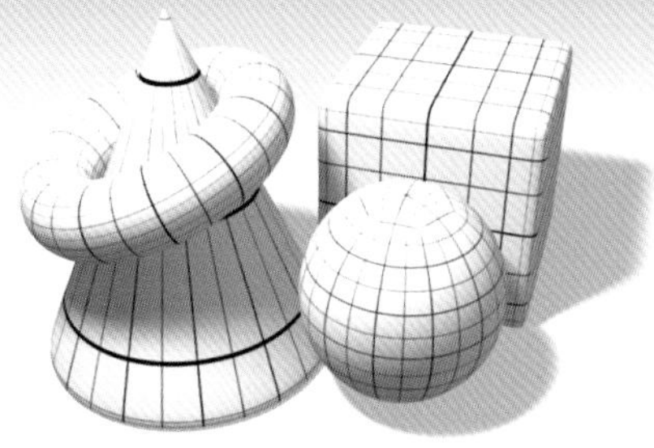

EON has three scriptable object types. You can refer to this appendix for information about their methods and properties. The three object types are:

- EON Base Object—for various functions related to EON
- EON Node Object—representing a node in the simulation tree
- EON Field Object—representing a field of a node

Methods or properties belong to each object. Each method ends in parentheses. Although VBScript does not insist on these parentheses unless they are necessary to enclose arguments to the method, JScript always requires the parentheses for methods, even if no arguments are required. Parentheses should not be used for properties because there is only one property—the Value property of the EON Field Object.

BEST PRACTICES

Use of Case in Scripting

Please note that the methods of EON Studio's objects do not need to be in a certain case; that is, you can use lowercase or uppercase or both. Usually, JScript will insist that methods use the same case every time. For example, if you want to use a method named parseInt in JScript, you cannot use parseint or ParseINT. But this is not true for methods belonging to EON objects. Therefore, you can use all of the following object names, and many others, interchangeably:

- getfieldbyname
- getFieldByName
- GETFieldByName

Throughout this appendix, we use mixed case for enhanced readability.

EON Base Object

The EON Base Object provides support for various functions related to the EON environment. This includes access to the simulation tree (Find, FindNode, GetNodeName, and GetNodePath), creating multiple value fields (such as MakeSFVec3f), and outputting text (Trace and MessageBox).

To access all of the methods of the EON Base Object, you type:

```
eon.
```

followed by the method name. For example:

```
set cam = eon.FindNode("Camera")
eon.Trace("object clicked")
p.value = eon.C(1, 2, 3)
```

Table B.1 provides details about the EON Base Object methods. For each method, the table provides an example of the syntax and notes about the syntax. Following the table, you will find numerous topics that provide additional information about how to use several of these methods.

tips+tricks

When you paste a node, it will become the last node under the *newParent*. In JScript, you can create a reference to the new node, as shown in the following example:

```
var treech = newParent.
    GetFieldByName
    ("TreeChildren");
var newnode = treech.
    GetMFElement(treech.
    GetMFCount()-1);
```

tips+tricks

Use the DeleteNode method with care. Deleting one node will remove all of its child nodes as well, and deleting important nodes may cause EON Studio to crash. If your script has a variable holding a node reference and the referred node is deleted, then you will see a script error because the value is no longer available from the variable.

TABLE B.1 EON Base Object Methods

Method	Description	Syntax Example	Syntax Details
CopyNode	Copies a node within the simulation tree.	eon. CopyNode(*node*, *newParent*)	eon is always required; it is the EON Base Object. *node* is required; it is a reference to an EON Node Object to copy. *newParent* is required; it is a reference to the EON Node Object in which the copied node should be placed.
DeleteNode	Deletes a node from the simulation tree.	eon. DeleteNode(*node*)	eon is always required; it is the EON Base Object. *node* is required; it is a reference to the node to be deleted.
Find	Returns a collection of EON Node Objects matching a given name or regular expression.	eon.Find(*node_exp* [, *root*][, *maxdepth*])	eon is always required; it is the EON Base Object. *node_exp* is either a string representing the whole name of the nodes to be found or it is a regular expression. *root* (optional) is a reference to an EON Node Object from which the search begins. If omitted, the highest node, which is the Simulation node, is used as the root node. The root node is always included in the search. *maxdepth* (optional) is the number of levels under the root node that the search should include. 0 means Find is only applied on the root node; 1 means only the root and its children nodes. Less than 0 will return an empty collection. If omitted, the search is applied to an unlimited number of levels. See the *Using the Find Method* section following this table.
FindNode	Returns a reference to an EON Node Object when given the name of the node.	eon.FindNode ([*parentnode1!*] [*parentnodeN!*]... *nodename*)	eon is always required; it is the EON Base Object. *parentnode1...parentnodeN* is optional; it identifies the names of the parent nodes to the nodename node. Using this option will narrow the search. Each node must be separated by the (!) exclamation mark. *nodename* is required; it is an expression that equates to a string and represents an existing node's name. See the *Using the FindNode Method* section following this table.

FindByProgID	Returns a collection of EON Node Objects matching the given name ProgID. It is similar to eon.Find, but the search is based on an exact match of ProgID instead of a name or regular expression.
	ProgID is an identifier of a node type, ProgID. See eon.GetNodeProgID.
		eon.FindByProgID (*progID*)
		eon.FindByProgID (*progID*, *root*)
		eon.FindByProgID (*progID*, *root*, *maxdepth*)
			eon is always required; it is the EON Base Object.
			progID is required; it is text identifying the node type.
			root is optional; it is a reference to an EON Node Object that will be the root for the search.
			maxdepth is optional; it is the maximum depth to search in the subtree.
			<u>JScript Example</u>
			// Turn off all lights in the simulation
			allLights = eon.FindByProgID("EonD3D.Light.2")
			for (var i=0; i<allLights.Count; i++)
			{
			allLights.item(i).GetFieldByName("Active").Value = false;
			}

(continued)

tips+tricks

The GetNodeName method can be useful for scripts that will access many nodes. For example, you may want to display the node name in the EON window to identify the active object or display the name of the node when reporting errors. In VBScript, the code would look like the following example:

```
childnode = this.
    GetFieldByName
  ("TreeChildren").
    GetMFElement(3)
scriptname = eon.
GetNodeName(childnode)
```

Note that it is not possible to set the name of the node.

TABLE B.1 EON Base Object Methods (*continued*)

Method	Description	Syntax Example	Syntax Details
FindAncestor-NodeByName	Returns an ancestor to the selected node. Searches all parents by name until the node is found.	eon.FindAncestor-NodeByName-(*node*, *name*)	eon is always required; it is the EON Base Object. *node* is required; it is a reference to an EON Node Object. *name* is required; it is the name of the ancestor to find.
FindAncestor-NodeByProgID	Returns an ancestor to the selected node. Searches all parents by ProgID until the node is found.	eon.FindAncestor-NodeByProgID-(*node*, *progid*)	eon is always required; it is the EON Base Object. *node* is required; it is a reference to an EON Node Object. *progid* is required; it is a ProgID string of the ancestor to find.
FindAncestor-SiblingNode-ByName	Returns a sibling to an ancestor of the selected node. Searches all parent siblings by name until the node is found.	eon.FindAncestor-SiblingNodeBy-Name(*node*, *name*)	eon is always required; it is the EON Base Object. *node* is required; it is a reference to an EON Node Object. *name* is required; it is a node name of the ancestors sibling to find.
FindAncestor-SiblingNode-ByProgID	Returns a sibling to an ancestor of the selected node. Searches all parent siblings by ProgID until the node is found.	eon.FindAncestor-SiblingNodeBy-ProgID(*node*, *progid*)	eon is always required; it is the EON Base Object. *node* is required; it is a reference to an EON Node Object. *progid* is required; it is a ProgID string of the ancestor sibling to find.
GetNodeName	Returns a string with the name of the node.	eon.GetNode-Name(*node*)	eon is always required; it is the EON Base Object. *node* is required; it is a reference to an EON Node Object.
GetNodePath	Returns a string with the full path to the node.	eon.GetNode-Path(*node*)	eon is always required; it is the EON Base Object. *node* is required; it is a reference to an EON Node Object.
GetNode-ProgId	Returns the ProgID of a node. The ProgID is an identifier of a node type.	eon.GetNode-ProgID(*node*)	eon is always required; it is the EON Base Object. *node* is required; it is a reference to an EON Node Object. JScript Example: var scene = eon.FindNode("Scene") var progID = eon.GetNodeProgID(scene) eon.Trace(progID); This will log the message *EonD3D.Frame.1*.

tips+tricks

When using the GetNodePath method, the path returned always starts with the Simulation node and shows each node's name in the node hierarchy, separated by a backslash. In VBScript, the code would look like the following example:

```
nodepath = eon.
GetNodePath(this)
eon.Trace("Error
occurred in script: "
  & nodepath)
```

where *this* represents the Script node. This script code may produce a result such as Simulation\Scene\Camera\Script.

tips+tricks

The GetScriptTimeout method is the same as the SetScriptTimeout() method, except that it only gets the value; it does not give a new value. The default timeout value is 6 (six seconds). The code would look like the following example:

```
t = eon.
GetScriptTimeout()
```

GetScript-Timeout	Returns the time in seconds that a script can be inactive before a message will appear offering to terminate the script.	eon.GetScript-Timeout()	eon is always required; it is the EON Base Object.
SetScript-Timeout	Sets the time in seconds that a script can be inactive before a message will appear offering to terminate the script. Returns the current timeout value.	eon.SetScript-Timeout(*exp1*)	eon is always required; it is the EON Base Object. *exp1* is required; it must be a positive number, representing a time in seconds. Using zero will effectively turn off this function. See the *Using the SetScriptTimeout Method* section following this table.
MakeSFColor	Returns a safe array that EON uses to represent the SFColor data type. The SFColor data type is a three-dimensional array of RGB values.	eon.MakeSFColor-(*red*, *green*, *blue*)	eon is always required; it is the EON Base Object. *red*, *green*, and *blue* (all required) represent values between 0 and 1 that collectively represent an RGB-defined color. Example: NewColor.value = eon.MakeSFColor(r, g, b)
MakeSF-Rotation	Returns a safe array that EON uses to represent the SFRotation data type. The SFRotation data type is a four-dimensional vector array.	eon.MakeSF-Rotation(*exp1*, *exp2*, *exp3*, *exp4*)	eon is always required; it is the EON Base Object. *exp1*, *exp2*, *exp3*, and *exp4* (all required) represent expressions that can equate to float data types. Example: MyOri.value = eon.MakeSFRotation(x, y, z, a)
MakeSFVec2f	Returns a safe array that EON uses to represent the SFVec2f data type. The SFVec2f data type is a two-dimensional vector array.	eon.MakeSF-Vec2f(*exp1*, *exp2*)	eon is always required; it is the EON Base Object. *exp1* and *exp2* (required) represent expressions that can equate to float data types. Example: TextBoxPos.value = eon.MakeSFVec2f(x, y)
MakeSFVec3f	Returns a safe array that EON uses to represent the SFVec3f data type. The SFVec3f data type is a three-dimensional vector array.	eon.MakeSF-Vec3f(*exp1*, *exp2*, *exp3*)	eon is always required; it is the EON Base Object. *exp1*, *exp2*, and *exp3* (all required) represent expressions that can equate to float data types. Example: Position.value = eon.MakeSFVec3f(x, y, z)
MessageBox	Displays a pop-up dialog box with a text message and title of your choice.	eon.Message-Box(*message*, *title*)	eon is always required; it is the EON Base Object. *message* is a string literal or a variable with a value that can equate to a string that is the main text in the message box. *title* is a string literal or a variable with a value that can equate to a string that will appear in the title bar of the message box. See the *Using the MessageBox Method* section following this table.

(*continued*)

TABLE B.1 EON Base Object Methods (*continued*)

Method	Description	Syntax Example	Syntax Details
Trace	Displays text in the EON Log window.	eon.Trace(*Logtext*)	eon is always required; it is the EON Base Object. *Logtext* is a string literal or a variable with a value that can equate to a string. See the *Using the Trace Method* section following this table.
Trace2	Provides an extended version of Trace.	eon.Trace2(*source, description, message*)	eon is always required; it is the EON Base Object. *source* is required; it is the text to be displayed in the "Source" field in the Log window. *description* is required; it is the text to be displayed in the "Description" field in the Log window. *message* is required; it is the text to be displayed in the "Message" field in the Log window. JScript Example: eon.Trace(eon.GetNodePath(eonthis), eon.GetNodeName(eonthis), "Some message") Note that the *eonthis* keyword refers to the Script node itself.
Transform-Position	Returns a position that has been transformed from one coordinate system to another.	eon.Transform-Position(*fromnode, x, y, z, tonode*)	eon is always required; it is the EON Base Object. *fromnode* and *tonode* represent Frame nodes (coordinate systems), where *fromnode* is the frame we are transforming from and *tonode* is the frame we are transforming to. *x, y,* and *z* are positions in the *fromnode* frame. All parameters are required, but *x, y,* and *z* may be 0. See the *Using the TransformPosition Method* section following this table.
Transform-Orientation	Returns an orientation that has been transformed from one coordinate system to another.	eon.Transform-Orientation (*fromnode, h, p, r, tonode*)	eon is always required; it is the EON Base Object. *fromnode* and *tonode* represent Frame nodes (coordinate systems), where *fromnode* is the frame we are transforming from and *tonode* is the frame we are transforming to. *h, p,* and *r* are orientations in the *fromnode* frame. All parameters are required, but *h, p,* and *r* may be 0. See the *Using the TransformOrientation Method* section following this table.
SaveSnapshot	Saves an image of the current rendered EON simulation window to a local file.	eon.SaveSnap-Shot(*filename, format, param*)	eon is always required; it is the EON Base Object. *filename* is required; it is the full path and filename, including extension. *format* is required; it is an integer that represents the format to be used for the saved file. (1 = PPM, 2 = PNG) *param* is reserved and should always be set to 0.

Using the Find Method

The Find method will return multiple nodes (all nodes that match the search criteria), whereas the FindNode method will return only the first node found that matches the search criteria. One or more arguments can be supplied:

- eon.Find(*name*)
- eon.Find(*name*, *root*)
- eon.Find(*name*, *root*, *maxdepth*)

The nodes in the collection are listed in sequence based on the hierarchy—that is, the root node if it was matched, then the nodes found among the children of the root node, then the grandchildren of the root node, and so on.

To determine whether any nodes found use the Count property of the collection object, use the following code:

In JScript:

```
mynodes = eon.Find("Frame")
if (mynodes.Count > 0)
{
   firstnode = mynodes.item(0)
   firstnode.GetFieldByName("SetRun").value = false
}
```

In VBScript:

```
set mynodes = eon.Find("Frame")
eon.Trace ("The find method found " & mynodes.Count & " nodes")
```

To access an individual node, use the item(*i*) property of the collection object. Note that the first item is accessed by item(0), the second item is accessed by item(1), and so on.

```
set mynodes = eon.Find("Frame")
if mynodes.Count > 0 then
   set firstnode = mynodes.item(0)
   firstnode.GetFieldByName("SetRun").value = false
end if
```

Using the FindNode Method

If a node with the required name is not found at runtime, an error will occur. If multiple nodes have the same name, then the method will return only the first node found.

First, EON Studio looks at all nodes of the same hierarchy level in the simulation tree before moving to the next lower hierarchy level. That is, EON looks among the children of the root node first, looks among the grandchildren of the root node next, and so on. To avoid mistakes, give a unique name to the node that you want to find. Increase the probability of the name's uniqueness by adding a prefix that includes the name of the parent node and an exclamation mark.

Example (JScript and VBScript):

```
eon.FindNode("Table2!Frame").GetFieldByName("SetRun").value =
true
Mynode.value = eon.FindNode("Simulation!Scene!MyScript")
```

Then, in JScript:

```
var aNode
aNode = eon.FindNode("UniqueScript")
```

Or, in VBScript:

```
dim aNode
set aNode = eon.FindNode("UniqueScript")
```

Here, *aNode* is an object variable that holds a reference to the UniqueScript node. VBScript requires the keyword *set* for variables that hold objects, but JScript does not.

In the previous examples, the node reference was stored in a variable. It can be stored in an SFNode field. To do that, type:

```
FoundNode.value = eon.FindNode("UniqueScript")
```

where *FoundNode* is the name of an SFNode script field.

Instead of storing the node reference, we can use the FindNode method as part of a process to find a field's value and store it in a script field like the following example:

```
CamPos.value = eon.FindNode("Camera").GetFieldByName
("Position").value
```

where *CamPos* is a script field with the data type SFVec3f.

To avoid runtime errors that occur when a node is not found, use error handling, as shown in the following example in VBScript:

```
On Error Resume Next ' turns on error handling
set mynode = eon.FindNode("ObjectNav")
if Err.Number <> 0 then
   Msgbox "Can't find the ObjectNav node. Check that it has the
   correct name!"
   Err.clear
end if
On Error GoTo 0 ' turns off error handling
```

Or, like this in JScript:

```
Try
{
   mynode = eon.FindNode("ObjectNav")
}
catch(e)
{
   eon.Trace("Can't find the ObjectNav node. Check that it has
   the correct name! ")
}
```

Using the MessageBox Method

The MessageBox method was added in EON Studio version 4.1. A message box–type function has always been available with VBScript with the built-in MsgBox() function, but this was not available in JScript. You may have thought that the alert(), confirm(), and prompt() functions are a part of JScript, but they are actually functions of the window object of Internet browsers.

The MessageBox method is useful for debugging your scripts. By adding a message box to your script, you can confirm that your script runs correctly. Also, to ensure that it is working the way you intend, you can display values produced by your script. You can use a message box as part of your finished application as a quick way of providing information to the users. The message box shown in Figure B.1, for example, provides information about an object the viewer clicked.

FIGURE B.1 MessageBox example

VBScript and JScript:

```
msg = "You have clicked on the conference room. The office con-
ference room seats up to 12 people and has an audiovisual sys-
tem for company presentations."
eon.MessageBox(msg, "Conference Room")
```

For VBScript, the parentheses are not used:

```
eon.MessageBox msg, "Conference Room"
```

To format your message text by forcing a new line, use Chr(13) in VBScript. In JScript, type a backslash and the letter n (\n) to force a new line.

VBScript:

```
msg = "Congratulations!" & Chr(13) & "Training Complete."
eon.MessageBox msg, "ECC Training"
```

JScript:

```
msg = "Congratulations!\nTraining Complete."
eon.MessageBox(msg, "ECC Training")
```

You can see the resulting message created by this code in Figure B.2.

FIGURE B.2 Message with forced new lines

tips+tricks

The MessageBox function stops the script from running until you click the OK button. If a script stops running for more than six seconds, a timeout message is displayed. To avoid displaying the timeout message, you should change the script timeout time. See the SetScriptTimeout Method in Table B.1 and in the following section, *Using the SetScriptTimeout Method.*

Using the SetScriptTimeout Method

EON has a default timeout of six seconds. This means that a message box will be displayed if a script has stopped running for longer than six seconds; it will ask whether you want to terminate the script. This method enables you to get out of an endless loop that has been scripted by mistake. In some situations, you may want to increase this six-second period or turn it off to allow more time for the script to do its work. When a message box is displayed, the script is paused until the user clicks the OK button. If the timeout value is not changed, the user will see this message box. To avoid displaying the message, set the timeout value to 0, which will turn off the timeout and reset it after the message box code.

```
tid = eon.SetScriptTimeout(0)
msgbox "Correct. Proceed to Question 5."
eon.SetScriptTimeout(tid)
```

Notice that the SetScriptTimeout(0) method also returns the current timeout value before setting it to 0. The old timeout value is saved in the *tid* variable and is returned in the last line.

In other situations, you may need to increase the timeout time or turn off the timeout function when performing time-consuming tasks such as accessing text files, using a database, or performing complicated calculations. However, if you see a timeout message, the script usually has an error. Typically, it means that the script is caught in an endless loop. Figure B.3 shows the warning message you will see when the script times out.

FIGURE B.3 Script timeout warning message

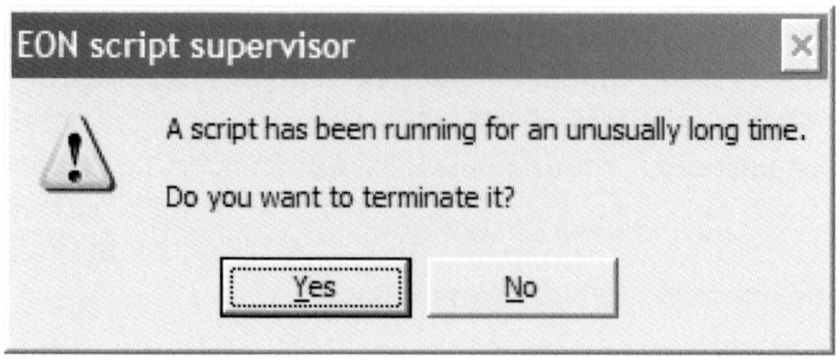

After the script is terminated, the location of the error is reported in another message box. See Figure B.4.

FIGURE B.4 Script error message

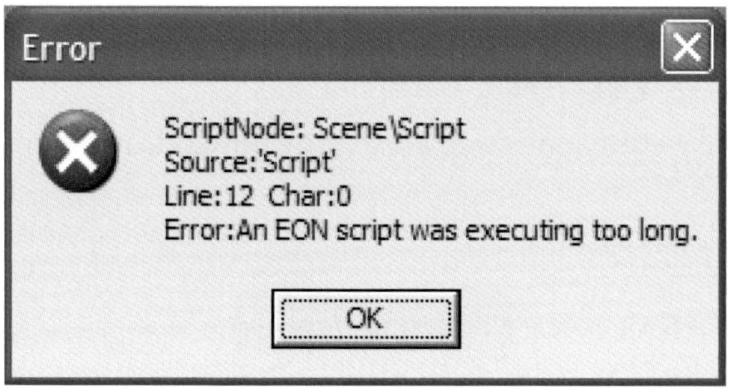

tips+tricks

You cannot avoid the timeout message by typing On Error Resume Next in your script.

Using the Trace Method

The Trace method will help you debug your scripts. Sending text to the Log window makes it possible to examine the values that are generated by your script to determine whether the correct value is generated at the correct time. In the following example, the text "Value ball = 9 !" will be displayed in the Log window. Make sure that Trace is turned on by right-clicking the Log window, choosing Set Filter from the pop-up menu, checking the Script Trace check box, and clicking OK.

In JScript:

```
eon.Trace("Value ball = " + ball + "!")
```

In VBScript:

```
eon.Trace("Value ball = " & ball & "!")
```

tips+tricks

For VBScript, the parentheses are optional. They can be left off, as shown in the following example:

```
eon.Trace "hello Eon"
```

Using the TransformOrientation Method

To understand the TransformOrientation method better, remember that WorldOrientation is an orientation expressed relative to the Scene node. If you want to calculate WorldOrientation, then the last parameter, *tonode,* would be the Scene node.

For example, suppose you have a moon orbiting Earth, which is orbiting the sun. Calculate the orientation of the moon relative to Earth.

```
var moonframe = eon.FindNode("Moon")
var earthframe = eon.FindNode("Earth")
var ori = eon.TransformPosition(moonframe, 0, 0, 0, earthframe)
```

Using the TransformPosition Method

To understand the TransformPosition method better, remember that WorldPosition is a position expressed relative to the Scene node. If you want to calculate WorldPosition, then the last parameter, *tonode,* would be the Scene node. The position returned is an array with three elements like the output of the MakeSFVec3f method.

For example, calculate the world position of a node's bounding box center and give it to OrbitNav.

```
var node = eon.FindNode("myobject")
var scene = eon.FindNode("Scene")
var OrbitNav = eon.FindNode("OrbitNav")
var bbc = node.GetFieldByName("BBoxCenter").value.toArray()
var wp= eon.TransformPosition(node, bbc[0], bbc[1], bbc[2], scene)
OrbitNav.GetFieldByName("ResetPivotPos").value = wp
```

EON Node Object

The syntax requires that these methods be preceded with a reference to an EON Node Object.

```
node.methodname()
```

You can get a reference to an EON Node Object in several ways:

- Use the Find and FindNode methods of the EON Base Object.
- In VBScript, the keyword *this* refers to the Script node itself as an EON Node Object.
- In both VBScript and JScript, the keyword *eonthis* refers to the Script node itself as an EON Node Object.
- Given a node reference, you can get a reference to its parent with the GetParentNode() method.
- Get the value of a field with the SFNode data type.
- Get an element of a field with the MFNode data type.

cross-reference

Right-click a node, choose the Copy as Link command, and then paste the link under another node to create a node reference. See Module 1 Lesson 2 or Module 7 Lesson 3 for more information about referenced links, which are also known as node references.

Each Node Object is a collection of fields. Four of the five methods of the Node Object relate to fields: getting the number of fields, getting a reference to a field by index number or name, and getting the name of a field by index number.

Every node has at least seven fields, which are the default fields of TreeChildren, Children, SetRun, SetRun_, OnRunFalse, OnRunTrue, and OnRunChanged with index numbers from 0 to 6. The TreeChildren field is an MFNode field that holds references to the children nodes. The Children field (also an MFNode field) is very similar to TreeChildren, but it can hold more children than the TreeChildren field. This is possible because referenced links or node references are included in this field, but not in the TreeChildren field.

Node Objects can be stored in SFNode type fields, but a Field Object cannot be stored in a field. There is no method (currently) that can get a reference directly to child nodes. Therefore, you must get a reference to the TreeChildren field and then get an element of it, which is a node. This process can be iterated to get references to grandchildren nodes and so on.

In the following VBScript example, GetField(0) will get the field with index number 0, which is always the TreeChildren field. GetMFElement(0) returns the first child node.

```
set cameranode = eon.FindNode("Simulation").GetField(0).
GetMFElement(0).

_

GetField(0).GetMFElement(0)
```

In VBScript, you can test whether one object is the same as another by using the keyword *is*.

```
set cam = eon.FindNode("Camera")
set parent = this.GetParentNode()
if cam is parent then
   eon.Trace("The parent node is the Camera node.")
end if
```

In JScript, the simple equality operator (==) can be used:

```
var cam, parent
cam = eon.FindNode("Headlight")
parent = thisNode.value.GetParentNode()
if (cam == parent)
eon.Trace("The parent node is the Camera node.")
```

Table B.2 provides details about the EON Node Object methods. For each method, you will find an example of the syntax and notes about the syntax listed in the table. Following the table, you will find topics that provide greater depth about the use of the GetField method and the GetParentNode method.

tips+tricks

The ID or index number of a field will always be at least 7 because the default fields are included in the count.

tips+tricks

If no field exists with the name that is being searched, then a runtime error occurs: Invalid procedure call or argument.

This method makes it possible to send values to a field. In this example, you can send a new value to the Viewport node's FieldOfView field:

```
eon.FindNode("Viewport").GetFieldByName
("FieldOfView").value = 80
```

tips+tricks

If no field exists with the name that is being searched, a runtime error occurs: Invalid procedure call or argument.

This example statement assigns id, the ID number of the Translation field in aNode:

id = aNode.GetIdOfName("Translation")

TABLE B.2 EON Node Object Methods

Method	Description	Syntax Example	Syntax Details
GetParentNode	Returns a reference to a node's parent node.	*node*.GetParentNode()	*node* is an EON Node Object. There are no parameters or arguments inside the parentheses of this method. See the *Using the GetParentNode Method* section following this table.
GetFieldCount	Returns an integer representing the number of fields belonging to a node.	*node*.GetFieldCount()	*node* is an EON Node Object. There are no parameters or arguments inside the parentheses of this method.
GetField	Returns a reference to an EON Field Object.	*node*.GetField(*index*)	*node* is always an EON Node Object. *index* is required; it is an integer representing the ID or index number of the field. See the *Using the GetField Method* section following this table.
GetFieldByName	Returns a reference to an EON Field Object.	*node*.GetFieldByName(*name*)	*node* is always an EON Node Object. *name* is required; it is a string representing the name of the field. Any case (upper, lower, or mixed) can be used.
GetIdOfName	Returns an integer representing the ID or index number of a field.	*node*.GetIdOfName(*name*)	*node* is always an EON Node Object. *name* is required; it is a string representing the name of the field. Any case (upper, lower, or mixed) can be used.

Using the GetParentNode Method

The GetParentNode method returns a reference to a node's parent node. An example of its use is:

```
set parent = boxnode.value.GetParentNode()
```

where *boxnode* is a name of a field of data type SFNode.

A script can be designed to affect its parent node. For example, a script can move and rotate or hide and display its parent Frame node.

In JScript:

```
function On_CurrentTime()
{
   var parent, h
   h = CurrentTime.value * 36
   parent = eonthis.GetParentNode()
   parent.GetFieldByName("Orientation").value = eon.
   MakeSFVec3f(h, 0, 0)
}
```

In VBScript:

```
sub On_CurrentTime()  ' inevent from a TimeSensor node
   dim h
   h = CurrentTime.value * 36
   set parent = eonthis.GetParentNode()
   parent.GetFieldByName("Orientation").value = eon.
   MakeSFVec3f(h, 0, 0)
end sub
```

In the previous VBScript example, the script will act like the Rotate node, affecting the Orientation field of the Script node's parent node.

Because this method returns a node as well as a method of a node, we can quickly get a reference to a great-grandfather node by repeating the method, as shown in the following example:

```
set rootnode = this.GetParentNode().GetParentNode().
GetParentNode()
```

Using the GetField Method

In this VBScript example, the SetRun field of the Rotate node will be set to true because the SetRun field always has an ID number of 2.

```
set SR = eon.FindNode("Rotate").GetField(2)
SR.value = true
```

If the supplied integer is negative or greater than the number of fields, then a runtime error occurs: Invalid procedure call or argument. Each field of a node has an ID number or index number. This is not displayed anywhere in EON Studio, but you can view a list of fields in the Fields dialog box, as shown in Figure B.5, or the Property Bar. The fields are always listed in ID number order. In this way, you can calculate a field's ID by starting at the top and counting down. Note that ID numbers start at 0 with the TreeChildren field.

FIGURE B.5 Fields dialog box

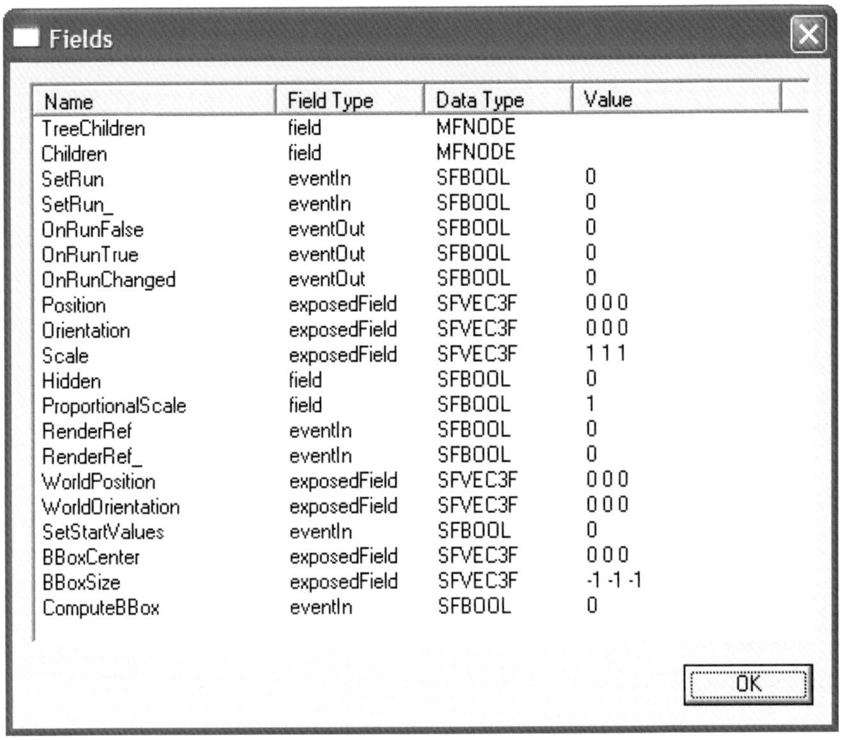

Name	Field Type	Data Type	Value
TreeChildren	field	MFNODE	
Children	field	MFNODE	
SetRun	eventIn	SFBOOL	0
SetRun_	eventIn	SFBOOL	0
OnRunFalse	eventOut	SFBOOL	0
OnRunTrue	eventOut	SFBOOL	0
OnRunChanged	eventOut	SFBOOL	0
Position	exposedField	SFVEC3F	0 0 0
Orientation	exposedField	SFVEC3F	0 0 0
Scale	exposedField	SFVEC3F	1 1 1
Hidden	field	SFBOOL	0
ProportionalScale	field	SFBOOL	1
RenderRef	eventIn	SFBOOL	0
RenderRef_	eventIn	SFBOOL	0
WorldPosition	exposedField	SFVEC3F	0 0 0
WorldOrientation	exposedField	SFVEC3F	0 0 0
SetStartValues	eventIn	SFBOOL	0
BBoxCenter	exposedField	SFVEC3F	0 0 0
BBoxSize	exposedField	SFVEC3F	-1 -1 -1
ComputeBBox	eventIn	SFBOOL	0

The GetField method can be a substitute for the GetFieldByName method, which also returns an EON Field Object. The latter is more useful because it is more common to ask for a field by its name rather than by its ID number. The former is useful because it requires less script code. Compare these two lines, which perform the same action. The first line uses the field's ID number. The second line uses the field's name.

```
var ch = anode.GetField(0)
var ch = anode.GetFieldByName("TreeChildren")
```

EON Field Object

The syntax of the EON Field Object methods requires that they be preceded with a reference to an EON Field Object.

```
field.methodname()
```

You can get a reference to an EON Field Object in two ways:

- If the field belongs to the Script node, then type the field's name.
- If the field belongs to another node, including other Script nodes, then using the GetField or GetFieldByName methods of the EON Node Object will return an EON Field Object.

EON Field Objects have a field type and data type. These are explained in the following sections.

Field Types

The field types are eventIn, eventOut, exposedField, and field. These names refer to how the fields can be connected in the Routes window. An eventIn type field will have its name in the list of fields that a route can be connected *to*, and an eventOut type field will have its name in the list of fields that a route can be connected *from*. ExposedField type fields can be connected to routes both ways. That is, they can have routes coming in and going out in the Routes window. The field type fields cannot have connections coming in or going out, so they are not available in the Routes window. When scripting, you can create your own fields. Therefore, you must decide which type of field is appropriate for your script.

Connections coming into the Script node usually affect the script you write or the node that receives the connection sent by the Script node. Connections going out of the Script node are the values created by your script. ExposedFields can receive and send connections. The field type usually stores values that are not intended to be changed during runtime. However, when scripting, these rules are much more flexible. Using script, you can send connections to fields of all types, and you can write a subroutine that handles an eventOut field that changes value.

Data Types

cross-reference

More details about these methods can be found in Table B.3.

Each field has a data type such as Boolean, string, float, integer, and so on. Furthermore, these data types fall into two groups: single-field (SF) type fields and multiple-field (MF) type fields. MF type fields are like an array or collection of SF type fields. To access MF type fields, you can use an MF method: GetMFCount, SetMFCount, GetMFElement, SetMFElement, AddMFElement, and RemoveMFElement.

SFNode and MFNode Data Types

In EON Studio, you will see that some nodes have yellow folder icons under them in the simulation tree to indicate that they hold fields of the SFNode or MFNode data type. These folders also can hold references to other nodes. The yellow folder icons with a red plus sign indicate that they are MFNode data types that can hold multiple node references. To place a reference to a node in a folder, right-click the node, select the Copy as Link option from the pop-up menu, right-click the yellow folder, and choose the Paste option from the pop-up menu.

TreeChildren and Children

Every node has two default fields that are named TreeChildren and Children. The fields are of MFNode data type, which have node references even though you do not see any yellow folders under them. These are special fields that are not like other MFNode fields because they actually hold the child nodes. The TreeChildren field holds the actual nodes, whereas the Children field holds a reference to them like normal MFNode fields.

In an SFNode field, you can enter the path to a node in the Script Properties dialog box for a Script node and click OK. A reference to the node will appear in the yellow folder. However, in your script, it is not possible to equate a string like "Scene\Camera\Walk" with an SFNode type or vice versa. To do this, you must use the eon.FindNode() method or the eon.GetNodePath() method.

Table B.3 provides details about the EON Field Object methods. For each method, an example of the syntax and notes about the syntax are provided. Following the table, you will find topics that provide greater depth about the use of several of these methods.

TABLE B.3 EON Field Object Methods

Method	Description	Syntax Example	Syntax Details
GetName	Returns the name of an EON Field Object.	*field*.GetName()	*field* is an EON Field Object. There are no parameters or arguments inside the parentheses of this method. See the *Using the GetNameMethod* section following this table.
GetType	Returns an integer representing the data type of the field.	*field*.GetType()	*field* is an EON Field Object. There are no parameters or arguments inside the parentheses of this method. See the *Using the GetType Method* section following this table.
GetMFCount*	Returns an integer representing the number of fields in a multiple-field (MF) type field.	*field*.GetMFCount()	*field* is an EON Field Object. There are no parameters or arguments inside the parentheses of this method. See the *Using the GetMFCount Method* section following this table.
SetMFCount*	Sets the number of fields in an MF type field, thereby deleting or adding fields.	*field*.SetMFCount(*count*)	*field* is an EON Field Object. *count* is a positive integer or 0 that represents the number of fields that will remain after this method. See the *Using the SetMFCount Method* section following this table.
GetMFElement*	Returns an element or value of an MF type field.	*field*.GetMFElement(*number*)	*field* is an EON Field Object. *number* is a positive integer or 0 that represents which of the values to be returned. 0 is the first element, 1 is the second element, and so on. See the *Using the GetMFElement Method* section following this table.
SetMFElement*	Sets (changes) an element or value of an MF type field.	*field*.SetMFElement(*number*, *value*)	*field* is an EON Field Object. *number* is a positive integer or 0 that represents which of the values to be set. 0 is the first element, 1 is the second element, and so on. *value* is any expression that has the same data type as *field*. If the value is not of the correct data type, a runtime script error (type mismatch) will occur. See the *Using the SetMFElement Method* section following this table.
AddMFElement*	Adds a new element or value to an MF type field.	*field*.AddMFElement(*value*)	*field* is an EON Field Object. *value* is any expression that has the same data type as *field*. If the value is not of the correct data type, a runtime script error (type mismatch) will occur. See the *Using the AddMFElement Method* section following this table.
RemoveMFElement*	Removes a specific element or value from an MF type field.	*field*.RemoveMFElement(*number*)	*field* is an EON Field Object. *number* is a positive integer or 0 that represents which of the values to be removed. 0 is the first element, 1 is the second element, and so on. See the *Using the RemoveMFElement Method* section following this table.
Value	Returns the value of an EON Field Object.	*field.value*	*field* is an EON Field Object. See the *Using the Value Property* section following this table.

*This method belongs to EON Field Objects that are of the MF type.

Using the GetName Method

Use this function to return a field name.

In JScript:

```
if (f.GetName() == "Width") f.Value = 100
```

In VBScript:

```
If f.GetName() = "Width" Then f.Value = 100
```

The statement checks whether the field f has the name Width before making the assignment.

Using the GetType Method

Use this function to identify the data type of a field.

```
if f.GetType() = 0 then f.value = true
if f.GetType() = 7 then f.value = "true"
```

These statements check whether the field f is of type SFBool or SFString before attempting to set it to true or "true."

The constants shown in Table B.4 are predefined for all EON data types. There are twenty-two data types. Eleven of them are single-field data types that start with SF, and the other eleven are corresponding multiple-field data types starting with MF.

TABLE B.4 Predefined Constants for EON Data Types

SF Data Type	Predefined Constant	MF Data Type	Predefined Constant
SFBool	0	MFBool	11
SFColor	1	MFColor	12
SFFloat	2	MFFloat	13
SFImage	3	MFImage	14
SFInt32	4	MFInt32	15
SFNode	5	MFNode	16
SFRotation	6	MFRotation	17
SFString	7	MFString	18
SFTime	8	MFTime	19
SFVec2f	9	MFVec2f	20
SFVec3f	10	MFVec3f	21

Using the GetMFCount Method

In the following example, the intent is to add the values of an MFFloat field and get the average. In this example, Times is an MFFloat field and Average is an SFFloat field.

In VBScript:

```
if Times.GetMFCount() = 0 then exit sub
dim total
total = 0
for i = 0 to Times.GetMFCount()-1
   total = total + Times.GetMFElement(i)
next
Average = total/Times.GetMFCount()
eon.Trace(Average)
```

In JScript:

```
if (Times.GetMFCount() == 0) return;
var total = 0
for (var i = 0; i < Times.GetMFCount(); i++)
{
   total = total + Times.GetMFElement(i)
}
Average.value = total/Times.GetMFCount()
eon.Trace(Average.value)
```

tips+tricks

If you want control over the values you add, use the AddMFElement() method.

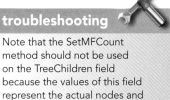

Using the SetMFCount Method

If an MF type field has eight fields and you use SetMFCount(3), then you delete the last five fields. If an MF type field has six fields and you use SetMFCount(10), then you effectively create four new fields. In this situation, the values of these fields are zeros. For an MFString field, blank strings are added.

The method is probably used most often to clear the whole field, setting the count to 0, before adding new values. In the following example, "Text" is an MFString field.

In VBScript:

```
sub On_Position()
   Text.SetMFCount(0)
   p = Position.value
   Text.AddMFElement("X = " & Round(p(0), 3))
   Text.AddMFElement("Y = " & Round(p(1), 3))
   Text.AddMFElement("Z = " & Round(p(2), 3))
   eon.FindNode("TextBox").GetFieldByName("Text").value = Text.
   value
end sub
```

In JScript:

```
function On_Position()
{
   Text.SetMFCount(0)
   p = Position.value.toArray()
   Text.AddMFElement("X = " + Math.round(p[0]*1000)/1000)
   Text.AddMFElement("Y = " + Math.round(p[1]*1000)/1000)
   Text.AddMFElement("Z = " + Math.round(p[2]*1000)/1000)
   eon.FindNode("TextBox").GetFieldByName("Text").value =
   Text.value
}
```

troubleshooting

Note that the SetMFCount method should not be used on the TreeChildren field because the values of this field represent the actual nodes and not just shortcuts to them like other MFNode fields. If you try to set the number of fields on the TreeChildren field, you may have no effect or a very negative effect. It is not possible to add nodes in this way, and EON is not designed to delete nodes in this way.

Using the GetMFElement Method

In this example, compare the method for returning a value of an SF type field and an MF type field:

```
b = singlefield.value
b = multiplefield.GetMFElement(0)
```

Remember that if the returned value is of data type SFNode, then you can only assign it to an object variable using the keyword *set* in VBScript; if assigning it to a field, then it must be an SFNode field.

troubleshooting

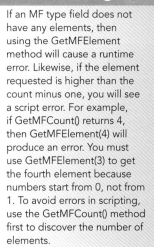

If an MF type field does not have any elements, then using the GetMFElement method will cause a runtime error. Likewise, if the element requested is higher than the count minus one, you will see a script error. For example, if GetMFCount() returns 4, then GetMFElement(4) will produce an error. You must use GetMFElement(3) to get the fourth element because numbers start from 0, not from 1. To avoid errors in scripting, use the GetMFCount() method first to discover the number of elements.

The GetMFElement() method is used in the following example to return a reference to the Camera node. The Camera node is assumed to be the first child node of the Scene node.

In VBScript:

```
set SceneNode = eon.FindNode("Scene")
set SceneTreeChildrenField = Scenenode.GetField(0)
set CameraNode = SceneTreeChildrenField.GetMFElement(0)
```

In the following example, we try to identify the top margin value of the TextBox node. The TextBox node has a Margins field of data type MFInt32, which has four elements. The sequence of the elements determines which margin it represents. Therefore, a value of 5 10 15 20 means leftmargin=5, rightmargin=10, topmargin=15, and bottom margin=20. The top margin is the third element, so we use 2 inside the parentheses.

In VBScript:

```
dim Margins, topmargin
set Margins = eon.FindNode("TextBox").GetFieldByName("Margins")
topmargin = Margins.GetMFElement(2)
```

In JScript:

```
var Margins, topmargin
Margins = eon.FindNode("TextBox").GetFieldByName("Margins")
topmargin = Margins.GetMFElement(2)
```

troubleshooting

If an MF type field does not have any elements, then using this method will cause a runtime error. Likewise, if the element requested is higher than the count minus one, you will see a script error. For example, if GetMFCount() returns 4, then GetMFElement(4) will produce an error. You must use GetMFElement(3) to get the fourth element because numbers start from 0, not from 1. To avoid errors in scripting, use the GetMFCount() method first to discover the number of elements.

Using the SetMFElement Method

Compare the method for setting a value of an SF type field and an MF type field in the following examples:

```
singlefield.value = b
multiplefield.SetMFElement(0, b)
```

In the following example, we try to set the top margin of a TextBox node to 30 pixels. The TextBox node has a Margins field of data type MFInt32, which has four elements. The sequence of the elements determines which margin it represents. Therefore, a value of 5 10 15 20 means leftmargin=5, rightmargin=10, topmargin=15, and bottom margin=20. The top margin is the third element, so we use 2 inside the parentheses.

In VBScript:

```
dim Margins
set Margins = eon.FindNode("TextBox").GetFieldByName("Margins")
Margins.SetMFElement(2, 30)
```

In JScript:

```
var Margins
Margins = eon.FindNode("TextBox").GetFieldByName("Margins")
Margins.SetMFElement(2, 30)
```

Using the AddMFElement Method

You can always add an element to an MF field. There is no theoretical limit. Practical limits arise because of the limitations of a computer's memory and speed. The value added is always added at the end of the MF field, thereby increasing its count by 1. In the following example, we are adding an x, y, z position to a field named Positions of type MFVec3f.

In JScript:

```
function On_Position()
{
    p = Position.value.toArray()
    Positions.AddMFElement(eon.MakeSFVec3f(p[0], p[1], p[2]))
}
```

In the following example, Text is an MFString field. Each time the AddMFElement(value) is used, it adds a line of text. After creating the values of the local Text field, the values are sent to the TextBox, which also has a field named Text, in which each element represents one line of text displayed.

In VBScript:

```
sub On_Position()
    Text.SetMFCount(0)
    p = Position.value
    Text.AddMFElement("X = " & Round(p(0), 3))
    Text.AddMFElement("Y = " & Round(p(1), 3))
    Text.AddMFElement("Z = " & Round(p(2), 3))
    eon.FindNode("TextBox").GetFieldByName("Text").value =
    Text.value
end sub
```

In JScript:

```
function On_Position()
{
    Text.SetMFCount(0)
    var p = Position.value.toArray()
    Text.AddMFElement("X = " + Math.round(p[0]*1000)/1000)
    Text.AddMFElement("Y = " + Math.round(p[1]*1000)/1000)
    Text.AddMFElement("Z = " + Math.round(p[2]*1000)/1000)
    eon.FindNode("TextBox").GetFieldByName("Text").value = Text.
    value
}
```

Using the RemoveMFElement Method

When you remove an element, you reduce the count of the field by one. All elements that were positioned after the removed element will be moved up one position. For example, if the field has eight elements and you remove the fifth element by using RemoveMFElement(4), then the old sixth element will become the fifth element, the old seventh element will become the sixth element, and so on.

troubleshooting

If you try to remove an element that does not exist, the script code is ignored. A script error does not occur.

In the following example, we attempt to calculate the frame rate by taking an average of the last five time intervals. An MFFloat field named Times holds the last five intervals. The last time interval is added. If the field has more than five elements, the first element is removed.

In JScript:

```
ct = CurrentTime.value
lt = LastTime.value
t = ct-lt
Times.AddMFElement(t)
while (Times.GetMFCount()>5)
{
   Times.RemoveMFElement(0)  //remove first element
}
for (var i=0; i<5; i++)
{
   t = t + Number(Times.GetMFElement(i))
}
Average.value = t/Times.GetMFCount()
FrameRate.value = 1/(Average.value)
LastTime.value = ct
```

Using the Value Property

The Value property returns the value of an EON Field Object. For example:

```
r = Radius.value
```

When the field is in the Script node and you are using VBScript, the .value part of the statement is not required unless the field is of data type SFNode. The .value is always required in JScript.

In VBScript:

```
r = Radius
if (Spinning.value) ...
```

In JScript:

```
r = Radius.value
if Spinning then ...
```

In the following example, the MFString field named Text of the TextBox node is given the value of an MFString field named "MyText" in the Script node itself.

```
eon.FindNode("TextBox").GetFieldByName("Text").value =
MyText.value
```

Therefore, .value can be used to get the value of the whole field of MF type fields. However, you need to use the GetMFElement() method to access individual values of an MF type field. For single-value type fields (SFBool, SFInt32, SFFloat, SFTime, SFString, and SFNode), the value returned can be assigned directly to a normal variable.

```
t = MyText.value
```

For the multiple-value type fields (MFVec2f, MFVec3f, MFColor, and MFRotation), the value returned will be a VB array. This can be assigned to an array variable in VBScript. However, in JScript, the VB array cannot be assigned to an array variable until it is converted by the toArray() method.

In JScript:

```
p = Position.value.toArray()
xpos = p[0]
```

In VBScript:

```
p = Position.value
'-or'
p = Position
xpos = p(0)
```

For the SFNode type field, the .value is always required, and it returns an EON Node Object. The following example uses an SFNode field named ViewportNode:

```
ViewportNode.value.GetFieldByName("FieldOfView").value = 60
```

If you omit the .value, as shown in the next example, a script error is displayed: Object doesn't support this property or method.

```
ViewportNode.GetFieldByName("FieldOfView").value = 60
// gives script error
```

tips+tricks

Note that .value is called a property and not a method because it should not have the parentheses after it as methods do.

Summary

In this appendix, you learned about EON's three scriptable object types. EON Base Object methods are used for various functions related to EON. The Node Object methods represent nodes in the simulation tree, and the EON Field Object methods represent a field of a node.

This appendix provides all of the information you need about methods and properties for EON Studio's scriptable object types. As you create simulations that include the scriptable object types in EON, you can use the tables and accompanying information in this appendix as a quick reference to supplement what you learned about scripting in Module 9.

Glossary

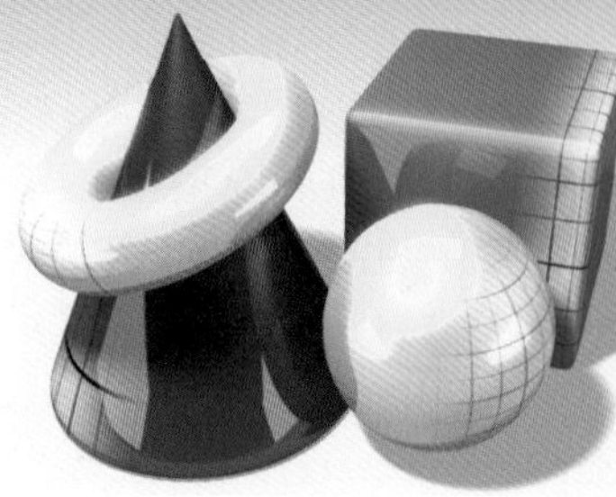

2DImage node Node that enables users to display bitmap images on top of the three-dimensional rendered EON window.

ActiveX control Places the necessary program code into a specific package to facilitate insertion into other programs known as host applications. See also *host application*.

Adapter prototype Prototype that converts data types, such as SFFloat to SFVec3F, to prevent problems caused by the need to share data that is of a different type.

Addition node Node that contains two float values (InValue1 and InValue2 fields) used to perform addition; results are placed in the OutValue field.

AfterParentTask node Nodes used to select paths (comparable to an IF statement in a programming language) or to divide the flow into two or more paths.

agent The active nodes of a simulation; nodes in the Agent Nodes library include the Gravitation, Latch, Rotate, and Spin nodes.

ambient light In OpenGL, the average volume of light created by the emission of light from all of the light sources surrounding (or located inside of) the lit area.

ambient light source In EON Studio, appears to illuminate all objects with equal intensity in all directions, like indirect sunlight.

amplitude Loudness of sound caused by the amount of pressure placed on the source of the sound by air molecules; also known as *volume*.

And node Node that compares two Boolean inEvents and sends a Boolean outEvent; the value of the outEvent will be true only if both inEvents are true.

animation Use of computer graphics to generate a sequence of frames that, when viewed in rapid succession, produces the illusion of a moving picture.

antialiasing Adjusts image quality to ensure a more realistic environment by smoothing an image's jagged edges when moving in the simulation.

application-oriented user interface Interface in which the main component is the application; the user runs the application and then brings other files into the application to accomplish a task.

attenuation 1. The gradual loss of intensity of light or sound as it moves further from its source. See Module 5 Lesson 1. See also *constant, linear,* and *quadratic*.
2. Conversion of the energy contained in acoustic waves into heat. See Module 7 Lesson 1.

AvatarCollision prototype Prototype that handles collisions between an avatar and the environment.

block In JScript, a group of statements enclosed in curly brackets.

bookmark Used to find a certain paragraph in a script; represented by a blue dot to the left of the line of script code.

BooleanSplitter prototype Prototype that allows users to send true or false events.

BooleanToIntegerConverter prototype Prototype that accepts fifty Boolean inEvents and sends a number between 1 and 50 as one integer outEvent.

bounding volume Bounding box, bounding sphere, or convex hull that is adjusted to wrap individual geometries or entire hierarchies of frames and geometries.

BoxSensor node Node that sends outEvents when the Position value of the Camera frame in the simulation moves the Camera frame into or out of a user-defined box.

BPButton prototype Prototype that provides a button (image) placed under the Camera node that can be positioned and sized using pixels. BP refers to BoxPosition, which is a typical field name used to position GUIControl nodes by pixels.

call Causing a function to run directly by specifying the function name.

camera Specific position and orientation in the three-dimensional world that determines what is rendered. See also *viewing plane*.

camera coordinate Camera's position and orientation.

Camera node Frame node that contains the Position and Orientation fields that provide values for the Viewport node to render the three-dimensional perspective of the viewing area.

Cartesian coordinate system Consists of three physical dimensions of space identified by the XYZ coordinates: width (X), length (Y), and height (Z).

Cg Programming language designed to allow simulation developers to control various aspects of a material's appearance in a high-level programmatic way. See also *shader*.

child node In the simulation tree hierarchy, nodes that are placed under a parent node.

child windows Windows within EON's main window that are used to access tasks needed when constructing EON simulations; the most important child windows are the

Cross-references are shown in italic text.

Simulation Tree window, Components window, Routes window, and Property Bar.

ClickSensor node Node that detects when an object has been clicked in the simulation window.

clipping plane One of the values used to specify the viewing frustum, which is the three-dimensional volume that is rendered; objects beyond a clipping plane are not rendered. See also *far clipping plane* and *near clipping plane*.

clone Creating a new prototype definition that is identical to an existing prototype.

code Content of a script.

CollisionManager node Node that holds global properties for a set of collision objects between which collisions should be tested.

CollisionObject node Node that holds properties and reports collisions for individual collision objects.

color field type Special kind of compound field used to store color values in RGB (Red, Green, Blue) format.

Colors prototype Prototype that converts Boolean inEvents to colors.

compilation Irreversible process that performs tasks such as polygon reduction, geometry compression, texture compression, and removal of other unnecessary information.

composability Interrelationships of three-dimensional components; considered to be an important requirement for developing the Virtual Reality Modeling Language (VRML). See also *extensibility* and *scalability*.

compound field type Field type containing a combination of several values; also known as a multiple value field.

compression Trading a smaller data file size for precision and quality by reducing textures and meshes to lower the requirements for memory and processor resources.

computer graphics Computational study of light and its effect on a geometric object.

computer simulation Discipline of designing a model of an actual or theoretical physical scenario, executing the model on a digital computer, and in some cases analyzing the output.

Computer-Assisted Virtual Environment (CAVE) Immersive virtual reality environment where projectors are directed to three, four, five, or six of the walls of a room-sized cube; also known as the EON ICUBE.

constant One of three coefficient values used to customize attenuation for lighting in a simulation; light intensity decreases as this value increases because light intensity is constant in relation to the distance from the light source. See also *attenuation*, *linear*, and *quadratic*.

Constant node Node that converts a Boolean inEvent to a number outEvent; sends a value stored in the Value (SFFloat) field when it receives the Trigger inEvent (SFBool).

convert Change the data type of information.

Convert 3.1 Visual Nodes tool Tool used to convert old 3.1 Mesh, Texture, and Material nodes to the 4.0 Visual Nodes set (Mesh2, Material2, Texture2, and Shape nodes).

Convert3DPosToScreenPos prototype Prototype that allows users to position two-dimensional elements over moving three-dimensional objects.

Converter node Node that allows users to convert data types.

Counter node Node that triggers another node when its counter value reaches a specified value.

culled Polygons selectively removed so that they will not be rendered.

culling Process of removing polygons so that they are not rendered.

customize Modifying a prototype instance by changing its field's values.

cycle When a limit is reached, move the value toward the opposite limit.

data manipulation Receiving, modifying, and sending the modified data; can include receiving data from multiple sources, performing calculations, and then sending the data in a more useful form.

decibel (dB) Unit of measurement that is used to measure the intensity or loudness of a sound.

default node fields Fields common to all EON nodes that are not shown in the Property Bar by default.

default value Exported field values at the time that a prototype is created.

DegreeOfFreedom node Defines a local coordinate system that can be used to transform underlying geometries; can limit the freedom of movement for its child nodes.

DelayTask node Node that can be used as a task that waits for an event to occur or for grouping several child tasks.

derivative prototype Prototype that is based on or derived from another prototype and typically maintains a close resemblance to the original prototype.

diffuse color Object's main color; one of a material's properties that defines an object's appearance.

diffuse light In OpenGL, light that has a specific position in space and comes from a single direction.

DirectDraw Surface (DDS) Standard graphics file format established for use with the DirectX SDK (software development kit); used to store surface and texture data and cubic environment maps with and without mipmap levels.

directional light source Linked to a Frame node, but appears to illuminate all objects with equal intensity in one direction, as if it were at an infinite distance from the scene; has orientation but no position—surfaces that are facing directly opposite this direction are illuminated the most.

DirectSound node Node that can play only .wav files; only EON-supplied node that can play three-dimensional sound.

DirectSound3D (DS3D) A component of Microsoft's DirectX library that allows software developers to write to a single standardized audio programming interface instead of writing code for each audio card manufacturer.

DirectX Audio DirectSound and Direct-Sound3D components of DirectX 8, collectively.

Display info of a node tool Tool used to display information about a node in the Log window, such as which nodes hold node references to the selected node; also known as the Node Info tool.

distribution file File format used specifically for the end user because it cannot be edited in EON authoring software; can be identified by the .edz file extension.

dither Combines different color pixels to estimate the correct color when a color cannot be displayed accurately in the current palette.

Cross-references are shown in italic text.

Division node Node that contains two float values (Numerator and Denominator fields) used to perform division; results are placed in the OutValue field.

Doppler effect Change in frequency and wavelength of a sound wave coming from a moving object toward a stationary observer.

downloading The process of getting the resource from the Internet to the local disk on a user's computer (Internet Cache folder).

DragManager prototype Prototype that allows drag-and-drop movement of objects; use with the DragSelector prototype.

DragSelector prototype Prototype used with the DragManager prototype to select an object to be positioned.

dynamic load Process of loading external resources after a simulation has started.

Dynamic Load Stand Alone license Type of EON Dynamic Load license used for computers that are not connected to the Internet.

dynamic prototype Prototype (.eop) library file loaded by EON Dynamic Load.

DynamicPrototype node Node that can download, load, unload, or swap any EON prototype during runtime (dynamically).

edutainment Educational entertainment with a focus on specific and intentional learning outcomes designed to achieve serious, measurable, sustained changes in performance and behavior.

emissive light In OpenGL, the type of light emitted by an object.

encapsulated Prototype that appears as one component in the simulation tree, although it actually contains various combinations of nodes, prototypes, and routes.

enumeration field type Field with a limited set of distinct values from which to choose.

EON Dependency Walker A program that allows users to view the components and component versions required by an EON simulation.

EON Dynamic Load license License required for accessing EON Dynamic Load functions.

EON Object Classes Objects that provide properties and methods for accessing and manipulating the simulation's environment, nodes, and fields in the nodes.

EON Server license Client-server–based solution for licensing the EON Dynamic Load function.

EON Software Development Kit (SDK) A software development kit used to construct custom EON nodes and modules; the same tool used by EON Reality to create standard nodes and modules.

EON-supplied prototype Prototype supplied by EON Studio that is found under the Prototypes tab in the Components window.

EON Viewer EON Reality's standalone software used to view .eoz and .edz files.

EON Viewer setup Installation program that allows users to install EON runtime software; includes all software needed to run most EON simulations.

EON Web Publisher Wizard Provides several default HTML templates that use JavaScript files to provide functionality for placing EonX controls (EON's ActiveX control) on a web page.

EonX ActiveX control used to display and control EON applications from other programs.

event Data sent between two nodes.

event handler Function that handles an event.

eventsProcessed Special event in script that will be triggered during every frame (related to frame rate) after all events have been processed, but only when at least one field of the script has changed its value since the last frame.

exported field Fields or properties available to a prototype when it is used as an instance; allows users to customize the prototype for use in a particular application, thereby increasing the usefulness of the prototype.

exposedField A field that can serve as both an outEvent and inEvent field.

extensibility Provides the ability to extend the capability of a language, such as the Virtual Reality Modeling Language (VRML), to serve a special purpose; considered to be an important requirement for developing VRML. See also *composibility* and *scalability*.

external event The inEvents and/or outEvents in a user's EON application that facilitate communication with host applications, such as a web page.

external field User-defined variable created in the Routes window that represents external events communicating with host applications.

external resource Content that comes from outside of the EON simulation file (.eoz); may be a prototype, geometry, texture, sound, or video.

external route Connection between an external field and an associated inEvent or OutEvent for a standard node.

Face Fixing tool Tool used to make manual corrections to the faces of certain types of imported three-dimensional data.

face validation Component of validation in computer simulation that measures whether a computer animation or a moving geometric model "looks good" to the viewer.

far clipping plane Objects that are farther away from the camera than this distance are not rendered; one of the values that determine the viewing frustum. See also *clipping plane, frustum,* and *near clipping plane.*

field of view Confined area of three-dimensional space defined by the camera's position and orientation, the field of view, and the near and far clipping planes; also known as the *viewing frustum.*

fields Used by nodes to store data and to communicate with other nodes.

file format importer Converts imported files, such as 3ds Max and LightWave files, to an internal EON database and builds an EON simulation tree.

file system object An ActiveX control object that allows scripting code to access the file system to perform tasks such as creating, opening, and saving text files as well as accessing file and folder information.

fixed screen size Interface that can be created quickly using 2DImage nodes and 2DEdit nodes if the ability to enter information is necessary.

FlashObject node Node that allows Flash files to be displayed on top of the EON simulation window; can be a method

Cross-references are shown in italic text.

for inserting media, but it also can be used to make an interface.

flat hierarchy In a modeling program or the EON simulation tree, each object is created on the same level as other objects. For example, the table top, the table legs, and the vase on the table are created in the same folder rather than grouping the table with the table legs and placing the vase in a separate folder. A flat hierarchy makes it difficult to locate objects and understand the structure.

floating point Numeric values that have a decimal point (i.e., real numbers).

frame rate Number of times the three-dimensional view is rendered per second.

frustum Confined area of three-dimensional space, with a rectangular pyramid shape, that has been intersected by two planes: a near plane at the front boundary of the area and a far plane at the rear boundary of the area. See also *far clipping plane* and *near clipping plane*.

Full-size Window mode Viewing mode used to maximize the simulation window to cover the entire desktop screen without any visible borders. See also *Normal Window mode*.

function Block of code (script or program statements) that performs a set of actions.

functional prototype Type of prototype that focuses on providing specific functionality such as navigation, making calculations, and converting or transforming data into a more usable form. See also *object prototype*.

geometry compression Reduces precision of the data used to define a polygon and other geometry data to reduce the file size and make the simulation perform as fast as possible without noticeably affecting quality.

geometry optimization Collective effort to reduce the size of the simulation through geometry compression and polygon reduction.

Geometry selection tool Tool used to find a Mesh2 node in the simulation tree by clicking a selected mesh in the rendered scene in the simulation window.

Gouraud shading Shading that is blended so that objects appear more rounded.

graphical user interface (GUI) User interface based on graphics instead of text.

Gravitation node Node that adds gravitational force to sibling nodes by modifying the parent Frame node's Z coordinate.

GroupGUINodes prototype Prototype that provides a time-saving function that moves and hides graphical user interface (GUI) nodes as a group while keeping their relative positions by changing the BoxPosition field.

haptic Based on the sense of touch. See also *tactile interface*.

heading Rotation around the z axis. See also *pitch*, *roll*, and *rotation*.

HexColor prototype Prototype that converts colors into a hexadecimal string for HTML use and vice versa.

Hidden Surface Removal (HSR) Process used to determine which surfaces (or parts of surfaces) are not visible from a certain viewpoint; necessary to render images correctly in virtual reality. Also known as Hidden Surface Determination (HSD) or Visible Surface Determination (VSD).

host application Application that can have an embedded EON application and the PrototypebaseURL property set; typically a web page run on a web browser, such as Internet Explorer or Mozilla Firefox, but can be any ActiveX-compliant software, including EON Viewer. See also *ActiveX control*.

host ID Number and/or letters found in network cards or hard disk drives that uniquely identify a specific computer.

host program environment Program in which an application or EON simulation is interpreted and executed, such as a web browser, EON Studio, or EON Viewer.

immersive Technology that enables users to interact with and manipulate a virtual world that matches what they would experience in a real environment like the one that has been simulated; the human-computer interaction is provided by various technological devices, such as head-mounted displays (HMDs), position sensors, and data gloves.

InactivitySensor prototype Prototype that triggers an event after a set time of mouse inactivity.

inEvent Type of field used to receive data.

instance Prototype that appears in the simulation tree that is based on a prototype definition in the Local Prototypes window.

instance counter Number of prototype instances in the simulation; displayed in brackets at the end of the prototype's name in the Local Prototypes window.

integer Numeric values that do not have a decimal point (i.e., whole numbers).

ISector node Node that emits a sensor ray along the y axis of its parent frame and detects when the ray is intersected by three-dimensional objects (Shape nodes or old Mesh nodes).

IterationTask node Node that repeats its child tasks a fixed number of times (comparable to a FOR loop in a programming language).

Joystick node Node that allows the user to navigate within a simulation using a joystick.

JScript® Microsoft object-oriented scripting language that is based on JavaScript®, a scripting language used for client-side web applications; contains blocks of program code called functions that must begin with the *function* keyword; used by the EON Script node.

KeyboardSensor node Node that detects when a specified key is pressed and generates events that can be routed to other nodes.

KeyFrame node Node that moves sibling nodes through predefined points, which consist of a timestamp, a position, and an orientation.

KeyMove node Node that provides a keyboard motion model and affects its parent node.

Latch node Node that holds a Boolean value and receives inEvents to set its Boolean value to true, clear its value to false, or toggle its value.

level of detail The complexity of a three-dimensional computer graphics object as measured by the number of polygons and the size and number of the textures.

Cross-references are shown in italic text.

library Category used to organize EON nodes or prototypes in the Components window; developers can create new libraries to organize new nodes or prototypes.

licensed EDZ application License inserted by EON Reality staff directly into the distribution file while it is being built.

light map Sampled light sources mapped on affected three-dimensional objects as a texture.

light mapping Computer graphics technique used to increase the speed of rendering three-dimensional objects with complex lighting; the contributions of the light sources are sampled and then mapped on the affected three-dimensional objects as a texture.

Light node Node used to illuminate objects in EON simulations.

linear One of three coefficient values used to customize attenuation for lighting in a simulation; light intensity decreases faster in relation to the distance from the light source as this value increases. See also *attenuation*, *constant*, and *quadratic*.

loading Process of moving a resource from the local file to the computer's memory.

local coordinate Coordinates associated with an individual parent object and all of its associated child objects within a model's hierarchy.

Local Prototypes window Area below the simulation tree where prototype definitions reside.

logic control nodes Nodes that help create logic structures, control the simulation flow, and activate other nodes when certain conditions are met.

logical hierarchy One of two methods to organize the simulation tree, this method places objects in the simulation tree according to their type or category. For example, a ClickSensor node would be placed with other ClickSensor nodes. See also *positional hierarchy*.

loop Continuously repeating sequence.

lossless Image quality is not lost for a certain pixel size in the image; examples include the image types PNG and DDS/DXT.

Make texture compression/resize permanent tool Tool used to make the resource compression of textures and meshes permanent.

map Second layer of surfacing that creates a more realistic surface by modifying the look and feel of an object; also known as a *texture*.

material First layer of surfacing that defines the appearance of the object; required for every object.

material definition Set of values that are applied uniformly over the entire surface of an object.

Material selection tool Tool that identifies the Material2 node in the simulation tree that provides the appearance for the object selected in the simulation window.

mathematical models Computerized, three-dimensional model consisting of XYZ coordinate values representing the surface geometry of a physical object.

media Sound and video, collectively.

MemoryTask node Node that stores important states (comparable to global variables in a programming language).

Merge Shapes with the same material tool Tool used to merge shapes/meshes into one large mesh; reduces the rendering cost for the Shape node.

method Function that belongs to an object; used to access and manipulate the associated object's properties.

Microsoft DirectShow® Multimedia framework and application programming interface (API) for software developers to perform various operations with media files or multimedia streams.

Microsoft DirectSound® Application programming interface (API) that supplies many useful capabilities, such as the ability to play multichannel sounds at high resolution.

Missile node Node that moves sibling nodes as if they were missiles, with user-defined acceleration at the beginning of the movement.

Motion node A node that moves one or more sibling nodes with user-defined velocity and acceleration and rotates them with user-defined angular velocity and angular acceleration.

MousePos3D prototype Prototype that provides the three-dimensional coordinates that identify the position of the mouse cursor when using an orthographic viewport.

MouseSensor node Node that detects the position of the mouse cursor and the location of the mouse clicks.

MouseToBoxPosition prototype Prototype that converts mouse position to BoxPosition (pixel values).

MouseToTextBoxPos prototype Prototype that converts mouse position into text box position for variously sized viewports.

Mover prototype Simple motion model that moves in the X, Y, Z, H, P, and R directions; requires KeyMover prototype to allow users to move objects using the arrow keys.

MoveRotateArrows3D prototype Prototype used to move and rotate objects in a simulation window by dragging or clicking arrows.

MovieTexture node Node that uses a movie file as its image source.

multimaterial In some three-dimensional modeling software, allows several different materials to be assigned to a single mesh; EON creates a MultiMaterial node when a multimaterial is imported.

multi-pass rendering Assigning certain components as part of the initial scene, or first rendering, in a simulation with other effects assigned to render as a second pass; allows Cg shaders to create effects, such as motion blur and distortion.

Multiple Document Interface (MDI) Windows that reside under a single parent window.

Multiplication node Node that contains two float values (InValue1 and InValue2 fields) used to perform multiplication; results are placed in the OutValue field.

near clipping plane Objects that are closer to the camera than this distance are not rendered; one of the values that determine the viewing frustum. See also *clipping plane*, *frustum*, and *far clipping plane*.

nested prototype Prototype within a prototype.

node Building blocks used to create EON simulations.

node reference Shortcut that enables users to reuse a node or prototype already in the simulation tree, including all of the property settings that have been changed from their defaults; also known as a *referenced link*.

Cross-references are shown in italic text.

Normal Window mode Default view that simply displays the EON simulation within a normal window. See also *Full-size Window mode.*

Not node Node that inverts a Boolean inEvent; if the inEvent is true, the value of the outEvent will be false, and vice versa.

numeric range field type Field that contains a slider that allows access to continuous field values within a limited range.

NURBS Non-uniform rational B-spline; represents a mathematical model commonly used in computer graphics for generating and representing curves and surfaces. See also *polygon reduction* and *tessellated.*

object Group of related properties, methods, and events.

Object Navigation model Allows users to zoom in or out and turn around the pivot point of the Scene frame.

object prototype Type of prototype that primarily holds three-dimensional object resources. See also *functional prototype.*

object-oriented programming A type of programming language in which a collection of objects are used and reused to create software applications.

object-oriented user interface (OOUI) Interface in which the user interacts only with objects that represent programming elements within the application.

opacity Transparent property of an object that determines the object's transparency; one of a material's properties that define an object's appearance.

OpenGL Standard application program interface (API) for defining two-dimensional and three-dimensional graphics.

operator Symbols that manipulate data values.

Opposites prototype Prototype that converts any data it receives and sends the opposite value.

Or node Node that compares two Boolean inEvents and sends a Boolean outEvent; if any inEvents are true, the value of the outEvent will be true.

OrbitNav prototype Provides a navigation system to rotate, zoom, and pan using a mouse; recommended for viewing a single object or a group of objects.

orthographic viewport Viewport without three-dimensional perspective; often referred to as a two-dimensional view.

outEvent Type of field used to send data.

Paint Material tool Tool used to assign materials in the simulation tree to objects in the simulation window.

parallel point light source In EON Studio, has a position and radiates light in all directions; the angle at which the light strikes an object is assumed to be parallel (like a directional light source) for all faces in the object.

parent node In the simulation tree hierarchy, a node that normally groups other nodes.

password-protected private resource Resources that will load only if referenced by a distribution file that has a matching password in the ResourcePasswords field of its Simulation node.

pitch 1. Rotation around the x axis. See Module 2 Lesson 1. See also *heading*, *roll*, and *rotation.*
2. Frequency of a sound wave. See Module 7 Lesson 1.

pivot point Position in an object that serves as the center of rotation and as the position reference; when an object rotates, it revolves around the pivot point.

Place node Node that moves sibling nodes to a new position and orientation within a user-defined time.

plug-in Small application that runs inside a larger application.

point light source Radiates light equally in all directions and requires the calculation of a new lighting vector for each facet it illuminates.

point source Sound with position but no orientation.

polygon reduction Trading a smaller data file size for precision and quality by reducing the number of polygons used to build a mesh so that the requirements for memory and processor resources are reduced. See also *NURBS* and *tessellated.*

PopupMenu node Node that provides the context-sensitive menu or right mouse button menu functionality that is common to other Windows programs.

PopupUnlimited prototype When used with a script, enables users to create pop-up menus with multiple levels and unlimited menu items; requires EON Professional.

positional hierarchy One of two methods used to organize the simulation tree, this method arranges elements in close proximity to the target elements they work with in a simulation. For example, a ClickSensor node and a Latch node that cooperate to turn a lamp on and off would be placed in the same Frame node. See also *logical hierarchy.*

PowerSwitch node Similar to the Switch node, but with extra inEvents so users can trigger certain child nodes with Boolean inEvents instead of using the integer value inEvent.

private resource External resource files that can only be used by the EON runtime software.

project plan Plan for all elements needed to create a finished project; can be a written outline, list, or drawing.

property Data field that stores a value; the set of properties for an object that collectively describe or define its state for a specific moment in time.

prototype Reusable, plug-and-play simulations that can be copied from an EON components library and placed into custom simulations.

prototype definition Contains all necessary information to construct a prototype instance, including a subtree hierarchy containing nodes and/or other prototypes, routes, data fields with designated default values, and any required graphics resource files (such as image maps and textures); displayed in the Local Prototypes window.

prototype instance An occurrence of a prototype in the simulation tree; created in the Simulation Tree window by copying the prototype definition from the Local Prototypes window or the Prototypes tab of the Components window.

prototype library Group of prototypes, based on similar functionality, that is displayed in the Components window in EON, providing long-term storage and easy access to many prototypes.

PrototypebaseURL Location where required files are hosted for EON Dynamic Load applications.

ProximitySensor node Sends outEvents when the simulation camera position moves into or out of a sphere with a user-defined radius.

public resource External resource files that can be opened in software other than the EON runtime software.

quadratic One of three coefficient values used to customize attenuation for lighting in a simulation; light intensity decreases faster in relation to the distance from the light source than linear values. See also *attenuation*, *constant*, and *linear*.

QuickPos prototype Prototype that allows users to display the Frame node's position information by pressing the Q key; the prototype must be placed under the Camera frame and the QuickPos prototype must contain a frame reference.

Raptor A 3ds Max plug-in that converts 3ds Max content to EON format and allows users to display and interact with 3ds Max content in real time with intuitive controls.

rasterization Conversion of three-dimensional vector graphic shapes (based on the final list of visible polygons) into two-dimensional raster images that can be drawn on a video display with minimal pixel redraw.

real-time rendering Immediate rendering and display of several frames per second in rapid succession in real time.

recursive function Function that calls itself.

referenced link Shortcut that enables users to reuse a node or prototype already in the simulation tree, including all of the property settings that have been changed from their defaults; also known as a *node reference*.

Remove duplicated resources tool Tool used to remove similar texture resources and improve file performance.

rendering Process of generating a two-dimensional snapshot image (or frame) of a three-dimensional model in computer graphics.

RenderTexture node Node that allows users to render a camera view to a texture and apply the texture to a material in the Scene frame. See also *Target node*.

RenderTree node Objects under this node will be rendered in the viewport.

reset In the OrbitNav prototype, refers to moving the camera without dragging the mouse.

Resolve resource references Function that creates a Group node named Resources under the Frame node and places copies of all of the resource nodes required by the Shape nodes found in the selected subtree.

resource node Nodes that hold references to geometry, image, sound, and video files.

resource sharing Use of specified external resources by multiple simulations.

RGB values Defines the amount of red, blue, and green in a color.

roll Rotation around the y axis. See also *heading*, *pitch*, and *rotation*.

Rotate node Node used to rotate sibling nodes; the user defines the direction and lap time of the rotation.

rotation Rotation around an axis expressed in H (heading), P (pitch), and R (roll) values. See also *heading*, *pitch*, and *roll*.

route Defines how information should be sent between nodes; simulation developers create a route by dragging nodes from the simulation tree hierarchy into the Routes window and connecting the nodes with a line, which represents a route.

RouteSwitch node Node that is used in the Routes window to allow events through only when the switch is on (when the Connected field is true); supports events of all EON data types.

SaveFrameValues prototype On shutdown, saves a Frame node's Position, Orientation, and Scale values as start values.

scalability Allows the creation of arbitrarily sized worlds; considered to be an important requirement for developing the Virtual Reality Modeling Language (VRML). See also *composibility* and *extensibility*.

scalable screen interface Preferred interface that enables users to create professional-looking products that run at different resolutions based on display resolution.

scope Location in which variables are visible; local variables disappear when the function is complete and global variables exist until the host program is shut down.

script Collection of instructions to be carried out by a computer.

Script node Node that is inserted to allow scripting in EON; an associated page is used to write script code.

scripting Activity of writing code.

scripting language System of symbols, keywords, and syntax rules that is used to communicate instructions to a computer.

SendEvent method Enables communication between an EON ActiveX control embedded within an external host application and a running EON application.

Sequence node Node that activates one of its children in a predetermined sequence at specified intervals.

serious game Software application developed with game technology and game design principles to run on personal computers or video game consoles, but for a primary purpose other than pure entertainment, such as training, advertising, simulation, or education; also known as instructional simulation and game for learning.

session Start of an EON application, usually when the end user goes to a web page containing an EON application.

SFNode field Field that contains a reference to another node.

shader Programmable material for which the appearance is defined by a short program in the Cg language; also known as a procedural material. See also *Cg*.

shape Three-dimensional object defined by a Mesh2 node (a basic geometric model) and a Material2 node (color and texture).

Shape selection tool Tool used to locate an object (Shape node) in the simulation tree by clicking the object in the Scene frame in the simulation tree.

simulation tree Hierarchical collection of nodes that creates an EON simulation.

SimultaneousSound prototype Prototype that plays sounds simultaneously when multiple DirectSound nodes are started in a short period of time.

SixButtons prototype Prototype that provides a set of six red and yellow buttons featuring all of the required supplementary functions.

Slider node Node that provides a vertical or horizontal slider control that appears on top of the three-dimensional rendered window.

SmoothOperator prototype Prototype that changes float values gradually; uses include fading sound in and out or increasing and decreasing transparency of objects so they fade away or become more visible.

sound cone Three-dimensional area in which a sound's volume is louder inside of the area than outside of the area; applies to three-dimensional sound with both position and orientation.

Sound node Older EON node that is still available because it is the only node that can play .midi sound files (in addition to .wav files).

specular light In OpenGL, the "bright spot," which is often white or light gray, on a curved surface that provides the shininess of an object.

specularity Highlight property of an object; one of a material's properties that defines an object's appearance.

Spin node Node that quickly revolves sibling nodes around the z axis at a given radius, speed, and height above the X–Y plane.

spot light source Light that illuminates only objects that are within a user-defined cone.

statement One line of code in JScript.

stereo Two separate pictures, one for each eye; special hardware is required to deliver the two pictures to each eye individually.

StickyMover prototype Enables users to move objects along the surface of other objects.

storyboard Graphic organizer that typically includes illustrations, images, and some text displayed in sequence or in the relationships as they will appear in the finished product.

streaming Ability to download and load external resources after the simulation has started.

sub stepping Process that increases the chance of detecting collisions between objects by testing for collisions at multiple positions (steps) between the new and previous positions of an object.

Subtraction node Node that contains two float values (InValue1 and InValue2 fields) used to perform subtraction; InValue2 is subtracted from InValue1 and the result is placed in the OutValue field.

subtree A portion of the EON simulation tree.

SuperMan prototype Prototype that provides a flying motion model.

surfacing Actions that affect the appearance of a finished geometry when rendered; consists of the material layer and the map layer. Also known as the texture layer.

Switch node Node that can turn on one child node while turning off the other child nodes.

tactile interface Interface that adds to or replaces other forms of output with haptic feedback methods that are based on the sense of touch. See also *haptic*.

Target node A node referenced by the Viewport node and used for Cg materials, for multi-pass rendering, and for the RenderTexture node. See also *RenderTexture node*.

task Individual items that can only be completed one at a time.

Task node Node used for a task that waits for an event to occur, as well as for grouping several child tasks.

tessellated In EON Studio, used to describe NURBS that have a checkered or tiled appearance after polygon reduction. See also *NURBS* and *polygon reduction*.

texture Second layer of surfacing that creates a more realistic surface by modifying the look and feel of an object; also known as a *map*.

texture compression Result of changing a texture's maximum width and height in pixels, its format, and its quality level to reduce the file size and make the simulation perform as fast as possible without noticeably affecting quality.

texture coordinates Coordinates that plot every vertex, or corner point of a polygon, of every face on a model to the UV coordinates on the bitmap to distribute the image over the surface of the model. The U coordinates run from left to right and the V coordinates run from bottom to top.

texture mapping Addition of detail, surface texture, and color to a graphic or three-dimensional model by adding one or more texture maps to a material and then applying that material to the surface area (a set of interconnected polygons) of the shape.

texture projection Method in which an image is mathematically projected onto the object; each coordinate in the image is assigned to the location on the model where it is "projected."

Texture selection tool Tool used to find a Texture2 node in the simulation tree by clicking an object in the simulation window that has textures mapped on its surface.

thumbnail Type of simple storyboard composed of rough sketches of what will be needed in each scene.

TimeSensor node Node that generates pulses (outEvents) at regular intervals to control the actions of other nodes.

toggle To switch between two values, such as swapping true to false or false to true.

tone Relative volume of different sound frequencies.

touch interface Graphical user interface that uses a touch-screen display as a combined input and output device instead of the keyboard, mouse, and monitor.

translation Movement within three-dimensional space that is expressed in (X, Y, Z) values.

transparency The property of an object that allows light to pass through the object so that objects beyond it are visible.

trigger Causing an event handler to run by assigning a value to a field.

Trigger node Node that signals when a value is outside a specified interval.

TVChannelSwitcher prototype Prototype that allows simulation users to click a TV or any three-dimensional object to change the "channel" (image displayed on the object); the channels can be links to different camera views from within the simulation or to movie files referenced by a MovieTexture node.

usability Extent to which the design of the user interface accounts for the "human" element and how effective and efficient it makes operating the system.

user interface Entire collection of elements that a user can access to complete a task; includes visual clues, static or dynamic information that impacts decision making or leads the user to actions, and elements that are manipulated (touched, pressed, turned, clicked, etc.) to cause change.

Cross-references are shown in italic text.

user-driven simulation Interactive simulation in which a user's actions and decisions determine the application's responses.

variable In script, the named memory locations used to temporarily store values needed for script.

VBScript Microsoft object-oriented scripting language based on the Visual Basic® programming language and used by the EON Script node, used by both client-side and server-side web applications, and within the Microsoft Windows® Script Host (WSH) environment; it has blocks of program code called subroutines that are enclosed between the *sub* and *end sub* keywords.

viewing frustum Confined area of three-dimensional space defined by the camera's position and orientation, the field of view, and the near and far clipping planes; also known as the *field of view.*

viewing plane Represents the three-dimensional area of a scene that is visible when viewed from the camera's position. See also *camera.*

viewport Area of the simulation window that displays a rendered scene.

virtual reality (VR) Form of human-computer interaction in which a real or imaginary environment is simulated.

Virtual Reality Modeling Language (VRML) Specification for displaying three-dimensional objects on the Internet.

Visual Nodes library Material-mesh system comprised of a set of nodes grouped together to enhance the expressiveness and flexibility of the visual system.

visualization Technique in which an image is used to communicate a message; use of visual imagery, diagrams, and animations as an effective way to communicate both abstract and concrete ideas.

volume Loudness of sound caused by the amount of pressure placed on the source of the sound by air molecules; also known as *amplitude.*

Walk Navigation model Allows users to navigate within a simulation using an intuitive behavior that is similar to walking through a simulated environment.

Walk node Node that implements the walk motion models found in many three-dimensional environments.

WalkAbout node Node that allows the user to navigate within a simulation using the keyboard.

Web Publisher template Pattern or example that includes a group of features from which users can choose functionality and appearance for their web publication.

world coordinate An object's position and orientation relative to the global virtual world environment or Scene frame.

XOR node Node that compares two Boolean inEvents and sends a Boolean outEvent; if the two inEvents have different values, the value of the outEvent will be true.

zero parallax Distance from the eye to the plane where the images from the left and right eye coincide; used for optimizing stereo for an object so that ideal three-dimensional effects can be created for the simulation file.

Zoom Extents tool Tool used to move the camera to locate three-dimensional objects in the Scene frame by clicking the object's node in the simulation tree.

Index